SIXTH CANADIAN EDITION

COST ACCOUNTING
A MANAGERIAL EMPHASIS

CHARLES T. HORNGREN • SRIKANT M. DATAR • GEORGE FOSTER • MADHAV V. RAJAN
Stanford University   Stanford University   Stanford University   Stanford University

CHRISTOPHER D. ITTNER • MAUREEN P. GOWING • STEVE JANZ
University of Pennsylvania   University of Windsor   Southern Alberta
Institute of Technology

Toronto

This text is dedicated to my family to thank them
and recognize their love and encouragement.

M.P.G.

I would like to thank those amazing students I have had the pleasure of
teaching over the past eight years, my talented colleagues, and my supportive
and inspiring friends and family.

S.J.

Vice-President, Editorial Director: Gary Bennett
Editor-in-Chief: Nicole Lukach
Acquisitions Editor: Megan Farrell
Marketing Manager: Jenna Wulff
Developmental Editor: Suzanne Simpson Millar
Lead Project Manager: Avinash Chandra
Manufacturing Manager: Susan Johnson
Production Editor: Leanne Rancourt
Copy Editor: Susan Bindernagel
Proofreader: Gail Copeland
Compositor: MPS Limited, a Macmillan Company
Technical Checkers: Jake Chazan and Elizabeth Zaleschuk
Photo Researcher/Permissions Editor: Lynn McIntyre
Art Director: Julia Hall
Cover and Interior Designer: Anthony Leung
Cover Image: Shutterstock Images

Credits and acknowledgments of material borrowed from other sources and reproduced,
with permission, in this textbook appear on the appropriate page within the text and on p. C-1.

If you purchased this book outside the United States or Canada, you should be aware that it has been imported
without the approval of the publisher or the author.

10 9 8 7 6 5 4 3 2   [CKV]

Library and Archives Canada Cataloguing in Publication

 Cost accounting : a managerial emphasis / Charles T.
Horngren ... [et al.]. — 6th Canadian ed.

Includes index.
ISBN 978-0-13-339288-3

 1. Cost accounting. 2. Costs, Industrial. I. Horngren,
Charles T., 1926-

HF5686.C8C68 2012   658.15'52   C2011-905517-1

ISBN 978-0-13-339288-3

BRIEF CONTENTS

TABLE OF CONTENTS

Studying cost accounting is one of the best business investments a student can make. Why? Because success in any organization—from the smallest corner store to the largest multinational corporation—requires the use of cost accounting concepts and practices. Cost accounting provides key data to managers for planning and controlling, as well as costing products, services, and customers. This book emphasizes how cost accounting helps managers make better decisions, along with a clear presentation of analytical procedures.

Cost accountants are a part of top-level management decision-making teams. Filtering relevant from irrelevant data remains an important theme in this text, to highlight that different decisions require different cost data and analyses. We recognize cost accounting as a powerful set of analytical tools that good managers use to select, implement, and evaluate business strategy. In this edition we emphasize both the development of skills using analytical tools in Excel, which future employers value, and also respect for human values and teamwork that make cost accountants effective in the workplace.

HALLMARK FEATURES

- ◆ Exceptionally strong emphasis on managerial uses of cost information
- ◆ Extensively revised content to promote clarity, readability, and understandability
- ◆ Excellent balance in integrating modern topics with existing content
- ◆ Emphasis on human behaviour aspects
- ◆ Balanced emphasis on both the preparation and use of cost information through extensive use of real-world examples
- ◆ Ability to teach chapters in different sequences
- ◆ Excellent quantity, quality, and range of assignment material

The first 13 chapters provide the essence of a one-term (quarter or semester) course. There is ample text and assignment material in the book's 24 chapters for a two-term course. This book can be used immediately after the student has had an introductory course in financial accounting. Alternatively, this book can build on an introductory course in managerial accounting.

Deciding on the sequence of chapters in a textbook is a challenge. Every instructor has a favourite way of organizing his or her course. Hence, we present a modular, flexible organization that permits a course to be custom tailored. *This organization facilitates diverse approaches to teaching and learning.*

As an example of the book's flexibility, the sixth edition now includes coverage of variance analysis for substitutable inputs at the end of Chapter 7, instead of the fifth edition's Chapter 16. Instructors can now cover Level 4 substitutable input variance analyses here, then move ahead to Chapter 8. If this material is excluded or left until Chapter 16, instructors can do this without any loss of continuity.

THE FIVE STEP DECISION-MAKING FRAMEWORK

Chapter 1 introduces a five-step decision-making process that managers use when making decisions. This framework is applied throughout the text to highlight the importance of using the results of any cost analysis to make business decisions:

1. **Identify the problem and uncertainties**

   For example, whether a newspaper should increase its advertising rate, and the effect this decision will have on advertising demand.

2. **Obtain information.**

   For example, review the effects on demand of past increases in advertising rates, or do market research on advertising rates charged by competing newspapers.

3. **Make predictions about the future**

   For example, how demand will be affected by different potential increases in advertising rates.

4. **Decide on and implement one of the available alternatives**.

   For example, choosing a new advertising rate

5. **Implement the decision, evaluate the performance, and learn**

   For example, informing potential advertisers about the new rates and comparing what actually happened against the plans.

A consistent application of the decision framework helps students understand why specific cost accounting tools described in each chapter are important to good management. The repetition of each step in the framework throughout the book gives instructors the opportunity to emphasize the importance of making business management decisions in a disciplined and rigorous way.

NEW CUTTING EDGE TOPICS

The pace of change in organizations continues to be rapid. The sixth Canadian edition of *Cost Accounting* reflects changes occurring in the role of cost accounting in organizations:

◆ Chapters 4 and 5 on traditional job cost allocation and ABC cost systems have been rewritten to emphasize the unequal distribution of benefits arising when common resources are not equally shared by users. The text also emphasizes the need to select good direct input measures to proxy the unequal use of indirect shared resources. A clear connection is now made between more consumption of indirect resources and value-added to an output for which a customer will pay.

◆ Chapter 10 expands on how to analyze past data from a traditional cost system to select the best direct input measure to proxy for the value-added from unequal use of indirect resources. The revised chapter also highlights the appropriate use of statistics reported by the linear regression program in Excel to make this decision. Within the decision framework, the best proxy will enable management teams to provide the most reliable predictions of future outcomes (step 3 of the decision framework). Instructors may choose to cover this material after Chapter 4, cover it later, or exclude statistical analyses using Excel without losing continuity.

◆ We introduce Dr. Michael Porter's framework to analyze the best match between the intensity of competition and the company's strategy. This framework fits with the value-added theme. When competition is intense, if customers do not perceive added value from the activities and inputs used to produce what they purchase, they will not pay and the costs will not be recovered in the price of the product.

◆ We also discuss the selection of strategy and use of balanced scorecard measures to track how well the strategy is being implemented by using key financial and nonfinancial measures of performance.

BUSINESS MATTERS

Each chapter opens with a vignette on a real company situation. The vignettes engage the reader in a business situation or dilemma. The vignette motivates and illustrates why and how the analytical tools of cost accounting, presented in the chapter, are relevant to good business management. For example, Chapter 1 describes how Research In Motion uses cost accounting to retain its competitive advantage by spending on innovation and new product introductions. Chapter 2 reports the consequences of GM's struggle and failure to meet the challenge of implementing a useful cost identification and control system. Chapter 3 explains how WestJet's ability to classify costs and know how costs behave contributes to success at profit management and reveals how much a last-minute passenger's seat should cost.

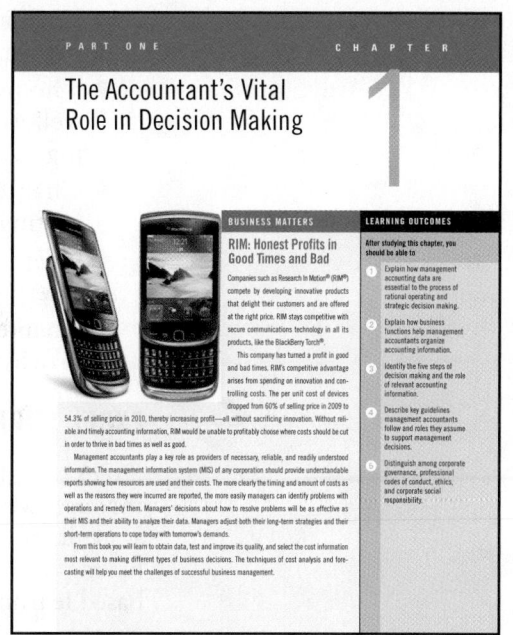

CONCEPTS IN ACTION

These boxes cover real-world cost accounting issues across a variety of industries, including automobile racing, defence contracting, entertainment, manufacturing, and retailing. The sixth edition streamlined these boxes into two types: Strategy and Governance.

Concepts in Action: Strategy   Strategy and good decisions set great managers apart, so these boxes highlight the importance of strategic decision making in real business situations. Students are given a real-world look into how companies use the concepts in the chapter to make decisions for the companies, an important skill as they enter the business world.

Concepts in Action: Governance   These boxes address the recent and increasing emphasis on issues of legal compliance and social justice or corporate social responsibility. Management teams must pursue the corporate mission and adhere to legal and ethical norms. The team must not only remain profitable but also fulfill its social responsibility to contribute to progress and justice. These boxes explore recent examples of behavioural and ethical issues and report on the consequences of good and bad decisions.

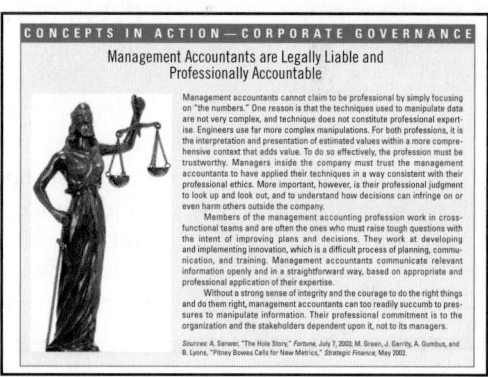

STREAMLINED PRESENTATION

A major thrust of this edition has been to simplify and streamline our presentation of various topics to make it as easy as possible for a student to learn the concepts, tools, and frameworks introduced in different chapters. For example:

◆ Learning Objectives now have a unified presentation to avoid confusion with the colour-coded Value Chain activities.

◆ The fifth edition's various boxed features have been reduced and streamlined into two *Concepts in Action* boxes, as discussed above.

◆ The end-of-chapter assignment material has been simplified and streamlined considerably to allow for further integration with chapter Learning Objectives and MyAccountingLab. Rather than Mastery Questions being separated out with its own gradation, organization, and competency levels, they are now integrated into the exercises and problems. This allows students to be able to work through the assignment material in order.

- In Chapter 2, the flow of revenues and costs for a manufacturing sector company has been improved.
- The procedure to calculate the indirect cost allocation rate in Chapter 4, as well as the accounting entries for a normal job-costing system in manufacturing, has been simplified and clarified.
- Chapter 9 now uses a single comprehensive example to integrate inventory costing and capacity concepts
- Chapter 10 presents how to conduct an Excel linear regression and correctly interpret the statistics.
- Chapters 17 and 18 use a simpler sequence for the five steps in process costing, providing more structure for students to follow

EXCEL SUPPORT

Excel templates for selected end-of-chapter exercises and problems are available through MyAccountingLab (www.myaccountinglab.com). These templates allow students to complete selected exercises and problems using Excel. The focus is on having students use Excel to understand and apply chapter content. This Excel-based learning is completely optional; therefore, students may choose to solve these exercises and problems manually.

The sixth edition also incorporates new material on the use of linear regression and Solver functions readily available in Excel. These programs can be installed within seconds and used to complete higher-level analyses of available data extremely quickly. Now, with the simplification of the arithmetic procedures required to obtain results, the text can provide in more depth an answer to the question, "What does knowing these numbers do for me?" Again, instructors may choose to include or exclude the Excel material without losing continuity because the end-of-chapter questions focus on interpreting the results, not invoking an Excel program.

SELECTED CHAPTER-BY-CHAPTER CONTENT CHANGES

Below is a detailed chapter-level overview of this revision and the changes that have been made.

Chapter 1 introduces a familiar five-step decision-making framework featured in each chapter of the book. It also introduces the necessity of developing a cost accounting system that reports on what actually occurred during a specific time period at the company. This concept of economic plausibility and truth in cost reporting recurs in the text. It reminds students that cost accounting must be truthful if the data are to be reliable and relevant to making important management decisions. The value chain of business functions is colour-coded, and the colours are used consistently in exhibits throughout the text to help visual learners associate material with the appropriate business function.

Chapter 2 has been rewritten to place cost accounting classification in the context of decisions on how to value inventory and cost of goods sold on the financial statements. The flow of costs to match the actual flow of production reminds students that economic plausibility or truth in reporting is central to both managerial and financial reports. The process of valuation is presented in four steps to simplify the content. The chapter exhibits have been completely revised so students can follow all the concepts, steps, and numbers on the exhibits themselves.

Chapter 3 has been reorganized. It starts with an example then relates the specific example to the decision framework. The content emphasizes the importance of predicting outcomes when key data is missing. The method of calculating breakeven revenue using the contribution margin percent is presented alongside the method of calculating breakeven quantities of production. The uncertainty of making predictions is quantified using probability. Sections on alternative fixed cost/variable cost structures, multiple product breakeven analysis, and contribution margin versus gross margin have been significantly revised and shortened.

Chapter 4 concepts are developed within the context of the five-step decision-making process introduced in Chapter 1. This allows for a richer managerial discussion of strategy, risk, and uncertainty. The unequal use and cost of shared indirect resources is a simple motivation for assigning these costs in an economically plausible way if they are to recover the costs in the price of the output. Value-added depends on the customer's willingness to pay. In this way, the strategic value of truthful cost assignment links good management of shared indirect resources to profitability.

Chapter 5 has been simplified, consistent with Chapter 4, to associate the benefits of a refined cost system with value-added from the customer's point of view. The revision associates design of the cost system and clearer identification of what the customer is willing to pay for. Costs of those activities that are non-value-added cannot be recovered in the price and will reduce profit.

Chapter 6 frames the budgeting process as a decision-making activity. Once again the emphasis is on accumulating data that truthfully reflects the economic facts of a company's activities. Issues such as budgetary slack and remuneration based on achievement of budget goals impede the collection and analysis of these data. This adds complexity and uncertainty to predicting the future.

Chapter 7 now includes material on variance analyses of substitutable inputs, Level 4 variance analysis. All techniques of variance analysis now appear in one chapter.

Chapter 8 introduces new exhibits to streamline and simplify the discussion of different levels of variance analysis. The management decision about the fixed capacity used to calculate the fixed overhead rate is linked to the need to reflect the economic fact of what capacity is available. Reflecting economic fact improves the reliability of variance information and the reliability of any management decisions to ignore or remedy an unfavourable production-volume variance.

Chapter 9 integrates the two parts of the chapter on inventory costing and denominator-level capacity concepts using a single comprehensive example.

Chapter 10 has replaced manual methods of calculating statistics with the use of the Excel linear regression program. This refocuses the content on answering the question, "What do these numbers do for me?" The emphasis is on how to interpret the basic statistics to decide on the best cost allocation base in a traditional costing system. The appendix to this chapter explains how other results from Excel are used to calculate the normal range within which a predicted overhead cost will fall. The benefit or value-added is to support management by exception. The analysis of quality improvement benefits through the learning curve has been moved to Chapter 19.

Chapter 11 introduces the use the Excel program Solver to make product mix decisions when capacity is constrained. The alternative to manual linear programming refocuses the discussion from how to calculate to how to interpret results. More realistic product mix problems have been added to the end-of-chapter material, which lets students practise how to solve more realistic profit maximization and cost minimization problems with multiple products and constraints.

Chapter 12 has been revised to place pricing within the context of the decision framework. The importance of gathering competitive information is highlighted and sets the foundation for new material on strategy presented in Chapter 13. Relevant information and decisions about adding or dropping customers has been moved to Chapter 16.

Chapter 13 presents one very widely used strategic framework created by Dr. Michael Porter. The new material makes clearer the need for multiple measures of performance. This motivates the new material on balanced scorecard measurement and enterprise resource planning as improved measures of strategic implementation. Chapter 13 emphasizes interdependence among the uncontrollable threats and opportunities in the external environment and the controllable strengths and weaknesses internal to the company. The revised material on strategy maps associates the strategic identification of core or unique competence with a reasonable plan to implement a cost or value leadership strategy that exploits the core competence.

Chapter 14 contains new exhibits that combine a graphic presentation of each support cost allocation method with the calculations of allocated costs. New material in this revised chapter explains how to use the Excel program Solver to calculate the solution to a reciprocal cost allocation problem. New end-of-chapter material has been added to let students solve more complex and realistic reciprocal cost allocation problems.

Chapter 15 discusses alternative methods of allocating shared production costs in contrast to shared indirect support costs. The decision to adopt a joint cost allocation method is guided by affordability, understandability, and which method best reflects the actual unequal proportion of joint inputs used by each distinct product. Economic plausibility means the allocation method will provide the management team with the most reliable assignment of joint costs upon which to make planning and control decisions.

Chapter 16 has been revised to sharpen its focus on revenue allocation and variance analysis. The related analyses for adding or dropping a customer, formerly in Chapter 12, are now here, and evaluation of customer profitability complete the new chapter content.

In Chapters 17 and 18, the sequence of the five-step procedure for process costing has been slightly revised. The new formats and exhibits are more structured to ease student learning.

Chapter 19 includes new content on the globalization of quality control standards by the International Standards Organization. These ISO standards, which initially applied to production systems, now apply to governance, corporate social responsibility, and financial risk management. Conformance with ISO standards has become a source of competitive advantage. Quality improvement from learning curve effects is now presented in this chapter to emphasize the links between learning and retention and improved profit.

Chapter 20 provides more depth on the discussion of just-in-time supply strategies and backflush costing. Economic plausibility determines how useful backflush costing is when accurate quantities of inputs, costs, scrap, and finished goods data are available in modern management information systems. With fast production cycles, backflush costing reflects best the economic facts of the production process for use in internal management decision making.

Chapters 21 and 22 include new material on the tax treatment of capital gains. The methods used by management teams in their pre- and post-tax consideration of cash flow are placed in the context of the decision framework.

Chapter 23 highlights the importance of management decisions on transfer pricing. The relevance of global tax regimes is emphasized as key to good corporate governance and saving on costs of litigation with tax authorities who must approve of the management teams transfer-price decision.

Chapter 24 has been revised to focus on the increased responsibility of the executives and board of directors for corporate governance. This chapter reviews the most recent legislation in Canada, the United States, and the European Union that intensify the scrutiny of how well the decisions of management teams comply with existing laws.

ASSIGNMENT MATERIAL

The sixth edition continues the widely applauded close connection between text and assignment material forged in previous editions. The end-of-chapter material has been thoroughly revised to reflect optimal support of the Learning Objectives, effective gradation from simple to complex, and an enhanced integration with MyAccountingLab, and above all else accuracy.

- ◆ *Short-Answer Questions* require students to understand basic concepts and the meaning of key terms.
- ◆ *Exercises* are short, structured assignments that test basic issues presented in the chapter. New to this edition is one terminology question per chapter targeting key terms in a fill-in-the-blank format.
- ◆ *Problems* are longer and more difficult assignments. Some problems span multiple chapters and test student comprehension of related issues.
- ◆ *Collaborative Learning Cases* require students to think critically about a particular problem or specific business situation.

Note that the Mastery Questions section from the previous edition has been removed and amalgamated into the sections listed above. This allows for a consecutive flow through the Learning Objectives as well as increasing difficulty throughout the end-of-chapter material. It also allows for a closer integration with MyAccountingLab.

TEACHING AND LEARNING SUPPORT

MyAccountingLab delivers **proven results** in helping individual students succeed. It provides **engaging experiences** that personalize, stimulate, and measure learning for each student. And it comes from a **trusted partner** with educational expertise and an eye on the future.

MyAccountingLab can be used by itself or linked to any learning management system. To learn more about how MyAccountingLab combines proven learning applications with powerful assessment, visit **www.myaccountinglab.com**.

MyAccountingLab

FOR INSTRUCTORS

Instructor's Resource CD-ROM (0-132-88051-2)

◆ *Instructor's Resource Manual* offers helpful classroom suggestions, teaching tips, and handouts, as well as chapter quizzes, text references to applicable assignment material, and writing/discussion exercises. Available in both Word and PDF formats.

◆ *Instructor's Solutions Manual* provides instructors with a complete set of solutions to all the end-of-chapter material in this text. Available in both Word and PDF formats.

◆ *Pearson TestGen*, the test bank for *Cost Accounting*, offers a comprehensive suite of tools for testing and assessment. TestGen allows educators to easily create and distribute tests for their courses, either by printing and distributing through traditional methods or by online delivery. The more than 2,200 items are linked to the Learning Objectives, gradated in difficulty.

◆ *Image Library* Includes the exhibits and illustrations from the text for use by instructors.

◆ *PowerPoint Lecture Slides* have been prepared for each chapter of the text. The interactive presentation offers helpful graphics that illustrate key figures and concepts from the text, chapter outlines, and additional examples. In addition, instructors can custom-create their own using a combination of these supplied slides and the Image Library of exhibits.

FOR STUDENTS

Student Solutions Manual (0-132-88667-7) Designed to enable students to monitor their progress, this supplement contains fully worked-out solutions for all of the even-numbered questions, exercises, and problems in the textbook. This supplement may be purchased with the instructor's permission.

Excel Templates Excel templates for selected end-of-chapter exercises and problems are available through MyAccountingLab (www.myaccountinglab.com). These templates allow students to complete selected exercises and problems using Excel. See page xviii for more information.

ACKNOWLEDGMENTS

Cost Accounting, Sixth Canadian Edition, is the product of a rigorous research process that included multiple reviews at various stages of its development to ensure a revision that meets the needs of Canadian students and instructors. The extensive feedback helped shape this edition into a clearer, more readable, and fully streamlined textbook—in both the chapter content and the assignment material.

We are indebted to those who provided their time, support, and feedback throughout this process:

Gillian Bubb *University of the Fraser Valley*	Karen Matthews *Okanagan College*
Mark Gandey *Bishops University*	Sheila McGillis *Laurentian University*
Connie Hahn *Southern Alberta Institute of Technology*	Mark Morpurgo *Northern Alberta Institute of Technology*
Sepand Jazzi *Kwantlen Polytechnic University*	Barbara Nudd *Okanagan College*
Jennifer Kao *University of Alberta*	Glen Stanger *Douglas College*
Darlene Lowe *Grant MacEwan University*	Helen Vallee *Kwantlen Polytechnic University*
Elin Maher *University of New Brunswick*	

We also want to thank our colleagues who helped us greatly by accuracy checking the text and supplements, including Jake Chazan. A special thank you to Elizabeth Zaleschuk of Douglas College and the following students for contributing valuable review feedback:

Sarah Biletski	Urszula Lipska
Navraj Brar	Matthew Pothecary
Crystine Fernandez	Umida Pulatova
Mario Lara Garzona	Sandhya Shingala
Bethany Hochstein	Colin Yi

We thank the people at Pearson Canada for their hard work and dedication, including Nicole Lukach who put together an awesome team. We extend special thanks to Suzanne Simpson Millar, Queen Bee at Simpson Editorial Services, who was the developmental editor on this edition. Suzanne took charge of this project and directed the project successfully across the finish line. Suzanne accomplished the impossible with grace, expertise, unceasing encouragement, and extraordinary skill. This book would not have been possible without her dedication and diplomacy. Leanne Rancourt and Susan Bindernagel added their substantive and copyediting talents to the quality, consistency, and accuracy of this edition. Avinash Chandra, Leanne Rancourt, and others expertly managed the production aspects of all the manuscript preparation with superb skill and tremendous dedication. We are deeply appreciative of their good spirits, loyalty, and ability to stay calm in the most hectic of times.

Appreciation also goes to the Certified General Accountants Association of Canada, the Society of Management Accountants of Canada, the Financial Executive Institute of America, the American Institute of Certified Public Accountants, the Institute of Management Accountants, and many other publishers and companies for their generous permission to quote from their publications.

We are grateful to the professors who contributed assignment material for this edition. Their names are indicated in parentheses at the start of their specific problems. We are also grateful for the development of Excel program material on Solver provided by Aaron Campbell and on use of Excel matrix commands by David Gowing.

Our task is to serve the learning needs of students and teaching needs of instructors as they surmount the challenge of the impossible—creating, managing, and controlling the profitability of future outcomes. We welcome your comments and suggestions on how to serve you better.

Maureen P. Gowing
Steve Janz

CHARLES T. HORNGREN was the Edmund W. Littlefield Professor of Accounting, Emeritus, at Stanford University. A Graduate of Marquette University, the late Professor Horngren received his MBA from Harvard University and his Ph.D. from the University of Chicago. He is also the recipient of honorary doctorates from Marquette University and DePaul University.

A Certified Public Accountant, Horngren served on the Accounting Principles Board for six years, the Financial Accounting Standards Board Advisory Council for five years, and the Council of the American Institute of Certified Public Accountants for three years. For six years he served as a trustee of the Financial Accounting Foundation, which oversees the Financial Accounting Standards Board and the Government Accounting Standards Board. Horngren is a member of the Accounting Hall of Fame.

A member of the American Accounting Association, Horngren has been its President and its Director of Research. He received its first Outstanding Accounting Educator Award. The California Certified Public Accountants Foundation gave Horngren its Faculty Excellence Award and its Distinguished Professor Award. He is the first person to have received both awards. The American Institute of Certified Public Accountants presented its first Outstanding Educator Award to Horngren. Horngren was named Accountant of the Year, Education, by the national professional accounting fraternity, Beta Alpha Psi.

Professor Horngren was also a member of the Institute of Management Accountants, from whom he received its Distinguished Service Award. He was also a member of the Institutes' Board of Regents, which administers the Certified Management Accountant examinations.

Horngren is the author of other accounting books published by Prentice Hall: *Introduction to Management Accounting*, 13th ed. (2005, with Sundem and Stratton); *Introduction to Financial Accounting*, 9th ed. (2005, with Sundem and Elliott); *Accounting*, 6th ed. (2005, with Harrison and Bamber); and *Financial Accounting*, 6th ed. (2005, with Harrison).

Horngren was the Consulting Editor for the Charles T. Horngren Series in Accounting.

GEORGE FOSTER is the Paul L. and Phyllis Wattis Professor of Management at Stanford University. He graduated with a university medal from the University of Sydney and has a Ph.D. from Stanford University. He has been awarded honorary doctorates from the University of Ghent, Belgium, and from the University of Vaasa, Finland. He has received the Outstanding Educator Award from the American Accounting Association. Foster has received the Distinguished Teaching Award at Stanford University and the Faculty Excellence Award from the California Society of Certified Public Accountants. He has been a Visiting Professor to Mexico for the American Accounting Association. Research awards Foster has received include the Competitive Manuscript Competition Award of the American Accounting Association, the Notable Contribution to Accounting Literature Award of the American Institute of Certified Public Accountants, and the Citation for Meritorious Contribution to Accounting Literature Award of the Australian Society of Accountants.

He is the author of *Financial Statement Analysis*, published by Prentice Hall. He is co-author of *Activity-Based Management Consortium Study* (APQC and CAM-I) and *Marketing, Cost Management and Management Accounting* (CAM-I). He is also co-author of two monographs published by the American Accounting Association—*Security Analyst Multi-Year Earnings Forecasts* and *The Capital Market and Market Microstructure and Capital Market Information Content Research*. Journals publishing his articles include *Abacus*, *The Accounting Review*, *Harvard Business Review*, *Journal of Accounting and Economics*, *Journal of Accounting Research*, *Journal of Cost Management*, *Journal of Management Accounting Research*, *Management Accounting*, and *Review of Accounting Studies*.

Foster works actively with many companies, including Apple, ARCO, BHP, Digital Equipment Corp., Exxon, Frito-Lay Corp., Hewlett-Packard, McDonald's Corp., Octel Communications, PepsiCo, Santa Fe Corp., and Wells Fargo. He also has worked closely with Computer Aided Manufacturing-International (CAM-I) in the development of a framework for modern cost management practices. Foster has presented seminars on new developments in cost accounting in North and South America, Asia, Australia, and Europe.

SRIKANT M. DATAR is the Arthur Lowes Dickinson Professor of Business Administration and Senior Associate Dean at Harvard University. A graduate with distinction from the University of Bombay, he received gold medals upon graduation from the Indian Institute of Management, Ahmedabad, and the Institute of Cost and Works Accountants of India. A Chartered Accountant, he holds two masters degrees and a Ph.D. from Stanford University.

Cited by his students as a dedicated and innovative teacher, Datar received the George Leland Bach Award for Excellence in the Classroom at Carnegie Mellon University and the Distinguished Teaching Award at Stanford University.

Datar has published his research in leading accounting, marketing, and operations management journals, including *The Accounting Review*, *Contemporary Accounting Research*, *Journal of Accounting, Auditing and Finance*, *Journal of Accounting and Economics*, *Journal of Accounting Research*, and *Management Science*. He has also served on the editorial board of several journals and presented his research to corporate executives and academic audiences in North America, South America, Asia, Africa, Australia, and Europe.

Datar is a member of the board of directors of Novartis A.G., ICF International, and KPIT Cummins Infosystems Ltd. and has worked with many organizations, including Apple Computer, AT&T, Boeing, Du Pont, Ford, General Motors, Hewlett-Packard, Kodak, Morgan Stanley, PepsiCo, Stryker, TRW, Visa, and the World Bank. He is a member of the American Accounting Association and the Institute of Management Accountants.

MADHAV V. RAJAN is the Gregor G. Peterson Professor of Accounting and area coordinator for Accounting at the Graduate School of Business, Stanford University. He is also Professor of Law (by courtesy) at Stanford Law School.

Rajan received his undergraduate degree in Commerce from the University of Madras, India, and his MS in Accounting, MBA, and Ph.D. degrees from the Graduate School of Industrial Administration at Carnegie Mellon University. In 1990, his dissertation won the Alexander Henderson Award for Excellence in Economic Theory.

Rajan's primary area of research interest is the economics-based analysis of management accounting issues, especially as they relate to internal control cost allocation, capital budgeting quality management, supply chain, and performance systems in firms. He has published his research in leading accounting and operations management journals including *The Accounting Review*, *Review of Financial Studies*, *Journal of Accounting Research*, and *Management Science*. In 2004, he received the Notable Contribution to Management Accounting Literature award.

Rajan has served as an editor of *The Accounting Review* for the past six years. He is an associate editor for both the Accounting and Operations areas for *Management*

Science, and for the *Journal of Accounting, Auditing and Finance*. He is a member of the Management Accounting section of the American Accounting Association and has twice been a plenary speaker at the AAA Management Accounting Conference.

Rajan has won several teaching awards at Wharton and Stanford, including the David W. Hauck Award, the highest undergraduate teaching honour at Wharton. Rajan teaches in a variety of executive education programs including the Stanford Executive Program, the National Football League for Managers, and the National Basketball Players Association Program.

CHRISTOPHER D. ITTNER is the Ernst & Young Professor of Accounting at The Wharton School of the University of Pennsylvania. A graduate of California State University, Long Beach, he received his MBA from UCLA and a Ph.D. in Business Administration from Harvard University.

Ittner has received a number of teaching awards from Wharton students, and teaches management accounting courses for doctoral students from throughout the United States and Europe.

His research has been published in leading accounting, marketing, and operations management journals, including *The Accounting Review*, *Journal of Accounting and Economics*, *Journal of Accounting Research*, *Management Science*, and *Operation Research*. Awards for his research include the American Accounting Association's Notable Contribution to Management Accounting Literature and Outstanding Dissertation in Management Accounting. He is also co-author of the book *Linking Quality to Profits: Quality-Based Cost Management* (ASQC and IMA). Ittner is an Associate Editor of *Accounting, Organizations and Society* and *Management Science* and serves on the editorial boards of a number of other accounting and operations management journals.

Ittner is a founding board member of the Performance Measurement Association and a member of the American Accounting Association, Institute of Management Science, and Production and Operations Management Society. He has worked with a large number of companies on cost accounting and performance measurement issues, including Capital One, EDS, Ernst & Young, General Motors, and Sunoco.

MAUREEN P. GOWING is an Assistant Professor in the Odette School of Business at the University of Windsor. Prior to being appointed at Odette, she worked as an Assistant Professor at the John Molson School of Business at Concordia University. She received her BA (psychology) from Carleton University, her MBA from the University of Toronto, and her Ph.D. from Queen's University. Gowing received the Award of Excellence from the Administrative Sciences Association of Canada for her doctoral dissertation.

She has co-authored many journal articles and has published in the *Journal of Business Ethics* and the *Canadian Journal of Higher Education*, among others. In addition to co-authoring, with Charles Horngren, George Foster, Srikant Datar, Madhav Rajan, Christopher Ittner, and Steve Janz *Cost Accounting: A Managerial Emphasis*, Sixth Canadian Edition, Gowing has also co-authored an introductory financial accounting textbook with Dr. George Kanaan.

Gowing obtained both her BA and MBA while working full time. She has worked as a financial analyst with an upstream oil exploration and development company that was controlled by Noranda, and a boutique Canadian investment banker, Pemberton Securities Ltd., now part of the Royal Bank. Her research portfolio of companies newly listed on the Toronto Stock Exchange included Westar, Ballard Technologies, and QLT Pharmaceuticals. She has also consulted for Discovery Foundation of British Columbia, and just prior to her return to university to obtain her Ph.D., she did forensic analysis for the Vancouver Stock Exchange.

STEVE JANZ is an Instructor in the School of Business at SAIT Polytechnic in Calgary. Janz received his Bachelor of Commerce from the University of Manitoba, CGA designation from the province of Alberta, and his MBA from Heriot-Watt

University in Scotland. Janz received a teaching excellence award in 2011 from the National Institute for Staff and Organizational Development (NISOD) for his use and implementation of technology within the classroom.

In addition to co-authoring, with Charles Horngren, George Foster, Srikant Datar, Madhav Rajan, Christopher Ittner, and Maureen Gowing, *Cost Accounting: A Managerial Emphasis*, Sixth Canadian Edition, Janz has co-authored the new Business Case 1 case (S&D Developments) for CGA Canada.

Janz has worked as a cost and financial analyst within the property management, education, and airline industries prior to his career as an Instructor at SAIT Polytechnic.

The Accountant's Vital Role in Decision Making

BUSINESS MATTERS

RIM: Honest Profits in Good Times and Bad

Companies such as Research In Motion® (RIM®) compete by developing innovative products that delight their customers and are offered at the right price. RIM stays competitive with secure communications technology in all its products, like the BlackBerry® Torch™ smartphone.

This company has turned a profit in good and bad times. RIM's competitive advantage arises from spending on innovation and controlling costs. The per unit cost of devices dropped from 60% of selling price in 2009 to 54.3% of selling price in 2010, thereby increasing profit—all without sacrificing innovation. Without reliable and timely accounting information, RIM would be unable to profitably choose where costs should be cut in order to thrive in bad times as well as good.

Management accountants play a key role as providers of necessary, reliable, and readily understood information. The management information system (MIS) of any corporation should provide understandable reports showing how resources are used and their costs. The more clearly the timing and amount of costs as well as the reasons they were incurred are reported, the more easily managers can identify problems with operations and remedy them. Managers' decisions about how to resolve problems will be as effective as their MIS and their ability to analyze their data. Managers adjust both their long-term strategies and their short-term operations to cope today with tomorrow's demands.

From this book you will learn to obtain data, test and improve its quality, and select the cost information most relevant to making different types of business decisions. The techniques of cost analysis and forecasting will help you meet the challenges of successful business management.

LEARNING OUTCOMES

After studying this chapter, you should be able to

1. Explain how management accounting data are essential to the process of rational operating and strategic decision making.

2. Explain how business functions help management accountants organize accounting information.

3. Identify the five steps of decision making and the role of relevant accounting information.

4. Describe key guidelines management accountants follow and roles they assume to support management decisions.

5. Distinguish among corporate governance, professional codes of conduct, ethics, and corporate social responsibility.

MANAGEMENT ACCOUNTING DATA: COST ACCOUNTING AND COST MANAGEMENT

Accounting systems take economic events and transactions, such as sales and materials purchases, and process the data into information helpful to managers. Costs and other data are part of **management information systems (MIS)**. An ideal MIS will include databases—sometimes called a data warehouse or infobarn—that consists of small, detailed bits of information that can be used for several purposes. New technologies such as the Cloud enable even small companies to lease affordable, pre-designed, sophisticated, and integrated MIS. Without high-quality, timely, reliable information effective management of costs could not occur. Details about dates, quantities, and cost per unit, reveal the flow of costs as the business activities of a company occur. The MIS database stores information in a way that allows sales, distribution, and production managers to access the information they need. Many companies build their own comprehensive database, called an **enterprise resource planning (ERP) system**. The ERP software integrates data and provides managers with reports that highlight the interdependence of different business activities.

Cost accounting measures and reports financial and nonfinancial information related to the costs of acquiring and using resources. Cost accounting reports show how costs accumulate as corporations use resources to produce and sell their products and services. Costs are recovered when customers purchase products and services.

Cost management includes the activities of identifying, reporting, and analyzing all costs of operations. Management decisions range from the quantity and quality of materials used to whether to shut down an entire company. As part of cost management, managers often deliberately incur additional costs in the short run—for example, in advertising and product modifications—to enhance revenues and profits in the long run. Cost management is an integral part of general management strategies and their implementation. Examples include programs that enhance customer satisfaction and product quality, research and development (R&D), and marketing programs to promote "blockbuster" new products.

Financial accounting focuses on reporting to external parties such as investors, government agencies, banks, and suppliers. The goal is to present fairly to external parties how the business activities during a specific time period affected the economic health of a company. This is called **economic substance**, which is the financial outcome of all the different types of business transactions that happened. Financial accountants report financial outcomes based on generally accepted accounting principles (GAAP) and standards. Reports formatted in a way similar to balance sheets, income statements, and statements of cash flows are common to both management accounting and financial accounting.

Management accounting measures, analyzes, and reports financial and non-financial information to internal managers. The goal is to use past performance to predict the future. The internal reports should plainly inform managers of the financial results of actual operations. The reports should also show how activities can be changed to affect and improve what will happen in the future. **Management accountants** reorganize and analyze financial and non-financial data using rigorous methods. The rigour of management accounting methods is intended to support managers in their efforts to decide on changes that will improve future financial success. The distinction between management accounting and cost accounting is not clear-cut, and we often use these terms interchangeably in the book.

Exhibit 1-1 summarizes the major differences between management accounting and financial accounting. Note, however, that reports such as balance sheets, income statements, and statements of cash flows are common to both management accounting and financial accounting.

OPERATING DECISIONS AND MANAGEMENT ACCOUNTING

Operations refer to the activities that convert various resources into a product or service ready for sale. Procuring and converting resources most efficiently, with a limited amount of money and time, is the economics of conducting business.

	Management Accounting	Financial Accounting
Purpose of information	Help managers make decisions to fulfill an organization's goals	Communicate organization's financial position to investors, banks, regulators, and other outside parties
Primary users	Managers of the organization	External users such as investors, banks, regulators, and suppliers
Focus and emphasis	Future-oriented (budget for 2012 prepared in 2011)	Past-oriented (reports on 2011 performance prepared in 2012)
Rules of measurement and reporting	Internal measures and reports do not have to follow GAAP but are based on cost-benefit analysis	Financial statements must be prepared in accordance with GAAP and be attested to by independent auditors
Time span and type of reports	Varies from hourly information to 15 to 20 years, with financial and nonfinancial reports on products, departments, territories, and strategies	Annual and quarterly financial reports, primarily on the company as a whole, and presented as consolidated financial statements
Behavioural implications	Designed to influence the behaviour of managers and other employees	Primarily reports economic events but also influences behaviour because manager's compensation is often based on reported financial results

Obtaining and converting resources, however, creates costs that cannot be recovered until a sale is made. Customers reimburse the company when they pay for a good or service. Customers may be governments, other businesses, or individuals. For-profit businesses strive to obtain more from customers than the costs the business incurred to obtain and convert resources, thereby making a profit.

Business operations are complex sets of activities, and to maximize profit considerable information, analyses, and decision making is required in advance of actual action. Nevertheless, once a plan is implemented most operations run with little intervention from managers. Operating decisions are needed when exceptions arise, such as supplies of a raw material fail to be delivered, workers go on strike, or machines break down. Decisions are needed when there are real alternatives that managers can choose from to deal with operating problems, which can include the decision to do nothing. The decision, however, is intended to remedy a short-term problem and return business to a routine state. Without high-quality information, business could not be conducted.

STRATEGIC DECISIONS AND MANAGEMENT ACCOUNTING

Strategy specifies how an organization matches its own capabilities with the opportunities in the marketplace and formally communicates how it will compete. One of two strategies is available: either cost leadership or value leadership by means of product (service) differentiation.[1] Companies such as LG generate growth and profits by providing the right combination of generic product features—quality and low price (cost leadership). Companies such as RIM generate growth and profits by offering unique, innovative products or services (value leadership). Customers who believe the features are valuable will pay a higher price for this type of product. Both LG and RIM understand that their customers are willing to spend their scarce resources on products where there is a value-added component—whether that's low price or innovation (or both). Pursuing the most appropriate strategy sustains competitive advantage for each type of company.

[1]Michael Porter (Harvard University) presented strategy as an interplay of internal and external factors. He distinguished the two generic strategies of differentiation and cost leadership.

Innovation in Business Models Requires Innovation in Strategy

E-business meant nothing a decade ago, and it is only through what companies have achieved using Internet capabilities that we now understand what the term means.

Companies such as RIM have been careful to use the web for a variety of business functions, none of which are critical to the company's success. These companies have adopted a strategy of *rational experimentation* to ensure they understand the downside of innovation before taking too much risk.

Other companies have pursued a strategy of *operational excellence*, such as Dell, which uses the Internet to complete almost all of its customer transactions electronically, from order taking through to payment. FedEx is a similar example. Via the web, FedEx gives customers full access to information about where their packages are in transit.

Finally, companies such as eBay, Facebook, and MySpace have used breakthrough strategies and invented services for new and profitable customer groups.

At the other extreme, some companies have used a strategy of new fundamentals to communicate old information via the web to reduce costs. For example, companies put information about employee benefits on their internal websites and post career opportunities on their external websites, reducing human resource and recruiting costs.

Sources: A. Hartman, J. Sifonis, and J. Kador, *Net Ready* (New York: McGraw Hill, 2000); Google Inc., S-1: Registration Statement, April 29, 2004 (Mountain View, CA: Google Inc., 2004); various company financial reports.

Deciding between these strategies is a critical part of what managers do. Management accountants work closely with managers in formulating strategy by providing information and helping them answer questions such as:

◆ Who are our most important customers, and how do we deliver value to them?

◆ What substitute products exist in the marketplace, and how do we attract customers to purchase our product instead of others?

◆ What are we particularly competent at doing? Innovating? Applying technology? Production? Multiple factors such as price, quality, and timely delivery drive the customer's perception of value. How do we decide to create that value in an affordable way?

◆ Will adequate cash be available to fund the strategy? If not, how can we acquire these additional funds?

The best-designed strategies and the best-developed capabilities are of no value unless they are executed well. In the next section, we describe a common framework within which managers take action to create value for their customers and how management accountants help them do it.

VALUE-CHAIN AND SUPPLY-CHAIN ANALYSIS AND KEY SUCCESS FACTORS

2 Explain how business functions help management accountants organize accounting information.

Customers demand more than a low price from companies. They expect a useful, quality product or service delivered in a timely way. These factors influence how customers experience their consumption of a product or service and assess its value-in-use. The more positive their experience, the higher is their perceived value added. Managers decide how best to create this value in an affordable way for the corporation.

VALUE-CHAIN ANALYSIS

Value chain is the sequence of business functions in which customer usefulness is added to products or services. The flow of costs incurred in a corporation can be classified into the value-adding activities of research and development (R&D),

EXHIBIT 1-2
The Value Chain of Business Functions and Costs

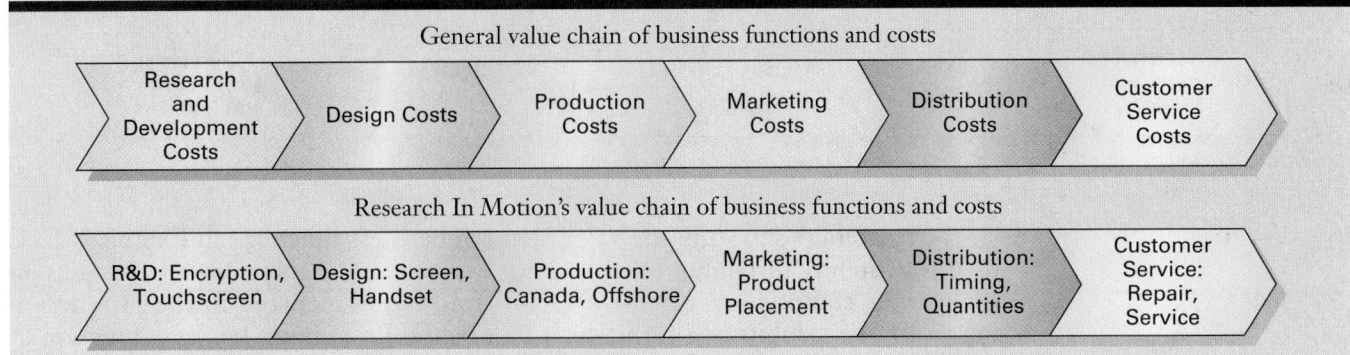

design, production, marketing, distribution, and customer service. From innovation through to verifying customer satisfaction, these costs accumulate and cannot be recovered, plus some reasonable profit, unless customers are willing to pay.

Exhibit 1-2 illustrates these functions using RIM's smartphone division as an example. The business functions are coordinated to make sure that the money being spent on R&D, for example, will provide features of a product that will satisfy customers and for which they will pay. Cost, quality, and the speed with which new products are developed require teamwork among managers across the business functions. For example, it may be worthwhile to increase spending on product design if it saves more on costs related to customer service.

1. **R&D**—Generating and experimenting with ideas related to new products, services, or processes. At RIM, this function includes research on backup systems to ensure reliable access to its communications system.

2. **Design of products, services, or processes**—Detailed planning and engineering of products, services, or processes. Design at RIM includes determining the number of component parts in a smartphone model and the effect of alternative product designs on quality and manufacturing costs.

3. **Production**—Acquiring, coordinating, and assembling resources to produce a product or deliver a service. Production of a RIM smartphone includes the acquisition and assembly of the electronic parts, the handset, and the packaging used for shipping.

4. **Marketing**—Promoting and selling products or services to customers or prospective customers. RIM markets its smartphones through the Internet, trade shows, and advertisements in newspapers and magazines.

5. **Distribution**—Delivering products or services to customers. Distribution systems to deliver RIM smartphones include shipping globally to mobile telecommunications providers, governments, retail outlets, and direct sales via the Internet.

6. **Customer service**—Providing after-sale support to customers. RIM provides customers both telephone and online help to set up and troubleshoot its smartphones.

Each of these business functions is essential to RIM keeping its customers satisfied (and loyal) over time. Companies use the term *customer relationship management (CRM)* to describe a strategy that integrates people and technology in all business functions to enhance relationships with customers, partners, and distributors. CRM initiatives use technology to coordinate all customer-facing activities (such as marketing, sales calls, distribution, and post-sales support) and the design and production activities necessary to get products to customers. The value chain is one way management accountants can track the costs incurred by each business function. One goal is to reduce costs in each category and improve efficiency without impairing value added. Cost information also helps managers make cost-benefit tradeoffs.

EXHIBIT 1-3
Supply Chain for RIM

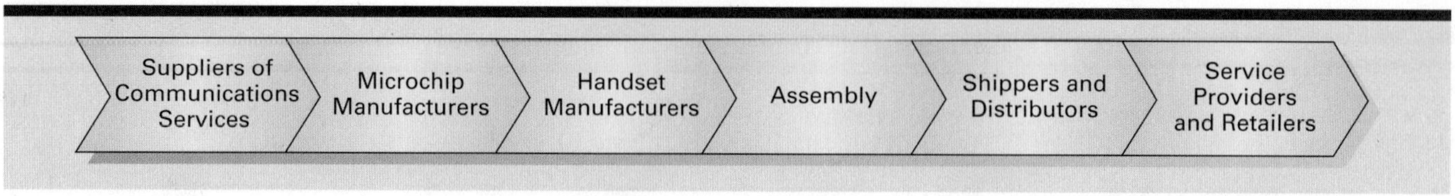

Suppliers of Communications Services	Microchip Manufacturers	Handset Manufacturers	Assembly	Shippers and Distributors	Service Providers and Retailers

The colours shown in the value chain of business functions in Exhibit 1-2 are used consistently throughout the text. For example, in Chapter 2, which focuses on the various components of cost of goods sold (costs incurred in the production function), the exhibits are in the same blue as the Production business function in Exhibit 1-2. The supply chain is an essential part of the Production business function, which is why the elements of this chain are all in blue (see Exhibit 1-3).

SUPPLY-CHAIN ANALYSIS

Supply-chain analysis is one way companies can implement strategy, cut costs, and create value. The term **supply chain** describes the flow of goods, services, and information from their initial sources to the delivery of products and services to consumers, regardless of whether those activities occur in one or more organizations. Consider RIM. Many companies play a role in bringing its smartphone products to consumers. Exhibit 1-3 presents an overview of RIM's supply chain with various global suppliers.

Cost management emphasizes integrating and coordinating activities across all companies in the supply chain, as well as across each business function in an individual company's value chain, to reduce costs. For example, RIM arranges for frequent delivery of small quantities of expensive materials like microchips directly to the production floor of its assembling companies around the world. This strategy reduces materials-handling costs from inventories held inside the factory.

KEY SUCCESS FACTORS (KSF)

Customers continue to demand that companies use the value chain and supply chain to deliver ever-improving levels of performance. **Key success factors** are those activities that are essential to successful corporate performance and include:

◆ **Cost and efficiency**—Companies such as IKEA set a target price and operating profit for a product first. Then, working together, managers and management accountants achieve the target cost by minimizing necessary activities and tasks in all value-chain business functions, from R&D through to customer service.

Increased global competition is placing even more pressure on companies to lower costs. North American and European companies often cut costs by outsourcing some of their business functions. RIM increasingly develops its software in Eastern Europe and India.

◆ **Quality**—Customers expect high levels of quality. Total quality management (TQM) directs attention toward simultaneously improving all operations throughout the value chain to deliver products and services that exceed customer expectations. TQM includes:
  ◆ Designing products or services to meet the needs and wants of customers.
  ◆ Producing products with zero (or minimal) defects and waste.
  ◆ Maintaining low inventories.

◆ **Time**—Every value-chain activity takes time. The increasing pace of technological innovation has led to the need for companies to bring new products out faster because of shorter product life cycles. Customer response time continues to increase in importance. Companies compete to meet or exceed customers' expectations of responsiveness in production, delivery, and after-sales service.

◆ **Innovation**—Constant flows of innovative products in response to customer demand result in ongoing growth and success. Management accountants help managers evaluate alternative investment decisions and R&D decisions.

Management accountants help managers track and compare a company's performance on key success factors relative to their competitors. Tracking what is happening in other companies serves as a benchmark and alerts managers to the changes their own customers are observing and evaluating. The goal is for a company to continuously improve its critical operations—for example, on-time arrival for WestJet, customer access for online auctions at eBay, and cost reduction at Sumitomo Electric. Sometimes more fundamental changes in operations—such as redesigning a manufacturing process to reduce costs—may be necessary.

Strategy requires careful analyses of information and a decision about the most appropriate alternative to assure long-term success. However, successful strategy implementation requires more than value-chain and supply-chain analysis and execution of key success factors. Central to success is a rigorous decision-making process. Managers can use a well-known framework to assist them in improving the quality of their decisions. The framework encourages objective analyses of evidence in a logical and disciplined process.

DECISION MAKING, PLANNING, AND CONTROL: THE FIVE-STEP DECISION-MAKING PROCESS

Identify the five steps of decision making and the role of relevant accounting information. **3**

We will apply and explain the five-step decision-making process using *Best News*, a fictional national newspaper, as an example. The five-step process is a robust and versatile framework within which to decide the best way to address a wide variety of operating and strategic challenges.

A key challenge for Nicole Simpson, the manager of *Best News*, was to increase revenues. To achieve this goal, Nicole worked through the five-step decision-making process.

1. **Identify the problem and uncertainties** Nicole's MIS reported a steady decline in revenue and Nicole, with her team, agreed they must increase revenue without a disproportionate increase in costs.

2. **Obtain information** Decisions cannot be reasonably made without relevant and reliable information to help managers understand the uncertainties. Nicole asked her marketing manager to talk to some representative readers to gauge how they might react to an increase in the newspaper's selling price. She asked her advertising sales manager to talk to current and potential advertisers to get a better understanding of the advertising market. She also reviewed the effect that past price increases had on readership. Ramon Sandoval, the management accountant at *Best News*, provided information about past increases or decreases in advertising rates and the subsequent changes in advertising revenues. He also collected and analyzed information on advertising rates charged by competing media outlets, including other newspapers.

3. **Make predictions about the future** On the basis of the information she obtained, Nicole can improve her predictions about the future. Her analysis of the marketing information indicates that readers would be quite upset if she increased prices. One result would be a significant drop in readership volume, which would make Nicole's problem worse, not better. But in contrast, after analyzing the information on advertising rates, it is clear Nicole would not lose any advertisers nor would the pages of advertising space sold decrease if she increased the rates. Ramon's information indicated a very likely market-wide increase in all media advertising rates. None of Nicole's predictions are certain, but she is confident enough to decide to raise advertising rates, and not subscription prices.

Good decisions require not only good information and good judgment when interpreting any analyses, but also careful reflection about other important non-financial and non-quantitative factors. For example, would readers continue to pay for online analyses of news, or would they prefer free access to facts they could analyze themselves? Was the website the most effective way to deliver the service, or would a new generation of readers prefer a blog or Twitter site?

4. Decide on one of the available alternatives Nicole communicated her decision to the sales department to increase advertising rates to $5,200 per page starting March 1, 2012—a 4% increase.

Steps 1 through 4 can be considered planning. **Planning** is a purposeful analysis of information to select and rank in importance the goals of an organization. Rigorous analyses are how managers make reasonable predictions about the best alternative set of actions to take to achieve goals. Through discussion and analyses, managers can develop ways to effectively communicate goals and the plan of how they will be achieved by coordinated action throughout the entire organization. Management accountants are partners in these planning activities because they can explain and interpret financial information to team members. Together, the team identifies value-added activities that create value and the key success factors.

The most important planning tool is a budget. A **budget** is the quantitative expression of management's proposed plan of action; it is an aid to coordinating what must be done and when to implement a successful plan. Budget preparation crosses business functions and forces coordination and communication throughout the company, as well as with the company's suppliers and customers.

5. Implement the decision, evaluate performance, and learn Managers at *Best News* take actions to implement the March 2012 budget. Management accountants collect information to follow through on how actual performance compares to planned or budgeted performance (also referred to as scorekeeping). The comparison of actual performance to budgeted performance is the control or post-decision role of information.

When exercising control, managers compare actual and targeted nonfinancial measures as well as financial measures and take corrective actions. **Control** comprises taking actions that implement the decision, measuring and evaluating performance, and providing feedback. Without feedback, managers cannot learn how to improve future performance. Having taken action, now managers need high-quality, timely, reliable information about actual results. Without information on the timing and magnitude of resources used, costs incurred, and costs recovered through sales, management is impossible.

Performance measures tell managers if subunits are performing as predicted. Rewards linked to achievement motivate managers, and rewards are both intrinsic (self-satisfaction for a job well done) and extrinsic (salary, bonuses, and promotions). A budget serves as both a control and planning tool since it is a comparison benchmark against actual performance.

Consider performance evaluation at *Best News*. During March 2012, the newspaper sold advertising, issued invoices, and received payments that were all recorded in the accounting system. Exhibit 1-4 shows *Best News'* performance report of advertising revenues for March 2012. This report indicates that 760 pages of advertising (40 pages fewer than the budgeted 800 pages) were sold. The average rate per page was $5,080, compared with the budgeted $5,200 rate, yielding actual advertising revenues of $3,860,800. The actual advertising revenues were $299,200 less than the budgeted $4,160,000. The performance report in Exhibit 1-4 spurs investigation and learning.

The data in this performance report would prompt the management accountant to raise several questions about the implementation of the plan. This is not about laying blame, but rather constructively directing the attention of managers to problems and opportunities. The information does not answer questions but rather raises questions that need answers. Did the marketing and sales department make sufficient efforts to convince advertisers that, even with the new higher rate of $5,200 per page, advertising in *Best News* was a good buy? Why was the actual

EXHIBIT 1-4
Performance Report of Advertising Revenues at *Best News* for March 2012

	Actual Result (1)	Budgeted Amount (2)	Difference: (Actual Result − Budgeted Amount) (3) = (1) − (2)	Difference as a Percentage of Budgeted Amount (4) = (3) ÷ (2)
Advertising pages sold	760 pages	800 pages	40 pages Unfavourable	5.0% Unfavourable
Average rate per page	$5,080	$5,200	$120 Unfavourable	2.3% Unfavourable
Advertising revenues	$3,860,800	$4,160,000	$299,200 Unfavourable	7.2% Unfavourable

average rate per page $5,080 instead of the budgeted rate of $5,200? Did economic conditions change and some competitors not raise rates? Did some sales representatives offer discounted rates? Are revenues falling because editorial and production standards have declined? Answers to these questions should prompt Nicole to take appropriate actions, such as changing her assumptions and predictions, altering the discount policy, or improving content. Good implementation requires the marketing, editorial, and production departments to coordinate their actions.

The management accountant could go further by identifying the specific advertisers that cut back or stopped advertising after the rate increase went into effect. Managers could then decide when and how sales representatives should follow up with these advertisers.

Learning arises from comparing actual performance (the control function) to expected performance (the planning function). The purpose for managers is to systematically explore how to make better-informed predictions, decisions, and plans in the future. Learning will lead to appropriate changes in goals, the ways decision alternatives are identified, and the range of information collected when making predictions—and occasionally, changes in managers.

The left side of Exhibit 1-5 provides an overview of the decision-making processes at *Best News*. The right side of the exhibit highlights how the management accounting system aids in decision making.

EXHIBIT 1-5
How Accounting Aids Decision Making, Planning, and Control at *Best News*

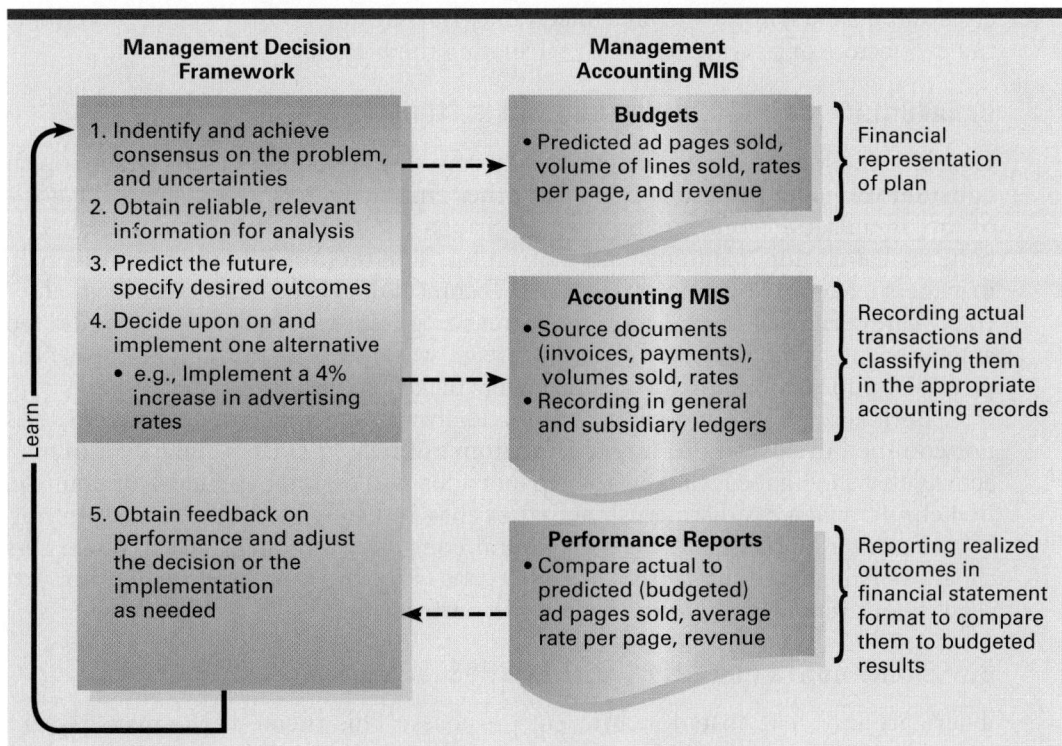

High-quality, reliable information is the foundation of management. Management accountants provide both financial and nonfinancial information to help managers implement strategy and improve operations. Action plans often include targets for market share, quality, new-product development, and employee satisfaction, but managers understand that plans must be flexible because the future and outcomes are always uncertain. Unforeseeable outcomes often arise, and flexibility ensures that managers can seize unforeseen opportunities and remedy unforeseen threats to success. The plan is not a guarantee of any outcome. For *Best News*, when an opportunity to cover a sensational news story not encompassed by the plan requires spending more with a high potential gain in sales, then the managers need flexibility to make the decision and take new action.

KEY MANAGEMENT ACCOUNTING GUIDELINES AND ORGANIZATION STRUCTURE

④ Describe key guidelines management accountants follow and roles they assume to support management decisions.

Three guidelines help management accountants provide the most value to their companies in strategic and operational decision making:

◆ Use a cost-benefit approach.
◆ Recognize both behavioural and technical considerations.
◆ Use different costs for different purposes.

COST-BENEFIT APPROACH

The **cost-benefit approach** (risk/return, downside risk/upside potential) is used to make resource allocations such that the expected benefits exceed the expected costs. The cost-benefit approach should be used to make resource-allocation decisions, such as whether to purchase a new software package or hire a new employee. This approach requires explicit comparisons of the financial costs and benefits of different alternatives. Often good ideas provide too little **upside potential** or benefit for the predicted costs that will be incurred. At other times the upside potential may be quite high, but the **downside risk** of failure is also quite high. When forecasting costs and benefits, managers take uncertainty into consideration when they combine the two factors of risk and return in calculating the benefits.

BEHAVOURIAL AND TECHNICAL CONSIDERATIONS

Consider the human (or behavioural) side of why budgeting is used. **Behavioural considerations** motivate managers and other employees to try to achieve the goals of the organization. Budgets improve decisions within an organization because of better collaboration, planning, and motivation. The **technical considerations** help managers make wise economic decisions. Technical data (e.g., costs in various value-chain categories) in an appropriate format (e.g., actual results versus budgeted amounts) and at the preferred frequency (e.g., weekly versus monthly) improve the quality of information upon which managers make decisions.

Both accountants and managers should always remember that management is not confined exclusively to technical matters. Management is primarily a human activity that should focus on how to help individuals do their jobs better—for example, by helping managers distinguish activities that add value from those that do not. When workers underperform, behavioural considerations suggest that managers should personally discuss with workers ways to improve performance and not just send them a report highlighting their underperformance.

DIFFERENT COSTS FOR DIFFERENT PURPOSES

There are different costs for different purposes. This theme is the management accountant's version of the "one size does *not* fit all" notion. A cost concept used for external reporting may not be appropriate for internal, routine reporting to managers.

Consider the advertising costs associated with RIM's launch of a major new product, the BlackBerry® PlayBook™ tablet. The product is expected to have a useful life of two years or more. For external reporting to shareholders, television advertising costs for this product are fully expensed in the income statement in the year they are incurred. This is required by GAAP for external reporting. In contrast, for internal purposes of evaluating management performance, the television advertising costs could be capitalized and then amortized or written off as expenses over the product's life cycle. RIM could capitalize these advertising costs if it believes doing so results in a more accurate and fairer measure of the performance of the managers who launched the new product.

ORGANIZATION STRUCTURE AND THE MANAGEMENT ACCOUNTANT

Most organizations distinguish between line and staff management. **Line management** is directly responsible for completing routine tasks that attain operating goals. These are the core activities that produce the good or service ready for sale. Line managers' goals can include achieving a specified amount of operating income plus targets for product (service) quality, safety, and legal compliance.

Staff management, including management accountants, human resources managers, and information technology staff, provide advice and assistance to line management. Organizations deploy teams that include both line and staff management so that all inputs into a decision are available simultaneously. As a result, the traditional distinctions between line and staff have become less clear-cut than they were a decade ago.

The Chief Financial Officer (CFO)   The **chief financial officer (CFO)**—also called the finance director—is the senior officer empowered to oversee the financial operations of an organization. In Canada the CFO is legally and personally responsible for the quality of financial information publicly reported. Responsibilities encompass the following five areas:

◆ **Controllership**—includes providing legal assurance of a high-quality internal control system. Controllers of companies with shares listed on a stock exchange are legally responsible for the design of this system to ensure that bribery, fraud, malfeasance, and misappropriation of assets are reasonably unlikely. This legal accountability is one way to be confident that high-quality financial information is provided in the internal reports to managers and external reports to investors.

◆ **Audit**—ensures internal and external audits are conducted as per the direction of the audit committee.

◆ **Treasury**—includes short- and long-term financing and investments, banking, cash management, foreign exchange, and derivatives management.

◆ **Taxation**—includes reporting and managing income taxes, sales taxes, and domestic and international tax planning.

◆ **Risk management**—includes analysis, evaluation, and minimization of external risks over which management has no control and internal risks over which management has control.

◆ **Investor relations**—includes responding to and interacting with shareholders.

The **controller** is responsible for the quality of the information supplied from the accounting department. The controller's line authority extends only over his or her own department. But controllers, through their professional expertise and experience, exercise a broader scope of corporate control. They produce reports and analyses of relevant data that influence and impel management toward improving each step of their decision making.

CORPORATE GOVERNANCE, ETHICS, AND CORPORATE SOCIAL RESPONSIBILITY

5 Distinguish among corporate governance, professional codes of conduct, ethics, and corporate social responsibility.

At no time has the focus on corporate governance, professional conduct, and ethical behaviour been sharper than it is today. Corporate scandals at Nortel, Livent, and Hollinger Inc. have seriously eroded the public's confidence in corporate honesty and fair dealing. **Corporate governance** comprises activities undertaken both to ensure legal compliance and that accountants fulfill their fiduciary responsibilities. Professional codes of conduct are not laws but publicly declare additional rules that members must comply with if they are to remain members. **Ethics** comprise agreed upon standards of honesty and fairness that apply to everyone in all their dealings with one another. Corporate social responsibility (CSR) is the integration of social and environmental with financial stewardship in the conduct of business.

CORPORATE GOVERNANCE

Exhibit 1-6 shows a legally compliant, generic corporate governance structure for a corporation listed on a stock exchange. The **Board of Directors (BOD)** is the independent group of external experts responsible for holding the external auditors, the **Chief Executive Officer (CEO)**, CFO, and **Chief Operating Officer (COO)** accountable for the quality of financial information and organizational outcomes. Legislation now permits people injured as a result of poor corporate governance to conduct lawsuits against alleged perpetrators, which includes not only the corporation but also these individuals personally.

EXHIBIT 1-6
Legal Corporate Governance and Accountability Structure

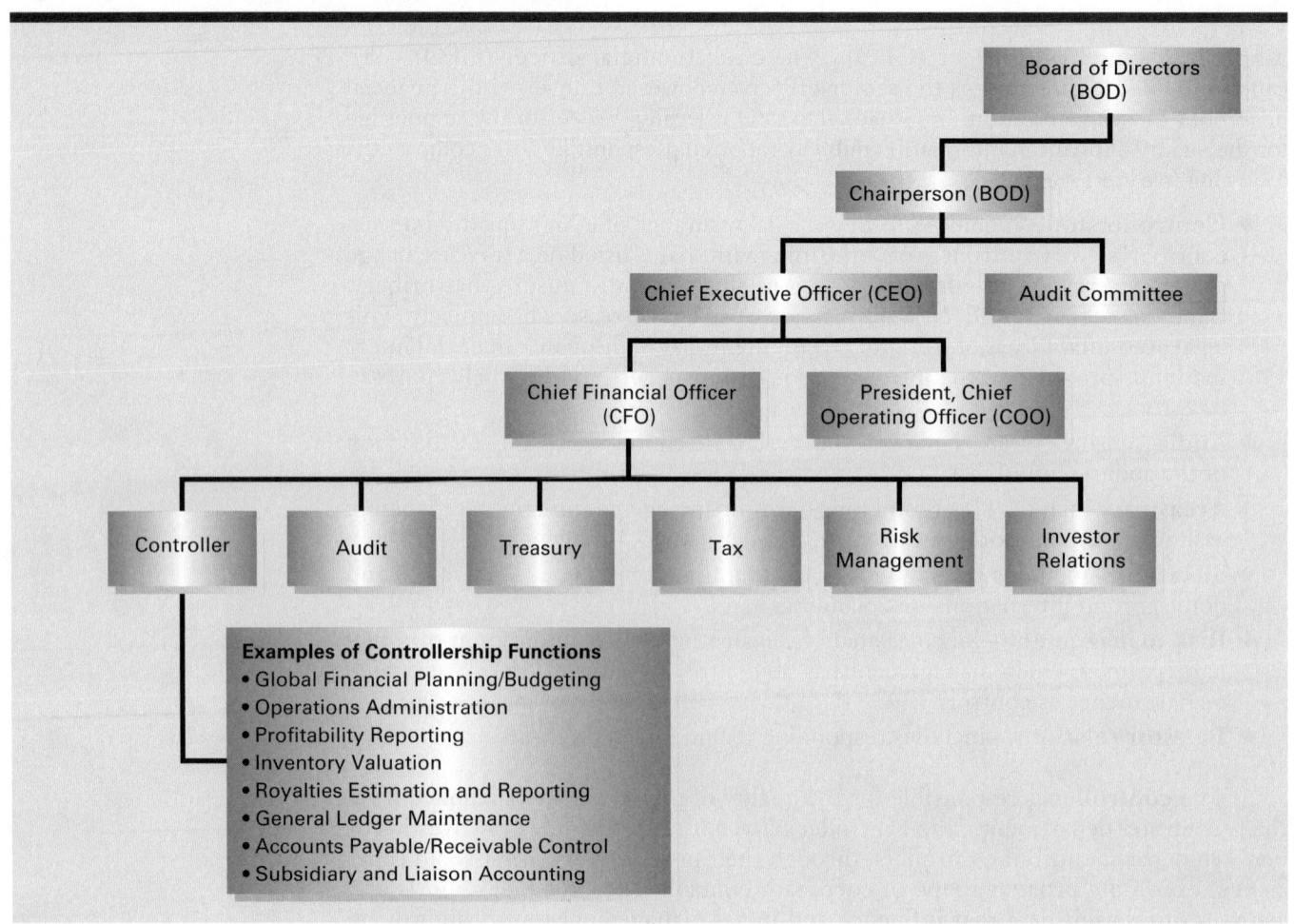

Examples of Controllership Functions
- Global Financial Planning/Budgeting
- Operations Administration
- Profitability Reporting
- Inventory Valuation
- Royalties Estimation and Reporting
- General Ledger Maintenance
- Accounts Payable/Receivable Control
- Subsidiary and Liaison Accounting

Management Accountants Are Legally Liable and Professionally Accountable

Management accountants cannot claim to be professional by simply focusing on "the numbers." One reason is that the techniques used to analyze data are not very complex, and technique does not constitute professional expertise. Engineers use far more complex dynamic models in analyses. For both professions, it is the interpretation and presentation of estimated values within a more comprehensive context that adds value. To do so effectively, the profession must be trustworthy. Managers inside the company must trust the management accountants to have applied their techniques in a way consistent with their professional ethics. More value arises from their professional judgment to look up and look out, and to plainly convey how decisions can infringe on or even harm others outside the company.

Members of the management accounting profession work in cross-functional teams and are often the ones who must raise tough questions with the intent of improving plans and decisions. They work at developing and implementing innovation, which is a difficult process of planning, communication, and training. Accountants communicate relevant information openly and in a straightforward way, based on appropriate and professional application of their expertise.

Without a strong sense of integrity and the courage to do the right things and do them right, accountants may succumb to pressures to reduce the quality of their information. The profession's commitment is to society, the employer, and the stakeholders dependent upon the profession, not to managers.

Sources: A. Serwer, "The Hole Story," *Fortune,* July 7, 2003; M. Green, J. Garrity, A. Gumbus, and B. Lyons, "Pitney Bowes Calls for New Metrics," *Strategic Finance,* May 2002.

The BOD is led by a chairperson, and its members must be independent from the CEO, COO, and CFO to assure no conflict of interest. The CEO is legally accountable to the board. The COO is accountable to the CEO for all operating results. In addition to these formal relationships, informal relationships also exist among people throughout the organization. Examples include friendships (professional or personal) among managers and the personal preferences of senior managers for the type of managers they choose to rely on in decision making.

Provincial, federal, and international laws that apply to all dimensions of business conduct comprise the body of laws that define corporate governance. For example, the Canadian Securities Administrators (CSA) generate provincial laws known as Multi-Lateral Instruments (MI) and federal laws known as National Instruments (NI). These laws govern publicly listed companies, their BOD, CEO, and CFO. Along with legal responsibilities specific to people in these roles come penalties for illegal activities.

For example, National Instrument 52-109 (NI 52-109) places full responsibility on the CEO and CFO for the quality and integrity of all voluntary and mandatory financial disclosure. NI and MI impose a higher threshold of legal compliance on both management and financial accountants, which includes most CFOs. Other CSA laws specify the composition of the BOD, its level of competence, span of control, the professional status of external auditors, and so on. Provincial and federal laws provide for both individual and class action lawsuits against corporations by aggrieved parties. As stewards of other people's wealth, accountants have special legal, professional, and ethical obligations. Recent legislation extends liability for individual wrongdoing within a corporation to include personal and unlimited liability for convicted parties, in particular for accountants.

PROFESSIONAL CODES OF CONDUCT

The profession of accounting is self-governing, which means it sets standards of practice and behaviour and enforces these standards internally to assure the public of its integrity. **Professional codes of conduct** specify how a profession must behave in professional practice. Codes are developed and enforced by licensing and certification bodies such as the **Society of Management Accountants of Canada (SMAC)**, the **Canadian Institute of Chartered Accountants (CICA)**, and the **Certified General Accountants (CGA)**, which post the codes on their websites. These professional codes, however, do not grant accountants an exemption from ethics, laws, and regulations. In fact, the professional codes subject accountants to an added layer of stringent scrutiny and accountability. Non-compliance can result in fines, a temporary or permanent loss of license to practice, and public censure. Both the professional codes and corporate governance laws require mandatory compliance, and equivalent legislation and professional codes exist worldwide.

For example, the Regulated Accounting Profession Act of Alberta lists 10 dimensions of unprofessional conduct.[2] Just a few examples of what is considered unprofessional are listed below:

- ◆ Conduct that is detrimental to the best interests of the public or harms the integrity of the accounting profession.
- ◆ Conduct that contravenes this Act, the regulations, or the bylaws.
- ◆ Conduct that displays a lack of competence.
- ◆ Failure or refusal to co-operate in a practice review.

Further protection for the public is assured by provincial legislation that limits self-governance and sets out governance criteria. These require, among other things, that members formally provide evidence they have updated their skills and knowledge to retain professional competence. Provinces can prosecute professional bodies should they fail to ensure that their members are complying.

ETHICAL GUIDELINES

Professional accounting organizations such as the SMAC promote high ethical standards, and exist in many countries around the world. Appendix B discusses professional organizations in Canada, the United States, Australia, Japan, and the United Kingdom. Some issue ethical guidelines to help their members reason through appropriate responses to ethical issues.

Professions are distinguished by specific characteristics, and understanding these characteristics helps explain why professional ethics are so important. These characteristics include (but are not limited to):

- ◆ A mastery of specific skills, techniques, and knowledge acquired by education and training.
- ◆ An acceptance of a duty to exceed, not just meet, the standards set by the professional accounting associations.
- ◆ An independent, objective, neutral perspective.
- ◆ A high standard in private and professional conduct.

Members of professions provide medical, legal, financial, or other services, not products. The public cannot assess either professional competence or conduct because the public lacks that specific training and knowledge. This is what sends the public to a professional in the first place, but is also what leaves the public vulnerable to misuse of professional knowledge. Expertise explains why members of a profession set and enforce their own standards and codes. Professions publicize both the enforcement process and its results to the public.

[2]Province of Alberta, Regulated Accounting Profession Act, Chapter R-12, section 91(1). 2010.

For example, SMAC is the largest association of management accountants in Canada, and provides programs leading to the **Certified Management Accountant (CMA)** certificate as well as assuring CMA competence. All graduates must be competent in their knowledge of the Professional Misconduct and Code of Professional Ethics. Exhibit 1-7 provides excerpts from the Certified Management Accountants of Ontario's Code, which not only refers to ethical practice, but also to ethical character and general behaviour.

EXHIBIT 1-7
Excerpts from the CMA of Ontario's "Professional Misconduct and Code of Professional Ethics"

All Members, Students, Firms, Public Accounting Firms and Professional Corporations will adhere to the following Code of Professional Ethics of CMA Ontario:

3.1 A Member, Student, Firm, Public Accounting Firm or Professional Corporation will act at all times with:
 (a) responsibility for and fidelity to public needs;
 (b) fairness and loyalty to such Member's, Student's, Firm's, Public Accounting Firm's or Professional Corporation's associates, clients and employers; and
 (c) competence through devotion to high ideals of personal honour and professional integrity.

3.2 A Member, Student, Firm, Public Accounting Firm or Professional Corporation will:
 (a) maintain at all times independence of thought and action;
 (b) not express an opinion on financial reports or statements without first assessing her, his or its relationship with her, his or its client to determine whether such Member, Student, Firm, Public Accounting Firm or Professional Corporation might expect her, his or its opinion to be considered independent, objective and unbiased by one who has knowledge of all the facts; and
 (c) when preparing financial reports or statements or expressing an opinion on financial reports or statements, disclose all material facts known to such Member, Student, Firm, Public Accounting Firm or Professional Corporation in order not to make such financial reports or statements misleading, acquire sufficient information to warrant an expression of opinion and report all material misstatements or departures from generally accepted accounting principles; and
 (d) comply with the requirements of the CMA Ontario Independence Regulation for Assurance, Audit and Review Engagements.

3.3 A Member, Student, Firm, Public Accounting Firm or Professional Corporation will:
 (a) not disclose or use any confidential information concerning the affairs of such Member's, Student's, Firm's, Public Accounting Firm's or Professional Corporation's employer or client unless authorized to do so or except when such information is required to be disclosed in the course of any defence of himself, herself or itself or any associate or employee in any lawsuit or other legal proceeding or against alleged professional misconduct by order of lawful authority of the Board or any Committee of CMA Ontario in the proper exercise of their duties but only to the extent necessary for such purpose and only as permitted by law;
 (b) obtain, at the outset of an engagement, written agreement from any party or parties to whom work is contracted not to disclose or use any confidential information concerning the affairs of such Member's, Student's, Firm's, Public Accounting Firm's or Professional Corporation's employer or client unless authorized to do so or except when such information is required to be disclosed in the course of any defence of himself, herself or itself or any associate or employee in any lawsuit or other legal proceeding but only to the extent necessary for such purpose and only as permitted by law;
 (c) inform his, her or its employer or client of any business connections or interests of which such Member's, Student's, Firm's, Public Accounting Firm's or Professional Corporation's employer or client would reasonably expect to be informed;
 (d) not, in the course of exercising his or her duties on behalf of such Member's, Student's, Firm's, Public Accounting Firm's or Professional Corporation's employer or client, hold, receive, bargain for or acquire any fee, remuneration or benefit without such employer's or client's knowledge and consent; and
 (e) take all reasonable steps, in arranging any engagement as a consultant, to establish a clear understanding of the scope and objectives of the work before it is commenced and will furnish the client with an estimate of cost, preferably before the engagement is commenced, but in any event as soon as possible thereafter.

(Continued)

EXHIBIT 1-7 *(continued)*

3.4 A Member, Student, Firm, Public Accounting Firm or Professional Corporation will:

(a) conduct himself, herself or itself toward Members, Students, Firms, Public Accounting Firms and Professional Corporations with courtesy and good faith;

(b) not commit an act discreditable to the profession;

(c) not engage in or counsel any business or occupation which, in the opinion of CMA Ontario, is incompatible with the professional ethics of a management accountant;

(d) not accept any engagement to review the work of a Member, Student, Firm, Public Accounting Firm or Professional Corporation for the same employer except with the knowledge of that Member, Student, Firm, Public Accounting Firm or Professional Corporation, or except where the connection of that Member, Student, Firm, Public Accounting Firm or Professional Corporation with the work has been terminated, unless the Member, Student, Firm, Public Accounting Firm or Professional Corporation reviews the work of others as a normal part of his or her responsibilities;

(e) not attempt to gain an advantage over Members, Students, Firms, Public Accounting Firms and Professional Corporations by paying or accepting a commission in securing management accounting or public accounting work;

(f) uphold the principle of adequate compensation for management accounting and public accounting work; and

(g) not act maliciously or in any other way which may adversely reflect on the public or professional reputation or business of a Member, Student, Firm, Public Accounting Firm or Professional Corporation.

3.5 A Member, Student, Firm, Public Accounting Firm or Professional Corporation will:

(a) at all times maintain the standards of competence expressed by the Board from time to time;

(b) disseminate the knowledge upon which the profession of management accounting is based to others within the profession and generally promote the advancement of the profession;

(c) undertake only such work as he, she or it is competent to perform by virtue of his, her or its training and experience and will, where it would be in the best interests of an employer or client, engage, or advise the employer or client to engage, other specialists;

(d) expose before the proper tribunals of CMA Ontario any incompetent, unethical, illegal or unfair conduct or practice of a Member, Student, Firm, Public Accounting Firm or Professional Corporation which involves the reputation, dignity or honour of CMA Ontario; and

(e) endeavour to ensure that a professional partnership, company or individual, with which such Member, Student, Firm, Public Accounting Firm or Professional Corporation is associated as a partner, principal, director, officer, associate or employee, abides by the Code of Professional Ethics and the Rules of Professional Conduct established by CMA Ontario.

Source: Professional Misconduct and Code of Professional Ethics, Certified Management Accountants of Ontario, http://www.cma-ontario.org/index.cfm?ci_id=7406&la_id=1, accessed December 22, 2010, with permission of Certified Management Accountants of Ontario.

Typical Ethical Challenges Ethical issues can confront management accountants in many ways. Here are two examples:

◆ **Case A:** A management accountant knows that reporting a loss for a software division will result in yet another "rightsizing initiative" (a gentler term for "layoffs"). He has concerns about the commercial potential of a software product for which development costs are currently being capitalized as an asset rather than being shown as an expense for internal reporting purposes. The division manager argues that showing development costs as an asset is justified because the new product will generate profits. However, the division manager presents little evidence to support his argument. The last two products from this division have been unsuccessful. The management accountant has many friends in the division and wants to avoid a personal confrontation with the division manager.

◆ **Case B:** A packaging supplier, bidding for a new contract, offers the management accountant of a purchasing company an all-expenses-paid weekend to Edmonton during the Grey Cup. The supplier does not mention the new contract when giving the offer. The accountant is not a personal friend of the supplier. She knows cost issues are critical in approving the new contract and is concerned that the supplier will ask for details about bids by competing packaging companies.

In each case, the management accountant is faced with an ethical dilemma. Case A involves competence, credibility, and integrity, whereas Case B involves confidentiality and integrity.

Ethical issues are not clear-cut. The management accountant in Case A should request that the division manager provide credible evidence that the new product is commercially viable. If the manager does not provide such evidence, expensing development costs in the current period is appropriate.

In Case B the supplier may have no intention of raising issues associated with the bid. But the appearance of a conflict of interest such as this is sufficient for many companies to prohibit employees from accepting "favours" from suppliers. The accountant in Case B should discuss the invitation with her immediate supervisor. If the visit is approved, the supplier should be informed that the invitation has been officially approved subject to her following corporate policy (which includes the confidentiality of information).

Worldwide, professional accounting organizations issue statements about professional ethics. However, small differences exist and it is the responsibility of, for example, a CMA from British Columbia to know the professional code of the jurisdiction in which she or he works. In the United Kingdom, the Chartered Institute of Management Accountants (CIMA) identifies the four principles of competency, confidentiality, integrity, and objectivity. The Institute of Management Accountants of the United States goes further and provides guidance on how to resolve ethical conflict.

CORPORATE SOCIAL RESPONSIBILITY (CSR)

Corporate social responsibility (CSR) is the voluntary integration of social and environmental concerns into business decisions.[3] One example is the proactive development of effective social programs that educate and improve the health, safety, and security of workers. Globally active companies have adopted guidelines to measure and achieve CSR goals on a global level, such as fair trade. Many multinational corporations refuse to do business with suppliers who endanger their workers or families. Consumers refuse to purchase products such as blood diamonds because the proceeds from their sale finance war. Some give away new health products that cure local diseases, while others pay for infrastructure such as roads to improve access for local people to new markets for their work. The overall goal is sustainable management of increasingly scarce or degraded resources.

In for-profit companies, CSR policies are controversial to shareholders in whose financial interests managers are supposed to act first. But recent research indicates that exercising CSR improves profitability, strengthens customer relationships, and increases employee commitment.[4] To fully inform external parties, many companies produce reports for each component of the **triple bottom line**, which includes GAAP-compliant reports of financial results, corporate governance, and CSR. The last two are neither standardized nor audited.

[3]D. Silberhorn and R.C. Warren, "Defining Corporate Social Responsibility," *European Business Review* (2007), 352–372.

[4]M.J. Polonsky and C. Jevons, "Understanding Issue Complexity When Building a Socially Responsible Brand," *Business Ethics: A European Review* (2006), 340–349.

PULLING IT ALL TOGETHER—PROBLEM FOR SELF-STUDY

(Try to solve this problem before examining the solution that follows.)

PROBLEM
The Campbell Soup Company incurs the following costs:
a. Purchase of tomatoes by the canning plant for Campbell's tomato soup products.
b. Materials purchased for redesigning Mr. Christie biscuit containers to make biscuits stay fresh longer.

c. Payment to Bates, the advertising agency for the Healthy Request line of soup products.

d. Salaries of food technologists researching feasibility of a Prego pizza sauce that has zero calories.

e. Payment to Sobeys for shelf space to display Campbell's food products.

f. Cost of a toll-free telephone line used for customer inquiries about possible taste problems with Campbell's soups.

g. Cost of gloves used by line operators on the Swanson Fiesta breakfast food production line.

h. Cost of hand-held computers used by Campbell Soup Company delivery staff serving major supermarket accounts.

REQUIRED

1. Identify two costs incurred most likely as a result of strategic decisions.
2. Classify each cost item (a) to (h) into a component of the value chain shown in Exhibit 1-2 (p. 5).
3. How would the treatment of (c) by a financial accountant differ from that by a management accountant?
4. How could Campbell Soup Company use corporate social responsibility to brand its products?

SOLUTION

1. Costs incurred for materials for redesign in (b) are likely the result of a strategic decision, as are those from (d).
2. The items should be classified as:
   a. Production
   b. Design of products, services, or processes
   c. Marketing
   d. Research and development
   e. Marketing
   f. Customer service
   g. Production
   h. Distribution
3. Advertising is an expense: a cost that financial accountants must record during the period it is incurred. For internal purposes of management evaluation, advertising costs are likely based on a strategic decision and would be capitalized by management accountants producing a performance report.
4. A strategy of corporate social responsibility would link the attributes of a product to the core values of the customers to whom the product is sold. Campbell's could advertise the wholesome method in which raw materials were produced (e.g., chicken for soup) or its use of organic vegetables. The strategy will only be effective, however, if it is true.

SUMMARY POINTS

The following question-and-answer format summarizes the chapter's learning outcomes. Each point presents a key question, and the guidelines are the answer to that question.

LEARNING OUTCOMES

1. What information does cost accounting provide?

GUIDELINES

Cost accounting measures, analyzes, and reports financial and nonfinancial information related to the cost of acquiring or using resources in an organization. Cost accounting provides information for both management and financial accounting. Management accountants contribute to both operating and strategic decisions by providing information about the sources of competitive advantage.

2. How do companies add value?	Companies add value through R&D; design of products, services, or processes; production; marketing; distribution; and customer service. Managers in all business functions of the value chain use management accounting information about the value chain. Customers expect companies to deliver performance through cost, efficiency, quality, timeliness, and innovation.
3. What role does relevant accounting information play in the five steps of decision making?	Planning is undertaken prior to action while control is an evaluation of how well plans have been implemented. Different reports and presentations of the same information are used to identify a problem, gather additional relevant information, predict the future, decide among alternatives, implement the decision, and evaluate results. This information identifies and is used to respond to strategic and operating problems.
4. What guidelines do management accountants use?	Three guidelines that help management accountants increase their value to managers are (a) employ a cost-benefit approach, (b) recognize behavioural as well as technical considerations, and (c) identify different costs for different purposes. Management accounting is an integral part of the controller's function in an organization. In most organizations, the controller reports to the chief financial officer, who is a key member of the top management team.
5. Of what importance for management accountants are corporate governance, codes of conduct, and ethics?	Management accountants must comply with all legislation, civil and criminal. This is a profession that must also comply with well-publicized codes of conduct and ethics. Laws are enforced by the relevant jurisdiction, but professional codes are enforced by the profession itself. Management accountants have ethical responsibilities that are related to competence, confidentiality, integrity, and objectivity.

TERMS TO LEARN

Each chapter will include this section. Like all technical terms, accounting terms have precise meanings. Learn the definitions of new terms when you initially encounter them. The meaning of each of the following terms is given in this chapter and in the Glossary at the end of this book.

behavioural considerations (p. 10)
board of directors (p. 12)
budget (p. 8)
Canadian Institute of Chartered Accountants (CICA) (p. 14)
Certified General Accountants (CGA) (p. 14)
Certified Management Accountant (CMA) (p. 15)
chief executive officer (CEO) (p. 12)
chief financial officer (CFO) (p. 11)
chief operating officer (COO) (p. 12)
control (p. 8)
controller (p. 11)
corporate governance (p. 12)
corporate social responsibility (CSR) (p. 17)
cost accounting (p. 2)

cost-benefit approach (p. 10)
cost management (p. 2)
customer service (p. 5)
design of products, services, or processes (p. 5)
distribution (p. 5)
downside risk (p. 10)
economic substance (p. 2)
enterprise resource planning (ERP) system (p. 2)
ethics (p. 12)
financial accounting (p. 2)
key success factors (p. 6)
learning (p. 9)
line management (p. 11)
management accountants (p. 2)
management accounting (p. 2)

management information system (MIS) (p. 2)
marketing (p. 5)
operations (p. 2)
planning (p. 8)
production (p. 5)
professional codes of conduct (p. 14)
research and development (R&D) (p. 5)
Society of Management Accountants of Canada (SMAC) (p. 14)
staff management (p. 11)
strategy (p. 3)
supply chain (p. 6)
technical considerations (p. 10)
triple bottom line (p. 17)
upside potential (p. 10)
value chain (p. 4)

SHORT-ANSWER QUESTIONS

1-1   How does management accounting differ from financial accounting?

1-2   "Management accounting should not fit the straitjacket of financial accounting." Explain and give an example.

1-3   How can management accountants help formulate strategy?

1-4   Describe the business functions in the value chain.

1-5   Explain the term *supply chain* and its importance to cost management.

1-6   "Management accounting deals only with costs." Do you agree?

1-7   How can management accountants help improve quality and achieve timely product deliveries?

1-8   Describe the five-step decision-making process.

1-9   Distinguish planning decisions from control decisions.

1-10 What three guidelines help management accountants provide the most value to managers?

1-11 "Knowledge of technical issues such as computer technology is necessary but not sufficient to becoming a successful accountant." Do you agree? Why?

1-12 As a new controller, reply to this comment by a plant manager: "As I see it, our accountants may be needed to keep records for shareholders and Canada Revenue Agency—but I don't want them sticking their noses in my day-to-day operations. I do the best I know how. No pencil-pushing bean counter knows enough about my responsibilities to be of any use to me."

1-13 What steps should a management accountant take if established written policies provide insufficient guidance on how to handle an ethical conflict?

EXERCISES

1-14 **Terminology.** A number of terms are listed below:

timely	management accounting
ethical guidelines	cost-benefit
technical	control
value chain	reliable
corporate social responsibility	strategy

REQUIRED

Select the terms from the above list to complete the following sentences.

1. Management of activities, businesses, or functional areas, which managers oversee and co-ordinate within the organization, require _____ and _____ information.
2. The _____ considerations help managers make wise economic decisions by providing them with the desired information in an appropriate format and at the preferred frequency.
3. _____ comprises taking actions that implement the planning decisions, deciding how to evaluate performance, and providing feedback to learn how to improve future decisions.
4. Many professional accounting organizations issue _____ to help their members reason through an appropriate response to an ethical issue.
5. _____ measures, analyzes, and reports financial and nonfinancial information to internal managers who use it to choose, communicate, and implement strategy and operational changes.

6. The _____ approach should be used to make resource-allocation decisions. Resources should be spent if the expected benefits to the company exceed the expected costs.

7. _____ specifies how an organization matches its own capabilities with the opportunities in the marketplace to accomplish its objectives.

8. _____ is the sequence of business functions in which customer usefulness is added to products or services.

9. _____ is the voluntary integration by companies of social and environmental concerns into their business operation.

1-15 Cost, management, and financial accounting. Financial accountants use estimates of financial value differently than either cost or management accountants. ①

REQUIRED
1. Identify two differences in use.
2. Identify a similarity among accountants.

1-16 Strategy. Strategy usually includes some formal processes. ①

REQUIRED
1. How can managers choose between different strategies?
2. How is strategy different from an operating decision?

1-17 Value chain and classification of costs, fast food restaurant. Burger King, a hamburger fast food restaurant, incurs the following costs: ②

1. Cost of oil for the deep fryer.
2. Wages of the counter help who give customers the food they order.
3. Cost of the costume for the King on the Burger King television commercials.
4. Cost of children's toys given away free with kids' meals.
5. Cost of the posters indicating the special "two cheeseburgers for $2."
6. Costs of frozen onion rings and French fries.
7. Salaries of the food specialists who create new sandwiches for the restaurant chain.
8. Cost of "to-go" bags requested by customers who could not finish their meals in the restaurant.

REQUIRED
Classify each of the cost items (1–8) as one of the business functions of the value chain shown in Exhibit 1-2 (p. 5).

1-18 Value chain and customer expectations. A Canadian biopharmaceutical company incurs the following costs: ②

1. Cost of redesigning blister packs to make drug containers more tamper-proof.
2. Cost of videos sent to doctors to promote sales of a new drug.
3. Cost of a toll-free telephone line used for customer inquiries about usage, side effects of drugs, and so on.
4. Equipment purchased by a scientist to conduct experiments on drugs awaiting approval by the government.
5. Payment to actors in an infomercial to be shown on television promoting Visudyne, a new treatment for age-related progressive blindness.
6. Labour costs of workers in the packaging area of a production facility.
7. Bonus paid to a salesperson for exceeding monthly sales quota.
8. Cost of the Purolator courier services to deliver drugs to hospitals.

REQUIRED
Classify each of the cost items (1–8) as one of the business functions of the value chain shown in Exhibit 1-2 (p. 5).

1-19 Planning and control decisions. Conner Company makes and sells brooms and mops. It takes the following actions, not necessarily in the order given below. ③

REQUIRED
For each action (1–5 below), state whether it is a planning decision or a control decision.
1. Conner asks its marketing team to consider ways to get back market share from its newest competitor, Swiffer.
2. Conner calculates market share after introducing its newest product.
3. Conner compares costs it actually incurred with costs it expected to incur for the production of the new product. ③

4. Conner's design team proposes a new product to compete directly with the Swiffer.

5. Conner estimates the costs it will incur to sell 30,000 units of the new product in the first quarter of the next fiscal year.

1-20 Five-step decision-making role of relevant accounting information. Garnicki Foods makes frozen dinners that it sells through grocery stores. Typical products include turkey dinners, pot roast, fried chicken, and meatloaf. The managers at Garnicki have recently introduced a line of frozen chicken pies. They take the following actions with regard to this decision.

REQUIRED

Classify each action (1–7 below) as a step in the five-step decision-making process (identify the problem and uncertainties; obtain information; make predictions about the future; decide on one of the available alternatives; implement the decision, evaluate performance, and learn). The actions below are not listed in the order they are performed.

1. Garnicki performs a taste test at the local shopping mall to see if consumers like the taste of its proposed new chicken pie product.
2. Garnicki sales managers estimate they will sell more meat pies in their northern sales territory than in their southern sales territory.
3. Garnicki managers discuss the possibility of introducing a new product.
4. Garnicki managers compare actual costs of making chicken pies with their budgeted costs.
5. Costs for making chicken pies are budgeted.
6. Garnicki decides to make chicken pies.
7. The purchasing manager calls a supplier to check the prices of chicken.

1-21 Five-step decision-making process, service firm. Brite Exteriors is a firm that provides house painting services. Robert Brite, the owner, is trying to find new ways to increase revenues. Mr. Brite performs the following actions, not in the order listed.

REQUIRED

Classify each action below according to its step in the five-step decision-making process (identify the problem and uncertainties; obtain information; make predictions about the future; decide on one of the available alternatives; implement the decision, evaluate performance, and learn).

1. Mr. Brite calls Home Depot to ask the price of paint sprayers.
2. Mr. Brite discusses with his employees the possibility of growing revenues of the firm.
3. One of Mr. Brite's project managers suggests that using paint sprayers instead of hand painting will increase productivity and thus revenues.
4. The workers who are not familiar with paint sprayers take more time to finish a job than they did when painting by hand.
5. Mr. Brite compares the expected cost of buying sprayers to the expected cost of hiring more workers who paint by hand, and estimates profits from both alternatives.
6. The project scheduling manager confirms that demand for house painting services has increased.
7. Mr. Brite decides to buy the paint sprayers rather than hire additional painters.

PROBLEMS

1-22 Strategic decisions and management accounting. A series of independent situations in which a firm is about to make a strategic decision follow.

DECISIONS

a. Roger Phones is about to decide whether to launch production and sale of a cell phone with standard features.
b. Computer Magic is trying to decide whether to produce and sell a new home computer software package that includes the ability to interface with a sewing machine and a vacuum cleaner. There is no such software currently on the market.
c. Christina Cosmetics has been asked to provide a "store brand" lip gloss that will be sold at discount retail stores.
d. Marcus Meats is entertaining the idea of developing a special line of gourmet bologna made with sun dried tomatoes, pine nuts, and artichoke hearts.

REQUIRED

1. For each decision, state whether the company is following a low price or a differentiated product strategy.

2. For each decision, discuss what information the management accountant can provide about the source of competitive advantage for these firms.

1-23 **Planning and control decisions.** Softmoc is a shoe retailing company. The majority of its sales are made at its own stores. These stores are often located in shopping malls or in the downtown shopping districts of cities. A small but increasing percentage of sales are made via its Internet shopping division.

The following five reports were recently prepared by the management accounting group at Softmoc:

a. Annual financial statements included in the annual report sent to its shareholders.

b. Weekly report to the vice-president of operations for each Softmoc store—includes revenue, gross margin, and operating costs.

c. Report to insurance company on losses Softmoc suffered at its new Toronto store resulting from a storm.

d. Weekly report to a new supplier on the sales of that supplier's products at both the Softmoc stores and by the Internet division.

e. Study for vice-president of new business development of the expected revenue and expected costs of the Softmoc Internet division selling foot-health products (arch supports, heel inserts, etc.) as well as shoes.

REQUIRED
For each report, identify how a manager would use it to make both a planning decision and a control decision (either at Softmoc or another company).

1-24 **Management accountants' guidelines and roles in a company.** Stephen Bergstrom is the new corporate controller of a multinational company that has just overhauled its organizational structure. The company is now decentralized. Each division is under an operating vice-president who, within wide limits, has responsibility and authority to run the division like a separate company.

Bergstrom has a number of bright staff members. One of them, Bob Garrett, is in charge of a newly created performance analysis staff. Garrett and staff members prepare monthly division performance reports for the company president. These reports are division income statements, showing budgeted performance and actual results, and they are accompanied by detailed written explanations and appraisals of variances. In the past, each of Garrett's staff members was responsible for analyzing one division; each consulted with division line and staff executives and became generally acquainted with the division's operations.

After a few months, Bill Whisler, vice-president in charge of Division C, stormed into the controller's office. The gist of his complaint follows:

"Your staff is trying to take over part of my responsibility. They come in, snoop around, ask hundreds of questions, and take up plenty of our time. It's up to me, not you and your detectives, to analyze and explain my division's performance to central headquarters. If you don't stop trying to grab my responsibility, I'll raise the whole issue with the president."

REQUIRED
1. What events or relationships may have led to Whisler's outburst?
2. As Bergstrom, how would you answer Whisler's contentions?
3. What alternative actions can Bergstrom take to improve future relationships?

1-25 **Professional ethics and end-of-year actions.** Janet Taylor is the new division controller of the snack-foods division of Gourmet Foods. Gourmet Foods has reported a minimum 15% growth in annual earnings for each of the past five years. The snack-foods division has reported annual earnings growth of more than 20% each year in this same period. During the current year, the economy went into a recession. The corporate controller estimates a 10% annual earnings growth rate for Gourmet Foods this year. One month before the December 31 fiscal year-end of the current year, Taylor estimates the snack-foods division will report an annual earnings growth of only 8%. Warren Ryan, the snack-foods division president, is not happy, but he notes that "the end-of-year actions" still need to be taken.

Taylor makes some inquiries and is able to compile the following list of end-of-year actions that were more or less accepted by the previous division controller:

a. Deferring December's routine monthly maintenance on packaging equipment by an independent contractor until January of next year.

b. Extending the close of the current fiscal year beyond December 31 so that some sales of next year are included in the current year.

c. Altering dates of shipping documents of next January's sales to record them as sales in December of the current year.

d. Giving salespeople a double bonus to exceed December sales targets.

e. Deferring the current period's advertising by reducing the number of television spots run in December and running more than planned in January of next year.

f. Deferring the current period's reported advertising costs by having Gourmet Foods' outside advertising agency delay billing December advertisements until January of next year or by having the agency alter invoices to conceal the December date.

g. Persuading carriers to accept merchandise for shipment in December of the current year although they normally would not have done so.

REQUIRED

1. Why might the snack-foods division president want to take these end-of-year actions?

2. The division controller is deeply troubled. Classify each of the end-of-year actions (a–g) as acceptable or unacceptable.

3. What should Taylor do if Ryan suggests that these end-of-year actions are taken in every division of Gourmet Foods and that she will greatly harm the snack-foods division if she does not cooperate and paint the rosiest picture possible of the division's results?

⑤ **1-26 Professional ethics and earnings management.** Harvest Day Corporation is a publishing company that produces trade magazines. The company's shareholders are awaiting the announcement of Harvest Day's earnings for the fiscal year, which ends on December 31. Market analysts have predicted earnings to be around $1.34 per share. The CEO of Harvest Day expects earnings to be only $1.20 per share, and knows this will cause the price of the stock to drop. The CEO suggests the following ideas to various managers to try to increase reported earnings by the end of the fiscal year:

a. Delaying recording of cancelled subscriptions for December until January.

b. Waiting until the new fiscal year to update the software on office computers.

c. Recognizing unearned subscription revenue (cash received in advance for magazines that will be sent in the future) as revenue when received in the current month (just before fiscal year end) instead of booking it as a liability.

d. Delaying recording purchases of office supplies on account until after year end.

e. Booking advertising revenues that relate to January in December.

f. Waiting until after fiscal year-end to do building repairs.

g. Switching from declining balance to straight line depreciation to reduce depreciation expense in the current year.

REQUIRED

1. Why would Harvest Day Corporation's CEO want to "manage" earnings?

2. Which of the items in a–g above are acceptable to Harvest Day's controller? Which are unacceptable?

3. What should the controller do about the CEO's suggestions? What should the controller do if the CEO refuses to change the suggestions?

⑤ **1-27 Professional ethics and corporate governance.** Janet Segato is division controller and Tom Maloney is division manager of the Sports Shoe Company. Segato has line responsibility to Maloney, but she also has staff responsibility to the company controller.

Maloney is under severe pressure to achieve budgeted division income for the year. He has asked Segato to book $240,000 of sales on December 31. The customers' orders are firm, but the shoes are still in the production process. They will be shipped on or about January 4. Maloney said to Segato, "The key event is getting the sales order, not shipping the shoes. You should support me, not obstruct my reaching division goals."

REQUIRED

1. Describe Segato's ethical responsibilities.

2. What should Segato do if Maloney gives her a direct order to book the sales?

⑤ **1-28 Professional ethics and corporate governance.** Jorge Michaels is the Winnipeg-based controller of Mexa Foods, a rapidly growing manufacturer and marketer of Mexican food products. Michaels is currently considering the purchase of a new cost management package for use by each of its six manufacturing plants and its many marketing personnel. Four major competing products are being considered by Michaels.

Horizon 1-2-3 is an aggressive software developer. It views Mexa as a target of opportunity. Every six months Horizon has a three-day users' conference in a Caribbean location. Each conference has substantial time left aside for "rest and recreation." Horizon offers Michaels an all-expenses-paid visit to the upcoming conference in Cancun, Mexico. Michaels accepts the offer, believing that it will be very useful to talk to other users of Horizon software. He is especially looking forward to the visit as he has close relatives in the Cancun area.

Before leaving, Michaels receives a visit from the president of Mexa. She shows him an anonymous letter sent to her. It argues that Horizon is receiving unfair favourable treatment in the Mexa software decision-making process. The letter specifically mentions Michaels's upcoming "all-expenses-paid trip to Cancun during Winnipeg's deep winter." Michaels is deeply offended. He says he has made no decision and believes he is very capable of making a software choice on the merits of each product. Mexa currently does not have a formal written code of ethics.

REQUIRED

1. Do you think Michaels faces an ethical problem regarding his forthcoming visit to the Horizon users' group meeting? Explain.
2. Should Mexa allow executives to attend users' meetings while negotiating with other vendors about a purchase decision? Explain. If yes, what conditions on attending should apply?
3. Would you recommend that Mexa develop its own code of ethics to handle situations such as this one? What are the pros and cons of having such a written code?

COLLABORATIVE LEARNING CASE

1-29 Global company, ethical challenges. In June 2012, the government of Vartan invited bids for the construction of a cellular telephone network. ZenTel, an experienced communications company, was eager to enter the growing field of cellular telephone networks in countries with poor infrastructures for land lines. If ZenTel won a few of these early contracts, it would be sought after for its field experience and expertise. After careful analysis, it prepared a detailed bid for the Communications Ministry of Vartan, building in only half of its usual profit margin and providing a contractual guarantee that the project would be completed in two years or less. The multimillion-dollar bid was submitted before the deadline, and ZenTel received notification that it had reached the Vartan government. Then, despite repeated faxes, emails, and phone calls to the ministry, there was no news on the bids or the project from the Vartan government.

Steve Cheng, VP of Global Operations for ZenTel, contacted the Canadian commercial attaché in Vartan, who told him that his best chance was to go to Vartan and try to meet the deputy minister of communications in person. Cheng prepared thoroughly for the trip, rereading the proposal and making sure that he understood the details.

At the commercial attaché's office in Vartan's capital, Cheng waited nervously for the deputy minister and his assistant. Cheng had come to Vartan with a clear negotiating strategy to try to win the bid. Soon the deputy minister and his staff arrived, introductions were made, and pleasantries were exchanged. The deputy minister asked a few questions about ZenTel and the bid and then excused himself, leaving his assistant to talk to Cheng. After clearly indicating that many other compelling bids had been made by firms from around the world, the assistant said, "Mr. Cheng, I guarantee that ZenTel's bid will be accepted if you pay a $1 million commission. Of course, your excellent proposal doesn't have to be altered in any way." It was clear to Cheng that the "commission" was, in fact, a bribe. Tactfully, he pointed out that Canadian laws and ZenTel's corporate policy prohibited such a payment. The assistant wished him a good day and a pleasant flight home and left.

REQUIRED

1. As a shareholder in ZenTel, would you prefer that ZenTel executives agree to the payment of the "commission"?
2. When Cheng described his experience to his friend Hank Shorn, who managed international business development for another company, Hank said that his own "personal philosophy" was to make such payments if they were typical in the local culture. Do you agree with Hank's point of view? Explain.
3. Why would ZenTel have a corporate policy against such payments?
4. What should Steve Cheng do next?

An Introduction to Cost Terms and Purposes

BUSINESS MATTERS

GM Struggles Under the Weight of Its Fixed Costs[1]

After 75 years of shrinking market share, General Motors Corporation (GMC) finally lost its title as the world's largest automaker to Japan's Toyota Motor Company just prior to the recession of 2007. GMC's profitability has always been affected by its fixed costs (costs that do not change with the number of cars made). To cover these fixed costs, GMC needed to sell far more cars than it actually did sell, before it started to turn any profit. Despite aggressive transfer of manufacturing into China and Eastern Europe, where costs are far lower, and a decade of belt-tightening to reduce costs of direct material and labour, it was too little, too late. GMC declared bankruptcy.

Its name became Motors Liquidation Company and GMC disappeared, along with all its shares. The U.S. government purchased the "new" GM Company's viable assets and hired Mr. E. Whitacre to run its operations. In 2010, GMC had turned around. At the time of writing this text, GM had issued shares, raising $23 billion to repay debt and reduce government ownership to only 33%.

The GMC story tells us that no company can ignore cost behaviour and survive in the long term. If the problem is excessive fixed costs, then reducing variable costs will not succeed as a cost leadership strategy. Managers must use relevant information and understand how costs behave to make sure their strategic response to a changing external environment is effective.

LEARNING OUTCOMES

After studying this chapter, you should be able to

1. Identify and distinguish between two manufacturing cost classification systems: direct and indirect, prime and conversion.

2. Differentiate fixed from variable cost behaviour and explain the relationship of cost behaviour to direct and indirect cost classifications.

3. Interpret unitized fixed costs appropriately when making cost management decisions.

4. Apply cost information to produce a GAAP-compliant income statement showing proper cost of goods sold and a balance sheet showing proper inventory valuation.

5. Explain cost identification, classification, and management systems and their use within the decision framework.

[1]*Sources:* http://www.gm.com/corporate/investor_information/, accessed August 9, 2010; David Welch, "GM's U.S. Blues," *BusinessWeek Online* (March 14, 2007); Sholnn Freeman and Albert B. Crenshaw, "GM to Cut White-Collar Retirement Benefits," *The Washington Post* (March 8, 2006), p. D01; "GM Chief Says Results Will Improve," *Bloomberg News* (January 14, 2006); A. Gary Shilling, "What's Bad for GM," *Forbes* (April 25, 2005); Alex Taylor III, "GM Hits the Skids," *Fortune* (April 4, 2005); David Welch and Kathleen Kerwin, "For GM, Sweet Deals Are Smarter Than They Look," *BusinessWeek Online* (August 26, 2002).

COSTS AND COST TERMINOLOGY

1 Identify and distinguish between two manufacturing cost classification systems: direct and indirect, prime and conversion.

What does the word *cost* mean to you? Is it a cash outflow from your pocket? A sacrifice you made to gain something of value? The loss of something? Is cost something that affects profitability? There are many different types of costs, but this text focuses almost exclusively on costs measured in dollars and cents. At different times, organizations put more or less emphasis on different types of financial costs. Managers require reliable and relevant cost information for products, services, departments, projects (such as upgrading an MIS), activities (such as quality control), training, and business development.

A **cost** is a resource sacrificed or forgone to achieve a specific objective. It is measured as the monetary amount that must be paid to acquire goods or services. An **actual cost** has been incurred in the past (historical). A **budgeted cost** is expected or predicted to occur in the future (forecast).

Answering the question "What does it cost?" requires knowing what "it" is and what problem the cost information will be applied to. "It" is a **cost object**, anything for which a measurement of costs is desired. Next, managers have to decide if the budgeted cost of a cost object or the actual cost or both is desired. Managers often need both when making decisions, since actual or past costs help managers predict future costs in a budget.

A typical cost management information system has two stages: cost accumulation and cost assignment. **Cost accumulation** is the collection (accumulation) of actual cost data in an organized way. Management accountants refer to accumulated costs as **cost pools**. This is not to be confused with what financial accountants collect in general ledger accounts, though on first glance they appear the same. Cost pools can include costs from *different* transactions, whereas costs accumulated in the general ledger are for *similar* transactions only. A cost pool, for example, could include all the material and labour costs for a cost object. At its Spartanburg plant, BMW accumulates actual costs in categories such as raw materials, different types of labour, equipment use, and supervision (see Exhibit 2-1).

Cost assignment systematically links a pool of actual costs to a distinct cost object. For example, managers and management accountants assign accumulated costs to different models of cars (the cost object). BMW managers use this cost information to help them determine the selling price for that particular model of car. They also use the information to motivate and influence employees by rewarding actions they take that reduce costs.

Some costs, such as material costs, are easier to assign to a cost object than others, such as supervision costs. One reason is that some costs pay for resources shared in completing many diverse cost objects. Assigning cost pools common to diverse cost objects is not as easy as assigning a cost pool used exclusively to complete a distinct cost object.

DIRECT COSTS AND INDIRECT COSTS

We now describe how costs are classified as direct or indirect and the methods used to assign these costs to cost objects.

EXHIBIT 2-1
Examples of Distinct Cost Objects at BMW

Cost Object	Illustration
Product	A BMW X5 sports activity vehicle
Service	Telephone hotline providing information and assistance to BMW dealers
Project	R&D project on enhancing the DVD system in BMW cars
Customer	Herb Chambers Motors, a BMW dealer that purchases a broad range of BMW vehicles
Activity	Setting up machines for production or maintaining production equipment
Department	Environmental, Health, and Safety Department

◆ **Direct costs** of a cost object are related to the distinct cost object and can be *traced* to it in a cost-effective way using manual or electronic documentation. For example, the cost of tires can be readily accumulated from invoices, payments, and requisitions from inventory. These documents provide a "paper trail" of costs that can be traced directly to a car model—for example, the BMW X5. The accumulated cost of tires for the BMW X5 is an example of a **direct materials (DM) cost**. BMW can also electronically trace any individual worker's time spent working on the X5 through time sheets. This is an example of a **direct manufacturing labour (DML) cost**. Through its management information system (MIS), BMW can trace sales commission costs for the X5. This is an example of a non-manufacturing **direct labour (DL) cost**. The company can also trace the quantity of machine hours used when a BMW X5 is manufactured, which is an example of **direct machine-hour (DMH) costs**. **Cost tracing** is the method of assigning direct costs to a distinct cost object.

◆ **Indirect costs** of a cost object are necessary but cannot be traced to a specific cost object in a cost-effective way because the benefits from use of the resources is shared among diverse cost objects. The cost of shared resources is common to many cost objects, but often the sharing is unequal. **Cost allocation** is the method used to divide up an indirect cost pool unequally and assign costs to diverse cost objects. Indirect costs may be either manufacturing or non-manufacturing costs.

Typical indirect manufacturing costs are often referred to as **manufacturing overhead (MOH)**. Collectively, these indirect costs can represent a far larger proportion of total production costs than total direct costs, which means a large percentage of total production costs are allocated rather than traced. Materials, such as machine lubricants, maintenance supplies, security systems, and janitorial supplies, provide benefits to all units manufactured, not just one distinct type of output. Some examples of typical MOH costs are

Indirect Materials	Indirect Manufacturing Overhead
Indirect supplies	Security (labour and supplies)
Indirect materials	Custodial (labour and supplies)
	Materials handling (labour, equipment, maintenance)
Indirect Labour	
All labour fringe benefits	Quality control (labour, equipment, supplies)
Rework of output	Maintenance in the plant (labour, supplies)
Overtime	All statutory fringe benefits (CPP, EI)
Idle time	Plant lease or plant amortization
	Equipment lease or equipment amortization
Machine maintenance	Utilities (for security, custodial, quality control, plant, equipment)
Supervisor salaries	Insurance (plant property, equipment, people)
Plant manager salaries	Tax (manufacturing plant, equipment)

Non-manufacturing costs are incurred either before production begins or after production ends. Costs incurred prior to production are often called **upstream costs** and those incurred after production are called **downstream costs**. Because a company can only be profitable if it recovers its full costs, non-manufacturing costs must be either traced or allocated to cost objects. Salaries for engineers who invent and design a new product are an example of an upstream indirect non-manufacturing cost; sales commission is an example of a downstream direct non-manufacturing cost.

To summarize, *cost assignment* is a general term that encompasses both (1) tracing direct costs to a distinct cost object and (2) allocating indirect costs among diverse cost objects. Exhibit 2-2 depicts upstream, production, and downstream direct and indirect costs with both forms of cost assignment: cost tracing and cost allocation. The cost object is one distinct output, the BMW X5. When the outputs are services, the provider will incur service rather than production costs.

EXHIBIT 2-2
Cost Assignment of Upstream, Production, and Downstream Business Function Costs

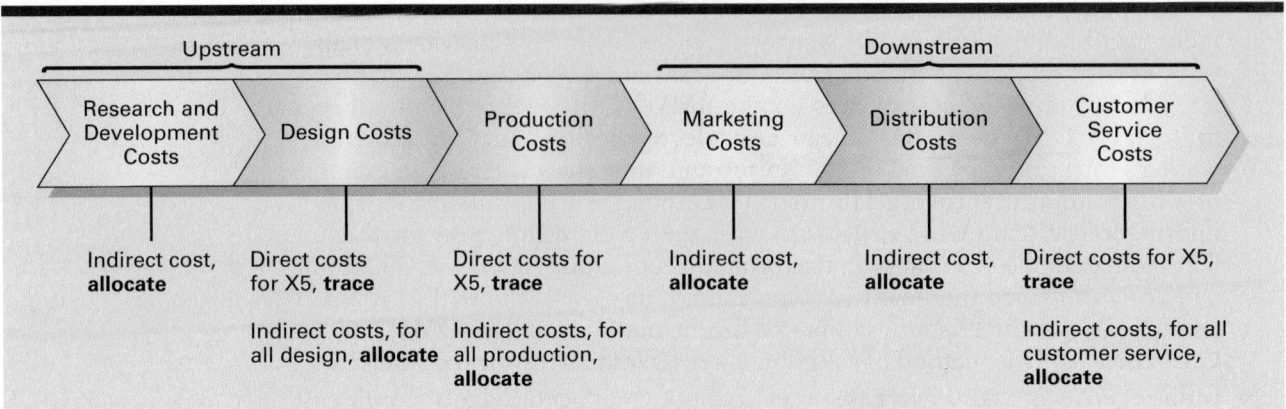

Each company determines how to accumulate, trace, allocate, and assign all its costs. Exhibit 2-2 illustrates *one* possible way to assign direct and indirect costs in the value chain using one model BMW X5 as the distinct cost object. The items listed in each business function would be very different if the cost object was the customer service department, or the activity of developing a special BMW promotion event at the Montreal Grand Prix Formula One Race.

FACTORS AFFECTING DIRECT/INDIRECT COST CLASSIFICATIONS

Distinguishing direct from indirect costs is not straightforward. Situations differ. Balancing several factors that influence cost classification requires professional judgment:

◆ **Selection of the distinct cost object.** Whether a cost pool is classified as direct or indirect will change depending on the cost object. For example, a BMW assembly-line supervisor's salary can be accumulated in the direct cost pool for the assembly department. This is a distinct cost object that benefits exclusively from the costs of the work done by the supervisor. But if the assembly line produces different models of BMW and some models require more attention than others, then the benefits of the assembly line supervisor's salary are shared among the various models. More than one model means the cost objects are diverse. The costs cannot be traced but must be allocated.

◆ **The materiality or significance of the cost in question.** The smaller the cost, the less likely it is economically feasible to trace that cost to a particular cost object. The cost of the colour of dye added to each plastic interior piece in a BMW is insignificant—less than a fraction of $0.01—and it costs more than this to trace the dye cost to a distinct model. It is cost effective to accumulate all costs of dye into one MOH account. Models benefiting significantly more (less) from this common resource will be assigned more (less) cost from the MOH cost pool. For financial accountants, *material* refers to the level of materiality, usually a difference of between 5% and 10% of the total dollar value of the cost pool.

◆ **Available information-gathering technology.** Integrated cost information systems access cost data electronically through bar codes and radio frequency identification. At BMW, component parts such as the different computer chips for its on-board computers are identified and can be scanned at every point in the production process. Software makes this cost data accessible to any authorized user in accounts receivable, R&D, customer service, or production.

◆ **Design of operations.** It's easier to classify and accumulate direct cost pools when one facility is used exclusively for a specific cost object, such as a specific product, model, activity, or customer. For example, GMC had a manufacturing plant dedicated solely to producing its Saturn models; DuPont has separate R&D facilities located in Mississauga, Ontario.

AN EXAMPLE OF COST ASSIGNMENT

Consider the cost to lease the BMW Spartanburg manufacturing plant. The lease is a fixed cost of using the property and building to build different models of cars. The Spartanburg lease will be allocated according to the space used by each model produced in the plant. Allocating costs of shared space would be done the same way in service industries. Instead of different car models, the type of service provided (activity) identifies the cost objects receiving benefits from using the space.

If the lease cost was $500,000 per year and production of the X5 occupied 10% of the space, then $50,000 would be allocated to the X5. This allocated cost for the lease would be added to other direct and indirect costs for the model X5 to ensure the assigned costs were reasonably accurate and recovered when this distinct model was sold. The measure of benefit is called the **cost allocation base**. Management accountants help develop an appropriate measure of benefit that will discover any inequality among distinct cost objects.

Allocating indirect costs for services provided from executive salaries at head office to the X5 is not as obvious because the benefits are intangible. Intangible benefits are extremely difficult to measure. Often the choice is to allocate based on a ratio of the total salary to the total business function activity's cost. The result tells a management team the executive salary dollars spent for every $1 of business function activity cost. This indirect non-manufacturing cost is unequally assigned to each activity.

Managers select cost allocation bases carefully to make sure these choices faithfully represent the value added from each business process. Otherwise, managers can unknowingly decide to increase production of unprofitable products while decreasing production of profitable products. Generally, managers are more confident about accuracy when tracing direct costs, such as the cost of steering wheels for the X5.

PRIME COSTS AND CONVERSION COSTS

Two terms describe cost classifications in the production function of the value chain: *prime costs* and *conversion costs*. Cost classification as prime or conversion requires professional judgment because these are not mutually exclusive categories in all situations. Making simplifying assumptions is helpful to explain the mechanics and benefits of these methods, but the goal of any cost classification system is to faithfully reflect the economic reality of each company in a useful, relevant way. Management accountants provide expert advice on how to select a costing system that best helps managers in their planning, control, and pricing decisions.

Prime costs are defined as direct manufacturing costs (DM, DML) *but* are not always classified according to the definition. If the BMW X5 plant accumulated $240,000 in DM and $260,000 in DML in one month, according to the definition prime costs would total $500,000. However, prime costs are assigned using an **average cost** per input used over a specific time period. The average cost, also called a **unit cost**, is calculated by dividing the total prime cost pool by physical units consumed. Cost assignment splits the prime cost pools between units fully complete and those remaining in work-in-process (WIP) inventory.

$$\text{Prime costs} = \text{Direct material costs} + \text{Direct manufacturing labour costs}$$
$$= \$240,000 + \$260,000 = \$500,000$$

There may also be additional prime costs. For example, if significant power costs are measured in specific areas of a plant and identified with distinct outputs, then prime costs would include direct materials, direct manufacturing labour, and direct metered power. If an assembly line and a plant are dedicated to the exclusive production of the BMW X5, then the depreciation on the plant and production equipment is a direct fixed manufacturing cost of this distinct model. It is readily traced to a distinct output and included in prime costs.

RIM, a computer software company as well as a manufacturer of smartphones and other mobile telecommunications equipment, may have a "purchased technology" cost item. This item includes payments to suppliers who develop software algorithms for one type of product. The cost is readily traced to one smartphone model and is a prime cost of the model.

Conversion costs are all non-prime costs and comprise the indirect MOH cost pool. Conversion costs are incurred during the process of transforming direct materials into outputs, finished goods ready for sale. But the cost classification as MOH is not black and white. If DML is an insignificant cost, then it may be accumulated in the conversion cost pool. In fact, in some costing systems DML can be accounted for in two different ways. The calculation of a conversion cost pool rate is discussed in Chapter 17.

In a two-part production costing system, the only prime cost is DM and all the other costs are classified as contributors to the MOH or conversion cost pool. In a three-part production costing system, DM and DML are separate prime cost pools, and all remaining costs are classified as contributors to the indirect MOH. For purposes of external reporting of cost of goods sold (COGS) and inventory valuation, both systems are GAAP-compliant.[2] For example, in a two-part costing system, if the BMW X5 plant incurred an additional $550,000 monthly in total MOH costs, then total monthly conversion costs would be $810,000 ($260,000 DML + $550,000 total MOH = $810,000).

$$\text{Conversion costs} = \frac{\text{Direct manufacturing}}{\text{labour costs}} + \frac{\text{Manufacturing}}{\text{overhead costs}} = \$260{,}000 + \$550{,}000 = \$810{,}000$$

Of course the *actual* total monthly manufacturing costs for the BMW X5 plant are $1,050,000 no matter how they are classified.

Usually DML is not accounted for in more than one way, but it is straightforward to make end-of-year adjustments for external reporting. The Problem for Self-Study at the end of this chapter illustrates how useful having more than one method to account for DML can be in constructing GAAP compliant valuations of inventory. The problem introduces students to the usefulness of ambiguity in cost classification to solve a practical problem with limited data.

COST-BEHAVIOUR PATTERNS: VARIABLE COSTS AND FIXED COSTS

2 Differentiate fixed from variable cost behaviour and explain the relationship of cost behaviour to direct and indirect cost classifications.

To clarify how costs behave, always focus on total cost and whether or not it changes as the quantity of the input purchased and used changes. Accounting systems record and accumulate costs of inputs acquired to complete business functions in the value chain over a specific time period. Some total costs change with the quantity of inputs purchased and used to complete outputs. These are variable costs. Other costs remain fixed regardless of the quantity of outputs produced within a specified relevant range. These are fixed costs.

VARIABLE COSTS

A **variable cost** (VC) changes in proportion to changes in the related level of total activity or volume within a relevant range, because the cost per unit is constant. **Relevant range** means that either below a minimum or above a maximum quantity the cost per unit of input changes. Many suppliers offer quantity discounts that decrease the variable cost per unit when quantity purchased in a single order exceeds some threshold. You may also hear this referred to as a *strictly* or *proportionately* variable cost.

For example, at the BMW Spartanburg plant, the relevant range is from 1 to 3,000 steering wheels. The steering wheel includes all the windshield wiper and Bluetooth controls, directional signals, and audio-visual controllers. Within this range, each steering wheel installed will cost $15,000 and the total variable cost will equal the variable cost per unit multiplied by the quantity of steering wheels purchased and installed. If the quantity increases 15%, so will the total variable cost. If no steering wheels are damaged during installation, then the total variable

[2]Generally Accepted Accounting Principles (GAAP) guide all financial accounting classifications and reporting to external parties. For Canadian companies listed on a stock exchange, financial disclosure at year-end must be IFRS–GAAP compliant. While standards may differ among countries (the US does not use IFRS), GAAP remain unchanged.

cost of steering wheels is one *part* of the total direct variable cost pool to produce a single X5 each month. It is precisely because the variable cost per steering wheel, column (2) in the table below, is the same for each steering wheel that the total variable cost of steering wheels, column (3), changes proportionately with the number of steering wheels purchased and used to produce X5s.

Number of X5s Produced (1)	Variable Cost per Steering Wheel (2)	Total Variable Cost of Steering Wheels (3) = (1) × (2)
1	$15,000	$ 15,000
1,000	15,000	15,000,000
3,000	15,000	45,000,000

Exhibit 2-3 presents the total of all direct and indirect variable costs for different quantities of BMW X5s produced in one month. The quantity never exceeds the relevant range of 3,000 steering wheels. In column (1) the total cost of the steering wheel includes direct materials of $2,400 per steering wheel and direct installation labour of $2,600 per steering wheel. To simplify, assume that one total indirect variable cost pool per BMW X5 amounts to $10,000. Column (2) lists different volumes of X5s produced in a month. Total variable costs are calculated in column (3). The graph illustrates the behaviour of total variable costs of production over the relevant range 0–100 BMW X5s.

EXHIBIT 2-3
Cost Behaviour of Monthly Total Variable Costs

Monthly Variable Cost Behaviour			
	Cost Information Per Unit (1)	Volume of X5s Produced (2)	Total VC (3) = (1) × (2)*
DM VC per steering wheel	$ 2,400	0	$ –
DML VC per X5	2,600	10	150,000
Indirect total VC per X5	10,000	20	300,000
Unit VC, direct and indirect	15,000	30	450,000
		40	600,000
		50	750,000
		60	900,000
		70	1,050,000
		80	1,200,000
		90	1,350,000
		100	1,500,000

*This formula applies only to the $15,000 amount in the row "Unit VC, direct and indirect."

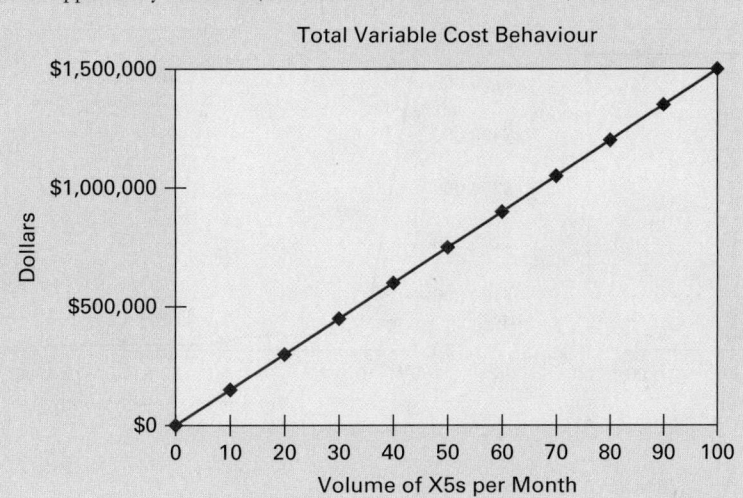

Total Variable Cost Behaviour

FIXED COSTS

In contrast, a **fixed cost** is constant within a relevant range of finished outputs produced. Assume the relevant range at Spartanburg is 0 to 100 vehicles. No matter how many BMW X5s are produced in one month to a maximum of 100, the lease cost will remain unchanged. For simplicity, assume the total monthly fixed MOH of the Spartanburg plant is $550,000, the lease cost listed in column (3) of Exhibit 2-4. The monthly fixed cost remains unchanged regardless of the volume of vehicles produced, listed in column (2), from 0 to 100 per month. If managers at Spartanburg needed to meet demand of 150 vehicles, then fixed cost would increase because this quantity of output exceeds the relevant range or capacity of the plant. BMW would have to expand the size of the plant, purchase additional equipment, hire more salaried staff, and so on.

Unitized fixed cost per vehicle is calculated as monthly fixed cost divided by the quantity of vehicles produced in the month, as listed in column (4). This is not an average cost because it is not constant. A unitized cost varies as the denominator changes from month to month. It is precisely because total fixed cost is constant that the unitized fixed cost decreases as the number of vehicles assembled increases.

Exhibit 2-5 illustrates the effect on *total* manufacturing costs when the monthly volume of X5s produced changes. This is an example of a **mixed cost**. A mixed costs pool comprises both variable and fixed costs. Notice that the sloped line no longer

EXHIBIT 2-4
Cost Behaviour of Monthly Fixed Costs

Monthly Fixed Cost Behaviour for the X5			
		Volume of X5s Produced (2)	Total FC (3)	Fixed Cost per X5 (4) = (3) ÷ (2)
Fixed MOH	$550,000	0	$550,000	$550,000
		10	550,000	55,000
		20	550,000	27,500
		30	550,000	18,333
		40	550,000	13,750
		50	550,000	11,000
		60	550,000	9,167
		70	550,000	7,857
		80	550,000	6,875
		90	550,000	6,111
		100	550,000	5,500

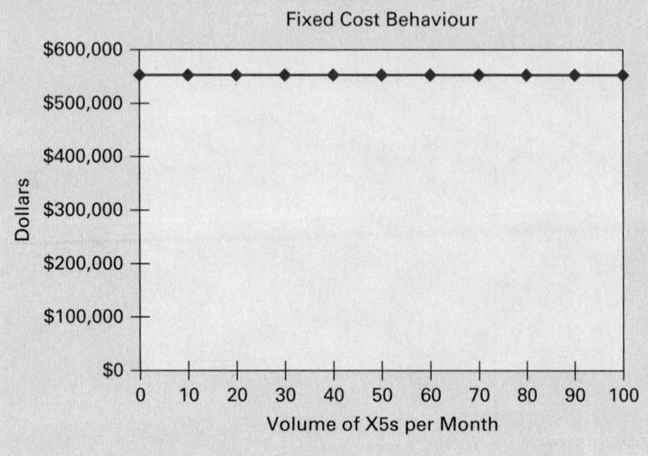

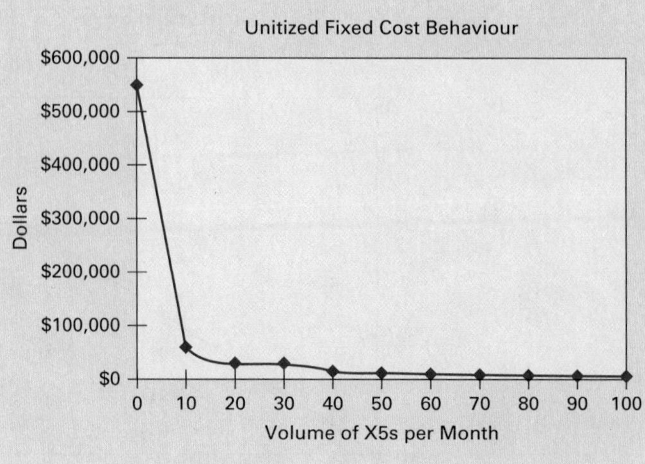

Fixed Cost Behaviour

Unitized Fixed Cost Behaviour

EXHIBIT 2-5
Cost Behaviour of Monthly Mixed Costs

	Monthly Variable Cost Behaviour			Monthly Fixed Cost Behaviour		Total Cost and Total Cost per Unit	
	Cost Information Per Unit (1)	Volume of X5s Produced (2)	Total VC (3) = (1) × (2)*	Total FC (4)	FC per X5 (5) = (4) ÷ (2)	Total Cost (6) = (3) + (4)	Total Cost per X5 (7) = (6) ÷ (2)
DM VC per steering wheel	$ 2,400	0	$ –	$550,000	$550,000	$ 550,000	$550,000
DML VC per X5	2,600	10	150,000	550,000	55,000	700,000	70,000
Indirect total VC per X5	10,000	20	300,000	550,000	27,500	850,000	42,500
Unit VC, direct and indirect	15,000	30	450,000	550,000	18,333	1,000,000	33,333
		40	600,000	550,000	13,750	1,150,000	28,750
Fixed MOH	550,000	50	750,000	550,000	11,000	1,300,000	26,000
		60	900,000	550,000	9,167	1,450,000	24,167
		70	1,050,000	550,000	7,857	1,600,000	22,857
		80	1,200,000	550,000	6,875	1,750,000	21,875
		90	1,350,000	550,000	6,111	1,900,000	21,111
		100	1,500,000	550,000	5,500	2,050,000	20,500

*This formula applies only to the $15,000 in the row "Unit VC, direct and indirect."

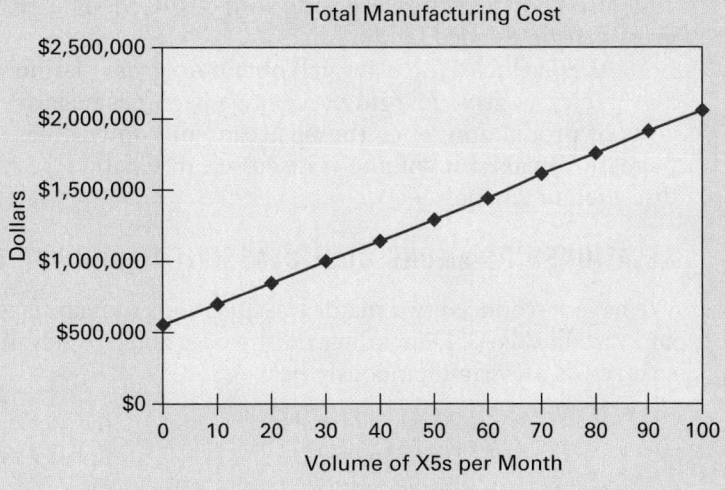

Total Manufacturing Cost

originates at $0 when 0 units are produced, as was the case in Exhibit 2-3. The sloped line originates at $550,000 when 0 vehicles are produced because even if no BMW X5s are produced in a month the plant will still cost $550,000. This behaviour can also be called *semi-fixed* or *semivariable*. You have probably experienced this mixed cost with your smartphone service. The phone service cost is fixed regardless of the number of calls sent or received, but the text service cost varies with the number of texts you send or receive. Mixed cost assignment is discussed more fully in Chapter 10.

The mixed cost pool calculations are based on volumes of resources purchased and used in one month. The effect of a unitized fixed cost is reported in column (7) of Exhibit 2-5. Notice that as the volume increases the total production cost per BMW X5 decreases. This explains why companies attempt to use equipment at its full capacity. Customers willing to pay a reasonable amount above $20,500 will not pay in excess of $70,000. Instead, they will simply purchase another vehicle with the features they prefer at a lower price than $70,000 when it is available.

If the price point is, for example, $26,000, then BMW will earn approximately 21% gross margin percentage [($26,000 − $20,500) ÷ $26,000] on every vehicle only if it produces 100 vehicles. The gross margin is revenue less total production

How AutoShare Reduces Business Transportation Costs

Transforming a fixed to a variable cost for a business is a good cost leadership strategy. AutoShare, founded by Kevin McLaughlin in 1998, operates in Toronto. It offers a car-sharing service to its members. This form of outsourcing is a pay-on-demand model for periods as short as one hour and as long as one year. Members reserve vehicles online or by phone, then retrieve the vehicle, swipe an electronic card over a sensor that unlocks the vehicle, and drive away. Corporate rates begin at $7.75/hour plus a one-time fee of $125 (to pay for insurance and credit checks) and a deposit of $250, refundable when membership terminates. The cars are picked up from and returned to specified locations.

Car sharing allows companies to convert the fixed costs of owning a company car to variable costs of using a car. If business slows, or a car isn't required to visit a client, AutoShare customers are not saddled with the fixed costs of car ownership. AutoShare's fleet is about 10% hybrid cars and the company claims its service takes 10 cars off the road for every AutoShare vehicle.

Sources: http://carsharingtoronto.com; http://www.zipcar.com/how/; http://www.thestar.com/business/article/974358—zipcar gears-up-for-ipo; http://torontoist.com/2006/09/the_car_sharing.php. All accessed April 14, 2011.

cost, also known as **cost of goods sold** (**COGS**). The gross margin percentage is the gross margin divided by the price.

At 50 vehicles the plant will obtain no gross margin percentage, and at less than 50 vehicles its gross margin percentage becomes negative. Given these costs are just costs of production, once the upstream and downstream costs are added the losses increase. Breakeven volume is discussed in Chapter 3, and capacity management is discussed in Chapter 9.

RELATIONSHIPS AMONG COST CLASSIFICATIONS AND COST BEHAVIOURS

We have introduced two major classifications of manufacturing costs: direct/indirect and variable/fixed. Depending on the cost object, relevant range, and specified time span, costs may simultaneously be:

Direct and variable	Indirect and variable
Direct and fixed	Indirect and fixed

Cost classification is not black and white. A particular cost pool can be variable with respect to one quantity of input but fixed with respect to another. For example, annual registration and licence costs for a fleet of planes owned by an airline company are variable with respect to the number of aircraft. But registration and licence costs for a specific aircraft are fixed whether it flies 0 or 1 million kilometres. Here are examples for the Spartanburg plant, where the BMW X5 cost object is one distinct model among others:

Classification of a Cost for Distinct Cost Object BMW X5

		Direct	Indirect
Cost-Behaviour Pattern	Variable Costs	Steering wheel used in vehicle assembly	Power cost for the Spartenburg plant
	Fixed Costs	Exclusive assembly line supervisor's salary	Plant monthly lease

COST DRIVERS

A **cost driver** is a variable, such as the level of activity or volume, that causally affects costs over a given time span. For direct costs there is a readily measured cause and effect relationship between the change in either the level of activity (hours of DML) or volume (kilograms of DM used) and a change in the total costs. For other production costs, such as the cost of plant security, which benefits all distinct cost objects, the measure of benefit may be the computer space required to store surveillance records of distinct areas in the plant. The larger the storage space, the higher the assumed benefit for the distinct cost object. The relationship is cost and benefit rather than cause and effect. Identifying the best cost and benefit relationship guides the selection of indirect cost drivers (see Chapters 4 and 5). In principle, this emphasizes the point that costs added throughout the various stages of the production function should also add value or benefit to a cost object.

In addition, costs that are fixed in the short run may be variable in the long run, which is why we specify a time period. For example, assume the quality control costs to HP for their printers are salary costs paid to the quality control workers. In the short run these are fixed by employment contracts, regardless of how many printers are tested. In the long run, however, HP could outsource this activity to a third party offshore. Fixed salary costs disappear and the contract could specify that HP pay a unit cost per printer tested. The quality control costs would now vary with the quantity of printers tested.

INTERPRETING UNITIZED FIXED COSTS

Interpret unitized fixed costs appropriately when making cost management decisions. ③

Failure to understand the variability of unitized cost rates causes poor decisions. For example, assume that the manager forecasting the Spartanburg budget for next year predicts volume will increase from 50 to 80 X5 units produced per month. If the manager doesn't change the unitized fixed cost, the resulting fixed cost assigned per vehicle will be wrong—with potentially disastrous effects, as illustrated in Exhibit 2-6. Assume that the desired gross margin percentage is 30%. The price depends on the total cost of the vehicle, and the difference between the price and total production cost needs to be 30%. If the unitized fixed cost per vehicle is not changed, the analysis will indicate that $11,000 ($550,000/50) is the fixed cost per X5 produced instead of the correct amount of $6,875 ($550,000/80). This type of error can lead managers into making very poor pricing and product decisions. In this example, managers may price the vehicle at ($15,000 + $11,000) ÷ (1 − 0.30) = $37,143[3] because they incorrectly believe the fixed cost amount per X5 is $11,000, a $4,125 error per unit ($11,000 − $6,875). The correct price is $31,250. The difference of $5,893 is approximately 16% ($5,893 ÷ $37,143) and may be enough to cause customers to switch from the X5 to a comparable GM vehicle.

A good analysis is done on the common basis of total variable and total fixed costs. As Exhibit 2-6 indicates, managers should think in terms of *total* variable costs, *total* fixed costs, and *total* outputs when they develop a pricing model. If customers switch, then the expansion in volume will lose money and the expected profit will not be realized. Increasing marketing and advertising to boost sales will not help. The problem is not customer awareness—the problem is product mispricing due to the misinterpretation of unitized fixed cost.

EXHIBIT 2-6
BMW Mispricing Based on Incorrect Unitized Cost

Total VC per X5 and FC	$15,000	$15,000	
Unitized Fixed MOH assigned	11,000	6,875	
Production cost	26,000	21,875	
Gross margin percentage	30%	30%	
Price	$37,143	$31,250	
Gross margin (GM = Price − Production Cost)	$11,143	$9,375	
Gross margin percentage (GM ÷ Price)	30%	30%	

[3]The gross margin on the correctly priced BMW X5 is $9,375 ($31,250 − $21,875) and the gross margin percentage is 30% ($9,375 ÷ $31,250).

4 Apply cost information to produce a GAAP-compliant income statement showing proper cost of goods sold and a balance sheet showing proper inventory valuation.

Now we will consider cost and inventory valuation for purposes of financial reporting. On the income statement, the cost of goods sold (COGS) must be reported in compliance with GAAP. The COGS refers only to the finished goods both produced *and* sold. Unsold finished goods are finished goods inventory. The **cost of goods manufactured (COGM)** is the cost of producing the total volume of finished goods in a specific time period, both sold and unsold. Of course, it is only through a sale that any company can recover its costs and some reasonable profit.

GAAP rules on inventory and COGS for Canadian companies trading on the Toronto Stock Exchange (TSX) are identical whether finished goods are produced in Canada, the US, or Europe. For the BMW X5, the COGS is assigned by multiplying the total costs of production by the volume of X5s produced and sold as shown in column (6) of Exhibit 2-5. To simplify, assume that the beginning inventory is zero and the manufacturing costs do not change month by month. Next month, the Spartanburg plant produces 50 X5s. The total monthly manufacturing costs, shown in column (6) of Exhibit 2-5, are $1,300,000. The unitized total cost shown in column (7) is $26,000. If all 50 vehicles are sold, then the COGS will be $1,300,000 and there will be no inventory of finished goods at the start of the next month.

The volume of goods sold, however, may differ from the volume of goods produced in any specific time period. To calculate the cost of goods manufactured (COGM), multiply the unitized total manufacturing cost by the quantity manufactured in a specific time period. In the example above, the COGM per unit is simply the total cost of production divided by the total volume of X5s manufactured in a one-month period. Clearly, from our previous discussion, the unitized total manufacturing cost depends on the volume of X5s produced; therefore, both COGS and COGM will vary with the volume manufactured each month.

$$\frac{\text{Total manufacturing costs}}{\text{Number of units manufactured}} = \frac{\$1,300,000}{50 \text{ units}} = \$26,000 \text{ per unit}$$

If 30 units are sold at a price of $37,143 each, and 20 units remain in finished goods ending inventory, the unitized cost helps the financial accountant report several important pieces of information to shareholders, banks, and the government. In this example, the information in Exhibit 2-7 is applied in financial accounting to produce a GAAP-compliant balance sheet and income statement (statement of profit and loss). Of course, in reality companies that sell shares must report every three months (quarterly). However, to make this concept clearer we used a simple monthly report.

With a sales price of $37,143 per vehicle, the gross margin for the month will be $11,143 per X5 sold ($37,143 unit price − $26,000 unitized cost = $11,143 per unit). From this information we can generate the first three lines of a normal income statement, shown coloured according to the production function of the value chain. The data from Exhibit 2-7 are illustrated in Exhibit 2-8 in GAAP format using financial accounting terms.

These are not the only costs incurred during the month, however, because there are other functions in the value chain that must be added to those of production.

EXHIBIT 2-7
Finished Goods Ending Inventory Valuation, COGM, and COGS for X5s (in $ millions)

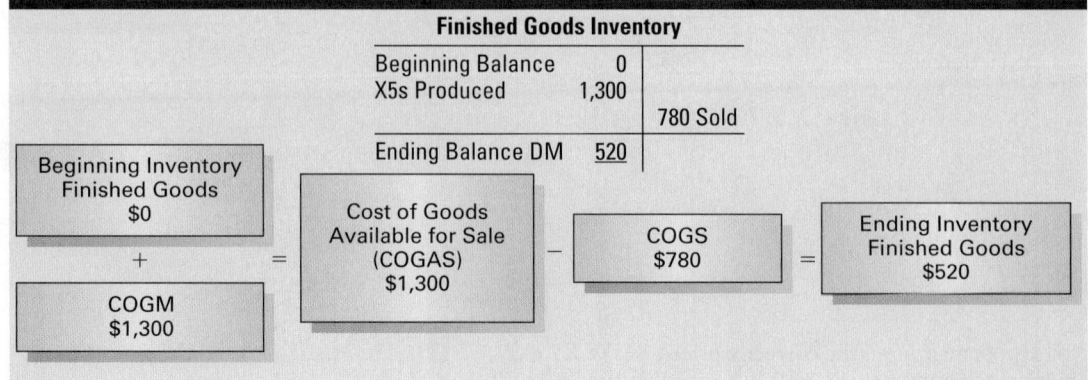

EXHIBIT 2-8
Gross Margin Percentage of 30%

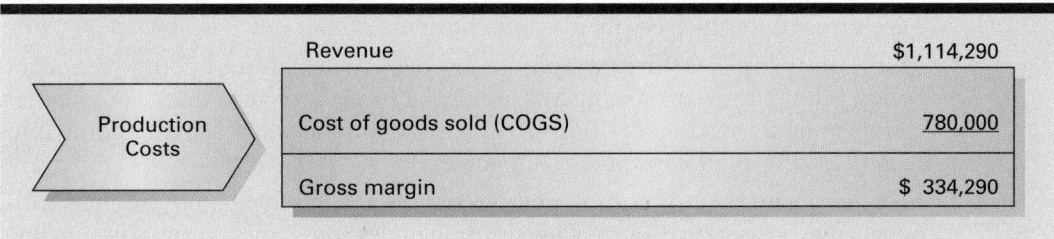

Revenue	$1,114,290
Cost of goods sold (COGS)	780,000
Gross margin	$ 334,290

EXHIBIT 2-9
Income Statement for One Month

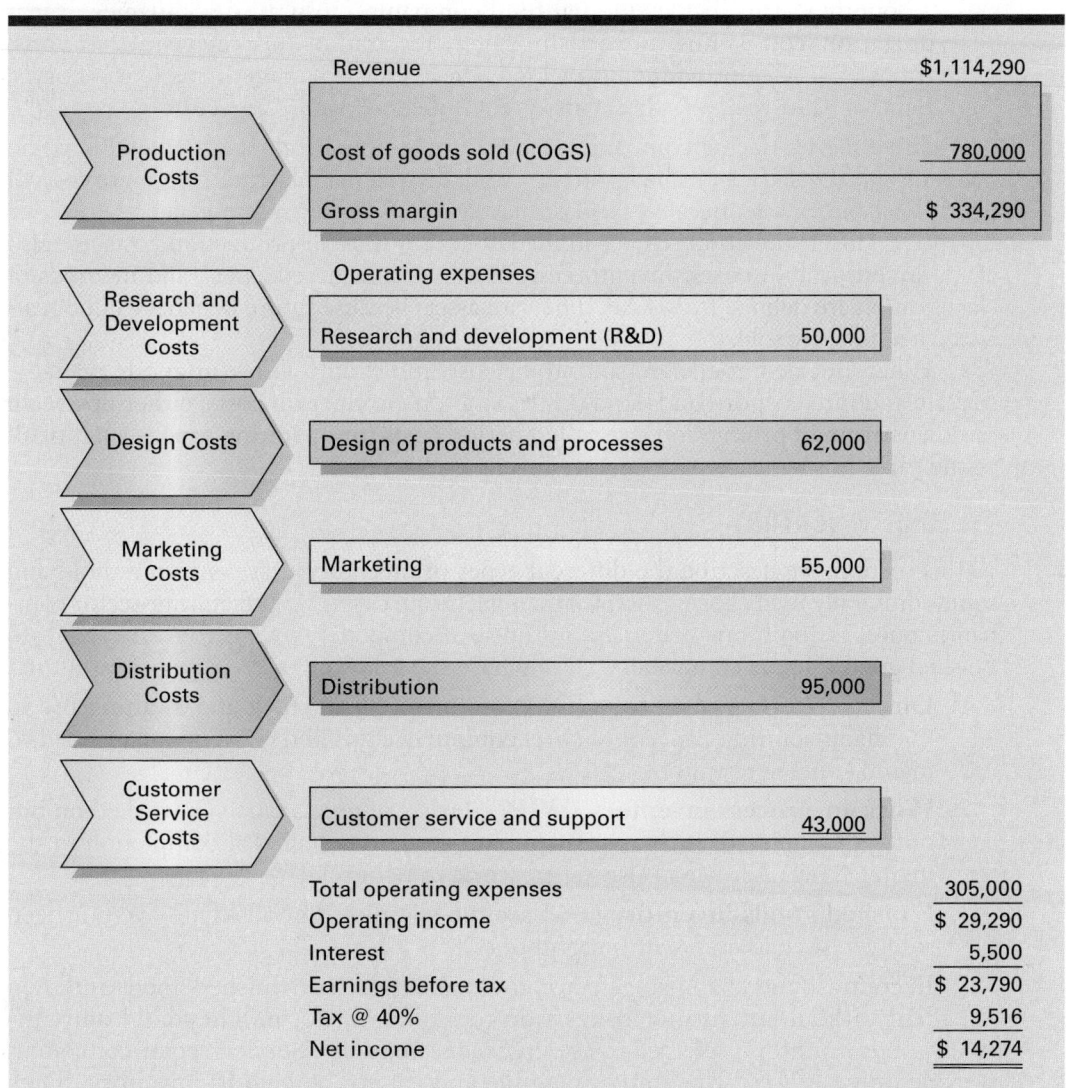

Revenue		$1,114,290
Cost of goods sold (COGS)		780,000
Gross margin		$ 334,290
Operating expenses		
Research and development (R&D)	50,000	
Design of products and processes	62,000	
Marketing	55,000	
Distribution	95,000	
Customer service and support	43,000	
Total operating expenses		305,000
Operating income		$ 29,290
Interest		5,500
Earnings before tax		$ 23,790
Tax @ 40%		9,516
Net income		$ 14,274

Unitized costs are also found in all business functions of the value chain, such as the unitized cost of product design, of sales visits, and of customer-service calls. By summing unitized costs throughout the value chain, managers calculate the total unitized cost of each product or service they deliver and determine the profitability of each product or service at full cost. Managers use this information, for example, to decide which products they should invest more resources in and the prices they should charge to cover all costs and earn a fair profit. Assuming that the non-manufacturing costs are given and the corporate tax rate is 40%, we can complete a GAAP-compliant report. Exhibit 2-9 shows the full financial statement for the Spartanburg plant for one month of production.

There are three economic sectors in which businesses operate:

1. **Manufacturing-sector companies** purchase materials and components and convert them into various finished goods. Examples are automotive companies, cellular phone producers, food-processing companies, and textile companies (e.g., RIM, Maple Leaf, Gildan Activewear).

2. **Merchandising-sector companies** purchase and then sell tangible products without changing their basic form. This sector includes companies engaged in retailing, distribution, or wholesaling (e.g., Indigo Books, Gildan, Canadian Diamonds).

3. **Service-sector companies** provide services (intangible products)—for example, legal advice or audits—to their customers. Examples are law firms, accounting firms, banks, mutual fund companies, insurance companies, transportation companies, advertising agencies, radio and television stations, Internet service providers, travel agencies, and brokerage firms (e.g., Tory's, Bank of Montreal, Via Rail, Cossette, Globe and Mail, Cogeco).

Since service-sector companies provide intangible products, they will have no inventoriable costs. If no finished goods are sold, then all manufacturing costs are costs of goods available for sale. Because the costs have yet to be recovered and generate revenue for the producer, the costs remain in inventory and thus all production costs are also called **inventoriable costs**. Inventoriable costs are considered assets, and methods of classification are defined by GAAP. They are assets because future benefits will be realized when they are sold.

When finished goods are sold, their costs move out of cost of goods available for sale and into cost of goods sold (COGS). Non-production costs, either upstream or downstream of production, are called period costs (or operating expenses). Not all of the three business sectors generate inventoriable costs.

TYPES OF INVENTORY

In this section, we describe the different types of inventory that companies hold and some commonly used classifications of manufacturing costs. Manufacturing-sector companies purchase both raw materials and finished components, then convert them into finished goods. These companies typically have the following three types of inventory:

1. **Direct materials inventory (DM)** are materials in stock and awaiting use in the manufacturing process, such as computer chips and components needed to manufacture smartphones.

2. **Work-in-process inventory (WIP)** consists of goods partially worked on but not yet completed, such as smartphones at various stages of completion in the manufacturing process. Also called **work in progress**.

3. **Finished goods inventory (FG)** are the completed goods that have not been sold yet, such as complete smartphones.

In contrast, merchandising-sector companies purchase finished goods and then sell them without any further conversion to a different form. They hold only finished goods inventory, referred to as *merchandise inventory*. Service-sector companies provide only services, which are intangible and cannot be held in inventory. They have no equivalent to either cost of sales or cost of goods sold.

COMMONLY USED CLASSIFICATIONS OF MANUFACTURING COSTS

Three terms commonly used when describing manufacturing costs are *direct material costs*, *direct manufacturing labour costs*, and *indirect manufacturing costs*.

1. *Direct material costs (DM)* are the acquisition costs of all materials that eventually become part of the cost object (work-in-process and then finished goods) and can be traced to the cost object in an economically feasible way. Acquisition costs of direct materials include freight-in (inward delivery) charges, sales taxes, and customs duties. Examples of direct material costs are the steel and tires used to make the BMW X5, and the computer chips used by RIM to make smartphones.

2. *Direct manufacturing labour costs (DML)* include the compensation of all manufacturing labour that can be traced to the cost object (work-in-process and then finished goods) in an economically feasible way. Examples include wages and fringe benefits paid to machine operators and assembly-line workers who convert direct materials purchased into finished goods.

3. *Indirect manufacturing costs*, also referred to as *manufacturing overhead costs (MOH)* or *factory overhead costs*, are all manufacturing costs that are related to the cost object (work-in-process and then finished goods) but cannot be traced to a cost object in an economically feasible way. Examples include amortization, maintenance supplies, and supervisors' salaries in a specific plant. We use *indirect manufacturing costs* and *manufacturing overhead costs* interchangeably in this book.

INVENTORIABLE COSTS

Inventoriable costs are all costs of a product that are considered as assets on the balance sheet when they are incurred. Inventoriable costs become cost of goods sold on the income statement when the product is sold. The cost of goods sold includes all three of the manufacturing costs (direct materials, direct manufacturing labour, and MOH) incurred to produce the goods that are sold. Inventoriable costs arise *only* for companies in the manufacturing sector.

For merchandising-sector companies like The Brick, inventoriable costs are usually called **cost of sales (COS)**. COS includes purchasing costs of the goods (that are eventually sold), incoming freight, insurance, and handling costs. The goods will undergo no further conversion. Service-sector companies provide something that can be experienced, an intangible, which cannot be inventoried. They do not incur any inventoriable costs of production or purchase. Typical costs classified as direct/indirect and variable/fixed for the distinct bank service of mortgage lending would be as follows:

Classification of a Cost for Distinct Cost Object Mortgage Loans

		Direct	Indirect
Cost-Behaviour Pattern	Variable Costs	Appraisal fees to value property	Internet service costs to transmit documents
	Fixed Costs	Mortgage division supervisor's salary	Sponsorship cost of annual charity events

PERIOD COSTS

Period costs are all costs in the income statement other than cost of goods sold. They are also referred to as *upstream and downstream costs, non-manufacturing costs, operating expenses,* and *non-inventoriable costs.* Because there is not sufficient evidence to conclude that any future benefit will arise from incurring these costs, they are not considered an asset. Under GAAP, period costs are expensed when incurred.

For merchandising-sector companies, period costs in the income statement are all costs *excluded* from COS. Examples of these period costs are labour costs of sales floor personnel, advertising, distribution, and customer-service costs. For service-sector companies, all costs on the income statement are period costs, because there are neither inventories nor inventoriable costs for these companies. Interest and tax are not operating expenses. They are financing and regulatory costs. They are reported as deductions below the total operating income line.

ILLUSTRATING THE FLOW OF INVENTORIABLE COSTS: A MANUFACTURING-SECTOR EXAMPLE

We can follow the flow of inventoriable costs through the income statement of a manufacturing company. Exhibit 2-10 shows the GAAP-compliant, audited income statement for RIM. As described earlier, inventoriable costs flow through the balance sheet accounts as direct materials are converted through work-in-process inventory, where labour and manufacturing overhead are added, and finished goods inventory before entering cost of goods sold in the income statement. This completes all the production transactions required to identify, accumulate, and assign costs of goods manufactured.

EXHIBIT 2-10
RIM Income Statement

File　Edit　View　Insert　Format　Tools　Data　Window　Help

	A	B	C	D
1	**PANEL A: INCOME STATEMENT**			
2	**RIM**			
3	**Income Statement**			
4	**For the Year Ended December 31 (in $ thousands)**			
5	Revenue		$ 210,000	
6	Cost of goods sold:			
7	Beginning finished goods inventory January 1	$ 22,000		
8	Cost of goods manufactured (COGM: see Panel B)	104,000 ◄		
9	Cost of goods available for sale (COGAS)	126,000		
10	Ending finished goods inventory December 31	(18,000)		
11	Cost of goods sold (COGS)		108,000	
12	Gross margin		$ 102,000	
13	Operating expenses:			
14	R&D, Design, Marketing, Distribution, Customer Service	(70,000)		
15	Total operating expenses		(70,000)	
16	Operating income		$ 32,000	
17				
18	**PANEL B: COST OF GOODS MANUFACTURED (COGM)**			
19	**RIM**			
20	**Schedule of Cost of Goods Manufactured***			
21	**For the Year Ended December 31 (in $ thousands)**			
22	Direct materials:			
23	Beginning inventory January 1	$ 11,000		
24	Purchases of direct materials	73,000		
25	Cost of direct materials available for use	84,000		
26	Ending inventory December 31	(8,000)		
27	Direct materials used		$ 76,000	
28	Direct manufacturing labour		9,000	
29	Manufacturing overhead:			
30	Indirect manufacturing labour	7,000		
31	Supplies	2,000		
32	Utilities	5,000		
33	Depreciation on manufacturing plant	2,000		
34	Manufacturing equipment lease costs	3,000		
35	Miscellaneous	1,000		
36	Total manufacturing overhead		20,000	
37	Manufacturing costs incurred		$ 105,000	
38	Beginning work-in-process inventory January 1		6,000	
39	Total manufacturing costs to account for		$ 111,000	
40	Ending work-in-process inventory December 31		(7,000)	
41	Cost of goods manufactured (COGM transferred to Income Statement)		$ 104,000	
42				

STEP 4 (rows 6–11)

STEP 1 (rows 23–26)

STEP 2 (rows 27–36)

STEP 3 (rows 37–41)

*Note: This schedule can become a Schedule of Cost of Goods Manufactured and Sold simply by including the beginning and ending finished goods inventory figures in the supporting schedule rather than in the body of the income statement.

Assuming all costs are given for RIM, the cost assignment to inventory and COGS is described in four steps; the results of the calculations in steps 1 to 4 are shown in income statement format in Panel A and the COGM schedule in Panel B of Exhibit 2-10. The costs to produce finished goods (COGM) are recovered when finished goods are sold and identified as cost of goods sold (COGS) on the income statement. Unsold finished goods inventory is reported on the balance sheet as one component of total manufacturing inventory. Note that companies are not required by GAAP to report their schedule of COGM, but external auditors need this schedule to assure no significant misstatement.

Step 1: Cost of direct materials used   Note how the costs never disappear in Exhibit 2-10 but flow through inventories until they are recovered when finished goods are sold. The correct terminology is transferred in when costs accumulate in an account, and transferred out when costs flow from one account into another. A way to think of this is that additional costs "fill up" an account as they transfer in and they "empty out" an account when they flow out.

Beginning DM inventory value for this year is $11,000. This year's direct material purchases, $73,000, "fill up" the DM inventory as cost of DM available for use. As DM is used, the cost of $76,000 "empties out" inventory, leaving a DM ending inventory value of $8,000 that becomes the beginning inventory value for the next year, as illustrated at the top of Exhibit 2-10.

Beginning inventory of direct materials, January 1	$11,000
+ Purchases of direct materials	73,000
− Ending inventory of direct materials, December 31	8,000
= Direct materials used	$76,000

Step 2: Total manufacturing costs incurred   Total manufacturing costs refers to all of RIM's direct material, labour, and manufacturing overhead costs incurred during conversion this year. Some costs remain in WIP for those goods that were not fully converted to finished foods (FG).

(i) Direct materials used (shaded blue in Exhibit 2-10, Panel B)	$ 76,000
(ii) Direct manufacturing labour (shaded blue in Exhibit 2-10, Panel B)	9,000
(iii) Manufacturing overhead costs (shaded blue in Exhibit 2-10, Panel B)	20,000
Total manufacturing costs incurred	$105,000

Step 3: Cost of goods manufactured   COGM refers to the cost of all goods completely converted from raw materials to finished goods during the year and transferred out to finished goods inventory. Beginning WIP inventory value of $6,000 and total manufacturing costs of $105,000 incurred this year "fill up" the WIP inventory box. Some of the manufacturing costs incurred remain in WIP as the ending work-in-process inventory value of $7,000. This becomes the beginning inventory value for the next year, and the COGM this year of $104,000 "empties out" the WIP inventory value, while "filling up" the finished goods inventory value.

Beginning work-in-process inventory, January 1	$ 6,000
+ Total manufacturing costs incurred	105,000
= Total manufacturing costs to account for	111,000
− Ending work-in-process inventory, December 31	7,000
= Cost of goods manufactured	$104,000

Steps 2 and 3 are combined in the illustration of the flow of costs in the middle of Exhibit 2-10 because in combination they lead to correct value for inventoriable cost assignment to either finished goods or WIP inventory.

Step 4: Cost of goods sold (COGS)   The COGS is the cost of only the finished goods inventory that has been sold to customers during the current year. The beginning inventory value of finished goods of $22,000 reports unsold inventory from last year. Adding the COGM this year of $104,000 "fills up" the finished goods inventory box. These two accumulated costs are the cost of goods available for sale (COGAS) of $126,000. Subtracting the COGS for this year of $108,000 "empties out" the finished goods inventory value to leave unsold goods of $18,000. COGS matches this year's revenues. RIM's smartphone COGS and ending inventory values are:

Beginning inventory of finished goods, January 1	$ 22,000
+ Cost of goods manufactured	104,000
− Ending inventory of finished goods, December 31	18,000
= Cost of goods sold	$108,000

Newcomers to cost accounting often assume that indirect costs such as utilities, telephone, and depreciation are always costs of the period in which they are incurred. This is not true. The classification depends on the business function where the costs were incurred. If they are incurred specifically in production, then they comprise MOH and, according to GAAP, are inventoriable. When incurred in other non-manufacturing business functions, they are period costs (expenses).

Interest expense is incurred during a specific time period, but it is a financing, not an operating, cost. The value-chain business functions exclude finance decisions. Finance decisions are closely coordinated with strategic and operating decisions, including production. Similarly, tax expense is not an operating expense despite being a period cost. It is a regulatory cost of doing business in any country.

INVENTORIABLE COSTS AND PERIOD COSTS FOR A MERCHANDISING COMPANY

Inventoriable costs and period costs flow through the income statement at a merchandising company similarly to the way costs flow at a manufacturing company. At a merchandising company, however, the flow of costs is much simpler to understand and track because the only inventory is finished goods. Purchased goods are held as merchandise inventory, the cost of which is shown as an asset in the balance sheet. As the goods are sold, their costs are shown in the income statement as cost of sales.

A merchandising-sector company also has a variety of period costs, such as marketing, distribution, and customer-service costs. In the income statement, period costs are deducted from revenues without ever having been included as part of inventory. In Exhibit 2-11, the top half distinguishes between inventoriable costs and period costs for a retailer or wholesaler who buys goods for resale. The bottom half distinguishes inventoriable and period costs for a manufacturer.

EXHIBIT 2-11
Merchandising Compared to Manufacturing Ledgers and Income Statement Terminology

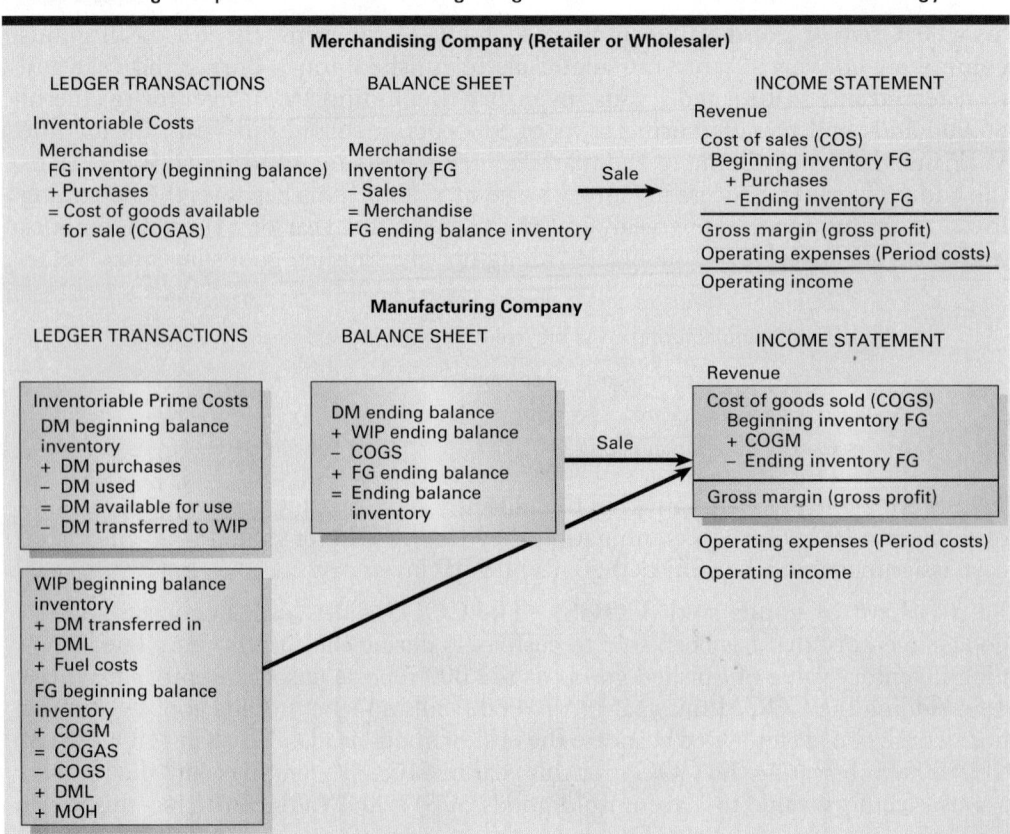

MEASURING AND CLASSIFYING COSTS REQUIRES JUDGMENT

Explain cost identification, classification, and management systems and their use within the decision framework.

⑤

Measuring costs requires judgment because costs can be defined and classified in alternative ways. Different companies and even different subunits within the same company may define and classify the same costs differently. Definition and classification of costs depends on the decision that needs to be made, the cost object, and the company. We illustrate this point with respect to labour cost measurement.

MEASURING LABOUR COSTS

Although manufacturing labour cost classifications vary among companies, most companies have the following categories:

- Direct manufacturing labour (labour that can be traced to individual products).
- Manufacturing overhead (examples of prominent indirect labour components of manufacturing overhead follow):
  - Maintenance labour costs.
  - Maintenance supplies costs (lubricants, etc.).
  - Materials handling labour costs (e.g., forklift truck operators).
- Plant janitors (custodial labour costs).
- Custodial supplies costs (cleansers, mops, floor cleaning machines, etc.).
- Plant guards (security labour costs).
- Security supplies (uniforms, server space for CCTV data or DVDs, dogs, etc.).
- Rework labour (response to quality control issues).
- Idle time labour (paid even though no work is done, response to scheduling issues).
- Unscheduled overtime labour.
- Managers', department heads', and supervisors' salaries for a factory.
- Payroll fringe costs (e.g., health care premiums and pension costs).

The list includes a variety of hourly wage and salaried indirect labour. *Indirect labour costs* comprise a wide range of hourly wages, which are variable costs, plus statutory benefits. Some indirect labour costs of setup, quality control, supervision, and management of the plant are fixed salary plus statutory benefits. Statutory benefits such as paid vacation, mandatory contributions by the company for employment insurance, health care, and pensions are significant. The reason these labour costs are in an indirect cost pool is that they are the costs incurred of shared resources used in the completion of diverse cost objects.

It is important to be alert regarding whether or not these costs are classified as indirect manufacturing costs is because there is some flexibility in GAAP when including costs in COGM and COGS. Management salaries may legitimately be classified as operating expenses when plant managers also spend time doing overall corporate work. This flexibility means the gross margin and gross margin percentage will differ among similar companies depending on how factory management salaries are classified.

Clear cost identification and classification enables all decision makers to avoid disputes among themselves and with external parties such as Canada Revenue Agency (CRA). One extremely significant cost of labour is *payroll fringe costs* (e.g., an employer's statutory contributions for employee benefits such as CPP, EI, and provincial medical care). Many employers also provide discretionary benefits (e.g., company pensions, extended medical care, disability and life insurance). Confusion arises if decision makers are unclear as to whether the company has classified these payments as direct or indirect labour.

For example, assume that direct labourers such as assembly-line workers earn gross wages of $20 an hour plus fringe benefits of $5 per hour. Some companies classify the $20 as direct manufacturing labour cost and the $5 as MOH. Other companies classify the entire $25 as direct manufacturing labour cost. The second approach is a more accurate report of the cost of direct labour resources because the stated wage and the fringe benefit costs always arise together. Achieving clarity avoids labour union contract disputes and disputes about cost-reimbursement contracts and income tax payments.

Overtime Premium and Idle Time   The purpose of classifying costs in detail is to associate an individual cost with a specific reason for why it was incurred. Two classes of indirect labour—overtime premium and idle time—need special mention. **Overtime premium** is the wage rate paid to workers for any labour in *excess* of their straight-time wage rates. Here's an example from the service sector. Ahmed does home repairs for Sears Appliance Services. He is paid $20 per hour for straight time and $30 per hour (time and a half) for overtime. His overtime premium is $10 per overtime hour. If he works 44 hours, including 4 overtime hours, in one week, his gross compensation would be classified as follows:

Direct service labour: 44 hours × $20 per hour	$880
Overtime premium: 4 hours × $10 per hour	40
Total compensation for 44 hours	$920

The overtime premium paid for direct labour is usually classified as MOH even when it can be traced to specific repair jobs. The reason is that scheduling repair jobs is often either random or done to minimize total travel time. For example, if five jobs are scheduled for one ten-hour day, two of which will be overtime, then the decision is to either trace the overtime premium to the last two jobs or average it and assign equal amounts to all jobs. Averaging or prorating the overtime premium does not unduly increase the cost of a particular job because it happened to fall during the overtime hours. Instead, the overtime premium is considered to be a result of the heavy overall volume of work. Its cost is regarded as part of service overhead, which is borne by all repair jobs. In contrast, if a particular customer demands a rush job that is the clear and only cause of overtime, then the overtime premium is regarded as a direct cost of that job.

Idle time is wages paid for unproductive time caused by lack of orders, machine breakdowns, material shortages, poor scheduling, or low customer traffic. If the Sears repair truck broke down for three hours, Ahmed's earnings would be classified as follows:

Direct service labour: 41 hours × $20/hour	$820
Idle time (service overhead): 3 hours × $20/hour	60
Overtime premium (service overhead): 4 hours × $10/hour	40
Total earnings for 44 hours	$920

When neither idle time nor overtime is caused by a particular job, under normal circumstances managers decide to classify them as indirect costs.

Another contentious area of labour costs is rework labour, which arises from quality failure or non-conformance with quality standards. The outputs can, with further work, be made ready for sale. Rates of quality failure are predictable but are usually random. This is because rework is not value-added from a customer's perspective. The company's quality control problem is not the customer's problem and, given the choice, customers will not pay a higher price to cover the costs of rework. Most companies do not want to incur unrecoverable costs of rework and therefore work hard to identify, reduce, or even eliminate quality control failures. Thus any failures are usually uncontrollable or random.

DECISION FRAMEWORK AND FLEXIBILITY OF COSTING METHODS

Many cost terms found in practice have ambiguous meanings. Consider the term *product cost*. A **product cost** is the sum of the costs assigned to a product to make a specific decision. Different decisions often require different measures of product cost, as the brackets on the value chain in Exhibit 2-12 show:

EXHIBIT 2-12
Different Product Costs for Different Purposes

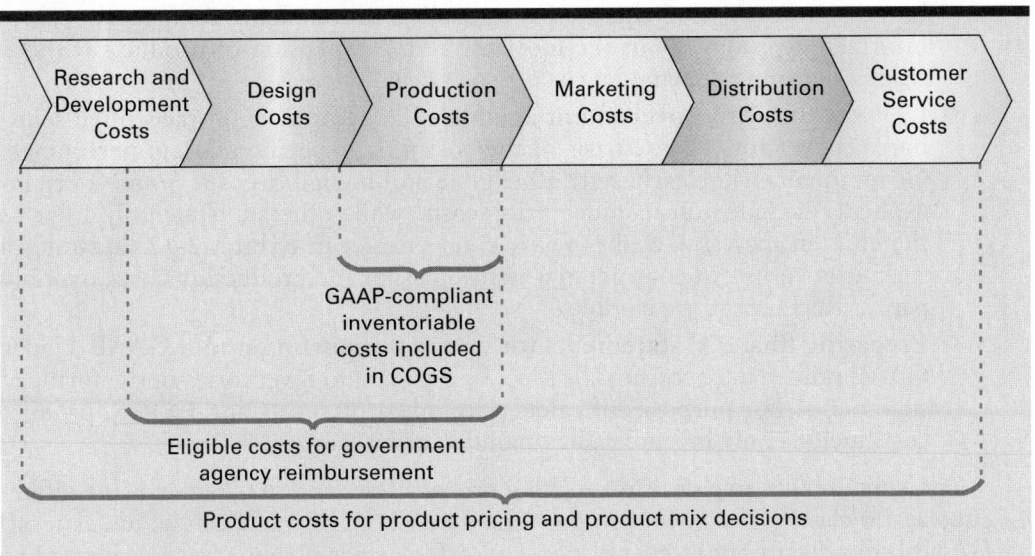

Research and Development Costs → Design Costs → Production Costs → Marketing Costs → Distribution Costs → Customer Service Costs

GAAP-compliant inventoriable costs included in COGS

Eligible costs for government agency reimbursement

Product costs for product pricing and product mix decisions

CONCEPTS IN ACTION—GOVERNANCE

Don't Overcharge the Government

Recently, after a normal audit, the US Pentagon identified in excess of US$1.03 billion billed by Haliburton's subsidiary Kellogg, Brown, and Root (KBR). Two former employees of KBR and a Kuwaiti businessman have been indicted and charged with ten counts of defrauding the US government of more than $3.5 million. Contracts were awarded by the US military for logistics support to front-line troops during the Iraq war.

But the fraud extended into the US military procurement process itself. Two civilian whistleblowers have testified at special Senate investigations that contracts were awarded without a bidding process. Furthermore, no oversight was extended by those accountable to do so. The logistics contracts awarded exceeded $7 billion, but one KBR employee testified that the government was being overcharged $1 million a month to launder the troop's clothing. And while the active military was being housed at $1.39 per month in leased tents, housing in Kuwait for KBR's employees cost $110 per day.

Defrauding of the government is a significant problem. On November 5, 2010, a different company was fined a total of $69.3 million in criminal and civil penalties. The company overcharged the US Agency for International Development for reconstruction work in Sudan, Iraq, and Afghanistan. The employee who blew the whistle has received a portion of the penalties as a reward for disclosing how the company padded its bills by adding indirect costs unrelated to the contracted projects. Two senior financial officers of the company pleaded guilty to fraud and may spend up to 37 months in jail.

Accounting systems are never intended to provide companies with a way to inflate actual costs or to make up imaginary costs. They are intended to disclose faithfully the costs of what was actually done—the economic reality. For accountants, public disgrace, crippling financial penalties, and loss of the right to practise are among the consequences of being found guilty of fraud. The Code of Professional Ethics states that management accountants must act with responsibility for and fidelity to public needs (see Chapter 1). This means accounting services are intended to serve both the public and the client. Government contracts are paid by taxpayers, so defrauding the government also defrauds the taxpaying citizens of a country.

Sources: http://www.cbsnews.com/stories/2004/08/17/eveningnews/main636644.shtml; http://www.c-spanvideo.org/program/188894-1; http://www.nytimes.com/2010/11/06/world/asia/06contractor.html?_r=1&ref=reconstruction; http://www.nj.com/news/index.ssf/2010/11/morristown_company_settles_in.html. All accessed April 17, 2011.

- **Pricing and product-mix decisions.** If the decision is how to price a product or which product among many earns the highest profit, then the issue is how to best assign total value-chain costs to each product. Using total costs enables informed decisions about the most profitable expansion of products without risking declining demand by customers if prices increase.
- **Contracting with government agencies.** Government contracts often reimburse contractors on the basis of the cost plus a specific markup percentage. Governments will clearly state all eligible and ineligible costs. Some contracts explicitly exclude non-manufacturing costs, while others include only a few of the costs in the value chain. The second bracket in Exhibit 2-12 illustrates a specific government contract in which all design and production costs, but only part of R&D costs, are eligible.
- **Preparing financial statements for external reporting under GAAP.** Under GAAP, only manufacturing costs can be assigned to inventories in the financial statements. For purposes of calculating inventory costs and COGS, product costs include only inventoriable (manufacturing) costs.

Using the five-step decision-making process described in Chapter 1, the different ways to classify costs depending on the decision to be made can be understood. GAAP limits flexibility in cost classification for external reporting purposes. For internal management decisions, management accountants can provide a customized costing method. This flexibility allows for faithful representation of the economic reality of any business by reporting relevant costs in an orderly way.

1. *Identify the problem and uncertainties.* Decisions to comply with GAAP for external reporting differ from those to determine eligibility for government reimbursement or to determine the most profitable product mix. Costing depends on the problem to be solved. General ledger cost pools are classified according to type of transaction, not the costing problem.

2. *Obtain information.* Identify and classify direct and indirect costs to match the decision that must be made. These data are usually available in the company's MIS, and the higher the data quality, its faithful representation, detail and timeliness, the more reliable and relevant the information will be. Managers also gather information about the economy, customers, competitors, and prices of substitute products from external sources.

Different Cost Classification Systems

1. Business function	3. Behaviour pattern in relation to the level of activity or volume
a. Research and development	
b. Design of products, services, or processes	a. Variable cost
c. Production	b. Fixed cost
d. Marketing	4. Aggregate or average
e. Distribution	a. Total cost
f. Customer service	b. Unit cost
2. Assignment to a cost object	5. Assets or expenses
a. Direct cost	a. Inventoriable cost
b. Indirect cost	b. Period cost

3. *Predict the future.* Estimate future costs of the cost object. This requires making predictions about the quantity of outputs that managers expect to sell and understanding fixed and variable cost behaviours as quantities of output change.

4. *Decide among alternatives.* Clarify both the definition and classification systems to more accurately assign costs that identify alternative courses of action, then make a choice.

5. *Implement the decision, evaluate performance, and learn.* Compare actual to predicted cost outcomes to learn from successes and remedy any shortfalls.

The concepts introduced in this chapter are the basis for understanding cost accounting and cost management. The concepts can be applied to many topics, such as strategy evaluation, customer profitability, and investment decisions. We develop and apply these concepts in the remainder of the book.

(Try to solve this problem before examining the solution that follows.)

PROBLEM

A distraught employee, Guy Arson, put a torch to a manufacturing plant on February 26. The resulting blaze completely destroyed the plant and its contents. Fortunately, some accounting records were kept in another building. They revealed the following for the period from January 1 to February 26:

Direct materials (DM) purchased in January	$ 192,000
Work in process, January 1	$ 40,800
Direct materials (DM), January 1	$ 19,200
Finished goods, January 1	$ 36,000
Indirect manufacturing costs	40% of conversion costs
Revenues	$ 600,000
Direct manufacturing labour (DML)	$ 216,000
Prime costs	$ 352,800
Gross margin percentage based on sales	20%
Cost of goods available for sale	$ 540,000

REQUIRED

1. Calculate the cost of finished goods inventory, February 26.
2. Calculate the cost of work-in-process inventory, February 26.
3. Calculate the cost of direct materials inventory, February 26.

SOLUTION

1. = $60,000
2. = $33,600
3. = $74,400

This problem is not as easy as it first appears. These answers are obtained by working from the known figures to the unknowns in the schedule below. Use the fact that DML overlaps in both prime and conversion costs. The basic relationships among the categories of costs are:

Prime costs (given)		$352,800
Direct materials used	= $352,800 − Direct manufacturing labour costs	
	= $352,800 − $216,000	$136,800
Total conversion costs	= Direct manufacturing labour + Indirect manuf. costs	
$0.4 \times$ Conversion costs	= Indirect manufacuring costs	
$0.6 \times$ Conversion costs	= Direct manufacturing labour	$216,000
Total conversion costs	= $216,000 ÷ 0.6	$360,000
Indirect manuf. costs	= 0.40 × $360,000	$144,000
	(or $360,000 − $216,000)	

It may be helpful to follow the key amounts through the work-in-process inventory, finished goods inventory, and cost of goods sold T-accounts. All amounts are in thousands of dollars:

Work-in-Process Inventory				Finished Goods Inventory				Cost of Goods Sold	
BI	40.8			BI	36				
DM used	136.8	COGM 504.0			→ 504	COGS 480		→ 480	
DML	216.0								
OH	144.0			(*Available*					
(*To account for*	537.6)			*for sale*	540)				
EI	33.6			EI	60			COGS	480

The following question-and-answer format summarizes the chapter's learning outcomes. Each point presents a key question, and the guidelines are the answer to that question.

LEARNING OUTCOMES	GUIDELINES
1. What distinguishes two manufacturing cost classification systems: direct and indirect, prime and conversion?	A direct cost is any cost that can be traced to the cost object in an economically feasible way. All direct costs are defined as prime costs. Indirect costs are related to a specific cost object but cannot be traced in an economically feasible way. All indirect manufacturing costs are conversion costs that may also include direct manufacturing labour. Classification of direct and indirect depends on the cost object.
2. How are variable and fixed costs different from one another and how do they relate to direct and indirect costs?	A variable cost changes in total in proportion to changes in the related level of total activity or volume. A fixed cost remains unchanged in total for a given time period over a relevant range of volume. A cost may be either direct and variable or direct and fixed. Another cost may be either indirect and variable or indirect and fixed.
3. Why are average costs different from unitized fixed costs?	Analysis requires a focus on total costs, not unit costs. An average cost rate is appropriate only when the quantity of identical units produced is constant. The unitized cost rate varies as the quantity of distinct units produced varies. The higher the quantity produced, the lower the unitized rate for a fixed cost pool.
4. What distinguishes inventoriable and period costs among manufacturing companies, merchandising companies, and service-sector companies?	Manufacturing-sector companies convert materials into finished goods. These costs are inventoriable under GAAP. The three manufacturing inventories depict stages in the conversion process: direct materials, work in process, and finished goods. Non-manufacturing costs are period costs, also called operating expenses. Merchandising-sector companies never convert what they purchase prior to sale. Service-sector companies provide their customers with an intangible experience of a service. Service companies carry no inventory.
5. Explain the usefulness of cost identification, classification, and management systems.	Judgment is needed to distinguish the relevant costs pertaining to each type of decision. Costs from all business functions of the value chain are relevant to pricing and product-mix decisions. Three activities common to all costing systems are (1) calculate the cost of products, services, and other cost objects; (2) obtain information to plan, control, and evaluate performance; (3) analyze relevant information for different types of decisions.

TERMS TO LEARN

This chapter contains many important basic terms. Do not proceed before you check your understanding of the following terms. Both the chapter and the Glossary at the end of the book contain definitions.

SHORT-ANSWER QUESTIONS

2-1 Define *cost object* and give three examples.

2-2 Define *direct costs* and *indirect costs*.

2-3 Why do managers consider direct costs to be more accurate than indirect costs?

2-4 Name three factors that affect the classification of a cost as direct or indirect.

2-5 What is a cost driver? Give one example.

2-6 What is the *relevant range*? What role does the relevant-range concept play in explaining how costs behave?

2-7 Explain why unit costs must often be interpreted with caution.

2-8 Describe how manufacturing-, merchandising-, and service-sector companies differ from each other.

2-9 What are three different types of inventory that manufacturing companies hold?

2-10 Do service-sector companies have inventoriable costs? Explain.

2-11 Describe the overtime-premium and idle-time categories of indirect labour.

2-12 Define product cost. Describe three different purposes for computing product costs.

2-13 Why do management accountants need to understand financial accounting?

EXERCISES

2-14 **Terminology.** A number of terms are listed below:

prime costs	fixed cost
inventoriable costs	period costs
indirect	conversion costs
variable cost	relevant cost

REQUIRED

Select the terms from the above list to complete the following sentences.

1. _____ are incurred during the process of transforming direct materials into finished goods ready for sale.
2. A _____ remains unchanged for a given time period, despite wide changes in the related level of total activity or volume of output.
3. _____ are all costs of a product that are considered as assets on the balance sheet when they are incurred.
4. _____are all direct manufacturing costs.
5. _____ are all costs in the statement of profit and loss other than cost of goods sold.
6. A_____ changes in proportion to changes in the related level of total activity or volume.
7. _____ costs of a cost object are related to the particular cost object but cannot be traced to it in an economically feasible (cost-effective) way.
8. _____ information is cost information that will change a decision. It is needed to identify and remedy different cost-management problems.

2-15 **Inventoriable costs versus period costs.** Each of the following cost items pertains to one of the following companies: Toyota (a manufacturing-sector company), Sobeys (a merchandising-sector company), and Google (a service-sector company):

1. Spring water purchased by Sobeys for sale to its customers.
2. Electricity used to provide lighting for assembly-line workers at a Toyota truck-assembly plant.
3. Amortization on computer equipment at Google used to update directories of websites.
4. Electricity used to provide lighting for Sobeys store aisles.

5. Amortization on computer equipment at Toyota used for quality testing of truck components during the assembly process.
6. Salaries of Sobeys marketing personnel planning local newspaper advertising campaigns.
7. Spring water purchased by Google for consumption by its software engineers.
8. Salaries of Google marketing personnel selling banner advertising.

REQUIRED

Classify each of the **(1–8)** cost items as an inventoriable cost or a period cost. Explain your answers.

2-16 Classification of costs, service sector. Consumer Focus is a marketing research firm that organizes focus groups for consumer-product companies. Each focus group has eight individuals who are paid $50 per session to provide comments on new products. These focus groups meet in hotels and are led by a trained, independent marketing specialist hired by Consumer Focus. Each specialist is paid a fixed retainer to conduct a minimum number of sessions and a per session fee of $2,000. A Consumer Focus staff member attends each session to ensure that all the logistical aspects run smoothly.

REQUIRED

Classify each of the following cost items as:

a. Direct or indirect (D or I) costs with respect to each individual focus group.

b. Variable or fixed (V or F) costs with respect to how the total costs of Consumer Focus change as the number of focus groups conducted changes. (If in doubt, select on the basis of whether the total costs will change substantially if there is a large change in the number of groups conducted.)

You will have two answers (D or I; V or F) for each of the following items:

Cost Item	D or I	V or F

A. Payment to individuals in each focus group to provide comments on new products.
B. Annual subscription of Consumer Focus to *Consumer Reports* magazine.
C. Phone calls made by Consumer Focus staff member to confirm individuals will attend a focus group session (records of individual calls are not kept).
D. Retainer paid to focus group leader to conduct 20 focus groups per year on new medical products.
E. Meals provided to participants in each focus group.
F. Lease payment by Consumer Focus for corporate office.
G. Cost of tapes used to record comments made by individuals in a focus group session (these tapes are sent to the company whose products are being tested).
H. Gasoline costs of Consumer Focus staff for company-owned vehicles (staff members submit monthly bills with no mileage breakdowns).

2-17 Classification of costs, merchandising sector. Home Entertainment Centre (HEC) operates a large store in Halifax. The store has both a DVD section and a music section (compact discs, MP3 players, etc.). HEC reports revenues for the DVD section separately from the music section.

REQUIRED

Classify each of the following cost items as

a. Direct or indirect (D or I) costs with respect to the DVD section.

b. Variable or fixed (V or F) costs with respect to how the total costs of the DVD section change as the number of DVDs sold changes. (If in doubt, select the cost type based on whether the total costs will change substantially if a large number of DVDs are sold.) You will have two answers (D or I; V or F) for each of the following items:

Cost Item	D or I	V or F

A. Annual retainer paid to a DVD distributor.
B. Electricity costs of HEC store (single bill covers entire store).
C. Costs of DVDs purchased for sale to customers.
D. Subscription to *DVD Trends* magazine.
E. Leasing of computer software used for financial budgeting at HEC store.
F. Cost of popcorn provided free to all HEC customers.
G. Fire insurance policy for HEC store.
H. Freight-in costs of DVDs purchased by HEC.

2-18 Classification of costs, manufacturing sector. The Fremont, California, plant of NUMMI (New United Motor Manufacturing, Inc.), a joint venture of General Motors and Toyota, assembles two types of cars (Corollas and Geo Prisms). A separate assembly line is used for each type of car.

REQUIRED

Classify each of the following cost items as
   a. Direct or indirect (D or I) costs with respect to the type of car assembled (Corolla or Geo Prism).
   b. Variable or fixed (V or F) costs with respect to how the total costs of the plant change as the number of cars assembled changes. (If in doubt, select the cost type based on whether the total costs will change substantially if a large number of cars are assembled.) You will have two answers (D or I, and V or F) for each of the following items:

Cost Item	D or I	V or F
A. Cost of tires used on Geo Prisms.		
B. Salary of public relations manager for NUMMI plant.		
C. Annual awards dinner for Corolla suppliers.		
D. Salary of engineer who monitors design changes on Geo Prism.		
E. Freight costs of Corolla engines shipped from Toyota City, Japan, to Fremont, California.		
F. Electricity costs for NUMMI plant (single bill covers entire plant).		
G. Wages paid to temporary assembly-line workers hired in periods of high production (paid on an hourly basis).		
H. Annual fire-insurance policy cost for NUMM1 plant.		

2-19 Variable costs, fixed costs, total costs. Ana Compo is getting ready to open a small restaurant. She is on a tight budget and must choose between the following long-distance phone plans:

Plan A: Pay 8 cents per minute of long-distance calling.

Plan B: Pay a fixed monthly fee of $16 for up to 300 long-distance minutes, and 5 cents per minute thereafter (if she uses fewer than 300 minutes in any month, she still pays $16 for the month).

Plan C: Pay a fixed monthly fee of $20 for up to 480 long-distance minutes and 4 cents per minute thereafter (if she uses fewer than 480 minutes, she still pays $20 for the month).

REQUIRED

Which plan should Compo choose if she expects to make 100 minutes of long-distance calls? 300 minutes? 500 minutes?

2-20 Total costs and unit costs. A student association has hired a musical group for a graduation party. The cost will be a fixed amount of $4,800.

1. Unit cost per person $9.60

REQUIRED

1. Suppose 500 people attend the party. What will be the total cost of the musical group; the unit cost per person?
2. Suppose 2,000 people attend. What will be the total cost of the musical group; the unit cost per person?
3. For prediction of total costs, should the manager of the party use the unit cost in requirement 1; the unit cost in requirement 2? What is the major lesson of this problem?

2-21 Total and unit costs, decision making. Graham's Glassworks makes glass flanges for scientific use. Materials cost $1 per flange, and the glass blowers are paid a wage rate of $20 per hour. A glass blower blows 10 flanges per hour. Fixed manufacturing costs for flanges are $20,000 per period. Period (non-manufacturing) costs associated with flanges are $10,000 per period, and are fixed.

1. The variable direct manufacturing unit cost, $3/flange

REQUIRED

1. Fred's Flasks sells flanges for $8.25 each. Can Graham sell below Fred's price and still make a profit on the flanges? Assume Graham produces and sells 5,000 flanges this period.
2. How would your answer to requirement 2 differ if Graham's Glassworks made and sold 10,000 flanges this period? Why? What does this indicate about the use of unit cost in decision making?

1 **4**

1. Supreme $1.75
Deluxe $1.3833
Regular $0.94

2-22 Computing and interpreting manufacturing unit costs. Maximum Office Products (MOP) produces three different paper products at its Vernon lumber plant—Supreme, Deluxe, and Regular. Each product has its own dedicated production line at the plant. MOP currently uses the following three-part classification for its manufacturing costs: direct materials, direct manufacturing labour, and indirect manufacturing costs. Total indirect manufacturing costs of the plant in May 2012 are $150 million ($20 million of which are fixed). This total amount is allocated to each product line on the basis of direct manufacturing labour costs of each line. Summary data (in millions) for May 2012 are

	Supreme	Deluxe	Regular
Direct materials cost	$84	$ 54	$ 62
Direct manufacturing labour costs	$14	$ 28	$ 8
Indirect manufacturing costs	$42	$ 84	$ 24
Kilograms produced	80	120	100

REQUIRED
1. Compute the total manufacturing cost per kilogram for each product produced in May 2012. Compute the total variable manufacturing cost per kilogram for each product produced in May 2012.
2. Suppose that in June 2012, production was 120 million kilograms of Supreme, 160 million kilograms of Deluxe, and 180 million kilograms of Regular. Why might the May 2012 information on total manufacturing costs per kilogram be misleading when predicting total manufacturing costs in June 2012?

3

1. Total variable cost per tonne of sand, $130/tonne

2-23 Variable costs and fixed costs. Consolidated Minerals (CM) owns the rights to extract minerals from beach sands on Fraser Island. CM has costs in three areas:

a. Payment to a mining subcontractor who charges $80 per tonne of beach sand mined and returned to the beach (after being processed on the mainland to extract three minerals: ilmenite, rutile, and zircon).

b. Payment of a government mining and environmental tax of $50 per tonne of beach sand mined.

c. Payment to a barge operator. This operator charges $150,000 per month to transport each batch of beach sand—up to 100 tonnes per batch per day—to the mainland and then return to Fraser Island (that is, 0 to 100 tonnes per day = $150,000 per month; 101 to 200 tonnes per day = $300,000 per month, and so on).

   Each barge operates 25 days per month. The $150,000 monthly charge must be paid even if fewer than 100 tonnes are transported on any day and even if CM requires fewer than 25 days of barge transportation in that month.

   CM is currently mining 180 tonnes of beach sands per day for 25 days per month.

REQUIRED
1. What is the variable cost per tonne of beach sand mined? What is the fixed cost to CM per month?
2. Plot a graph of the variable costs and another graph of the fixed costs of CM. Your graphs should be similar to Exhibit 2-3 (p. 33), and Exhibit 2-4 (p. 34). Is the concept of relevant range applicable to your graphs? Explain.
3. What is the unit cost per tonne of beach sand mined (a) if 180 tonnes are mined each day and (b) if 220 tonnes are mined each day? Explain the difference in the unit-cost figures.

3 **4**

1. Annual relevant range of output, 0 to 48,000 jawbreakers

2-24 Variable costs, fixed costs, relevant range. Yumball Candies manufactures jaw-breaker candies in a fully automated process. The machine that produces candies was purchased recently and can make 4,000 per month. The machine costs $6,000 and is depreciated using straight-line depreciation over ten years assuming zero residual value. Rent for the factory space and warehouse, and other fixed manufacturing overhead costs total $1,000 per month.

Yumball currently makes and sells 3,000 jaw-breakers per month. Yumball buys just enough materials each month to make the jaw-breakers it needs to sell. Materials cost 10 cents per jawbreaker.

Next year Yumball expects demand to increase by 100%. At this volume of materials purchased, it will get a 10% discount on price. Rent and other fixed manufacturing overhead costs will remain the same.

1. What is Yumball's current annual relevant range of output?
2. What is Yumball's current annual fixed manufacturing cost within the relevant range? What is the variable manufacturing cost?
3. What will Yumball's relevant range of output be next year? How will total fixed and variable manufacturing costs change next year?

2-25 Using unit costs for making decisions. Rhonda Heninger is a well-known software engineer. Her specialty is writing software code used in maintaining the security of credit card information. Heninger is approached by the Electronic Commerce Group (ECG). They offer to pay her $120,000 for the right to use her code under licence in their e-procurement software package. Heninger rejects this offer because it provides her with no additional benefits if the e-procurement package is a runaway success. Both parties eventually agree to a contract in which ECG pays Heninger a flat fee of $120,000 for the right to use her code in up to 10,000 packages. If e-procurement sells more than 10,000 packages, Heninger receives $9.60 for each package sold beyond the 10,000 level.

4

1. a. $60/package

REQUIRED

1. What is the unit cost of ECG for Heninger's software code included in its e-procurement package if it sells (a) 2,000, (b) 6,000, (c) 10,000, and (d) 20,000 packages? Comment on the results.
2. For prediction of ECG's total cost of using Heninger's software code in e-procurement, which unit cost (if any) of (a) to (d) in requirement 1 would you recommend ECG use? Explain.

2-26 Computing cost of goods manufactured and cost of goods sold. The following are account balances relating to 2013 (in thousands):

2

1. Cost of goods manufactured, $250,800

Property tax on plant building	$ 3,600
Marketing, distribution, and customer-service costs	44,400
Finished goods inventory, January 1, 2013	32,400
Plant utilities	20,400
Work-in-process inventory, December 31, 2013	31,200
Amortization of plant building	10,800
General and administrative costs (nonplant)	51,600
Direct materials used	104,400
Finished goods inventory, December 31, 2013	40,800
Amortization of plant equipment	13,200
Plant repairs and maintenance	19,200
Work-in-process inventory, January 1, 2013	24,000
Direct manufacturing labour	40,800
Indirect manufacturing labour	27,600
Indirect materials used	13,200
Miscellaneous plant overhead	4,800

REQUIRED

Compute cost of goods manufactured and cost of goods sold.

2-27 Income statement and schedule of cost of goods manufactured. The Howell Corporation has the following account balances (in millions):

2

1. Cost of goods manufactured, $774

For Specific Date		**For Year 2013**	
Direct materials, January 1, 2013	$18	Purchases of direct materials	$ 390
Work in process, January 1, 2013	12	Direct manufacturing labour	120
Finished goods, January 1, 2013	84	Amortization—plant, building, and equipment	96
Direct materials, December 31, 2013	24	Plant supervisory salaries	6
Work in process, December 31, 2013	6	Miscellaneous plant overhead	42
Finished goods, December 31, 2013	66	Revenues	1,140
		Marketing, distribution, and customer-service costs	288
		Plant supplies used	12
		Plant utilities	36
		Indirect manufacturing labour	72

Prepare an income statement and a supporting schedule of cost of goods manufactured for the year ended December 31, 2013.

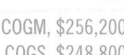
COGM, $256,200
COGS, $248,800

2-28 Computing cost of goods manufactured and cost of goods sold. The following are account balances relating to 2013 (in thousands):

Property tax on plant building	$ 4,200
Marketing, distribution, and customer-service costs	44,400
Finished goods inventory, January 1, 2013	37,400
Plant utilities	20,400
Work-in-process inventory, December 31, 2013	32,200
Amortization of plant building	14,700
General and administrative costs (nonplant)	51,600
Direct materials used	106,800
Finished goods inventory, December 31, 2013	44,800
Amortization of plant equipment	14,700
Plant repairs and maintenance	19,200
Work-in-process inventory, January 1, 2013	25,000
Direct manufacturing labour	38,400
Indirect manufacturing labour	27,600
Indirect materials used	12,200
Miscellaneous plant overhead	5,200

REQUIRED

Compute cost of goods manufactured and cost of goods sold.

a. COG Purchased,
$152,000

b. COS, $145,000

2-29 Computing cost of goods purchased and cost of sales. The data below are for Marvin Department Store. The account balances (in thousands) are for 2013.

Marketing, distribution, and customer-service costs	$ 37,000
Merchandise inventory, January 1, 2013	27,000
Utilities	17,000
General and administrative costs	43,000
Merchandise inventory, December 31, 2013	34,000
Purchases	155,000
Miscellaneous costs	4,000
Transportation in	7,000
Purchase returns and allowances	4,000
Purchase discounts	6,000

REQUIRED

Compute (a) cost of goods purchased and (b) cost of sales.

1. Accounting representative cost driver, number of transactions processed

2-30 Cost drivers and functions. The list of representative cost drivers in the right column of this table are randomized with respect to the list of functions in the left column. That is, they do not match.

Function	Representative Cost Driver
1. Accounting	A. Number of invoices sent
2. Human resources	B. Number of purchase orders
3. Data processing	C. Number of research scientists
4. Research and development	D. Hours of computer processing unit (CPU)
5. Purchasing	E. Number of employees
6. Distribution	F. Number of transactions processed
7. Billing	G. Number of deliveries made

REQUIRED

1. Match each function with its representative cost driver.
2. Give a second example of a cost driver for each function.

PROBLEMS

2-31 Labour cost, overtime, and idle time. Len Lippart is a line worker in the assembly department of Maxart Manufacturing. He normally earns $12 per hour, but gets time and a half ($18 per hour) for overtime, over 40 hours per week. He earns double time if he works holidays even if he has not worked 40 hours that week.

Sometimes the assembly-line equipment goes down and Len has to wait for the mechanics to repair the equipment or there is a scheduling mix-up. Len is paid for this time and Maxart considers this idle time.

In May, Len worked two 42-hour weeks, one 43-hour week, and the last week he worked 40 hours, but one of those days was a national holiday. During regular hours, the assembly-line equipment was down 4.2 hours in May, and Len had one hour of idle time because of a scheduling mix-up.

1

1. a. $1,941.60

REQUIRED

1. Calculate (a) direct manufacturing labour, (b) idle time, (c) overtime holiday premium, and (d) total earnings for Len in May.
2. Is idle time and overtime premium a direct or indirect cost of the jobs that Len worked on in May? Explain.

2-32 Direct costs versus indirect costs. Gwen Benson, Ian Blacklaw, and Eduardo Cabrera are sales representatives for Electronic Manufacturing Inc. (EMI). EMI specializes in low-volume production orders for the research groups of major companies. Each sales representative receives a base salary plus a bonus based on 20% of the actual profit (gross margin) of each order they sell. Before this year, the bonus was 5% of the revenues of each order they sold. Actual profit in the revised system was defined as actual revenue minus actual manufacturing cost. EMI uses a three-part classification of manufacturing costs—direct materials, direct manufacturing labour, and indirect manufacturing costs. Indirect manufacturing costs are determined as 200% of actual direct manufacturing labour cost.

5

1. Gross margin percentage BBC, 6.3%

Benson receives a report on an EMI job for BBC Inc. She is dismayed by the low profit on the BBC job. She prided herself on not discounting the price BBC would pay by convincing BBC of the quality of EMI's work. Benson discussed the issue with Blacklaw and Cabrera. They share with her details of their most recent jobs. Summary data are as follows:

Customer	Westec	La Electricidad	BBC
Sales representative	Blacklaw	Cabrera	Benson
Revenues	$504	$984	$576
Direct materials	300	492	324
Direct manufacturing labour	48	120	72
Indirect manufacturing	96	240	144
Direct labour-hours	2 hours	5 hours	2 hours

Benson asks Hans Brunner, EMI's manufacturing manager, to explain the different labour costs charged on the Westec and BBC jobs, given both used two direct labour-hours. She was told the BBC job was done in overtime and the actual rate ($36) was 50% higher than the $24 per hour straight-time rate. Benson noted that she brought the BBC order to EMI one week ago and there was no rush order on the job.

In contrast, the Westec order was a "hot-hot" one with a request it be done by noon the day after the order was received. Brunner said that the "actual cost" he charged to the BBC job was the $24 per hour straight-time rate.

REQUIRED

1. Using both the actual straight-time and overtime rates paid for direct labour, what is the actual profit EMI would report on each of the three jobs?
2. Assume that EMI charges each job for direct labour at the $24 straight-time rate (and that the indirect-manufacturing rate of 200% includes an overtime premium). What would be the revised profit EMI would report on each of the three jobs? Comment on any differences from requirement 1.
3. Discuss the pros and cons of charging the BBC job the $36 labour rate per hour.
4. Why might EMI adopt the 20% profit incentive instead of the prior 5% of revenue incentive? How might EMI define *profit* to reduce possible disagreements with its sales representatives?

❶ ❷ ❸

1. $1,400

2-33 **Comprehensive problem on unit costs, product costs.** Soo Office Equipment manufactures and sells metal shelving. It began operations on January 1, 2013. Costs incurred for 2013 are as follows (V stands for variable; F stands for fixed):

Direct materials used costs	$140,000 V
Direct manufacturing labour costs	30,000 V
Plant energy costs	5,000 V
Indirect manufacturing labour costs	10,000 V
Indirect manufacturing labour costs	16,000 F
Other indirect manufacturing costs	8,000 V
Other indirect manufacturing costs	24,000 F
Marketing, distribution, and customer-service costs	122,850 V
Marketing, distribution, and customer-service costs	40,000 F
Administrative costs	50,000 F

Variable manufacturing costs are variable with respect to units produced. Variable marketing, distribution, and customer-service costs are variable with respect to units sold.
Inventory data are as follows:

	Beginning, January 1, 2013	Ending, December 31, 2013
Direct materials	0 kilograms	2,000 kilograms
Work in process	0 units	0 units
Finished goods	0 units	? units

Production in 2013 was 100,000 units. Two kilograms of direct materials are used to make one unit of finished product.

Revenues in 2013 were $436,800. The selling price per unit and the purchase price per kilogram of direct materials were stable throughout the year. The company's ending inventory of finished goods is carried at the average unit manufacturing costs for 2013. Finished goods inventory at December 31, 2013, was $20,970.

REQUIRED
1. Calculate direct materials inventory, total cost, December 31, 2013.
2. Calculate finished goods inventory, total units, December 31, 2013.
3. Calculate selling price per unit in 2013.
4. Calculate operating income for 2013 (show your computations).

❷

1. 125,000 units

2-34 **Budgeted income statement (continuation of 2-33).** Assume management predicts that the selling price per unit and variable cost per unit will be the same in 2014 as in 2013. Fixed manufacturing costs and marketing, distribution, and customer-service costs in 2014 are also predicted to be the same as in 2013. Sales in 2014 are forecast to be 122,000 units. The desired ending inventory of finished goods, December 31, 2014, is 12,000 units. Assume zero ending inventories of both direct materials and work in process. The company's ending inventory of finished goods is carried at the average unit manufacturing costs for 2014. The company uses the first-in, first-out inventory method. Management has asked that you prepare a budgeted income statement for 2014. On December 31, 2013, finished goods inventory is 9,000 units.

REQUIRED
1. Calculate the units of finished goods produced in 2014.
2. Prepare a budgeted income statement for 2014.

❷

1. COGM, $136,000

2-35 **Cost of goods manufactured.** Consider the following account balances (in thousands) for the Canseco Company:

	Beginning of 2013	End of 2013
Direct materials inventory	$22,000	$26,000
Work-in-process inventory	21,000	20,000
Finished goods inventory	18,000	23,000
Purchases of direct materials		75,000
Direct manufacturing labour		25,000
Indirect manufacturing labour		15,000
Plant insurance		9,000
Amortization—plant building and equipment		11,000
Repairs and maintenance—plant		4,000
Marketing, distribution, and customer-service costs		93,000
General and administrative costs		29,000

1. Prepare a schedule of cost of goods manufactured for 2013.
2. Revenues in 2013 were $300 million. Prepare the 2013 income statement.

2-36 Flow of inventoriable costs. Hofstra Plastics Inc.'s selected data for the month of August 2013 are presented below (in millions):

1. Direct materials
inventory, $75

Work-in-process inventory, August 1, 2013	$ 200
Direct materials inventory, August 1, 2013	90
Direct materials purchased	360
Direct materials used	375
Variable manufacturing overhead	250
Total manufacturing overhead	480
Total manufacturing costs incurred during August 2013	1,600
Cost of goods manufactured	1,650
Cost of goods sold	1,700
Finished goods inventory, August 1, 2013	125

REQUIRED
Calculate the following costs:

1. Direct materials inventory on August 31, 2013.
2. Fixed manufacturing overhead costs for August.
3. Direct manufacturing labour costs for August.
4. Work-in-process inventory on August 31, 2013.
5. Cost of goods available for sale in August.
6. Finished goods inventory on August 31, 2013.

2-37 Income statement and schedule of cost of goods manufactured. The Powell Corporation has the following account balances (in millions):

Operating income, $75
COGM, $762

For Specific Date		**For Year 2013**	
Direct materials, January 1, 2013	$15	Purchases of direct materials	$ 390
Work in process, January 1, 2013	10	Direct manufacturing labour	120
Finished goods, January 1, 2013	70	Amortization—plant building and equipment	96
Direct materials, December 31, 2013	20	Plant supervisory salaries	6
Work in process, December 31, 2013	5	Miscellaneous plant overhead	42
Finished goods, December 31, 2013	55	Revenues	1,140
		Marketing, distribution, and customer-service costs	288
		Plant supplies used	12
		Plant utilities	36
		Indirect manufacturing labour	60

REQUIRED
Prepare an income statement and a supporting schedule of cost of goods manufactured for the year ended December 31, 2013.

2-38 Interpretation of statements (continuation of 2-37). Refer to the preceding problem.

4. Unit cost for direct
materials, $385

REQUIRED
1. How would the answer to the preceding problem be modified if you were asked for a schedule of cost of goods manufactured and sold instead of a schedule of cost of goods manufactured? Be specific.
2. Would the sales manager's salary (included in marketing, distribution, and customer-service costs) be accounted for differently if the Powell Corporation were a merchandising company instead of a manufacturing company? Describe how the wages of an assembler in the plant would be accounted for in this manufacturing company.
3. Plant supervisory salaries are usually regarded as indirect manufacturing costs. Under what conditions might some of these costs be regarded as direct manufacturing costs? Give an example.

4. Suppose that both the direct materials used and the plant amortization were related to the manufacture of 1 million units of product. What is the unit cost for the direct materials assigned to those units? What is the unit cost for plant building and equipment amortization? Assume that yearly plant amortization is computed on a straight-line basis.

5. Assume that the historical, actual cost behaviour patterns in requirement 4 persist—that is, direct materials costs behave as a variable cost and amortization behaves as a fixed cost. Repeat the computations in requirement 4, assuming that the costs are being predicted for the manufacture of 1.2 million units of product. How would the total costs be affected?

6. As a management accountant, explain concisely to the president why the unit costs differed in requirements 4 and 5.

 2-39 Prime costs versus conversion costs. The following items (in millions) pertain to the Chan Corporation:

For Specific Date		For Year 2013	
Work in process, January 1, 2013	$12.00	Plant utilities	$ 6.00
Direct materials, December 31, 2013	6.00	Indirect manufacturing labour	24.00
Finished goods, December 31, 2013	14.40	Amortization—plant, building, and equipment	10.80
Accounts payable, December 31, 2013	24.00	Revenues	420.00
Accounts receivable, January 1, 2013	60.00	Miscellaneous manufacturing overhead	12.00
Work in process, December 31, 2013	2.40	Marketing, distribution, and customer-service costs	108.00
Finished goods, January 1, 2013	48.00	Purchases of direct materials	96.00
Accounts receivable, December 31, 2013	36.00	Direct manufacturing labour	48.00
Accounts payable, January 1, 2013	48.00	Plant supplies used	7.20
Direct materials, January 1, 2013	36.00	Property taxes on plant	1.20

Chan's manufacturing cost system uses a three-part classification of manufacturing costs. There are two prime costs and one conversion cost: direct materials, direct manufacturing labour, and indirect manufacturing costs.

REQUIRED
1. Identify the prime costs. Identify the conversion costs.
2. Prepare an income statement and a supporting schedule of cost of goods manufactured.

 **2-40** Foxwood Company is a metal- and wood-cutting manufacturer selling products to the home construction market. Consider the following data for the year 2013:

Sandpaper	$ 2,000
Materials-handling costs	70,000
Lubricants-handling costs	5,000
Miscellaneous indirect manufacturing labour	40,000
Direct manufacturing labour	300,000
Direct materials, January 1, 2013	40,000
Direct materials, December 31, 2013	50,000
Finished goods January 1, 2013	100,000
Finished goods December 31, 2013	150,000
Work in process, January 1, 2013	10,000
Work in process, December 31, 2013	14,000
Plant leasing costs	54,000
Amortization—plant equipment	36,000
Property taxes on plant equipment	4,000
Fire and casualty insurance on plant equipment	3,000
Direct materials purchased in 2013	460,000
Revenue	1,360,000
Marketing and promotion	60,000
Marketing salaries	100,000
Shipping costs	70,000
Customer-service costs	100,000

1. Prepare an income statement with a separate supporting schedule of cost of goods manufactured. For all manufacturing items, indicate by V or F whether each is basically a variable cost or a fixed cost (where the cost object is a product unit). If in doubt, decide on the basis of whether the total cost will change substantially over a wide range of production output.
2. Suppose that both the direct materials and plant leasing costs are tied to the production of 900,000 units. What is the direct materials cost assigned to each output unit produced? Assume that the plant leasing costs are a fixed cost. What is the unit cost of the plant leasing costs?
3. Repeat the computation in requirement 2 for direct materials and plant leasing costs assuming that the costs are being predicted for the manufacturing of 1 million units next year. Assume no changes in the historical or actual cost behaviour patterns.
4. As a management consultant, explain concisely to the president why the direct materials cost per output unit did not change in requirements 2 and 3 but the plant leasing costs per output unit did change.
5. Calculate what direct manufacturing labour (DML) cost is as a percentage of total cost of goods sold (COGS). In your opinion is this a material cost? Provide your reason(s). Consistent with your opinion, would you classify DML as a prime or a conversion cost?

2-41 Inventory decision, opportunity costs. Lawnox, a manufacturer of lawn mowers, predicts that it will purchase 240,000 spark plugs next year. Lawnox estimates that 20,000 spark plugs will be required each month. A supplier quotes a price of $9 per spark plug. The supplier also offers a special discount option: If all 240,000 spark plugs are purchased at the start of the year, a discount of 4% off the $9 price will be given. Lawnox can invest its cash at 10% per year. It costs Lawnox $200 to place each purchase order.

1. Opportunity cost, $94,680

1. What is the opportunity cost of interest forgone from purchasing all 240,000 units at the start of the year instead of in 12 monthly purchases of 20,000 units per order?
2. Would this opportunity cost be recorded in the accounting system? Why?
3. Should Lawnox purchase 240,000 units at the start of the year or 20,000 units each month? Show your calculations.

COLLABORATIVE LEARNING CASES

2-42 Finding unknown balances. An auditor for Canada Revenue Agency is trying to reconstruct some partially destroyed records of two taxpayers. For each case in the accompanying list, find the unknowns designated by capital letters (figures are in thousands).

A = $20,700

	Case 1	Case 2
Accounts receivable, December 31, 2013	$ 6,000	$ 2,100
Cost of goods sold	A	20,000
Accounts payable, January 1, 2013	3,000	1,700
Accounts payable, December 31, 2013	1,800	1,500
Finished goods inventory, December 31, 2013	B	5,300
Gross margin	11,300	C
Work in process, January 1, 2013	0	800
Work in process, December 31, 2013	0	3,000
Finished goods inventory, January 1, 2013	4,000	4,000
Direct materials used	8,000	12,000
Direct manufacturing labour	3,000	5,000
Indirect manufacturing costs	7,000	D
Purchases of direct material	9,000	7,000
Revenues	32,000	31,800
Accounts receivable, January 1, 2013	2,000	1,400

2-43 Labour-cost ethics, governance. XKY Manufacturing has recently opened a plant in Costa Melon in order to take advantage of certain tax benefits. In order to qualify for these tax benefits, the company's direct manufacturing labour costs must be at least 20% of total manufacturing costs for the period.

XKY Manufacturing normally classifies direct manufacturing labour wages as direct manufacturing labour, but classifies fringe benefits, overtime premiums, idle time, and vacation time and sick leave as indirect manufacturing labour.

During the first period of operations in Costa Melon, XKY incurs a total of $2,500,000 in manufacturing costs. Of that, $410,000 is direct manufacturing labour wages, $45,000 is overtime premium, $86,000 is fringe benefits, $20,500 is vacation time and sick leave, and $10,900 is idle time.

REQUIRED
1. Will XKY's direct manufacturing labour costs qualify them for the tax benefit?
2. Buyoung Kim, the manager of the new Costa Melon plant, is concerned that she will not get a bonus this year because the plant will not get the tax benefit. What might she ask the plant controller to do to make sure XKY gets the tax benefit? How might these accounting changes be rationalized?
3. Should the plant controller do what the manager has asked in requirement 2? Why or why not?

2-44 Classifying costs for managerial decisions. Kamal Diamond is the owner of the Galaxy chain of four-star prestige hotels. These hotels are in Chicago, London, Los Angeles, Montreal, New York, Seattle, Tokyo, and Vancouver. Diamond is currently struggling to set weekend rates for the Vancouver hotel (the Vancouver Galaxy). From Sunday through Thursday, the Galaxy has an average occupancy rate of 90%. On Friday and Saturday nights, however, average occupancy declines to less than 30%. Galaxy's *major customers* are business travellers who stay mainly Sunday through Thursday.

The current room rate at the Galaxy is $180 a night for single occupancy and $216 a night for double occupancy. These rates apply seven nights a week. For many years, Diamond has resisted having rates for Friday and Saturday nights that are different from those for the remainder of the week. Diamond has long believed that price reductions convey a "nonprestige" impression to his guests. The Vancouver Galaxy highly values its reputation for treating its guests as "royalty."

Most room costs at the Galaxy are fixed on a short-stay (per-night) basis. Diamond estimates the variable costs of servicing each room to be $24 a night per single occupancy and $26.40 a night per double occupancy.

Many prestige hotels in Vancouver offer special weekend rate reductions (Friday and/or Saturday) of up to 50% of their Sunday-through-Thursday rates. These weekend rates also include additional items such as a breakfast for two, a bottle of champagne, and discounted theatre tickets.

REQUIRED
1. Would you recommend that Diamond reduce room rates at the Vancouver Galaxy on Friday and Saturday nights? What factors to protect the value proposition should be considered in his decision?
2. In six months' time, the Grey Cup is to be held in Vancouver. Diamond observes that several four-star prestige hotels have already advertised a Friday-through-Sunday rate for Grey Cup weekend of $360 a night. Should Diamond charge extra for the Grey Cup weekend? Explain.

2-45 Cost analysis, litigation risk, governance. Sam Nash is the head of new product development of Forever Young (FY). Nash is currently considering Enhance, which would be FY's next major product in its beauty/cosmetics line and its estimated unit cost is currently $144. Enhance represents a new direction for FY. All FY's current products are cosmetics applied to the skin by the consumer. In contrast, Enhance is inserted via needle into the skin by a nurse after an initial meeting with a doctor. FY planned to sell Enhance at cost plus 20% to physicians. FY used an estimated treatment cost to patients of $432 to provide a financial incentive to physicians. Each treatment will last three months. Enhance is an animal-based product that fills out the skin so that fewer wrinkles are observable.

Nash, however, questions the economics of this product because FY has failed to budget for any litigation costs, which Nash estimated as $132 per unit. At present, the costs recognized are research and development, manufacturing by a third party, marketing, distribution, and a small amount for customer support. Nash's main concern is with recognizing in the current costing proposal potential future litigation costs (such as the costs of lawyers and expert witnesses in defending lawsuits against Enhance). He points to the litigation with breast implants and notes that a settlement of more than $4.8 billion is being discussed in the press. He also notes the tobacco company litigation and those proposed billion-dollar settlements. Elisabeth Savage, the CEO and president of the company, disagrees with Nash. She maintains that she has total confidence in her medical research team and directs Nash not to include any dollar amount for potential litigation cost in his upcoming presentation to the board of directors on the economics and pricing of the Enhance product. Nash was previously controller of FY and has a strong background in finance. His current job represents his first nonfinance position, and he views himself as potential CEO material.

REQUIRED

1. What reasons might Savage have for not wanting Nash to record potential future litigation costs on the product in a presentation on Enhance's economics and pricing?
2. Suppose Savage asks Nash to give her an "off-the-record" presentation on the possible magnitude of the potential litigation costs of Enhance. What is the new unit cost including the estimated litigation costs? What should the new selling price to physicians be to maintain the triple-the-cost target? What is the percentage decrease in the margin physicians could expect per unit assuming the cost to the patient cannot be changed?
3. After hearing Nash's presentation (see requirement 2), Savage directs Nash to drop any further discussion of the litigation issue. He is to focus on making Enhance the blockbuster product that field research has suggested it will be. Nash is uneasy with this directive. He tells Savage it is an "ostrich approach" (head-in-the-sand) to a real problem that could potentially bankrupt the company. Savage tells Nash to go and think about her directive. What should Nash do next?

Cost-Volume-Profit Analysis

BUSINESS MATTERS

Cost-Volume-Profit (CVP)

Knowing how to classify costs and how costs behave is essential to managing profit. WestJet, for example, can combine information about the price and cost per seat, volume of seats sold, and profit using a technique called cost-volume-profit (CVP) analysis. The benefit is that WestJet can use this technique to calculate how many seats must be sold at what price to cover all costs of operating an aircraft during each flight. For WestJet, once the flight takes off with empty seats there is no chance to earn more revenue for that flight. At the last minute, when an unexpected passenger appears, what should the price for a seat be? The cost of carrying one more passenger with luggage is very small. However, if all last-minute passengers were charged a very deeply discounted price, progressively fewer passengers would reserve seats and total revenue would decrease. CVP analyses help managers analyze and solve this dilemma.

LEARNING OUTCOMES

After studying this chapter, you should be able to

1. Identify the essential elements of cost-volume-profit analysis and calculate the breakeven point (BEP).

2. Apply the CVP model to calculate a target operating profit before interest and tax.

3. Distinguish among contribution, gross, operating, and net income margins, and apply the CVP model to calculate target net income.

4. Apply the CVP model in decision making and explain how sensitivity analyses can help managers both identify and manage risk.

5. Interpret the results of CVP analyses in complex multi-product and multiple cost driver situations.

The purpose of this chapter is to introduce and apply a sweeping financial overview of the planning process using cost-volume-profit (CVP) analysis. Knowledge of cost behaviour is the foundation of planning and controlling profit, especially when business circumstances change from what was predicted. Management teams can use their initial analyses to predict the profit outcomes from a range of foreseeable changes. Based on foreseeable outcomes, managers can develop agility by putting plans in place to minimize foreseeable losses.

ESSENTIALS OF CVP ANALYSIS

1 Identify the essential elements of cost-volume-profit analysis and calculate the breakeven point (BEP).

Cost-volume-profit (CVP) analysis is a model to analyze the behaviour of net income in response to changes in total revenue, total costs, or both. In reality, businesses operate in a complex environment; a *model* reduces that complexity by using simplifying assumptions to focus on only the relevant relationships. The most important elements in a model affect one another in a predictable way. In this chapter, when we determine the breakeven point (BEP), we include *all* business function costs in the value chain, not just those of production. The **breakeven point (BEP)** is the point at which total revenue minus total business function costs is $0.

The CVP model identifies only the relevant relationships. The model depends on understanding the effects of cost behaviour on profit. The following assumptions identify relevant information required to complete a CVP analysis:

- Changes in the sales volume and production (or purchase) volume are identical (purchase volume would apply to a merchandiser). The ending balances in all inventories are zero. Everything purchased is used in production; everything produced is sold. For a merchandiser, the sales volume of finished goods purchased for resale is identical to the sales volume sold.
- All costs are classified as either fixed (FC) or variable (VC) with no mixed costs. The fixed costs include *both* manufacturing *and* non-manufacturing fixed costs. The total variable costs include both manufacturing and non-manufacturing variable costs.
- All cost behaviour is linear (a straight line) within the relevant volume range.
- The sales price per unit, variable costs per unit, and total fixed costs and sales (or production) volume are known. The MIS provides all of this information.
- Either the product sold or the product mix remains constant, although the volume changes.
- All revenue and costs can be calculated and compared without considering the time-value of money.

We know that fixed costs comprise part of total cost. We know that total revenue is the product of total sales volume or quantity (Q) of units sold multiplied by the price per unit. We also know that total variable cost is the product of total Q units produced multiplied by the cost per unit. Based on the simplifying assumption that Q sold = Q produced, the relationship among relevant elements of the CVP model upon which the BEP can be calculated is:

$$\text{Operating income} = (\text{Unit sales price} \times Q) - (\text{Unit variable cost} \times Q) - (\text{fixed costs}) \quad (1)$$

CVP ANALYSIS: AN EXAMPLE

Decision Framework   We will begin by looking at an example based on known information about operating income (net income before interest and taxes). Then we will analyze a straightforward decision based on calculating the required combination of Q and unit sales price to breakeven. In the CVP analysis, only one factor, sales volume (Q), changes.

Example: Wei Shao is considering selling Do-All Software, a home-office software package, at a computer convention in Vancouver. Wei knows she can purchase this software from a computer software wholesaler at $120 per package, with the privilege of returning all unsold packages and receiving a full $120 refund per package. She also knows that she must pay Computer Conventions, Inc. $2,000 for the booth rental at the convention. She will incur no other costs. Should she rent a booth?

Wei faces an uncertain future as she analyzes the information she has at hand. The decision framework presented in Chapter 1 can be applied in this situation:

1. **Identify the problem and uncertainties.** Wei has to resolve two important uncertainties—the unit sales price she can charge and the number of packages (Q) she can sell at that price. Unfortunately, the actual effect of her choices on operating income will not be known until after the convention. Therefore, her actual outcome is uncertain.

2. **Obtain information.** Wei obtains the relevant information on the variable and fixed costs to attend the conference and purchase the software. She uses her own information on sales volume and her previous experience at a similar convention in Seattle four months ago. Wei also gathers published industry information. She realizes that customers may purchase their software from competitors and wants to match her volume and purchase price to customer demand.

3. **Predict the future.** Wei predicts that she can charge $200 for Do-All Software. She is confident of the straight line or linear relationship between volume, price, and total revenue within her relevant range of 30 to 60 units. However, even with her past experience in Seattle, Wei remains uncertain. Have there been important changes in customer demand over the last four months? Her regular sales in the last couple of months have been lower than she expected. Is she too optimistic or biased in her predictions? Will a lot of potential customers attend a convention in the same region held so soon after the one in Seattle?

4. **Make decisions by choosing among alternatives.** Wei will use the CVP relationship to help her decide among alternatives available for pricing and quantity sold.

5. **Implement the decision, evaluate performance, and learn.** If Wei attends the convention then she will know her outcome or actual profit. This is important feedback to compare with her predicted profit. Wei can learn from this comparison how to make better decisions in the future.

Cost-Volume-Profit Analysis   Wei knows that the booth-rental cost of $2,000 is a fixed cost because it must be paid even if she sells nothing. Wei's variable cost per Do-All Software package is $120 for quantities between 30 and 60 packages. Wei sorts her data into classifications of revenue and total variable cost, then tests two volumes of sales shown in the spreadsheet:

	Wei Sells 5 Packages	Wei Sells 40 Packages
Revenue	$ 1,000 ($200 per package × 5 packages)	$8,000 ($200 per package × 40 packages)
Total variable cost	600 ($120 per package × 5 packages)	4,800 ($120 per package × 40 packages)
Contribution margin	$ 400	$3,200

The relevant relationship is the **contribution margin**, which equals revenue minus variable costs. The contribution margin is the amount remaining from revenue obtained after *all variable* costs have been paid. It is the amount available to contribute to or pay for all fixed costs and provide some reasonable profit:

Revenue − Total variable cost = Contribution margin

What is the breakeven price (BEP) in sales volume Q, where operating income = $0? Wei does not yet know her predicted operating income, nor does she know what her minimum Q must be to cover her costs. By including the fixed cost of $2,000 in her analysis, Wei can calculate how operating income changes as Q changes. If she sells only 5 packages, then she will suffer an operating loss of $1,600 ($400 − $2,000) and operating income < $0. If she sells 40 packages then she will enjoy a positive operating income of $1,200 ($3,200 − $2,000) and operating income > $0.

	Wei Sells 5 Packages	Wei sells 40 Packages
Revenue	$ 1,000 ($200 per package × 5 packages)	$ 8,000 ($200 per package × 40 packages)
Total variable cost	600 ($120 per package × 5 packages)	4,800 ($120 per package × 40 packages)
Contribution margin	$ 400	$ 3,200
Fixed cost	2,000	2,000
Operating income	$(1,600)	$ 1,200

But rather than simply using trial and error, Wei can exploit the assumption that

$$Q \text{ sold} = Q \text{ purchased for sale}$$

and simplify the CVP model (Equation 1). If Wei assumes that operating income = $0, she can easily calculate the sales volume Q at which she will break even:

$$\$0 = Q \times (\text{unit price} - \text{unit variable cost}) - \text{fixed cost} \tag{2}$$

Based on the information she has, Wei can substitute the financial values and complete her calculation as follows:

$$\$0 = Q \times (\$200 - \$120) - \$2,000$$
$$\$0 = Q \times (\$80) - \$2,000$$
$$\$2,000 = 80Q$$
$$\frac{\$2,000}{\$80} = Q$$
$$25 = Q$$

Contribution margin per unit is the difference between selling price and variable cost per unit. In the Do-All Software example, contribution margin per unit is $80 per unit ($200 price per unit − $120 variable cost per unit). Simplifying her model further:

$$\$0 = Q \times (\text{contribution margin per unit}) - \text{fixed cost} \tag{3}$$

This form of the CVP model exploits the methodical way in which revenue and total variable costs change together as the common factor, Q, changes. When the unit sales price is $200, Wei knows that each unit sold covers the variable cost of $120 per unit and provides $80 ($200 − $120) that can be used to cover her fixed cost of $2,000. By substituting the known amounts into the formula, Wei can calculate the BEP of 25 units ($2000 ÷ $80):

$$\$0 = Q \times (\$80) - \$2,000$$
$$\$2,000 = 80Q$$
$$\frac{\$2,000}{\$80} = Q$$
$$25 = Q$$

Exhibit 3-1 shows the result of calculating the BEP in two formats. On the right is the familiar financial income statement format. On the left is a **contribution income statement**, which groups costs as either variable or fixed according to their behaviour. The format of the report does not affect the dollar value of the operating income, since the revenue and total costs are identical. What has changed is the classification system used to report the results.

EXHIBIT 3-1
Contribution Statement Compared to Financial Statement Format

	Quantity Purchased and Sold = 25		
Contribution Format		**Financial Income Statement Format**	
Revenue ($200 × 25)	$5,000	Revenue ($200 × 25)	$5,000
− Total variable cost ($120 × 25)	3,000	− Total cost of sales (COS)	3,000
Total contribution margin	2,000	Gross margin	2,000
− Fixed costs (always a total)	2,000	− Total period cost	2,000
Operating income	$ −	Operating income	$ −

   Exhibit 3-2 illustrates the importance of assuming the linear relationship of cost and revenue to volume when Q purchased = Q sold. By varying the amount of Q, each line slopes methodically upward between 30 and 60 units (the relevant range). The rate of change is only $120 per unit for the total variable costs, while the rate of change is $200 per unit for the revenue shown on the right.

   The different rates of change in total cost and revenue is what causes the slopes of the two lines to differ: The slower the rate of change, the flatter is the line. Another reason is that when the Q purchased is 0, the total cost begins or originates at $2,000, but the total revenue originates at $0. Different slopes mean the two lines, when plotted on the same graph, will intersect. Note in Exhibit 3-3 that the two lines intersect at the breakeven point (BEP), where Q = 25 units.

EXHIBIT 3-2
Contribution Income Statement Format for Different Volumes of Do-All Software Packages Sold

Contribution Format		**Q of Software Units Sold**				
	Inputs	0	10	25	40	60
Revenue	$ 200 per package	$ −	$ 2,000	$5,000	$8,000	$12,000
Total variable costs	120 per package	−	1,200	3,000	4,800	7,200
Contribution margin	80 per package	$ −	$ 800	$2,000	$3,200	$ 4,800
Fixed costs	$2,000	2,000	2,000	2,000	2,000	2,000
Operating income		$ (2,000)	$(1,200)	$ −	$1,200	$ 2,800

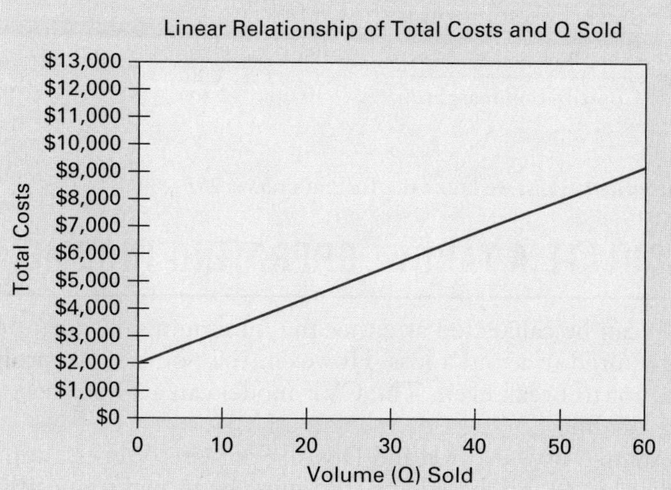

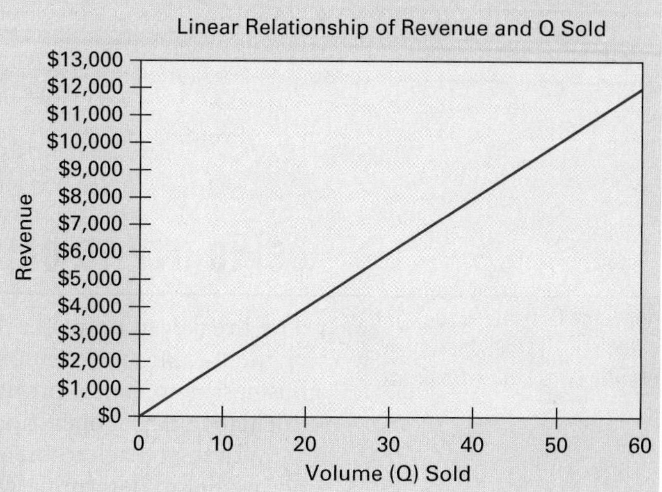

Linear Relationship of Total Costs and Q Sold

Linear Relationship of Revenue and Q Sold

EXHIBIT 3-3
Cost-Volume Graph for Do-All Software

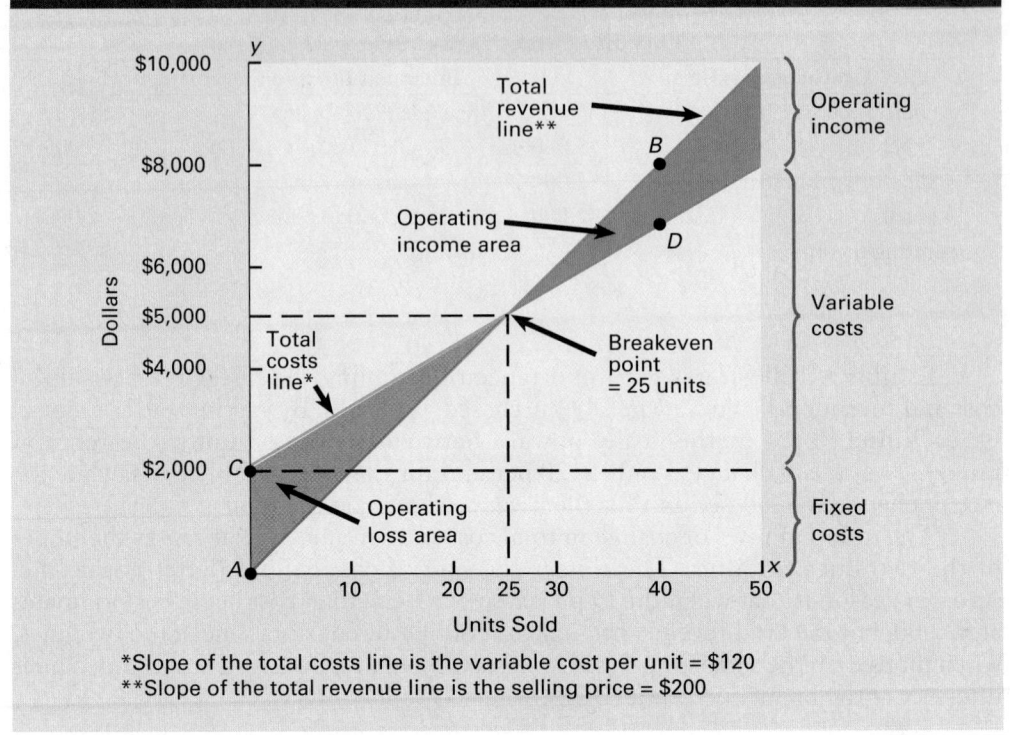

*Slope of the total costs line is the variable cost per unit = $120
**Slope of the total revenue line is the selling price = $200

CONTRIBUTION MARGIN PERCENTAGE: BREAKEVEN POINT IN REVENUE

Instead of expressing contribution margin as a dollar amount per unit, we can also express it as a percentage. **Contribution margin percentage** (also called **contribution margin ratio**) equals the contribution margin per unit divided by the selling price per unit:

$$\text{Contribution margin percentage} = \frac{\$80}{\$200} = 0.40, \text{ or } 40\%$$

The contribution margin percentage tells us how many pennies per $1.00 of revenue contribute to paying fixed costs. For example, a contribution margin percentage of 40% means for each $1.00 a customer pays for Do-All Software, $0.40 contributes to paying fixed cost.

The contribution margin percentage enables us to solve for values with partial data. For example, how do you calculate the breakeven point in revenue when you do not know the sales price per unit? The solution is shown below:

$$\frac{\text{Breakeven}}{\text{revenue}} = \frac{\text{Fixed costs}}{\text{Contribution margin \%}} = \frac{\$2,000}{0.40} = \$5,000$$

Proof: $5,000 ÷ $200 = 25 units

From previous calculations, we know the BEP in units is 25.

USING CVP TO CALCULATE A TARGET OPERATING INCOME

2 Apply the CVP model to calculate a target operating profit before interest and tax.

The breakeven point (BEP) can be calculated as either the minimum sales quantity or the minimum revenue required to avoid a loss. However, the point of for-profit business is to earn a profit, not to break even. The CVP model can also be used to calculate a target operating income.

Let's go back to the example of Wei Shao and Do-All Software. Wei can apply her model to determine what her Q purchased and sold must be to make a positive operating income. Instead of setting Operating income = $0, it is set to equal a non-zero amount. The method of calculating this target Q is identical to the method already described. Wei selects $1,500 as her target operating income.

$$\$1,500 = Q \times (\text{unit sales price} - \text{unit variable cost}) - \text{fixed cost}$$

$$Q \times (\$200 - \$120) - \$2,000 = \$1,500$$

$$\$80 \times Q = \$2,000 + \$1,500$$

$$Q = \$3,500 \div \$80 \text{ per unit} = 43.75 \text{ units}$$

Alternatively, Wei knows the contribution margin per unit and can calculate the Q required to achieve a target operating income of $1,500 by starting at the second line of the solution, treating the target operating income as if it were a fixed cost. This is exactly what we have done when adding the $1,500 to the $2,000 to obtain $3,500. The $80 is the contribution margin per unit. Dividing $3,500 by the contribution margin per unit gives the identical answer of Q = 43.75 units:

$$\frac{\text{Volume of units}}{\text{required to be sold}} = \frac{\text{Fixed costs} + \text{Target operating income}}{\text{Contribution margin per unit}} \tag{4}$$

$$\frac{\text{Volume of units}}{\text{required to be sold}} = \frac{\$2,000 + \$1,500}{\$80 \text{ per unit}} = 43.75 \text{ units}$$

Proof:

Revenue, $200 per unit × 43.75 units	$8,750
Variable costs, $120 per unit × 43.75 units	5,250
Contribution margin, $80 per unit × 43.75 units	3,500
Fixed costs	2,000
Operating income	$1,500

Of course, Wei cannot sell 75% of one Do-All package. If she rounds down to Q = 43 units she will bring in only $3,440, which is less than the $3,500 she needs to cover her $2,000 fixed cost plus a target operating income of $1,500. Wei must round up to Q = 44 units to reach her target.

Finally, Wei can use different information—fixed cost, target operating income, and the contribution margin percentage of 40%—to calculate her target revenue without first calculating her target Q. She will simply divide the sum of fixed cost plus her target operating income by the contribution margin percentage to obtain the target revenue required, as shown:

$$\text{Revenue needed to earn } \$1,500 = \frac{\$2,000 + \$1,500}{0.40} = \frac{\$3,500}{0.40} = \$8,750$$

CONTRIBUTION MARGIN, GROSS MARGIN, OPERATING MARGIN, AND NET INCOME MARGIN

The CVP model enables us to clearly distinguish the contribution margin, which provides information for CVP analysis. Recall that there are two formats in which costs can be classified: the contribution and the financial format. Both formats report identical costs, but the costs are classified differently. The difference between contribution and gross margin is shown in the two equations below:

Distinguish among contribution, gross, operating, and net income margins and apply the CVP model to calculate a target net income.

$$\text{Revenue} - \text{Cost of goods sold} = \text{Gross margin}$$

$$\text{Revenue} - \text{Total variable costs} = \text{Contribution margin}$$

Gross margin is a measure of competitiveness—how much a company can charge for its products over and above the cost of either purchasing (cost of sales) or producing them (cost of goods sold). The size of the gross margin depends on the successful competitive strategy of a company. The gross margin can be expressed as a total, as an amount per unit, or as a percentage (called **gross margin percentage**).

Gross margin is a financial accounting term, and non-accountants sometimes refer to gross margin as gross profit. But *gross profit* is an ambiguous term also used to identify operating margin. It is crucial to verify what people with no accounting training mean when they use the ambiguous term *gross profit*.

Contribution margin indicates how much of a company's sales price per unit is available to cover total fixed costs after variable costs are paid. Consider the distinction between gross margin and contribution margin in the context of manufacturing companies. In the manufacturing sector, contribution margin and gross margin differ in two respects: fixed manufacturing costs and variable non-manufacturing costs. The following example illustrates this difference:

Contribution Income Statement Emphasizing Contribution Margin (in $ thousands)			Financial Accounting Income Statement Emphasizing Gross Margin (in $ thousands)	
Revenue		$1,000	Revenue	$1,000
Variable manufacturing costs	$250		Cost of goods sold ($250 + $160)	410
Variable non-manufacturing costs	270	520		
Contribution margin		480	Gross margin	590
Fixed manufacturing costs	160		Non-manufacturing costs	
Fixed non-manufacturing costs	138	298	($270 + $138)	408
Operating income		$ 182	Operating income	$ 182

Fixed manufacturing costs of $160,000 are not deducted from revenue when computing contribution margin but are deducted when computing gross margin. Variable non-manufacturing costs (such as commissions paid to salespersons) of $270,000 are deducted from revenue when computing contribution margin but are not deducted when computing gross margin.

Operating margin has the same meaning as operating income. It is the result of deducting all business function costs from revenue. Neither interest nor tax expense are considered business function costs. The operating margin percentage is simply the operating income divided by revenue. It does not matter what format is used to report costs—because total costs are identical, the reported operating income will be identical. The **operating margin percentage** (sometimes called **gross profit percentage**) in the above example is 18.2% ($182 ÷ $1,000).

Net income margin is an alternative technical term for net income. The non-technical term that is readily recognized is *net profit margin*. The **net income margin percentage** is calculated by dividing net income by revenue. People with no accounting training often refer to net income margin percentage as simply net profit and drop the word *percentage*. Using non-technical terms, however, is quite confusing and it is far more sensible to use accounting terminology to clearly distinguish among all four types of margins and margin percentages. Notice that when calculating the gross, contribution, operating, and net income margin percentages, revenue is the common denominator.

TARGET NET INCOME AND INCOME TAXES

So far we have ignored the effect of income taxes when calculating the sales volume required to achieve a target income. The after-tax profit, however, is what matters to any business. Targets are set in terms of net income. In a real situation, managers must gather information on tax. In our example we will assume a corporate tax rate of 40%.

Let's return to the Do-All Software example. Wei's new problem is to calculate the required sales volume Q to earn a *net* income of $960, assuming an income tax rate of 40%. Using the contribution margin format:

$$\text{Target operating income} = \text{Revenue} - \text{Total variable costs} - \text{Fixed costs}$$

Assuming there is no interest expense, a 40% tax rate means that for every $1.00 of operating income earned, the company will pay CRA $0.40 and it will retain $0.60. In short, the company retains 60% of its operating income. The company's net income = Operating income × (1 – tax rate), or simply:

$$\frac{\text{Net income}}{1 - \text{Tax rate}} = \text{Operating income}$$

It is now straightforward to calculate the number of units that must be sold to achieve a target net income based on a target operating income. We have already seen three ways to do this calculation. First, using the relationship between revenue and total costs, both variable and fixed:

$$\frac{\text{Target net income}}{1 - \text{Tax rate}} = \text{Revenue} - \text{Total variable costs} - \text{Fixed costs}$$

Substituting numbers from our Do-All Software example:

$$\frac{\$960}{1 - 0.40} = (\$200 \times Q) - (\$120 \times Q) - \$2,000$$

$$\$1,600 = (\$200 \times Q) - (\$120 \times Q) - \$2,000$$

$$\$80 \times Q = \$3,600$$

$$Q = \$3,600 \div \$80 \text{ per unit} = 45 \text{ units}$$

Alternatively, we can exploit the contribution margin and calculate Q as shown:

$$\frac{\text{Target net income}}{1 - \text{Tax rate}} = \text{Target operating income}$$

$$\frac{\text{Fixed costs} + \dfrac{\text{Target net income}}{1 - \text{Tax rate}}}{\text{Contribution margin per unit}} = \text{Volume of units required to be sold}$$

$$\frac{\$2,000 + \dfrac{\$960}{1 - 0.40}}{\$80} = \frac{\$2,000 + \$1,600}{\$80 \text{ per unit}} = 45 \text{ units} = \frac{\text{Volume of units}}{\text{required to be sold}}$$

Proof:

Revenue, $200 per unit × 45 units	$9,000
Variable costs, $120 per unit × 45 units	5,400
Contribution margin	3,600
Fixed costs	2,000
Operating income	1,600
Income taxes, $1,600 × 0.40	640
Net income	$ 960

Recall that when we needed to calculate Q to achieve a target operating income, we obtained the rounded-up value of Q = 44 units. This is not enough, however, to achieve our target net income. But focusing the analysis on target net income instead of target operating income will never change the BEP. This is because, by definition, operating income at the breakeven point is $0, and no income taxes are paid when there is no operating income.

USING CVP ANALYSIS TO MAKE MORE COMPLEX DECISIONS

CVP models are very versatile. We are going to add complexity to our model by changing two or more factors at once. Wei has already made important strategic decisions to be a merchandiser, not a producer, and she understands customers can purchase from among several sellers. This means, all other things being equal, that reducing her costs will improve her profitability relative to her competitors. This is called a *cost leadership strategy*.[1]

Wei now wants to calculate the outcome of additional changes to her plan. For example, Wei would like to calculate the effect on her operating income if she decides to advertise. Wei would also like to calculate the effect on her operating income if at the same time she decides to change her sales price. Wei also thinks she has an opportunity to select among contracts to rent space. The contracts have

> **4**
> Apply the CVP model in decision making and explain how sensitivity analyses can help managers both identify and manage risk.

---

[1]Michael Porter of Harvard University first presented strategy as an appropriate matching of internal to external factors and distinguished two successful strategies as cost leadership and value leadership (product differentiation).

different cost structures: purely variable, purely fixed, and mixed. Using CVP analysis she can calculate the most profitable choice among the alternative contracts given the amount of risk she is willing to take.

DECISION TO ADVERTISE

Wei anticipates she will sell 40 units if she attends the convention. At 40 units, her operating income will be $1,200. However, if Wei pays $500 for an advertisement in the convention brochure, then she anticipates her sales volume will increase to 44 units. Advertising is a fixed cost because it must be paid even if Wei sells no units at all. Will her operating profit increase? The following table presents the CVP analysis:

	40 Packages Sold with No Advertising (1)	44 Packages Sold with Advertising (2)	Difference (3) = (2) − (1)
Revenue ($200 × 40; $200 × 44)	$8,000	$8,800	$800
Variable costs ($120 × 40; $120 × 44)	4,800	5,280	480
Contribution margin ($80 × 40; $80 × 44)	3,200	3,520	320
Fixed costs	2,000	2,500	500
Operating income	$1,200	$1,020	$(180)

Operating income decreases from $1,200 to $1,020. Clearly, if the goal is to increase operating income, this is not the correct decision. Notice that this conclusion can be seen in the third column, which predicts the difference with and without advertising. If Wei advertises, then contribution margin will increase by $320 (revenue, $800 − variable costs, $480), *and* fixed costs will increase by $500, resulting in a $180 decrease in operating income ($320 − $500).

As you become more familiar with CVP analysis, it is more effective to evaluate the financial results of different alternatives based only on those values that differ. It is the differences that affect your decision. Differences are *relevant* information about the consequences of each choice.

DECISION TO REDUCE SELLING PRICE

Wei now wonders if it's a good idea to reduce the selling price to $175 instead of $200. At this price, Wei anticipates she will sell 50 units instead of 40 units. The software wholesaler who supplies Do-All Software will sell the packages to Wei for $115 per unit instead of $120. Should Wei reduce the selling price? The following analysis tells Wei the answer is no:

Contribution margin from lowering price to $175: ($175 − $115) per unit × 50 units	$3,000
Contribution margin from maintaining price at $200: ($200 − $120) per unit × 40 units	3,200
Change in contribution margin from lowering price	$ (200)

The contribution margin decreases by $200. The fixed costs of $2,000 will not change under either option; therefore, operating income will decrease by $200.

Wei could also ask, "At what price can I sell 50 units (purchased at $115 per unit) and continue to earn a pre-tax target operating income of $1,200?" The CVP analysis works backwards, from the bottom to the top line of the contribution margin statement. Wei simply inserts all the values she knows. The targeted selling price per unit is $179.

Target operating income	$1,200
Add fixed costs	2,000
Target contribution margin	$3,200
Divided by number of units sold	÷50 units
Target contribution margin per unit	$ 64
Add variable cost per unit	115
Target selling price	$ 179

Proof:

Revenue, $179 per unit × 50 units	$8,950
Variable costs, $115 per unit × 50 units	5,750
Contribution margin	3,200
Fixed costs	2,000
Operating income	$1,200

Wei should examine the effects of other decisions, such as simultaneously increasing advertising costs and lowering sales prices. What effect would that have on operating income? After completing her analysis, Wei should choose the alternative with the highest operating income.

MARGIN OF SAFETY AND RISK

The **margin of safety** is the amount at which either expected or actual revenue exceeds breakeven revenue. Expressed in units, it is calculated as budgeted sales quantity Q minus the breakeven quantity (Q − BEP Q). If the result is zero, then there is no margin of safety. Wei can choose her margin of safety by changing predicted sales quantity; generally, the larger the margin of safety the less likely it is Wei will endure an operating loss. She can use the margin of safety to answer questions such as what the consequences are if revenue decreases below budget. How far can they fall below budget before the breakeven point is reached? Such a fall could be the result of the introduction of a competitor's product at the conference, taking away a portion of her budgeted sales volume.

Assume that Wei has fixed costs of $2,000, a selling price of $200, and variable cost per unit of $120. The budgeted revenue is $8,000, budgeted sales volume is 40 units, and the budgeted operating income is $1,200. Wei has already calculated that 25 units is the breakeven point for this set of assumptions and breakeven revenue is $5,000 ($200 per unit × 25 units). Wei can determine the margin of safety using the following relationship expressed in equation form:

$$\text{Margin of safety} = \frac{\text{Budgeted}}{\text{revenue}} - \frac{\text{Breakeven}}{\text{revenue}} = \$8,000 - \$5,000 = \$3,000$$

$$\frac{\text{Margin of}}{\text{safety (in units)}} = \frac{\text{Budgeted}}{\text{sales (units)}} - \frac{\text{Breakeven}}{\text{sales (units)}} = 40 - 25 = 15 \text{ units}$$

Sometimes margin of safety is expressed as a percentage, and once again the denominator is revenue:

$$\text{Margin of safety percentage} = \frac{\text{Margin of safety in dollars}}{\text{Budgeted (or actual) revenue}}$$

In our example, the margin of safety percentage is $= \dfrac{\$3,000}{\$8,000} = 37.5\%$

This result means revenue would have to decrease substantially, by 37.5%, to reach breakeven revenue. The high margin of safety gives Wei confidence that she is unlikely to suffer a loss. What if Wei had predicted a sales volume of 30 units? Then, budgeted revenue would be $6,000 and the margin of safety would be as follows:

$$\text{Budgeted revenue} - \text{Breakeven revenue} = \$6,000 - \$5,000 = \$1,000$$

$$\frac{\text{Margin of}}{\text{safety percentage}} = \frac{\text{Margin of safety in dollars}}{\text{Budgeted (or actual) revenue}} = \frac{\$1,000}{\$6,000} = 16.67\%$$

This result means that if revenue decreases by more than 16.67%, Wei would suffer a loss. A lower margin of safety increases the risk of a loss.

Wei has just performed a **sensitivity analysis**, which is a "what-if" technique that managers use to examine how an outcome will change if the original predicted data are not achieved or if an underlying assumption changes. In this case, it reveals how changes to budgeted revenue affect Wei's margin of safety. Sensitivity analysis is a simple approach to recognizing **risk**—the possibility that actual future results will differ from expected results. If Wei does not have the tolerance for this level of risk, she will prefer not to rent a booth at the convention. **Risk tolerance** is the risk of loss measured in percent that a person or team is willing to take. The lower the percentage, the lower the tolerance for risk.

ALTERNATIVE FIXED- AND VARIABLE-COST STRUCTURES

Computer Conventions has presented Wei with three booth rental options. Her first option is to rent the booth for the fixed amount of $2,000. Her second option is to pay a fixed amount of $800 and an additional $30 charge (15% of her $200 selling price per unit) for every unit she sells. Her third option is to pay a $50 charge (25% of her $200 selling price per unit) for every unit she sells. The third option does not have a fixed amount. Exhibit 3-4 graphically depicts the profit-volume relationship for each option. The lines represent the relationship between units sold and operating income. We are already familiar with Option 1; this is a fully fixed-cost contract. If Wei fails to sell a single unit, she still must pay $2,000 for the booth.

The line representing Option 2 shows fixed costs of $800 and a contribution margin per unit of $50 ($200 − $120 − $30). The arithmetic indicates that at 16 units Wei will cover her fixed cost ($800 ÷ $50 = 16 units)

The line representing Option 3 has fixed costs of $0 and a contribution margin per unit of $30 ($200 − $120 − $50). If Wei sells 0 units, it costs her nothing to rent the booth. The graph shows that under each contract, the breakeven point (BEP) is either 25, 16, or 0 units. You can read these values where each sloped line crosses the horizontal axis.

Wei's reaction to the different BEPs will depend on how much downside risk she is willing to accept. In the worst case, when she sells nothing, she could lose $2,000, $800, or nothing. The return or upside potential is that if she sells more than

EXHIBIT 3-4
Profit-Volume Graph for Alternative Rent Contract Options for Do-All Software

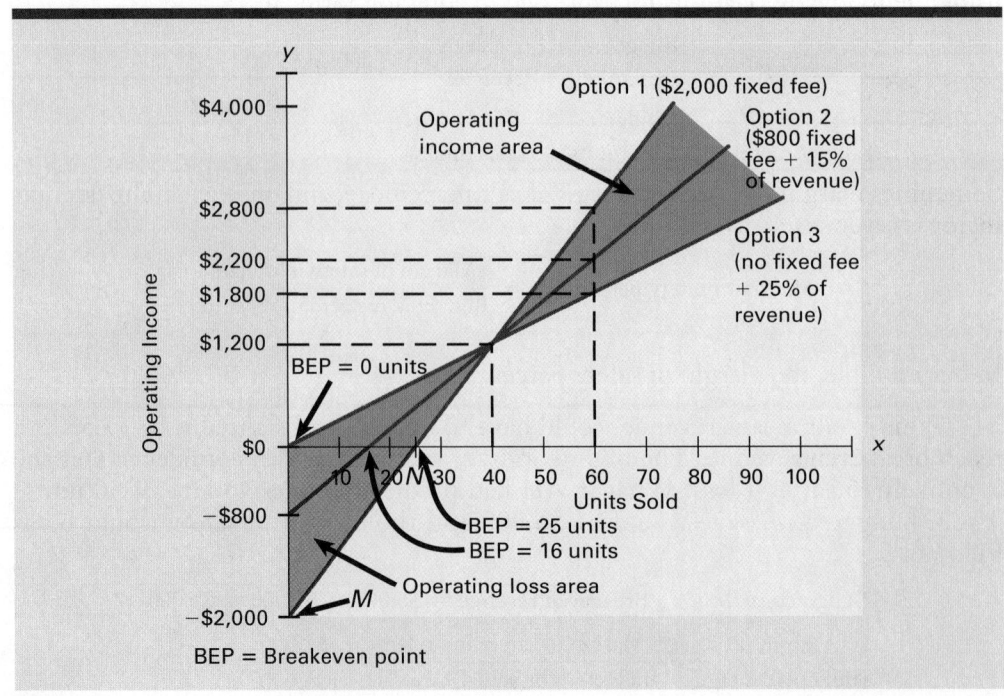

the BEP in Option 1, revenue from each unit sold above the BEP goes straight to operating income at the rate of $80 per unit. In Option 2 her BEP is lower, but so too is her upside potential. Revenue from each unit sold above the BEP goes to operating income at the rate of $50 per unit. In Option 3 her BEP is as low as possible. Her upside potential, however, is only $30 per unit sold above that BEP.

OPERATING LEVERAGE

The risk-return trade-off across alternative cost structures can be measured as operating leverage. **Operating leverage** describes the effects that fixed costs have on changes in operating income as changes occur in units sold and contribution margin. Organizations with a high proportion of fixed costs in their cost structures, as is the case under Option 1, have high operating leverage. The line representing Option 1 in Exhibit 3-4 is the steepest of the three lines. Small increases in sales lead to large increases in operating income; small decreases in sales result in relatively large decreases in operating income, leading to a greater risk of operating losses.

$$\frac{\text{Degree of}}{\text{operating leverage}} = \frac{\text{Contribution margin}}{\text{Operating income}}$$

The following table shows the **degree of operating leverage** at sales of 40 units for the three alternative rent contracts:

	Option 1	Option 2	Option 3
1. Contribution margin per unit	$ 80	$ 50	$ 30
2. Contribution margin (Row 1 × 40 units)	$3,200	$2,000	$1,200
3. Operating income (from Exhibit 3-4)	$1,200	$1,200	$1,200
4. Degree of operating leverage (Row 2 ÷ Row 3)	$\frac{\$3,200}{\$1,200} = 2.67$	$\frac{\$2,000}{\$1,200} = 1.67$	$\frac{\$1,200}{\$1,200} = 1.00$

When sales are 40 units, a 1 percentage change in sales and contribution margin will result in 2.67 times that percentage change in operating income for Option 1. This is why the term *leverage* is used. Under Option 2, for example, the leverage decreases to 1.67 times any 1 percentage change in sales.

Consider, for example, a sales increase of 50% from 40 to 60 units. Contribution margin will increase by 50% under each alternative. However, operating income will increase from $1,200 to $2,800 [($1,200) + (2.67 × 50% × $1,200)] in Option 1. In Option 3 operating income will only increase from $1,200 to $1,800 [($1,200) + (1.00 × 50% × $1,200)]. The degree of operating leverage at a given level of sales helps managers calculate the effect of fluctuations in sales on operating income.

In the presence of fixed costs, the degree of operating leverage is different at different levels of sales. For example, at sales of 60 units, the degree of operating leverage under each of the three options is as follows:

	Option 1	Option 2	Option 3
1. Contribution margin per unit	$ 80	$ 50	$ 30
2. Contribution margin (Row 1 × 60 units)	$4,800	$3,000	$1,800
3. Operating income (from Exhibit 3-4)	$2,800	$2,200	$1,800
4. Degree of operating leverage (Row 2 ÷ Row 3)	$\frac{\$4,800}{\$2,800} = 1.71$	$\frac{\$3,000}{\$2,200} = 1.36$	$\frac{\$1,800}{\$1,800} = 1.00$

The degree of operating leverage decreases from 2.67 (at sales of 40 units) to 1.71 (at sales of 60 units) under Option 1 and from 1.67 to 1.36 under Option 2. In general, whenever there are fixed costs, the degree of operating leverage decreases as the level of sales increases beyond the breakeven point. If fixed costs are $0, as in Option 3, contribution margin equals operating income and the degree of operating leverage equals 1.00 at all sales levels.

Sky-High Fixed Costs Trouble XM Satellite Radio

Fixed costs, unlike variable costs, do not automatically decrease as volume declines. XM Satellite Radio, once the market leader in satellite radio broadcasting, learned a hard lesson on the important effect of cost structure.

In 2001 the upfront costs for a broadcast license, two space satellites, and other infrastructure was over $1 billion. Once in operation XM spent billions more on fixed costs to purchase content, satellite transmission space, and R&D. XM's variable costs were minimal, mainly artists' royalty fees, customer service, and billing. This business model had high operating leverage. XM's breakeven revenue comprised both fees from millions of subscribers and advertising revenue. The competitive disadvantage of this highly leveraged business model soon became apparent. By 2002 Sirius Satellite radio began business, competing head-to-head with XM. Other competitors included traditional free radio, which had a huge share of the market. Then the iPod entered the market.

For a fee, iPod users could customize their entertainment and endure no commercial interruptions at all. The cost structure around the iPod had much lower operating leverage. Apple's R&D and purchase of various applications and content provided service to any iMac, MacBook, iPhone, or iPod user. Any additional or marginal costs were primarily tied to manufacturing and distribution

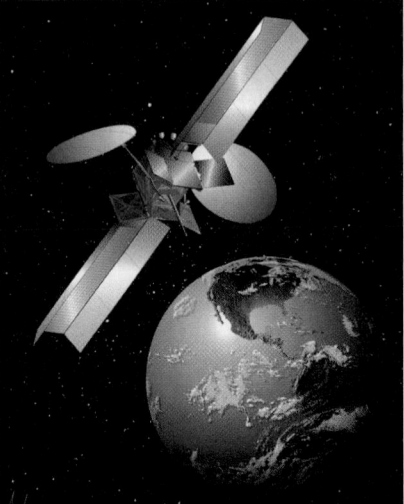

of the iPod. The breakeven sales volume for this product was far below that of any satellite radio station.

XM began spending extravagantly. They spent over $650 million for exclusive programming content, such as Major League Baseball and Oprah Winfrey. Sirius responded by inking an exclusive deal with the National Football League and paying "shock-jock" Howard Stern nearly $500 million to move to Sirius. This increased the operating leverage for both companies.

By 2006, despite its nearly 8 million subscribers, XM had never turned a profit and most analysts and observers felt that neither XM nor Sirius (with 6 million subscribers) would ever be able to recover their high fixed costs . . . and they were almost right. In 2007 XM merged with Sirius and the new CEO acknowledged that high operating leverage killed both companies and forced the merger. He vowed to look for "synergies on every line of the income statement."

Sources: "XM Satellite Radio (A)," Harvard Business School Case No. 9-504-009; "Satellite Radio: An Industry Case Study," Kellogg School of Management (Northwestern University) Case No. 5-206-255; Testimony of Sean Buston, CFA, before the Copyright Royalty Board of the Library of Congress (October 2006); Justin Fox, "The 'stop us before we spend again' merger," Time.com, February 20, 2007. time-blog.com/curious_capitalist/2007/02/the_stop_us_before_we_spend_ag.html; Various analysts reports.

Cost structure is a long-term decision because fixed costs usually pay for capacity. Companies with a high percentage of fixed costs in their cost structure are often called **capital intensive companies**. Industries such as airlines, mobile communications, and gold mining are very capital intensive. When sales volume exceeds the breakeven point, each additional sale will contribute a large proportion of revenue to operating income. But when sales volumes fail to exceed breakeven, the debt associated with fixed costs must still be repaid, creating financial distress. For example, as the airline and car manufacturing industries accumulated losses from 2001 through 2007, many companies could not sell enough to cover fixed costs and declared bankruptcy.

Managers cannot avoid difficulties arising from a high fixed cost structure if their industry is capital intensive. High fixed cost simultaneously increases the risk of losses if demand is weak, and magnifies profit if demand is strong. A high fixed cost structure requires financing through either debt or equity. Debt carries a mandatory interest payment that shelters profit from tax only as long as there is a profit. If demand drops, the mandatory debt payments increase losses. This is why it is important to carefully evaluate how the level of fixed costs and variable costs will affect the risk-return trade-off.

Other companies may be labour intensive and reduce costs by transferring manufacturing facilities from Europe and North America to lower-cost countries such as Mexico and China. Companies may also substitute high fixed costs with lower variable costs when they purchase products from lower-cost suppliers instead of manufacturing products themselves. General Electric and Hewlett-Packard recently began offshoring service functions, such as post-sales customer service, to countries like India where costs are lower. These alternatives reduce both costs and operating leverage but are controversial. Some argue that outsourcing helps to keep costs and therefore prices low, which means North American and European companies can remain globally competitive. Others argue that outsourcing reduces job opportunities at home and diminishes the capability of families to purchase finished goods.

EXPECTED VALUE

The tool best suited to help Wei make a decision is a calculation of expected value. **Expected value** is the sum of the risk-weighted average of the outcomes of each choice. In this example the outcome is the operating income. **Expected monetary value** is a more precise term that is used when the outcomes are measured in dollars. The mathematical notation for each alternative contract is a_1, a_2, and a_3.

Assume Wei can say she is 60% sure she will sell 30 units and 40% sure she will sell 60 units at the convention.[2] The 60% and 40% are measures of risk or probability (p_i). The sales volumes are events. Her weighted sales are the most likely events, a combination of $0.60 \times 30 = 18$ units and $0.40 \times 60 = 24$ units respectively. The notation for 60% is $p_1 = (0.60)$; the notation for 40% is $p_2 = (0.40)$. The mathematical notation for the possible sales volumes are $Q_1 = 30$ and $Q_2 = 60$. The expected or risk-weighted sales volume is calculated as the sum of the risk-weighted volumes:

$$(p_1 \times Q_1) + (p_2 \times Q_2) = \text{expected sales volume}$$

$$(0.6 \times 30) + (0.4 \times 60) = \text{expected sales volume}$$

$$= 42 \text{ units}$$

The outcomes x_1, x_2, and x_3 are the three expected monetary values of operating income.

Exhibit 3-5 illustrates how Wei can calculate her expected operating income using the expected sales volume of 42 units.

Interpreting Results from an Expected Value Analysis Under a_1 for the Vancouver convention, Wei will earn operating income of either $2,800 if she sells 60 units (high), or $400 if she sells 30 units (low). Under a_2 for the Vancouver convention, Wei will earn operating income of either $2,200 if she sells 60 units (high) or $700, if she sells 30 units (low). Under a_3 for the Vancouver convention, Wei will earn operating income of either $1,800 if she sells 60 units (high) or $900, if she sells 30 units (low).

What direction should Wei go? Wei could select rental option a_3, which is the safe option. If Wei is wrong about selling 30 units and sells nothing, she loses nothing. However, if she chooses this option Wei has failed to consider her upside potential and has focused only on her downside risk. Her upside potential for a_3 is the lowest at $30 per unit sold. Low risk tolerance is called **risk aversion**: the downside risk of loss matters more to the decision maker than the upside potential gain. This is a form of bias.

If Wei is highly tolerant of risk, she will prefer a_1, where the upside is the highest at $80 per unit sold. Unfortunately, if she is wrong, she could lose up to $2,000. High risk tolerance is called **risk loving**: the upside potential matters more to the decision maker than the downside risk of loss.[3] This is also a form of bias.

[2]To interpret the expected value, or risk-weighted average of all operating incomes, imagine Wei chooses contract alternative a_1. Assume Wei attends many conventions. The probabilities remain unchanged for each event. She will expect to earn $400 operating income 60% of the time (at 60 conventions), and $2,800 operating income 40% of the time (at 40 conventions), for a total expected operating income of $136,000 ($400 × 60 + $2,800 × 40). The expected value of $1,360 is the average operating income per convention ($136,000 ÷ 100). In the real world Wei will not have the luxury of attending 100 conventions to verify her judgment about the probabilities and the quantity of sales. Her decision will be one-time and short-term. But even in these circumstances, expected value clarifies Wei's incorporation of risk into her decision model.

[3]For more formal approaches, refer to J. Moore and L. Weatherford, *Decision Modeling with Microsoft Excel*, 6th ed. (Upper Saddle River, NJ: Prentice Hall, 2001).

EXHIBIT 3-5
Decision Table for Do-All Software

Inputs	Alternative a_1	Alternative a_2	Alternative a_3
Event, sales volume Q_i		30	60
Probability (p_i)		0.60	0.40
Expected sales volumes		18	24
Total expected sales volumes $= (p_1) \times (Q_1) + (p_2) \times (Q_2)$	42		
Alternative contracts: fixed cost	$2,000	$ 800	$ –
Alternative contracts: total variable cost as a % of revenues	0%	15%	25%
CVP analysis	**Alternative a_1**	**Alternative a_2**	**Alternative a_3**
Sales price per unit	$ 200	$ 200	$ 200
Variable cost per unit (including rental)	120	150	170
Contribution margin	80	50	30
Expected value analysis			
Expected revenues ($200 × 42)	$8,400	$8,400	$8,400
Expected total variable cost	5,040	6,300	7,140
Expected contribution margin	3,360	2,100	1,260
Fixed cost	2,000	800	–
Expected operating income (outcome x_1, x_2, x_3)	$1,360	$1,300	$1,260

If Wei is **risk neutral**, she will simply look at the expected operating income under each alternative contract. *Risk neutral* means the decision maker will feel as much pain at losing a dollar as joy at gaining a dollar. Wei will simply select the highest expected operating income. This is Wei's rational choice.

Making a decision is not the end of business planning and control. If Wei makes the decision to attend the convention, she has done so on the basis of predicted outcomes. As a good manager, Wei will conclude by comparing her actual operating income to her expected operating income. Exhibit 3-6 illustrates how the decision framework applies to making a decision using expected values.

EXHIBIT 3-6
Expected Value Decision Model

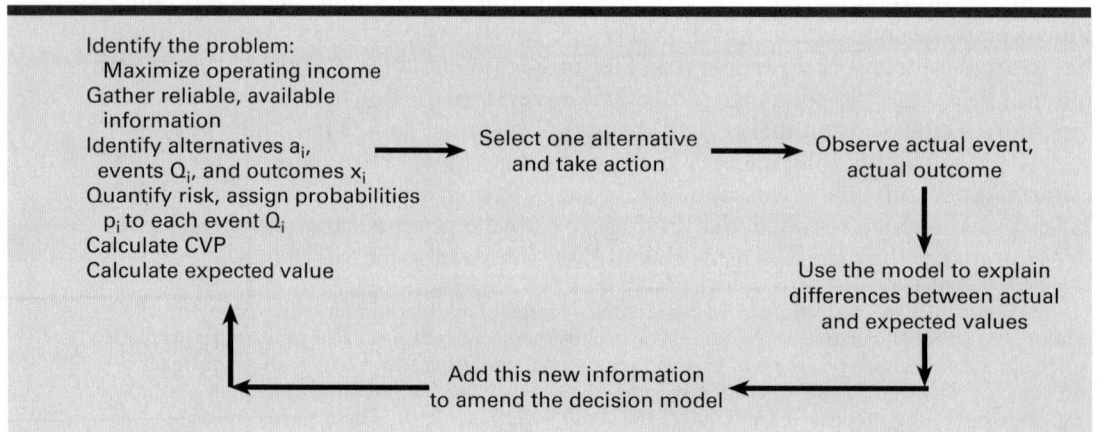

EFFECTS OF SALES MIX ON INCOME

Interpret the results of CVP analyses in more complex multi-product and multiple cost driver situations.

⑤

Sales mix is the quantities of various products (or services) that in sum are the total sales volume of a company. Each product or service is a proportion of the total sales volume measured either as units or revenue.

Suppose Wei looks to the future and budgets the following for a conference in Toronto where she expects to sell different quantities of two products, Do-All Software and Superword:

	Do-All	Superword	Total
Expected sales	60	40	100
Revenue, $200 and $100 per unit	$12,000	$4,000	$16,000
Total variable costs ($120 × 60; $70 × 40)	7,200	2,800	10,000
Contribution margin ($80 × 60; $30 × 40)	$ 4,800	$1,200	6,000
Fixed costs			4,500
Operating income			$ 1,500

What is the BEP? The total sales volume to break even in a multi-product company depends on the sales mix—the combination of the number of units of Do-All sold and the number of units of Superword sold. We assume that the budgeted sales mix is 3:2 (60:40), because Wei expects to sell 3 (60 out of the 100) units of Do-All for every 2 (40 out of the 100) units she sells of Superword. To simplify her planning, Wei assumes this will not change at different quantities of each product sold. In fact, Wei is selling a bundle composed of three units of Do-All and two units of Superword. The two products are not physically bundled, but for planning purposes (budgeting), it is easier to work with a bundle of five units in total sales volume.

Each bundle yields a contribution margin of $300, calculated as follows:

	Sales Volume per Product in Each Bundle	Contribution Margin per Unit for Do-All and Superword	Contribution Margin of the Bundle
Do-All	3	$80	$240
Superword	2	30	60
Total			$300

With the contribution margin for each bundle, Wei can now calculate the breakeven sales volume in bundles:

$$\text{Breakeven sales volume in bundles} = \frac{\text{Fixed costs}}{\text{Contribution margin per bundle}} = \frac{\$4,500}{\$300 \text{ per bundle}} = 15 \text{ bundles}$$

The breakeven point for each product using the 3:2 ratio is calculated by multiplying the breakeven sales volume of bundles first by 3 for Do-All, then 2 for Superword:

Do-All: 15 bundles × 3 units of Do-All per bundle	45 units
Superword: 15 bundles × 2 units of Superword per bundle	30 units
Breakeven sales volume in units	75 units

Breakeven point in dollars for Do-All and Superword is:

Do-All: revenue ($200 × 45)	$9,000
Superword: 30 units × $100 per unit	3,000
Breakeven revenue	$12,000

We can also calculate the breakeven point in revenue for the multi-products situation as follows:

	Sales Volume in Each Bundle	Sales Price per Unit	Revenue of the Bundle
Do-All	3	$200	$600
Superword	2	100	200
Total			$800

$$\begin{matrix} \text{Contribution} \\ \text{margin} \\ \text{percentage for} \\ \text{the bundle} \end{matrix} = \frac{\text{Contribution margin of the bundle}}{\text{Revenue of the bundle}} = \frac{\$300}{\$800} = 0.375 \text{ or } 37.5\%$$

$$\begin{matrix} \text{Breakeven} \\ \text{revenue} \end{matrix} = \frac{\text{Fixed costs}}{\text{Contribution margin \% for the bundle}} = \frac{\$4,500}{0.375} = \$12,000$$

$$\begin{matrix} \text{Breakeven} \\ \text{sales volume in} \\ \text{bundles} \end{matrix} = \frac{\text{Breakeven revenue}}{\text{Revenue per bundle}} = \frac{\$12,000}{\$800 \text{ per bundle}} = 15 \text{ bundles}$$

Recall that in all our calculations we have assumed that the budgeted sales mix (3 units of Do-All for every 2 units of Superword) will not change at different levels of total unit sales.

Of course, there are many different sales mixes (in units) that result in a contribution margin of $4,500 and cause Wei to break even, as the following table shows:

Sales Mix (Units)		Contribution Margin from		
Do-All (1)	Superword (2)	Do-All (3) = $80 × (1)	Superword (4) = $30 × (2)	Total Contribution Margin (5) = (3) + (4)
48	22	$3,840	$ 660	$4,500
36	54	2,880	1,620	4,500
30	70	2,400	2,100	4,500

If, for example, the sales mix changes to 3:7, or 3 units of Do-All for every 7 units of Superword, you can see in the preceding table that the breakeven sales volume in bundles increases from 75 units to 100 units. The breakeven quantity increases because the new sales mix shifted to the product with the lower contribution margin per unit ($30 rather than $80). Generally, if the problem is how to maximize operating income, Wei should shift her sales mix to increase the sales volume of the higher contribution margin product. Companies adjust their sales mix to respond to demand changes. For example, as gasoline prices increase and customers want smaller cars, auto companies shift their production mix to produce additional smaller cars.

MULTIPLE COST DRIVERS

Throughout this chapter, we have assumed that the sales volume Q was exactly the same as the production (or acquisition) volume. This single volume was the only **revenue driver** and the only cost driver. A more complicated problem arises if this assumption is wrong. The CVP analysis can be adapted if there are multiple cost drivers. To simplify, we will examine the situation where there is a single product.

Suppose Wei will incur a variable cost of $10 for preparing documents (including an invoice) for each customer who buys Do-All Software. The cost driver of document-preparation costs is the number of customers who buy Do-All Software. Wei's operating income can then be expressed in terms of revenue and these costs:

$$\begin{matrix} \text{Operating} \\ \text{income} \end{matrix} = \text{Revenue} - \begin{pmatrix} \text{Variable} \\ \text{cost per} \times \begin{matrix}\text{Quantity of} \\ \text{packages} \end{matrix} \\ \text{unit} \quad \text{sold} \end{pmatrix} - \begin{pmatrix} \text{Variable cost} \\ \text{of documents} \times \begin{matrix}\text{Quantity of} \\ \text{customers}\end{matrix} \\ \text{per customer} \end{pmatrix} - \text{Fixed costs}$$

If Wei sells 40 units to 15 customers, then operating income is:

Operating income = ($200 per unit × 40 units) − ($120 per unit × 40 units)
  − ($10 per customer × 15 customers) − $2,000
  = $8,000 − $4,800 − $150 − $2,000 = $1,050

If Wei sells 40 units to 40 customers, then operating income is:

Operating income = ($200 × 40) − ($120 × 40) − ($10 × 40) − $2,000
  = $8,000 − $4,800 − $400 − $2,000 = $800

The number of packages sold is not the only factor that affects Wei's operating income. If sales volume is constant but the quantity of customers increases, then Wei's operating income will decrease. The costs depend on two cost drivers, both the sales volume and the number of customers.

With multiple cost drivers, there is no unique breakeven point. Wei will break even if her sales volume is either 26 packages to 8 customers or 27 packages to 16 customers as shown:

$$(\$200 \times 26) - (\$120 \times 26) - (\$10 \times 8) - \$2,000 = \$5,200 - \$3,120 - \$80 - \$2,000 = \$0$$
$$(\$200 \times 27) - (\$120 \times 27) - (\$10 \times 16) - \$2,000 = \$5,400 - \$3,240 - \$160 - \$2,000 = \$0$$

CVP ANALYSIS IN NON-PROFIT ORGANIZATIONS

So far our CVP analysis has focused on a merchandising company. CVP can also be applied to manufacturing, service, and non-profit organizations. In fact, the key goal of a non-profit company is to break even, not to maximize profit. To apply CVP analysis in service and non-profit organizations we need to focus on measuring their output. Service and social welfare outputs are measured differently from products sold by manufacturing and merchandising companies. Examples of output measures in various service and non-profit industries are as follows:

Industry	Measure of Output
Airlines	Passenger miles
Hotels/motels	Room-nights occupied
Hospitals	Patient days
Universities	Student credit-hours

Consider a community care agency that has government support of $900,000 (its revenues) for 2012. This non-profit agency's purpose is to assist disabled people seeking employment. On average, the agency supplements each individual's annual income by $5,000. The agency's only other costs are fixed costs of rent and administrative salaries equal to $270,000. The agency manager wants to know how many people can be assisted in 2012. We can use CVP analysis here by setting operating income to $0. Let Q be the number of disabled people to be assisted:

$$\text{Revenue} - \text{Variable costs} - \text{Fixed costs} = \$0$$
$$\$900,000 - \$5,000\,Q - \$270,000 = \$0$$
$$\$5,000\,Q = \$900,000 - \$270,000 = \$630,000$$
$$Q = \$630,000 \div \$5,000 \text{ per person} = 126 \text{ people}$$

Suppose the manager is concerned that the total budget appropriation for 2012 will be reduced by 15% to $765,000 ($900,000 \times (1 - 0.15) = $765,000). How many disabled people could be assisted (with $5,000) on this reduced budget?

$$\$765,000 - \$5,000\,Q - \$270,000 = \$0$$
$$\$5,000\,Q = \$765,000 - \$270,000 = \$495,000$$
$$Q = \$495,000 \div \$5,000 \text{ per person} = 99 \text{ people}$$

Note the following two characteristics of the CVP relationships in this non-profit situation:

1. The percentage drop in the number of people assisted, $(126 - 99) \div 126$, or 21.4%, exceeds the 15% reduction in the budget. The reason is that the $270,000 in fixed costs must still be paid. In a lower total budget, less money remains to assist people. The percentage drop in service exceeds the percentage drop in budgeted revenue from the government.

2. Given the reduced revenue of $765,000, the manager can adjust operations to stay within this appropriation in at least one of three basic ways: (a) reduce the number of people assisted from the current 126, (b) reduce the variable cost of assistance from $5,000 per person, or (c) reduce the total fixed costs from the current $270,000.

(Try to solve this problem before examining the solution that follows.)

PROBLEM

The following problem illustrates how to use relevant information from both the financial accounting income statement and the contribution income statement to calculate the breakeven point. Wei wants to know how to calculate her breakeven sales volume and her breakeven sales revenue. (R. Lambert, adapted)

Wei has gathered the following information: Operating income for Wei Shao Inc. (WSI) for the year 2012 on production and sales volume (Q) of 200,000 units was summarized in the financial accounting operating income statement below. Additional accounting information was also provided regarding the inventoriable fixed costs and the period (non-manufacturing, operating expenses) variable costs per unit shown below the operating income:

Wei Shao Inc. Operating Income Statement Year Ended 2012	
Sales revenue	$3,120,000
Cost of goods sold (COGS)	1,920,000
Gross margin	1,200,000
Operating expenses	1,380,000
Operating income (loss)	$ (180,000)
Fixed cost (inventoriable)	$ 600,000
Variable cost per unit (non-manufacturing)	$ 6.00

REQUIRED

1. Calculate WSI's variable manufacturing costs per unit in 2012.
2. Calculate WSI's fixed marketing and distribution costs in 2012.
3. Because WSI's gross margin per unit is $6 ($1,200,000 ÷ 200,000 units), Wei believes that if WSI had produced and sold 230,000 units, it would have covered the $1,380,000 of marketing and distribution costs ($1,380,000 ÷ $6 = 230,000) and enabled WSI to break even for the year. Calculate WSI's operating income if production and sales volume had been Q = 230,000 units. Explain briefly why Wei is wrong.
4. Calculate the breakeven point for the year 2012 in both sales volume and revenue.
5. Calculate both the sales volume required to achieve operating income of $100,000 and the operating profit margin percentage.
6. Calculate total fixed and total variable cost as a proportion of total cost. What is Wei's cost structure and her risk/return tradeoff?
7. Wei has been following market demand closely and believes there is a 35% probability that sales volume will be 300,000 units in 2013, a 25% probability that sales volume will be 320,000 units, and a 40% probability that sales volume will be 280,000 units. Calculate the risk-weighted expected sales volume in 2013. Can Wei expect to earn her targeted operating income calculated in requirement 5?
8. Calculate Wei's margin of safety in dollars and percentage. How does adding risk as a factor improve Wei's CVP analysis?
9. If Wei had to pay an additional variable cost of $5 per customer order, calculate her best alternative to maximize operating income. Alternative 1 is to sell 297,000 units to 15,000 customers. Alternative 2 is to sell 293,334 to 9,500 customers.

SOLUTION

1. Calculate unit variable cost (inventoriable)

Total inventoriable costs (COGS)	$1,920,000
Fixed cost (inventoriable)	600,000
Total variable cost (inventoriable) = COGS − Fixed cost inventoriable	$1,320,000
Q produced and sold	200,000
Variable cost per unit (inventoriable) = Total variable cost ÷ Q =	$ 6.60

2. Calculate fixed cost (period or non-manufacturing operating expenses)

Total operating expenses	$1,380,000
Total variable cost (Variable cost per unit × Q) = $6.00 × 200,000	1,200,000
Fixed cost (Operating expenses − Total variable non-manufacturing cost) =	$ 180,000

3. Calculate operating income

Sales price per unit for Q produced and sold = Revenue ÷ Q	200,000	$ 15.60
Contribution margin per unit = (Sales price per unit − Total variable cost per unit)		$ 3.00
Revenue for Q produced and sold =	230,000	$3,588,000
Contribution margin for total Q produced and sold =		690,000
Total fixed cost (inventoriable and non-manufacturing)		780,000
Operating income (Contribution margin – Total fixed cost)		$ (90,000)

Wei has confused gross with total contribution margin. She assumed that the COGS comprised only variable costs and that non-manufacturing costs comprised only fixed costs. Wei does not distinguish that cost behaviour is independent of cost classification. Both manufacturing and non-manufacturing costs comprise both fixed and variable costs.

4. Calculate breakeven point in sales volume Q and revenue

Breakeven point, Q = (FC ÷ Contribution margin per unit = $780,000 ÷ $3.00)
$$= 260,000$$

Breakeven point, Revenue = (Breakeven volume Q × Contribution margin per unit)
$$= \$ 4,056,000$$

Alternatively use CM% = (Contribution margin per unit ÷ Sales price per unit) = 19.231%*

Breakeven point, Revenue = (Fixed cost ÷ CM% or $3,120,000 ÷ 0.19231)   = $ 4,056,000

*Exactly this percentage can also be obtained from Contribution margin ÷ Revenue using amounts from requirement 3.

5. Calculate a target operating income

Contribution margin per unit	$ 3.00
Target operating income	$ 100,000
Fixed costs	$ 780,000
Sales volume = $\dfrac{\text{(Fixed costs + Target operating income)}}{\text{Contribution margin per unit}}$ =	293,333.3
Revenue	$4,576,011 (rounded)
Operating profit margin percentage	2.2%

Note that Wei cannot make ⅓ of a sale therefore her targeted sales volume must be rounded up to 293,334.0.

6. Calculate total fixed and total variable costs as a proportion of total costs

	Cost	%
Total fixed costs	$ 780,000	23.6%
Total variable costs	2,520,000	76.4%
Total costs	$ 3,300,000	

7. Calculate the risk-weighted expected sales volume in 2012.

	Q	Probability	Risk Weighted
Sales volume 1	300,000	0.35	105,000
Sales volume 2	320,000	0.25	80,000
Sales volume 3	280,000	0.40	112,000
Risk-weighted total expected sales volume			297,000

Including risk as a quantitative factor makes it clear to Wei and others if she has a biased view of future demand. Should Wei choose to explain her assumptions, it would be very easy. She can also readily show very pessimistic and very optimistic "what if" expected sales volumes. Based on this model, Wei can also calculate her margin of safety relative to her expected sales volume.

Wei can expect to achieve her targeted operating income of $100,000 because the expected sales volume exceeds the sales volume required to achieve her target.

8. Calculate the margin of safety in dollars and % using the expected operating income.

	Expected	Breakeven	Margin of Safety
Margin of safety = Budgeted (expected revenue) = Breakeven revenue	$4,633,200	$4,056,000	$577,200
Margin of safety percentage = Margin of safety ÷ Expected revenue			12.46%

9. Calculate the alternative with the highest operating income.

	Q = Quantity	Sales price	Variable cost	Fixed costs	Operating income
Alternative 1					
Sales in units	297,000	$15.60	$12.60		
Sales to customers	15,000		5.00		
Totals:		4,633,200	3,817,200	$780,000	$ 36,000
Alternative 2					
Sales in units	293,334	$15.60	$12.60		
Sales to customers	9,500		5.00		
Totals:		4,576,011	3,743,508	$780,000	$ 52,502

Wei's operating income is higher under alternative 2 and this is the alternative she would prefer. She has 2 cost drivers but only 1 revenue driver. The fewer customer orders, the lower is her total variable cost. Her operating leverage is low and so too is her contribution margin. This information can help Wei market her product to increase the Q or increase the quantity of units per customer order, rather than just focus on increasing Q.

SUMMARY POINTS

The following question-and-answer format summarizes the chapter's learning outcomes. Each point presents a key question, and the guidelines are the answer to that question.

LEARNING OUTCOMES	GUIDELINES
1. How can CVP analysis assist managers?	CVP analysis requires managers to distinguish cost behaviour from cost classification in an accurate model of relationships among factors critical to maximize profit. While an income statement provides reliable information, managers use a different contribution margin format for CVP models. The values of relevant cost, volume, and profit factors change among alternatives.
2. How do managers determine the breakeven point or the output needed to achieve a target operating income?	These two analyses differ with respect to one factor: the value assigned to operating income. At the breakeven point, the target operating income = $0. Any target operating income > $0 requires a sales volume higher than the breakeven point.
3. How should companies incorporate income taxes into CVP analysis?	Income taxes can be incorporated into CVP analysis by using target net income rather than target operating income. The breakeven point is unaffected by income taxes because no income taxes are paid when operating income = $0.
4. How should companies cope with risk, to explain how cost structure affects decisions?	Expected value uses probability to make the effect of failure on operating income clear. The decision among alternatives requires understanding how cost structure affects both the downside risk and the upside potential effects on operating income.
5. How can CVP analysis be applied to a company producing multiple products (revenue drivers) and multiple cost drivers?	CVP analysis can be applied to a company producing multiple products by assuming the sales mix of products sold remains constant as the total quantity of units sold changes. The basic concepts of CVP analysis can be applied to multiple cost driver situations, but there is no unique breakeven point.

This chapter and the Glossary at the end of the book contain definitions of the following important terms:

breakeven point (BEP) (p. 66)
capital intensive companies (p. 78)
contribution income statement (p. 68)
contribution margin (p. 67)
contribution margin percentage
    (p. 70)
contribution margin per unit (p. 68)
contribution margin ratio (p. 70)
cost-volume-profit (CVP) analysis
    (p. 66)

degree of operating leverage (p. 77)
expected monetary value (p. 79)
expected value (p. 79)
gross margin (p. 71)
gross margin percentage (p. 71)
gross profit percentage (p. 72)
margin of safety (p. 75)
net income margin (p. 72)
net income margin percentage (p. 72)
operating leverage (p. 77)

operating margin (p. 72)
operating margin percentage (p. 72)
revenue driver (p. 82)
risk (p. 76)
risk aversion (p. 79)
risk loving (p. 79)
risk neutral (p. 80)
risk tolerance (p. 76)
sales mix (p. 81)
sensitivity analysis (p. 76)

MyAccountingLab Make the grade with MyAccountingLab: The questions, exercises, and problems marked in red can be found on MyAccountingLab at **www.myaccountinglab.com**. You can practise them as often as you want, and most feature step-by-step guided instructions to help you find the right answer. Exercises and problems with an Excel icon in the margin have an accompanying Excel template on MyAccountingLab.

SHORT-ANSWER QUESTIONS

3-1 Describe the assumptions underlying CVP analysis.

3-2 Distinguish between operating income and net income.

3-3 "CVP is both simple and simplistic. If you want realistic analysis to underpin your decisions, look beyond CVP." Do you agree? Explain.

3-4 How does an increase in the income tax rate affect the breakeven point?

3-5 Describe sensitivity analysis. How has spreadsheet software affected its use?

3-6 Give an example of how a manager can decrease variable costs while increasing fixed costs.

3-7 Give an example of how a manager can increase variable costs while decreasing fixed costs.

3-8 What is operating leverage? How is knowing the degree of operating leverage (DOL) helpful to managers?

3-9 How can a company with multiple products compute its breakeven point?

EXERCISES

3-10 **Terminology.** A number of terms are listed below:

contribution margin   cost-volume-profit analysis
capital intensive   operating leverage
gross margin   sales mix
contribution margin percentage   breakeven point
risk aversion   risk-loving
margin of safety

Select the terms from the above list to complete the following sentences.

1. A term for a company with a high percentage of fixed costs in its cost structure is _____.

2. _____ is a model to analyze the behaviour of net income in response to change in total revenues, total costs, or both.

3. The _____ in units is the quantity of units sold to attain an operating income of zero.

4. _____ describes the effects that fixed costs have on changes in operating income as changes occur in units sold and contribution margin.

5. _____ is where the upside potential matters more to the decision maker than the downside risk of loss.

6. The _____ is equal to revenue less variable costs.

7. The _____ equals the contribution margin per unit divided by the selling price per unit.

8. The _____ equals revenues less cost of goods sold.

9. The _____ is the quantities of various products (or services) that in sum are the total sales volume of a company.

10. _____ is where the downside risk of loss matters more to the decision maker than the upside potential gain.

11. The _____ is the amount by which expected (or actual) revenues exceed breakeven revenues.

3-11 CVP analysis computations. The following partial information is available. Complete the table by filling in all the blanks. Each case is independent.

Case a. CM%, 23.67%

Case	Revenues	Variable Costs	Fixed Costs	Total Costs	Operating Income	Contributing Margin Percentage
a	$ 3,000	$ —	$ 250	$ —	$ 460	—
b	—	7,400	—	8,700	9,800	—
c	10,600	—	3,200	—	—	30%
d	9,450	—	2,500	8,170	—	—

3-12 CVP analysis computations. Fill in the blanks for each of the following independent cases.

Case b. unit selling price, $87

Case	Unit Selling Price	Unit Variable Operating Costs	Number of Units Sold	Total Contribution Margin	Total Fixed Costs	Operating Income
a	$ 70	$25	—	$ 900,000	$ —	$200,000
b	—	62	15,000	—	250,000	125,000
c	250	—	30,000	4,500,000	—	900,000
d	150	—	24,000	1,728,000	1,500,000	—

3-13 CVP computations. Patel Manufacturing sold 200,000 units of its product for $30 per unit in 2012. Variable cost per unit is $25 and total fixed costs are $800,000.

1. a. Contribution margin, $1,000,000

REQUIRED

1. Calculate (a) contribution margin and (b) operating income.

2. Patel's current manufacturing process is labour intensive. Kate Schoenen, Patel's production manager, has proposed investing in state-of-the-art manufacturing equipment, which will increase the annual fixed costs to $2,400,000. The variable costs are expected to decrease to $16 per unit. Patel expects to maintain the same sales volume and selling price next year. How would acceptance of Schoenen's proposal affect your answers to (a) and (b) in requirement 1?

3. Should Patel accept Schoenen's proposal? Explain.

1. 40 cars

3-14 CVP analysis, income taxes. Diego Motors is a small car dealership. On average it sells a car for $26,000, which it purchases from the manufacturer for $22,000. Each month, Diego Motors pays $60,000 in rent and utilities and $70,000 for salespeople's salaries. In addition to their salaries, salespeople are paid a commission of $500 for each car they sell. Diego Motors also spends $10,000 each month for local advertisements. Its tax rate is 40%.

1. How many cars must Diego Motors sell each month to break even?
2. Diego Motors has a target monthly net income of $63,000. What is its target operating income? How many cars must be sold each month to reach the target monthly net income of $63,000?

3-15 CVP analysis, income taxes. (J. Watson) Orillia Equipment sells riding lawn mowers. The average price for a lawn mower is $16,000. Orillia purchases these mowers from the manufacturers at an average cost of $12,200. Orillia's monthly fixed costs are $28,000 in rent, $45,000 in salaries, $5,600 in advertising and promotion, and $1,200 in other operating expenses. It has a corporate tax rate of 25%.

1. 21 mowers

REQUIRED

1. How many mowers must Orillia Equipment sell each month to break even?
2. How many mowers must be sold each month if Orillia Equipment has a target net income of $42,750?

3-16 CVP analysis, income taxes. The Rapid Meal has two restaurants that are open 24 hours a day. Fixed costs for the two restaurants together total $450,000 per year. Service varies from a cup of coffee to full meals. The average sales check per customer is $8.00. The average cost of food and other variable costs for each customer is $3.20. The income tax rate is 30%. Target net income is $105,000.

1. Revenue, $1,000,000

REQUIRED

1. Compute the revenue needed to earn the target net income.
2. How many customers are needed to earn net income of $105,000? How many customers are needed to break even?
3. Compute net income if the number of customers is 150,000.

3-17 Gross margin and contribution margin. The Museum of Art is preparing for its annual appreciation dinner for contributing members. Last year, 500 members attended the dinner. Tickets for the dinner were $20 per attendee. Last year's income statement was as follows:

1. Contribution margin, $4,500

Ticket sales	$10,000
Cost of dinner	11,000
Gross margin	(1,000)
Invitations and paperwork	3,000
Profit (loss)	$(4,000)

This year the dinner committee does not want to lose money on the dinner. To help achieve its goal, the committee analyzed last year's costs. Of the $11,000 total cost of the dinner, it was determined that $6,000 were fixed costs and $5,000 were variable costs. Of the $3,000 for invitations and paperwork, $2,500 were fixed and $500 were variable.

REQUIRED

1. Prepare last year's profit report using the contribution-margin format.
2. The committee is considering expanding this year's dinner invitation to include volunteer members (in addition to contributing members). If the committee expects attendance to double, calculate the effect this will have on the profitability of the dinner.

3-18 Athletic scholarships, CVP analysis. Huron University is committed to improving access to higher education. Each year it makes $4,500,000 available for scholarships for students based on financial needs and academic achievement. The scholarship covers the full annual tuition (based on a full course load) for the recipients. Tuition fees are based on credit hours ($400 per credit hour), and a full-time student takes 30 credit hours per year. Fixed costs of administering the scholarship program are $600,000 per year.

1. 325 scholarships

REQUIRED

1. How many athletic scholarships can Huron University offer each year?
2. Suppose the total budget for the following year is reduced by 20%. Fixed costs are to remain the same. Calculate the number of scholarships that Huron can offer in the following year.
3. As in requirement 2, assume a budget reduction of 20%. Fixed costs are to remain the same. If Huron wanted to offer the same number of scholarships as it did in requirement 1, how much reduction in tuition would it be able to offer to each student who receives a scholarship?

1. a. 489 tickets

2. CM%, 40%

1. a. Operating income, $120,000

3-19 CVP analysis, changing revenues and costs. Sunshine Tours is a travel agency specializing in cruises between Miami and Jamaica. It books passengers on Carib Cruises. Sunshine's fixed costs are $22,000 per month. Carib charges passengers $1,000 per round trip ticket.

REQUIRED
Calculate the number of tickets Sunshine must sell each month to (a) break even and (b) make a target operating income of $10,000 per month in each of the following independent cases.

1. Sunshine's variable costs are $35 per ticket and Carib Cruises pays Sunshine 8% commission on the ticket price.
2. Sunshine's variable costs are $29 per ticket. Carib Cruises pays Sunshine 8% commission on the ticket price.
3. Sunshine's variable costs are $29 per ticket. It receives a $48 commission per ticket from Carib Cruises. Comment on the results.
4. Sunshine's variable costs are $29 per ticket. It receives a $48 commission per ticket from Carib Cruises. It charges customers a delivery fee of $5 per ticket. Comment on the results.

3-20 Contribution margin, gross margin, and margin of safety. Mirabel Cosmetics manufactures and sells a face cream to small family-run stores in the greater Montreal area. It presents the monthly operating income statement shown here to François Laval, a potential investor in the business. Help Mr. Laval understand Mirabel's cost structure.

Mirabel Cosmetics
Operating Income Statement
For the Month of June 2013

Units sold		10,000
Revenue		$100,000
Cost of goods sold		
Variable manufacturing costs	$55,000	
Fixed manufacturing costs	20,000	
Total		75,000
Gross margin		25,000
Operating costs		
Variable marketing costs	5,000	
Fixed marketing and administration costs	10,000	
Total operating costs		15,000
Operating income		$ 10,000

REQUIRED
1. Recast the income statement to emphasize contribution margin.
2. Calculate the contribution margin percentage and breakeven point in units and revenues for June 2013.
3. What is the margin of safety (in units) for June 2013?
4. If sales in June were only 8,000 units and Mirabel's tax rate is 30%, calculate its net income.

3-21 CVP computations. The Doral Company manufactures and sells pens. Present sales output is 5,000,000 units per year at a selling price of $0.60 per unit. Fixed costs are $1,080,000 per year. Variable costs are $0.36 per unit.

REQUIRED
(Consider each case separately.)
1. a. What is the present operating income for a year?
   b. What is the present breakeven point in revenue?
2. Compute the new operating income for each of the following changes:
   a. A $0.048 per unit increase in variable costs.
   b. A 10% increase in fixed costs and a 10% increase in units sold.
   c. A 20% decrease in fixed costs, a 20% decrease in selling price, a 10% decrease in variable costs per unit, and a 40% increase in units sold.
3. Compute the new breakeven point in units for each of the following changes:
   a. A 10% increase in fixed costs.
   b. A 10% increase in selling price and a $24,000 increase in fixed costs.

3-22 CVP exercises. (J. Watson) Beans Unlimited sells specialty coffees in 1-kilogram packages. Fixed costs are budgeted at $730,000 per year. For the upcoming year, revenues are forecasted to be $3,240,000 (selling price is $36 per kilogram) and the company has an average contribution margin percentage of 48%.

④

1. Budgeted OI, $825,200

REQUIRED
1. What is the budgeted operating income given the sales forecast?
2. Beans is considering reducing its fixed costs by 15%. This would result in a lowering of the contribution margin percentage to 42%. What would be the new forecasted operating income?
3. Another alternative Beans is considering is raising its selling price by 10%. It estimates this would result in a reduction in sales volume of 5%. There would be no changes to variable or fixed costs. What would be the forecasted operating income with the new selling price and volume? What is the new contribution margin percentage?
4. Which strategy would you recommend for the company? Explain.

3-23 Operating leverage. Charles Rothman is an importer of silver cuff bracelets from Mexico. He has a three-month agreement with the local coffee shop, Dellano's, to set up a booth to exhibit the jewellery. Rothman is under no obligation to keep any unsold items and can return them to the Mexican silversmith at no personal cost. The average selling price of the bracelets is $125 and it costs Rothman $80 to purchase each piece. Dellano's has proposed two payment alternatives for the use of space.

④

1. a. 29 bracelets

◆ Option 1: A fixed payment of $435 per month.
◆ Option 2: 12% of the total revenues earned during the agreement.

REQUIRED
1. Calculate the breakeven point in units for (a) option 1 and (b) option 2.
2. At what level of sales revenue will Rothman earn the same operating income under either option?
3. a. For what range of unit sales will Rothman prefer option 1?
   b. For what range of unit sales will Rothman prefer option 2?
4. Calculate the degree of operating leverage at sales of 150 units for the two alternative rental options.
5. Briefly explain and interpret your answer in requirement 4.

3-24 Gross margin and contribution margin, making decisions. Saunders' Electronics had the following results for the year just ended:

②

1. CM, $288,000

Revenues		$800,000
Cost of goods sold (48% of sales)		384,000
Gross margin		416,000
Operating costs		
Salaries fixed	$212,000	
Sales commissions (12% of sales)	96,000	
Amortization of equipment and fixtures	19,200	
Store rent ($5,100 per month)	61,200	
Other operating costs	72,300	460,700
Operating income (loss)		$ (44,700)

Mr. Saunders, the owner of the store, is unhappy with the operating results. An analysis of other operating costs reveals that it includes $32,000 variable costs, for which the cost driver is sales volume, and $40,300 fixed costs.

REQUIRED
1. Compute the contribution margin of Saunders' Electronics.
2. Compute the contribution margin percentage for the company.
3. Mr. Saunders estimates he can increase revenues by 25% by incurring additional advertising costs of $24,300. Calculate the impact on operating income of this action.

3-25 CVP, revenue mix. (J. Watson) Burdon Snowboards sells two models of snowboards: the Men's Dominator and the Ladies' Luxury. Information on the two models of snowboards follows:

⑤

2. Weighted-average CM, $243.70

Product	Unit Selling Price	Unit Variable Cost	Sales Commission
Dominator	$750	$475	$25
Luxury	$640	$390	$21

Of Burdon's total sales, 70% are for the Men's Dominator model. The company's annual fixed costs are $180,000.

REQUIRED

1. Compute the unit contribution margin for each model of snowboard.
2. Compute the weighted-average contribution margin assuming a constant sales mix.
3. If the company's target operating income is $115,000, how many units of each model of snowboard must be sold to achieve the company's goals?

1. a. India unit CM, $20.50

3-26 CVP, international cost structure differences. Kaleden Inc. is considering three countries for the sole manufacturing site of its new product: India, China, and Canada. The product will be sold to retail outlets in Canada at $47.50 per unit. These retail outlets add their own markup when selling to final customers. The three countries differ in their fixed costs and variable costs per product.

	Annual Fixed Costs	Variable Manufacturing Costs per Unit	Variable Marketing and Distribution Costs per Unit
India	$ 6.4 million	$ 5.20	$21.80
China	4.4 million	9.50	18.40
Canada	10.2 million	19.30	6.20

REQUIRED

1. Compute the breakeven point of Kaleden Inc. in both (a) units sold and (b) revenues for each of the three countries considered.
2. If Kaleden Inc. sells 1,350,000 units in 2013, what is the budgeted operating income for each of the three countries considered?
3. What level of sales (in units) would be required to produce the same operating income in China and in Canada? What would be the operating income in India at that volume of sales?

1. 6,000 hectares

3-27 CVP, not for profit. The Sunrise Group (SG) is an environmentally conscious organization that buys land with the objective of preserving the natural environment. SG receives private contributions and takes no assistance from the government. Fixed costs of operating the organization are $1,000,000 per year. Variable costs of purchasing the land (including environmental impact reports, title searches, etc.) average $3,000 per hectare. For the next budget year, SG expects to receive private contributions totalling $19,000,000. All contributions in excess of costs will be used to purchase land.

REQUIRED

1. How many hectares will SG be able to purchase next year?
2. SG is considering participating in a new government program that will provide $1,000 per hectare to subsidize the purchase of environmentally sensitive land. If SG participates in this program, it estimates the organization will lose $5,000,000 in contributions from supporters who believe that accepting money from the government is not consistent with its mission. If SG does participate in the program, and its forecasts are accurate, how many hectares of land will it be able to purchase? On financial considerations alone, should SG participate in the government program?
3. SG is worried that contributions may decrease by more than the $5,000,000 it has estimated if it takes the subsidy. By how much can contributions decrease for SG to be able to buy the same amount of land if it takes the government subsidy or rejects it? (i.e., what is the point of indifference between the two options?)

1. BEP in total units, 517,956

3-28 CVP, revenue mix. (J. Watson) Zyrcon Ltd. is a computer games manufacturer. It currently has two games on the market: Alien Predators and Vegas Pokermatch. Data regarding the two products are as follows:

	Alien Predators	Vegas Pokermatch
Selling price	$89	$59
Variable manufacturing costs	$18	$12
Variable marketing costs	$27	$16

The fixed costs of Zyrcon are $18,750,000, and the current sales mix is 40% Alien Predators and 60% Vegas Pokermatch.

REQUIRED

1. Assuming no change in sales mix, costs, or revenues, what is the breakeven point in total units? How many units of Alien Predators and how many units of Vegas Pokermatch are sold at the breakeven point?
2. Assume the following sales mix: 25% Alien Predators and 75% Vegas Pokermatch. Calculate the breakeven point under this sales mix assumption.
3. For the two possible sales mixes (in requirements 1 and 2), determine operating income if total unit sales are 750,000.

3-29 Alternate cost structures, uncertainty, and sensitivity analysis. Edible Bouquets (EB) makes and sells flower bouquets. EB is considering opening a new store in the local mall. The mall has several empty shops and EB is unsure of the demand for its product. The mall has offered EB two alternative rental agreements. The first is a standard fixed-rent agreement where EB will pay the mall $5,000 per month. The second is a royalty agreement where the mall receives $10 for each bouquet sold. EB estimates that a bouquet will sell for $50 and have a variable cost of $30 to make (including the cost of the flowers and commission for the sales-person).

③ ④

1. BEP for assumption 1 is 250 bouquets

REQUIRED

1. What is the breakeven point in units under each assumption?
2. For what range of sales levels will EB prefer (a) the fixed-rent agreement and (b) the royalty agreement?
3. If EB signs a sales agreement with a local flower stand, it will save $5 in variable costs per bouquet. How would this affect your answer in requirement 2?
4. EB estimates that the store is equally likely to sell 200, 400, 600, 800, or 1,000 arrangements. Using information from the original problem, prepare a table that shows the expected profit at each sales level under each rental agreement. What is the expected value of each rental agreement? Which rental agreement should EB choose?

3-30 CVP analysis, multiple cost drivers. (J. Watson) Clarke Ltd. is a manufacturer of promotional items. The majority of its revenues is from the production of promotional pens. Clarke imports these pens from China and then imprints them with corporate names. These pens are then distributed to customers, suppliers, etc., for promotional purposes. The pens are purchased in batches of 100 and each batch costs Clarke $95. Imprinting costs $0.35 per pen. Fixed costs average $275,000 per year. In addition to the variable imprinting costs, Clarke incurs setup charges for each customer. Setup costs average $120 per setup, regardless of the number of pens imprinted on that production run. The selling price is $4.50 per pen. Clarke requires a minimum order of 50 pens and typically sells to customers in batches of 50, 100, 250, or 500 units.

⑥

1. OI, $425,000

REQUIRED

1. Assuming that Clarke anticipates it will sell 350,000 pens during the year and that the average order size will be 100 pens, calculate Clarke's operating income and operating margin.
2. Calculate Clarke's operating income and operating margin assuming it will sell 350,000 pens, but that the average order size will be 250 pens.
3. Calculate the breakeven points (in terms of number of orders) assuming the various batch sizes of 50, 100, 250, and 500 units.

3-31 Uncertainty. Angela King is the Las Vegas promoter for professional fighter Randy Couture. King is promoting a new Octagon world championship fight for Couture. The key area of uncertainty is the size of the cable pay-per-view TV market. King will pay Couture a fixed fee of $3.2 million and 25% of net cable pay-per-view revenue. Every cable TV home receiving the event pays $45, of which King receives $27. King pays Couture $6.75, 25% of the $27.

④

1. Expected value, $6,220,625

King estimates the following probability distribution for homes purchasing the pay-per-view event:

Demand	Probability
250,000	0.05
300,000	0.10
350,000	0.20
400,000	0.40
500,000	0.15
1,000,000	0.10

1. What is the expected value of the payment King will make to Couture?
2. Assume the only uncertainty is over cable TV demand for the fight. King wants to know the breakeven point given her own fixed costs of $1.3 million and her own variable costs of $2.25 per home. (Also include King's payments to Couture in your answer.)

PROBLEMS

3-32 Effects on operating income, pricing decision. Teguchi Manufacturing is a manufacturer of electronics components. Income data for one of the products (XT-107) for the month just ended are as follows:

1. Contribution margin, $85,500

Sales, 220,000 units at average price of $125		$27,500,000
Variable costs:		
Direct materials at $48 per unit	$10,560,000	
Direct manufacturing labour at $16 per unit	3,520,000	
Variable manufacturing overhead at $8 per unit	1,760,000	
Sales commissions at 12% of sales	3,300,000	
Other variable costs at $7 per unit	1,540,000	
Total variable costs		20,680,000
Contribution margin		6,820,000
Fixed costs		4,620,000
Operating income		$ 2,200,000

Teguchi has capacity to produce 250,000 units each month, and its current average sales level is 175,000 units per month.

Recently Andrews Ltd. approached one of Teguchi's sales representatives and asked if Teguchi could supply a one-time order of 5,000 of the XT-107. Its current supplier is moving to a new factory and has temporarily suspended production. Andrews has offered a selling price of $98 per unit. Sales commissions on this order can be negotiated at a flat fee of $9,500, instead of the normal 12% of sales. All other costs would behave as with regular production.

REQUIRED

1. From a financial perspective, should Teguchi accept the order? (Calculate the change in monthly operating income if the order is accepted.)
2. The general manager of Teguchi is concerned about accepting the order at the $98 selling price. He is afraid of the precedent that might be set by cutting the price and that Andrews might expect the same price concessions in the future. He has stated that he believes the sales representative should quote the regular price of $125 and argues that the $98 is below the full cost (excluding the commission) of $100 per unit. Do you agree with the general manager? Explain.

3-33 CVP, executive teaching compensation. David Hutchinson is an internationally known Canadian professor specializing in consumer marketing. In 2012, Hutchinson and United Kingdom Business School (UKBS) agreed to conduct a one-day seminar at UKBS for marketing executives. Each executive would pay $350 to attend. The non–speaker-related fixed costs for UKBS conducting the seminar would be:

1. a. 72 attendees

Advertising in magazines	$5,200
Mailing of brochures	2,500
Administrative labour at UKBS	3,700
Charge for UKBS lecture auditorium	1,800

The variable costs to UKBS for each participant attending the seminar would be

Food service	$38
Printed materials and binders	37

The dean at UKBS initially offered Hutchinson its regular compensation package of (a) business-class airfare and accommodation ($3,800 maximum) and (b) a $2,750 lecture fee. Hutchinson views the $2,750 lecture fee as providing him no upside potential (that is, no sharing in the potential additional operating income that arises if the seminar is highly attended). He suggests instead that he receive 50% of the operating income to UKBS (if positive) from the one-day seminar and no other payments. The dean of UKBS quickly agrees to Hutchinson's proposal after confirming that Hutchinson is willing to pay his own airfare and accommodation and deliver the seminar irrespective of the number of executives signed up to attend.

1. What is UKBS's breakeven point (in number of executives attending) if
    a. Hutchinson accepts the regular compensation package of $3,800 expenses and a $2,750 lecture fee.
    b. Hutchinson receives 50% of the operating income to UKBS (if positive) from the one-day seminar and no other payments.
       Comment on the results for (a) and (b).
2. Hutchinson gave the one-day seminar at UKBS in 2009 (60 attended), 2010 (75 attended), and 2011 (120 attended). How much was Hutchinson paid by UKBS for the one-day seminar under the 50% of UKBS's operating income compensation plan in (a) 2009, (b) 2010, and (c) 2011? (Assume that the $350 charge per executive attending and UKBS's fixed and variable costs are the same each year.)
3. After the 2011 seminar, the dean at UKBS suggested to Hutchinson that the 50%–50% profit-sharing plan was resulting in Hutchinson getting excessive compensation and that a more equitable arrangement to UKBS be used in 2012. How should Hutchinson respond to this suggestion?

3-34 CVP computations with sensitivity analysis—Advanced. Hoot Washington is the newly elected charismatic leader of the Western Party. He is the darling of the right-wing media. His "take no prisoners" attitude has left many an opponent on a talk show feeling run over by a Mack truck.

1. Breakeven number in units, 252,708 copies (rounded)

    Media Publishers is negotiating to publish Hoot's *Manifesto*, a new book that promises to be an instant bestseller. The fixed costs of producing and marketing the book will be $600,000. The variable costs of producing and marketing will be $4.80 per book. These costs are before any payments to Hoot. Hoot negotiates an up-front payment of $3.60 million plus a 15% royalty rate on the net sales price of each book. The net sales price is the listed bookstore price of $36 minus the margin paid to the bookstore to sell the book. The normal bookstore margin of 30% of the listed bookstore price is expected to apply.

REQUIRED
1. How many copies must Media Publishers sell to (a) break even and (b) earn a target operating profit of $2.4 million?
2. Examine the sensitivity of the breakeven point to the following changes:
    a. Decreasing the normal bookstore margin to 20% of the listed bookstore price of $36.
    b. Increasing the listed bookstore price to $48 while keeping the bookstore margin at 30%.

3-35 CVP analysis, service firm. Wildlife Escapes generates average revenue of $9,200 per person on its five-day package tours to wildlife parks in Kenya. The variable costs per person are

1. 450 package tours

Airfare	$3,500
Hotel accommodations	1,200
Meals	480
Ground transportation	920
Park tickets and other costs	240

Annual fixed costs total $1,287,000.

REQUIRED
1. Calculate the number of package tours that must be sold to break even.
2. Calculate the revenue needed to earn a target operating income of $214,500.
3. If fixed costs increase by $40,500, what decrease in variable costs must be achieved to maintain the breakeven point calculated in requirement 1?

3-36 CVP, target operating and net income. (J. Watson) Carumba Inc.'s 2012 budget includes the following items:

1. BEP, $34.75

Sales	80,000 units
Production	80,000 units
Direct materials used	$600,000
Direct labour	400,000
Variable overhead	720,000
Fixed overhead	400,000
Variable selling costs	260,000
Fixed selling costs	250,000
Administrative costs (all fixed)	150,000

The company's tax rate is 30%.

1. At what price would the company break even?
2. If the company were to sell only 60,000 units, what price would produce a before-tax profit of 20% of sales?
3. Majestix Inc. has offered to supply Carumba with 80,000 units at a price of $28/unit. Should Carumba accept the offer? Explain.
4. What price would produce an after-tax profit of $350,000?

3-37 CVP, target income, service firm. Teddy Bear Daycare provides daycare for children Mondays through Fridays. Its monthly variable costs per child are

Lunch and snacks	$ 100
Educational supplies	75
Other supplies (paper products, toiletries, etc.)	25
Total	$ 200

Monthly fixed costs consist of

Rent	$2,000
Utilities	300
Insurance	300
Salaries	2,500
Miscellaneous	500
	$5,600

Teddy Bear charges each parent $600 per child.

REQUIRED

1. Calculate the breakeven point.
2. Teddy Bear's target operating income is $10,400 per month. Compute the number of children that must be enrolled to achieve the target operating income.
3. Teddy Bear lost its lease and had to move to another building. Monthly rent for the new building is $3,000. At the suggestion of parents, Teddy Bear plans to take children on field trips. Monthly costs of the field trips are $1,000. By how much should Teddy Bear increase fees per child to meet the target operating income of $10,400 per month, assuming the same number of children as in requirement 2?

3-38 CVP and income taxes. R. A. Ro and Company, a manufacturer of quality handmade walnut bowls, has experienced a steady growth in sales for the past five years. However, increased competition has led Mr. Ro, the president, to believe that an aggressive marketing campaign will be necessary next year to maintain the company's present growth.

To prepare for next year's marketing campaign, the company's controller has prepared and presented Mr. Ro with the following data for the current year, 2013:

Variable costs (per bowl):	
Direct manufacturing labour	$ 9.60
Direct materials	3.90
Variable overhead (manufacturing, marketing, distribution, customer service, and administration)	3.00
Total variable costs	$ 16.50
Fixed costs:	
Manufacturing	$ 30,000
Marketing, distribution, and customer service	48,000
Administrative	84,000
Total fixed costs	$162,000
Selling price per bowl	$30.00
Expected revenues, 2013 (20,000 units)	$600,000
Income tax rate	40%

REQUIRED

1. What is the projected net income for 2013?
2. What is the breakeven point in units for 2013?
3. Mr. Ro has set the revenue target for 2014 at a level of $660,000 (or 22,000 bowls). He believes an additional marketing cost of $13,500 for advertising in 2014, with all other costs remaining constant, will be necessary to attain the revenue target. What will be the net income for 2014 if the additional $13,500 is spent and the revenue target is met?

4. What will be the breakeven point in revenues for 2014 if the additional $13,500 is spent for advertising?

5. If the additional $13,500 is spent for advertising in 2014, what is the required 2014 revenue for 2014's net income to equal 2013's net income?

6. At a sales level of 22,000 units, what maximum amount can be spent on advertising if a 2014 net income of $72,000 is desired?

3-39 CVP, income taxes, manufacturing decisions. (J. Watson) Prairie Ltd. currently manufactures a single product in its Saskatoon factory. Last year's results (based on sales volume of 25,000 units) were

④ ⑤
1. BEP, 15,433 units

Sales		$1,350,000
Variable costs	$ 742,500	
Fixed costs	375,000	1,117,500
Operating income		232,500
Income taxes (40%)		93,000
Net income		$ 139,500

REQUIRED

1. Using last year's data, calculate Prairie's breakeven point in units and calculate the margin of safety in dollars.

2. How many units of product would Prairie have had to sell last year if it wished to earn $225,000 in net income?

3. In an attempt to improve its product quality, Prairie is considering replacing one of its current component parts. This part costs $7.50 (one component per finished unit), and Prairie is evaluating a new and better part that has a cost of $9.80 per unit. The company would simultaneously expand its production by investing in a machine that costs $25,000. This machine has no salvage value and would be amortized on a straight-line basis over five years (assume this is acceptable for both financial-statement and tax purposes). If these changes are made and selling price is held constant:

   a. Calculate the new breakeven point in units.

   b. Determine how many units of product must be sold next year to achieve the same net income after taxes as last year.

4. Instead of the changes in requirement 3, the company is considering adding a higher-quality product to its sales mix. This new product would sell for $95 and variable costs per unit would increase by 60% over the old product. Total unit sales are forecast to increase to 50,000 units (which is in the company's current capacity—no additional fixed costs are needed) and the sales mix is estimated to be 3:2 (old product to new product). If Prairie introduces this new product at the planned sales mix, calculate the new breakeven point in sales dollars.

3-40 CVP, shoe stores. The Walk Rite Shoe Company operates a chain of shoe stores. The stores sell ten different styles of inexpensive men's shoes with identical unit costs and selling prices. A unit is defined as a pair of shoes. Each store has a store manager who is paid a fixed salary. Individual salespeople receive a fixed salary and a sales commission. Walk Rite is trying to determine the desirability of opening another store, which is expected to have the following revenue and cost relationships:

③
1. a. BEP, 40,000 units

Selling price	$ 30.00
Unit variable cost per pair:	
Cost of shoes	$ 19.50
Sales commissions	1.50
Total variable costs	$ 21.00
Annual fixed costs:	
Rent	$ 60,000
Salaries	200,000
Advertising	80,000
Other fixed costs	20,000
Total fixed costs	$360,000

REQUIRED

(Consider each question independently.)

1. What is the annual breakeven point in (a) units sold and (b) revenues?

2. If 35,000 units are sold, what will be the store's operating income (loss)?

3. If sales commissions were discontinued for individual salespeople in favour of an $81,000 increase in fixed salaries, what would be the annual breakeven point in (a) units sold and (b) revenues?

4. Refer to the original data. If the store manager were paid $0.30 per unit sold in addition to his current fixed salary, what would be the annual breakeven point in (a) units sold and (b) revenues?

5. Refer to the original data. If the store manager were paid $0.30 per unit commission on each unit sold in excess of the breakeven point, what would be the store's operating income if 50,000 units were sold? (This $0.30 is in addition to both the commission paid to the sales staff and the store manager's fixed salary.)

1. 54,000 units

3-41 CVP, shoe stores (continuation of 3-40). Refer to requirement 3 of 3-40. In this problem assume the role of the owner of Walk Rite.

REQUIRED

1. Calculate the number of units sold where the operating income under (a) a fixed-salary plan and (b) a lower fixed-salary-and-commission plan (for salespeople only) would be equal. Above that number of units sold, one plan would be more profitable than the other; below that number of units sold, the reverse would occur.

2. As owner, which sales compensation plan would you choose if forecasted annual sales of the new store were at least 55,000 units? What do you think of the motivation aspects of your chosen compensation plan?

3. Suppose the target operating income is $168,000. How many units must be sold to reach the target under (a) the fixed-salary plan and (b) the lower fixed-salary-and-commission plan?

4. You open the new store on January 1, 2013, with the original salary-plus-commission compensation plan in place. Because you expect the cost of the shoes to rise due to inflation, you place a firm bulk order for 50,000 shoes and lock in the $19.50 per unit price. But, toward the end of the year, only 48,000 pairs of shoes are sold, and you authorize a markdown of the remaining inventory to $18 per unit. Finally all units are sold. Salespeople, as usual, get paid a commission of 5% of revenues. What is the annual operating income for the store?

2. Current system expected cost, $20,600,000

3-42 Uncertainty and expected costs. Dawmart Corp., an international retail giant, is considering implementing a new business-to-business (B2B) information system for processing purchase orders. The current system costs Dawmart $1,000,000 per month and $40 per order. Dawmart has two options: a partially automated B2B and a fully automated B2B system. The partially automated B2B system will have a fixed cost of $5,000,000 per month and a variable cost of $30 per order. The fully automated B2B system will have fixed costs of $10,000,000 per month and variable costs of $20 per order.

Based on data from the last two years, Dawmart has determined the following distribution on monthly orders:

Monthly Number of Orders	Probability
300,000	0.10
400,000	0.25
500,000	0.40
600,000	0.15
700,000	0.10

REQUIRED

1. Prepare a table showing the cost of each plan for each quantity of monthly orders.
2. What is the expected cost of each plan?
3. In addition to the information systems costs, what other factors should Dawmart consider before deciding to implement a new B2B system?

1. BEP, 25,600 units

3-43 CVP analysis, decision making. (M. Rajan, adapted) Tocchet Company manufactures CB1, a citizens' band radio that is sold mainly to truck drivers. The company's plant in Camden has an annual capacity of 75,000 units. Tocchet currently sells 60,000 units at a selling price of $148. It has the following cost structure:

Variable manufacturing costs per unit	$ 63
Fixed manufacturing costs	$1,012,000
Variable marketing and distribution costs per unit	$ 15
Fixed marketing and distribution costs	$ 780,000

REQUIRED

(Consider each question separately.)

1. Calculate the breakeven volume in units and in dollars.
2. The marketing department indicates that decreasing the selling price to $140 would stimulate sales to 70,000 units. This strategy will require Tocchet to increase its fixed costs, although variable costs per unit will remain the same as before. What is the *maximum* increase in fixed costs for which Tocchet will find it worthwhile to reduce the selling price?
3. The manufacturing department proposes changes in the manufacturing process to add new features to the CB1 product. These changes will increase fixed manufacturing costs by $150,000 and variable manufacturing costs per unit by $3.20. At its current sales quantity of 60,000 units, what is the *minimum* selling price above which Tocchet will find it worthwhile to add these new features?

3-44 Revenue mix, two products. The Goldman Company retails two products, a standard and a deluxe version of a luggage carrier. The budgeted income statement is as follows:

1. BEP, 160,000 total units

	Standard Carrier	Deluxe Carrier	Total
Units sold	150,000	50,000	200,000
Revenues @ $20 and $30 per unit	$3,000,000	$1,500,000	$4,500,000
Variable costs @ $14 and $18 per unit	2,100,000	900,000	3,000,000
Contribution margins @ $6 and $12 per unit	$ 900,000	$ 600,000	1,500,000
Fixed costs			1,200,000
Operating income			$ 300,000

REQUIRED

1. Compute the breakeven point in units, assuming that the planned revenue mix is maintained.
2. Compute the breakeven point in units (a) if only standard carriers are sold and (b) if only deluxe carriers are sold.
3. Suppose 200,000 units are sold, but only 20,000 are deluxe. Compute the operating income. Compute the breakeven point if these relationships persist in the next period. Compare your answers with the original plans and the answer in requirement 1. What is the major lesson of this problem?

3-45 CVP, movie production. Panther Productions has just finished production of the most recent sequel in its Illinois Jones series. The film cost $22 million to produce. Most production personnel and actors were paid a fixed salary (included in the $22 million); however, the two major stars of the film, Chevy Harrison and Sean Connelly, as well as the director and producer, Stephen Lucas and George Spielberg, all received equity interests in the film. In addition, the distributor of the film, Parimont Productions, receives royalties in exchange for its investment of $6.5 million to promote the film. The actors each receive 4% of revenues, the director and producer each receive 8% of revenues, and Parimont receives 12% of the revenues. Panther receives 65% of the total box office receipts, and out of this amount it pays the royalties to the actors, director, producer, and promoter.

1. a. BEP, $34,375,000

REQUIRED

1. What is the breakeven point on the film to Panther Productions expressed in terms of (a) revenues received by Panther and (b) total box office receipts?
2. Assume that, in its first year of release, the box office receipts for the movie total $320 million. What is the operating income to Panther from the movie in its first year?

3-46 CVP, cost structure differences, movie production (continuation of 3-45). Panther Productions is negotiating the next sequel to its Illinois Jones series. This negotiation is proving more difficult than for the original movie. There is a risk that the series may have peaked and the total box office receipts will drop. The budgeted production cost (excluding royalty payments) is $32 million. The agent negotiating for Harrison and Connelly proposes either of two contracts:

2. Contract A, $38,120,000
Contract B, $69,200,000

◆ Contract A. Fixed salary component of $50 million for both (combined) with no residual interest in the revenues.

◆ Contract B. Fixed salary component of $8 million for both (combined) plus a residual of 3% each of the revenues.

The promoter, Parimont Productions, will invest a minimum of $12 million of its own money, and because of its major role in the success of the last film, it will now be paid 18% of the revenues received from the total box office receipts. Panther continues to receive 65% of the total box office receipts (out of which comes the royalty payments).

REQUIRED

1. What is the breakeven point for Panther Productions expressed in terms of (a) revenues received by that company and (b) total box office receipts—for contracts A and B? Explain the difference between the breakeven points for contracts A and B.
2. Assume the sequel achieves $280 million in box office revenues. What is the operating income to Panther under each of the contracts? Comment on the results.

1. BEP, 7,800 units

3-47 Multi-product breakeven, decision making. Bonavista Cribs manufactures baby cribs. It currently produces one model, the Surrey crib, and it is priced at $600. Variable manufacturing costs are $210 per unit and variable shipping costs are $60 per unit. Fixed costs are $2,574,000. In 2011, it sold 9,800 units of the Surrey crib. One of Bonavista's customers, Dover Corporation, has asked if Bonavista could manufacture a new style of crib, the Shilo, for 2012. Dover will pay $350 for the Shilo. The variable costs to produce the new crib are estimated to be $180 per unit and Dover will pay for the shipping. Bonavista has sufficient manufacturing capacity and will not incur any additional fixed costs. Bonavista estimates that in 2012, it will sell 10,000 units of Surrey and 4,000 units of Shilo.

The president of Bonavista checked the impact of accepting the Dover order on the breakeven sales revenues for 2012 and was surprised to find that the dollar sales revenues required to break even using the sales mix for 2012 appeared to increase. He was not sure that his numbers were correct, but if they were, he felt inclined to reject the Dover order. He has asked for your advice.

REQUIRED

1. Calculate the breakeven point in units and sales dollars for 2011.
2. Calculate the breakeven point in units and sales dollars for 2012 at the expected sales mix.
3. Explain why the breakeven points in sales dollars calculated in requirements 1 and 2 are different.
4. What would you advise the president to do? Support your recommendations.

1. CM% using own sales agents, 37%
CM% using own sales force, 45%

3-48 Choosing between compensation plans, operating leverage. (CMA, adapted) Marston Corporation manufactures pharmaceutical products that are sold through a network of sales agents. The agents are paid a commission of 18% of sales. The income statement for the year ending December 31, 2011, under two scenarios, is as follows:

Marston Corporation
Income Statement
For the Year Ending December 31, 2011

	Using Sales Agents		Using Own Sales Force	
Sales		$26,000,000		$26,000,000
Cost of goods sold				
Variable	$11,700,000		$11,700,000	
Fixed	2,870,000	14,570,000	2,870,000	14,570,000
Gross margin		11,430,000		11,430,000
Marketing costs				
Commissions	$ 4,680,000		$ 2,600,000	
Fixed costs	3,420,000	8,100,000	5,500,000	8,100,000
Operating income		$ 3,330,000		$ 3,330,000

Marston is considering hiring its own sales staff to replace the network of agents. Marston will pay its salespeople a commission of 10% and incur additional fixed costs of $2,080,000.

REQUIRED

1. Calculate Marston Corporation's 2011 contribution margin percentage, breakeven revenues, and degree of operating leverage under each of the two scenarios. (You will first have to recast the 2011 income statement assuming Marston had hired its own sales staff.)
2. Describe the advantages and disadvantages of each type of sales alternative.
3. In 2012, Marston uses its own salespeople who demand a 15% commission. If all other cost behaviour patterns are unchanged, how much revenue must the salespeople generate in order to earn the same operating income as in 2011?

3-49 Special-order decision. Manitoba Production Corporation (MPC) specializes in the manufacture of one-litre plastic bottles. The plastic moulding machines are capable of producing 100 bottles per hour. The firm estimates that the variable cost of producing a plastic bottle is 25 cents. The bottles are sold for 55 cents each.

1. Additional income, $46,000

Management has been approached by a local toy company that would like the firm to produce a moulded plastic toy for it. The toy company is willing to pay $3.40 per unit for the toy. The unit variable cost to manufacture the toy will be $2.70. In addition, MPC would have to incur a cost of $24,000 to construct the mould required exclusively for this order. Because the toy uses more plastic and is of a more intricate shape than a bottle, a moulding machine can produce only 40 units per hour. The customer wants 100,000 units. Assume that MPC has a total capacity of 10,000 machine hours available during the period in which the toy company wants delivery of the toys. The firm's fixed costs, *excluding* the costs to construct the toy mould, during the same period will be $220,000.

REQUIRED

1. Suppose the demand for its bottles is 750,000 units, and the special toy order has to be either taken in full or rejected totally. Should MPC accept the special toy order? Explain your answer.
2. Suppose the demand for its bottles is 850,000 units, and the special toy order has to be either taken in full or rejected totally. Should MPC accept the special toy order? Explain your answer.
3. Suppose the demand for its bottles is 900,000 units, and the special toy order has to be either taken in full or rejected totally. Should MPC accept the special toy order? Explain your answer.

3-50 CVP, sensitivity analysis. Technology of the Past (TOP) produces old-fashioned simple corkscrews. Last year was not a good year for sales but TOP expects the market to pick up this year. Last year's income statement showed

1. OI, $5,000

Sales revenues ($4 per corkscrew)	$40,000
Variable cost ($3 per corkscrew)	30,000
Contribution margin	10,000
Fixed cost	6,000
Operating income	$ 4,000

To take advantage of the anticipated growth in the market, TOP is considering various courses of action:

1. Do nothing. If TOP does nothing, it expects sales to increase by 10%.
2. Spend $2,000 on a new advertising campaign that is expected to increase sales by 50%.
3. Raise the price of the corkscrew to $5. This is expected to decrease sales quantities by 20%.
4. Redesign the classic corkscrew and increase the selling price to $6 while increasing the variable costs by $1 per unit. The sales level is not expected to change from last year.

REQUIRED
Evaluate each of the alternatives considered by TOP. What should TOP do?

3-51 Non-profit institution. The City of Vancouver makes an $850,000 lump-sum budget appropriation to run a safe injection site for a year. All the appropriation is to be spent. The variable costs average $16 per patient visit. Fixed costs are $500,000 per year.

1. 21,875 patient visits

REQUIRED
1. Compute the number of patient visits that the budget allocation will cover.
2. Suppose the total budget for the following year is reduced by 10%. Fixed costs are to remain the same. The same level of service on each patient visit will be maintained. Compute the number of visits that could be provided in a year.
3. As in requirement 2, assume a budget reduction of 10%. Fixed costs are to remain the same. By how much would variable costs have to decline in order to provide the same number of visits?

3-52 CVP, non-profit event planning. The Windsor Chamber of Commerce is planning its annual event. There are two possible plans:

1. a. BEP, 180 tickets

a. Hold the event at a local hotel. The fixed rental cost would be $2,700 and the charge for meals would be $110 per person.

b. Hold the event at the University of Windsor. The fixed rental fee for the facility would be much higher at $7,000, and the Chamber would also spend another $500 in permits. However, the Chamber could use the local caterer and the per-unit charge for meals would drop to $75 per person.

The Chamber of Commerce budgets $5,000 for administration and marketing. Entertainment will cost $4,000 regardless of the venue chosen. Tickets to the event will be $175 per person. All other costs, such as door prizes and drinks, will be paid for by corporate sponsors.

REQUIRED

1. Compute the breakeven point for each plan in terms of tickets sold.
2. For each plan, compute the operating income of the event (a) if 100 people attend, (b) if 250 people attend. Comment on your results.
3. At what level of tickets sold will the two plans have the same operating income?

1. a. Probability of breaking even, 66.6%

3-53 CVP under uncertainty. (J. Patell) In your new position as supervisor of product introduction, you have to decide on a pricing strategy for a talking doll specialty product with the following cost structure:

Variable costs per unit	$ 60
Fixed costs	$240,000

The dolls are manufactured upon receipt of orders, so the inventory levels are insignificant. Your market research assistant is very enthusiastic about probability models and has presented the results of his price analysis in the following form:

a. If you set the selling price at $120 per unit, the probability distribution of revenues is uniform between $360,000 and $720,000. Under this distribution, there is a 0.50 probability of equalling or exceeding revenues of $540,000.

b. If you lower the selling price to $84 per unit, the distribution remains uniform, but it shifts up to the $720,000–$1,080,000 range. Under this distribution, there is a 0.50 probability of equalling or exceeding revenues of $900,000.

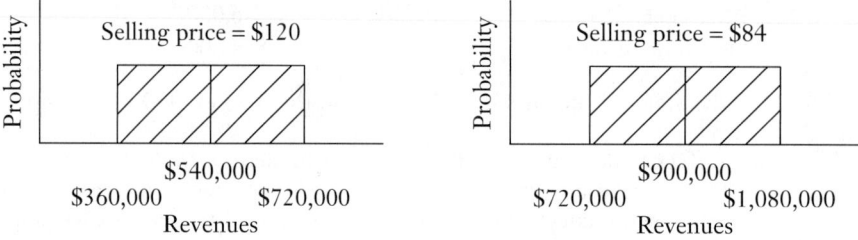

REQUIRED

1. This is your first big contract and, above all, you want to show an operating income. You decide to select the strategy that maximizes the probability of breaking even or earning a positive operating income.
   a. What is the probability of at least breaking even with a selling price of $120 per unit?
   b. What is the probability of at least breaking even with a selling price of $84 per unit?
2. Your assistant suggests that maximum expected operating income might be a better objective to pursue. Which pricing strategy would result in the higher expected operating income? (Use the expected revenues under each pricing strategy when making expected operating-income computations.)

1. BE revenues, $8,478,261

3-54 Governance, CVP analysis. Athabaska Ltd. produces a lens used for webcams. Summary data from its year 2011 income statement are as follows:

Revenues	$8,000,000
Variable costs	4,320,000
Fixed costs	3,900,000
Operating income	$ (220,000)

The president of Athabaska, Roberta Klein, is very concerned about the company's operations. She has discussed the situation with the Operations Manager, Roland Bell, and the controller, Clara Walton.

After two weeks, Roland returns with a proposal. After researching various component parts, he advises that he can reduce variable costs to 48% of revenues by changing both the direct materials and the production process. The downside of this proposal is that the new direct material (although cheaper) results in more waste and is more toxic to the environment. Currently, waste produced in the production process does not require any special treatment and is disposed of normally. Roland points out that there are no current specific laws governing the disposal of this waste created by the use of the new material, and therefore production costs can be cut by using this material. Clara is concerned that this would expose the company to potential environmental liabilities. She believes that these potential future costs need to be estimated and included in the analysis. Roland disagrees and reiterates that there are no laws being violated and replies, "There is some possibility that we may have to incur costs in the future, but if we bring it up now, this proposal will not go through because our senior management always assumes these costs to be larger than they are. The market is very tough and we are in danger of shutting down the company. We don't want all our colleagues to lose their jobs. The only reason our competitors are making money is because they are doing exactly what I am proposing."

REQUIRED

1. Calculate Athabaska's breakeven revenues for the year 2011.
2. Calculate Athabaska's breakeven revenues if variable costs are 48% of revenues.
3. Calculate Athabaska's operating income in 2011 if variable costs had been 48% of sales.
4. What should Roberta Klein do?

3-55 Governance, CVP, cost analysis. Ahmed Diba is the controller of the Body Products Division of World Wide Drugs (WWD). It is located in Winnipeg, which is also the headquarters of WWD. Diba is helping develop a proposal for a new product to be called Vital Hair. This product is a cream to be rubbed on the scalp to restore hair growth. Cheryl Kelly, president of the division, and Diba are scheduled to make a presentation to the WWD executive committee on the expected profitability of Vital Hair. The fixed costs associated with the development, production, and marketing of Vital Hair are $25,000,000. Each customer will pay a doctor $98 per monthly treatment, of which $68 is paid to WWD. Diba estimates WWD's variable costs per treatment to be $28.50. Included in this $28.50 is $9.25 for potential product litigation costs. Kelly is livid at Diba for including the $9.25 estimate. She argues that it is imperative to get the R&D funds approved (and quickly) and that any number that increases the breakeven point reduces the likelihood of the Vital Hair project being approved. She notes that WWD has had few successful lawsuits against it, in contrast to some recent "horrendous" experiences of competitors with breast implant products. Moreover, she is furious that Diba put the $9.25 amount in writing. "How do we know there will be any litigation problem?" She suggests Diba redo the report excluding the $9.25 litigation risk cost estimate. "Put it on the chalkboard in the executive committee room, if you insist, but don't put it in the report sent to the committee before the meeting. You can personally raise the issue at the executive committee meeting and have a full and frank discussion."

Diba takes Kelly's "advice." He reports a variable cost of $19.25 per treatment in the proposal. Although he feels uneasy about this, he is comforted by the fact that he will flag the $9.25 amount to the executive committee in his forthcoming oral presentation.

One month later, Kelly walks into Diba's office. She is in a buoyant mood and announces she has just come back from an executive committee meeting that approved the Vital Hair proposal. Diba asks why he was not invited to the meeting. Kelly says the meeting was held in Toronto, and she decided to save the division money by going alone. She then says to Diba that it "was now time to get behind the new venture and help make it the success the committee and her team members believe it will be."

REQUIRED

1. What is the breakeven point (in units of monthly treatments) when WWD's variable costs (a) include the $9.25 estimate and (b) exclude the $9.25 estimate for potential product litigation costs?
2. Should Diba have excluded the $9.25 estimate in his report to the executive committee of WWD? Explain your answer.
3. What should Diba do in response to Kelly's decision to make the Vital Hair presentation on her own?

1. a. 632,912 monthly treatments

1. BEP for Peona plant,
   73,500 units

3-56 **Deciding where to produce.** (CMA, adapted) Domestic Engines Company produces the same power generators in two plants, a newly renovated, automated plant in Peona, and an older, less automated plant in Modine. The following data are available for the two plants:

	Peona		Modine	
Selling price		$150.00		$150.00
Variable manufacturing cost per unit	$72.00		$88.00	
Fixed manufacturing cost per unit	30.00		15.00	
Variable marketing and distribution cost per unit	14.00		14.00	
Fixed marketing and distribution cost per unit	19.00		14.50	
Total cost per unit		135.00		131.50
Operating income per unit		$ 15.00		$ 18.50
Production rate per day		400 units		320 units
Normal annual capacity usage		240 days		240 days
Maximum annual capacity		300 days		300 days

All unit fixed costs are calculated based on a normal year of 240 working days. When the number of working days exceeds 240, variable manufacturing costs increase by $3.00 per unit in Peona and $8.00 per unit in Modine.

Domestic Engines is expected to produce and sell 192,000 generators during the coming year. Wanting to maximize the higher unit profit at Modine, Domestic Engines' production manager has decided to manufacture 96,000 units at each plant. This production plan results in Modine operating at capacity (320 units per day 300 days) and Peona operating at its normal volume (400 units per day 240 days).

REQUIRED
1. Determine the breakeven point for the Peona and Modine plants in units.
2. Calculate the operating income that would result from the division production manager's plan to produce 96,000 units at each plant.
3. Determine how the production of the 192,000 units should be allocated between Peona and Modine to maximize operating income for Domestic Engines. Show your calculations.

COLLABORATIVE LEARNING CASE

1. BEP units, 150,000

3-57 **CVP analysis and revenue mix.** Ronowski Company has three product lines of belts, A, B, and C, with contribution margins of $3.60, $2.40, and $1.20 respectively. The president forecasts sales of 200,000 units in the coming period, consisting of 20,000 units of A, 100,000 units of B, and 80,000 units of C. The company's fixed costs for the period are $306,000.

REQUIRED
1. What is the company breakeven point in units, assuming that the given revenue mix is maintained?
2. If the mix is maintained, what is the total contribution margin when 200,000 units are sold? What is the operating income?
3. What would operating income become if 20,000 units of A, 80,000 units of B, and 100,000 units of C were sold? What is the new breakeven point in units if these relationships persist in the next period?

Job Costing

What Does It Cost to Do the Job?

Each summer about 7,500 forest fires burn an average of 250,000 square kilometres of Canadian wilderness. A ferocious force of nature, wildfires cost Canadian taxpayers approximately $417 million per year to suppress. Fires cause evacuations of entire cities, destroy property, create economic hardship, and kill wildlife and people. In May 2011, almost half of Slave Lake in northern Alberta was destroyed by wildfire. But forest fires also renew the forests. In its aftermath, the minerals in the soil are revitalized and the sun penetrates to the forest floor.

The cost to suppress a forest fire depends on how accessible the fire is. Unfortunately, the most inaccessible wildfires are the most destructive and expensive to suppress. These fires are fought primarily using aircraft and fire retardant chemicals. The firefighters are delivered to the site by parachuting in (smoke jumpers) or rapelling in by rope from helicopters. On average, the cost to suppress a Canadian wildfire is approximately $60,000 per fire. Provincial governments use careful job-costing procedures to refine and improve their cost estimates for fire suppression. Governments need a reliable job-costing system so they can account to the taxpayers when asked how money was spent.

After studying this chapter, you should be able to

1. Identify and explain the elements of an effective job-costing system.

2. Apply the decision framework in a seven-step method to assign total actual costs to a distinct service.

3. Apply the decision framework in a seven-step method to assign total actual costs to a distinct product.

4. Distinguish among three methods—actual, budgeted, and normal—to calculate job-cost allocation rates and assign indirect costs to a distinct job.

5. Analyze the flow of costs from direct and indirect cost pools to inventory accounts, including adjustments for over- and underallocated costs.

BUILDING-BLOCK CONCEPTS OF COSTING SYSTEMS

1 Identify and explain the elements of an effective job-costing system.

All companies need to have an effective costing system. Management teams use information from their MIS to cost various types of cost objects, especially those that will generate revenue plus some reasonable profit when they are sold. We will use the generic term *jobs* to represent a cost object that will be sold. Job costing gives management teams the added ability to predict or budget for future improved profitability by planning to accept the most profitable types of jobs. For manufacturers, there are also external benefits. When reporting to external parties, GAAP compliance requires that indirect support costs of production (MOH) be included in cost of goods sold.

When companies produce distinct types of customized jobs, the job-costing system distinguishes costs of unequally shared resources used to customize each distinct type of job. This also allows companies to select the most profitable types of customized jobs. Job costing exploits the relationship between the quantity of inputs used and the change in the costs of those inputs. The team must decide on the best way to measure the unequal benefits provided to each job. What makes one job distinct from another is often the unequal quantities of shared inputs used. The difference in quantities used will be reflected in the assignment of different costs among different types of jobs.

To simplify the development of the costing system, we will assume the quality of inputs and the cost per unit is constant. Managers often combine cost information with non-cost information such as quantity of rework or volume of customer complaints. This helps ensure that key success factors won't be sacrificed in the long term for short-term profitability. This chapter focuses on assigning costs to a job that is either a tangible output (e.g., the BMW X5) or a less tangible outcome (e.g., suppressing a wildfire).

We assume that the actual cost of inputs and the quantities used have already been accumulated in the general ledger accounts of the company (MIS). We also assume that the finished jobs differ in the quantities of shared inputs (and accompanying costs) used to complete the job. If this were not true, a simple average cost of all jobs would be sufficient to set prices and budget for the future.

We also assume that the different quantity of inputs used is a good measure of different benefit or value added to the type of job. This is called a *proxy* or indirect measure of the benefit to a job. If the quantities of inputs used differ from one type of job to another, then it makes sense to make sure each type of job bears its fair share of indirect costs and that customers pay for this added value. The costs of shared inputs used by each type of job will be assigned according to the quantity of inputs used.

ASSIGNING DIRECT AND INDIRECT COSTS

An important management accounting task is to reclassify the job costs as direct or indirect manufacturing costs (MOH) and distinguish them from non-manufacturing costs.[1] Once this classification is done, then a job-costing system can be created. Direct costs can be traced to each job by the quantity of direct inputs used for each job. Three direct costs are direct materials (DM), direct labour-hours (DLH), and direct machine hours (DMH).

Indirect costs cannot be traced to one job because they are common costs incurred to support finishing all jobs. As you recall from Chapter 2 (p. 29), there are many indirect costs. In a traditional job-costing system, all of these are accumulated into one cost pool and an average **indirect cost allocation rate** is calculated. The indirect cost pool is then assigned to each type of job in a multi-stage process that is described in this chapter.

The key elements of a job-costing system are as follows:

◆ The distinct type of job is the cost object.
◆ Direct cost pools are accumulated separately from the indirect cost pool of the same distinct type of job.

[1]Assignment of non-manufacturing costs will be discussed in Chapter 14.

◆ Quantities of inputs (shared resources used) to complete the job generate all the cost pools, and these inputs are called *cost drivers* (also called a *cost allocation base*).

◆ The *cost driver rate* (also called *cost allocation rate*) is the result of dividing the indirect cost pool by the total quantity of shared inputs used (the cost driver) to complete the job.

Direct costs of DM, DLH, and DMH can be readily identified against a job, either electronically or manually, by giving the job a code and entering the code each time direct inputs are used for that particular job. Documentation ensures the direct cost will be traced to one cost object, the finished job. Because we assumed the cost rate per unit of input is constant, as each unit of direct input is used to complete the job the direct costs will rise with the quantity used. As we learned in Chapter 2, this is the distinguishing feature of a variable cost. The accumulation of total variable DM costs for a job is called a DM **cost pool**. DLH and DMH cost pools are named similarly.

Examples of indirect costs include custodial, maintenance, and security costs, rework, and fringe benefits, all of which vary with the hours worked. Of course the cost rate to pay for janitorial labour will be different from that paid for maintenance labour. Both of these different costs are variable and often summed together with fringe benefit costs in the same indirect cost pool. Fixed costs such as insurance and property rental fees are also indirect and added to the same cost pool as the variable indirect costs. The indirect cost pool is a mix of fixed and variable costs from many sources.

The problem is how to divide up the indirect cost pool among the jobs, knowing each job uses inputs common to them all in different quantities. This task is called **cost allocation**, and it is a method to estimate the cost of common inputs used in different quantities by different jobs. Recall from Chapter 2 that managers assign the direct cost pool by tracing, and the indirect cost pool by allocating the costs to each job. These relationships are illustrated in Exhibit 4-1.

To assign the single *indirect* cost pool to jobs, a link needs to be made that can methodically and consistently explain how a change in the use of one input can explain changes to the costs assigned to the job. The assumption is that the more of an input that is used, the higher the benefit or value added to the job will be. The input use is the reason why one job costs more or less than another. The link is called a **cost allocation base (cost driver)**. The selection of this input is difficult since an MIS usually records the quantity of direct inputs, not the indirect inputs. Many small businesses cannot afford to keep track of every quantity of every indirect input, nor would it make sense to spend the money required to do so. This is a proxy measure of benefit.

EXHIBIT 4-1
Generic Job-Costing System

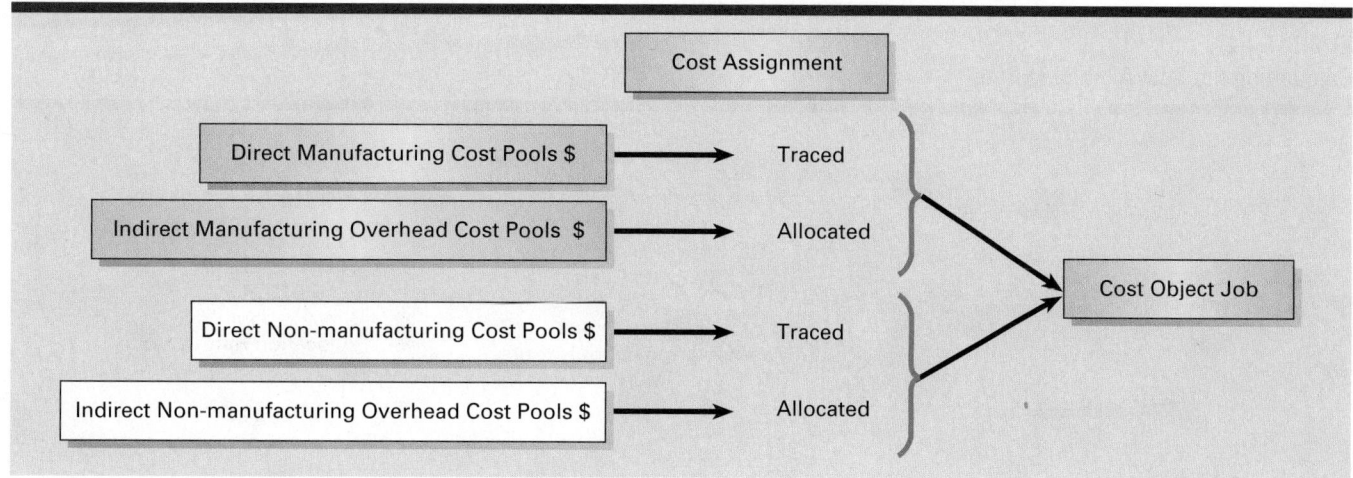

For manufacturing jobs the management team has three choices for a cost allocation base: quantity of DM, DMLH, or DMH. The goal is to make sure that the economic fact of how much a job costs is captured in the choice of the cost allocation base. Managers assume that their choice of a direct input used in different quantities by different jobs is a good signal of the proportion of common indirect resources each distinct job consumes. For example, if job 1 consumes more DMH than job 2, then it will also consume more common resources. If true, then the costing system will represent the real cost of the job completion process faithfully. Using more machine hours means more of the maintenance and property insurance costs should be assigned to job 1. The recovery of all direct and indirect costs for job 1 means the customer will pay more for this job than for job 2.

Clearly, the use of DMH does not explain how the costs of direct materials should be assigned to each job because these depend on costs per unit of DM. But remember that job costing is a GAAP-compliant, inexpensive way to *estimate* differences in job costs and assign these costs in a reasonable way. One guideline to help managers make this choice is whether the conversion of inputs into finished goods is more machine or labour intensive. If it is more machine intensive, then DMH would be a better choice as a cost allocation base than DMLH, and vice versa for a job that is more labour intensive.

In this chapter we will specify the cost allocation base, but in reality this is a difficult management task. Interestingly, the measurement of a quantity of inputs can be either non-financial, such as hours of direct labour, or financial, such as total cost of direct labour used. There is nothing stopping managers from selecting more than one pair of indirect cost pools and cost allocation bases when it is appropriate to the business decision that must be made. The larger the number of indirect cost pools, the more refined the job-costing system will be (which is described further in Chapter 5).

The **cost allocation rate** is the result of dividing the indirect cost pool by the cost allocation base (see Exhibit 4-2). This is the simple average indirect cost per cost object. Even though the cost allocation base is a direct input quantity, the indirect cost allocation rate is never the same as any direct cost rate. The reason, of course, is that the indirect cost pool is the result of common use of the same support resources by all jobs. If the cost object is one customized BMW X5 and the cost allocation base is the total number of *direct* manufacturing labour hours (DMLH), then the indirect cost allocation rate is the *indirect* cost per DMLH. This is a cost per unit of benefit to the job.

The cost allocation rate and the quantity of DMLH per customized BMW X5 are used to *assign* the indirect cost per customized BMW X5. Multiplying the indirect cost allocation rate by the quantity of DMLH per customized BMW X5 equals the total indirect cost per customized BMW X5.

EXHIBIT 4-2
Calculating the Cost Allocation Rate

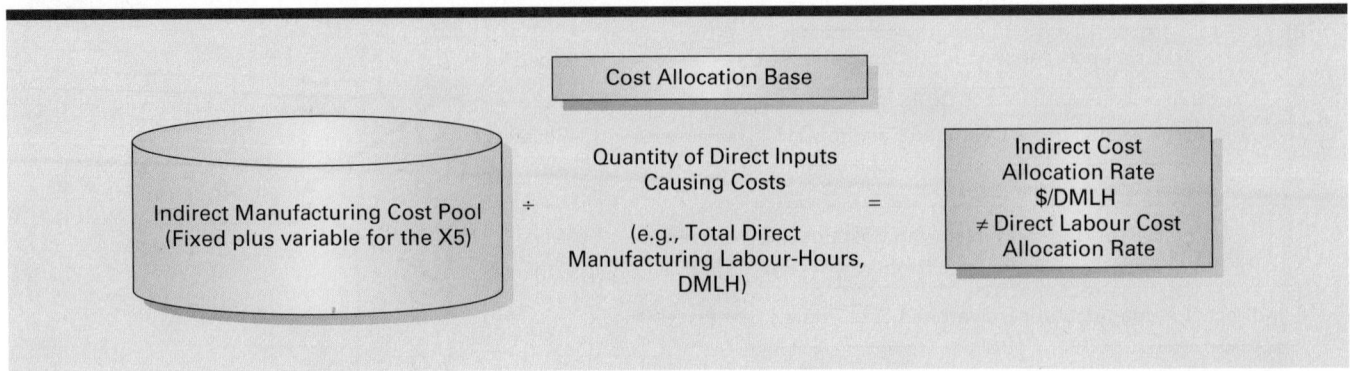

EXHIBIT 4-3
Cost Assignment Systems

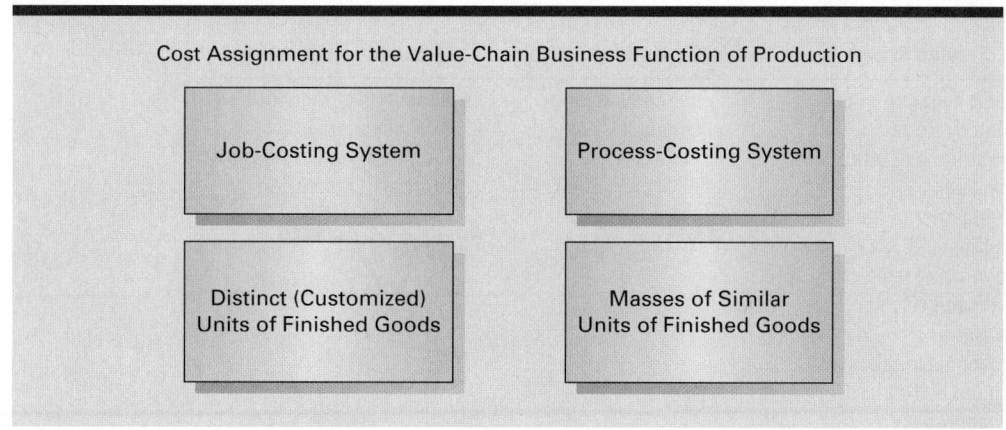

Cost Assignment for the Value-Chain Business Function of Production

Job-Costing System	Process-Costing System
Distinct (Customized) Units of Finished Goods	Masses of Similar Units of Finished Goods

JOB-COSTING AND PROCESS-COSTING SYSTEMS

Management accountants use two basic types of costing systems to assign costs to products or services (see Exhibit 4-3):

1. **Job-costing system.** In this system, the cost object is a distinct product or service called a **job**. For example, an advertising campaign produced by Cossette for Bombardier executive jets will be a service both unique and distinct from advertising campaigns for other clients. Job costing is also used to cost units of a distinct product, such as the costs incurred by Bombardier to customize an executive jet for a customer. Job-costing systems accumulate costs separately for each product or service.

2. **Process-costing system.**[2] In this system, the cost object is masses of identical units. For example, RBC Financial provides the same service to all its customers when processing ATM customer deposits, withdrawals, and bill payments. Customers of Maple Leaf all receive packages of the same processed meat. In each specified time period, process-costing systems use a cost allocation base called equivalent units to calculate an average prime cost and a separate average conversion or indirect cost rate. Averages are appropriate because each unit of finished goods consumes the same resources in the same quantities as all other units.

Companies have costing systems with elements of both job- and process-costing systems. Exhibit 4-4 shows a list of job-costing and process-costing examples in the service, merchandising, and manufacturing sectors. These two types of costing systems are best considered as opposite ends of a continuum; in between, one type of system can blur into the other to some degree. To provide information about the real costs of production in some time period, costing systems need to be tailored to the underlying production activities. For example, Kellogg Corporation uses job costing to calculate the total cost to manufacture each of its different and distinct types of products—such as frozen Eggos or boxes of Corn Flakes—but process costing to calculate the per-unit cost of producing each identical box of Corn Flakes. In this chapter, we focus on a job-costing system.

In this system, the cost object is at least one finished unit of a distinct product or service called a job. The finished product or service is customized such that its cost is distinct from the cost of other finished products or services. Customizing different jobs means using different quantities of inputs. For example, the cost of the legal service to defend Conrad Black of Hollinger in the United States differed from the cost of the legal service to defend Garth Drabinsky of Livent here in Canada.

---

[2]Process costing is discussed in detail in Chapter 17.

EXHIBIT 4-4

Examples of Job Costing and Process Costing in the Service, Merchandising, and Manufacturing Sectors

	Service Sector	**Merchandising Sector**	**Manufacturing Sector**
Job Costing Used	• Audit engagements done by Price Waterhouse Coopers • Consulting engagements done by McKinsey & Co. • Advertising-agency campaigns run by Cossette • Individual legal cases argued by Hale & Dorr • Computer-repair jobs done by Future Shop • Movies produced by Universal Studios	• Lululemon sending individual items by mail order • Special promotion of new products by Wal-Mart	• Assembly of individual executive jets at Boeing • Construction of bridges at Stantec Engineering
Process Costing Used	• Bank-cheque clearing at RBC • Postal delivery (standard items) by Canada Post	• Grain dealing by Arthur Daniel Midlands • Lumber dealing by Weyerhauser	• Oil refining by Canadian National Resources Limited • Beverage production by PepsiCo

A generic production function, shown in blue to match the value-chain assignment of production costs, is shown in Exhibit 4-5. The costs of DM and manufacturing overhead (MOH) are exclusive to the production function because they represent the direct and indirect costs of production. Rarely are 100% of direct materials converted in a specific time period, though, which is why both the work-in-process and finished goods inventory are included in blue to signify a production output. The cost of goods manufactured (COGM) includes direct materials and conversion. The other business functions in the value-chain are non-manufacturing costs and have no signifying colour. They are never included in COGM.

EXHIBIT 4-5

Generic Process Cost Allocation

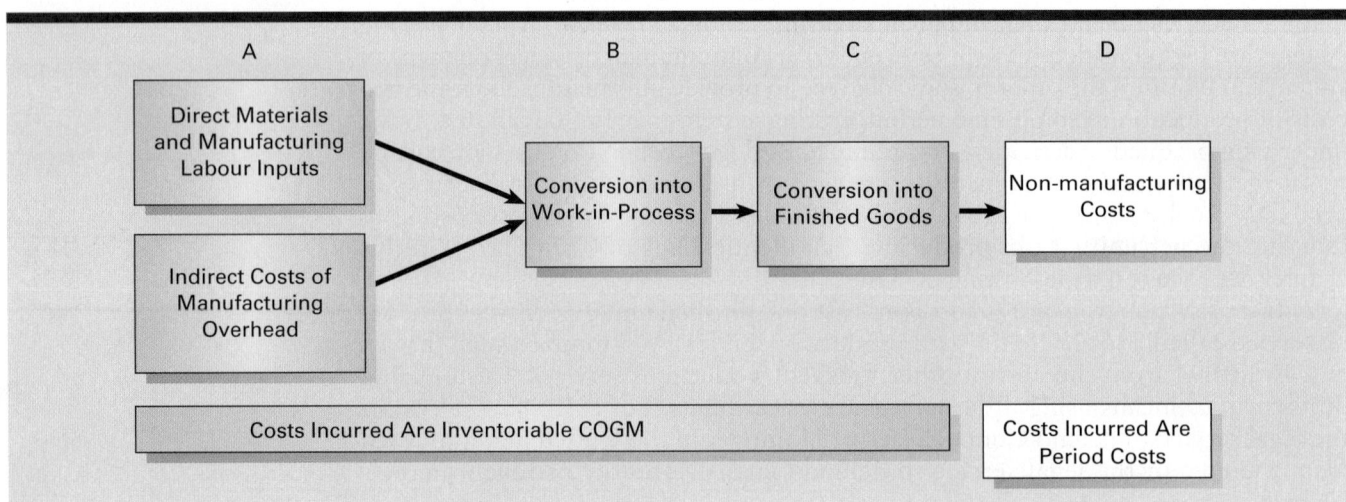

ASSIGNING COSTS TO JOBS

In general, there are seven steps in assigning costs to jobs (we will revisit these seven steps later in this chapter to assign total actual costs to a distinct service and a distinct product). To simplify these steps, we will ignore the difficulties in the decisions about what the cost object will be, the number of indirect cost pools, and the identification of appropriate cost drivers used to calculate the cost allocation rate.

Step 1: Identify the Distinct Job That Is the Cost Object Examples of a job would be the construction of a machine to a customer's specification or the production of a custom kitchen. For professional services, the job could be the audit of RIM. **Source documents**, which are original records (such as a labour time card) that support journal entries in the accounting system, provide relevant information because they link the quantity of a resource consumed to a distinct job.

All costs are accumulated in a distinct **job-cost record**, also called a **job-cost sheet**. The job-cost sheet accumulates all the costs assigned to a distinct job. Cost accumulation is done electronically, and information is available to authorized managers through the company's management information system.

Step 2: Identify the Direct Costs of the Distinct Job The relevant direct and indirect cost pools are identified according to the characteristics of a job. When the job output is a product such as a smartphone, direct materials for specific computer chips and software will generate significant costs. The trace for direct materials will be materials requisition records for each job or service that contain the quantity and cost of the materials.

Customizing products often takes considerable additional direct manufacturing labour. In this case, customers who request the customization should be willing to pay for the added value, which includes bearing a larger proportion of indirect costs like fringe benefits. The more direct labour used in a customized job, the higher the indirect cost of fringe benefits. It makes sense to reflect this economic fact by having this customer pay more indirect costs of finishing the product than another customer who has not demanded additional customization.

When the job output is a service such as an audit, the direct professional labour will generate significant costs. This pattern of costs is typical of the professional service industry, which is labour intensive. **Labour intensive** means that labour costs are a significant proportion of total costs. Accounting for direct labour also requires either a hardcopy or electronic trace of the labour time used, the cost per hour, and the distinct job. There may be many different types of direct labour used, depending on the job requirements. Each type, volume, and cost of direct labour-hour must be identified.

Step 3: Select the Cost Allocation Base to Use for Allocating the Indirect Cost Pool to a Distinct Job Indirect costs are incurred because some common inputs are necessary to do all jobs, such as maintenance, utilities, custodial services, and rework. These common costs must be allocated or divided up among all jobs because they are not incurred equally for all types of jobs. The cost allocation base is a quantity of direct inputs because this is measured in a company's MIS and is a reasonable measure of benefit or value added to distinct types of jobs.

Step 4: Identify and Add All the Indirect Costs into One Indirect Cost Pool All the MOH or indirect production costs associated with the use of common inputs are summed into one MOH cost pool. These costs will be recovered when the customer pays for the finished job. At the time of sale, the distinct job production costs become cost of goods sold (COGS). Sometimes companies will base a job-costing system on more than one indirect cost pool—one for machine- and one for labour-intensive jobs. The company would choose a machine-related input as the cost allocation base for the machine cost pool and a labour-related input for the labour cost pool.

Step 5: Compute the Indirect Cost Allocation Rate For each MOH cost pool, the **actual indirect cost allocation rate** is calculated by dividing the actual MOH cost pool (determined in Step 4) by the actual total quantity of the cost allocation base (determined in Step 3). The result is the average cost per unit of shared resources used by all types of jobs (see Exhibit 4-2).

Step 6: Compute the Indirect Cost Assigned to the Distinct Job The indirect costs of a distinct type of job are computed by multiplying the indirect cost rate by the actual quantity of the allocation base used in completing the distinct job.

Step 7: Compute the Total Cost of the Distinct Job by Adding All Direct and Indirect Costs Assigned to the Job The job cost is the *sum* of all direct and indirect costs assigned to the distinct job. The direct cost pools have been traced and the indirect costs have been allocated to each type of job.

JOB COSTING: ACTUAL COST ASSIGNMENT TO A DISTINCT SERVICE

> **②** Apply the decision framework in a seven-step method to assign total actual costs to a distinct service.

Now that we know the steps involved in assigning costs to jobs, let's go through these steps to assign total actual costs to a distinct service.

Lukach, Sulky, and Associates Ltd. (LSAL) is a public accounting firm. Using the decision framework, LSAL has identified their key problem as how to rank their audit jobs from most to least profitable. Gathering information already available internally on last year's actual costs, they identified relevant cost pools. Relevant cost pools distinguish the resources that are consumed differently by different types of audit jobs.

LSAL then predicted next year's budgeted operating income. What remains to be completed is the seven-step job-cost analysis to assign costs to jobs. Then the different types of audit jobs can be ranked from most to least profitable. This analysis will guide the firm in both future marketing plans and performance management. LSAL plans to continuously monitor and compare next year's actual performance to the predicted performance in the budget. Based on this feedback, managers will be able to identify the critical success factors for their most profitable audits. The firm can then choose the most profitable service mix and focus their efforts and resources on increasing those types of audit jobs.

LSAL may also decide that it is in their best economic interests to refuse less profitable types of audit jobs, or even discontinue providing services to existing low-profit clients. The reason is that LSAL has a limited number of 180 professionals working 1,600 direct labour hours per year at $300/DLH. LSAL will lose profitable opportunities when the hours are consumed by low-profit audits. This is called an **opportunity cost**, which is the contribution to income lost or foregone by not using a limited resource in its best alternative use.

We can follow the decision framework to solve LSAL's problem of how to rank different types of audit jobs. The most recent year-end statement of income and the budgeted statement of income for the coming year are presented in Exhibit 4-6.

There are a couple of notable features to this summary. First, LSAL predicts a drop in profitability from $20,408 to $18,390 million next year. This suggests that LSAL needs to improve profitability. Second, the professional labour costs were $82,260,000. General and administrative labour costs were $24,040,000. Total labour operating expenses were $106,300,000 ($82,260,000 + $24,040,000). More than 77% ($82,260,000 ÷ $106,300,000) of all labour costs pay the professional auditors. Overall, LSAL is very labour intensive.

SEVEN-STEP JOB COST ASSIGNMENT OF COSTS TO A DISTINCT SERVICE

Exhibit 4-7 graphically illustrates the key concepts and how they relate in creating an actual job-costing system for a service company. This is a visual tool for you to use when you analyze the data provided for a job-costing system. The Exhibit distinguishes between the allocation of MOH (Steps 1–6), the tracing of direct costs (at the bottom of the Exhibit), and the assignment of both costs to each job (Step 7). The varying sizes of the cost boxes signify that indirect and direct costs assigned to each distinct job vary. If this were not true, then job costing would not be useful and costs should simply be averaged across all jobs because they use identical quantities of shared inputs and must incur costs at an identical rate.

EXHIBIT 4-6
Lukach, Sulky, and Associates Actual and Budgeted Operating Income

Lukach, Sulky, and Associates (in $ thousands)				
	Actual 2011		Budget 2012	
Operating revenue		$168,120		$177,360
Operating expenses				
Professional labour		82,260		86,400*
General and administrative	$11,040		$12,180	
Administrative support	9,180		9,600	
Information systems	3,000		3,960	
Other administrative	820	24,040	1,038	26,778
Operating income after labour expenses		$61,820		$64,182
Non-labour operating expenses				
Liability insurance	8,826		12,960	
Professional development	3,240		5,280	
Rent	11,478		12,000	
Office services	7,980		8,580	
Travel	4,308		4,620	
Other non-labour	5,580	41,412	2,352	45,792
Operating income		$20,408		$18,390

$$\frac{180 \text{ professionals} \times 1,600 \text{ billable hours} \times \$300/\text{DLH}}{\$1,000} = \$86,400$$

Step 1: Identify the Distinct Type of Job That Is the Cost Object   The job is the audit of Simpson's Editorial Services, a very successful professional service. All costs of this audit must be assigned to the job before its profitability can be ranked among other types of audit jobs.

Step 2: Identify the Direct Costs of the Distinct Job   The direct costs were 800 professional labour hours at $300/DLH for a total of $240,000.

Step 3: Select the Cost Allocation Base to Use for Allocating the Indirect Cost Pool to a Distinct Job   There is only one category of direct costs, professional labour. LSAL managers assume that changes in professional labour-hours will explain a sufficient proportion of the change in the total indirect cost pool. The cost allocation base will be the total professional labour-hours actually consumed by LSAL last year. Exhibit 4-6 reports that the total professional labour cost at $300/DLH was $82,260,000, so the total DLH must have been 274,200 hours ($82,260,000 ÷ $300).

Step 4: Identify and Add All the Indirect Costs into One Indirect Cost Pool
In Exhibit 4-6, the actual total operating expenses have already been calculated as $147,712,000 ($82,260,000 + $24,040,000 + $41,412,000), of which actual direct professional labour costs were $82,260,000. The indirect cost pool must be $65,452,000 ($147,712,000 − $82,260,000).

Step 5: Compute the Indirect Cost Allocation Rate   Ways to resolve disputes over what quantity of what input should be in the cost allocation base are discussed in Chapter 10. Changes in the indirect cost pool should be reasonably explained by changes in the quantity of inputs in the cost allocation base. In this way, LSAL will assign costs in a way that reflects the economic facts of completing the job. The cost allocation rate for the single indirect cost pool using the cost allocation base of quantity of actual professional labour-hours is $65,452,000 ÷ 274,200 DLH = $238.7017/DLH (4 decimals).

EXHIBIT 4-7
Job-Costing Overview for Assigning Actual Total Costs of Three Service Jobs

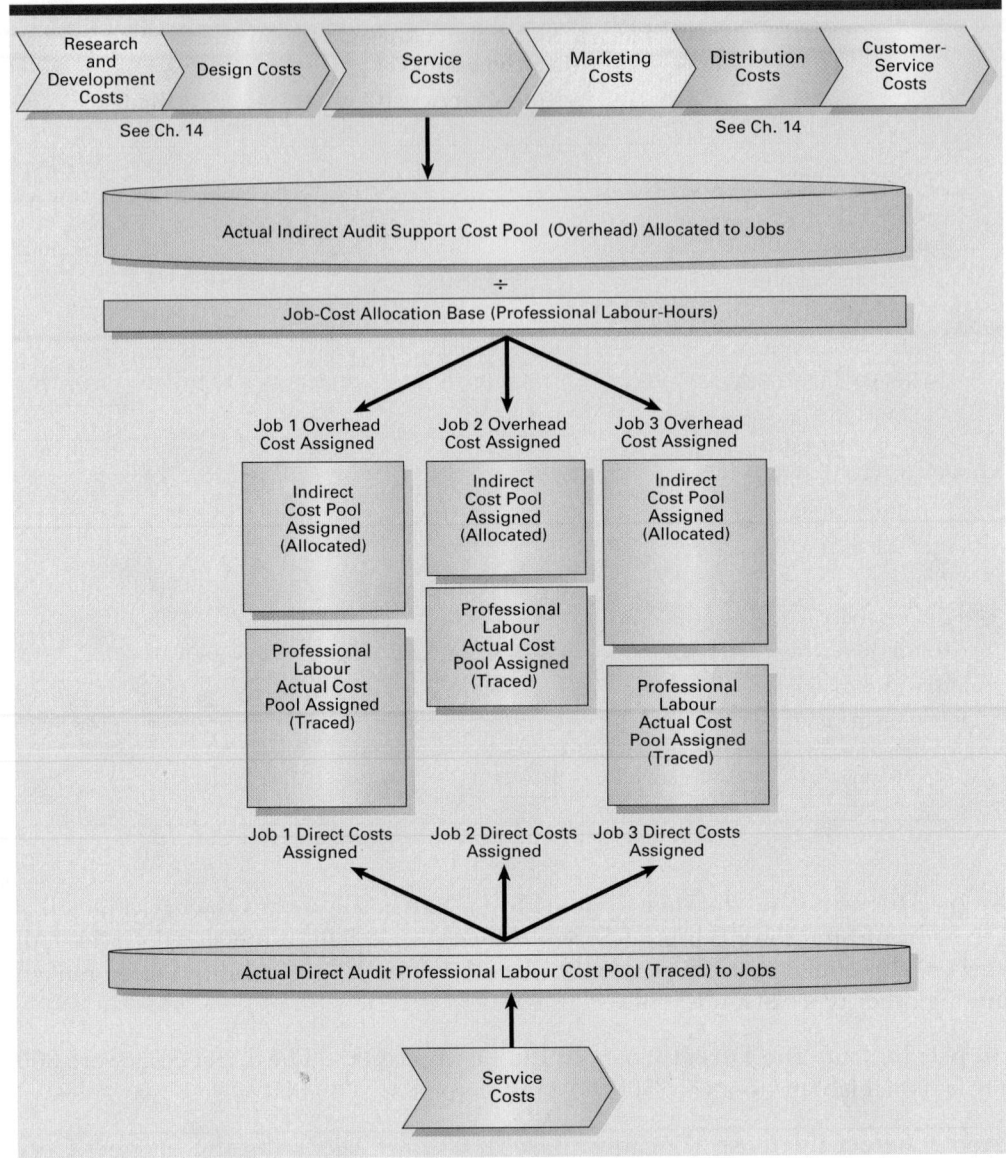

Step 6: Compute the Indirect Cost Assigned to the Distinct Job   The Simpson Editorial Services audit consumed 800 professional labour-hours. The total indirect cost assigned to this job at the cost allocation rate of $238.7017/DLH is $190,961 (rounded).

Step 7: Compute the Total Cost of the Distinct Job by Adding All Direct and Indirect Costs Assigned to the Job   Having spent time choosing a cost allocation base and calculating the cost allocation rate, managers must not forget to add the direct costs of the job to the allocated indirect costs to obtain the total job cost. The total cost of the Simpson Editorial Services audit was $430,961, as summarized in the table below:

Simpson Editorial Services Audit

	Professional Labour-Hours (1)	Direct Professional Labour Rate (2)	Direct Professional Labour Cost Pool (3) = (1) × (2)
Direct cost pool— professional labour	800	$300	$240,000
Indirect cost pool— audit support	800	$238.7017	190,961
Total job cost			$430,961

JOB COSTING: ACTUAL COST ASSIGNMENT TO A DISTINCT PRODUCT

Apply the decision framework in a seven-step method to assign total actual costs to a distinct product.

We can use the same decision framework to assign total actual costs to a distinct product. Robinson Company manufactures and installs customized machinery for the paper-making industry. In early 2012, BC Pulp and Paper Company (BCPP) sent Robinson a request for a proposal (RFP). Robinson will be among many competitors bidding to manufacture and install a new paper-making machine for BCPP. The RFP has both a product and service component because Robinson must install the completed machine.

The problem is determining whether Robinson's successful bid will be profitable. The profitability of the BCPP job depends on its cost and how low Robinson must bid to successfully obtain the job. The managers at Robinson have gathered relevant information on the specifications of the BCPP machine, the likely competitors and their resources, and the internal strengths and weaknesses at Robinson. After analyzing this information, they decided that the BCPP job fit the profile of a profitable job for Robinson and succeeded in the bid of $10,000 plus a profit of 50%, or $5,000 ($10,000 × 0.5 = $5,000), so $15,000 altogether. Robinson will monitor the BCPP job closely to obtain feedback comparing actual to budgeted costs. Cost overruns will be investigated, explained, and hopefully remedied to allow Robinson to realize its $5,000 expected profit.

SEVEN-STEP JOB COST ASSIGNMENT OF COSTS TO A DISTINCT PRODUCT

The seven steps to assign costs will be applied to the completed job, BCPP. The manual record for the BCPP job is part of Robinson's MIS and summarizes all costs for the distinct job as shown in Exhibit 4-8. These data are the basis for the assignment of costs to BCPP.

Step 1: Identify the Distinct Job That Is the Chosen Cost Object The cost object is job BCPP, manufacturing a paper-making machine for the BC Pulp and Paper Company in 2012. Throughout the BCPP job, Robinson's managers and management accountants gather information from source documents and job-cost records with the BCPP identification code.

Step 2: Identify the Direct Costs of the Distinct Job Robinson identifies direct materials and direct manufacturing labour cost pools. As required by the specifications, Robinson's manufacturing engineer will issue requisitions for direct materials. The basic source document, a **materials-requisition record**, lists the cost of direct materials used on each specific job in a specific department. The $112 actual total cost also appears on the BCPP job-cost record in Exhibit 4-8 in the Direct Materials section. The actual total direct materials cost was $4,606.

The second direct cost pool is direct manufacturing labour. The source document is called a **labour-time record (time sheet or time card)**. This record lists the amount of labour-time in direct manufacturing labour hours (DMLH) for the BCPP job, the date, the employee identification, the hourly rate in $/DMLH, and the total cost of each type of labour used. Notice that two different employees worked on this job for two different time periods and were paid two different hourly rates.

There is corroborating detail about both the direct materials and direct manufacturing labour resources consumed by the BCPP job. Panel A of Exhibit 4-9 shows the materials-requisition record that specifies what quantity of what material was requisitioned, the cost per unit, and the total direct materials cost. Panel B shows the labour-time for employee LT232 (the first DMLH record in Exhibit 4-8).

Notice that G.L. Cook worked on two jobs during the week. The 25 DMLH worked on BCPP is shown in detail day by day. The hourly rate is $18/DMLH and the total cost assigned to BCPP was $450, as shown in line 18 of Exhibit 4-8 under the heading Direct Manufacturing Labour. G.L. Cook, however, also performed 3 DMLH of maintenance. Maintenance is not traced to either job JL 256 or BCPP.

EXHIBIT 4-8
Source Documents at Robinson Company: Job-Cost Record BCPP

	File Edit View Insert Format Tools Data Window Help				
	A	B	C	D	E
1			JOB-COST RECORD		
2	JOB NO:	BCPP		CUSTOMER:	BC Pulp and Paper
3	Date Started:	Feb. 4, 2012		Date Completed:	Feb. 28, 2012
4					
5					
6	**DIRECT MATERIALS**				
7	Date	Materials-		Quantity	Unit	Total
8	Received	Requisition No.	Part No.	Used	Cost	Costs
9	Feb. 4, 2012	2012: 198	MB 468-A	8	$14	$ 112
10	Feb. 4, 2012	2012: 199	TB 267-F	12	63	756
11						•
12						•
13	Total					$ 4,606
14						
15	**DIRECT MANUFACTURING LABOUR**					
16	Period	Labour-Time	Employee	Hours	Hourly	Total
17	Covered	Record No.	No.	Used	Rate	Costs
18	Feb. 4-10, 2012	LT 232	551-87-3076	25	$18	$ 450
19	Feb. 4-10, 2012	LT 247	287-31-4671	5	19	95
20						•
21						•
22	Total					$ 1,579
23						
24	**MANUFACTURING OVERHEAD***					
25		Cost Pool		Allocation-Base	Allocation-	Total
26	Date	Category	Allocation-Base	Quantity Used	Base Rate	Costs
27	Dec. 31, 2012	Manufacturing	Direct Manufacturing	88 hours	$45	$ 3,960
28			Labour-Hours			
29						
30	Total					$ 3,960
31	**TOTAL MANUFACTURING COST OF JOB**					$10,145
32						
33						
34	*The Robinson Company uses a single manufacturing overhead cost pool. The use of multiple overhead cost pools					
35	would mean multiple entries in the "Manufacturing Overhead" section of the job-cost record.					
36						

EXHIBIT 4-9
Source Documents at Robinson Company: Materials-Requisition Record and Labour-Time Record

PANEL A:

MATERIALS-REQUISITION RECORD

Materials-Requisition Record No.			2012: 198	
Job No. BCPP		Date:	FEB. 4, 2012	
Part	Part		Unit	Total
No.	Description	Quantity	Cost	Cost
MB 468-A	Metal Brackets	8	$14	$112

Issued By: B. Clyde   Date: Feb. 4, 2012
Received By: L. Daley   Date: Feb. 4, 2012

PANEL B:

LABOUR-TIME RECORD

Labour-Time Record No: LT 232
Employee Name: G. L. Cook   Employee No: 551-87-3076
Employee Classification Code: Grade 3 Machinist
Hourly Rate: $18
Week Start: Feb. 4, 2012   Week End: Feb. 10, 2012

Job. No.	M	T	W	Th	F	S	Su	Total
BCPP	4	8	3	6	4	0	0	25
JL 256	3	0	4	2	3	0	0	12
Maintenance	1	0	1	0	1	0	0	3
Total	8	8	8	8	8	0	0	40

Supervisor: R. Stuart   Date: Feb. 4, 2012

Step 3: Select the Cost Allocation Base to Use for Allocating the Indirect Cost Pool to a Distinct Job Indirect manufacturing costs are costs that are necessary to do a job but cannot be traced to a specific job. Different jobs require different quantities of indirect resources. For example, Exhibit 4-9 shows that Mr. Cook's maintenance is not the same each day of the week. The objective is to allocate the actual total costs of indirect resources in a systematic way to their related jobs.

Robinson chooses direct manufacturing labour-hours as the allocation base for linking all actual indirect MOH to jobs. In its labour-intensive environment, Robinson believes that when the quantity of direct manufacturing labour-hours consumed changes, it will also explain a sufficient amount of change in the quantity of indirect costs consumed by each job. Robinson recorded a *total* of 27,000 actual direct manufacturing labour-hours for all jobs.

Step 4: Identify and Add All the Indirect Costs into One Indirect Cost Pool Actual total indirect manufacturing overhead costs have been accumulated as $1,215,000 for all jobs undertaken in the year.

Step 5: Compute the Indirect Cost Allocation Rate For each cost pool, the actual indirect cost rate is calculated by dividing actual total indirect costs in the pool (determined in Step 4 as $1,215,000) by the actual total quantity of the cost allocation base (determined in Step 3 as 27,000 DMLH). The cost allocation rate is:

$$\text{Actual manufacturing overhead rate} = \frac{\text{Actual manufacturing overhead costs}}{\text{Actual total quantity of cost allocation base}}$$

$$= \frac{\$1,215,000}{27,000 \text{ direct manufacturing labour-hours}}$$

$$= \$45 \text{ per direct manufacturing labour-hour}$$

Step 6: Compute the Indirect Cost Assigned to the Distinct Job Robinson's actual cost records for the year show that the total BCPP direct labour-hours consumed was 88 DMLH. The total MOH was $3,960 ($45/DMLH × 88 DMLH = $3,960).

Step 7: Compute the Total Cost of the Distinct Job by Adding All Direct and Indirect Costs Assigned to the Job From Exhibit 4-8, the actual total of direct and indirect costs for the BCPP job was $10,145.

Direct manufacturing costs		
Direct materials	$4,606	
Direct manufacturing labour	1,579	$ 6,185
Manufacturing overhead costs		
($45 per direct manuf. labour-hour × 88 hours)		3,960
Total manufacturing costs of job BCPP		$10,145

Recall that Robinson bid a price of $15,000 for the job. At that revenue, the actual-costing system shows a gross margin of $4,855 ($15,000 − $10,145) and a gross-margin percentage of 32.4% ($4,855 ÷ $15,000 = 0.324).

Robinson's manufacturing managers and sales managers can use the gross margin and gross-margin percentage calculations to compare the profitability of different jobs to understand the reasons why, for example, the BCPP job failed to meet its expected gross margin of $5,000 ($15,000 − $10,000) and gross-margin percentage of 33.3% ($5,000 ÷ $15,000). Overall, without a job-costing system, managers would have a very difficult time determining the profitability of specific jobs and identifying areas for improvement.

ADDITIONAL POINTS TO CONSIDER WHEN CALCULATING JOB-COST ALLOCATION RATES

Information technology simplifies the tracing of costs to jobs. If direct manufacturing labour-hours is used as the cost allocation base, very refined systems can trace direct manufacturing labour in minutes or longer intervals to each job. Employees simply scan their identification card and select the job identification code when they begin and again when they end their task. The computer then reports not only the

Job Costing on the Next-Generation Military Fighter Plane

Northrop Grumman, Inc. is a leading provider of systems and technologies for the US Department of Defense. Competitive bidding processes and increased public and congressional oversight make understanding costs critical in pricing decisions, as well as in winning and retaining government contracts. Each job must be estimated individually because the distinct outputs consume different amounts of Northrop Grumman's resources.

A project team of Northrop Grumman, Lockheed Martin, and BAE Systems was awarded the System Design and Demonstration contract to build the F-35 Lightning II aircraft—also known as the Joint Strike Fighter—in late 2001. This project, worth over $200 billion, will create a family of supersonic, multi-role fighter airplanes designed for the militaries of the United States, United Kingdom, Italy, The Netherlands, Turkey, Canada, Australia, Denmark, and

Norway. In December 2006, the F-35 Lightning II successfully completed its first test flight; it appears in this photograph during subsequent testing at Edwards Air Force Base, California, in 2009.

The project team for the F-35 Lightning II uses a job-costing system. There are two direct cost pools, material and manufacturing labour. The remaining costs are accumulated in one overhead cost pool. The cost allocation base is the total budgeted direct materials cost. This job-costing system allows managers to assign costs to processes and projects. Managers use this system to actively manage costs. Program representatives from the Department of Defense and members of Congress have access to clear, concise, and transparent costing data when they complete their audits.

Sources: Conversations with Northrop Grumman, Inc. management, www.jsf.mil, and various program announcements and press releases.

DMLH spent, but also the indirect costs of fringe benefits and rework for each job. For fixed cost allocation, when the cost object is a job it is sensible to collect the fixed costs incurred during the entire time period of the job.

Robinson Company computes indirect cost rates in Step 5 of the job-costing system (p. 117) on an annual basis. There are two reasons for using longer periods, such as a year, to calculate indirect cost rates:

- **Seasonal patterns.** The shorter the period is, the greater the influence of seasonal patterns on the amount of costs. For example, if indirect cost rates were calculated each month, then heating costs would be charged to production only during the winter months. An annual period incorporates the effects of all four seasons into one annual indirect cost rate.

- **Unitized fixed costs.** Longer periods to produce jobs mean that the unitized fixed cost portion of the machine and other fixed cost pools will be spread out more evenly. Even if output varies from month to month for a single job, the point is to cost the job, not the time period.

An audit firm has a highly seasonal workload. Tax advice accounts for more than 80% of the workload from January through April. Given the following mix of costs for a high-output month such as April and a low-output month such as July, actual indirect cost allocation rates fluctuate by almost 300%. If the low cost allocation rate were charged in April, then clients would be very pleased. If the high cost allocation rate were charged in July, then clients would leave. If costs are allocated and charged at the time they are incurred, then July clients are not paying a fair share of fixed resources for an identical job in April. July clients are penalized for the time of year the resources are consumed. Ultimately the firm could not cover its total annual fixed indirect costs.

	Indirect Costs			Professional Labour-Hours	Allocation Rate per Professional Labour-Hour
	Variable (1)	Fixed (2)	Total (3)	(4)	(5) = (3) ÷ (4)
High-output month	$40,000	$60,000	$100,000	3,200	$31.25
Low-output month	10,000	60,000	70,000	800	87.50

METHODS AVAILABLE TO CALCULATE COST RATES AND ASSIGN JOB COSTS

Exhibit 4-10 summarizes three methods that are available to calculate cost rates and assign job costs: actual, budgeted, and normal. The methods illustrate three GAAP-compliant combinations of actual and budgeted values used to calculate cost allocation rates and *assign* costs to distinct jobs. The methods differ in the use of either the budgeted or actual quantity of the cost allocation base used when assigning costs to distinct jobs. Standard costing, which is discussed in Chapters 9 and 17, differs from budgeted costing and includes normal levels of materials, supplies, labour, efficiency, and capacity utilization. The standard costs are kept current through a regular process of revision.

ACTUAL COSTING

Actual costing is a costing system that traces direct costs to a distinct type of job by using the actual direct cost rates. The direct rates are calculated by dividing the actual direct job cost pools by the actual quantity of direct inputs. The actual indirect cost pool is divided by the actual quantity of the direct input chosen as the cost allocation base to calculate the actual indirect cost allocation rate. To assign some amount of the indirect cost pool to one distinct type of job, the actual quantity of the direct cost allocation base used to complete the job is multiplied by the actual indirect cost allocation rate.

This method looks backwards to historical information as part of Step 5 in the decision framework. It is best used to provide feedback information to assess the profitability of each job in comparison to its expected profitability. The benefit of using an actual cost system is that the job-costing information accurately reflects economic facts.

However, the accounting cycle produces a lag between when the cost was incurred and when it was paid. In addition, there is often a wait for the actual information to be recorded within the accounting system, and data entry may be inaccurate. Finally, the job has to be finished before the final cost information is known. Unfortunately for many jobs, such as the construction of the Confederation Bridge, which links Prince Edward Island to New Brunswick, cost information to assess profitability was needed long before job-completion at the end of four years. Timeliness is an important characteristic that defines relevant information.

In addition, historical information may not be the best indicator of future costs. For example, the worldwide 2007 recession decreased profits in all industries worldwide. Fixed costs could not be reduced fast enough to keep pace with falling demand. Unsold inventory built up based on normally expected demand and profit fell because no one was buying. Managers need better than a 90- to 365-day-old set of information based on business as usual to adequately respond to these unpredicted threats to profit. As uncertainty and risk escalate, predictions or budgets need to

EXHIBIT 4-10
Methods to Calculate Cost Rates and Assign Job Costs

	Direct Cost Pools	Indirect Cost Pool
ACTUAL COSTING	Actual rate × Actual Q/Job	Actual indirect cost allocation rate × Actual Q/Job
BUDGET COSTING	Budgeted rate × Actual Q/Job	Budgeted indirect cost allocation rate × Actual Q/Job
NORMAL COSTING	Actual rate × Actual Q/Job	Budgeted indirect cost allocation rate × Actual Q/Job

Actual indirect cost allocation rate = Actual indirect cost pool ÷ Actual Q of direct inputs used

Budgeted indirect cost allocation rate = Budgeted cost pool ÷ Budgeted Q of direct inputs used

The Q of direct inputs used to allocate the Indirect Cost Pool was selected by managers as the cost allocation base.

change to reflect the economic reality outside a company. This is at least as important as gathering internal cost information from the company itself on the profitability of a distinct type of finished job.

BUDGETED COSTING

Budgeted job cost assignment is useful in service industries because bonuses, an indirect labour cost, are awarded after year-end when all professional billable hours are known. The indirect cost rate will be mismatched to actual economic events. Peak-period overtime worked in, for example, an audit company such as LSAL, is not a predictable amount and, for service companies who are growing their client base, is not readily budgeted. Nevertheless, overtime services provided to complete jobs during peak period is an additional input consumed by some jobs but not others. The customer requiring the overtime should pay for it; therefore, LSAL must use job costing to allocate indirect labour costs appropriately.

LSAL accumulates direct professional labour costs in one cost pool and direct professional labour-hours (DLH) in its MIS. These amounts are used to calculate the direct labour cost rate. Overtime and bonuses arise from business growth and are accumulated with other common costs in one indirect cost pool. In 2012, LSAL budgeted total direct labour costs of $14,400,000, total indirect costs of $12,960,000, and total DLH of 288,000 for the year. In this case, the rate is:

$$\text{Budgeted direct labour cost rate} = \frac{\text{Budgeted total direct labour costs}}{\text{Budgeted total direct labour–hours}}$$

$$= \frac{\$14,400,000}{288,000} = \$50/\text{DLH}$$

Assuming only one indirect cost pool and total DLH as the cost allocation base, the indirect cost allocation rate is:

$$\text{Budgeted indirect cost rate} = \frac{\text{Budgeted total costs in the indirect costs pool}}{\text{Budgeted total quantity of cost allocation base}}$$

$$= \frac{\$12,960,000}{288,000 \text{ DLH}} = \$45/\text{DLH}$$

Suppose an audit of LSAL's client Tracy Transport, completed during the peak period in March 2012, uses 800 DLH. LSAL calculates the direct costs of the Tracy Transport audit by multiplying the budgeted direct cost rate by the actual quantity of the DLH for the job. LSAL allocates indirect costs to the Tracy Transport audit by multiplying the budgeted indirect cost allocation rate by the actual quantity of the cost allocation base used in this job. On this basis, the cost of the Tracy Transport audit is:

Direct labour costs, $50 × 800	= $40,000
Indirect costs allocated, $45 × 800	= $36,000
Total	= $76,000

At the end of the year, the direct costs traced to jobs using budgeted rates will rarely equal the actual direct costs because the actual and budgeted rates are developed at different points in time using different information. End-of-period adjustments for underallocated or overallocated direct costs must be made in the same way that adjustments are made for underallocated or overallocated indirect costs. Three methods for making these adjustments—adjusted allocation rate, proration, and write-off—are discussed at the end of this chapter.

NORMAL COSTING

Normal costing is more complex than an actual job-costing system. The normal method differs from the actual method in the way indirect costs are assigned to a distinct job. A normal job-costing system still traces direct costs to a distinct type of job by multiplying the actual direct cost rates by the actual quantities of the direct cost inputs, but indirect costs are allocated based on the *budgeted (predetermined)* indirect cost allocation rates multiplied by the actual direct input quantity of the cost allocation base used by each distinct type of job. The difference is that the indirect cost allocation rate is calculated using a budgeted indirect cost pool divided by an indirect quantity of the cost allocation base used for all jobs. Source documents identify the actual quantities of direct materials, equipment, and labour used as each distinct type of job is completed.

We illustrate normal costing for the Robinson Company example using the seven-step procedure presented earlier. The following budgeted data for 2012 are for its manufacturing operations:

	Budget
Total manufacturing overhead costs	$1,120,000
Total direct manufacturing labour-hours	28,000

Steps 1 and 2 are exactly as before: Step 1 identifies BCPP as the cost object; Step 2 calculates actual direct material costs of $4,606, and actual direct manufacturing labour costs of $1,579. Recall from Step 3 that Robinson uses a single cost allocation base, direct manufacturing labour-hours, to allocate all manufacturing overhead costs to jobs. The budgeted quantity of direct manufacturing labour-hours for 2012 is 28,000 hours. In Step 4, Robinson groups all the indirect manufacturing costs into a single manufacturing overhead cost pool. In Step 5, the budgeted manufacturing overhead rate for 2012 is calculated as:

$$\frac{\text{Budgeted manufacturing}}{\text{overhead rate}} = \frac{\text{Budgeted annual manufacturing indirect costs}}{\text{Budgeted annual quantity of the cost allocation base}}$$

$$= \frac{\$1,120,000}{28,000 \text{ direct manufacturing labour-hours}}$$

$$= \$40 \text{ per direct manufacturing labour-hour}$$

In Step 6, under a normal costing system, the allocated MOH costs are $3,520:

$$\frac{\text{Manufacturing overhead costs}}{\text{allocated to BCPP}} = \frac{\text{Budgeted manufacturing}}{\text{overhead rate}} \times \frac{\text{Actual quantity of direct}}{\text{manufacturing labour-hours}}$$

$$= \frac{\$40 \text{ per direct manuf.}}{\text{labour-hour}} \times \frac{88 \text{ direct manufacturing}}{\text{labour-hours}}$$

$$= \$3,520$$

In Step 7, the cost of the job under normal costing is $9,705:

Direct manufacturing costs		
Direct materials	$4,606	
Direct manufacturing labour	1,579	$6,185
Manufacturing overhead costs		
($40 per direct manufacturing labour-hour × 88 actual direct manufacturing labour-hours)		3,520
Total manufacturing costs of job		$9,705

The manufacturing cost of the BCPP job is $440 lower under normal costing ($9,705) than it is under actual costing ($10,145) because the budgeted indirect cost rate is $40 per hour, whereas the actual indirect cost rate is $45 per hour. The difference in rates, ($45 − $40) × 88 actual direct manufacturing labour-hours = $440.

As we discussed previously, manufacturing costs of a job are available much earlier under a normal costing system. Consequently, Robinson's manufacturing and sales managers can evaluate the profitability of different jobs, the efficiency with which the jobs are done, and the pricing of different jobs as soon as the jobs are completed, while the experience is still fresh in everyone's mind. Another advantage of normal costing is that corrective actions can be implemented much sooner. At the end of the year, though, costs allocated using normal costing will not, in general, equal actual costs incurred. If material, adjustments will need to be made so that the cost of jobs and the costs in various inventory accounts are based on actual rather that normal costing.

A NORMAL JOB-COSTING SYSTEM AND COST FLOW

5 Analyze the flow of costs from direct and indirect cost pools to inventory accounts, including adjustments for over- and underallocated costs.

We now explain cost flow for a company with a normal job-costing system, Robinson Company. The following illustration considers events that occurred in February 2012. Exhibit 4-11 illustrates a broad framework for understanding the flow of costs and inventory valuation in job costing.

The upper part of Exhibit 4-11 shows the inventoriable costs from the purchase of materials and other manufacturing inputs, which flow during conversion into work-in-process and finished goods inventory. The sale of BCPP triggers the transfer of these costs from cost of goods manufactured (COGM) to the cost of goods sold (COGS) account.

Direct materials used and direct manufacturing labour can be easily traced to BCPP through the electronic source documents. These costs do not disappear even if they are paid. Rather, these costs are transferred to work-in-process inventory on the balance sheet. These direct costs are expended to transform or convert raw materials into finished goods inventory. As the goods are converted, value is added, which is why the work-in-process is a current asset. With more conversion, work-in-process inventory will provide future benefit in the form of revenue in a time period of less than 12 months.

Robinson also incurs MOH (including indirect materials and indirect manufacturing labour). These indirect support costs cannot be readily traced to BCPP because the inputs are common and used in different amounts by all of Robinson's jobs. First MOH is accumulated in an MOH ledger account and then allocated and

EXHIBIT 4-11
Flow of Costs in Job Costing

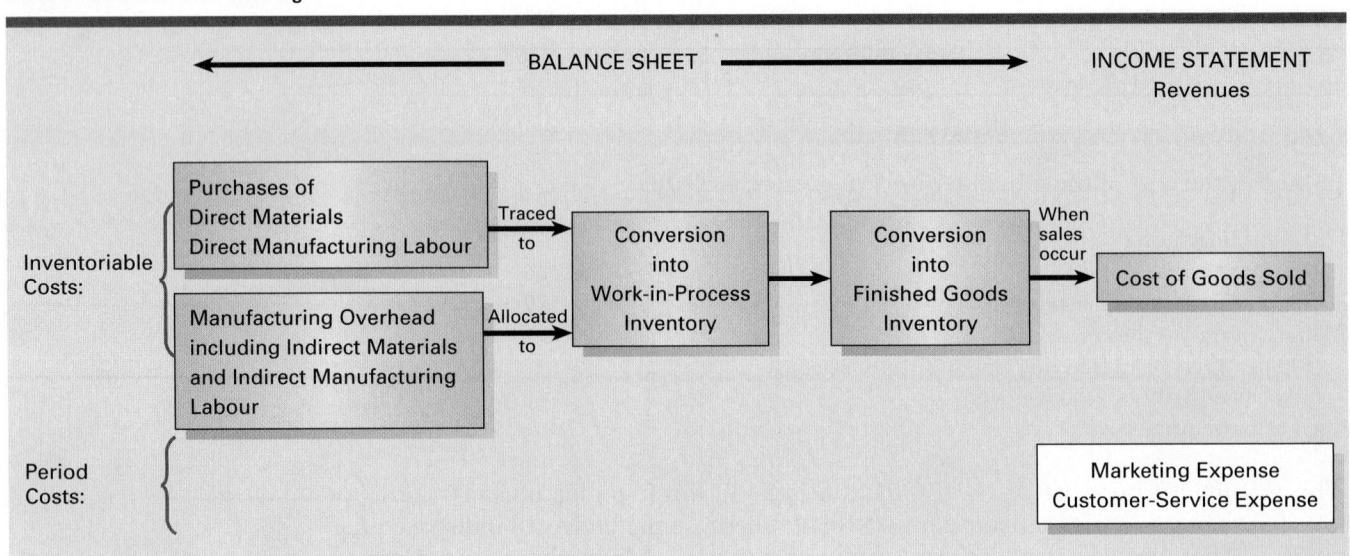

assigned to individual jobs. Once assigned to a job, MOH is transferred to the work-in-process inventory account. But Robinson is using a normal costing method and a budgeted indirect cost allocation rate, although it is using actual direct manufacturing labour-hours per job to assign the MOH to each job. Normal costing will create a discrepancy for which an accounting adjustment must be made, between what is recorded as the job is completed and the actual costs incurred.

Once complete, all assigned BCPP costs are transferred to the finished goods inventory account on the balance sheet. Only when finished goods are sold is an expense, cost of goods sold, recognized in the income statement and matched against revenue earned from sales.

GENERAL LEDGER

You know by this point that a job-costing system has a separate job-cost record for each job. A summary of the job-cost record is typically found in a subsidiary ledger. The general ledger account Work-in-Process Control presents the total of these separate job-cost records pertaining to all unfinished jobs. The job-cost records and Work-in-Process Control account track job costs from when jobs start until they are complete.

Exhibit 4-12 shows T-account relationships for Robinson Company's general ledger. The general ledger gives a "bird's-eye view" of the costing system. The amounts shown in Exhibit 4-12 are based on the transactions and journal entries that

EXHIBIT 4-12
Normal Job Costing for BCPP: Diagram of General Ledger Relationships for February 2012

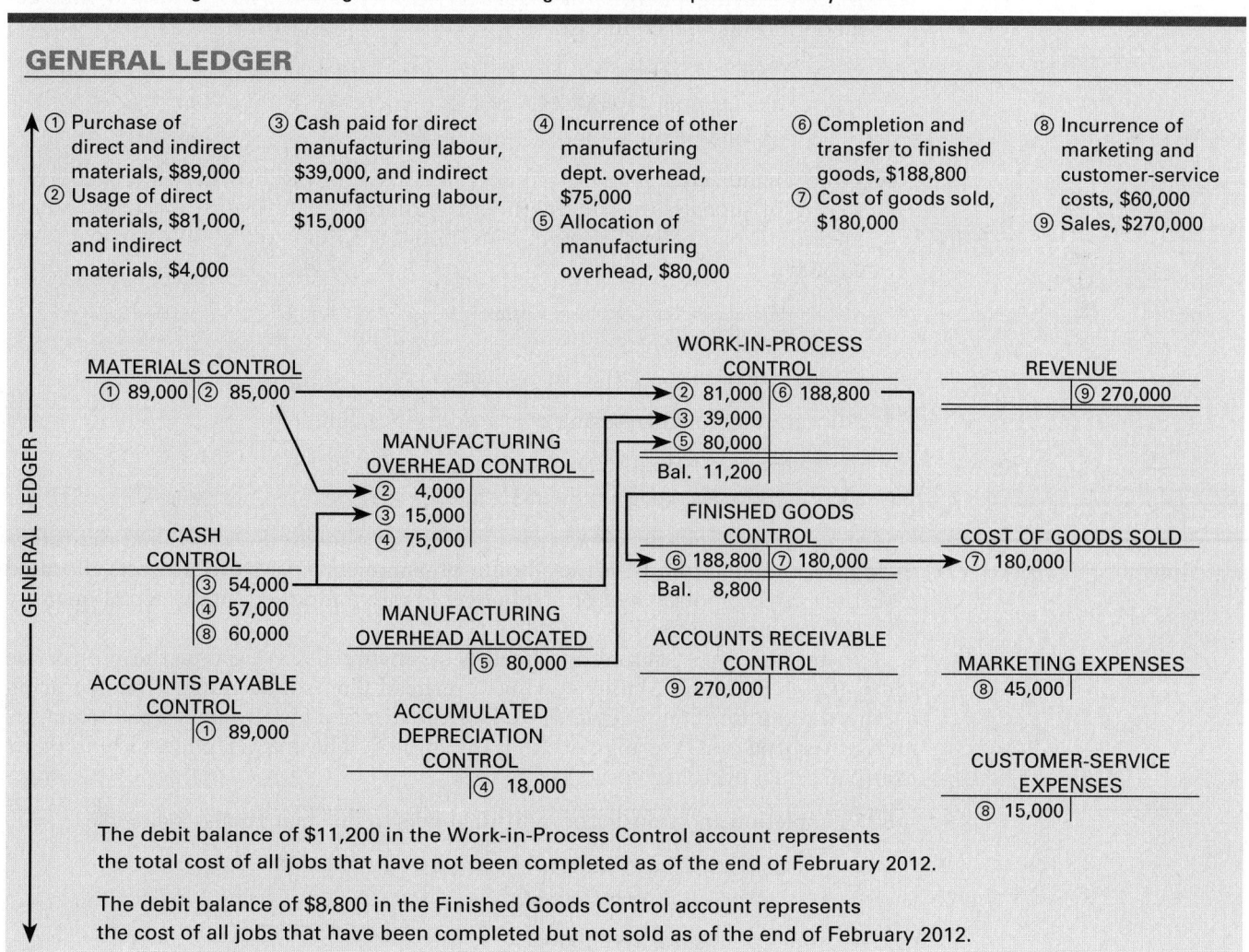

follow. As you go through each journal entry, use Exhibit 4-12 to see how the various entries being made come together. General ledger accounts with "Control" in the titles (for example, Materials Control and Accounts Payable Control) have underlying subsidiary ledgers that contain additional details, such as each type of material in inventory and individual suppliers that Robinson must pay.

A general ledger should be viewed as only one of many tools that assist management in planning and control. To control operations, managers rely on not only the source documents used to record amounts in the subsidiary ledgers, but also nonfinancial information such as the percentage of jobs requiring rework.

EXPLANATIONS OF TRANSACTIONS

We next look at a summary of Robinson Company's transactions for February 2012 and the corresponding journal entries for those transactions.

1. Purchases of materials (direct and indirect) on credit, $89,000.

Materials Control	89,000	
Accounts Payable Control		89,000

2. Usage of direct materials, $81,000, and indirect materials, $4,000.

Work-in-Process Control	81,000	
Manufacturing Overhead Control	4,000	
Materials Control		85,000

3. Manufacturing payroll for February: direct labour, $39,000, and indirect labour, $15,000, paid in cash.

Work-in-Process Control	39,000	
Manufacturing Overhead Control	15,000	
Cash Control		54,000

4. Other manufacturing overhead costs incurred during February, $75,000, consisting of supervision and engineering salaries, plant utilities, repairs, insurance, and plant depreciation. The non-cash item, plant depreciation, was $18,000.

Manufacturing Overhead Control	75,000	
Cash Control		57,000
Accumulated Depreciation Control		18,000

5. Allocation of manufacturing overhead to jobs, $80,000.

Work-in-Process Control	80,000	
Manufacturing Overhead Allocated		80,000

Under normal costing, **manufacturing overhead allocated**—also called **manufacturing overhead applied**—is the amount of manufacturing overhead costs allocated to distinct types of jobs based on the budgeted rate multiplied by the actual quantity of the allocation base used.

In transaction 4, actual overhead costs incurred throughout the month are added (debited) to the Manufacturing Overhead Control account. Manufacturing overhead costs are added (debited) to Work-in-Process Control *only when* manufacturing overhead costs are allocated in transaction 5. The amount allocated will differ from the actual overhead costs.

6. Completion and transfer of individual jobs to finished goods, $188,800.

Finished Goods Control	188,800	
Work-in-Process Control		188,800

7. Cost of goods sold, $180,000.

Cost of Goods Sold	180,000	
Finished Goods Control		180,000

8. Marketing costs for February, $45,000, and customer-service costs for February, $15,000, paid in cash.

Marketing Expenses	45,000	
Customer-Service Expenses	15,000	
Cash Control		60,000

9. Sales revenues, all on credit, $270,000.

Accounts Receivable Control	270,000	
Revenues		270,000

SUBSIDIARY LEDGERS

Exhibits 4-13 and 4-14 present subsidiary ledgers that contain the underlying details—the "worm's-eye view" as opposed to the "bird's-eye view" of the general ledger—such as each type of materials in inventory and costs accumulated in individual jobs. The sum of all entries in underlying subsidiary ledgers equals the total amount in the corresponding general ledger control accounts.

Material Records by Type of Materials The subsidiary ledger for materials at Robinson Company—called *Materials Records*—keeps a continuous record of quantity received, quantity issued to jobs, and inventory balances for each type of material. Panel A of Exhibit 4-13 shows the Materials Record for Metal Brackets (Part No. MB 468-A). Source documents supporting the receipt and issue of materials are scanned into a computer. Software programs then automatically update the

EXHIBIT 4-13
Subsidiary Ledger for Materials, Labour, and Manufacturing Department Overhead 2012*

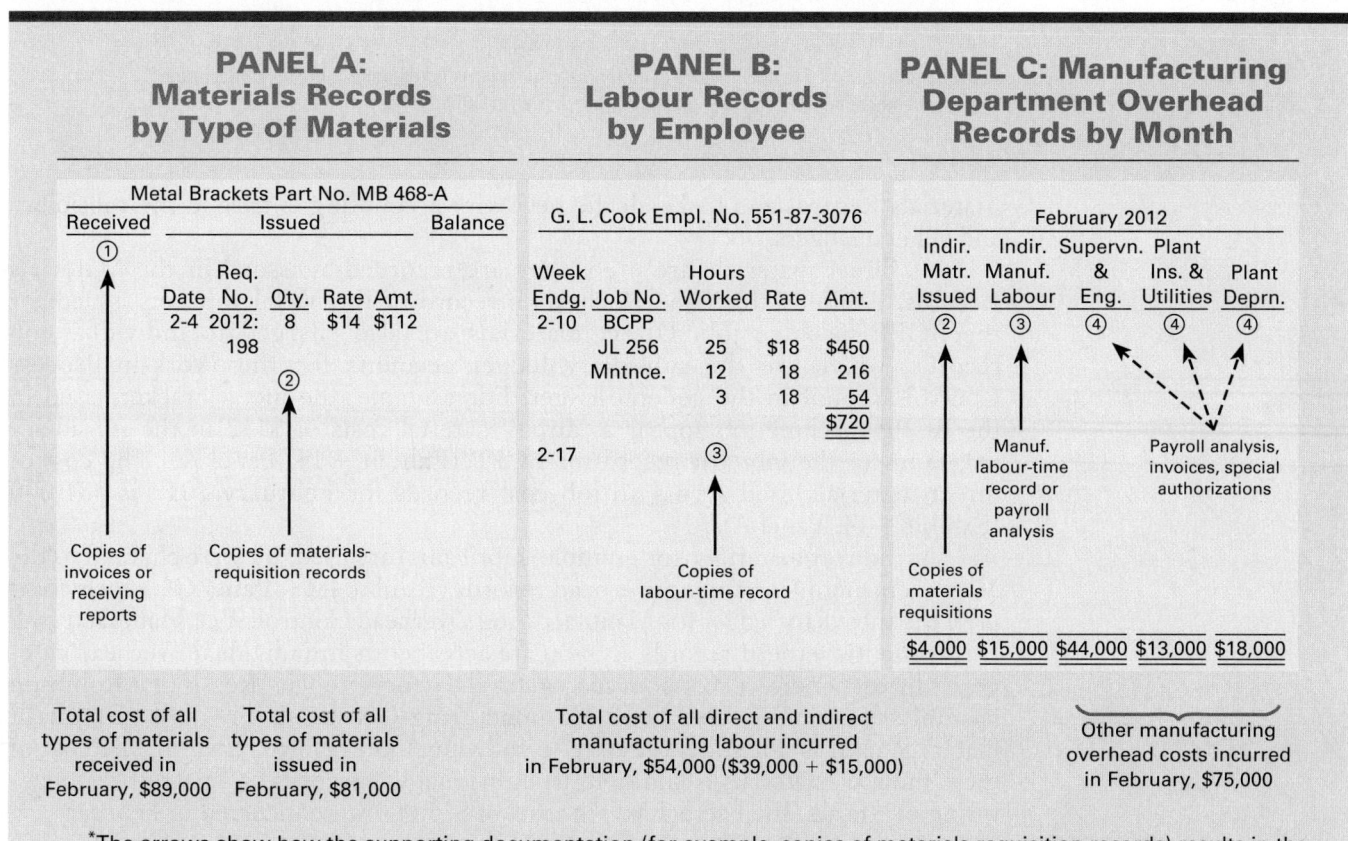

*The arrows show how the supporting documentation (for example, copies of materials-requisition records) results in the journal entry number shown in circles (for example, journal entry number 2) that corresponds to the entries in Exhibit 4-12.

EXHIBIT 4-14
Subsidiary Ledger for Individual Jobs 2012*

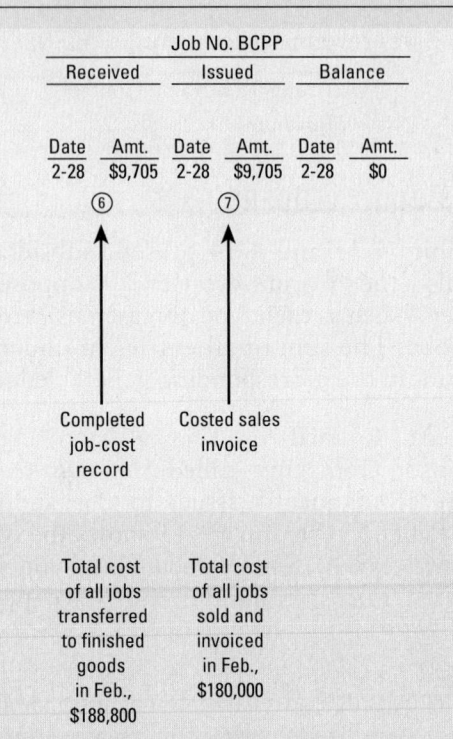

PANEL A: Work-in-Process Inventory Records by Jobs

Job No. BCPP

		In-Process			Completed		Balance	
Date	Direct Materials	Direct Manuf. Labour	Allocated Manuf. Overhead	Total Cost	Date	Total Cost	Date	Total Cost
2-4	$ 112			$ 112				
2-10		$ 450		$ 450				
	•	•		•				
2-28	$4,606 ②	$1,579 ③	$3,520 ⑤	$9,705	2-28	$9,705 ⑥	2-28	$0

Copies of materials-requisition records (②)

Copies of labour-time records (③)

Budgeted rate × actual direct manuf. labour-hours (⑤)

Completed job-cost record (⑥)

Total cost of direct materials issued to all jobs in Feb., $81,000

Total cost of direct manuf. labour used on all jobs in Feb., $39,000

Total manuf. overhead allocated to all jobs in Feb., $80,000

Total cost of all jobs completed and transferred to finished goods in Feb., $188,800

PANEL B: Finished Goods Inventory Records by Job

Job No. BCPP

Received		Issued		Balance	
Date	Amt.	Date	Amt.	Date	Amt.
2-28	$9,705 ⑥	2-28	$9,705 ⑦	2-28	$0

Completed job-cost record (⑥)

Costed sales invoice (⑦)

Total cost of all jobs transferred to finished goods in Feb., $188,800

Total cost of all jobs sold and invoiced in Feb., $180,000

*The arrows show how the supporting documentation (for example, copies of materials-requisition records) results in the journal entry number shown in circles (for example, journal entry number 2) that corresponds to the entries in Exhibit 4-12.

Materials Records and make all the necessary accounting entries in the subsidiary and general ledgers.

As direct materials are used, they are recorded as issued in the Materials Records. Exhibit 4-13, Panel A shows a record of the Metal Brackets issued for the BCPP machine job. Direct materials are also charged to individual job records, which are the subsidiary ledger accounts for the Work-in-Process Control account in the general ledger. For example, the metal brackets used in the BCPP machine job appear as direct material costs of $112 in the subsidiary ledger under the job-cost record for BCPP (Exhibit 4-14, Panel A). The cost of direct materials used across all job-cost records for February 2012 is $81,000 (Exhibit 4-14, Panel A).

As indirect materials (for example, lubricants) are used, they are charged to the Manufacturing Department overhead records (Exhibit 4-13, Panel C), which comprise the subsidiary ledger for Manufacturing Overhead Control. The Manufacturing Department overhead records accumulate actual costs in individual overhead categories by each indirect cost pool account in the general ledger. Recall that Robinson has only one indirect cost pool: Manufacturing Overhead. The cost of indirect materials used is not added directly to individual job records. Instead, the cost of these indirect materials is allocated to individual job records as a part of manufacturing overhead. Total actual MOH costs of $75,000 were incurred in February.

Labour Records by Employee Labour-time records shown in Exhibit 4-13, Panel B, are the trace for direct manufacturing labour to individual jobs. These records also contain indirect cost information that is accumulated in Manufacturing Department overhead records (Exhibit 4-13, Panel C). The subsidiary ledger for employee labour records shows the different jobs that G. L. Cook worked on and the $720 of wages owed to G. L. Cook for the week ending February 10. The sum of total wages owed to all employees for February 2012 is $54,000. The job-cost record for BCPP shows direct manufacturing labour costs of $450 for the time G. L. Cook spent on the BCPP machine job (Exhibit 4-14, Panel A). Total direct manufacturing labour costs recorded in all job-cost records (the subsidiary ledger for Work-in-Process Control) for February 2012 is $39,000.

G. L. Cook's employee record shows $54 for maintenance, which is an indirect manufacturing labour cost. The total indirect manufacturing labour costs of $15,000 for February 2012 appear in the Manufacturing Department overhead records in the subsidiary ledger (Exhibit 4-13, Panel C). These costs, by definition, are not traced to an individual job. Instead, they are allocated to individual jobs as a part of manufacturing overhead.

Manufacturing Department Overhead Records by Month   The Manufacturing Department overhead records (Exhibit 4-13, Panel C) that make up the subsidiary ledger for Manufacturing Overhead Control show details of different categories of overhead costs such as indirect materials, indirect manufacturing labour, supervision and engineering, plant insurance and utilities, and plant depreciation. The source documents for these entries include invoices (for example, a utility bill) and special schedules (for example, a depreciation schedule) from the responsible accounting officer.

Work-in-Process Inventory Records by Jobs   The job-cost record for each individual job in the subsidiary ledger will be debited by the cost of direct materials and direct manufacturing labour used by individual jobs. The job-cost record for each individual job in the subsidiary ledger will also be debited for manufacturing overhead allocated for the actual direct manufacturing labour-hours used in that job. For example, the job-cost record for Job BCPP (Exhibit 4-14, Panel A) shows Manufacturing Overhead Allocated of $3,520 (budgeted rate of $40 per labour-hour × 88 actual direct manufacturing labour-hours used). We assume 2,000 actual direct manufacturing labour-hours were used for all jobs in February 2012, resulting in a total manufacturing overhead allocation of $40 per labour-hour × 2,000 direct manufacturing labour-hours = $80,000.

Finished Goods Inventory Records by Jobs   Exhibit 4-14, Panel A, shows that Job BCPP was completed at a cost of $9,705. Job BCPP also simultaneously appears in the finished goods records of the subsidiary ledger. Given Robinson's use of normal costing, cost of goods completed consists of actual direct materials, actual direct manufacturing labour, and manufacturing overhead allocated to each job based on the budgeted manufacturing overhead rate multiplied by the actual direct manufacturing labour-hours. Exhibit 4-14, Panel B, indicates that Job BCPP was sold and delivered to the customer on February 28, 2012.

Other Subsidiary Records   Robinson maintains employee labour records in subsidiary ledgers for marketing and customer-service payroll as well as records for different types of advertising costs (print, television, and radio). An accounts receivable subsidiary ledger is also used to record the February 2012 amounts due from each customer, including the $15,000 due from the sale of Job BCPP.

Exhibit 4-15 provides Robinson's income statement for February 2012 using information from entries 7, 8, and 9. If desired, the cost of goods sold calculations can be further subdivided and presented in the format of Exhibit 2-10 (p. 42).

Non-manufacturing Costs and Job Costing   Chapter 2 (pp. 46–48) pointed out that companies use product costs for different purposes. The product costs reported as inventoriable costs to shareholders may differ from product costs reported for government contracting and may also differ from product costs reported to managers for guiding pricing and product-mix decisions. Remember, even though marketing and customer-service costs are expensed when incurred for financial

EXHIBIT 4-15

Robinson Company Income Statement for the Month Ending February 2012

Revenue		$270,000
Cost of goods sold ($180,000 + $14,000*)		194,000
Gross margin		76,000
Operating costs		
Marketing costs	$45,000	
Customer-service costs	15,000	
Total operating costs		60,000
Operating income		$ 16,000

*Cost of goods sold has been increased by $14,000, the difference between the Manufacturing Overhead Control account ($94,000) and the Manufacturing Overhead Allocated ($80,000). In a later section of this chapter, we discuss this adjustment, which represents the amount by which actual manufacturing overhead cost exceeds the manufacturing overhead allocated to jobs during February 2012.

accounting purposes, companies often trace or allocate these costs to individual jobs for pricing, product-mix, and cost-management decisions.

To identify marketing and customer-service costs of individual jobs, Robinson can use the same approach to job costing described earlier in this chapter in the context of manufacturing. Assume marketing and customer-service costs have the same cost allocation base, revenues, and are included in a single cost pool. Robinson can then calculate a budgeted indirect cost rate by dividing budgeted indirect marketing and customer-service costs by budgeted revenues. Robinson can use this rate to allocate these indirect costs to jobs. For example, if this rate were 15% of revenues, Robinson would allocate $2,250 to Job BCPP (0.15 × $15,000, the revenue from the job). By assigning both manufacturing costs and non-manufacturing costs to jobs, Robinson can compare all costs against the revenues that different jobs generate.

BUDGETED INDIRECT COSTS AND END-OF-ACCOUNTING-YEAR ADJUSTMENTS

Using budgeted indirect cost rates and normal costing instead of actual costing has the advantage that indirect costs can be assigned to individual jobs on an ongoing and timely basis, rather than only at the end of the fiscal year when actual costs are known. However, budgeted rates are unlikely to equal actual rates because they are based on estimates made up to 12 months before actual costs are incurred. We now consider adjustments that are needed when, at the end of the fiscal year, indirect costs allocated differ from actual indirect costs incurred.

Underallocated indirect costs occur when the allocated amount of indirect costs in an accounting period is less than the actual amount. **Overallocated indirect costs** occur when the allocated amount of indirect costs in an accounting period is greater than the actual amount.

Underallocated (overallocated) indirect costs = Actual indirect costs incurred − Indirect costs allocated

Consider the manufacturing overhead indirect cost pool at Robinson Company. There are two indirect cost accounts in the general ledger that have to do with manufacturing overhead:

1. Manufacturing Overhead Control, the record of the actual costs in all the individual overhead categories (such as indirect materials, indirect manufacturing labour, supervision, engineering, utilities, and plant depreciation).

2. Manufacturing Overhead Allocated, the record of the manufacturing overhead allocated to individual jobs on the basis of the budgeted rate multiplied by actual direct manufacturing labour-hours.

Assume the following annual data for the Robinson Company:

Manufacturing Overhead Control		Manufacturing Overhead Allocated	
Bal. Dec 31, 2012 1,215,000			Bal. Dec 31, 2012 1,080,000

The $1,080,000 credit balance in Manufacturing Overhead Allocated results from multiplying the 27,000 actual direct manufacturing labour-hours worked on all jobs in 2012 by the budgeted rate of $40 per direct manufacturing labour-hour.

The $135,000 difference (a net debit) is an underallocated amount because actual manufacturing overhead costs are greater than the allocated amount. This difference arises from two reasons related to the computation of the $40 budgeted hourly rate:

1. **Numerator reason (indirect cost pool).** Actual manufacturing overhead costs of $1,215,000 are greater than the budgeted amount of $1,120,000.

2. **Denominator reason (quantity of allocation base).** Actual direct manufacturing labour-hours of 27,000 are fewer than the budgeted 28,000 hours.

There are three main approaches to account for the $135,000 underallocated manufacturing overhead amount: (1) adjusted allocation-rate approach, (2) proration approach, and (3) write-off to cost of goods sold approach.

ADJUSTED ALLOCATION-RATE APPROACH

The **adjusted allocation-rate approach** restates all overhead entries in the general ledger and subsidiary ledgers using actual cost rates rather than budgeted cost rates. First, the actual manufacturing overhead rate is computed at the end of the fiscal year. Then, the manufacturing overhead costs allocated to every job during the year are recomputed using the actual manufacturing overhead rate (rather than the budgeted manufacturing overhead rate). Finally, end-of-year closing entries are made. The result is that at year-end, every job-cost record and finished goods record—as well as the ending Work-in-Process Control, Finished Goods Control, and Cost of Goods Sold accounts—represent actual manufacturing overhead costs incurred.

The widespread adoption of computerized accounting systems has greatly reduced the cost of using the adjusted allocation-rate approach. Consider the Robinson example. The actual manufacturing overhead ($1,215,000) exceeds the manufacturing overhead allocated ($1,080,000) by 12.5% [($1,215,000 – $1,080,000) ÷ $1,080,000]. At year-end, Robinson could increase the manufacturing overhead allocated to each job in 2012 by 12.5% using a single software command. The command would adjust both the subsidiary ledgers and the general ledger.

Consider the British Columbia Pulp and Paper machine job, BCPP. Under normal costing, the manufacturing overhead allocated to the job is $3,520 (the budgeted rate of $40 per direct manufacturing labour-hour × 88 hours). Increasing the manufacturing overhead allocated by 12.5%, or $440 ($3,520 × 0.125), means the adjusted amount of manufacturing overhead allocated to Job BCPP equals $3,960 ($3,520 + $440). Note from page 117 that, using actual costing, manufacturing overhead allocated to this job is also $3,960 (the actual rate of $45 per direct manufacturing labour-hour × 88 hours). Making this adjustment under normal costing for each job in the subsidiary ledgers ensures that all $1,215,000 of manufacturing overhead is allocated to jobs.

The adjusted allocation-rate approach yields the benefits of both the *timeliness and convenience of normal costing during the year and the allocation of actual manufacturing overhead costs at year-end*. Each individual job-cost record and the end-of-year account balances for inventories and cost of goods sold are adjusted to actual costs. After-the-fact analysis of actual profitability of individual jobs provides managers with accurate and useful insights for future decisions about job pricing, which jobs to emphasize, and ways to manage job costs.

PRORATION APPROACH

Proration spreads underallocated overhead or overallocated overhead among ending work-in-process inventory, finished goods inventory, and cost of goods sold. Materials inventory is not included in this proration because no manufacturing overhead costs have been allocated to it. In our Robinson example, end-of-year proration is made to the ending balances in Work-in-Process Control, Finished Goods Control, and Cost of Goods Sold. Assume the following actual results for Robinson Company in 2012:

	A	B	C
1	Account	Account Balance (Before Proration)	Allocated Manufacturing Overhead Included in Each Account Balance (Before Proration)
2	Work-in-process control	$ 50,000	$ 16,200
3	Finished goods control	75,000	31,320
4	Cost of goods sold	2,375,000	1,032,480
5		$2,500,000	$1,080,000

Robinson prorates the underallocated amount of $135,000 at the end of 2012. The proration method is done on the basis of the total amount of manufacturing overhead allocated in 2012 (before proration) in the ending balances of Work-in-Process Control, Finished Goods Control, and Cost of Goods Sold. The $135,000 underallocated overhead is prorated over the three affected accounts in proportion to their total amount of manufacturing overhead allocated (before proration) in column 2 of the following table, resulting in the ending balances (after proration) in column 5 at actual costs.

	A	B	C	D	E	F	G
10		Account Balance (Before Proration)	Allocated Manufacturing Overhead Included in Each Account Balance (Before Proration)	Allocated Manufacturing Overhead Included in Each Account Balance as a Percent of Total	Proration of $135,000 of Underallocated Manufacturing Overhead		Account Balance (After Proration)
11	Account	(1)	(2)	(3) = (2) / $1,080,000	(4) = (3) x $135,000		(5) = (1) + (4)
12	Work-in-process control	$ 50,000	$ 16,200	1.5%	0.015 x $135,000 =	$ 2,025	$ 52,025
13	Finished goods control	75,000	31,320	2.9%	0.029 x 135,000 =	3,915	78,915
14	Cost of goods sold	2,375,000	1,032,480	95.6%	0.956 x 135,000 =	129,060	2,504,060
15	Total	$2,500,000	$1,080,000	100.0%		$135,000	$2,635,000

Prorating on the basis of the manufacturing overhead allocated (before proration) results in allocating manufacturing overhead based on actual manufacturing overhead costs. Recall that the actual manufacturing overhead ($1,215,000) in 2012 exceeds the manufacturing overhead allocated ($1,080,000) in 2012 by 12.5%. The proration amounts in column 4 can also be derived by multiplying the balances in column 2 by 0.125. For example, the $3,915 proration to Finished Goods is $0.125 \times \$31,320$. Adding these amounts effectively means allocating manufacturing overhead at 112.5% of what had been allocated before. The journal entry to record this proration is:

Work-in-Process Control	2,025	
Finished Goods Control	3,915	
Cost of Goods Sold	129,060	
Manufacturing Overhead Allocated	1,080,000	
Manufacturing Overhead Control		1,215,000

If manufacturing overhead had been overallocated, the Work-in-Process Control, Finished Goods Control, and Cost of Goods Sold accounts would be decreased (credited) instead of increased (debited).

This journal entry closes (brings to zero) the manufacturing overhead-related accounts and restates the 2012 ending balances for Work-in-Process Control, Finished Goods Control, and Cost of Goods Sold to what they would have been if actual manufacturing overhead rates had been used rather than budgeted manufacturing overhead rates. This method reports the same 2012 ending balances in the general ledger as the adjusted allocation-rate approach.

WRITE-OFF TO COST OF GOODS SOLD APPROACH

Under this approach, the total under- or overallocated manufacturing overhead is included in this year's Cost of Goods Sold. For Robinson, the journal entry would be:

Cost of Goods Sold	135,000	
Manufacturing Overhead Allocated	1,080,000	
Manufacturing Overhead Control		1,215,000

Robinson's two Manufacturing Overhead accounts are closed with the difference between them included in cost of goods sold. The Cost of Goods Sold account after the write-off equals $2,510,000, the balance before the write-off of $2,375,000 *plus the underallocated manufacturing overhead amount* of $135,000.

CHOICE AMONG APPROACHES

The write-off to Cost of Goods Sold is the simplest approach for dealing with under- or overallocated overhead. If the amount of under- or overallocated overhead is insignificant relative to total operating income or some other measure of materiality, then a write-off yields a good approximation to the more complex approaches. Managers must be guided by cost/benefit. Companies have become more stringent in inventory control and work to minimize inventory quantities. As a result, cost of goods sold tends to be higher in relation to the dollar amount of work-in-process and finished goods inventories. Also, the inventory balances of job-costing companies are usually small because goods are often made in response to customer orders. Consequently, writing off, instead of prorating, under- or overallocated overhead will usually not cause a material misstatement in the financial statements.

Regardless of which of the three approaches is used, the underallocated overhead is not carried in the overhead accounts beyond the end of the fiscal year. The reason is that ending balances in Manufacturing Overhead Control and Manufacturing Overhead Allocated are closed to zero when transferred to Work-in-Process Control, Finished Goods Control, and Cost of Goods Sold at year-end.

PULLING IT ALL TOGETHER—PROBLEM FOR SELF-STUDY

(Try to solve this problem before examining the solution that follows.)

PROBLEM

You are asked to bring the following incomplete accounts of Endeavour Printing, Inc., up to date through January 31, 2013. Consider the data that appear in the T-accounts as well as the following information in items (a) through (j).

Endeavour's normal costing system has two direct cost categories (direct material costs and direct manufacturing labour costs) and one indirect cost pool (manufacturing overhead costs, which are allocated using direct manufacturing labour costs).

Materials Control		Wages Payable Control	
12-31-2012 Bal. 15,000			1-31-2013 Bal. 3,000

Work-in-Process Control		Manufacturing Overhead Control	
		1-31-2013 Bal. 57,000	

Finished Goods Control		Costs of Goods Sold	
12-31-2012 Bal. 20,000			

ADDITIONAL INFORMATION

a. Manufacturing overhead is allocated using a budgeted rate that is set every December. Management forecasts next year's manufacturing overhead costs and next year's direct manufacturing labour costs. The budget for 2013 is $600,000 for manufacturing overhead costs and $400,000 for direct manufacturing labour costs.

b. The only job unfinished on January 31, 2013, is No. 419, on which direct manufacturing labour costs are $2,000 (125 direct manufacturing labour-hours) and direct material costs are $8,000.

c. Total direct materials issued to production during January 2013 are $90,000.

d. Cost of goods completed during January is $180,000.

e. Materials inventory as of January 31, 2013, is $20,000.

f. Finished goods inventory as of January 31, 2013, is $15,000.

g. All plant workers earn the same wage rate. Direct manufacturing labour-hours used for January total 2,500 hours. Other labour costs total $10,000.

h. The gross plant payroll paid in January equals $52,000. Ignore withholdings.

i. All "actual" manufacturing overhead incurred during January has already been posted.

j. All materials are direct materials.

REQUIRED

Calculate the following:

1. Materials purchased during January.
2. Cost of Goods Sold during January.
3. Direct manufacturing labour costs incurred during January.
4. Manufacturing Overhead Allocated during January.
5. Balance, Wages Payable Control, December 31, 2012.
6. Balance, Work-in-Process Control, January 31, 2013.
7. Balance, Work-in-Process Control, December 31, 2012.
8. Manufacturing Overhead Underallocated or Overallocated for January 2013.

SOLUTION

Letters alongside entries and in T-accounts correspond to letters in the preceding additional information. Numbers alongside entries in T-accounts correspond to numbers in the requirements above. Amounts from the T-accounts are labelled "(T)."

1. From Materials Control T-account, Materials purchased: $90,000 (c) + $20,000 (e) − $15,000 (T) = $95,000

2. From Finished Goods Control T-account, Cost of Goods Sold: $20,000 (T) + $180,000 (d) − $15,000 (f) = $185,000

3. Direct manufacturing wage rate: $2,000 (b) ÷ 125 direct manufacturing labour-hours (b) = $16 per direct manufacturing labour-hour

   Direct manufacturing labour costs: 2,500 direct manufacturing labour-hours (g) × $16 per hour = $40,000

4. Manufacturing overhead rate: $600,000 (a) ÷ $400,000 (a) = 150%

   Manufacturing Overhead Allocated: 150% of $40,000 = 1.50 × $40,000 (see 3) = $60,000

5. From Wages Payable Control T-account, Wages Payable Control, December 31, 2012: $52,000 (h) + $3,000 (T) − $40,000 (see 3) − $10,000 (g) = $5,000

6. Work-in-Process Control, January 31, 2013: $8,000 (b) + $2,000 (b) + 150% of $2,000 (b) = $13,000 (This answer is used in item 7.)

7. From Work-in-Process Control T-account, Work-in-Process Control, December 31, 2012: $180,000 (d) + $13,000 (see 6) − $90,000 (c) − $40,000 (see 3) − $60,000 (see 4) = $3,000

8. Manufacturing overhead overallocated: $60,000 (see 4) − $57,000 (T) = $3,000.

Materials Control

December 31, 2012 Bal.	(given)	15,000			
	(1)	95,000*	(c)	90,000
January 31, 2013 Bal.	(e)	20,000			

Work-in-Process Control

December 31, 2012 Bal.	(7)	3,000	(d)	180,000
Direct materials	(c)	90,000		
Direct manufacturing labour	(b) (g) (3)	40,000		
Manufacturing overhead allocated	(3) (a) (4)	60,000		
January 31, 2013 Bal.	(b) (6)	13,000		

Finished Goods Control

December 31, 2012 Bal.	(given)	20,000	(2)	185,000
	(d)	180,000		
January 31, 2013 Bal.	(f)	15,000		

Wages Payable Control

	(h)	52,000	December 31, 2012 Bal.	(5)	5,000
				(g) (3)	40,000
				(g)	10,000
			January 31, 2013	(given)	3,000

Manufacturing Overhead Control

Total January charges	(given)	57,000		

Manufacturing Overhead Allocated

			(3) (a) (4)	60,000

Cost of Goods Sold

(d) (f) (2)	185,000		

*Can be computed only after all other postings in the account have been found.

SUMMARY POINTS

The following question-and-answer format summarizes the chapter's learning outcomes. Each point presents a key question, and the guidelines are the answer to that question.

LEARNING OUTCOMES

1. How do cost object, direct costs, indirect costs, cost pools, and cost allocation bases link to one another?

2. How does the decision framework apply to service job costing?

GUIDELINES

These concepts link together in a systematic way to produce a job-costing system. The cost object is a distinct job. All direct (prime) costs, both fixed and variable, comprise one or more cost pools. All indirect costs arise when all jobs use common inputs but in different amounts. All indirect fixed and variable costs comprise one or more indirect cost pools. The direct costs are assigned to each job by using source documents to trace the costs of inputs used directly to the job that used them. The indirect costs are assigned to jobs by using cost allocation.

Service industries are usually labour intensive. Managers begin by identifying the problem as how to rank order their service jobs from most to least profitable. They gather and analyze relevant information such as costs that differ from job to job because each job uses different amounts of inputs. This is the reason for a job-costing system. Knowing the actual total cost of jobs is the basis on which managers can improve predicted profitability by expanding the most profitable types of service jobs undertaken and monitor the profitability on a continuous basis.

3. How does the decision framework apply to product job costing?	Manufacturing industries are usually machine or capital intensive. The decision framework applies in the same way to product job costing as it does to service job costing. Many manufacturing processes are machine or capital intensive rather than labour intensive. This affects the identification of cost pools and cost allocation bases. The assignment of costs in a product job-costing system requires the same seven steps.
4. How do you distinguish actual, budgeted, and normal costing methods?	The difference among these three is in how the cost allocation rate is calculated and the quantity of the cost allocation base (actual or budgeted) used to assign the indirect cost to each distinct job.
5. When are transactions recorded in a job-costing system and what methods are available to adjust for over- and underallocation of indirect costs?	A job-costing system records the flow of inventoriable costs: (a) acquisition of all inputs, (b) their conversion into work-in-process, (c) their conversion into finished goods or services, and (d) the sale of finished goods or services. Year-end adjustments are made to over- or under-allocated support costs. The over- or underallocation is either prorated or if the difference is not significant, written off to cost of goods sold.

TERMS TO LEARN

This chapter and the Glossary at the end of the book contain definitions of the following important terms:

actual costing (p. 119)
actual indirect cost allocation rate (p. 111)
adjusted allocation-rate approach (p. 129)
cost allocation (p. 107)
cost allocation base (p. 107)
cost allocation rate (p. 108)
cost driver (p. 107)
cost pool (p. 107)

indirect cost allocation rate (p. 106)
job (p. 109)
job-cost record (p. 111)
job-cost sheet (p. 111)
job-costing system (p. 109)
labour intensive (p. 111)
labour-time record (p. 115)
manufacturing overhead allocated (p. 124)
manufacturing overhead applied (p. 124)

materials-requisition record (p. 115)
normal costing (p. 121)
opportunity cost (p. 112)
overallocated indirect costs (p. 128)
process-costing system (p. 109)
proration (p. 129)
source document (p. 111)
underallocated indirect costs (p. 128)

ASSIGNMENT MATERIAL

SHORT-ANSWER QUESTIONS

4-1 How does a job-costing system differ from a process-costing system?

4-2 What is the benefit of creating more than one manufacturing overhead cost pool?

4-3 Why might an advertising agency use job costing for an advertising campaign by Pepsi, whereas a bank might use process costing to determine the cost of chequing account deposits?

4-4 Describe the seven steps in job costing.

4-5 What are the two major types of organizational elements that managers focus on in companies using job costing?

4-6 Describe the three major source documents used in job-costing systems.

4-7 What is the main concern about source documents used to prepare job-cost records?

4-8 Give two reasons why most organizations use an annual period rather than a weekly or monthly period to compute budgeted indirect cost allocation rates.

4-9 How does actual costing differ from normal costing?

4-10 Describe two ways in which a house-construction company may use job-cost information.

4-11 Comment on the following statement: "In a normal costing system, the amounts in the Manufacturing Overhead Control account will always equal the amounts in the Manufacturing Overhead Allocated account."

4-12 Describe three different debit entries in the Work-in-Process Control general ledger T-account.

4-13 Describe three alternative ways to dispose of underallocated or overallocated indirect costs.

4-14 When might a company use budgeted costs rather than actual costs to compute direct labour rates?

4-15 Describe briefly why modern technology such as Electronic Data Interchange (EDI) is helpful to managers.

EXERCISES

4-16 Terminology. A number of terms are listed below:

source document   actual
cost tracing   cost allocation rate
proration   opportunity cost
cost pool

REQUIRED
Select the terms from the above list to complete the following sentences.

1. _____ spreads underallocated overhead or overallocated overhead among ending work-in-process inventory, finished goods inventory, and cost of goods sold.
2. The benefits of using a(n) _____ cost system is that your costing information is very accurate.
3. The _____ is the result of dividing the indirect cost pool by the cost allocation base.
4. A _____ is an original record that supports journal entries in an accounting system.
5. A(n) _____ is the contribution to income lost or forgone by not using a limited resource in its next-best alternative use.
6. _____ is the assigning of direct costs to the chosen cost object.
7. A _____ is a grouping of individual cost items.

4-17 Job costing, process costing. In each of the following situations, determine whether job costing or process costing would be more appropriate.

a. A CA firm
b. An oil refinery
c. A custom furniture manufacturer
d. A tire manufacturer
e. A textbook publisher
f. A pharmaceutical company
g. An advertising agency
h. An apparel manufacturing factory
i. A flour mill
j. A paint manufacturer
k. A medical care facility

l. A landscaping company
m. A cola-drink-concentrate producer
n. A movie studio
o. A law firm
p. A commercial aircraft manufacturer
q. A management consulting firm
r. A breakfast cereal company
s. A catering service
t. A paper mill
u. An auto repair garage

4-18 Actual costing, normal costing, manufacturing overhead. Destin Products uses a job-costing system with two direct cost categories (direct materials and direct manufacturing labour) and one manufacturing overhead cost pool. Destin allocates manufacturing overhead costs using direct manufacturing labour costs. Destin provides the following information:

1. Budget is 85% of direct labour costs.

	Budget for Year 2013	Actuals for Year 2013
Direct manufacturing labour costs	$2,600,000	$2,540,000
Direct manufacturing overhead costs	$2,210,000	$2,311,400
Direct materials costs	$1,800,000	$1,740,000

REQUIRED
1. Compute the actual and budgeted manufacturing overhead rates for 2013.
2. During March, the cost record for Job 626 contained the following:

Direct materials used	$38,000
Direct manufacturing labour costs	$27,000

Compute the cost of Job 626 using (a) an actual costing system and (b) a normal costing system.
3. At the end of 2013, compute the underallocated or overallocated manufacturing overhead under Destin's normal costing system. Why is there no underallocated or overallocated overhead under Destin's actual costing system?
4. Comment briefly on the advantages and disadvantages of actual costing systems and normal costing systems.

4-19 Job costing; actual, normal, and variation of normal costing. Chirac & Partners is a Quebec-based public accounting partnership specializing in audit services. Its job-costing system has a single direct cost category (professional labour) and a single indirect cost pool (audit support, which contains all the costs in the Audit Support Department). Audit support costs are allocated to individual jobs using actual professional labour-hours. Chirac & Partners employs ten professionals who are involved in their auditing services.

Budgeted and actual amounts for 2013 are as follows:

Budget for 2013	
Professional labour compensation	$960,000
Audit support department costs	$720,000
Professional labour-hours billed to clients	16,000 hours

Actual results for 2013	
Audit support department costs	$744,000
Professional labour-hours billed to clients	15,500 hours
Actual professional labour cost rate	$58 per hour

REQUIRED
1. Identify the direct cost rate per professional labour-hour and the indirect cost rate per professional labour-hour for 2013 under (a) actual costing, (b) normal costing, and (c) variation of normal costing that uses budgeted rates for direct costs.
2. The audit of Pierre & Company done in 2013 was budgeted to take 110 hours of professional labour time. The actual professional labour time on the audit was 120 hours. Compute the 2013 job cost using (a) actual costing, (b) normal costing, and (c) variation of normal costing that uses budgeted rates for direct costs. Explain any differences in the job cost.

4-20 Job costing; actual, normal, and variation from normal costing. Thanatos & Hades (T&H) is a law firm that specializes in writing wills. Its job-costing system has one direct cost pool, professional labour, and a single indirect cost pool that includes all supporting costs of running the law office. The support costs are allocated to clients on the basis of professional labour-hours. In addition to the two senior partners at T&H, there are six associates who work directly with clients. Each of the eight lawyers is expected to work for approximately 2,500 hours per year.

Budgeted and actual costs for 2012 were:

Budgeted professional labour costs	$1,100,000
Budgeted support costs	$2,000,000
Actual professional labour costs	$1,320,000
Actual support costs	$2,400,000
Actual total professional hours	22,000 hours

1. Compute the direct cost rate and the indirect cost rate per professional labour-hour under:

   a. Actual costing.
   b. Normal costing.
   c. Variation from normal costing that uses budgeted rates for direct costs.

2. The will for a rich tycoon, Ari Roos, was very complex and took four lawyers at the firm 1,000 hours each to prepare. What would be the cost of writing this will under each of the costing methods in requirement 1?

4-21 **Job costing, normal, and actual costing.** Anderson Construction assembles residential homes. It uses a job-costing system with two direct cost categories (direct materials and direct labour) and one indirect cost pool (assembly support). The allocation base for assembly support costs is direct labour-hours. In December 2012, Anderson budgets 2013 assembly support costs to be $8,000,000 and 2013 direct labour-hours to be 160,000.

1a. $50 per direct labour-hour;
b. $42 per direct labour-hour

At the end of 2013, Anderson is comparing the costs of several jobs that were started and completed in 2013. Information for a couple of jobs follows.

Construction Period	Laguna Model February–June 2013	Mission Model May–October 2013
Direct materials	$106,450	$127,604
Direct labour	$ 36,276	$ 41,410
Direct labour-hours	900	1,010

Direct materials and direct labour are paid for on a contract basis. The costs of each are known when direct materials are used or direct labour-hours are worked. The 2013 actual assembly support costs were $6,888,000, while the actual direct labour-hours were 164,000.

REQUIRED

1. Compute the (a) budgeted and (b) actual indirect cost rate. Why do they differ?
2. What is the job cost of the Laguna Model and the Mission Model using (a) normal costing and (b) actual costing?
3. Why might Anderson Construction prefer normal costing over actual costing?

4-22 **Normal costing, manufacturing overhead.** (J. Watson) Trenton Ltd. uses a normal job-costing system and applies manufacturing overhead to products on the basis of machine hours. At the beginning of 2012, the company controller budgeted annual overhead at $1,500,000. She also forecast that machine hours would total 48,000. Actual costs were as follows:

1. $31.25 per machine hour

Direct material (DM) used	$ 340,000
Direct labour	$ 875,000
Manufacturing overhead (MOH)	$1,605,000

Actual machine hours worked during the year were 49,200. Trenton adjusts any underallocated or overallocated overhead to cost of goods sold. The company's records show that total sales for the year were $2,938,000 and cost of goods sold (before adjustment) equalled $2,260,000.

REQUIRED

1. Determine the company's budgeted overhead rate.
2. Determine the amount of underallocated or overallocated overhead for the year.
3. Compute the company's cost of goods sold.

4-23 **Job costing, accounting for manufacturing overhead, budgeted rates.** Lynn Company uses a job-costing system at its Mississauga plant. The plant has a Machining Department and an Assembly Department. Its job-costing system has two direct cost categories (direct materials and direct manufacturing labour) and two manufacturing overhead cost pools (the Machining Department, allocated using actual machine hours (MH), and the Assembly Department, allocated using actual direct manufacturing labour cost). The 2013 budget for the plant is as follows:

1. Total MOH allocated to Job 494, $99,000

	Machining Department	Assembly Department
Manufacturing overhead (MOH)	$1,800,000	$3,600,000
Direct manufacturing labour cost	$1,400,000	$2,000,000
Direct manufacturing labour-hours (DMLH)	100,000	200,000
Machine hours (MH)	50,000	200,000

The company uses a budgeted overhead rate for allocating overhead to production orders on a machine-hour basis in Machining and on a direct-manufacturing-labour-cost basis in Assembly.

REQUIRED

1. During February, the cost record for Job 494 contained the following:

	Machining Department	Assembly Department
Direct materials used	$45,000	$70,000
Direct manufacturing labour cost	$14,000	$15,000
Direct manufacturing labour-hours (DMLH)	1,000	1,500
Machine hours (MH)	2,000	1,000

Compute the total manufacturing overhead costs of Job 494.

2. At the end of 2013, the actual manufacturing overhead costs were $2,100,000 in Machining and $3,700,000 in Assembly. Assume that 55,000 actual machine hours were used in Machining and that actual direct manufacturing labour costs in Assembly were $2,200,000. Compute the overallocated or underallocated manufacturing overhead for each department.

1. Unit cost, $64.81

4-24 Job costing, budgeted rates, unit costs. (J. Watson) Lytton Ltd. uses a normal job-costing system with two direct cost categories (direct materials and direct labour) and one indirect cost pool. It allocates manufacturing overhead to jobs using a predetermined overhead rate based on direct labour-hours. At the start of the year, the company estimated that manufacturing overhead would be $632,000, and direct labour-hours were estimated at 32,000 hours for the year. In November, Job #X905 was completed. Materials costs on the job totalled $13,200 and labour costs totalled $10,120 at $22 per hour. At the end of the year, it was determined that the company worked 34,100 direct labour-hours for the year and incurred $656,125 in actual manufacturing overhead costs.

REQUIRED

1. Job #X905 contained 500 units. Determine the unit cost that would appear on the job-cost sheet.
2. Assuming Lytton prices its products to achieve a 25% margin, what would be the selling price of Job X905?
3. Determine the underallocated or overallocated overhead for the year.

2a. Hansen operating income, $275.

4-25 Computing indirect cost rates, services. Mike Rotundo, the president of Tax Assist, is examining alternative ways to compute indirect cost rates. He collects the following information from the budget for 2013:

◆ Budgeted variable indirect costs: $12 per hour of professional labour time
◆ Budgeted fixed indirect costs: $60,000 per quarter
  The budgeted billable professional labour-hours per quarter are:

January–March	24,000 hours
April–June	12,000 hours
July–September	4,800 hours
October–December	7,200 hours

Rotundo pays all tax professionals employed by Tax Assist on an hourly basis ($36 per hour, including all fringe benefits).

Tax Assist's job-costing system has a single direct cost category (professional labour at $36 per hour) and a single indirect cost pool (office support that is allocated using professional labour-hours).

Tax Assist charges clients $78 per professional labour-hour.

REQUIRED

1. Compute budgeted indirect cost rates per professional labour-hour using
   a. Quarterly budgeted billable hours as the denominator.
   b. Annual budgeted billable hours as the denominator.
2. Compute the operating income for the following four customers using
   a. Quarterly based indirect cost rates.
   b. An annual indirect cost rate.
      ◆ Stan Hansen: 10 hours in February.
      ◆ Lelani Kai: 6 hours in March and 4 hours in April.

♦ Ken Patera: 4 hours in June and 6 hours in August.
♦ Evelyn Stevens: 5 hours in January, 2 hours in September, and 3 hours in November.
3. Comment on your results in requirement 2.

4-26 Job costing, journal entries. The University of Toronto Press is wholly owned by the university. It performs the bulk of its work for other university departments, which pay as though the Press were an outside business enterprise. The Press also publishes and maintains a stock of books for general sale. A job-costing system is used to cost each job. There are two direct cost categories (direct materials and direct manufacturing labour) and one indirect cost pool (manufacturing overhead, allocated based on direct labour costs).

1. Overallocation, $130

The following data (in thousands) pertain to 2013:

Direct materials and supplies purchased on account	$ 800
Direct materials used	710
Indirect materials issued to various production departments	100
Direct manufacturing labour	1,300
Indirect manufacturing labour incurred by various departments	900
Amortization on building and manufacturing equipment	400
Miscellaneous manufacturing overhead* incurred by various departments	
(ordinarily would be detailed as repairs, photocopying, utilities, etc.)	550
Manufacturing overhead allocated at 160% of direct manufacturing labour costs	?
Cost of goods manufactured	4,120
Revenues	8,000
Cost of goods sold	4,020
Inventories, December 31, 2012:	
Materials control	100
Work-in-process control	60
Finished goods control	500

*The term *manufacturing overhead* is not used uniformly. Other terms that are often encountered in printing companies include *job overhead* and *shop overhead*.

REQUIRED

1. Prepare general journal entries to summarize 2013 transactions. As your final entry, dispose of the year-end overallocated or underallocated manufacturing overhead as a direct write-off to Cost of Goods Sold. Number your entries. Explanations for each entry may be omitted.
2. Show posted T-accounts for all inventories, Cost of Goods Sold, Manufacturing Overhead Control, and Manufacturing Overhead Allocated.

4-27 Job costing, journal entries. Duchess Ltd. manufactures and installs kitchen cabinetry. It uses normal job costing with two direct cost categories (direct materials and direct manufacturing labour) and one indirect cost pool for manufacturing overhead (MOH), applied on the basis of machine hours (MH). At the beginning of the year, the company estimated that it would work 980,000 MH and had budgeted $73,500,000 for MOH. The following data (in $ millions) pertain to operations for the year 2013:

1. WIP ending balance, $17.40

Materials control (beginning balance), December 31, 2012	$6.0
Work-in-process control (beginning balance), December 31, 2012	1.8
Finished goods control (beginning balance), December 31, 2012	7.2
Materials and supplies purchased on account	238
Direct materials used	194
Indirect materials (supplies) issued to various production departments	27
Direct manufacturing labour	123
Indirect manufacturing labour incurred by various departments	19
Amortization on plant and manufacturing equipment	21
Miscellaneous manufacturing overhead incurred (credit Various Liabilities;	
ordinarily would be detailed as repairs, utilities, etc.)	9
Manufacturing overhead allocated (972,000 actual MH)	?
Cost of goods manufactured	374.3
Revenues	512
Cost of goods sold	368.4

1. Prepare general journal entries. Number your entries. Post to T-accounts. What is the ending balance of Work-in-Process Control?
2. Show the journal entry for disposing of overallocated or underallocated manufacturing overhead directly as a year-end write-off to Cost of Goods Sold. Post the entry to T-accounts.

3 5

1. $551,500

4-28 Job costing, unit cost, ending work-in-process. Coakwell Company worked on only two jobs during May. Information on the jobs is given below:

	Job A701	Job A702
Direct materials	$ 80,000	$ 92,000
Direct labour	287,000	219,000
Direct manufacturing labour-hours (DMLH)	20,500	14,600

At the beginning of the year, annual manufacturing overhead (MOH) was budgeted at $3,780,000 and Coakwell budgeted 35,000 DMLH per month. Job A701 was completed in May.

REQUIRED

1. Compute the total cost of Job A701.
2. Calculate per unit cost for Job A701 assuming it has 2,500 units.
3. Make this journal entry transferring Job A701 to Finished Goods.
4. Determine the ending balance in the Work-in-Process account.

3 5

1a. $25 per direct labour-hour

4-29 Job costing, various cost drivers. (J. Watson) Rochester Ltd. has budgeted $435,000 for manufacturing overhead for the upcoming year. It forecast that 72,500 machine hours will be used in the factory, and budgeted direct labour-hours were 17,400. The average direct labour rate is budgeted to be $20. Actual data for the year were:

Actual manufacturing overhead	$434,300
Actual machine hours	73,010
Actual direct labour wage rate	$ 19.60
Actual direct labour-hours worked	17,630

REQUIRED

1. Compute the budgeted manufacturing overhead rate under each of the following cost drivers:
   a. Direct labour-hours
   b. Direct labour cost
   c. Machine hours
2. Compute the amount of underallocated or overallocated manufacturing overhead under each of the cost drivers listed in requirement 1.

3 5

2. Overallocation, $16,000

4-30 Job costing, journal entries, T-accounts, source documents. Production Company produces gadgets for the coveted small appliance market. The following data reflect activity for the most recent year, 2012:

Costs incurred	
Purchases of direct materials (net) on account	$124,000
Direct manufacturing labour cost	80,000
Indirect labour	54,500
Amortization, factory equipment	30,000
Amortization, office equipment	7,000
Maintenance, factory equipment	20,000
Miscellaneous factory overhead	9,500
Rent, factory building	70,000
Advertising expense	90,000
Sales commissions	30,000

Beginning and ending inventories for the year were as follows:

	January 1, 2012	December 31, 2012
Direct materials	$9,000	$11,000
Work-in-process	6,000	21,000
Finished goods	69,000	24,000

Production Company uses a normal job-costing system and allocates overhead to work-in-process at a rate of $2.50 per direct manufacturing labour dollar. Indirect materials are insignificant, so there is no inventory account for indirect materials.

REQUIRED

1. Prepare journal entries to record the 2012 transactions including an entry to close out over-allocated or underallocated overhead to cost of goods sold. For each journal entry, indicate the source document that would be used to authorize each entry. Also note which subsidiary ledger, if any, should be referenced as backup for the entry.
2. Post the journal entries to T-accounts for all of the inventories, Cost of Goods Sold, Manufacturing Overhead Control, and Manufacturing Overhead Allocated accounts.

4-31 Accounting for manufacturing overhead. Consider the following selected cost data for KYM Inc. for 2013.

1. $22 per MH

Budgeted manufacturing overhead (MOH)	$4,180,000
Budgeted machine hours (MH)	190,000
Actual manufacturing overhead (MOH) ending balance	$4,230,000
Actual machine hours (MH)	192,000

KYM's job-costing system has a single manufacturing overhead cost pool (allocated using a budgeted rate based on actual MH). Any amount of underallocation or overallocation is immediately written off to cost of goods sold.

REQUIRED

1. Compute the budgeted manufacturing overhead (MOH) rate.
2. Journalize the allocation of manufacturing overhead (MOH).
3. Compute the amount of underallocation or overallocation of MOH. Is the amount significant? Journalize the disposition of this amount based on the ending balances in the relevant accounts.

4-32 Proration of overhead. The Ride-On-Water (ROW) Company produces a line of non-motorized boats. ROW uses a normal job-costing system and allocates manufacturing overhead costs using direct manufacturing labour cost. The following data are available for 2012:

1. 50% of direct manufacturing labour costs

Budgeted manufacturing overhead costs	$100,000
Budgeted direct manufacturing labour cost	$200,000
Actual manufacturing overhead costs	$106,000
Actual direct manufacturing labour cost	$220,000

Inventory balances on December 31, 2012 were:

Account	Ending Balance	2012 Direct Manufacturing Labour Cost in Ending Balance
Work-in-process	$ 50,000	$ 20,000
Finished goods	$240,000	$ 60,000
Cost of goods sold	$560,000	$140,000

REQUIRED

1. Calculate the budgeted manufacturing overhead rate.
2. Calculate the amount of underallocated or overallocated manufacturing overhead.
3. Calculate the ending balances in work-in-process, finished goods, and cost of goods sold if underallocated or overallocated overhead is:
   a. Written off to cost of goods sold
   b. Prorated based on ending balances (before proration) in each of the three accounts
   c. Prorated based on the overhead allocated in 2012 in the ending balances, before proration, in each of the three accounts.
4. Which disposition method do you prefer in requirement 3? Explain.

a. $653,000

4-33 Job costing, solving for unknowns. (J. Watson) Osprey Ltd. manufactures designer purses. During the year, it recorded direct materials used of $684,000. Total manufacturing costs of $1,482,000 were incurred during the year. Osprey uses one indirect cost pool for all overhead costs and allocates overhead at a rate of 60% of direct labour dollars.

	January 1	December 31
Direct materials inventories	$193,000	$162,000
Work-in-process inventories	204,000	107,000
Finished goods inventories	225,000	248,000

REQUIRED

Prepare a Schedule of Cost of Goods Manufactured and Sold for the year. You will need to solve for the following unknowns:

a. Direct materials purchased.

b. Direct labour costs.

c. Manufacturing overhead allocated.

d. Cost of goods manufactured.

e. Cost of goods sold.

PROBLEMS

1

1. Taylor operating
margin, 2.5%

4-34 Job-costing procedures. Broadway Printers operates a printing press with a monthly capacity of 2,000 machine hours (MH). Broadway has two main customers, Taylor Corporation and Kelly Corporation. Data on each customer for January follow:

	Taylor Corporation	Kelly Corporation	Total
Revenues	$132,000	$88,000	$220,000
Variable costs	46,200	52,800	99,000
Fixed costs (allocated on the basis of revenues)	66,000	44,000	110,000
Total operating costs	112,200	96,800	209,000
Operating income (loss)	$ 19,800	$(8,800)	$ 11,000
Machine hours (MH) required	1,500 hours	500 hours	2,000 hours

Each of the following requirements refers only to the preceding data; there is *no connection* between the requirements.

REQUIRED

1. Fixed costs arise because equipment and other capacity have been purchased. What would the allocation of fixed costs and what would be the operating income and operating margin for each job if the fixed MOH cost allocation base were machine hours instead of revenue?
2. Should Broadway drop the Kelly Corporation business? If Broadway drops the Kelly Corporation business, its total fixed costs will decrease by 20%.
3. Kelly Corporation indicates that it wants Broadway to do an *additional* $88,000 worth of printing jobs during February. These jobs are identical to the existing business Broadway did for Kelly in January in terms of variable costs and machine hours required. Broadway anticipates that the business from Taylor Corporation in February will be the same as that in January. Broadway can choose to accept as much of the Taylor and Kelly business for February as it wants. Assume that total fixed costs for February will be the same as the fixed costs in January. What should Broadway do? What will Broadway's operating income be in February?

5

1. Underallocated, $35,000

4-35 Disposition of underallocated or overallocated overhead. (J. Watson) Princeton Manufacturing budgeted $325,000 and incurred $337,000 of overhead costs in the past year. During the year, it allocated $302,000 to its production. An extract from the company's financial records showed the following account balances:

Allocated MOH in Work-in-Process Inventory	$52,246
Allocated MOH in Finished Goods Inventory	$75,802
Allocated MOH in Cost of Goods Sold	$173,952

1. Calculate the amount of underallocated or overallocated manufacturing overhead for the year.
2. Prepare the journal entry to dispose of this underallocated or overallocated overhead amount using
   a. Immediate write-off to Cost of Goods Sold.
   b. Proration based on the manufacturing overhead allocated (before proration) in Work-in-Process Inventory, Finished Goods Inventory, and Cost of Goods Sold.
3. Which method do you recommend for this company?

4-36 Job costing, law firm. Keating & Partners is a law firm specializing in labour relations and employee-related work. It employs 25 professionals (5 partners and 20 managers) who work directly with its clients. The average budgeted total compensation per professional for 2013 is $104,000. Each professional is budgeted to have 1,600 billable hours to clients in 2013. Keating is a highly respected firm, and all professionals work for clients to their maximum 1,600 billable hours available. All professional labour costs are included in a single direct cost category and are traced to jobs on a per-hour basis.

   All costs of Keating & Partners other than professional labour costs are included in a single indirect cost pool (legal support) and are allocated to jobs using professional labour-hours as the allocation base. The budgeted level of indirect costs in 2013 is $2.2 million.

2 4

1. $65 per professional labour-hour

REQUIRED

1. Compute the 2013 budgeted professional labour-hour direct cost rate.
2. Compute the 2013 budgeted indirect cost rate per hour of professional labour.
3. Keating & Partners is considering bidding on two jobs:
   a. Litigation work for Richardson Inc. that requires 100 budgeted hours of professional labour.
   b. Labour contract work for Punch Inc. that requires 150 budgeted hours of professional labour.

   Prepare a cost estimate for each job.

4-37 Job costing with two direct cost and two indirect cost categories, law firm (continuation of 4-36). Keating has just completed a review of its job-costing system. This review included a detailed analysis of how past jobs used the firm's resources and interviews with personnel about what factors drive the level of indirect costs. Management concluded that a system with two direct cost categories (professional partner labour and professional manager labour) and two indirect cost categories (general support and administration support) would yield more accurate job costs. Budgeted information for 2013 related to the two direct cost categories is as follows:

2 4

1a. $125 per hour
b. $50 per hour

	Professional Partner Labour	Professional Manager Labour
Number of professionals	5	20
Hours of billable time per professional	1,600 per year	1,600 per year
Total compensation (average per professional)	$200,000	$80,000

Budgeted information for 2013 relating to the two indirect cost categories is

	General Support	Administration Support
Total costs	$1,800,000	$400,000
Cost allocation base	Professional labour-hours	Partner labour-hours

REQUIRED

1. Compute the 2013 budgeted direct cost rates for (a) professional partners and (b) professional managers.
2. Compute the 2013 budgeted indirect cost rates for (a) general support and (b) administration support.

3. Compute the budgeted job costs for the Richardson and Punch jobs, given the following information:

	Richardson Inc.	Punch Inc.
Professional partners	60 hours	30 hours
Professional managers	40 hours	120 hours

4. Comment on the results in requirement 3. Why are the job costs different from those computed in Problem 4-36?

1. $2,875,000

4-38 Normal costing, overhead allocation, working backwards. Gaston Ltd. uses a normal job-costing system with two direct cost categories—direct materials and direct manufacturing labour—and one indirect cost category—manufacturing overhead. At the beginning of 2013, Gaston had $236,000 in work-in-process inventory. The company allocates manufacturing overhead at the rate of 180% of direct manufacturing labour costs. Total allocated manufacturing overhead for the year was $5,175,000. Manufacturing costs incurred for the year were $9,732,500 and the cost of goods manufactured for the year totalled $9,612,200.

REQUIRED

1. What was the total direct labour cost in 2013?
2. What was the total cost of direct materials used in 2013?
3. What was the dollar amount of work-in-process inventory on December 31, 2013?

2. Machining Department:
Overallocation, $510,000;
Assembly Department:
Underallocation, $170,000

4-39 Disposition of overhead overallocation or underallocation, two indirect cost pools. Glavine Corporation manufactures precision equipment made to order for the semiconductor industry. Glavine uses two manufacturing overhead cost pools—one for the overhead costs incurred in its highly automated Machining Department and another for overhead costs incurred in its labour-based Assembly Department. Glavine uses a normal costing system. It allocates Machining Department overhead costs to jobs based on actual machine hours using a budgeted machine hour overhead rate. It allocates Assembly Department overhead costs to jobs based on actual direct manufacturing labour-hours using a budgeted direct manufacturing labour-hour rate.

The following data are for the year 2013:

	Machining Department	Assembly Department
Budgeted overhead	$5,850,000	$7,812,000
Budgeted machine hours (MH)	90,000	0
Budgeted direct manufacturing labour-hours (DMLH)	0	124,000
Actual manufacturing overhead costs	$5,470,000	$8,234,000

Machine hours and direct manufacturing labour-hours and the ending balances (before proration of underallocated overhead) are as follows:

	Actual Machine Hours	Actual Direct Manufacturing Labour-Hours	Balance before Proration, December 31, 2013
Cost of Goods Sold	69,000	83,200	$21,600,000
Finished Goods	6,900	12,800	2,800,000
Work-in-Process	16,100	32,000	7,600,000

REQUIRED

1. Compute the budgeted overhead rates for the year in the Machining and Assembly Departments.
2. Compute the underallocated or overallocated overhead in *each* department for the year. Dispose of the underallocated or overallocated amount in *each* department using:
   a. Immediate write-off to Cost of Goods Sold.
   b. Proration based on ending balances (before proration) in Cost of Goods Sold, Finished Goods, and Work-in-Process.

c. Proration based on the allocated overhead amount (before proration) in the ending balances of Cost of Goods Sold, Finished Goods, and Work-in-Process.

3. Which disposition method do you prefer in requirement 2? Explain.

4-40 Job costing, normal versus actual under/over applied overhead. (J. Watson) The following information relates to the activities of King Ltd. for the year 2013:

③ ④ ⑤
1. Underallocated, $21,100

Advertising Costs	$ 62,500	Beginning Work-in-Process	$ 34,000
Direct Labour	320,000	Beginning Direct Materials	52,000
Indirect Labour	61,400	Factory Amortization	162,000
Factory Equipment Maintenance	13,300	Ending Work-in-Process	45,000
Ending Direct Materials	42,500	Factory Utilities	26,000
Office Amortization	13,000	Sales Commissions	24,000
Purchases of Direct Materials	156,000	Corporate Salaries	289,000
Factory Supplies	4,400	Insurance on Factory	22,600

The company uses normal costing and applies overhead on the basis of machine hours (MH). The company had calculated its overhead rate to be $4.25 per MH on the basis of 60,000 budgeted MH. Actual MH worked in the plant were 63,200.

REQUIRED

1. Compute the amount of overallocated or underallocated overhead for the year.

2. Prepare the journal entry to record the disposition of the amount of overallocated or underallocated overhead assuming the company writes off the difference to Cost of Goods Sold.

3. Identify and briefly outline an alternative treatment (from requirement 2) for disposing of overallocated or underallocated overhead.

4. Prepare a Schedule of Cost of Goods Manufactured for the year.

5. Briefly explain the differences between actual and normal costing, and state how the Schedule of Cost of Goods Manufactured would differ under actual costing.

4-41 Job costing and governance. Jack Halpern is the owner and CEO of Aerospace Comfort, a firm specializing in the manufacture of seats for air transport. He has just received a copy of a letter written to the Auditor General of the Canadian government. He believes it is from an ex-employee of Aerospace.

④
1. $820.30 per seat

Dear Sir,

Aerospace Comfort in 2013 manufactured 100 X7 seats for the Canadian Forces. You may be interested to know the following:

1. Direct materials cost billed for the 100 X7 seats was $40,000.

2. Direct manufacturing labour cost billed for 100 X7 seats was $8,400. This cost includes 16 hours of setup labour at $50 per hour, an amount included in the manufacturing overhead cost pool as well. The $8,400 also includes 15 hours of design time at $120 an hour. Design time was explicitly identified as a cost the Canadian Forces was not to reimburse.

3. Manufacturing overhead cost billed for 100 X7 seats was $14,700 (175% of direct manufacturing labour costs). This amount includes the 16 hours of setup labour at $50 per hour that is incorrectly included as part of direct manufacturing labour costs.

You may also want to know that over 40% of the direct materials is purchased from Frontier Technology, a company that is 51% owned by Jack Halpern's brother.

For obvious reasons, this letter will not be signed.

c.c.: *The Globe and Mail*
Jack Halpern, CEO of Aerospace Comfort

Aerospace Comfort's contract states that the Canadian Forces reimburses Aerospace at 130% of manufacturing costs.

REQUIRED

Assume that the facts in the letter are correct as you answer the following questions.

1. What is the cost amount per X7 seat that Aerospace Comfort billed the Canadian Forces? Assume that the actual direct materials costs are $40,000.

2. What is the amount per X7 seat that Aerospace Comfort should have billed the Canadian Forces? Assume that the actual direct materials costs are $40,000.

3. Based on the problems highlighted in the letter, what should the Canadian Forces do to tighten its procurement procedures to reduce the likelihood of such situations recurring?

4-42 **Allocation of manufacturing overhead and disposition of overallocation or underallocation.** (SMA, heavily adapted) Nicole Limited is a company that produces machinery to customer order. Its job-costing system (using normal costing) has two direct cost categories (direct materials and direct manufacturing labour) and one indirect cost pool (manufacturing overhead, allocated using a budgeted rate based on direct manufacturing labour costs). The budget for 2013 was:

Direct manufacturing labour	$630,000
Manufacturing overhead	$441,000

At the end of 2013, two jobs were incomplete: No. 1768B (total direct manufacturing labour costs were $15,000) and No. 1819C (total direct manufacturing labour costs were $48,000). Machine time totalled 318 hours for No. 1768B and 654 hours for No. 1819C. Direct materials issued to No. 1768B amounted to $30,600. Direct materials for No. 1819C came to $56,800.

Total charges to the Manufacturing Overhead Control account for the year were $406,200. Direct manufacturing labour charges made to all jobs were $650,000, representing 25,000 direct manufacturing labour-hours (DMLH).

There were no beginning inventories. In addition to the ending work-in-process, the ending finished goods showed a balance of $204,500 (including a direct manufacturing labour cost component of $60,000). Sales for 2013 totalled $3,124,000, cost of goods sold was $2,200,000, and marketing costs were $523,900.

Nicole prices on a cost-plus basis. It currently uses a guideline of cost plus 40% of cost.

REQUIRED

1. Prepare a detailed schedule showing the ending balances in the inventories and cost of goods sold (before considering any underallocated or overallocated manufacturing overhead). Show also the manufacturing overhead allocated to these ending balances.
2. Compute the underallocated or overallocated manufacturing overhead for 2013.
3. Prorate the amount computed in requirement 2 on the basis of:
   a. The ending balances (before proration) of work-in-process, finished goods, and cost of goods sold.
   b. The allocated overhead amount (before proration) in the ending balances of work-in-process, finished goods, and cost of goods sold.
4. Assume that Nicole decides to immediately write off to Cost of Goods Sold any underallocated or overallocated manufacturing overhead. Will operating income be higher or lower than the operating income that would have resulted from the proration in requirements 3(a) and 3(b)?
5. Calculate the cost of job No. 1819C if Nicole Limited had used the adjusted allocation rate approach to disposing of underallocated or overallocated manufacturing overhead in 2013.

4-43 **General ledger relationships, underallocation and overallocation.** (S. Sridhar, adapted) Northley Industries is a manufacturer of sailboats. The following partial information for 2013 is available:

Material Control		
1-1-2013	32,000	403,000
	431,000	

Work-in-Process Control		
1-1-2013	18,000	
Direct Manufacturing Labour		
	380,000	

Finished Goods Control		
1-1-2013	12,250	1,280,000
	1,307,250	

Manufacturing Overhead Allocated	

Manufacturing Overhead Control	
543,000	

Cost of Goods Sold	

1. Direct manufacturing labour wage rate was $16 per hour.
2. Manufacturing overhead (MOH) is allocated at $25 per direct manufacturing labour-hour (DMLH).
3. During the year, sales revenues were $1,664,000, and marketing and distribution expenses were $199,700.

REQUIRED
1. What was the amount of direct materials issued to manufacturing during the year?
2. What was the amount of manufacturing overhead allocated to jobs during the year?
3. What was the cost of jobs completed during the year?
4. What was the balance in work-in-process inventory on December 31, 2013?
5. What was the cost of goods sold before any proration of underallocated or overallocated overhead?
6. What was the underallocated or overallocated manufacturing overhead for the year?
7. Dispose of the underallocated or overallocated manufacturing overhead using:

   a. Immediate write-off to Cost of Goods Sold.

   b. Proration based on ending balances (before proration) in Work-in-Process, Finished Goods, and Cost of Goods Sold.

8. Using each of the disposition methods in requirement 7, calculate operating income for the year.
9. Which disposition method in requirement 7 do you recommend Northley use? Explain your answer briefly.

4-44 Normal costing, departments. (J. Watson) Kalor Ltd. uses a normal job-costing system with two direct cost categories, direct materials and direct labour, and one indirect cost pool. Manufacturing overhead is allocated based on direct labour costs. Any overallocated or underallocated overhead is written off to Cost of Goods Sold. Each product goes through two departments, Fabrication and Assembly. The Fabrication process is automated whereas the Assembly Department is highly labour intensive. Kalor's budget for 2013 was as follows:

③ ④

1. $17,829,625

Budgeted	Fabrication	Assembly
Direct Materials (DM)	$3,500,000	$2,100,000
Direct Labour	$ 735,000	$3,825,000
Factory Overhead	$6,450,000	$1,530,000
Machine Hours (MH)	2,580,000	250,000

Kalor started the year without any work-in-process. During the year it had the following results:

Actual	Fabrication	Assembly
Direct Materials (DM)	$3,350,000	$2,200,000
Direct Labour	$ 750,000	$3,750,000
Factory Overhead	$6,390,000	$1,590,000
Machine Hours (MH)	2,610,000	260,000

At December 31, 2013, the company had only two jobs still in process, #Z438 and #Q917. Job #Z438 had $7,000 of direct materials and $1,500 of direct labour and had used 3,400 MH in fabrication. It had not yet been transferred to the Assembly Department. Job #Q917 had incurred $4,000 and $6,000 of direct materials costs in Fabrication and Assembly, respectively. It had used 1,800 MH in Fabrication and 800 MH in Assembly. Labour charges in the two departments were $9,000 and $18,000 for Fabrication and Assembly, respectively.

REQUIRED
1. Calculate Cost of Goods Manufactured for the year ended December 31, 2013, assuming the company uses its current overhead costing method.
2. Under the current costing system, what is the amount of overallocated or underallocated overhead?
3. What would be the amount of overallocated or underallocated overhead at the end of the year if the company had used departmental overhead rates with the most appropriate base for each department?

1. $60 per machine hour

4-45 **Disposition of underallocated or overallocated overhead—Advanced.** (Z. Iqbal, adapted) Naf Radiator Company uses a normal costing system with a single manufacturing overhead (MOH) cost pool and machine hours (MH) as the cost allocation base. The following data are for 2013:

Budgeted manufacturing overhead (MOH)	$4,800,000
Overhead allocation base	machine hours (MH)
Budgeted machine hours (MH)	80,000
Manufacturing overhead (MOH) incurred	$4,900,000
Actual machine hours (MH)	75,000

Machine-hours data and the ending balances (before proration of underallocated or overallocated overhead) are as follows:

	Actual Machine Hours (MH)	2013 End-of-Year Balance
Cost of Goods Sold	60,000	$8,000,000
Finished Goods Control	11,000	1,250,000
Work-in-Process Control	4,000	750,000

REQUIRED

1. Compute the budgeted manufacturing overhead rate for 2013.
2. Compute the underallocated or overallocated manufacturing overhead of Naf Radiator in 2013. Dispose of this underallocated or overallocated amount using:
   a. Write-off to Cost of Goods Sold.
   b. Proration based on ending balances (before proration) in Work-in-Process Control, Finished Goods Control, and Cost of Goods Sold.
   c. Proration based on the allocated overhead amount (before proration) in the ending balances of Work-in-Process Control, Finished Goods Control, and Cost of Goods Sold.
3. Which method do you prefer in requirement 2? Explain.

COLLABORATIVE LEARNING CASES

1. $12 per direct labour-hour

4-46 **Normal job costing, unit costs.** (J. Watson) Pearson Ltd. uses a normal job-costing system and applies overhead on the basis of direct labour-hours. At the beginning of the year, the company estimated that total overhead costs for the year would be $180,000, and it budgeted total labour-hours of 15,000. Actual labour-hours worked for the period January 1 to November 30 were 13,750.

On December 1, the company had three jobs in process:

Work-in-Process at December 1

Job Number	815	817	822
Direct Materials (DM)	$1,400	$2,500	$1,700
Direct Labour (DL)	$1,200	$2,400	$ 600
Overhead (OH)	$ 600	$1,350	$ 450
Total	$3,200	$6,250	$2,750

During the month of December the following costs were incurred by job:

Job #	815	817	822	823	824
DM	$500	$ 700	$1,300	$1,250	$1,500
DL	$900	$1,440	$3,060	$3,960	$5,940
DL hours	50 hours	80 hours	170 hours	220 hours	330 hours

In addition, the company incurred the following costs during the month of December (these costs have not yet been recorded in the books):

DM purchases	$7,800	Advertising expense	$5,200
Plant amortization	2,490	Factory repairs and maintenance	1,500
Factory utilities	1,800	Factory supplies	1,800
Production supervisor salary	2,200	Sales personnel salaries	9,700
Administrative salaries	3,450	Interest expense	1,400

ADDITIONAL INFORMATION

1. The balance in the Overhead Control account on December 1 was $195,010.
2. There were no jobs in Finished Goods as of December 1.
3. Jobs # 815, 822, 823, and 824 were completed during December.
4. Job 824 is the only job in Finished Goods as of December 31.
5. The company's pricing policy is 200% of total manufacturing cost.

REQUIRED

1. Calculate the budgeted overhead rate used by Pearson.
2. Calculate the unit cost of ending work-in-process inventory assuming that the number of units in the job(s) total 250 units.
3. Calculate the cost of goods manufactured and the unadjusted gross margin for the month of December.
4. Calculate the amount of overallocated or underallocated overhead for the year.

4-47 Job costing, service industry. Michael Scott books tours for new bands, and arranges to print T-shirts and produce demo CDs to sell on the tour. Scott's agency uses a normal costing system with two direct cost pools, labour and materials, and one indirect cost pool, general overhead. General overhead is allocated to each tour at 150% of labour cost. The following information relates to the agency for 2013:

② ④
1. $2,100

1. As of June 1, there were tours in progress for two bands: Grunge Express and Different Strokes.
2. During June, both bands finished their tours.
3. New tours were started for three bands, As I Lay Dying, Ask Me Later, and Maybe Tomorrow. Of these bands, only Maybe Tomorrow finished its tour by the end of June.

All costs incurred during the planning stage for a tour are gathered in a balance sheet account called "Tours In Process (TIP)". When a tour is completed, the costs are transferred to an income statement account called "Cost of Completed Tours (CCT)."

The following cost information is for June:

	From Beginning TIP		Incurred in June	
	Materials	Labour	Materials	Labour
Grunge Express	$400	$600	$ 0	$100
Different Strokes	$300	$400	$175	$300
As I Lay Dying	$ 0	$ 0	$250	$400
Ask Me Later	$ 0	$ 0	$350	$200
Maybe Tomorrow	$ 0	$ 0	$275	$400

Actual overhead in June was $2,500.

REQUIRED

1. Calculate the TIP for the end of June.
2. Calculate CCT for June.
3. Calculate underallocated or overallocated overhead at the end of June.
4. Calculate the ending balances in work-in-process and cost of goods sold if the underallocated or overallocated overhead amount is:
   a. Written off to CCT.
   b. Prorated using the ending balances (before proration) in TIP and CCT.
   c. Prorated based on the overhead allocated in June in the ending balances of TIP and CCT (before proration).
5. Which of the methods in requirement 4 would you choose? Explain.

Activity-Based Costing and Management

BUSINESS MATTERS

Accurate Assignment = Better Profit

How much does a large double-double from Tim Hortons cost to produce? What about a venti latte from Starbucks? Both companies sell hundreds of millions of cups of coffee, beverages, mugs, and food each year. As customers, we know the price. Managers must know the costs. Coffee beans (the raw materials) cost little compared to the indirect and overhead costs of converting them into products to sell at a price where customers will buy. In the extremely competitive world of coffee, the more accurate the assignment of indirect costs, the more likely managers will remain profitable.

LEARNING OUTCOMES

After studying this chapter, you should be able to

1. Identify the basic elements of activity-based costing systems as distinguished from traditional systems, and explain how preventable undercosting and overcosting of products and services affects profitability.

2. Identify and explain the problem of preventable over- and undercosting.

3. Apply the cost hierarchy to develop an activity-based costing (ABC) system.

4. Assign costs using activity-based costing (ABC).

5. Explain the benefits of activity-based costing (ABC) systems for activity-based management (ABM).

So far we've discussed the cost pool, cost allocation base, cost allocation rate, and traditional cost assignment of a single indirect cost pool to distinct cost objects. The reliability of the financial and nonfinancial data in the MIS limits the choice of a single cost allocation base to a quantity of direct inputs used. Cost allocation is a second-best solution, chosen in part because it is *not* cost-beneficial to improve on cost assignment accuracy by tracing indirect costs to distinct jobs. In Chapter 5, we assume that it *would* be cost-beneficial to generate better measures of the unequal benefits from support activities shared among distinct types of goods or services. Costing more accurately will require more than one indirect cost pool and cost driver (allocation) base.

Improving indirect cost assignment requires classifying the scope of the cost effects of activities. An **activity** is an event or task, or series of related tasks, that provide a measurable benefit in the completion of goods or services ready for sale. Some activities transform inputs to a single unit of output, such as brewing and pouring a venti mocha latte. Some activities transform many similar inputs to larger quantities of similar outputs called a batch, such as mixing, baking, and glazing ten dozen double-chocolate doughnuts. Some activities transform inputs for an entire product, such as manufacturing Tim Hortons thermal mugs. The indirect costs of an activity become a cost pool that supports production at the unit, batch, or product level. A focus on the scope of the effects of support activities results in an activity-based costing (ABC) system.

ACTIVITY-BASED COSTING: BUILDING BLOCK CONCEPTS

1 Identify the basic elements of activity-based costing systems as distinguished from traditional systems, and explain how preventable undercosting and overcosting of products and services affects profitability.

The discipline of management decision making begins with an awareness that there is a decision to be made: Keep doing what we're doing, or start doing something differently? If change is desirable, then how do we proceed? The decision framework introduced in Chapter 1 is one tool for ensuring that the change process is disciplined. While it is rare that a team of decision makers will proceed easily from one step to the next, the framework is a way to make sure that, eventually, the team takes all the steps in an orderly way. Having recognized there is a decision to be made, the management team proceeds to gather information and filter out relevant data.

The MIS within the company is the source of internal quantitative data. Successful companies also gather important data about their business environment. This will help make decisions that improve the competitiveness of a company, given the threats and opportunities posed by the environment. Management teams need to sort out the relevant from the irrelevant data pertaining to the problem at hand. For example, in any pricing decision, teams must understand costs. Some costs are controllable and relevant, especially variable costs that increase when the quantity of finished goods increases. Costing techniques that reveal the variable cost behaviour of direct and indirect cost pools increase the scope of data in the MIS that will be relevant. Based on a rigorous analysis of relevant data, alternatives can be identified and reliable predictions can be made. No decision is certain in its outcomes, but the more rigorous the strategic analysis and more disciplined the selection of alternatives, the more probable it is the predicted outcomes will be achieved. This is the heartbeat of business management—set realistic goals, achieve the goals.

The basic elements of activity-based costing are similar to those defined in the job-costing system in Chapter 4. More than most techniques, the design of an ABC system relies on the relationship between activities and the increased value added from customizing the output, for which customers will pay. It is only fair that if resources are not equally shared when customizing outputs, customers who obtain no added value are not asked to pay more. ABC systems distinguish more accurately the outputs that cost more from the outputs that cost less. Knowing this, the management team can price more accurately to assure a reliable profit from customized outputs. The team can also make wiser selections among outputs to increase the market share for the most profitable.

If indirect activity costs are a small proportion of total costs, then ABC systems are not cost-beneficial. If the difference in benefits of indirect activities in support of completing different types of finished goods is uniform, then **traditional costing** (also known as **cost smoothing process,** or **peanut butter costing**) is the appropriate approach to cost assignment. In this case traditional costing represents the economic fact of the production process and simply spreads the single indirect overhead cost pool over each job in proportion to one quantity of one direct input used.

Activity-based costing (ABC) is a technique to improve the reliability of cost assignment from indirect cost pools to distinct types of outputs. One indirect cost pool comprises mixed costs. Included in one pool are costs of different types of indirect supplies and labour that many distinct, completed goods and services share, but that they do not share equally. ABC is a way to disclose the unequal benefits provided by shared indirect support activities. ABC also draws attention to the inter-relationships among common activities across the entire value-chain of business functions. This helps managers make strategic decisions about how to reduce costs.

The **activity cost pool** is the accumulation of all costs required to pay for a defined activity (or set of related activities) that indirectly supports the completion of all outputs. The benefits of indirect activities, while shared among distinct types of goods or services, are not shared equally. This means the activity cost pool should not be divided equally among the distinct outputs because it fails to reflect the economic facts of completing the outputs.

The **activity cost driver** is a proxy measure of the benefits from using support activities common to all outputs. While all distinct outputs benefit from the costs of shared support activities, they do not do so equally. The selected cost driver should vary with the quantity of benefit received by each distinct good or service. When the benefit is intangible, another method can be used to divide up (allocate) the indirect support activity cost pool.

The **activity cost rate** is the result of dividing the activity cost pool by the total quantity of the activity cost driver (the benefit). The result is a rate per unit of benefit received. As the quantity of activity increases, the quantity of the activity cost driver should increase and the cost of the activity to customize an output should increase. In practice, this link between the change in the activity cost driver and the change in the activity cost pool is called **explanatory power**. Explanatory power means that a change in the quantity of an activity cost driver will explain the change in cost of a distinct type of output. Once the quantity of activity cost driver (a measure of benefit) used by each cost object and the activity cost driver rate is known, the indirect activity cost pool is assigned. The activity cost driver rate is multiplied by the quantity of the activity cost driver consumed by each distinct type of output.

An **activity level** identifies the scope of the effect of any changes in an activity's cost. The scope may be as broad as an entire organization, such as quantity of total POs completed or quantity of information technology support hours provided, or as narrow as a group of single units, such as quality control of maple-flavoured bacon packaged on Wednesday afternoons. For example, the activity of purchasing is common to all business functions in the value-chain, from R&D to customer service. Assume all the costs of this shared purchasing support activity are accumulated in a separate purchasing activity cost pool. The benefit to all business functions can be measured by the quantity of purchase orders (PO) completed in a timely way. As the quantity of POs increases, the total costs of the purchasing activities also increase. This activity cost will also decrease directly as the quantity of POs completed decreases.

ABC provides a straightforward cost-benefit analysis of the unequally shared benefits of a support activity. The technique also clearly discloses the scope of business functions where cost control will have a positive effect. Identification of the scope of cost control focused on different activity levels should lead to:

◆ Increased reliability of the costs and benefits measures of various support activities.

◆ Deeper understanding of interdependencies among costs and activities throughout the value chain.

◆ Clearer diagnoses of costing problems and identification of more effective remedies.

◆ Refined, more reliable predicted (budgeted) future costs.

◆ Superior methods to predict (budget) future outcomes, particularly profitability.

ACTIVITY-BASED MANAGEMENT

ABC is the foundation of **activity-based management (ABM)**. ABC is a strategy to eliminate non-value-added activities for which customers will not pay. When outputs are customized they use inputs in different amounts depending on the customization. Matching the cost of customization to a customer's willingness to pay is a value-leadership strategy. But in highly competitive business environments, many companies compete for the same customer by offering a range of customized products, such as different blends of coffee.

With many retailers to choose from and little difference in quality and availability, customers will make their purchase decisions based on price. Charge too much for a kilogram of ground coffee or a venti latte and your customer will switch to a different source. In this intensely competitive environment, cost leadership drives profitability. The company that has the best costing for its distinct products and services will have the competitive edge in pricing to assure it retains customers and achieves a predicted level of profit. With a cost leadership strategy, lower overall costs mean that the price of finished goods and services can be lowered while still maintaining a constant profit.

Going back to our purchasing example, knowing the scope of benefits from a specific indirect activity reveals to managers where changes in methods of purchasing could lower costs across the entire value chain. Reducing activity cost per PO without impairing timely delivery and price of materials is a strategic decision that benefits the entire company. In the production business function, operating decisions such as changing a production schedule to extend production runs could reduce the frequency of ordering materials and the quantity of POs, thereby reducing the indirect activity cost of purchasing in production. ABC systems help managers discover and exploit these relationships between benefits and costs.

UNDERCOSTING AND OVERCOSTING

When customization results in a distinct type of output, activities to customize production of the output differ. For example, a small cup of black coffee poured from a carafe costs less to prepare and serve than an individually prepared small-sized cup of cappuccino. One reason is that cappuccino requires more labour time to produce versus a carafe of coffee. However, what if a company assigned an almost identical cost for each cup based on the quantity of coffee beans used (simple average)? This approach ignores the added training costs (indirect) for a barista who can quickly create an appealing cappuccino. The cappuccino will be significantly undercosted relative to the cost of pouring a cup of black coffee from a carafe. By assuming the costs of training are uniform for both distinct products, you would end up with the following:

◆ **Output level undercosting**. A unit, batch, or product (cappuccino) consumes a relatively high level of support activity, but is reported to have a relatively low total cost.

◆ **Output level overcosting**. A unit, batch (carafe of coffee), or product consumes a relatively low level of indirect activity, but is reported to have a relatively high total cost.

The ABC method of assigning costs will help managers reach a more reliable cost per distinct output than a simple average. The product pricing will be more accurate based on the economic fact of unequal distribution of the benefits of indirect activities that support the completion of all finished goods and services.

Unintentional Cost Cross-Subsidization   Unfortunately, when a simple average method is used, one output, batch, or product will be undercosted and at least one output, batch, or product will be overcosted. This is referred to as **cross-subsidization**. Some companies deliberately provide product or service bundles with cross-subsidized elements as a strategy to increase market share. But this is a management decision; it

EXHIBIT 5-1
Cross-Subsidization of Costs—Costs Not Borne by One Must Be Assigned to the Other

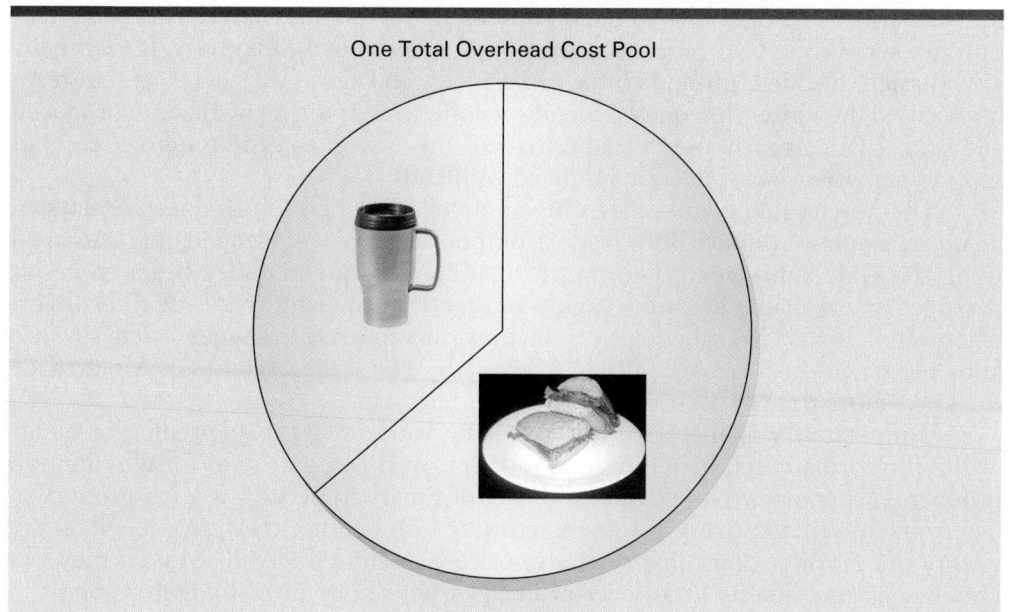

One Total Overhead Cost Pool

does not occur by accident. Unintentional cross-subsidization is not a management decision and it will impair profits or, at the extreme, result in bankruptcy.

You most likely have experienced cross-subsidization if you have gone out for the evening with some friends. You agree in advance to simply average the bill for food and drinks among you equally. This method does not trace direct costs to each "unit," but rather assigns total costs on the basis of a single cost pool (the bill) and a single cost driver (the total number of people enjoying food and drink).

For example, at the restaurant Matt, Hussain, Lincoln, and Shuye order dinner. Matt is bulking up because he is on the university's weightlifting team. He orders a large meat dinner, dessert, and a couple of drinks that total $42. Hussain does not drink alcohol, but he too enjoys an entree (a full-course vegetarian dinner), dessert, and fresh juice that total $27. Lincoln cannot tolerate sweets but enjoys soup, a calamari pasta dinner, and drinks totalling $31. Shuye orders a fresh fish dinner and a drink that total $22. The grand total on the cheque (the cost pool) comes out to $122. The simple average cost per person will be $30.50. Hussain and Shuye actually consumed resources that cost only $27 and $22, respectively, so their contributions of $30.50 were overcosted and they have cross-subsidized the undercosted night out for Lincoln and Matt.

In Exhibit 5-1, the coffee mugs are clearly distinct products from sandwiches. The quantity of common indirect activities to support sales of coffee mugs differ from the quantity used to support sandwich sales. Tim Hortons sells millions of each distinct type of product each day and can't afford to accidentally overcost a less-expensive product, which then subsidizes an undercosted but expensive one. There are hundreds of other coffee shops competing for sales of almost identical products. Customers will not overpay for a Tim Hortons sandwich and will simply substitute one from Mr. Sub, Couche Tard, or even the local gas station. The pressure of competition means Tim Hortons remains an industry leader by knowing its costs, controlling its cost drivers, and remedying pricing problems when they arise. Overall, ABC is intended to more accurately assign overhead costs and avoid unintentional cross-subsidization.

IDENTIFYING PREVENTABLE OVER- AND UNDERCOSTING

Identifying over- and undercosting situations is important because it leads to the over- and underpricing of products or services, which affects profitability. Let's look at an example to illustrate how preventable over- and undercosting can be identified and resolved through a more refined costing system.

Identify and explain the problem of preventable over- and undercosting. ②

Coffee Bean Inc. (CBI) takes green coffee beans and then roasts, blends, grinds, and distributes different blends to retail customers. The green coffee beans are sold by each farmer's co-operative to the highest bidder through a central worldwide auction market. While CBI purchases green coffee beans in 100 kg bags, it eventually sells roasted, blended, ground coffee in 1 kg bags and tins. CBI's management team has focused their attention on two blends of coffee out of the many that are produced and sold. CBI currently uses a traditional costing system to assign indirect costs of support activities shared in completing all its blends.

The Mocha Loa blend sells in high volume. The newly introduced Malaysian blend sells in low volume. Both distinct outputs are roasted, blended, and packaged using the same equipment. The transformation from green coffee beans to goods packaged and available for sale is highly automated, requiring very little direct manufacturing labour. CBI schedules production runs to produce larger batches (more kilos per batch) of Mocha Loa than Malaysian. The larger batches of Mocha Loa each take more time to roast than a batch of Malaysian.

With its traditional costing system, CBI's management team predicts or budgets its pro forma costs, including one indirect overhead cost pool for all common production support activities, then adds a profit markup of 30% to each product to determine its selling price. Customers return to CBI because they can depend on the quality of the coffee. Customers are also price-conscious and will switch if they can obtain the same quality at a lower price elsewhere. The 2012 budget reports the totals in these three cost pools of the traditional system, one of which is *total* indirect costs (overhead) of $7,875,400 (column 3).

| | Costs per Unit | | |
	Mocha Loa (1)	Malaysian (2)	Total (3)
Direct materials (per kg)	$5.04	$3.84	$ 7,200,000
Direct manufacturing labour (per DLH)	0.36	0.36	1,575,080
Total direct costs	$5.40	$4.20	$ 8,775,080
Indirect costs			7,875,400
Total			$16,650,480

The single MOH cost pool will change in an ABC system, replaced by six identifiable support activity cost pools, common to manufacturing all blends of coffee. Measures of benefit from the activities, the cost drivers, will be used in the cost driver base to calculate the cost driver rate for each activity cost pool. Distinct blends of coffee will be assigned unequal proportions of each activity cost pool depending on the amount of benefit received, as measured by the cost driver.

From the table you can readily calculate that the overhead cost pool is the highest proportion of total costs, exceeding 47% ($7,875,400 ÷ 16,650,480). The traditional cost allocation rate uses the ratio of two cost pools. It is the total pro forma value of the overhead cost pool divided by the total pro forma direct manufacturing labour (DML) cost pool:

$$\text{Traditional overhead allocation rate} = \frac{\text{Budgeted overhead cost pool}}{\text{Budgeted direct manufacturing labour cost pool}}$$

$$= \frac{\$7,875,400}{\$1,575,080}$$

$$= \$5.00 \text{ per direct manufacturing labour dollar}$$

The cost allocation *base*, or denominator, for the single MOH cost pool is budgeted direct manufacturing labour cost. The ratio means that for every direct manufacturing labour dollar spent to produce 1 kg of either Mocha Loa or Malaysian coffee, CBI will allocate $5.00 of overhead. Then, the pro forma direct cost to produce 1 kg of Mocha Loa is $5.04/kg for the green coffee beans used in this blend and 0.36/kg for direct labour. For every $1 DLH the MOH rate is $5.00, therefore the MOH cost for 1 kg of Mocha Loa is $0.36 × $5.00 = $1.80/kg. Total cost of Mocha Loa is

$7.20/kg plus a markup of 30% for a sales price of $10.29/kg ($7.20 ÷ 1 − 0.30 = $10.29). **Cost plus pricing** means the gross margin of $3.09 ($10.29 − $7.20) equals 30% of the price. Similarly, the current price of 1 kg of Malaysian is $8.57/kg using the traditional costing method:

		Costs per Unit	
		Mocha Loa (1)	Malaysian (2)
Direct materials (per kg)		$ 5.04	$3.84
Direct manufacturing labour (per DLH)		0.36	0.36
Total direct costs		5.40	4.20
Indirect cost allocation rate per $1.00 DLH	$5.00		
Indirect costs assigned (0.36 DLH × $5.00)		1.80	1.80
Total unit cost per kg		$ 7.20	$6.00
Markup 30%	30.0%		
Pro forma price per kilogram (unit cost per kg/0.70)		$10.29	$8.57

The controller believes that the current traditional cost assignment method overcosts Mocha Loa, meaning that this popular blend is overpriced. Malaysian, however, may be undercosted and therefore underpriced. If true, then CBI is impairing its profits and could charge less for Mocha Loa but more for Malaysian. Knowing that in a competitive market the correct quality and price tradeoff is CBI's competitive advantage, the controller decides to refine the costing system before repricing the two blends.

Providing more reliable information to guide managers in pricing decisions will improve the competitive pricing of products without impairing profit. This mispricing of products is preventable and manageable with a more refined costing system. As we've learned, the ABC system is an improvement only when the distinct types of outputs derive unequal benefit from the unequal use of indirect activities common to producing all outputs.

COST HIERARCHIES

A **cost hierarchy** classifies cost drivers (allocation base) by the *number of business functions* in the value chain to which the activities provide benefits. This scope of benefits provided across the value chain is the activity level in the cost hierarchy. In this chapter, the ABC system has four different activity levels. From broadest to most narrow they are: facilities, product, batch, and distinct type of output (blend of roasted coffee).

Management accountants provide the important service of identifying costly support activities and classifying them by activity level. There must be a way to measure the benefits from the activity in a reasonable and reliable way. For example, a measure of benefits arising from a purchasing activity is quantity of purchase orders (POs) completed in a timely way. The measure of benefit is the activity cost driver, because as the quantity of benefits changes it explains changes in the activity cost pool value.

Facility-Sustaining Costs   **Facility-sustaining costs** are the broadest scope of costs. These costs arise from an activity that benefits all business functions of the value chain. Facilities-sustaining cost pools include items like executive salaries. The benefits of facilities-level activity are usually intangible and uncountable. When this is the case we may simply use a ratio of facilities-sustaining activity cost divided by total costs to calculate an activity cost driver rate. Often different facilities-level activities sustain one another's activities, such as IT services and Purchasing.

Product-Sustaining Costs   **Product-sustaining (or service-sustaining) costs** accumulate from activities that support entire product or service lines. In the manufacturing sector, GAAP requires their classification as cost of goods sold (COGS), not operating expenses. In the merchandising sector, GAAP requires their classification as cost of sales (COS). In the service sector, GAAP requires their classification as operating expenses. The product or service is the cost object that benefits from the product-sustaining activities.

In our example, CBI produces several blends of coffee. Each is a distinct product. A change from one blend to another requires that a routine set of product-sustaining activities be undertaken. Inventory is moved from the warehouse to the machine roasting and blending area. The raw beans must be unpackaged and placed on conveyors; the machines must be reset to roast and blend the beans at the correct temperature for the correct time. Now the production line is set up to convert the new blend of beans into a saleable product.

Notice that there are different identifiable activities that comprise the setup for a product. Some may be manual labour, such as pouring different types of beans into a blender, and will vary according to the labour-hours consumed. Others, such as moving and opening the sacks of green coffee beans, may be done by robots and other equipment. These are fixed costs. This is typical of an activities indirect cost pool where costs of several related setup activities are accumulated in one cost pool separate from the costs of other unrelated activities.

One measure of the benefit of these activities to each distinct product is the total quantity of setups. This is observable and measurable, and as the quantity of setups increases, so too will the cost. Quantity of setups is the cost driver for this activity cost pool. The costs of all setup activities accumulated in the setup activity cost pool divided by the total quantity of setups results in the setup activity cost driver rate. The cost per setup multiplied by the total setups for the distinct blend results in the total setup cost for the distinct product. It is the relationship between the different quantity of setups for different products that determine that this cost pool is a product-sustaining cost.

Batch-Level Costs **Batch-level costs** accumulate from activities that sustain a group of outputs of one distinct blend. In our example, CBI doesn't roast a single bean or even a single kilo of coffee but rather a specific quantity of different coffee beans for each blend. Ensuring reliable quality is a competitive advantage, which means the blending and roasting of each batch of Mocha Loa must be consistent. The quality control indirect cost pool comprises testing activities. Testing *each* batch after blending and roasting assures reliable taste before the product is ground and packaged for sale by the kilo. The benefit is measured by number of batches tested.

Machine capacity determines the quantity of kilos per batch for each blend. The larger the quantity of kilos per batch, the fewer batches that need to be run to achieve a target production level of kilos of the finished product. The greater the number of batches blended and roasted per product, the higher the number of tests and the higher the cost of quality assurance activities. The batch is the cost driver. The cost driver rate is total testing costs divided by total batches tested. The quantity of batches per blend multiplied by the cost per batch results in the total testing cost per blend.

Output Unit-Level Costs **Output unit-level costs** accumulate from those activities that sustain a single distinct type of service or output. In our example, CBI sells its finished goods by the kilo; therefore, the cost object is total kilos of coffee of each blend. Ultimately, the goal is to refine an *economically feasible* cost system that is reliable because it mirrors the reality of how costs flow through the production process for each blend. The ABC focus is on important and relevant costs. If measures of the benefits from activities causing the costs are controlled, then the costs will be controlled.

ACTIVITY-BASED COSTING SYSTEMS

③ Apply the cost hierarchy to develop an activity-based costing (ABC) system.

ABC refines the method of cost assignment. The refined method can unlock cost savings opportunities hidden by the traditional costing method. While accountants often lead the redesign of costing systems, it is the managers who must use their expertise to identify activities, their scope, and their measurement. This is the data-gathering phase of the decision-making process. These data will be the basis for deciding how many ABC indirect cost pools are necessary and their appropriate measures of benefit (cost drivers). Managers strive to obtain the greatest improvement in reliable costing with the minimum number of added cost pools. This improves the understandability of the new ABC system by reducing the complexity.

Assume CBI's managers have identified six activities for which controlling costs are critical: purchasing, materials handling, quality control, roasting, blending, and packaging. These will become the new indirect activity cost pools separated out from the total indirect cost pool. The manager of purchasing noted that as the number of purchase orders (POs) increased, the cost of the purchasing activity increased. This meant that the number of POs was an activity cost driver of the indirect activity cost pool, purchasing.

Total Pro Forma Indirect Actvity

Activity (1)	Cost Pool (2)	Mocha Loa	Malaysian
Purchasing (activity cost pool)	$2,777,600		
PO for all blends (activity cost driver)	448		
PO activity cost driver rate ($2,777,600 ÷ 448)	$ 6,200		
Total sales volumes (kg)		1,050,000	350,000
Purchase (PO) order size		25,000	5,000
PO quantity for Mocha Loa		42	
PO quantity for Malaysian			70
PO activity cost per blend ($6,200 × 42 POs; 70 POs)		$ 260,400	$434,000

The budgeted purchasing activity cost driver rate at $6,200 per PO is a very high cost activity and reducing the number of POs processed would generate cost savings. The cost of the purchasing activity was not uniformly distributed because the benefits to each blend are different. The marketing manager's forecast sales is 1,050,000 kg of Mocha Loa, but each PO size will be 25,000 kg. The quantity of Mocha Loa POs will be 42 (1,050,000 kg ÷ 25,000 kg per PO). In comparison, the Malaysian blend forecast sales is 350,000 kg. The budgeted PO size is only 5,000 kg, therefore the number of POs will be 70. The benefits of the purchasing activity cost more for Malaysian than for Mocha Loa.

For Mocha Loa, the assigned product-level purchasing activity cost is $260,400 ($6,200 × 42 POs), and for Malaysian the assigned product-level purchasing cost is $434,000 ($6,200 × 70 POs). Because the benefits differ, the quantity of activity cost driver consumed for each blend differs. For such a high cost activity, CBI benefits from knowing that ultimately it needs to price Malaysian to recover a higher proportion of purchasing costs than Mocha Loa. By defining activities, measuring the benefits, and identifying the costs of performing each activity, ABC systems provide a greater level of detail to understand how an organization uses its common inputs differently for distinct products. As we describe cost assignment refinement, keep in mind three features:

1. *Direct cost tracing.* A feature of ABC systems is to identify some indirect activities and accumulate their costs in a separate cost pool. The measure of benefits from the activity will directly drive cost pool changes. To make the effort and cost of an ABC system worthwhile, the activities costs identified should generate a high proportion of total indirect costs.

2. *Indirect cost pools.* The ABC system of cost assignment creates smaller indirect activity cost pools (numerators) that vary with the measure of benefit from the specific activity. Because quantity of benefits increases quantity of activities, the costs in the activity cost pool change with the measure of benefits, the cost driver. The benefit directly drives activities costs but remains an indirect cost of the distinct output. In the CBI example, purchasing did not result in kilograms of ground coffee, but without purchasing direct materials, there would be nothing to produce.

3. *Activity cost drivers.* For each activity cost pool there is an indirect cost. A measure of the activity performed is required. It is the denominator that is divided into the indirect cost pool to calculate the activity cost driver rate. In the CBI example, the output from the purchasing activity was measured as the quantity of purchase orders generated in a year. The rate was the cost per PO completed.

With a refined ABC system, the managers can now see that the cost of ordering direct materials for the Malaysian coffee beans is far higher than Mocha Loa. The difference is $173,600 ($434,000 − $260,400). The evidence so far indicates that the price of Mocha Loa is cross-subsidizing the purchasing activity costs incurred by Malaysian. The managers at CBI would not have detected this effect had they not applied the ABC method.

On the basis of only this information, the managers at CBI should suspect that Malaysian is undercosted and underpriced while Mocha Loa is overcosted and overpriced. A competitor who has implemented an ABC system of assigning indirect costs would know more accurately the costs of each blend. This competitor could reduce the price of coffee of similar quality and taste as Mocha Loa substantially and still earn a 30% profit. CBI would lose sales because they lacked the information needed to become price-competitive.

The goal in the CBI example, however, is not to calculate the cost per purchase order (activity cost driver), but rather the cost per kilogram of ground coffee sold for each blend, either Mocha Loa or Malaysian. Calculating the cost per purchase order—the activity cost rate—is simply an intermediate step that is necessary because different quantities of purchase orders are issued for each blend. This means the purchasing activity (and cost) is not uniformly consumed. In fact, this is true of each activity identified by CBI's managers.

Cost assignment requires that the total indirect purchasing activity cost pool derived from the ABC system be assigned to each kilogram of Mocha Loa and Malaysian produced. This links the indirect cost to the kilogram or unit of distinct finished goods that CBI will sell to its customers. The kilogram package of coffee is the cost object. Adjustments are also made for underallocated or overallocated indirect costs for each distinct output, using the methods described in Chapter 4 (write-off, proration, or adjusted allocation rate).

IMPLEMENTING AN ABC COST-ASSIGNMENT SYSTEM

④ Assign costs using activity-based costing (ABC).

Now the ABC system will be applied using all six cost pools and activity cost driver measures to improve CBI's pricing. Having identified the activities, scope or level of each, and the measures of benefit, six activity cost driver rates were calculated, as shown in Exhibit 5-2.

Purchasing   Purchasing is an extremely expensive benefit at $6,200 for each PO completed in a timely manner for the distinct blends. CBI produces many other blends of coffee that generate the total purchasing support activity cost pool of $2,777,600. Of all 448 POs completed, together Mocha Loa and Malaysian blends account for only 112 POs. Of the total activity cost pool, only $694,400 has been budgeted and assigned to each of the two distinct blends: $260,400 has been assigned to Mocha Loa (42 PO × $6,200/PO) and $434,000 to Malaysian (70 PO × $6,200/PO). This is also the case for the remaining five activity cost pools. Together, Mocha Loa and Malaysian use only part of the total indirect support activities for all blends sold by CBI.

The amount to be recovered for the purchasing activity is $0.2480/kg for Mocha Loa ($260,400 ÷ 1,050,000 kg) and $1.24/kg for Malaysian ($434,000 ÷ 350,000 kg). When pricing Mocha Loa there is far less purchasing activity cost to be recovered than for Malaysian. The difference of $0.992/kg is a concern because the budgeted price of Malaysian is $1.20/kg lower than for Mocha Loa. On this basis only, the controller appears to be correct and the blends are mispriced. But there are five other activity costs plus the direct costs to be assigned to each blend. In Exhibit 5-3 the measures of benefit from each indirect activity are identified in the far right column. The order of the rows indicates the level in the cost hierarchy.

EXHIBIT 5-2
Activity Cost Pools, Cost Drivers, Activity Cost Rates, and Activity Level for CBI's Activity Cost Pools

Activity (1)	Total Pro Forma Indirect Activity Cost Pool (2)	Total Pro Forma Activity Cost Driver Quantity (3)	Activity Cost Rate (4) = (2) ÷ (3)	Activity Cost Driver	Cost Hierarchy Activity Level	Relationship of the Activity Cost Driver to the Total Activity Cost
Purchasing	$2,777,600	448	$6,200.00	per PO	Product	Purchasing costs increase with number of POs.
Material handling	3,465,000	15,400	225.00	per setup-hour	Batch	Indirect setup costs increase with setup-hours.
Quality control	687,800	1,900	362.00	per batch	Batch	Indirect quality control costs increase with the batches inspected.
Roasting	182,000	9,100	20.00	per roasting-hour	Batch	Indirect roasting costs increase with the hours of roasting.
Blending	273,000	9,100	30.00	per blending-hour	Batch	Indirect blending costs increase with the hours of blending.
Packaging	490,000	49,000	10.00	per packaging-hour	Unit	Indirect packaging costs increase with the packaging-hours.
Total activity costs	$7,875,400					

EXHIBIT 5-3
CBI's Assigned Costs from its ABC System for Two Distinct Blends, Mocha Loa and Malaysian

Activity Used Unequally by Distinct Blends	Mocha Loa	Malaysian	Activity Cost Rate	Measure of Benefit or Cost Driver
Purchasing	42	70	$6,200.00	PO
Material handling	2,100	1,750	$ 225.00	setup-hour
Quality control	300	175	$ 362.00	batch
Roasting	525	350	$ 20.00	roasting-hour
Blending	210	175	$ 30.00	blending-hour
Packaging	10,500	1,750	$ 10.00	packaging-hour
Pro forma marketing demand, kg	1,050,000	350,000		

	Assigned Activity Cost Pools		Activity Cost per kg	
Activity cost assigned	Mocha Loa	Malaysian	Mocha Loa	Malaysian
Purchasing ($6,200 × 42; 70)	$260,400	$434,000	$0.2480	$1.2400
Material handling ($225 × 2,100; 1,750)	472,500	393,750	0.4500	1.1250
Quality control ($362 × 300; 175)	108,600	63,350	0.1034	0.1810
Roasting ($20 × 525; 350)	10,500	7,000	0.0100	0.0200
Blending ($30 × 210; 175)	6,300	5,250	0.0060	0.0150
Packaging ($10 × 10,500; 1,750)	105,000	17,500	0.1000	0.0500
Total assigned activity costs	$963,300	$920,850	$0.917	$2.631

The quantities of each cost driver measuring the benefit to the distinct blends are also reported for Mocha Loa and Malaysian. This verifies that from the indirect activities listed, the two blends derive unequal benefit. For example, the purchasing activity supports 70 POs for Malaysian but only 42 for Mocha Loa. At a rate of $6,200/PO, the activities cost is almost double for Malaysian than for Mocha Loa. But knowing the ABC rate is not the objective. The objective is to assign costs per kilogram of a package of each blend. Each activity cost pool for each blend must be divided by the total kilos produced in a year for that blend to obtain the activity cost per kilogram.

Material Handling   Assume the maximum number of kilograms CBI's equipment can process at any single time (the batch size) is 500 kg for Mocha Loa and 200 kg for Malaysian. To produce 1,050,000 kg of Mocha Loa, CBI would require 2,100 setups. To produce 350,000 kg of Malaysian, CBI would require 1,750 setups. Overall, a total number of 3,850 setups would be needed annually to produce 1,400,000 kg of the two distinct blends. The benefit of setup activities arises when the batches of each blend are completed and production of a new blend begins. The setup benefits are measured in setup-hours per batch. As you recall, most of the setup is done by equipment and involves moving the green coffee beans from storage to the production area, opening the bags, and placing the correct amount for a batch on the conveyor belts. This is known as materials handling.

Each day, the production manager knows the setup equipment handles enough coffee beans for 6 batches of Mocha Loa and 5 batches of Malaysian. Dividing the total budgeted materials handling activity cost pool by total setups, results in an activity cost rate of $225 per setup ($3,465,000 ÷ 15,400 setups). The materials handling activity cost assigned to Mocha Loa will be $472,500 ($225/setup × 2,100 setups) and for Malaysian will be $393,750 ($225/setup × 1,750 setups). On a cost-per-kilogram basis, the materials handling activity costs will be $0.4500/kg for Mocha Loa ($472,500 ÷ 1,050,000 kg) and $1.1250/kg for Malaysian ($393,750 ÷ 350,000 kg).

Now the unequal distribution of the benefits of setups for each kilogram of each blend sold is clear. The activity cost that must be recovered in the price of Mocha Loa is only $0.45/kg whereas it is $1.125/kg for Malaysian. On the basis of only setup cost/kg, the price of Malaysian should be $0.675/kg higher than for Mocha Loa. This would account for more than half the budgeted price difference between the two of $1.20/kg.

Quality Control   CBI's quality control policy is to test every 7 batches of Mocha Loa and every 10 batches of Malaysian. In one year, there would be 300 quality control tests for Mocha Loa and 175 quality control tests for Malaysian, for a total of 475 tests. The indirect quality control activity cost pool pro forma value was $687,800, and the activity cost rate per batch tested was $362 per batch ($687,800 ÷ 1,900 batches). The quality control activity costs assigned to Mocha Loa would be $108,600 ($362/batch × 300 batches) and to Malaysian would be $63,350 ($362/batch × 175 batches) for the year. On a cost-per-kilogram basis, the quality control activity costs will be $0.1034/kg for Mocha Loa ($108,600 ÷ 1,050,000 kg) and $0.1810/kg for Malaysian ($63,350 ÷ 350,000 kg).

Roasting   The costs included in the activity cost pool of roasting hours included utilities to power the roaster and vent the fumes, and standardized computer checks of temperature and colour. The standard time to roast a 500-kg batch of Mocha Loa was 15 minutes and for a 200-kg batch of Malaysian was 12 minutes. In total, running 6.5 hours per day for 350 days, there is a roasting capacity of 2,275 roasting-hours for each of CBI's four roasters. A total of 9,100 roasting-hours (2,275 roasting-hours × 4 roasters) are available. The benefit of the roasting activity for Mocha Loa is budgeted at 525 roasting-hours, and for Malaysian at 350 roasting-hours.

The total indirect roasting activity cost pool is budgeted at $182,000 and the activity cost rate at $20/roasting-hour ($182,000 ÷ 9,100 roasting-hours). Budgeted roasting activity cost assigned to Mocha Loa was $10,500 ($20/roasting-hour × 525 roasting-hours). For Malaysian, the pro forma activity cost assigned was $7,000

($20/roasting-hour $\times$ 350 roasting-hours). On a cost-per-kilogram basis, then, the roasting activity costs will be $0.0100/kg for Mocha Loa ($10,500 $\div$ 1,050,000 kg) and $0.0200/kg for Malaysian ($7,000 $\div$ 350,000 kg).

Blending The costs included in the activity cost pool of blending-hours included utilities to power the blender and the conveyor belt moving the blended beans from the roaster to the blender. Moving the beans in the open air allows them to cool properly and stop the roasting process. One conveyor serviced each roaster and blender pair, and if the conveyor stopped the batch could be spoiled. The combined time to move and blend the beans limits CBI's processing capacity, but the entire process consumes only six minutes, or 0.10 of an hour, per batch. The remaining time until the next batch moves along the conveyor is spent inspecting and either informing the roaster not to start the next batch or switching to another conveyor-blender pair.

During the year, CBI had budgeted to process 2,100 batches of Mocha Loa and 1,750 batches of Malaysian. Of the total blending-hours of capacity, Mocha Loa consumed 210 blending-hours (2,100 batches $\times$ 0.10 blending-hours per batch) and Malaysian 175 blending-hours (1,750 batches $\times$ 0.10 blending-hours per batch) per year. The blending activity cost rate was based on full capacity of 9,100 hours and the pro forma blending activity cost pool was $273,000. The blending activity cost rate was $30/blending-hour ($273,000 $\div$ 9,100 blending-hours). The blending activity cost assigned to Mocha Loa was $6,300 ($30/blending-hour $\times$ 210 blending-hours), and the amount assigned to Malaysian was $5,250 ($30/blending-hour $\times$ 175 blending-hours). On a cost-per-kilogram basis, the blending activity costs will be $0.0060/kg for Mocha Loa ($6,300 $\div$ 1,050,000 kg) and $0.0150/kg for Malaysian ($5,250 $\div$ 350,000 kg).

Packaging The total indirect packaging activity cost pool was budgeted at $490,000 and it takes approximately 36 seconds, or 0.01 hours/kg, to fill each package of Mocha Loa blend. It takes approximately 18 seconds, or 0.005 hours/kg, to fill each package of Malaysian blend. Each packaging process uses a different sealing method, which accounts for the time difference. CBI has six packaging machines.

Note that in the exercise of refining the cost-assignment system, this was the only unit activity cost identified. The indirect cost pool value changes as the measure of benefits, the quantity of packaging hours used, changes. CBI's budgeted capacity is 49,000 packaging hours; therefore, the activity cost rate is $10 per packaging-hour ($490,000 $\div$ 49,000 packaging hours). The total time to package Mocha Loa's 1,050,000 kg was 10,500 hours (1,050,000 kg $\times$ 0.01 packaging-hour per kg) and for Malaysian's 350,000 kg was 1,750 hours (350,000 kg $\times$ 0.005 packaging-hour per kg). The total packaging activity cost assigned to Mocha Loa was $105,000 ($10/packaging-hour $\times$ 10,500 packaging- hours) and to Malaysian was $17,500 ($10/packaging-hour $\times$ 1,750 packaging-hours). On a cost-per-kilogram basis, the packaging activity costs will be $0.1000/kg for Mocha Loa ($105,000 $\div$ 1,050,000 kg) and $0.0500/kg for Malaysian ($17,500 $\div$ 350,000 kg).

Summary Exhibit 5-4 illustrates how the budgeted amounts in the six activity cost pools are unequally shared between the two distinct blends. The calculations of these amounts were reported in Exhibit 5-3. The two direct cost pools are assigned by tracing to each distinct blend and are illustrated at the bottom of Exhibit 5-4. The activity costs pertain only to the business function of production and are in blue.

It takes a tremendous amount of information, both financial and nonfinancial, to refine this costing system to only six activity cost pools. Managers will only spend their time gathering data at this level of detail if they are convinced it is important to the company's short- and long-term success. The use of the cost hierarchy as the basis for an ABC system is a strategic decision, not an operating decision, because it affects the long-term understanding of how activities across the value chain interact to increase or decrease the costs of each unit of distinct output. Generally speaking, high activity cost rates will provide a good initial signal to managers of where to begin with cost-control efforts. Those efforts will succeed

EXHIBIT 5-4
Budgeted Activity-Based Cost Assignment at CBI for Mocha Loa and Malaysian Blends

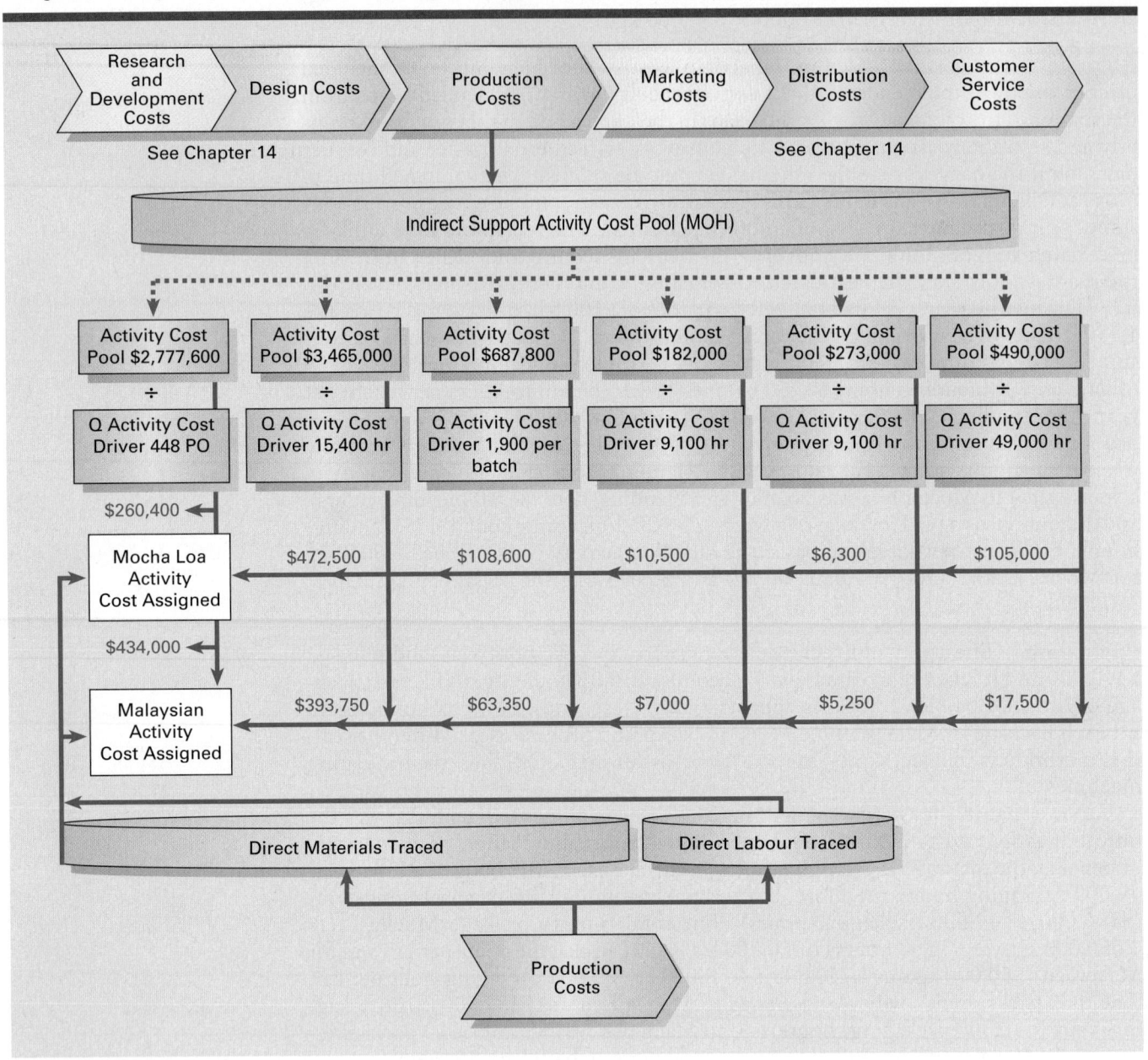

either if they reduce the activity cost rate or they decrease the volume of activity undertaken (the multiplier).

COMPARING PRICES UNDER ABC AND TRADITIONAL COSTING SYSTEMS

Exhibit 5-5 reports the difference between the cost assignment and price per kilo for Mocha Loa and Malaysian using the traditional method to the price under the ABC system. The more refined ABC system tells CBI that its Mocha Loa blend is overpriced in a very competitive market. If this is not remedied, customers could switch to a brand they perceive as being equally high in quality but of lower cost.

 The analyses show that CBI can reduce its Mocha Loa price to $9.02 and, all other things being equal, retain its 30% profit. Just as important, CBI also knows now that it is losing more than $1/kg it sells of Malaysian ($9.76 − $8.57). CBI can either increase the unit price of Malaysian to achieve its 30% markup, or leave the price as it is and be satisfied with a profit of $1.739/kg ($8.57/kg − $6.831/kg) or

EXHIBIT 5-5
CBI's Costing and Pricing Using Traditional and ABC Systems

Traditional Costing				ABC Costing		
	Costs per Unit				**Costs per Unit**	
	Mocha Loa (1)	Malaysian (2)			Mocha Loa (1)	Malaysian (2)
Direct materials (per kg)	$ 5.04	$3.84	Direct materials (per kg)		$5.0400	$3.8400
Direct manufacturing labour (per DLH)	0.36	0.36	Direct manufacturing labour (per DLH)		0.3600	0.3600
Total direct costs	5.40	4.20	Total direct costs		5.4000	4.2000
Indirect cost allocation rate per $1.00 DLH	$5.00		Activity costs			
			Purchasing		0.2480	1.2400
Indirect costs assigned (0.36 DLH × $5.00)	1.80	1.80	Materials handling		0.4500	1.1250
			Quality control		0.1034	0.1810
Total unit cost per kg	$ 7.20	$6.00	Roasting		0.0100	0.0200
Markup 30%	30.0%		Blending		0.0060	0.0150
Pro forma price per kilo			Packaging		0.1000	0.0500
(unit cost per kg ÷ 0.70)	$10.29	$8.57	Total indirect costs		0.9174	2.6310
			Total cost		6.3174	6.8310
			Markup	30.0%		
			Pro forma price per kilo			
			(unit cost per kg ÷ 0.70)		$ 9.02	$ 9.76

25.46% profit ($1.739/kg ÷ $8.57/kg). Pricing decisions can now be made with considerable assurance that a targeted (predicted) profit level will be achieved.

COMPARING ABC TO DEPARTMENT-RATE COSTING SYSTEMS

Companies often use costing systems that include some features of ABC systems (e.g., multiple cost pools, multiple cost allocation bases), but that don't emphasize individual activities. One example is a departmental costing system. In this costing system, benefits from using departmental services are shared unequally by distinct types of outputs. A refined costing system will prevent cost and price distortion and the long-run impairment of a company's profitability.

Separate indirect pools for each department are accumulated into one departmental cost pool, such as IT Services, Purchasing, or Production Quality Control. A measure of benefit is chosen as the cost allocation base. Often benefit is measured by a departmental resource used such as IT labour-hours. By dividing the departmental cost pool by the total in the cost allocation base, managers can calculate a departmental indirect cost rate. In this section, we compare ABC systems and department-rate costing systems.

In the CBI example, the entire purchasing department constituted one activity cost pool. The decision team calculated the purchasing activity cost rate by dividing total purchasing department costs by a measure of benefit, in this case purchase orders. CBI did not find it worthwhile to calculate separate activity rates within the purchasing department because the electronic, standard method to complete a PO resulted in a uniform cost per PO. It does not matter in CBI who raised the request for inputs or what the inputs were because there is no significant difference in the cost of filling the PO in a timely way.

In contrast, in the production department CBI identified different activity cost pools—for example, a materials handling cost pool and a quality control cost pool—rather than using a single production department indirect cost pool. There are two reasons for this. First, each of these activities of production incurs significant costs and consumes different common inputs. Materials handling costs are driven by the time required to move and open sacks of green coffee beans and then pour the contents onto the conveyor each time a setup changes; roasting costs are driven by the roasting time per batch. Second, the Mocha Loa and Malaysian blends do not use

Effective Cost Assignment: It's the Law

Fiduciary duty is a legal term that means managers act on behalf of the owners of assets under management control. This is the basis of a large body of business law called corporate governance.

ABC cost assignment should only be undertaken when there is adequate reason to believe the benefits will outweigh the costs for the owners of the business. One benefit of ABC systems is that they make the flow of costs more transparent, thereby exposing wasteful use of inputs and excessive costs. Identifying costs that are disproportionate to the benefit received is one step toward cost control.

Increased transparency in an internal cost control system also provides reasonable assurance that fraud and misappropriation of assets will not occur. One important task for accountants is to design internal control systems that provide this assurance. Failure to do so can result in a costly investigation and trial that may ultimately end an accountant's career.

ABC systems apply when a large proportion of activities shared unequally distinguish the costs of one output from another. In principle, the burdens and benefits of shared resources should be borne fairly rather than equally. The cost-benefit relationship exploited by the ABC system of indirect support cost pool assignment is more relevant than a cause/effect relationship. It is precisely because there is no identifiable cause/effect relationship that shared activities costs are indirect rather than direct cost pools.

Behaviourally, change is often difficult to justify and implement because it may threaten the remuneration of some managers and enhance the remuneration of others. Less resistance will arise if everyone potentially affected by change receives full information about the new ABC system. An effective response is to establish incentive plans wherein employees obtain a percentage of cost savings achieved because of their suggestions. Reducing resistance to change will not only reduce costs of implementation but improve the probability that profitability will increase.

---

resources from these two activity areas in the same proportion of available hours. Using a single activity cost driver would result in overcosting one blend and undercosting the other.

It is appropriate to use a single department indirect cost rate to allocate costs to products if:

◆ A single activity, like contacting suppliers, accounts for a material amount of the department's costs.

◆ Significant costs are incurred on different activities within a department but each activity has the same cost allocation base.

or

◆ Products use resources from the different activity areas in the same proportions.

If any one of these three conditions are true, a departmental costing system is adequate. If none of the conditions hold, emphasizing activities leads to more focused and homogeneous cost pools. This aids in identifying activity cost drivers with clearer benefit relationships to the costs incurred in the respective activity cost pools. But an ABC system is costly to design, sometimes difficult to implement, and has little relevance for companies that specialize in only one service or product.

Improved costing systems are intended to more faithfully reveal the relationships between the benefits received by distinct outputs from their unequal but shared use of common activities. Ultimately, a for-profit company succeeds if the costs of activities plus some reasonable profit are recovered through sale of these outputs to customers. But for most companies, the management team is acting on behalf of its owners. Business law requires managers to make decisions that are in the best interests of the owners. Accountants employed by a company must also comply with this fiduciary duty.

ABC: THE FOUNDATION OF ABM

Explain the benefits of activity-based costing (ABC) systems for activity-based management (ABM).

⑤

The emphasis of this chapter so far has been on how ABC systems identify preventable over- and undercosting and the mispricing of distinct outputs that occurs as a result. For CBI, it seems clear that an ABC system will help the company improve and control its profit. These profits can be reinvested in CBI to grow the company. However, if the ABC system is adopted, some measure of its benefit is required to provide essential feedback on how well the change has achieved CBI's profitability goals.

Using activity-based costing information to guide management decisions is referred to as *activity-based management (ABM)*. ABM is a strategic approach to cost control that avoids impairing the activities of customization for which customers are willing to pay. An ABC system is one building block of ABM. The second building block is the ability of managers to understand that the demand for output is central to profitability. CBI must produce blends that are desirable to its customers at a desirable price. In principle, all activities should not only add cost but also add value to outputs.

Value added is always considered from the customers' perspective. The outcome of **value-added activities** is that the costs plus some predictable profit will be fully recovered when the output is sold. Customers pay for features they perceive as desirable. In contrast, **non-value-added activities** add costs that fail to improve desirability and for which customers will not pay. ABM focuses cost control on reducing non-value-added activities. The management accountant's role is to apply the ABC system and distinguish value from non-value-added activities. Effective ABM will:

- Increase effective coordination among business function activities.
- Reduce costs of non-value-added activities.
- Improve selection of process activities to enhance profit.
- Match the company's use of resources to customer demand.
- Achieve planned growth.

Increase Effective Co-ordination among Business Function Activities   The repricing of Mocha Loa and Malaysian for CBI has already been discussed, but the company must make longer-term product decisions. Based on the information from traditional cost assignment, it appears that the more kilograms sold of Mocha Loa, the higher the revenue. This could lead CBI to spend more on marketing and advertising of Mocha Loa, anticipating it could simply increase the unit price to cover the additional cost. The cost hierarchy refinement, however, signals to CBI that the opposite is true.

Mocha Loa is already overpriced in the market, posing a threat to CBI that its customers will switch if the price is increased. Added marketing and advertising activity will be non-value added and it does not correct the basic problem of inaccurate costing and overpricing. This decision results in costs of a non-value-added activity being added to an already overpriced product.

CBI would be more successful if the management team increased revenue by reducing the unit price of Mocha Loa to stimulate higher sales volume. The team now knows it can reduce price as much as $1.27/kg and still retain its 30% gross margin. How much to reduce the price will depend on what competitors charge for coffee blends of similar quality. CBI also knows that in the long run, if the market will not accept a price increase of almost $1/kg on Malaysian, then CBI must make the hard decision to either drop this blend to retain its profit margin of 30% or reduce its profit expectations to lower than 30%.

Select Non-Value-Added Activities to Reduce Costs   The largest activity cost rate at CBI, purchasing, is very large indeed. At $6,200 per PO, this rate is almost 28 times higher than the next highest rate! This fact alone is attention-getting, and managers at CBI need to investigate ways to reduce the purchasing activity cost without impairing benefits of timely completion for users. The expensive purchasing process is unlikely to be perceived by customers as value added. Managers should focus on redesigning the purchasing process to eliminate non-value-added activities and their costs without reducing timely completion.

One question that must be asked is, given the expense of a single PO, why is an order of Malaysian only 5,000 kg while an order of Mocha Loa is 25,000 kg? Unless there would be some deterioration in quality of raw Malaysian coffee beans, then it may be less expensive to reduce the number of POs by increasing the quantity ordered each time and incur the extra inventory costs.

Select Process Activities to Enhance Value Added for Customers and Profitability
The activity cost pools were selected by CBI managers because these activities were critical to the company's success. Doing less but achieving the same outcome improves efficiency. Each activity comprised a set of related activities. Generally, streamlining a process to reduce the total number of activities or repetitions will reduce the activity cost pool. For example, the number of daily setups in the production process is quite high due to the capacity constraints imposed by the equipment. It may be worthwhile to purchase higher-capacity equipment to reduce the number of daily setup-hours and decrease the materials handling activity cost pool. This requires CBI managers to recognize that preventable redundance is non-value added to both the internal users of this common support activity and to customers.

One benefit of ABC systems of cost assignment is that only the capacity used is included in operating costs. Thus, the long-run cost of excess capacity is not assigned to current production. If managers receive bonuses for reducing the costs of existing processes, this approach provides a financial incentive to seek and implement appropriate process improvements in a timely way.

Change to one part of an internal production process often requires other changes to avoid bottlenecks in the rest of the process. It is also difficult, however, to cost-effectively match the production capacity in every stage of transformation. For example, increasing the batches blended and roasted in a specific time period may overwhelm the capacity of quality control to test each batch. While the cost of setups may decrease, cost of quality control may increase.

By inspecting Exhibit 5-5, we can see that the cost per kilogram of materials handling, the setup activity, for Mocha Loa is $0.45/kg, approximately 4.4 times higher than for quality control at only $0.1034. This gives CBI's managers important data to predict the likely outcome of any increase in quality control activity to debottleneck production. Overall, if the total cost of all value-added activities decreases when the production process is redesigned, change will help CBI grow and improve its profits.

Select Output Designs to Match Customer Perceptions of Value Added
Management can improve performance by evaluating how product and process designs affect activities and costs. Companies can then work with their customers to evaluate the costs and prices of alternative design choices. At CBI, creative design decisions that decrease the complexity of blends will affect how many types of beans are included in each blend. Each type of bean may require different roasting times, which will increase the number of setups.

If CBI used its traditional system to choose among alternative designs of their blends, the company would favour the ones that reduce direct manufacturing labour-hours the most, because the cost system sends an erroneous signal that reducing direct manufacturing labour-hours reduces overhead costs. In fact, the cost-benefit relationship between direct manufacturing labour-hours used and CBI's total overhead costs is not faithful to economic facts. Therefore, reducing direct manufacturing labour-hours would have no effect on CBI's indirect costs. Moreover, without ABC the opportunity to perceive value added from the customer's perspective is lost.

Select a Plan to Achieve Growth
Growth can be a haphazard outcome of good luck or a predictable result of good management. While a little good luck cannot hurt CBI's growth, it is not value added by management activities. Planned growth requires rigorous strategic analysis by the decision team to ensure the decisions will achieve predicted growth and profitability. An ABC system based on the careful analysis of actual activities costs improves decisions when distinct outputs used enjoy unequal benefits from shared inputs.

If Only Everything Did Not Depend on Everything Else

A tremendous benefit of refined costing systems is that they reveal the complex dependencies between customer demand and supply of distinct products and services. Successful companies match their use of value-added activity to produce outputs that customers desire and for which they will pay. Observing how types and quantities of shared support activity affect cost also clarifies how to reduce the variety of types and quantities of activity. Complexity is not the same as confusion. Instead of confusion, an ABC system, ironically, leads to clarity in understanding costs and benefits of complex sets of activities.

The cost hierarchy "chunks" financial information into one of four cost pools. The logic is simple—classify a cost according to the scope of business functions that benefit from it. Determine a common measure of benefit and develop a cost rate per unit of benefit. ABC systems are an example of the strategy of simplicity. This strategy can be applied in any business when the objective is to improve the relevance of information used to make business decisions.

Source: Mintzberg, Ahlstrand, and Lampel, *Strategy Bites Back*, (London: Prentice Hall, 2005).

The ABC system itself, augmented by ABM, will improve the value added of management activities. The team will make better decisions on how to coordinate different business function activities, identify and reduce costs of non-value-added activities, improve effectiveness of process activities, match the company's resources to customer demand, and achieve planned growth.

REFINED COSTING SYSTEMS

A **refined costing system** improves the measure of non-uniformity in the use of an organization's shared resources. Managing complex technology and producing diverse products requires committing an increasing amount of resources for various support functions, such as production scheduling, product and process design, and engineering. As the activities increase in their interdependence, companies install business software such as SAP to reconfigure activities and reduce costs. Refinements are costly because they require more data gathering and more analysis. But benefits include opportunities for improved forecasting, performance measurement, control, and a faster, more focused strategic response. At the end of the day, though, the ABC benefits must outweigh the costs of the system refinements.

ABC SYSTEMS IN MERCHANDISING AND SERVICE COMPANIES

Although many of the early examples of ABC originated in manufacturing, it can be as effectively applied in the merchandising and service areas. Merchandising companies, which resell products without changing them, such as Indigo and Amazon.com, have also implemented ABC and ABM.

The general approach to ABC in service and even non-profit organizations is very similar to the approach described in this chapter. Service and non-profit organizations also have to confront the problems of accumulating activity cost pools and identifying the cost drivers that best measure benefit or value added from sharing common resources. Companies in banking, insurance, accounting, and consulting industries have implemented ABC systems to define profitable service mixes. For example, banks combine free automated debit-card transactions with more costly wealth management advice to select customers willing to pay a premium price for this value-added service. Similarly, some of the federal government's service providers (for example, Environment Canada, the Meteorological Service, and Citizenship and Immigration) have implemented ABC and ABM.

(Try to solve this problem before examining the solution that follows.)

PROBLEM

Family Supermarkets (FS) has decided to increase the size of its St. John's store. It wants information about the profitability of individual product lines: soft drinks, fresh produce, and packaged food.

Operating personnel at FS provide the following data for each product line:

	Soft Drinks	Fresh Produce	Packaged Food
Revenue	$317,400	$840,240	$483,960
Cost of goods sold	$240,000	$600,000	$360,000
Cost of bottles returned	$ 4,800	$ 0	$ 0
Number of purchase orders placed	144	336	144
Number of deliveries received	120	876	264
Hours of shelf-stocking time	216	2,160	1,080
Items sold	50,400	441,600	122,400

FS also provides the following information for the year 2012:

Activity (1)	Description of Activity (2)	Total Costs (3)	Cost Allocation Base (4)		
Bottle returns	Returning empty bottles to store	$ 4,800	Direct tracing to soft-drink line		
Ordering	Placing orders for purchases	$ 62,400	purchase orders	=	624
Delivery	Physical delivery and receiving of merchandise	$100,800	deliveries	=	1,260
Shelf-stocking	Stocking and restocking merchandise	$ 69,120	hours stocking	=	3,456
Customer support	Assistance provided for customers	$122,880	items sold	=	614,400
Total		$360,000			

REQUIRED

①

1. FS currently allocates store support costs (all costs other than cost of goods sold) to product lines based on cost of goods sold of each product line. Calculate the operating income and operating income as a percentage of revenues for each product line.

②③④

2. If FS allocates store support costs (all costs other than cost of goods sold) to product lines using an activity-based costing (ABC) system, calculate the operating income and operating income as a percentage of revenues for each product line.

⑤

3. Comment on your answers to requirements 1 and 2.

SOLUTION

1. The following table shows the operating income and operating margin (operating income as a percentage of revenues). All store support costs (that is, costs other than cost of goods sold) are allocated to product lines using cost of goods sold of each product line as the cost allocation base. Total store support costs equal $360,000 (cost of bottles returned, $4,800 + cost of purchase orders, $62,400 + cost of deliveries, $100,800 + cost of shelf-stocking, $69,120 + cost of customer support, $122,880). If cost of goods sold is the cost allocation base, the allocation rate for store support costs = $360,000 ÷ $1,200,000 = $0.30 per dollar of cost of goods sold. To allocate support costs to each product line, FS multiplies the cost of goods sold of each product line by 0.30. Operating income for each product line is as follows:

	Soft Drinks	Fresh Produce	Packaged Food	Total
Revenue	$317,400	$840,240	$483,960	$1,641,600
Cost of goods sold	240,000	600,000	360,000	1,200,000
Store support cost ($240,000; $600,000; $360,000 × 0.30)	72,000	180,000	108,000	360,000
Total costs	312,000	780,000	468,000	1,560,000
Operating income	$ 5,400	$ 60,240	$ 15,960	$ 81,600
Operating margin (Operating income ÷ Revenue)	1.70%	7.17%	3.30%	4.97%

2. Under an ABC system, FS identifies bottle return costs as a direct cost since these costs can be traced easily to the soft drink product line. FS then calculates cost allocation rates for each activity area. The activity rates are as follows:

Activity (1)	Cost Hierarchy (2)	Total Costs (3)	Quantity of Cost Allocation Base (4)	Overhead Allocation Rate (5) = (3) ÷ (4)
Ordering	Batch level	$ 62,400	624 purchase orders	$ 100 per purchase order
Delivery	Batch level	$100,800	1,260 deliveries	$ 80 per delivery
Shelf-stocking	Unit level	$ 69,120	3,456 hours stocking	$ 20 per hour stocking
Customer support	Unit level	$122,880	614,400 items sold	$0.20 per item sold

Store support costs for each product line by activity are obtained by multiplying the total quantity of the cost allocation base for each product line by the activity cost rate. Operating income for each product line is as follows:

	Soft Drinks	Fresh Produce	Packaged Food	Total
Revenue	$317,400	$840,240	$483,960	$1,641,600
Cost of goods sold	240,000	600,000	360,000	1,200,000
Bottle-return costs	4,800	–	–	4,800
Ordering costs (144; 336; 144) PO × $100	14,400	33,600	14,400	62,400
Delivery costs (120; 876; 264) del. × $80	9,600	70,080	21,120	100,800
Shelf-stocking costs (216; 2,160; 1,080) hr × $20	4,320	43,200	21,600	69,120
Customer support costs (50,400; 441,600; 122,400) items × $0.20	10,080	88,320	24,480	122,880
Total costs	283,200	835,200	441,600	1,560,000
Operating income	$ 34,200	$ 5,040	$ 42,360	$ 81,600
Operating margin (Operating income ÷ Revenue)	10.78%	0.60%	8.75%	4.97%

3. Managers believe the ABC system is more credible than the previous costing system. It distinguishes the different types of activities at FS more precisely. It also tracks more accurately how individual product lines use their resources. Rankings of relative profitability (the percentage of operating income to revenues) of the three product lines under the previous costing system and under the ABC system are as follows:

Simple Costing System		ABC System	
1. Fresh produce	7.17%	1. Soft drinks	10.78%
2. Packaged food	3.30%	2. Packaged food	8.75%
3. Soft drinks	1.70%	3. Fresh produce	0.60%

The percentage of revenues, cost of goods sold, and activity costs for each product line are as follows:

	Soft Drinks	Fresh Produce	Packaged Food
Revenue	19.335%	51.184%	29.481%
Cost of goods sold	20.000%	50.000%	30.000%
Bottle-return costs	100.000%	0.000%	0.000%
Ordering costs	23.077%	53.846%	23.077%
Delivery costs	9.524%	69.524%	20.952%
Shelf-stocking costs	6.250%	62.500%	31.250%
Customer support costs	8.203%	71.875%	19.922%

Soft drinks consume less of all resources. Soft drinks have fewer deliveries and require less shelf-stocking than does either fresh produce or packaged food. Most major soft-drink suppliers deliver merchandise to the store shelves and stock the shelves themselves. In contrast, the fresh produce area has the most deliveries and consumes a large percentage of shelf-stocking time. It also has the highest number of individual sales items. The previous costing system assumed that each product line used the resources in each activity area in the same ratio as their respective individual cost of goods sold to total cost of goods sold ratio. Clearly, this assumption was inappropriate. The previous costing system was a classic example of broad averaging via cost smoothing.

FS managers can use the ABC information to guide decisions on how to allocate the planned increase in floor space. An increase in the percentage of space allocated to soft drinks is warranted. Note, however, that ABC information should be but one input into decisions about shelf space allocation. FS may have minimum limits on the shelf space allocated to fresh produce because of shoppers' expectations that supermarkets will carry merchandise from this product line.

Pricing decisions can also be made in a more informed way with the ABC information. For example, suppose a competitor announces a 5% reduction in soft-drink prices. Given the 10.78% margin FS currently earns on its soft-drink product line, it has flexibility to reduce prices and still make a profit on this product line. In contrast, the previous costing system erroneously implied that soft drinks only had a 1.70% margin, leaving little room to counter a competitor's pricing initiatives.

SUMMARY POINTS

The following question-and-answer format summarizes the chapter's learning outcomes. Each point presents a key question, and the guidelines are the answer to that question.

LEARNING OUTCOMES	GUIDELINES
1. When does product undercosting or product overcosting occur?	Product undercosting (overcosting) occurs when a product or service consumes a high (low) level of shared support activities but is reported to have a low (high) cost. Traditional, or peanut butter, costing is a common cause of undercosting or overcosting. This method uniformly assigns costs based on a simple average for all products. It is not effective when products obtain unequal benefit from unequal use shared inputs common to complete distinct types of products. Product cost cross-subsidization exists when one undercosted (overcosted) product results in at least one other product being overcosted (undercosted).
2. How does traditional cost assignment differ from the activities cost hierarchy?	The activities cost hierarchy separates a single total indirect cost pool into as many as four "chunks" according to the scope of benefits from the activity. The smallest scope of activity is the unit of output level and the largest is the facilities level. The second smallest is a batch level and the next largest is the product level. Traditional costing separates costs into manufacturing and non-manufacturing cost pools without regard to the scope of benefits.

3. How are cost assignment systems refined using ABC?	The refinement of cost assignment systems should only be undertaken when shared inputs give rise to indirect costs that are both significant relative to total costs and not used equally to complete a distinct type of output unit. Managers identify activities and their scope of benefits, and identify a measure of benefit from the activity common throughout its scope. The measure is called an *activity cost driver*. It reliably explains how the total activity cost pool changes when the quantity of the cost driver changes.
4. How are costs assigned using ABC?	Once the indirect activity cost pools and measures of the activity cost drivers are identified, an activity cost driver rate can be calculated. For activity cost pools at the batch, product, and facilities levels, calculating the activity cost driver rates is an intermediate step that allows costs to be assigned per batch or product or facility. The final step is to assign costs per batch, product, or facility to each unit of a distinct output.
5. How can ABC systems be used to manage better?	Activity-based management (ABM) describes management decisions based on ABC information to satisfy customers and improve profits. ABC systems are used for such management decisions as pricing, product-mix, cost reduction, process improvement, product and process redesign, and planning and managing activities.

TERMS TO LEARN

This chapter and the Glossary at the end of the book contain definitions of the following important terms:

activity (p. 152)
activity-based costing (ABC) (p. 153)
activity-based management (ABM) (p. 154)
activity cost driver (p. 153)
activity cost pool (p. 153)
activity cost rate (p. 153)
activity level (p. 153)
batch-level cost (p. 158)

cost hierarchy (p. 157)
cost plus pricing (p. 157)
cost smoothing (p. 153)
cross-subsidization (p. 154)
explanatory power (p. 153)
facility-sustaining cost (p. 157)
non-value-added activity (p. 167)
output level overcosting (p. 154)

output level undercosting (p. 154)
output unit-level cost (p. 158)
peanut butter costing (p. 153)
product-sustaining cost (p. 157)
refined costing system (p. 169)
service-sustaining cost (p. 157)
traditional costing (p. 153)
value-added activity (p. 167)

ASSIGNMENT MATERIAL

SHORT-ANSWER QUESTIONS

5-1   Define cost smoothing and describe the consequences it can have on costs.

5-2   Why should managers worry about product overcosting or undercosting?

5-3   What is costing system refinement? Describe three guidelines for such refinement.

5-4   What is an activity-based approach to refining a cost assignment system?

5-5   Describe four levels of a cost hierarchy.

5-6   Why is it important to classify costs into a cost hierarchy?

5-7   What are the key reasons for product cost differences between traditional costing systems and ABC systems?

5-8 Describe four decisions for which ABC information is useful.

5-9 "Department indirect cost rates are never activity cost rates." Do you agree? Explain.

5-10 Describe four ways that help indicate when ABC systems are likely to provide the most benefits.

5-11 What are the main costs and limitations of implementing ABC systems?

5-12 "ABC systems apply only to manufacturing companies." Do you agree? Explain.

5-13 "Activity-based costing is the wave of the present and the future. All companies should adopt it." Do you agree? Explain.

5-14 "Increasing the number of indirect cost pools is guaranteed to sizably increase the accuracy of product or service costs." Do you agree? Why?

5-15 The controller of a retailer has just had a $50,000 request to implement an ABC system quickly turned down. A senior vice-president involved in rejecting the request noted, "Given a choice, I will always prefer a $50,000 investment in improving things a customer sees or experiences, such as our shelves or our store layout. How does a customer benefit by our spending $50,000 on a supposedly better accounting system?" How should the controller respond?

EXERCISES

5-16 Terminology.

activity-based costing system (ABC)	batch	activity cost driver
activity cost pools	output	cross-subsization
non-value-added activity	peanut butter	product (or service)
refinement	value-added activity	facility sustaining
activity-based management	cost plus	

REQUIRED

Select the terms from the above list to complete the following sentences.

One common _____ to a traditional or _____ _____ costing system is called an _____-_____ _____ (___) system. The single MOH cost pool is separated into different _____ ___ _____ distinguished from one another by their measure of benefits provided, or the _____ ____ _____. Benefits provided unequally to distinct types of outputs provide value added to customers, for which customers are willing to pay. This is the basic concept that guides the approach to cost reduction and control called _____-_____ _____(___). The management team identifies and eliminates ___-_____ _____ and its costs and reorganizes the _____-_____ _____ to minimize costs. There are four levels of activities in a cost hierarchy. From narrowest to broadest in scope they are _____, _____, _____ (or _____), and _____-_____ cost.

When a management team fails to develop a cost management system that reports faithfully the unequal benefits (and costs) of value-added activities there is a high risk of mispricing distinct types of outputs. If managers use _____-_____ pricing, an overcosted output will be priced too high and an undercosted product will be priced too low relative to the economic value added. The result is preventable _____-_____ of costs of the lower-priced by the higher-priced product.

5-17 **Cost hierarchy.** Teledor Inc. manufactures boomboxes (music systems with radio, MP3, and compact disc players) for different well-known companies. The boomboxes differ significantly in their complexity and the batch sizes in which they are manufactured. The following costs were incurred in 2012:

a. Indirect manufacturing labour costs such as supervision that supports direct manufacturing labour, $1,200,000.

b. Procurement costs of placing purchase orders, receiving materials, and paying suppliers that are related to the number of purchase orders placed, $600,000.

c. Cost of indirect materials, $350,000.

d. Costs incurred to set up machines each time a different product needs to be manufactured, $700,000.

e. Designing processes, drawing process charts, making engineering process changes for products, $900,000.

f. Machine-related overhead costs such as amortization, maintenance, production engineering, $1,200,000. These resources are related to the activity of running the machines.

g. Plant management, plant rent, and insurance, $950,000.

REQUIRED

1. Classify each of the preceding costs as output unit-level, batch-level, product-sustaining, or facility-sustaining. Explain your answers.

2. Consider two boomboxes made by Teledor Inc. One boombox is complex to make and is made in many batches. The other boombox is simple to make and is made in a few batches. Suppose that Teledor needs the same number of machine-hours to make either boombox. If Teledor allocated all overhead costs using machine-hours as the only allocation base, how, if at all, would the boomboxes be miscosted? Briefly explain why.

3. How is the cost hierarchy helpful to Teledor in managing its business?

5-18 Cost hierarchy classification. (J. Watson) The following outlines a number of activities related to operations at Nordan Manufacturing Ltd.:

a. Engineers design new products.
b. Production workers set up machines.
c. Completed goods are inspected for quality assurance.
d. Direct materials are moved from inventory to the production line.
e. Raw materials are received from the supplier.
f. Regular equipment maintenance is performed.
g. The inventory management software is updated.

REQUIRED
1. Classify each of the preceding activities as output unit-level, batch-level, product-sustaining, or facility-sustaining. Explain your answers.
2. Identify a possible appropriate cost driver for each of the activities listed.

5-19 Apply the logic of an ABC cost hierarchy. Huey Parker produces mathematical and financial calculators. Data related to the two products are presented below.

2. $6 per machine hour

	Mathematical	Financial
Annual production in units	50,000	100,000
Direct materials costs	$180,000	$360,000
Direct manufacturing labour costs	$ 60,000	$120,000
Direct manufacturing labour-hours	2,500	5,000
Machine hours	25,000	50,000
Number of production runs	50	50
Inspection hours	1,000	500

Both products pass through Department 1 and Department 2. The departments' combined manufacturing overhead costs are:

	Total
Machining costs	$450,000
Setup costs	144,000
Inspection costs	126,000

REQUIRED
1. Compute the manufacturing overhead cost for each product.
2. Compute the manufacturing cost for each product.

5-20 Plantwide indirect cost rates. Automotive Products (AP) designs, manufactures, and sells automotive parts. Actual variable manufacturing overhead costs for 2012 were $308,600. AP's simple costing system allocates variable manufacturing overhead to its three customers based on machine hours and prices its contracts based on full costs. One of its customers has regularly complained of being charged non-competitive prices, so AP's controller, Devon Smith, realizes that it is time to examine the consumption of resources more closely. AP has three main operating departments: design, engineering, and production.

2. Total variable MOH, $308,600

♦ Design—the design of parts, using state-of-the-art, computer-aided design (CAD) equipment.
♦ Engineering—the prototyping of parts and testing of their specifications.
♦ Production—the manufacture of parts.

Interviews with the department personnel and examination of time records yield the following detailed information:

Department	Cost Driver	Variable MOH in 2012	Use of Cost Drivers by Customer		
			United Motors	Holden Motors	Leland Motors
Design	CAD design hours	$ 39,000	110	200	80
Engineering	Engineering hours	29,600	70	60	240
Production	Machine hours	240,000	120	2,800	1,080
Total		$308,600			

REQUIRED

1. Using the simple costing system, compute the plantwide variable manufacturing overhead rate for 2012 and the variable manufacturing overhead allocated to each contract in 2012.
2. Compute the variable manufacturing overhead rate for 2012 and the variable manufacturing overhead allocated to each contract in 2012 using department-based variable overhead rates.
3. Comment on your answers in requirements 1 and 2. Which customer do you think was complaining about being overcharged in the simple system? If the new department-based rates are used to price contracts, which customer(s) will be unhappy? How would you respond to these concerns?
4. How else might AP use the information available from its department-by-department analysis of variable manufacturing overhead costs?
5. AP's managers are wondering if they should further refine the department-by-department costing system into an ABC system by identifying different activities within each department. Under what conditions would it not be worthwhile to further refine the department costing system into an ABC system?

2. Price of floor model, $89.60

5-21 ABC, product cross-subsidization. (J. Watson) Noble Industries manufactures two models of tiffany-style lamps, a table-top model and a floor model. Summary data for the two products for the most recent fiscal year showed the following:

	Table-Top Model	Floor Model
Unit Costs:		
Direct material	$28	$34
Direct labour (@ $14/hour)	7	14
Manufacturing overhead	8	16

Under the company's current costing, manufacturing overhead is allocated on the basis of direct labour-hours. The company president is concerned that the use of a single overhead cost pool does not result in accurate costing of the two product lines and is wondering whether the company should implement activity-based costing (ABC).

The overhead for the year has been estimated at a total of $1,600,000. Further analysis of the overhead costs resulted in the following classification:

Materials handling	$450,000
Setups	750,000
General factory overhead	400,000

The company has identified the appropriate cost driver for each activity. Materials handling will be allocated using number of parts, setups will be allocated based on number of setups, and general factory overhead will be allocated using direct labour-hours. The company has budgeted for the production of 40,000 units of the table-top model and 80,000 units of the floor model. Consumption of the cost drivers, based on this production volume, is estimated as follows:

Cost Driver	Table-Top Model	Floor Model	Total
Number of parts	160,000	240,000	400,000
Number of setups	500	250	750
Direct labour-hours	20,000	80,000	100,000

The company currently prices its products by adding a 40% markup to the total manufacturing cost.

1. Compute the per-unit cost and selling price of both models of lamps based on the current costing system.
2. Compute the per-unit cost and selling price of both models of lamps using an ABC costing system.
3. Compare and briefly outline the significance of your results from requirements 1 and 2.

5-22 **Explain undercosting and overcosting of services.** The Wolfson Group (WG) provides tax advice to multinational firms. WG charges clients for (a) direct professional time (at an hourly rate), and (b) support services (at 30% of the direct professional costs billed). The three professionals in WG and their rates per professional hour are as follows:

1. WG amount billed to Tokyo Enterprises, $6,802

Professional	Billing Rate per Hour
Myron Wolfson	$600
Naomi Ku	144
John Anderson	96

WG has just prepared the May 2012 bills for two clients. The hours of professional time spent on each client are as follows:

	Hours per Client	
Professional	Winnipeg Dominion	Tokyo Enterprises
Wolfson	15	2
Ku	3	8
Anderson	22	30
Total	40	40

REQUIRED

1. What amounts did WG bill to Winnipeg Dominion and Tokyo Enterprises for May 2012?
2. Suppose support services were billed at $60 per professional labour-hour (instead of 30% of professional labour costs). How would this change affect the amounts WG billed to the two clients for May 2012? Comment on the differences between the amounts billed in requirements 1 and 2.
3. How would you determine whether professional labour costs or professional labour-hours is the more appropriate allocation base for WG's support services?

5-23 **Contrast the logic of two cost assignment systems.** Niagara Winery makes two different grades of wine—regular wines and specialty wines. Recently, Niagara has shown small profits on its regular wines and large profits on its specialty wines. As a result, management is considering getting out of the regular wine business and concentrating on specialty wines. This is a difficult decision because Niagara had been very profitable in regular wines, its original business. In fact, the profitability of regular wines dipped substantially only after Niagara got into the specialty wine business. Before making a decision, Niagara wants to be sure that it understands what it costs to make and sell the regular and specialty wines. This question focuses on costs in the distribution area.

2. b. Distribution cost per regular case, $11.10

Niagara distributes the regular wines and the specialty wines through completely different distribution channels. It distributes 120,000 cases of the regular wines through 10 provincial distributors and 80,000 cases of the specialty wines through 30 specialty distributors. Niagara incurs $2,636,000 in distribution costs. Under its existing costing system, Niagara allocates distribution costs to products based on cases shipped.

To understand better the demands on its resources in the distribution area, Niagara identifies three activities and related activity costs:

1. Promotional activity including advertising and point-of-sales material at each distributor. Niagara estimates it incurs $9,600 per distributor.
2. Order handling costs including costs to confirm and input the order into the order-entry system, set aside the correct number of cases, organize shipment and delivery, verify order packing, ensure delivery, send invoices, and follow up for payments. Niagara estimates costs of $360 for performing all the activities pertaining to each order. Niagara's records show that distributors of regular wine placed an average of 10 orders per year, while distributors of specialty wine placed an average of 20 orders per year.
3. Distribution costs of $10 per case for freight.

1. Calculate the total distribution costs and distribution cost per case for the regular wine and the specialty wine using Niagara's existing costing system.
2. a. For each activity, classify the cost of the activity as an output unit-level, batch-level, product-sustaining, service-sustaining, or facility-sustaining cost. Explain your answers.

   b. Calculate the total distribution costs and distribution cost per case for the regular wine and the specialty wine using Niagara's activity-based costing (ABC) system.
3. Explain the cost differences and the accuracy of the product costs calculated using the existing and the ABC systems. How might Niagara's management use the information from the ABC system to manage its business better?

5-24 **Allocation of costs to activities, unused capacity.** Harmon Academy, a private school, serves 500 students: 200 in the middle school (grades 6 to 8) and 300 in the high school (grades 9 to 12). Each school group has its own assistant principal, and there is one principal, Brian Smith, for the academy. For any single student, almost all of Harmon's costs are indirect. Harmon currently has five indirect cost categories, which are listed in the following table. Smith wants to develop an activity-based costing system for the school. He identifies four activities—academic instruction, administration, sports training, and community relationships—related to the educational enterprise.

1. Overall cost, $15,600 per student.

Smith and his team identify number of students as the cost driver of academic instruction and administration costs, and the number of team sports offered by the school as the driver of sports training costs. The cost of maintaining community relationships—dealing with the town council and participating in local activities—is a facility-sustaining cost that the school has to incur each year. The table shows the percentage of costs in each line item used by each activity.

Percentage of Costs Used by Each Activity

Indirect Cost	Academic Instruction	Administration	Sports Training	Community Relationships	2012 Expenditures
Teachers' salaries/benefits	60%	20%	8%	12%	$4,000,000
Principals' salaries and benefits	10%	60%	5%	25%	400,000
Facilities	35%	15%	45%	5%	2,600,000
Office staff salaries and benefits	5%	60%	10%	25%	300,000
Sports program staff salaries and benefits	35%	10%	45%	10%	500,000

REQUIRED

1. What is the overall cost of educating each student? Of this cost, what percentage is the cost of academic instruction? Of administration?
2. Smith is dismayed at the high cost of sports training. Further examination reveals that $300,000 of those costs are for ice hockey, a sport pursued by a total of 40 students. What would be the overall cost of educating each student if the ice hockey program is eliminated and its cost saved?
3. For the 2013 school year, Harmon charges an annual fee of $1,000 for any student who wants to play ice hockey. As a result, 10 of the less-motivated students drop the sport. Assuming the costs of the school in 2013 are the same as in 2012, what is the overall cost of educating each student in 2013?
4. Consider the costs of the academic instruction activity and assume they are fixed in the short run. At these costs, Harmon could serve 600 students. What is the cost of the academic instruction resources used by Harmon's current 500 students? What is the cost of unused academic instruction capacity? What actions can Smith take to reduce the cost of academic instruction per student in the short run? In the long run?

1. Operating income increase, $190,000

5-25 **Special order, activity-based costing.** (CMA, adapted) The Medal Plus Company manufactures medals for winners of athletic events and other contests. Its manufacturing plant has the capacity to produce 12,000 medals each month; current production and sales are 9,000 medals per month. The company normally charges $200 per medal. Cost information for the current activity level is as follows:

Variable costs (vary with units produced):		
Direct materials		$ 360,000
Direct labour		405,000
Variable costs (vary with number of batches):		
Setups, materials handling, quality control		126,000*
Fixed manufacturing costs		325,000
Fixed marketing costs		224,000
Total costs		$1,440,000

*Costs of $126,000 are based on 180 batches at $700 per batch

Medal Plus has just received a special one-time-only order for 2,500 medals at $168 per medal. Accepting the special order would not affect the company's regular business. Medal Plus makes medals for its existing customers in batch sizes of 50 medals (180 batches × 50 medals per batch = 9,000 medals). The special order requires Medal Plus to make the medals in 25 batches of 100 each.

REQUIRED
1. Should Medal Plus accept this special order? Explain briefly.
2. Suppose plant capacity was only 10,000 medals instead of 12,000 medals each month. The special order must either be taken in full or rejected totally. Should Medal Plus accept the special order?
3. As in requirement 1, assume that monthly capacity is 12,000 medals. Medal Plus is concerned that if it accepts the special order, its existing customers will immediately demand a price discount of $11 in the month in which the special order is being filled. They would argue that Medal Plus's capacity costs are now being spread over more units and that existing customers should get the benefit of these lower costs. Should Medal Plus accept the special order under these conditions? Show all calculations.

5-26 **ABC, product cost cross-subsidization.** PEI Potatoes processes potatoes into potato cuts at its highly automated plant. For many years, it processed potatoes for only the retail consumer market where it had a superb reputation for quality. Recently, it started selling potato cuts to the institutional market, which includes hospitals, cafeterias, and university dormitories. Its penetration into the institutional market has been slower than predicted.

1. Current cost, $1.548 per kg

PEI's existing costing system has a single direct cost category (direct materials, which are the raw potatoes) and a single indirect cost pool (production support). Support costs are allocated on the basis of kilograms of potato cuts processed. Support costs include packaging material. The 2012 total actual costs for producing 1,000,000 kilograms of potato cuts (900,000 for the retail market and 100,000 for the institutional market) are:

Direct materials used	$ 250,000
Production support	1,298,000

The existing costing system does not distinguish between potato cuts produced for the retail or the institutional markets.

At the end of 2012, PEI unsuccessfully bid for a large institutional contract. Its bid was reported to be 30% above the winning bid. This came as a shock, as PEI included only a minimum profit margin on its bid. Moreover, the PEI plant was widely acknowledged as the most efficient in the industry.

As part of its lost contract bid review process, PEI decided to explore several ways of refining its costing system. First, it identified that $260,000 of the $1,298,000 pertains to packaging materials that could be traced to individual jobs ($238,000 for retail and $22,000 for institutional). These will now be classified as a direct material. The $250,000 of direct materials used were classified as $225,000 for retail and $25,000 for institutional. Second, it used activity-based costing (ABC) to examine how the two products (retail potato cuts and institutional potato cuts) used the support area differently. The finding was that three activity areas could be distinguished and that different usage occurred in two of these three areas. The indirect cost per kilogram of finished product at each activity area is as follows:

Activity Area	Retail Potato Cuts	Institutional Potato Cuts
Cleaning	$0.18	$0.18
Cutting	0.30	0.20
Packaging labour	0.60	0.28

There was no beginning or ending amount of any inventory (materials, work-in-process, or finished goods).

1. Using the current costing system, what is the cost per kilogram of potato cuts produced by PEI?
2. Using the refined costing system, what is the cost per kilogram of (a) retail market potato cuts, and (b) institutional market potato cuts?
3. Comment on the cost differences shown between the two costing systems in requirements 1 and 2. How might PEI use the information in requirement 2 to make better decisions?

Chain 1 contribution to profit, $4,200

5-27 **ABC, wholesale, customer profitability.** Ames Wholesalers sells furniture items to four department-store chains. Mr. Ames commented, "We apply ABC to determine profit line profitability. The same ideas apply to customer profitability, and we should find out our customer profitability as well." Ames Wholesalers sends catalogues to the corporate purchasing departments on a monthly basis. The customers are entitled to return unsold merchandise within a six-month period from the purchase date and receive a full purchase-price refund. The following data were collected from last year's operations:

	Chain 1	Chain 2	Chain 3	Chain 4
Gross sales	$50,000	$30,000	$100,000	$70,000
Sales returns:				
Number of items	100	26	60	40
Amount	$10,000	$ 5,000	$ 7,000	$ 6,000
Number of orders:				
Regular	40	150	50	70
Rush	10	50	10	30

Ames has calculated the following activity rates:

Activity	Cost Driver Rate
Regular order processing	$20 per regular order
Rush order processing	$100 per rush order
Returned items processing	$10 per item
Catalogues and customer support	$1,000 per customer

REQUIRED

Determine the contribution to profit from each chain last year. Cost of goods sold is 80% of net sales. Comment on your solution.

1. MOH allocation rate for equipment setup, $550 per setup

5-28 **ABC, product line costing.** (J. Watson) PTech Ltd. manufactures two models of cordless phones. The Family Friend model has features designed for a multiple-user family, including the ability to have multiple ringtones and caller ID. The Office Assistant model is designed for use in home offices. Data regarding the two product lines are as follows:

	Family Friend	Office Assistant
Expected production	50,000 units	150,000 units
Direct material cost	$12.14 per unit	$28.64 per unit
Direct labour cost	$10.86 per unit	$10.86 per unit

PTech is considering implementing an activity-based costing (ABC) system in its plant and has identified four primary activities. Data on these activities are as follows:

	Family Friend	Office Assistant	Budgeted Cost
Equipment setup	50 setups	30 setups	$ 44,000
Machine processing	30,000 machine-hours	220,000 machine-hours	$875,000
Quality control	5,000 inspection-hours	10,000 inspection-hours	$630,000
Packaging/shipping	125 shipments	75 shipments	$ 80,000

REQUIRED

1. Calculate the manufacturing overhead allocation rate for each activity using ABC.
2. Compute the unit cost of each model of phone using ABC.
3. Assume the company currently allocates overhead on the basis of direct labour costs. Compute the unit cost of each model of phone using this method.
4. Compare the unit costs of each model calculated in requirements 2 and 3. Comment on your results.

5-29 ABC, product costing at banks, cross-subsidization. First International Bank (FIB) is examining the profitability of its Premier Account, a combined savings and chequing account. Depositors receive a 6% annual interest rate on their average deposit. FIB earns an interest rate spread of 2.5% (the difference between the rate at which it lends money and the rate it pays depositors) by lending money for residential home loan purposes at 8.5%. Thus, FIB would gain $250 on the interest spread if a depositor has an average Premier Account balance of $10,000 in 2012 ($10,000 × 2.5% = $250).

1. 2012 profitability of Robinson account, $321.90 operating loss

The Premier Account allows depositors unlimited use of services such as deposits, withdrawals, chequing account, and foreign currency drafts. Depositors with Premier Account balances of $2,500 or more receive unlimited free use of services. Depositors with minimum balances of less than $2,500 pay a $35 monthly service fee for their Premier Account.

FIB recently conducted an activity-based costing study of its services. It assessed the following costs for six individual services. The use of these services in 2012 by three Premier Account customers is as follows:

	ABC Cost per Transaction	Account Usage		
		Robinson	Skerrett	Farrel
Deposits/withdrawals with teller	$ 4.00	45	55	10
Deposits/withdrawals at ATM	1.20	12	24	18
Prearranged monthly deposit/withdrawal	0.80	0	15	60
Cheques written	11.25	10	5	4
Foreign currency drafts	12.50	4	1	7
Account balance inquiries	2.50	12	20	11
Average cash balance		$2,600	$1,200	$40,000

Assume Robinson and Farrel always maintain a balance above $2,500 while Skerrett always has a balance below $2,500 in 2012.

REQUIRED

1. Compute the 2012 profitability of the Robinson, Skerrett, and Farrell Premier Accounts at FIB.
2. What evidence is there of cross-subsidization across Premier Accounts? Why might FIB worry about this cross-subsidization if the Premier Account product offering is profitable as a whole?
3. What changes at FIB would you recommend for its Premier Account?

5-30 ABC, costs of quality. (J. Watson) Stanford Industries currently uses a normal job-costing system with a single overhead cost pool. It supplies parts to the aeronautic industry and, as a result, quality control is paramount. It currently applies the indirect costs of quality control on the basis of direct labour cost at a rate of 150%. Most of the company's work is awarded by bidding on cost-plus contracts. Recently, Stanford has come under increasing pressure to justify its costs. It is concerned that its single allocation rate may be distorting some of its product bids.

1. a. Overhead allocated to contract, $700,500

In an analysis of its quality-control costs, it has determined that there are four activities, and it has determined the following cost drivers and rates based on annual projections:

Activity	Cost Driver	Activity Rate
Incoming materials testing and inspection	Number of types of part	$36 per type
In-process testing and inspection	Number of units produced	$6 per unit produced
Final product testing and inspection	Number of units inspected	$25 per unit inspected
Testing supplies	Direct materials (DM) cost	30% of DM cost

Stanford has decided to review one of its recently completed contracts. Direct labour on the job was $467,000 and the direct material cost was $392,000. A review of the job's activities showed that:

◆ 50 different types of parts were used.
◆ A total of 40,000 units were produced.
◆ 30% of all units produced were inspected upon completion.

REQUIRED

1. Calculate the amount of overhead that would be allocated to the contract:
   a. Using the current costing system that allocates overhead on the basis of direct labour cost.
   b. Using an ABC system.
2. Do you recommend a switch to ABC? Why or why not?

PROBLEMS

5-31 Job costing with single direct-cost category, single indirect-cost pool, law firm. Wigan
Associates is a recently formed law partnership. Ellery Hanley, the managing partner of
Wigan Associates, has just finished a tense phone call with Martin Offiah, president of Widnes
Coal. Offiah complained about the price Wigan charged for some legal work done for
Widnes Coal.

Hanley also received a phone call from its only other client (St. Helen's Glass), who said it
was very pleased with both the quality of the work and the price charged on its most recent case.

Wigan Associates operates at capacity and uses a cost-based approach to pricing
(billing) each job. Currently it uses a single direct-cost category (for professional labour-
hours) and a single indirect-cost pool (general support). Indirect costs are allocated to cases
on the basis of professional labour-hours per case. The case files show the following:

	Widnes Coal	St. Helen's Glass
Professional labour	104 hours	96 hours

Professional labour costs at Wigan Associates are $70 an hour. Indirect costs are allo-
cated to cases at $105 an hour. Total indirect costs in the most recent period were $21,000.

REQUIRED
1. Why is it important for Wigan Associates to understand the costs associated with individual cases?
2. Compute the costs of the Widnes Coal and St. Helen's Glass cases using Wigan's simple
   costing system.

5-32 Job costing with multiple direct-cost categories, single indirect-cost pool, law firm
(continuation of 5-31). Hanley asks his assistant to collect details on those costs included in
the $21,000 indirect-cost pool that can be traced to each individual case. After further analy-
sis, Wigan is able to reclassify $14,000 of the $21,000 as direct costs:

Other Direct Costs	Widnes Coal	St. Helen's Glass
Research support labour	$1,600	$ 3,400
Computer time	500	1,300
Travel and allowances	600	4,400
Telephones/faxes	200	1,000
Photocopying	250	750
Total	$3,150	$10,850

Hanley decides to calculate the costs of each case had Wigan used six direct-cost pools
and a single indirect-cost pool. The single indirect-cost pool would have $7,000 of costs and
would be allocated to each case using the professional labour-hours base.

REQUIRED
1. What is the revised indirect cost allocation rate per professional labour-hour for Wigan
   Associates when total indirect costs are $7,000?
2. Compute the costs of the Widnes and St. Helen's cases if Wigan Associates had used its
   refined costing system with multiple direct-cost categories and one indirect-cost pool.
3. Compare the costs of the Widnes and St. Helen's cases in requirement 2 with those in
   requirement 2 of Problem 5-31. Comment on the results.

5-33 Job costing with multiple direct-cost categories, multiple indirect-cost pools, law firm
(continuation of 5-31 and 5-32). Wigan Associates has two classifications of professional staff—
partners and managers. Hanley asks his assistant to examine the relative use of partners and managers on the recent Widnes Coal and St. Helen's cases. The Widnes case used 24 partner-hours
and 80 manager-hours. The St. Helen's case used 56 partner-hours and 40 manager-hours.

Hanley decides to examine how the use of separate direct-cost and indirect-cost pools
for partners and managers would have affected the costs of the Widnes and St. Helen's cases.
Indirect costs in each cost pool would be allocated based on total hours of that category of
professional labour.

The rates per category of professional labour are as follows:

Category of Professional Labour	Direct Cost per Hour	Calculation	Indirect Cost per Hour
Partner	$100.00	$4,600/80 hours	$57.50
Manager	$ 50.00	$2,400/120 hours	$20.00

- ③ 2. Widnes Coal costs, $18,200
- ④ 1. Revised indirect cost-allocation rate, $35 per professional labour-hour
- ⑤ Widnes Coal costs, $12,530

182 | CHAPTER 5

Compute the costs of the Widnes and St. Helen's cases with Wigan Associates' further refined system, with multiple direct-cost categories and multiple indirect-cost pools.

5-34 Contrast the logic of two cost assignment systems. Halifax Test Laboratories does heat testing (HT) and stress testing (ST) on materials. Under its current costing system, Halifax aggregates all operating costs of $1,440,000 into a single overhead cost pool. Halifax calculates a rate per test-hour of $18 ($1,440,000 ÷ 80,000 total test-hours). HT uses 50,000 test-hours and ST uses 30,000 test-hours. Gary Celeste, Halifax's controller, believes that there is enough variation in test procedures and cost structures to establish separate costing and billing rates. The market for test services is very competitive, and without this information, any miscosting and mispricing could cause Halifax to lose business. Celeste breaks down Halifax's costs into four activity-cost categories.

2. Cost of heat testing, $20.16 per hour

1. Direct labour costs, $288,000. These costs can be directly traced to HT, $216,000, and ST, $72,000.
2. Equipment-related costs (rent, maintenance, energy, and so on), $480,000. These costs are allocated to HT and ST based on test-hours.
3. Setup costs, $420,000. These costs are allocated to HT and ST based on the number of setup hours required. HT requires 13,500 setup-hours and ST requires 4,000 setup-hours.
4. Costs of designing tests, $252,000. These costs are allocated to HT and ST based on the time required to design the tests. HT requires 2,800 hours and ST requires 1,400 hours.

REQUIRED

1. Classify each of the activity costs as output unit-level, batch-level, product- or service-sustaining, or facility-sustaining. Explain your answers.
2. Calculate the cost per test-hour for HT and ST using activity-based costing (ABC). Explain briefly the reasons why these numbers differ from the $18 per test-hour that Halifax had calculated using its existing costing system.
3. Explain the cost differences and the accuracy of the product costs calculated using the existing and the ABC systems. How might Halifax's management use the cost hierarchy and ABC information to manage its business better?

5-35 Use ABC systems for ABM. Family Supermarkets (FS) found that its ABC analysis (see p. 170) provided important insights. FS extends the analysis to cover three more product lines: baked goods, milk and fruit juice, and frozen products. It identifies four activities and activity cost rates for each activity as:

2. Operating margin percentage for baked goods, 13.33%

Ordering	$120 per purchase order
Delivery and receipt of merchandise	$96 per delivery
Shelf-stocking	$24 per hour
Customer support and assistance	$0.24 per item sold

The revenues, cost of goods sold, store support costs, and activity area usage of the three product lines are as follows:

	Baked Goods	Milk and Fruit Juice	Frozen Products
Financial data:			
Revenues	$68,400	$75,600	$62,400
Cost of goods sold	45,600	56,400	42,000
Store support	13,680	16,920	12,600
Activity area usage (cost driver):			
Ordering (purchase orders)	30	25	13
Delivery (deliveries)	98	36	28
Shelf-stocking (hours)	183	166	24
Customer support (items sold)	15,500	20,500	7,900

There are no bottle returns for any of these three product lines.

REQUIRED

1. Use the previous costing system (support costs allocated to products at the rate of 30% of cost of goods sold) to compute a product line profitability report for FS.
2. Use the ABC system (ordering at $120 per purchase order, delivery at $96 per delivery, shelf-stocking at $24 per hour, and customer support at $0.24 per item sold) to compute a product line profitability report for FS.
3. What new insights does the ABC system in requirement 2 provide to FS managers?

④ ⑤

1. Budgeted cost for service,
$56.16 per X-ray

5-36 Department and activity cost rates, service sector. Radhika's Radiology Centre (RRC) performs X-rays, ultrasounds, CT scans, and MRIs. RRC has developed a reputation as a top radiology centre in the area. RRC has achieved this status because it constantly re-examines its processes and procedures. RRC has been using a single, facility-wide overhead allocation rate. The VP of Finance believes that RRC can make better process improvements if it uses more disaggregated cost information. She says, "We have state-of-the-art medical imaging technology. Can't we have state-of-the-art accounting technology?"

The following budgeted information is available:

Radhika's Radiology Centre
Budgeted Information
For the Year Ending May 30, 2013

	X-Rays	Ultrasound	CT Scan	MRI	Total
Technician labour	$ 61,440	$105,600	$ 96,000	$ 105,000	$ 368,040
Amortization	32,240	268,000	439,000	897,500	1,636,740
Materials	22,080	16,500	24,000	31,250	93,830
Administration					20,610
Maintenance					247,320
Sanitation					196,180
Utilities					134,350
Totals	$115,760	$390,100	$559,000	$1,033,750	$2,697,070
Number of procedures	3,840	4,400	3,000	2,500	
Minutes to clean after each procedure	5	5	15	35	
Minutes for each procedure	5	15	20	45	

RRC operates at capacity. The proposed allocation bases for overhead are as follows:

Administration	Number of procedures
Maintenance (including parts)	Capital cost of equipment (amortization)
Sanitation	Total cleaning minutes
Utilities	Total procedure minutes

REQUIRED

1. Calculate the budgeted cost per service for X-rays, ultrasounds, CT scans, and MRIs using the direct technician labour as the cost allocation base.
2. Calculate the budgeted cost per service for X-rays, ultrasounds, CT scans, and MRIs if RRC allocated overhead costs using activity-based costing (ABC).
3. Explain how the disaggregation of information could be helpful to RRC's intention to continuously improve its services.

⑤

1. General supermarket chains gross margin percentage, 2.91%

5-37 Activity-based costing, merchandising. Pharmacare Inc. specializes in the distribution of pharmaceutical products. Pharmacare operates at capacity and has three main market segments:

a. General supermarket chains
b. Drugstore chains
c. "Mom and Pop" single-store pharmacies

Rick Flair, the new controller of Pharmacare, reported the following data for August 2012:

	General Supermarket Chains	Drugstore Chains	"Mom and Pop" Single Stores	Pharmacare
Revenues	$3,708,000	$3,150,000	$1,980,000	$8,838,000
Cost of goods sold	3,600,000	3,000,000	1,800,000	8,400,000
Gross margin	$ 108,000	$ 150,000	$ 180,000	438,000
Other operating costs				301,080
Operating income				$ 136,920

For many years, Pharmacare has used gross margin percentage [(Revenue – Cost of goods sold) ÷ Revenue] to evaluate the relative profitability of its different groupings of customers (distribution outlets).

Flair recently attended a seminar on activity-based costing (ABC) and decides to consider using it at Pharmacare. Flair meets with all the key managers and many staff members. People generally agree that there are five key activity areas at Pharmacare:

Activity Area	Cost Driver
Order processing	Number of customer purchase orders
Line-item processing	Number of line items ordered by customers
Delivering to stores	Number of store deliveries
Cartons shipped to store	Number of cartons shipped
Stocking of customer store shelves	Hours of shelf-stocking

Each customer order consists of one or more line items. A line item represents a single product (such as Extra-Strength Tylenol Tablets). Each product line item is delivered in one or more separate cartons. Each store delivery entails the delivery of one or more cartons of products to a customer. Pharmacare's staff stacks cartons directly onto display shelves in customers' stores. Currently, there is no additional charge to the customer for shelf-stocking, and not all customers use Pharmacare for this activity. The level of each activity in the three market segments and the total cost incurred for each activity in 2012 are shown below:

Activity	General Supermarket Chains	Drugstore Chains	"Mom and Pop" Single Stores	Total Cost of Activity in 2012
Number of orders processed	140	360	1,500	$80,000
Number of line items ordered	1,960	4,320	15,000	$63,840
Number of store deliveries made	120	360	1,000	$71,000
Number of cartons shipped to stores	36,000	24,000	16,000	$76,000
Shelf stocking (hours)	360	180	100	$10,240

REQUIRED

1. Compute the August 2012 gross margin percentage for each of Pharmacare's three market segments.
2. Compute the August 2012 per-unit cost driver rate for each of the five activity areas.
3. Use the activity-based costing (ABC) information to allocate the $301,080 of "other operating costs" to each of the market segments. Compute the operating income for each market segment.
4. Comment on the results. What new insights are available with the activity-based information?

5-38 ABC, product cross-subsidization. Cartwright Ltd. manufactures two models of saddles, the Jordan and the Shenandoah. The Jordan is a more basic model and sells for $750. The Shenandoah is a professional-model saddle and sells for $1,600. At the beginning of the year, the following budgeted data were available:

1. Cost of Jordan, $163.86 per unit

	Jordan	Shenandoah
Expected production (units)	15,000	5,000
Machine time (hours)	2,000	2,000
Direct material unit cost	$ 100	$ 200
Direct labour-hours	30,000	30,000
Receiving (number of orders processed)	150	650
Setups (number of setups)	15	100
Direct labour average wage rate (per hour)	$ 20	$ 20
Purchasing (number of requisitions)	50	110
Inspection (% of units inspected)	10%	20%
Maintenance hours	450	950
Design and production support (hours)	100	400

The following are the budgeted indirect costs for the year:

Equipment maintenance	$140,000
Utilities	48,000
Purchasing materials	50,000
Indirect materials	60,000
Receiving goods	35,000
Factory rental	96,000
Setting up equipment	13,800
Inspection costs	148,000
Design	50,000
Production support	75,000

Facility-level costs are allocated on the basis of machine hours.

REQUIRED
1. Calculate the cost per unit for each product assuming the company uses a single overhead allocation rate based on direct labour-hours.
2. Form homogeneous cost pools and select appropriate cost drivers. Explain the rationale behind each of your groupings. Calculate the activity rates.
3. Using the activity rates calculated in requirement 2, calculate the per-unit cost for each product.
4. Compare your results from requirements 1 and 3, and comment on your results.

5-39 Choosing cost drivers, activity-based costing, activity-based management. (J. Watson) Pumpkin Bags (PB) is a designer of high-quality backpacks and purses. Each design is made in small batches. Each spring, PB comes out with new designs for the backpack and for the purse. They use these designs for one year and then move on to the next trend. The bags are all made on the same fabrication equipment that is expected to operate at capacity. The equipment must be switched over to a new design and set up to prepare for the production of each new batch of products. When completed, each batch of products is immediately shipped to a wholesaler. Shipping costs vary with the number of shipments. Budgeted information for the year is as follows:

3. Cost for setup, $320 per batch

Pumpkin Bags

Budgeted Costs and Activities for the Year Ending February 28, 2013

Direct materials—purses	$ 362,000
Direct materials—backpacks	427,000
Direct labour—purses	98,000
Direct labour—backpacks	115,597
Setup	64,960
Shipping	72,065
Design	167,000
Plant utilities and administration	225,000
Total	$1,531,622

Other information:

	Backpacks	Purses	Total
Number of bags	6,000	3,150	9,150
Hours of production	1,560	2,600	4,160
Number of batches	133	70	203
Number of designs	3	2	5

REQUIRED
1. Identify the cost hierarchy level for each cost category.
2. Identify the most appropriate cost driver for each cost category. Explain briefly your choice of cost driver.
3. Calculate the cost per unit of cost driver for each cost category.
4. Calculate the total costs and cost per unit for each product line.
5. Explain how you could use the information in requirement 4 to reduce costs.

5-40 Make or buy, activity-based costing, opportunity costs. (N. Melumad and S. Reichelstein, adapted) Ace Bicycle Company produces bicycles. This year's expected production is 10,000 units. Currently, Ace makes the chains for its bicycles. Ace's accountant reports the following costs for making the 10,000 bicycle chains:

5

1. Difference in relevant costs, $6,000

	Costs per unit	Costs for 10,000 units
Direct materials	$6	$60,000
Direct labour	3	30,000
Variable manufacturing overhead (utilities)	2	20,000
Inspection, setup, materials handling		2,500
Equipment rental		3,500
Allocation of fixed plant facility costs (insurance, administration, etc.)		34,000

Ace has received an offer from an outside vendor to supply any number of chains Ace requires at $12.20 per chain. The following additional information is available:

a. Inspection, setup, and materials-handling costs vary with the number of batches in which the chains are produced. Ace produces chains in batch sizes of 1,000 units. Ace estimates that it will produce the 10,000 units in ten batches.

b. Ace rents the machine used to make the chains. If Ace buys all its chains from the outside vendor, it does not need to pay rent on this machine.

REQUIRED

1. Assume that, if Ace purchases the chains from the outside supplier, the facility where the chains are currently made will remain idle. Should Ace accept the outside supplier's offer at the anticipated production (and sales) volume of 10,000 units?

2. For this question, assume that if the chains are purchased outside, the facilities where the chains are currently made will be used to upgrade the bicycles by adding mud flaps and reflectors. As a consequence, the selling price on bicycles will be raised by $25. The variable per-unit cost of the upgrade would be $20.50, and additional tooling costs of $18,500 would be incurred. Should Ace make or buy the chains, assuming that 10,000 units are produced (and sold)?

3. The sales manager at Ace is concerned that the estimate of 10,000 units may be high and believes that only 6,400 units will be sold. Production will be cut back, and this opens up work space, which can be used to add the mud flaps and reflectors whether Ace goes outside for the chains or makes them in-house. At this lower output, Ace will produce the chains in eight batches of 800 units each. Should Ace purchase the chains from the outside vendor?

5-41 ABC, implementation, governance. (CMA, adapted) Applewood Electronics, a division of Elgin Corporation, manufactures two large-screen television models: the Monarch, which has been produced since 2008 and sells for $1,700, and the Regal, a new model introduced in early 2008, which sells for $2,200. Based on the following income statement for the year ended November 30, 2012, senior management at Elgin have decided to concentrate Applewood's marketing resources on the Regal model and begin to phase out the Monarch model.

5

1. Profitability of Regal model, $436,760 gross margin

Applewood Electronics
Income Statement
For the Year Ended November 30, 2012

	Monarch	Regal	Total
Sales	$30,600,000	$4,400,000	$35,000,000
Cost of goods sold	19,890,000	3,080,000	22,970,000
Gross margin	10,710,000	1,320,000	12,030,000
Selling and administrative expense	8,032,500	925,000	8,957,500
Operating income	$ 2,677,500	$ 395,000	$ 3,072,500
Units sold	18,000	2,000	
Operating income per unit sold	$148.75	$ 197.50	

Unit costs for the Monarch and Regal are as follows:

	Monarch	Regal
Direct materials	$ 540.00	$1,089.00
Direct labour		
Monarch (2.5 hours × $18 per hr)	45.00	
Regal (7.0 hours × $18 per hr)		126.00
Machine costs*		
Monarch (8 hours × $25 per hr)	200.00	
Regal (5 hours × $25 per hr)		125.00
Other manufacturing overhead**	320.00	200.00
Total	$1,105.00	$1,540.00

*Machine costs include leasing of the machine, repairs, and maintenance.
**Other manufacturing overhead is allocated on the basis of machine hours at a rate of $40 per machine hour.

Applewood's controller, Susan Benzo, is advocating the use of activity-based costing (ABC) and activity-based management (ABM), and has gathered the following information about the company's manufacturing overhead costs for the year ended November 30, 2012.

		Units of Cost Driver	
Activity Centre	Total Activity Costs	Monarch	Regal
Soldering (number of solder points)	$1,872,400	1,296,000	214,000
Shipments (number of shipments)	1,480,000	1,500	500
Quality control (number of inspections)	1,749,600	54,000	18,000
Purchase orders (number of POs)	582,400	16,640	4,160
Machine power (machine hours)	61,600	144,000	10,000
Machine setups (number of setups)	414,000	360	100
Total manufacturing overhead	$6,160,000		

After completing her analysis, Benzo showed the results to Filipe Figueira, the Applewood Division President. Figueira did not like what he saw. "If you show headquarters this analysis, they are going to ask us to phase out the Regal line, which we have just introduced. This whole costing thing has been a major problem for us. First Monarch was not profitable and now Regal.

"Looking at the ABC analysis, I see two problems. We do many more activities than the ones you have listed. If you had included all activities, maybe your conclusions would have been different. Second, you used number of setups and number of inspections as allocation bases. The numbers would have been different had you used setup hours and inspection hours instead. I know that measurement problems precluded you from using these other cost allocation bases, but at least you ought to make some adjustments to our current numbers to compensate for these issues. I know you can do better. We can't afford to phase out either product."

Benzo knew her numbers were fairly accurate. On a limited sample, she had calculated the profitability of Regal and Monarch using different allocation bases. The set of activities and activity rates she had chosen resulted in numbers that approximated closely those based on more detailed analyses. She was confident that headquarters, knowing that Regal was introduced only recently, would not ask Applewood to phase it out. She was also aware that a sizable portion of Figueira's bonus was based on division sales. Phasing out either product would adversely affect the bonus. Still, she felt some pressure from Figueira to do something.

REQUIRED
1. Using activity-based costing (ABC), calculate the profitability of the Regal and Monarch models.
2. Explain briefly why these numbers differ from the profitability of the Regal and Monarch models calculated using Applewood's existing costing system.
3. Comment on Figueira's concerns about the accuracy and limitations of ABC.
4. How might Applewood find the ABC information helpful in managing its business?
5. What should Susan Benzo do?

COLLABORATIVE LEARNING CASE

5-42 Using ABC for activity-based management (ABM). As you've seen in this chapter, activity-based costing (ABC) systems are useful in helping companies make better decisions about pricing, product mix, and cost management related to product design and efficiency. In fact, General Mills used ABC to identify and analyze the costs associated with the different channels used to market its Colombo frozen yogurt products.

⑤
1. New Impulse location net income, $714,000

Before performing ABC analysis, General Mills charged the same prices and provided the same promotions—$3 per case—to its customers, whether the customer was in the grocery channel (food purchased for later consumption or preparation at home) or the food-service (outside of home, immediate consumption) channel. Upon closer examination of the food-service channel, General Mills discovered segments within food service: destination yogurt shops or restaurants and impulse locations, located in business cafeterias and on college campuses and military bases. General Mills also noticed that sales dollars for frozen yogurt products were relatively constant, but profits were declining. The company sensed that destination yogurt shops might be more profitable than impulse locations, but it didn't have the information about profit differences to make changes. General Mills' logic was: Destination shops/restaurants focus on maximizing profit per square foot and managing guest cheque averages. However, impulse locations focus on cost per serving, and this segment of the business was growing at a much faster rate than the destination shop segment.

The case sales data and income statements for last year, by segment, looked like this:

Category	Impulse Location	Yogurt Shops	Total
Sales in cases	1,200,000	300,000	1,500,000
Sales revenue	$23,880,000	$5,970,000	$29,850,000
Less: Promotions	3,600,000	900,000	4,500,000
Net sales	20,280,000	5,070,000	25,350,000
Cost of goods sold	13,800,000	3,450,000	17,250,000
Gross margin	6,480,000	1,620,000	8,100,000
Less: Merchandising	1,380,000	345,000	1,725,000
Less: Selling, general, and admin. expenses	948,000	237,000	1,185,000
Net income	$ 4,152,000	$1,038,000	$ 5,190,000

Cost of goods sold includes $14,250,000 for ingredients, packaging, and storage, and $3,000,000 for picking, packing, and shipping. The product is the same across segments, so cost to produce is the same. However, picking, packing, and shipping costs vary if the order is for a full pallet. Full pallets cost $75 to pick and ship, where individual orders cost $2.25 per case. There are 75 cases in a pallet, with pallet and case usage by segment shown here:

	Segment		
	Impulse Location	Yogurt Shops	Total
Cases in full pallets	60,000	240,000	300,000
Individual cases	1,140,000	60,000	1,200,000
Total cases	1,200,000	300,000	1,500,000

For merchandising, costs consist mainly of kits selling for $500 each. A total of 3,450 kits were delivered in the period, 90 of them to yogurt shops. For selling, general, and administration, costs were allocated to products based on gross sales dollars. When a random sample of the sales force was asked to keep diaries for 60 days, the resulting data revealed they spent much more time per sales dollar on yogurt sales than other General Mills products they represented. Thus, when selling, general, and administration costs were allocated based on time, the total allocation to yogurt products jumped from $1,185,000 to $3,900,000. Of the total time spent on selling Colombo frozen yogurt, only 1% of that time was spent in shops.

REQUIRED

1. How do the two segments identified by General Mills for Colombo frozen yogurt sales differ from each other?
2. Using ABC analysis, restate the income statements above to show new net income (*hint:* add a line item for shipping). What is "per case" net income?
3. Based on your analysis in requirement 2, what changes should General Mills make?

(IMA adapted; "Colombo Frozen Yogurt," John Guy and Jane Saly, *Cases from Management Accounting Practice*, Vol. 15, Institute of Management Accountants, 2000.) © IMA. Reprinted with permission from the Institute of Management Accountants, Montvale, N.J., www.imanet.org.)

PART TWO

Master Budget and Responsibility Accounting

BUSINESS MATTERS

Budgets Communicate Choices

Chrysler's budget forecasts how changes in the business and economic environment are likely to affect Chrysler's financial health. Chrysler has limited resources, and its budgets represent choices about where those resources will be used, based both on experience from the past and assumptions about the future. A budget reports pro forma, or expected, financial results in standard financial statement format. The pro forma financial reports are performance targets that Chrysler's managers have committed to achieve.

LEARNING OUTCOMES

After studying this chapter, you should be able to

1. Distinguish the long-term from the short-term benefits of budgets (pro forma financial statements).

2. Prepare a master operating budget and all supporting budgets or schedules.

3. Prepare a cash budget.

4. Distinguish among sensitivity analysis, Kaizen budgeting, and activity-based budgeting.

5. Contrast responsibility against controllability.

Budgets quantify, coordinate, communicate, and motivate future activities. The actual, historical results are the foundation upon which budgets are built. But in just looking to the past, managers can lose track of change, which means the future will not resemble history in important ways. New opportunities and threats abound in for-profit environments, which are dynamic and turbulent.

Financial budgets such as pro forma statements of income, statements of cash flow, and the balance sheet report expected results in GAAP-compliant formats. **Nonfinancial budgets** report on both the timing and quantity of resources required to achieve predicted financial results. The key purpose of nonfinancial budgets is coordination of all business functions in the value chain. With coordination comes control. Once in place, the predicted outcomes can be compared against actual outcomes with the goal of improving on any unfavourable actual performance relative to what was expected in the budget. As one observer has said, "Few businesses plan to fail, but many of those that flop failed to plan."

This chapter presents the budgeting process used to create an operating budget (reported as a pro forma income statement) and a cash budget (presented as a statement of operating cash flow). The statement of operating cash flow uses the direct method. These pro forma statements are predictions, not historical outcomes; therefore, they are never audited.

THE DECISION FRAMEWORK AND BUDGETS

1 Distinguish the long-term from the short-term benefits of budgets (pro forma financial statements).

A **budget** is a quantitative expression of a proposed (future) plan of action by management for a set time period. It is because resources are constrained that choices must be made to obtain the maximum benefit of the resources available for use. The **budget constraints** describe the combination of limitations on nonfinancial and financial resources within a company's management control.

The **master budget** summarizes all the financial and nonfinancial plans into a single document. The financial predictions are reported according to GAAP standards and are supported by nonfinancial schedules. The term *master* in master budget means it is a comprehensive, coordinated organization-wide set of schedules and a budget.

The terminology used to describe budgets varies among organizations. For example, budgeted financial statements are sometimes called **pro forma statements**. Some organizations refer to budgeting as targeting. Indeed, to give a more positive thrust to budgeting, many organizations—for example, Nissan Canada and Bombardier—describe the budget as a *profit plan*.

Budgets are the result of a simultaneous set of complex *decision processes*.

Step 1: Identify the Problem and Uncertainties All corporations must both plan and control their activities and costs to meet their budget resource constraints. The problem is how to maximize profit and thrive in the long term. Like all well-disciplined team decision making, the process begins with discussion to identify and understand any control and planning issues. Once key issues are identified and ordered in priority as either external threats and opportunities, or internal strengths and weaknesses, the management team can begin the budget process as a coordinated response to the issues.

Step 2: Obtain Information Evidence to justify various opinions must be gathered both internally from the MIS and externally from the economic, social, political, technological, and industrial context. There will be meticulous and detailed gathering of information upon which to create the various schedules that will justify the final budget. Throughout the process, however, many decisions will be made about resource allocation to support the core production process of a company.

Step 3: Make Predictions About the Future Budgets themselves are predictions about the future that represent choices among alternative uses of available resources. Intelligent assumptions, based on the management team's understanding of its own strengths and weaknesses as well as the external opportunities and threats, are central to budgets. Most of this chapter illustrates and describes how the available information is analyzed into a coordinated forecast and reported as a pro forma income statement (see Exhibit 6-7 on p. 210).

Step 4: Decide on and Implement One of the Available Alternatives Implementation in well-managed organizations usually follows four steps in the **budgeting cycle:**

1. Plan the performance of organizational sub-units and coordinate into a whole. The entire management team must agree with what is expected and commit to achieving the budget targets.

2. Provide a frame of reference—a set of specific expectations against which actual results can be compared. Budget targets are not discretionary but mandatory achievements. If one sub-unit fails, then failure will cascade through all the rest.

3. Investigate variations from plans. If necessary, corrective action follows investigation so the plan will be met in the future.

4. Plan again, based on feedback from changed conditions and actual performance.

The prevalence of budgets in companies of all sizes is evidence that the benefits of budgeting processes outweigh their costs. Executive support is especially critical for obtaining active line participation in the formulation of budgets and for successful administration of budgets. The "garbage in, garbage out" maxim applies to budgets. At all levels in a company, managers must understand and support both the budget and the control it imposes on their decision making.

Budgets need to be somewhat flexible, because changing conditions call for changes in plans. A manager may commit to the budget, but opportunities often develop where some special repairs or a special advertising program would better serve the interests of the organization. Deferring the repairs or the advertising to meet the budget is foolish if it will hurt the organization in the long run. Attaining the budget is never an end in itself.

Often, but not always, budgeted amounts are also standards. A **standard** is a carefully predetermined price, cost, or quantity used for judging performance. The term is frequently used to refer to amounts estimated from either engineering or time-motion studies. Standard amounts are usually expressed on a per-unit basis (e.g., per hour, per square metre, per task, per output, etc.). Not all budgeted costs, however, are standard costs. Many budgeted costs are based on assuming historical data will characterize future performance. Managers can use time series linear regression (see Chapter 10), but this approach fails to examine whether history represents the best or even good performance levels in any competitive situation.

There is a danger when companies rely entirely on internal data to set standards. Their more successful competitors clearly have achieved higher standards. To improve their own performance, companies need to look outside the firm to the best achieved performance. This type of standard is often referred to as a **benchmark**. It arises from a broader scope of information sought outside the company. Benchmarks encourage the setting of **stretch goals**, those that challenge managers to achieve excellent performance rather than maintain the status quo.

Step 5: Implement the Decision, Evaluate Performance, and Learn Probably the most disliked application, but at the same time the most important, is the evaluation of actual against predicted or budgeted performance. Actual outcome that falls short of expectations indicates a problem in implementation. Often managers are paid bonuses for exceeding, not for failing to meet, expectations. Without feedback, however, there is no basis upon which to analyze how the failure occurred and remedy it.

ADVANTAGES OF BUDGETS

Budgets are a major feature of most management-control systems. When administered intelligently, budgets

◆ Compel planning and monitoring of the implementation of plans.
◆ Provide reliable performance assessment criteria.
◆ Promote communication and coordination within the organization.

Budgeting is most useful when it is part of a company's strategic analysis.[1] **Strategic analysis** is the evaluation of how well the organization has matched its own capabilities with the relevant features of the competitive environment to progress toward its future success. For the strategy to succeed, the company also needs to match its activities to the strategy in a reliable way. For example, if cost control is the strategy, then the company needs cross-functional teams. Members from different business functions of the value chain can seek major cost reductions. By streamlining activities higher in the cost hierarchy, teams can reduce the quantities of common cost drivers consumed in unequal proportions by many users.

OPERATING AND STRATEGIC PERFORMANCE ASSESSMENT

Budgeted performance measures can overcome two key limitations of using past performance as a basis for judging actual results. For example, past results incorporate past miscues and substandard performance. There is clearly a problem if past sales records are used when the departed employees selling the product did not understand their customers. Using the sales records of those departed employees would set the performance bar for knowledgeable salespeople far too low.

Another limitation of past performance is that the anticipated future may be very different from the past. Suppose the company had a 20% revenue increase in 2013, compared with a 10% increase in 2012. But in November 2012, an industry trade association forecast that the 2013 growth rate in industry revenue would be 40%. Moreover, in 2013 the actual growth rate in industry revenue was 50%. The company's 20% actual revenue gain in 2013, although it exceeds the 2012 actual growth rate of 10%, remains well below the actual industry gain of 50%. Use of the 40% figure as the budgeted rate provides a better way to evaluate the 2013 sales performance than the use of the 2012 actual rate of 10%.

Exhibit 6-1 illustrates the strategic analysis and planning processes. The dual-directional arrows indicate the interdependence among these activities and outcomes. The budgets, expressed in financial format, are outcomes of plans. The cycle of planning and budgeting is continuous as actual results provide feedback regarding how well managers forecast future results. When the feedback is negative, it is sensible for managers to reassess their long-run and short-run plans to determine where changes can be made to improve the achievement of their financial and nonfinancial goals.

EXHIBIT 6-1
Strategic Analysis in the Formulation of Long-Run and Short-Run Budgets

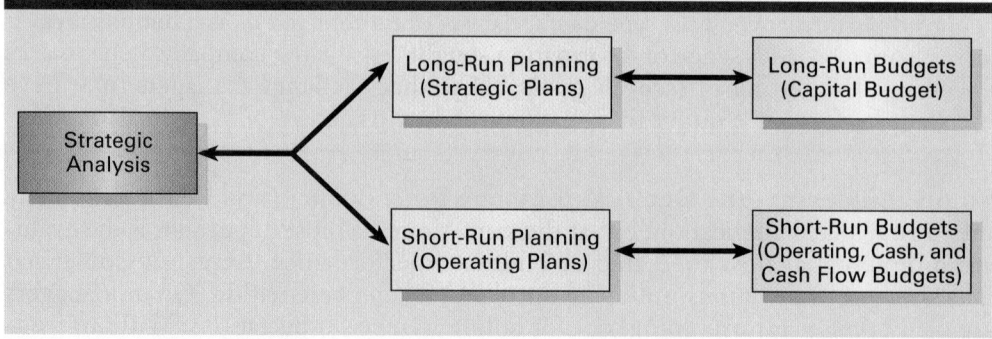

[1]See J. Hope and R. Fraser, *Beyond Budgeting* (Boston, MA: Harvard Business School Press, 2003) for several examples.

A company's internal budget is not the only threshold of year-to-year accomplishment that can be used to evaluate performance. Companies must also consider their own performance relative both to their peers in the industry and the overall industry's annual performance. When companies evaluate accomplishment exclusively on their internal performance, the situation is ripe for "gaming," whereby managers set easily achieved targets;[2] but those to whom they report know this game. In turn, they set more challenging targets and negotiating begins among the levels of the company's managers to decide what the budget will be. General Electric's former CEO Jack Welch maintained that demanding, yet achievable, goals created anxiety for managers but improved corporate performance. He perceived "stretch" goals as a way to motivate creative change and progress in existing processes of each business function.

COORDINATION AND COMMUNICATION

Coordination is the meshing and balancing of all factors of production or service and of all the departments and business functions so that the company can meet its objectives. *Communication* is getting those objectives understood and accepted by all employees.

Coordination forces executives to think of relationships and interdependencies among individual operations, departments, and the company as a whole. As we learned in Chapter 5, purchasing officers make material purchase plans based on either production, service, or merchandising requirements. Reduction in purchasing costs can improve profitability in other value-chain functions because of interdependence. In a manufacturing setting, after marketing managers forecast future demand, production managers plan personnel and machinery needs to produce the number of products necessary to meet revenue forecasts.

How does a budget lead to coordination? Consider Snapple Beverage Corporation. Production managers, who are evaluated on maximizing output while keeping unit costs per bottle low, would prefer long production runs with very few changeovers of flavours. But if the output cannot be sold, Snapple may find itself awash in a costly inventory buildup of Mango Madness. The budget achieves coordination by constraining production managers to produce only what marketing forecasts. This may entail doing a changeover from Mango Madness to Lemonade partway through a production shift. It may be inconvenient, but it is cost-beneficial because the COGS will only be recovered when the outputs are sold.

Communication is key to coordination. Production managers must know the sales plan, purchasing managers must know the production plans, and so on. A formal document, such as the budget, is an effective way to communicate a consistent set of plans to the organization as a whole. Within a company, the value-chain managers must produce a budget of benefit to the entire company.

THE MASTER OPERATING BUDGET

TIME COVERAGE

The purpose(s) for budgeting should guide the time period chosen for the budget. Consider budgeting for a new Harley-Davidson 500-cc motorcycle. If the purpose is to budget for the total profitability of this new model, a five-year period (or more) may be appropriate because it covers design, manufacture, sales, and after-sales support. In contrast, consider budgeting for a Christmas play. If the purpose is to estimate all cash outlays, a six-month period from the planning to staging of the play may be adequate.

The most frequently used budget period is one year. The annual budget is often subdivided by months for the first quarter and by quarters for the remainder of

Prepare a master operating budget and all supporting budgets or schedules.

---

[2]For a more detailed discussion, see R. Varnick, G. Wu, and C. Heath, "Raising the Bar on Goals," *Graduate School of Business Publication*, University of Chicago, Spring, 1999.

the year. The budgeted data for a year are frequently revised as the year unfolds. For example, at the end of the first quarter, the budget for the next three quarters is changed in light of new information gathered from actual experience.

Businesses increasingly use rolling budgets. A **rolling budget** is a budget or plan that is always available for a specified future period by adding a month, quarter, or year in the future as the current month, quarter, or year is completed. Thus, a 12-month rolling budget for the March 2012 to February 2013 period becomes a 12-month rolling budget for the April 2012 to March 2013 period the next month, and so on. This way there is always a 12-month budget in place. Rolling budgets motivate managers to look forward 12 months, regardless of the month at hand. Companies also frequently use rolling budgets when developing five-year budgets for long-run planning.

STEPS IN DEVELOPING AN OPERATING BUDGET

Budgeting, like swimming, is best learned by doing. We will move through the development of an actual master budget because it provides a comprehensive picture of the entire budgeting process. Our example is a mid-sized, owner-managed manufacturer of aircraft replacement parts, Halifax Engineering. Its job-costing system for manufacturing costs (see Chapter 4) has two direct cost categories, direct materials and direct manufacturing labour, as well as one indirect cost pool, manufacturing overhead. Manufacturing overhead (both variable and fixed) is allocated to output units using direct manufacturing labour-hours as the allocation base. The company manufactures specialized parts for the aerospace industry.

Exhibit 6-2 illustrates the flow among the various parts of the master budget for Halifax Engineering. The master budget summarizes the anticipated financial outcomes of all the organization's individual budgets. The result is a set of related financial statements for a set time period, usually a year. The schedules in Exhibit 6-2 illustrate the logical flow among budgets that together are often called the *operating budget*. The **operating budget** presents the results of operations in many value-chain business functions prior to financing and taxes. Later in this chapter you will learn how the remaining budget information is produced to create a budgeted or pro forma income statement.

The operating budget and pro forma income statement, new elements introduced in this chapter, are coloured green, as is the arrow indicating all the schedules required to produce the operating budget.

The dual-direction arrows in Exhibit 6-2 indicate interdependencies among elements. For example, the operating budget will be amended to include added amortization if the demand forecast indicates that a permanent increase in production is required. A permanent increase in production means the purchase of long-term assets would be recorded in the capital budget. Financing the purchase and the interest incurred would be recorded in the cash budget and would affect the pro forma income statement. If Halifax Engineering cannot access the financing to increase its capacity, then production must be decreased and the operating budget changed. Similarly, if the interest expense on the cash budget indicates that Halifax Engineering will be "in the red" with a negative net profit, the company may decide to postpone its expansion plans.

The financial budget is that part of the master budget that comprises the capital budget, cash budget, budgeted balance sheet, and budgeted cash flow statement. This set of budgets is coloured yellow in Exhibit 6-2. Notice the dual-direction arrow between the financial and operating budget. This signifies that Halifax Engineering must be able to afford its operating and investing plans. The final master budget is often the result of several iterations. Each draft involves interaction across the various business functions of the value chain.

The master budget reports a large amount of nonfinancial data from various value-chain functions. The managers at the company use these data to create forecasts of the drain on or contribution to financial resources each quarter.

EXHIBIT 6-2
Overview of the Master Budget for Halifax Engineering

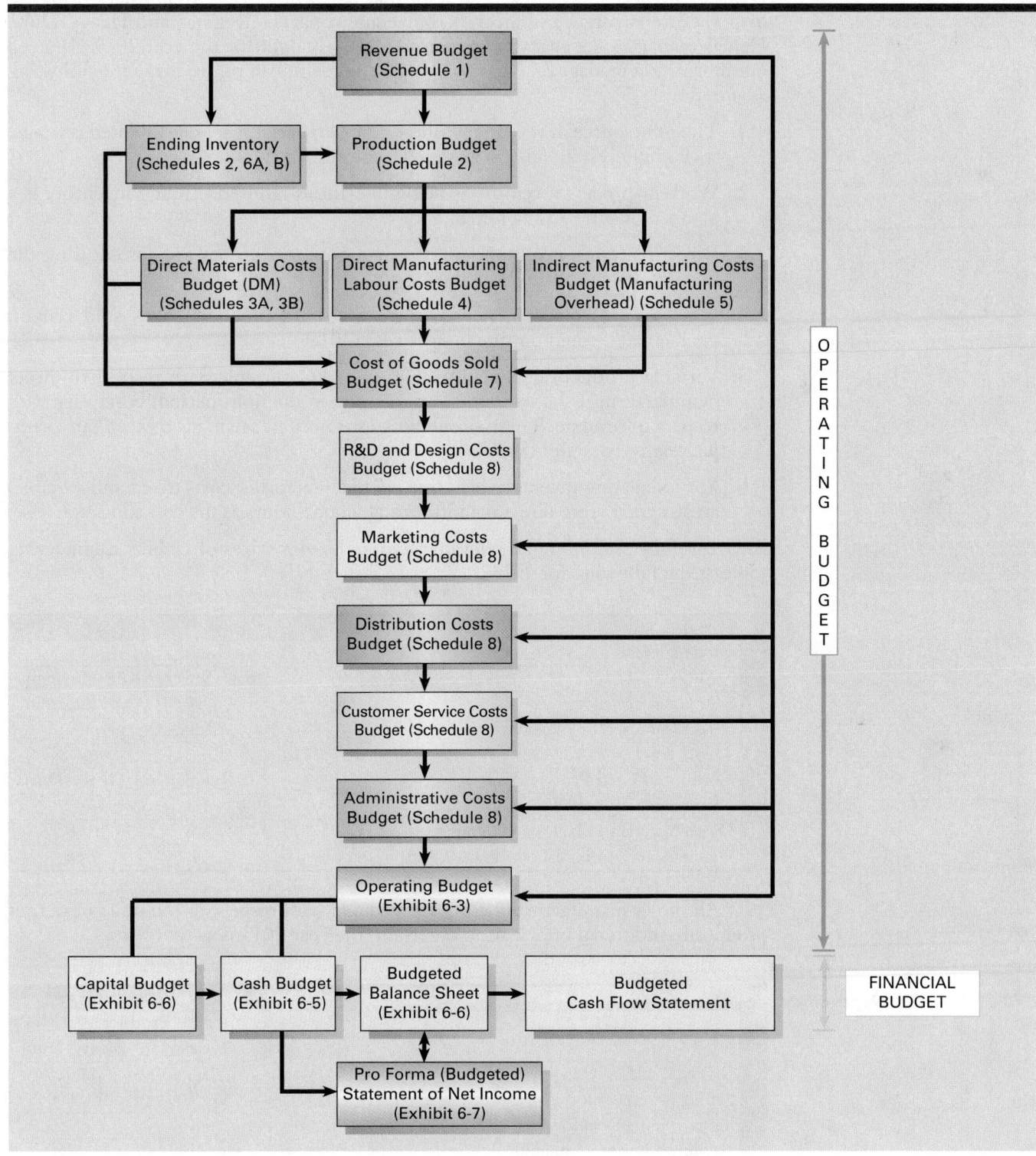

The dual-direction arrow between the pro forma or budgeted income statement and the budgeted or pro forma balance sheet indicates familiar interdependencies. For example, net income is one of the financial elements included in owners' equity on the balance sheet. While budgeting is not financial accounting, the quality of the financial-accounting data in the management information system is crucial to good budgeting. Moreover, the structure of financial-accounting statements enables communication and coordination among managers using a familiar and common financial language.

BASIC DATA AND REQUIREMENTS

Halifax Engineering is a machine shop that uses skilled labour and metal alloys to manufacture two types of aircraft replacement parts—Regular and Heavy-Duty. Halifax managers are ready to prepare a master budget for the year 2013. To keep our illustration manageable for clarifying basic relationships, we make the following assumptions:

1. The only source of revenue is sales of the two parts. Non-sales-related revenue, such as interest income, is assumed to be zero.

2. Work-in-process inventory is negligible and is ignored. Ending inventory is a planned quantity, not a remainder.

3. Direct materials inventory and finished goods inventory are costed using the first-in, first-out (FIFO) method.

4. Unit costs of direct materials purchased and finished goods sold remain unchanged throughout the budget year (2013).

5. Variable production (inventoriable) costs are variable with respect to direct manufacturing labour-hours. Variable nonproduction (period) costs vary with respect to revenue. These simplifying assumptions are made to keep our example relatively straightforward.

6. For calculating inventoriable costs, *all* manufacturing costs (fixed and variable) are assigned using direct manufacturing labour-hours as the cost allocation base.

After carefully examining all relevant factors, the executives of Halifax Engineering forecast the following for 2013:

	A	B	C
1	Direct materials:		
2	Material 111 alloy	$ 7	per kilogram
3	Material 112 alloy	$10	per kilogram
4	Direct manufacturing labour	$20	per hour
5			
6	**Content of Each Product Unit**	**Regular**	**Heavy-Duty**
7	Direct materials 111 alloy—kilograms	12	12
8	Direct materials 112 alloy—kilograms	6	8
9	Direct manufacturing labour-hours (DLH)	4	6

All direct manufacturing costs are variable with respect to the units of output produced. Additional information regarding the year 2013 is as follows:

	A	B	C
1		**Product**	
2		**Regular**	**Heavy-Duty**
3	Expected sales in units	5,000	1,000
4	Selling price per unit	$ 600	$ 800
5	Target ending inventory in units*	1,100	50
6	Beginning inventory in units	100	50
7	Beginning inventory value in dollars	$38,400	$26,200
8			
9		**Direct Materials**	
10		**111 Alloy**	**112 Alloy**
11	Beginning inventory in kilograms	7,000	6,000
12	Target ending inventory in kilograms*	8,000	2,000
13			
14	*Target inventories depend on expected sales, expected variation in demand for products, and management philosophies such as just-in-time (JIT) inventory management.		

At the anticipated output levels for the Regular and Heavy-Duty aircraft parts, management believes the manufacturing overhead costs will be incurred as shown below. Notice that amortization of the manufacturing plant and equipment is included on COGS. There is no remaining amortization expense reported in the non-inventoriable (period costs) schedule.

	A	B	C
1	**Manufacturing Overhead Costs**		
2	Variable:		
3	Supplies	$ 90,000	
4	Indirect manufacturing labour	190,000	
5	Direct and indirect manufacturing labour fringe costs @ 15.4% (rounded)	121,689	
6	Power	120,000	
7	Maintenance	60,000	$581,689
8	Fixed:		
9	Amortization	220,000	
10	Property taxes	50,000	
11	Property insurance	10,000	
12	Supervision	100,000	
13	Power	22,000	
14	Maintenance	18,000	420,000
15	Total		$1,001,689

The period or nonproduction overhead costs are:

	A	B	C
1	**Other (Non-manufacturing or Period) Costs**		
2	Variable:		
3	R&D/product design	$ 56,000	
4	Marketing	92,600	
5	Distribution	66,500	
6	Customer service	47,600	
7	Administrative	78,000	$340,700
8	Fixed:		
9	R&D/product design	45,000	
10	Marketing	35,000	
11	Distribution	28,000	
12	Customer service	16,870	
13	Administrative	100,000	224,870
14	Total		$565,570

Our task at hand is to prepare a budgeted or pro forma income statement for the year 2013. As shown in Exhibit 6-2 (p. 197), this is one component of Halifax's master budget. Other components of the master budget—the budgeted or pro forma balance sheet and the cash budget—are discussed in the next section of this chapter.

The following supporting budget schedules will be prepared when developing Halifax's budgeted income statement:

1. Revenue budget.

2. Production budget (in units).

3. Direct materials usage budget and direct materials purchases budget.

4. Direct manufacturing labour budget.

5. Manufacturing overhead budget (includes manufacturing plant and equipment amortization. This amortization expense is also included in the cost of goods sold budget).

6. Ending inventory budget.

7. Cost of goods sold (COGS) budget.

8. Other (nonproduction) costs budget.

Some companies prepare budget manuals; while details differ among organizations, the sequence of events outlined below is common for developing a budgeted income statement. Beginning with the revenue budget, each budget is developed in logical fashion. In most cases, computer software speeds the budget calculations.

PREPARING A MASTER OPERATING BUDGET

◆ **Schedule 1**: *Revenue budget.* The revenue budget (Schedule 1) is the usual starting point for budgeting. The reason is that production (and hence costs) and inventory levels generally depend on the forecasted level of revenue.

	A	B	C	D
1		Schedule 1: Revenue Budget		
2		For the Year Ended December 31, 2013		
3			Selling	Total
4		Units	Price	Revenues
5	Regular	5,000	$600	$3,000,000
6	Heavy-Duty	1,000	800	800,000
7	Total			$3,800,000

The $3.8 million is the amount of revenue in the budgeted income statement. The revenue budget results from elaborate information gathering and intense discussions among sales managers and field sales representatives.

Pressures can exist for budgeted revenue to be either overestimates or underestimates of the expected amounts. Some firms set "stretch" or "challenge" targets for revenue. These targets are actually overestimates of expected revenue and are intended to motivate employees to put in extra effort and achieve higher performance.

Pressure for employees to underestimate budgeted revenue can occur when a company uses the difference between actual and budget amounts to evaluate managers. These managers may respond by giving highly conservative forecasts. **Padding** the budget or introducing **budgetary slack** refers to underestimating budgeted revenue (or overestimating budgeted costs) to make budgeted targets easier to achieve. From the marketing manager's standpoint, budgetary slack hedges against unexpected downturns in demand.

Occasionally, revenue is limited by available production capacity. For example, unusually heavy market demand, shortages of labour or resources, or strikes may cause a company to exhaust its finished goods inventory completely. Additional sales cannot be made because no stock of the product is available. In such cases, the production capacity—the factor that limits revenue—is the starting point for preparing the revenue budget.

◆ **Schedule 2**: *Production budget (in units).* After revenue is budgeted, the production budget (Schedule 2) can be prepared. The total finished goods units to be produced depends on planned sales and expected changes in inventory levels:

$$\text{Budgeted production (units)} = \text{Budgeted sales (units)} + \text{Target ending finished goods inventory (units)} - \text{Beginning finished goods inventory (units)}$$

	A	B	C
1	**Schedule 2: Production Budget**		
2	**For the Year Ended December 31, 2013**		
3		**Product**	
4		**Regular**	**Heavy-Duty**
5	Budgeted sales (schedule 1)	5,000	1,000
6	Add: Target ending finished goods inventory	1,100	50
7	Total requirements	6,100	1,050
8	Deduct: Beginning finished goods inventory	(100)	(50)
9	Units to be produced	6,000	1,000

When unit sales are not stable throughout the year, managers must decide whether (1) to adjust production levels periodically to minimize inventory held, or (2) to maintain constant production levels and let inventory rise and fall. Increasingly, managers are choosing to adjust production.

◆ **Schedule 3**: *Direct materials usage budget and direct materials purchases budget.* The decision on the quantity of each type of output unit produced (Schedule 2) provides the data required to calculate the quantities of direct materials used. Information from purchasing will provide the cost data to produce Schedule 3A.

	A	B	C	D	E
1	**Schedule 3A: Direct Materials Usage Budget in Kilograms and Dollars**				
2	**For the Year Ended December 31, 2013**				
3		**Materials**			
4		**111 Alloy**	**112 Alloy**	**Total**	
5	Direct materials to be used in production of Regular parts (6,000 units) × 12 and 6 kilograms	72,000	36,000		see Schedule 2
6	Direct materials to be used in production of Heavy-Duty (1,000 units) × 12 and 8 kilograms	12,000	8,000		see Schedule 2
7	Total direct materials to be used (in kilograms)	84,000	44,000		
8	Direct materials to be used from beginning inventory (assume FIFO cost flow)	7,000	6,000		
9	Multiply by: Cost per kilogram of beginning inventory	$ 7	$ 10		
10	Cost of direct materials to be used from beginning inventory	$ 49,000	$ 60,000	$ 109,000	(a)
11	Direct materials to be used from purchases (84,000 − 7,000; 44,000 − 6,000)	77,000	38,000		
12	Multiply by: Cost per kilogram of purchased materials	$ 7	$ 10		
13	Cost of direct materials to be used from purchases	$539,000	$380,000	$ 919,000	(b)
14	Total costs of direct materials to be used (a) + (b)	$588,000	$440,000	$1,028,000	

Schedule 3B computes the budget for direct materials purchases, which depends on the budgeted direct materials to be used, the beginning inventory of direct materials, and the target ending inventory of direct materials:

Purchases of direct materials	=	Usage of direct materials	+	Target ending inventory of direct materials	−	Beginning inventory of direct materials

	A	B	C	D
1	**Schedule 3B: Direct Materials Usage Budget in Kilograms and Dollars**			
2	**For the Year Ended December 31, 2013**			
3		**Materials**		
4		**111 Alloy**	**112 Alloy**	**Total**
5	Direct materials to be used in production (in kilograms)	84,000	44,000	
6	Add: Target ending direct materials inventory	8,000	2,000	
7	Total requirements (in kilograms)	92,000	46,000	
8	Deduct: Beginning direct materials inventory	(7,000)	(6,000)	
9	Direct materials to be purchased (in kilograms)	85,000	40,000	
10	Multiply by: Cost per kilogram of purchased materials	$ 7	$ 10	
11	Total direct materials purchase costs	$595,000	$400,000	$995,000

◆ **Schedule 4:** *Direct manufacturing labour budget.* These costs depend on wage rates, production methods, and hiring plans. The computations of budgeted direct manufacturing labour costs appear in Schedule 4.

	A	B	C	D	E	F
1		**Schedule 4: Direct Manufacturing Labour Budget**				
2		**For the Year Ended December 31, 2013**				
3		**Output**	**Direct**			
4		**Units**	**Manufacturing**		**Hourly**	
5		**Produced**	**Labour-Hours**	**Total**	**Wage**	
6		**(Schedule 2)**	**per Unit**	**Hours**	**Rate**	**Total**
7	Regular	6,000	4	24,000	$20	$480,000
8	Heavy-Duty	1,000	6	6,000	$20	120,000
9	Total			30,000		$600,000

◆ **Schedule 5:** *Manufacturing overhead budget.* The total of these costs depends on how individual overhead costs vary with the assumed cost allocation base, direct manufacturing labour-hours. The calculations of budgeted manufacturing overhead costs appear in Schedule 5. Notice that manufacturing equipment and

	A	B	C	D
1	**Schedule 5: Manufacturing Overhead Budget***			
2	**For the Year Ended December 31, 2013**			
3		**At Budgeted Level of 30,000 Direct**		
4		**Manufacturing Labour-Hours**		
5	Variable manufacturing overhead costs:			
6	Supplies	$ 90,000		
7	Indirect manufacturing labour	190,000		
8	Direct and indirect manufacturing labour fringe costs @ 15.4% (rounded)	121,689		
9	Power	120,000		
10	Maintenance	60,000	$581,689	
11	Fixed:			
12	Amortization	220,000		
13	Property taxes	50,000		
14	Property insurance	10,000		
15	Supervision	100,000		
16	Power	22,000		
17	Maintenance	18,000	420,000	
18	Total		$1,001,689	
19				
20	*The annual amortization expense becomes part of Cost of Goods Sold (Schedule 7).			

plant amortization has been transferred from the schedule of Manufacturing Overhead Costs (p. 199) and included in this budget. This means some amortization expense is included in the Cost of Goods Sold (COGS) budget and is allocated to each unit of output. The remaining amortization, if any, of nonproduction long-term assets is included in fixed non-inventoriable or period costs, a separate schedule.

Schedule 5 reports two costs, power and maintenance, as both variable and fixed costs. This suggests that most of these two manufacturing overhead cost pools vary with some common input measure. Managers at Halifax Engineering have decided that the $22,000 of fixed power costs and $18,000 of fixed maintenance costs are material and should be reported separately as a fixed manufacturing overhead cost pool. Halifax treats all MOH as inventoriable costs and does not separate variable from fixed in this cost pool.[3]

◆ **Schedule 6:** *Ending inventory budget.* Schedule 6A shows the computation of unit costs for the two products. These unit costs are used to calculate the costs of target ending inventories of direct materials and finished goods in Schedule 6B.

	A	B	C	D	E	F
1	**Schedule 6A: Computation of Units Costs of Manufacturing**					
2				**Product**		
3				**Regular**	**Heavy-Duty**	
4		**Cost per Unit**				
5		**of Input***	**Inputs***	**Amount**	**Inputs***	**Amount**
6	Material 111 alloy	$ 7	12	$ 84	12	$ 84
7	Material 112 alloy	$10	6	60	8	80
8	Direct manufacturing labour	$20[†]	4	80	6	120
9	Manufacturing overhead	$33[‡]	4	134	6	200
10	Total			$358		$484
11						
12	*In kilograms or hours					
13	[†]Data are from p. 202.					
14	[‡]Direct manufacturing labour-hours is the sole allocation base for manufacturing overhead (both variable and fixed). The budgeted manufacturing overhead rate per direct manufacturing labour-hour of $33 was calculated in schedule 5.					

	A	B	C	D	E
1	**Schedule 6B: Ending Inventory Budget**				
2	**For the Year Ended December 31, 2013**				
3			**Cost per**		
4		**Kilograms**	**Kilogram**		**Total**
5	Direct materials				
6	111 alloy	8,000*	$ 7	$ 56,000	
7	112 alloy	2,000*	$10	20,000	$ 76,000
8			**Cost per**		
9		**Units**	**Unit**		
10	Finished goods				
11	Regular	1,100[†]	$358[‡]	$393,314	
12	Heavy-Duty	50[†]	$484[‡]	24,217	$417,531
13	Total Ending Inventory				$493,531
14					
15	*Data are from p. 198.				
16	[†]Data are from p. 198.				
17	[‡]From schedule 6A: this is based on 2013 costs of manufacturing finished goods because, under the FIFO costing method, the units in finished goods ending inventory consist of units that are produced during 2013.				

[3]This inventory costing method is termed *full absorption costing* because the costs of production, including fixed manufacturing overhead, are recorded in COGS and recovered in the price of the outputs sold (see Chapter 9).

◆ **Schedule 7:** *Cost of goods sold budget.* The information from Schedules 1 to 6 leads to Schedule 7:

	A	B	C	D
1	**Schedule 7: Cost of Goods Sold Budget**			
2	**For the Year Ended December 31, 2013**			
3		**From Schedule**		**Total**
4	Beginning finished goods inventory, January 1, 2013	Given		$ 64,600
5	Direct materials used	3A	$1,028,000	
6	Direct manufacturing labour	4	600,000	
7	Manufacturing overhead	5	1,001,689	
8	Cost of goods manufactured			2,629,689
9	Cost of goods available for sale			2,694,289
10	Deduct: Ending finished goods inventory,			
11	December 31, 2013	6B		(417,531)
12	Cost of goods sold			$2,276,758
13				
14	*Note:* The annual amortization expense has been included in manufacturing overhead and therefore is part of Cost of Goods Sold.			

Note that the following holds:

$$\text{Cost of goods sold} = \text{Beginning finished goods inventory} + \text{Cost of goods manufactured} - \text{Ending finished goods inventory}$$

◆ **Schedule 8:** *Other (nonproduction) costs budget.* Schedules 2 to 7 cover budgeting for Halifax's production area of the value chain. For brevity, other areas of the value chain are combined into a single schedule.

	A	B	C	D	E
1	**Schedule 8: Other (Nonproduction) Costs Budget**				
2	**For the Year Ended December 31, 2013**				
3					
4	Variable costs:				
5	R&D/product design	$ 56,000			
6	Marketing	92,600			
7	Distribution	66,500			
8	Customer service	47,600			
9	General and administrative	78,000	$340,700		
10	Fixed costs:				
11	R&D/product design	45,000			
12	Marketing	35,000			
13	Distribution	28,000			
14	Customer service	16,870			
15	General and administrative	100,000	224,870		
16	Total costs		$565,570		

◆ **Schedule 9:** *Budgeted income statement.* Schedules 1, 7, and 8 provide the necessary information to complete the budgeted operating income statement, shown in Exhibit 6-3. Of course, more details could be included in the income statement and then fewer supporting schedules would be prepared.

EXHIBIT 6-3
Budgeted Income Statement for Halifax Engineering for the Year Ended December 31, 2013

	A	B	C	D
1	**Budgeted Operating Income Statement for Halifax Engineering**			
2	**For the Year Ended December 31, 2013**			
3	Revenue	Schedule 1		$3,800,000
4	Costs:			
5	Cost of goods sold	Schedule 7		2,314,758
6	Gross margin			1,485,242
7	Operating (period) costs			
8	R&D/product design costs	Schedule 8	$101,000	
9	Marketing costs	Schedule 8	127,600	
10	Distribution costs	Schedule 8	94,500	
11	Customer service costs	Schedule 8	64,470	
12	Administrative costs	Schedule 8	178,000	565,570
13	Operating income			$ 919,672
14				
15	*Note:* Unlike financial accounting, this budgeted income statement contains the non-cash annual amortization expense in Cost of Goods Sold (see Schedule 5 and Schedule 7).			

Remember that a budget is a forecast of anticipated future performance—it can be changed. Exhibit 6-3 illustrates a pro forma operating income statement. Almost all companies own long-term assets that generate amortization, depreciation, or depletion, which is reported on the income statement. But Halifax Engineering reports no amortization expense under its period costs. The reason is clear if you refer to the Manufacturing Overhead Costs and the Other (Non-manufacturing) Costs data (p. 199), which are reported as Schedule 5 (p. 202) and Schedule 8 (p. 204), respectively. All amortization for Halifax Engineering, a machine shop, is for the manufacturing plant and equipment. This non-cash cost has been correctly reported, in full GAAP compliance, as an inventoriable cost and included in the Cost of Goods Sold amount in Exhibit 6-3. This is why there is no amortization expense reported in the Operating (Period) Cost section.

Top management's strategies for achieving revenue and operating income goals influence the costs planned for the different business functions of the value chain. In particular, all direct variable costs will change as volumes change, while all indirect variable costs will change as the quantities of common inputs consumed change. If a large expansion is planned, then the amortization expense as well as fixed costs, such as insurance and taxes, will also change. The actual financial results will be compared to budgeted results. Management can then evaluate whether their operating plan has been successful and change the plan if necessary.

PREPARING THE CASH BUDGET

3 Prepare a cash budget.

So far this chapter has featured the operating budget, which reports the expected inventoriable and period costs for Halifax Engineering but does not report the interest expense, tax expense, or net income. Without these estimates, the company will not be able to complete any of its financial budgets. In this section we focus on developing the cash budget. The **cash budget** is a schedule of *expected* cash receipts and disbursements, and is essential for forecasting any expected interest expense. Once interest expense has been estimated, Halifax Engineering can prepare a pro forma income statement in proper financial format.

The budgeted quarterly cash flows, shown below, will differ from actual cash flows. All cash flows from operations shown in a cash budget will differ from the revenue, COGS, and operating expenses in the supporting schedules. This is because there is a time lag between when sales are made and accounts are paid by purchasers. At year end, there is always some revenue that has not been realized as a cash payment by customers. There is also a time lag between when companies are invoiced and when they pay the invoice. At the end of the year, some bills owing have not been paid in cash. Accrual accounting in compliance with GAAP results in these discrepancies arising from timing differences between when a benefit or obligation must be reported and when the cash inflow or outflow actually occurs.

| | Quarters | | | | |
	(1)	(2)	(3)	(4)	Total
Collections from customers	$800,000	$700,000	$950,000	$918,400	$3,368,400
Disbursements:					
Direct materials	350,000	230,000	200,000	230,000	1,010,000
Payroll	380,000	295,000	276,000	282,000	1,233,000
Income taxes	50,000	47,912	47,912	47,912	193,736
Other costs	195,000	185,000	180,000	183,000	743,000
Machinery purchase	—	—	—	35,080	35,080

The actual balance sheet for Halifax Engineering for the year ended December 31, 2012, is reported in Exhibit 6-4; these will be the opening balances for the 2013 cash budget. The cash budget for 2013 will affect all the amounts except that reported for land. The preparation of a capital budget, which is necessary for the preparation of the pro forma balance sheet, is covered in Chapters 21 and 22.

Halifax Engineering has always budgeted for a $35,000 minimum cash balance at the end of each quarter. The company can borrow or repay exactly the amount required at an annual interest rate of 2%. The terms of its agreement with the bank call for the company to repay total interest owed and as much of the principal outstanding as possible at the end of each quarter. Interest each quarter is on a quarterly rate of 0.5% per quarter (0.02 ÷ 4 months = 0.005, or 0.5% per quarter). Assume that borrowing and repayment occur at the end of the quarters in question.

EXHIBIT 6-4
Balance Sheet for Halifax Engineering as of December 31, 2012

	A	B	C
1	**Assets**		
2	Current Assets		
3	Cash	$ 30,000	
4	Accounts receivable	100,000	
5	Direct materials	109,000	
6	Finished goods	64,600	$ 303,600
7	Property, plant, and equipment		
8	Land	100,000	
9	Building and equipment	6,200,000	
10	Accumulated amortization	(3,100,000)	3,200,000
11	Total Assets		$3,503,600
12			
13	**Liabilities and Shareholders' Equity**		
14	Current Liabilities		
15	Accounts payable	50,000	
16	Income taxes payable	50,000	100,000
17	Shareholders' Equity:		
18	Common shares, no par value 25,000 I/OS	2,150,000	
19	Retained earnings	1,253,600	3,403,600
20	Total Liabilities and Shareholders' Equity		$3,503,600
21	*Note:* Many adjustments must be made to the assure GAAP compliance. These create discrepancies between the cash budget and, for example, collections remaining in the year and the Accounts Receivable on the balance sheet.		

Interest is calculated to the nearest dollar. Tax expense has been rounded to the nearest dollar, using a 40% tax rate.

There are three facts to remember when preparing cash budgets:

◆ The ending balance (EB) of the previous quarter must be the beginning balance (BB) of the next quarter, *except*

◆ The "Year as a Whole" column reports the total cash receipts and disbursements for four quarters. This is because the BB for quarter 1 is the *year-end* balance for 2012, which becomes the BB for the *year* 2013. The EB for this "Year as a Whole" column must be the same as the EB for quarter 4 because there is no further activity in cash inflow or outflow.

◆ Amortization is not a cash disbursement and is therefore not reported in the cash budget. A sophisticated approach would be to use the actual capital cost allowance (CCA) and estimated taxes. These refinements are presented in Chapters 21 and 22.

The company must now prepare the cash budget in a logical flow:

1. Prepare a statement of cash receipts and disbursements by quarters, including details of borrowing, repayment, and interest expense.

2. Prepare a budgeted balance sheet.

3. Prepare a budgeted income statement, including the effects of interest expense and income taxes. Assume that income taxes for 2013 (at a tax rate of 40%) are $193,736.

PREPARATION OF THE CASH BUDGET

1. The cash budget (Exhibit 6-5) details expected cash receipts and disbursements quarter by quarter. It predicts the effects on the cash position at a given level of

EXHIBIT 6-5
Cash Budget for Halifax Engineering for the Year Ended December 31, 2013

	A	B	C	D	E	F
1		Quarters				
2		(1)	(2)	(3)	(4)	Annual
3	Cash balance, beginning	$ 30,000	$ 35,000	$ 35,000	$ 40,182	$ 30,000
4	Add: Receipts					
5	Collections from customers	800,000	700,000	950,000	918,400	3,368,400
6	Total cash available for needs: (a)	830,000	735,000	985,000	958,582	3,398,400
7	Deduct: Disbursements					
8	Direct materials	350,000	230,000	200,000	230,000	1,010,000
9	Payroll	380,000	295,000	276,000	282,000	1,233,000
10	Income taxes	50,000	47,912	47,912	47,912	193,736
11	Other costs	195,000	185,000	180,000	183,000	743,000
12	Machinery purchase	—	—	—	35,080	35,080
13	Total disbursements (b)	975,000	757,912	703,912	777,992	3,214,816
14	Cash balance before borrowing (a) – (b)	(145,000)	(22,912)	281,088	180,590	
15	Minimum cash balance desired (c)	35,000	35,000	35,000	35,000	
16	Additional cash available (needed)	180,000	57,912	—	—	
17	Loan repayment excluding interest 2%/year	—	—	240,006	—	
18	Interest repayment		900	1,194		2,094
19	Cash balance end of quarter or year after interest	$ 35,000	$ 35,000	$ 40,182	$180,590	$ 180,590
20	Financing					
21	Borrowing (at end of each quarter)	$ 180,000	$ 58,812	$ —		
22	Repayment (at end of next quarter)	—		240,006		
23	Interest (at 2% per year or 0.50% per quarter)*	—	900	1,194		
24	Total effects of financing	$ 180,000	$ 59,712	$ 241,200		
25	Cash balance end of quarter (after repayments)	$ 35,000	$ 35,000	$ 40,182		
26	*Annualized interest = 2% per year ÷ 4 = 0.50% per quarter					

operations. Each quarter, this budget clearly shows the impact of cash-flow timing on bank loans and their repayment. In practice, monthly—and sometimes weekly—cash budgets are helpful for cash planning and control, depending on the company's needs. Cash budgets help avoid unnecessary idle cash and unexpected cash deficiencies. Ordinarily, the cash budget has the following main sections:

a. The *beginning cash balance* plus cash receipts equals the total cash available for needs. Cash receipts depend on collections of accounts receivable, cash sales, and miscellaneous recurring sources such as rental or royalty receipts. Information on the prospective collectibility of accounts receivable is needed for accurate predictions. Key factors include bad debt (uncollectible accounts) experience and average time lag between sales and collections.

b. *Cash disbursements* include the following items:

   i. Direct materials purchases, which depend on credit terms extended by suppliers and bill-paying patterns of the buyer.

   ii. Direct labour and other wage and salary outlays, which depend on payroll dates.

   iii. Other costs that depend on timing and credit terms. Amortization is *not* a cash outlay.

   iv. Other disbursements are cash outlays for property, plant, and equipment, as well as long-term investments.

c. *Financing requirements* depend on how the cash balance before borrowing, keyed as (a) – (b) in Exhibit 6-5, line 14, compares with the minimum cash balance desired, keyed as (c), line 15. The financing plans will depend on the relationship between the cash balance before borrowing and the minimum cash balance desired. If there is excess cash, loans may be repaid or temporary investments made. The outlays for interest expense are usually shown in this section of the cash budget.

d. *Ending cash balance* reports the net effect of the financing decisions on the cash budget. When the amount is negative as it is at the end of the first quarter $(145,000)$, the company must borrow enough to cover this shortfall plus $35,000 to achieve its desired ending balance for the quarter. From the cash budget, Halifax managers can forecast their annual interest payment and proceed to calculate pre-tax income and estimate tax at 40% on their budgeted income statement for 2013.

The cash budget in Exhibit 6-5 shows the short-term *self-liquidating cycle* of cash loans. Seasonal peak load on production or sales often result in heavy cash disbursements for purchases, payroll, and other operating outlays as the products are produced and sold. Cash receipts from customers typically lag behind sales. The loan is self-liquidating in the sense that the borrowed money is used to acquire resources that are combined for sale, and the proceeds from sales are used to repay the loan. This **self-liquidating cycle**—sometimes called the **working capital cycle, cash cycle,** or **operating cycle**—is the movement of cash from producing inventories to receivables from sales and back to cash from collections.

2. The budgeted balance sheet is presented in Exhibit 6-6. Each item is projected in light of the details of the business plan as expressed in all the

EXHIBIT 6-6
Halifax Engineering: Budgeted Balance Sheet as of December 31, 2013

	A	B	C	D
1	**Assets**			
2	Current Assets			
3	Cash (from Exhibit 6-5)	$ 180,590		
4	Accounts receivable (1)	431,600		
5	Direct materials (2)	76,000		
6	Finished goods (2)	417,531		$1,105,721
7	Property, plant, and equipment			
8	Land (3)		100,000	
9	Building and equipment (4)	6,235,080		
10	Accumulated amortization (5)	3,321,754	2,913,326	3,013,326
11	Total Assets			$4,119,047
12				
13	**Liabilities and Shareholders' Equity**			
14	Current Liabilities			
15	Accounts payable (6)		$ 75,000	
16	Income taxes payable (7)		91,492	$ 166,492
17	Shareholders' Equity			
18	Common shares, no par value 25,000 I/OS (8)		2,150,000	
19	Retained earnings (9)		1,802,554	3,952,554
20	Total Liabilities and Shareholders' Equity			$4,119,047
21				
22	*Notes:*			
23	Beginning balances from Exhibit 6-4 are used as the starting point for most of the following computations:			
24	(1) $100,000 + $3,800,000 revenue − $3,368,400 receipts (Exhibit 6-5) = $531,600.			
25	(2) From schedule 6B, p. 203.			
26	(3) From beginning balance sheet (Exhibit 6-4).			
27	(4) $6,200,000 + $35,080 purchases = $6,235,080.			
28	(5) $3,100,000 + $220,000 (schedule 5, p. 202) plus incremental amortization of $1,754 Exhibit 6-7.			
29	(6) $50,000 + $1,035,000 (schedule 3B, p. 202) − $1,010,000 (Exhibit 6-5) = $75,000.			
30	(7) 25% of total tax, $365,970, quarterly payments have been made.			
31	(8) From beginning balance sheet (Exhibit 6-4).			
32	(9) $1,253,600 + $548,954 net income (Exhibit 6-7) = $1,802,554.			

EXHIBIT 6-7
Budgeted Income Statement for Halifax Engineering for the Year Ended December 31, 2013

	A	B	C	D
1	Revenue	Schedule 1		$3,800,000
2	Costs:			
3	Cost of goods sold	Schedule 7		2,314,758
4	Gross margin			1,485,242
5	Period costs:			
6	R&D and product design costs	Schedule 8	$101,000	
7	Marketing costs	Schedule 8	127,600	
8	Distribution	Schedule 8	94,500	
9	Customer service	Schedule 8	64,470	
10	Administration costs	Schedule 8	178,000	
11	Amortization on new purchase*		1,754	567,324
12	Operating income			917,918
13	Interest expense			2,994
14	Income before tax			914,924
15	Income tax at 40%			365,970
16	Net income			$ 548,954
17				
18	*Amortization on the new purchase was excluded from the initial estimate of manufacturing overhead and cost of goods sold. Incremental expense has been calculated by applying the half-year rule, assuming a useful life of ten years and no residual value.			

previous budget schedules. The beginning balances for this pro forma balance sheet for 2013 were, of course, the ending balances for the actual balance sheet for 2012.[4]

3. The budgeted income statement is presented in Exhibit 6-7. It is merely the budgeted operating income statement in Exhibit 6-3 (p. 205) expanded to include interest expense and income taxes. It would have been impossible to forecast the interest expense without the cash budget, and without that estimate Halifax could not calculate its pre-tax income. Once the cash budget is complete, Halifax can not only forecast its net income but also use that value to calculate retained earnings for the budgeted year 2013. The managers begin with the actual ending balance in retained earnings in 2012 and add the forecast income for 2013 to obtain the forecast 2013 retained earnings. A similar process can be followed using other information in the schedules to derive the 2013 budget.

Amortization is reported as a period cost in Exhibit 6-7. With the added information available from the cash budget, there is an anticipated new purchase. This expected acquisition of a long-term asset must not be manufacturing plant or equipment because the amortization is reported as a period cost and there has been no change in the total COGS reported.

For simplicity, the cash receipts and disbursements were given explicitly in this illustration of a cash budget. Frequently, there are lags between the items reported on the accrual basis of accounting in an income statement and their related cash receipts and disbursements. In the Halifax Engineering example, collections from customers are derived under two assumptions: (1) In any month, 10% of sales are cash sales and 90% of sales are on credit, and (2) half the total credit sales are collected in each of the two months subsequent to the sale, as illustrated for the third quarter in the following table:

---

[4]Technically the cash budget should include capital cost allowance (CCA) and other Canada Revenue considerations. These give rise to both short- and long-term deferred tax liabilities or assets on the balance sheet. CCA is discussed in Chapter 22, while balance sheet items are discussed in advanced financial accounting texts.

	A	B	C	D	E	F	G
1							**Cash Collections**
2							**in 3rd Quarter**
3		**May Actual**	**June Actual**	**July Forecast**	**August Forecast**	**September Forecast**	**as a Whole**
4	Monthly revenue budget for Halifax assumes the following revenue flows:						
5	Credit sales, 90%	$252,494	$301,253	$285,000	$285,000	$285,000	
6	Cash sales, 10%	42,516	31,591	31,667	31,667	31,667	
7	Total sales (or revenue)	$295,010	$332,844	$316,667	$316,667	$316,667	
8	Cash collections from:						
9	Cash sales this month			$ 31,667	$31,667	$ 31,667	
10	Credit sales last month			150,627	142,500	142,500	
11	Credit sales two months ago			126,247	150,627	142,500	
12	Total collection			$308,540	$324,793	$316,667	$950,000
13							
14	Assume credit is 90% of all revenue						
15	Collection is 50% of sales revenue the month after the sale and the remaining 50% two months after the sale.						
16	For example: July credit sales collection from June = 50% × $301,253 = $150,627						
17	July credit sales collections from May = 50% × $252,494 = $126,247						

The revenue budget requires detailed analysis of different ways in which customers can pay for their purchases. Halifax managers have assumed that 10% of their monthly sales will be paid cash. They assume the remaining 90% of their total monthly sales will be on credit with a 30-day payment date. Therefore, in June, 90% of May's credit sales will be collected. Managers have assumed no default on credit payments and that the remaining 10% of credit sales will be collected two months after the month of sale. Therefore the remainder of May's sales will be collected in July.

Of course, such schedules of cash collections depend on credit terms, collection histories, and expected bad debts. Similar monthly schedules can be prepared for operating costs and their related cash disbursements.

THREE BUDGET STRATEGIES: SENSITIVITY ANALYSIS, KAIZEN BUDGETING, AND ACTIVITY-BASED BUDGETS

Exhibit 6-1 (p. 194) illustrated the interrelationships among strategic analysis, planning, and budgeting. The value of budgets to managers in their strategic analysis and planning is enhanced by conducting sensitivity analysis. Sensitivity analysis is a *what-if* technique that examines how a result will change if the original predicted data are not achieved or if an underlying assumption changes. A hand-held calculator is adequate to do the basic budget calculations. Commercial software packages such as Microsoft FRx, however, make important tests such as sensitivity analysis, continuous improvement planning, and activity-based budgeting accessible even to small owner-managed enterprises.

The financial planning model from which the master budgets and schedules were calculated for Halifax Engineering assumes the following:

Distinguish among sensitivity analysis, Kaizen budgeting, and activity-based budgeting.

◆ Direct materials and direct manufacturing labour costs vary proportionately with the quantities of Regular and Heavy-Duty parts produced.

◆ Variable manufacturing overhead costs vary with direct manufacturing labour-hours.

◆ Variable non-manufacturing costs vary with revenue dollars.

◆ Target ending inventories remain unchanged.

SENSITIVITY ANALYSIS: A FORM OF STRATEGIC ANALYSIS

The budget and schedules are simply quantified reports of expectations; they are not actual achievements. Some assumptions are more critical to the company's success than others. Recall that one tool for strategic analysis requires identifying critical

EXHIBIT 6-8
Effect of Changes in Budget Assumptions on Budgeted Income for Halifax Engineering

What-if Scenario	Units Sold		Selling Price		Direct Materials Cost*		Budgeted Operating Income	
	Regular	Heavy-Duty	Regular	Heavy-Duty	111 Alloy	112 Alloy	Dollars	Change from Master Budget
Master budget	5,000	1,000	$600	$800	$7.00	$10.00	$486,000†	—
Scenario 1	5,000	1,000	582	776	7.00	10.00	386,250	20.52% decrease
Scenario 2	4,800	960	600	800	7.00	10.00	438,562	9.76% decrease
Scenario 3	5,000	1,000	600	800	7.35	10.50	448,380	7.74% decrease

*Per kilogram.
†From Exhibit 6-7, p. 210

factors. Exhibit 6-8 presents the budgeted operating income for three changes in each of three critical factors for Halifax Engineering:

◆ Scenario 1: A 3% decrease in the selling price of the Regular part and a 3% decrease in the selling price of the Heavy-Duty part.

◆ Scenario 2: A 4% decrease in units sold of the Regular part and a 4% decrease in units sold of the Heavy-Duty part.

◆ Scenario 3: A 5% increase in the price per kilogram of 111 alloy and a 5% increase in the price per kilogram of 112 alloy.

Exhibit 6-8 indicates that, relative to the master budget, budgeted operating income decreases by 21% under scenario 1, by 10% under scenario 2, and by 8% under scenario 3. Managers can use this information to plan actions if faced with these scenarios, rather than scrambling in a crisis if such changes occur.

KAIZEN BUDGETING: IMPLEMENTING CONTINUOUS QUALITY IMPROVEMENT STRATEGIES

Chapter 1 noted how continuous improvement is one of the key issues facing management today. **Kaizen budgeting** implements a strategy of systematic elimination of waste in every business process.[5] A key assumption is that attention is focused on eliminating activities that create cost but add no value. The improvements gained through Kaizen budgeting arise from many small changes made during the budget period as a result of employees' suggestions. Kaizen is most closely identified with Toyota and the strategy of lean management.

Consider our Halifax Engineering example in Schedule 4 (p. 202). The 2013 budget assumes that it will take 4.0 and 6.0 manufacturing labour-hours respectively for each Regular and Heavy-Duty aircraft part. A Kaizen budgeting approach would incorporate continual reduction in these manufacturing labour-hour requirements during 2013. Assume Halifax budgets the following labour-hour amounts:

	Budgeted Amounts (Labour-Hours)	
	Regular	Heavy-Duty
January–March 2014	4.00	6.00
April–June 2014	3.90	5.85
July–September 2014	3.80	5.70
October–December 2014	3.70	5.55

[5]For an overview of Japanese management accounting, see R. Cooper, "Japanese Cost Management Practices," *CMA Magazine*, October 1994.

Unless Halifax meets these continuous improvement goals, unfavourable variances will be reported. Note that in the Halifax budget, the implications of these direct labour-hour reductions would extend to reductions in variable manufacturing overhead costs, given that direct manufacturing labour-hours is the driver of these costs.

ACTIVITY-BASED BUDGETING

Chapter 5 explained how activity-based cost (ABC) assignment systems can lead to improved decision making. ABC principles also extend to budgeting. **Activity-based budgeting (ABB)** is a strategy that focuses on the cost of activities necessary to produce and sell products and services. A survey of U.K. managers reported the following ranking of the benefits from activity-based budgeting: (1) ability to set more realistic budgets, (2) better identification of resource needs, (3) linking of costs to outputs, (4) clearer linking of costs with staff responsibilities, and (5) identification of budgetary slack[6] (see the Governance box on p. 219).

The example in Exhibit 6-2 (p. 197) assumed a budget was produced for business functions in the value chain. You will recall from Chapter 5 that activities, especially those at the batch, product, and facilities levels, will cross boundaries among business functions and highlight interdependencies among them. A new company, Bradford Aerospace, illustrates how activity-based budgeting requires schedules and budgets for different activities rather than different business functions.

The key difference between the two approaches is that in ABB, the operating loop must be completed first within the resource-budget constraints. Then the financial budget is produced.[7] Both approaches begin with the forecast demand for outputs. Managers using ABB focus their efforts on matching forecast demand to the rates at which different *activities* are consumed at specified activity levels to fulfill a single unit of demand. Recall that these are conversion activities and that cost drivers measure the resources consumed during conversion. In this approach, the measure of the quantities of cost drivers will be the basis for calculating the costs of activities. The second stage is the financial loop, the goal of which is to match various measures of rates of return (e.g., net profit, operating profit, return on assets) with the demanded rate of return.

Activity-based budgeting also follows a logical order:

- ◆ Determine the budgeted costs of performing each unit of activity for each activity area.
- ◆ Determine the demand for each individual activity at the product level based on, for example, budgeted new-product R&D, production, marketing, and so on. Budgets and schedules are also needed for existing products. Adding or dropping a product will change both the activity and the cost pool.
- ◆ Calculate the costs of performing each activity.
- ◆ Describe the budget as costs of performing various activities (rather than budgeted costs of functional or conventional value-chain spending categories).

This approach highlights imbalances among demand for and supplies of resources at the unit, batch, product (or service), and facilities levels that are not readily apparent from the traditional approach. As with the ABC costing approach, ABB ensures that managers will not focus on individual business functions but rather on the interdependencies among the functions.

Consider activity-based budgeting for the R&D/product design parts of the value chain at Bradford Aerospace. Four activity areas and their cost drivers have

---

[6]J. Innes and F. Mitchell, "A Survey of Activity-Based Costing in the U.K.'s Largest Companies," *Management Accounting Research*, 6: 137–53.

[7]Stephen C. Hansen, David T. Otley, and Wim A. Van der Stede, "Recent Developments in Budgeting: An Overview and Research Perspective," *Journal of Management Accounting Research*, 15 (2003): 95–116.

EXHIBIT 6-9
Activity-Based Budget for R&D/Product Design Costs of Bradford Aerospace: January to December 2013

Activity Area	Budgeted Usage of Driver		Budgeted Rate per Cost Driver	Budgeted Activity Costs
Computer-aided design	200	hours	$80	$16,000
Manual design	70	hours	50	3,500
Prototype development	80	hours	60	4,800
Testing	280	hours	40	11,200
Procurement	120	purchase orders	25	3,000
Total				$38,500

been identified. The budgeted 2013 rates for the costs in each activity area are as follows:

Activity	Cost Driver/Budgeted Cost Rate
Computer-aided design (CAD)—using computer software to design aircraft parts	CAD hours, $80 per hour
Manual design—manually designing aircraft parts	Manual design hours, $50 per hour
Prototype development—building actual versions of aircraft parts	Prototyping hours, $60 per hour
Testing—examining how new aircraft parts "perform" in different operating conditions	Testing hours, $40 per hour
Procurement—purchasing supplies and component parts	Purchase orders, $25 per purchase order

Exhibit 6-9 presents the activity-based budget for January to December 2013. Bradford budgets usage of the cost driver in each activity area based on budgeted production and new-product development. This budgeted usage of the cost driver for each activity is multiplied by the respective budgeted cost rates per activity to obtain the budgeted activity costs. The budgeted total costs for R&D/product design is the sum of the budgeted costs of the individual activities in that part of the value chain.

The activity-based budget in Exhibit 6-9 is for one part of Bradford's value chain. In many cases, the same activity will appear in more than one part of the value chain. For example, procurement activities such as purchase ordering and supplier payment are found in most areas of the value chain. Companies using activity-based budgeting may choose to present their budgets at either the individual value-chain level or at some more basic activity level, such as procurement, by combining budgeted procurement costs from different parts of the value chain.

RESPONSIBILITY VERSUS CONTROLLABILITY

5 Contrast responsibility against controllability.

ORGANIZATIONAL STRUCTURE AND RESPONSIBILITY

Organizational structure is the arrangement of centres of responsibility within an entity. A company like Petro-Canada may be organized primarily by business function: exploration, refining, and marketing. Another company like Procter & Gamble, a household-products giant, may be organized by product or brand line. The managers of the individual divisions (toothpaste, soap, and so on) would each have decision-making authority concerning all the business functions (manufacturing, marketing, etc.) within that division.

Managers and executives are assigned responsibility and held accountable for achieving specific financial and nonfinancial performance targets. A **responsibility centre** is a part, segment, or sub-unit of an organization whose manager is accountable for a specified set of activities. The higher the manager's level, the broader the responsibility centre he or she manages and, generally, the larger the number of subordinates who report to him or her. **Responsibility accounting** is a system that measures the plans (by budgets) and actions (by actual results) of each responsibility centre. The complexity of the processes in a company often requires decentralizing both authority and responsibility. Four major types of responsibility centres are as follows:

1. **Cost centre.** The manager is accountable for costs only, not revenue lost or gained. Some managers may have authority over subordinate managers responsible for the outcomes of quantity, price, and scheduling decisions; others may not. The scope of authority, and therefore decentralization, will depend on the organizational structure.

2. **Revenue centre.** The manager is accountable for revenue only, not costs incurred to generate the revenue. Some managers of revenue centres may have authority over subordinate managers responsible for the outcomes of quantity and unit price decisions; others may not.

3. **Profit centre.** The manager is accountable for revenue and costs and has some authority over others who decide upon key factors affecting both revenue and cost. A profit-centre manager can coordinate among those responsible for either costs or revenue; however, this increases centralization.

4. **Investment centre.** The manager is accountable for investments, revenue, and costs.

The maintenance department of a Delta hotel is a cost centre if the maintenance manager is responsible only for costs; the budget would also emphasize costs. The sales department of the hotel is a revenue centre if the sales manager is responsible only for revenue, and the budget would emphasize revenue. The hotel manager might be in charge of a profit centre if he or she is accountable for both revenue and costs, and the budget would then emphasize both. The regional manager responsible for investments in new hotel projects and for revenue and costs could be in charge of an investment centre; revenue, costs, and the investment base would be emphasized in the budget for this manager.

Responsibility accounting affects behaviour. Consider the following incident:

The sales department requests a rush production run. The plant scheduler argues that it will disrupt production and will cost a substantial, though not clearly determined, amount of money. The answer coming from sales is, "Do you want to take responsibility for losing X Company as a customer?" Of course, the production scheduler does not want to take such a responsibility and gives up, but not before a heavy exchange of arguments and the accumulation of a substantial backlog of ill feeling.

The controller proposes an innovative solution. He analyzes the payroll in the assembly department to determine the costs involved in getting out rush orders. This information eliminates the cause for argument. Henceforth, any rush order is accepted by the production scheduler, "no questions asked." The extra costs are duly recorded and charged to the sales department.

As a result, the tension created by rush orders disappears, and the number of rush orders requested by the sales department is progressively reduced to an insignificant level.[8]

Responsibility accounting assigns accountability to:

◆ The individual who has the best knowledge about why the costs arose.
◆ The individual undertaking the activity that caused the costs.

[8]R. Villers, "Control and Freedom in a Decentralized Company," *Harvard Business Review*, 32.2: 95.

In this incident, the cause was the sales activity, and the resulting costs were charged to the sales department. If rush orders occur regularly, the sales department might have a budget for such costs, and the department's actual performance would then be compared against the budget.

FEEDBACK

When applied to budgets, responsibility accounting provides feedback to top management about the performance of different responsibility-centre managers relative to the budget. Differences between actual results and budgeted amounts—also called variances—if properly used, can be helpful in three ways:

1. *Early warning.* Variances alert managers early to events neither easily nor immediately evident. Managers can then take corrective actions or exploit the available opportunities. For example, is a small decline in sales this period an indication of an even steeper decline to follow later in the year, or an opportunity to design a higher value-added and more competitive product?

2. *Performance evaluation.* Variances inform managers about how well the company has performed in implementing its strategies. Were materials and labour used efficiently? Was R&D spending increased as planned? Did product warranty costs decrease as planned?

3. *Evaluating strategy.* Variances sometimes signal to managers that their strategies are ineffective. For example, a company seeking to compete by reducing cost and improving quality may find that it is achieving these goals but with little effect on sales and profits. Top management may then want to reevaluate the strategy.

DEFINITION OF CONTROLLABILITY

Controllability is the degree of authority that a specific manager has over costs, revenue, or other items in question. A **controllable cost** is any cost that is primarily subject to the authorization of a specific manager of a specific responsibility centre for a specific time span. A responsibility accounting system could either exclude all uncontrollable costs from a manager's performance report or segregate such costs from the controllable costs.

Recall the separation of variable from fixed costs of manufacturing overhead. Fixed costs comprised items such as insurance, taxes, lease costs or amortization, and management salaries. These costs are rarely controllable. Insurance companies set premiums with executives of corporations rather than plant managers; and cities, provinces, and countries set tax policies independent of corporations (not to mention individuals). While some negotiation of insurance premiums may be possible year to year, governments do not negotiate tax increases. Other examples include foreign currency exchange rates, commodity prices, and interest rates. All are important factors over which individual companies have no control.

Within a corporation, for example, a machining supervisor's performance report might be confined to quantities (not costs) of direct materials, direct manufacturing labour, power, and supplies. Unless the machining supervisor has the authority to set the price at which materials are procured, this approach is fair to the supervisor. Assume the purchasing manager has the authority to decide at what price materials will be purchased. The problem of cost control arises because the supervisor may order a lower quantity than required, or incur more than the expected level of waste in a time period. To meet customer demand, the supervisor will request a rush order. The purchasing manager has no authority to refuse and knows the cost of a rush order is higher than orders with a normal delivery time. Who is responsible for any cost overrun: the supervisor who needs the materials or the purchasing manager who negotiates prices with suppliers?

In practice, controllability is difficult to pinpoint:

1. Few costs are clearly under the sole influence of one manager. For example, costs of direct materials may be influenced by a purchasing manager, but such costs also depend on market conditions beyond the manager's control. Quantities used may be influenced by a production manager, but it also depends on the quality of materials purchased. Moreover, managers often work in teams. How can individual responsibility be evaluated in a team decision?

2. With a long enough time span, all costs will come under somebody's control. However, most performance reports focus on periods of a year or less. A current manager may have inherited problems and inefficiencies from his or her predecessor. For example, current managers may have to work under undesirable contracts with suppliers or labour unions that were negotiated by their predecessors. How can we separate what the current manager actually controls from the results of decisions made by others? Exactly what is the current manager accountable for? Answers to such questions may not be clear-cut.

Senior managers differ in how they embrace the controllability notion when evaluating those reporting to them. For example, a newly appointed president took his management team on a cruise and commented, "I expect everybody to meet their budget targets no matter what happens, and those who don't should stand a little closer to the railing." Other presidents believe that a more risk-sharing approach with managers is preferable, where noncontrollable factors are taken into account when making judgments about the performance of managers who miss their budgets.

EMPHASIS ON INFORMATION AND BEHAVIOUR

Responsibility accounting focuses on information and knowledge, not control. To succeed, however, other incentive systems must be aligned to the goal of free exchange of accurate information. The key question is: Who is the best informed? To put it another way: Who is the person that can tell us the most about the specific item in question, regardless of that person's ability to exert personal control? For instance, purchasing managers may be held accountable for total purchase costs, not because of their ability to affect market prices but because of their ability to predict uncontrollable prices and explain uncontrollable price changes. Similarly, managers at a Tim Hortons store may be held responsible for the operating income of their units, even though they do not fully control selling prices or the costs for many food items and have minimal flexibility as to which items to sell or their ingredients. These unit managers are in the best position to explain variances between their actual operating income and their budgeted operating income.

Performance reports for responsibility centres may also include uncontrollable items because this approach could change behaviour for the better. For example, some companies have changed cost centres to profit centres to motivate a change in managers' decisions and actions. A cost centre manager may emphasize production efficiency and deemphasize the pleas of sales personnel for faster service and rush orders. In a profit centre, the manager is responsible for both costs and revenue. Although the manager still has no control over sales personnel, the manager will now more likely weigh the impact of his or her decisions on costs *and* revenue rather than solely on costs.

HUMAN ASPECTS OF BUDGETING

Why did we cover three major topics—master budgets, cash budgets, and responsibility accounting—in the same chapter? Primarily to emphasize that human factors are crucial aspects of budgeting. The budgeting techniques themselves are free of emotion; however, their administration requires education, persuasion, and intelligent interpretation. To be effective, budgeting requires honest communication about the business from subordinates and lower-level managers to their bosses. But subordinates may try to build in budgetary slack to hedge against unexpected adverse circumstances. The budgetary slack could mislead top management about the true profit potential of the company.

What can top management do to obtain accurate budget forecasts from lower-level managers? There are several options.

To explain one approach, let's consider the plant manager of a beverage bottler who is suspected by top management of understating the productivity potential of the bottling lines in his forecasts for the coming year. His presumed motivation is to increase the likelihood of meeting next year's production bonus targets. Suppose top management could purchase a consulting firm's study that reports productivity levels—such as the number of bottles filled per hour—at a number of comparable plants owned by other bottling companies. This report would show that their own plant manager's productivity forecasts are well below actual productivity levels being achieved at other comparable plants.

Top management could share this independent information source with their plant manager and ask him to explain why his productivity differs from that at other comparable plants. They could also base part of the plant manager's compensation on his plant's productivity relative to other "benchmark" plants rather than on the forecasts he provided. Using external benchmark performance measures reduces a manager's ability to set budget levels that are easy to achieve.[9]

Another approach to reducing budgetary slack is for managers to involve themselves regularly in understanding what their subordinates are doing. Such involvement should not result in managers dictating the decisions and actions of subordinates. Rather, a manager's involvement should take the form of providing support, challenging in a motivational way the assumptions subordinates make, and enhancing mutual learning about the operations. Regular interaction with subordinates allows managers to become knowledgeable about the operations and diminishes the ability of subordinates to create slack in their budgets.

Part of top management's responsibility is to improve organization commitment to a set of core values and norms. The values and norms describe what constitutes acceptable and unacceptable behaviour. Companies such as General Electric and Johnson & Johnson have developed values and a culture that discourage budgetary slack.

Some companies, such as IBM and Kodak, have designed innovative performance-evaluation measures that reward managers based on the subsequent accuracy of the forecasts used in preparing budgets. For example, the *higher and more accurate* the budgeted profit forecasts of division managers, the higher their incentive bonuses.

Many of the best-performing companies set "stretch" or "challenge" targets. *Stretch targets* are actually overestimates of expected performance, intended to motivate employees to exert effort and attain better performance.

Many managers regard budgets negatively. To them, the word *budget* is about as popular as *downsizing, layoff,* or *strike.* Top managers must convince their subordinates that the budget is a tool designed to help them set and reach goals. But budgets are not remedies for weak management talent, faulty organization, or a poor accounting system.

The management style of executives is also a factor in how budgets are perceived in companies. Some CEOs argue that "numbers always tell the story." An executive once noted that "you can miss your plan once, but you wouldn't want to miss it twice." Other CEOs believe that too much focus on making the numbers in a budget can lead to poor decision making.

---

[9]For an excellent discussion of these issues, see Chapter 14 ("Formal Models in Budgeting and Incentive Contracts") of R. S. Kaplan and A. A. Atkinson, *Advanced Management Accounting*, 3rd ed. (Upper Saddle River, NJ: Prentice Hall, 1998).

Management Accounting and the Corporate Governance Laws

An accurate budget is essential to a company's success. But when it comes time to discuss the budget, some managers approach the negotiation process with an eye toward protecting their own interests. If managers make their budgets—or, better, improve on them—financial rewards generally come their way. So managers may intentionally ask for budget amounts that will help them achieve their targets but that will not maximize the company's overall profits. Addressing this issue of budgetary slack may be the most difficult role for management accountants because they must be able to deal with conflict and argue persuasively for more realistic targets.

The CMA code of ethics states:

(3.1) A Member, Student, Firm, Public Accounting Firm or Professional Corporation will act at all times with: (a) responsibility for and fidelity to public needs; (b) fairness and loyalty to such Member's, Student's, Firm's, Public Accounting Firm's or Professional Corporation's associates, clients and employers; and (c) competence through devotion to high ideals of personal honour and professional integrity. (3.2) A Member, Student, Firm, Public Accounting Firm or Professional Corporation will: (a) maintain at all times independence of thought and action . . .

It is not only sensible to persuade managers to act in the best interests of the organization but also required by the professional code of ethics. Members of the CMA are expected to fulfill their fiduciary duty to the public, act with fairness and loyalty toward employers, and act independently.

Sources: L. Gray, "Why Budgeting Kills Your Company," *Working Knowledge*, Harvard Business School, August 11, 2003; Professional Misconduct and Code of Professional Ethics, Certified Management Accountants of Ontario, http://www.cma-ontario.org/index.cfm/ci_id/7409/la_id/1.htm, accessed December 22, 2010, with permission of Certified Management Accountants of Ontario.

BUDGETING: A PROCESS IN TRANSITION

Many areas of management accounting are subject to ongoing debate. Budgeting is no exception. Advocates of new proposals invariably include criticisms of so-called "traditional budgeting." These criticisms are often exaggerations of "current worst practice." Exhibit 6-10 summarizes six proposals designed to improve traditional budgeting systems. Few of the negative features cited in the left-hand column are new; they have long been singled out for criticism. Indeed, earlier sections of this chapter have mentioned the importance of avoiding many of these problems. Nonetheless, major changes that address these problems are currently being examined by managers.

EXHIBIT 6-10
Criticisms of Traditional Budgeting and Proposals for Change

Criticism of Traditional Budgeting	Proposal for Change
Excessive reliance on extrapolating past trends	Link budgeting explicitly to strategy.
Making across-the-board fixed percentage cuts when early iterations of a budget provide "unacceptable results"	Use activity-based budgeting to identify areas for cost reduction.
Examining individual functional areas as if they are independent (so-called silos, to use a farming analogy)	Explicitly adopt a cross-functional approach where interdependencies across business function areas of the value chain are recognized.
Myopically overemphasizing a fixed time horizon such as a year Viewing annual cost targets as a key task to be accomplished	Tailor the budget cycle to the purpose of budgeting. Events beyond current period are recognized as important when evaluating current actions. Value creation is given paramount importance.
Being preoccupied with financial aspects of events in the budget period	Balance financial aspects with nonfinancial (such as quality and time) aspects.
Not using budgets to evaluate performance until end of budget period	Signal to all employees the need for continuous improvement of performance (such as revenue enhancement and cost reduction) within the budget period.

Source: Adapted from "Advanced Budgeting Study Group Report for CAM-I," *Management Accounting* (U.K.).

(Try to solve this problem before examining the solution that follows.)

PROBLEM

Consider the Halifax Engineering example described in this chapter. Suppose Halifax Engineering managers conducted sensitivity analyses not only on the cash budget (see Exhibit 6-8, p. 212) but also on the effect of a 10% price increase in material 112 alloy from $10 to $11; a 12% increase in the variable supplies cost; a 22% increase in power costs to account for an unexpected jump in oil prices; and a corresponding 22% increase in distribution costs to account for ground and air transportation cost increases in concert with an oil-price increase.

REQUIRED

1. What are the benefits of budgeting for these specific changes now?
2. Before preparing a budgeted income statement, identify the supporting budget schedules that will *not* change as a result of this sensitivity analysis.
3. Prepare the budgeted operating income statement, including all necessary supporting schedules.
4. Discuss the results. Focus on any important changes that can be planned should the increases described above be realized in the coming year.
5. Discuss how responsibility and controllability will affect Halifax Engineering's response to the events noted in the sensitivity analysis.

SOLUTION

1. In the short term, the budget constraints for Halifax have changed. Only by recalculating the affected schedules can the company's managers understand what remedies may be available to reduce the effects of these cost increases. The team can agree in advance what responses may be made to sustain operating profits. The managers are already anticipating how to protect the company from external threats over which the company itself has no control.

    In the long run, the managers can assess if their current strategy will respond to these changes in the critical success factors of their environment. If the management team believes that key input prices can increase by such a large percentage, one strategic response may be to change how its products are distributed. In the long run, existing transportation contracts can be amended to share the risk of fuel price increases and managers can undertake hedging strategies. Halifax may also be able to renegotiate contracts with its purchasers to place the burden of transportation costs on them.

2. The revenue, production, and direct manufacturing labour budgets (Schedules 1, 2, and 4, p. 200, 201, and 202) will not change as a result of this sensitivity analysis.
3. The change in the cost of 112 alloy is shown in Schedule 3A. In total, the costs of direct materials to be used has increased from $1,028,000 to $1,066,000.

	A	B	C	D	E
1	Schedule 3A: Direct Materials Usage Budget in Kilograms and Dollars				
2	For the Year Ended December 31, 2013				
3		Materials			
4		111 Alloy	112 Alloy	Total	
5	Direct materials to be used in production of Regular parts (6,000 units) × 12 and 6 kilograms	72,000	36,000		see Schedule 2
6	Direct materials to be used in production of Heavy-Duty (1,000 units) × 12 and 8 kilograms	12,000	8,000		see Schedule 2
7	Total direct materials to be used (in kilograms)	84,000	44,000		

(continued)

8	Direct materials to be used from beginning inventory (assume FIFO cost flow)	7,000	6,000		
9	Multiply by: Cost per kilogram of beginning inventory	$ 7	$ 10		
10	Cost of direct materials to be used from beginning inventory	$ 49,000	$ 60,000	$ 109,000	(a)
11	Direct materials to be used from purchases (84,000 − 7,000; 44,000 − 6,000)	77,000	38,000		
12	Multiply by: Cost per kilogram of purchased materials	$ 7	$ 11		
13	Cost of direct materials to be used from purchases	$539,000	$418,000	$ 957,000	(b)
14	Total costs of direct materials to be used (a) + (b)	$588,000	$478,000	$1,066,000	

Changes to Schedule 3B, below, reflect the increase in cost of 112 alloy. The direct materials purchase cost for this alloy has increased from $400,000 to $440,000. Overall, the total direct materials purchase cost has also increased $40,000.

	A	B	C	D
1	**Schedule 3B: Direct Materials Usage Budget in Kilograms and Dollars**			
2	**For the Year Ended December 31, 2013**			
3		**Materials**		
4		**111 Alloy**	**112 Alloy**	**Total**
5	Direct materials to be used in production (in kilograms)	84,000	44,000	
6	Add: Target ending direct materials inventory	8,000	2,000	
7	Total requirements (in kilograms)	92,000	46,000	
8	Deduct: Beginning direct materials inventory	(7,000)	(6,000)	
9	Direct materials to be purchased (in kilograms)	85,000	40,000	
10	Multiply by: Cost per kilogram of purchased materials	$ 7	$ 11	
11	Total direct materials purchase costs	$595,000	$440,000	$1,035,000

In Schedule 5, the variable manufacturing overhead supplies has increased from $90,000 to $100,800 and the total manufacturing overhead budget has also increased $37,200 to $1,035,724:

	A	B	C	D
1	**Schedule 5: Manufacturing Overhead Budget**			
2	**For the Year Ended December 31, 2013**			
3		**At Budgeted Level of 30,000 Direct**		
4		**Manufacturing Labour-Hours**		
5	Variable manufacturing overhead costs:			
6	Supplies (12% increase)	$100,800		
7	Indirect manufacturing labour	190,000		
8	Direct and indirect manufacturing labour fringe costs @ 15%	118,524		
9	Power (22% increase)	146,400		
10	Maintenance	60,000	$ 615,724	
11	Fixed:			
12	Amortization	220,000		
13	Property taxes	50,000		
14	Property insurance	10,000		
15	Supervision	100,000		
16	Power	22,000		
17	Maintenance	18,000	420,000	
18	Total		$1,035,724	

The change in Schedule 6A reflects both the change in direct materials and in variable manufacturing overhead:

	A	B	C	D	E	F
1	**Schedule 6A: Computation of Unit Costs of Manufacturing**					
2				Product		
3				Regular	Heavy-Duty	
4		Cost per Unit				
5		of Input*	Inputs*	Amount	Inputs*	Amount
6	Material 111 alloy	$ 7	12	$ 84	12	$ 84
7	Material 112 alloy	$11	6	66	8	88
8	Direct manufacturing labour	$20†	4	80	6	120
9	Manufacturing overhead	$41.24‡	4	165	6	247
10	Total			$395		$539
11						
12	*In kilograms or hours					
13	†Data are from p. 202.					
14	‡Direct manufacturing labour-hours is the sole allocation base for manufacturing overhead (both variable and fixed). The budgeted manufacturing overhead rate per direct manufacturing labour-hour is $41.24 ($1,035,724 ÷ 30,000 budgeted direct manufacturing labour-hours).					

The change in Schedule 6B also reflects the change in direct materials on the value of total ending inventory:

	A	B	C	D	E
1	**Schedule 6B: Ending Inventory Budget**				
2	**For the Year Ended December 31, 2013**				
3			Cost per		
4		Kilograms	Kilogram		Total
5	Direct materials				
6	111 alloy	8,000*	$ 7	$ 56,000	
7	112 alloy	2,000*	$11	22,000	$ 78,000
8			Cost per		
9		Units	Unit		
10	Finished goods				
11	Regular	1,100†	$395	$434,500	
12	Heavy-Duty	50†	$539	26,950	$461,450
13	Total Ending Inventory				$539,450
14					
15	*Data are from pp. 198 and 220.				
16	†Data are from p. 198.				

The changes to inventoriable costs result in the following Cost of Goods Sold Budget, Schedule 7:

	A	B	C	D
1	**Schedule 7: Cost of Goods Sold Budget**			
2	**For the Year Ended December 31, 2013**			
3		From Schedule		Total
4	Beginning finished goods inventory, January 1, 2013	Given*		$ 64,600
5	Direct materials used (10% increase)	3A	$1,172,600	
6	Direct manufacturing labour	4	600,000	
7	Manufacturing overhead	5	1,035,724	
8	Cost of goods manufactured			2,808,324
9	Cost of goods available for sale			2,872,924
10	Deduct: Ending finished goods inventory,			
11	December 31, 2013	6B		(461,450)
12	Cost of goods sold			$2,411,474
13				
15	*Given in the description of basic data and requirements (Regular $38,400, Heavy-Duty $26,200) on p. 198.			

The change to distribution costs is reflected in the non-manufacturing costs budget, Schedule 8:

	A	B	C	D	E
1	**Schedule 8: Other (Non-manufacturing or Period) Costs**				
2					
3					
4	Variable:				
5	R&D/product design	$ 56,000			
6	Marketing	92,600			
7	Distribution (22% increase)	74,480			
8	Customer service	47,600			
9	Administrative	78,000	$348,680		
10	Fixed:				
11	R&D/product design	45,000			
12	Marketing	35,000			
13	Distribution	34,160			
14	Customer service	16,870			
15	Administrative	100,000	231,030		
16	Total		$579,710		

The result of these changes on operating income for Halifax Engineering is:

	A	B	C	D
1	**Budgeted Operating Income Statement for Halifax Engineering**			
2	**For the Year Ended December 31, 2013**			
3	Revenue	Schedule 1		$3,800,000
4	Costs:			
5	Cost of goods sold	Schedule 7		2,411,474
6	Gross margin			1,388,526
7	Operating (period) costs			
8	R&D/product design costs	Schedule 8	$101,000	
9	Marketing costs	Schedule 8	127,600	
10	Distribution costs	Schedule 8	108,640	
11	Customer service costs	Schedule 8	64,470	
12	Administrative costs	Schedule 8	178,000	579,710
13	Operating income			$ 808,816
14			**Original**	**Sensitivities**
15	Operating income percentage		24.23%	21.28%

4. The operating margin percentage without the sensitivity was approximately 24% ($922,342 ÷ $3,800,000) while after the sensitivities it decreased to about 21% ($808,816 ÷ $3,800,000). This is unsurprising given all the sensitivities were cost increases. A close comparison of the Ending Inventory Budget and the Cost of Goods Sold Budget provides the answer. The increase in direct materials, while only $1 per kilogram, increases the value of ending inventory from $448,600 to $461,450. This is a deduction from the cost of goods available for sale resulting in a larger cost of goods sold. Revenue has remained constant, therefore the gross margin decreases from $1,487,912 to $1,388,526.

The results illustrate the importance of sensitivity analysis. In the immediate one-year period, the effect is positive; however, the following year will present problems. All other things equal, and without further projected cost increases, Halifax must recover the additional costs in ending inventory of $191,400; otherwise its operating profit will decline in the second year and years following. The sensitivity analysis directs the managers to look beyond the short term.

5. Halifax changed its assumptions about the purchase price of direct materials. If an ongoing increase in prices is forecast and if Halifax has no special bargaining power with suppliers, it has no control over price. Those people in purchasing will have the greatest knowledge about likely future prices and sources of supply. In the short term, they can advise Halifax of the availability of long-term contracts and the likelihood of new suppliers entering the market for alloy 112.

The production engineers, however, will have the greatest knowledge about the current performance and safety specifications that require the use of alloy 112. The engineers can advise Halifax about the likelihood of switching to a less expensive direct material input, or of redesigning the part to use less of this alloy without jeopardizing performance and safety.

Those in the marketing function will have the greatest knowledge about the needs of customers such as Boeing. The engineering specifications in a contract require Boeing to take extreme care prior to making changes because the company sells its finished product, aircraft, to purchasers. Before Boeing can change its parts specification it must receive authorization not only from the Boeing aeronautical engineers but also from its customers. Finally, the federal government inspects all aircraft, which must conform in all respects to safety laws. The specification change process can easily take over a year to complete.

Halifax must communicate across the functions in the value chain to obtain the best advice from marketing, engineering, and purchasing. The responsibility for developing a plan to respond to the potential increase in direct materials price is spread throughout the company. The sensitivity analysis should direct Halifax to begin the consultation process and involve each responsibility centre in assessing the best strategic response.

The other changes in the sensitivity analysis to variable supplies and fuel costs, which affect costs of power and distribution, will also require input from several responsibility centres.

SUMMARY POINTS

The following question-and-answer format summarizes the chapter's learning outcomes. Each point presents a key question, and the guidelines are the answer to that question.

LEARNING OUTCOMES	GUIDELINES
1. What are the long-term and short-term benefits of budgets?	Budgets look forward to the future to anticipate financial and nonfinancial achievements of the company. In the long term, an annual budget cycle is integral to strategic analysis—the evaluation of how well the company fits with its environment. In the short term, budgets provide financial targets and a framework for operating performance measurement and control.
2. Why is a master budget useful?	A master budget summarizes all the projections (plans) of the managers in different areas of the company. It presents in a familiar and standardized financial-statement format how the financial future of a company will arise, quarter by quarter, month by month, or even week by week. The familiar format coordinates and communicates where the company is, where it wants to go, and how it will get there. The output from a master budget is an operating budget.
3. What is a cash budget and why is it useful?	A cash budget summarizes the timing and amount of cash inflows and outflows for a company over a specified time period. The cash budget depends on the facts summarized in the operating budget. One result of the cash budget is anticipated interest expense, which enables companies to produce a pro forma or budgeted income statement. Input into the cash budget includes any capacity expansion requiring the acquisition of long-term assets reported in the capital budget. Together, these budgets lead to the pro forma or budgeted balance sheet and cash flow statement.

4. How do the strategies of sensitivity analysis, Kaizen budgeting, and activity-based budgeting differ?	Sensitivity analysis is a way to alter the assumptions of the master budget. This analysis permits managers to establish plans in advance of possible adverse events. Kaizen budgeting is incremental cost reduction through elimination of waste in various business processes. Activity-based budgeting is the reduction of non-value-added activities that fail to contribute to the customers' value proposition. They are all long-term strategies to reduce costs.
5. How does responsibility differ from controllability?	Responsibility refers to holding accountable for achievement of performance targets those people who know best how to do so. The complexity of most organizations means one person cannot be responsible for every decision without slowing decision making to a halt. It is a decentralized type of budgeting that should converge with both incentives and compensation and organizational structure. Individuals responsible for achievement of organizational targets rarely control all the factors contributing toward that achievement. Controllability means the decisions about different key factors affecting cost, revenue, investment, or some combination of the three are within an individual's control, even though the individual may not be responsible for them.

TERMS TO LEARN

This chapter and the Glossary at the end of the book contain definitions of the following important terms:

activity-based budgeting (ABB) (p. 213)
benchmark (p. 193)
budget (p. 192)
budget constraint (p. 192)
budgetary slack (p. 200)
budgeting cycle (p. 193)
cash budget (p. 206)
cash cycle (p. 209)
controllability (p. 216)
controllable cost (p. 216)

cost centre (p. 215)
financial budget (p. 192)
investment centre (p. 215)
Kaizen budgeting (p. 212)
master budget (p. 192)
nonfinancial budget (p. 192)
operating budget (p. 196)
operating cycle (p. 209)
organizational structure (p. 214)
padding (p. 200)
profit centre (p. 215)

pro forma statements (p. 192)
responsibility accounting (p. 215)
responsibility centre (p. 215)
revenue centre (p. 215)
rolling budget (p. 196)
self-liquidating cycle (p. 209)
standard (p. 193)
strategic analysis (p. 194)
stretch goals (p. 193)
working capital cycle (p. 209)

ASSIGNMENT MATERIAL

MyAccountingLab   Make the grade with MyAccountingLab: The questions, exercises, and problems marked in red can be found on MyAccountingLab at **www.myaccountinglab.com.** You can practise them as often as you want, and most feature step-by-step guided instructions to help you find the right answer. Exercises and problems with an Excel icon in the margin have an accompanying Excel template on MyAccountingLab.

SHORT-ANSWER QUESTIONS

6-1 What are the four elements of the budgeting cycle?

6-2 Define *master budget*.

6-3 If actual results do not match the budget, what should managers do?

6-4 "Strategy, plans, and budgets are unrelated to one another." Do you agree? Explain.

6-5 "Budgeted performance is a better criterion than past performance for judging managers." Do you agree? Explain.

6-6 How might a company benefit by sharing its own internal budget information with other companies?

6-7 Define *rolling budget*. Give an example.

6-8 Outline the steps in preparing an operating budget.

6-9 "The revenue budget is the cornerstone for budgeting." Why?

6-10 How can the use of sensitivity analysis increase the benefits of budgeting?

6-11 Define *Kaizen budgeting*.

6-12 Describe how non-output-based cost drivers can be incorporated into budgeting.

6-13 Explain how the choice of the responsibility centre type (cost, revenue, profit, or investment) affects budgeting.

6-14 When governments reduce their funding to hospitals and universities, often the executives respond with a demand for an equal percentage reduction in costs by all business functions. Is this the best strategic approach?

EXERCISES

6-15 Terminology. A number of terms are listed below:

budget constraint(s)	budgetary slack
cash cycle	controllable cost
investment budget	operating cycle
rolling budget	self-liquidating cycle

REQUIRED

Select the terms from the above list to complete the following sentences.

A _____, also known as an _____, is the movement of cash arising from business functions to inventories, to receivables, and back to cash when outputs are sold. It is a _____ where all costs of a corporation are recovered when output is sold. _____ is the practice of underestimating revenue and overestimating costs to make the _____ less challenging. Once the corporate budget is produced, all managers make a commitment to reach budget targets. They are responsible for _____ that must be at or below the budget constraint during each reporting time period. Some companies produce a _____ that adds a reporting time period as one is completed. An _____ _____ affects the flow in and out of cash either to make the investment or to pay to finance it.

⑤

6-16 Responsibility and controllability. Consider each of the following independent situations:

1. A very successful salesman at Amcorp Computers regularly ignores the published sales catalogue and offers lowered prices to his customers in order to close sales. The VP of sales notices that revenue is substantially lower than budgeted.

2. Every "special deal" offered to a customer by any salesperson at Amcorp Computers has to be cleared by the VP of sales. Revenue for the second quarter has been lower than budgeted.

3. The shipping department of Amcorp has limited capacity, and sales orders are being cancelled by customers because of delays in delivery. Revenue for the past month has been lower than budgeted.

4. At Planetel Corp., a manufacturer of telecommunications equipment, the production supervisor notices that a significantly larger number of direct manufacturing labour-hours were used than had been budgeted. Investigation revealed that it was due to a decline in educational standards required by the Human Resources department when it interviewed applicants for hourly production jobs six months earlier.

5. At Planetel Corp., a relatively new production supervisor finds that more direct manufacturing labour-hours were used than had been budgeted. Interviews revealed that workers were unhappy with the supervisor's management style and were intentionally working slowly and inefficiently.

6. At Planetel Corp., the production supervisor traces the excessive consumption of direct materials (relative to the budget) to the fact that waste was high on machines that had not been properly maintained.

REQUIRED

For each situation described, determine where (that is, with whom) (a) responsibility and (b) controllability lie. Suggest what might be done to solve the problem or to improve the situation.

6-17 Budgeting; direct material usage, manufacturing cost, and gross margin. Xerxes Manufacturing Company manufactures blue rugs, using wool and dye as direct materials. All other materials are indirect. At the beginning of the year Xerxes has an inventory of 349,000 skeins of wool at a cost of $715,450 and 5,000 gallons of dye at a cost of $24,850. Target ending inventory of wool and dye is zero. Xerxes uses the FIFO inventory cost flow method.

1. Wool direct materials used this period, $6,017,450

One blue rug is budgeted to use 30 skeins of wool at a cost of $2 per skein and 1/2 gallon of dye at a cost of $5 per gallon.

Xerxes blue rugs are very popular and demand is high, but because of capacity constraints the firm will produce only 100,000 blue rugs per year. The budgeted selling price is $2,000 each. There are no rugs in beginning inventory. Target ending inventory of rugs is also zero.

Xerxes makes rugs by hand, but uses a machine to dye the wool. Thus, overhead costs are accumulated in two cost pools—one for weaving and the other for dyeing. Weaving overhead is allocated to product based on direct manufacturing labour-hours (DMLH). Dyeing overhead is allocated to product based on machine-hours (MH).

There is no direct manufacturing labour cost for dyeing. Xerxes budgets 56 direct manufacturing labour-hours to weave a rug at a budgeted rate of $15 per hour. It budgets 0.15 machine hours to dye each skein in the dyeing process.

The following table presents the budgeted overhead costs for the dyeing and weaving cost pools:

	Dyeing (based on 450,000 MH)	Weaving (based on 5,600,000 DMLH)
Variable costs		
Indirect materials	$ 0	$11,200,000
Maintenance	4,950,000	2,240,000
Utilities	5,400,000	1,680,000
Fixed costs		
Indirect labour	239,000	1,300,000
Depreciation	1,900,000	52,000
Other	320,000	2,380,000
Total budgeted costs	$12,809,000	$18,852,000

REQUIRED
1. Prepare a direct material usage budget in both units and dollars.
2. Calculate the budgeted overhead allocation rates for weaving and dyeing.
3. Calculate the budgeted unit cost of a blue rug for the year.
4. Prepare a revenue budget for blue rugs for the year, assuming Xerxes sells (a) 100,000 or (b) 95,000 blue rugs (that is, at two different sales levels).
5. Calculate the budgeted cost of goods sold for blue rugs under each sales assumption.
6. Find the budgeted gross margin for blue rugs under each sales assumption.

6-18 Sales budget, service setting. In 2013, McGrath & Sons, a small environmental-testing firm, performed 11,000 radon tests for $250 each and 15,200 lead tests for $200 each. Because newer homes are being built with lead-free pipes, lead-testing volume is expected to decrease by 10% next year. However, awareness of radon-related health hazards is expected to result in a 5% increase in radon-test volume each year in the near future. Jim McGrath feels that if he lowers his price for lead testing to $190 per test, he will have to face only a 5% decline in lead-test sales in 2014.

1. Total revenue, $5,623,500

REQUIRED
1. Prepare a 2014 sales budget for McGrath & Sons assuming that McGrath holds prices at 2013 levels.
2. Prepare a 2014 sales budget for McGrath & Sons assuming that McGrath lowers the price of a lead test to $190. Should McGrath lower the price of a lead test in 2014 if its goal is to maximize sales revenue?

6-19 Sales and production budget. The Armondo Company expects 2013 sales of 135,000 units of serving trays. Armondo's beginning inventory for 2013 is 9,700 trays; target ending inventory: 16,300 trays.

Total requirements, 151,300

Compute the number of trays budgeted for production in 2013.

Total requirements
(bottles), 2,155,000

6-20 Direct materials budget. The wine-producing company Lebeau Vineyard expects to produce 2.1 million 3-litre bottles of Chablis in 2013. Lebeau purchases empty glass bottles from a reliable supplier. The target ending inventory of such bottles is 55,000; the beginning inventory is 23,700. For simplicity, ignore loss due to breakage.

REQUIRED

Compute the number of bottles to be purchased in 2013.

54,350 production units

6-21 Budgeting material purchases. In the preparation of the sales budget for the next three-month period, the Westing Company determined that 52,250 finished units would be needed to fulfill sales obligations. The company has an inventory of 27,300 units of finished goods on hand at December 31 and has a target finished goods inventory of 29,400 units at the end of the succeeding quarter.

It takes three litres of direct materials to make one unit of finished product. The company has an inventory of 117,350 litres of direct materials at December 31 and has a target ending inventory of 110,000 litres.

REQUIRED

How many litres of direct materials should be ordered for delivery during the three months ending March 31?

1. Total revenue,
$18,660,000

6-22 Sales and production budget. From its company-owned natural spring in northern Ontario, Fountain Springs Inc. bottles and distributes mineral water worldwide. Fountain Springs markets its product in 1-litre disposable plastic bottles and in 16-litre reusable plastic containers.

REQUIRED

1. For the year 2013, Northern marketing managers project monthly sales of 520,000 1-litre and 185,000 16-litre units. Average selling prices are estimated at $0.50 per 1-litre unit and $7.00 per 16-litre unit. Prepare a revenue budget for Fountain Springs Inc. for the year ending December 31, 2013.
2. Fountain Springs begins 2013 with 1,275,000 1-litre units in inventory (that is, beginning inventory). The VP of operations requests that 1-litre ending inventory on December 31, 2013, be no fewer than 976,000 units. Based on sales projections as budgeted above, what is the minimum number of 1-litre units Fountain Springs must produce during 2013?
3. The VP of operations requests that ending inventory of 16-litre units on December 31, 2013, be 265,000 units. If the production budget calls for Fountain Springs to produce 2,090,000 16-litre units during 2013, what is the beginning inventory of 16-litre units on January 1, 2013?

Gross margin for
November, $16,231

6-23 Budgeting revenue, cost of sales, and gross margin. Madeline Franks, the owner of a small gift and souvenir shop, expects cash sales of $14,000 for October, $16,300 for November, and $21,100 for December. In addition, she expects credit card sales of $9,800 during October and $11,200 and $15,800, respectively, during November and December. Sales returns and allowances, being historically nonexistent, can be ignored. Credit card companies such as Visa and MasterCard charge 4% on credit card sales; thus, the net sales will be 96%. Cost of goods sold traditionally averages 40% of net sales.

REQUIRED

Ms. Franks, operating under the business name Whimsy Gifts, asks you to prepare a schedule of budgeted revenue, cost of goods sold, and gross margin for each month of the last quarter. Also, she requires you to show totals for the quarter.

2. Total production,
948,000 units

6-24 Revenue, production, and purchases budget. The Suzuki Company in Japan has a division that manufactures two-wheel motorcycles. Its budgeted sales for Model G in 2013 is 985,000 units. Suzuki's target ending inventory is 115,000 units, and its beginning inventory is 152,000 units. The company's budgeted selling price to its distributors and dealers is 505,000 yen (¥) per motorcycle.

Suzuki buys all its wheels from an outside supplier. No defective wheels are accepted. (Suzuki's needs for extra wheels for replacement parts are ordered by a separate division of the company.) The company's target ending inventory is 28,000 wheels and its beginning inventory is 19,000 wheels. The budgeted purchase price is ¥21,300 per wheel.

REQUIRED
1. Compute the budgeted revenue in yen.
2. Compute the number of motorcycles to be produced.
3. Compute the budgeted purchases of wheels in units and in yen.

6-25 **Budgets for production and direct manufacturing labour.** (CMA, adapted) The All Frame Company makes and sells artistic frames for pictures of weddings, graduations, and other special events. Martin Flack, the company controller, is responsible for preparing the master budget and has accumulated the following information for 2013:

$595,900 Total DL cost

	2013				
	January	**February**	**March**	**April**	**May**
Estimated sales in units	10,000	12,000	8,000	9,000	9,000
Selling price	$54.00	$51.50	$51.50	$51.50	$51.50
Direct manufacturing labour-hours per unit	2.0	2.0	1.5	1.5	1.5
Wage per direct manufacturing labour-hour	$10.00	$10.00	$10.00	$11.00	$11.00

Direct manufacturing labour-related costs include pension contributions of $0.50 per hour, workers' compensation insurance of $0.15 per hour, employee medical insurance of $0.40 per hour, and employment insurance, in addition to wages. Assume that as of January 1, 2013, the employment insurance rates are 7.5% of wages for employers and 7.5% of wages for employees. The cost of employee benefits paid by All Frame for its employees is treated as a direct manufacturing labour cost.

All Frame has an employee labour contract that calls for a wage increase to $11.00 per hour on April 1, 2013. New labour-saving machinery has been installed and will be fully operational by March 1, 2013.

The controller has been informed that the company expects to have 16,000 frames on hand on December 31, 2012, and has a policy of carrying an end-of-month inventory of 100% of the following month's sales plus 50% of the second following month's sales.

REQUIRED
Prepare a production budget and a direct manufacturing labour budget for the All Frame Company by month and for the first quarter of 2013. The direct manufacturing labour budget should include labour-hours and show the details for each labour cost category.

6-26 **Cash flow analysis.** (CMA, adapted) TabComp Inc. is a retail distributor for MZB-33 computer hardware and related software and support services. TabComp prepares annual sales forecasts of which the first six months for 2013 are presented here. Cash sales account for 25% of TabComp's total sales, 30% of the total sales are paid by bank credit card, and the remaining 45% are on open account (TabComp's own charge accounts). The cash sales and cash from bank credit-card sales are received in the month of the sale. Bank credit-card sales are subject to a 4% discount deducted at the time of the daily deposit. The cash receipts for sales on open account are 70% in the month following the sale and 28% in the second month after the sale. The remaining accounts receivable are estimated to be uncollectible.

1. $429,400

TabComp's month-end inventory requirements for computer hardware units are 30% of the next month's sales. A one-month lead time is required for delivery from the manufacturer. Thus, orders for computer hardware units are placed on the 25th of each month to assure that they will be in the store by the first day of the month needed. The computer hardware units are purchased under terms of n/45 (payment in full within 45 days of invoice), measured from the time the units are delivered to TabComp. TabComp's purchase price for the computer units is 60% of the selling price.

TabComp Inc.
Sales Forecast for First Six Months of 2013

| | Hardware Sales | | Software Sales and Support | Total Revenues |
	Units	Dollars		
January	130	$ 390,000	$160,000	$ 550,000
February	120	360,000	140,000	500,000
March	110	330,000	150,000	480,000
April	90	270,000	130,000	400,000
May	100	300,000	125,000	425,000
June	125	375,000	225,000	600,000
Total	675	$2,025,000	$930,000	$2,955,000

REQUIRED

1. Calculate the cash that TabComp Inc. can expect to collect during April 2013. Be sure to show all of your calculations.
2. TabComp Inc. is determining how many MZB-33 computer hardware units to order on January 25, 2013.

   a. Determine the projected number of computer hardware units that will be ordered.

   b. Calculate the dollar amount of the order that TabComp will place for these computer hardware units.

3. As part of the annual budget process, TabComp prepares a cash budget by month for the entire year. Explain why a company such as TabComp would do this.

6-27 Activity-based budgeting. The Chelsea location of Family Supermarket (FS), a chain of small neighbourhood grocery stores, is preparing its activity-based budget for January 2013. FS has three product categories: soft drinks, fresh produce, and packaged food. The following table shows the four activities that consume indirect resources at the Chelsea store, the cost drivers and their rates, and the cost driver amount budgeted to be consumed by each activity in January 2013.

| Activity | Cost Driver | January 2013 Budgeted Cost Driver Rate | January 2013 Budgeted Amount of Cost Driver Used | | |
			Soft Drinks	Fresh Produce	Packaged Food
Ordering	Number of purchase orders	$ 90	14	24	14
Delivery	Number of deliveries	$ 82	12	62	19
Shelf-stocking	Hours of stocking time	$ 21	16	172	94
Customer support	Number of items sold	$0.18	4,600	34,200	10,750

REQUIRED

1. What is the total budgeted indirect cost at the Chelsea store in January 2013? What is the total budgeted cost of each activity at the Chelsea store for January 2013? What is the budgeted indirect cost of each product category for January 2013?
2. Which product category has the largest fraction of total budgeted indirect costs?
3. Given your answer in requirement 2, what advantage does FS gain by using an activity-based approach to budgeting over, say, allocating indirect costs to products based on cost of goods sold?

6-28 Kaizen approach to activity-based budgeting (continuation of 6-27). Family Supermarkets (FS) has a Kaizen (continuous improvement) approach to budgeting monthly activity area costs for each month of 2013. Each successive month, the budgeted cost driver rate decreases by 0.2% relative to the preceding month (so, for example, February's budgeted cost driver rate is 0.998 times January's budgeted cost driver rate, and March's budgeted cost driver rate is 0.998 times the budgeted February 2013 rate). FS assumes that the budgeted amount of cost driver usage remains the same each month.

REQUIRED
1. What is the total budgeted cost for each activity and the total budgeted indirect cost for March 2013?
2. What are the benefits of using a Kaizen approach to budgeting? What are the limitations of this approach, and how might FS management overcome them?

PROBLEMS

6-29 **Revenue and production budgets.** (CPA, adapted) Two products are manufactured by the Burlington Northern Corporation: Widget and Thingamajig. In July 2013, the controller of Burlington Northern, upon instructions from senior management, had the budgeting department gather the following data in order to prepare budgets for 2014:

2. Production Widgets, 65,000 units

Thingamajigs, 41,000 units

2014 Projected Sales

Product	Units	Price
Widget	60,000	$198
Thingamajig	40,000	$300

2014 Inventories in Units

Product	Expected January 1, 2014	Target December 31, 2014
Widget	22,000	27,000
Thingamajig	10,000	11,000

The following direct materials are used to produce one unit of Widget and Thingamajig:

Direct Material	Unit	Amount Used per Unit	
		Widget	Thingamajig
A	Kilograms	4	5
B	Kilograms	2	3
C	Each	0	1

Projected data for 2014 with respect to direct materials are as follows:

Direct Material	Anticipated Purchase Price	Expected Inventories, January 1, 2014	Target Inventories, December 31, 2014
A	$14	32,000 kilograms	36,000 kilograms
B	$ 7	29,000 kilograms	32,000 kilograms
C	$ 5	6,000 units	7,000 units

Projected direct manufacturing labour requirements and rates for 2014 are as follows:

Product	Hours per Unit	Rate per hour
Widget	2	$15
Thingamajig	3	$19

Manufacturing overhead is allocated at the rate of $24 per direct manufacturing labour-hour.

REQUIRED

Based on the preceding projections and budget requirements for Widgets and Thingamajigs, prepare the following budgets for 2014:

1. Revenue budget (in dollars).
2. Production budget (in units).
3. Direct materials purchases budget (in quantities).
4. Direct materials purchases budget (in dollars).
5. Direct manufacturing labour budget (in dollars).
6. Budgeted finished goods inventory at December 31, 2014 (in dollars).

Operating income, $843

6-30 Budgeted income statement. (CMA, adapted) Easecom Company is a manufacturer of video-conferencing products. Regular units are manufactured to meet marketing projections, and specialized units are made after an order is received. Maintaining the video-conferencing equipment is an important area of customer satisfaction. With the recent downturn in the computer industry, the video-conferencing equipment segment has suffered, leading to a decline in Easecom's financial performance. The following income statement shows results for 2012.

Easecom Company
Income Statement
For the Year Ended December 31, 2012 (in $ thousands)

Revenues:		
Equipment	$6,000	
Maintenance contracts	1,800	
Total revenues		$7,800
Cost of goods sold		4,600
Gross margin		3,200
Operating costs:		
Marketing	600	
Distribution	150	
Customer maintenance	1,000	
Administration	900	
Total operating costs		2,650
Operating income		$ 550

1. Selling prices of equipment are expected to increase by 10% as the economic recovery begins. The selling price of each maintenance contract is expected to remain unchanged from 2012.
2. Equipment sales in units are expected to increase by 6%, with a corresponding 6% growth in units of maintenance contracts.
3. Cost of each unit sold is expected to increase by 3% to pay for the necessary technology and quality improvements.
4. Marketing costs are expected to increase by $250,000, but administration costs are expected to remain at 2012 levels.
5. Distribution costs vary in proportion to the number of units of equipment sold.
6. Two maintenance technicians are to be hired at a total cost of $130,000, which covers wages and related travel costs. The objective is to improve customer service and shorten response time.
7. There is no beginning or ending inventory of equipment.

REQUIRED

Prepare a budgeted income statement for the year ending December 31, 2013.

1. Total budgeted
revenue, $1,654,560

6-31 Comprehensive review of budgeting. Prepare a master operating budget; budget schedules for manufacturer. Sierra Furniture is an elite desk manufacturer. It manufactures two products:

◆ Executive desks: 0.91 m × 1.5 m oak desks = 1.365 m²
◆ Chairperson desks: 1.8 m × 1.2 m red oak desks = 2.16 m²

The budgeted direct cost inputs for each product in 2013 are as follows:

	Executive Line	Chairperson Line
Direct materials:		
Oak top	1.5 square metres	—
Red oak top	—	2.3 square metres
Oak legs	4 legs	—
Red oak legs	—	4 legs
Direct manufacturing labour	3 hours	5 hours

Unit data pertaining to the direct materials for March 2013 are as follows:

Actual Beginning Direct Materials Inventory
(March 1, 2013)

	Product	
	Executive Line	Chairperson Line
Oak top	29.8 square metres	—
Red oak top	—	13.9 square metres
Oak legs	100 legs	—
Red oak legs	—	40 legs

Target Ending Direct Materials Inventory
(March 31, 2013)

	Product	
	Executive Line	Chairperson Line
Oak top	17.9 square metres	—
Red oak top	—	18.6 square metres
Oak legs	80 legs	—
Red oak legs	—	44 legs

Unit cost data for direct cost inputs pertaining to February 2013 and March 2013 are:

	February 2013 (Actual)	March 2013 (Budgeted)
Oak top (per square metre)	$21.60	$24.00
Red oak top (per square metre)	27.60	30.00
Oak legs (per leg)	13.20	14.40
Red oak legs (per leg)	20.40	21.60
Manufacturing labour cost per hour	36.00	36.00

Manufacturing overhead (both variable and fixed) is allocated to each desk based on budgeted direct manufacturing labour-hours per desk. The budgeted variable manufacturing overhead rate for March 2013 is $42 per direct manufacturing labour-hour. The budgeted fixed manufacturing overhead for March 2013 is $51,000. Both variable and fixed manufacturing overhead costs are allocated to each unit of finished goods.

Data relating to finished goods inventory for March 2013 are:

	Executive Line	Chairperson Line
Beginning inventory	20 units	5 units
Beginning inventory in dollars (cost)	$12,576	$5,820
Budgeted ending inventory	30 units	15 units

Budgeted sales for March 2013 are 740 units of the Executive Line and 390 units of the Chairperson Line. The budgeted selling prices per unit in March 2013 are $1,224 for an Executive Line desk and $1,920 for a Chairperson Line desk.

Assume the following in your answer:

a. Work-in-process inventories are negligible and ignored.

b. Direct materials inventory and finished goods inventory are costed using the FIFO method.

c. Unit costs of direct materials purchased and finished goods are constant in March 2013.

REQUIRED

Prepare the following budgets for March 2013:

1. Revenue budget.
2. Production budget in units.
3. Direct materials usage budget and direct materials purchases budget.
4. Direct manufacturing labour budget.
5. Manufacturing overhead budget.
6. Ending inventory budget.
7. Cost of goods sold budget and gross margin calculation.

1. Total revenue, $54,260,000

6-32 Comprehensive review of budgeting. Prepare a master operating budget; budget schedules for manufacturer. Dinettes Inc. operates at capacity and makes glass-topped dining tables and wooden chairs that are typically sold as sets of four chairs with one table. However, some customers purchase replacement or extra chairs, and others buy some chairs or a table only, so the sales mix is not exactly 4:1. Dinettes Inc. is planning its annual budget for fiscal year 2013. Information for 2013 follows:

Input prices

Direct materials	
Wood	$1.60 per board foot
Glass	$12 per sheet
Direct manufacturing labour	$15 per direct manufacturing labour-hour

Input quantities per unit of output

	Chairs	Tables
Direct materials		
Wood	5 board feet	7 board feet
Glass	—	2 sheets
Direct manufacturing labour	4 hours	8 hours
Machine hours (MH)	3 MH	5 MH

Inventory information, direct materials

	Wood	Glass
Beginning inventory	109,200 board feet	8,750 sheets
Target ending inventory	117,500 board feet	9,000 sheets
Cost of beginning inventory	$170,352	$109,375

Dinettes Inc. accounts for direct materials using a FIFO cost flow.

Sales and inventory information, finished goods

	Chairs	Tables
Expected sales in units	172,000	45,000
Selling price	$80	$900
Target ending inventory in units	8,500	2,250
Beginning inventory in units	8,000	2,100
Beginning inventory in dollars	$760,000	$477,000

Dinettes Inc. uses a FIFO cost flow assumption for finished goods inventory.

Chairs are manufactured in batches of 500, and tables are manufactured in batches of 50. It takes three hours to set up for a batch of chairs, and two hours to set up for a batch of tables.

Dinettes Inc. uses activity-based costing and has classified all overhead costs as shown in the table below:

Cost type	Budgeted variable	Budgeted fixed	Cost driver/ Allocation base
Manufacturing:			
Materials handling	$342,840	$ 600,000	Number of board feet used
Setup	97,000	300,740	Setup hours
Processing	789,250	5,900,000	Machine hours
Non-manufacturing:			
Marketing	2,011,200	4,500,000	Sales revenue
Distribution	54,000	380,000	Number of deliveries

Delivery trucks transport units sold in delivery sizes of 500 chairs or 500 tables.

REQUIRED
Do the following for the year 2013:
1. Prepare the revenue budget.
2. Use the revenue budget to:
   a. Find the budgeted allocation rate for marketing costs.
   b. Find the budgeted number of deliveries and allocation rate for distribution costs.
3. Prepare the production budget in units.

6-33 **Comprehensive budget, fill in schedules; prepare a cash budget.** The following information is for the Newport Stationery Store.

3

1. Total for November, $68,400

Balance Sheet Information as of September 30

Current assets:	
Cash	$ 14,400
Accounts receivable	12,000
Inventory	76,320
Equipment, net	120,000
Liabilities	None

Recent and Anticipated Sales

September	$48,000
October	57,600
November	72,000
December	96,000
January	43,200

◆ **Credit sales.** Sales are 75% for cash and 25% on credit. Assume that credit accounts are all collected in the month following the sale. The accounts receivable on September 30 are the result of the credit sales for September (25% of $48,000). Gross margin averages 30% of sales. Newport treats cash discounts on purchases in the income statement as "other income."

◆ **Operating costs.** Salaries and wages average 15% of monthly sales; rent, 5%; other operating costs, excluding amortization, 4%. Assume that these costs are disbursed each month. Amortization is $1,200 per month.

◆ **Purchases.** Newport keeps a minimum inventory of $36,000. The policy is to purchase additional inventory each month in the amount necessary to provide for the following month's sales. Terms on purchases are 2/10, n/30: a 2% discount is available if the payment is made within ten days after purchase; no discount is available if payment is made beyond ten days after purchase; and the full amount is due within thirty days. Assume that payments are made in the month of purchase and that all discounts are taken.

◆ **Light fixtures.** The expenditures for light fixtures are $720 in October and $480 in November. These amounts are to be capitalized.

Assume that a minimum cash balance of $9,600 must be maintained. Assume also that all borrowing is effective at the beginning of the month and all repayments are made at the end of the month of repayment. Loans are repaid when sufficient cash is available. Interest is paid only at the time of repaying principal. The interest rate is 18% per year. Management does not want to borrow any more cash than is necessary and wants to repay as soon as cash is available.

Schedule A
Budgeted Monthly Cash Receipts

Item	September	October	November	December
Total sales	$48,000	$57,600	$72,000	$96,000
Credit sales	12,000	14,400		
Cash sales				
Receipts:				
Cash sales		$43,200		
Collections on accounts receivable		12,000		
Total		$55,200		

Schedule B
Budgeted Monthly Cash Disbursements for Purchases

Item	October	November	December	4th Quarter
Purchases	$50,400			
Deduct: 2% cash discount	1,008			
Disbursements	$49,392			

Schedule C
Budgeted Monthly Cash Disbursements
for Operating Costs

Item	October	November	December	4th Quarter
Salaries and wages	$ 8,640			
Rent	2,880			
Other cash operating costs	2,304			
Total	$13,824			

Schedule D
Budgeted Total Monthly Cash
Disbursements

Item	October	November	December	4th Quarter
Purchases	$49,392			
Cash operating costs	13,824			
Light fixtures	720			
Total	$63,936			

Schedule E
Budgeted Cash Receipts
and Disbursements

Item	October	November	December	4th Quarter
Receipts	$ 55,200			
Disbursements	63,936			
Net cash increase (decrease)	$ (8,736)			

Schedule F
Financing Required

Item	October	November	December	Total
Beginning cash balance	$14,400			
Net cash increase				
Net cash decrease	8,736	____	____	____
Cash position before borrowing	5,664			
Minimum cash balance required	9,600	____	____	____
Excess/(deficiency)	(3,936)			
Borrowing required	4,000			
Interest payments				
Borrowing repaid				
Ending cash balance	$ 9,664	____	____	____

REQUIRED

1. Based on the preceding facts, complete schedule A.
2. Complete schedule B. Note that purchases are 70% of next month's sales.
3. Complete schedule C.
4. Complete schedule D.
5. Complete schedule E.
6. Complete schedule F. (Assume that borrowings must be made in multiples of $1,000.)
7. What do you think is the most logical type of loan needed by Newport? Explain your reasoning.
8. Prepare a budgeted income statement for the fourth quarter and a budgeted balance sheet as of December 31. Ignore income taxes.
9. Some simplifications have been introduced in this problem. What complicating factors would be met in a typical business situation?

6-34 **Prepare a cash budget.** On December 1, 2013, the Itami Wholesale Company is attempting to project cash receipts and disbursements through January 31, 2014. On January 31, 2014, a note will be payable in the amount of $120,000. This amount was borrowed in September to carry the company through the seasonal peak in November and December.

Ending cash balance, December 2013, $2,580

The trial balance on December 1 shows in part the following information:

Cash	$ 12,000	
Accounts receivable	336,000	
Allowance for bad debts		$ 18,960
Inventory	105,000	
Accounts payable		110,400

Sales terms call for a 2% discount if payment is made within the first ten days of the month after purchase; after that, the full amount is due by the end of the month after purchase. Experience has shown that 70% of the billings will be collected within the discount period, 20% by the end of the month after purchase, 8% in the following month, and 2% will be uncollectible. There are no cash sales.

The average selling price of the company's products is $120 per unit. Actual and projected sales are as follows:

October actual	$ 216,000
November actual	300,000
December estimated	360,000
January estimated	180,000
February estimated	144,000
Total estimated for year ended June 30, 2014	1,800,000

All purchases are payable within 15 days. Thus, approximately 50% of the purchases in a month are due and payable in the next month. The average unit purchase cost is $84. Target ending inventories are 500 units plus 25% of the next month's unit sales.

Total budgeted marketing, distribution, and customer service costs for the year are $480,000. Of this amount, $180,000 is considered fixed (and includes amortization of $36,000). The remainder varies with sales. Both fixed and variable marketing, distribution, and customer service costs are paid as incurred.

REQUIRED

Prepare a cash budget for December and January. Supply supporting schedules for collections of receivables, payments for merchandise, and marketing, distribution, and customer-service costs. Will there be enough cash available on January 31, 2014 to repay the $120,000 note?

④
5. Budgeted unit cost,
$74.80

6-35 Activity-based budget; Kaizen improvements. Korna Company manufactures a product, gizmo, that uses the following direct inputs:

	Price	Quantity	Cost per unit of output
Direct materials	$4 per gram	10 grams per unit	$40 per unit
Direct manufacturing labour-hours (DMLH)	$15 per DMLH	2 DMLH per unit	$30 per unit

Korna has no direct materials inventory. All manufacturing overhead costs are variable costs. The manufacturing overhead cost is comprised of two activities: setup and operations. The cost driver for setup is setup hours, and the cost driver for operations is direct manufacturing labour-hours. Korna allocates setup cost at a rate of $80 per setup-hour, and each setup takes two hours. Korna Company makes gizmos in batches of 100 units. Operations costs are allocated at a rate of $1.60 per direct manufacturing labour-hour.

REQUIRED

1. Korna plans to make and sell 20,000 gizmos in the first quarter of next year. The selling price for the product is $120. Prepare the revenue budget for the first quarter.
2. Prepare the direct material usage budget for the first quarter of next year.
3. Prepare the direct manufacturing labour usage budget for the first quarter of next year.
4. Prepare the manufacturing overhead cost budget for each activity for the first quarter of next year.
5. Compute the budgeted unit cost of a gizmo for the first quarter of next year.
6. Prepare the cost of goods sold budget for the first quarter of next year. Assume Korna budgets 1,000 units of beginning finished goods inventory at a cost of $72 per unit. Korna uses the LIFO cost flow assumption for finished goods inventory. Korna expects to sell all 20,000 gizmos made in the first quarter.
7. Calculate the budgeted gross margin for the first quarter of next year.
8. Korna Company managers want to implement Kaizen costing. They budget a 1% decrease in materials quantity and direct manufacturing labour-hours and a 3% decrease in setup time per unit for each subsequent quarter. Calculate the budgeted unit cost and gross margin for quarters two and three. Assume no change in budgeted output.
9. Refer to requirement 8 above. How could the reduction in materials and time be accomplished? Are there any problems with this plan?

④
2. Production units:
Cat-allac, 520
Dog-eriffic, 285

6-36 Comprehensive problem with ABC costing. Pet Transport Company makes two pet carriers, the Cat-allac and the Dog-eriffic. They are both made of plastic with metal doors, but the Cat-allac is smaller. Information for the two products for the month of April is given in the following tables:

Input prices

Direct materials	
Plastic	$4 per kilogram
Metal	$3 per kilogram
Direct manufacturing labour	$10 per direct manufacturing labour-hour

Input quantities per unit of output

	Cat-allac	Dog-eriffic
Direct materials		
Plastic	4 kilograms	6 kilograms
Metal	0.5 kilograms	1 kilogram
Direct manufacturing labour-hours (DMLH)	3 hours	5 hours
Machine hours (MH)	10 MH	18 MH

Inventory information, direct materials

	Plastic	Metal
Beginning inventory	250 kilograms	60 kilograms
Target ending inventory	380 kilograms	55 kilograms
Cost of beginning inventory	$950	$180

Pet Transport accounts for direct materials using a FIFO cost flow assumption.

Sales and inventory information, finished goods

	Cat-allac	Dog-eriffic
Expected sales in units	500	300
Selling price	$ 160	$ 250
Target ending inventory in units	35	15
Beginning inventory in units	15	30
Beginning inventory in dollars	$1,500	$5,580

Pet Transport uses a FIFO cost flow assumption for finished goods inventory.

Pet Transport uses an activity-based costing system and classifies overhead into three activity pools: Setup, Processing, and Inspection. Activity rates for these activities are $100 per setup hour, $5 per machine hour, and $16 per inspection hour. Other information follows:

Cost driver information

	Cat-allac	Dog-eriffic
Number of units per batch	20	15
Setup time per batch	1.5 hours	1.75 hours
Inspection time per batch	0.5 hour	0.6 hour

Nonproduction fixed costs for March equal $36,000, of which half are salaries. Salaries are expected to increase by 5% in April. The only variable nonproduction cost is sales commission, equal to 1% of sales revenue.

REQUIRED

Prepare the following for April:

1. Revenue budget.
2. Production budget in units.
3. Direct material usage budget and direct material purchases budget.
4. Direct manufacturing labour cost budget.
5. Manufacturing overhead cost budgets for each of the three activities.
6. Budgeted unit cost of ending finished goods inventory and ending inventories budget.
7. Cost of goods sold budget.
8. Non-manufacturing costs budget.
9. Budgeted income statement (ignore income taxes).

6-37 **Cash budget.** (Continuation of 6-36) Assume the following: Pet Transport (PT) does not make any sales on credit. PT sells only to the public, and accepts cash and credit cards. Of its sales, 90% are to customers using credit cards, for which PT gets the cash right away, less a 3% transaction fee.

Ending cash balance, $20,740

Purchases of materials are on account. PT pays for half the purchases in the period of the purchase and the other half in the following period. At the end of March, PT owes suppliers $8,500. PT plans to replace a machine in April at a net cash cost of $13,700. Labour, other production costs, and nonproduction costs are paid in cash in the month incurred except, of course, amortization, which is not a cash flow. For April, $20,000 of the production cost and $10,000 of the nonproduction cost is amortization.

PT currently has a $2,000 loan at an annual interest rate of 12%. The interest is paid at the end of each month. If PT has more than $10,000 cash at the end of April, it will pay back the loan. PT owes $5,000 in income taxes that need to be remitted in April. PT has cash of $5,360 on hand at the end of March.

REQUIRED

Prepare a cash budget for April for Pet Transport.

6-38 Responsibility and controllability. (Adapted from a description by R. Villers) Francois Chenier is the purchasing agent for Highlight Manufacturing Company. Marge Belvedere is head of the production planning and control department. Every six months, Belvedere gives Chenier a general purchasing program. Chenier gets specifications from the engineering department. He then selects suppliers and negotiates prices. When he took this job, Chenier was informed very clearly that he bore responsibility for meeting the general purchasing program once he accepted it from Belvedere.

During week 24, Chenier was advised that Part No. 1234—a critical part—would be needed for assembly on Tuesday morning of week 32. He found that the regular supplier could not deliver. He called everywhere and finally found a supplier in the West and accepted the commitment.

He followed up by mail. Yes, the supplier assured him, the part would be ready. The matter was so important that on Thursday of week 31, Chenier checked by phone. Yes, the shipment had left on time. Chenier was reassured and did not check further. But on Tuesday of week 32, the part had not arrived. Inquiry revealed that the shipment had been misdirected by the railroad and was stuck in Winnipeg.

REQUIRED

What department should bear the costs of time lost in the plant? Why? As the purchasing agent, do you think it fair that such costs be charged to your department?

6-39 Budgeting and governance. Delma Company manufactures a variety of products in a variety of departments, and evaluates departments and departmental managers by comparing actual costs and outputs relative to their budgets. Departmental managers help create the budgets and usually provide information about input quantities for materials, labour, and overhead costs. Wert Mimble is the manager of the department that produces Product Z. Wert has estimated these inputs for Product Z:

Input	Budget Quantity per Unit of Output
Direct material	3 kilograms
Direct manufacturing labour	20 minutes
Machine time	10 minutes

The department produces about 100 units of Product Z each day. Wert's department always gets excellent evaluations, sometimes exceeding budgeted production quantities. Each 100 units of Product Z uses, on average, about 32 hours of direct manufacturing labour (four people working eight hours each), 295 kilograms of material, and 16.5 machine hours.

Top management of Delma Company has decided to implement budget standards that will challenge the workers in each department and it has asked Wert to design more challenging input standards for Product Z. Wert provides top management with the following input quantities:

Input	Budget Quantity per Unit of Output
Direct material	2.95 kilograms
Direct manufacturing labour	19.2 minutes
Machine time	9.9 minutes

REQUIRED

Discuss the following:

1. Are these challenging standards for Wert's department?
2. Why do you suppose Wert picked these particular standards?
3. What steps can Delma Company top management take to make sure Wert's standards really meet the goals of the firm?

1. Total revenues, $648,000

6-40 Prepare a master operating budget. Slopes Inc. manufactures and sells snowboards. Slopes manufactures a single model, the Pipex. In the summer of 2012, Slopes's accountant gathered the following data to prepare budgets for 2013. These units are standard in the lumber industry. Wage rate = $25/hr.

Materials and Labour Requirements

Direct materials	
Wood	5 board-feet per snowboard
Fibreglass	6 yards per snowboard
Direct labour	5 hours per snowboard

Slopes's CEO expects to sell 1,200 snowboards during 2013 at an estimated retail price of $540 per board. Further, she expects 2013 beginning inventory to be 100 boards and would like to end 2013 with 200 snowboards in stock. The company follows FIFO for inventory flow.

Direct Material Inventories

	Beginning Inventory January 1, 2013	Ending Inventory December 31, 2013
Wood	2,000 feet	1,500 feet
Fibreglass	1,000 yards	2,000 yards

The beginning inventory of wood was purchased at $34 per board foot and fibreglass was purchased at $5.80 per yard. Prices have now risen to $36 per board foot of wood and $6 per yard of fibreglass. Variable manufacturing overhead is allocated at the rate of $8.40 per direct manufacturing labour-hour. Fixed manufacturing overhead costs are budgeted at $78,000 for 2013. Variable marketing costs are allocated at the rate of $300 per sales visit, and the marketing plan calls for 36 sales visits during 2013. Finally, fixed non-manufacturing costs are budgeted at $36,000 for 2013.

REQUIRED

Based on the data and projections supplied by Slopes's managers,

1. Prepare the 2013 revenue budget (in dollars).
2. Prepare the 2013 production budget (in units).
3. Prepare direct materials usage and purchases budgets for 2013.
4. Prepare a direct manufacturing labour budget for 2013.
5. Prepare a manufacturing overhead budget for 2013.
6. What is the budgeted manufacturing overhead rate?
7. What is the budgeted manufacturing overhead cost per output unit?
8. Calculate the cost of a snowboard in finished goods inventory at the end of 2013.
9. Prepare an ending inventory budget for 2013.
10. Prepare a cost of goods sold budget for 2013. (Opening finished goods inventory is $44,976.)
11. Prepare the budgeted income statement for Slopes Inc. for 2013.

6-41 **Responsibility versus controllability; fixing responsibility.** (Adapted from a description by H. Bierman, Jr.) The city of Mountainvale hired its first city manager four years ago. She favoured a "management by objectives" philosophy and accordingly set up many profit responsibility centres, including a sanitation department, a utility department, and a repair shop.

Lost contribution margin is rarely accounted for in ordinary accounting systems.

For many months, the sanitation manager had been complaining to the utility manager about overhead wires being too low at one point along a city road. There was barely clearance for large sanitation trucks. The sanitation manager asked the repair shop to make changes in the clearance. The repair shop manager asked, "Should I charge the sanitation or the utility department for the $2,400 cost of making the adjustment?" Both departments refused to accept the charge, so the repair department refused to do the work.

Late one day, the top of a sanitation truck caught the wires and ripped them down. The repair department made an emergency repair at a cost of $3,120. Moreover, the city lost $1,200 of utility revenue (net of variable costs) because of the disruption of service.

Investigation disclosed that the sanitation truck had failed to clamp down its top properly. The extra two inches of height caused the wire to be caught.

Both the sanitation manager and the utility manager argued strenuously about who should bear the $3,120 cost. Moreover, the utility manager demanded reimbursement from the sanitation department of the $1,200 of lost utility income.

REQUIRED

As the city controller in charge of the responsibility accounting system, how would you favour accounting for these costs? Specifically, what would you do next? What is the proper role of responsibility accounting in assigning cost in this situation?

COLLABORATIVE LEARNING CASES

6-42 Comprehensive budgeting problem; activity-based costing, operating and financial budgets. Yummi-Lik makes really big lollipops in two sizes, large and giant. Yummi-Lik sells these lollipops to convenience stores, fairs, schools for fundraisers, and in bulk on the Internet. Summer is approaching and Yummi-Lik is preparing its budget for the month of June. The lollipops are handmade, mostly out of sugar, and attached to wooden sticks. Expected sales are based on past experience. This company uses pounds of material as its standard measure.

Other information for the month of June follows:

Input prices

Direct materials	
Sugar	$0.50 per pound (lb)
Sticks	$0.30 each
Direct manufacturing labour	$8 per direct manufacturing labour-hour

Input quantities per unit of output

	Large	Giant
Direct materials		
Sugar	0.25 lb	0.50 lb
Sticks	1	1
Direct manufacturing labour-hours (DMLH)	0.20 hours	0.25 hours
Setup hours per batch	0.08 hours	0.09 hours

Inventory information, direct materials

	Sugar	Sticks
Beginning inventory	125 lb	350
Target ending inventory	240 lb	480
Cost of beginning inventory	$64	$105

Yummi-Lik accounts for direct materials using a FIFO cost flow assumption.

Sales and inventory information, finished goods

	Large	Giant
Expected sales in units	3,000	1,800
Selling price	$3	$4
Target ending inventory in units	300	180
Beginning inventory in units	200	150
Beginning inventory in dollars	$500	$474

Yummi-Lik uses a FIFO cost flow assumption for finished goods inventory.

All the lollipops are made in batches of ten. Yummi-Lik incurs manufacturing overhead costs, and marketing and general administration costs, but customers pay for shipping. Other than manufacturing labour costs, monthly processing costs are very low. Yummy-Lik uses activity-based costing and has classified all overhead costs for the month of June as shown in the following chart:

Cost Type	Denominator Activity	Rate
Manufacturing:		
Setup	Setup hours	$20 per setup hr
Processing	Direct manufacturing labour-hours (DMLH)	$1.70 per DMLH
Non-manufacturing:		
Marketing and general administration	Sales revenue	10%

REQUIRED

1. Prepare each of the following for June:
   a. Revenue budget.
   b. Production budget in units.
   c. Direct material usage budget and direct material purchases budget.

d. Direct manufacturing labour cost budget.

e. Manufacturing overhead cost budgets for processing and setup activities.

f. Budgeted unit cost of ending finished goods inventory and ending inventories budget.

g. Cost of goods sold budget.

h. Marketing and general administration costs budget.

2. Yummi-Lik's balance sheet for May 31 follows. Use it and the following information to prepare a cash budget for Yummi-Lik for June.

- ◆ 80% of sales are on account, of which half are collected in the month of the sale, 49% are collected the following month, and 1% are never collected and written off as bad debts.
- ◆ All purchases of materials are on account. Yummi-Lik pays for 70% of purchases in the month of purchase and 30% in the following month.
- ◆ All other costs are paid in the month incurred.
- ◆ Yummi-Lik is making monthly interest payments of 1% (12% per year) on a $20,000 long-term loan.
- ◆ Yummi-Lik plans to pay the $500 of taxes owed as of May 31 in the month of June. Income tax expense for June is zero.
- ◆ 40% of processing and setup costs, and 30% of marketing and general administration costs are amortization.

Yummi-Lik
Balance Sheet
May 31

Assets

Cash		$ 587
Accounts receivable	$ 4,800	
Less: Allowance for bad debts	96	4,704
Inventories:		
Direct materials		169
Finished goods		974
Fixed assets	190,000	
Less: Accumulated amortization	55,759	134,241
Total assets		$140,675

Liabilities and Equity

Accounts payable		$ 696
Taxes payable		500
Interest payable		200
Long-term debt		20,000
Common shares		10,000
Retained earnings		109,279
Total liabilities and equity		$140,675

3. Prepare a budgeted income statement for June and a budgeted balance sheet for Yummi-Lik as of June 30.

6-43 University department, budget revision options. Gary Gemst is the athletics director of Pacific University (PU). He has been director for more than ten years. PU is a men's football and basketball powerhouse. The women's athletics program, however, has had less success. Last year, the women's basketball team finally had more wins than losses.

Gemst has just had a meeting with Laura Medley, the newly appointed president of PU. It did not go well. Medley and Gemst discussed what she called "Draft I" of the 2013 athletics department budget. He had believed it was the final draft. Medley expressed four grave concerns about Draft I in particular and about the PU athletics program in general:

- ◆ **Concern 1.** The athletics department was budgeting a loss of more than $3.6 million in 2013. Given the tight fiscal position of the university, this was unacceptable. A budgeted loss of $1.2 million was the most she would tolerate for 2013. Draft II of the 2013 budget was due in two weeks' time. By 2014, the athletics department had to operate with a balanced budget. She told Gemst this was nonnegotiable.
- ◆ **Concern 2.** There was very little money allocated to the women's athletics program. Frontline, a tabloid television show, recently ran a program titled "It's a Man's World at the Pacific University Athletics Program." Medley said Gemst was treating female athletes as "third-class citizens."

- ◆ **Concern 3.** The men's football athletes, many of whom had full scholarships, had poor academic performance. Medley noted that the local TV news recently ran an interview with three football team students, none of whom "exemplified the high academic credentials she wanted Pacific to showcase to the world." She called one student "incoherent" and another "incapable of stringing sentences together."
- ◆ **Concern 4.** The salary paid to Bill Madden, the football coach, was outrageous. Medley noted it was twice that of the highest-paid academic on campus, a Nobel Prize winner! Moreover, Madden received other payments from his "Football the Pacific Way" summer program for high-school students.

Exhibit 6-11 is a summary of the Draft I athletics department budget for 2013.

INSTRUCTIONS
Form groups of two or more students to complete the following requirement.

REQUIRED
Your group should discuss the concerns noted both from quantitative and qualitative perspectives. What should be addressed in preparing Draft II of the athletics department's 2013 budget? This draft will form the basis of a half-day meeting Gemst will have with key officials of the athletics department.

EXHIBIT 6-11
Pacific University 2013 Athletics Department Budget (in $ millions)

Revenues:		
Men's athletics programs	$12.420	
Women's athletics programs	0.936	
Other (endowment income, gifts)	4.080	$ 17.436
Costs:		
Men's athletics programs	$13.248	
Women's athletics programs	3.360	
Other (not assigned to programs)	4.440	21.048
Operating income		$ (3.612)

Men's Athletics Programs

	Football	Basketball	Swimming	Other	Total
Revenues	$10.320	$1.800	$0.120	$0.180	$12.420
Costs	8.880	3.240	0.360	0.768	13.248
Full student scholarships	37	21	6	4	68

Women's Athletic Programs

	Basketball	Swimming	Other	Total
Revenues	$ 0.720	$0.096	$0.120	$ 0.936
Costs	2.160	0.240	0.960	3.360
Full student scholarships	11	4	2	17

Flexible Budgets, Variances, and Management Control: I

BUSINESS MATTERS

Keeping It Real

At McDonald's, "Would you like fries with that?" is "cross selling." If diners say "yes," then the larger sale contributes to the restaurant's sales targets and profitability. Managers track both actual sales and costs. Budgeted food and labour costs are compared to actual restaurant performance. Any significant differences between the budgeted and actual results must be explained. If the differences are unfavourable, variance analyses help managers find the appropriate remedies. Managers can then quickly implement them so that goals and objectives to which managers committed in their budget will be achieved in the future.

LEARNING OUTCOMES

After studying this chapter, you should be able to

1. Distinguish between a static budget and a flexible budget.

2. Develop flexible budgets, and calculate flexible-budget Level 2 and Level 3 variances for direct manufacturing costs.

3. Distinguish between Levels 3 and 4 variance analyses for substitutable inputs, and calculate Level 4 direct mix and yield variances.

4. Undertake variance analysis in activity-based costing systems.

5. Describe how managers use variance analyses.

6. Appendix. Distinguish among standards, budgets, benchmarks.

Managers quantify their operating and strategic plans for the future in the form of budgets, which summarize a series of complex decisions. A **variance** is the difference between the budgeted (predicted) results and the actual results. **Variance analysis** is an exceptions-based approach to management that provides feedback. It is a management control tool that enables **management by exception**, the practice of focusing management attention on areas where performance fails to meet expectations. By analyzing the exceptions, managers can explain why actual results failed to meet the budget and act to remedy and control what has gone wrong.

Assume that the operating income is the *point of reference* from which variances are assessed as favourable or unfavourable. A **favourable (F) variance** will result in an actual operating income that *exceeds* the budgeted amount. An **unfavourable (U) variance** will result in an actual operating income that is *less* than the budgeted amount. The logic of variance analysis is clear. All other things being equal, when either actual revenue is less than or actual expenses are more than pro forma, the operating income will decrease relative to the budgeted operating income. These are unfavourable variances.

THE DECISION FRAMEWORK AND VARIANCE ANALYSES

The first step in any decision process is to identify or frame the problem. Usually the results of variance analyses focus on failure, but a management team can also learn from success and then intentionally repeat it. Variance analysis depends on the availability and communication of timely, reliable financial-accounting information reported in good form. The MIS supplies the basic budgeted and actual data; then the management team analyzes it to produce a variance report. These reports are feedback on how well the company achieved its predicted targets.

Because the future is uncertain, the one sure thing about budgeted values is that they will be wrong. The question is whether or not the inaccuracies are tolerable. If the variances threaten the economic health of the company, then managers must identify what caused the failures and find remedies.

Unfavourable variances indicate that actual results *failed* to meet what was budgeted. In some cases the remedy is to change expectations and revise the budget. Usually, however, an unfavourable variance indicates the need to regain control of costs by changing operations. Quick identification of the cause of unfavourable variances improves results and allows the management team to learn from its past mistakes.

STATIC AND FLEXIBLE BUDGETS

1 Distinguish between a static budget and a flexible budget.

This chapter compares actual results to both static and flexible budgets. A **static budget** is a budget that is based on one level of output. It is not adjusted or altered after it is set. Unfortunately, the static-budget variance analysis has limited use. For example, if the volume of sales is higher than expected, all other things being equal the variance will be favourable.

All other things, however, are not equal because some costs vary directly with the quantity produced and sold. This change in total variable costs is perfectly predictable. The actual direct material costs, for example, will most certainly be greater than the budgeted direct material costs because an increased quantity was both produced and sold. Higher variable costs are caused by the higher sales volume, not by some inefficiency in the purchase and use of direct materials.

To avoid wasting time investigating predictable variances, the **flexible budget** is more effective than the static-budget analysis largely because it is dynamic. After each time period, the budgeted variable costs and budgeted revenue amounts will be adjusted according to changes in actual quantity produced and sold. A flexible budget enables managers to calculate a more informative set of variances to provide more effective feedback.

Budgets, both static and flexible, can differ in their level of detail. In this text, the term *Level* followed by a number denotes the amount of detail indicated by the variance(s) isolated. Level 0 reports the least detail; Levels 1, 2, 3, and 4 offer progressively more detailed information. Detail is also referred to as **fineness** in financial accounting. Fineness is a characteristic of reliable information that identifies cause with effect and cost with benefit. The finer the detail and the clearer the cause-effect and cost-benefit relationships, the more readily costs can be controlled.

THE COSTING SYSTEM AT WEBB COMPANY

Webb Company's costing system will illustrate static and flexible budgets. Webb manufactures and sells a single product, a distinctive jacket, which is wholesaled to independent clothing stores and retail chains. Production of the finished goods requires different raw materials, tailoring, and hand and machine operations. Webb's costing system classifies the direct and indirect costs of manufacturing into four cost pools as shown. The non-manufacturing costs are represented by the two downstream cost pools for marketing; one is direct and the other is indirect.

	Direct Costs	Indirect Costs
Manufacturing	Direct materials	Variable manufacturing overhead
	Direct manufacturing labour	Fixed manufacturing overhead
Marketing	Direct marketing labour	Variable marketing overhead
		Fixed marketing overhead

Based on this straightforward costing system, Webb's marketing division has estimated budgeted revenue (budgeted selling price × budgeted units sold) for the year and per month. Other operating division managers have estimated budgeted costs for the year and per month. Once a flexible budget is developed, this cost MIS provides Webb's management team with all the relevant information required to do a very fine level of variance analysis.

We make three simplifying assumptions: First, the monthly estimates are $\frac{1}{12}$ of the annual amounts; second, each jacket consumes identical amounts of both labour and machine time; and third, the quantity (Q) produced equals the quantity sold, or zero finished goods inventory at the end of each month. The variable costs and revenue have an identical driver, Q. These simplifying assumptions are the basis for our discussion about flexible budgeting.

The traceable costs per jacket are direct materials (DM) purchased *and* used. This means there will be zero DM ending inventory. The DM is purchased in square metres (m²). The direct manufacturing labour hours (DMLH) and direct marketing labour hours (DLH) are traced to each jacket produced and sold. The direct machine hours (DMH) are not traced but are useful in fixed cost allocation and indirect variance analysis discussed in Chapter 8. The variable manufacturing overhead costs (VMOH) are allocated using DMH as the cost driver, while the variable period or non-manufacturing overhead costs (VPOH) are allocated using the cost driver marketing DLH. Exhibit 7-1 reports data available in Webb's costing MIS.

Period costs include downstream marketing costs, which are traced to each jacket. The downstream distribution, customer service, and advertising costs, form the variable period overhead cost pool and are allocated. The relevant range for both the manufacturing and period cost drivers is from 8,000 to 16,000 units.

STATIC-BUDGET VARIANCES

Webb's actual results and the *static*-budget amounts for operating income in April 2013, in contribution margin format, are as follows:

LEVEL 0 Variance Analysis

	Actual	Static-Budget Variance	Static-Budget Amount
Operating income	$25,000	$(237,000) U	$262,000

EXHIBIT 7-1
Webb Company's Accounting System Data

	Budgeted	Actual		
Unit sales price per jacket	$180.00	$185.00		
Q = Relevant range of jackets produced and sold	8,000–16,000	10,000		

Cost Category per Jacket	Budgeted Cost Driver	Budgeted Q Cost Driver per Jacket	Budgeted Cost per Input Unit	Budgeted Cost per Jacket
Direct material (DM) measured in square metres (m²)	m²	2.000	$30.00	$60.00
Direct manufacturing labour (DMLH)	DMLH	0.800	20.00	16.00
Variable manufacturing overhead (VMOH*)	DMH	0.400	30.00	12.00
Total budgeted variable manufacturing costs per jacket				$88.00
Direct marketing labour upstream (DLH)	DLH	0.250	24.00	6.00
Variable marketing overhead upstream (VPOH**)	DLH	0.125	40.00	5.00
Total budgeted variable period costs per jacket				$11.00
Total budgeted variable costs per unit				$99.00
Fixed costs of production (FMOH*)	$276,000			
Fixed period costs (FPOH**)	434,000			
Total budgeted fixed costs	$710,000			

*VMOH and FMOH refer to manufacturing overhead for variable and fixed costs.
**VPOH and FPOH refer to period overhead for variable and fixed non-manufacturing overhead costs.

Interpretation of Level 0 Results Webb's managers have received almost no useful feedback from this Level 0 variance analysis report. All that is clear is that the actual performance failed to meet the budget, but there is no indication as to why. The *static-budget variance* is based on the actual result of $25,000 less the operating income of $262,000 that was forecast. Level 0 variance analysis provides a signal but no insight to the management team about how the large unfavourable variance arose.

Using more of the data available in the MIS, Webb can improve the quality of feedback by using the contribution margin format as shown:

	Actual Results	Static-Budget Amounts
Jackets Q sold	10,000	12,000
Total revenue	$1,850,000	$2,160,000
Total variable costs	1,120,000	1,188,000
Contribution margin	730,000	972,000
Fixed costs	705,000	710,000
Operating income	$ 25,000	$ 262,000

This format encourages a line-by-line variance analysis that provides the management team with a bit of insight about why they fell short of the budget. This is a Level 1 variance analysis. The Level 0 and 1 variance analyses are compared in Exhibit 7-2.

When Q produced is equal to Q sold, the reason for the variance of $310,000 is Webb's failure to sell the predicted sales of Q = 12,000 jackets. The reason for the favourable total variable cost variance of $68,000 is Webb's failure to produce Q = 12,000 jackets. Because fixed costs should remain unchanged over the relevant range of 8,000 to 16,000 jackets, the favourable fixed cost variance must have arisen from an unexpected change, such as lower than expected insurance payments.

It is worthwhile to consider the difference between the arithmetic meaning of the variances, which are all negative, and what each difference or variance means. The negative result in each line simply means the numbers in the first column are smaller than those in the last column. In the first line, the actual revenue is less than the predicted revenue by $(310,000). Webb's actual revenue is under budget. All other things equal the result is bad news because less cash will flow in from sales. There will be a decrease in and the effect is U, on operating income.

EXHIBIT 7-2
Comparison of Levels 0 and 1 Static-Budget Variance Analysis*

LEVEL 0 Analysis

	Actual Results	Static-Budget Variance	Static-Budget Amount
Operating income	$25,000	$(287,000) U	$262,000

LEVEL 1 Variance Analysis

	A	B	C	D
		Actual	Static-Budget	Static-Budget
		Results	Variance	Amount
		(1)	(2)	(3)
4	Jackets Q sold	10,000	2,000 U	12,000
5	Total revenue	$1,850,000	$310,000 U	$2,160,000
6	Total variable costs	1,120,000	68,000 F	1,188,000
7	Contribution margin	730,000	(242,000) U	972,000
8	Fixed costs	705,000	5,000 F	710,000
9	Operating income	$ 25,000	$(237,000) U	$ 262,000
10				
11			$(237,000) U	
12			Total static-budget variance	
13				
14	*F = favourable effect on operating income; U = unfavourable effect on operating income.			

In the second line, the total actual variable costs are less than the predicted variable costs by $(68,000). Webb's actual costs are under budget. All other things equal, the result is good news because less cash will flow out from paying for materials, labour and machine use. There will be an increase in, and the effect is F on, operating income. Although both variances are arithmetically negative, one has the opposite effect on operating income from the other.

In the third line, the actual contribution margin is less than the predicted contribution margin by $(242,000). Webb's actual contribution margin is under budget (see Chapter 3). All other things equal, the result is bad news because there is less cash from operations available to pay fixed costs. This means there will be a decrease in, and the effect is U on, operating income because the decrease in total revenue exceeds the decrease in total variable costs. Of course this must be true. The price per unit must exceed the total variable cost per unit or the company would be on the path to bankruptcy.

In the fourth line, the actual fixed costs are less the predicted fixed costs by $(5,000). The actual costs are under budget. All other things equal, the result is good news because less cash will flow out from paying for leasing manufacturing equipment, insurance premium payments, and taxes. Webb's actual fixed costs are under budget. There will be an increase in, and the effect will be F on, operating income.

In the final line, the actual operating income is less than the predicted operating income by $(237,000). To obtain this result, the $(5,000) F for fixed costs reduces the $(242,000) U in contribution margin to $(237,000) U in operating income. This is a strong signal that Webb's operations are proceeding according to the plan. In the rest of the exhibits, brackets will not be used. The variance will be signified only by U or F.

Interpretation of Level 1 Results   At Level 1, the variance analysis in Exhibit 7-2 reveals additional interesting information. The actual unit sales price per jacket must have been $185 ($1,850,000 ÷ 10,000 jackets), not the budgeted $180 per jacket shown in Exhibit 7-1. The total variable costs were actually $112 per jacket, ($1,120,000 ÷ 10,000 jackets), not the budgeted $99 per jacket shown in Exhibit 7-1. On a per jacket basis, the revenue per jacket was $5 favourable and the variable cost per jacket was $13 unfavourable.

EXHIBIT 7-3
Relationship between Cost Variance Analysis Levels 0 and 1

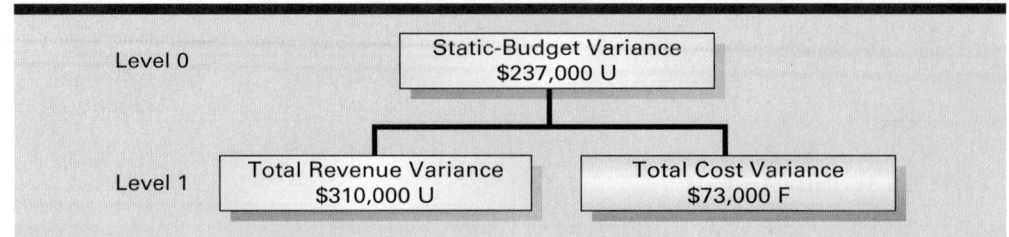

The budgeted contribution margin percentage of 45.0% ($972,000 ÷ $2,160,000) decreases to 39.5% ($730,000 ÷ $1,850,000) for the actual results. This is, in fact, the most important information provided—it answers the question of what effect the net change of actual performance had on operating income. Unfortunately, it does not tell management what caused a significant unfavourable variance. To do so requires more data and the creation of a more dynamic budget, the flexible budget. The reconciliation of the Level 0 and Level 1 variance analyses is illustrated in Exhibit 7-3. The two values in Level 1 add to the value in Level 0.

DEVELOPING A FLEXIBLE BUDGET FROM THE COST MIS

② Develop flexible budgets, and calculate flexible budget Level 2 and Level 3 variances for direct manufacturing costs.

Webb's MIS report in Exhibit 7-1 summarizes relevant data from the budget schedules, but not very much of what is available has been used to give the management team feedback. Exhibit 7-4 demonstrates how, by using more of the data available in the cost MIS, the management team can develop a *flexible budget* and improve the feedback to a finer or more detailed Level 2 variance analysis. Instead of multiplying by only Q = 12,000 produced and sold, the price per jacket and each cost per jacket are multiplied by three

EXHIBIT 7-4
Flexible-Budget Data for Webb Company for April 2013

	A	B	C	D	E	F
1		**Budgeted**	**Flexible-Budget Amounts for**			**Actual Results**
2		**Amount**	**Alternative Levels of Output Units Sold**			**Results for**
3	**Line Item**	**Per Unit**	**10,000**	**12,000**	**16,000**	**10,000 units**
4	(1)	(2)	(3)	(4)	(5)	(6)
5						
6	Revenue	$180	$1,800,000	$2,160,000	$2,880,000	$1,850,000
7	Variable costs					
8	Direct materials	60	600,000	720,000	960,000	688,200
9	Direct manufacturing labour	16	160,000	192,000	256,000	198,000
10	Direct marketing labour	6	60,000	72,000	96,000	57,600
11	Variable manufacturing overhead	12	120,000	144,000	192,000	130,500
12	Variable marketing overhead	5	50,000	60,000	80,000	45,700
13	Total variable costs	99	990,000	1,188,000	1,584,000	1,120,000
14	Contribution margin	$ 81	$ 810,000	$972,000	$1,296,000	$ 730,000
15	Fixed costs					
16	Manufacturing overhead		276,000	276,000	276,000	285,000
17	Marketing overhead		434,000	434,000	434,000	420,000
18	Total fixed costs		710,000	710,000	710,000	705,000
19	Total costs		1,700,000	1,898,000	2,294,000	1,825,000
20	Operating income		$ 100,000	$ 262,000	$ 586,000	$ 25,000

different Q in turn. The three Q are within the relevant range of 8,000 to 16,000 jackets produced and sold.[1] The results of Q = 10,000 is reported in column (3), Q = 12,000 in column (4), and Q = 16,000 in column (5). *Actual* results are reported in column (6).

Having developed the flexible-budget amounts and included the actual results, the management team will focus on only the contribution margin data. This begins the Level 2 analysis.

FLEXIBLE-BUDGET VARIANCES AND SALES-VOLUME VARIANCES

The Level 2 flexible-budget variance analysis will help Webb Company identify where the unfavourable difference of $237,000 between actual and budgeted costs arose. The Level 2 results are compared to the Level 0 static-budget variance analysis Exhibit 7-5. Only the lines in the contribution format of the income statement have been analyzed.

The total Level 0 unfavourable static-budget variance has two sources. The first is the **flexible-budget variance**, which is the total of the differences between the *actual results* and the flexible-budget amounts. In Exhibit 7-4, subtracting the last amount in column (3) from the last amount in column (6) equals the flexible-budget variance. These variances arise because the actual Q = 10,000 produced and sold was less than budgeted Q = 12,000 produced and sold:

$$\text{Flexible-budget variance} = \text{Actual results} - \text{Flexible-budget amount}$$
$$= \$25,000 - \$100,000$$
$$= \$75,000 \text{ U}$$

The second source of static-budget variance is the **sales-volume variance**. The sales-volume variance is the total of the differences between the flexible-budget and *static-budget amounts*. These variances arise because the actual units *sold*, Q = 10,000, was lower than the static-budget quantity of Q = 12,000:

$$\frac{\text{Sales-volume}}{\text{variance}} = \frac{\text{Flexible-budget}}{\text{amount}} - \frac{\text{Static-budget}}{\text{amount}}$$
$$= \$100,000 - \$262,000$$
$$= \$162,000 \text{ U}$$

Using contribution margin information available at Level 2, the third line in Exhibit 7-5 indicates that there are three sources of flexible-budget variance of $(75,000) U. The first is the difference between actual and flexible-budget revenue arising from the difference in selling price.

$$\frac{\text{Selling-price}}{\text{variance}} = \left(\frac{\text{Actual selling}}{\text{price}} - \frac{\text{Budgeted}}{\text{selling price}} \right) \times \frac{\text{Actual units}}{\text{sold}}$$
$$= (\$185 - \$180) \times 10,000$$
$$= \$50,000 \text{ F}$$

EXHIBIT 7-5
Relationship between Cost Variance Analysis Levels 0 and 2

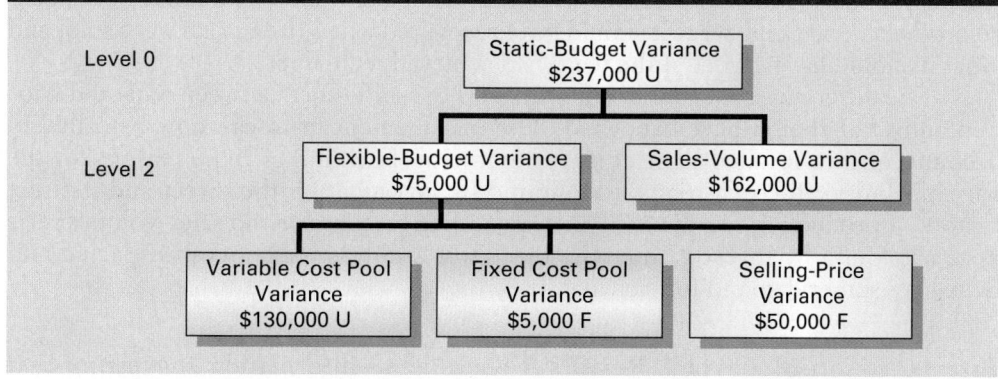

[1] At a Q produced and sold of 10,000 jackets, the flexible-budget revenue is $180 per jacket × 10,000 jackets = $1,800,000 and total manufacturing costs are $99 per jacket × 10,000 = $990,000.

	A	B	C	D	E	F
		Actual	Flexible-Budget	Flexible	Sales-Volume	Static
		Results	Variances	Budget	Variances	Budget
		(1)	(2) = (1) − (3)	(3)	(4) = (3) − (5)	(5)
4	Units sold	10,000	—	10,000	2,000 U	12,000
5	Revenue	$1,850,000	$ 50,000 F	$1,800,000	$360,000 U	$2,160,000
6	Variable costs	1,120,000	$130,000 U	990,000	198,000 F	1,188,000
7	Contribution margin	730,000	80,000 U	$ 810,000	162,000 U	972,000
8	Fixed costs	705,000	5,000 F	710,000	—	710,000
9	Operating income	$ 25,000	$ 75,000 U	$ 100,000	$162,000 U	$ 262,000
10						
11			$ 75,000 U		$162,000 U	
12			Total flexible-budget variance		Total sales-volume variance	
13						
14				$237,000 U		
15				Total static-budget variance		

LEVEL 2 Variance Analysis

Note: Pay careful attention because the variances in columns (2) and (4) depend on how the variance affects Operating income.

The second and third sources contributing to the total flexible-budget variance are the variable and fixed cost pool variances. In Exhibit 7-4 the total actual variable cost is $1,120,000 (column 6) and the total flexible-budget variable cost is $990,000 (column 3). The difference is

$$\text{Variable cost variance} = (\text{Actual variable cost} - \text{Flexible-budget variable cost})$$
$$= \$1,120,000 - \$990,000$$
$$= \$130,000 \text{ U}$$

For the fixed costs, the difference between the total actual fixed costs of $705,000 and the flexible-budget fixed costs of $710,000 is

$$\text{Fixed cost variance} = \text{Actual fixed cost} - \text{Flexible-budget fixed cost}$$
$$= \$705,000 - \$710,000$$
$$= \$5,000 \text{ F}$$

The two sets of variance calculations are in columns (2) and (4) of Exhibit 7-6. The actual results are in column (1). In column (3), all the flexible budgeted values are reported as if managers could tell the future perfectly and budget for Q = 10,000 jackets produced and sold in April. The values indicate what Webb should have paid to produce the jackets, what it should have recovered when the jackets were sold, and what it should have earned if the team had achieved its budget.

The difference reported in column (2) is the difference between what did happen and what should have happened. The management team can now be called to account for how it failed to meet its commitment. In column (2) the reasons for the variable and fixed cost variances are found by investigating the direct and indirect factors of production for the 10,000 jackets. The reasons for the sales-volume variance are found by investigating why there was a difference between expected and actual consumer demand for jackets.

Interpretation of Level 2 Results   There is no information suggesting that Webb's jackets are differentiated from others by especially desirable attributes for which customers will pay more. Customers set the price for the product and Webb, along with its competitors, is a price taker. Webb's profitability depends on cost leadership. By keeping a sharp focus on controlling its costs, Webb will squeeze more profit from each jacket at $180 than its competitors with less focus on cost control. It is possible that Webb's customers simply switched from the jacket costing $185 to purchase similar jackets costing $180. It is the task of the marketing division to investigate this possibility.

It is interesting that Webb's actual fixed costs were less than the flexible-budget amount. Insurance premiums or perhaps property taxes decreased unexpectedly. This change is likely to persist and the budget should be revised. Alternatively, perhaps a salaried manager resigned in April. In this case the unexpected change is temporary until a replacement is hired and no change should be made to the budget.

Webb also exceeded its flexible budgeted variable costs by approximately 13% ($130,000 ÷ $990,000). The Level 2 analysis has helped clarify how the overall $237,000 U static-budget variance came about. But better feedback is needed to identify what changes happened to the quantities and unit rates generating the variable costs. Webb must use more of the information already reported in its MIS. Important non-financial data are also reported in Exhibit 7-1 on the budgeted quantities of different inputs purchased and used as well as cost allocation bases for the indirect costs. The level of detail in the existing MIS is fine enough to isolate the effect of changes in quantities from changes in cost per input and provide feedback sufficient to do a Level 3 analysis.

DIRECT VARIABLE RATE AND EFFICIENCY VARIANCES

The value added of a Level 3 analysis is to direct the management team's attention to specific elements of production that are out of control. Conventional terms may be somewhat confusing at first. We can refer to the cost per unit of input as its rate, input rate, or rate per unit. A **rate variance** is the difference between the actual rate and the budgeted rate multiplied by the actual quantity of input in question (such as direct materials purchased or used). This is sometimes referred to as an **input price variance**. It is a confusing term that is not used in this text.

The price per unit of finished goods sold *by* Webb to its customers is a cash inflow. The price per unit of direct materials sold *to* Webb by a supplier is a cash outflow. It is more straightforward to think of the direct materials sold to Webb in terms of a cost per unit or a rate per unit, that always indicates a cash outflow.

An **efficiency variance** is the difference between the actual quantity of input used (such as metres of cloth in direct materials) and the budgeted quantity of input that should have been used, multiplied by the budgeted rate to obtain the flexible-budget value. *Efficiency variances* are sometimes called **input-efficiency variances** or **usage variances**.

The relationship of these two components of direct variances to those variable costs we have already discussed for Webb is shown in Exhibit 7-7. The manufacturing costs are in the boxes shaded blue, the colour of the production business function. The non-manufacturing costs are shaded yellow, the colour of the marketing function in the value chain. Indirect variances (variable and fixed) are analyzed in Chapter 8.

In reality, managers are responsible for controlling efficiency variances and have the authority to do so. This is not usually the case with rate variances. Unless the company is a very large consumer (a monopsony) of direct materials, it has no power to affect the cost per unit of those materials. This is especially true if there is only one supplier (a monopoly). The company depends on astute negotiation with the supplier to obtain the lowest possible rate per unit at the right quality level and at the right time. Managers remain responsible for explaining rate variance but have little control over it.

AN ILLUSTRATION OF RATE AND EFFICIENCY VARIANCES FOR INPUTS

Consider Webb's three direct-cost categories of materials, manufacturing labour, and marketing labour. For simplicity, assume that direct materials used is equal to direct materials purchased; therefore, there will be no ending inventory. At this point in our analysis, we do not want to complicate the variance analyses with questions of

EXHIBIT 7-7
Detailed Variable-Cost Sources of Variance

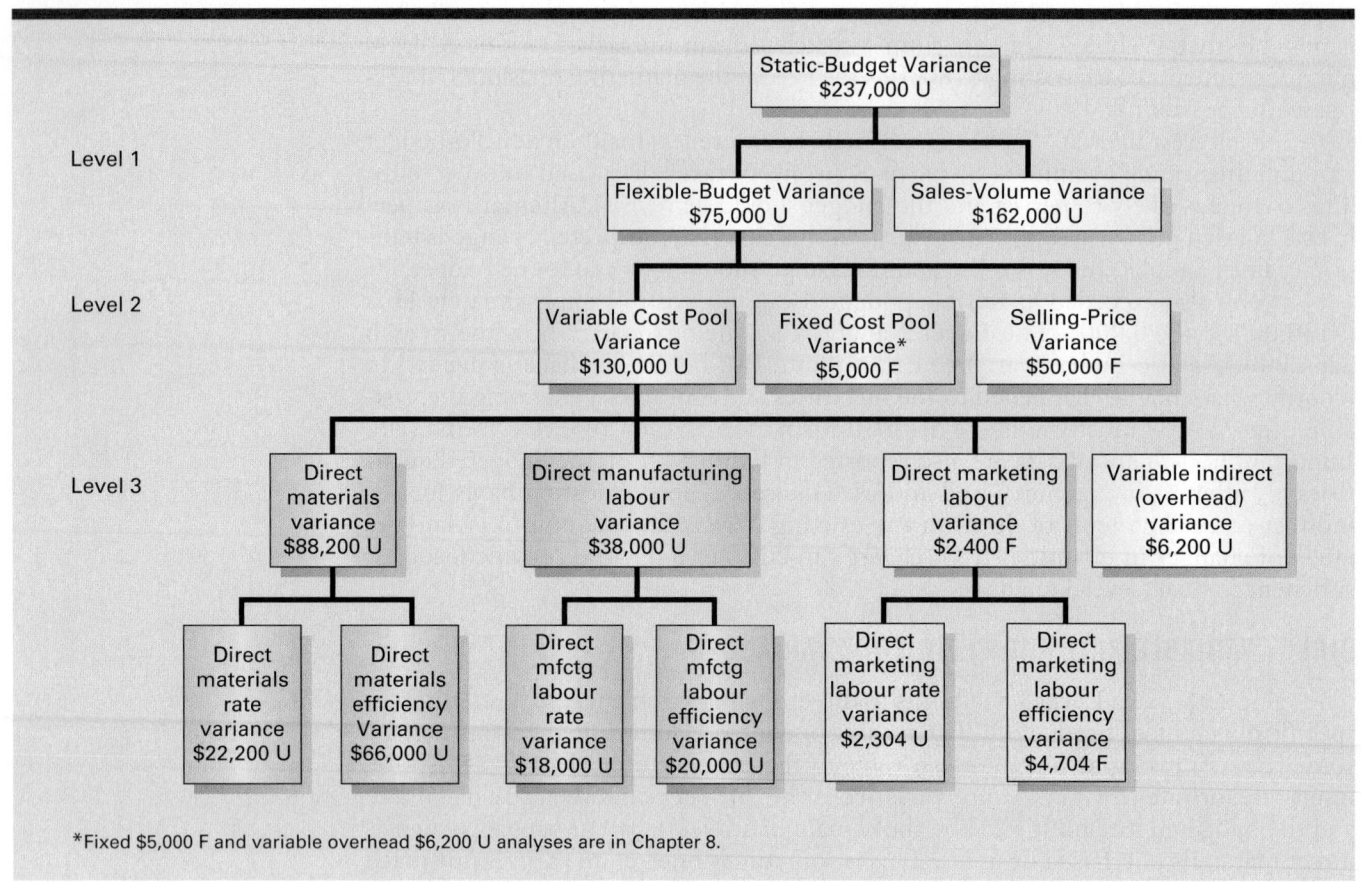

Level 1 — Static-Budget Variance $237,000 U

Flexible-Budget Variance $75,000 U — Sales-Volume Variance $162,000 U

Level 2 — Variable Cost Pool Variance $130,000 U — Fixed Cost Pool Variance* $5,000 F — Selling-Price Variance $50,000 F

Level 3 — Direct materials variance $88,200 U — Direct manufacturing labour variance $38,000 U — Direct marketing labour variance $2,400 F — Variable indirect (overhead) variance $6,200 U

Direct materials rate variance $22,200 U — Direct materials efficiency Variance $66,000 U — Direct mfctg labour rate variance $18,000 U — Direct mfctg labour efficiency variance $20,000 U — Direct marketing labour rate variance $2,304 U — Direct marketing labour efficiency variance $4,704 F

*Fixed $5,000 F and variable overhead $6,200 U analyses are in Chapter 8.

inventory valuation. By expanding the data in Exhibit 7-1 to include actual results, Exhibit 7-8 shows the basis for a Level 3 analysis.[2]

We can summarize the data for all direct inputs that are the first stage of a Level 2 analysis as follows:

	Actual Results (1)	Flexible Budget Variances (2) = (1) − (3)	Flexible Budget (3)	
Direct materials (22,200 × $31/m²)	$688,200	$ 88,200 U	$600,000	(20,000 × $30/m²)
Direct manufacturing labour (9,000 × $22/DMLH)	198,000	38,000 U	160,000	(8,000 × $20/DMLH)
Direct marketing labour (2,304 × $25/DLH)	57,600	(2,400) F	60,000	(2,500 × $24/DLH)
Total	$943,800	$ 123,800 U	$820,000	

But this tells us only how the flexible-budget variances are distributed among the three direct inputs; we do not know what caused the variances. Was it rates, efficiency, or a combination of both? The data summarized in Exhibit 7-8 are sufficient to more sharply focus the attention of Webb's management team on what items require the most immediate attention to bring their costs back under control, the costs per unit or the quantities used.

RATE VARIANCES

The formula for computing a rate variance is

$$\text{Price variance} = \left(\begin{array}{c} \text{Actual price} \\ \text{of input} \end{array} - \begin{array}{c} \text{Budgeted price} \\ \text{of input} \end{array} \right) \times \begin{array}{c} \text{Actual quantity} \\ \text{of input} \\ \text{purchased} \end{array}$$

[2]Detail on non-manufacturing variances is presented in the Appendix to this chapter.

EXHIBIT 7-8
Detailed Variable-Cost Sources of Variance

LEVEL 2 ANALYSIS

	A	B	C	D	E	F	G	H
1				**Budgeted**		**Actual**		
2	Unit sales price per jacket			$ 180.00		$ 185.00		
3	Q = Relevant range of jackets Produced and sold			8,000–16,000		10,000		
4	**Cost Category per Jacket**	**Budgeted Cost Driver (0)**	**Budgeted Q Cost Driver per Jacket (1)**	**Budgeted Cost per Input Unit (2)**	**Budgeted Cost per Jacket (1) × (2)**	**Actual Q Cost Driver per Jacket (3)**	**Actual Cost per Input Unit (4)**	**Actual Cost per Jacket (3) × (4)**
5	Direct material (DM) measured in square metres (m²)	m²	2.000	$ 30	$60	2.2200	$ 31.00	$ 68.82
6	Direct manufacturing labour (DMLH)	DMLH	0.800	20	16	0.9000	22.00	19.80
7	Variable manufacturing overhead (VMOH)*	DMH	0.400	30	12	0.4500	29.00	13.05
8	Total budgeted variable manufacturing costs per jacket				$88			$ 101.67
9	Direct marketing labour (DLH)	DLH	0.250	24.00	6	0.2304	25.00	5.76
10	Variable marketing overhead (VPOH)†	DLH	0.125	40.00	5	0.1828	25.00	4.57
11	Total budgeted variable period costs per jacket				11			$ 10.33
12	Total budgeted variable costs per unit				$99			$ 112.00
13	Fixed costs of production (FMOH)	$276,000				$285,000		
14	Fixed period costs (FPOH)	434,000				420,000		
15	Total budgeted fixed costs	$710,000				$705,000		

*Budgeted VMOH is $12/jacket or $144,000 ÷ 12,000 jackets. The standard of 0.40 DMH/jacket at a rate of $30/DMH is derived in Chapter 8.
†Non-manufacturing cost allocation is discussed in Chapter 14.

Based on the formula, the rate variances for each of Webb's three direct cost categories are as follows:

	Actual less Budgeted Rate Per Unit (1)	Actual Quantity of Input Units Purchased (2)	=	Input Rate Variance (1) × (2)
Direct materials ($31/m² – $30/m²) × 22,200 m²	$1.00	22,200	=	$ 22,200 U
Direct manufacturing labour ($22/DMLH – $20/DMLH) × 9,000 DMLH	$2.00	9,000	=	18,000 U
Direct marketing labour ($25/DLH – $24/DLH) × 2,304 DLH	$1.00	2,304	=	2,304 U
				$ 42,504 U

All three rate variances are unfavourable (they reduce operating income) because the actual direct rate per input unit exceeds the budgeted rate. In total, Webb incurred more direct cost per input unit than was budgeted.

Interpretation of Level 3 Result of Rate Variance Analyses Generally speaking, the management team's attention will be directed to the largest U variance, the direct materials rate variance. But more investigation is needed because there are many potential reasons for the rate variance:

◆ Budgeted purchase rates for Webb's materials were set without careful analysis of its suppliers.

- Webb's purchasing manager negotiated less skillfully than was committed to in the budget.
- Webb's purchasing manager bought in smaller lot sizes than budgeted, even though quantity discounts were available for the larger lot sizes.
- Materials rates unexpectedly increased because of unanticipated increases in market demand or unanticipated increases in costs of transportation from the supplier to Webb.
- The specified quality of materials required was discontinued by suppliers. Quality of materials purchased exceeded the production specifications, leading to higher rates.

The first step is to identify the cause, which will affect the remedy to bring the direct materials rate back under control. If Webb identifies the reason as poor negotiating by its purchasing officer, then the remedy may be to invest more in training this officer in negotiation. Alternatively, Webb may decide to hire a more skillful purchasing officer. Another alternative is to negotiate long-term fixed rate contracts to ensure no future unfavourable rate variance for the life of the contract.

EFFICIENCY VARIANCES

For any actual level of output, the efficiency variance is the difference between the actual and budgeted quantity of inputs multiplied by the budgeted rate per unit. Holding the rate constant isolates the effect of variance in quantity purchased and used from any change in rate:

$$\frac{\text{Efficiency}}{\text{variance}} = \left(\frac{\text{Actual quantity}}{\text{of input used}} - \frac{\text{Budgeted quantity of input allowed}}{\text{for actual output units achieved}} \right) \times \frac{\text{Budgeted rate}}{\text{of input}}$$

The idea here is that an organization is inefficient if it uses more inputs than budgeted for the actual output units achieved, and it is efficient if it uses fewer inputs than budgeted for the actual output units achieved.

The efficiency variances for each of Webb's direct cost categories are as follows:

	Actual less Budgeted Quantity Per Input Unit (1)	×	Budgeted Rate per Unit Purchased (2)	= =	Input Efficiency Variance (1) × (2)
Direct materials [22,200 m² − (10,000 units of output × 2 m²)] × $30/m²	2,200	×	$30.00	=	$66,000 U
Direct manufacturing labour [9,000 − (10,000 units of output × 0.80)] × $20/DMLH	1,000	×	$20.00	=	20,000 U
Direct marketing labour [2,304 − (10,000 units of output × 0.25)] × $24/DLH	196	×	$24.00	=	4,704 F
Total					$81,296 U

The two manufacturing-efficiency variances (direct materials and direct manufacturing labour) are both unfavourable because more input was used than was budgeted, resulting in a decrease in operating income. The marketing-efficiency variance is favourable because less input was used than was budgeted, resulting in an increase in operating income.

Interpretation of Level 3 Result of Efficiency Variance Analyses   Like the rate variance, the largest efficiency variance also arises from direct materials. But the management team must consider a range of intertwined reasons for efficiency variances. The direct materials variance could be influenced by the unfavourable direct manufacturing labour variance. For example, Webb's unfavourable direct materials variance could be due to one or more of the following reasons:

- ◆ Webb's human resources manager hired underskilled workers or their training was inadequate.
- ◆ Webb's production process was reorganized or a new machine has been installed, creating additional direct manufacturing labour time per jacket as workers learn the new process.
- ◆ Webb's production scheduler inefficiently scheduled work, resulting in more direct manufacturing labour time per jacket.
- ◆ Webb's marketing department promised early deliveries to clients, which created too many rush-order interruptions that led to overtime.
- ◆ Webb's maintenance department did not properly maintain machines, resulting in additional direct manufacturing labour time per jacket to avoid damage done by the machines.
- ◆ Webb's jacket design became obsolete, leading to a new, more complicated design requiring more direct manufacturing labour time.
- ◆ Budgeted time standards were set without careful analysis of the operating conditions and employees' skills.

The first step is to identify the cause of the unfavourable variance. If the cause was poor machine maintenance, then one reasonable response is to create a team consisting of plant machine engineers and machine operators who will develop a new maintenance schedule so that there will be less materials spoilage. Another alternative is to remove any incentives in the marketing area to place rush orders. Perhaps allocating a portion of overtime costs would eliminate any interruption in routine maintenance and reduce spoilage. A third alternative is to penalize the maintenance department by allocating a portion of overtime and material spoilage costs to that department to keep them to the schedule. Finally, it may be time for Webb to invest in replacing obsolete machines to reduce spoilage and maintenance hours.

PRESENTATION OF RATE AND EFFICIENCY VARIANCES FOR INPUTS

Note how the sum of the rate variance and the efficiency variance equals the flexible-budget variance:

	Input Rate Variances	Input Efficiency Variances	Flexible-Budget Variance
Direct materials	$22,200 U	$66,000 U	$ 88,200 U
Direct manufacturing labour	$18,000 U	$20,000 U	$ 38,000 U
Direct marketing labour	$ 2,304 U	$(4,704) F	$ (2,400) F
Total	$42,504 U	$81,296 U	$123,800 U

	Input Price Variances	Input Efficiency Variances	Flexible-Budget Variance
Direct materials	17.93% U	53.31% U	71.24% U
Direct manufacturing labour	14.54% U	16.16% U	30.70% U
Direct marketing labour	1.86% U	−3.80% F	−1.94% F
Total	34.33% U	65.67% U	100.00% U

Exhibit 7-9 integrates the actual and budgeted input information used to compute the rate and efficiency variances for direct materials when materials purchased equals materials used.

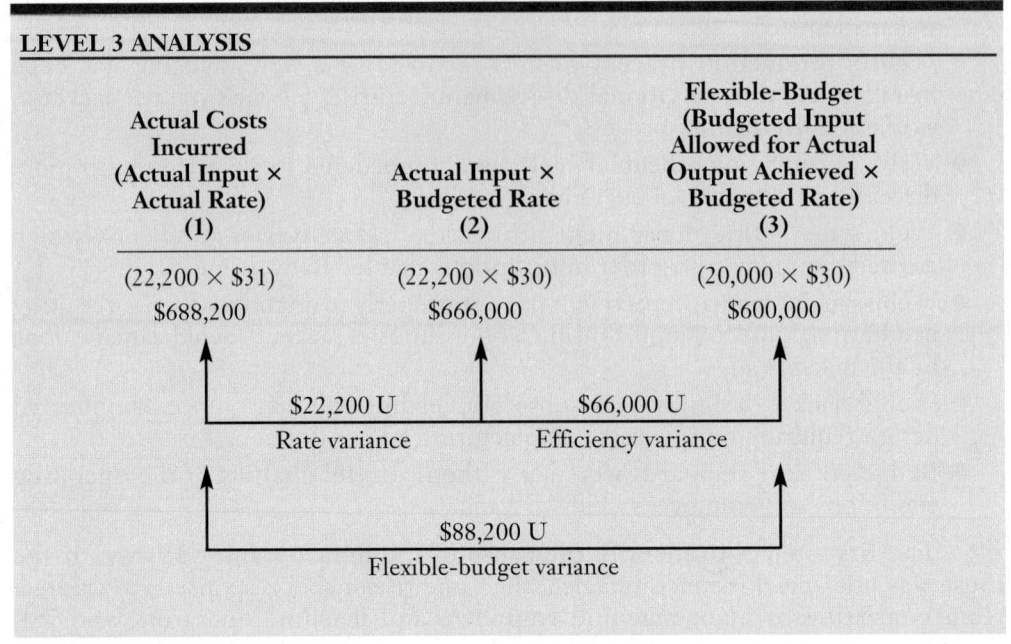

LEVEL 3 ANALYSIS

Actual Costs Incurred (Actual Input × Actual Rate) (1)	Actual Input × Budgeted Rate (2)	Flexible-Budget (Budgeted Input Allowed for Actual Output Achieved × Budgeted Rate) (3)
(22,200 × $31)	(22,200 × $30)	(20,000 × $30)
$688,200	$666,000	$600,000

$22,200 U $66,000 U
Rate variance   Efficiency variance

$88,200 U
Flexible-budget variance

A comparison of the fineness among three levels of variance analyses are reported. Notice that as the fineness increases, the insight with respect to what has caused the variance becomes clearer. But Webb's value-added activities in its chain of business functions are not separate but rather interdependent on one another. What explains one variance may explain several.

LEVEL 0 Variance Analysis

	Actual	Static-Budget Variance	Static Budget
Operating income	$25,000	$237,000 U	$262,000

LEVEL 1 Variance Analysis

	Actual	Static-Budget Variance	Static Budget
Jackets Q sold	10,000	2,000 U	12,000
Total revenue	$1,850,000	$310,000 U	$2,160,000
Total variable costs	1,120,000	68,000 F	1,188,000
Contribution margin	730,000	242,000 U	972,000
Fixed costs	705,000	5,000 F	710,000
Operating income	$ 25,000	$237,000 U	$ 262,000

$237,000 U

Total static-budget variance

LEVEL 2 Variance Analysis*

	Actual Results (1)	Flexible-Budget Variances (2) = (1) − (3)	Flexible Budget (3)	Sales-Volume Variances (4) = (3) − (5)	Static Budget (5)
Units sold	10,000	—	10,000	2,000 U	12,000
Revenue	$1,850,000	$50,000 F	$1,800,000	$360,000 U	$2,160,000
Variable costs	1,120,000	130,000 U	990,000	198,000 F	1,188,000
Contribution margin	730,000	80,000 U	$ 810,000	162,000 U	972,000
Fixed costs	705,000	5,000 F	710,000	—	710,000
Operating income	$ 25,000	$75,000 U	$ 100,000	$162,000 U	$ 262,000

$75,000 U ← Total flexible-budget variance

$162,000 U ← Total sales-volume variance

$87,000 U — Total static-budget variance

*Pay careful attention because the variances reported in columns (2), (4) depend on how the variance affects Operating income.

LEVEL 3 Variance Analysis*

	Actual Results (1)	Flexible-Budget Variances (2) = (1) − (3)	Flexible Budget (3)	Sales-Volume Variances (4) = (3) − (5)	Static Budget (5)
Units sold	10,000	—	10,000	2,000 U	12,000
Revenue	$1,850,000	$50,000 F	$1,800,000	$360,000 U	$2,160,000
Variable costs		—		—	
Direct materials	$ 688,200	88,200 U	600,000	120,000 U	720,000
Direct manufacturing labour	198,000	38,000 U	160,000	32,000 F	192,000
Direct marketing labour	57,600	2,400 F	60,000	12,000 F	72,000
Variable manufacturing overhead	130,500	10,500 U	120,000	24,000 F	144,000
Variable marketing overhead	45,700	4,300 F	50,000	10,000 F	60,000
Total variable costs	$1,120,000	$80,000 U	$ 990,000	$198,000 F	$1,188,000
Contribution margin	$ 730,000	$80,000 U	$ 810,000	$162,000 F	$ 972,000
Fixed manufacturing costs	285,000	9,000 U	276,000	—	276,000
Fixed marketing costs	420,000	14,000 F	434,000	—	434,000
Operating income	$ 25,000	$75,000 U	$ 100,000	$162,000 U	$ 262,000

*Total variable overhead variance is $6,200 U ($4,300 F − $10,500 U).

MIX AND YIELD LEVEL 4 VARIANCES FOR SUBSTITUTABLE INPUTS

For most mass production manufacturing processes—for example, refining oil—the barrel of oil from one Hibernia well is the same as the barrel of oil from a different Hibernia well. These are called **substitutable inputs** because the manufacturer can readily replace one with the other. Substitutability enables a more detailed analysis of the direct materials efficiency variance. Both materials and labour inputs may be substitutable in either manufacturing, merchandising, or service industries.

But sometimes the output is distinguished by its taste—for example, wine or ketchup. The taste difference is due to the **input mix**, which is the determination of the *standard* combination and proportion of very similar direct material inputs that may be substituted for one another (see the Appendix to this chapter for a discussion of standards). For ketchup, a combination of different tomatoes leads to the distinctive

> Distinguish between Levels 3 and 4 variance analyses for substitutable inputs, and calculate Level 4 direct mix and yield variances.
>
> ③

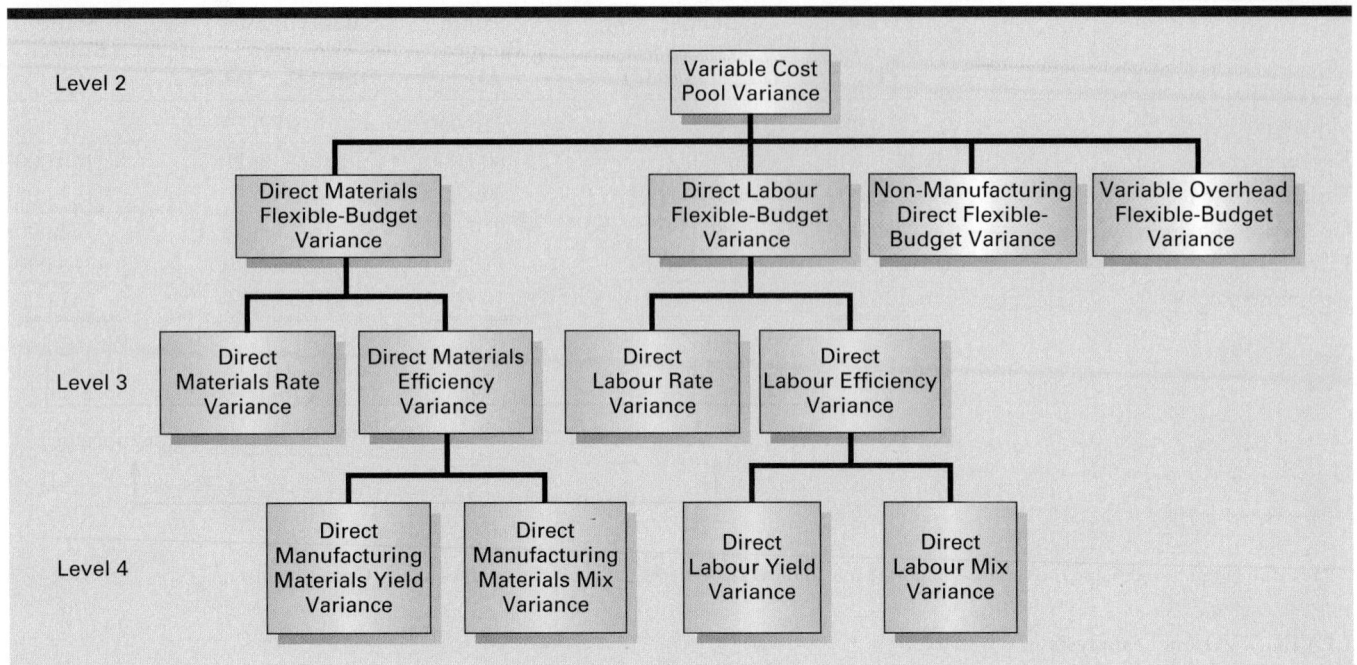

taste that distinguishes one brand from another. Small differences in the input mix that do not affect taste can reduce costs. The managers are given some discretion about the proportions of different tomatoes used to give them the flexibility necessary to exercise good cost leadership.

In changing the input mix, however, managers must ensure that the quantity of output is unchanged. It is only by selling the finished ketchup that all the costs of inputs can be recovered. The **yield** is the proportion of output obtained from a specified quantity of input. It is measured in the same units as inputs. Yield is calculated as the total quantity of output units divided by the total quantity of input units. **Mix variance** measures the variance of actual from expected input mix. The **yield variance** measures the variance of the actual from expected yield of outputs obtained from expected quantity of inputs. The relationship among the variance components of the direct materials and labour mix and yield variances are shown in Exhibit 7-10.

THE DECISION FRAMEWORK AND SUBSTITUTABLE INPUTS

The problem is to select the best combination of substitutable inputs. For example, Del Monte can combine direct material inputs (such as pineapples, cherries, and grapes) in varying proportions for its cans of fruit salad. The decisions managers make will have financial implications for profitability, which are highlighted by the presentation of mix and yield variances. These variances separate the components of the direct materials and direct labour efficiency variances obtained from a Level 3 variance analysis. The Level 4 variance analyses provide feedback to managers regarding the effect on profitability of their decisions to substitute one direct materials or labour input for another.

Assume the information required to complete a Level 4 variance analysis can be gathered from an existing MIS. This detailed feedback will give the management team information on which they can more readily predict the outcomes of various combinations of substitutable inputs. The value-added of a Level 4 analysis is to isolate the effects of combinations of different inputs on the flexible-budget efficiency variance from those of the yield.

SUBSTITUTABLE DIRECT MATERIALS INPUTS

To illustrate mix and yield variances, let's examine Delpino Corporation, which makes tomato ketchup. Our example focuses on direct material inputs and substitution among three of these inputs, but the same approach can be used to examine substitutable direct labour inputs. To produce ketchup of the desired consistency, colour, and taste, Delpino mixes three types of tomatoes grown in three different regions—Latin American tomatoes (Latoms), California tomatoes (Caltoms), and Florida tomatoes (Flotoms). Delpino's production standards require 1.60 tonnes of tomatoes to produce 1 tonne of ketchup, with 50% of the tomatoes being Latoms, 30% Caltoms, and 20% Flotoms. The direct materials input standards to produce 1 tonne of ketchup are:

0.80 (50% of 1.6) tonne of Latoms at $70 per tonne	$ 56.00
0.48 (30% of 1.6) tonne of Caltoms at $80 per tonne	38.40
0.32 (20% of 1.6) tonne of Flotoms at $90 per tonne	28.80
Total standard cost of 1.6 tonnes of tomatoes	$123.20

Budgeted average cost per tonne of tomatoes is $123.20 ÷ 1.60 tonnes = $77.00 per tonne. The total quantity of inputs is 1.60 tonnes regardless of the type of tomato.

Because Delpino uses fresh tomatoes to make ketchup, no inventories of tomatoes are kept. Purchases are made as needed. All rate variances relate to tomatoes purchased and used. Actual results for June 2013 show that a total of 6,500 tonnes of tomatoes were used to produce 4,000 tonnes of ketchup:

3,250	tonnes of Latoms at actual cost of $70 per tonne	$227,500
2,275	tonnes of Caltoms at actual cost of $82 per tonne	186,550
975	tonnes of Flotoms at actual cost of $96 per tonne	93,600
6,500	tonnes of tomatoes	$507,650
	Standard cost of 4,000 tonnes of ketchup at $123.20	492,800
	Total variance to be explained	$ 14,850 U

Given the standard ratio of 1.60 tonnes of tomatoes to 1 tonne of ketchup, 6,400 tonnes of tomatoes should be used to produce 4,000 tonnes of ketchup. At the standard mix, the quantities of each type of tomato required are as follows:

Latoms	0.50 × 6,400 = 3,200 tonnes
Caltoms	0.30 × 6,400 = 1,920 tonnes
Flotoms	0.20 × 6,400 = 1,280 tonnes

DIRECT MATERIALS RATE AND EFFICIENCY VARIANCES

The direct materials rate and efficiency variances are calculated separately for each input material and then added together. The variance analysis prompts Delpino to investigate the unfavourable rate and efficiency variances—why did they pay more for the tomatoes and use greater quantities than they should have? Causes could include a higher market rate for tomatoes or poor negotiation by the purchasing department. One is uncontrollable, the other is controllable. Inefficiency could also have been due to poor-quality tomatoes with too much water content or issues with the processing. To calculate the efficiency and rate variances:

$$\text{Efficiency variance} = \left(\begin{array}{c} \text{Actual quantity} \\ \text{of input used} \end{array} - \begin{array}{c} \text{Budgeted quantity of input allowed} \\ \text{for actual output units achieved} \end{array} \right) \times \begin{array}{c} \text{Budgeted rate} \\ \text{of input} \end{array}$$

The results are shown in Exhibit 7-11. The management team will focus on how to explain the $4,450 U efficiency variance in terms of input mix or yield variance.

EXHIBIT 7-11
Direct Materials Rate and Efficiency Variances for the Delpino Corporation for June 2013

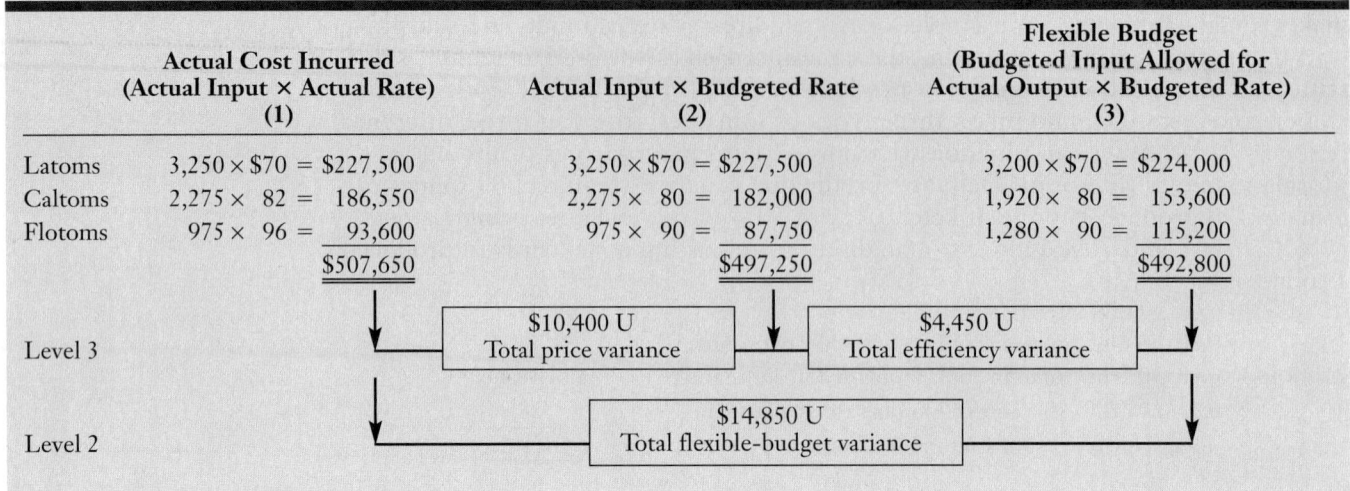

	Actual Cost Incurred (Actual Input × Actual Rate) (1)	Actual Input × Budgeted Rate (2)	Flexible Budget (Budgeted Input Allowed for Actual Output × Budgeted Rate) (3)
Latoms	3,250 × $70 = $227,500	3,250 × $70 = $227,500	3,200 × $70 = $224,000
Caltoms	2,275 × 82 = 186,550	2,275 × 80 = 182,000	1,920 × 80 = 153,600
Flotoms	975 × 96 = 93,600	975 × 90 = 87,750	1,280 × 90 = 115,200
	$507,650	$497,250	$492,800

Level 3 — $10,400 U Total price variance — $4,450 U Total efficiency variance

Level 2 — $14,850 U Total flexible-budget variance

DIRECT MATERIALS MIX AND DIRECT MATERIALS YIELD VARIANCES

Managers sometimes have discretion to substitute one material for another. For example, the manager of Delpino's ketchup plant has some leeway in combining Latoms, Caltoms, and Flotoms without affecting quality. We will assume that to maintain quality, the mix percentages of each type of tomato can vary only up to 5% from the standard mix. For example, the percentage of Caltoms in the mix can vary between 25% and 35% (30% ± 5%).

When inputs are substitutable, direct materials efficiency improvements relative to budgeted costs can come from two sources: (1) using a cheaper mix to produce a given quantity of output or (2) using less input to achieve a given quantity of output. The direct materials yield and mix variances divide the efficiency variance into two variances: the mix variance focuses on how the multiple types of substitutable materials or labour are combined, and the yield variance focuses on how much of those inputs are used.

Holding constant the actual total quantity of all direct materials inputs used, the total **direct materials mix variance** is the difference between two amounts: (1) the budgeted cost for the actual mix of the total quantity of direct materials used, and (2) the budgeted cost of the budgeted mix of the actual total quantity of direct materials used. Signify each input as x_i and calculate the variance as:

$$\text{Direct materials mix variance} = \sum_{i=1}^{n} (\text{Actual} - \text{Budgeted input mix } x_i) \times \text{Budgeted rate } x_i$$

The details of the calculation are shown in column format in Exhibit 7-12.

Holding the budgeted input mix constant, the **direct materials yield variance** is the difference between two amounts: (1) the budgeted cost of direct materials based on the actual total quantity of all direct materials inputs used, and (2) the flexible-budget cost of direct materials based on the budgeted total quantity of direct materials inputs for the actual output. Again, with each input signified as x_i, the variance is calculated as:

$$\text{Direct yield variance} = \sum_{i=1}^{n} (\text{Actual } x_i \times [\text{Actual} - \text{Budgeted input mix \% } x_i] \times \text{Budgeted rate } x_i)$$

Exhibit 7-12 presents the calculation of total direct materials mix and yield variances for the Delpino Corporation.

Interpretation of Direct Materials Mix Variance   Compare columns 1 and 2 in Exhibit 7-12. Both columns calculate cost using the actual total quantity of all inputs used (6,500 tonnes) and budgeted input rates (Latoms, $70; Caltoms, $80; and Flotoms, $90). The *only* difference is that column 1 uses *actual input mix* (Latoms, 50%; Caltoms, 35%; Flotoms, 15%), and column 2 uses *budgeted input mix* (Latoms, 50%; Caltoms, 30%; and Flotoms, 20%). The difference in costs between the two columns is the total direct materials mix variance, attributable solely to differences in the mix of inputs used. The total direct materials mix variance is the sum of the direct materials mix variances for each input:

Latoms	$(0.50 - 0.50) \times 6{,}500 \times \$70 = 0.00 \times 6{,}500 \times \$70$	$= \$ \quad 0$
Caltoms	$(0.35 - 0.30) \times 6{,}500 \times \$80 = 0.05 \times 6{,}500 \times \$80$	$= 26{,}000$ U
Flotoms	$(0.15 - 0.20) \times 6{,}500 \times \$90 = 0.05 \times 6{,}500 \times \$90$	$= \underline{29{,}250}$ F
Total direct materials mix variance		$\underline{\$ 3{,}250}$ F

Interpretation of Level 4 Direct Materials Yield Variance   Compare columns 2 and 3 of Exhibit 7-12. Column 2 calculates costs using the budgeted input mix and the budgeted rates. Column 3 calculates the flexible-budget cost based on the budgeted cost of the total quantity of all inputs used (6,400 tonnes of tomatoes) for the actual output achieved (4,000 tonnes of ketchup) times the budgeted input mix (Latoms, 50%; Caltoms, 30%; Flotoms, 20%).

The only difference in the two columns is that column 2 uses the actual total quantity of all inputs used (6,500 tonnes), while column 3 uses the budgeted total quantity of all inputs used (6,400 tonnes). Hence, the difference in costs between the two columns is the total direct materials yield variance, due solely to differences in actual and budgeted total input quantity used. The total direct materials yield variance is the sum of the direct materials yield variances for each input:

Latoms	$(6{,}500 - 6{,}400) \times 0.50 \times \$70 = 100 \times 0.50 \times \$70 = \$3{,}500$ U
Caltoms	$(6{,}500 - 6{,}400) \times 0.30 \times \$80 = 100 \times 0.30 \times \$80 = \quad 2{,}400$ U
Flotoms	$(6{,}500 - 6{,}400) \times 0.20 \times \$90 = 100 \times 0.20 \times \$90 = \quad \underline{1{,}800}$ U
Total direct materials yield variance	$\underline{\$7{,}700}$ U

The total direct materials yield variance is unfavourable because Delpino used 6,500 tonnes of tomatoes rather than the 6,400 tonnes it should have used to produce 4,000 tonnes of ketchup. Holding the budgeted mix and budgeted rates of tomatoes constant, the budgeted cost per tonne of tomatoes in the budgeted mix is $77 per tonne. The unfavourable yield variance represents the budgeted cost of using 100 more tonnes of tomatoes: $(6{,}500 - 6{,}400) \times \$77 = \$7{,}700$ U. The direct materials variances can be summarized as shown in Exhibit 7-13.

The Level 4 direct materials variance analyses of mix and yield extends efficiency and effective analysis to substitutable inputs. For perishable food processing such as ketchup, olive oil, and imperishable processing of ethanol from corn, an inescapable economic fact is that the higher the yield, the lower the costs of finished goods. This is because the finished goods are also substitutable. All other things equal, people will find one litre of ketchup the same as another.

EXHIBIT 7-12
Total Direct Materials Mix and Yield Variances for the Delpino Corporation for June 2013

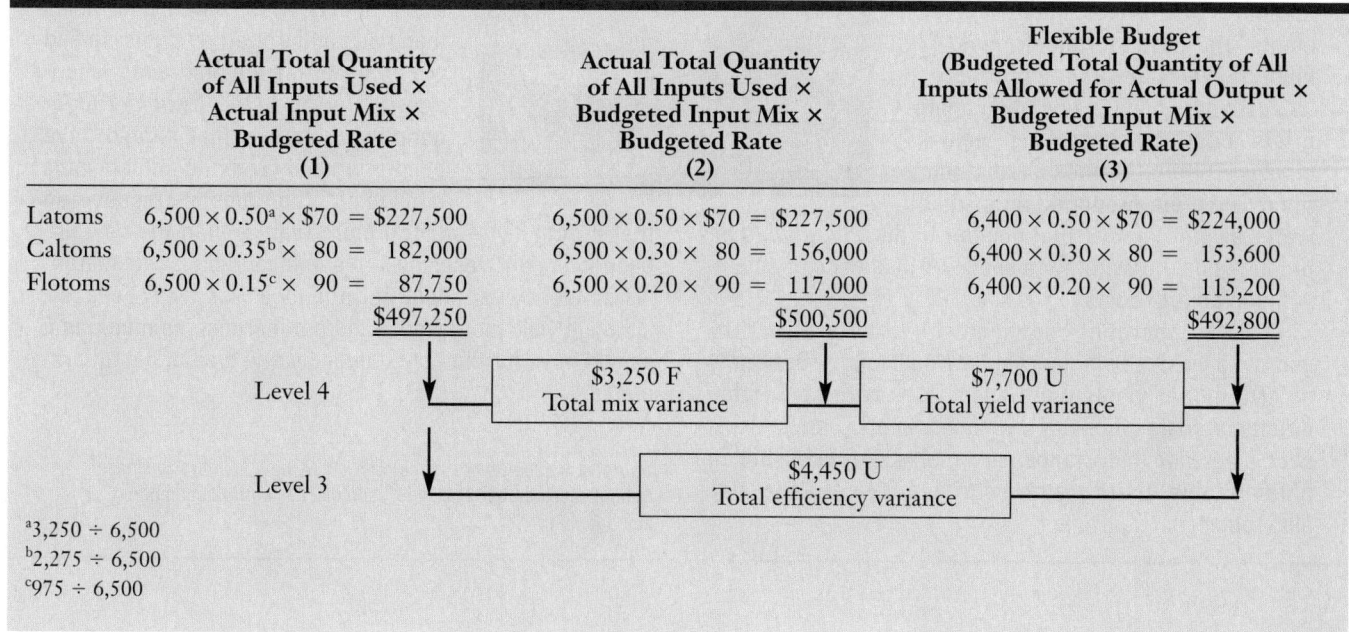

	Actual Total Quantity of All Inputs Used × Actual Input Mix × Budgeted Rate (1)	Actual Total Quantity of All Inputs Used × Budgeted Input Mix × Budgeted Rate (2)	Flexible Budget (Budgeted Total Quantity of All Inputs Allowed for Actual Output × Budgeted Input Mix × Budgeted Rate) (3)
Latoms	$6{,}500 \times 0.50^a \times \$70 = \$227{,}500$	$6{,}500 \times 0.50 \times \$70 = \$227{,}500$	$6{,}400 \times 0.50 \times \$70 = \$224{,}000$
Caltoms	$6{,}500 \times 0.35^b \times 80 = 182{,}000$	$6{,}500 \times 0.30 \times 80 = 156{,}000$	$6{,}400 \times 0.30 \times 80 = 153{,}600$
Flotoms	$6{,}500 \times 0.15^c \times 90 = \underline{87{,}750}$	$6{,}500 \times 0.20 \times 90 = \underline{117{,}000}$	$6{,}400 \times 0.20 \times 90 = \underline{115{,}200}$
	$\underline{\$497{,}250}$	$\underline{\$500{,}500}$	$\underline{\$492{,}800}$

Level 4 — $3,250 F Total mix variance — $7,700 U Total yield variance

Level 3 — $4,450 U Total efficiency variance

$^a 3{,}250 \div 6{,}500$
$^b 2{,}275 \div 6{,}500$
$^c 975 \div 6{,}500$

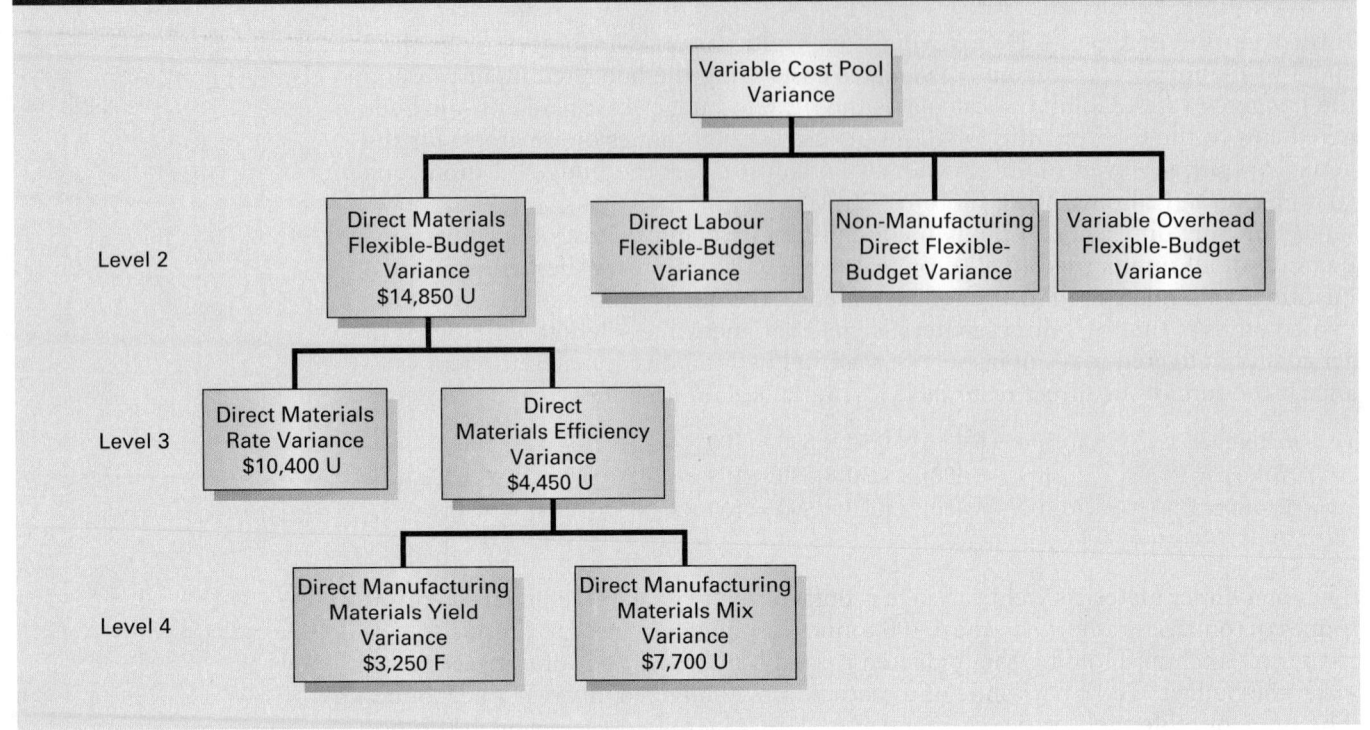

Almost Fooled: Analyzing Efficiency and Yield

Analog Devices, Inc. (ADI) produces integrated circuits and systems used in computer disc drives, medical instruments, and customer electronics. ADI must deliver high-quality products to its customers on time and at an appropriate cost. By improving yield (a measure of effectiveness)—the quantity of good die produced on a silicon wafer divided by the total number of die that *should* be produced on the wafer for a specified quantity of inputs—ADI can control costs.

ADI's operating managers believed that if they improved yield, an efficiency gain would follow. Ordinarily at ADI, higher yields were associated with favourable direct materials efficiency variances. In one period, however, a puzzling thing happened—yields increased, but an unfavourable direct materials efficiency variance was also reported.

In the relevant period, ADI had changed to producing more standardized products, which have higher yields than nonstandardized products. To find out if performance improved, managers referred to the *flexible-budget* quantity of wafers that should have been produced given the actual inputs consumed. The company discovered that it actually produced more wafers than the flexible-budget amount, resulting in the unfavourable direct materials efficiency variance. Performance was *weak* because, although yield increased, it did not increase as much as it should have for the actual quantity and type of output produced.

Sources: Analog Devices: The Half-Life System, Harvard Business School case number 9–190–061, and discussions with company management.

FLEXIBLE BUDGETING AND ACTIVITY-BASED COSTING

Activity-based costing (ABC) systems focus on individual activities that occur throughout the value-chain functions. ABC systems classify the costs of various activities into a cost hierarchy—output unit-level costs, batch-level costs, product-sustaining costs, and facility-sustaining costs. The two common direct cost categories—direct materials costs and direct manufacturing labour costs—are examples of output unit-level costs. In this section, we focus on batch-level costs to show how the basic principles and concepts of flexible budgets and variance analysis can be applied to other levels of the cost hierarchy. Batch-level costs are the costs of activities related to a group of units of products or services rather than to each individual unit of product or service.

Undertake variance analysis in activity-based costing systems.

4

RELATING BATCH COSTS TO PRODUCT OUTPUT

Consider Lyco Brass Works, which manufactures Jacutaps, a line of decorative brass faucets for home spas. Lyco produces Jacutaps in batches. For each product line, Lyco dedicates material-handling labour to bring materials to the manufacturing area, transport work in process from one work centre to the next, and take the finished product to the shipping area. Hence, material-handling labour costs are direct costs of Jacutaps. Because the materials for a batch are moved together, material-handling labour costs vary with the number of batches rather than with the number of units in a batch. Material-handling labour costs are variable direct batch-level costs.

Information regarding Jacutaps for 2013 is as follows:

	Static-Budget Amounts	Actual Amounts
1. Units of Jacutaps produced and sold	180,000	151,200
2. Batch size (units per batch)	150	140
3. Number of batches (Line 1 ÷ Line 2)	1,200	1,080
4. Material-handling labour-hours per batch	5	5.25
5. Total material-handling labour-hours (Line 3 × Line 4)	6,000	5,670
6. Cost per material-handling labour-hour	$ 14	$ 14.50
7. Total material-handling labour costs	$ 84,000	$ 82,215

To prepare the flexible budget for material-handling labour costs, Lyco starts with the actual units of output produced, 151,200 units, and proceeds as follows:

◆ *Using budgeted batch size, calculate the number of batches that should have been used to produce the actual output.* At the budgeted batch size of 150 units per batch, Lyco should have produced the 151,200 units of output in 1,008 batches (151,200 units ÷ 150 units per batch).

◆ *Using budgeted material-handling labour-hours per batch, calculate the number of material-handling labour-hours that should have been used.* At the budgeted quantity of 5 hours per batch, 1,008 batches should have required 5,040 material-handling labour-hours (1,008 batches × 5 hours per batch).

◆ *Using budgeted cost per material-handling labour-hour, calculate the flexible-budget amount for material-handling labour-hours.* The flexible-budget amount is 5,040 material-handling labour-hours × $14 budgeted cost per material-handling labour-hour = $70,560.

Note how the flexible-budget calculations for material-handling costs focus on batch-level quantities (material-handling labour-hours) rather than on output unit-level amounts (such as material-handling labour-hours per unit of output). The flexible-budget variance for material-handling costs can then be calculated as:

Flexible-budget variance = Actual costs − Flexible-budget costs
= (5,670 hours × $14.50 per hour) − (5,040 hours × $14 per hour)
= $82,215 − $70,560
= $11,655, or $11,655 U

The unfavourable variance indicates that material-handling labour costs were $11,655 higher than the flexible-budget target.

RATE AND EFFICIENCY VARIANCES

We can get some insight into the possible reasons for this $11,655 unfavourable variance by examining the rate and efficiency components of the flexible-budget variance:

$$\begin{array}{rl} \text{Rate} \atop \text{variance} & = \left(\begin{array}{l} \text{Actual rate} \\ \text{of input} \end{array} - \begin{array}{l} \text{Budgeted rate} \\ \text{of input} \end{array} \right) \times \begin{array}{l} \text{Actual quantity} \\ \text{of input} \end{array} \\ & = (\$14.50 \text{ per hour} - \$14 \text{ per hour}) \times 5,670 \text{ hours} \\ & = \qquad\quad \$0.50 \text{ per hour} \qquad\quad \times 5,670 \text{ hours} \\ & = \$2,835, \text{ or } \$2,835 \text{ U} \end{array}$$

The $14.50 actual cost per material-handling labour-hour exceeds the $14.00 budgeted cost, indicating an unfavourable rate variance for material-handling labour. This variance could be due, for example, to (1) Lyco's human resources manager negotiating less skillfully than was planned in the budget or (2) unexpected wage rate increases due to scarcity of labour.

There is also an unfavourable efficiency variance:

$$\begin{array}{rl} \text{Efficiency} \atop \text{variance} & = \left(\begin{array}{l} \text{Actual quantity} \\ \text{of input used} \end{array} - \begin{array}{l} \text{Budgeted quantity of input} \\ \text{allowed for actual output} \end{array} \right) \times \begin{array}{l} \text{Budgeted rate} \\ \text{of input} \end{array} \\ & = \qquad (5,670 \text{ hours} - 5,040 \text{ hours}) \qquad \times \$14 \text{ per hour} \\ & = \qquad\qquad\quad 630 \text{ hours} \qquad\qquad \times \$14 \text{ per hour} \\ & = \$8,820, \text{ or } \$8,820 \text{ U} \end{array}$$

The 5,670 actual material-handling labour-hours exceeded the 5,040 material-handling labour-hours that Lyco should have used for the number of units it produced, indicating an unfavourable efficiency variance. Two reasons for the unfavourable efficiency variance are:

◆ Smaller actual batch sizes of 140 units, instead of the budgeted batch sizes of 150 units, resulting in Lyco producing the 151,200 units in 1,080 batches instead of 1,008 (151,200 ÷ 150) batches.

◆ Higher actual material-handling labour-hours per batch of 5.25 hours instead of budgeted material-handling labour-hours of 5 hours.

Reasons for smaller-than-budgeted batch sizes could include:

◆ Quality problems if batch sizes exceed 140 faucets.
◆ High costs of carrying inventory.

Reasons for higher actual material-handling labour-hours per batch could include:

◆ Inefficient layout of the Jacutap production line relative to the layout proposed in the budget.
◆ Material-handling labour having to wait at work centres before picking up or delivering materials.
◆ Unmotivated, inexperienced, or underskilled employees.
◆ Standards for material-handling time that are too tight.

Identifying the reasons for the efficiency variance will help Lyco's managers develop a plan for improving material-handling labour efficiency.

FOCUS ON HIERARCHY

The greatest improvement in control will arise if managers focus the flexible-budget quantity computations at the appropriate level of the cost hierarchy. For example, because material handling is a batch-level cost, the flexible-budget quantity calculations are made at the batch level—the quantity of material-handling labour-hours that Lyco should have used based on the number of batches it should have taken to produce the actual quantity of 151,200 units. If a cost had been a product-sustaining cost—such as product design—the flexible-budget quantity computations would focus on the product-sustaining level, for example, by evaluating the actual complexity of product design relative to the budget.

MANAGERIAL USES OF VARIANCE ANALYSES

PERFORMANCE EVALUATION

Describe how managers use variance analyses. ⑤

Some managers refer to the task of proceeding through successively more detailed data as "drilling down" (or "peeling the onion"). The growing use of online data collection is increasing the number of databases that have this drill-down capability. A key use of variance analysis is in performance evaluation. Two attributes of performance are commonly measured:

◆ **Effectiveness:** The degree to which a predetermined objective or target is met.
◆ **Efficiency:** The relative amount of inputs used to achieve a given level of output.

To illustrate the difference, consider that killing a fly with a sledgehammer will be effective (if you hit the fly), but not efficient, since you will expend a lot of extra energy. Killing a fly with a fly swatter is both effective and efficient.

Managers must be careful to understand the cause(s) of a variance before using it as a performance measure. Assume that a Webb purchasing manager has just negotiated a deal resulting in a favourable rate variance for materials. The deal could have achieved a favourable variance for any or all of three reasons:

◆ The purchasing manager bargained effectively with suppliers.
◆ The purchasing manager accepted lower-quality materials at a lower rate.
◆ The purchasing manager secured a discount for buying in bulk. However, he or she bought higher quantities than necessary for the short run, which resulted in excessive inventories.

If the purchasing manager's performance is evaluated solely on materials rate variances, only the first reason will be considered acceptable, and the evaluation will be positive. The second and third reasons will be considered unacceptable and will likely cause the company to incur additional costs, such as higher inventory storage costs, higher quality inspection costs, higher costs to repair or replace defects, and higher materials scrap costs. *Managers should not automatically interpret a favourable variance as "good" news.*

FINANCIAL AND NONFINANCIAL PERFORMANCE MEASURES

Almost all organizations use a combination of financial and nonfinancial performance measures rather than relying exclusively on either type. Control is often exercised by focusing on nonfinancial measures like combining the least expensive quantities in a product mix. But overall cost leadership is not a simple matter. Managers are evaluated on financial measures of results. This introduces conflict of interest. Depending on the level of the cost hierarchy of an activity, cutting a volume of input to the benefit of one business function may increase costs throughout the entire value chain.

Performance measures should focus managers' attention on reducing the total costs incurred by the entire company. When a single performance measure (for example, a materials-mix variance) receives excessive emphasis, managers tend to make decisions that will maximize their own reported performance based on favourable materials-mix variance. A focus on cost control for functions at a high level in the hierarchy will motivate decisions to benefit the entire company.

Ironically, long-term profitability and cost control often mean more costs in the short run to achieve long-run benefit. A small increase in quality of product mix, for example, may generate a cost increase but improve the yield. More quantity of finished goods are available for sale, and consumer demand may also increase. The costs will be recovered through increased sales volume without increasing the sales price per unit. Additional cost reductions may also be realized if there are fewer returns, meaning customer service function costs will decrease.

WHEN TO INVESTIGATE VARIANCES

Exhibit 7-14 illustrates all four levels of variance analyses possible within a very simple costing system for products with substitutable inputs. This type of production process is most recognizable in industrial food processing and resource refining. It seems almost inevitable that for any specific time period there will be an unfavourable variance somewhere. When to use expensive and scarce management time to investigate and explain variances depends on the situation. Usually this feedback directs attention to the largest U variance first.

For critical items, however, a small variance may prompt follow-up. For other items, a minimum dollar variance or a specific percentage of variance from budget may prompt investigations. Of course, a 4% variance in direct materials costs of $1,000,000 may deserve more attention than a 20% variance in repair costs of $10,000. Therefore, rules such as "investigate all variances exceeding $5,000 or 25% of budgeted cost, whichever is lower" are common. Variance analysis is not a "blame game" tool that initiates a search for a scapegoat. This is an abuse of credible information intended to improve the foundation of all management decisions. The foundation is good information in and good feedback out that will motivate learning and progress.

EXHIBIT 7-14
Flexible-Budget Variable Direct Variances, Levels 0, 1, 2, 3, and 4

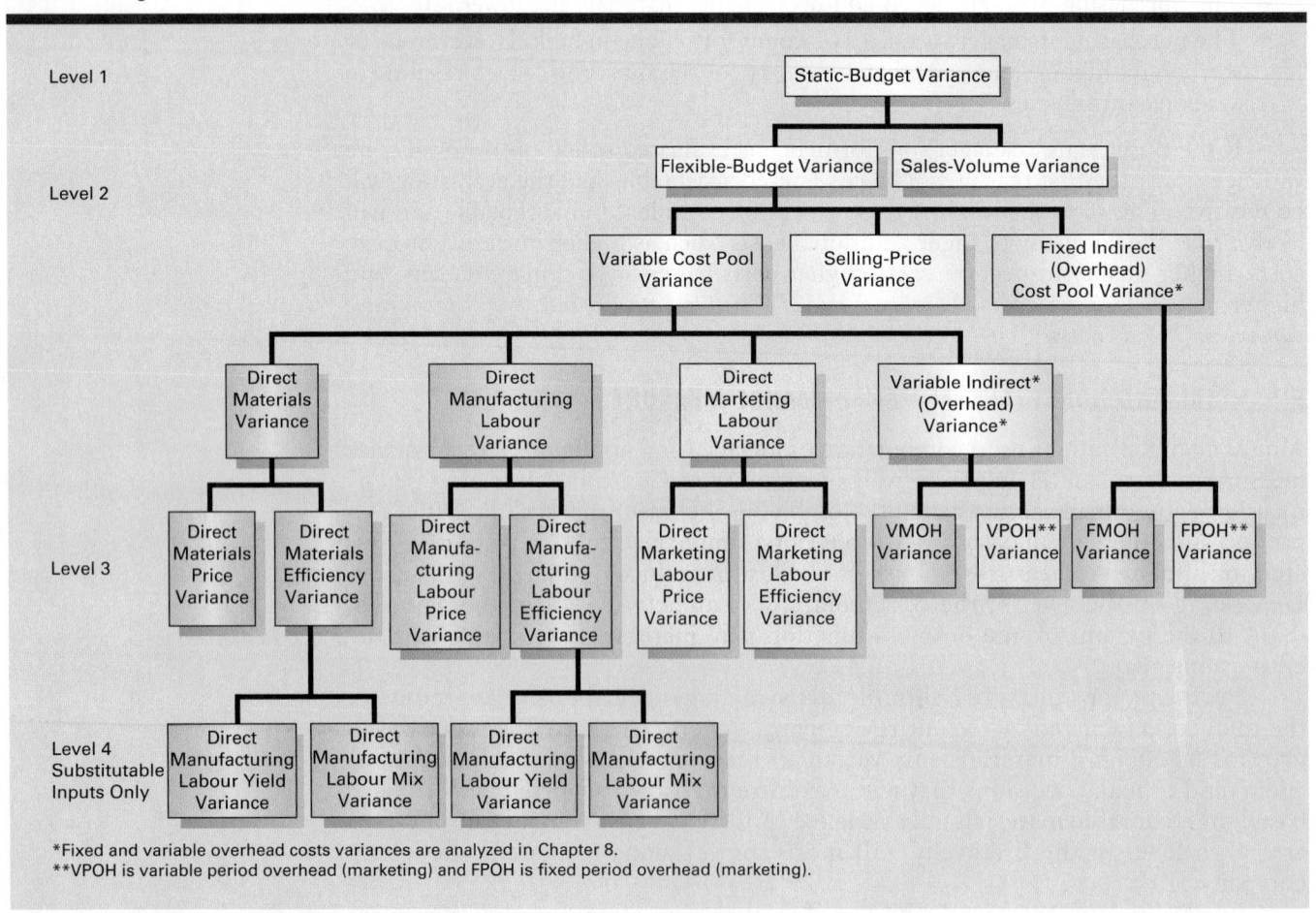

*Fixed and variable overhead costs variances are analyzed in Chapter 8.
**VPOH is variable period overhead (marketing) and FPOH is fixed period overhead (marketing).

Learn, Don't Blame

The performance-evaluation aspect of variance analysis causes anxiety for managers because they are responsible for the commitment made to achieving budgeted targets—for being effective. If targets are not met, however, the objective should be to learn how to become more effective and efficient. The benefit can emerge only if accountants report the unbiased variances and persuade managers to be realistic about performance. Learning from past mistakes and implementing corrective action plans happens quickly when the information gathered to make decisions is faithful to economic facts.

At Starbucks, for example, managers must make sure that each new store's sales meet or exceed expectations. Management accountants at the company are intimately involved in establishing budgeted performance and monitoring actual performance for each of the company's stores. The variance analyses provide managers with clear and precise explanations for variances in a thoughtful, constructive, and helpful way.

Sources: Allison Linn, "Starbucks Lays Out Aggressive Growth Plans," *Seattle Post-Intelligence*, March 30, 2004; "Schaeffer's Market Observation Features Starbucks: SBUX," *Businesswire.com*, April 1, 2004; Andy Serwer, "Starbucks to Go," *Fortune*, January 26, 2004.

Management-accounting systems have incorrectly been interpreted as a tool to communicate budgeted performance as if it were a single point of measurement. In reality, managers realize that a budgeted amount is an estimate of a band or range of possible acceptable outcomes. Statistics provide the tools to examine whether or not observed variances are within control (see the Chapter 10 Appendix). Managers expect actual outcomes to vary from predicted because they know they cannot foretell the future. Good managers know in advance of receiving any variance reports when there are control problems because that is their job. Often the variance analyses simply confirm an issue exists. Exhibit 7-14 presents a comprehensive road map of where we have been. The overhead variance analyses of the indirect manufacturing and non-manufacturing cost pools are presented in Chapter 8.

CONTINUOUS IMPROVEMENT

The most important task in variance analysis is to interpret and learn from variance analyses. At each opportunity for feedback, small improvements can be made to control variances. **Continuous improvement** is a budgeted cost that is successively reduced over succeeding time periods. Improvement opportunities can be easier to identify at the initial stages of production, but for mature internal processes this becomes more difficult. Some companies use Kaizen budgeting to target explicit amounts of reductions in budgeted costs over successive periods.

For example, the budgeted direct materials cost for each jacket that Webb Company manufactured in April 2013 is $60 per unit. The budgeted cost for variance analysis for subsequent periods could be based on a targeted 1% reduction each period:

Month	Prior Month's Amount	Reduction in Budgeted Amount	Revised Budgeted Amount
April 2013	—	—	$60.00
May 2013	$60.00	$0.600 (0.01 × $60.00)	59.40
June 2013	59.40	0.594 (0.01 × $59.40)	58.81
July 2013	58.81	0.588 (0.01 × $58.81)	58.22

The source of the 1% reduction in budgeted direct materials costs could be efficiency improvements or rate reductions. By using continuous improvement budgeted costs, an organization signals the importance of constantly seeking ways to reduce total costs. For example, managers could avoid unfavourable materials efficiency variances by continuously reducing materials waste.

IMPACT OF INVENTORIES

Our Webb Company illustration assumed the following:

◆ All units are manufactured and sold in the same accounting period. There are no work-in-process or finished goods inventories at either the beginning or the end of the accounting period.

◆ All direct materials are purchased and used in the same accounting period. There is no direct materials inventory at either the beginning or the end of the period.

Both assumptions can be relaxed without changing the key concepts introduced in this chapter. However, changes in the computation or interpretation of variances would be required when beginning or ending inventories exist. Suppose direct materials are purchased some time before their use and the beginning direct materials inventories are almost always non-zero. The direct materials purchased do not equal the direct materials used. Managers typically want to pinpoint variances at the earliest possible time to regain control over costs quickly.

For direct materials rate variances, the purchase date will almost always be the earliest possible time to isolate a variance. As a result, many organizations compute direct materials rate variances using the quantities purchased in an accounting period. The Problem for Self-Study below illustrates how to use two different times (purchase time and use time) to pinpoint direct materials variances.

PULLING IT ALL TOGETHER—PROBLEM FOR SELF-STUDY

(Try to solve this problem before examining the solution that follows.)

PROBLEM

O'Shea Company manufactures ceramic vases. It uses its standard costing system when developing its flexible-budget amounts. In April 2013, 2,000 finished units were produced. The following information is related to its two direct manufacturing cost categories of direct materials and direct manufacturing labour.

Direct materials used were 4,400 kilograms. The standard direct materials input allowed for one output unit is 2 kilograms at $15 per kilogram, and 5,000 kilograms of materials were purchased at $16.50 per kilogram, for a total of $82,500.

Actual direct manufacturing labour-hours were 3,250 at a total cost of $66,300. Standard manufacturing labour time allowed is 1.5 hours per output unit, and the standard direct manufacturing labour cost is $20 per hour.

REQUIRED

2 1. Calculate the direct materials rate and efficiency variances and the direct manufacturing labour rate and efficiency variances. The direct materials rate variance will be based on a flexible budget for actual quantities purchased, but the efficiency variance will be based on a flexible budget for actual quantities used.

2 2. Prepare journal entries for a standard-costing system that isolates variances as early as feasible.

5 3. Based on these results, list in order from most to least important the variances you would investigate. Explain briefly what you considered in your ranking.

4. Give three alternative explanations for the most important variance.

5. Give reasons why the flexible-budget variance analysis is more helpful than a static-budget variance analysis for O'Shea.

6. O'Shea likely produces vases in a variety of shapes and colours. What advantages might arise from using the strategy of ABC budgeting and variance analysis?

SOLUTION

1. Exhibit 7-15 shows how the columnar presentation of variances introduced in Exhibit 7-13 can be adjusted for the difference in timing between the purchase and use of materials. In particular, note the two sets of computations in column 2 for direct materials. The $75,000 pertains to the direct materials purchased; the $66,000 pertains to the direct materials used.

EXHIBIT 7-15
Columnar Presentation of Variance Analysis: Direct Materials and Direct Manufacturing Labour*

LEVEL 3 ANALYSIS

	Actual Costs Incurred (Actual Input × Actual Price) (1)	Actual Input Budgeted Price (2)	Flexible Budget (Budgeted Input Allowed for Actual Output Achieved × Budgeted Price) (3)
Direct materials	(5,000 kg × $16.50/kg) $82,500	(5,000 kg × $15/kg) $75,000 (4,400 kg × $15/kg) $66,000	(2,000 units × 2 kg/unit × $15/kg) $60,000
	↑___ $7,500 U* ___↑ Price variance	↑___ $6,000 U ___↑ Efficiency variance	
Direct manufacturing labour	(3,250 hrs × $20.40/hr) $66,300	(3,250 hrs × $20/hr) $65,000	(2,000 units × 1.5 hrs/unit × $20/hr) $60,000
	↑___ $1,300 U ___↑ Price variance	↑___ $5,000 U ___↑ Efficiency variance	

*F = favourable effect on operating income; U = unfavourable effect on operating income.

2.

Materials Control		
(5,000 kilograms × $15/kg)	$75,000	
Direct Materials Price Variance		
(5,000 kilograms × $1.50/kg)	$ 7,500	
Accounts Payable Control		
(5,000 kilograms × $16.50/kg)		$82,500
Work-in-Process Control		
(2,000 units × 2 kg/unit × $15/kg)	$60,000	
Direct Materials Efficiency Variance		
(400 kilograms × $15/kg)	$ 6,000	
Materials Control		
(4,400 kilograms × $15/kg)		$66,000
Work-in-Process Control		
(2,000 units × 1.5 hrs/unit × $20/hr)	$60,000	
Direct Manufacturing Labour Price Variance		
(3,250 hours × $0.40/hr)	$ 1,300	
Direct Manufacturing Labour Efficiency Variance		
(250 hours × $20/hr)	$ 5,000	
Wages Payable Control		
(3,250 hours × $20.40/hr)		$66,300

3. In order, the most important variances from most to least important are direct materials rate variance of $7,500 U; direct materials efficiency variance of $6,000 U; direct manufacturing labour efficiency variance of $5,000 U; and direct manufacturing labour rate variance of $1,300 U. No guidelines are provided; therefore, the only reason for this ranking is the level of materiality—the highest unfavourable variance first followed by the lower unfavourable variances, in order.

4. The direct materials rate variance could have several explanations. The rate variance is accompanied by an almost equally high efficiency variance, which suggests the two may be linked. An explanation could be poor scheduling of production that led to emergency orders of additional material that cost more per unit. The rate variance is also accompanied by a labour efficiency variance, which means more labour was consumed than was budgeted. Of course, the purchasing department may have simply failed to negotiate an appropriate rate or failed to order appropriate quantities on time.

   The value of the variance itself is a good signal of potential problems but provides no conclusive explanation of what caused the unfavourable variances. If the variances are beyond what O'Shea considers normal, an investigation is needed.

5. A static-budget analysis may have shown a variable cost variance without comparing the actual to budgeted quantity of output produced and sold. If the actual quantity produced and sold was higher than the pro forma amounts, then variable costs must increase relative to the pro forma amounts. This level of analysis fails to signal when actual performance is outside of an expected range.

6. ABC requires a focus on activities that occur throughout a set of value-chain functions. The activities are undertaken to obtain batches of similar outputs and different products. ABC budgeting would help O'Shea understand the interdependencies among value-chain functions, and how these contribute to favourable or unfavourable variances.

APPENDIX: BUDGETS, BENCHMARKS, AND STANDARDS

6 Distinguish among standards, budgets, benchmarks.

In our analyses we referred to the static- and flexible-budget data. Webb's budget data were the result of careful planning. The management team used its experience to examine all the amounts used to create the budget schedules. Then the team made a commitment to use quantities of inputs at established rates to achieve targeted quantities of outputs for sale at an established price. Typically budgets are set every year, but depending on the results of variance analyses, budgets may change.

Budgeted amounts are predictions based on past actual input rates and quantities. These past amounts can be used for the budgeted amounts in a flexible budget. Past data are available at a relatively low cost from the company's management information system (MIS). The limitations of using this source are (1) past data include past inefficiencies and (2) past data do not incorporate any planned changes that are expected to occur in the budget period.

BENCHMARKING

An ideal rather than average performance may be chosen as the budgeted threshold. A **benchmark** is the best possible performance achieved anywhere in any industry using a similar process. Unless, however, external and internal conditions match those in the benchmarked company, this standard cannot be achieved. Using a benchmark requires commitment to internal change. If this is absent then, inevitably, Webb would report unfavourable variances and part of the explanation would always be that ideal conditions did not prevail.

Benchmarking reports are based on the costs of other companies and may be developed for many activities and products. For example, Webb Company could estimate (possibly with the aid of consultants) the materials cost of the jackets manufactured by its competitors. The materials cost estimate of the lowest-cost competitor could be used as the budgeted amounts in its variance computations. An unfavourable materials-efficiency variance would signal that Webb has a higher materials cost than "best cost practice" in its industry. The magnitude of the cost difference would be of great interest to Webb. It could prompt Webb to do an extensive search into how to bring its own cost structure in line with that of the lowest in the industry.

STANDARDS

A **standard** is a carefully predetermined amount based on investigation of external performance achieved by similar processes. A standard is usually expressed on a per-unit basis and communicates an average amount indicating what *should* be achieved by any similar process each time period that performance measures are taken. Once a standard is set it remains unchanged over time. Standards differ from budget amounts because budget amounts change from one time period to the next. Standards differ from benchmarks because they are average, not ideal, amounts.

Assume Webb uses industry time-and-motion and engineering studies to determine its standard amounts. Each task involved in making a jacket, for example, is assigned a standard amount of time based on work by an experienced operator using equipment operating in an efficient manner.

Advantages of using average external standards are that (1) they can exclude past inefficiencies that Webb can control and (2) they can take into account expected changes in the budget period. An example of (1) for direct materials is a supplier making dramatic improvements in its ability to consistently meet Webb's demanding quality requirements for the cloth used to make jackets. An example of (2) is the acquisition of new cutting machines that operate at a faster speed yet enable work to be done with lower reject rates. For internal efficiencies in the conversion process, an example of (1) is a new process designed to eliminate unnecessary steps in production and reduce the labour hours per unit. An example of (2) is the purchase of newer equipment that would replace some labourers during the budgeted time period.

If the industry or the company itself is innovative and changes are rapid, then Webb would have to review its standards more often than if the industry and the company were very stable. The standards could not be ideal because the best internal and external conditions would change too frequently. If change is very rapid, it might be better for Webb to avoid standards and use internal data and assumptions to calculate its budgeted amounts summarized in Exhibit 7-1.

Webb has developed standard inputs and standard costs per unit for each of its variable cost items. A **standard input** is a predetermined average quantity of inputs (such as kilograms of materials or hours of labour time) required for one unit of output. A **standard cost** method is based on either a predetermined average cost per input or a predetermined average total input cost per unit of output. Webb's budgeted cost for each variable cost item is computed using the following formula:

Standard inputs allowed for one output unit × Standard cost per input unit

And the variable cost items are

- ◆ **Direct materials:** a standard of 2 square metres (m²) of cloth input allowed per output unit (jacket) manufactured, at $30 standard cost per square metre:

  Standard cost = 2 × $30 = $60 per output unit manufactured

- ◆ **Direct manufacturing labour:** 0.80 manufacturing labour-hours of input allowed per output unit manufactured, at $20 standard cost per hour:

  Standard cost = 0.80 × $20 = $16 per output unit manufactured

- ◆ **Direct marketing labour:** 0.25 marketing labour-hours of input allowed per output unit sold, at $24 standard cost per hour:

  Standard cost = 0.25 × $24 = $6 per output unit sold

◆ **Variable manufacturing overhead:** Allocated based on 0.40 machine-hours per output unit manufactured at $30 standard cost per machine-hour:

Standard cost = 0.40 × $30 = $12 per output unit manufactured

◆ **Variable marketing overhead:** Allocated based on 0.125 direct marketing labour-hours per output unit sold at $40 standard rate per hour:

Standard cost = 0.125 × $40 = $5 per output unit sold

These standard cost calculations reconcile to Exhibit 7-8.

The breakdown of the flexible-budget variance into its rate and efficiency components is important when evaluating individual managers. At Webb, the production manager is responsible for the efficiency variance, while the purchasing manager is responsible for the rate variance. Judgments about efficiency (the quantity of inputs used to produce a given level of output) are not affected by whether actual input rates differ from budgeted input rates. A word of caution, however, is that causes of rate and efficiency variances can be interrelated. For this reason, it is unwise to interpret these variances in isolation from each other.

STANDARD COSTING AND INFORMATION TECHNOLOGY

Modern information technology greatly facilitates the use of standard costing systems for product costing and control. The company's MIS can readily store barcode scanner or RFID (radio frequency identification) information to record the receipt of materials, immediately costing each material using its stored standard rate. The receipt of materials is matched with the purchase order to record Accounts Payable and to isolate the direct materials rate variance.

As output is completed, the standard quantity of direct materials that should have been used is computed and compared with the actual quantity requested for direct materials that was input into the MIS by an operator on the production floor. This difference is multiplied by the standard direct material rate to obtain the direct materials efficiency variance. Labour variances are calculated as employees log into production floor terminals and punch in their employee numbers, start and end times, and the quantity of the product they helped produce. Managers use this instantaneous feedback on variances to initiate immediate corrective action, as needed.

MULTIPLE CAUSES OF VARIANCES

Often the causes of variances are interrelated. For example, an unfavourable materials-efficiency variance can be related to a favourable materials rate variance because a purchasing officer purchased lower-cost, lower-quality materials. It is always best to consider possible interdependencies because variances can arise from different parts of the value chain in one organization. Consider an unfavourable materials-efficiency variance in the production area of Webb. Possible causes of this variance across the value chain of the organization include:

◆ Poor design of products or processes.
◆ Poor work quality in the manufacturing area.
◆ Inadequate training of the labour force.
◆ Inappropriate assignment of labour or machines to specific jobs.
◆ Congestion due to scheduling a large number of rush orders required by Webb marketing representatives.
◆ Webb's suppliers do not manufacture cloth materials of uniformly high quality.

An even broader perspective is to consider actions taken in the *supply chain* of an organization. A **supply chain** is an integrated system of suppliers, subcontractors, manufacturers, distributors, and retailers collaborating with the purpose of adding value to the output for the customer.[3] The supply chain for Webb Company (the manufacturer) includes

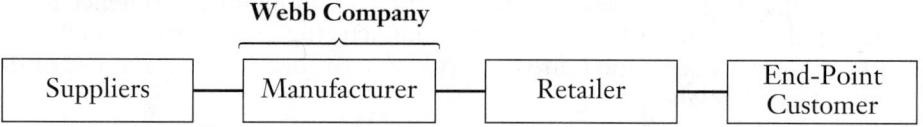

Webb Company

| Suppliers | — | Manufacturer | — | Retailer | — | End-Point Customer |

For example, actions taken by Webb's suppliers could cause unfavourable material-efficiency variances at Webb. The causes of variance covered in this text are far from exhaustive. However, they are broad enough in scope to indicate that the cause of a variance in one part of the value chain (production in our example) can be due to actions taken in other parts of the value chain (for example, product design or marketing). Note how improvements in early stages of the supply chain or value chain can sizably reduce the magnitudes of variances in subsequent stages.

CONTROL FEATURE OF STANDARD COSTS

We will now illustrate journal entries when standard costs are used. For illustrative purposes, we will focus on direct materials and direct manufacturing labour and continue with the data from the Webb Company illustration with one exception. Assume that during April 2013 Webb purchases 25,000 m² of materials. The actual quantity used is 22,200 m² and the standard quantity allowed for the actual output achieved is 20,000 m². The actual purchase cost was $31 per m², while the standard rate was $30 m². In fact, *contrary* to the budget assumption, Webb had a DM ending inventory of 2,800 m².

If Webb's managers were well-informed when they generated the budget, the performance in April generated unnecessary expense in two ways. First, actual cost exceeded budget, although we do not know why. Second, the quantity of DM purchased was 25% more than expected (25,000 m² − 20,000 m² ÷ 20,000 m²) and 11% more was used than expected (22,200 m² − 20,000 m² ÷ 20,000 m²). Note that in each of the following entries, unfavourable cost variances are always debits because they reduce operating income. Favourable cost variances are always credits because they increase operating income.

◆ **Entry 1(a).** Isolate the direct materials rate variance at the time of purchase by debiting Materials Control at standard rates. This is the earliest date possible to isolate this variance.

1. a.	Materials Control		
	(25,000 m² × $30/m²)	$750,000	
	Direct Materials Price Variance		
	(25,000 m² × $1/m²)	25,000	
	Accounts Payable Control		775,000

To record direct materials purchased.

◆ **Entry 1(b).** Isolate the direct materials efficiency variance at the time of usage by debiting Work-in-Process Control at standard input quantities allowed for actual output units achieved at standard input rates. This approach is consistent with Chapter 4 where, under the actual and normal cost methods, the direct costs are calculated using actual unit costs.

1. b.	Work-in-Process Control		
	(20,000 m² × $30/m²)	$600,000	
	Direct Materials Efficiency Variance		
	(2,200 m² × $30/m²)	66,000	
	Materials Control		
	(22,200 m² × $30/m²)		666,000

To record direct materials used.

[3]J.W.K. Chan and N.D. Burn, "Benchmarking Manufacturing Planning and Control (MPC) Systems: An Empirical Study of Hong Kong Supply Chains," *Benchmarking: An International Journal*, 9.3 (2002): 256–77.

♦ **Entry 2.** Isolate the direct manufacturing labour rate and efficiency variances at the time this labour is used by debiting Work-in-Process Control at standard quantities allowed for actual output units achieved at standard input rates. Note that Wages Payable Control measures the payroll liability and hence is always at actual wage rates. Because direct manufacturing labour can never be inventoried, there is only one journal entry for both the purchase and use of direct manufacturing labour.

2. Work-in-Process Control
    (8,000 hours × $20/hr) $160,000

    Direct Manufacturing Labour Price Variance
    (9,000 hours × $2/hr)   18,000

    Direct Manufacturing Labour Efficiency Variance
    (1,000 hours × $20/hr)   20,000

            Wages Payable Control
            (9,000 hours × $22/hr)   198,000

To record liability for direct manufacturing labour costs.

A major advantage of this standard costing system is its emphasis on the control feature of standard costs. All variances are isolated at the earliest possible time, when managers can make informed decisions based on those variances.

END-OF-PERIOD ADJUSTMENTS

Chapter 4 discussed approaches to recognizing the underallocated or overallocated manufacturing overhead at the end of a period:

♦ The adjusted allocation rate approach, which adjusts every job cost record for the difference between the allocated and actual indirect cost amounts.

♦ The proration approach, which makes adjustments to one or more of the following end-of-period account balances: materials, work-in-process, finished goods, and cost of goods sold.

Rate and efficiency variances can also be disposed of using these same two approaches.

BENCHMARKING AND VARIANCE ANALYSIS

If a benchmark is the best possible performance, then theoretically a favourable variance will be impossible. Competitive benchmarking, as it is now known, is only one form of strategic management accounting.

Benchmarking is also a useful way to set internal performance standards, especially for large multinational companies. Companies also benchmark key competencies, quality, product or service attributes, customer profitability, intellectual capital, and environmental sustainability.[4] Benchmarking involves continuous change within a company in an effort to match or exceed the best performance in some domain. Changes in the outputs offered, design processes, speed of innovation, target markets, and customers served are often needed to achieve or exceed a benchmark. Management's choice to benchmark can either support an existing corporate mission and strategy, or signal a change. The answer to whether or not benchmarking is the best remedy depends on careful reconsideration of existing strategic choices.

The strategy of adopting excellence as a goal implies widespread change in many organizations. Simply establishing what a best practice or performance threshold *is* means little without understanding if and how an organization can change to achieve it. The broader the scope of a benchmarking target, the more dispersed the relevant data will be. For example, benchmarking a specific manufacturing process

---

[4]W.P. Wong and K.Y. Wong, "A Review on Benchmarking of Supply Chain Performance Measures," *Benchmarking: An International Journal*, 15.1 (2008): 25–51.

for one product is of narrower scope than benchmarking the most ecologically friendly packaging process for all products. The first is limited to applying change to a specific value-chain function within an organization. The second is almost unbounded in terms of the factors that must be considered to define and achieve the best packaging process.

The benchmarking team may discover that the most important data are only available from competitors. The problem is that sharing some competitive information is illegal if it leads to price fixing or discourages competition in a market. If, legally, the data cannot be shared, then the company must analyze any available information as best it can. When information can be shared—for example, in not-for-profit industries—organizations may collaborate on data analysis to achieve a better performance for all. In Canada, for example, hospitals gather U.S. data on performance benchmarks, then collaborate amongst themselves to obtain improvements.

NOT-FOR-PROFIT BENCHMARKING

The Canadian government has benchmarked its own performance in terms of trust, change, corporate development strategy, tasks, progress, and quality. The following example refers to a provincial government ministry of health initiative. The initiative was designed to allocate the total amount of tax revenue available to hospitals for health care in a different way.

HayGroup is a global human resources consulting organization. HayGroup, among other things, collects and analyzes cost information submitted by hospitals to provincial and federal governments to comply with financial and nonfinancial reporting regulations. From this and other data HayGroup collects privately, the target hospital can prepare benchmark reports. These reports show how costs to treat case-mix groups (CMG) in a target hospital differ from those of other comparable hospitals. CMG is an imaginary cost object that refers to a set of related medical diagnoses—for example, stroke, respiratory disorders, etc.

Standard lengths of stay per CMG have been calculated. From these, standard costs have been estimated per length of stay for each CMG. A standard cost, however, is not a benchmark. A benchmark is the lowest cost per length of stay achieved by any hospital for treatment of a particular CMG. If a hospital's actual costs per CMG are higher than a standard cost for comparable hospitals, it will certainly be higher than the benchmark cost per CMG in that same group of hospitals.

Exhibit 7-16 illustrates a typical report for a client hospital. Panel A reports that the target hospital's cost per CMG is 10% above the average for comparable hospitals. Note that the benchmark hospital is Hospital E and the target hospital's costs are 59% higher than this benchmark. Panel B reports costs for three specific CMGs. Focus for now on the costs per CMG for stroke. The problem for the target hospital is that the government that funds treatment of patients in this CMG will only pay the average amount. If the target hospital cannot reduce its costs, it will show an operating deficit.

The government has the power to replace managers of the hospital with others appointed by the government. It may be true that higher CMG costs can be justified because those admitted are more seriously ill than at other hospitals, or the treatment provided is superior, but this is rare. Moreover, the costs per CMG are adjusted for severity levels and hospitals must report these severity levels in the normal course of complying with government reporting requirements. Cost reports like Exhibit 7-16 provide an external benchmark that forces the administrator to ask *why* cost levels differ between hospitals and *how* best practices can be transferred from the more efficient to the less efficient hospitals.

Evaluating the overall performance of a hospital or hospital personnel requires analyzing other factors in addition to costs. These factors include the perceived quality of service to patients; the success rate of operations (for example, how many patients with strokes survive?); and the morale of the doctors, nurses, and other staff. In many

EXHIBIT 7-16
Cost Benchmark Reports for a Client Hospital

PANEL A: COST COMPARISONS AT HOSPITAL LEVEL

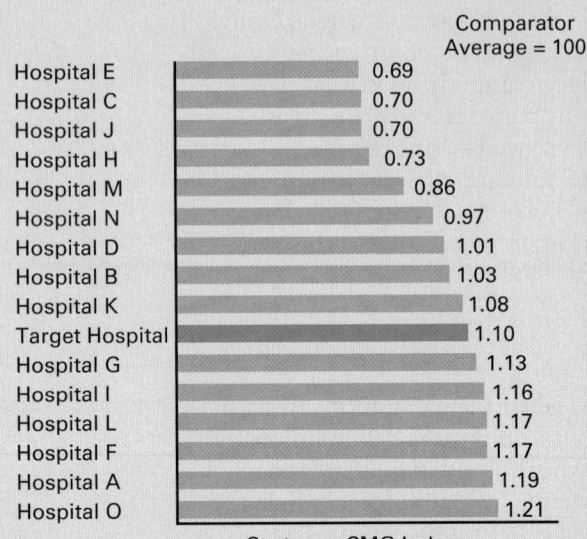

	Comparator Average = 100
Hospital E	0.69
Hospital C	0.70
Hospital J	0.70
Hospital H	0.73
Hospital M	0.86
Hospital N	0.97
Hospital D	1.01
Hospital B	1.03
Hospital K	1.08
Target Hospital	1.10
Hospital G	1.13
Hospital I	1.16
Hospital L	1.17
Hospital F	1.17
Hospital A	1.19
Hospital O	1.21

Costs per CMG Index

HOW TO READ THIS CHART:

This chart shows the target hospital's relative-case costs performance versus that of comparable hospitals. The target hospital is benchmarked with the average-case costs of its peers at the CMG level for funding purposes.

EXAMPLE:

On an overall costs per case basis, after adjusting for case mix, the target hospital's cost is 10% higher than the comparable group average. There are nine hospitals that have lower overall case costs than the target hospital.

PANEL B: COST COMPARISONS AT DIAGNOSTIC GROUP LEVEL

Case-Mix Group	Target Hospital	Group Average	25th Percentile	Average of Lowest Cost Quartile (0–25th)
Stroke	$33,700	$31,300	$21,900	$20,500
Respiratory disorders	66,800	53,700	44,400	38,400
Simple pneumonia	37,100	29,500	23,300	22,000

Source: Market Insights (San Francisco, California).

cases, however, cost factors have been given too little weighting in the past, in part because of the lack of reliable information on cost relationships in this sector of the economy.

While those managing hospitals are responsible for prudent fiscal management, their overriding concern is for the safety of their patients. That is why the managers of hospitals must exercise caution when they change their treatment processes to become more cost-efficient. Safe treatment of patients is made more complex because many patients are not admitted until they are very close to death.

Simply changing one or two activities may reduce the costs of activities but not the treatment processes as a whole. Costs saved by changing one set of activities can easily drive up the costs of a second interlinked and more expensive set of activities. The result may be higher rather than lower overall costs per CMG. It is also the case that hospitals are funded to provide effective and safe medical treatment, not spend the money paying for sophisticated costing systems. Despite these potential shortcomings, benchmarking does give managers the opportunity to investigate different, equally safe treatment processes that also reduce costs.

The following question-and-answer format summarizes the chapter's learning outcomes. Each point presents a key question, and the guidelines are the answer to that question.

LEARNING OUTCOMES	GUIDELINES
1. How do flexible budgets differ from static budgets, and why should companies use flexible budgets?	A static budget is based on the level of output planned at the start of the budget period. A flexible budget is adjusted (flexed) to recognize the actual output level of the budget period. Flexible budgets help managers gain more insight into the causes of variances.
2. How can you develop a flexible budget and compute the flexible-budget variance and the efficiency variance?	The various supporting documents for the master budget give revenue and cost driver quantities, unit rates and costs, and cost allocation rates for all inventoriable and period variable costs. Variable costs increase or decrease with the actual quantities produced and sold. Rate variance reveals differences among actual and budgeted input rates. Efficiency variance reveals differences among actual and the budgeted quantities of input for the actual output.
3. What is a substitutable product and how do input mix and yield variances improve control?	Continuous processes such as ketchup manufacturing use different varieties of tomatoes that are almost identical. Varieties are substitutable one for the other. The mix of varieties is specified. A significant departure from the mix affects both cost and yield. Yield variance is the difference between actual quantity of finished goods obtained and predicted quantity that should have been obtained.
4. How can variance analysis be used with an activity-based costing system?	Variance analysis can be applied to activity costs (such as setup costs) to gain insight into why actual activity costs differ from activity costs in the static budget or in the flexible budget. Interpreting cost variances for different activities requires understanding whether the costs are output unit-level, batch-level, product-sustaining, or facility-sustaining costs.
5. What does variance analysis contribute to the critical function of management control?	Variance analysis is feedback that highlights exceptional performance. Unfavourable variances indicate consumption of resources in excess of those available. The processes exceed a range of outcomes that would indicate they are within control. Variance analyses at a high level of fineness permit managers to identify causes of variance and control them. The feedback is essential to improve decisions.
6. What is benchmarking and why is it useful?	Benchmarking is a strategy to calculate standard costs based on the best performance of competitors. This strategy implies the company will undertake the continuous process of comparing its level of performance in producing products and services and executing activities against the best levels of performance. Benchmarking measures how well a company and its managers are doing relative to others.

This chapter and the Glossary at the end of the book contain definitions of the following important terms:

benchmark (p. 272)
benchmarking reports (p. 272)
continuous improvement (p. 269)
direct materials mix variance (p. 262)
direct materials yield variance (p. 262)
effectiveness (p. 267)
efficiency (p. 267)
efficiency variance (p. 253)
favourable (F) variance (p. 246)
fineness (p. 247)
flexible budget (p. 246)

flexible-budget variance (p. 251)
input mix (p. 259)
input price variance (p. 253)
input-efficiency variance (p. 253)
management by exception (p. 246)
mix variance (p. 260)
rate variance (p. 253)
sales-volume variance (p. 251)
standard (p. 273)
standard cost (p. 273)
standard input (p. 273)

static budget (p. 246)
substitutable inputs (p. 259)
supply chain (p. 274)
unfavourable (U) variance (p. 246)
usage variance (p. 253)
variance (p. 246)
variance analysis (p. 246)
yield (p. 260)
yield variance (p. 260)

SHORT-ANSWER QUESTIONS

7-1 How does static-budget variance analysis mislead those assessing actual performance against pro forma performance indicators?

7-2 What is the relationship between *management by exception* and *variance analysis*?

7-3 Distinguish between a *favourable variance* and an *unfavourable variance*.

7-4 What is the key difference between a *static budget* and a *flexible budget*?

7-5 Describe the steps in developing a flexible budget.

7-6 List four reasons for using standard costs.

7-7 List three causes of a favourable materials price variance.

7-8 Describe why direct materials price variance and direct materials efficiency variance may be computed with reference to different points in time.

7-9 Describe three reasons for an unfavourable direct manufacturing labour efficiency variance.

7-10 Distinguish between processes where the inputs are nonsubstitutable and where they are substitutable.

7-11 Explain how the direct materials mix and direct materials yield variances provide additional information about the direct materials efficiency variance.

7-12 How does variance analysis help in continuous improvement?

7-13 Why might an analyst examining variances in the production area look beyond that business function for explanations of those variances?

7-14 Comment on the following statement made by a plant supervisor: "Meetings with my plant accountant are frustrating. All he wants to do is pin the blame for the many variances he reports."

EXERCISES

7-15 Terminology. A number of terms are listed below:

direct materials mix variance	fineness	management by exception
favourable (F) variance	input mix	input price variance
flexible-budget variance	sales-volume variance	efficiency variance
rate variance	unfavourable (U) variance	flexible budget
substitutable inputs	yield variance	mix variance
yield	variance analysis	static budget
direct materials yield variance	static budget variance	variance

REQUIRED

Select the terms from the above list to complete the following sentences.

The question is whether or not the actual results met expectations, exceeded expectations or failed to meet expectations and a _____ _____ will respond to this question. A _____ is the result of subtracting the budgeted or predicted outcome from the actual outcome. A _____ (_) _____ means the effect of the variance is to increase operating income. An _____ (_)_____ means the effect of the variance is to decrease operating income. A _____ _____ _____ simply fails to reflect the routine effect of changes in quantity produced and sold on the revenue and the variable costs. A _____ _____ does reflect the routine changes to be expected when the quantity produced and sold fluctuates from what was predicted. The _____ _____ permits more _____ in the report of non-routine variances and _____ __ _____. The _____ _____ _____ plus the _____ _____ _____ equals the _____ _____ _____.

When quantities of direct materials purchased and used differs from budget the variance can be the result of either a ____ _____ (_____ _____ _____) arising in an unexpected difference in the cost/unit or an *efficiency variance* arising from an unexpected difference in the quantity of the input used, or a combination of both. When a direct materials _____ ___ has _____ _____ both the _____ _____ ____ _____ and the _____ _____ _____ _____ become important. These elements of a level 4 analysis permit the managers to assess how changes from what was expected affected the _____.

7-16 Flexible budget. Brabham Enterprises manufactures tires for the Formula I motor racing circuit. For August 2013, it budgeted to manufacture and sell 3,000 tires at a variable cost of $74 per tire and total fixed costs of $54,000. The budgeted selling price was $110 per tire. Actual results in August 2013 were 2,800 tires manufactured and sold at a selling price of $112 per tire. The actual total variable costs were $229,600, and the actual total fixed costs were $50,000.

1. Total sales-volume variance, $7,200 U

REQUIRED
1. Prepare a performance report (akin to Exhibit 7-6, p. 252) that uses a flexible budget and a static budget.
2. Comment on the results in requirement 1.

7-17 Flexible budget. Connor Company's budgeted prices for direct materials, direct manufacturing labour, and direct marketing (distribution) labour per attaché case are $40, $8, and $12, respectively. The president is pleased with the following performance report:

Flexible-budget variance, $24,000 U

	Actual Costs	Static Budget	Variance
Direct materials	$364,000	$400,000	$36,000 F
Direct manufacturing labour	78,000	80,000	2,000 F
Direct marketing (distribution) labour	110,000	120,000	10,000 F

Actual output was 8,800 attaché cases. Assume all three direct cost items above are variable costs.

REQUIRED
Is the president's pleasure justified? Prepare a revised performance report that uses a flexible budget and a static budget.

7-18 Materials and manufacturing-labour variances. Consider the following data collected for Great Homes Inc.:

Direct manufacturing labour efficiency variance, $6,000 U

	Direct Materials	Direct Manufacturing Labour
Costs incurred: Actual inputs × actual prices	$200,000	$90,000
Actual inputs × standard prices	214,000	86,000
Standard inputs allowed for actual outputs × standard prices	225,000	80,000

REQUIRED
Compute the price, efficiency, and flexible-budget variances for direct materials and direct manufacturing labour.

7-19 Price and efficiency variances. Peterson Foods manufactures pumpkin scones. For January 2013, it budgeted to purchase and use 16,000 kilograms of pumpkin at $1.11 per kilogram; budgeted output was 60,000 scones. Actual purchases and use for January 2013 was 17,000 kilograms at 0.99 per kilogram; actual output was 60,800 scones.

2. Price variance, $2,040 F

REQUIRED
1. Calculate the flexible-budget variance.
2. Calculate the price and efficiency variances
3. Comment on the results in requirements 1 and 2.

7-20 Flexible-budget and sales-volume variances. Marron, Inc. produces the basic fillings used in many popular frozen desserts and treats—vanilla and chocolate ice creams, puddings, meringues, and fudge. Marron uses standard costing and carries over no inventory from one month to the next. The ice-cream product group's results for June 2013 were:

2. Flexible-budget variance, $105,000 U

	File Edit View Insert Format Tools Data Window Help		
	A	B	C
1	Performance Report, June 2013		
2		Actual Results	Static Budget
3	Units (pounds)	525,000	500,000
4	Revenue	$3,360,000	$3,250,000
5	Variable manufacturing costs	1,890,000	1,750,000
6	Contribution margin	$1,470,000	$1,500,000

Ted Levine, the business manager for ice-cream products, is pleased that more pounds of ice cream were sold than budgeted and that revenues were up. Unfortunately, variable manufacturing costs went up too. The bottom line is that contribution margin declined by $30,000, which is less than 1% of the budgeted revenues of $3,250,000. Overall, Levine feels that the business is running fine.

REQUIRED

1. Calculate the static-budget variance in units, revenues, variable manufacturing costs, and contribution margin. What percentage is each static-budget variance relative to its static-budget amount?
2. Break down each static-budget variance into a flexible-budget variance and a sales-volume variance.
3. Calculate the selling-price variance.
4. Assume the role of management accountant at Marron. How would you present the results to Ted Levine? Should he be more concerned? If so, why?

1. Total flexible-budget variance, $8,672 F

7-21 Comprehensive variance analysis. Sol Electronics, a fast-growing electronic device producer, uses a standard costing system, with standards set at the beginning of each year.

In the second quarter of 2013, Sol faced two challenges: it had to negotiate and sign a new short-term labour agreement with its workers' union, and it also had to pay a higher rate to its suppliers for direct materials. The new labour contract raised the cost of direct manufacturing labour relative to the company's 2013 standards. Similarly, the new rate for direct materials exceeded the company's 2013 standards. However, the materials were of better quality than expected, so Sol's management was confident that there would be less waste and less rework in the manufacturing process. They also speculated that the per-unit direct manufacturing labour cost might decline as a result of the materials' improved quality.

At the end of the second quarter, Sol's CFO, Terence Shaw, reviewed the following results:

Variable Costs	Standard		Variable Costs per Unit First-Quarter 2013 Actual Results		Second-Quarter 2013 Actual Results	
Direct materials	2.2 kg at $5.70/kg	$12.54	2.3 kg at $5.80/kg	$13.34	2.0 kg at $6.00/kg	$12.00
Direct manufacturing labour	0.5 hrs at $12/hr	$ 6.00	0.52 hrs at $12/hr	$ 6.24	0.45 hrs at $14/hr	$ 6.30
Other variable costs		$10.00		$10.00		$ 9.85
		$28.54		$29.58		$28.15

	Static Budget for Each Quarter Based on 2013	First-Quarter 2013 Results	Second-Quarter 2013 Results
Units	4,000	4,400	4,800
Selling price per unit	$ 70	$ 72	$ 71.50
Sales	$280,000	$316,800	$343,200
Variable costs:			
Direct materials	50,160	58,696	57,600
Direct manufacturing labour	24,000	27,456	30,240
Other variable costs	40,000	44,000	47,280
Total variable costs	114,160	130,152	135,120
Contribution margin	165,840	186,648	208,080
Fixed costs	68,000	66,000	68,400
Operating income	$ 97,840	$120,648	$139,680

Shaw was relieved to see that the anticipated savings in material waste and rework seemed to have materialized. But, he was concerned that the union would press hard for higher wages, given that actual unit costs came in below standard unit costs and operating income continued to climb.

1. Prepare a detailed variance analysis of the second-quarter results relative to the static budget. Show how much of the improvement in operating income arose due to changes in sales volume and how much arose for other reasons. Calculate variances that isolate the effects of price and usage changes in direct materials and direct manufacturing labour.
2. Use the results of requirement 1 to prepare a rebuttal to the union's anticipated demands in light of the second-quarter results.
3. Terence Shaw thinks that the company can negotiate better if it changes the standards. Without performing any calculations, discuss the pros and cons of immediately changing the standards.

7-22 **Flexible-budget preparation and analysis.** Bank Management Printers Inc. produces luxury chequebooks with three cheques and stubs per page. Each chequebook is designed for an individual customer and is ordered through the customer's bank. The company's operating budget for September 2013 included these data:

Number of chequebooks	15,000
Selling price per book	$ 20
Variable costs per book	$ 8
Total fixed costs for the month	$145,000

The actual results for September 2013 were

Number of chequebooks produced and sold	12,000
Average selling price per book	$ 21
Variable costs per book	$ 7
Total fixed costs for the month	$150,000

The executive vice-president of the company observed that the operating income for September was much less than anticipated, despite a higher-than-budgeted selling price and a lower-than-budgeted variable cost per unit. You have been asked to provide explanations for the disappointing September results.

Bank Management develops its flexible-budget-based budgeted revenue per output unit and variable costs per output unit without a detailed analysis of budgeted inputs.

REQUIRED
1. Prepare a Level 1 analysis of the September performance.
2. Prepare a Level 2 analysis of the September performance.
3. Why might Bank Management find the Level 2 analysis more informative than the Level 1 analysis? Explain your answer.

7-23 **Flexible budget, working backward.** The Clarkson Company produces engine parts for car manufacturers. A new accountant intern at Clarkson has accidentally deleted the calculations on the company's variance analysis calculations for the year ended December 31, 2013. The following table is what remains of the data.

File	Edit	View	Insert	Format	Tools	Data	Window	Help		
	A		B	C		D		E		F
1				Performance Report, Year Ended December 31, 2013						
2										
3			Actual Results	Flexible-Budget Variances	Flexible Budget		Sales-Volume Variances		Static Budget	
4	Units sold		130,000						120,000	
5	Revenue (sales)		$715,000						$420,000	
6	Variable costs		515,000						240,000	
7	Contribution margin		200,000						180,000	
8	Fixed costs		140,000						120,000	
9	Operating income		$ 60,000						$ 60,000	

1. Calculate all the required variances. (If your work is accurate, you will find that the total static-budget variance is $0.)
2. What are the actual and budgeted selling prices? What are the actual and budgeted variable costs per unit?
3. Review the variances you have calculated and discuss possible causes and potential problems. What is the important lesson learned here?

7-24 Material cost variances, use of variances for performance evaluation. Katharine Stanley is the owner of Better Bikes, a company that produces high-quality cross-country bicycles. Better Bikes participates in a supply chain that consists of suppliers, manufacturers, distributors, and elite bicycle shops. For several years Better Bikes has purchased titanium from suppliers in the supply chain. Better Bikes uses titanium for the bicycle frames because it is stronger and lighter than other metals and therefore increases the quality of the bicycle. Earlier this year, Better Bikes hired Michael Scott, a recent graduate from Key University, as purchasing manager. Michael believed that he could reduce costs if he purchased titanium from an online marketplace at a lower price.

Better Bikes established the following standards based upon their experience with their previous suppliers. The standards are

Cost of titanium	$20 per kg
Titanium used per bicycle	8 kg

Actual results for the first month using the online supplier of titanium are:

Bicycles produced	500
Titanium purchased	6,000 kg for $108,000
Titanium used in production	5,000 kg

REQUIRED

1. Compute the direct materials price and efficiency variances.
2. What factors can explain the variances identified in requirement 1? Could any other variances be affected?
3. Was switching suppliers a good idea for Better Bikes? Explain why or why not.
4. Should Michael Scott's performance evaluation be based solely on price variances? Should the production manager's evaluation be based solely on efficiency variances? Why it is important for Katharine Stanley to understand the causes of a variance before she evaluates performance?
5. Other than performance evaluation, what reasons are there for calculating variances?
6. What future problems could result from Better Bikes' decision to buy a lower quality of titanium from the online marketplace?

7-25 Materials and manufacturing labour variances, standard costs. Dunn Inc. is a privately held furniture manufacturer. For August 2013, Dunn had the following standards for one of its products, a wicker chair:

	Standards per Chair
Direct materials	2 square metres of input at $5 per square metre
Direct manufacturing labour	0.5 hours of input at $10 per hour

The following data were compiled regarding actual performance: actual output units (chairs) produced, 2,000; square metres of input purchased and used, 3,700; price per square metre, $5.10; direct manufacturing labour costs, $8,820; actual hours of input, 900; labour price per hour, $9.80.

REQUIRED

1. Show your computations on the price and efficiency variances for direct materials and for direct manufacturing labour. Give a plausible explanation of why the variances occurred.
2. Suppose 6,000 square metres of materials were purchased (at $5.10 per square metre) even though only 3,700 square metres were used. Suppose further that variances are identified with their most likely control point; accordingly, direct materials price variances are isolated and traced to the purchasing department rather than to the production department. Compute the price and efficiency variances under this approach.

1. Price variance, $12,000 F

1. Direct materials price variance, $370 U

7-26 Journal entries and T-accounts (continuation of 7-25). Prepare journal entries and post them to T-accounts for all transactions in Exercise 7-25, including requirement 2. Summarize how these journal entries differ from the normal costing entries described in Chapter 5.

7-27 Flexible budget (continuation of 7-25 and 7-26). Suppose the static budget was for 2,500 units of output. Actual output was 2,000 units. The variances are shown in the following report:

Direct materials efficiency variance, $1,500 F

	Actual Results	Static Budget	Variance
Direct materials	$18,870	$25,000	$6,130 F
Direct manufacturing labour	8,820	12,500	3,680 F

REQUIRED

What are the price, efficiency, and sales-volume variances for direct materials and direct manufacturing labour? Based on your results, explain why the static budget was not achieved.

7-28 Direct materials efficiency, mix, and yield variances. (CMA, adapted) The Energy Products Company produces a gasoline additive, Gas Gain, that increases engine efficiency and improves gasoline mileage. The actual and budgeted quantities (in litres) of materials required to produce Gas Gain and the budgeted prices of materials in August 2013 are as follows:

1. Echol actual mix percentage, 0.28

Chemical	Actual Quantity	Budgeted Quantity	Budgeted Price
Echol	24,080	25,200	$0.22
Protex	15,480	16,800	0.47
Benz	36,120	33,600	0.17
CT-40	10,320	8,400	0.32

REQUIRED

1. Calculate the total direct materials efficiency variance for August 2013.
2. Calculate the total direct materials mix and yield variances for August 2013.
3. What conclusions would you draw from the variance analysis?

7-29 Direct materials rate, efficiency, mix, and yield variances. Greenwood Inc. manufactures apple products such as apple jelly and applesauce. It makes applesauce by blending Tolman, Golden Delicious, and Ribston apples. Budgeted costs to produce 100,000 kilograms of applesauce in November 2013 are as follows:

1. Tolman direct materials price variance, $1,240 F

45,000 kilograms of Tolman apples at $0.32 per kilogram	$14,400
180,000 kilograms of Golden Delicious apples at $0.28 per kilogram	50,400
75,000 kilograms of Ribston apples at $0.24 per kilogram	18,000

Actual costs in November 2013 are

62,000 kilograms of Tolman apples at $0.30 per kilogram	$18,600
155,000 kilograms of Golden Delicious apples at $0.28 per kilogram	43,400
93,000 kilograms of Ribston apples at $0.22 per kilogram	20,460

REQUIRED

1. Calculate the total direct materials price and efficiency variances for November 2013.
2. Calculate the total direct materials mix and yield variances for November 2013.
3. Comment on your results in requirements 1 and 2.

PROBLEMS

7-30 Variance analysis, non-manufacturing setting. Stevie McQueen has run Lightning Car Detailing for the past ten years. His static-budget and actual results for June 2013 are provided below. Stevie has one employee who has been with him for all ten years that he has been in business. He has not been as lucky with his second and third employees. Stevie is hiring new employees in those positions almost every second month. It usually takes 2 hours to detail a

2. Flexible-budget variance for labour, $300 F

vehicle. It takes as long for the seasoned employee as for the new ones, as the former tends to put more into the job. Stevie pays his long-term employee $20 per hour and the other two employees $10 per hour. Stevie pays all employees for 2 hours of work on each car, regardless of how long the work actually takes them. There were no wage increases in June.

Lightning Car Detailing
Actual and Budgeted Income Statements
For the Month Ending June 30, 2013

	Budget	Actual
Cars detailed	200	225
Revenue	$30,000	$ 39,375
Variable costs:		
Costs of supplies	1,500	2,250
Labour	5,600	6,000
Total variable costs	7,100	8,250
Contribution margin	22,900	31,125
Fixed costs	9,500	9,500
Operating income	$13,400	$ 21,625

REQUIRED

1. Prepare a statement of the static-budget variances that Stevie would be interested in.
2. Compute any flexible-budget variances that you believe would be appropriate.
3. What information, in addition to that provided in the income statements, would you want Stevie to gather if you wanted to improve operational efficiency?
4. How many cars, on average, did Stevie budget for each employee? How many cars did they actually detail?
5. What advice would you give Stevie about motivating his employees?

7-31 Direct-materials variances, long-term agreement with supplier. For its manufacturing facility in Montreal, Quebec, Metalmoulder has a long-term contract with Osaka Metals. Metalmoulder manufactures large-scale machining systems that are sold to other industrial companies. Each machining system has a sizable direct materials cost, consisting primarily of the purchase price for a metal compound. Osaka will supply to Metalmoulder up to 2,400 kilograms of metal per month at a fixed purchase price of $144 per kilogram for each month in 2013. For purchases above 2,400 kilograms in any month, Metalmoulder renegotiates the price for the additional amount with Osaka Metals (or another supplier). The standard price per kilogram is $144 for each month in the January to December 2013 period.

Production data, direct materials actual usage in dollars, and direct materials actual price per kilogram for the January to May 2013 period, are as follows:

	Number of Machining Systems Produced	Total Actual Direct Materials Usage	Average Actual Direct Materials Purchase Price per Kilogram of Metal
January	10	$290,880	$144.00
February	12	343,872	144.00
March	18	530,712	151.20
April	16	474,317	153.60
May	11	304,128	144.00

The average actual direct materials purchase price is for all units purchased in that month. Assume that (a) the direct materials purchased in each month are all used in that month and (b) each machining system is started and completed in the same month.

The Montreal facility is one of three plants that Metalmoulder operates to manufacture large-scale machining systems. The other plants are in Worcester, U.K., and Tokyo, Japan.

1. Assume that Metalmoulder's standard materials input per machining system is 198 kilograms of metal. Compute the direct materials price variance and direct materials efficiency variance for each month of the January to May 2013 period.
2. How does the signing of a long-term agreement with a supplier—an agreement that includes a fixed-purchase-price clause—affect the interpretation of a materials price variance?

7-32 Variance procedures; price and efficiency variances, journal entries. The Monroe Corporation manufactures lamps. It has set up the following standards per finished unit for direct materials and direct manufacturing labour:

1. Direct materials efficiency variance, $2,002 F

Direct materials: 10 kg at $4.50 per kg	$45.00
Direct manufacturing labour: 0.5 hour at $30 per hour	15.00

The number of finished units budgeted for January 2013 was 10,000; 9,850 units were actually produced.

Actual results in January 2013 were:
Direct materials: 98,055 kg used
Direct manufacturing labour: 4,900 hours $154,350

Assume that there was no beginning inventory of either direct materials or finished units.
During the month, materials purchases amounted to 100,000 kg, at a total cost of $465,000. Input price variances are isolated upon purchase. Input-efficiency variances are isolated at the time of usage.

REQUIRED

1. Compute the January 2013 price and efficiency variances of direct materials and direct manufacturing labour.
2. Prepare journal entries to record the variances in requirement 1.
3. Comment on the January 2013 price and efficiency variances of Monroe Corporation.
4. Why might Monroe calculate direct materials price variances and direct materials efficiency variances with reference to different points in time?

7-33 Direct materials and manufacturing labour variances, solving unknowns. (CPA, adapted) On May 1, 2013, Bovar Company began the manufacture of a new Internet paging device known as Dandy. The company installed a standard costing system to account for manufacturing costs. The standard costs for a unit of Dandy are as follows:

1. Standard DMLH for actual output achieved, 2,000 hours

Direct materials (3 kg at $5 per kg)	$15.00
Direct manufacturing labour (0.5 hours at $20 per hour)	10.00
Manufacturing overhead (75% of direct manufacturing labour costs)	7.50
	$32.50

The following data were obtained from Bovar's records for the month of May:

	Debit	Credit
Revenues		$125,000
Accounts payable control		
(for May's purchases of direct materials)		68,250
Direct materials price variance	$3,250	
Direct materials efficiency variance	2,500	
Direct manufacturing labour price variance	1,900	
Direct manufacturing labour efficiency variance		2,000

Actual production in May was 4,000 units of Dandy, and actual sales in May were 2,500 units. The amount shown for direct materials price variance applies to materials purchased during May. There was no beginning inventory of materials on May 1, 2013.

REQUIRED

Compute each of the following items for Bovar for the month of May. Show your computations.

1. Standard direct manufacturing labour-hours (DMLH) allowed for actual output achieved.
2. Actual direct manufacturing labour-hours (DMLH) worked.
3. Actual direct manufacturing labour wage rate.
4. Standard quantity of direct materials allowed (in kg).
5. Actual quantity of direct materials used (in kg).
6. Actual quantity of direct materials purchased (in kg).
7. Actual direct materials price per kg.

1. Direct manufacturing labour price variance, $16,000 F

7-34 Direct manufacturing labour and direct materials variances, missing data. (CMA, adapted) Morro Bay Surfboards is a California company that manufactures fibreglass surfboards. The standard cost of direct materials and direct manufacturing labour is $100 per board. This includes 20 pounds of direct materials, at the budgeted price of $2 per pound, and 5 hours of direct manufacturing labour, at the budgeted rate of $12 per hour. Following are additional data for the month of July:

Units completed	6,000 units
Direct material purchases	150,000 pounds
Cost of direct material purchases	$292,500
Actual direct manufacturing labor-hours	32,000 hours
Actual direct-labor cost	$368,000
Direct materials efficiency variance	$ 12,500 U

There were no beginning inventories.

REQUIRED

1. Compute direct manufacturing labour variances for July.
2. Compute the actual pounds of direct materials used in production in July.
3. Calculate the actual price per pound of direct materials purchased.
4. Calculate the direct materials price variance.

1. Price variance for the wool, $395 U

7-35 Direct materials and manufacturing labour variances, journal entries. Shayna's Smart Shawls Inc. is a small business that Shayna developed while in college. She began hand-knitting shawls for her dorm friends to wear while studying. As demand grew, she hired some workers and began to manage the operation. Shayna's shawls require wool and labour. She experiments with the type of wool that she uses, and she has great variety in the shawls she produces. Shayna has bi-modal turnover in her labour—she has some employees who have been with her for a very long time and others who are new and inexperienced.

Shayna uses standard costing for her shawls. She expects that a typical shawl should take 3.5 hours to produce, and the standard wage rate is $10.50 per hour. An average shawl uses 12 skeins of wool. Shayna shops around for good deals and expects to pay $3.00 per skein.

Shayna uses a just-in-time inventory system, as she has clients tell her what type and colour of wool they would like her to use.

For the month of April, Shayna's workers produced 230 shawls using 836 hours and 2,633.5 skeins of wool. Shayna bought wool for $8,295.50 (and used the entire quantity), and incurred labour costs of $7,814.50.

REQUIRED

1. Calculate the price and efficiency variances for the wool, and the price and efficiency variances for direct manufacturing labour.
2. Record the journal entries for the variances incurred.
3. Discuss logical explanations for the combination of variances that Shayna experienced.

1. a. Selling-price variance, $54,000 U

7-36 Comprehensive variance analysis. (CMA, adapted) Aunt Molly's Old Fashioned Cookies bakes cookies for a chain of retail stores. The company's best-selling cookie is Chocolate Nut Supreme, which is marketed as a gourmet cookie and regularly sells for $9.60 per kilogram. The standard input cost per kilogram of Chocolate Nut Supreme, based on Aunt Molly's normal monthly production of 400,000 kilograms, is calculated as follows:

Cost Item	Standard Quantity	Unit Cost	Total Cost
Direct materials:			
Cookie mix	625 g	$0.384 per kg	$0.24
Milk chocolate	312.5 g	$2.88 per kg	0.90
Almonds	62.5 g	$9.60 per kg	0.60
1,000 g = 1 kg			$1.74
Direct labour			
Mixing	1 minute	$17.28 per hour	$0.288
Baking	2 minutes	$21.60 per hour	0.720
			$1.008

Aunt Molly's management accountant, Karen Blair, prepares monthly budget reports based on these standard costs. Presented here is April's report, which compares budgeted and actual performance.

Performance Report
April 2013

	Budget	Actual	Variance
Units (in kilograms)*	400,000	450,000	50,000 F
Revenue	$3,840,000	$4,266,000	$ 426,000 F
Direct material	$ 696,000	$1,017,365	$ 321,365 U
Direct labour	$ 403,200	$ 453,600	$ 50,400 U

*Units produced and sold

Usage Report
April 2013

Cost Item	Quantity	Actual Cost
Direct materials:		
Cookie mix	290,000 kg	$111,360
Milk chocolate	161,720 kg	$621,005
Almonds	29,688 kg	$285,000
1,000 g = 1 kg		
Direct labour		
Mixing	450,000 minutes	$129,600
Baking	800,000 minutes	$288,000

REQUIRED

1. Compute the following variances:
   a. Selling-price variance.
   b. Material-price variance.
   c. Material-efficiency variance.
   d. Labour-price variance.
   e. Labour-efficiency variance.
2. What explanations might exist for the variances in requirement 1?

7-37 Comprehensive variance analysis, responsibility issues. (CMA, adapted) Styles Inc. manufactures a full line of well-known sunglasses frames and lenses. Styles uses a standard costing system to set attainable standards for direct materials, labour, and overhead costs. Styles reviews and revises standards annually, as necessary. Department managers, whose evaluations and bonuses are affected by their department's performance, are held responsible to explain variances in their department performance reports.

Recently, the manufacturing variances in the Image prestige line of sunglasses have caused some concern. For no apparent reason, unfavourable materials and labour variances have occurred. At the monthly staff meeting, Jack Barton, manager of the Image line, will be

1. a. Selling-price variance, $14,550 F

expected to explain his variances and suggest ways of improving performance. Barton will be asked to explain the following performance report for 2013:

	Actual Results	Static-Budget Amounts
Units sold	7,275	7,500
Revenue	$596,550	$600,000
Variable manufacturing costs	$351,965	$324,000
Fixed manufacturing costs	$108,398	$112,500
Gross margin	$136,187	$163,500

Barton collected the following information:

Three items comprised the standard variable manufacturing costs in 2013:

◆ Direct materials: Frames. Static-budget cost of $49,500. The standard input for 2013 is 3.00 g per unit.
◆ Direct materials: Lenses. Static-budget costs of $139,500. The standard input for 2013 is 6.00 g per unit.
◆ Direct manufacturing labour: Static-budget costs of $135,000. The standard input for 2013 is 1.20 hours per unit.

Assume there are no variable manufacturing overhead costs.

The actual variable manufacturing costs in 2013 were:

◆ Direct materials: Frames. Actual costs of $55,872. Actual grams used were 3.20 g per unit.
◆ Direct materials: Lenses. Actual costs of $150,738. Actual grams used were 7.00 g per unit.
◆ Direct manufacturing labour: Actual costs of $145,355. The actual labour rate was $14.80 per hour.

REQUIRED

1. Prepare a report that includes:
   a. Selling-price variance.
   b. Sales-volume variance and flexible-budget variance for operating income in the format of the analysis in Exhibit 7-6.
   b. Price and efficiency variances for:
      ◆ Direct materials: frames.
      ◆ Direct materials: lenses.
      ◆ Direct manufacturing labour.
2. Give three possible explanations for each of the three price and efficiency variances at Styles in requirement 1c.

 **7-38 Comprehensive variance analysis review.** Memflash Inc. manufactures 500 megabyte flash drives that are compatible with a popular portable storage device. Memflash sells flash drives directly to computer retail chains and to direct marketing organizations that resell flash drives under their house brands. The flash drives retail for an average of $9.60 per unit, and compete with well-known brands that retail for between $12.00 and $14.40 per flash drive.

2. Total static-budget variance, $652,280 U

Memflash's CFO has provided you with the following budgeted standards for the month of February 2013:

Budgeted average wholesale selling price per unit	$4.80
Total direct material standard cost per drive	$1.02
Direct manufacturing labour	
Direct manufacturing labour standard cost per hour	$18.00
Average labour productivity (drives per hour)	300
Direct marketing cost per unit	$0.36
Total fixed overhead	$1,080,000

The VP of Marketing forecasts sales of 1,660,500 units for the month.

On March 7, the VP of Planning and Control meets with the executive committee to discuss February results. He reports as follows:

◆ Unit sales totalled 1,400,000 units.
◆ Actual average selling price declined to $4.86.
◆ Productivity dropped to 280 drives/hour; however, because of favourable market conditions, the actual price per unit dropped to $0.94.
◆ Fixed costs came in $33,000 below plan.
◆ All other costs were incurred at their standard rates.

As the senior financial analyst, you are asked to calculate the following:
1. Static-budget and actual operating income.
2. Total static-budget variance.
3. Flexible-budget operating income.
4. Total flexible-budget variance.
5. Total sales-volume variance.
6. Price and efficiency variances.
7. What is the material-price variance? What is the labour-price variance?
8. What is the material-efficiency variance? What is the labour-efficiency variance?

7-39 **Materials variances: price, efficiency, mix, and yield.** PDS Manufacturing makes wooden furniture. One of their products is a wooden dresser. The exterior and some of the shelves are made of oak, a high-quality wood, but the interior drawers are made of pine, a less expensive wood. The budgeted direct materials quantities and prices for one dresser are

③

1. Cost per dresser, $72

	Quantity	Price per Unit of Input	Cost for One Dresser
Oak	8 board feet	$6 per board foot	$48
Pine	12 board feet	2 per board foot	24

That is, each dresser is budgeted to use 20 board feet of wood, comprised of 40% oak and 60% pine, although sometimes more pine is used in place of oak with no obvious change in the quality or function of the dresser.

During the month of May, PDS manufactures 3,000 dressers. Actual direct materials costs are:

Oak (23,180 board feet)	$141,398
Pine (37,820 board feet)	68,076
Total actual direct materials cost	$209,474

REQUIRED
1. What is the budgeted cost of direct materials for 3,000 dressers?
2. Calculate the total direct materials price and efficiency variances.
3. For the 3,000 dressers, what is the total actual amount of oak and pine used? What is the actual direct materials input mix percentage? What is the budgeted amount of oak and pine that should have been used for the 3,000 dressers?
4. Calculate the total direct materials mix and yield variances. How do these numbers relate to the total direct materials efficiency variance? What do these variances tell you?

7-40 **Product input mix and yield variance.** Tropical Fruits Inc. processes tropical fruit into a fruit salad mix, which it sells to a food-service company. Tropical Fruits has in its budget the following standards for the direct materials inputs to produce a batch of 80 kilograms of tropical fruit salad:

③

1. Direct materials price variance, $2,590 F

50 kilograms of pineapple at $1.05 per kilogram	$52.50
30 kilograms of watermelon at $0.55 per kilogram	16.50
20 kilograms of strawberries at $0.80 per kilogram	16.00
100	$85.00

Note that 100 kilograms of input quantities are required to produce 80 kilograms of fruit salad. No inventories of direct materials are kept. Purchases are made as needed, so all price variances are related to direct materials used. The actual direct materials inputs used to produce 54,000 kilograms of tropical fruit salad for October were:

36,400 kilograms of pineapple at $0.95 per kilogram	$34,580
18,200 kilograms of watermelon at $0.65 per kilogram	11,830
15,400 kilograms of strawberries at $0.75 per kilogram	11,550
70,000	$57,960

REQUIRED

1. Compute the total direct materials price and efficiency variances in October.
2. Compute the total direct materials mix and yield variances for October.
3. Comment on your results in requirements 1 and 2.
4. How might the management of Tropical Fruits Inc. use information about the direct materials mix and yield variances?

7-41 Possible causes for price and efficiency variances. You are a student preparing for a job interview with a large Canadian consumer products manufacturer. You are applying for a job in the Finance Department. This company is known for its rigorous case-based interview process. One of the students who successfully obtained a job with the company upon graduation last year advised you to "know your variances cold!" When you inquired further, she told you that she had been asked to pretend that she was investigating wage and materials variances. Per her advice, you have been studying the causes and consequences of variances. You are excited when you get to the interview and find that the first case you are presented with deals with variance analysis. You are given the following data for May for a detergent bottling plant:

Actual

Bottles filled	360,000
Direct materials used in production	60,000,000 g
Actual direct material cost	$2,125,000
Actual direct manufacturing labour-hours	22,040 hours
Actual direct labour cost	$ 664,940

Standards

Purchase price of direct materials	$ 0.035 per g
Bottle materials used	150 g
Wage rate	$29.30 per hour
Bottles per minute	0.5

REQUIRED

Please respond to the following questions as if you were in an interview situation:

1. Calculate the materials efficiency and price variance, and the wage and labour efficiency variances for the month of May.
2. You are given the following context: "Union organizers are targeting our detergent bottling plant for a union." Can you provide a better explanation for the variances that you have calculated on the basis of this information?

7-42 Variance analysis with activity-based costing and batch-level direct costs. Electric Eels Company produces high-quality electric eels for Museums and Aquaria to sell in their gift shops. It accounts for the production of these eels with an ABC system. For 2013, Electric Eels expected to produce and sell 16,000 units, but actual output was only 15,000 units.

You are a new management accountant at the company. You been asked to calculate the variances for the batch-level costs. The two main batch-level costs are setup and quality inspection. Quality inspection is driven by inspection hours, and setup is driven by the number of setup-hours.

		Setup	Quality Inspection
Static Budget:	Batch size (units per batch)	100	120
	Cost driver (hours) per batch	8	10
	Cost per hour	$10.75	$17.50
Actual Result:	Batch size (units per batch)	75	100
	Cost driver (hours) per batch	7	9
	Cost per hour	$12.00	$15.50

REQUIRED

1. Calculate the flexible-budget, price, and efficiency variances for both batch activities.
2. Write a short memo to your boss, the controller, explaining the variances that you calculated.

Left margin notes:

4
1. Direct materials price variance, $25,000 U

4
1. Efficiency variance, $2,150 U

7-43 Variance procedures; flexible-budget preparation, service sector. Meridian Finance helps prospective homeowners of substantial means to find low-cost financing and assists existing homeowners in refinancing their current loans at lower interest rates. Meridian works only for customers with excellent borrowing capacity. Hence, Meridian is able to obtain a loan for every customer with whom it decides to work.

2. Operating income for 120 loan applications, $33,360

Meridian charges clients 0.5% of the loan amount it arranges. In 2011, the average loan amount per customer was $238,800. In 2012, the average loan amount was $240,252. In its 2013 flexible-budgeting system, Meridian assumes the average loan amount will be $240,000. Budgeted cost data per loan application for 2013 are:

- Professional labour: 6 budgeted hours at a budgeted rate of $48 per hour
- Loan filing fees: budgeted at $120 per loan application
- Creditworthiness checks: budgeted at $144 per loan application
- Courier mailings: budgeted at $60 per loan application

Office support (the costs of leases, administrative staff, and others) is budgeted to be $37,200 per month. Meridian Finance views this amount as a fixed cost.

REQUIRED

1. Prepare a static budget for November 2013 assuming 90 loan applications.
2. Actual loan applications in November 2013 were 120. Other actual data for November 2010 were:
   - Professional labour: 7.2 hours per loan application at $50.40 per hour
   - Loan filing fees: $120 per loan application
   - Creditworthiness checks: $150 per loan application
   - Courier mailings: $64.80 per loan application

   Office support costs for November 2013 were $40,200. The average loan amount for November 2013 was $268,800. Meridian received its 0.5% fee on all loans. Prepare a Level 2 variance analysis of Meridian Finance for November 2013. Meridian's output measure in its flexible-budgeting system is the number of loan applications.

7-44 Benchmarking, hospital cost comparisons. Julie Leung is the newly appointed president of Provincial University. Provincial University Hospital (PUH) is a major problem for her because it is running large deficits. While it is not-for-profit, the province will reduce funding if hospitals fail to meet their budgets. Sam Horn, the chairperson of the hospital, tells Leung that he and his staff have cut costs to the bare bone. Any further cost cutting, he argues, would destroy the culture of the hospital. He also argues that the use of detailed cost studies is totally inappropriate for a medical institution because of (a) the inability to have well-defined relationships between inputs and outputs and (b) the problem of defining what a good output for a hospital is. He notes that he is "fed up with people equating continuous improvement at PUH with continued cost reduction. This is only a cost accountant's view of the world. Our top priority is to help doctors save lives and to help people recover their health."

5
2. Ratio of PUH 25th percentile angina, chest pain, 1.33

Leung hears about a new benchmark cost analysis service offered by Market Insights (MI). She asks Horn to hire Market Insights to provide a benchmark cost report that pertains to PUH. Horn is not enthusiastic about doing so, but he complies with her request. The report includes the following:

a. Aggregate Hospital Cost Comparison
(average = 1.00)

Hospital E	0.69
Hospital C	0.70
Hospital J	0.70
⋮	⋮
Hospital A	1.19
Provincial University Hospital	1.20
Hospital O	1.21

b.

Diagnostic Group Cost Comparison

Diagnostic Group	Provincial University Hospital	Market Average	25th Percentile	Average of Best Quartile (0–25th)
Angina, chest pain	$27,600	$24,600	$20,760	$18,360
Asthma, bronchitis	18,480	15,720	12,480	10,800
Skin disorders, cellulitis	11,520	11,040	7,800	6,960
Renal failure and dialysis	9,120	6,600	5,040	4,320
Diabetes	8,040	6,120	4,440	3,720
Gastroenteritis	14,400	22,200	19,200	15,360

REQUIRED

1. Do you agree with Horn that the use of detailed cost studies at PUH is totally inappropriate? Explain your answer and comment on Horn's reasoning.
2. What inferences can you draw from the MI benchmark cost report on PUH?
3. What use might Leung make of the MI benchmark cost report?
4. What criticisms might you anticipate Horn would make of the MI benchmark cost report?
5. What factors other than cost might Leung consider in evaluating Horn's performance and that of PUH?

COLLABORATIVE LEARNING CASES

5

1. Hergonia purchase price variance, $400,000 U

7-45 Procurement costs, variance analysis, governance. Rashid Daley is the manager of the athletic shoe division of Raider Products. Raider is a European-based company that has just purchased Fastfoot, a leading European shoe company. Fastfoot has long-term production contracts with suppliers in two East European countries: Hergonia and Tanista. Daley receives a request from Kevin Neal, president of Raider Products. Daley and his controller, Brooke Mullins, are to make a presentation to the next board of directors' meeting on the cost competitiveness of its Fastfoot subsidiary. This should include budgeted and actual procurement costs for 2013 at its Hergonia and Tanista supply sources.

Mullins decides to visit the two supply operations. The budgeted average procurement cost for 2013 was $14 per pair of shoes. This includes payments to the shoe manufacturer and all other payments to conduct business in each country. Mullins reports the following to Daley:

◆ **Hergonia.** Total 2013 procurement costs for 250,000 pairs of shoes were $3,900,000. Payment to the shoe manufacturer was $3,108,000. Very few receipts exist for the remaining $792,000. Kickback payments are viewed as common in Hergonia.
◆ **Tanista.** Total 2013 procurement costs for 900,000 pairs of shoes were $12,300,000. Payment to the shoe manufacturer was $10,136,000. Receipts exist for $827,000 of the other costs, but Mullins is skeptical of their validity. Kickback payments are a "way of business" in Tanista.

At both the Hergonia and Tanista plants, Mullins is disturbed by the employment of young children (many of them under 15 years). She is told that all major shoe-producing companies have similar low-cost employment practices in both countries.

Daley is uncomfortable about the upcoming presentation to the board of directors. He was a leading advocate of the acquisition. A recent business magazine reported that the Fastfoot acquisition would make Raider Products the global low-cost producer in its market lines. The stock price of Raider Products jumped 21% the day the Fastfoot acquisition was announced. Mullins, likewise, is widely identified as a proponent of the acquisition. She is seen as a rising star due for promotion to a division management post in the near future.

REQUIRED

1. What summary procurement cost variances could be reported to the board of directors of Raider Shoes?
2. What ethical issues do (a) Daley and (b) Mullins face when preparing and making a report to the board of directors?
3. How should Mullins address the issues you identify in requirement 2?

7-46 Price and efficiency variances, problems in standard-setting, benchmarking. New Fashions Inc. manufactures shirts for retail chains. Andy Jorgenson, the controller, is becoming increasingly disenchanted with New Fashions' standard costing system. The budgeted and actual amounts for direct materials and direct manufacturing labour for June 2012 were as follows:

② ⑤
1. Direct-materials price variance, $306 F

	Budgeted Amounts	Actual Amounts
Shirts manufactured	6,000	6,732
Direct material costs	30,000	$30,294
Direct material units (rolls of cloth)	600	612
Direct manufacturing labour costs	$27,000	$27,693
Direct manufacturing labour-hours (DMLH)	1,500	1,530

There were no beginning or ending inventories of materials.

Standard costs are based on a study of the operations conducted by an independent consultant six months earlier. Jorgenson observes that, since that study, he has rarely seen an unfavourable variance of any magnitude. He notes that even at their current output levels, the workers seem to have a lot of time for sitting around and gossiping. Jorgenson is concerned that the production manager, Charlie Fenton, is aware of this but does not want to tighten up the standards because the lax standards make his performance look good.

REQUIRED

1. Compute the price and efficiency variances of New Fashions for direct materials and direct manufacturing labour in June 2013.
2. Describe the types of actions the employees at New Fashions may have taken to reduce the accuracy of the standards set by the independent consultant. Why would employees take those actions? Is this behaviour ethical?
3. If Jorgenson does nothing about the standard costs, will his behaviour violate any of the ethical conduct characteristics described in Chapter 1?
4. What actions should Jorgenson take?
5. Jorgenson can obtain benchmarking information about the estimated costs of New Fashions' major competitors from Benchmarking Clearing House (BCH). Discuss the pros and cons of using the BCH information to compute the variances in requirement 1.

Flexible Budgets, Variances, and Management Control: II

8

BUSINESS MATTERS

Tracking Performance

Manufacturing and non-manufacturing overhead comprise a large proportion of total costs. For extraction industries such as oil, gold, and iron ore, the costs of exploration, development, and refining are in the hundreds of millions. For service industries like airline transportation, one new aircraft can cost at least $40 million. These fixed assets are used for many years and their costs are called fixed overhead costs of either service or production.

Barrick Gold Corporation, a Canadian gold producer and largest in the world, explores for, refines, and produces gold, all of which are capital intensive activities. In Barrick's 2010 annual report, its property, plant, and equipment was valued at more than $17.7 billion. Barrick's long-term profit depends on recovering the costs of both its fixed assets and annual costs of operation as it sells each troy ounce of gold. Barrick cannot control gold price, but it can control costs as long as it knows the fixed and variable overhead costs per troy ounce produced.

LEARNING OUTCOMES

After studying this chapter, you should be able to

1. Assign MOH fixed costs, then calculate and analyze flexible-budget variances.

2. Establish variable overhead cost allocation rates; calculate and analyze flexible-budget variances.

3. Calculate ABC overhead variances.

4. Integrate the fixed and variable overhead cost variance analyses to reconcile the actual overhead incurred with overhead allocated.

5. Analyze non-manufacturing variances.

This chapter completes the Level 3 flexible-budget variance for both fixed and variable manufacturing overhead. Fixed manufacturing overhead (FMOH) costs include taxes, amortization, lease expenses, insurance, and salaries. Some fixed costs are locked in by legal contracts for terms as short as one year, such as salaries and insurance. Others are locked in by far longer-term contracts to purchase or lease plant and equipment. Taxes are inevitable as long as the company earns profits. These FMOH costs are assigned to each unit of output because companies have only one way to recover the costs—charge a reasonable price when they sell output.

Variable manufacturing overhead (VMOH) costs also contribute to overhead. These VMOH costs of shared resources are assigned to each unit of output in proportion to the benefit received by distinctive types of output. VMOH costs can only be recovered in the price charged when output is sold, which is why both FMOH and VMOH costs are assigned to units of output.

FLEXIBLE-BUDGET MOH COST VARIANCES

1 Assign MOH fixed costs, then calculate and analyze flexible-budget variances.

Continuing our analysis of Webb Company begun in Chapter 7, we simplify the example by examining only inventoriable costs or MOH. Recall that MOH are defined by GAAP and used to estimate both cost of goods sold and inventory values. Referring back to Exhibit 7-4, p. 250, this discussion includes only the VMOH of $120,000 budgeted for the 10,000-jackets level of output and FMOH of $276,000 budgeted for the relevant range including 10,000 jackets. The task is to explain the FMOH cost pool variance of $6,000 U ($276,000 − $285,000) and the VMOH cost pool variance of $10,500 U ($120,000 − $105,500).

Webb's cost structure illustrates the importance of management planning and control of manufacturing overhead costs. The following percentages of total static-budget costs of $1,898,000 (column (4) of Exhibit 7-4, p. 250) are based on Webb's static budget for 12,000 jackets for April:

	Variable Overhead Costs	Fixed Overhead Costs	Total Overhead Costs
Manufacturing[1]	7.59%	14.54%	22.13%
Marketing	3.16	22.87	26.03
Total	10.75%	37.41%	48.16%

Total overhead costs are significant and amount to almost half (48.16%) of Webb's total budgeted costs at 12,000 output units per month ($914,000 ÷ $1,898,000). Based on its fixed costs as a percentage of total costs of approximately 37.41% ($710,000 ÷ $1,898,000) relative to variable costs of 10.75% ($204,000 ÷ $1,898,000), Webb may be classified as a high operating leverage company. The variable costs consume only $0.1075 from every revenue dollar earned. After Webb breaks even, $0.8925 of every revenue dollar earned will contribute to paying for fixed costs and the remainder to operating income.

Based on the static budget, the contribution margin percentage is 45% ($972,000 ÷ $2,160,000) and the **BEP in revenue** is approximately $15,778. In Q of jackets produced and sold the **BEP in volume** is 8,766 ($15,778 ÷ 0.45 ≈ 8,765.43). If Webb achieves its budgeted sales Q produced *and* sold its operating income will be approximately $582,120 (12,000 jackets − 8,766 jackets ≈ 3,234 jackets × $180). When Webb sold only 10,000 jackets, its operating income would have been $222,120 (10,000 jackets − 8,766 jackets ≈ 1,234 jackets × $180). Webb's recovery of FMOH per jacket sold and its profit depend on meeting its budget.

---

[1]VMOH as a percentage of total costs is $144,000 ÷ $1,898,000 = 7.59% and FMOH is $276,000 ÷ 1,898,000 = 14.54%. Total manufacturing overhead is $420,000 ÷ $1,898,000 = 22.13%. Similar calculations will result in the percentages shown for marketing overhead costs. The total variable marketing and manufacturing overhead costs as a percentage of total costs is ($144,000 + $60,000) ÷ $1,898,000 = 10.75%.

Shortfalls in quantity produced and sold reduce revenue and the total contribution that will pay for fixed costs. Management teams like Webb's are very careful when they invest in their equipment. The total fixed costs will remain unchanged whether jackets are sold or 16,000 jackets are sold. What changes is Webb's total operating income, its operating profit. The decision at the centre of long-term profitability is how much to spend on equipment that provides the capacity to supply jackets to meet consumer demand and still be profitable.

THE DECISION FRAMEWORK AND FIXED OVERHEAD COSTS

Effective planning of fixed overhead costs is basically a capacity planning issue. **Capacity** refers to the quantity of outputs that can be produced from long-term resources available to the company. The alternatives that managers consider in capacity decisions are covered in Chapter 9. However, regardless of the alternative chosen, capacity is acquired through the purchase or lease of long-term assets. This means decisions about capacity are *strategic* decisions. Decisions would include consideration of current capacity, forecasted future demand and risks, potential alternative uses of idle capacity, and ease of disposal of excess capacity.

The fixed overhead issue is that either the lease or acquisition cost of capacity must be recovered through the sale of outputs (goods or services). But Webb is a price-taker; consumers have set the price they are willing to pay for a jacket at $180. If the management team leased or purchased too many machines relative to demand for the jackets, Webb would have unutilized or idle capacity. This unutilized capacity cost must be recovered, but Webb cannot simply increase its price to cover idle capacity cost per jacket. Competitors may not have any or as much idle capacity and, all other things being equal, will achieve higher profitability per jacket at $180 than Webb.

This means Webb needs to be right when it forecasts consumer demand and sets its price per jacket. The marketing business function is accountable for these estimates. The sales division is responsible for reaching the estimates of quantity sold. The production business function is responsible for completing the appropriate quantity of jackets each month within the cost per jacket they have committed to.

Capacity cost is a fixed manufacturing overhead cost. Webb's cost system is not an ABC system and the company collects all FMOH into a single indirect cost pool. While this chapter focuses on inventoriable capacity costs, period capacity costs also exist. It is often more readily apparent in manufacturing than in service industries what is the most informative grouping of capacity costs into overhead cost pools.

It may seem strange, but idle capacity occurs in well-managed and well-planned companies. In reality, machines require maintenance to refurbish and repair the wear and tear arising from normal use. Without scheduled idle or down time for maintenance, the machines would break down. Also, government regulations in many industries (such as the airline industry) legislate scheduled maintenance at specific times, which companies must comply with or face large legal penalties. Good capacity management requires excess capacity to minimize output lost during both scheduled maintenance and unexpected breakdowns.

In service industries, period overhead costs arise when the same building houses both those whose activities generate revenue as well as those who engage in all service-support activities. Capacity is related to the people and their intangible skills rather than to tangible equipment and property. These intangible skills may be referred to as *human capital*. The labour expense can be recorded, but the benefit is shared throughout the business. GAAP prohibits accounting for costs of this type in inventory. Period support costs, however, must still be recovered when the service is provided or the product is sold. Management accountants may use one of five methods (see Chapter 14) to assign period costs to distinct output units based on the proportion of benefit to the unit.

ASSIGNING FIXED MANUFACTURING OVERHEAD AT WEBB

The data in Exhibit 8-1 are available from Webb's MIS. The FMOH cost allocation rate and cost assigned per jacket can be readily calculated as shown in the exhibit.

EXHIBIT 8-1
FMOH Cost Assignment

		Flexible- and Static-Budgeted Amounts for the Year			
FMOH* (1)	**DMH/Year** (2)	**Rate per DMH** (3) = (1) ÷ (2)	**Q Jackets/year** (4)	**DMH/Jacket** (5) = (2) ÷ (4)	**Rate per Jacket** (6) = (3) × (5)
$3,312,000	57,600	$57.50	144,000	0.40	$23.00

*Anual FMOH = $276,000 × 12

The fixed cost pools do not change when the volume of output changes; therefore, the static budget is also the flexible budget. The assignment of budgeted, unitized FMOH costs to units of output depends on the quantity of output in the denominator. FMOH arises because equipment has been leased or purchased. But first the FMOH cost pool is allocated in Webb's traditional system using direct machine hours (DMH) as the cost allocation base. The economic reality should be that the higher the DMH used for a distinct type of jacket, the higher the cost per jacket and the higher the value added or benefit to the customer. But a **production denominator level** (or **volume**) that will be divided into the FMOH cost pool to calculate the rate per jacket is a measure of capacity *available*, not *actual* customer demand or capacity *used*. From four potential choices, Webb's management team has chosen the amount that is Canada Revenue Agency (CRA) compliant for tax reporting purposes. The alternative denominators are discussed in detail in Chapter 9.

The equipment *input* capacity budgeted for the year is 57,600 DMH and the total volume of output for the year is budgeted at 144,000 jackets. On a per unit basis, the rate of use is 0.40 DMH/jacket, (57,600 DMH ÷ 144,000 jackets). The budget for one month of output is 4,800 DMH/month (0.40 DMH × 12,000 jackets). The fixed MOH cost pool is budgeted at $276,000/month, so the budgeted FMOH rate will be $57.50/jacket ($276,000 ÷ 4,800 DMH).

$$\text{Budgeted fixed overhead rate per unit of allocation base} = \frac{\text{Budgeted fixed overhead costs}}{\text{Budgeted quantity of allocation base units}}$$

$$= \$276,000 \div 4,800 \text{ DMH}$$

$$= \$57.50 \text{ per DMH}$$

FIXED OVERHEAD COST VARIANCE CALCULATION AND ANALYSIS

The actual results for fixed manufacturing overhead are shown in Exhibit 7-4 (p. 250). The static-budget amount for fixed manufacturing overhead is based on 12,000 output units. Given that it is for a fixed cost, this same $276,000 would be the budgeted amount for all output levels in the relevant range. There is no "flexing" of fixed costs. The Level 1 static-budget variance for Webb's FMOH is $9,000 U:

$$\text{Fixed overhead static-budget variance} = \text{Actual results} - \text{Static-budget amount}$$

$$= \$285,000 - \$276,000$$

$$= \$9,000 \text{ U}$$

Webb spent more on fixed manufacturing overhead in April than the lump sum pro forma budgeted amount, and the result was a $9,000 decrease in the month's expected gross margin and operating income. All other things being equal, the operating income will also decrease by $9,000. This is why it is called a **fixed overhead rate variance**. This $9,000 is an opportunity cost. The $9,000 is, however, only part of the total flexible-budget overhead variance; there is another source of fixed overhead variance as well as all variable manufacturing overhead variances.

The FMOH flexible-budget variance is the same as the fixed overhead static-budget variance because there is no flex in a fixed cost. Moreover, for Level 3 analysis (decomposing the flexible-budget variance into its efficiency and rate components), the total flexible-budget variance is attributed to rate variance because volume does not affect FMOH. The quantity of DMH in the cost allocation base remains unchanged over a relevant range of quantity produced.

Unless the actual quantity produced exceeds the relevant range, any difference in DMH consumed compared to the quantity in the cost-allocation base is irrelevant. Exceeding the relevant range implies new equipment must be acquired or leased, which is a decision with long-term implications.

Interpretation of Fixed Overhead Rate Variance   The arithmetic involved here is trivial—the value of variance analysis arises from finding the cause or causes of the variance. Reasons for the unfavourable FMOH rate variance could include:

◆ An unplanned salary increase to retain the plant manager.
◆ Increased equipment lease or amortization rates.
◆ Increased insurance premiums.
◆ Increased taxes.

Assume Webb investigated and determined that there was a $9,000 per month unexpected increase in its equipment leasing costs. However, management concluded that the new lease rates were competitive with lease rates available elsewhere. If the rate had not been competitive, then the management team could have looked elsewhere to lease equipment from other suppliers. The increase was not controllable by individual managers and it is a permanent increase in FMOH. The appropriate response is to change the FMOH budgeted cost pool. Unfortunately, there is no value added to a customer when it costs more to run the same equipment and it is very unlikely that Webb can increase the cost per jacket without losing sales. To achieve the budgeted gross margin, the management team must find ways to reduce other controllable costs.

Exhibit 8-2 shows a summary of the Levels 1, 2, and 3 variance analyses for Webb's fixed manufacturing overhead in April, but it is not consistent with Exhibit 7-4 because neither the production-volume variance nor the variable overhead variances have been analyzed. Together, the rate and production-volume variances sum to the flexible-budget fixed overhead variance.

Budgeted fixed costs are, by definition, unaffected by sales-volume changes. Sales and production volumes are assumed to be identical. Within a relevant range, there will never be a sales-volume variance because the sales-volume variance arises only for costs affected by changes in the volume of sales. Managers cannot be more or less efficient in dealing with a fixed overhead cost pool and a relevant range of outputs.

EXHIBIT 8-2
Static-Budget and Flexible-Budget for Fixed Manufacturing Overhead Rate Variance

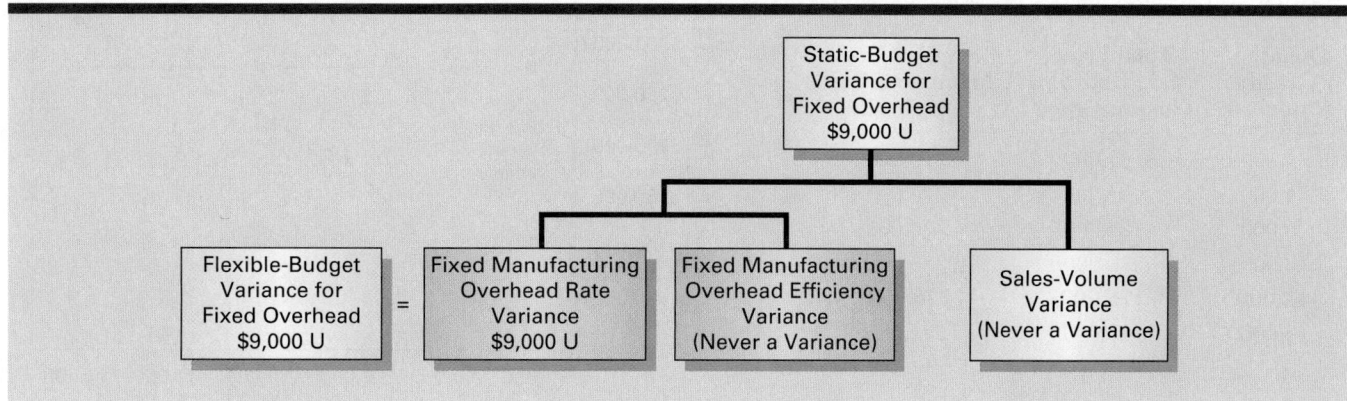

PRODUCTION-VOLUME VARIANCE CALCULATION AND ANALYSIS

The production-volume variance (PVV) analysis reveals the variance arises because of a misallocation of FMOH from using the method of normal costing in a traditional system. Normal cost assignment multiplies actual quantities by budgeted rates (Chapter 4). The **production-volume variance** is the difference between budgeted fixed overhead ($23/jacket for 12,000 jackets) and the fixed overhead that *should* have been assigned for the *actual* quantity of outputs. The rate is constant, but the multiplier changes. Other terms for this variance are **denominator-level variance** and **output-level overhead variance**. The management team can now analyze the PVV to identify how the difference of $55,000 U arose between the actual and budgeted costs. Exhibit 8-3 illustrates the fixed overhead variance relationships.

The production-volume variance analysis applies what you learned about unitized fixed cost behaviour, as illustrated in Exhibit 8-4. The second column in Exhibit 8-4 lists the allocation of FMOH using normal costing, and the unfavourable variance of $55,000 is overallocated. Had the variance been favourable, the FMOH would have been underallocated.

The graph in Exhibit 8-4 compares the total fixed cost behaviour based on the unitized FMOH rate of $23/jacket with total fixed manufacturing overhead. The quantities of jackets produced and sold are reported in the first column, and what the total FMOH *should* be at a rate of $23/jacket is in the second column. The actual total FMOH is $276,000. The budgeted FMOH cost pool at Q = 12,000 jackets

EXHIBIT 8-3
Analysis of Fixed Manufacturing Overhead Costs

```
                                    ┌─────────────────────┐
                                    │ Fixed Manufacturing │
                                    │  Overhead Variance   │
                                    │       (FMOH)         │
                                    │     $55,000 U        │
                                    └─────────────────────┘
                                              │
                        ┌─────────────────────┴─────────────────────┐
┌──────────────────────┐      ┌──────────────────┐      ┌──────────────────────┐
│ Both Static- and     │      │   FMOH Rate      │      │ FMOH Production-     │
│ Flexible-Budget       │  =   │   Variance       │      │ Volume Variance      │
│ Variance for          │      │   $9,000 U       │      │    $46,000 U         │
│ FMOH $9,000 U*        │      └──────────────────┘      └──────────────────────┘
└──────────────────────┘
```

*This refers to only fixed manufacturing overhead variance—the total manufacturing overhead variance would have to include the additional variable manufacturing overhead variance.

EXHIBIT 8-4
Production-Volume Assigned Total Cost Behaviour

Fixed overhead allocation rate per jacket: $23.00

Quantity Actually Produced	Total Fixed Manufacturing Cost Assigned	Budgeted Fixed Manufacturing Overhead
1,000	$ 23,000	$276,000
4,000	92,000	276,000
8,000	184,000	276,000
10,000	230,000	276,000
12,000	**276,000**	**276,000**
14,000	322,000	276,000

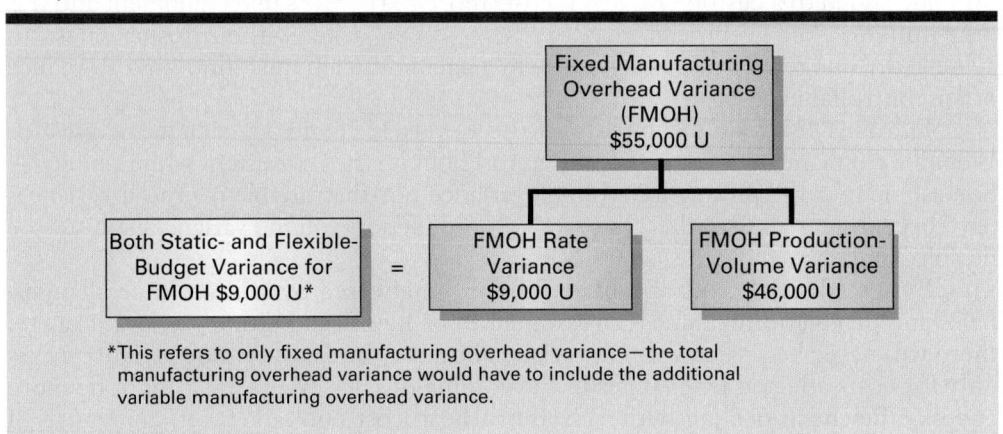

produced and sold is the straight line at the top of the graph. The sloped line indicates what the total FMOH *should* have been if Webb could have matched its capacity available as actual Q produced and sold varied. At Q = 10,000 produced and sold the assigned amount Webb *should* have spent is $230,000/month using the budgeted rate. But the total FMOH is fixed, irrespective of the Q actually produced, at $276,000/month.

The gap between the point on the sloped line and the horizontal line is the production volume variance. When the points on the sloped line are below the horizontal line, the variance is unfavourable. The actual FMOH cost for the actual output is higher than what the actual output *should* have cost. Where the actual and budgeted Q are equal, the sloped and horizontal lines intersect and the production-volume variance is zero. Where the sloped line exceeds the horizontal line, the actual cost of $276,000 incurred is less than what the actual output should have cost. The calculation of production-volume variance is as follows:

$$\begin{array}{l} \text{Production-volume} \\ \text{variance} \end{array} = \begin{array}{c} \text{Budgeted} \\ \text{fixed} \\ \text{overhead} \end{array} - \left(\begin{array}{c} \text{Total fixed} \\ \text{overhead assigned} \\ \text{for actual output} \end{array} \times \begin{array}{c} \text{Budgeted fixed} \\ \text{overhead rate} \end{array} \right)$$

$$= \$276,000 - (0.40 \text{ MH per jacket} \times 10,000 \text{ jackets} \times \$57.50 \text{ per MH})$$

$$= \$276,000 - (4,000 \text{ MH} \times \$57.50 \text{ per MH})$$

$$= \$276,000 - \$230,000$$

$$= \$46,000 \text{ U}$$

The total FMOH cost pool is the budgeted fixed overhead of $276,000. Assigned fixed overhead is calculated using the data in Exhibit 8-1. The budgeted DMH rate per jacket is multiplied by the actual quantity of jackets produced and sold. The result is then multiplied by the FMOH budgeted cost per direct machine hour. Unfortunately, Webb cannot vary the capacity available. It has paid for capacity at Q = 12,000 produced and sold. Exhibit 8-5 shows the Level 3 variance analysis for Webb Company for the month of April.

Interpretation of Production-Volume Variance   Inevitably, there will almost always be a production-volume variance reported. The capacity level to calculate the fixed overhead rate is the budgeted value selected from among four alternatives.

EXHIBIT 8-5
Flexible-Budget Level 3 Variance Analysis for Webb Company for April 2013

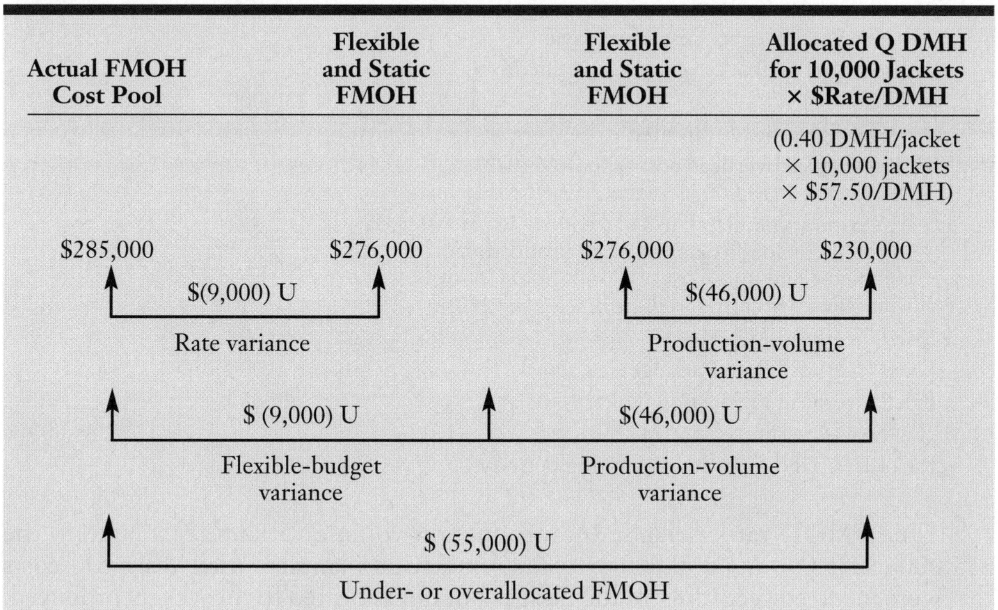

Actual FMOH Cost Pool	Flexible and Static FMOH	Flexible and Static FMOH	Allocated Q DMH for 10,000 Jackets × $Rate/DMH
			(0.40 DMH/jacket × 10,000 jackets × $57.50/DMH)
$285,000	$276,000	$276,000	$230,000
	$(9,000) U		$(46,000) U
	Rate variance		Production-volume variance
	$ (9,000) U		$(46,000) U
	Flexible-budget variance		Production-volume variance
		$ (55,000) U	
		Under- or overallocated FMOH	

The fixed manufacturing overhead rate is the FMOH cost pool divided by capacity, assumed in this example to be Q = 12,000 jackets. Production-volume variance is an opportunity cost. Webb paid for the opportunity, the benefit from producing and selling 12,000 jackets in April, and produced and sold only Q = 10,000.

Webb's management team must determine why this occurred. Perhaps the sales price of $185/jacket instead of $180/jacket affected demand and that is why the amount produced and sold was less than what the management team committed to in the budget. If true, and the team at Webb ignores this variance, then the gross margin will continue to be lower than expected. Refusing to adjust the sales price to match the price consumers are willing to pay impairs, not maximizes, operating income. Webb's cost of equipment is a sunk cost and the investment was made in anticipation of meeting monthly consumer demand with capacity to produce 12,000 jackets. Overpricing will cause a persistent shortfall in profit.

Perhaps there was an unexpected equipment malfunction that caused both idle time while repairs were made and overtime to make up volume when equipment was operational again. We already know there was an unfavourable price and efficiency variance for direct labour, and equipment malfunction could explain all three variances. This is temporary and the management team would have less cause for concern. It may be that Webb's management team increased the price per jacket in the hope it would minimize impairment to operating income. In this case the team made a good decision and profit from an extra $5.00/jacket could persist.

Imagine that Webb only had capacity to produce 8,000 jackets and needed to increase capacity to meet an anticipated growth in demand of 10,000 jackets in the first quarter of the year, increasing gradually to 12,000 jackets by the middle of next year. If capacity can only be added in 4,000-jacket increments, then Webb's expansion will increase its practical capacity to 12,000 jackets. GAAP requires this amount be used to calculate FMOH values of inventory and cost of goods sold. In this case there will automatically be a production volume variance until actual demand and production grow to 12,000.

JOURNAL ENTRIES FOR FIXED OVERHEAD COSTS AND VARIANCES

The journal entries are illustrated below for the month of April using the Fixed Overhead Control and the contra account Fixed Overhead Allocated. These data are identical to those in Exhibit 8-12 Panel B. The fixed manufacturing overhead variances are the same as those shown in Exhibit 8-3. The reconciliation of the two data sets will be explained by the variable cost variances in the next section.

1. Fixed Overhead Control	285,000	
Salaries, lease, tax, insurance payable		285,000
To record actual fixed overhead costs incurred		
2. WIP Control	230,000	
Fixed Overhead Allocated		230,000
To record fixed overhead costs allocated (0.40 MH/jacket × 10,000 jackets × $57.50/MH)		
The costs accumulated in WIP control are transferred to Finished Goods Control when production is completed and into Cost of Goods Sold Control when the goods are sold (Ch. 4)		
3. Fixed Overhead Allocated	230,000	
Fixed Overhead Rate Variance	9,000	
Fixed Overhead Production-Volume Variance	46,000	
Fixed Overhead Control		285,000
Records variances for the accounting period		

The FMOH rate variance and production-volume variance reconcile to the $55,000 ($285,000 − $230,000 = $55,000) of fixed manufacturing overhead costs that were incurred according to the budget but not allocated to the jackets produced. These are the underallocated fixed overhead costs from normal costing (introduced in Chapter 4).

How the FMOH variance is treated at the end of the fiscal year depends on its materiality. If it is immaterial, it may be either written off to Cost of Goods Sold or prorated among the Work-In-Process Control, Finished Goods Control, and Cost of Goods Sold accounts on the basis of the fixed overhead allocated to these accounts. This process was described in detail in Chapter 4 in Learning Objective 5. Some companies combine the write-off and proration methods. They write off the portion of variance arising from inefficiency that could have been avoided, and then prorate the portion that was unavoidable. If the balance in the Fixed Overhead Rate Variance account at the end of April is also the year-end balance in December and is immaterial, then the following journal entry records the write-off to Cost of Goods Sold:

Cost of Goods Sold	9,000	
Fixed Overhead Rate Variance		9,000

Also assume that the balance in the Fixed Overhead Rate Variance account at the end of April remains unchanged and is the year-end balance in December. Assume there is some WIP and finished goods inventory at December 31. There is some argument about the appropriate treatment of an unfavourable production-volume variance. Some accountants contend that the $46,000 U measures the cost of resources expended in anticipation of 2,000 jackets that were not produced ($23/jacket × 2,000 jackets = $46,000). Prorating would inappropriately allocate fixed overhead costs incurred for jackets not produced to those that were produced. In principle, the jackets produced already bear their fair share of the burden of overhead incurred during the year. This interpretation favours charging the unfavourable production-volume variance against the year's revenue to ensure that the fixed costs of unused capacity are not carried in the WIP and finished goods inventories. This avoids an understatement of cost of goods sold from an overstated inventory valuation.

Alternatively, some accountants look at the choice of a denominator level as merely an estimate of the fixed capacity needed to produce jackets. Unforeseen events happen randomly, which can cause the actual capacity to differ from the denominator level. Such random events in April led to the production of 10,000 jackets rather than the planned 12,000. We know this because there is no systematic and repeated unfavourable production-volume variance in months leading to year-end. The budgeted $276,000 supported the cost of manufacturing the 10,000 jackets. Therefore, it is appropriate to prorate this fixed overhead cost to the jackets to properly allocate the costs to the remaining WIP and finished goods inventories.

Favourable production-volume variances could also arise. Assume Webb had manufactured and sold 13,800 jackets in April:

$$\text{Production-volume variance} = \text{Budgeted fixed overhead} - \text{Fixed overhead allocated using the budgeted cost per output unit overhead allowed for the actual output produced}$$

$$= \$276,000 - (\$23/\text{jacket} \times 13,800 \text{ jackets})$$

$$= \$276,000 - \$317,400$$

$$= \$41,400 \text{ F}$$

The fixed overhead costs of $276,000 in this situation supported the production of all 13,800 jackets and must be allocated to the actual production volume. The more conservative approach is to prorate the favourable production-volume variance of $41,400 to reduce the value of WIP and finished goods inventories because this will increase the cost of goods sold, which reduces the reported gross margin and in turn the operating income. Crediting the entire amount to cost of goods sold would result in a higher reported operating income.

Recall that the process of setting standards used for a budget is complex, and if variances were always written off to cost of goods sold there would be temptation for managers to set standards to affect financial reports rather than to improve operating and strategic management decisions. The denominator level could be chosen to increase (for financial-reporting purposes) or decrease (for tax purposes) the reported operating income. Webb could generate a favourable (or unfavourable) production-volume

Cost Allocation Base Denominator Decision: There Is a Right Way

A lower capacity level avoids unfavourable variances that reduce operating income. If Webb's management team had chosen 48,000 instead of 57,600 direct machine hours, then the FMOH cost allocation rate would have been applied to 10,000 jackets per month, not 12,000. But equipment capacity is a fact, not a choice. To be relevant, data such as FMOH rates need to be unbiased or the managers' decisions will be biased.

The CMA code of ethics requires (in part) that "A Member will act at all times with: (i) responsibility for and fidelity to public needs." The investing public needs unbiased reports of net income to make rational investing decisions. A biased allocation rate will temporarily understate cost of goods sold, gross margin, and inventory values. Bias can result in material misstatement of the actual economic strength of a company.

variance by setting the denominator level to allocate fixed overhead costs either low (or high) to either increase (or decrease) reported operating income.

Each approach has its strengths and weaknesses and the procedure is a matter of professional judgment assessed case by case. If Webb wrote off the production-volume variance to Cost of Goods Sold, the journal entry would be:

Fixed Overhead Production-Volume Variance	41,400	
Cost of Goods Sold		41,400

FLEXIBLE-BUDGET VARIABLE OVERHEAD VARIANCES

② Establish variable overhead cost allocation rates; calculate and analyze flexible-budget variances.

Among Webb's variable manufacturing overhead costs are energy, machine maintenance, engineering support, indirect materials, and indirect manufacturing labour.

Webb's management team uses direct machine hours as the cost allocation base and a single variable overhead cost pool budgeted at $1,728,000 for the year. Monthly variable overhead has been budgeted at $144,000, given the same budgeted Q = 12,000 jackets produced and sold.

VARIABLE OVERHEAD COST VARIANCE CALCULATIONS AND ANALYSES

The Webb Company summary information for April is as shown:

Overhead Category	Actual Results	Flexible-Budget Amount (for 10,000 Output Units)	Static-Budget Amount (for 12,000 Output Units)
Variable manufacturing overhead	$130,500	$120,000	$144,000
Variable marketing overhead	45,700	50,000	60,000

The variable manufacturing overhead (VMOH) cost per input unit is \$30.00/DMH (\$1,728,000 ÷ 57,600 DMH). Webb's cost per output is \$12/jacket (at \$30.00/DMH × 0.40 DMH/jacket). This rate will be used both in the static budget and the monthly performance reports:

Flexible- and Static-Budgeted Amounts for the Year

VMOH* (1)	DMH/Year (2)	Rate per DMH (3) = (1) ÷ (2)	Q Jackets/ year (4)	DMH/ Jacket (5) = (2) ÷ (4)	Rate per Jacket (6) = (3) × (5)
\$ 1,728,000	57,600	\$ 30.00	144,000	0.40	\$ 12.00

*Annual VMOH = \$144,000 × 12

The budgeted variable manufacturing overhead and the actual rate per jacket in April has been reported as:

Item	Actual Results	Flexible-Budget Amount (for 10,000 output units)	Static-Budget Amount (for 12,000 output units)
1. Variable overhead costs	\$130,500	\$120,000	\$144,000
2. DMH	4,500	4,000	4,800
3. Output, jackets	10,000	10,000	12,000
4. DMH/jacket (2 ÷ 3)	0.45	0.40	0.40
5. Variable overhead cost (1 ÷ 2)	\$ 29.00	\$ 30.00	\$ 30.00
6. Variable overhead rate/DMH (1 ÷ 2)	\$ 13.05	\$ 12.00	\$ 12.00

The Level 0 static-budget variance is not sufficiently informative; therefore, this discussion begins with the Level 1 static-budget variance for Webb's VMOH, which is \$13,500 F:

$$\text{Variable overhead}\atop\text{static-budget variance} = {\text{Actual}\atop\text{results}} - {\text{Static-budget}\atop\text{amount}}$$

$$= \$130,500 - \$144,000$$

$$= \$13,500 \text{ F}$$

Unfortunately, the result of a simple subtraction provides no insight into what caused the variance. More insight is gained by analyzing the relationships among the Levels 2 and 3 variances, as illustrated in Exhibit 8-6.

EXHIBIT 8-6
Flexible-Budget Level 1, 2, 3 Variable Manufacturing Overhead Analyses

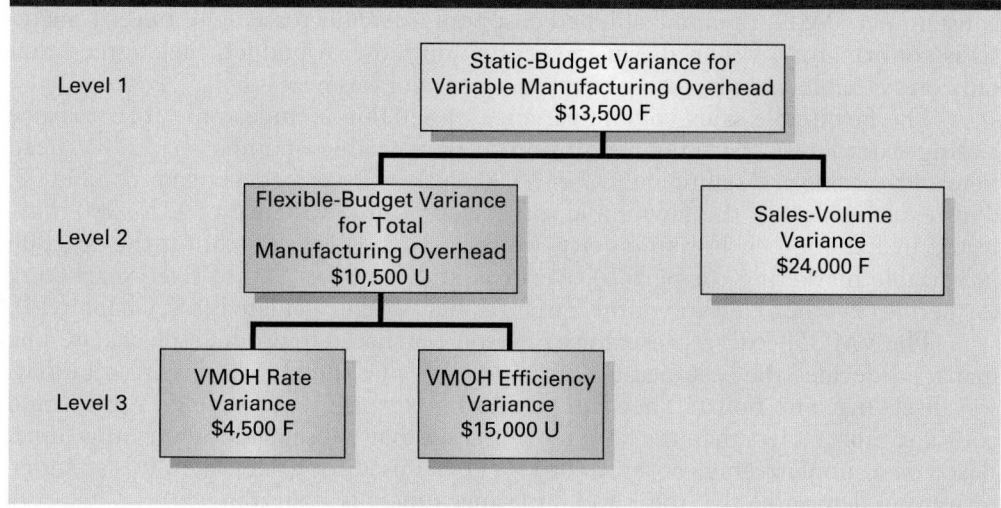

EXHIBIT 8-7
Static-Budget and Flexible-Budget Analysis of Variable Manufacturing Overhead Costs

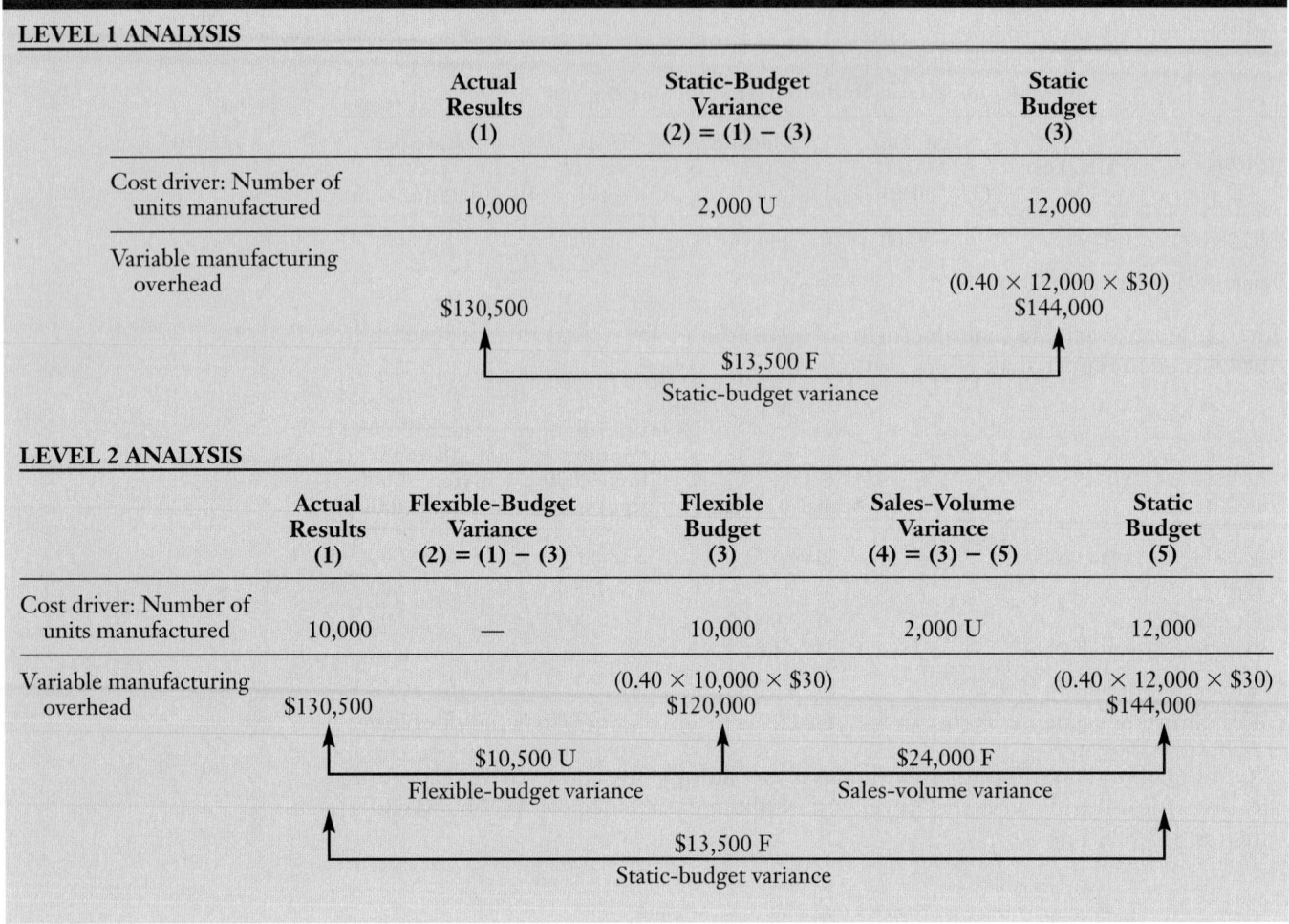

LEVEL 1 ANALYSIS

	Actual Results (1)	Static-Budget Variance (2) = (1) − (3)	Static Budget (3)
Cost driver: Number of units manufactured	10,000	2,000 U	12,000
Variable manufacturing overhead	$130,500		(0.40 × 12,000 × $30) $144,000

$13,500 F
Static-budget variance

LEVEL 2 ANALYSIS

	Actual Results (1)	Flexible-Budget Variance (2) = (1) − (3)	Flexible Budget (3)	Sales-Volume Variance (4) = (3) − (5)	Static Budget (5)
Cost driver: Number of units manufactured	10,000	—	10,000	2,000 U	12,000
Variable manufacturing overhead	$130,500		(0.40 × 10,000 × $30) $120,000		(0.40 × 12,000 × $30) $144,000

$10,500 U
Flexible-budget variance

$24,000 F
Sales-volume variance

$13,500 F
Static-budget variance

The Level 2 flexible-budget analysis will get the attention of the management team. The April flexible budget for variable manufacturing overhead is $120,000 $(0.4 \times 10{,}000 \times \$30)$. This is the amount Webb should have incurred to produce and sell $Q = 10{,}000$ jackets, as shown in Exhibit 8-7.

Interpretation of the Level 1 Variance Analysis   It is entirely to be expected that, when there is a reduction in quantity of jackets produced, the total variable manufacturing overhead cost will decrease, all other things being equal. Because the direct machine-hours decrease while the variable manufacturing overhead rate remains constant per DMH, the total assigned cost pool *should* decrease. The Level 1 analysis is confirmatory. When the managers committed to a budget, they agreed that only one variable manufacturing overhead cost pool was necessary.

The favourable sales-volume variance of $24,000 includes only that variance arising from lower shared consumption of the variable manufacturing overhead items. Producing and selling only $Q = 10{,}000$ jackets generated a savings of $24,000. This explains part of the favourable total sales-volume variance of $162,000 illustrated in Exhibit 7-5. For simplicity, we have excluded discussion of the $50,000 in variable marketing (or period) overhead and the $434,000 of fixed marketing (or period) overhead, although the variances have been calculated (see Chapter 14).

The VMOH costs represent use of resources shared to produce all jackets. The managers decided the best measure of benefit or value added from sharing all inputs was direct machine-hours. They had no reason to expect that jackets in April would consume more or less than the 0.40 DMH/jacket than those made at any other time. Based on a simple average cost rate of $30/DMH used for each jacket, it is straightforward to determine that the Level 1 variance report is misleading.

If Webb's use of common production resources had been for Q = 12,000 jackets produced and sold then the Level 1 analysis would be more useful. But this is a "what if" approach rather than a "what is" approach. The better alternative is to compare what the variable manufacturing cost *should* have been when Q = 10,000 jackets to what they actually were in April. Webb's managers need to work with their economic reality. This is particularly important when the cost pool being analyzed is a variable cost pool.

LEVEL 2 VARIABLE MANUFACTURING OVERHEAD VARIANCE ANALYSIS

The Level 2 analysis reports that what *should* have been spent on variable manufacturing overhead was $120,000. This amount is the result of the VMOH rate of $12/jacket (0.40 DMH/jacket × $30/DMH) to which managers committed when they approved the budget, multiplied by the actual Q = 10,000 jackets produced and sold. The actual amount spent on variable manufacturing overhead was higher:

$$\frac{\text{Variable overhead}}{\text{flexible-budget variance}} = \frac{\text{Actual}}{\text{result}} - \frac{\text{Flexible-budget}}{\text{amount}}$$

$$= \$130,500 - \$120,000$$

$$= \$10,500 \text{ U}$$

Interpretation of the Level 2 Variance Analysis   The consumption of common resources per jacket exceeded what it *should* have been by $10,500. The economic reality is that Webb failed to earn what it should have in operating income in April. Either the DMH/jacket or the rate per DMH exceeded the amount the managers had committed to spend. Webb's management team now knows that the operations in April were economically poor. Something is out of control in production, and a Level 3 analysis will give managers insight into why they failed.

LEVEL 3 VARIABLE MANUFACTURING OVERHEAD EFFICIENCY AND RATE VARIANCES

At Level 3, Webb's management team will isolate the VMOH variance arising from using too many DMH per jacket from the variance arising from paying too high a rate per DMH. Recall that overall this company fell short of budget by a total of $237,000, only $162,000 of which can be explained by the lower output level and of that, $24,000 or about 15% in savings came from VMOH ($24,000 ÷ $162,000). Of the remaining $75,000 ($237,000 − $162,000), approximately 14% ($10,500 ÷ $75,000) can be attributed to the variable manufacturing overhead variance. It is a significant source of unfavourable variance.

The **variable overhead efficiency variance** measures the efficiency with which the DMH have been used to produce jackets. It is a way to measure yield. The budgeted 0.40 DMH/jacket multiplied by 10,000 jackets is multiplied by budgeted rate of $30/DMH and the result is the $15,000 U efficiency variance shown in the first calculation.

The **variable overhead rate variance** is the difference between actual cost per unit for the DMH and budgeted cost per unit of $30/DMH (cost allocation base), or what *should* have been used. The result of the subtraction is then multiplied by the actual quantity of DMH used to produce actual output:

$$\frac{\text{Variable overhead}}{\text{efficiency variance}} = \begin{pmatrix} \text{Actual units of} & \text{Budgeted units of} \\ \text{variable overhead} & \text{variable overhead} \\ \text{cost allocation base} - \text{cost allocation base} \\ \text{used for actual output} & \text{allowed for actual} \\ \text{units achieved} & \text{output units achieved} \end{pmatrix} \times \begin{array}{c} \text{Budgeted} \\ \text{variable overhead} \\ \text{cost allocation rate} \end{array}$$

$$= [4{,}500 \text{ DMH} - (10{,}000 \text{ units} \times 0.40 \text{ DMH/unit})] \times \$30 \text{ per DMH}$$

$$= (4{,}500 \text{ DMH} - 4{,}000 \text{ DMH}) \times \$30 \text{ per DMH}$$

$$= 500 \text{ DMH} \times \$30 \text{ per DMH}$$

$$= \$15{,}000 \text{ U}$$

$$\begin{array}{c}\text{Variable overhead} \\ \text{rate variance}\end{array} = \begin{pmatrix}\text{Actual variable} \\ \text{overhead cost} \\ \text{per unit of cost} \\ \text{allocation base}\end{pmatrix} - \begin{pmatrix}\text{Budgeted variable} \\ \text{overhead cost per} \\ \text{unit of cost} \\ \text{allocation base}\end{pmatrix} \times \begin{pmatrix}\text{Actual quantity of variable} \\ \text{overhead cost allocation} \\ \text{base used for actual} \\ \text{output units achieved}\end{pmatrix}$$

$$= (\$29 \text{ per DMH} - \$30 \text{ per DMH}) \times 4{,}500 \text{ DMH}$$

$$= -\$1 \text{ per DMH} \times 4{,}500 \text{ DMH}$$

$$= \$4{,}500 \text{ F}$$

It is important to remember that although the Level 3 direct and indirect variances are called the same, the VMOH is not caused by nor is it explained by the DMH consumed. The VMOH inputs include janitorial labour and supplies, maintenance labour and supplies, and fringe benefits. These inputs are shared throughout the production of all jackets. The measure of benefit provided to all jackets is a decision made by Webb's managers. They have decided that the best measure of benefit is direct machine-hours, DMH.

As the DMH/jacket changes, the total VMOH cost pool assigned to each jacket will change because of the arithmetic relationship between cost and benefit created by the managers. In their judgment this is the best measure of economic reality at Webb. There is no direct relationship between the DMH cost driver and the total amount in the VMOH cost pool. The relationship is not causal but rather one of cost and benefit. In columnar format, Exhibit 8-8 reconciles the Levels 2 and 3 variance analyses.

Interpretation of the Level 3 Variance Analysis   Webb's unfavourable efficiency variance of $15,000 means that actual DMH used per jacket exceeded budget. The yield or quantity of jackets produced was too low for the DMH used. In fact, at $12/jacket, Webb should have produced 11,250 jackets for sale ($135,000 ÷ $12/jacket). Possible causes for the deterioration in the relationship between shared input and shared benefit are as varied as the resource costs accumulated in this single variable manufacturing overhead cost pool. For example, the efficiency variance may have arisen because of any of the following reasons:

◆ Machine malfunction because of poor maintenance resulting in more time per jacket than 0.40 DMH.

EXHIBIT 8-8
Columnar Presentation of Variance Analysis: Variable Manufacturing Overhead for Webb Company

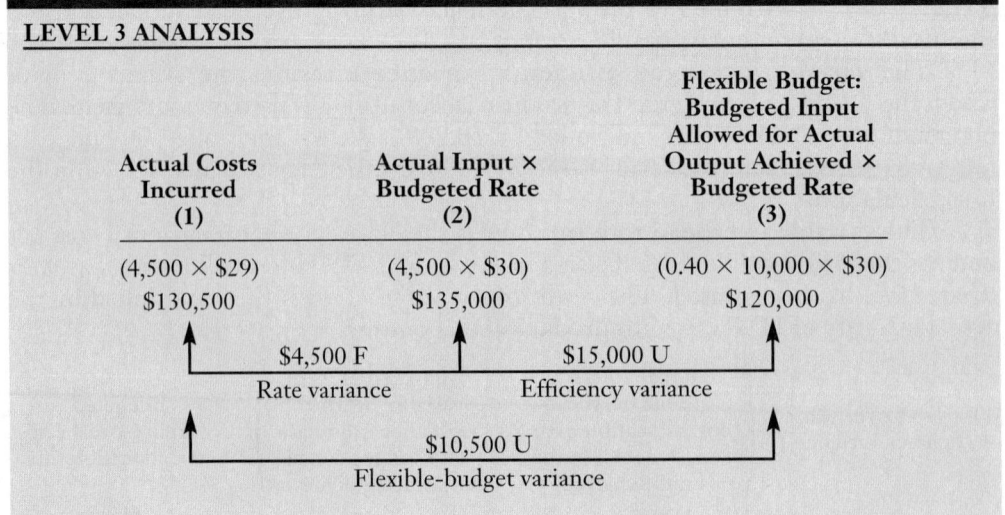

- Poor production scheduling resulting in too much idle time waiting for the materials to be cut and moved to the sewing area.
- Poor coordination between sales and production resulting in displacement of normal batches by rush orders and excessive setup times.
- Poor quality of materials resulting in downtime to clean the machines of debris when the materials disintegrated during sewing.

In the analysis of the production volume variance, the difference in the capacity purchased and the capacity used could be explained in part by neglecting machine maintenance. It is reasonable to expect that DMH actually used per jacket would be unfavourably affected by downtime. In fact, what the four potential causes have in common is that they interrupt access to the benefits provided by well-working machinery.

The favourable rate variance may arise from the manufacturing labour portion of VMOH, any variable utilities costs, or reduction in quantities of supplies purchased and used, for example:

- Probationary workers receive no paid leave for idle time and no other discretionary benefits resulting in lower fringe benefit costs.
- Statutory holidays resulting in lower custodial costs from fewer cleaning hours paid and lower quantity of cleaning supplies used.
- Statutory holidays resulting in lower consumption of utilities.
- Change in classification of an input from an indirect to a direct cost.

If the turnover is high at Webb and there is a probation period, then new hires may receive no pay for idle time and no discretionary medical or dental fringe benefits. Therefore, the $4,500 F in the rate variance could be attributed to the turnover.

The actual costs of individual items included in variable manufacturing overhead cost pools, for example, cleaning or security supplies, could have been lower than expected in April. The favourable rates could be the result of skillful negotiation on the part of the purchasing manager or oversupply in the market.

The actual usage of individual items included in variable overhead differs from the budgeted use. If the actual energy consumed was 32,400 kilowatt-hours (kWh) compared to a flexible budget amount of 30,000 kWh, then the 8% increase [(32,400 kWh – 30,000 kWh) ÷ 30,000 kWh = 8%] powered a 12.5% increase in DMH [(4,500 DMH – 4,000 DMH) ÷ 4,000 DMH = 12.5%]. The cost of additional energy supported proportionally more DMH, which gave rise to the favourable rate variance.

The use of cotton thread for sewing jackets illustrates the difference between the efficiency variance for direct cost inputs and the efficiency variance for variable overhead cost categories. If Webb classifies garment patch labels as a direct cost item, the direct materials efficiency variance will indicate whether more patch labels per jacket were used than was budgeted for the actual output achieved. If Webb classifies patch labels as an indirect cost, then cost of patch label use will not affect the VMOH efficiency variance. Variance in the cost of patch label use will be shown in the VMOH rate variance.

Based on their analysis of the situation, the key cause of Webb's unfavourable flexible-budget manufacturing overhead variance is that the actual use of machine-hours is higher than budgeted. Webb's managers decided to reduce some capacity use but had to maintain excess capacity, which could perhaps be used for production outsourced to them by other manufacturers. Exhibit 8-9 excludes all direct and non-manufacturing overhead variances.[2]

Webb's costing system distinguished between variable and fixed overhead cost pools. Some companies do not segregate their overhead costs this way. For these

---

[2]Reconciling to Chapter 7, Exhibit 7-7, from data in Exhibit 7-4, non-manufacturing overhead is $14,000 F ($420,000 – $434,000) while the FMOH is $9,000 U for net total fixed cost variance of $5,000 F. Variable non-manufacturing overhead is $4,300 F ($45,700 – $50,000) while the VMOH is $10,500 U for a net total variable cost variance of $6,200 U ($4,300 – $10,500).

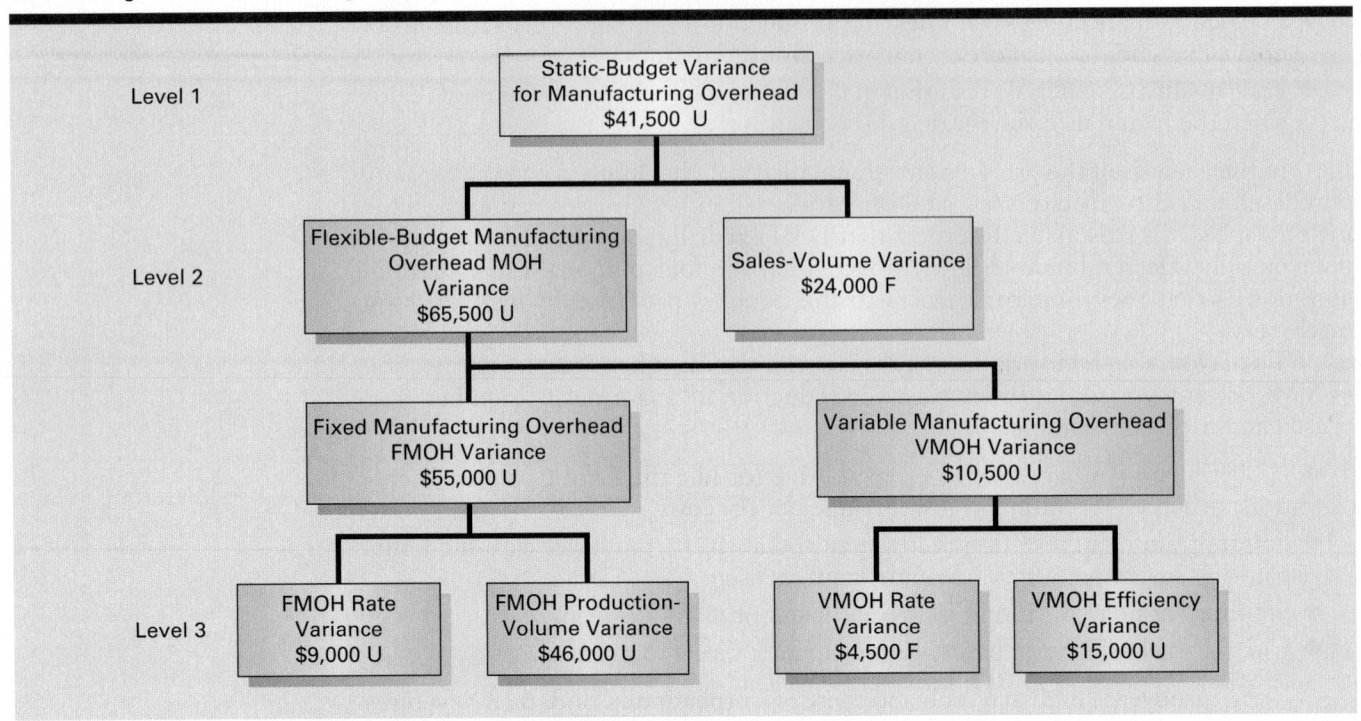

companies, all overhead costs are assumed to be fixed when conducting variance analyses. Any interpretation of the variance analysis for these companies will be limited because of the selection of this type of cost system.

JOURNAL ENTRIES FOR VARIABLE OVERHEAD COSTS AND VARIANCES

Variable Overhead Control and the contra account Variable Overhead Allocated are used for the journal entries for April (Exhibit 8-7):

1. Variable Overhead Control 130,500
       Utilities, wages, and other accounts payable 130,500
   Records actual variable overhead costs incurred

2. WIP Control 120,000
       Variable Overhead Allocated 120,000
   To record variable overhead costs allocated
       (0.40 DMH/jacket × 10,000 jackets × $30/DMH)

   The costs accumulated in WIP control are transferred
   to Finished Goods Control when production is completed
   and into Cost of Goods Sold Control when the goods
   are sold (Ch. 4).

3. Variable Overhead Allocated 120,000
   Variable Overhead Efficiency Variance 15,000
       Variable Overhead Control 130,500
       Variable Overhead Rate Variance 4,500
   Records variances for the accounting period

The variances arise because of underallocated or overallocated variable overhead costs. At the end of the fiscal year, the treatment of a variance depends on whether it is significant or not. If the variances are not significant, then the variance accounts are written off to cost of goods sold. If the variances are significant, then they are prorated among WIP Control, Finished Goods Control, and Cost of Goods Sold accounts on the basis of the variable overhead allocated to these accounts (see Chapter 4). Only the unavoidable costs are prorated and all avoidable variances are written off in the period. Assume that the April variances are also those at the end of the fiscal year and are not significant. The following journal entry records the write-off of the variance accounts to cost of goods sold:

Cost of Goods Sold	10,500	
Variable Overhead Rate Variance	4,500	
Variable Overhead Efficiency Variance		15,000

ACTIVITY-BASED COSTING AND VARIANCE ANALYSIS

Calculate ABC overhead variances. ③

ABC systems classify costs of various activities into a cost hierarchy: output-unit level, batch level, product sustaining, and facility sustaining. The basic principles and concepts for variable and fixed manufacturing overhead costs presented earlier in this chapter can be extended to ABC systems. In this section, we illustrate variance analysis for variable and fixed batch-level setup overhead costs. Batch-level costs are resources sacrificed on activities that are related to a group of units of product(s) or service(s) rather than to each individual unit of product or service.

Let's continue our example from Chapter 7 of Lyco Brass Works, which manufactures Jacutaps, a line of decorative brass faucets for Jacuzzis. Lyco manufactures Jacutaps in batches. To manufacture a batch of Jacutaps, Lyco must set up the machines and moulds to ensure the correct colour is injected into each batch. Setup is a skilled activity. Hence, a separate department is responsible for setting up machines and moulds for different types of Jacutaps. Lyco regards setup costs as overhead costs of products. Furthermore, set up requires that the machines be idle; machines cannot be set up for batches of, say, black taps when they are being used to produce batches of white taps.

Lyco wants to ensure that the cost of productive capacity is appropriately assigned according to benefit for distinct outputs. Lyco cannot run batches of different coloured taps unless they idle the machines to set them up. The benefit of setups is shared among all taps, and setup costs are incurred each time a new batch of product is going to be produced. In the ABC cost hierarchy, setup cost is a batch rather than a product cost.

Setup costs consist of some costs that are variable and some costs that are fixed with respect to the number of setup-hours. Variable costs of setup consist of hourly wages paid to setup labour and indirect support labour, costs of maintenance of setup equipment, and costs of indirect materials and energy used during setups. Fixed setup costs consist of salary costs of engineers, supervisors, and setup equipment leases.

Information regarding Jacutaps for 2013 follows:

	Static-Budget Amounts	Actual Amounts
1. Units of Jacutaps produced and sold	180,000	151,200
2. Batch size (units/batch)	150	140
3. Number of batches (Line 1 ÷ Line 2)	1,200	1,080
4. Setup-hours per batch	6	6.25
5. Total setup-hours (Line 3 × Line 4)	7,200	6,750
6. Variable overhead rate per setup hour	$ 20	$ 21
7. Variable setup overhead costs (Line 5 × Line 6)	$144,000	$141,750
8. Total fixed setup overhead costs	$216,000	$220,000

THE DECISION FRAMEWORK AND ABC VARIANCE ANALYSES

To prepare the flexible budget for variable setup overhead costs, Lyco starts with the actual units of output produced (151,200 units), then undertakes a series of inter-dependent processes. Development of ABC systems is a complex process. The management team at Lyco has carefully considered and chosen the best cost driver or measure of benefit for its batches of taps. The batch size (number of coloured taps) has also been selected as well as what variable and fixed costs will accumulate in the batch cost pool.

Now Lyco's managers can calculate the budgeted variable overhead setup cost driver rate per setup-hour. They can also calculate how many batches are required to produce an actual quantity of output units (e.g., blue taps) during a specified time period.

Lyco should have manufactured the 151,200 units of output in 1,008 batches (151,200 ÷ 150). Based on the quantity of setups, Lyco's managers calculate the quantity of setup-hours (cost driver) that should have been consumed for the actual number of batches during a specified time period. At the budgeted quantity of 6 setup hours per batch, 1,008 batches should have required 6,048 setup-hours (1,008 batches × 6 setup hours/batch). Notice that this is a flexible-budgeting approach to establishing variable overhead cost variances. What has changed is that the unit of measure is a different level in the cost hierarchy.

At this stage in the process, it is relatively straightforward to multiply the variable overhead setup cost driver rate by the budgeted (standard or benchmark) flexible quantity of setup hours for the actual output produced. The flexible-budget amount is 6,048 setup-hours × $20/setup-hour = $120,960.

$$\begin{array}{rl} \text{Flexible-budget} \\ \text{variance for variable} & = \dfrac{\text{Actual}}{\text{costs}} - \dfrac{\text{Flexible-budget}}{\text{costs}} \\ \text{setup overhead costs} \end{array}$$

$$= \begin{array}{c} 6{,}750 \text{ setup-hours} \\ \times\ \$21/\text{setup-hour} \end{array} - \begin{array}{c} 6{,}048 \text{ setup-hours} \\ \times\ \$20/\text{setup-hour} \end{array}$$

$$= \$141{,}750 - \$120{,}960$$

$$= \$20{,}790\ \text{U}$$

Exhibit 8-10 presents the variances for variable setup overhead costs in columnar form.

The flexible-budget variance for variable setup overhead costs can be subdivided into efficiency and rate variances.

$$\begin{array}{l} \text{Variable setup} \\ \text{overhead efficiency} \\ \text{variance} \end{array} = \left(\begin{array}{c} \text{Actual units of} \\ \text{variable overhead} \\ \text{cost allocation base} \\ \text{used for actual output} \end{array} - \begin{array}{c} \text{Budgeted units of} \\ \text{variable overhead cost} \\ \text{allocation base allowed} \\ \text{for actual output} \end{array} \right) \times \begin{array}{c} \text{Budgeted} \\ \text{variable} \\ \text{overhead rate} \end{array}$$

$$= (6{,}750 \text{ setup-hours} - 6{,}048 \text{ setup-hours}) \times \$20/\text{setup-hour}$$

$$= 702 \text{ setup-hours} \times \$20/\text{setup-hour}$$

$$= \$14{,}040\ \text{U}$$

EXHIBIT 8-10
Columnar Presentation of Variable Setup Overhead Variance Analysis for Lyco Brass Works for 2013

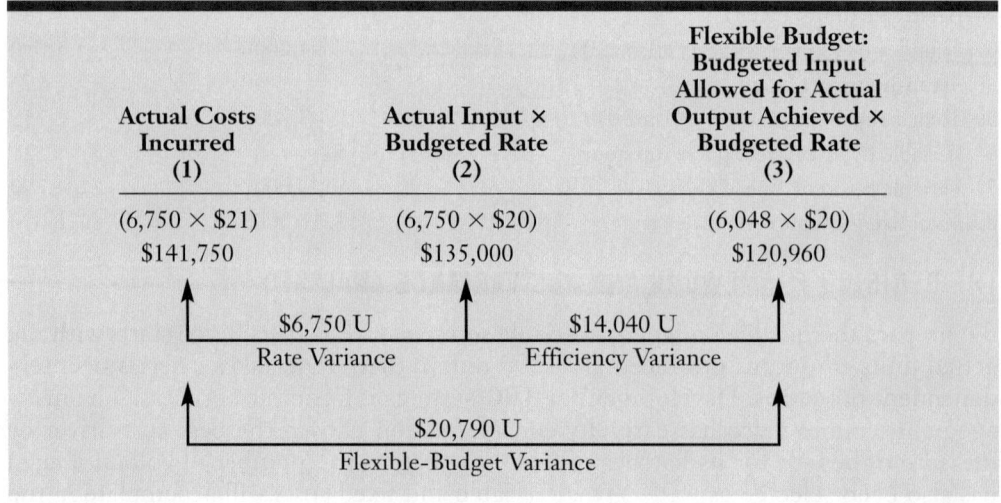

Interpretation of Variable Setup Overhead Efficiency Variance The unfavourable variable setup overhead efficiency variance of $14,040 arises because the actual number of setup-hours (6,750) exceeds the number of setup-hours that Lyco should have used (6,048) for the number of units it produced.

Two reasons for the unfavourable efficiency variance are (1) smaller actual batch sizes of 140 units instead of budgeted batch sizes of 150 units, which results in Lyco producing the 151,200 units in 1,080 batches instead of 1,008 batches, and (2) higher actual setup-hours per batch of 6.25 hours instead of the budgeted setup-hours per batch of 6 hours.

Explanations for smaller-than-budgeted batch sizes could include (1) quality problems if batch sizes exceed 140 faucets or (2) high costs of carrying inventory. Explanations for longer actual setup-hours per batch could include (1) problems with equipment, (2) unmotivated or inexperienced employees, or (3) inappropriate setup-time standards.

$$\begin{pmatrix} \text{Variable setup} \\ \text{overhead rate} \\ \text{variance} \end{pmatrix} = \begin{pmatrix} \text{Actual variable} & \text{Budgeted variable} \\ \text{overhead cost} & \text{overhead cost per} \\ \text{per unit of cost} - \text{unit of cost} \\ \text{allocation base} & \text{allocation base} \end{pmatrix} \times \begin{pmatrix} \text{Actual quantity of variable} \\ \text{overhead cost allocation} \\ \text{base used for actual output} \\ \text{units achieved} \end{pmatrix}$$

$$= (\$21/\text{setup-hour} - \$20/\text{setup-hour}) \times 6{,}750 \text{ setup-hours}$$

$$= \$1/\text{setup-hour} \times 6{,}750 \text{ setup-hours}$$

$$= \$6{,}750 \text{ U}$$

Interpretation of Variable Setup Overhead Rate Variance The unfavourable rate variance indicates that Lyco operated in 2013 with higher-than-budgeted variable overhead cost per setup-hour. Two main reasons that could contribute to the unfavourable rate variance are (1) the actual prices of individual items included in variable overhead, such as setup labour, indirect support labour, or energy, are higher than the budgeted prices, and (2) the actual quantity usage of individual items such as energy increases more than the increase in setup-hours, due perhaps to setups becoming more complex because of equipment problems. Thus, equipment problems could lead to an unfavourable efficiency variance because setup-hours increase, but they could also lead to an unfavourable rate variance because each setup-hour requires more resources from the setup-cost pool than the budgeted amounts. Identifying the reason for the variances is important because it helps managers plan for and take action to regain control. Let's now consider fixed setup overhead costs.

ABC VARIANCE ANALYSIS FOR FIXED MANUFACTURING OVERHEAD COST

For fixed setup overhead costs, the flexible-budget amount equals the static-budget amount of $216,000; there is no "flexing" of fixed costs over a relevant range of production.

$$\begin{array}{c} \text{Fixed setup overhead} \\ \text{flexible-budget variance} \end{array} = \begin{array}{c} \text{Actual} \\ \text{costs} \end{array} - \begin{array}{c} \text{Flexible-budget} \\ \text{costs} \end{array}$$

$$= \$220{,}000 - \$216{,}000$$

$$= \$4{,}000 \text{ U}$$

The fixed setup overhead rate variance is the same amount as the fixed overhead flexible-budget variance (because fixed overhead costs have no efficiency variance).

$$\begin{array}{c} \text{Fixed setup overhead} \\ \text{rate variance} \end{array} = \begin{array}{c} \text{Actual} \\ \text{costs} \end{array} - \begin{array}{c} \text{Flexible-budget} \\ \text{costs} \end{array}$$

$$= \$220{,}000 \text{ U} - \$216{,}000$$

$$= \$4{,}000$$

Interpretation of Fixed Setup Overhead Rate Variance The unfavourable fixed setup overhead rate variance could be due to lease costs of new setup equipment or higher salaries paid to engineers and supervisors. Lyco may have incurred these costs to alleviate some of the difficulties it was having in setting up machines.

Next Lyco will calculate its production volume variance. The budgeted cost allocation rate for fixed overhead setup costs for the year used MIS data. The annual budgeted setup-hours are 7,200. The budgeted fixed overhead cost pool for setups is $216,000. The fixed overhead rate is $30/setup-hour ($216,000 ÷ 7,200 setup-hours = $30/setup-hour).

$$\begin{array}{c} \text{Budgeted fixed setup} \\ \text{overhead rate} \end{array} = \frac{\text{Budgeted total costs in overhead cost pool}}{\text{Budgeted total quantity of cost allocation base}} = \frac{\$216,000}{7,200 \text{ setup-hours}}$$

During 2013, Lyco planned to produce 180,000 units of Jacutaps but actually produced only 151,200 units. The unfavourable production-volume variance measures the amount of extra fixed setup costs that Lyco incurred for setup capacity it planned to use but did not.

$$\begin{array}{c} \text{Production-volume} \\ \text{variance for fixed} \\ \text{setup overhead costs} \end{array} = \begin{array}{c} \text{Budgeted fixed} \\ \text{setup overhead} \\ \text{costs} \end{array} - \begin{array}{c} \text{Fixed setup overhead allocated} \\ \text{using budgeted input allowed for} \\ \text{actual output units produced} \end{array}$$

$$= \$216,000 - (1,008 \text{ batches} \times 6 \text{ hours per batch}) \times \$30/\text{setup-hour}$$

$$= \$216,000 - (6,048 \text{ setup-hours} \times \$30/\text{setup-hour})$$

$$= \$216,000 - \$181,440$$

$$= \$34,560 \text{ U}$$

Exhibit 8-11 presents and reconciles the ABC variance analyses of fixed setup overhead in columnar form.

Interpretation of Production Volume Variance One interpretation is that the unfavourable $34,560 production-volume variance represents inefficient utilization of setup capacity. However, Lyco may have earned higher operating income by selling 151,200 units at a higher price than what it would have earned by selling 180,000 units at a lower price. The production-volume variance should be interpreted cautiously based on full information.

EXHIBIT 8-11
Columnar Presentation of Fixed Setup Overhead Variance Analysis

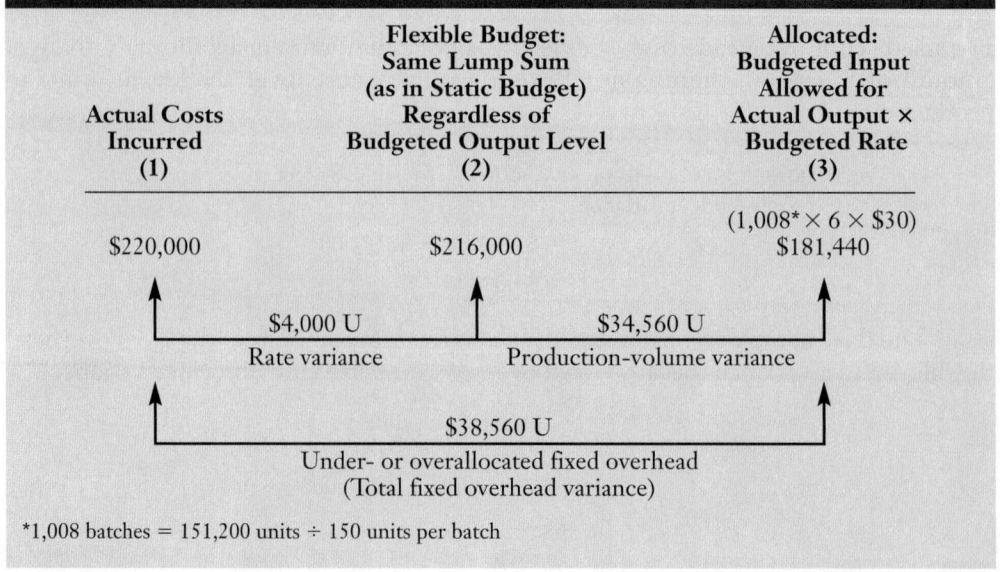

*1,008 batches = 151,200 units ÷ 150 units per batch

SUMMARY OF ALL OVERHEAD COST VARIANCES

All of these variances can be summarized in a simple table that eliminates unnecessary overhead variances from the model. A variable manufacturing overhead cost pool can never incur a production-volume variance. A fixed manufacturing overhead cost pool can never incur an efficiency variance. This simplifies Webb's presentation considerably. In total, the overhead manufacturing cost variance is $65,500 U, of which the majority is opportunity cost arising from underuse of capacity.

Integrate the fixed and variable overhead cost variance analyses to reconcile the actual overhead incurred with overhead allocated.

4

Four-Variance Analysis

	Rate Variance	Efficiency Variance	Production-Volume Variance
Variable manufacturing overhead	$4,500 F	$15,000 U	(Never a variance)
Fixed manufacturing overhead	$9,000 U	(Never a variance)	$46,000 U

The variances relate to the flexible-budget variance as shown in Exhibit 8-12: Panel A summarizes relationships among variable manufacturing overhead variances and Panel B summarizes those among fixed manufacturing overhead cost variances. In total, the flexible-budget variance for overhead costs is $65,500 U, the sum of the $10,500 U variable overhead variance and the $55,000 U fixed overhead variance.

Reporting overhead variances at this level of detail assists managers in large and complex businesses to focus attention on where actual or realized results did not meet expectations. In smaller and less complex businesses, managers might choose not to distinguish the variable from fixed overhead because they are very familiar with the causes of cost overruns.

The $65,500 unfavourable total manufacturing overhead variance for Webb Company in April 2013 is largely the result of the $46,000 unfavourable production-volume variance. Using the four-variance analysis presentation, the next-largest amount is the $15,000 unfavourable variable overhead efficiency variance. This variance arises from the additional 500 direct machine-hours used in April above the 4,000 direct machine-hours allowed to manufacture the 10,000 jackets. The two rate variances ($4,500 F and $9,000 U) partially offset each other. At this point the management team simply knows that some combination of changes to expected variable inputs included in the variable cost pool was favourable. The unexpected changes to fixed cost were, on balance, unfavourable during April.

Webb's variances may not be caused by independent events. For example, the company may have purchased lower-quality lubricants that caused a favourable variable overhead rate variance. Perhaps one result, however, was increased direct machine-hours per jacket, since the sewing needles moved more slowly, and an unfavourable variable overhead efficiency variance. In turn, this may have led to a smaller quantity of jackets produced, causing an unfavourable production-volume variance. This brief analysis highlights the interdependencies among factors of production, even in a simple jacket manufacturing company like Webb.

Panel A in Exhibit 8-12 illustrates the sources of flexible-budget variable overhead variance. The amount of variable overhead is always the flexible-budget amount because that is the definition of a variable cost. There is no production-volume variance arising from an actual cost allocation base consumption different from a denominator-level capacity choice. Variable overhead arises from use of shared resources. The benefit is measured by direct machine-hours but changes in the use of hours does not cause any change to the variable manufacturing cost pool.

In the next table, the two *rate* variances from the four-variance analysis have been combined to produce a three-variance analysis in the table. The only loss of information in the three-variance analysis is in the overhead rate variance area—only one rate variance is reported instead of separate variable and fixed overhead rate variances. Three-variance analysis is sometimes called **combined-variance analysis** because it combines variable-cost and fixed-cost variances when reporting overhead cost variances. Mixed costs have both a fixed and variable component. It would not

EXHIBIT 8-12
Columnar Presentation of Total Manufacturing Overhead Variance Analyses at Webb Company

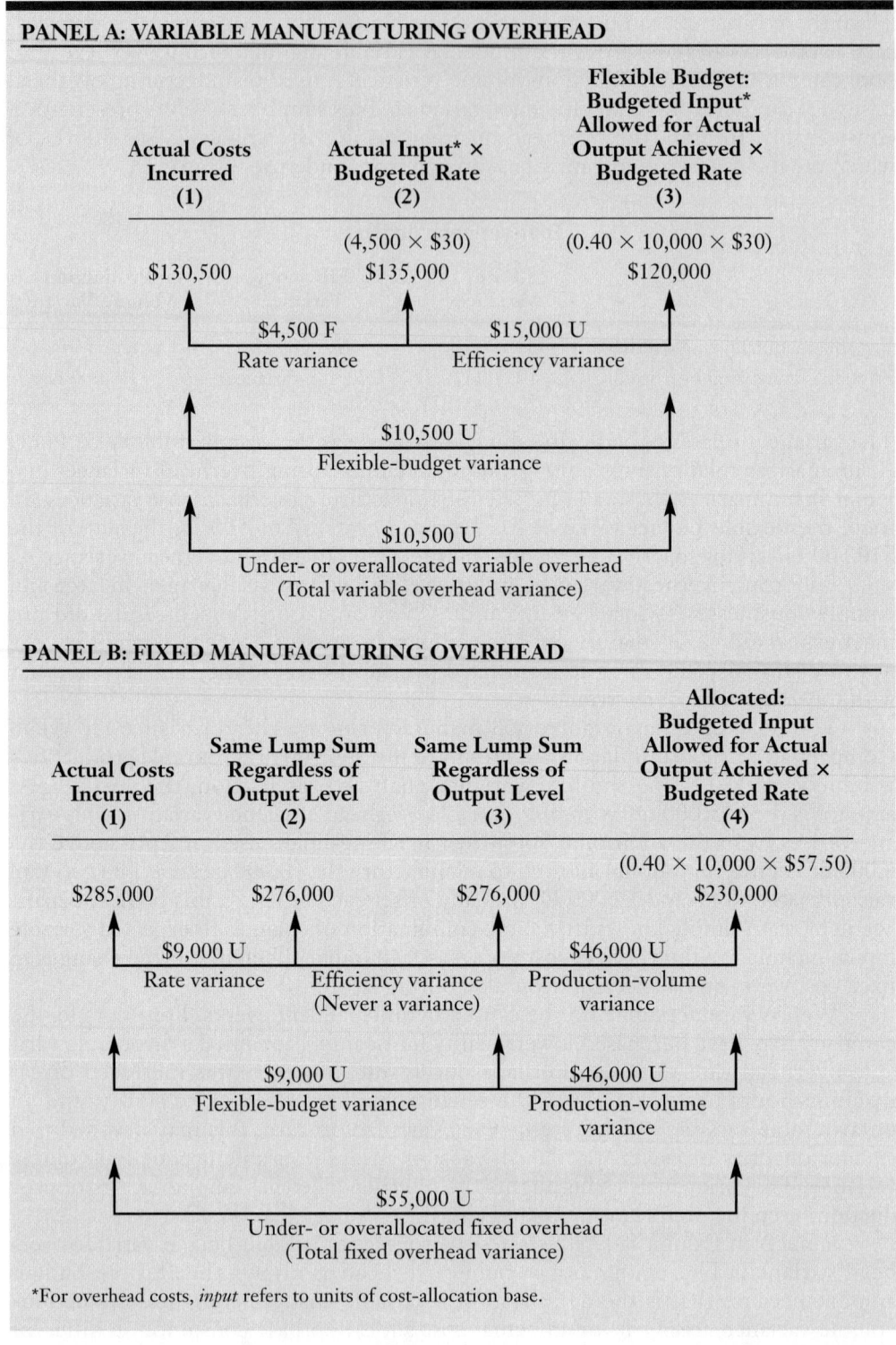

PANEL A: VARIABLE MANUFACTURING OVERHEAD

Actual Costs Incurred (1)	Actual Input* × Budgeted Rate (2)	Flexible Budget: Budgeted Input* Allowed for Actual Output Achieved × Budgeted Rate (3)
	(4,500 × $30)	(0.40 × 10,000 × $30)
$130,500	$135,000	$120,000

$4,500 F — Rate variance $15,000 U — Efficiency variance

$10,500 U — Flexible-budget variance

$10,500 U — Under- or overallocated variable overhead (Total variable overhead variance)

PANEL B: FIXED MANUFACTURING OVERHEAD

Actual Costs Incurred (1)	Same Lump Sum Regardless of Output Level (2)	Same Lump Sum Regardless of Output Level (3)	Allocated: Budgeted Input Allowed for Actual Output Achieved × Budgeted Rate (4)
			(0.40 × 10,000 × $57.50)
$285,000	$276,000	$276,000	$230,000

$9,000 U — Rate variance Efficiency variance (Never a variance) $46,000 U — Production-volume variance

$9,000 U — Flexible-budget variance $46,000 U — Production-volume variance

$55,000 U — Under- or overallocated fixed overhead (Total fixed overhead variance)

*For overhead costs, *input* refers to units of cost-allocation base.

be worthwhile to separate the components of these semivariable or semi-fixed costs, so combining them is sensible. This may well explain why the two overhead rate variances were combined.

Three-Variance Analysis

	Rate Variance	Efficiency Variance	Production-Volume Variance
Total manufacturing overhead	$4,500 U	$15,000 U	$46,000 U

The table below combines the rate and efficiency variances from the three-variance analysis into a two-variance analysis. The first cost pool includes the variable overhead rate and efficiency variances as well as the fixed overhead rate variance. In constructing these variances, it is not necessary to know the actual machine-hours because no efficiency variance is calculated.

Two-Variance Analysis

	Flexible-Budget Variance	Production-Volume Variance
Total manufacturing overhead	$19,500 U	$46,000 U

The single variance of $65,500 U in one-variance analysis is the sum of the flexible-budget variance and the production-volume variance under two-variance analysis. This simply reports the flexible-budget variance between the $415,500 ($130,500 + $285,000 = $415,500) total manufacturing overhead actually realized in April and the $350,000 ($120,000 + $230,000 = $350,000) budgeted manufacturing overhead allocated to produce 10,000 jackets (actual output) during that month.

One-Variance Analysis

	Total Overhead Variance
Total manufacturing overhead	$65,500 U

A **value-added cost** is one that, if eliminated, would reduce the value customers obtain from using the product or service. A **non-value-added cost** is one that, if eliminated, would not reduce the value customers obtain from using the product or service. For example, to offset problems that arise if suppliers fail to meet their delivery schedule, Webb inventories rolls of cloth in its warehouse. To the customer, a jacket sewn from cloth stored in a warehouse is no different from a jacket sewn from cloth delivered by a supplier directly to the production floor. Therefore, the activity of storing cloth is non-value-added for the customer, and managers view the manufacturing overhead costs associated with warehousing as non-value-added costs. There is a continuum between value-added costs and non-value-added costs. Many overhead cost items are in a grey, uncertain area between value-adding and non-value-adding costs.

As Webb's management team works through a plan to bring costs back under control the focus should be on eliminating non-value-added costs first. This is a strategic cost management approach to ensure that most of Webb's costs are value-added and therefore may be recovered when the jacket is sold.

CONCEPTS IN ACTION—STRATEGY

Interdependencies and Shared Benefits

Webb's attention has, so far, been directed by the most significant unfavourable variance. Yes, direct machine-hours is certainly a measurable and required resource, but in the value chain there are business functions beyond production. The team must be aware of a broader scope of effects than simply maximizing jackets produced per direct machine-hour.

The reason Webb is successful is beyond its corporate boundaries. It succeeds because it meets its customers' expectations of value in use from the jacket. Customer cost management views Webb's business function value chain through the eyes of the customer. Webb's team may also look out to those who do similar tasks best and replace a "do the best we can" with "do the best that can be done" cost management policy. These approaches to strategic cost management require an external perspective.

DIFFERENT PURPOSES OF MANUFACTURING OVERHEAD COST ANALYSIS

Different types of cost analysis may be appropriate for different purposes. Webb's variable manufacturing overhead is shown in Exhibit 8-4 as being variable, with respect to output units (jackets) produced, for both the planning and control purpose (p. 302) and the inventory costing purpose. The greater the number of output units manufactured, the higher the budgeted total variable manufacturing overhead costs and the amount allocated to output units.

Exhibit 8-4 also shows that, for the planning and control purpose, fixed overhead costs do not change in the 1,000- to 14,000-unit output range. Consider a monthly leasing cost of $20,000 for a building under a three-year leasing agreement. Managers control this fixed leasing cost at the time the lease is signed. During any month in the leasing period, management can do little to change this $20,000 lump sum payment. Contrast this description of fixed overhead with how these costs are depicted for the inventory costing purpose. Under GAAP, fixed manufacturing costs are capitalized as part of inventory on a unit-of-output basis. Every output unit that Webb manufactures will increase the fixed overhead allocated to products by $23/jacket ($57.50/DMH × 0.40 DMH/jacket). Managers should not use this unitization of fixed manufacturing overhead costs for their planning and control.

NON-MANUFACTURING VARIANCE ANALYSIS

⑤ Analyze non-manufacturing variances.

The overhead variances discussed in this chapter have been examples of *financial* performance measures. Services ranging from passenger air transportation to recuperative health care to management accounting are also provided by for-profit companies. A customer's **value proposition** is the satisfaction or value added the customer expects to receive from purchasing the product or service. Value propositions change quickly for service providers. To retain customers and remain profitable, service providers must respond quickly and appropriately to changes in both what their customers value and attributes for which they will pay.

NONFINANCIAL PERFORMANCE MEASURES

Nonfinancial performance measures include market share, on-time delivery performance (e.g., Purolator), customer acquisition rate, customer retention rate, and order time to completion. These measures will vary from one service industry to another. In the hospitality industry, a hotel would track nonfinancial measures of satisfaction with hotel location; room availability and reservations; check-in; room security, quietness, cleanliness, and amenities; restaurant and bar services; spa services; entertainment; and concierge services.[3] While the core services of a hotel are lodging and food, other ancillary services contribute to the customer's positive experience and satisfaction.

Effective and efficient customer response or **agility** implies a process of service design, implementation, and delivery with flexible performance indicators. It seems that at least four standards are required—quality, timeliness, customization, and cost—to capture measures of agility. The agile service company has the ability to excel simultaneously in quality, delivery time, customization, and cost in a coordinated way.[4]

Crucial for a profitable service provider is the customer's satisfaction. Where the value proposition is the customer's view of cost and benefit, what brings the customer back is satisfaction, a nonfinancial measure of value. Management accountants have applied cost estimation techniques to identify and measure nonfinancial factors contributing most to customers' satisfaction. Within the service sector, the selection

[3]A. Cuigini, A. Carù, and F. Zerbini, "The Cost of Customer Satisfaction: A Framework for Strategic Cost Management in Service Industries," *European Accounting Review*, 16.3 (2007): 499–530.
[4]L.J. Menor, A.V. Roth, and C.H. Mason, "Agility in Retail Banking: A Numerical Taxonomy of Strategic Service Groups," *Manufacturing and Service Operations Management*, 3.4 (Fall 2001): 273–292.

of standards is difficult to reconcile with the need for agility. Standards make for straightforward comparisons between customer segments but they are, by definition, constant. Ironically, agility requires solutions to problems that were not imagined when the standards were chosen. The challenge for management accountants is to provide excellent measures of a service company's economic reality that reflect a dynamic value proposition.

Strategically, service companies often must both customize their service and exercise cost leadership strategies to maintain profitability. Service companies may respond by segmenting their services based on types of customers. Satisfaction may arise from flexible responses by the provider to purchasing preference (rush orders, standing contracts), delivery (face-to-face, electronic), range of services (core, facilitating, peripheral), service provision (the vice-president, managers), and after-sale support. Overall, service companies can also examine a value chain beginning with the business acquisition and marketing, development of relationships, customer account maintenance, and customer account administration overhead. Non-manufacturing overhead or backroom operations would include contract management, billing, collections, and general administration such as technical and legal support.

Starbucks, for example, lost its place as first in customer loyalty in 2007 to Dunkin' Donuts. After analysis of the competition, Starbucks decided that its strategic approach had been inappropriate. The company had removed the roasting process and had automated espresso and cappuccino delivery, which reduced the time customers spent chatting with baristas. The relentless focus on controlling costs by changing internal processes did not conform to the value proposition of customers: Starbucks customers wanted the coffee "experience" rather than fast-food delivery.[5] Starbucks had improved the time and cost of service delivery but the quality of its service from the customers' point of view had deteriorated. One analytical approach is shown below:

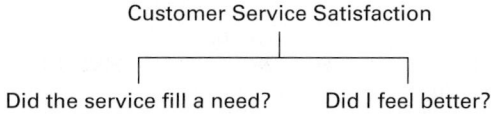

The two dimensions of satisfaction include a thoughtful or cognitive dimension and an emotional or affective dimension. For a Starbucks' customer, a cognitive response to satisfaction could be that a beverage quenched thirst in the anticipated way. The affective response could be delight, happiness, or contentment from being pampered at an affordable price. The chairman of Revlon once said, "We don't sell cosmetics; we sell hope" in an attempt to characterize the difference between the cognitive and affective dimensions of Revlon's products.

Service attributes such as timeliness appeal to cognitive satisfaction, while those such as quality and customization appeal to affective satisfaction. The smell of roasting and fresh ground coffee delighted the Starbucks customers who left to quench their thirst elsewhere when this perk was eliminated. More careful analysis of the multidimensional nature of what a cup of Starbucks meant to customers could have given managers information relevant to their decision, which changed the experience and meaning of purchasing a cup of Starbucks coffee.

Even in manufacturing environments, nonfinancial measures have proven value as indicators of benefit. Webb Company identified the following:

◆ Actual indirect materials usage in metres per machine-hour, compared with budgeted indirect materials usage in metres per machine-hour.

◆ Actual energy usage per machine-hour, compared with budgeted energy usage per machine-hour.

◆ Actual machining time per job, compared with budgeted machining time per job.

[5]K.A. Gjerde and S.B. Hughes, "Tracking Performance: When Less is More," *Management Accounting Quarterly*, 9.1 (2007): 1–12.

The measures all focused on the efficient use of capacity, Webb's most expensive and uncontrollable committed cost of production. But the importance of capacity management also extends to service industries such as telecommunications and transportation.

A service company such as an airline would likely analyze nonfinancial measures of satisfaction with the personal space per seat, seat comfort, food, and baggage handling, as well as flight availability, on-time take-off and arrival, and convenient connections with other flights. Few costs can be traced to these outputs in a cost-effective way. The majority of costs are fixed overhead costs (for example, costs of equipment, buildings, and staff). Using capacity effectively is the key to profitability, and fixed overhead variances can help managers in this task. For airlines, the non-financial capacity measure is available seat miles (ASM) while the financial measures are revenue per ASM (RASM) and costs per ASM (CASM).

Consider the following data for WestJet from 2006 to 2010. Available seat miles (ASM) are the actual seats in a plane multiplied by the distance travelled. One measure of capacity management is the operating income per ASM (RASM − CASM), which tells managers what WestJet's annual operating income has been, given its total capacity of ASM.

WestJet Annual Report 2010

Year	Total ASMs (billions) (1)	Revenue per ASM (2)	Cost per ASM (3)	Operating Income per ASM (4) = (2) − (3)
2010	19.535	$0.1336	$0.1209	$0.0127
2009	17.588	$0.1297	$0.1177	$0.0120
2008	17.139	$0.1488	$0.1317	$0.0171
2007	14.139	$0.1462	$0.1236	$0.0226
2006	12.524	$0.1398	$0.1210	$0.0188

The global recession hit in 2007, yet despite a dramatic drop in demand for air travel, WestJet managed to sustain an improved operating profit. In part this resulted from negotiating flexible delivery dates for aircraft. The company also increased the distance travelled per flight. Relative to the cost of keeping the aircraft aloft, takeoffs and landings comprise almost all the operating costs per flight (especially fuel). By lengthening the distances per flight the costs of takeoff and landing were diluted over more ASM. WestJet kept its CASM almost constant while RASM increased slightly. It could charge slightly more because it was flying passengers farther, a feature for which they were willing to pay. The financial result was a large increase in operating income per ASM from 2006 to 2007.

In an industry as equipment intensive as an airline, cost management extends to the fourth decimal place. Once committed to lease and purchasing contracts, the company cannot change the fixed cost per ASM. The $0.1209/ASM capacity cost in 2010 is a sunk cost that will not change. That is why WestJet enjoys great benefit from either a very small increase in RASM or decrease in CASM relative to budgeted values. Fractions of a cent will generate a large favourable variance in operating income. The management team has also kept its fleet to a single aircraft type to reduce maintenance expenses and cabin and flight crew training costs and to retain a negotiating advantage with its supplier. WestJet implements its cost leadership strategy through a relentless focus on reducing its cost of capacity use.

Moreover, the airline's passengers have similar in-flight experiences whether they fly short business or long destination flights. They are familiar with WestJet's value proposition as a low-cost provider and have set the price they are willing to pay. WestJet and its competitors are price takers. Any mistakes in management control cannot be passed on through increases in price. As a provider of bare-bones transportation, WestJet does not have a lot of opportunities to reduce any service amenities. For this service provider, variance analyses reports give the management team information that is crucial to remaining profitable.

In different environments, for example, competitive contract bidding, variance analysis of fixed non-manufacturing overhead costs is also important. Most companies bid on a full project cost-plus basis—that is, the purchaser pays all actual project costs plus an additional fixed percentage of total costs. Careful cost assignment clarifies the scope and intensity of use of resources shared by many distinct projects. The bidder can reduce uncertainty around what the actual costs will be. Timely variance analyses reports of non-manufacturing fixed overhead cost pools will improve the responsiveness of the management team to unforeseen excessive use of these shared resources.

PULLING IT ALL TOGETHER—PROBLEM FOR SELF-STUDY

(Try to solve this problem before examining the solution that follows.)

Dawn Smith is the newly appointed president of Laser Products. She is examining the May 2013 results for the Aerospace Products division. This division manufactures wing parts for satellites. Smith's current concern is with manufacturing overhead costs at the Aerospace Products division. Both variable and fixed manufacturing overhead costs are allocated to the wing parts based on laser-cutting-hours. The budgeted cost rates are variable manufacturing overhead of $200 per hour and fixed manufacturing overhead of $240 per hour. The budgeted laser-cutting time per wing part is 1.50 hours. Budgeted production and sales for 2013 are 5,000 wing parts. Budgeted fixed manufacturing overhead costs for May 2014 are $1,800,000.

Wing parts produced and sold	4,800 units
Laser-cutting-hours used	8,400 units
Variable manufacturing overhead costs	$1,478,400
Fixed manufacturing overhead costs	$1,832,200

REQUIRED

1. Compute the rate variance and the efficiency variance for variable manufacturing overhead. ①

2. Compute the rate variance and the production variance for fixed manufacturing overhead. ②

3. Give explanations for the variances in requirements 1 and 2 to illustrate how fixed and variable overhead cost variances provide integrated relevant information. ④

4. What nonfinancial variables could Laser Products use as performance measures? ⑤

5. What customer-satisfaction measures would be important to Laser Products? ⑤

SOLUTION

1. and 2. See Exhibit 8-13.

3. a. Variable manufacturing overhead rate variance ($201,600 F). One possible reason is that the actual prices of individual items included in variable overhead (such as utilities cost) are lower than the budgeted prices. A second possible reason is that the percentage increase in the actual quantity usage of individual items in the variable overhead cost pool is less than the percentage increase in machine-hours compared to the flexible budget.

   b. Variable manufacturing overhead efficiency variance ($240,000 U). One possible reason is inadequate maintenance of laser machines, causing them to take more laser time per wing part. A second possible reason is use of less-trained workers with the laser-cutting machines, resulting in longer laser time per wing part.

EXHIBIT 8-13
Columnar Presentation of Integrated Variance Analysis: Laser Products

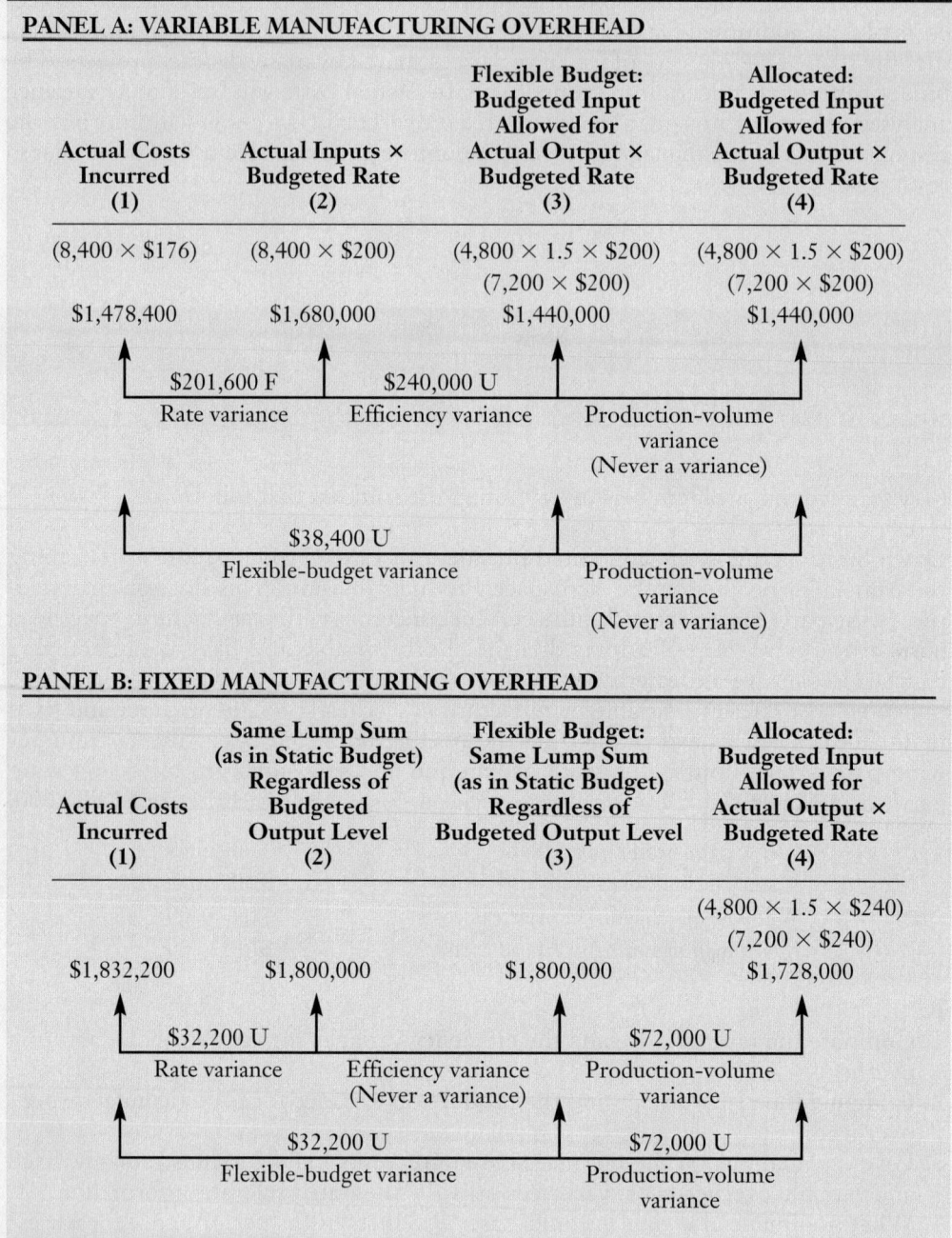

PANEL A: VARIABLE MANUFACTURING OVERHEAD

Actual Costs Incurred (1)	Actual Inputs × Budgeted Rate (2)	Flexible Budget: Budgeted Input Allowed for Actual Output × Budgeted Rate (3)	Allocated: Budgeted Input Allowed for Actual Output × Budgeted Rate (4)
(8,400 × $176)	(8,400 × $200)	(4,800 × 1.5 × $200)	(4,800 × 1.5 × $200)
		(7,200 × $200)	(7,200 × $200)
$1,478,400	$1,680,000	$1,440,000	$1,440,000

$201,600 F ← Rate variance

$240,000 U ← Efficiency variance

Production-volume variance (Never a variance)

$38,400 U ← Flexible-budget variance

Production-volume variance (Never a variance)

PANEL B: FIXED MANUFACTURING OVERHEAD

Actual Costs Incurred (1)	Same Lump Sum (as in Static Budget) Regardless of Budgeted Output Level (2)	Flexible Budget: Same Lump Sum (as in Static Budget) Regardless of Budgeted Output Level (3)	Allocated: Budgeted Input Allowed for Actual Output × Budgeted Rate (4)
			(4,800 × 1.5 × $240)
			(7,200 × $240)
$1,832,200	$1,800,000	$1,800,000	$1,728,000

$32,200 U ← Rate variance

Efficiency variance (Never a variance)

$72,000 U ← Production-volume variance

$32,200 U ← Flexible-budget variance

$72,000 U ← Production-volume variance

c. Fixed manufacturing overhead rate variance ($32,200 U). One possible reason is that the actual prices of individual items in the fixed-cost pool unexpectedly increased from those budgeted (such as an unexpected increase in the manager's salary). Overhead also includes maintenance supplies and labour, inspection labour, taxes, and insurance costs. It could be that an unanticipated increase in taxes or inspection time caused the rate variance for the month.

d. Production-volume variance ($72,000 U). Actual production of wing parts is 4,800 units compared with the 5,000 units budgeted. One possible reason is demand factors, such as a decline in the aerospace program that led to a decline in the demand for satellite wings. What is known with certainty is that the use of the laser time exceeded what would have been budgeted for 4,800 wing parts. An actual inefficiency may have caused this increased consumption of laser hours or the company could have chosen an inappropriate denominator level. The increased use of laser hours could have several causes, from ill-trained operators who took more time and caused waste to an improperly functioning machine. It may also have been a smart decision by the company not to produce 5,000 wing parts if quality control was an issue or if demand had fallen.

4. Laser Products is already measuring nonfinancial variables when it measures the actual quantity consumed of the cost allocation base. Other nonfinancial variables that could be important would depend upon the competitive environment. If, for example, the environment is becoming increasingly competitive, Laser Products may want to plan ways of becoming more agile. For a manufacturing company, this could involve cross-training equipment operators, and some measure of hours of training would be needed. As those purchasing Laser Products parts become more demanding and request more customization, the company may choose to analyze the types of customers it may be able to serve according to the attributes of the products they demand such as physical size, fragility, complexity, and so on.

5. Customers for wing parts are unlikely to have an affective response to receiving these products. They are focused on how useful the product is, how well it meets engineering specifications, and if it is delivered on time within the costs stated in the contract. These are cognitive measures of customer satisfaction appropriate to this manufacturing setting.

SUMMARY POINTS

The following question-and-answer format summarizes the chapter's learning outcomes. Each point presents a key question, and the guidelines are the answer to that question.

LEARNING OUTCOMES	GUIDELINES
1. How do managers budget pro forma fixed overhead cost rates and analyze fixed overhead variances?	Managers combine internal experience and external information about competitors to set a budgeted cost rate per unit of equipment input. They estimate the quantity of input needed to produce a single output unit to calculate an overhead cost rate per output unit. Fixed cost variances can arise from unforeseen changes in items such as taxes or salaries of production supervisors. The former is persistent and uncontrollable; the latter is usually temporary and controllable. Production volume variance is an opportunity cost of poor capacity management that reports a misallocation of overhead fixed costs to output units actually made.
2. How do managers analyze and interpret variable overhead variances?	Variable overhead variances reflect a difference in the actual compared to the pro forma relationship between variable costs of shared resources and the benefits to distinctive outputs from sharing resources. Either the budgeted cost per unit of shared resource or the quantity of benefit to the output unit, or both, differed from actual amounts.
3. Can the flexible-budget variance approach for analyzing overhead costs be used in activity-based costing?	Flexible budgeting in ABC systems gives insight into why actual overhead activity costs differ from budgeted overhead activity costs. The relationship remains one between the cost for shared activities and a measure of benefit to the output unit.
4. How does increasing detail of variance analyses help reconcile actual with budgeted overhead costs?	A four-variance analysis presents rate and efficiency variances for variable overhead costs, as well as rate and production-volume variances for fixed overhead costs. By analyzing these variances together, managers can reconcile the actual overhead costs with the amount of overhead allocated to output produced during a period.

Indirect cost pools can also be separated by either business function or department, and separate cost allocation bases selected. These are two alternatives to using ABC to refine costing systems. |
| 5. Of what use are nonfinancial and non-manufacturing performance measures? | Increasingly, companies must simultaneously manage costs, quality, customization, and timely delivery. The separation of cost from value leadership by differentiating either products or outputs will not accomplish this goal. Nonfinancial measures of customer satisfaction and comparisons to some pro forma amounts are relevant to important management decisions that will affect revenue. |

This chapter and the Glossary at the end of the book contain definitions of the following important terms:

agility (p. 320)
BEP in revenue (p. 298)
BEP in volume (p. 298)
capacity (p. 299)
capacity cost (p. 299)
combined-variance analysis (p. 317)
denominator-level variance (p. 302)

fixed overhead rate variance (p. 300)
non-value-added cost (p. 319)
output-level overhead variance (p. 302)
production denominator level
   (or volume) (p. 300)
production-volume variance (p. 302)
value-added cost (p. 319)

value proposition (p. 320)
variable overhead efficiency
   variance (p. 309)
variable overhead rate
   variance (p. 309)

ASSIGNMENT MATERIAL

MyAccountingLab Make the grade with MyAccountingLab: The questions, exercises, and problems marked in red can be found on MyAccountingLab at **www.myaccountinglab.com**. You can practise them as often as you want, and most feature step-by-step guided instructions to help you find the right answer. Exercises and problems with an Excel icon in the margin have an accompanying Excel template on MyAccountingLab.

SHORT-ANSWER QUESTIONS

8-1 How do managers plan for variable overhead costs?

8-2 How does the planning of fixed overhead costs differ from the planning of variable overhead costs?

8-3 How do standard and actual costing differ?

8-4 What are the steps in developing a budgeted variable overhead cost allocation rate?

8-5 The rate variance for variable manufacturing overhead is affected by several factors. Explain.

8-6 Assume variable manufacturing overhead is allocated using machine-hours. Give three possible reasons for a $30,000 favourable variable overhead efficiency variance.

8-7 Describe the difference between a direct materials efficiency variance and a variable manufacturing overhead efficiency variance.

8-8 What are the steps in developing a budgeted fixed overhead rate?

8-9 Why is the flexible-budget variance the same amount as the rate variance for fixed manufacturing overhead?

8-10 Explain how the analysis of fixed overhead costs differs for (a) planning and control on the one hand and (b) inventory costing for financial reporting on the other.

8-11 Provide one caution that will affect whether a production-volume variance is a good measure of the economic cost of unused capacity.

8-12 The production-volume variance should always be written off to "Cost of Goods Sold." Do you agree? Explain.

8-13 Explain how four-variance analysis differs from one-, two-, and three-variance analysis.

8-14 "Overhead variances should be viewed as interdependent rather than independent." Give an example.

EXERCISES

8-15 **Terminology.** A number of terms are listed below:

agility	value-added cost
capacity	capacity cost
non-value-added cost	denominator-level variance
fixed overhead rate variance	production-volume variance
variable overhead efficiency variance	variable overhead rate variance

REQUIRED

Select the terms from the above list to complete the following sentences.

Interpretation of variances strategically means management teams must place their internal performance relative to their competitors and to what their customers value. Decisions about _____ incur _____ of ownership and maintenance for the long term. To the customer, however, the cost of unused capacity is a _____ for which they will not pay. This cost arises because the quantity produced is less than the capacity available. The cost is fixed therefore the burden assigned to each actual unit produced is higher than it should be. This unfavourable outcome is a _____. It is also referred to as the _____ and is an underallocation of capacity costs that will persist until consumer demand, actual production, and available capacity intersect. But fixed costs also include contractual costs such as salaries and regulatory costs of taxes. These costs can change unexpectedly and will result in a _____. Equipment also requires maintenance which, along with custodial and security costs, are required and shared resources that benefit all outputs. When the actual measure of benefit provided exceeds the budget, what arises is an unfavourable _____. When the actual cost per unit of benefit provided exceeds budget, there arises an unfavourable _____. Both are underallocations of variable overhead cost.

8-16 **Variable manufacturing overhead, variance analysis.** Esquire Clothing is a manufacturer of designer suits. The cost of each suit is the sum of three variable costs (direct materials costs, direct manufacturing labour costs, and manufacturing overhead costs) and one fixed-cost category (manufacturing overhead costs). Variable manufacturing overhead cost is allocated to each suit based on budgeted direct manufacturing labour-hours (DMLH) per suit. For June 2013, each suit is budgeted to take 4 labour-hours. Budgeted variable manufacturing overhead costs per labour-hour are $12.00. The budgeted number of suits to be manufactured in June 2013 is 1,040.

1. Flexible-budget variance, $324 U

Actual variable manufacturing overhead costs in June 2013 were $52,164 for 1,080 suits started and completed. There was no beginning or ending inventory of suits. Actual direct manufacturing labour-hours for June were 4,536 DMLH.

REQUIRED

1. Compute the flexible-budget variance, the rate variance, and the efficiency variance for variable manufacturing overhead.
2. Comment on the results.

8-17 **Fixed manufacturing overhead variance analysis (continuation of 8-16).** Esquire Clothing allocates fixed manufacturing overhead to each suit using budgeted direct manufacturing labour-hours (DMLH) per suit. Data pertaining to fixed manufacturing overhead costs for June 2013 are $62,400 budgeted and $63,916 actual.

1. Rate variance, $1,516 U

REQUIRED

1. Compute the rate variance for fixed manufacturing overhead. Comment on these results.
2. Compute the production-volume variance for June 2013. What inferences can Esquire Clothing draw from this variance?

8-18 **Variable manufacturing overhead variance analysis.** French Bread Company has two direct-cost categories: direct materials and direct manufacturing labour. Variable manufacturing overhead is allocated to products on the basis of standard direct manufacturing labour-hours (DMLH).

1. Denominator level, 76,000 hours

Baguettes are baked in batches of 100 loaves. Following are some pertinent data for French Bread Company:

Direct manufacturing labour use	2.00 DMLH per batch
Variable manufacturing overhead	$4.00 per DMLH

French Bread Company recorded the following additional data for the year ended December 31, 2013:

Planned (budgeted) output	3,840,000 baguettes
Actual production	3,360,000 baguettes
Direct manufacturing labour	50,400 DMLH
Actual variable MOH	$326,400

REQUIRED

1. What is the denominator level used for allocating variable manufacturing overhead? (That is, for how many direct manufacturing labour-hours is French Bread budgeting?)
2. Prepare a variance analysis of variable manufacturing overhead. Use Exhibit 8-6 (p. 307) for reference.
3. Discuss the variances you have calculated and give possible explanations for them.

8-19 Fixed manufacturing overhead variance analysis. French Bread Company also allocates fixed manufacturing overhead to products on the basis of standard direct manufacturing labour-hours. For 2013, fixed manufacturing overhead was budgeted at $4.00 per direct manufacturing labour hour. Actual fixed manufacturing overhead incurred during the year was $272,000.

REQUIRED
1. Prepare a variance analysis of fixed manufacturing overhead costs.
2. Is fixed overhead underallocated or overallocated? By how much?
3. Comment on your results. Discuss the various variances and explain what may be driving them.

8-20 Manufacturing overhead, variance analysis. Solutions Corporation is a manufacturer of centrifuges. Fixed and variable manufacturing overhead cost pools are allocated to each centrifuge using budgeted assembly hours. Budgeted assembly time is two hours per unit. The following table shows the budgeted amounts and actual results related to overhead for June 2013.

Solutions Corporation (June 2013)	Actual Results	Static Budget
Number of centrifuges assembled and sold	216	200
Hours of assembly time	411	
Variable manufacturing overhead cost per hour of assembly time		$ 30.00
Variable manufacturing overhead costs	$12,420	
Fixed manufacturing overhead costs	$20,560	$19,200

REQUIRED
1. Prepare an analysis of all variable manufacturing overhead and fixed manufacturing overhead variances using the columnar approach in Exhibit 8-12, p. 318.
2. Prepare journal entries for Solutions' June 2013 variable and fixed manufacturing overhead costs and variances; write off these variances to cost of goods sold for the quarter ended June 30, 2013.
3. How does the planning and control of variable manufacturing overhead costs differ from the planning and control of fixed manufacturing overhead costs?

8-21 Four-variance analysis, fill in the blanks. Pandom Inc. produces chemicals for large biotech companies. It has the following data for manufacturing overhead costs during August 2013:

	Variable	Fixed
Actual costs incurred	$35,700	$18,000
Costs allocated to products	27,000	14,400
Flexible budget: Budgeted input allowed for actual output produced × budgeted rate	27,000	15,000
Actual input × budgeted rate	31,500	15,000

REQUIRED
Fill in the variances in the table below. Use F for favourable and U for unfavourable.

	Variable	Fixed
1. Rate variance	$_____	$_____
2. Efficiency variance	$_____	$_____
3. Production-volume variance	$_____	$_____
4. Flexible-budget variance	$_____	$_____
5. Underallocated (overallocated) manufacturing overhead	$_____	$_____

8-22 Straightforward four-variance overhead analysis. Lopez Company uses a standard cost system in its manufacturing plant for auto parts. The standard cost of a particular auto part, based on a denominator level of 4,000 output units per year, included 6 machine-hours of variable manufacturing overhead at $8 per hour and 6 machine-hours of fixed manufacturing overhead at $15 per hour. Actual output achieved was 4,400 units. Variable manufacturing overhead incurred was $245,000. Fixed manufacturing overhead incurred was $373,000. Actual incurred machine-hours were 28,400.

REQUIRED

1. Prepare an analysis of all variable manufacturing overhead and fixed manufacturing overhead variances, using the four-variance analysis in Exhibit 8-12, p. 318.
2. Prepare journal entries using the four-variance analysis.
3. Describe how individual variable manufacturing overhead items are controlled from day to day. Also, describe how individual fixed manufacturing overhead items are controlled.

8-23 **Straightforward coverage of manufacturing overhead, standard cost system.** The Singapore division of a Canadian telecommunications company uses a standard cost system for its machine-based production of telephone equipment. Data regarding production during June are as follows:

Variable manufacturing overhead costs incurred	$186,120
Variable manufacturing overhead costs allocated (per standard machine-hour allowed for actual output achieved)	$ 14.40
Fixed manufacturing overhead costs incurred	$481,200
Fixed manufacturing overhead budgeted	$468,000
Denominator level in machine-hours	15,600
Standard machine hours allowed per unit of output	0.30
Units of output	49,200
Actual machine-hours used	15,960
Ending work-in-process inventory	0

REQUIRED

1. Prepare an analysis of all manufacturing overhead variances. Use the four-variance analysis framework illustrated in Exhibit 8-12, p. 318.
2. Prepare journal entries for manufacturing overhead without explanations.
3. Describe how individual variable manufacturing overhead items are controlled from day to day. Also, describe how individual fixed manufacturing overhead items are controlled.

8-24 **Overhead variances, service sector.** Meals on Wheels (MOW) operates a meal home-delivery service. It has agreements with 20 restaurants to pick up and deliver meals to customers who phone or fax orders to MOW. MOW allocates variable and fixed overhead costs on the basis of delivery time. MOW's owner, Josh Carter, obtains the following information for May 2013 overhead costs:

Meals on Wheels (May 2013)	Actual Results	Static Budget
Output units (number of deliveries)	8,800	10,000
Hours per delivery		0.70
Hours of delivery time	5,720	
Variable overhead cost per hour of delivery time		$ 1.50
Variable overhead costs	$10,296	
Fixed overhead costs	$38,600	$35,000

REQUIRED

1. Compute rate and efficiency variances for MOW's variable overhead in May 2013.
2. Compute the rate variance and production-volume variance for MOW's fixed overhead in May 2013.
3. Comment on MOW's overhead variances and suggest how Josh Carter might manage MOW's variable overhead differently from its fixed overhead costs.

8-25 **Total overhead, three-variance analysis.** Furniture Inc. specializes in the production of futons. It uses standard costing and flexible budgets to account for the production of a new line of futons. For 2013, budgeted variable overhead at a level of 3,200 standard monthly direct labour-hours was $25,600; budgeted total overhead at 4,000 standard monthly direct labour-hours was $79,040. The standard cost allocated to each output included a total overhead rate of 120% of standard direct labour costs. For October, Furniture Inc. incurred total overhead of $99,600 and direct labour costs of $80,976. The direct labour price variance was $3,856 unfavourable. The direct labour flexible-budget variance was $5,776 unfavourable. The standard labour price was $16 per hour. The production-volume variance was $5,600, favourable.

1. Compute the direct labour efficiency variance, and the rate and efficiency variances for overhead. Also, compute the denominator level.
2. Describe how individual variable overhead items are controlled from day to day. Also, describe how individual fixed overhead items are controlled.

④

8-26 Overhead variances, missing information. Dvent budgets 18,000 machine hours for the production of computer chips in August 2013. The budgeted variable overhead rate is $6 per machine-hour. At the end of August there is a $375 favourable rate variance for variable overhead and a $1,575 unfavourable rate variance for fixed overhead. For the computer chips produced, 14,850 machine-hours are budgeted and 15,000 machine-hours are actually used. Total actual overhead costs are $120,000.

REQUIRED

1. Compute efficiency and flexible-budget variances for Dvent's variable overhead in August 2013. Will variable overhead be overallocated or underallocated? By how much?
2. Compute production-volume and flexible-budget variances for Dvent's fixed overhead in August 2013. Will fixed overhead be overallocated or underallocated? By how much?

④

8-27 Identifying favourable and unfavourable variances. Purdue Inc. manufactures tires for large auto companies. It uses standard costing and allocates variable and fixed manufacturing overhead based on machine-hours.

REQUIRED

For each independent scenario given, indicate whether each of the manufacturing variances will be favourable or unfavourable or, in case of insufficient information, indicate "cannot be determined."

Scenario	Variable Overhead Rate Variance	Variable Overhead Efficiency Variance	Fixed Overhead Rate Variance	Fixed Overhead Production-Volume Variance
Production output is 5% more than budgeted, and actual fixed manufacturing overhead costs are 6% more than budgeted				
Production output is 10% more than budgeted; actual machine-hours are 5% less than budgeted				
Production output is 8% less than budgeted				
Actual machine hours are 15% greater than flexible-budget machine-hours				
Relative to the flexible budget, actual machine-hours are 10% greater, and actual variable manufacturing overhead costs are 15% greater				

④

8-28 Flexible-budget variances, review of Chapters 7 and 8. David James is a cost accountant and business analyst for Doorknob Design Company (DDC), which manufactures expensive brass doorknobs. DDC uses two direct cost categories: direct materials and direct manufacturing labour. James feels that manufacturing overhead is most closely related to material usage. Therefore, DDC allocates manufacturing overhead to production based upon kilograms of materials used.

At the beginning of 2013, DDC budgeted production of 100,000 doorknobs and adopted the following standards for each doorknob:

	Input	Cost/Doorknob
Direct materials (brass)	0.5 kg @ $20/kg	$10.00
Direct manufacturing labour	0.25 hours @ $30/hour	7.50
Manufacturing overhead:		
Variable	$10/kg × 0.5 kg	5.00
Fixed	$ 5/kg × 0.5 kg	2.50
Standard cost per doorknob		$25.00

1. Variable MOH rate (spending) variance, $375

First scenario: Variable overhead rate variance, cannot be determined

1. a. Direct materials price variance, $100,000 U

Actual results for April 2013 were:

Production	95,000 doorknobs
Direct materials purchased	50,000 kg at $22/kg
Direct materials used	45,000 kg
Direct manufacturing labour	20,000 hours for $650,000
Variable manufacturing overhead	$400,000
Fixed manufacturing overhead	$350,000

REQUIRED

1. For the month of April, compute the following variances, indicating whether each is favourable (F) or unfavourable (U).
   a. Direct materials price variance (based on purchases).
   b. Direct materials efficiency variance.
   c. Direct manufacturing labour price variance.
   d. Direct manufacturing labour efficiency variance.
   e. Variable manufacturing overhead rate variance.
   f. Variable manufacturing overhead efficiency variance.
   g. Production-volume variance.
   h. Fixed manufacturing overhead rate variance.

2. Can James use any of the variances to help explain any of the other variances? Give examples.

PROBLEMS

8-29 Comprehensive variance analysis. Kitchen Whiz manufactures premium food processors. The following is some manufacturing overhead data for Kitchen Whiz for the year ended December 31, 2013.

④

1. Budgeted DMH, 1,776

Manufacturing Overhead	Actual Results	Flexible Budget	Amount Allocated
Variable	$ 76,608	$ 76,800	$ 76,800
Fixed	350,208	348,096	376,320

Budgeted number of output units: 888
Planned allocation rate: 2 machine-hours per unit
Actual number of machine-hours used: 1,824
Static-budget variable manufacturing overhead costs: $71,040

REQUIRED

Compute the following quantities (you should be able to do so in the prescribed order):

1. Budgeted number of machine-hours planned.
2. Budgeted fixed manufacturing overhead costs per machine-hour.
3. Budgeted variable manufacturing overhead costs per machine-hour.
4. Budgeted number of machine-hours allowed for actual output achieved.
5. Actual number of output units.
6. Actual number of machine-hours used per output unit.

8-30 Journal entries (continuation of 8-29). Refer to Problem 8-29.

① ② ④

REQUIRED

1. Prepare journal entries for variable and fixed manufacturing overhead (you will need to calculate the various variances to accomplish this).
2. Overhead variances are written off to the Cost of Goods Sold (COGS) account at the end of the fiscal year. Show how COGS is adjusted through journal entries.

8-31 Graphs and overhead variances. Fresh Inc. is a manufacturer of vacuums and uses standard costing. Manufacturing overhead (both variable and fixed) is allocated to products on the basis of budgeted machine-hours. In 2013, budgeted fixed manufacturing overhead cost was $18,000,000. Budgeted variable manufacturing overhead was $9 per machine-hour. The denominator level was 1,000,000 machine-hours.

① ②

2. Variable MOH rate variance, $475,000 U

REQUIRED

1. Prepare a graph for fixed manufacturing overhead. The graph should display how Fresh Inc.'s fixed manufacturing overhead costs will be depicted for the purposes of (a) planning and control and (b) inventory costing.

2. Suppose that 875,000 machine-hours were allowed for actual output produced in 2013, but 950,000 actual machine-hours were used. Actual manufacturing overhead was $9,025,000, variable, and $18,050,000, fixed. Compute (a) the variable manufacturing overhead rate and efficiency variances and (b) the fixed manufacturing overhead rate and production-volume variances. Use the columnar presentation illustrated in Exhibit 8-12, p. 318.

3. What is the amount of the underallocated or overallocated variable manufacturing overhead and the underallocated or overallocated fixed manufacturing overhead? Why are the flexible-budget variance and the underallocated or overallocated overhead amount always the same for variable manufacturing overhead but rarely the same for fixed manufacturing overhead?

4. Suppose the denominator level were 750,000 rather than 1,000,000 machine-hours. What variances in requirement 2 would be affected? Recompute them.

Case A FMOH rate variance,
$1,500 U

8-32 Fixed overhead variance. Consider each of the following situations—cases A, B, and C— independently. Data refer to operations for April 2013. For each situation, assume standard costing. Also assume the use of a flexible budget for control of variable and fixed manufacturing overhead based on machine-hours.

	Cases		
	A	**B**	**C**
1. Fixed manufacturing overhead incurred	$26,500	—	$30,000
2. Variable manufacturing overhead incurred	$15,000	—	—
3. Denominator level in machine-hours	1,250	—	2,750
4. Standard machine-hours allowed for actual output achieved	—	1,625	—
5. Fixed manufacturing overhead (per standard machine-hour)	—	—	—
Flexible-budget data:			
6. Variable manufacturing overhead (per standard machine-hour)	—	$ 8.50	$ 5.00
7. Budgeted fixed manufacturing overhead	$25,000	—	$27,500
8. Budgeted variable manufacturing overhead[a]	—	—	—
9. Total budgeted manufacturing overhead[a]	—	$31,313	—
Additional data:			
10. Standard variable manufacturing overhead allocated	$18,750	—	—
11. Standard fixed manufacturing overhead allocated	$25,000	—	—
12. Production-volume variance	—	$ 1,250 U	$ 1,250 F
13. Variable manufacturing overhead rate variance	$ 4,875 F	$ 0	$ 875 U
14. Variable manufacturing overhead efficiency variance	—	$ 0	$ 250 U
15. Fixed manufacturing overhead rate variance	—	$ 750 F	—
16. Actual machine-hours used	—	—	—

[a]For standard machine-hours allowed for actual output produced.

REQUIRED
Fill in the blanks under each case. [Hint: Prepare a worksheet similar to that in Exhibit 8-12, p. 318. Fill in the knowns and then solve for the unknowns.]

3. FMOH rate variance
$6,000 U

8-33 Flexible budgets, four-variance analysis. (CMA, adapted) Nolton Products uses standard costing. It allocates manufacturing overhead (both variable and fixed) to products on the basis of standard direct manufacturing labour-hours (DLH). Nolton develops its manufacturing overhead rate from the current annual budget. The manufacturing overhead budget for 2013 is based on budgeted output of 720,000 units, requiring 3,600,000 DLH. The company is able to schedule production uniformly throughout the year.

A total of 66,000 output units requiring 315,000 DLH was produced during May 2013. Manufacturing overhead (MOH) costs incurred for May amounted to $375,000. The actual costs, compared with the annual budget and ½ of the annual budget, are as follows:

Annual Manufacturing Overhead Budget 2013

	Total Amount	Per Output Unit	Per DLH Input Unit	Monthly MOH Budget May 2013	Actual MOH Costs for May 2013
Variable MOH					
Indirect manufacturing labour	$ 900,000	$1.25	$0.25	$ 75,000	$ 75,000
Supplies	1,224,000	1.70	0.34	102,000	111,000
Fixed MOH					
Supervision	648,000	0.90	0.18	54,000	51,000
Utilities	540,000	0.75	0.15	45,000	54,000
Depreciation	1,008,000	1.40	0.28	84,000	84,000
Total	$4,320,000	$6.00	$1.20	$360,000	$375,000

REQUIRED

Calculate the following amounts for Nolton Products for May 2013:

1. Total manufacturing overhead costs allocated.
2. Variable manufacturing overhead rate variance.
3. Fixed manufacturing overhead rate variance.
4. Variable manufacturing overhead efficiency variance.
5. Production-volume variance.

Be sure to identify each variance as favourable (F) or unfavourable (U).

8-34 Variable overhead variance. Sarah Beth's Art Supply Company produces various types of paints. Actual direct manufacturing labour-hours (DMLH) in the factory that produces paint have been higher than budgeted hours for the last few months and the owner, Sarah B. Jones, is concerned about the effect this has had on the company's cost overruns. Because variable manufacturing overhead is allocated to units produced using DMLH, Sarah feels that the mismanagement of labour will have a twofold effect on company profitability. Following are the relevant budgeted and actual results for the second quarter of 2013.

2. Variable MOH efficiency variance, $32,500 U

	Budget Information	Actual Results
Paint set production	10,000	13,000
Direct manufacturing labour-hours (DMLH) per paint set	0.5 DMLH	0.75 DMLH
Direct manufacturing labour rate	$20.00/DMLH	$20.20/DMLH
Variable manufacturing overhead rate	$ 10/DMLH	$ 9.75/DMLH

REQUIRED

1. Calculate the direct manufacturing labour price and efficiency variances and indicate whether each is favourable (F) or unfavourable (U).
2. Calculate the variable manufacturing overhead rate and efficiency variances and indicate whether each is favourable (F) or unfavourable (U).
3. For both direct manufacturing labour and variable manufacturing overhead, do the price/rate variances help Sarah explain the efficiency variances?
4. Is Sarah correct in her assertion that the mismanagement of labour has a twofold effect on cost overruns? Why might the variable manufacturing overhead efficiency variance not be an accurate representation of the effect of labour overruns on variable manufacturing overhead costs?

8-35 Causes of indirect variances. Heather's Horse Spa (HHS) is an establishment that boards, trains, and pampers horses while their owners are on vacation. Heather sells her service as an "enchanting vacation experience for your horse while you vacation elsewhere." Horse feed, shampoos, ribbons, and other supplies are treated as variable indirect costs. Consequently, there are no direct materials involved in the vacation service. Other overhead costs, including indirect labour, amortization on the barn, and advertising, are fixed. Both variable and fixed overhead are allocated to each horse guest-week using the weight of the horse in pounds (lbs) as the basis of allocation.

2. Variable MOH rate variance, $280 U

HHS budgeted amounts for August 2013 were:

Horse guest-weeks	40
Average weight per horse	900 lbs
Variable overhead cost per pound of horse	$0.20/lb
Fixed overhead rate	$1.50/lb

Actual results for August 2013 were:

Horse guest-weeks	38
Average weight per horse	950 lbs
Actual variable overhead	$ 7,500
Actual fixed overhead	$50,000

REQUIRED

1. Calculate the variable overhead rate and efficiency variances and indicate whether each is favourable (F) or unfavourable (U).
2. Calculate the fixed overhead rate and production-volume variances and indicate whether each is favourable (F) or unfavourable (U).
3. Explain what the variable overhead rate variance means. What factors could have caused it?
4. What factors could have caused the variable overhead efficiency variance?
5. If fixed overhead is, in fact, fixed, how could a fixed overhead rate variance occur?
6. What caused the fixed overhead production-volume variance? What does it mean? What are the negative implications, if any, of the production-volume variance?

1. Static-budget number of crates, 20,000

8-36 Activity-based costing, batch-level variance analysis. Rica's Fleet Feet Inc. produces dance shoes for stores all over the world. While the pairs of shoes are boxed individually, they are crated and shipped in batches. The shipping department records both variable and fixed overhead costs. The following information pertains to shipping costs for 2013.

	Static-Budget Amounts	Actual Results
Pairs of shoes shipped	240,000	180,000
Average number of pairs of shoes per crate	12	10
Packing hours per crate	1.2 hours	1.1 hours
Variable overhead cost per hour	$20	$21
Fixed overhead cost	$60,000	$55,000

REQUIRED

1. What is the static-budget number of crates for 2013?
2. What is the flexible-budget number of crates for 2013?
3. What is the actual number of crates shipped in 2013?
4. Assuming fixed overhead is allocated using crate-packing hours, what is the predetermined fixed overhead allocation rate?
5. For variable overhead costs, compute the rate and efficiency variances.
6. For fixed overhead costs, compute the rate and the production-volume variances.

1. Static-budget number of setups, 400

8-37 Activity-based costing, batch-level variance analysis. Jo Nathan Publishing Company specializes in printing specialty textbooks for a small but profitable college market. Due to the high setup costs for each batch printed, Jo Nathan holds the book requests until demand for a book is approximately 500. At that point Jo Nathan will schedule the setup and production of the book. For rush orders, Jo Nathan will produce smaller batches for an additional charge of $700 per setup.

Budgeted and actual costs for the printing process for 2013 were:

	Static-Budget Amounts	Actual Results
Number of books produced	200,000	216,000
Average number of books per setup	500	480
Hours to set up printers	6 hours	6.5 hours
Variable overhead cost per setup-hour	$ 100	$ 90
Total fixed setup overhead costs	$72,000	$79,000

1. What is the static-budget number of setups for 2013?
2. What is the flexible-budget number of setups for 2013?
3. What is the actual number of setups in 2013?
4. Assuming fixed setup overhead costs are allocated using setup-hours, what is the predetermined fixed setup overhead allocation rate?
5. Does Jo Nathan's charge of $700 cover the budgeted variable overhead cost of an order? The budgeted total overhead cost?
6. For variable setup overhead costs, compute the rate and efficiency variances.
7. For fixed setup overhead costs, compute the rate and the production-volume variances.
8. What qualitative factors should Jo Nathan consider before accepting or rejecting a special order?

8-38 Production-volume variance analysis and sales-volume variance. Dawn Floral Creations Inc. makes jewellery in the shape of flowers. Each piece is hand-made and takes an average of 1.5 hours to produce because of the intricate design and scrollwork. Dawn uses direct labour-hours to allocate the overhead cost to production. Fixed overhead costs, including rent, amortization, supervisory salaries, and other production expenses, are budgeted at $9,000 per month. These costs are incurred for a facility large enough to produce 1,000 pieces of jewellery a month.

1. Fixed overhead rate variance, $200 U

During the month of February, Dawn produced 600 pieces of jewellery and actual fixed costs were $9,200.

REQUIRED

1. Calculate the fixed overhead rate variance and indicate whether it is favourable (F) or unfavourable (U).
2. If Dawn uses direct labour-hours available at capacity to calculate the budgeted fixed overhead rate, what is the production-volume variance? Indicate whether it is favourable (F) or unfavourable (U).
3. An unfavourable production-volume variance is a measure of the underallocation of fixed overhead cost caused by production levels at less than capacity. It therefore could be interpreted as the economic cost of unused capacity. Why would Dawn be willing to incur this cost? Your answer should separately consider the following two unrelated factors:

   a. Demand could vary from month to month while available capacity remains constant.

   b. Dawn would not want to produce at capacity unless it could sell all the units produced. What does Dawn need to do to raise demand and what effect would this have on profit?

4. Dawn's budgeted variable cost per unit is $25 and it expects to sell the jewellery for $55 apiece. Compute the sales-volume variance and reconcile it with the production-volume variance calculated.

8-39 Comprehensive review of Chapters 7 and 8, working backward from given variances. Mancusco Company uses a flexible budget and standard costs to aid planning and control of its machining manufacturing operations. Its costing system for manufacturing has two direct cost categories (direct materials and direct manufacturing labour—both variable) and two overhead cost categories (variable manufacturing overhead and fixed manufacturing overhead, both allocated using direct manufacturing labour-hours (DMLH)).

1. a. Total direct materials purchased, 160,000 kg

At the 40,000 budgeted DMLH level for August, budgeted direct manufacturing labour is $800,000, budgeted variable manufacturing overhead is $480,000, and budgeted fixed manufacturing overhead is $640,000.

The following actual results are for August:

Direct materials price variance (based on purchases)	$176,000 F
Direct materials efficiency variance	69,000 U
Direct manufacturing labour costs incurred	522,750
Variable manufacturing overhead flexible-budget variance	10,350 U
Variable manufacturing overhead efficiency variance	18,000 U
Fixed manufacturing overhead incurred	597,460
Fixed manufacturing overhead rate variance	42,540 F

The standard cost per kilogram of direct materials is $11.50. The standard allowance is three kilograms of direct materials for each unit of product. During August, 30,000 units of product were produced. There was no beginning inventory of direct materials. There was no beginning or ending work-in-process. In August, the direct materials price variance was $1.10 per kilogram.

In July, labour unrest caused a major slowdown in the pace of production, resulting in an unfavourable direct manufacturing labour efficiency variance of $45,000. There was no direct manufacturing labour price variance. Labour unrest persisted into August. Some workers quit. Their replacements had to be hired at higher wage rates, which had to be extended to all workers. The actual average wage rate in August exceeded the standard average wage rate by $0.50 per hour.

REQUIRED

1. Compute the following for August:

   a. Total kilograms of direct materials purchased.

   b. Total number of kilograms of excess direct materials used.

   c. Variable manufacturing overhead rate variance.

   d. Total number of actual DMLH used.

   e. Total number of standard DMLH allowed for the units produced.

   f. Production-volume variance.

2. Describe how Mancusco's control of variable manufacturing overhead items differs from its control of fixed manufacturing overhead items.

④

2. a. Direct materials price variance, $5,000 U

8-40 Review of Chapters 7 and 8, three-variance analysis. (CPA, adapted) Beal Manufacturing Company's costing system has two direct cost categories: direct materials and direct manufacturing labour. Manufacturing overhead (both variable and fixed) is allocated to products on the basis of standard direct manufacturing labour-hours (DMLH). At the beginning of 2013, Beal adopted the following standards for its manufacturing costs:

	Input	Cost per Output Unit
Direct materials	3 kg at $5 per kg	$ 15
Direct manufacturing labour	5 hours at $15 per hour	75
Manufacturing overhead:		
Variable	$6 per DMLH	30
Fixed	$8 per DMLH	40
Standard manufacturing cost per output unit		$160

The denominator level for total manufacturing overhead per month in 2013 is 40,000 DMLH. Beal's flexible budget for January 2013 was based on this denominator level. The records for January indicate the following:

Direct materials purchased	25,000 kg at $5.20/kg
Direct materials used	23,100 kg
Direct manufacturing labour	40,100 hours at $14.60/hour
Total actual manufacturing overhead (variable and fixed)	$600,000
Actual production	7,800 output units

REQUIRED

1. Prepare a schedule of total standard manufacturing costs for the 7,800 output units in January 2013.

2. For January 2013, compute the following variances, indicating whether each is favourable (F) or unfavourable (U):

   a. Direct materials price variance, based on purchases.

   b. Direct materials efficiency variance.

   c. Direct manufacturing labour price variance.

   d. Direct manufacturing labour efficiency variance.

   e. Total manufacturing overhead rate variance.

   f. Variable manufacturing overhead efficiency variance.

   g. Production-volume variance

⑤

1. Efficiency Variance, 10 hrs U

8-41 Nonfinancial and non-manufacturing variances. Daisy Canine Products produces high-quality dog food distributed only through veterinary offices. To ensure that the food is of the highest quality and has taste appeal, Daisy has a rigorous inspection process. For quality-control purposes, Daisy has a standard based on the number of kilograms inspected per hour and the number of kilograms that pass or fail the inspection.

Daisy expects that for every 10,000 kilograms of food produced, 1,000 kilograms of food will be inspected. Inspection of 1,000 kilograms of dog food should take 1 hour. Daisy also expects that 2% of the food inspected will fail the inspection. During the month of May, Daisy produced 2,250,000 kilograms of food and inspected 200,000 kilograms of food in 210 hours. Of the 200,000 kilograms of food inspected, 3,500 kilograms of food failed to pass the inspection.

REQUIRED

1. Compute two variances that help determine whether the time spent on inspections was more or less than expected. (Follow a format similar to the one used for the variable overhead rate and efficiency variances, but without prices.)
2. Compute two variances that can be used to evaluate the percentage of the food that fails the inspection.

8-42 Nonfinancial performance measures. Rollie Manufacturing makes, among other things, wheels for roller skates. Manufacturing Department B receives plastic wheel casings from Manufacturing Department A and puts them on axles along with some ball bearings. The wheel casings have been inspected in Department A and should be free from major defects.

Most of the work in Department B is done by machine, but before the wheels are sent to the Packaging Department they are inspected for defects. Poorly made wheels are disassembled by hand and sent back to the beginning of the Department B line for rework. Thus any wheel that was made incorrectly and fixed takes more than twice as long to finish as a wheel that was made correctly the first time. Any wheels still not useable after rework are thrown away.

The same amount of ball bearings is requisitioned from the materials storeroom daily. Any leftover ball bearings at the end of the day are discarded. Ball bearings are measured by weight.

The machines in Department B are serviced only at night after the manufacturing run is over to save on intentional downtime. There are three machines in Department B, so if one does go down during processing there are still two workable machines until the next day. Rollie's goal in Department B is to produce 400 usable wheels per day.

REQUIRED

1. Under what circumstance would you consider ball bearings indirect rather than direct materials? Would you consider them direct materials or overhead in this problem?
2. What nonfinancial measures can Rollie use in Department B to control overhead costs?
3. Suggest some ways Rollie can better plan for and reduce overhead costs, given your answer to requirement 2.

8-43 Overhead variances, governance. Zuller Company uses standard costing. The company prepared its static budget for 2013 at 2,500,000 machine-hours for the year. Total budgeted overhead cost is $31,250,000. The variable overhead rate is $10 per machine-hour ($20 per unit). Actual results for 2013 follow:

1. a. Budgeted fixed overhead, $6,250,000

Machine-hours	2,400,000 hours
Output	1,245,000 units
Variable overhead	$25,200,000
Fixed overhead rate variance	$ 1,500,000 U

REQUIRED

1. Compute for the fixed overhead:
   a. Budgeted amount.
   b. Budgeted cost per machine-hour.
   c. Actual cost.
   d. Production-volume variance.
2. Compute the variable overhead rate variance and the variable overhead efficiency variance.
3. Jack Remich, the controller, prepares the variance analysis. It is common knowledge in the company that he and Ronald Monroe, the production manager, are not on the best of terms. In a recent executive committee meeting, Monroe had complained about the lack of usefulness of the accounting reports he receives. To get back at him, Remich manipulated the actual fixed overhead amount by assigning a greater-than-normal share of allocated costs to the production area. And, he decided to amortize all of the newly acquired production equipment using the double-declining-balance method rather than the straight-line method, contrary to company practice. As a result, there was a sizable unfavourable fixed overhead rate variance. He boasted to one of his confidants, "I am just returning the favour." Discuss Remich's actions and their ramifications.

8-44 ABC overhead variances. Asma Surgical Instruments Inc. makes a special line of forceps, SFA, in batches. Asma randomly selects forceps from each SFA batch for quality-testing purposes. Quality-testing costs are batch-level costs. A separate quality-testing section is responsible for SFA quality testing.

Quality-testing costs consist of some variable and some fixed costs in relation to the quality-testing hours. The following information is for 2013:

	Static-Budget Amounts	Actual Amounts
Units of SFA produced and sold	21,000	22,000
Batch size (number of units per batch)	500	550
Testing hours per batch	5.5	5.4
Variable overhead cost per testing hour	$ 48.00	$ 50.40
Total fixed testing overhead costs	$32,650.00	$32,659.00

REQUIRED
1. For variable testing overhead costs, compute the efficiency and rate variances. Comment on the results.
2. For fixed testing overhead costs, compute the rate and the production-volume variances. Comment on the results.

8-45 ABC overhead variances. CellOne is a cellular phone service reseller, contracting with major cellular operators for airtime in bulk and then reselling service to retail customers. Having adopted an ABC system last year, CellOne has defined the following activity areas— contracting, marketing, technical service, and customer service.

The technical service area has one major cost driver—technical support hours. One hour of technical support is budgeted for every 5,000 minutes of airtime sold. For the month ended August 31, 2013, CellOne budgeted to sell 6,850,000 minutes; however, actual minutes sold totalled 7,350,000. During August 2013, 1,500 actual technical support hours were logged. Some additional data follow:

	Actual	Budget
Variable technical service activity cost	$37,800	$39,456
Fixed technical service activity costs	$81,000	$83,844

Budgeted input allowed for actual output achieved totalled 1,470 hours of technical support.

REQUIRED
1. What is the actual variable technical service activity area cost per technical support hour? Budgeted cost per hour?
2. What is the allocated fixed technical service area overhead?
3. Calculate the rate variance, the efficiency variance, and the flexible-budget variance for variable overhead costs. Explain these variances based on the data provided.
4. Has CellOne management underallocated or overallocated fixed overhead for August 2013? Show how you calculate the underallocation or overallocation.

8-46 Integrate and reconcile all overhead variances. FlatScreen manufactures flat-panel LCD displays. The displays are sold to major PC manufacturers. Following are some manufacturing overhead data for FlatScreen for the year ended December 31, 2013:

	Actual	Flexible Budget	Allocated Amount
Variable manufacturing overhead	$1,838,592	$1,843,200	$1,843,200
Fixed manufacturing overhead	$8,404,992	$8,354,304	$9,031,680

FlatScreen's budget was based on the assumption that 17,760 units (panels) will be manufactured during 2013. The planned allocation rate was two machine-hours per unit. FlatScreen uses machine-hours as the cost driver. Actual number of machine-hours used during 2013 was 36,480. The budgeted variable manufacturing overhead costs equal $1,704,960.

REQUIRED

Compute the following quantities (you should be able to do so in the prescribed order):

1. Budgeted number of machine-hours planned.
2. Budgeted fixed manufacturing overhead costs per machine-hour.
3. Budgeted variable manufacturing overhead costs per machine-hour.
4. Budgeted number of machine-hours allowed for actual output achieved.
5. Actual number of output units.
6. Actual number of machine-hours used per panel.
7. Allocated amount for fixed manufacturing overhead.

8-47 Integrate and reconcile all overhead variances. (Continuation of 8-46).

REQUIRED

1. Prepare appropriate journal entries for variable and fixed manufacturing overhead (you will need to calculate the different variances to accomplish this).
2. Overhead variances may be used to reconcile the Cost of Goods Sold account at the end of the fiscal year. Cost of goods sold (COGS) is then entered on the income statement. Show how COGS is reconciled through journal entries.

8-48 Overhead analysis. The following information for 2013 is for Morgan Corporation, which uses standard costing:

Static-budget machine-hours	33,000
Fixed overhead budget costs	$ 5,940,000
Fixed overhead actual costs	$ 5,400,000
Variable overhead actual costs	$11,520,000
Variable overhead rate per machine-hour	$ 360
Actual machine hours used	30,000
Budgeted machine-hours allowed for actual output	35,000

REQUIRED

1. Calculate variable overhead rate variance and efficiency variance.
2. Compute fixed overhead rate variance and production-volume variance.

COLLABORATIVE LEARNING CASES

8-49 Overhead variances, four-variance analysis. A large metropolitan health-care complex, General Hospital, has had difficulty controlling its accounts receivable. Costs currently available from the information system are inaccurate and have led to gross errors in reports to the various government funding agencies, which have indicated that the hospital appears to be operating at a deficit. The hospital administration is concerned that the poor quality of information could lead to their replacement.

With the participation of the billing department, a set of standard costs and standard amounts was developed for 2013. These standard costs can be used in a flexible budget with separate variable cost and fixed cost categories. The output unit is defined to be a single bill.

The accountant of General Hospital provides you with the following for April 2013:

1. 1,600 hours

Variable overhead costs, allowance per standard hour	$ 12
Fixed overhead flexible budget variance	$ 240 F
Total budgeted overhead costs for the bills prepared	$ 27,000
Production-volume variance	$ 1,080 F
Variable cost rate variance	$ 2,400 U
Variable cost efficiency variance	$ 2,400 F
Standard hours allowed for the bills prepared	1,800 labour-hours

REQUIRED

Compute the following:

1. Actual hours of input used.
2. Fixed overhead budget.
3. Fixed overhead allocated.
4. Budgeted fixed overhead rate per hour.
5. Denominator level in hours.

8-50 Standard setting, benchmarking, governance. (Continuation of 8-49) Ira Stone, the president of General Hospital, has a meeting with the Medical Economics Group (MEG). MEG is a consulting firm in the health services sector. It reports that General's billing operations are grossly inefficient. Its standard costing per bill is above 90% of the 130 hospitals MEG tracks in its benchmark.

Stone suspects the billing group deliberately "padded" its standard costs and standard amounts. Despite large investment in new information systems, the standards for 2013 were not below actual results for 2012. Stone does not want to institute a witch hunt, but he does want to eliminate the fat in General's cost structure.

REQUIRED

1. How might General's billing operations group have "padded" its standard costs and standard amounts? Why might they do this padding?
2. What steps should Stone take to "reduce the fat" in the overhead costs of the billing operations at General Hospital?

Income Effects of Denominator Level on Inventory Valuation

9

BUSINESS MATTERS

Capacity-Level Choices

Intel is a high-operating-leverage company. When it operates at full capacity, the higher the production output, the lower the fixed-cost rate per unit. There is, however, a limit or constraint on just how many chips Intel can produce without purchasing more capacity.

The cost of goods sold includes only the fixed costs of units sold, not units produced, and the difference remains in the valuation of finished goods inventory. The decision about what capacity will be in the denominator level used to calculate the fixed-cost manufacturing overhead rate affects the reported operating income because it affects both the inventory values and cost of goods sold.

LEARNING OUTCOMES

After studying this chapter, you should be able to

1. Identify the factors important to choosing the denominator level used to calculate fixed overhead allocation rates.

2. Explain how the choice of denominator affects capacity management, costing, pricing, and performance evaluation.

3. Distinguish absorption from variable costing; prepare and explain the differences in operating income under each costing policy.

4. Distinguish throughput costing from variable costing and absorption costing, and explain differences in operating income under each costing policy.

5. Explain productivity measurement under each of the three costing policies.

In this chapter we examine the capacity choices available to managers who decide on the denominator level used to calculate fixed overhead rates. The capacity choice managers make will be the denominator level. This decision affects product costing and pricing, capacity management, governance (compliance with external reporting regulations), and performance evaluation. This is one of the most strategically important and complex decisions managers face.

The decision to acquire too much capacity relative to demand will incur idle, unproductive capacity costs that often cannot be recovered. Too little capacity relative to demand means companies will incur the opportunity cost of lost market share as competitors serve their customers, who may never return.

DENOMINATOR LEVELS: A COMPLEX DECISION WITH COMPLEX EFFECTS

Each of the four choices for denominator level constrains output. The first two denominator-level choices constrain output because of the supply that can be provided by existing capacity:

◆ **Theoretical capacity** is the amount of output theoretically possible if there were never any delays or interruptions in production—a 24/7/365 quantity.

◆ **Practical capacity** is the amount of output practically possible after taking into account required idle time for maintenance, safety inspections, holidays, and other relevant factors.

Theoretical capacity must always be greater than practical capacity because practical capacity excludes any volume lost through idle time.

The following two denominator-level choices constrain output produced because of the existing demand level for the output:

◆ **Normal capacity** is the level of output that will satisfy average customer demand over a specified time period and complies with GAAP.

◆ **Master-budget capacity** is the level of output that will satisfy customer demand for a single budget cycle and complies with Canada Revenue Agency (CRA) for tax purposes.

Exhibit 9-1 illustrates the four potential choices of capacity and the implications of using each capacity option as the denominator level. The decision process itself is in purple, and there are two pairs of denominator-level choices: The pair of choices based on production capacity is illustrated in blue, and the pair based on non-production factors is in gold.

The issues arising from the selection of the denominator level based on either a supply or demand measure of capacity affect both the balance sheet and the income statement. Although high-operating-leverage companies rely more heavily on machines (or capital) than labour in the production process, the capacity level will also entail changes to labour supply.

Assume that managers have good business intelligence about the level of demand (market size) in the industry and how well their competitors do (market share). The first decision is whether to acquire all the forecast capacity required to supply growth in the company's market share, or to make acquisitions as the need arises. Bear in mind that most capacity is purchased in large increments on the basis that it will provide net cash inflow from sales of output. This will sum to a return on investment over the useful life of the capacity. This means, for acquisition purposes, capacity costs are semi-fixed. The demand, however, is usually a continuous growth curve that peaks, then tapers off as the life cycle of the product ends. There is no perfect capacity choice to ensure a perfect denominator level because the behaviours of fixed costs, demand, and inventory values differ.

Managers have two sets of objectives to consider and four different capacity measures to choose from—theoretical, practical, normal, and master-budget capacity. Bushells Company produces labelled bottles of iced tea for Tazo. The company uses absorption costing (discussed below) for monthly internal reporting and for

EXHIBIT 9-1
Stage in the Denominator Level Choice Process

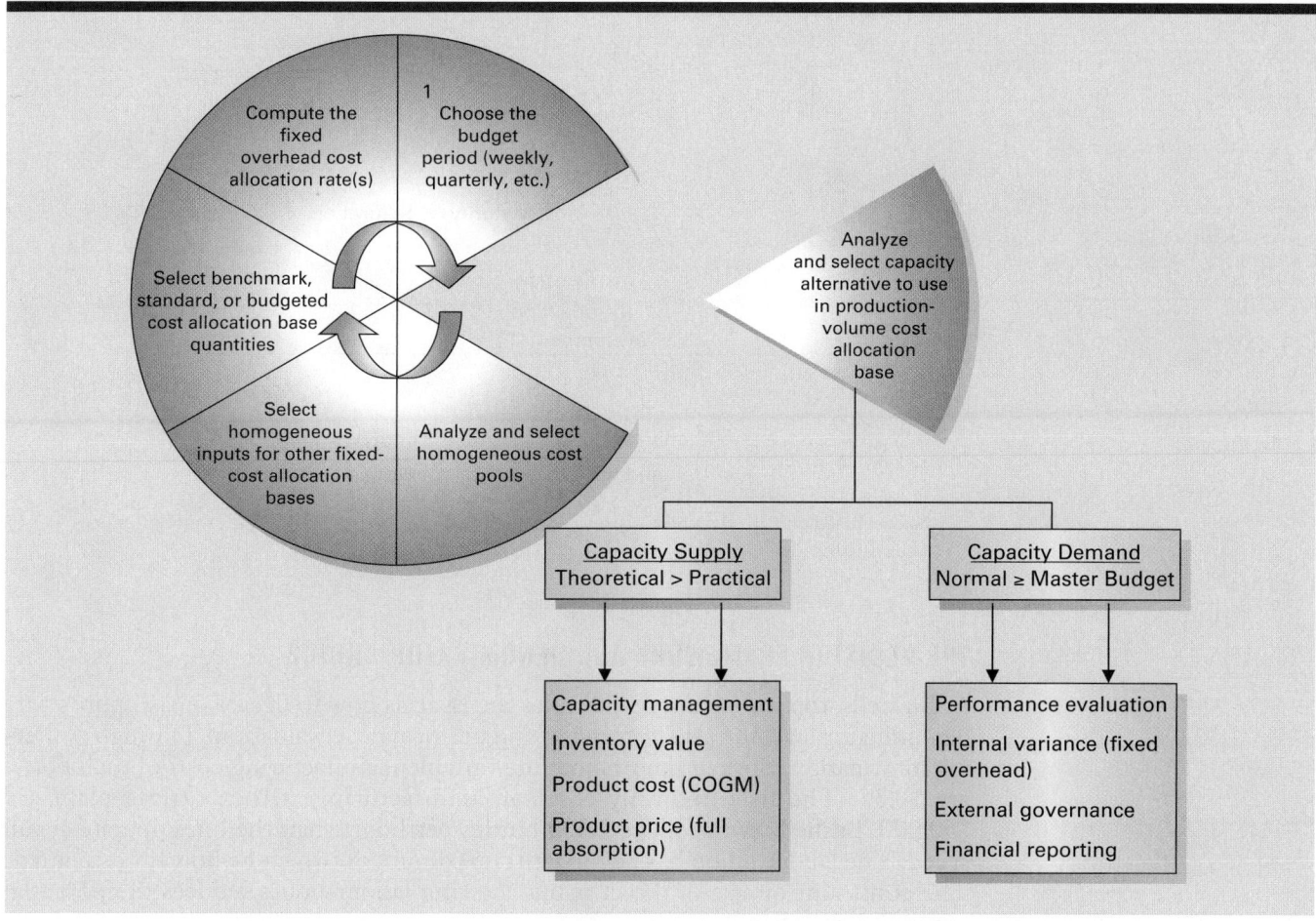

financial reporting to shareholders. Capacity is measured as bottles of iced tea. The management team determines that for external reporting purposes there is no choice. The denominator required by Canada Revenue Agency (CRA) when fixed costs are allocated to cost of goods sold and inventory is the master-budget capacity. Income tax rules effectively prohibit using either theoretical capacity or practical capacity denominator levels. Both typically result in companies taking writeoffs of fixed manufacturing overhead as tax deductions more quickly than desired by the CRA. To receive a clean audit on disclosure presented externally, however, there is no choice and practical capacity must be the denominator used. The master-budget capacity is a short-term forecast of anticipated demand for output, and it is assumed that use of capacity will closely match demand.

Notice that two of the choices are measures of supply of capacity and two are measures of demand by customers. The quantity demanded by customers will influence the amount of unused capacity. Exhibit 9-2 illustrates two types of rates of change. The blue dashed line is a stepped or discontinuous rate of change for capacity. The curved gold line is the rate of change in demand assumed over time for the product life cycle. The different rates and patterns of change make it unlikely the lines will intersect. This means that corporations will almost always have a production-volume variance. For internal management purposes, the dollar value of that production-volume variance will depend on the capacity measure—the denominator level—chosen by managers.

Notice in Exhibit 9-2 that, where the horizontal lines shorten on the stepped growth of capacity, the demand curve line is steeper. The distance between the demand growth curve and the semi-fixed capacity growth visually represents the presence of production-volume variance. We have assumed that the company has decided the cost of temporary excess capacity throughout the growth stage is bearable to sustain growth in market share, which is why the demand curve never crosses the semi-fixed costs.

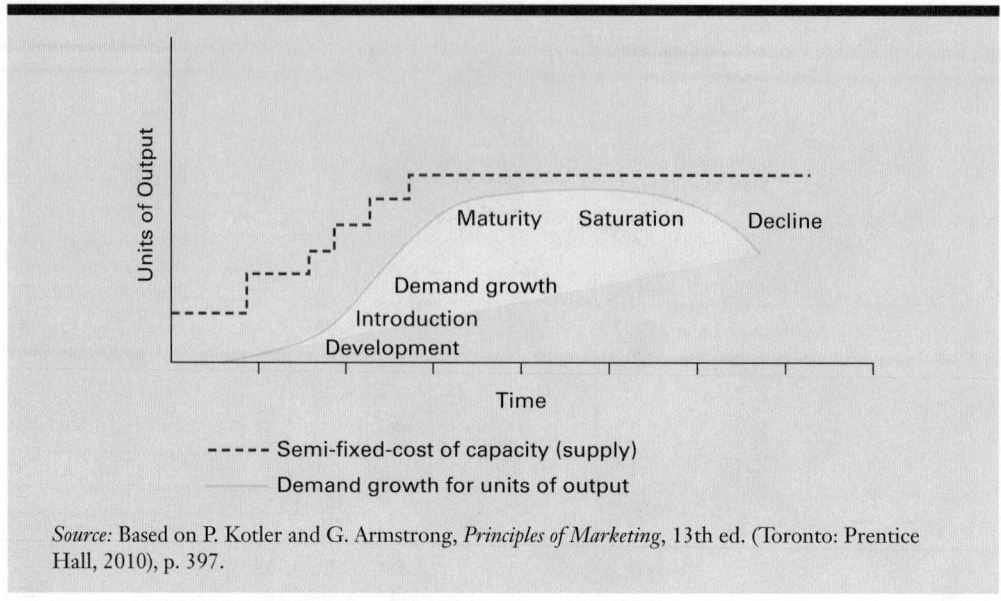

Source: Based on P. Kotler and G. Armstrong, *Principles of Marketing*, 13th ed. (Toronto: Prentice Hall, 2010), p. 397.

THE DECISION FRAMEWORK AND DENOMINATOR CHOICE

At Bushells, top management identifies the issue as how to decide on an appropriate denominator level for *internal* pricing and performance evaluation. Through gathering information, Bushells knows that the variable manufacturing costs of each bottle are $0.35. The fixed monthly costs of manufacturing at the bottling plant are $50,000. Bushells can produce 2,400 bottles per hour when the lines operate at full speed. The labour union has negotiated a maximum of two eight-hour shifts per day. The constraint on use of direct manufacturing labour-hours reduces the potential output for the plant.

Supply Measures: Theoretical Capacity or Practical Capacity? Theoretical capacity is theoretical in the sense that it does not allow for any plant maintenance or interruptions from bottle breakages on the filling lines or a host of other factors. Although it is a rare plant that is able to operate at theoretical capacity, it can represent a goal or target level of usage. The strategic tradeoff here is that scheduled idle time for maintenance can lengthen the useful life of equipment and the long-term total output, or it can improve short-term cost savings. Bushells' theoretical monthly capacity is:

$$2,400 \text{ bottles per hour} \times 16 \text{ hours per day} \times 30 \text{ days} = 1,152,000 \text{ bottles}$$

Assume that the financial-accounting reporting method is used to estimate cost of goods manufactured and sold, which includes fixed overhead costs as well as variable manufacturing costs. This is called absorption costing or full absorption costing (see p. 352 for further discussion). No idle time results in the highest possible supply-side denominator level, the lowest fixed overhead cost rate, and the lowest inventory valuation. If, however, actual production is less than theoretical capacity because there is no demand or production is interrupted, the production-volume variance will be high and indicates the opportunity cost of idle productive capacity. This is a non-value added cost to the customer and for which a customer will not pay.

Practical capacity reduces theoretical capacity for unavoidable operating interruptions such as scheduled maintenance time, shutdowns for holidays, safety inspections, and so on. This type of scheduled idle capacity is often called **off-limits idle capacity**. Strategically, companies might schedule off-limits idle capacity to comply with regulations and safety legislation. For example, the board of directors would require Bushells to shut down for maintenance and inspection to comply with specific occupational health and safety legislation.

Transport Canada requires companies in the airline industry to comply with numerous safety regulations. After an aircraft has flown a specified number of air miles, taken off and landed a specified number of times, and so on, Transport Canada requires the aircraft be grounded and its systems, such as wiring and hydraulics, must be rebuilt. The goal of these procedures is to minimize risk to passengers. After a rebuild, the aircraft must undergo inspection by an Transport Canada agent before it can be airborne again.

The U.S. has similar laws. You may remember that in 2008, American Airlines cancelled 2,500 flights after a surprise inspection by U.S. government authorities revealed poor maintenance. Wiring in the landing gear was a potential fire hazard and the planes were grounded. American subsequently scrapped 570 aircraft in its fleet. For example, Southwest Airlines was fined $10.2 million for failing to comply with inspection schedules. This illustrates why companies in some industries must plan for off-limits idle capacity.

Practical capacity is not constant over the life of equipment. Process redesign can improve labour efficiency, wait time for materials, and scheduling, which would increase practical capacity. At Bushells, assume that the practical hourly production rate including non-productive and off-limits idle capacity is 2,000 bottles an hour and that the plant can operate 25 days a month. The practical monthly capacity is:

$$2,000 \text{ bottles per hour} \times 16 \text{ hours} \times 25 \text{ days} = 800,000 \text{ bottles}$$

Corporations cannot purchase long-term capacity in small increments. Investment in capacity to meet long-term anticipated normal demand is often made well in advance of actually reaching this level. But investments are made to retain and expand market share, understanding the risk that normal demand may never be realized. Practical capacity excludes off-limits idle capacity, during which scheduled maintenance occurs.[1] Often, the difference between theoretical and practical capacity is off-limits idle capacity.

Another cause of downtime is setups, and at a bottling company like Bushells customers use differently sized and shaped bottles with different labels. This is **non-productive idle capacity**. This type of capacity is not off limits because it can be minimized with excellent scheduling or used to accomplish other value-added activities. Bushells may also acquire idle capacity to provide some excess resources required if there are unexpected delays in obtaining materials or unscheduled interruptions to fill rush orders.

Engineers at the Bushells plant can provide input on the technical capabilities of machines for filling bottles. Human safety factors are also important, such as increased risk of injury when the line operates at faster speeds. The likelihood of bottles shattering and the hazard of bottling broken glass with the tea also increases as the line speed increases. In some cases, an increase in capacity may be technically possible but not economically sound. For example, the labour union may actually permit a third shift per day but only at unusually high wage rates that clearly do not make financial sense in the bottling market.

Demand Measures: Normal Capacity or Master-Budget Capacity? Normal capacity utilization and master-budget capacity utilization measure the denominator level in terms of demand for the output. In many cases, demand is well below the capacity or supply available, as was illustrated in Exhibit 9-2. In such cases, the semi-fixed costs do not intersect the demand line, indicating the presence of idle non-productive capacity. Bushells' senior management believes that over the next one to three years, the normal monthly production level will be 500,000 bottles. This also explains the distance between the demand and semi-fixed cost lines in Exhibit 9-2. External reporting requires the use of normal capacity in the denominator, taking into account off-limits idle capacity. Unallocated overhead (variance) is

---

[1]Parvez, R. Sopariwala, "Capacity Utilization: Using the CAM-I Capacity Model in a Multi-Hierarchical Manufacturing Environment," *Management Accounting Quarterly*, 7.2 (Winter 2006): pp. 17–34.

recognized in the time period incurred. GAAP also permits the use of actual production level if it is not materially different from normal capacity.

Strategically, Bushells' managers have likely concluded that the excess non-productive capacity can be used in other revenue-generating ways (see Chapters 11 and 12) until demand growth accelerates. Increased demand by customers may not only be for product, but also for services customized to their needs. Bushells may also have made this decision as an agility-response strategy: The managers may have seen the ability to provide faster delivery (using increased capacity) as a competitive advantage in acquiring new customers and considered the benefit greater than the cost of excess capacity.

Normal capacity utilization is based on the level of capacity utilization that satisfies average customer demand over a period (say, of two to three years) that includes seasonal, cyclical, or other trend factors. Master-budget capacity utilization is based on the anticipated level of capacity utilization for the next operating budget period of a month, a quarter, or a year. The key difference is the *time period* under consideration, long (normal) or short (master) term. These two denominator levels will differ when an industry has cyclical periods of high and low demand or when management believes that the budgeted production for the coming period is unrepresentative of "long-term" demand.

Consider our Bushells example. The master budget for 2013 is based on production of 400,000 bottles per month. Hence, the master budget denominator level is 400,000 bottles, which is a short-term estimate of market share for the year 2013.

EFFECTS ON REPORTING, COSTING, PRICING, AND EVALUATION

2 Explain how the choice of denominator affects capacity management, costing, pricing, and performance evaluation.

Bushells has budgeted fixed manufacturing costs of $50,000 per month. Assume the actual costs are also $50,000. To keep this example simple, we assume all fixed manufacturing costs are indirect. Bushells' top management team must now forecast the outcomes from using the different capacity alternatives in the denominator.

Bushells' budgeted fixed manufacturing overhead rates in May 2013 for the four alternative capacity denominator levels are as follows:

Capacity Concept (1)	Budgeted Fixed Manufacturing Overhead per Month (2)	Budgeted Capacity Level (in Bottles) (3)	Budgeted Manufacturing Overhead Cost Rate (4) = (2) ÷ (3)
Theoretical capacity	$50,000	1,152,000	$0.0434
Practical capacity	50,000	800,000	0.0625
Normal capacity utilization	50,000	500,000	0.1000
Master-budget capacity utilization	50,000	400,000	0.1250

The budgeted fixed manufacturing overhead rate based on master-budget capacity utilization ($0.1250) represents an increase of more than 188% from the rate based on theoretical capacity ($0.0434). The fixed-cost pool is $50,000 over the relevant range of 400,000 to 1,152,000 bottles.

Exhibit 9-3 illustrates the four possible fixed overhead cost rates per bottle as the denominator-level choice changes. If the managers decide to use only one system for both internal management and external financial reporting purposes, then they will choose 500,000 as the denominator level. This will guarantee a short-run 2013 unfavourable production-volume variance. But the company will also be consistent with GAAP and use full absorption costing to estimate inventory value and cost of goods sold. This will lead to applying the full cost of $0.1000 of all idle capacity of 752,000 bottles (1,152,000 − 400,000 bottles) when pricing each of the 400,000 bottles actually sold.

Deciding on the denominator level requires more quantitative input about how the choices will affect performance assessment. Assume now that Bushells' actual production in May 2013 is 460,000 bottles. Actual sales are 420,000 bottles. Also

EXHIBIT 9-3
Fixed-Cost Overhead Rate per Bottle at Bushells

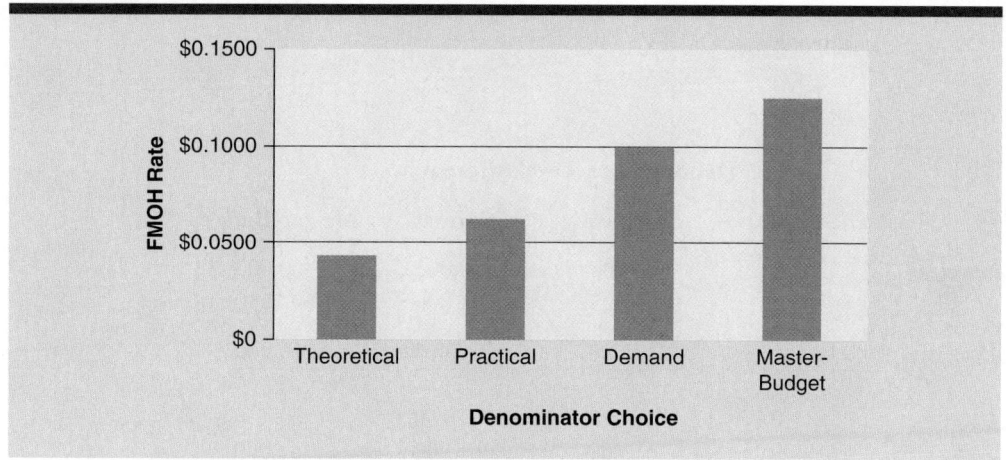

assume no beginning inventory on May 1, 2013, and no price, rate, or efficiency variances for May 2013. The manufacturing plant sells bottles of iced tea to another division for $0.50 per bottle. Its only costs are variable manufacturing costs of $0.35 per bottle and $50,000 per month for fixed manufacturing overhead. Bushells writes off all variances to cost of goods sold each month.

The budgeted manufacturing costs per bottle of iced tea for each capacity concept are the sum of $0.35 in variable manufacturing costs and the budgeted fixed manufacturing overhead costs (shown from the preceding table):

Capacity Concept (1)	Variable Manufacturing Costs (2)	Fixed Manufacturing Overhead Cost Rate (3)	Total Manufacturing Costs (4) = (2) + (3)
Theoretical capacity	$0.3500	$0.0434	$0.3934
Practical capacity	0.3500	0.0625	0.4125
Normal capacity utilization	0.3500	0.1000	0.4500
Master-budget capacity utilization	0.3500	0.1250	0.4750

Each capacity concept will result in a different production-volume variance:

$$\text{Production-volume variance} = \left(\begin{array}{c} \text{Denominator} \\ \text{level in} \\ \text{output units} \end{array} - \begin{array}{c} \text{Actual} \\ \text{output units} \end{array} \right) \times \begin{array}{c} \text{Budgeted fixed} \\ \text{manufacturing overhead} \\ \text{rate per output unit} \end{array}$$

$$\text{Theoretical capacity} = (1,152,000 - 460,000) \times \$0.0434$$
$$= \$30,033 \text{ U}$$

$$\text{Practical capacity} = (800,000 - 460,000) \times \$0.0625$$
$$= \$21,250 \text{ U}$$

$$\text{Normal capacity utilization} = (500,000 - 460,000) \times \$0.1000$$
$$= \$4,000 \text{ U}$$

$$\text{Master-budget capacity utilization} = (400,000 - 460,000) \times \$0.1250$$
$$= 7,500 \text{ F}$$

Exhibit 9-4 shows how the choice of a denominator affects Bushells' operating income for May 2013. Using the master-budget denominator will mean assigning the highest amount of fixed manufacturing overhead costs per bottle to the 40,000 bottles in ending inventory. Accordingly, operating income is highest using the master-budget capacity utilization denominator. Recall that Bushells had no beginning inventory on May 1, 2013, production in May of 460,000 bottles, and sales in May of 420,000 bottles. Hence, the ending inventory on May 31 is 40,000 bottles. The differences between the operating incomes for the four denominator-level concepts in

EXHIBIT 9-4
Bushells Company Income Statement Effects of Alternative Denominator Levels for May 2013

Actual sales volume (bottles)	420,000			
Actual output (bottles)	460,000			
Variable manufacturing overhead rate	$0.3500			

	Denominator-Level Alternatives			
	Theoretical	**Practical**	**Normal**	**Master-Budget**
Capacity alternative (denominator level)	1,152,000	800,000	500,000	400,000
Fixed overhead cost rate	$0.0434	$0.0625	$0.1000	$0.1250
Sales, $0.50 × 420,000	$210,000	$210,000	$210,000	$210,000
Cost of goods sold (COGS)				
Beginning inventory	0	0	0	0
Variable manufacturing costs*	161,000	161,000	161,000	161,000
Fixed manufacturing overhead costs†	19,964	28,750	46,000	57,500
Cost of goods available for sale	180,964	189,750	207,000	218,500
Ending inventory‡	15,736	16,500	18,000	19,000
Total COGS (at standard)	165,228	173,250	189,000	199,500
Adjustments for variances§	30,033U	21,250U	4,000U	(7,500)F
Total COGS	195,261	194,500	193,000	192,000
Gross margin	14,739	15,500	17,000	18,000
Marketing, other expenses	10,000	10,000	10,000	10,000
Operating income	$ 4,739	$ 5,500	$ 7,000	$ 8,000

*$0.35 × 460,000 = $161,000

†Fixed manufacturing overhead costs

Production		Rate		Cost
460,000	×	$0.0434	=	$19,964
460,000	×	$0.0625	=	$28,750
460,000	×	$0.1000	=	$46,000
460,000	×	$0.1250	=	$57,500

‡Ending inventory costs

Variable		Fixed		Production		Sales		Value
($0.3500	+	$0.0434)	×	(460,000	−	420,000)	=	$ 15,736
($0.3500	+	$0.0625)	×	(460,000	−	420,000)	=	$ 16,500
($0.3500	+	$0.1000)	×	(460,000	−	420,000)	=	$ 18,000
($0.3500	+	$0.1250)	×	(460,000	−	420,000)	=	$ 19,000

§The production-volume variance is calculated on p. 347. It is the only variance Bushells incurred in May 2013.

Exhibit 9-4 are due to different amounts of fixed manufacturing overhead costs being inventoried:

Fixed Manufacturing Overhead May 31, 2012 Pro Forma Inventory Valuation

Denominator Level (1)	Pro Forma Quantity (2)	Fixed Overhead Rate (3)	Pro Forma Inventory (4) = (2) × (3)
Theoretical	40,000	$0.0434	$1,736
Practical	40,000	0.0625	2,500
Normal	40,000	0.1000	4,000
Master-budget	40,000	0.1250	5,000

Thus, in Exhibit 9-4 the difference in operating income between the master-budget capacity utilization concept and the normal capacity utilization concept of

$1,000 ($8,000 − $7,000) is due to the difference in fixed manufacturing overhead inventoried ($5,000 − $4,000 = $1,000).

PRODUCT COSTING

Cost data from a standard-costing system are often used in pricing or product-mix decisions. As the Bushells example illustrates, the use of theoretical capacity results in an unachieveably small fixed manufacturing overhead cost per bottle because it is based on an unattainable level of capacity utilization. Theoretical capacity is rarely used as the denominator because it departs significantly from the real capacity available to a company.

Many companies favour practical capacity as the denominator to calculate the budgeted fixed manufacturing cost per bottle. Practical capacity in the Bushells example represents the maximum number of bottles that Bushells intends to produce per year. If Bushells had consistently planned to produce fewer bottles of iced tea, it would have built a smaller plant and incurred lower costs. The drawback is that neither GAAP nor CRA accept this denominator for external reporting purposes. For internal performance measurement and product pricing, this denominator level is superior to the others at predicting recoverable costs. It is also appropriate to assess production managers' performances. It is not, however, appropriate to assess the marketing function because marketing managers have no control over production functions.

Bushells budgets $0.0625 in fixed manufacturing overhead cost per bottle based on the $50,000 it costs to acquire the capacity to produce 800,000 bottles. This plant capacity is acquired well before Bushells uses the capacity and even before Bushells knows how much of the capacity it will actually use. That is, the budgeted fixed manufacturing cost of $0.0625 per bottle measures the *cost per bottle of supplying the capacity*.

Demand for Bushells' iced tea bottles in 2013 is expected to be 400,000 bottles lower than practical capacity. The cost of *supplying* the capacity needed to make bottles is still $0.0625 per bottle. That's because capacity is acquired in "lumpy" amounts, and it costs $50,000 per year to acquire the capacity to make 800,000 bottles. The capacity and its cost are fixed in the *short run*; the capacity supplied cannot be reduced to match the capacity needed in 2013. As a result, not all of the capacity supplied at $0.0625 per bottle will be needed or used in 2013.

Using practical capacity will include the cost of idle capacity in the fixed overhead cost rate. Highlighting the cost of capacity acquired but not used directs managers' attention to managing unused capacity, perhaps by designing new products to fill unused capacity or leasing out unused capacity to others. In contrast, using either of the capacity levels based on the demand for Bushells' iced tea bottles—master-budget capacity utilization or normal capacity utilization—hides the amount of unused capacity.

If Bushells had used the master-budget capacity utilization as the capacity level to conform with CRA, it would have calculated the budgeted fixed manufacturing cost per bottle as $0.1250 ($50,000 ÷ 400,000 bottles). This calculation does not use data about practical capacity, so it does not separately identify the cost of unused capacity. Note, however, that the cost of $0.1250 per bottle includes a charge for unused capacity—the $0.0625 fixed manufacturing resource that would be used to produce each bottle at practical capacity plus the cost of unused capacity allocated to each bottle, $0.0625 per bottle.

The next section illustrates how the use of normal capacity utilization or master-budget capacity utilization results in setting selling prices that are not competitive.

PRODUCT PRICING: THE DOWNWARD DEMAND SPIRAL

The easiest way to understand the downward demand spiral is by an example. The **downward demand spiral** is a progressive reduction in capacity use, which leads to an increase in the fixed overhead rate. As sales decrease, the actual capacity used also decreases to control the amount in ending inventory. This means that the realized quantity in the master-budget denominator of any fixed overhead cost rate decreases, but the fixed-cost pool remains constant.

Denominator-Level Choice Reflects Recoverable Costs in Strategic Pricing

If Bushells has adequate business intelligence data to benchmark its fixed overhead to become at least as good as or better than its competitors, the $0.0625 rate is more aggressive than the $0.1250 master-budget rate yet remains possible to achieve, which the $0.0434 theoretical rate is not. Practical capacity focuses on the supply constraint on production and does not include any non-productive idle capacity cost. It is, by definition, a long-term estimate of what Bushells will need in the long run to meet demand. But often corporations control growth by purchasing capacity before master-budget demand requires it.

In a competitive market where gross margins are very slim, the cost of idle capacity is non-value added to the customer who expects Bushells to either manage its capacity or bear the costs of ineffectiveness. Customers are very sensitive to price, and if Bushells tries to recover non-value added from customers they will simply purchase a less expensive product from a competitor. In the long run, Bushells must recover all costs in its sales price if it is to be profitable. Until actual capacity use reaches practical capacity, the difference in cost per unit that cannot be recovered will erode gross margin.

The master-budget fixed overhead rate increases each time the master-budget denominator decreases. This does not mean, however, that the increased unitized fixed cost can be recovered by increasing the price. A decreased quantity of forecast sales must bear higher costs per unit—which leads to an increased unit sales price to cover full costs. In a competitive market, all else being equal, this will further decrease sales. At the extreme, if Bushells sold only one bottle, its share of fixed overhead cost would be $50,000. This is a drawback of using master-budget capacity as the denominator level.

Assume Bushells uses master-budget capacity utilization of 400,000 bottles for full product costing in 2013. The resulting manufacturing cost is $0.4750 (0.35 + 0.125) per bottle. Assume in December 2013 that a competitor, Lipton Iced Tea, offers to supply a major customer of Bushells at $0.45 per bottle. Bushells' forecast of sales to this customer was 100,000 bottles in 2013. The Bushells manager, not wanting to show a loss on the account of $0.025 per bottle and wanting to recoup all costs in the long run, does not match the competitor's price and the account is lost. The lost account means budgeted fixed manufacturing costs of $50,000 will be spread over the remaining master-budget volume of 300,000 bottles. This means the unitized rate will increase to $0.167 ($50,000 ÷ 300,000 bottles) from $0.125 ($50,000 ÷ 400,000). The variable MOH rate remains at $0.35. The new full absorption cost, all other things being equal, will be $0.517 per bottle ($0.35 + $0.167 = $0.517).

Suppose then another customer of Bushells—also accounting for 100,000 bottles of budgeted volume—receives a bid from a competitor priced at $0.45. The Bushells manager compares this bid with his revised unit cost of $0.517, declines to match the competition, and the account is lost. The planned output would shrink further to 200,000 units. The budgeted fixed manufacturing cost per unit for the remaining 200,000 now would be $0.25 ($50,000 ÷ 200,000 bottles). With the variable costs remaining at $0.35, the new full absorption cost will be $0.60.

The use of practical capacity as the denominator to calculate the budgeted fixed manufacturing cost per bottle avoids the recalculation of unit costs when expected demand levels change. This is an example of standard rates used in budgeting and variance analysis. The fixed-cost rate is calculated based on the standard or practical capacity available rather than the capacity used to meet demand. Managers who use reported unit costs in a mechanical way to set prices are less likely to promote a downward demand spiral when they use practical capacity concepts because this quantity remains unchanged regardless of demand. Use of either normal capacity or master-budget capacity utilization can promote the downward demand spiral as capacity used decreases.

PERFORMANCE EVALUATION

Consider how the choice between normal capacity utilization, master-budget capacity utilization, and practical capacity affects how a marketing manager is evaluated.

Normal capacity utilization is often used as a basis for long-term plans. The normal capacity utilization depends on the time span selected and the forecasts made for each year. However, *normal capacity utilization is an average that provides no meaningful feedback to the marketing manager for a particular year.* Using normal capacity utilization as a reference for judging current performance of a marketing manager is an example of misusing a long-run measure for a short-run purpose.

Obtaining feedback after implementation is also something that Bushells needs to consider. None of the denominator levels is suitable to all purposes. The master-budget capacity utilization, rather than normal capacity utilization or practical capacity, is what should be used for evaluating a marketing manager's performance in the current year. This is because the master budget is the principal short-run planning and control tool. Managers feel more obligated to reach the levels specified in the master budget, which should have been carefully set in relation to the maximum opportunities for sales in the current year.

When large differences exist between practical capacity and master-budget capacity utilization, companies routinely classify part of the large difference as *planned unused capacity*. One reason they do so is performance evaluation. At Bushells, for example, the managers in charge of capacity planning usually do not make pricing decisions. Top management decided to build an iced-tea plant with 800,000 bottles of practical capacity, focusing on demand over the next five years. Bushells' marketing managers, who are mid-level managers, make the pricing decisions. This group believes it should be held accountable only for the manufacturing overhead costs related to the potential customer base in 2013. The master-budget capacity utilization suggests a customer base in 2013 of 400,000 bottles. Using responsibility accounting principles, part of the budgeted total fixed manufacturing costs would be attributed to the fixed capacity costs of meeting 2013 demand. The remaining costs would be separately shown as the capacity cost of meeting long-run demand increases expected to occur beyond 2013.

CAPACITY COSTS AND DENOMINATOR-LEVEL ISSUES

The choice of any denominator level introduces rigidity into the budgeting and costing system. Standard cost systems do not recognize fluctuations and uncertainty. The managers must make a choice despite their knowledge that they will almost certainly be wrong. GAAP requires frequent updating because standards may change quickly over time. Managers know that both supply of and demand for capacity is uncertain, if only because of random events. Bushells' plant has an estimated practical capacity of 800,000 bottles. The estimated master-budget capacity utilization for 2013 is 400,000 bottles. These estimates are uncertain. To deal with uncertainty, Bushells more than likely built its current plant with an 800,000-bottle practical capacity in part to provide the capability to meet unexpected surges in growth in demand. For example, consumers are increasingly aware of the waste from plastic bottles and producers are switching back to glass despite the increased weight, fragility, and transportation costs.

Challenging issues also arise in measuring the numerator, the fixed-cost pool. For example, deregulation of the electric utility industry has resulted in many electric utilities becoming unprofitable. This situation has led to write-downs in the values of their plant and equipment. The write-downs reduce the numerator via the amortization used to compute fixed capacity cost per kilowatt-hour of electricity produced.

In non-manufacturing value-chain functions, capacity costs also arise. Bushells may acquire a fleet of vehicles capable of distributing the output of its iced-tea plant. When actual production is below the practical capacity, there will be unused capacity cost issues with the distribution function as well as with the manufacturing function.

As you saw in Chapter 8, capacity cost issues are prominent in many service-sector companies, such as airlines, hospitals, railroads, and banks, even though these companies carry no inventory and have no inventory-costing issues. For example, in calculating the fixed overhead cost per patient-day in its obstetrics and gynecology department, a hospital must decide what denominator to use—practical capacity, normal utilization, or master-budget utilization. Its decision may have implications for capacity management as well as performance evaluation.

The Bushells example assumed that all fixed manufacturing overhead costs had a single cost driver: bottles of iced tea produced. As you saw in Chapter 5, ABC systems have multiple overhead cost pools at the output-unit, batch, product-sustaining, and facility-sustaining levels, each with its own cost driver. In calculating the activity cost rates (for setups and materials handling, say), management must choose a capacity level for the quantity of the cost driver (setup-hours or loads moved). Should it use practical, normal, or master-budget capacity utilization? For all the reasons described in the chapter, most proponents of ABC argue that practical capacity should be used as the denominator to calculate activity cost rates.

DENOMINATOR LEVEL AND INVENTORY VALUATION

3 Distinguish absorption from variable costing; prepare and explain the differences in operating income under each costing policy.

From the standpoint of Canadian and international financial accounting standards, both standard costing based on practical capacity and full absorption based on the normal-capacity denominator level are acceptable. It is the most conservative of the three overhead cost assignment and inventory valuation policy choices available for internal management purposes. Inventory must also be valued on a first-in, first-out (FIFO) basis. For internal management purposes, the two most commonly encountered methods of inventory valuation are variable costing and absorption costing. A third option is throughput costing.

ABSORPTION AND VARIABLE INVENTORY VALUATION ASSUMPTIONS

Throughout this chapter, we assume that the chosen allocation base for calculating the variable and fixed manufacturing overhead allocation rates is a production-output-related variable—for example, direct labour-hours or direct machine-hours per unit of output produced. The variable and fixed manufacturing overhead cost pools are assumed to be reasonably associated with a benefit measured using a direct manufacturing input. This association is what permits managers to explain variances in cost on the basis of changes in the consumption of the cost allocation base, making it sensible to calculate efficiency and production-volume variances.

Absorption costing (also called **full absorption costing**) is a method of inventory valuation in which inventory "absorbs" both variable and fixed *manufacturing* costs as inventoriable costs, but classifies all non-manufacturing costs as period costs, which are excluded. A variety of costs such as tax, insurance premiums, and amortization of manufacturing plant and equipment will be included in the fixed overhead cost rate assigned to each unit remaining in inventory. The important event transferring costs of production from the inventory on the balance sheet to the cost of goods sold (COGS) expense on the income statement is a sale. The timing of recognition of COGS is matched to incoming revenue.

Variable costing is a method of inventory valuation in which only *variable manufacturing* costs are included as inventoriable costs. All fixed and all non-manufacturing costs are classified as period costs expensed during the specific time period they are incurred. Under variable costing, for example, no amortization of manufacturing plant and equipment will be included in the overhead rate assigned to each unit remaining in inventory. These costs will be recognized as period costs when incurred as cost of goods available for sale. The important event transferring fixed costs of production from inventory on the balance sheet to period expenses on the income statement is the end of the budget period.

The key distinguishing factors of these two valuation policies are:

◆ The classification of fixed manufacturing overhead as an inventoriable (COGS) or a period cost.
◆ The classification of variable non-manufacturing overhead as an inventoriable (COGS) or period cost.
◆ The event that triggers recognition of fixed overhead expense.
◆ The timing of expensing fixed manufacturing overhead.

We will illustrate differences between the two costing methods using Radius Company, which manufactures specialty industrial belts. Radius allocates costs using a normal costing system. That is, its direct costs are traced to products using actual prices multiplied by the actual inputs used, but its indirect (overhead) costs are allocated using budgeted indirect cost rate(s) multiplied by actual inputs used. The allocation base for all manufacturing costs is units of output produced. The allocation base for all marketing costs is units of output sold. We assume the following for 2013:

◆ The budgeted equals the actual number of units produced (1,100,000 units).
◆ The budgeted equals the actual number of units sold (1,000,000 units).
◆ The budgeted equals actual fixed costs.
◆ Work in process is minimal.
◆ There is no beginning inventory on January 1, 2013.
◆ All variable costs are driven by an output-unit–related variable. (We assume, for example, batch-level and product-sustaining costs are zero.)

With 2013 production of 1,100,000 units and sales of 1,000,000 units, the ending inventory on December 31, 2013, is 100,000 units. The per unit and total actual costs for 2013 are as follows:

	Per Unit	Total Costs
Variable costs:		
Direct materials	$3.50	$3,850,000
Direct manufacturing labour	1.60	1,760,000
Indirect manufacturing costs	0.90	990,000
Manufacturing costs	6.00	6,600,000
Direct marketing costs	0.80	800,000
Indirect marketing costs	1.60	1,600,000
Marketing costs	2.40	2,400,000
Total variable costs	$8.40	$9,000,000
Fixed costs:		
Direct manufacturing costs	$0.30	$ 330,000
Indirect manufacturing costs	1.70	1,870,000
Manufacturing costs	2.00	2,200,000
Direct marketing costs	2.10	2,100,000
Indirect marketing costs	3.40	3,400,000
Marketing costs	5.50	5,500,000
Total fixed costs	$7.50	$7,700,000

The heart of the difference between variable and absorption costing for financial reporting is accounting for fixed manufacturing and variable non-manufacturing costs. There is no difference in how variable manufacturing overhead costs are recognized, which is as inventoriable (COGS) expenses. A direct manufacturing cost could be supervision of production of a product line, but the supervisors' salaries are fixed regardless of the quantity of individual outputs produced. This is a fixed direct cost of production. The straight-line amortization expense on a machine is also a fixed cost, but it is an indirect cost of producing the output that is established based on useful life, not quantity of outputs produced.

		Direct	Indirect
Same under Both Methods	} Variable	Direct manufacturing cost	Indirect manufacturing cost
Differs under the Two Methods	} Fixed	Direct manufacturing cost	Indirect manufacturing cost

In budgeting (Chapter 6), all the fixed overhead manufacturing costs including amortization of plant and equipment used exclusively in converting raw materials to finished goods were included in COGS. In variance analysis (Chapter 8), this was also true for budgeting the pro forma fixed-cost manufacturing overhead rate for the static budget. The static budget assumed an unvarying output, the denominator level used to calculate the fixed-cost manufacturing overhead rate. The denominator level could have been the theoretical, normal, practical, or master-budget level.

The important point is that the denominator level for the static budget be used to calculate the pro forma fixed overhead rate. The internal inventory valuation policy is a choice of where and when to recognize the fixed manufacturing overhead, the overallocated or underallocated fixed manufacturing overhead (the variance), and the variable non-manufacturing costs as an expense. If included in COGS, they are inventoriable; if included in period costs, they are not inventoriable. Notice that by including fixed manufacturing overhead and variance in the COGS, managers slow down the timing of recognizing this expense and capitalize this dollar value according to the rate at which units are sold.

Both absorption and variable inventory valuation methods capitalize all fixed costs (both manufacturing and non-manufacturing). *Capitalizing* means acquisition costs are recorded as an asset on the balance sheet when incurred. This value is methodically decreased as amortization, most often via the units-of-production or the straight-line method. The dollar value, amortization (an expense), is methodically transferred to the income statement. Under the absorption valuation method, there is a second stage of capitalization of fixed manufacturing overhead. This value is capitalized according to the units of finished goods sold using FIFO. The variable costing method deducts the amortization expense associated with fixed costs (both manufacturing and non-manufacturing) as a period cost of the period in which they are incurred.

An example of a fixed indirect manufacturing cost is the annual lease cost of a building where multiple products are assembled. The lease cost is allocated over the different products. If the building had been used for manufacturing only one product, it would be a fixed direct cost of that product.

Inspecting the classification of inventoriable costs under the two methods for Radius, as shown below, makes it clear that under absorption costing the total unit inventoriable cost is higher than under the variable costing method. Accurately classifying the costs determines both the appropriate inventory valuation and estimates of cost of goods sold expense using each method.

	Variable Costing		Absorption Costing	
Variable manufacturing costs:				
Direct materials	$3.50		$3.50	
Direct manufacturing labour	1.60		1.60	
Indirect manufacturing costs	0.90	$6.00	0.90	$6.00
Fixed manufacturing costs:				
Direct manufacturing costs	–		0.30	
Indirect manufacturing costs	–	–	1.70	2.00
Total inventoriable costs		$6.00		$8.00

Exhibit 9-5 presents the variable costing and absorption costing income statements for Radius Company in 2013. The absorption costing income statement uses the gross margin format introduced in Chapter 2. The variable costing income statement uses the contribution format introduced in Chapter 3.

The contribution format highlights the distinction between variable and fixed costs, whereby all fixed costs are period costs and excluded from calculating the variable cost of goods sold. The gross-margin format highlights the distinction between manufacturing and non-manufacturing costs, whereby all non-manufacturing costs are period costs and excluded from calculating the absorption cost of goods sold. Many companies using absorption costing find it unnecessary to design a cost accounting system that distinguishes between variable and fixed costs.

EXHIBIT 9-5

Comparison of Variable Costing and Absorption Costing Income Statements for the Year Ended December 31, 2013, for Radius Company (quantity of units and dollar values are reported in thousands)

	A	B	C
1	**PANEL A: VARIABLE COSTING**		
2	Revenues $17 × 1,000 units (in thousands)		$17,000
3	Variable costs:		
4	Beginning inventory	$ 0	
5	Variable manufacturing costs: $6 × 1,100 units	6,600	
6	Cost of goods available for sale	6,600	
7	Deduct ending inventory: $6 × 100 units	(600)	
8	Variable cost of goods sold	6,000	
9	Variable marketing costs: $2.40 × 1,000 units sold	2,400	
10	Adjustment for variable cost variances	0	
11	Total variable costs		8,400
12	Contribution margin		8,600
13	Fixed costs:		
14	Fixed manufacturing costs $2 × 1,100	2,200	
15	Fixed marketing costs $5.50 × 1,000 units sold	5,500	
16	Adjustment for fixed-cost variances	0	
17	Total fixed costs		7,700
18	Operating income		$ 900
19			
20	**PANEL B: ABSORPTION COSTING**		
21	Revenues $17 × 1,000 units (in thousands)		$17,000
22	Cost of goods sold:		
23	Beginning inventory	$ 0	
24	Variable manufacturing costs: $6 × 1,100 units	6,600	
25	Allocated fixed manufacturing costs $2 × 1,100	2,200	
26	Cost of goods available for sale	8,800	
27	Deduct ending inventory: $8 × 100 units	(800)	
28	Adjustment for manufacturing variances	0	
29	Cost of goods sold		8,000
30	Gross margin		9,000
31	Marketing costs:		
32	Variable marketing costs $2.40 × 1,000 units sold	2,400	
33	Fixed marketing costs $5.50 × 1,000 units sold	5,500	
34	Adjustment for marketing variances	0	
35	Total marketing costs		7,900
36	Operating income		$ 1,100

Let's look more closely at the fixed manufacturing costs of $2,200,000 in Exhibit 9-5. The income statement under variable costing deducts the $2,200,000 lump sum as a period cost in 2013. In contrast, the income statement under absorption costing regards each finished unit as absorbing $2 of fixed manufacturing costs. Under absorption costing, the $2,200,000 is initially capitalized as an inventoriable cost in 2012. Given the preceding data for Radius, $2,000,000 subsequently becomes an expense in 2013, and $200,000 remains an asset—part of ending finished goods inventory (100,000 units × $2) at December 31, 2013. The variable manufacturing costs are accounted for in the same way in both income statements in Exhibit 9-5.

In comparing sales of 900,000, 1,000,000, and 1,100,000 units by Radius Company in 2013, fixed manufacturing costs would be included in the 2013 expense as follows:

	Fixed Manufacturing Costs Treated as an Expense in 2013
Variable costing, where	
◆ Sales are 900,000, 1,000,000, or 1,100,000 units	$2,200,000
Absorption costing, where	
◆ Sales are 900,000 units, $400,000 (200,000 × $2) held back in inventory	$1,800,000
◆ Sales are 1,000,000 units, $200,000 (100,000 × $2) held back in inventory	$2,000,000
◆ Sales are 1,100,000 units, $0 held back in inventory	$2,200,000

Some companies use the term **direct costing** to inaccurately describe the inventory costing method we call *variable costing*. This is unfortunate terminology:

◆ Variable and absorption inventory valuation treat direct *manufacturing variable* costs identically as COGS expense.

◆ Variable inventory valuation includes direct non-manufacturing and variable non-manufacturing costs as COGS expense.

◆ Variable inventory valuation excludes both direct *fixed* manufacturing and non-manufacturing costs (such as general administration) from COGS.

COMPARISON OF STANDARD VARIABLE COSTING AND ABSORPTION COSTING

Our next example explores the implications of accounting for fixed manufacturing costs in more detail. Stassen Company manufactures and markets telescopes for military use. Stassen uses a standard costing system for both its manufacturing and its marketing costs.[2] Stassen began business on January 1, 2013, and it is now March 2013. The president asks you to prepare comparative income statements for January 2013 and February 2013. The following simplified data are available:

	A	B	C
1	**Unit Data**	**January 2013**	**February 2013**
2	Beginning inventory	0	200
3	Production	600	650
4	Sales	400	750
5	Ending inventory	200	100
6	**Other data**		
7	Selling price	$ 99	per unit sold
8	Standard variable unit manufacturing costs	$ 20	per unit produced
9	Standard variable unit marketing costs	$ 19	per unit sold
10	Standard fixed monthly manufacturing costs	$12,800	
11	Standard fixed monthly marketing costs	$10,400	
12	Budgeted denominator level of monthly production	800	output units

The total standard variable manufacturing costs per unit of $20 includes $11 for direct materials. For simplicity, we assume all fixed manufacturing costs are indirect product costs.

---

[2]For simplicity, we assume that Stassen Company uses a standard-costing system for all its operating costs—that is, it uses standards for both variable and fixed costs in both its manufacturing and marketing.

Prorate or Writeoff: CRA versus Internal Evaluation

Good governance is in part about adopting costing policies that comply with external reporting standards and legislation. But managers also require relevant cost information to inform important managerial decisions. Strategic choices have practical implications. The strategic choice to undertake ABC and use either theoretical or practical denominator levels as appropriate to the activities measured by the cost driver will lead to overallocation and underallocation.

CRA requires the use of the master-budget denominator level for tax purposes. GAAP requires the use of the normal capacity denominator. Overallocations or underallocations, which will show as variances, must be prorated according to the CRA and GAAP—but each requires a different denominator. This will lead to a tax COGS estimate and an estimate of inventory values that differs from the GAAP COGS estimate and the estimate of inventory values. For internal purposes, writing off even material variances may provide more relevant information for strategic and operating decisions than proration. Management accountants are often called upon to provide the cost estimates and to translate the benefits of, for example, ABC into dollar values. The common language of benefit and cost is dollars, and by doing this in a thoughtful way, management accountants contribute relevant information crucial to choosing the denominator level and other financial policy decisions.

Answers to denominator-level policy and costing policy issues are not clear-cut. Managers can still make choices that increase (or sometimes decrease) operating income. Between 1999 and 2001, Bristol-Myers Squibb (BMS) endured decreasing sales. Under absorption costing the inventory did not affect operating income. But BMS went much further, by offering incentives to wholesalers to build their inventories and then BMS recorded deliveries to wholesalers as revenues—an illegal practice called channelling. This step allowed BMS to meet its quarterly revenue forecasts.

The U.S. Department of Justice and the Securities and Exchange Commission (SEC) investigated BMS and 695 other companies to restore trust in financial disclosure. The SEC concluded that the loading of inventories onto wholesalers could not be recognized as revenue. BMS was charged with overstating revenues by US$2.5 billion from 1999 through 2001. The change in inventory valuation resulted in a writedown on March 12, 2003, which had been publicly alluded to in its financial report of January 29, 2003. The company also changed its discount and incentive policies to wholesalers. In a 2004 interview, chief financial officer Andrew Bonfield stated that the company was working to "improve the transparency and quality of its financial disclosures." The board of directors failed in its corporate governance duty to BMS, but this does not remove responsibility from management accountants who also had a professional obligation not to produce misleading reports.

Sources: Barbara Martinez, "Bristol-Myers Again Restates Results," *Wall Street Journal*, March 16, 2004; Robert Steyer, "Bristol-Myers Squibb Restates Earnings Again," *The Street*, March 15, 2004, www.thestreet.com/story/10148799/1html; Reed Abelson "Bristol-Myers Lowers Revenue By $2.5 Billion in Restatement," *The New York Times*, March 11, 2003; Michael Schroeder, "Under the Gun from the SEC, Firms Divulge Accounting Issues," *Wall Street Journal Online*, August 15, 2002, www.happinessonline.org/infectiousGreed/p23.htm.

We assume work in process is minimal. There were no beginning or ending inventories of materials. On January 1, 2013, there was no beginning inventory of finished goods. To highlight the effect of the production-volume variance, we assume there were no price, efficiency, or rate variances for any costs in either January or February of 2013. The standard fixed manufacturing cost per unit is $16 ($12,800 ÷ 800). Thus, the key standard cost data per units of denominator-level capacity are:

Variable costs:	
Standard variable manufacturing costs	$20
Standard variable marketing costs	19
Total variable costs	$39
Manufacturing costs:	
Standard variable manufacturing costs	$20
Standard fixed manufacturing costs ($12,800 ÷ 800)	16
Total manufacturing costs	$36

Stassen expenses all variances to cost of goods sold in the accounting period in which they occur.

Assume that managers at Stassen receive a bonus based on reported monthly income. The following sections illustrate how the choice between variable and absorption costing will affect Stassen's reported monthly income and hence the bonuses its managers will receive.

COMPARATIVE INCOME STATEMENTS

Exhibit 9-6 contains the comparative income statements under variable costing (Panel A) and absorption costing (Panel B) for Stassen Company in January 2013 and February 2013. The operating income numbers are:

	January 2013	February 2013
(1) Absorption costing	$4,000	$20,200
(2) Variable costing	800	21,800
(3) Difference = (1) − (2)	$3,200	$(1,600)

In Panel A, Variable Costing, all variable-cost line items are at standard cost except the adjustment for variances. This item would include all price, rate, and efficiency variances related to variable cost items (which are zero in our Stassen example).

In Panel B, Absorption Costing, all cost of goods sold line items are at standard cost except the adjustment for variances. This item includes all manufacturing cost variances—price, rate, efficiency, and production-volume variances. Only the production-volume variance is nonzero in our Stassen example.

Keep the following points about absorption costing in mind as you study Panel B of Exhibit 9-6:

◆ The inventoriable costs are $36 per unit, not $20, because fixed manufacturing costs ($16) as well as variable manufacturing costs ($20) are assigned to each unit of product.

◆ The $16 fixed manufacturing cost rate was based on a denominator level of 800 units per month ($12,800 ÷ 800 = $16). Whenever actual *production* (not sales) volume varies from the denominator level of 800 units, a production-volume variance arises. This variance is the difference between actual and denominator-level volumes multiplied by $16, the rate.

◆ The production-volume variance, which relates to fixed manufacturing overhead, exists only under absorption costing and not under variable costing because fixed costs are not allocated in the variable costing method. All other variances exist under both absorption costing and variable costing.

◆ The absorption costing income statement classifies costs primarily by *business function*, such as manufacturing and marketing. In contrast, the variable costing income statement features *cost behaviour* (variable or fixed) as the basis of classification. Absorption costing income statements need not differentiate between the variable and fixed costs. Exhibit 9-6 makes this distinction for Stassen Company to highlight how individual line items are classified differently under variable and absorption costing formats.

EXPLAINING DIFFERENCES IN OPERATING INCOME

If the inventory level increases during an accounting period, the value of total ending inventory increases more under the absorption than variable valuation policy. The period cost, however, will be lower under the absorption than variable valuation policy. The difference between operating income under absorption costing and variable costing can be computed by Formula 1, which is illustrated with Exhibit 9-6 data:[3]

---

[3]This formula assumes that the amounts used for beginning and ending inventory are after proration of manufacturing overhead variances.

EXHIBIT 9-6
Comparison of Variable Costing and Absorption Costing Income Statements for January 2013 and February 2013 for Stassen Company

	A	B	C
1	**PANEL A: VARIABLE COSTING**		
2		**January 2013**	**February 2013**
3	Revenue $99 × 400; 750 units	$39,600	$74,250
4	Variable costs:		
5	Beginning inventory $20 × 0; 200 units	0	4,000
6	Variable cost of goods manufactured $20 × 600; 650 units	12,000	13,000
7	Cost of goods available for sale	12,000	17,000
8	Ending inventory $20 × 200; 100 units	(4,000)	(2,000)
9	Variable manufacturing cost of goods sold	8,000	15,000
10	Variable marketing costs $19 × 400; 750 units	7,600	14,250
11	Total standard variable costs	15,600	29,250
12	Contribution margin (standard)	24,000	45,000
13	Adjustment for variable cost variances to COGS	0	0
14	Total variable costs	15,600	29,250
15	Contribution margin	24,000	45,000
16	Fixed costs:		
17	Fixed manufacturing costs	12,800	12,800
18	Fixed marketing costs	10,400	10,400
19	Total standard fixed costs	23,200	23,200
20	Adjustment for fixed-cost variances	0	0
21	Total fixed costs	23,200	23,200
22	Operating income	$ 800	$21,800
23			
24	**PANEL B: ABSORPTION COSTING**		
25		**January 2013**	**February 2013**
26	Revenue $99 × 400; 750 units	$39,600	$74,250
27	Cost of goods sold		
28	Beginning inventory $36 × 0; 200 units	0	7,200
29	Variable manufacturing costs $20 × 600; 650 units	12,000	13,000
30	Allocated fixed manufacturing costs $16 × 600; 650 units	9,600	10,400
31	Cost of goods available for sale	21,600	30,600
32	Deduct ending inventory: $36 × 200; 100 units	(7,200)	(3,600)
33	Total standard cost of goods sold	14,400	27,000
34	Gross margin at standard	25,200	47,250
35	Adjustment for manufacturing variances to COGS*	3,200 U	2,400 U
36	Cost of goods sold	17,600	29,400
37	Gross margin	22,000	44,850
38	Marketing costs:		
39	Variable marketing costs $19 × 400; 750 units sold	7,600	14,250
40	Fixed marketing costs	10,400	10,400
41	Total standard marketing costs	18,000	24,650
42	Adjustment for marketing variances	0	0
43	Total marketing costs	18,000	24,650
44	Operating income	$ 4,000	$20,200
45			
46	*Production volume variance for January $16 × 200 where the denominator of 800 units exceeds the volume produced and the allocation rate is $12,800 ÷ 800 = $16/unit. Similarly, the production-volume variance for February is $16 × 150.		

Formula 1

$$\begin{pmatrix} \text{Absorption costing} \\ \text{operating} \\ \text{income} \end{pmatrix} - \begin{pmatrix} \text{Variable costing} \\ \text{operating} \\ \text{income} \end{pmatrix} = \begin{pmatrix} \text{Fixed manufacturing} \\ \text{costs in} \\ \text{ending inventory} \end{pmatrix} - \begin{pmatrix} \text{Fixed manufacturing} \\ \text{costs in} \\ \text{beginning inventory} \end{pmatrix}.$$

January 2013 $\$4,000 - \$800 = (200 \times \$16) - (0 \times \$16)$
$$\$3,200 = \$3,200$$

February 2013 $\$20,200 - \$21,800 = (100 \times \$16) - (200 \times \$16)$
$$-\$1,600 = -\$1,600$$

Fixed manufacturing costs in ending inventory are a current-period expense under variable costing that absorption costing defers to future periods.

Two alternative formulas can be used if we assume that all manufacturing variances are written off as period costs, that no change occurs in work-in-process inventory, and that no change occurs in the budgeted fixed manufacturing overhead rate between accounting periods:

Formula 2

$$\begin{pmatrix} \text{Absorption costing} \\ \text{operating} \\ \text{income} \end{pmatrix} - \begin{pmatrix} \text{Variable costing} \\ \text{operating} \\ \text{income} \end{pmatrix} = \begin{pmatrix} \text{Units} \\ \text{produced} - \begin{matrix} \text{Units} \\ \text{sold} \end{matrix} \end{pmatrix} \times \begin{pmatrix} \text{Budgeted fixed} \\ \text{manufacturing} \\ \text{cost rate} \end{pmatrix}$$

January 2013 $\$4,000 - \$800 = (600 - 400) \times \$16$
$$\$3,200 = \$3,200$$

February 2013 $\$20,200 - \$21,800 = (650 - 750) \times \$16$
$$-\$1,600 = -\$1,600$$

Formula 3

$$\begin{pmatrix} \text{Absorption costing} \\ \text{operating} \\ \text{income} \end{pmatrix} - \begin{pmatrix} \text{Variable costing} \\ \text{operating} \\ \text{income} \end{pmatrix} = \begin{pmatrix} \text{Ending} \\ \text{inventory} \\ \text{in units} - \begin{matrix} \text{Beginning} \\ \text{inventory} \\ \text{in units} \end{matrix} \end{pmatrix} \times \begin{pmatrix} \text{Budgeted fixed} \\ \text{manufacturing} \\ \text{cost rate} \end{pmatrix}.$$

January 2013 $\$4,000 - \$800 = (200 - 0) \times \$16$
$$\$3,200 = \$3,200$$

February 2013 $\$20,200 - \$21,800 = (100 - 200) \times \$16$
$$-\$1,600 = -\$1,600$$

EFFECT OF SALES AND PRODUCTION ON OPERATING INCOME

The period-to-period change in operating income under variable costing is driven solely by changes in the unit level of sales, given a constant contribution margin per unit. Consider for Stassen the variable costing operating income in February 2013 versus that in January 2013:

$$\begin{matrix} \text{Change in} \\ \text{operating income} \end{matrix} = \begin{matrix} \text{Contribution} \\ \text{margin} \end{matrix} \times \begin{matrix} \text{Change in unit} \\ \text{sales level} \end{matrix}$$
$$\$21,800 - \$800 = (\$99 - \$39) \times (750 - 400)$$
$$\$21,000 = \$60 \times 350$$
$$\$21,000 = \$21,000$$

Note that under variable costing, Stassen managers cannot increase operating income (and hence their bonuses) by producing to increase inventory.

Under absorption costing, however, period-to-period change in operating income is driven by variations in *both* the unit level of sales and the unit level of production. Exhibit 9-7 illustrates this point by showing how absorption costing operating income for February 2013 changes as the production level in February 2013 changes. This exhibit assumes that all variances (including the production-volume variance) are written off to cost of goods sold at the end of each accounting period. The beginning inventory in February 2013 of 200 units and the February sales of

EXHIBIT 9-7
Stassen Company: Effect on Absorption Costing Operating Income of Different Production Levels Holding the Unit Sales Level Constant—Data for February 2013 with Sales of 750 Units

	February 2013 Production Level				
	550	**650**	**700**	**800**	**850**
Unit data:					
Beginning inventory	200	200	200	200	200
Production	550	650	700	800	850
Goods available for sale	750	850	900	1,000	1,050
Sales	750	750	750	750	750
Ending inventory	0	100	150	250	300
Income statement:					
Revenues	$74,250	$74,250	$74,250	$74,250	$74,250
Beginning inventory ($36/unit)	7,200	7,200	7,200	7,200	7,200
Variable manufacturing (production) costs*	11,000	13,000	14,000	16,000	17,000
Fixed manufacturing costs†	8,800	10,400	11,200	12,800	13,600
Cost of goods available for sale	27,000	30,600	32,400	36,000	37,800
Ending inventory‡	0	3,600	5,400	9,000	10,800
Cost of goods sold (at standard cost)	27,000	27,000	27,000	27,000	27,000
Adjustment for manufacturing variances§	4,000 U	2,400 U	1,600 U	0	800 F
Total cost of goods sold	31,000	29,400	28,600	27,000	26,200
Gross margin	43,250	44,850	45,650	47,250	48,050
Total marketing and administrative costs	24,650	24,650	24,650	24,650	24,650
Operating income	$18,600	$20,200	$21,000	$22,600	$23,400

*$20 per unit.
†Assigned at $16 per unit.
‡$36 per unit.
§(Production in units − 800) × $16. All written off to cost of goods sold at end of the accounting period.

750 units are unchanged. Exhibit 9-7 shows that production of only 550 units meets February 2013 sales of 750. Operating income at this production level (column 1) is $18,600. By producing more than 550 units in February 2013, Stassen increases absorption costing operating income.

Each unit in February 2013 ending inventory will increase February operating income by $16. For example, if 800 units are produced, ending inventory will be 250 units and operating income will be $22,600. This amount is $4,000 more than what operating income is with zero ending inventory (250 units × $16 = $4,000) at the end of the month. Recall that Stassen's managers receive a bonus based on monthly operating income. Absorption costing enables them to increase operating income (and hence their bonuses) by producing to increase inventory.

Managers whose performance evaluation and compensation are based on absorption costing income have incentives to increase production solely to increase reported income. But this will increase the costs of doing business without an attendant increase in revenue obtained from additional sales. Each additional unit produced absorbs fixed manufacturing costs that would otherwise have been written off as a cost of the period.

PERFORMANCE EVALUATION: UNDESIRABLE BUILDUP OF INVENTORIES

Absorption costing is the required inventory valuation method for external reporting in Canada, and to avoid any internal confusion that could arise by using a different valuation method for internal planning and control, most companies use one method for both internal and external purposes. Using the same method for valuation and performance evaluation helps avoid situations wherein managers take action that enhances their individual evaluation but harms overall corporate performance.

EXHIBIT 9-8
Comparative Income Effects of Variable Costing and Absorption Costing

Question	Variable Costing	Absorption Costing	Comment
Are fixed manufacturing costs inventoried?	No	Yes	Basic theoretical question when these costs should be expensed as period costs.
Is there a production-volume variance?	No	Yes	Choice of denominator level affects measurement of operating income under absorption costing only.
How are the other variances treated?	Same	Same	Highlights that the basic difference is the accounting for fixed manufacturing costs, not the accounting for any variable manufacturing costs.
Are classifications between variable and fixed costs routinely made?	Yes	Not always	Absorption costing can be easily modified to obtain subclassifications for variable and fixed costs, if desired (for example, see Exhibit 9-5, Panel B).
How do changes in unit inventory levels affect operating income?			
Production = sales	Equal	Equal	Differences are attributable to the timing of when fixed manufacturing costs become period costs
Production > sales	Lower*	Higher†	
Production < sales	Higher	Lower	
What are the effects on cost-volume-profit relationships?	Driven by unit sales level	Driven by unit sales level and unit production level	Management control benefit: Effects of changes in production level on operating income are easier to understand under variable costing.

*That is, lower operating income than under absorption costing.
†That is, higher operating income than under variable costing.

Absorption costing includes all production costs when valuing inventory that has been sold and better informs the long-run pricing and product mix decisions. In the long run, the revenue must cover total costs plus generate profit if a company is to thrive.

Unfortunately, absorption costing can lead managers to increase operating income in the short run by increasing the production schedule independent of customer demand. In practice this is a well-known possibility and can be controlled either by monitoring the inventory levels or choosing a variable cost method for internal performance evaluation based on the efficiency and effectiveness of manufacturing activities. The added advantage of variable costing is to reveal the cost-volume-profit relationships that improve the quality of information upon which managers make short-run decisions. Exhibit 9-8 compares the key differences between variable and absorption costing.

The undesirable effects of an increase in production to increase operating income in the short run may be sizable, and they can arise in several ways, as the following examples show:

◆ A plant manager may switch production to those orders that absorb the highest amount of fixed manufacturing costs, regardless of the customer demand for these products (called "cherry picking" the production line). Some difficult-to-manufacture items may be delayed, resulting in failure to meet promised customer delivery dates.

◆ A plant manager may accept a particular order to increase production, even though another plant in the same company is better suited to handle that order.

◆ To meet increased production, a manager may defer maintenance beyond the current accounting period. Although operating income may increase now, future operating income will probably decrease because of increased repairs and less-efficient equipment.

Early criticisms of absorption costing concentrated on whether fixed manufacturing overhead qualified as an asset under GAAP. However, current criticisms of absorption costing have increasingly emphasized its potentially undesirable incentives for managers. Indeed, one critic labels absorption costing as "one of the black holes of cost accounting," in part because it may induce managers to make decisions against the long-run interests of the company.

Proposals for Revising Performance Evaluation Critics of absorption costing have made a variety of proposals for revising how managers are evaluated:

1. *Change the accounting system.* As discussed previously and will be shown later in this chapter, both variable and throughput costing reduce the incentives of managers to build up inventory.

2. *Careful budgeting and inventory planning* to reduce management's freedom to build up excess inventory. For example, the budgeted monthly balance sheets have estimates of the dollar amount of inventories. If actual inventories exceed these dollar amounts, top management can investigate the inventory buildups.

3. *Incorporate a carrying charge for inventory* in the internal accounting system. For example, an inventory carrying charge of 1% per month could be assessed for the investment tied up in inventory and for spoilage and obsolescence when evaluating a manager's performance.

4. *Change the time period used to evaluate performance.* Critics of absorption costing give examples where managers take actions that maximize quarterly or annual income at the potential expense of long-run income. By evaluating performance over a three- to five-year period, the incentive to take short-run actions that reduce long-term income is reduced.

5. *Include nonfinancial as well as financial variables in the measures used to evaluate performance.* Companies currently are using nonfinancial variables, such as the following, drawn from the Stassen data:

(a) $\dfrac{\text{Ending inventory in units February 2013}}{\text{Beginning inventory in units February 2013}} = \dfrac{100}{200} = 0.5$

(b) $\dfrac{\text{Units produced in February 2013}}{\text{Units sold in February 2013}} = \dfrac{650}{750} = 0.867$

A good report of manufacturing performance would show not only stable inventory ratios of outputs over time for each product, but also a production to sales-volume ratio very close to 1 to indicate all production and inventory was sold during the period it was produced. Of course, these nonfinancial ratios would also be interpreted in light of, for example, fluctuations due to seasonal demand, perishability, and other factors appropriate to a specific manufacturing situation.

THROUGHPUT: SUPER-VARIABLE COSTING

Some critics of existing costing systems maintain that even variable costing materially overstates operating income and provides a perverse incentive to produce more inventory to decrease the COGS expense. They argue that only direct materials are "truly variable" with respect to volume (quantity) of units produced and, ideally, the quantity of units produced should meet the quantity demanded by customers. Production managers can rarely control direct materials and labour prices or fixed manufacturing overhead, but they can control direct materials efficiency variances by matching volumes produced as closely as possible to volumes demanded.

To reward efficient and effective production, **throughput costing** (also called **super-variable costing**) treats all costs except variable direct materials (which are inventoriable) as period costs that are expensed when they are incurred. All overhead and labour costs are not considered as a source of future benefit for internal planning and control purposes. All other things being equal, this method is most conservative and leads to the lowest internally reported operating income in comparison to either

Distinguish throughput costing from variable costing and absorption costing, and explain differences in operating income under each costing policy.

EXHIBIT 9-9
Throughput Costing for Stassen Company

	A	B	C
		January 2013	February 2013
1			
2	**Unit Data Production:**	**600**	**650**
3	**Unit Data Sales:**	**400**	**750**
4	Income Statement:		
5	Revenue $99 × 400; 750	$39,600	$74,250
6	Variable direct materials costs:		
7	Beginning inventory $11 × 0; 200 units	0	2,200
8	Direct materials in goods manufactured $11 × 600; 650	6,600	7,150
9	Cost of goods available for sale	6,600	9,350
10	Ending inventory $11 × 200; 100	(2,200)	(1,100)
11	Direct materials standard cost	4,400	8,250
12	Adjustment for direct materials variances	0	0
13	Total variable direct materials costs	4,400	8,250
14	Throughput contribution*	35,200	66,000
15	Other costs:		
16	Manufacturing $12,800 + ($9 × 600; 650)	18,200	18,650
17	Marketing $10,400 + ($19 × 400; 750)	18,000	24,650
18	Adjustment for variances	0	0
19	Total other costs	36,200	43,300
20	Operating income	$ (1,000)	$22,700
21			
22	*Throughput contribution is the difference between revenues and variable direct materials costs.		

variable or absorption costing. As you can see from Exhibit 9-9, each unsold unit reduces the throughput contribution by $88, a decrease of $11 in cost, but a larger decrease of $99 in lost revenue for a net loss of $88. It is the difference in rate of change of revenue and cost that reduces operating income by another $88. It is a sensible choice when there is no inventory, which is the case when a just-in-time manufacturing system is in place.

When innovation cycles are very short, obsolescence can occur almost overnight and the assumption that unsold production is unlikely to produce future benefit may be appropriate. In situations such as this, achieving expected profit targets requires an intense focus on minimizing period costs incurred caused by the production of unsold units. This is a more recently designed method of inventory valuation, matching a just-in-time manufacturing policy. It is GAAP compliant if it is based on standard, actual, or normal costing methods.[4]

Exhibit 9-9 is the throughput costing income statement for Stassen Company. Compare the operating income amounts reported with those for absorption and variable costing:

	Absorption Costing	Variable Costing	Throughput Costing
January 2013	$ 4,000	$ 800	$ (1,000)
February 2013	20,200	21,800	22,700

Only the $11 direct materials cost per unit is inventoriable under throughput costing (compared with $36 for absorption costing and $20 for variable costing).

[4]See E. Goldratt, *The Theory of Constraints* (New York: North River Press, 1990); E. Noreen, D. Smith, and J. Mackey, *The Theory of Constraints and Its Implications for Management Accounting* (New York: North River Press, 1995).

Where production exceeds sales (as in January 2013), throughput costing results in the largest amount of costs being expensed to the current period. Throughput contribution in Exhibit 9-9 is revenues minus all variable direct materials costs.

Advocates of throughput costing maintain there is reduced incentive for building up excess inventories compared to when variable or (especially) absorption costing is used. Reducing inventory levels means less funds are tied up in inventory and hence more funds are available to invest in productive outlets. Moreover, reducing inventory levels typically means reducing inventory spoilage and obsolescence costs.

OVERVIEW OF THREE COSTING POLICIES

Variable costing, absorption costing, and throughput costing may be combined with actual, normal, or standard costing. Exhibit 9-10 presents a capsule comparison of a job-costing record under nine alternative inventory costing systems:

Variable Costing	Absorption Costing	Throughput Costing
1. Actual costing	4. Actual costing	7. Actual costing
2. Normal costing	5. Normal costing	8. Normal costing
3. Standard costing	6. Standard costing	9. Standard costing

The data in Exhibit 9-10 represent the debits to job-costing account(s) (that is, the amounts assigned to products) under alternative inventory costing systems.

Variable costing has been a controversial subject among accountants—not so much because there is disagreement about the need for delineating between variable and fixed costs for management planning and control, but because there is a question about using variable costing for external reporting. Those favouring variable costing for external reporting maintain that the fixed portion of manufacturing costs is more closely related to the capacity to produce than to the production of specific units. Supporters of absorption costing maintain that inventories should carry a fixed manufacturing cost component. Why? Since both variable and fixed manufacturing costs

EXHIBIT 9-10
Capsule Comparison of Alternative Inventory Costing Systems

			Actual Costing	Normal Costing	Standard Costing
Absorption Costing	Variable Costing	Throughput Costing	**Variable Direct Materials Costs**	Actual prices × Actual quantity of inputs used	Actual prices × Actual quantity of inputs used	Standard prices × Standard quantity of inputs allowed for actual output achieved
			Variable Direct Conversion* Costs	Actual prices × Actual quantity of inputs used	Actual prices × Actual quantity of inputs used	Standard prices × Standard quantity of inputs allowed for actual output achieved
			Variable Manufacturing Overhead Costs	Actual variable overhead rate × Actual quantity of cost allocation bases used	Budgeted variable overhead rates × Actual quantity of cost allocation bases used	Standard variable overhead rates × Standard quantity of cost allocation bases allowed for actual output achieved
			Fixed Direct Manufacturing Costs	Actual prices × Actual quantity of inputs used	Actual prices × Actual quantity of inputs used	Standard prices × Standard quantity of inputs allowed for actual output achieved
			Fixed Manufacturing Overhead Costs	Actual fixed overhead rates × Actual quantity of cost-allocation bases used	Budgeted fixed overhead rates × Actual quantity of cost-allocation bases used	Standard fixed overhead rates × Standard quantity of cost-allocation bases allowed for actual output achieved

*Conversion costs are all manufacturing costs minus direct materials costs.

are necessary to produce goods, both types of costs should be inventoriable, regardless of their having different behaviour patterns.

Absorption costing (or variants close to it) is the method required to achieve the external regulatory purpose of accounting systems. For example, when companies whose shares are traded on the Toronto Stock Exchange report financial results to the Ontario Securities Commission, generally accepted accounting principles as stated in the *CICA Handbook* must be followed. Thus, all manufacturing costs plus some product overhead must be included as inventoriable costs. Overhead costs must be allocated between those costs related to manufacturing activities (inventoriable costs) and those not related to manufacturing activities. For external reporting to shareholders, companies around the globe tend to follow the generally accepted accounting principle that all manufacturing overhead is inventoriable.

Throughput costing is not permitted for external reporting purposes if it results in materially different numbers to those reported by absorption costing. Full absorption costing requires the use of either actual or normal cost allocation methods for indirect manufacturing costs. Advocates of throughput costing emphasize the *internal* purposes of management accounting data because this method best reflects the economic facts of the actual production process.

PRODUCTIVITY UNDER EACH COST POLICY

⑤ Explain productivity measurement under each of the three costing policies.

Chapter 3 introduced cost-volume-profit analysis. If variable costing is used, the breakeven point (operating income of $0) is computed in the usual manner. There is only one breakeven point in this case, and it is a function of:

◆ fixed costs,
◆ contribution margin per unit, and
◆ unit level of sales.

Holding fixed cost and unit contribution margin constant, operating income rises as the level of sales rises. The formula for computing the breakeven point with variable costing is a special case of the more general target operating income formula from Chapter 3 (p. 71):

$$Q = \frac{\text{Total fixed costs} + \text{Target operating income}}{\text{Contribution margin per unit}}$$

= Number of units sold to earn the target operating income

Breakeven occurs when the target operating income is $0. In our Stassen illustration for 2013 (see p. 359):[5]

$$Q = \frac{(\$12,800 + \$10,400) + \$0}{\$99 - (\$20 + \$19)} = \frac{\$23,200}{\$60}$$

= 387 units (rounded)

If absorption costing is used, the required number of units sold to achieve a specific target operating income is not unique because of the number of variables involved.

---

[5] Operating income is not $0 because the breakeven number of units is rounded up to 387 from 386.67.

Proof of breakeven point:

Revenues, $99 × 387	$38,313
Variable costs, $39 × 387	15,093
Contribution margin, $60 × 387	23,220
Fixed costs	23,200
Operating income	$ 20

The following formula highlights the factors that will affect the target operating income under absorption costing:

$$Q = \frac{\begin{array}{c}\text{Total} \\ \text{fixed} \\ \text{costs}\end{array} + \begin{array}{c}\text{Target} \\ \text{operating} \\ \text{income}\end{array} + \left[\begin{array}{c}\text{Fixed} \\ \text{manufacturing} \\ \text{cost rate}\end{array} \times \left(\begin{array}{c}\text{Breakeven} \\ \text{sales} \\ \text{in units}\end{array} - \begin{array}{c}\text{Units} \\ \text{produced}\end{array}\right)\right]}{\text{Contribution margin per unit}}$$

This formula has three terms in the numerator compared with two terms in the numerator of the variable-costing formula stated earlier. In this formula, total fixed costs include all manufacturing and non-manufacturing fixed costs. The extra term added to the numerator under absorption costing is as follows:

$$\left[\begin{array}{c}\text{Fixed manufacturing} \\ \text{cost rate}\end{array} \times \left(\begin{array}{c}\text{Breakeven sales} \\ \text{in units}\end{array} - \begin{array}{c}\text{Units} \\ \text{produced}\end{array}\right)\right]$$

This term captures the additional amount of target operating income in the numerator caused by absorption costing, which moves fixed manufacturing costs to inventory from cost of goods sold for all units produced that exceed the breakeven sales quantity. This formula shows that under absorption costing there is still a unique breakeven point for each quantity of units produced.

There is also an inverse relationship (as one goes up the other goes down) between the quantity of units produced and the required quantity of units sold to break even. The higher the quantity of units produced, the higher the level of fixed manufacturing overhead costs absorbed into finished goods inventory and the higher the COGS. The period costs remain unchanged; therefore, the quantity of units that must be sold to cover these costs too (and break even) will decrease.

Consider Stassen Company in 2013. One breakeven point under absorption costing for production of 500 units is as follows:

$$Q = \frac{(\$12{,}800 + \$10{,}400) + \$0 + [\$16(Q - 500)]}{\$99 - (\$20 + \$19)}$$

$$= \frac{\$23{,}200 + \$16Q - \$8{,}000}{\$60}$$

$$\$60Q = \$15{,}200 + \$16Q$$

$$\$44Q = \$15{,}200$$

$$Q = 346 \text{ (rounded)}$$

The breakeven point under absorption costing depends on the:

◆ fixed costs,
◆ contribution margin per unit,
◆ unit level of sales,
◆ unit level of production, and
◆ overhead cost rate.

For Stassen in 2013, a combination of 346 units sold, 500 units produced, and an 800-unit denominator level would result in an operating income of $0.[6] Note, however, that there are many combinations of these five factors that would give an operating income of $0. For example, a combination of 291 units sold, 650 units produced, and an 800-unit denominator level also results in an operating income of $0 under absorption costing.

Suppose in our illustration that actual production in 2013 were equal to the denominator level, 800 units. Also suppose that there were no units sold and no fixed operating costs. All the production would be placed in inventory, so all the fixed manufacturing overhead would be included in inventory; there would be no production-volume variance. Thus, the company would break even with no sales whatsoever! In contrast, under variable costing the operating loss would be equal to the fixed manufacturing costs of $12,800.

[6]Operating income is not exactly $0 because the breakeven number of units is rounded up to 346 from 345.45.

(Try to solve this problem before examining the solution that follows.)

PROBLEM

Suppose that Bushells Company from our chapter example is computing the operating income for May 2012. This month is identical to May 2013, the results of which are in Exhibit 9-4 (p. 348), except that master-budget capacity utilization for 2012 is 600,000 bottles per month instead of 400,000 bottles. There was no beginning inventory on May 1, 2012, and no variances other than the production-volume variance. Bushells writes off this variance to cost of goods sold each month.

REQUIRED

1. Identify the four potential denominator levels and calculate each fixed overhead rate.
2. Calculate the new production-volume variance for the new master-budget denominator level and explain the CRA effect of the production-volume variance.
3. How would the financial results in Exhibit 9-4 for Bushells Company be different if the month were May 2012 rather than May 2013? Show your computations.
4. Explain what the higher master-budget denominator level means.
5. What changes would adopting a variable inventory valuation method mean to the internal reports of COGS and period expense?
6. What change would adopting a throughput inventory valuation method mean to the internal reports of COGS and period expense?
7. Calculate a breakeven for Bushells (there is no unique solution).

SOLUTION

1. The four possible levels are theoretical, practical, normal, and master budget. The rates are calculated by dividing $50,000 by 1,152,000, 800,000, 500,000, and 600,000. All but the master-budget rate are in Exhibit 9-4. The rates are $0.0434, $0.0625, $0.1000, and $0.0833.

$$\frac{\$50,000}{600,000 \text{ bottles}} = \$0.0833 \text{ per bottle}$$

2. The manufacturing cost per bottle becomes $0.4333 ($0.3500 + $0.0833). In turn, the production volume variance for May 2012 becomes:

$$(600,000 - 460,000) \times (\$0.0833) = \$11,662 \text{ U}$$

The master-budget level conforms with CRA regulations. The unfavourable production-volume variance must be prorated over the inventory remaining in finished goods. The unfavourable variance increases the finished goods inventory value, which is subtracted from COGS. A lower COGS will be reported for tax purposes and therefore a higher taxable income.

3. The income statement for May 2012 is now

Revenue	$210,000
Cost of goods sold:	
Beginning inventory	0
Variable manufacturing costs:	
$0.35 × 460,000	161,000
Fixed manufacturing costs:	
$0.0833 × 460,000	38,318
Cost of goods available for sale	199,318
Ending inventory:	
$0.4333 × (460,000 − 420,000)	17,332
Total cost of goods sold (at standard costs)	181,986
Adjustment for variances	11,662 U
Total cost of goods sold	193,648
Gross margin	16,352
Marketing, other expenses	10,000
Operating income	$ 6,352

4. The higher denominator level in the 2012 master budget means that a temporary set of circumstances has led Bushells to expect a higher than normal denominator-level of sales and production in 2012. The normal denominator level is based on a longer-term expected average demand.

5. For purposes of external reporting, the use of variable inventory valuation does not comply either with GAAP or with CRA, which both require absorption inventory valuation. Variable inventory valuation collects all manufacturing and non-manufacturing costs incurred during a production time period and allocates this total variable cost pool to each unit remaining in finished goods inventory. All fixed manufacturing and non-manufacturing costs are deducted as period expenses. This method will make it easier for Bushells to calculate a breakeven volume.

6. Throughput inventory valuation collects only the direct materials costs during a production time period and these are traced to each unit of output remaining in finished goods inventory. All other costs are treated as period costs. Very likely, the immediate recognition of all variable and fixed-cost pools during the period they were incurred will reduce the internally reported operating income.

7. There is no *unique* solution—the answer will depend on assumptions made.

SUMMARY POINTS

The following question-and-answer format summarizes the chapter's learning outcomes. Each point presents a key question, and the guidelines are the answer to that question.

LEARNING OUTCOMES	GUIDELINES
1. What are the various capacity levels a company can use to calculate budgeted fixed manufacturing cost rate?	Capacity levels can be measured in terms of what a plant can supply—theoretical capacity or practical capacity. Capacity can also be measured in terms of demand for the output of a plant—normal capacity utilization or master-budget capacity utilization. When the chosen capacity level exceeds the actual production level, there will be an unfavourable production-volume variance; when the chosen capacity level is less than the actual production level, there will be a favourable production-volume variance.
2. What are the major factors managers consider when choosing the capacity level to compute the budgeted fixed overhead cost rate?	The major factors managers consider when choosing the capacity level to compute the budgeted fixed manufacturing cost per unit are (a) the effect on product costing and capacity management, (b) the effect on pricing decisions, (c) the effect on performance evaluation, (d) the effect on financial statements, (e) regulatory requirements, and (f) difficulties in forecasting chosen capacity-level concepts.
3. How do level of sales and level of production affect operating income under variable costing and absorption costing?	Under variable costing, operating income is driven by the unit level of sales. Under absorption costing, operating income is driven by the unit level of production, as well as by the unit level of sales.
4. How does throughput costing differ from variable costing and absorption costing?	Throughput costing treats all costs except direct materials as costs of the period in which they are incurred. Throughput costing results in a lower amount of manufacturing costs being inventoried than either variable or absorption costing.
5. How is a breakeven calculation affected by using absorption costing?	The target operating income at breakeven is $0 and there is no unique solution because a number of values change at the same time, including fixed costs, contribution margin per unit, sales quantity, production quantity, and the overhead cost rates. Many values for these factors can combine to give an operating income of $0.

This chapter contains definitions of the following important terms:

absorption costing (p. 352)
direct costing (p. 356)
downward demand spiral (p. 349)
full absorption costing (p. 352)
master-budget capacity (p. 342)

non-productive idle capacity (p. 345)
normal capacity (p. 342)
off-limits idle capacity (p. 344)
practical capacity (p. 342)
super-variable costing (p. 363)

theoretical capacity (p. 342)
throughput costing (p. 363)
variable costing (p. 352)

ASSIGNMENT MATERIAL

MyAccountingLab Make the grade with MyAccountingLab: The questions, exercises, and problems marked in red can be found on MyAccountingLab at **www.myaccountinglab.com**. You can practise them as often as you want, and most feature step-by-step guided instructions to help you find the right answer. Exercises and problems with an Excel icon in the margin have an accompanying Excel template on MyAccountingLab.

SHORT-ANSWER QUESTIONS

9-1 "Differences in operating income between variable and absorption costing are due solely to accounting for fixed costs." Do you agree? Explain.

9-2 Why is the term *direct costing* a misnomer for variable costing?

9-3 Do companies in either the service sector or the merchandising sector make choices about absorption costing versus variable costing?

9-4 Explain the main conceptual issue under variable and absorption costing regarding the proper timing for the release of fixed manufacturing overhead as expense.

9-5 "Companies that make no variable-cost/fixed-cost distinctions must use absorption costing and those that do make variable-cost/fixed-cost distinctions must use variable costing." Do you agree? Explain.

9-6 "The main trouble with variable costing is that it ignores the increasing importance of fixed costs in modern manufacturing." Do you agree? Why?

9-7 Give an example of how, under absorption costing, operating income could fall even though the unit sales level rises.

9-8 What are the factors that affect the breakeven point under (a) variable costing and (b) absorption costing?

9-9 Critics of absorption costing have increasingly emphasized its potential for promoting undesirable incentives for managers. Give an example.

9-10 What are two ways of reducing the negative aspects associated with using absorption costing to evaluate the performance of a plant manager?

9-11 Describe the downward demand spiral and its implications for pricing decisions.

9-12 Will the financial statements of a company always differ when different choices at the start of the period are made regarding the denominator-level capacity concept?

9-13 Which denominator-level concepts emphasize what a plant can supply? Which denominator-level concepts emphasize what customers demand for products produced by a plant?

9-14 "The difference between practical capacity and master-budget capacity utilization is the best measure of management's ability to balance the costs of having too much capacity and having too little capacity." Do you agree? Explain.

EXERCISES

9-15 Terminology. A number of terms are listed below:

absorption costing	super-variable costing
theoretical capacity	practical capacity
normal capacity	master budget capacity
non-productive idle capacity	off-limits idle capacity

Select the terms from the above list to complete the following sentences.

When the full costs of production are included this is called _____, but it is sometimes more appropriate to use either variable costing or to include only direct materials called throughput or _____. The two types of demand capacity that can be used in the denominator to calculate a unitized fixed-cost rate are long-term demand _____ or short-term demand called _____. The only acceptable measure for CRA is _____, while the only GAAP compliant measure to value inventory and COGS is _____ capacity. The two supply side measures that may be used in the denominator to calculate a unitized fixed-cost rate are long-term measures. The first is unrealistic and excludes any allowance for _____. It is a 24/7/365 measure called _____. The second includes allowance for scheduled maintenance and but not for _____. It is called. _____.

9-16 Variable and absorption costing; explaining operating-income differences. Zippy Motors assembles and sells motor vehicles, and uses standard costing. Actual data relating to April and May 2012 are

1. a. Operating income, April 2012, $1,250,000

	April	May
Unit data:		
Beginning inventory	0	150
Production	500	400
Sales	350	520
Variable costs:		
Manufacturing cost per unit produced	$10,000	$10,000
Operating (marketing) cost per unit sold	3,000	3,000
Fixed costs:		
Manufacturing costs	$2,000,000	$2,000,000
Operating (marketing) costs	600,000	600,000

The selling price per vehicle is $24,000. The budgeted level of production used to calculate the budgeted fixed manufacturing cost per unit is 500 units. There are no price, efficiency, or rate variances. Any production-volume variance is written off to cost of goods sold in the month in which it occurs.

REQUIRED
1. Prepare April and May 2012 income statements for Zippy Motors under (a) variable costing and (b) absorption costing.
2. Prepare a numerical reconciliation and explanation of the difference between operating income for each month under variable costing and absorption costing.

9-17 Throughput costing (continuation of 9-16). The variable manufacturing costs per unit of Zippy Motors are:

1. Operating income, April 2012, $755,000

	April	May
Direct material cost per unit	$6,700	$6,700
Direct manufacturing labour cost per unit	1,500	1,500
Manufacturing overhead cost per unit	1,800	1,800

REQUIRED
1. Prepare income statements for Zippy Motors in April and May of 2012 under throughput costing.
2. Contrast the results in requirement 1 with those in requirement 1 of Exercise 9-16.
3. Give one motivation for Zippy Motors to adopt throughput costing.

9-18 Variable and absorption costing, explaining operating-income differences. BigScreen Corporation manufactures and sells 50-inch television sets and uses standard costing. Actual data relating to January, February, and March of 2013 are:

	January	February	March
Unit data:			
Beginning inventory	0	300	300
Production	1,000	800	1,250
Sales	700	800	1,500
Variable costs:			
Manufacturing cost per unit produced	$900	$900	$900
Operating (marketing) cost per unit sold	600	600	600
Fixed costs:			
Manufacturing costs	$400,000	$400,000	$400,000
Operating (marketing) costs	140,000	140,000	140,000

The selling price per unit is $3,000.

REQUIRED
1. Present income statements for BigScreen Corporation in January, February, and March of 2013 under (a) variable costing and (b) absorption costing.
2. Explain the difference in operating income for January, February, and March under variable costing and absorption costing.

9-19 Throughput costing (continuation of 9-18). The variable manufacturing costs per unit of BigScreen Corporation are:

	January	February	March
Direct material cost per unit	$500	$500	$500
Direct manufacturing labour cost per unit	100	100	100
Manufacturing overhead cost per unit	300	300	300
	$900	$900	$900

REQUIRED
1. Prepare income statements for BigScreen Corporation in January, February, and March of 2012 under throughput costing.
2. Contrast the results in requirement 1 with those in requirement 1 of Exercise 9-18.
3. Give one motivation for BigScreen to adopt throughput costing.

9-20 Absorption and variable costing. (CMA) Osawa Inc. planned and actually manufactured 200,000 units of its single product in 2013, its first year of operation. Variable manufacturing cost was $20 per unit produced. Variable operating (non-manufacturing) cost was $10 per unit sold. Planned and actual fixed manufacturing costs were $600,000. Planned and actual fixed operating (non-manufacturing) costs totalled $400,000. Osawa sold 120,000 units of product at $40 per unit.

REQUIRED
1. Osawa's 2013 operating income using absorption costing is (a) $440,000, (b) $200,000, (c) $600,000, (d) $840,000, or (e) none of these. Show supporting calculations.
2. Osawa's 2013 operating income using variable costing is (a) $800,000, (b) $440,000, (c) $200,000, (d) $600,000, or (e) none of these. Show supporting calculations.

9-21 Comparison of actual costing methods. Rehe Company sells its razors at $3 per unit. The company uses a first-in, first-out actual costing system. A fixed manufacturing cost rate is computed at the end of each year by dividing the actual fixed manufacturing costs by the actual production units. The following data are related to its first two years of operation:

	2012	2013
Sales	1,000 units	1,200 units
Production	1,400 units	1,000 units
Costs:		
Variable manufacturing	$ 700	$ 500
Fixed manufacturing	700	700
Variable operating (marketing)	1,000	1,200
Fixed operating (marketing)	400	400

1. Prepare income statements based on variable costing for each of the two years.
2. Prepare income statements based on absorption costing for each of the two years.
3. Prepare a numerical reconciliation and explanation of the difference between operating income for each year under absorption costing and variable costing.
4. Critics have claimed that a widely used accounting system has led to undesirable buildups of inventory levels. (a) Is variable costing or absorption costing more likely to lead to such buildups? Why? (b) What can be done to counteract undesirable inventory buildups?

9-22 Absorption versus variable costing. Electron Inc. is a semiconductor company based in Winnipeg. In 2013, it produced a new router system for its corporate clients. The average wholesale selling price of the system is $1,200 each. For 2013, Electron estimates that it will sell 10,000 router systems and so produces 10,000 units. Actual 2013 sales are 8,960 units. Electron's actual 2013 costs are:

1. Operating income, $2,531,520

Variable costs per unit:	
Manufacturing cost per unit produced	
Direct materials	$ 55
Direct manufacturing labour	45
Manufacturing overhead	120
Marketing cost per unit sold	75
Fixed costs:	
Manufacturing costs	$1,471,680
R&D	981,120
Marketing	3,124,480

REQUIRED

1. Calculate the operating income under variable costing.
2. Each router unit produced is allocated $165 in fixed manufacturing costs. If the production-volume variance is written off to cost of goods sold, and there are no price, rate, or efficiency variances, calculate the operating income under absorption costing.
3. Explain the differences in operating incomes obtained in requirement 1 and requirement 2.
4. Electron's management is considering implementing a bonus for the supervisors based on gross margin under absorption costing. What incentives will this create for the supervisors? Do you think this new bonus plan is a good idea? Explain briefly.

9-23 Capacity management, denominator-level capacity concepts.

① ②

1. a, b

REQUIRED

Match each of the following numbered items with one or more of the denominator-level capacity concepts by putting the appropriate letter(s) by each item:
a. Theoretical capacity
b. Practical capacity
c. Normal capacity utilization
d. Master-budget capacity utilization

1. Measures the denominator level in terms of what a plant can supply
2. Is based on producing at full efficiency all the time
3. Represents the expected level of capacity utilization for the next budget period
4. Measures the denominator level in terms of demand for the output of the plant
5. Takes into account seasonal, cyclical, and trend factors
6. Should be used for performance evaluation
7. Represents an ideal benchmark
8. Highlights the cost of capacity acquired but not used
9. Should be used for long-term pricing purposes
10. Hides the cost of capacity acquired but not used
11. If used as the denominator-level concept, would avoid the restatement of unit costs when expected demand levels change

9-24 **Variable versus absorption costing.** The Zwatch Company manufactures trendy, high-quality moderately priced watches. As Zwatch's senior financial analyst, you are asked to recommend a method of inventory costing. The CFO will use your recommendation to prepare Zwatch's 2013 income statement. The following data are for the year ended December 31, 2013:

Beginning inventory, January 1, 2013	85,000 units
Ending inventory, December 31, 2013	34,500 units
2013 sales	345,400 units
Selling price (to distributor)	$22.00 per unit
Variable manufacturing cost per unit, including direct materials	$5.10 per unit
Variable operating (marketing) cost per unit sold	$1.10 per unit sold
Fixed manufacturing costs	$1,440,000
Denominator-level machine-hours	6,000
Standard production rate	50 units per machine-hour
Fixed operating (marketing) costs	$1,080,000

Assume standard costs per unit are the same for units in beginning inventory and units produced during the year. Also, assume no price, rate, or efficiency variances. Any production-volume variance is written off to cost of goods sold in the month in which it occurs.

REQUIRED
1. Prepare income statements under variable and absorption costing for the year ended December 31, 2013.
2. What is Zwatch's operating income as percentage of revenues under each costing method?
3. Explain the difference in operating income between the two methods.
4. Which costing method would you recommend to the CFO? Why?

PROBLEMS

9-25 **Downward demand spiral.** Network Company is a large manufacturer of optical storage systems based in British Columbia. Its practical annual capacity is 7,500 units, and, for the past few years, its budgeted and actual sales and production volume have been 7,500 units per year. Network's budgeted and actual variable manufacturing costs are $100 per unit, and budgeted and actual total fixed manufacturing costs are $2,250,000 per year. Network calculates full manufacturing cost per unit as the sum of the variable manufacturing cost per unit and the fixed manufacturing costs allocated to the budgeted units produced. Selling price is set at a 100% markup to full manufacturing cost per unit.

REQUIRED
1. Compute Network's selling price.
2. Recent competition from abroad has caused a drop in budgeted production and sales volume to 6,000 units per year, and analysts are predicting further declines. If Network continues to use budgeted production as the denominator level, calculate its new selling price.
3. Comment on the effect that changes in budgeted production have on selling price. Suggest another denominator level that Network might use for its pricing decision. Justify your choice.
4. Network has received an offer to buy identical storage units for $400 each instead of manufacturing the units in-house. Shutting down the manufacturing plant would reduce fixed costs to $450,000 per year. At what level of expected annual sales (in units) should Network accept this offer? Explain your answer.

9-26 **Absorption costing and production-volume variance—alternative capacity bases.** Earth Light First (ELF), a producer of energy-efficient light bulbs, expects that demand will increase markedly over the next decade. Due to the high fixed costs involved in the business, ELF has decided to evaluate its financial performance using absorption costing income. The production-volume variance is written off to cost of goods sold. The variable cost of production is $2.50 per bulb. Fixed manufacturing costs are $1,000,000 per year. Variable and fixed selling and administrative expenses are $0.25 per bulb sold and $250,000, respectively.

Because its light bulbs are currently popular with environmentally conscious customers, ELF can sell the bulbs for $9.00 each.

ELF is deciding whether to use, when calculating the cost of each unit produced:

Theoretical capacity	800,000 bulbs
Practical capacity	500,000 bulbs
Normal capacity	250,000 bulbs (average production for the next three years)
Master-budget capacity	200,000 bulbs produced this year

REQUIRED

1. Calculate the inventoriable cost per unit using each level of capacity to compute fixed manufacturing cost per unit.
2. Calculate the production-volume variance using each level of capacity to compute the fixed manufacturing overhead allocation rate and this year's production of 220,000 bulbs.
3. Assuming ELF has no beginning inventory, calculate operating income for ELF using each type of capacity to compute fixed manufacturing cost per unit and this year's sales of 200,000 bulbs.

9-27 Operating income effects of denominator-level choice and disposal of production-volume variance (continuation of 9-26).

1. Theoretical operating income, $125,000

REQUIRED

1. If ELF sells all 220,000 bulbs produced, what would be the effect on operating income of using each type of capacity as a basis for calculating manufacturing cost per unit?
2. Compare the results of operating income at different capacity levels when 200,000 bulbs are sold and when 220,000 bulbs are sold. What conclusion can you draw from the comparison?
3. Using the original data (that is, 220,000 units produced and 200,000 units sold), if ELF had used the proration approach to allocate the production-volume variance, what would operating income have been under each method? (Assume that there is no ending work in process.)

9-28 Throughput. (CMA) Byrd Company is a manufacturer of appliances for both residential and commercial use. The company's accounting and financial reporting system is primarily designed to meet external reporting requirements in accordance with generally accepted accounting principles. For inventory costing purposes, Byrd uses the absorption costing method in conjunction with a standard costing system. Costs are allocated to products on a units-produced basis. The denominator of fixed manufacturing costs is normal capacity utilization in production units. Relevant information on Byrd's steam cooker appliance for the last two years is as follows:

1. Operating Income 2013
Throughput costing, $126,420

Unit Data	2012	2013
Beginning inventory	900	1,400
Production	2,000	400
Sales	1,500	1,700
Normal capacity utilization	2,000	2,000

The standard costs for this product are the same in 2012, 2013, and 2014.

Financial Data	2012	2013
Selling price per unit	$ 120	$ 120
Standard variable direct manufacturing costs per unit*	48.70	48.70
Standard variable indirect manufacturing costs per unit	15	15
Variable marketing costs per unit sold	1	1
Total budgeted (and actual) fixed manufacturing costs	10,000	10,000
Total fixed marketing costs	3,000	3,000
Net unfavourable variance† pertaining to variable manufacturing costs	1,000	1,000

*Standard variable direct materials costs are $28 per unit.
†All variances are written off to cost of goods sold in the period incurred.

Currently, Byrd evaluates the performance of its product-line managers and calculates their bonuses based on operating income computed on an absorption-costing basis. It has been suggested that the use of variable costing for internal reporting purposes would more accurately reflect the performance of each product-line manager.

REQUIRED

1. Calculate Byrd Company's operating income on its steam cooker appliance line for 2012 and 2013 using (a) absorption costing, (b) variable costing, and (c) throughput costing.
2. Discuss the features of variable costing that allow it to reflect the performance of Byrd's product-line managers more accurately. Be sure to include in your discussion how absorption costing may influence a product-line manager's behaviour differently from the way variable costing would.
3. What are the pros and cons of adopting throughput costing?

3. Reconciliation, $16,000

9-29 Denominator-level choices, changes in inventory levels, effect on operating income. Koshu Corporation is a manufacturer of computer accessories. It uses absorption costing based on standard costs and reports the following data for 2013:

	A	B	C
1	Theoretical capacity	144,000	units
2	Practical capacity	120,000	units
3	Normal capacity utilization	96,000	units
4	Selling price	$ 30	per unit
5	Beginning inventory	10,000	units
6	Production	104,000	units
7	Sales volume	112,000	units
8	Variable budgeted manufacturing cost	$ 3	per unit
9	Total budgeted fixed manufacturing costs	$1,440,000	
10	Total budgeted operating (non-manuf.) costs (all fixed)	$ 400,000	

There are no price, rate, or efficiency variances. Actual operating costs equal budgeted operating costs. The production-volume variance is written off to cost of goods sold. For each choice of denominator level, the budgeted production cost per unit is also the cost per unit of beginning inventory.

REQUIRED

1. What is the production-volume variance in 2013 when the denominator level is (a) theoretical capacity, (b) practical capacity, and (c) normal capacity utilization?
2. Prepare absorption costing-based income statements for Koshu Corporation using theoretical capacity, practical capacity, and normal capacity utilization as the denominator levels.
3. Why is the operating income under normal capacity utilization lower than the other two scenarios?
4. Reconcile the difference in operating income based on theoretical capacity and practical capacity with the difference in fixed manufacturing overhead included in inventory.

3. Operating income for 2011, 2012 = $0

9-30 Variable and absorption costing, sales, and operating-income changes. Headsmart, a three-year-old company, has been producing and selling a single type of bicycle helmet. Headsmart uses standard costing. After reviewing the income statements for the first three years, Stuart Weil, president of Headsmart, commented, "I was told by our accountants—and in fact, I have memorized—that our breakeven volume is 50,000 units. I was happy that we reached that sales goal in each of our first two years. But, here's the strange thing: in our first year, we sold 50,000 units and indeed we broke even. Then, in our second year we sold the same volume and had a positive operating income. I didn't complain, of course . . . but here's the bad part. In our third year, we sold 20% more helmets, but our operating income fell by more than 80% relative to the second year! We didn't change our selling price or cost structure over the past three years and have no price, efficiency, or rate variances . . . so what's going on?!"

Absorption Costing	2011	2012	2013
Sales (units)	50,000	50,000	60,000
Revenues	$2,100,000	$2,100,000	$2,520,000
Cost of goods sold:			
Beginning inventory	0	0	380,000
Production	1,900,000	2,280,000	1,900,000
Available for sale	1,900,000	2,280,000	2,280,000
Deduct ending inventory	0	(380,000)	0
Adjustment for production-volume variance	0	(240,000)	0
Cost of goods sold	1,900,000	1,660,000	2,280,000
Gross margin	200,000	440,000	240,000
Selling and administrative expenses (all fixed)	200,000	200,000	200,000
Operating income	$ 0	$ 240,000	$ 40,000
Beginning inventory	0	0	10,000
Production (units)	50,000	60,000	50,000
Sales (units)	50,000	50,000	60,000
Ending inventory	0	10,000	0
Variable manufacturing cost per unit	$14	$14	$14
Fixed manufacturing overhead costs	$1,200,000	$1,200,000	$1,200,000
Fixed manufacturing costs allocated per unit produced	$24	$24	$24

REQUIRED
1. What denominator level is Headsmart using to allocate fixed manufacturing costs to the bicycle helmets? How is Headsmart disposing of any favourable or unfavourable production-volume variance at the end of the year? Explain your answer briefly.
2. How did Headsmart's accountants arrive at the breakeven volume of 50,000 units?
3. Prepare a variable-costing-based income statement for each year. Explain the variation in variable costing operating income for each year based on contribution margin per unit and sales volume.
4. Reconcile the operating incomes under variable costing and absorption costing for each year, and use this information to explain to Stuart Weil the positive operating income in 2012 and the drop in operating income in 2013.

9-31 **Denominator-level problem.** Speedy Inc. is a manufacturer of the very popular G36 motorcycles. The management at Speedy has recently adopted absorption costing and is debating which denominator level concept to use. The G36 motorcycles sell for an average price of $8,500. Budgeted fixed manufacturing overhead costs for 2013 are estimated at $4,000,000. Speedy Inc. uses subassembly operators that provide component parts. The following are the denominator-level options that management has been considering:

1. Theoretical budgeted fixed manufacturing overhead cost rate, $1,388.89

a. Theoretical capacity—based on two shifts, completion of four motorcycles per shift, and a 360-day year—$2 \times 4 \times 360 = 2,880$.
b. Practical capacity—theoretical capacity adjusted for unavoidable interruptions, break-downs, and so forth—$2 \times 3 \times 320 = 1,920$.
c. Normal capacity utilization—estimated at 1,200 units.
d. Master-budget capacity utilization—the growing popularity of motorcycles have prompted the Marketing Department to issue an estimate for 2013 of 1,500 units.

REQUIRED
1. Calculate the budgeted fixed manufacturing overhead cost rates under the four denominator-level concepts.
2. What are the benefits to Speedy Inc. of using either theoretical capacity or practical capacity?
3. Under a cost-based pricing system, what are the negative aspects of a master-budget denominator level? What are the positive aspects?

9-32 Cost allocation, downward demand spiral. Deli One operates a chain of 10 retirement homes in the Toronto area. Its central food-catering facility, Deliman, prepares and delivers meals to the retirement homes. It has the capacity to deliver up to 1,460,000 meals a year. In 2012, based on estimates from each retirement home controller, Deliman budgeted for 1,022,000 meals a year. Budgeted fixed costs in 2012 were $1,533,000. Each retirement home was charged $6.00 per meal—$4.50 variable costs plus $1.50 allocated budgeted fixed cost.

Recently, the retirement homes have been complaining about the quality of Deliman's meals and their rising costs. In mid-2012, Deli One's president announces that all Deli One retirement homes and support facilities will be run as profit centres. Retirement homes will be free to purchase quality-certified services from outside the system. Ron Smith, Deliman's controller, is preparing the 2013 budget. He hears that three retirement homes have decided to use outside suppliers for their meals; this will reduce the 2013 estimated demand to 876,000 meals. No change in variable cost per meal or total fixed costs is expected in 2013.

REQUIRED
1. How did Smith calculate the budgeted fixed cost per meal of $1.50 in 2012?
2. Using the same approach to calculating budgeted fixed cost per meal and pricing as in 2012, how much would retirement homes be charged for each Deliman meal in 2013? What would their reaction be?
3. Suggest an alternative cost-based price per meal that Smith might propose and that might be more acceptable to the retirement homes. What can Deliman and Smith do to make this price profitable in the long run?

9-33 Effects of differing production levels on absorption costing income: Metrics to minimize inventory buildups. University Press produces textbooks for university courses. They recently hired a new editor, Leslie White, to handle production and sales of books for an introduction to accounting course. Leslie's compensation depends on the gross margin associated with sales of this book. Leslie needs to decide how many copies of the book to produce. The following information is available for the fall semester 2013:

Estimated sales	10,000 books
Beginning inventory	0 books
Average selling price	$100 per book
Variable production costs	$60 per book
Fixed production costs	$120,000 per semester

The fixed-cost allocation rate is based on expected sales and is therefore equal to $120,000 ÷ 10,000 books = $12 per book.

REQUIRED
Leslie must decide whether to produce 10,000, 12,000, or 16,000 books.
1. Calculate expected gross margin if Leslie produces 10,000, 12,000, or 16,000 books. (Make sure you include the production-volume variance as part of cost of goods sold.)
2. Calculate ending inventory in units and in dollars for each production level.
3. Managers who are paid a bonus that is a function of gross margin may be inspired to produce product in excess of demand to maximize their own bonus. The chapter suggested metrics to discourage managers from producing products in excess of demand. Do you think the following metrics will accomplish this objective? Show your work.
   a. Incorporate a charge of 10% of the cost of the ending inventory as an expense for evaluating the manager.
   b. Include nonfinancial measures (such as the ones recommended on p. 363) when evaluating management and rewarding performance.

9-34 Variable costing and absorption costing, The All-Fixed Company. (R. Marple, adapted) It is the end of 2013. The All-Fixed Company began operations in January 2012. The company is so named because it has no variable costs. All its costs are fixed.

All-Fixed is located on the bank of a river and has its own hydroelectric plant to supply power, light, and heat. The company manufactures a synthetic fertilizer from air and river water and sells its product at a price that is not expected to change. It has a small staff of employees, all hired on a fixed annual salary. The output of the plant can be increased or decreased by adjusting a few dials on a control panel.

Management adopted the policy, effective January 1, 2013, of producing only as much product as was needed to fill sales orders. During 2013, sales were the same as 2012 and were filled entirely from beginning inventory at the start of 2013.

The following are data regarding the operations of The All-Fixed Company:

	2012	2013
Sales (tonnes)	10,000	10,000
Production (tonnes)	20,000	0
Selling price per tonne	$30	$30
Costs (all fixed):		
Manufacturing	$280,000	$280,000
Marketing and administrative	$40,000	$40,000

REQUIRED

1. Prepare income statements with one column for 2012, one column for 2013, and one column for the two years together, using (a) variable costing and (b) absorption costing.
2. What is the breakeven point under (a) variable costing and (b) absorption costing?
3. What inventory costs would be carried on the balance sheets at December 31, 2012, and 2013, under each method?
4. Assume that the performance of the top manager of the company is evaluated and rewarded largely on the basis of reported operating income. Which costing method would the manager prefer? Why?

9-35 **Variable and absorption costing, and breakeven points.** Shasta Hills, a winery in British Columbia, manufactures a premium white cabernet and sells primarily to distributors. Wine is sold in cases of one dozen bottles. In the year ended December 31, 2013, Shasta Hills sold 242,400 cases at an average selling price of $112.80 per case. The following additional data are for Shasta Hills for the year ended December 31, 2013 (assume constant unit costs and no price, rate, or efficiency variances):

3. b. Q = 252,647 (rounded up)

Beginning inventory, January 1, 2013	32,600 cases
Ending inventory, December 31, 2013	24,800 cases
Fixed manufacturing overhead	$4,504,320
Fixed operating costs	$7,882,560
Variable costs per case:	
Direct materials	
Grapes	$19.20 per case
Bottles, corks, and crates	$12.00 per case
Direct labour	
Bottling	$7.20 per case
Winemaking	$16.80 per case
Aging	$2.40 per case

On December 31, 2013, the unit costs per case for closing inventory are $55.20 for variable costing and $73.20 for absorption costing.

REQUIRED

1. Calculate cases of production for Shasta Hills in 2013.
2. Find the breakeven point (number of cases) in 2013:
   a. Under variable costing.
   b. Under absorption costing.
3. Grape prices are expected to increase 25% in 2014. Assuming all other data remain constant, what is the minimum number of cases Shasta Hills must sell in 2014 to break even? Calculate the breakeven point:
   a. Under variable costing.
   b. Under absorption costing.
4. Assume the owners of Shasta Hills want to increase 2014 operating income 10% over 2013 levels. Using the same data as in requirement 3, recalculate the target quantity of cases under variable and absorption costing. Use approximation method re absorption costing.

3. Difference in Operating income, $(380,000)

9-36 Comparison of variable costing and absorption costing. Hinkle Company uses standard costing. Tim Bartina, the new president of Hinkle Company, is presented with the following data for 2013:

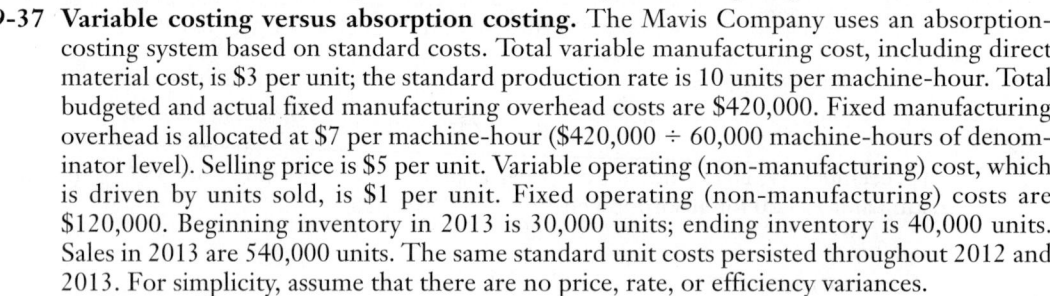

		Variable Costing	Absorption Costing
1	**Hinkle Company**		
2	**Income Statements for the Year Ended December 31, 2013**		
3		**Variable**	**Absorption**
4		**Costing**	**Costing**
5	Revenue	$9,000,000	$9,000,000
6	Cost of goods sold (at standard costs)	4,680,000	5,860,000
7	Fixed manufacturing overhead (budgeted)	1,200,000	—
8	Fixed manufacturing overhead variances (all unfavourable):		
9	Rate	100,000	100,000
10	Production volume	—	400,000
11	Total marketing and administrative costs (all fixed)	1,500,000	1,500,000
12	Total costs	7,480,000	7,860,000
13	Operating income	$1,520,000	$1,140,000
14			
15	Inventories (at standard costs)		
16	December 31, 2012	$1,200,000	$1,720,000
17	December 31, 2013	66,000	206,000

REQUIRED

1. At what percentage of denominator level was the plant operating during 2013?
2. How much fixed manufacturing overhead was included in the 2012 and the 2013 ending inventory under absorption costing?
3. Reconcile and explain the difference in 2013 operating incomes under variable and absorption costing.
4. Tim Bartina is concerned. He notes that despite an increase in sales over 2012, 2013 operating income has actually declined under absorption costing. Explain how this occurred.

1. Operating income, $7,000

9-37 Variable costing versus absorption costing. The Mavis Company uses an absorption-costing system based on standard costs. Total variable manufacturing cost, including direct material cost, is $3 per unit; the standard production rate is 10 units per machine-hour. Total budgeted and actual fixed manufacturing overhead costs are $420,000. Fixed manufacturing overhead is allocated at $7 per machine-hour ($420,000 ÷ 60,000 machine-hours of denominator level). Selling price is $5 per unit. Variable operating (non-manufacturing) cost, which is driven by units sold, is $1 per unit. Fixed operating (non-manufacturing) costs are $120,000. Beginning inventory in 2013 is 30,000 units; ending inventory is 40,000 units. Sales in 2013 are 540,000 units. The same standard unit costs persisted throughout 2012 and 2013. For simplicity, assume that there are no price, rate, or efficiency variances.

REQUIRED

1. Prepare an income statement for 2013 assuming that the production-volume variance is written off at year-end as an adjustment to cost of goods sold.
2. The president has heard about variable costing. She asks you to recast the 2013 statement as it would appear under variable costing.
3. Explain the difference in operating income as calculated in requirements 1 and 2.
4. Graph how fixed manufacturing overhead is accounted for under absorption costing. That is, there will be two lines: one for the budgeted fixed manufacturing overhead (which is equal to the actual fixed manufacturing overhead in this case) and one for the fixed manufacturing overhead allocated. Show how the production-volume variance might be indicated in the graph.
5. Critics have claimed that a widely used accounting system has led to undesirable buildups of inventory levels. (a) Is variable costing or absorption costing more likely to lead to such buildups? Why? (b) What can be done to counteract undesirable inventory buildups?

9-38 Effects of denominator—Elementary. Shen Company is a manufacturer of MP3 players. It implemented standard costs and a flexible budget on January 1, 2013. The president has been pondering how fixed manufacturing overhead should be allocated to products. Machine-hours have been chosen as the allocation base. Her remaining uncertainty is the denominator level for machine-hours. She decides to wait for the first month's results before making a final choice of what denominator level should be used from that day forward.

In January 2013, the actual units of output had a standard of 28,000 machine-hours allowed. If the company used practical capacity as the denominator level, the fixed manufacturing overhead rate variance would be $4,000, unfavourable, and the production-volume variance would be $14,400, unfavourable. If the company used normal capacity utilization as the denominator level, the production-volume variance would be $8,000, favourable. Budgeted fixed manufacturing overhead was $48,000 for the month.

REQUIRED

1. Compute the denominator level, assuming that the normal-capacity-utilization concept is chosen.
2. Compute the denominator level, assuming that the practical-capacity concept is chosen.
3. Suppose you are the executive vice-president. You want to maximize your 2013 bonus, which depends on 2013 operating income. Assume that the production-volume variance is written off to cost of goods sold at year end. Which denominator level would you favour? Why?

9-39 Cost allocation, responsibility accounting, ethics (continuation of 9-32). In 2013, only 806,840 Deliman meals were produced and sold to the hospitals. Smith suspects that hospital controllers had systematically inflated their 2013 meal estimates.

REQUIRED

1. Recall that Deliman uses the master-budget capacity utilization to allocate fixed costs and to price meals. What was the effect of production-volume variance on Deliman's operating income in 2013?
2. Why might hospital controllers deliberately overestimate their future meal counts?
3. What other evidence should Deli One's controller seek to investigate Smith's concerns?
4. Suggest two specific steps that Deli One's controller might take to reduce hospital controllers' incentives to inflate their estimated meal counts.

9-40 Variable and absorption costing, and breakeven points. Tammy Cat Tree Co. (TCTC) builds luxury cat trees and sells them through the Internet to cat owners who want to provide their cats with a more natural environment. At the start of 2013, TCTC carried no inventory. During the year, it produced 1,000 cat trees and sold 800 cat trees for $300 each. Fixed production costs were $100,000 and variable production costs were $75 per cat tree. Fixed advertising, website, and other general and administrative expenses were $50,000 and variable shipping costs were $25 per tree.

REQUIRED

1. Prepare an income statement assuming TCTC uses:
   a. Variable costing.
   b. Absorption costing.
2. Compute the breakeven point in units assuming TCTC uses:
   a. Variable costing.
   b. Absorption costing.
3. Due to recent changes in local conservation laws, the price of the wood used in the cat trees is expected to increase by $25 for each tree. What effect would this have on the breakeven points calculated above?
4. Using the original data in the problem and the breakeven/target income formulas, show that it would be necessary to sell 800 cat trees to earn the income calculated in requirements 1a and 1b above.

COLLABORATIVE LEARNING CASE

9-41 Absorption, variable, and throughput costing. EnRG Inc. produces trail mix packaged for sale in convenience stores across Canada. At the beginning of April 2012, EnRG has no inventory of trail mix. Demand for the next three months is expected to remain constant at 50,000 bags per month. EnRG plans to produce to demand, 50,000 bags in April. However, many of the employees take vacation in June, so EnRG plans to produce 70,000 bags in May and only 30,000 bags in June.

1. Allocated MOH, $56,000

1. Production volume variance, $121,030 U

1. a. Operating income, $10,000

1. Operating income for April, $75,000

Costs for the three months are expected to remain unchanged. The costs and revenues for April, May, and June are expected to be:

Sales revenue	$6.00 per bag
Direct material cost	$0.80 per bag
Direct manufacturing labour cost	$0.45 per bag
Variable manufacturing overhead cost	$0.30 per bag
Variable selling cost	$0.15 per bag
Fixed manufacturing overhead cost	$105,000 per month
Fixed administrative costs	$ 35,000 per month

Suppose the actual costs, market demand, and levels of production for April, May, and June are as expected.

REQUIRED

1. Compute operating income for April, May, and June under variable costing.
2. Compute operating income for April, May, and June under absorption costing. Assume that the denominator level for each month is that month's expected level of output.
3. Compute operating income for April, May, and June under throughput costing.
4. Discuss the benefits and problems associated with using throughput costing.

1. Theoretical budgeted fixed manufacturing overhead rate per barrel, $9.51

9-42 **Capacity-level (denominator) choices.** Lucky Lager recently purchased a brewing plant from a bankrupt company. It was constructed only two years ago. The plant has budgeted fixed manufacturing overhead of $50 million per year ($4.167 million each month) in 2012. Paul Vautin, the controller of the brewery, must decide on the denominator-level concept to use in its absorption costing system for 2012. The options available to him are:

a. Theoretical capacity: 600 barrels an hour for 24 hours a day for 365 days = 5,256,000 barrels

b. Practical capacity: 500 barrels an hour for 20 hours a day for 350 days = 3,500,000 barrels

c. Normal capacity utilization for 2012: 400 barrels an hour for 20 hours a day for 350 days = 2,800,000 barrels

d. Master-budget capacity utilization for 2012 (separate rates computed for each half-year):
   ◆ January to June 2012 budget—320 barrels an hour for 20 hours a day for 175 days = 1,120,000 barrels
   ◆ July to December 2012 budget—480 barrels an hour for 20 hours a day for 175 days = 1,680,000 barrels

Variable standard manufacturing costs per barrel are $51.40 (variable direct materials, $38.40; variable manufacturing labour, $6.00; and variable manufacturing overhead, $7.00). The brewery "sells" its output to the sales division of Lucky Lager at a budgeted price of $82.00 per barrel.

In 2012, the brewery of Lucky Lager showed these results:

Unit data in barrels:	
Beginning inventory, January 1, 2012	0
Production	2,600,000
Ending inventory, December 31, 2012	200,000

The brewery had actual costs of

Cost data:	
Variable manufacturing	$144,456,000
Fixed manufacturing overhead	$ 48,758,400

The sales division of Lucky Lager purchased 2,400,000 barrels in 2012 at the $82 per barrel rate. All manufacturing variances are written off to cost of goods sold in the period in which they are incurred.

REQUIRED

1. Compute the budgeted fixed manufacturing overhead rate using each of the four denominator-level concepts for (a) beer produced in March 2012 and (b) beer produced in September 2012. Explain why any differences arise.
2. Explain why the theoretical capacity and practical capacity concepts are different.
3. Which denominator-level concept would the plant manager of the brewery prefer when senior management of Lucky Lager is judging plant manager performance during 2012? Explain.
4. Compute the operating income of the brewery using the following: (a) theoretical capacity, (b) practical capacity, and (c) normal capacity utilization denominator-level capacity concepts. Explain any differences between (a), (b), and (c).
5. What denominator-level concept would Lucky Lager prefer for income tax reporting? Explain.
6. Explain the ways in which the Canada Revenue Agency might restrict the flexibility of a company like Lucky Lager, which uses absorption costing to reduce its reported taxable income.

Quantitative Analyses of Cost Functions

BUSINESS MATTERS

Objectivity in Cost Estimation and Cost Control

Elegant Rugs may have either a machine-intensive or a labour-intensive carpet-manufacturing process. Wall-to-wall carpet is manufactured primarily by machines that dye, tuft, knot, shear, and carve the yarn on rolls four to five metres wide. Carpets from Asia and the Middle East are smaller, one-of-a-kind, and made by hand. Controlling direct costs of production is straightforward because there is an observable cause-effect relationship. This is not true for indirect costs, because the indirect resources used in production are shared unequally in the production of two distinct types of outputs. Indirect resources essential to support production are shared unequally when distinct types of outputs are produced. The relationship is assumed to be one of cost-benefit between the value added to the output and the use of a greater amount of indirect resources.

Controlling indirect costs is difficult because it is neither feasible nor cost effective to measure indirect inputs that generate each manufacturing overhead cost. Management teams with traditional cost systems have scant data, a single indirect cost pool, accompanied by quantity and cost data of only direct resources used.

The management team at Elegant Rugs must assume that a change to the quantity of a selected direct input will explain most of the change to the value of the total overhead cost pool. If true, then the change in use of direct input that explains the greatest proportion of change in the overhead cost pool is the best measure of the cost-benefit relationship. To predict the future value of the indirect overhead cost pool, the team needs to select the most affordable, reliable, and practical method of prediction that best reflects the economic reality of the actual use of indirect resources in manufacturing at Elegant Rugs.

LEARNING OUTCOMES

After studying this chapter, you should be able to

1. Use standard mathematical notation to specify a cost function that can be graphed as a straight line.

2. Understand the various methods of cost estimation and use historical data to predict future costs.

3. Apply OLS linear regression to analyze goodness of fit and the values of *a* and *b* to predict the MOH cost pool.

4. Explain ways to clean up dirty data.

5. Appendix. Use statistics reported from a simple linear regression to reliably and confidently predict the range within which total value of the cost pool will fall. Use multiple linear regression to determine how more than one cost driver (X_i) improves the prediction of the MOH cost pool value (*y*).

The management team at Elegant Rugs faces a series of difficult decisions when generating predictions of future manufacturing overhead (MOH). According to the decision framework, the team needs to collect relevant past data and predict future cost behaviour based on these data. The quality of the data will, in large part, determine the quality of the team's predictions, but so too will the quality of the method the team chooses to make these predictions.

Assume the team must work with a traditional costing system. The team's problem is how to select the best method to predict the one MOH cost pool value in an unbiased way. They can only use the data available about quantities of direct inputs that are reported in the traditional costing system to predict the future MOH values. A reliable and large enough set of information is essential. With enough good data, the management team can choose a method of analysis, an appropriate method of prediction, and report on how confident they are about their prediction.

This chapter describes and compares the available methods to predict the future value of an indirect manufacturing overhead (MOH) cost pool within the limitations of a traditional costing system. The various methods of analysis and prediction are all quantitative, but their rigour differs.

GENERAL ISSUES IN ESTIMATING COST FUNCTIONS

1 Use standard mathematical notation to specify a cost function that can be graphed as a straight line.

There are four methods available to select the cost driver that could best be used to reliably calculate an indirect manufacturing overhead (MOH) cost rate and predict the total future value of the indirect MOH cost pool. This rate was called the *indirect cost allocation rate* in Chapter 4 and the *cost driver rate* in Chapter 5. This rate measures the cost per unit of benefit received by each distinct type of output from an unequal use of the same resources.

The MOH costs are accumulated together into one cost pool, but the causes of these MOH costs, the amount or quantity of shared resources used, are not recorded in a traditional costing system.[1] The benefit provided to those sharing MOH resources may be measured as, for example, direct manufacturing labour-hours (DMLH) already reported in the traditional costing system. Clearly DMLH is not an indirect cost driver at all, but the data are available. GAAP-compliant indirect resources shared, the costs of which generate the MOH cost pool, are limited to:

Indirect Manufacturing Overhead (MOH)

Security (labour and supplies)	All direct manufacturing idle time
Custodial (labour and supplies)	All direct manufacturing overtime
Materials handling (labour, equipment, maintenance)	Plant lease or plant amortization
Quality control (labour, equipment, supplies)	Equipment lease or equipment amortization
Maintenance in the plant (labour, supplies)	Utilities (for security, custodial, quality control (QC), plant, equipment)
All statutory (CPP, EI) and fringe (sick leave, vacation) benefits	Insurance (plant property, equipment, people)
All direct manufacturing rework labour	Tax (manufacturing plant, equipment)

Capacity purchased for long-term use generates purely fixed, shared, and GAAP-compliant MOH costs such as amortization or lease costs, HST, federal and provincial corporate income tax, property and asset tax, and property insurance premiums paid. The dollars paid remain unchanged regardless of the quantity of distinctive outputs produced. Other essential support resources shared such as security, custodial, and maintenance labour paid hourly, will generate variable costs. A single cost pool total that includes many different costs is a **heterogeneous cost pool**.

---

[1]You will recall from Chapter 5 that many activity levels that create costs in the MOH can be reported if the traditional costing system is refined and becomes an ABC system. But the assumption is that this is not an alternative available to the management team of Elegant Rugs.

In the example of Elegant Rugs, a traditional system is currently in place. The management team already knows how different MOH costs behave in the single MOH cost pool; their task is to choose one measure of benefit from the alternatives, reported by the existing MIS, not to restructure the cost system. But there is no single measure of benefit from shared resource use that will explain changes in all MOH costs. The reason the best measure of benefit is necessary is that the managers want assurance that if they change the quantity used in the measurement of benefit, there will be a corresponding and systematic change in the cost pool.

The goal is to choose a method to use to describe the cost-benefit relationship that best reflects the unequal sharing of common MOH resources between distinct types of outputs. The management team should start by *specifying* or expressing the known cost-benefit relationship in equations, as we did in Chapter 3. Assume all quantities of potential measures of benefit, such as DMLH, and the total value of the MOH cost pool are reliable and available from the MIS, and that the management team knows which MOH costs are fixed, variable, or a combination of both.

LINEAR AND CURVILINEAR COST FUNCTIONS

A **linear cost function** for MOH can be graphed when the reported amount of quantity of benefit received (X) can be paired with the corresponding dollar value of the cost pool (Y), an (X,Y) data pair. The use of capital letters here for X and Y signals that the values are historical, actual values. But remember that not all cost functions are linear. The fourth graph in Exhibit 10-1, of a unitized fixed-cost behaviour, is a **curvilinear cost function**, which means that when the data points are joined they form a curve. Curvilinear cost functions are discussed in Chapter 19.

To better understand linear and curvilinear cost functions and to see the role of cost functions in business decisions, consider the negotiations between Cannon

EXHIBIT 10-1
Examples of Linear (Variable, Fixed, and Mixed) and Curvilinear Cost Functions

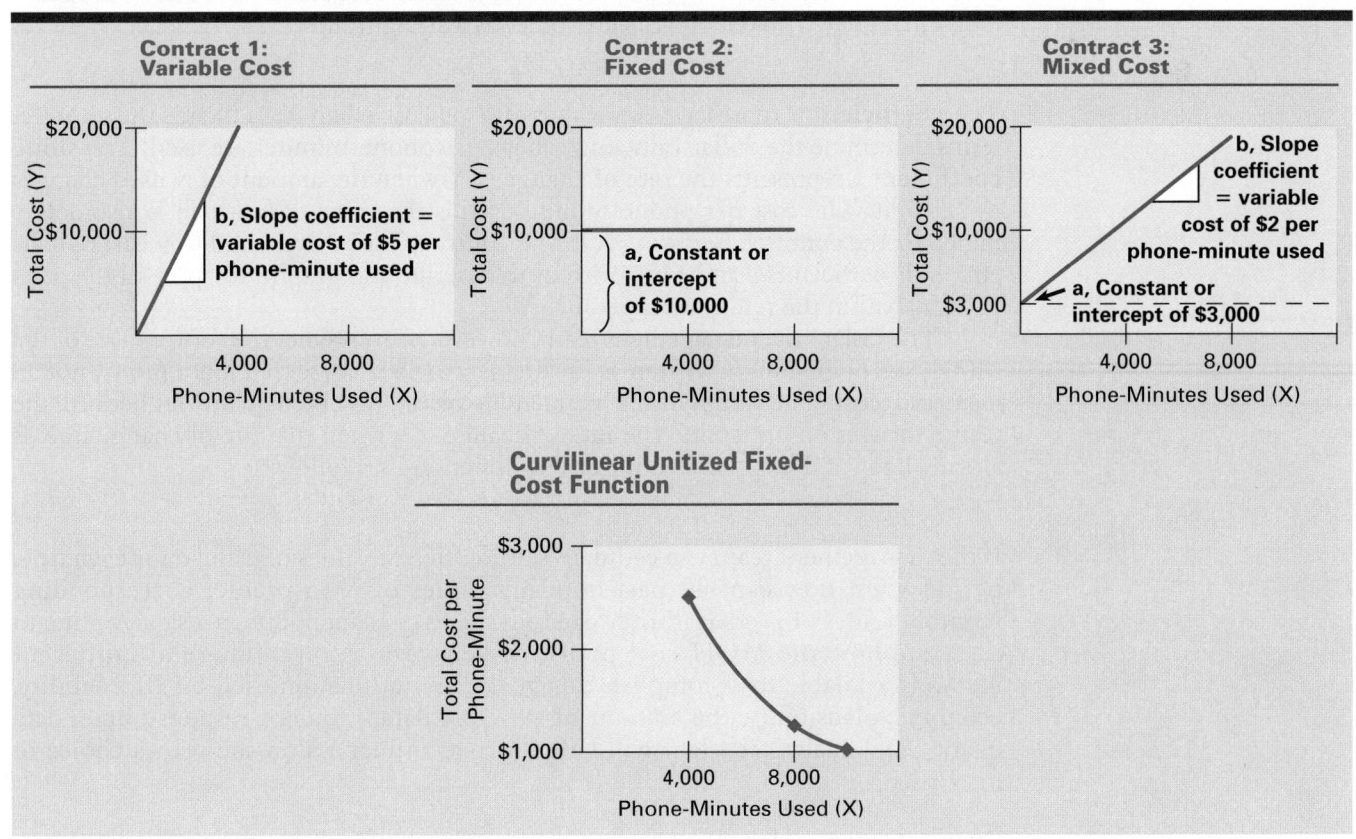

Service and World Wide Communications (WWC) for exclusive use of a telephone between Vancouver and Tokyo. Exhibit 10-1 shows three types of linear cost functions plus a curvilinear cost function. Contract 1 represents a *variable cost* for Cannon; Contract 2 represents a *fixed cost*; Contract 3 represents a *mixed cost*. The curvilinear graph shows the average fixed-cost function for Cannon.

The phone-minutes used by Cannon provide value to the users in different business functions in Cannon's value chain. Users share the benefits of this common resource, but different users in the business value chain do not consume phone-minutes in equal quantity. For the purpose of full absorption pricing, the management team wants to isolate *only* that proportion of phone costs that provided an essential support benefit to the business function of production. This is the proportion of the total phone cost that will be GAAP-compliant MOH.

The equation of a straight line, based on historically observed actual values of (X,Y), tells managers how changes in X correspond to changes in Y in an orderly or systematic way. The changes in X drive or explain, but do not cause, the changes in Y, the heterogeneous total MOH cost. Management accountants select relevant actual data, analyze it, and use the results to assess how orderly the relationship is between X and Y. The goal of the analysis is to illustrate how well change in the benefits that result from the costs match the change in actual quantities of one resource used. The closer the match, the more likely a change in the quantities of a resource used will explain a lot of the change in the MOH cost pool. This is referred to as a **correlation** between cost and the measure of a shared resource used. Correlation is the orderly association of changes in one quantity that explains but does not cause changes in another quantity. The choice of the quantity of a direct resource as the best measure of benefit is assessed based on its **economic plausibility**. The better the method of analysis matches the value added from the physical production process, the greater the improvement to reliability and confidence in predicting the value of the MOH cost pool.

The benefit of the linear cost function is that it can be applied to predict future costs for all linear cost behaviour. The terms of each telephone contract shown in Exhibit 10-1 may differ, but each describes a linear cost function[2]. The cost behaviour when the (X, Y) data points are joined is a straight line:

$$Y = a + bX \tag{1}$$

The **coefficient** a represents any value of Y or cost when X = 0, and the contract terms determine the dollar value of a when zero phone-minutes are used. The **slope coefficient** b represents the rate of change in Y when the amount of X used changes by *one* unit. The cost per phone-minute used is the value of b, which is also determined by the contract. Knowing X (the quantity of cost driver used to measure benefit) and coefficients a and b is sufficient to describe and graphically plot all the pairs of (X,Y) within the relevant range of X.

The task of the management team, however, is to predict the future value of the MOH cost pool. This is written as lowercase y to emphasize that it is a *future*, not an historical, cost. The values of X remain at historical, observed quantities because the team's focus is on predicting the rate of change in y when the rate of change in X is already known. The predicted linear cost function is as follows:

$$y = a + bX \tag{2}$$

If the management team can estimate the coefficient values of a and b for each time period, then they can use past monthly values of X to predict corresponding monthly values of y—that is, they can join the (X, y) data points in a straight line to illustrate how the MOH cost pool will behave in future. There are different methods available to accomplish this goal. Limitations imposed by affordability, economic plausibility, the amount of available data, required response time, data quality, and analytical talent will be important influences on the team's choice of method.

---

[2]Note that the unitized fixed cost does not represent a contract at all, but rather is a general model of curvilinear cost behaviour. The curve forms because the slope changes throughout the relevant range.

VARIABLE, FIXED, AND MIXED LINEAR COST FUNCTIONS

Now we will compare and contrast the three possible linear contracts Cannon Services and WWC are negotiating in more detail. The linear relationship between phone-minutes used (X) and the cost of service (Y), illustrated in Exhibit 10-1, is fully defined by one of three contracts:

◆ Contract 1: $5 per phone-minute used:

$$Y = \$5X$$

Clearly, when X = 0 minutes, Y = $0. The value of Y when X = 0 is called the *intercept value*, or the point where the line intersects with the vertical axis, Y. The linear equation also tells managers that when X increases by 1 minute, the total cost pool value of Y will increase by $5.00.

◆ Contract 2: Total cost will be $10,000 per month, regardless of the number of phone-minutes used:

$$Y = \$10,000$$

The fixed-cost pool of $10,000 is the dollar value of coefficient a, which is constant regardless of the value of X. In Exhibit 10-1, notice that the slope coefficient, b, is zero for Contract 2, indicating there is no rate of change in this cost pool as the cost driver X changes.

◆ Contract 3: $3,000 per month plus $2 per phone-minute used:

$$Y = \$3,000 + \$2X$$

When X = 0, a = $3,000 and b = $2.00/minute, according to the contract.

Understanding cost-behaviour patterns and the most probable use of phone minutes, Cannon's managers can make the best decision among the three alternatives. If managers forecast normal use of the cost driver at X = 4,000 phone-minutes per month, then the total cost pool (y) predicted from each of the three contracts would be as follows:

◆ Contract 1 cost y_1: $20,000 ($5 per phone-minute × 4,000 phone-minutes)
◆ Contract 2 cost y_2: $10,000
◆ Contract 3 cost y_3: $11,000 [$3,000 + ($2 per phone-minute × 4,000 phone-minutes)]

Clearly, when X = 4,000 phone-minutes, the predicted cost from contracts 2 and 3 are less costly to Cannon than contract 1.

COST FUNCTION ESTIMATION BASED ON QUANTITATIVE DATA ANALYSIS

Returning to our opening example of Elegant Rugs, the management team is faced with the problem of how to identify the cost driver (a quantity of direct inputs) that best explains changes in the indirect MOH cost pool using data from their traditional costing system. To organize, plan, and control costs, the management team at Elegant Rugs needs an MIS that reports the historical MOH costs and the quantity of direct resources consumed that will be the measure of benefit. These are all quantities, hence the term *quantitative data analysis*. Choosing from methods of analysis includes several steps.

Step 1   From the available data, identify the value of the indirect MOH cost pool and potential measures of *direct* resources used that may best measure the unequal benefit from sharing the common indirect resources used. Usually these data are reported monthly. **Time-series data** is a set of data reported at regular intervals during a specified time period. These data must be accurate, up to date, and represent the amounts and dollar values arising during normal or routine production processes.

Step 2 Gather existing data on actual cost driver quantities (X) and the corresponding actual indirect cost pool values (Y) that have occurred in the past. Carefully inspect the data for reliability and accuracy. In a column, report the orderly sequence of different amounts of X used each time period, such as each month. These values of X are often denoted as X_i, where the i will be a letter or number identifying the month. Beside the first set of X_i, report the quantities of the alternative cost driver (there must be at least two potential cost drivers or there will be no choice required). Repeat this step for all alternative cost drivers, then report the unique value of Y, the cost pool, for each month corresponding to the monthly value of all X_i.

Step 3 Test whether these data match three basic assumptions:

1. Economic plausibility is reflected in the relevant range of X observed and reported and in Y, the actual costs reported. To have value added, any prediction of a cost function $y = a + bX$ has to reflect a real situation that has occurred and will recur in an orderly way. For example, if direct manufacturing labour-hours (DMLH) are reported, then each distinct type of output must use DMLH. If this is not true then there is no economic plausibility.

2. The systematic relationship between orderly changes in some quantities of direct resources used and corresponding orderly changes in cost can be defined as linear. As Exhibit 10-1 illustrates, not all systematic relationships between X and Y are linear. The methods of analysis discussed in this chapter do not apply unless the cost behaviour is linear.

3. The data pairs (X,Y) represent a continuous change between one set of data points and the next. This is why we can join the space between data points with a continuous straight line. Not all relationships between (X,Y) are continuous. The methods of analysis discussed in this chapter do not apply unless the cost behaviour is continuous.

Step 4 Graph either the economically plausible data of available (X,Y) pairs of data or the (X, y) pairs, depending on the method of prediction used. Analyze the straight-line results for each cost driver and evaluate the best choice of cost driver.

Step 5 Estimate the continuous, linear cost function using the best cost driver, and if the analytical method permits, estimate the normal range (the variance) within which future MOH amounts are likely to occur.

INDIRECT MANUFACTURING OVERHEAD COST POOLS (MOH)

The more orderly the actual monthly changes in X and the corresponding actual monthly changes to the MOH cost pool (Y), the more accurate the explanation and prediction of cost changes will be. The reason there exists an indirect MOH cost pool with several contributors (fixed, variable, supplies, labour, and so on) is that there is no economically plausible association of the cost drivers of these many costs to the unit of output sold. For example, assume that a smartphone manufacturer uses animal security. How many cans of dog food are used each month per smartphone produced? Knowing the cans of food per hour of security provided and the associated costs has no effect on the quantity of smartphones produced in one month. Nevertheless, these costs provide a benefit and must be budgeted, controlled, and recovered in the price of the finished output that is sold.

In contrast, either a direct machine or a direct labour cost pool matches the economic reality that one cost driver, direct machine-hours (DMH), generates some of the total indirect MOH costs of materials handling, maintenance supplies, and labour over some time period. The same is true of the direct manufacturing labour cost pool and its cost driver, direct manufacturing labour-hours (DMLH). Recall that idle time, rework time, overtime, and statutory fringe benefits accrue at a rate per DMLH but accumulate in the MOH cost pool. Therefore,

DMLH is an economically plausible measure of benefit from sharing MOH resources used.

There can exist an economically plausible relationship between direct and indirect resources consumed. For example, as the quantity of DMH changes one could anticipate changes in machine maintenance labour and supplies cost and perhaps even janitorial service costs and insurance. As the quantity of DMLH changes, one could anticipate changes in fringe benefits, idle time, rework, and overtime costs. The question is the proportion of orderly change in the total indirect MOH that is explained by orderly changes in either of these cost drivers.

The more capital- or machine-intensive a production process, the more likely it is that maintenance and supplies to keep the machines in working order will be an important contributor to an indirect MOH cost pool. The more labour-intensive a manual production process, the more likely it is that statutory fringe benefits, rework, overtime, and idle time will be the most important contributor to an indirect MOH cost pool. At Elegant Rugs, if managers must choose only one of these cost drivers, which one best predicts the future value of the MOH cost pool?

Managers face two important problems: selecting the best cost driver among the alternatives available and testing their decision rigorously enough to provide evidence the choice was indeed the best. Then managers can use the relationship between changes in the consumed quantity of the chosen cost driver to reliably predict (budget) a total indirect cost pool value. But predictions are never certain. It would be extraordinary, even suspicious, if there were no variance between the actual and budgeted value of an indirect MOH cost pool.

One prediction method—statistics—extends beyond just predicting future values of the cost pool (y). The statistical method gives managers information to also predict the normal variance—unfavourable (U) or favourable (F)—around the predicted value of y. In addition this method provides indicators of when the costs have increased beyond the routine level of variation around the predicted y. This signals that the resource use is out of control and a remedy is needed. Management effort to explain predictable variance decreases because the report directs attention to non-routine variances. This is management by exception. The limitation on this method is that an adequate quantity of high-quality data points that report on routine production must be available. In addition, most people are not familiar enough with statistics to interpret the results correctly.

COST ESTIMATION METHODS USING HISTORICAL DATA

Cost estimation follows a standard pattern, but the management team's decisions are extremely difficult. Once the team has made a decision, it must then be able to explain the decision to others, and for some methods this task is more difficult than for others. To begin, managers can use the five steps of quantitative analysis outlined on pages 389 to 390 to choose an appropriate cost driver.

Step 1 At Elegant Rugs, managers know the quantity of DMH and DMLH used as well as the indirect MOH costs accumulated weekly for the past 12 weeks. The managers of Elegant Rugs have decided that changes in either of these two cost drivers could be useful when budgeting weekly values of indirect MOH for the next 12 weeks.

Step 2 The management team has reported the 12 values of X on either side of the MOH cost pool Y. Notice that the production process shuts down for the eighth week. This is reassuring, because it means there is a real economic event, X = 0, and there is an actual value of $Y when X = 0. This is the a coefficient and can be read quite easily from the following report for Elegant Rugs as $480:

Week	Direct Machine-Hours Alternative (X₁)	Indirect-Manufacturing Overhead Costs (Y)	Direct Manufacturing Labour-Hours Alternative (X₂)
1	70	$ 1,200	30
2	93	1,231	35
3	66	1,004	36
4	76	920	20
5	64	765	57
6	102	1,473	47
7	82	1,192	49
8	—	480	—
9	87	1,345	70
10	98	1,146	38
11	72	767	39
12	52	978	41
Total	862	$12,501	462

Using these data, managers may be able to learn something from analyzing if and how the cost driver changes affect cost pool changes. For example, how much of the increase of $31 in the indirect MOH from week 1 to week 2 can be best explained by either the change of 23 DMH or the change of 5 DMLH? The same question can be posed for each weekly change.

One important weakness of this set of data is that there are very few data points. The fewer the data points, the less confident managers can be that a routine or normal set of costs and quantities has been reported. This quarter may have been either an exceptionally cost-efficient or an exceptionally wasteful quarter for any number of reasons. If this were true, then predicting the future based on a non-routine data set would not be reliable.

Step 3   There are several analytical methods from which to choose, but first managers must test the data against the three basic assumptions of economic plausibility, linearity, and continuity. Affordability and understandability are also important in this selection.

Step 4   Graph the economically plausible data of available (X,Y) pairs, as shown in Exhibit 10-2, as a basis to do preliminary tests of the three basic assumptions.

EXHIBIT 10-2
Graph of the Elegant Rugs Actual Data for Each Cost Driver and the Indirect MOH Cost Pool

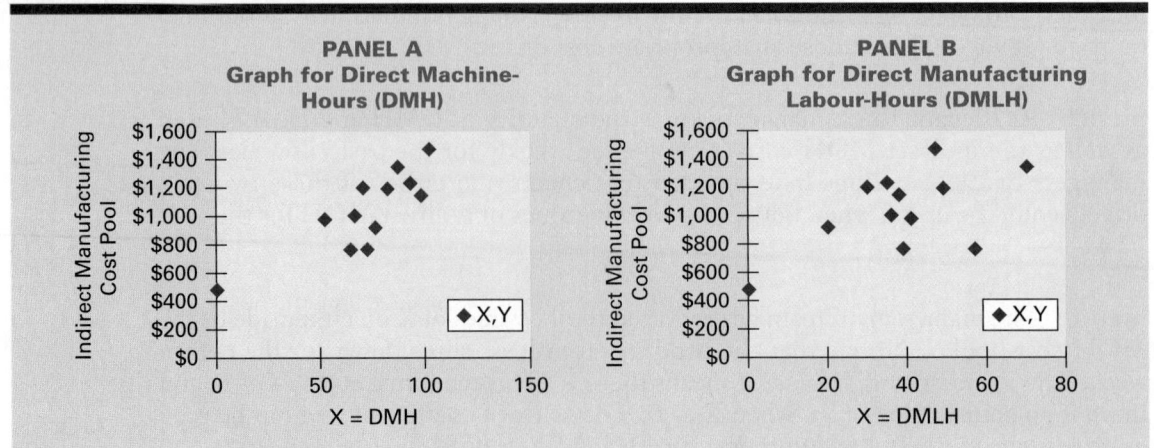

◆ Economic plausibility depends on the real consumption of both DMH and DMLH in the quantities recorded and the corresponding changes in indirect MOH during the same weekly time periods. Managers know that in week 8 the plant shuts down for scheduled maintenance. This happens once every 90 days. All machines shut down, and all those people on the direct manufacturing assembly lines did not come into work.

◆ Linearity can be assessed either quantitatively or qualitatively, depending on the analytical method chosen. In this case, the managers simply used an Excel spreadsheet to input and chart a graph of these data and looked at it to assess if it was a curve. Fortunately, neither graph is indicating a curved shape to the data. This reassures the managers that the orderly changes in X and the corresponding changes in Y can be estimated as a linear cost function.

◆ Continuity can also be tested by comparing the graph in Exhibit 10-1 to those in Exhibit 10-3, which illustrate three types of discontinuous cost functions. A **discontinuous cost (step fixed cost) function** arises when, within the relevant range of production inputs, the graph of total costs with a single resource consumed does not form a straight line with a constant slope.

An indirect MOH example would be a quantity discount available on indirect materials like lubricants, as shown in Panel A of Exhibit 10-3. For quantities between 1 and 1,000 units of machine lubricants purchased, the rate of change in the cost per unit is $25. For quantities between 1,001 and 2,000 units purchased, there is a quantity discount and the rate of change in cost per unit is $15. The rate of change in cost of this indirect material is, of course, the slope b in a linear equation. At each quantity point where the unit price decreases, the total cost for indirect materials rises, but at a slower rate. The result is a straight line with varying slopes. There is a systematic relationship between changes in X and changes in Y, but it is not correctly expressed as a simple equation of a straight line.

Panel B of Exhibit 10-3 illustrates a **step variable-cost function**, which is a function in which the cost is constant over various ranges of capacity, but the cost increases by discrete amounts (that is, in steps) as the range of the resource consumed changes from one relevant range to another. When capacity is acquired in discrete amounts (e.g., one person at a time) but used in fractional amounts (e.g., 3.5 hours per day instead of 8 hours per day), the result is a step variable-cost function.

Panel C in Exhibit 10-3 illustrates a step fixed (or discontinuous) cost function, which is similar to a step variable-cost function except for the capacity and time horizon. A steel company operating heat treatment furnaces to harden steel parts acquires each furnace at $300,000 with a capacity of 7,500 heating hours. For the

EXHIBIT 10-3
Three Examples of Discontinuous Cost Functions

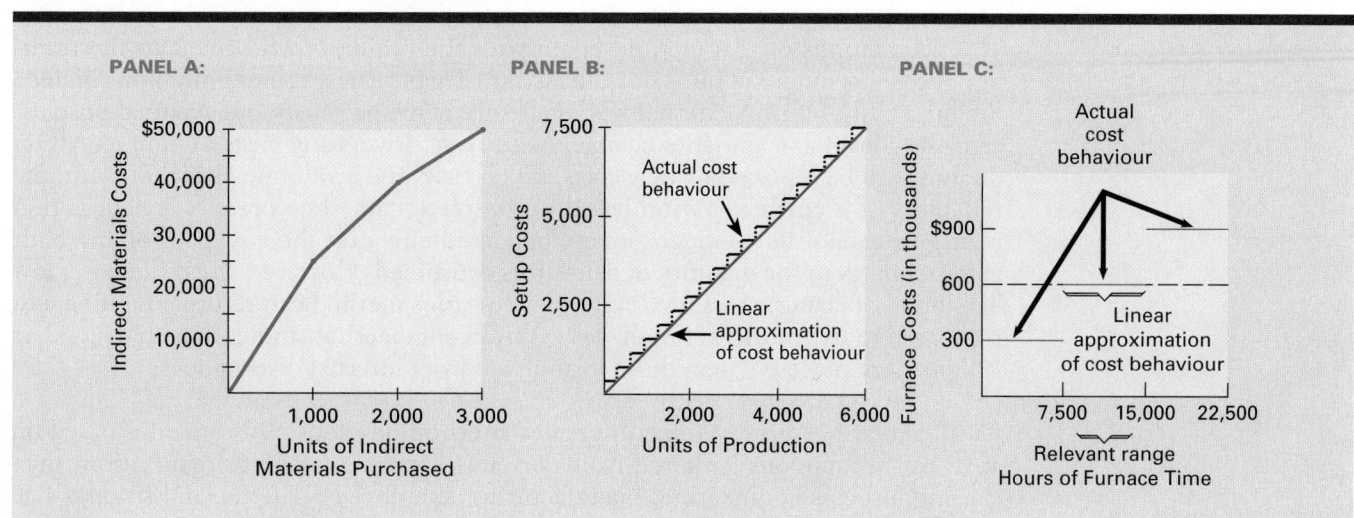

relevant range of 7,500 to 15,000 hours of furnace time required, the company expects to operate with two furnaces at a cost of $600,000. Any hours required beyond 15,000 heating hours (e.g., 19,500 hours) will incur a purchase cost of $300,000 to provide only 4,500 additional hours.

What all three examples have in common is that the relationship of rate of change in units consumed and rate of change in costs is discontinuous. The scatter-plots in Exhibit 10-2 do not indicate that the cost function is discontinuous. Having tested the basic assumptions, managers at Elegant Rugs can choose from four methods of analysis (outlined in the next section) to add meaning to the data available.

Step 5 Estimate the continuous, linear cost function using the best cost driver, and if the analytical method permits, estimate the normal variation.

METHODS OF COST ESTIMATION

There are four alternative approaches to cost estimation:

♦ Industrial engineering method.
♦ Conference method.
♦ Account analysis method.
♦ Quantitative analyses (High-Low, Ordinary Least Squares Linear Regression).

These approaches differ in the costs of conducting the analysis, the reliability of the estimated cost function, the balance of quantitative and qualitative data used, and limitations of the analysis. They are not mutually exclusive, and many organizations use a combination of these approaches.

Industrial Engineering Method The **industrial engineering method** (also called the **work measurement method**) begins with an analysis of the relationship between quantities of physical inputs and physical outputs. This means someone must be able to observe (or at least count) these quantities. Inputs for Elegant Rugs would include cotton, wool, synthetics, dyes, DMLH, and DMH. Production output is square metres of carpet (m^2). Assume a time-and-motion study is used to analyze the time and materials required to perform the various conversion activities to produce the carpets. The industrial engineering study concludes that 20 m^2 of carpet requires two bales of cotton and 11 litres of dye.

Assume the new measure is named a bale-litre. The combined measure can be used as a cost driver, and the costs of two different inputs, the bales of cotton and litres of dye can be combined into one cost pool. Dividing the cost pool by the quantity of the total bale-litres consumed results in a standard unit cost measured as $/bale-litre. When multiplied by the m^2 per carpet, Elegant Rugs can forecast part of the materials cost of any carpet.

Limitations of this method begin with the required refinement to the traditional costing system. This is not the task at Elegant Rugs. Other limitations include the high cost of hiring external work-measurement specialists and eventual obsolescence as conversion activities change. As the cost drivers and costs in indirect MOH disappear to be replaced by new costs, it decreases the economic plausibility and the reliability of a cost estimation based on obsolete data. The practical result is that managers cannot be confident in any budgeted effect on the cost pool of any budgeted changes to the quantity of bale-litres consumed. However, when there is a low likelihood of changes to a production process, this method can return a high benefit compared to its cost. In addition, results from engineering studies done by outsiders will be more objective than those formulated from internal discussion.

Conference Method The **conference method** develops cost estimates based on analysis and opinions gathered from various departments of an organization (purchasing, process engineering, manufacturing, employee relations, and so on). The benefit is the use of the intelligence and experience of a specific organization to solve its specific data collection problems. The Co-operative Bank in the United Kingdom develops cost functions for its retail banking products (e.g., current accounts, VISA, mortgages) from a consensus of estimates of managers who are considered experts in the relevant departments. This method allows quick development of cost functions and cost estimates. Accuracy, however, depends on the care and attention paid by the people providing the estimates.[3]

Limitations of this method are that a potential conflict of interest can exist between what a specific manager can use as a measure and the measure best suited to the corporation as a whole. The emphasis on qualitative data opens the door for bias that will favour what is best for one business function or manager over what is best for the entire organization.

There is the potential for paralysis by analysis as managers delay their actions to wait for more and more information. Systematic relationships can be identified, but there is a risk that the best systematic relationships will remain concealed. No additional consulting costs are sustained, but the paid time managers spend on this project generates an opportunity cost because that time could be spent reducing costs instead of talking about reducing costs.

Account Analysis Method   The **account analysis method** classifies cost accounts in the general ledger as variable, fixed, or mixed with respect to the cost driver. Typically, qualitative rather than quantitative analysis is used in making these classification decisions. The account analysis approach is widely used.[4] The strength of this approach is that any limitations to the quality of the data would be readily explained by a financial accountant. The financial data are reported according to CICA standards. The inventory valuation standard determines all the direct and indirect costs of materials and conversion. The audit may reveal material misstatement. After appropriate adjustments are made, the management team can be reasonably assured of the quality of the input data they use.

One limitation, however, is that many managers cannot readily grasp the limitations imposed by GAAP-compliant reporting. This restricts the consultative process to those who can or will cause additional costs as people are trained to interpret the ledger accounts correctly. Another limitation is that several general ledger accounts may have to be adjusted to match the timeliness of current nonfinancial information. There is often a lag between incurring a cost and paying it. This means that an accrual is reported prior to the full use of the resource or cost driver. There is still an orderly relationship between a change in the quantity of cost driver consumed and the change in cost, but the resource use lags the reported cost.

Quantitative Analysis: High-Low Method   The **high-low method** is a quantitative approach that depends on using actual data reported from past events. To determine the high-low cost equation for Elegant Rugs, the management team must select the highest and lowest driver observations from the past 12 weeks. If we use direct machine-hours as our driver, we will select week 6 (102 machine-hours and $1,473 indirect MOH) as our highest and week 8 (0 machine-hours and $480 indirect MOH) as our lowest. It is important that we select the highest and lowest cost driver (machine-hours), not the highest and lowest indirect MOH costs. The changes in the cost driver quantity will, ideally, explain and predict corresponding changes in the MOH cost pool. The cost driver (X) is the **predictor variable**. The predicted value of the MOH cost pool (y) is the **outcome variable**.

To calculate the high-low cost equation, the team must determine the differences in machine-hours and indirect costs between the two weekly observations. The difference in indirect costs is $993 ($1,473 − $480), and the difference in machine-hours is 102 (102 − 0). If we divide these differences, we can determine the variable component b

---

[3]The conference method is further described in W. Winchell, *Realistic Cost Estimating for Manufacturing*, 2nd ed. (Dearborn, Mich.: Society for Manufacturing Engineers, 1991).

[4]Survey evidence appears in M. M. Mowen, *Accounting for Costs as Fixed and Variable* (Montvale, N.J.: National Association of Accountants, 1986).

of our high-low cost equation as $9.735 ($993 ÷ 102). To determine the final component of our equation (the fixed cost − a), we substitute our variable cost value into either of our high or low cost equation observations and solve for the fixed cost. For example, if we use the high observation, our original equation is:

$$\$1,473 = a + b(102)$$

Substitute the calculated value of $9.735 for b and solve for a:

$$\$1,473 = a + \$9.735(102)$$

$$a = \$480$$

Now, we have our high-low cost equation:

$$Y = \$480 + \$9.735(X)$$

The management team at Elegant Rugs can use this cost function to estimate future indirect manufacturing labour costs. For example, if they anticipate 90 machine-hours in week 13, budgeted indirect manufacturing labour costs will equal $1,356.15 [$480 + ($9.735 × 90)]. It is important to realize that this equation is not perfect. The reason is that unexpected events that are not likely to recur introduce unexpected but random costs into the total actual MOH. The equation ignores this error term because it is unpredictable. Budgeting is an estimating process, not a precise process.

However, the method relies on extreme instead of routine data points. What if the extremes are not reasonable or representative of a normal range of cost driver use and MOH costs? It is entirely possible because the data points could have arisen because of very rare and unexpected events. These are not be the best points to consider when determining the normal or routine equation of cost behaviour. The statistical method of analysis, called ordinary least squares (OLS) linear regression, overcomes that obstacle by considering an error term and all the data points. OLS will therefore generate a more accurate equation to use in the budgeting process. The data table, calculations, and a chart of data points illustrate the high-low method when the predictor variable, or cost driver is DMH:

High-Low Method

	High	Low	Difference
Y	$1,473	$480	$993
DMH	102	—	102
Rate of change (slope) b per DMH =		$993/102 =	$9.735/DMH
Constant a =	$1,473 −	($102 ×	$9.735) = $ 480.00
Constant b =	$480 −	(− ×	$9.735) = $ 480.00
Y = a + bX (High-Low)	90 $480 +	($9.735 ×	90) = $1,356.18

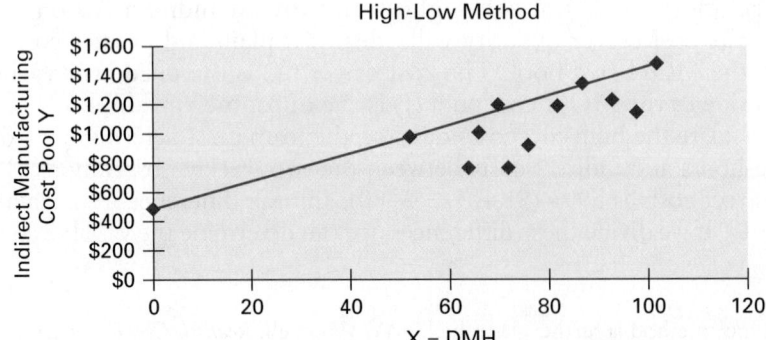

ORDINARY LEAST SQUARES LINEAR REGRESSION

Ordinary least squares (OLS) linear regression is a statistical method of cost estimation used to identify and assess the strength of a linear relationship between changes to one cost driver (X) and one *predicted* indirect MOH cost pool (y). The specific name for this method of data analysis is **simple linear regression analysis.**[5] *Simple* means the effects of changes in one cost driver on the indirect MOH cost pool are analyzed one at a time, not together. *Regression* is the mathematical manipulations of the data to provide the statistics used to identify the cost driver with the highest explanatory power. **Explanatory power** is measured as the percentage of change in y that can be reliably explained by a change in X. This method provides information about the limitations to the reliability of the prediction of y based on changes in each cost driver. This additional information allows the management team to decide on the most reliable predictor of changes to y.

Apply OLS linear regression to analyze goodness of fit and the values of *a* and *b* to predict the MOH cost pool.

3

OLS IS A TOOL TO IMPROVE ON HOW TO CHOOSE A COST DRIVER

Using the five-step process for cost estimation outlined above, steps 1 to 3 remain the same when using OLS analysis. Please bear in mind that 12 data points is a very small set of data. Consider your own behaviour during the year you graduated from high school. It was a very poor predictor of what your behaviour would be during your first year of university. The same is true in the life of a business. The objective of gathering data is to reflect a routine economic outcome and it may take far more than 12 weeks of data to achieve that goal. The management team must use judgment because the OLS simple linear regression program in Excel has no judgment. The program will run a regression on any data set, whether it has 1,000 or only two independent data points.

Beginning at step 4, the graphic results of the OLS analysis for Elegant Rugs are shown in Exhibit 10-4. The original data points are from Exhibit 10-2, and the predicted relationship (the red line) results from the OLS analysis. The red line is also called the regression line. Just looking at the spread of actual (X,Y) data points around the regression line joining the predicted (X, y) points, there is no distinctive curvilinear pattern. So it is safe to assume that the relationships between both cost driver alternatives and the MOH cost pool are linear.

Standard software packages, including Excel, PASW, and SAS, make this type of rigorous analysis straightforward, quick, affordable, and available even to very small companies.

EXHIBIT 10-4
Graphic Results of OLS: Actual Past (X, Y) in Blue Compared to Predicted (X, y) Joined in a Red Straight Line

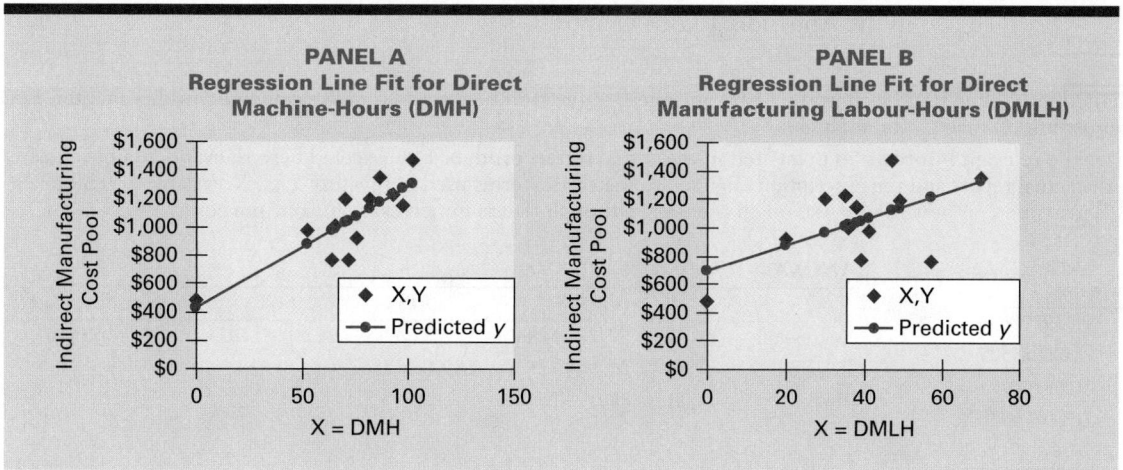

[5]In early versions of Excel, the linear regression program is installed from the Data Analysis selection on the Tools drop-down menu. In later versions of Excel, the program is installed by clicking on the MS Office icon, selecting Excel options then Add-Ins from the pop-up menu, and then Analysis ToolPak. When the tool is installed you will see a new button appear on the toolbar called Data Analysis, from which you can run linear regression.

EXHIBIT 10-5
Summary of Statistics from Excel Results of an OLS Simple Linear Regression

Regression Statistics	PANEL A				PANEL B			
	DMH	Std Error	*t*-Stat	P-value	DMLH	Std Error	*t*-Stat	P-value
R Square	0.6886				0.3310			
Observations	12.0				12.0			
df	11.0				11.0			
Intercept *a*	$425.4229	139.3356	3.0532	0.0122	$691.4157	172.0383	4.0190	0.0024
Slope *b*	$8.5800	$1.8248	4.7019	0.0008	$9.0996	4.0906	2.2245	0.0503
Confidence	95.0%		95.0%		95.0%		95.0%	
Critical Value df = 11	2.201		2.201		2.201		2.201	

Step 5 in the cost estimation process is to select the best cost driver and, if the analytical method permits, estimate the normal variance around each predicted cost. The change in resource consumption (X) with the greatest reliable effect on *y* will be the best choice for a cost driver.

The results of an OLS simple linear regression analysis allow managers to establish **goodness of fit**. The explanatory power of each cost driver can be quantified and compared by using a specific measurement called the **coefficient of determination** also called r^2 (or as Excel reports it, the R Square). The r^2 for each cost driver directly compares the percentage of change in the predicted MOH cost pool *y* from one week to the next that can be explained by changes from one week to the next in each cost driver, either DMH or DMLH. All other things being equal, managers would prefer a higher r^2.

Notice from Exhibit 10-5[6] that the r^2 of the cost driver DMH is 0.6886, or approximately 69%, in comparison with 0.3310 or 33% for the cost driver DMLH. This means that any change in DMH from one time period to the next explains 69% of the change in the predicted cost pool value of *y* in comparison with an explanatory power of only 33% for changes in the cost driver DMLH. This suggests that the real production process at Elegant Rugs is not as labour intensive as it is capital or machine intensive.

The **confidence level** for both DMH and DMLH was selected by the management team prior to doing the analysis. The team decided they wanted to be 95% confident that, when they replaced the *a* and *b* coefficients with reported values and selected an X, their prediction of (*y*) would be right 95% of the time. Their alternative choice was 99% and reasons for choosing a lower confidence level will be discussed in the Appendix to this chapter.[7]

---

[6] The other values presented in Exhibit 10-5, such as the *t*-Stat and the P-value, will be discussed in the Appendix to this chapter. For now, the r^2 value is of most importance to our analysis.

[7] Exhibit 10-5 summarizes the relevant information presented in the actual report produced by Excel. These relevant data have been boxed by solid lines in the actual report and the description changed to match the terms used in this text (e.g., X Variable 1 to Slope *b*). Any statistics text will instruct you on how to understand all the data, although that is unnecessary for our purposes.

SUMMARY OUTPUT

Regression Statistics	
Multiple R	0.829790636
R Square	0.6885525
Adjusted R Square	0.65740775
Standard Error	163.6779538
Observations	12

ANOVA

	df	SS	MS	F	Significance F
Regression	1	592287.5244	592287.5244	22.10814024	0.000839107
Residual	10	267904.7256	26790.47256		
Total	11	860192.25			

	Coefficients	Standard Error	*t*-Stat	P-value	Lower 95%	Upper 95%
Intercept	425.422857	139.3355926	3.053224585	0.012184495	114.963811	735.8819031
X Variable 1	8.579960227	1.824774357	4.701929417	0.000839107	4.514109604	12.64581085

Knowledge Improves the Implementation of a Cost-Leadership Strategy

Not everyone managing a company is both aware of and understands the power of statistical analyses. Management accountants who know the assumptions and limitations of OLS linear regression can provide unbiased statistical evidence that justifies the choice of one direct resource rather than another as a cost driver. In a highly competitive environment, knowing with a 99% or even a 95% confidence level that future actual costs will range within well-specified limits provides practical cost leadership advantages in both pricing and budgeting.

Statistical analyses can reduce costs in several ways:

■ Less wasted time on arguments over the selection of a cost driver to allocate indirect costs.
■ Increased probability of actually reducing costs in the indirect cost pool by reducing the consumption of the appropriate cost driver.
■ Improved identification of and control over variances in the indirect cost pools.
■ Justification of important decisions based on unbiased and quantitative statistical evidence.
■ Identification of weaknesses in reliability of quantitative data in existing management information systems.
■ Prediction of a normal variance (U or F) in each week to avoid costs of unnecessary investigations.

Cost leadership is a successful strategy for the first mover (the first entrant into a market) when it can be sustained. If the cost savings are passed on to buyers, then keeping a steady profit margin while reliably decreasing costs makes it difficult for new entrants who lack knowledge to compete. Management accountants who understand the power and limitations of OLS linear regression can gather and use data to achieve and retain cost leadership.

Elegant Rugs' management team can use the summary output information from DMH to determine the manufacturing overhead cost function. To determine the cost function, the intercept *a* value is $425.42 and the slope *b* value is $8.58. The team can infer that when no DMH are used, it still costs Elegant Rugs approximately $425.42 even though there is no output produced. The team can also infer that, for every change in 1 DMH consumed, there will be a corresponding change of $8.58 in the MOH cost pool. Management will be able to use the following equation to estimate future overhead costs:

$$y = \$425.42 + \$8.58(X)$$

For example, if the team anticipates 76 machine-hours in week 13, budgeted indirect manufacturing labour costs will equal $1,077.50 [$425.42 + (8.58 × 76)]. As you may recall from the data above, in week 4, 76 machine-hours were actually used and indirect manufacturing labour costs equalled $920.00 that week, not $1,077.50. But random events may have happened in week 4 that will not recur. Budgeting is an estimating process, not a precise process.

CLEANING UP DIRTY DATA

One of the simplest ways to improve budgeting is to clean up dirty, unreliable data. When management teams use dirty historical data, they cannot provide a good predicted cost estimate. Teams can choose either to collect historical data about the same process over a long time horizon (time-series data) or systematically collect data simultaneously at many different locations (**cross-sectional data**). Once the data are available, managers need to test their quality. The result of any linear regression analysis is only as *reliable* as the historical data input.

Explain ways to clean up dirty data.

The ideal database for estimating cost functions quantitatively has two characteristics:

1. It contains at least 31 reliably measured observations of the predictor variable (direct input quantity X) and the outcome variable (predicted MOH cost pool value Y). An explanation of the number 31 is provided in the Appendix to this chapter.

2. It includes values for the predictor variable over a wide range. Using only a few values that are grouped closely together considers too small a segment of the relevant range and reduces the confidence in the estimates obtained.

Unfortunately, management accountants rarely have the advantage of working with a database that has both characteristics. This section outlines some frequently encountered data problems and steps a management accountant can take to overcome them.

◆ The time period for measuring the outcome variable (for example, indirect manufacturing costs) does not match the period for measuring the predictor variable(s) (for example, DMH and DMLH). This problem often arises when financial accounting records are cash based rather than accrual based. Assume that lubricants are purchased sporadically and stored for regular, scheduled use. On a cash basis, the cost of sporadic purchase rather than regular use of the lubricant will be recorded. If records are kept on an accrual basis, the reported cost of lubricants actually used throughout the time periods will reflect the economic substance of the physical fact of their use.

◆ Fixed costs are allocated as if they were variable (see Chapter 2 for a full discussion of unitized costs). Costs such as amortization, insurance, or rent may be allocated to products to calculate costs per unit of output as if they were variable. Apparent variability is the result of multiplying a unit fixed cost based on a specific quantity of input units by a different quantity of input units. In fact, over a relevant range the total fixed cost does not vary, but the unit fixed cost does. Applying knowledge of cost behaviour means dividing total fixed costs by the actual input in the relevant range, then adding unit variable costs to arrive at a total cost per output unit.

◆ Data are either unavailable for all observations or not uniformly reliable. Missing and erroneous data entry are more likely to arise when different departments input to the management information system. The data quality improves as more care is taken to provide accurate input. In some systems, data are still recorded manually rather than electronically, resulting in a higher percentage of errors and missing observations. Closer supervision of routine manual data entry or a switch to electronic methods will improve data quality.

◆ Extreme values of observations, or outliers, occur from errors in recording costs (for example, a misplaced decimal point), from a period in which an unusual major machine breakdown occurred, or from observations outside the relevant range. These data need to be cleaned up by adjusting or eliminating outliers before estimating a cost function to reduce the effect of outliers on the residual values and standard error and to decrease the range of budgeted values for the indirect cost pool. Care is required to make sure the adjustments do not bias the input, because outliers can also signal undetected difficulties.

◆ There is no causal, economically plausible relationship between the individual cost items in a heterogeneous mixed pool and a single cost driver. There may, however, exist a systematic, economically plausible relationship between changes in consumption of one cost driver and changes in the value of a heterogeneous indirect cost pool. The ABC solution reveals causality between cost drivers and their respective cost pools, which leads to separating out some cost pools from a larger indirect cost pool.

◆ The accounting cycle affects when costs are recorded in the general ledger accounts that make up the various direct and indirect cost pools. Often companies providing goods and services wait for a specific date of the month to bill their clients. If that happens to be a month-end, most contracts permit a grace period up to 30 days before interest is charged. This means that payments for costs incurred in one time period may not be recorded in the cost pools until the next period. The relationship between a cost driver for an indirect cost pool may lag by one time period.

◆ The relationship between predictor and outcome variables is not stationary. The underlying process that generated the observations of (X,Y) data pairs does not remain stable over time (for example, if the data cover a period in which new technology was introduced). One test of whether the relationship is stationary is to split the sample into two parts and estimate separate cost relationships for each time period before and after the technology was introduced. If the estimated coefficients for regression lines during the two periods are similar, then the management accountant can pool all the data to estimate a single cost relationship. If they are not similar, then the relationship is discontinuous and a basic assumption of the cost function does not hold true. In this case, none of the methods we have discussed so far will be appropriate.

◆ Inflation affects the outcome variable, the predictor variable(s), or both. Inflation is not controllable by managers. Inflation may systematically affect cost pools even when there is no change in the quantity of cost driver consumed. Residual value analysis such as the Durbin-Watson d calculation (see the Appendix to this chapter) will reveal a systematic relationship of costs and inflation. One remedy is to respecify the cost function to include inflation as a second variable and conduct a multiple linear regression analysis.

PULLING IT ALL TOGETHER—PROBLEM FOR SELF-STUDY

(Try to solve this problem before examining the solution that follows.)

PROBLEM
Mr. Dan Wong is examining customer service costs in the Southern Region of Capitol Products. Capitol Products has over 200 separate electrical products that are sold with a six-month guarantee of full repair or replacement with a new product. When a product is returned by a customer, a service report is made. This service report includes details of the problem and the time and cost of resolving the problem.

Each product manager shares the services of the customer service department, a separate business function in the company. The total costs of this support service are all pooled in one traditional overhead cost pool. The management team wants to determine what the cost per service request is and to predict future values of the cost pool without refining the entire cost system.

In the following table of data pairs for the most recent 16-week period, X is the quantity of customer service requests and Y is the actual service support cost for the customer service department in each week. Notice that there is a shutdown in week 11 for audit purposes when no requests are received.

Week	Customer Service Department Costs	Customer Service Requests
1	$16,614	201
2	24,750	276
3	15,530	122
4	22,142	386
5	17,810	274
6	26,268	436
7	20,198	321

(Continued)

Week	Customer Service Department Costs	Customer Service Requests
8	25,715	328
9	21,920	243
10	20,198	161
11	6,500	—
12	15,325	185
13	19,522	300
14	17,120	250
15	19,300	300
16	20,050	315
Total	$308,962	

REQUIRED

1. Plot the relationship between the number of service reports and customer service costs. Is the relationship economically plausible?
2. What variables, in addition to number of service reports, might be cost drivers of monthly service costs of Capitol Products?
3. Use the high-low method to compute (predict) the value of the customer service indirect cost pool when the the number of service reports X = 436.
4. Using the statistical results from the Excel OLS simple linear regression, calculate (predict) the value of the customer service indirect cost pool when the number of customer service reports X = 436.
5. Dan predicts that, 11 weeks in the future, the number of service reports will equal 425. Estimate the customer service costs of 425 service reports using the results of the calculation of the high-low and regression cost functions.
6. Why is the OLS simple linear regression analysis cost function usually the more accurate cost function?
7. What is the importance of a sufficient *quality* of actual data?
8. What is the importance of a sufficient *quantity* of historical data? (Appendix)

SOLUTION

1. There is a positive relationship between the number of service reports and the customer service department costs. This relationship is economically plausible because as quantity of defective output changes so too will the requests to return the product. Ultimately the defective output will be either scrapped or reworked. Thus, the cost to process customer returns is a support cost of production that must be recovered in the price. If it is not recovered in the price, then the company must bear the cost itself and profit will decrease.

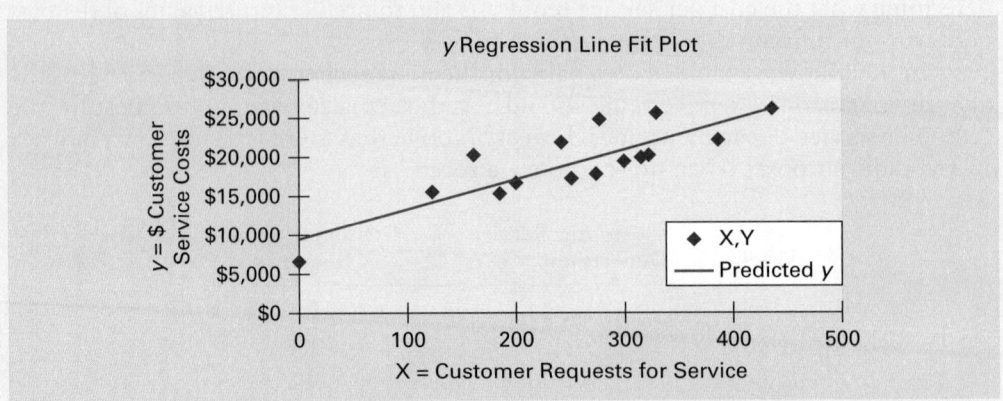

2. Other possible cost drivers of customer service department costs are:
   a. Number of products replaced with a new product (and the dollar value of the new products charged to the customer service department).
   b. Number of products repaired and the time and cost of repairs.

3. The predicted value of the indirect customer service cost pool at X = 436 is:

High-Low Method	High	Low	Difference		
Y = Service costs	$26,268	$6,500	$19,768		
X = Customer requests	436	—	436		
Rate of change (slope) b	$45.339	$45.339	/request		
High constant a	$26,268 − ($45.339	×	436)	=	$ 6,500.00
Low constant a	$6,500 − ($45.339	−	−)	=	$ 6,500.00
y = a + bX where X =	$6,500 + ($45.339	×	436)	=	$26,268

4. Using the Excel report (rounded) the value of the indirect customer service cost pool is:

Regression Statistics	Service Requests	Std Error	t-Stat	P-value
R Square	0.7061			
Observations	16.0			
df	15.0			
Intercept a	$9,549.909	1,812.1184	5.2700	0.0001
Slope b	$38.107	6.5701	5.8001	0.0000

The prediction of the future value of the customer service overhead cost pool is expressed as a linear cost function:

$$y = \$9,549.909 + \$38.107(436) = \$26,164.561$$

5. High-Low Estimate = $6,500 + $45.339(425) = $25,769.075
Regression Estimate = $9,549.909 + $38.107(425) = $25,745.384

6. The regression equation uses information from all observations, whereas the high-low method relies only on the observations that have the highest and lowest values of the cost driver. These high and low observations are generally not representative of all the data. Therefore, the regression equation is usually the more accurate cost function.

7. Of course the data must be reported accurately and must reliably reflect the actual, economically plausible relationship between changes in a cost driver and changes in the MOH cost pool. The relationship needs to be stationary or have a constant slope over the time period for which these data were reported. Finally, where there are either missing or extreme data points (outliers), the management team must make a hard decision about whether to adjust or exclude these data. If the reason(s) for the extreme values is highly unlikely to recur, then the team is more justified in adjusting or excluding these data.

8. The reason the quantity of X,Y actual data pairs is important is that the management team must be reasonably sure the data set represent the normal economic reality of what happens in the company. A single year of monthly observations might be a special year, either extremely cost-efficient or extremely resource wasteful, or any combination of the two. The management team wants to predict a routine future MOH cost, and to do that needs a data set that has enough observations to report a routine past. The regression line is mathematically the most likely future, but the actual outcome will almost certainly differ, though not by too much, from the predicted point on the regression line.

The reason $n = 31$ is set as a minimum quantity of observations is found in calculation of the t-Stat (Appendix p. 405) and the comparison to the critical value (Appendix Exhibit 10-6).

APPENDIX: REGRESSION ANALYSIS[8]

Look again at Exhibit 10-5. In addition to the r^2, there are several other statistics reported in that exhibit. Together, these statistics provide objective evidence from the OLS linear regression analysis for the management team to consider before they make their decision to select a cost driver. In fact, once the team completes the analysis of all the evidence, it will be able to both budget a monthly future value y for the MOH cost pool and the range or variance (see Chapter 8) within which most actual future values of Y should fall. The team will be able to place what actually occurs in the future into a context of what normally should occur with either 95% or 99% confidence. This added capability is an example of a sensitivity analysis based on statistics. The t-Stat, P-value, and standard error of the estimates of a and b will be used to make these predictions.

It is important to understand the limitations of any statistical analysis. The use of quantitative evidence may persuade the team that one measure of benefit or value added from shared resource use is more useful than another to predict costs. But no amount of statistical evidence proves there is any cause-effect relationship between changes in the quantity of direct resources used and changes in the total monthly MOH.

The OLS method depends on correlation, an orderly association of changes, not on causality. If the measures of direct input quantities bear no relationship in economic fact of how distinct outputs benefit from using shared MOH resources, then the statistics cannot be helpful. The experience of the team and its collective common sense are the basis upon which to judge whether the statistics are reporting a useful correlation or just a repetitive but useless coincidence. This coincidence is often referred to as a **spurious correlation**.

Now we will begin our assessment of the other results reported in the remaining statistics in Exhibit 10-5. Recall that the OLS simple linear regression is $y = a + bX$. Management teams need evidence that the values of a and b reported by the OLS are not just guesses but that they are reliable. In the report there is an error term e (standard error), also called the residual. Analysis of this term will help the team to determine if e arises from random events. A management team wants the term e to be unpredictable or due to random events, to be reassured that the coefficients of a and b are reliable. If the coefficient values are not reliable, then the team cannot use the equation to predict future values of y with confidence. Ironically, if the e is changing in an orderly way, the team has missed identifying an explanatory variable when the cost function was defined.

STATISTICAL SIGNIFICANCE: THE t-STAT

Managers can explain the importance of statistical significance using the **t-Stat (Student's t)**, or **test of statistical significance**. Statistical significance is a good thing because it means the values of a and b are not just random. If they are random, then managers cannot say with any confidence what either the a (future unexplained values of changes in y) or b (the rate of change in MOH when the cost driver changes by one unit) will be. A computer program will do the math based on any data set, but statistical significance reports the usefulness of the results.

Mathematically, the t-Stat is calculated as the coefficient value divided by its standard error, shown in the second column of Exhibit 10-5 (see equation 3 below). Notice that the denominator (the standard error) is also a value calculated by dividing a statistic σ, called the standard deviation, by $\sqrt{n}$. This means the larger the number of observations the larger $\sqrt{n}$ will be. As this number increases, the standard error will decrease.

---

[8]Please refer to the online tutorial for instructions on how to complete the menu to correctly run the regression analysis in Excel.

EXHIBIT 10-6
Table of Critical Values: *t*-Stat

Degrees of Freedom	95% Confidence Interval	99% Confidence Interval
1	12.706	63.657
2	4.303	9.925
3	3.182	5.841
4	2.776	4.604
5	2.571	4.032
6	2.447	3.707
7	2.365	3.499
8	2.306	3.355
9	2.262	3.250
10	2.228	3.169
11	2.201	3.106
12	2.179	3.055
15	2.131	2.947
16	2.120	2.921
17	2.110	2.898
18	2.101	2.878
19	2.093	2.861
20	2.086	2.845
25	2.060	2.787
30	2.042	2.750
40	2.021	2.704
60	2.000	2.660
∞	1.960	2.576

Source: Abrami, Philip C.; Cholmsky, Paul; Gordon, Robert, *Statistical Analysis for the Social Sciences*: *An Interactive Approach*, 1st ed. © 2001. Reprinted with permission of Pearson Education, Inc., Upper Saddle River, NJ.

All other things being equal, the *t*-Stat will also increase. The larger the *t*-Stat, the more likely it will exceed the critical value in Exhibit 10-6[9]. The reason is that the larger *n* (the number of data points) is, the smaller the critical value is. When the *t*-Stat exceeds the critical value, it is more likely the values of *a* and *b* are not just guesses. The values of each coefficient are more likely to be reliable and therefore the linear equation is more likely to be a reliable prediction of the behaviour of (*y*) based on actual past changes in (X).

$$t = \frac{\bar{x} - \mu}{\sigma/\sqrt{n}}$$

Exhibit 10-6 is a table of critical values for the *t*-Stat reporting different values at different **degrees of freedom (df)** and confidence levels. A significant *t*-Stat is a strength when evaluating the explanatory power of one cost driver compared to another. The reported values in Exhibit 10-5 have been rounded; therefore, the value of the *t*-Stat calculated manually may be slightly different from the value reported, but not enough to mislead the management team and cause it to come to a wrong conclusion.

[9]Examine Exhibit 10-6 and you will notice that the critical value decreases as the number of data pairs (*n*) increases. But the rate of decrease slows. For example, the difference in the critical value if df = *n* − 1 = 1 compared to df = *n* − 1 = 2 is huge. The difference between df = *n* − 1 = 25 and df = *n* − 1 = 30 appears only at the third and fourth decimal place. The change in the critical value between df = *n* − 1 = 30 and df = *n* – 1 = 60 is very small. That is why a reasonable and achievable *n* = 31 is the recommended minimum. It is affordable, takes a reasonable amount of time, and not much value added will arise from increasing to *n* = 61. The *t*-Stat is not likely to change enough to make it worth the wait to obtain 5 years of monthly observations instead of 3.5 years—after all, the point is to predict the future, not wait for it.

The practical use of the *t*-Stat is that it provides objective evidence. The arithmetic behind calculating the *a* and *b* values is determined regardless of how sensible the correlation of (X,Y) might be. That is the most profound limitation of computer programs. Give the program any data set and it will apply the formulae to generate the values of *a* and *b*; the question answered by analyzing the *t*-Stat is whether or not these values are just a random result of the arithmetic or if they have meaning and can be replicated?

If the team can successfully explain a past outcome (Y) based on (X), then it can repeat that outcome in future, because there is a real relationship between the (X,Y) values used to calculate *a* and *b*. Not only can the team explain the past but has evidence the past can be used to reliably predict the future. In practice, the management accountant can assure users that the results were not good luck arising from the data points used.

Statistical significance is determined by comparing the *t*-Stat to a threshold called **critical value** (shown in Exhibit 10-5) of each *a* and *b* value given the confidence level and degrees of freedom. When the *t*-Stat reported exceeds the critical value, there is evidence that the values of *a* and *b* are statistically significant, not random, and are therefore are economically plausible.

The table of critical values in Exhibit 10-6 is standard and will not change regardless of the relationship between outcome and predictor variables being tested. For Elegant Rugs, reading down the column for the confidence level of 95% and across the row for df = 11, the critical value is 2.201. Simple inspection of the *t*-Stat of 3.0532 for the *a* value of DMH and 4.0190 for the *a* value of DMLH indicates that neither value is random. Statistical significance is an all-or-nothing comparison—the *t*-Stat either exceeds the critical value at 95% confidence and df = 11 or it does not. Simple inspection of the *t*-Stat for the *b* value of DMH and the *b* value of DMLH indicates they, too, are both statistically significant.

The importance of selecting the confidence level first is illustrated in the output of the *t*-Stat for both pairs of *a* and *b* values. Notice that had the managers selected the 99% confidence level, the critical value would have been 3.106. The table below indicates that the *t*-Stat for the value of *a* for DMH fails to exceed the critical value although the *t*-Stat for the value of *b* does. The reverse is true because the value of *a* for DMLH does exceed the critical value while the value of *b* does not. If the managers had chosen the 99% confidence rate, the choice of the better cost driver, based only on the *t*-Stat, will be unclear.

Regression Statistics	DMH	*t*-Stat	DMLH	*t*-Stat
Intercept *a*	425.42	3.05	691.42	4.02
Slope *b*	8.58	4.70	9.10	2.22
Confidence	99.0%		99.0%	
Critical value df = 11	3.301		3.301	

If managers select DMH at the 99% confidence interval, they have no evidence that the future observed and unexplained change of *y* will fall within any range of error calculated by using the standard error of the estimate of *a*. If they select DMLH, they have no evidence that the observed future rate of change in *y* will fall within any range of error calculated using the standard error of the estimate for *b*. This type of result is common when so few observations of actual data are available. The selection of a cost driver under these conditions becomes subjective rather than objective. Both estimates produce a non-significant value of either *a* or *b*, so there is no evidence that predicting a *y* based on these values is any better than a guess.

One obvious remedy is to wait until 20 or more observations are available. The table of critical values indicates that the threshold value for confidence level 99% and df = 19 is only 2.861, far lower than 3.301. The results of a new OLS simple linear regression with more observations will provide clearer evidence of which cost driver is consistently better based on all the statistical evidence. But if there is no time to wait, the management team at Elegant Rugs might be better off choosing a simpler method, such as the conference or high-low methods, until the added data can be gathered.

ESTABLISHING LIMITATIONS OF THE ANALYSIS: THE P-VALUE

The **P-value** is the probability that, regardless of the statistical significance of the t-Stat, we are wrong to conclude that either a or b are not random. Recall the ambiguity around the cost driver choice had managers selected a confidence level of 99%. When this happens, the P-value may help managers choose. All other things being equal, a manager would prefer a very small to a larger probability of being wrong in accepting the pairs of a and b that are not random. At a 95% confidence level, managers want that P-value to be less than or equal to 0.05.

We interpret the results by assuming we have far more than 12 observations and that these 12 are only a sample. If we took many samples from the same large pool of observations, how often would we be wrong in accepting that the OLS simple linear regression results for a and b are not random? The smaller the P-value, the smaller the probability we came to the wrong conclusion despite the statistical significance of the t-Stats.

The P-value for DMH (see Exhibit 10-5) for the value of a is 0.0122, which means that accepting that a is not random will be the wrong conclusion 1 out of 100 times. The P-value for DMH for the value of b is 0.0008, which means that accepting that b is not random will be the wrong conclusion 8 out of 1,000 times. The corresponding values for DMLH for the value of a is 0.0024 (accepting a is not random will be the wrong conclusion 24 times in 1,000), and for the value of b the P-value is 0.0503 (accepting b is not random will be the wrong conclusion 5 times out of 100).

The reason we have used various methods to test the effect of orderly changes of X on corresponding changes in y is that it is often difficult to tell what causes what—the classic chicken and egg problem. OLS linear regression can never define what is causing what[10]—accountants use cost tracing to accomplish that. Linear regression is a waste of time for direct cost pools and is appropriate only when heterogeneous indirect cost pools must be allocated. For a heterogeneous cost pool, managers have alternative cost drivers from which to choose. Linear regression is a tool to improve decisions about this choice.

THE RESIDUAL ERROR OR DISTURBANCE TERM

Now that we have ensured that the values of a and b are not random, we want to make sure that the values of e, the residual error or disturbance term, *is* random. Exhibit 10-7 shows the residuals as calculated by the Excel OLS simple linear regression program. If you subtract the predicted y in week 1, \$1,026.0201, from the actual Y, \$1,200, you obtain the residual value of \$173.9799. But in this form, these data are not very useful.

EXHIBIT 10-7
Results of Calculations of the Residuals e Derived $(Y - y)$ for Each Outcome Variable

Week	RESIDUAL OUTPUT			
	Predicted y	Residuals	Predicted y	Residuals
1	1,026.0201	173.9799	964.4035	235.5965
2	1,223.3592	7.6408	1,009.9014	221.0986
3	991.7002	12.2998	1,019.0010	(15.0010)
4	1,077.4998	(157.4998)	873.4075	46.5925
5	974.5403	(209.5403)	1,210.0925	(445.0925)

[10]The Granger causality test can be used to assess the direction of causality. A full explanation can be found in advanced statistics textbooks.

EXHIBIT 10-8
Scatterplot of the Residuals *e* for DMH and DMLH

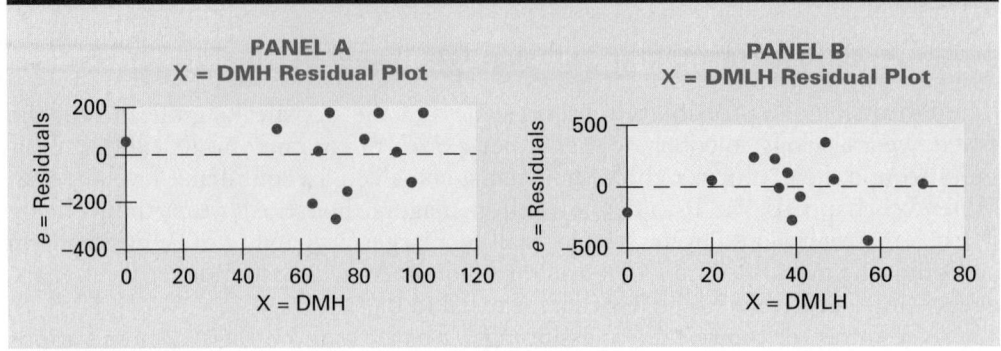

The **residual (error, disturbance)** term *e* is only supposed to arise when random events occur that are not likely to happen repeatedly. Some examples are the costs of repair from an unexpected shutdown of machines or a wildcat strike. Just because this happens in one week does not mean it will happen again. By definition, although random events do not often recur, any random event is equally likely to occur. The positive and negative residuals of *e* therefore should sum to 0 for any specific set of observations.[11]

When users request a graphic report of the residuals, they receive output resembling that shown in Exhibit 10-8. The scatter of red points around the horizontal straight line for both DMH and DMLH does not seem to have a pattern. This provides evidence of uniform distribution of positive and negative residuals around the horizontal straight line. Statistically, this balance of positive and negative variation distinguishes a random distribution from a non-random distribution of outcomes.

Because there seems to be no pattern, managers at Elegant Rugs can also be reassured that error terms in one time period (e.g., week 3) do not affect the error terms in either week 1 or week 4. The events giving rise to the *e* are in fact independent of one another, a characteristic of random events. Dependence means predictability between events. This independence is also evidence that the scatter of all residuals over many samples of 12 weeks would resemble a normal or bell-shaped curve. Further analysis can be done by calculating the *Durbin-Watson statistic, d,* which provides mathematical evidence of normality.[12]

The timing of events can affect the pattern of the residuals. For example, the accounting cycle can result in costs being recorded in a time period, denoted as *t* + 1, after the input was purchased. But, in fact, the actual resource consumption has already occurred in time *t*. This is called **autocorrelation** because the values of X_i depend on one another. In specifying a cost function this is called a **lagged relationship**. Occasionally the opposite is true, and expenses are prepaid, denoted as *t* − 1, when the actual consumption of the resource will not occur until time *t*. This is called a **leading relationship**. Do not confuse the notation for a time period with the *t*-Stat.

In Exhibit 10-9, the residuals from an initial OLS simple linear regression for a different data set of DMH (shown in Panel A) indicate a series that forms a funnel that widens from the left to the right. There are fewer positive residuals located above the horizontal line compared to the negative residuals below the line. The distance between the horizontal line and the data points above it is larger than the distance between the horizontal line and the data points below it. This suggests some non-random event is giving rise to more positive than negative *e* terms.

In Panel B, the residuals are split into two groups. There are fewer positive residuals located above the horizontal line than below it. Once again, it seems the distance between the horizontal line and the data points above it is larger than the

---

[11]For a full explanation of random normal distributions, please refer to Abrami, P., Cholmsky, P., and Gordon, R. *Statistical Analysis for the Social Sciences, an Interactive Approach* (2001), Chapter 4, pp. 85–117: Pearson Education Company.

[12]A full discussion of how to calculate and interpret a Durbin-Watson d statistic can be found in any advanced statistics text.

EXHIBIT 10-9
Scatterplot of the Residuals *e* for DMH and DMLH

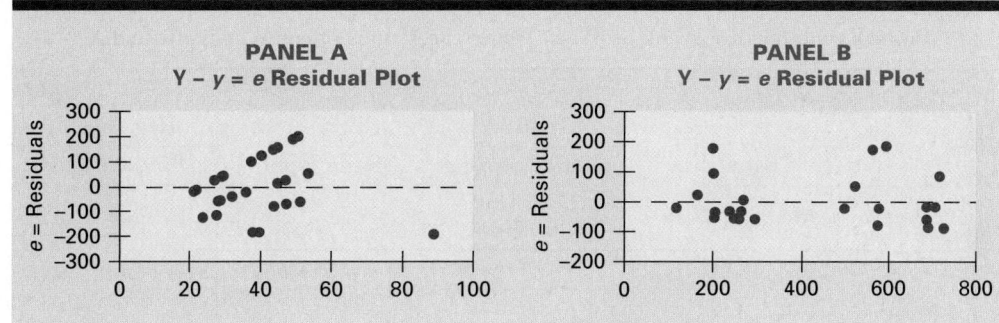

distance between the horizontal line and the data points below it. The patterns in both panels indicate that the error term *e* is not random. The variance is increasing in an orderly way in Panel A, and in Panel B there seems to be an S-shape to the residuals, or **serial correlation**, typically observed when the error term of the last period (t_0) affects the size of the error term in this period (t_1). An explanatory variable is missing from this OLS simple linear regression model, which is the cause of the orderly change in the error term.

PRACTICAL APPLICATION: BUDGET THE FUTURE VALUES AND VARIANCE OF *y*

Now that the different statistics have been discussed, there are two practical applications. The first requires replacing the actual values of X and the calculated values of *a* and *b* into *y* = *a* + *b*X to calculate the budgeted values of *y* for the next 12 weeks. This is somewhat helpful, but ignores the additional information available from the standard error terms. The second practical application is an adjustment to the point estimates from the simple linear equation to include additional information from the analysis of *e*:

$$y = a + bX + e \tag{3}$$

By using these adjustments, we can also budget for ordinary or expected variance between the predicted *y* and actually observed future Y.

Budget Cost Pool Values of *y*   By simply replacing the values of *a*, *b*, and X in each linear regression, we can budget the cost pool values of *y*. A point estimate of the predicted *y* for the next 12 weeks and the total is shown in Exhibit 10-10. These predicted values are the centre of the range we will calculate to adjust for *e*.

We can now use the critical value, the standard error of the estimate of *a* and *b*, respectively, and the square root of the observations ($\sqrt{n}$), all of which come from Exhibit 10-5, to calculate a range of values for *y* (Exhibit 10-11). If either *a* or *b* are not statistically significant, this range will not be reliable and managers cannot use the regression results to budget the future value of the indirect MOH cost pool with any confidence. If both *a* and *b* are statistically significant, managers know that, at their chosen confidence level, future actual observed values of Y will fall within the calculated range of *y*. The critical value changes, all else being equal, if the confidence interval changes. Pair the high with the low values of *a* and then do the same for *b*, and the arithmetic formulae for the adjustment to the point estimates of *y*, beginning with the high, are:

a + (critical value × standard error of *a*/$\sqrt{n}$) calculates the high or U variance

b + (critical value × standard error of *b*/$\sqrt{n}$) calculates the high or U variance

a − (critical value × standard error of *a*/$\sqrt{n}$) calculates the low or F variance

b − (critical value × standard error of *b*/$\sqrt{n}$) calculates the low or F variance

EXHIBIT 10-10
Budgeted $y = a + bX$ Using Actual DMH and DMLH

Point Estimates of y Week by Week Using the Values of a and b and Actual X

	A	B	C	D	E
1			Indirect	Regression	Regression
2		Cost Driver:	Manufacturing	Prediction of	Prediction of
3	Week	Machine-Hours	Overhead Cost Pool	Cost Pool DMH	Cost Pool DMLH
4		(X)	(Y)	$y = a + bX$	$y = a + bX$
5	1	70	$1,200	$1,026.02	$ 964.40
6	2	93	1,231	1,223.36	1,009.90
7	3	66	1,004	991.70	1,019.00
8	4	76	920	1,077.50	873.41
9	5	64	765	974.54	1,210.09
10	6	102	1,473	1,300.58	1,119.10
11	7	82	1,192	1,128.98	1,137.30
12	8	—	480	425.42	691.42
13	9	87	1,345	1,171.88	1,328.39
14	10	98	1,146	1,266.26	1,037.20
15	11	72	767	1,043.18	1,046.30
16	12	52	978	871.58	1,064.50
17			$12,501	$12,501.00	$12,501.01

EXHIBIT 10-11
The High and Low Values of Pairs of a and b for DMH and DMLH

RANGE OF COEFFICIENT VALUES

Cost Driver DMH		95.0% df = 11	$\sqrt{n} = 3.464$			
			Critical Value	Standard Error	High	Low
Intercept a	$425.4229		2.201	139.3356	$513.95	$336.89
Slope b	$ 8.5800		2.201	1.8248	$ 9.74	$ 7.42

Cost Driver DMLH		95.0% df = 11				
			Critical Value	Standard Error	High	Low
Intercept a	$691.4157		2.201	172.0383	$800.72	$582.11
Slope b	$ 9.0996		2.201	4.0906	$ 11.6986	$ 6.5006

As you increase your number of observations n, the value of $\sigma/\sqrt{n}$ will decrease. Both the t-Stat and the critical value will decrease. This is why it is important to use a larger rather than smaller number of observations, because the range of potential values of a and b around the reported estimates will shrink. The smaller the range within which actual future values will occur 95 out of 100 times, the smaller the budget slack.

Exhibit 10-12 reports the range and calculates the expected variance for the weekly budgeted indirect MOH cost pool. The budget slack using DMH will be approximately ± $2,062, whereas for DMLH it will be approximately ± $2,512. This final result is consistent with the analysis of all the other statistics, and managers at Elegant Rugs can conclude that DMH is superior to DMLH as a choice of cost driver for this indirect MOH cost pool.

EXHIBIT 10-12
Range of Budgeted Values of the Total Indirect Cost Pool

	RANGE OF BUDGETED VALUES OF THE TOTAL INDIRECT COST POOL: $y = a + bX + e$			
	Cost Driver X = DMH		Alternative X = DMLH	
Week	High $e = \sigma^2$ (U)	Low $e = \sigma^2$ F	High $e = \sigma^2$ (U)	Low $e = \sigma^2$ F
1	$ 1,195.71	$ 856.33	$ 1,151.68	$ 777.11
2	1,419.71	1,027.00	1,210.18	809.63
3	1,156.75	826.65	1,221.87	816.13
4	1,254.15	900.85	1,034.70	712.12
5	1,137.27	811.81	1,467.55	952.64
6	1,507.37	1,093.79	1,350.56	887.63
7	1,312.58	945.38	1,373.96	900.63
8	513.95	336.89	800.72	582.11
9	1,361.28	982.48	1,619.63	1,037.15
10	1,468.41	1,064.11	1,245.27	829.13
11	1,215.19	871.17	1,256.97	835.63
12	1,020.40	722.76	1,280.37	848.63
Total	$14,562.78	$10,439.22	$15,013.46	$9,988.54
Y =	$12,501.00		$12,501.00	
σ^2	$ (2,061.78)	$ 2,061.78	$ (2,512.46)	$2,512.46

COMPARISON OF HIGH-LOW AND OLS SIMPLE LINEAR REGRESSION

Compare the regression equation for DMH, $y = \$425.42 + \$8.58X$, with the initial high-low equation, $Y = \$480 + \$9.735X$. For X = 66 DMH, the rounded forecast cost based on the high-low equation is $\$480 + (\$9.735 \times 66) = \$1,122.53$. Based on the linear regression, however, the forecast is only $991.70 (see Exhibit 10-10).

Assume that over the next 12-week period, Elegant Rugs runs its machines for 90 hours each week for three weeks and incurs average indirect machine-hour costs for those three weeks of $3,250. Based on the rounded high-low forecast of $3,368 ($1,122.53 × 3), Elegant Rugs would conclude it has performed well with a favourable variance of $118. When compared to the rounded linear regression forecast of $2,975 ($991.70 × 3), however, Elegant Rugs has incurred an unfavourable variance of $(275). Exhibit 10-13 summarizes all of this information.

The variance analysis should be a reliable signal to managers that draws their attention to overconsumption of resources. Not only does the high-low method report

High-Low Method		High		Low		Difference	
Y		$ 1,473	$	480	$	993	
DMH Week 6		102		—		102	
Rate of change (slope) b per DMH =			$993/102		= $	9.735 /DMH	
Constant in Week 8 a =		$ 1,473	− ($	102 × $	9.735)	= $	480.00
$Y = a + bX$ (Week 3 DMH for X)	66 $	480	+ ($	9.735 × $	66)	= $ 1,122.53	
$Y = a + bX$ (High X week 6)		—					
OLS Simple Linear Regression							
$y = a + bX$ (Week 3 DMH for X)	66 $	425.4	+ ($	8.58 ×	66)	= $	991.70
Calculate ordinary variance U (Exh 10-10)	$ (165.05)	= $		991.70 −	1,156.75)	= $	(165.05)
Calculate ordinary variance F (Exh 10-10)	$ 165.05	= $		991.70 −	826.65)	= $	165.05

the variance inaccurately, but it also gives no signal about whether this would be expected or not. In contrast, the OLS simple linear regression provides a more justifiable estimate of y and the expected, routine variance of ($165) U when the cost driver X = 66 DMH. Managers can tell that the actual variance not only is unfavourable but requires investigation. The actual use of indirect MOH cost pool resources in a future week 3 exceeds what would ordinarily be expected by approximately 67% [($165 − $275) ÷ $165].

The improvement in reliability from using the OLS simple linear regression method will lead managers to correct decisions about whether or not their consumption of resources is in or out of control. In this example, the small favourable variance of 3.5% ($118 ÷ $3,368) under the high-low method contrasted to an unfavourable variance of approximately 9% ($275 ÷ $2,975) under the simple linear regression method will lead managers to opposite conclusions about whether their actual operations improved or hindered the achievement of a forecast operating margin.

METHODS TO IMPROVE BUDGETING: MULTIPLE LINEAR REGRESSION

To improve their cost allocation system, managers may decide to create more than one indirect cost pool. Each cost pool where changes are driven by a different cost driver could be generated quite quickly using OLS linear regression. Of course, they may also choose the alternative of switching to an ABC allocation system and use the results of this analysis as evidence to support the change. The results of this analysis at least define the limitations of their current cost allocation system.

At Elegant Rugs, the management team has been working with only 12 observations. To improve the reliability and neutrality of the input data and clean it up, the managers may also decide to collect more data. The managers might be able to accomplish this simply by returning to their existing management information system and retrieving a finer data set of daily instead of weekly data. The risk here is that there may exist serial correlation from day to day that is not present week to week. We will discuss other ways to clean up the data in the following sections.

It is also possible that another cost driver would be a better alternative to the two under consideration, or that adding a second predictor (cost driver) would make the systematic change to the indirect cost pool clearer as both cost drivers change. This requires multiple linear regression analysis.

MULTIPLE LINEAR REGRESSION

For linear regression to provide the best information, there should be only a few unrelated or independent predictor variables that affect the value of the outcome variable. Independence means that the presence of and change in the value of one predictor variable has no effect on the change in value of a second predictor variable. If this is true, then each predictor variable independently measures a different effect on the outcome variable. **Multiple linear regression** is the technique used to measure the strength of relationships between at least two predictor variables and the outcome variable. An example would be inflation and DMH as predictors of indirect cost. The quantity of DMH consumed is not influenced by inflation, although the total indirect MOH cost will be.

In the Elegant Rugs example, many different types of labour arose as a consequence of the machine and labour-time directly consumed when the factory was in production. Each type of labour caused some portion of the indirect MOH cost pool to increase. Depending on how well the consumption of either direct labour- or direct machine-hours explained the change in the size of the indirect MOH cost pool, it could be worthwhile for the management accountant to seek a second or third predictor variable. Multiple regression analysis is extremely useful for estimating total costs when different levels of the cost hierarchy are involved. Our example below uses number of machine-hours (an output unit-level cost driver) and number of production batches (a batch-level cost driver).

Multiple Regression and Cost Hierarchies   In some cases, a satisfactory estimation of a cost function may be based on only one predictor variable, such as machine-hours. In many cases, however, basing the estimation on more than one predictor variable is economically plausible and improves the reliability of the linear

EXHIBIT 10-14
Weekly Indirect MOH Costs, DMH, DMLH, and Number of Production Batches for
Elegant Rugs

	A	B	C	D	E
1			Number of	Direct	Indirect
2			Production	Manufacturing	MOH
3	Week	Machine-Hours	Batches	Labour-Hours	Cost Pool
4		(X_1)	(X_2)		(Y)
5	1	68	12	30	$ 1,190
6	2	88	15	35	1,211
7	3	62	13	36	1,004
8	4	72	11	20	917
9	5	60	10	47	770
10	6	96	12	45	1,456
11	7	78	17	44	1,180
12	8	46	7	38	710
13	9	82	14	70	1,316
14	10	94	12	30	1,032
15	11	68	7	29	752
16	12	48	14	38	963
17	Total	862	144	462	$12,501

regression. The most widely used equations to express relationships between two or more predictor variables and an outcome variable are linear in form:

$$y = a + b_1X_1 + b_2X_2 + \cdots + e$$

where:

y = the cost pool or outcome X variable

$X_1, X_2, \cdots$ = predictorF variables on which the estimate of the outcome variable is based

$a, b_1, b_2, \cdots$ = estimated coefficients of the regression model

e = the residual term that includes the net effect of other factors not in the model and measurement errors in the predictor and outcome variables

Consider the Elegant Rugs data in Exhibit 10-14. Indirect manufacturing labour costs include sizable costs incurred for setup and changeover when production on one carpet batch is stopped and production on another batch is started. Management believes that, in addition to machine-hours (an output-unit-level cost driver), indirect manufacturing labour costs are also affected by the number of different batches of carpets produced during each week (a batch-level driver).

Exhibit 10-14 presents results for the following multiple regression model, using slightly different data that assumes no shutdown of the plant:

$$y = \$42.58 + \$7.60X_1 + \$37.77X_2$$

where X_1 is the number of DMH and X_2 is the number of production batches. It is economically plausible that both DMH and production batches would help explain variations in indirect MOH costs at Elegant Rugs. The r^2 of 0.6886 for the simple regression using DMH (Exhibit 10-5) increases to 0.72 with the multiple regression in Exhibit 10-14. The t-Stats suggest that the predictor variable coefficients of both machine-hours and production batches are significantly different from zero ($t = 2.74$ for the coefficient on DMH, and $t = 2.48$ for the coefficient on production batches).

The multiple regression model in Exhibit 10-15 satisfies both economic and statistical criteria, and it explains much greater variation in indirect MOH costs than does the simple regression model using only machine-hours as the independent variable. The information in Exhibit 10-15 indicates that both DMH and production batches are important cost drivers of monthly indirect MOH costs at Elegant Rugs.

EXHIBIT 10-15
Multiple Regression Results with Indirect MOH Costs and Two Independent Variables or Cost Drivers (DMH and Production Batches) for Elegant Rugs

	A	B	C	D	E	F	G
1		Coefficients	Standard Error	t-Statistic			
2		(1)	(2)	(3) = (1) ÷ (2)			
3	Intercept	$42.58	$213.91	0.20			
4	Independent variable 1: Machine-hours (X_1)	$ 7.60	$ 2.77	2.74 →	= Coefficient/Standard Error = B4/C4 = 7.60/2.77		
5	Independent variable 2: Number of production batches (X_2)	$37.77	$ 15.25	2.48			
6							
7	Regression Statistics						
8	R Square	0.72					
9	Durbin-Watson Statistic	2.49					

In Exhibit 10-15, the slope coefficients—$7.60 for DMH and $37.77 for production batches—measure the change in indirect MOH costs associated with a unit change in a predictor variable (assuming that the other predictor variable is held constant). For example, indirect MOH costs increase by $37.77 when one more production batch is added, assuming that the number of DMH is held constant.

An alternative approach would be to create two separate cost pools—one for costs tied to DMH and another for costs tied to production batches. Elegant Rugs would then estimate the relationship between the cost driver (predictor variable) and indirect MOH separately for each cost pool. The difficulty under that approach would be properly dividing indirect MOH costs into the two cost pools.

MULTICOLLINEARITY

A major concern that arises with multiple linear regression is multicollinearity. **Multicollinearity** exists when two or more predictor variables are highly correlated with each other. The rule of thumb is if the correlation between X_1 and X_2 is 0.70, then there is no issue of correlated predictor variables. If the correlation is ≥ 0.70, then one of the predictor variables must be dropped. Multicollinearity increases the standard errors of the coefficients of the individual predictor variables. The result is that there is greater uncertainty about the underlying value of the coefficients of each predictor variable. That is, variables that are economically and statistically significant will appear insignificant.

The coefficients of correlation between the potential predictor variables for Elegant Rugs in Exhibit 10-15 are as follows:

Coefficient of Pairwise Combinations	Correlation
Machine-hours and direct manufacturing labour-hours	0.12
Machine-hours and production batches	0.40
Direct manufacturing labour-hours and production batches	0.31

These results indicate that multiple regressions using any pair of the independent variables in Exhibit 10-15 are not likely to encounter multicollinearity problems. If severe multicollinearity exists, try to obtain new data that do not suffer from multicollinearity problems. Do not drop a predictor variable (cost driver) that should be included in a model because it is correlated with another predictor variable. Omitting such a variable will cause the estimated coefficient of the predictor variable included in the model to be biased away from its true value.

The following question-and-answer format summarizes the chapter's learning outcomes. Each point presents a key question, and the guidelines are the answer to that question.

LEARNING OUTCOMES	GUIDELINES
1. What two key assumptions are frequently made when estimating a cost function?	The first assumption is that changes in either the use of a single resource or amount of single activity will explain changes in a total cost pool. The second assumption is that the cost function representing cost behaviour is linear within the relevant range of the resource or activity being considered.
2. What purpose is there to estimating cost functions?	If past data on changes in resource consumption and cost change is of high quality, and the changes are orderly, then these pairs of historical data points can be used to predict future costs. Many methods of prediction are available. Selecting the best method depends on data quality, the number of data points, the continuity of the cost function and its linearity, cost, and understandability. Of most importance is to select the method that best represents the reality of what happens day to day in the company.
3. What methods of predicting future costs are quantitative methods?	All four methods are quantitative methods to some extent because the data used is quantitative data. The four methods are industrial engineering, conference, account analysis, and ordinary least squares (OLS) simple linear regression. The most objective of the four methods, which relies least on opinion and other qualitative input, is the OLS method. But this method is not appropriate unless sufficient data are available.
4. What concept is central to understanding OLS simple linear regression?	The key concept is explanatory power. OLS is useful in predicting MOH where there is a cost-benefit and not a cause-effect relationship between a cost driver and cost pool. The purpose of OLS is to select from many possible cost drivers the one with highest explanatory power. The issue of dirty data means the available information is not reliable. The mathematics of OLS cannot compensate for poor data quality—garbage in, garbage out. Irrespective of the content of the statistical report, the prediction will be unreliable.
5. What is the usefulness of the standard error of the estimate and the t-Stat?	If the coefficient values of a and b are statistically significant, then the t-Stat for each coefficient will equal or exceed a critical value. Using arithmetic, the standard error of the estimated value of each coefficient will help a management team not only predict the most likely value of MOH but also a normal range within which that future value should fall, 95% of the time. The benefit of knowing the range of expected variance (U) or (F) means the team will investigate only the actual outcome that falls beyond this range, known as management by exception.

This chapter and the Glossary at the end of the book contain definitions of the following important terms:

account analysis method (p. 395)
autocorrelation (p. 408)
coefficient (p. 388)
coefficient of determination (p. 398)
conference method (p. 394)
confidence level (p. 398)
correlation (p. 388)
critical value (p. 406)
cross-sectional data (p. 399)
curvilinear cost function (p. 387)
degrees of freedom, df (p. 405)
discontinuous cost function (p. 393)
economic plausibility (p. 388)
explanatory power (p. 397)

goodness of fit (p. 398)
heterogeneous cost pool (p. 386)
high-low method (p. 395)
industrial engineering method (p. 394)
lagged relationship (p. 408)
leading relationship (p. 408)
linear cost function (p. 387)
multicollinearity (p. 414)
multiple linear regression (p. 412)
ordinary least squares (OLS) linear
    regression (p. 397)
outcome variable (p. 395)
predictor variable (p. 395)
P-value (p. 407)

r^2 (p. 398)
residual (error, disturbance) (p. 408)
serial correlation (p. 409)
simple linear regression analysis (p. 397)
slope coefficient (p. 388)
spurious correlation (p. 404)
step fixed-cost function (p. 393)
step variable-cost function (p. 393)
test of statistical significance (p. 404)
time-series data (p. 389)
t-Stat (p. 404)
work measurement method (p. 394)

SHORT-ANSWER QUESTIONS

10-1 What two assumptions are frequently made when estimating a linear cost function?

10-2 What is a linear cost function? Describe three alternative linear cost functions.

10-3 What is the first step in any statistical analysis?

10-4 "High correlation between two variables means that one is the cause and the other is the effect." Do you agree? Explain.

10-5 What is a discontinuous linear cost function? What types of analyses can be done to improve cost control when the data sets indicate a discontinuous linear cost function?

10-6 Name four approaches to estimating a cost function.

10-7 Discuss the conference method for estimating a cost function. What are advantages of this method?

10-8 When using the high-low method, should you base the high and low observations on the outcome variable or on the predictor variable?

10-9 What is the goal of an OLS linear regression?

10-10 Describe three criteria for evaluating cost functions and choosing cost drivers.

10-11 What is the difference between the coefficient of determination, r^2, and the goodness of fit?

10-12 "All independent variables in a cost function estimated with regression analysis are cost drivers." Do you agree?

10-13 Discuss four frequently encountered problems when collecting cost data on variables included in a cost function.

EXERCISES

10-14 Terminology. A number of terms are listed below:

account analysis method	conference method	correlation
economic plausibility	explanatory power	goodness of fit
high-low method	industrial engineering method	linear cost function
ordinary least squares (OLS)	simple linear regression	outcome variable
predictor variable	method	r^2
t-Stat	P-value	time-series

REQUIRED

Select the terms from the above list to complete the following sentences.

There are several methods of quantitative analysis that a management team can use to predict the value of a single overhead cost pool in a traditional costing system. The methods are
_____ _____ _____, _____ _____, ___-___ _____, _____ _____ _____, _____ ____ _____(___), and_____ _____ _____ _____. There are different criteria to consider when choosing a method of analysis which are: affordability, understandability, data availability and quality, _____ _____, and _____ _____.

      The change in quantity of resources used must be a good measure of change in benefit. The relationship must be a _____ ____ _____ if OLS simple linear regression analysis is to be used. Ideally, the OLS will be based on at least 25 data points observed and reported in the past as a _____. If insufficient data are available then the other methods of analysis will help the management team predict the value of the indirect cost pool. When true, the orderly change in the quantity of resource used will explain a large proportion of the change in the indirect cost pool. This is called_____. A high explanatory power indicates a high _____between the change in the measure of benefit or the _____ variable, X, and the change in the predicted indirect cost pool or _____, y. You can observe this in the

_____ between the predicted (X, y) line and the actual data points (X, Y) from which the prediction was made. The measure of goodness of fit is called _____. Other important statistics that assess the reliability of the predicted regression line are the _____ and _____. While the OLS is a very rigorous analysis and can predict future values at a specific _____, it is not appropriate for all situations.

10-15 Estimating a cost function. The controller of the Ijiri Company wants you to estimate a cost function from the following two observations in a general ledger account called Maintenance:

Month	Machine-Hours	Maintenance Costs Incurred
January	6,000	$4,000
February	10,000	5,400

REQUIRED

1. Estimate the cost function for maintenance.
2. Can the constant in the cost function be used as an estimate of fixed maintenance cost per month? Explain.

10-16 Discontinuous linear cost functions. (CPA, adapted) Select the graph that matches the numbered manufacturing cost data. Indicate by letter which of the graphs best fits each of the situations or items described.

The vertical axes of the graphs represent total dollars of cost, and the horizontal axes represent production output during a calendar year. In each case, the zero point of dollars and production is at the intersection of the two axes. The graphs may be used more than once.

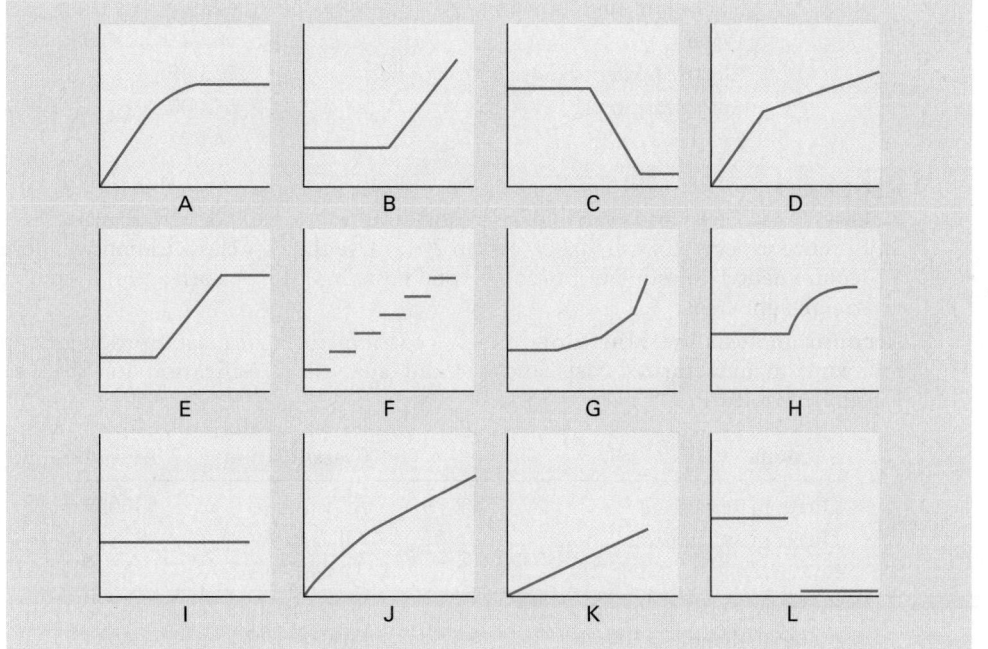

1. Annual amortization of equipment, where the amount of amortization charged is computed by the machine-hours method.
2. Electricity bill—a flat fixed charge, plus a variable cost after a certain number of kilowatt-hours are used, where the quantity of kilowatt-hours used varies proportionately with quantity of production output.
3. City water bill, which is computed as follows:

First 1,000,000 litres or less	$1,000 flat fee
Next 10,000 litres	$0.003 per litre used
Next 10,000 litres	$0.006 per litre used
Next 10,000 litres	$0.009 per litre used
And so on	And so on

The litres of water used vary proportionately with the quantity of production output.

4. Cost of lubricant for machines, where cost per unit decreases with each kilogram of lubricant used (for example, if one kilogram is used, the cost is $10; if two kilograms are used, the cost is $19.98; if three kilograms are used, the cost is $29.94) with a minimum cost per kilogram of $9.20.

5. Annual amortization of equipment, where the amount is computed by the straight-line method. When the amortization rate was established, it was anticipated that the obsolescence factor would be greater than the wear-and-tear factor.

6. Rent on a manufacturing plant donated by the city, where the agreement calls for a fixed fee payment unless 200,000 labour-hours are worked, in which case no rent need be paid.

7. Salaries of repair personnel, where one person is needed for every 1,000 machine-hours or less (that is, 0 to 1,000 hours requires one person, 1,001 to 2,000 hours requires two people, etc.).

8. Cost of direct materials used (assume no quantity discounts).

9. Rent on a manufacturing plant donated by the county, where the agreement calls for rent of $100,000 reduced by $1 for each direct manufacturing labour-hour worked in excess of 200,000 hours, but a minimum rental fee of $20,000 must be paid.

2. Total costs, $573,500

10-17 Account analysis method. Lorenzo operates a brushless car wash. Incoming cars are put on an automatic, continuously moving conveyor belt. Cars are washed as the conveyor belt carries the car from the start station to the finish station. After the car moves off the conveyor belt, the car is dried manually. Workers then clean and vacuum the inside of the car. Lorenzo serviced 80,000 cars in 2012. Lorenzo reports the following costs for 2012:

Account Description	Costs
Car wash labour	$260,000
Soap, cloth, and supplies	42,000
Water	38,000
Electric power to move conveyor belt	72,000
Amortization	64,000
Salaries	46,000

REQUIRED

1. Classify each account as variable or fixed with respect to cars washed. Explain.

2. Lorenzo expects to wash 90,000 cars in 2013. Use the cost classification you developed in requirement 1 to estimate Lorenzo's total costs in 2013. Amortization is computed on a straight-line basis.

1. Total variable costs in 2013, $716,000

10-18 Account analysis method. Gower Inc., a manufacturer of plastic products, reports the following manufacturing costs and account analysis classification for the year ended December 31, 2012.

Account	Classification	Amount
Direct materials	All variable	$300,000
Direct manufacturing labour	All variable	225,000
Power	All variable	37,500
Supervision labour	20% variable	56,250
Materials-handling labour	50% variable	60,000
Maintenance labour	40% variable	75,000
Amortization	0% variable	95,000
Rent, property taxes, and administration	0% variable	100,000

Gower Inc., produced 75,000 units of product in 2012. Gower's management is estimating costs for 2013 based on 2012 numbers. The following additional information is available for 2013:

a. Direct materials prices in 2013 are expected to increase by 5% compared with 2012.

b. Under the terms of the labour contract, direct manufacturing labour wage rates are expected to increase by 10% in 2013 compared with 2012.

c. Power rates and wage rates for supervision, materials-handling, and maintenance are not expected to change from 2012 to 2013.

d. Amortization costs are expected to increase by 5%, and rent, property taxes, and administration costs are expected to increase by 7%.

e. Gower, Inc. expects to manufacture and sell 80,000 units in 2013.

REQUIRED

1. Prepare a schedule of variable, fixed, and total manufacturing costs for each account category in 2013. Estimate total manufacturing costs for 2013.
2. Calculate Gower's total manufacturing cost per unit in 2012 and estimated total manufacturing cost per unit in 2013.
3. How can you get better estimates of fixed and variable costs? Why would these better estimates be useful to Gower?

10-19 Linear cost approximation. Sandy Smith, managing director of the Calgary Consulting Group, is examining how overhead costs behave with changes in monthly professional labour-hours billed to clients. Assume the following historical data:

2. a. At 5,000 hours, costs overstated by $8,000

Total Overhead Costs	Professional Labour-Hours Billed to Clients
$340,000	3,000
400,000	4,000
435,000	5,000
477,000	6,000
529,000	7,000
587,000	8,000

REQUIRED

1. Compute the linear cost function, relating total overhead cost to professional labour-hours, using the representative observations of 4,000 and 7,000 hours. Plot the linear cost function. Does the constant component of the cost function represent the fixed overhead costs of the Calgary Consulting Group? Why?
2. What would be the predicted total overhead costs for (a) 5,000 hours and (b) 8,000 hours using the cost function estimated in requirement 1? Plot the predicted costs and actual costs for 5,000 and 8,000 hours.
3. Smith had a chance to accept a special job that would have boosted professional labour-hours from 4,000 to 5,000 hours. Suppose Smith, guided by the linear cost function, rejected this job because it would have brought a total increase in contribution margin of $38,000, before deducting the predicted increase in total overhead cost, $43,000. What is the actual total contribution margin forgone?

10-20 Cost-volume-profit and regression analysis. Garvin Corporation manufactures a children's bicycle, model CT8. Garvin currently manufactures the bicycle frame. During 2012, Garvin made 30,000 frames at a total cost of $900,000. Ryan Corporation has offered to supply as many frames as Garvin wants at a cost of $28.50 per frame. Garvin anticipates needing 36,000 frames each year for the next few years.

1. a. Average cost per frame, $30

REQUIRED

1. **a.** What is the average cost of manufacturing a bicycle frame in 2012? How does it compare to Ryan's offer?
   b. Can Garvin use the answer in requirement 1a to determine the cost of manufacturing 36,000 bicycle frames? Explain.
2. Garvin's cost analyst uses annual data from past years to estimate the following regression equation with total manufacturing costs of the bicycle frame as the dependent variable and bicycle frames produced as the independent variable:

$$y = \$432{,}000 + \$15X$$

During the years used to estimate the regression equation, the production of bicycle frames varied from 28,000 to 36,000. Using this equation, estimate how much it would cost Garvin to manufacture 36,000 bicycle frames. How much more or less costly is it to manufacture the frames rather than to acquire them from Ryan?
3. What other information would you need to be confident that the equation in requirement 2 accurately predicts the cost of manufacturing bicycle frames?

10-21 OLS simple linear regression analysis in Excel; regression analysis, service company. (CMA, adapted) Dave Ladouceur owns a catering company that prepares banquets and parties for both individual and business functions throughout the year. Mr. Ladouceur's business is seasonal, with a heavy schedule during the summer months and the year-end holidays and a light schedule at other times. During peak periods there are extra costs. He shuts down in January to repair and maintain and clean.

One of the major events Mr. Ladouceur's customers request is a cocktail party. He offers a standard cocktail party and has developed the following cost structure on a per-person basis.

	Time/Person	Cost/hour	Total Cost
Food and beverages (direct materials)			$ 15.00
Labour (in hours)	0.50	$12.00	6.00
Average overhead (in hours)	0.60	15.70	9.42
Total costs per person			30.42

Mr. Ladouceur is quite certain about his estimates of the food, beverages, and labour costs but is not as comfortable with the overhead estimate. This estimate was based on the actual data for the past 12 months, presented below. These data indicate that overhead expenses vary with the direct labour-hours expended. The $15.70-per-hour estimate was determined by dividing total overhead expended for the 12 months by total labour-hours.

Mr. Ladouceur has recently become aware of regression analysis. He estimated the following regression equation with overhead costs as the dependent variable (y) and labour-hours as the independent variable (X):

$$y = \$31{,}886 + \$9.45X + e$$

REQUIRED
1. Using Excel and the data provided in the table, complete a regression analysis at a confidence level of 95%.
2. What important information is presented in the r^2, t-Stat, and P-values?
3. What is the range within which Mr. Ladouceur can be confident of the values of a and b?
4. Mr. Ladouceur has been asked to prepare a bid for a 200-person cocktail party to be given next month. Determine the minimum bid price that Mr. Ladouceur would be willing to submit to earn a positive contribution margin using his estimate and the results of the linear regression analysis.
5. Explain Mr. Ladouceur's problem with using the linear regression results.
6. What further information does the chart of the residuals provide?

Months	Labour-Hours	Overhead Costs
January	—	$2,500
February	2,700	70,800
March	3,000	72,000
April	4,200	76,800
May	7,500	92,400
June	5,500	85,200
July	6,500	88,800
August	4,500	80,400
September	7,000	90,000
October	4,500	81,600
November	3,100	74,400
December	6,500	87,600
Total	57,500	902,500

10-22 Regression analysis, activity-based costing, choosing cost drivers. Jill Goldstein has been collecting data over the last year in an effort to understand the cost drivers of distribution costs at Waterloo Corporation, a manufacturer of brass door handles. Distribution costs include the costs of organizing different shipments as well as physically handling and moving packaged units. Goldstein believes that, because the product is heavy, number of units moved will affect distribution costs significantly but she is not certain that this is the case.

Goldstein collects the following monthly data for the past 12 months:

Months	Distribution Costs	Number of Units	Number of Shipments
January	$ 33,600	51,000	200
February	24,000	43,000	210
March	8,000	0	50
April	38,400	67,000	315
May	48,000	73,000	335
June	28,800	54,000	225
July	26,400	37,000	190
August	42,000	72,000	390
September	50,400	71,000	280
October	27,600	56,000	360
November	39,600	52,000	380
December	26,400	45,000	270
Total	$393,200	621,000	3,205

Goldstein estimates the following regression equations:

$$y = \$5,187.72 + (\$0.533 \times \text{Number of packaged units moved})$$
$$y = \$9,073.11 + (\$88.71 \times \text{Number of shipments made})$$

REQUIRED

1. Using Excel, produce plots of the monthly data and the regression lines underlying each of the following cost functions:
   a. Predicted distribution costs $y = a + bX$ (where X = Number of packaged units moved)
   b. Predicted distribution costs $y = a + bX$ (where X = Number of shipments made)

   Which cost driver for support overhead costs would you choose? Explain your answer briefly based on the graphs and statistics provided by the analysis.
2. Goldstein anticipates moving 40,000 units in 220 shipments next month. Using the cost function you chose in requirement 1, what distribution costs should Goldstein budget?
3. If Ms. Goldstein chose the wrong cost function—the cost function other than the one you chose in requirement 1—and 40,000 units were moved in 220 shipments, would you expect actual costs to be lower than, to be greater than, or to closely approximate the predictions made using the "wrong" cost driver and cost function? Explain your answer briefly and discuss any other implications of choosing the "wrong" cost driver and cost function.
4. What problem is common to both estimations of predicted cost pool values based on changes in either cost driver and what can Goldstein do now?

PROBLEMS

10-23 OLS and high-low method. Ken Howard, financial analyst at JVR Corporation, a manufacturer of precision parts, is examining the behaviour of quarterly maintenance costs for budgeting purposes. Ken collects data on machine-hours worked and maintenance costs for the past 26 quarters. The data are as follows:

Quarter	Machine Hours	Maintenance
1	90,000	$282,000
2	110,000	222,000
3	100,000	264,000
4	120,000	240,000
5	85,000	288,000
6	105,000	204,000
7	95,000	258,000
8	115,000	234,000
9	95,000	282,000
10	115,000	228,000
11	105,000	270,000
12	125,000	216,000
13	90,000	283,500
14	112,000	221,800

(Continued)

Quarter	Machine Hours	Maintenance
15	98,000	267,000
16	122,000	235,000
17	89,000	287,500
18	107,000	207,500
19	92,000	257,800
20	118,000	233,400
21	94,000	284,300
22	113,000	221,000
23	103,000	263,500
24	125,500	224,100
25	87,500	279,500
26	111,500	219,500
	2,722,500	$6,473,400

REQUIRED

1. a. Using Excel, do a regression analysis to estimate and plot the quarterly data underlying the cost function: Maintenance costs $y = a + bX + e$ (where X = 100,000 Direct machine-hours).

   b. Estimate the cost function for the data represented by the plots in requirement 1a using the high-low method.

   c. How well does each cost function fit the data?

2. a. After considering the accounting cycle, Ken realizes that maintenance costs are not even invoiced to the company until the month following the completion of the work. Work done at the end of March will not be invoiced and paid until April. This delays payment of the cost of maintenance completed in quarter 1 into quarter 2, when the payment is recorded in the maintenance cost pool. Ken then uses Excel to complete an OLS regression to estimate and plot the quarterly data relating machine-hours in a quarter (such as t) to maintenance costs in the following quarter ($t + 1$). That is, plot machine-hours in quarter 1 against maintenance costs in quarter 2, machine-hours in quarter 2 against maintenance costs in quarter 3, and so on.

   b. Estimate the cost function for the data represented by the plots in requirement 2a using the high-low method.

   c. How well does each cost function fit the data?

③ ④ ⑤

1. a. Predicted revenue, $50,144

10-24 OLS simple linear regression analysis. (CIMA, heavily adapted) Lisa Aoli, the financial manager at the Casa Real restaurant is working with Megan Dryden, the marketing manager, to establish if there is any relationship between the newspaper advertising expense and the sales revenue at the restaurant each month. The table below reports the actual data for the past 10 months.

Based on these data the two partners will compare the predicted revenue based on a linear relation which they have assumed depicts the economic substance of any systematic change in revenue due to a change in advertising expense. The specification will be $Y = a + bX$ for the two methods based on actual data and $y = a + bX + e$ for the linear regression. The partners obtain their linear regression results in less than five minutes from Excel. Their account analyses take longer, but they determine that the fixed monthly revenue from longstanding and regular customers is $5,000. They want to predict revenue when the advertising expense X = $1,900.

Month	Revenues	Advertising Expense
March	$60,000	$2,400
April	84,000	3,600
May	66,000	1,800
June	78,000	4,200
July	66,000	1,200
August	78,000	2,400
September	54,000	1,800
October	96,000	4,800
November	66,000	3,000
December	72,000	3,000
	$720,000	$28,200

REQUIRED

1. Determine the predicted total revenue using (a) account analysis, (b) high-low method and (c) the output from the linear regression.
2. Calculate the range within which the value of y when X = $1,900 is likely to fall.
3. Comment on the results of the OLS simple linear regression and begin with the data quality.
4. Would you recommend the use of the OLS simple linear regression results to predict monthly revenue?

10-25 OLS linear regression. Below are the input and results of an OLS linear regression. The president of a specialty fruit juice company believed that for every single degree change in average temperature during the summer months, the profit would decline 3%. This information was used to prepare budgets. The president obtained forecasts of the average summer temperature then requested the budget be adjusted. The table of values presents the raw data for temperatures (Predictor Variable X) and net income (Outcome Variable Y).

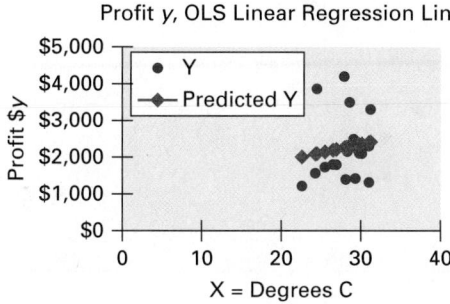

Profit y, OLS Linear Regression Line

X = Degrees C

Regression Statistics	Degrees C	Std Error	t-Stat	P-value
R Square	0.017029265			
Observations	19			
df	18			
Intercept a	$943.84316	2440.03187	0.386816	0.70369
Slope b	$47.12590	86.8375498	0.54269	0.59439
Confidence	95.00%	95.00%		
Critical value of df = 18	2.101	2.101		

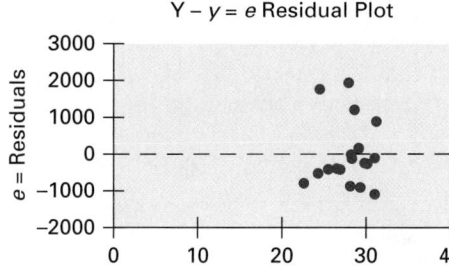

Y − y = e Residual Plot

Original Data Set:

Observations	X = Degrees C	Profit Y
1993	22.6	$1,219
1994	24.3	1,568
1995	25.5	1,731
1996	28.1	1,395
1997	29.3	1,421
1998	31.0	1,320
1999	30.1	2,101
2000	26.9	1,795
2001	31.0	2,300
2002	28.3	2,152
2003	29.1	2,487
2004	29.8	2,104
2005	31.2	3,307
2006	28.6	3,502
2007	24.5	3,862
2008	27.9	4,200
2009	26.5	1,800
2010	28.2	2,265
2011	29.1	2,475

REQUIRED

1. What do the coefficients of the OLS linear regression line: $y = a + bX + e$ (where a = $943.843 and b = $47.126) tell you about the relationship between these two sets of data?
2. What does the R Square (r^2) tell you about the explanatory power of temperature to predict net income?
3. What does the t-Stat and the P-value tell you about whether or not the coefficients a and b could arise by accident?
4. What recommendations would you make to the president?

10-26 Specification of a linear cost function. Martin Goretsky examines the output and data from an OLS simple linear regression, what does the plot of the residuals tell Mr. Goretsky?

X Monthly Produced Q = Q Sold	Y Indirect Manufacturing Cost Pool
37.8	252
39.6	264
88.7	591
43.8	398
23.8	216
27.7	252
51.0	464
47.2	429
32.0	355
28.6	318
47.1	523
44.6	496
35.8	398
28.1	312
53.4	593
40.3	576
21.1	301
44.8	640
37.2	532
29.5	422
21.8	311
43.4	620
49.1	701
29.1	415
27.0	386
50.6	723

Y – y = e Residual Plot

COLLABORATIVE LEARNING CASES

10-27 Account analysis, high-low method, alternative regression functions. M&S Java, run by two graduates of the university, have just opened their take-out coffee and snack bar on the university campus. At the end of their first month of operations they want to understand which cost driver to choose of two available that they already track in their management information system. The first alternative is kilograms of coffee used each day and the second alternative is cups. M&S Java shuts down completely one day each month to clean and test all equipment thoroughly to make sure they will pass any health inspections.

INSTRUCTIONS
Form groups of two or more students to complete the following requirements:

REQUIRED
1. Using the account analysis method, knowing the fixed cost is $572 for the month, what is the forecast value of consuming 65 kg of coffee beans?
2. If M&S Java use 65 kg of coffee beans, then what is the forecast indirect cost for using the high-low method based on actual values provided in the table?
3. If M&S Java chose linear regression to predict the future MOH costs, then examining the line graphs and the statistics what is the better choice of cost driver for this indirect cost pool and what justifies that choice?
4. If M&S Java use 65 kg of coffee beans, then contrast the results from this requirement to those of requirement 3 and comment on the difference.

Days	Cost Driver Kg Coffee Beans	Outcome Actual $Y	Cost Driver Cups
1	70	$155	485
2	63	150	462
3	72	180	460
4	60	135	460
5	66	156	455
6	70	168	465
7	74	178	461
8	65	160	372
9	62	132	375
10	67	145	373
11	69	140	368
12	65	152	359
13	67	153	361
14	64	141	316
15	63	138	356
16	—	20	—
17	25	65	112
18	48	100	286
19	59	129	322
20	63	129	420
21	67	150	443
22	70	148	453
23	68	145	380
24	65	140	327
25	61	138	418
26	66	142	311
	1,589	$3,589	9,600

Regression Statistics	KG Coffee	Std Error	t-Stat	P-value
R Square	0.9283			
Observations	26.0			
df	25.0			
Intercept a	$13.323	7.2915	1.8272	0.0801
Slope b	2.041	0.0270	17.6303	0.0000
Confidence	95.0%			
Critical value df	2.0600			

Regression Statistics	Cups	Std Error	t-Stat	P-value
R Square	0.8069			
Observations	26.0			
df	25.0			
Intercept a	$38.332	10.3702	3.6963	0.0011
Slope b	0.270	0.0270	10.0147	0.0000
Confidence	95.0%			
Critical value df	2.060			

y = Regression Line Fit Plot Kg Beans

y = Regression Line Fit Plot Cups

Y − y = e Residual Plot

Y − y = e Residual Plot

10-28 Evaluating alternative simple regression models, not-for-profit. (Chapter Appendix) Kathy Hanks, executive assistant to the president of Eastern University, is concerned about the overhead costs at her university. Cost pressures are severe, so controlling and reducing overhead is very important. Hanks believes overhead costs incurred are generally a function of the number of different academic programs (including different specializations, degrees, and majors) that the university has and the number of enrolled students. Both have grown significantly over the years. She collects the following data:

Year	Overhead Costs (in thousands)	Number of Programs	Enrolled Students
1	$16,200	29	3,400
2	23,040	36	5,000
3	20,160	49	2,600
4	24,120	53	4,700
5	23,400	54	3,900
6	27,720	58	4,900
7	28,440	88	5,700
8	24,120	72	3,900
9	27,360	83	3,500
10	35,640	73	3,700
11	37,440	101	5,600
12	45,720	103	7,600

♦ **Regression 1.** Overhead costs = a + (b × number of academic programs)

Variable	Coefficient	Standard Error	t-Value
Constant	$8,553.30	$4,002.41	2.14
Independent variable 1: number of academic programs	$ 288.76	$ 56.80	5.08

$r^2 = 0.72$; Durbin-Watson statistic = 2.07
The adjusted $r^2 = 0.693$

♦ **Regression 2.** Overhead costs = a + (b × number of enrolled students)

Variable	Coefficient	Standard Error	t-Value
Constant	$7,190.10	$6,081.45	1.18
Independent variable 1: number of enrolled students	$ 4.53	$ 1.29	3.52

$r^2 = 0.55$; Durbin-Watson statistic = 0.82
The adjusted $r^2 = 0.509$

INSTRUCTIONS

Form groups of two or more students to complete the following requirements:

REQUIRED

1. Plot the relationship between overhead costs and each of the following variables: (a) number of academic programs and (b) number of enrolled students.
2. Compare and evaluate the two simple regression models estimated by Hanks. Use the comparison format employed in Exhibit 10-12 (p. 411).
3. What insights do the analyses provide about controlling and reducing overhead costs at the university?
4. What are two important issues that would suggest the predictions are unreliable?

⑤ **10-29 Evaluating multiple regression models, not-for-profit** (continuation of 10-28).

INSTRUCTIONS

Form groups of two or more students to complete the following requirements:

REQUIRED

1. Given your findings in Problem 10-28, should Hanks use multiple regression analysis to better understand the cost drivers of overhead costs? Explain your answer.
2. Hanks decides that the simple regression analysis in Problem 10-28 should be extended to a multiple regression analysis. She finds the following result:

♦ **Regression 3.** Overhead costs = a + (b_1 × number of academic programs) + (b_2 × number of enrolled students)

Variable	Coefficient	Standard Error	t-Value
Constant	$3,335.54	$4,344.06	0.77
Independent variable 1: number of academic programs	$ 214.04	$ 61.84	3.46
Independent variable 2: number of enrolled students	$ 2.24	$ 1.11	2.02

$r^2 = 0.81$; Durbin-Watson statistic = 1.91
The adjusted $r^2 = 0.766$

The coefficient of correlation between number of academic programs and number of students is 0.60. Use the format in Exhibit 10-13 (p. 411) to evaluate the multiple regression model. (Assume linearity, and constant variance and normality of residuals.) Should Hanks choose the multiple regression model over the two simple regression models of Problem 10-28?

3. How might the president of Eastern University use these regression results to manage overhead costs?

Decision Making and Relevant Information

Different Information for Different Decisions

Gildan Activewear is a multinational company that markets and manufactures various kinds of apparel. The company sells clothing to wholesale distributors as "blanks," which are then decorated by screenprinters with designs and logos. Consumers ultimately purchase Gildan's products in places such as sporting goods stores, entertainment venues, and tourism destinations. The company is also a leading supplier of private-label and Gildan-branded socks to mass-market retailers.

The company's managers require excellent cost information to make decisions common to most businesses: accepting or rejecting one-time only orders; insourcing or outsourcing services, parts, and supplies; replacing or refurbishing equipment, to name just a few.

After studying this chapter, you should be able to

1. Contrast relevant and irrelevant costs and revenue as well as quantitative and qualitative information influencing decisions.

2. Identify the differences among relevant costs for short-term and long-term production output decisions.

3. Explain why opportunity cost is relevant and book value is irrelevant in decision making.

4. Identify key concepts and apply them to product mix decisions.

5. Explain how to reduce the negative effects and conflicts arising in relevant-cost analyses.

Accountants serve as technical experts, gathering and analyzing data, predicting future outcomes, and recommending the best alternative available to resolve an issue. Reliable and relevant information is essential to good decision making, but it does not guarantee good decisions. The ability to distinguish relevant from irrelevant data and analyze systematic relationships (see Chapter 10) are fundamental skills needed for making reasonable business decisions. Some managers do not understand the limitations of data quality or analytic techniques, or they ignore recommendations and take impulsive actions. With objective use of high-quality data and readily used techniques of analyses, managers will make informed assumptions to predict future outcomes (see Chapter 3).

Forecasting outcomes is the heart of a decision, but it is quite normal that the most relevant information is missing. There will almost always be a gap between what was expected and what is actually realized because no one can predict the future with accuracy. A good decision process includes a post-implementation assessment and explanation of the key causes of differences between expected and actual outcomes. This is how managers learn from their experiences.

DECISION FRAMEWORK: CHOOSE ONLY RELEVANT COSTS

1 Contrast relevant and irrelevant costs and revenue as well as quantitative and qualitative information influencing decisions.

What distinguishes good from bad decision processes is the discipline of decision making described in the decision model applied throughout this textbook. If perfect and complete information were available, no decision would be necessary—it would be obvious what should be done. Decisions are future based, because nothing can alter the past; hard, reliable data are historical. There may be several sources of data:

◆ Quantitative data from either electronic or hardcopy source documents.

◆ Qualitative data from relevant past experience or relevant stories of past experience from others.

◆ Executive, managerial, and line expertise about processes and outcomes.

◆ Analyses of both current and historical internal MIS quantitative data.

◆ Analyses of both current and historical external data about uncontrollable factors in the competitive environment.

◆ Advice and forecasts of experts in an area.

Quantitative data can be measured numerically. Examples include the costs of direct materials, direct manufacturing labour, and marketing. Some **quantitative factors** can be readily expressed in financial terms, whereas others are measured numerically but are not expressed in financial terms. Examples include amounts of labour-hours, direct materials, or units produced.

Relevant data can be distinguished from irrelevant data. If the data will change a decision, they are relevant. This means any data, such as revenue or costs, that differ between the available choices are relevant. Remember, however, that it is forecast *future* revenue and costs upon which a decision is made, not historical revenue and costs. Management teams usually assume that past data are a reliable signal of the future. What is certain about the future is that it will actually be a surprise. No one can accurately forecast the future, so managers expect they will be wrong in their forecasts. That does not mean they make wrong decisions; rather, the actual outcomes of a decision differ from the budgeted or predicted outcomes.

ANALYZING RISK

The reliability of historical costs and the likelihood the future will unfold as the past did will contribute to the relevance of historical cost. In situations where sudden changes to business as usual occur, the future will not unfold as the past did. The way to incorporate this common knowledge into any forecast is to build into the forecast the risk that the forecast will be wrong (see Chapters 3, 10). Quantifying risk helps bring clarity to situations where either fear or overconfidence would lead managers to make decisions detrimental to the company. The measure of known risk is *probability*. Unknown risk remains unimagined and, of course, cannot be quantified.

The use of probabilities not only helps a team calculate the financial consequences, but also records assumptions about the future that can be checked at a later date. As discussed in Chapter 3, probabilities (p) permit estimation of a range of predicted outcomes and identification of the most likely to occur, the **expected value**, which is the sum of the risk-weighted outcomes (called *sumprod* in Solver, which is explained later in this chapter; see pp. 448–450). **Risk-weights** are measured as probabilities in decimal format, while outcomes are usually measured as financial payouts from pursuing a specific course of action. The management decision, however, is to discuss and achieve a consensus on expected values of different choices, not merely on the probabilities themselves.

Often the straightforward discipline of attaching numbers to expectations leads to very fruitful discussions to justify the probabilities and helps team members think more clearly about what future outcomes are more and less probable. Once a quantity is attached to the probability, discussions often become less emotional, because while people have strong commitment to their beliefs they don't tend to have strong commitments to numbers. This is especially helpful if a company is having difficulty remaining profitable.

Risk analysis will result in a number from 0 to 1 that represents how likely it is that a particular risk will occur. A measure of risk like p = 0.01 is an example of a rare outcome compared to p = 0.87, which is a near certain outcome. If a decision is "highly risky," it usually means there is either a high probability of (near certain) loss, or there is a small probability of a very large loss. A management team will focus on ways to reduce this loss or downside risk. A high return usually refers to either a highly improbable but large upside return or a near certain return. As circumstances change, assumptions about probability, negative and positive financial outcomes, and their magnitudes can be readily changed in a spreadsheet and new expected values calculated. Expected value is a solid quantitative basis upon which to discuss and decide the best response to business situations.

It is important to understand that risky decisions can also be the best decisions to make in a specific situation. Generally, the higher the risk of a course of action, the higher the return or payout expected from being right. Exceptional managers do not try to avoid risk but rather try to take sensible risks. One criterion of a sensible risk is that the expected return will be higher than the other, less risky choices. It would be a rare and desperate management team who would knowingly "bet the farm" and choose an alternative which, if it fails, carries the risk of destroying the company, unless analysis indicates it is the only alternative.

While analyzing risk is important, action must be taken or nothing will change. **Paralysis by analysis** describes situations where managers decide to wait and wait for more information. The danger is that the opportunity to actually remedy problems can disappear faster than relevant information can appear. If the decision is good, failure to achieve the expected improvement can happen at the action stage because of poor implementation (or execution). Top managers must decide when to take action despite risk, absence of relevant information, and presence of low-quality information.

RELEVANT VERSUS IRRELEVANT COSTS

We will look at an example to illustrate the differences between relevant and irrelevant costs when making decisions. We will simplify the decision process by presenting a complete and perfect set of information, and we will hold most outcomes constant (all other things being equal).

Exhibit 11-1 provides all the relevant information required to calculate the financial outcomes of each of two alternatives for Precision Sporting Goods: (1) do nothing and keep things the same or (2) reorganize the production line by purchasing a new machine, rearranging the production process, and laying off workers who are not required in the new process. This combination of actions is often referred to as restructuring. The costing system source documents indicate under the current situation (Alternative 1: Do Nothing), the managers can forecast a sales volume of Q = 25,000 units at a price per unit of $250 with no forecast change. Precision Sports locks in most of its sales volume in long-term contracts.

EXHIBIT 11-1
Budgeted Income Statement for August, Absorption-Costing Format, for Precision Sporting Goods

Precision Sporting Goods

Output Q in units	25,000	Workers	20	15	
Price per unit	$ 250	Cost/DMLH	$16	$16	

	All Revenues and Costs		Relevant Revenues and Costs	
	Alternative 1: **Do Nothing**	**Alternative 2:** **Rearrange**	**Alternative 1:** **Do Nothing**	**Alternative 2:** **Rearrange**
Revenue[a]	$6,250,000	$6,250,000	$ —	$ —
Costs:				
Direct materials[b]	1,250,000	1,250,000	$ —	$ —
Manufacturing labour[c, d]	640,000	480,000	640,000	480,000 F
Manufacturing overhead	750,000	750,000	—	—
Marketing	2,000,000	2,000,000	—	—
Rearrangement costs	—	90,000	—	90,000 U
Total costs	4,640,000	4,570,000 F	$(640,000)	$(570,000) F
Operating income	$1,610,000	$1,680,000 F		
Difference in operating income		$ 70,000 F		$ (70,000)
		(Operating income is higher)		(Costs are lower)

[a]25,000 units × $250/unit = $6,250,000   [c]20 workers × 2,000 hr/worker × $16/DMLH = $640,000
[b]25,000 units × $50/unit = $1,250,000   [d]15 workers × 2,000 hr/worker × $16/DMLH = $480,000

Revenue does not change between the two alternatives and is *irrelevant* because this information will not change the decision. **Relevant revenue** is the forecast future revenue that *differs* because of a decision; where data are identical, disciplined decision makers will be indifferent. **Incremental revenue** is any additional total revenue from one alternative, whereas **differential revenue** is the difference between the total revenue of two or more alternatives. The variance or difference (U) or (F) is relative to the decreasing or increasing effect of each choice on operating income.

The current cohort of 20 workers work 2,000 direct manufacturing labour hours (DMLH) per year at a rate of $16/DMLH. The manufacturing and non-manufacturing overhead are given. Under Alternative 2 to rearrange the production line, direct materials costs are forecast to remain constant because longer-term contracts are in place. Similarly, the labour contract continues for a few more years but the cohort of workers decreases to 15 at the same wage rate per DMLH.

The labour DMLH rate is *irrelevant* because the alternative to purchase the new machine will not change the DMLH rate. It will, however, change the total DMLH cost of production. The total labour cost is *relevant* because it differs between the two alternatives—these projected savings will persist year after year. The overhead costs of each alternative are *irrelevant* because they are identical in the two alternatives. There are one-time implementation costs that are *relevant* because they differ between the two alternatives. The first two columns of the table list all costs while the last two columns highlight only the **relevant costs**.

The difference between total and relevant costs is identical. There is a total saving of $70,000 to Precision Sporting Goods if managers choose Alternative 2. There is a $90,000 one-time added or incremental cost. An **incremental cost** (also known as either **out-of-pocket**, **outlay**, or **differential cost**) is the difference between two alternative relevant costs. The ongoing savings of $160,000 in direct manufacturing labour cost more than pays for the $90,000 incremental cost. The incremental saving minus the incremental cost is the **net relevant cost** of $70,000 saved.

It is important to realize, however, that the numbers do not dictate the decision. This is only one of many relevant pieces of information that must be considered by the management team. Having the forecast of financial values helps, but managers need to carefully assess any interdependencies within their enterprise. Reflection on the indirect consequences (for example, low employee morale, absenteeism, turnover) that could increase costs of Alternative 2 will help the enterprise avoid unintended and negative consequences. Some unintended consequences can also be very positive. An improvement in profitability is, nevertheless, a persuasive but not a decisive indication of a reasonable course of action.

ADDITIONAL RELEVANT CONSIDERATIONS: TIME VALUE, TAX, AND QUALITATIVE FACTORS

So far our analysis has ignored both the time value of money and income tax. A full discussion of the considerable influence of both of these quantitative factors is undertaken in Chapters 21 and 22. The time value of money in particular would be important to Precision Sporting Goods because the cost savings will be ongoing. It is also often the case that managers can predict the increase in corporate taxes as their pre-tax income increases from one tax bracket to the next.

Qualitative factors are outcomes that cannot be measured in numerical terms. Examples include ineffective training, employee morale, and incorrect assumptions made by top management. Most experienced decision makers know their expected outcome is only as good as its assumptions as well as the data. Management accountants often make an extremely important contribution by developing rough measures of qualitative information like morale using scales such as +1 (very low) through +5 (very high). Gathering information directly from surveys of employees, it is straightforward to estimate average scores for the survey questions.

Precision decides to reorganize the production line and purchase the new equipment. Actual results will provide feedback, and it turns out to be bad news. The realized new manufacturing labour costs are reported as $550,000, not $480,000. The forecast saving from reorganization is zero ($550,000 + $90,000 = $640,000). The value added comes from finding out why the implementation has failed. Assuming all other things are equal, the relevant information is unfavourable manufacturing labour costs:

◆ The skills of remaining workers did not match those required for the new process; the result was overtime, which suggests a failure in recruitment, training, placement, or perhaps all three.

◆ The training programs failed to provide adequate opportunity for workers to learn new skills; the result was lower-than-expected productivity, which suggests a human resources failure or a failure to communicate new training needs.

◆ The equipment installation did not go well and the batch sizes had to be reduced until repairs could be made; the result was excess nonproductive idle time for setups and overtime for workers, which suggests a failure to foresee and fulfill the need for process improvement.

◆ The layoffs affected morale and productivity; the result was that more workers had to be hired to meet production commitments, which suggests a failure to foresee and fulfill human resource management needs.

◆ The assumptions top management used in their forecast were incorrect, which suggests weakness in either performance measurement or in strategic processes.

The unexpected $70,000 labour cost overrun ($550,000 − $480,000 = $70,000 U) could then be divided by the average score (ranging from +1 to +5) assigned to the qualitative factors—for example, +1. If low morale from the layoffs was the problem and the goal was +5 on the scale, then it cost Precision approximately $17,500 per lost morale point ($70,000 ÷ [5 − 1] = $17,500). The remedy to ensure the savings are realized in the future is to undertake a program to restore morale. Quantifying the qualitative factor of morale into a rough estimate of financial value provides relevant information to assist in the reassessment of the decision.

Some factors, such as health and safety, are not priced by corporations. Insurance companies do price these factors and provide the benefit of insurance to spread the risk of loss, if companies are willing to pay the price. Responsible management teams will go to experts outside their enterprise to help them more clearly understand the risks a particular decision may pose to their employees, customers, and other stakeholders without assessing financial value. The idea of putting a price or a cost on safety and health is often enough to make the decision team aware that it will not sacrifice safety, regardless of the financial benefits of doing so.

Managers must at times give more weight to either qualitative or nonfinancial quantitative factors than to financial factors. For example, Precision Sporting Goods may, upon further investigation, determine that it can purchase preassembled materials from an outside supplier at a price that is lower than what it costs to manufacture them in-house. The company may still choose to manufacture in-house because it feels that the supplier is unlikely to meet the demanding delivery schedule—a quantitative nonfinancial factor—and because purchasing the part from outside may adversely affect employee morale—a qualitative factor. Trading off nonfinancial and financial considerations is seldom easy.

CHANGE OUTPUT LEVEL: SHORT- AND LONG-TERM DECISIONS

2 Identify the differences among relevant costs for short-term and long-term production output decisions.

Managers often make decisions that affect output levels. For example, managers must choose whether to introduce a new product or sell more units of an existing product. All production output decisions involve identifying differences among relevant costs, but some decisions are short term and some are long term in nature.

Short-term production output decisions have no capacity-management effects, such as accepting or rejecting one-time-only special orders when there is idle production capacity and when the order has no long-run implications. Consider the following example of Surf Gear, a company that produces towels. To simplify this short-term decision process and the identification of relevant costs, assume:

◆ No variable marketing costs are incurred to obtain the special one-time order.

◆ All costs can be classified as either variable with respect to a single driver (units of output) or fixed.

◆ All outcome data have already been weighted by their respective probabilities (risks).

Under these assumptions, fixed costs are irrelevant. They must be paid whether the special order is accepted or not. Full absorption costing is inappropriate to the pricing of the finished goods (see Chapter 9). Only the incremental variable costs are relevant, and those costs must be recovered plus some profit. Variable (and in some cases throughput) costing is appropriate to pricing the finished goods. When there is idle capacity, the effect of a special order on operating income depends on the customer accepting the contract, not on full absorption cost recovery.

Recall the discussion on unitized fixed costs. Any increase in output will reduce the unitized fixed cost for all output. But total fixed costs must be paid even if production or sales, or both, is zero. As long as there is capacity available, there are no opportunity costs. As long as all variable costs plus some profit are recovered, the special order will be an additional contribution to cover fixed costs. There is no other opportunity available; therefore, accepting the special order is the best use of available excess resources.

Example 1: At the top of Exhibit 11-2 are the facts of the special order for Surf Gear towels. The monthly practical production capacity is 48,000, but expected monthly production is 30,000 towels (normal capacity). This means that this month Surf Gear has expected idle capacity of 18,000 towels. The expected value of monthly operating income is $30,000. All expected costs are based on historical data. The expected manufacturing cost of $12 per unit and the marketing cost of $7 per unit include both variable and fixed costs. The expected full absorption or full product costs are $19 per unit. The expected variable direct material, direct manufacturing labour, and variable MOH per unit sum to $7.50 per unit.

EXHIBIT 11-2
Budgeted Income Statement for August, Full Absorption-Costing Format, for Surf Gear[a]

		Full Absorption Costing	
Capacity/month	48,000	Total manufacturing cost/unit	$12.00
Current production/month	30,000	Total non-manufacturing cost/unit	$ 7.00
Direct material/unit	$6.00	Direct manufacturing labour/unit	$ 0.50
Variable MOH/unit	$1.00	Fixed direct manufacturing labour/unit	$ 1.50
Fixed MOH/unit	$3.00		
Fixed Marketing/unit	$2.00		

	Per Unit	Total
Units sold		30,000
Revenue	$20.00	$600,000
Cost of goods sold (COGS)		
Variable manufacturing costs[b]	7.50	225,000
Fixed manufacturing costs[c]	4.50	135,000
Total COGS	12.00	360,000
Marketing costs		
Variable marketing costs	5.00	150,000
Fixed marketing costs	2.00	60,000
Total marketing costs	7.00	210,000
Full costs of the product	19.00	570,000
Operating income	$ 1.00	$ 30,000

[a]Surf Gear incurs no R&D, product-design, distribution, or customer-service costs.

[b]Variable manufacturing = Direct material + Direct manufacturing + Variable
    cost per unit   cost per unit   labour cost per unit   overhead per unit
        = $6.00 + $0.50 + $1.00 = $7.50

[c]Fixed manufacturing   = Fixed direct manufacturing + Fixed manufacturing
   cost per unit   labour cost per unit   overhead per unit
        = $1.50 + $3.00 = $4.50

As a result of a strike at its existing towel supplier, a luxury hotel chain has offered to buy 5,000 towels from Surf Gear in August at $11 per towel. This is $8 per unit less than full absorption, but $3.50 per unit more than total variable costs. No subsequent sales to this hotel chain are anticipated. The additional 5,000 towels are within the relevant range of practical capacity of 48,000 towels (see Chapter 9). Fixed manufacturing costs will not change regardless of whether Surf Gear accepts the special order or not. Surf Gear will use existing idle capacity to produce the 5,000 towels.

No other incremental costs will be incurred because the customer has already approached Surf Gear. Exhibit 11-3 summarizes the facts. Surf Gear uses a variable costing policy to analyze the effects of each decision (reject or accept) on contribution margin, and therefore on operating income. Fixed costs are irrelevant; each additional dollar of contribution margin will flow directly to operating income.

At this point in the decision-making process, Surf Gear has assumed that taking on this order at a price of $11/unit will not affect the price its long-term customers are willing to pay. No marketing costs are incurred, so the price of $19/unit is not appropriate. But the $11/unit price offered is $1.00 less than the full-absorption manufacturing cost of $12/unit. To decide whether or not to accept this order, based on relevant data, Surf Gear managers need to compare the expected operating income if they accept or if they reject the special order.

The capacity costs (fixed costs) are **sunk costs** and cannot be retrieved. The fixed marketing costs are also the result of market share decisions made in the past and are committed costs that can not be retrieved in the short run, whether this

EXHIBIT 11-3
Comparative Budgeted Income Statement for August, Contribution Statement Format, for Surf Gear

	Variable Costing Policy: Reject the Special Order		Variable Costing Policy: Accept the Special Order		
	Per unit	Total	Per unit	Total	Difference
Output level		30,000		35,000	5,000
Sales	$20.00	$600,000	$11.00	$655,000	$55,000 F
Costs:					
Variable costs:					
Manufacturing[a]	7.50	225,000	7.50	262,500	37,500 U
Marketing[b]	5.00	150,000	5.00	150,000	—
Total variable costs	12.50	375,000	12.50	412,500	37,500 U
Contribution margin	7.50	225,000		242,500	17,500 F
Fixed costs:					
Manufacturing[c]	5.00	150,000		150,000	—
Marketing	2.00	60,000		60,000	—
Total fixed costs	7.00	210,000		210,000	—
Operating income	$ 0.50	$ 15,000		$ 32,500	$17,500 F

[a]Variable manufacturing costs = direct materials ($6) + direct manufacturing labour ($0.50) + manufacturing overhead ($1) = $7.50

[b]No additional (incremental) variable marketing costs are incurred for the special order of 5,000 towels at a price of $11/towel.

[c]Fixed manufacturing costs = fixed direct manufacturing labour ($1.50) + manufacturing overhead ($3) = $4.50. These are unaffected by the special order.

special order is accepted or not. Finally, although there are variable marketing costs, they too are irrelevant because the special order incurs no *incremental* variable costs of marketing. The incremental costs of $7.50 per unit that Surf Gear will incur if it accepts the special order for 5,000 towels would be avoided if Surf Gear did not accept the special order.

The appropriate technique is a contribution margin and variance analysis, because it is the net outcome of *differences*, or variance, between the two alternatives that will matter to the choice. If accepting the special order is the appropriate choice then the operating income variance will be favourable. Relevant costs include only the total expected variable manufacturing (incremental) costs of $37,500, total revenue of $55,000, (5,000 × $11 per unit), and total contribution margin of $17,500 (5,000 × [($11 − $7.50]). If Surf Gear accepts the special order then expected operating income increases as indicated in Exhibit 11-3 by the favourable contribution margin variance.

OUTSOURCING—MAKE OR BUY—AND IDLE FACILITIES

Another type of output-level decision is long term in nature. This is the decision either to expand existing capacity to **insource**, and produce more output in-house, or to **outsource** the additional production externally. Another term to describe this decision is a **make/buy decision**. Kodak prefers to manufacture its own digital cameras (insourcing) but has IBM do its data processing (outsourcing). British Airways outsources almost all its activities, including reservations, food services, baggage handling, information technology, and legal services. It even leases aircraft with pilots, ground crew, and maintenance. Dell Computers must buy the Pentium chip for its personal computers from Intel (outsourcing) because it does not have the expertise and technology to make the chips itself.

Insourcing implies a strategy of **vertical integration**, which means a company grows by including as much of the production function as possible within itself, from direct materials to finished goods. The oil and gas industry is made up of the very different activities of oil and gas exploration, extraction, refining, and retailing.

Suncor, for example, is a vertically integrated company that controls all of these various activities. It explores for new raw materials, extracts them, and transports them to its own refineries where the direct materials are inputs for gasoline, home heating oil, and other petroleum products. It sells gasoline and other automotive products at its Sunoco stations.

Sometimes a company decides to protect its competitive advantage by protecting the secure supply of key inputs. For other companies, making the product in-house retains control of the product and technology. For example, to safeguard Coca-Cola's formula, the company does not outsource the manufacture of its concentrate. What are the most important factors in the make/buy decision? Surveys of company practices indicate they are quality, dependability of supplies, and cost.

Example 2: The Windsor-Essex Company manufactures a digital flat-screen television system, which includes an MP3 player with a spectacular sound system. Currently, materials-handling and setup activities occur each time a batch of MP3 players is made. Windsor-Essex produces 1,000,000 MP3 players in 2,500 batches, with 400 units in each batch. The number of batches is the cost driver for these costs. Total materials-handling costs and setup costs equal $1,750,000: fixed costs of $500,000 plus variable costs of $500 per batch [$500,000 + (2,500 batches × $500 per batch) = $1,750,000].

Windsor-Essex has decided to produce MP3 players in smaller batch sizes. Windsor-Essex's managers forecast producing the 1,000,000 MP3 players next year in 5,000 batches of 200 units per batch. Through continuous improvement, the company expects to reduce variable costs for materials handling and setup to $300 per batch. No other changes in variable cost per unit or fixed costs are forecast.

Another manufacturer offers to sell Windsor-Essex 1,000,000 MP3 players next year for $16 per unit on as flexible a delivery schedule as Windsor-Essex wants. Assume that financial factors will be the basis of this make/buy decision. Should Windsor-Essex make or buy the MP3 players?

Columns 3 and 4 of Exhibit 11-4 summarize these data and a decision analysis of the expected operating income from both alternatives. Materials-handling and setup costs are expected to increase, even with no change in total production quantity. That's because these costs will vary with the number of batches, not the number of units produced. Total materials-handling costs and setup costs are expected to be $2,000,000 [$500,000 + (5,000 batches × the cost per batch of $300)]. Windsor-Essex expects fixed manufacturing overhead costs to remain the same.

EXHIBIT 11-4
Windsor-Essex Analyses of Historical and Expected Values

Windsor-Essex	Historical	Expected	Total Historical	Total Expected
Output Q	1,000,000	1,000,000		
Batches	2,500	5,000		
Units per batch	400	200		
MOH per batch	$ 500.00	$ 300.00		
Direct materials	$ 9.00	$9.00	$ 9,000,000	$ 9,000,000
DMLH	2.40	2.40	2,400,000	2,400,000
VMOH power, utilities	1.60	1.60	1,600,000	1,600,000
FMOH setup and materials*	1.75	2.00	1,750,000	2,000,000
FMOH equipment	3.00	3.00	3,000,000	3,000,000
Total cost per unit	$ 17.75	$ 18.00	$17,750,000	$18,000,000

*The cost object is setups and these vary with the total batches not the total units produced. The expected unit cost per batch for setup and materials handling will decrease to $300 from $500 but expected total batches increases to 5,000. Total fixed cost remains at $500,000 for MOH setup and materials handling.

   Total MOH becomes = $500,000 + 5,000 × $300
                     = $2,000,000

MOH per unit, expected = $2.00

The expected manufacturing cost per unit for next year is $18. At first glance, it appears that the company should buy the MP3 players because the expected $18 per-unit cost of making the MP3 player is more than the $16 per unit to buy it. But often a make/buy decision is not quite so obvious. A good decision depends on the answer to the question "What is the difference in *relevant costs* between the alternatives?" Assume:

◆ The capacity now used to make the MP3 players *will become idle* next year if the MP3 players are purchased.
◆ The $3,000,000 of fixed manufacturing overhead will continue to be incurred next year, regardless of the decision made.
◆ The $500,000 in fixed salaries to support materials handling and setup will *not be incurred* if the manufacture of MP3 players is completely shut down.

Exhibit 11-5 presents the relevant cost computations. Note that Windsor-Essex will save $1,000,000 by making the MP3 players rather than buying them from the outside supplier, so making the MP3 players is the preferred alternative. The values in Exhibit 11-5 are valid only if the released facilities remain idle. There is a different analysis needed if the MP3 player is bought from the outside supplier and the released facilities can potentially be used for other, more profitable purposes.

More generally, then, the issue or problem is how best to use available capacity, not whether to make or buy. The notation of U or F beside the difference in the final column indicates the effect on operating income. In this case, operating income would decrease by $1,000,000 if the company outsourced. We use relevance to assess which costs to consider, as noted below.

◆ Current cost data in the Historical and Forecast columns (Exhibit 11-4) play no role in the analysis in Exhibit 11-5 because for next year's make/buy decision these costs are past. Their usefulness lies in helping to forecast expected future costs.

EXHIBIT 11-5
Relevant (Incremental) Items for Make/Buy Decision for MP3 Players at Windsor-Essex

Insource (Make)	Historical	Forecast		
Fixed setup and materials handling	$ 500,000	$500,000	Output Q =	1,000,000
Variable batch setup and materials handling	$ 500	$ 300	Batches =	5,000
Total setup and materials handling[a]	$1,750,000	$2,000,000	Units per batch	200

Outsource (Buy)	Quantity (Q)	Unit Price	Total Cost
Purchase	1,000,000	$16.00	$16,000,000

	Total Relevant Costs: Make		Total Relevant Costs: Buy		
Total units	1,000,000				
	Per unit	Total	Per unit	Total	Difference
Purchase (buy)	—	—	$16.00	$16,000,000	$16,000,000 U
Direct materials (make)	$ 9.00	$ 9,000,000	—	—	9,000,000 F
Direct labour (make)	2.40	$ 2,400,000	—	—	2,400,000 F
Direct MOH (make)	1.60	$ 1,600,000	—	—	1,600,000 F
Mixed handling and setup	2.00	$ 2,000,000	—	—	2,000,000 F
Totals[b]	$15.00	$15,000,000	$16.00	$16,000,000	$ 1,000,000 U

[a]Total setup and materials handling (Historical = $500,000 + $500/batch × 2,500 batches), Forecast = $500,000 + $300/batch × 5,000 batches).
[b]The $3,000,000 of plant-lease, insurance, and administration costs could be included under both alternatives. But these costs remain unchanged irrespective of the decision that is made. Therefore they are not relevant costs. One reason managers may prefer to see this $3,000,000 is to have a complete set of costs to be reassured of those that remain unchanged between the alternatives.

◆ Exhibit 11-5 shows $2,000,000 of future materials-handling and setup costs under the make alternative but not under the buy alternative. Buying MP3 players rather than manufacturing them will eliminate $2,000,000 in future variable costs per batch and avoidable fixed costs of nonproductive idle capacity incurred during setups. The $2,000,000 represents future costs that differ between the alternatives; it is relevant to the make/buy decision.

◆ Exhibit 11-5 excludes the $3,000,000 of plant-lease, insurance, and administration costs under both alternatives. These future fixed manufacturing overhead costs will not differ between the alternatives; they are irrelevant.

In this example, the incremental cost of making the MP3 players is the additional full-absorption cost of $15,000,000 that Windsor-Essex will incur if it decides to manufacture rather than outsource the players. Similarly, the incremental cost of outsourcing the MP3 players is the additional variable cost of $16,000,000 that Windsor-Essex will incur from the buy decision. A *differential cost* is the difference in total cost between two alternatives. In Exhibit 11-5, the differential cost ($16,000,000 − $15,000,000) is $1,000,000 higher. Note that *incremental* and *differential cost* are sometimes used interchangably in practice. When these terms are used, ensure you know what they mean.

CONCEPTS IN ACTION—STRATEGY

The Changing Benefits and Costs of "Offshoring"

The rapidly evolving practice of "offshoring" differs from outsourcing. Outsourcing usually means relocating routine production and customer service functions to a country where labour is very cheap relative to Canadian salaries. Latin America, India, China, and the Phillipines require a small fraction of what labourers obtain for the same jobs in North America and Europe.

Offshoring is the transfer of entire production sites from one country to another, then importing the output for use in the home country. The practice is not new. It indicates that countries that used to specialize in the value chain for specific products now specialize in specific business functions within the value chain. Today many strategic service functions are located offshore. Companies such as British Airways offshore their software research and development, accounting, and information systems support. Canada itself is a strong competitor and benefits from offshoring by U.S. companies. Highly repetitive work such as accounting, predictable work such as customer service, and work that can be segmented such as software development are candidates for offshoring.

Economic studies have concluded that countries such as Canada, the U.S., and the European Union will benefit from this stimulus to their economies. But this is an extremely controversial conclusion. In 2010, when IBM laid off over 10,000 workers in the U.S., the union blamed offshoring for the increase in U.S. unemployment. But the shifting of work away from math-based rules to custom work that requires deep local knowledge creates natural limits to offshoring. IBM's work with Center Point Energy, a Texas utility, to install computerized meter-readers and a "smart" grid could not be outsourced. The team had to become familiar with and integrate the new technology with local power and telecommunications lines.

McKinsey & Company, a consulting firm, has noted that the growing complexity of all economic activity has driven the phenomenon of increasing specialization of labour. For example, globalization requires far more complex logistics to assemble all essential resources where and when they are required. Global supply-chain managers must be multilingual and familiar with a wide variety of technologies to effectively coordinate resource deliveries.

Sources: http://www2parl.gc.ca/content/lop/researchpublications/prb0459-e.htm, http://www.careerplanner.com/Career-Articles/Offshoring-jobs.cfm, http://www.mckinsey.com/mgi/reports/pdf/changing_fortunes/Changing_fortunes_ofAmericas_workforce.pdf, http://www.computerworld.com/s/article/9164379/IBM_layoffs_blamed_on_offshoring, all accessed April 7, 2011; S. Lohr, "At IBM, A Smarter Way to Outsource," *The New York Times*, July 5, 2007.

OPPORTUNITY COST AND BOOK VALUE—ONE RELEVANT, ONE IRRELEVANT

3 Explain why opportunity cost is relevant and book value is irrelevant in decision making.

The calculations in Exhibit 11-5 assumed that the capacity currently used to make MP3 players will remain idle if Windsor-Essex purchases the parts from the outside manufacturer. But what if the released capacity could be used for other, more profitable purposes? Now the problem for Windsor-Essex managers is how best to use available production capacity.

Deciding to use a resource in a particular way causes a manager to give up the opportunity to use the resource in alternative ways. The lost opportunity is a cost that the manager must take into account when making a decision. However, you will never find a general ledger account called Opportunity Costs. In financial accounting a transaction must occur, and since rejected alternatives do not produce transactions they are not recorded. **Opportunity cost** is a management accounting concept of costs relevant to capacity utilization decisions.

Example 3: Suppose that if Windsor-Essex decides to buy the MP3 players for its HDTVs from the outside supplier, then the best use of the capacity that becomes available is to produce 500,000 standalone converters that convert input from low-definition DVDs and TV cable into a viewing format that fills the screen. Assume the quantity Q produced is completely sold out at a unit sales price of $16.00. The decision criterion will be determined by the lowest relevant cost. In Exhibit 11-6, Aléxandre Ouelette, the management accountant, summarizes the following expected relevant cost changes based on information from the managers. Which one of the following three alternatives should Windsor-Essex choose?

1. Make MP3 players and do not make HD converters.

2. Buy MP3 players and do not make HD converters.

3. Buy MP3 players and make HD converters.

Exhibit 11-6, Panel A, summarizes the "total-alternatives" approach—the incremental expected future costs and expected future revenue for all alternatives. Alternative 3, buying MP3 players and using the available capacity to make and sell HD converters, is the preferred alternative because the total relevant cost is lowest in the third column of Panel A. The forgone incremental operating income from selling HD converters is treated as a reduction to the incremental cost of alternative 3. In Panel B it is treated as the forgone cost savings that add to total relevant costs. In the final column of Panel B, where the HD converters are sold, there are no added costs because we have indeed sold these converters. The lowest cost is still alternative 3, regardless of how the analysis is completed.

The key difference between Windsor-Essex and Surf Gear is that Windsor-Essex can put its idle capacity to long-term use. If Windsor-Essex fails to do so it incurs the opportunity cost of not using this idle capacity. Surf Gear had no alternative use for its idle capacity.

Panel B highlights the idea that when capacity is constrained, the relevant revenue and costs of any alternative *must* include the opportunity cost. But, when more than two alternatives are being considered simultaneously, it is generally easier to use the total-alternatives approach. Recognizing the opportunity cost of $2,500,000 always leads to the conclusion that it is preferable to buy the MP3 players.

Suppose Windsor-Essex has sufficient capacity to make HD converters even if it makes MP3 players. In this case, there is a fourth alternative: make MP3 players *and* make HD converters. There is no opportunity cost of making MP3 players because there is enough capacity to make both. The relevant costs are $15,000,000 (incremental costs of $15,000,000 plus opportunity cost of $0). Under these conditions, Windsor-Essex would prefer to make the MP3 players rather than buy them, and also make HD converters.

Besides quantitative considerations, the make/buy decision should consider strategic and qualitative factors as well. If Windsor-Essex decides to buy MP3 players from an outside supplier and make the HD converters, it should consider factors

EXHIBIT 11-6
Total-Alternatives Approach and Opportunity-Cost Approach to Make/Buy Decisions for Windsor-Essex Company

	Forecast per Unit		Totals
Q HD converters produced/sold	500,000		
Sales price per unit		$16.00	$8,000,000
DM	$ 6.80		
DMLH	$ 2.00		
VMOH	$ 1.20		
Materials handling and setup	1.00		
Total cost per unit		$11.00	$5,500,000
Contribution margin		$ 5.00	$2,500,000

Alternatives for Windsor-Essex: Make or Buy

	PANEL A: Incremental-Cost Approach			PANEL B: Opportunity-Cost Approach		
Relevant items	Make MP3s Do not make HD converters	Buy MP3s Do not make HD converters	Buy MP3s Make HD converters	Make MP3s Do not make HD converters	Buy MP3s Do not make HD converters	Buy MP3s Make HD converters
All incremental future costs*	$15,000,000	$16,000,000	$16,000,000	$15,000,000	$16,000,000	$16,000,000
Forgone future operating income from not selling HD converters	—	—	(2,500,000)	2,500,000	2,500,000	—
Total relevant costs	$15,000,000	$16,000,000	$13,500,000	$17,500,000	$18,500,000	$16,000,000

The $3,000,000 in total fixed costs are sunk costs and will not change the effect of ± $2,500,000 on operating income.

*The differences in costs across the Panel A columns are the same as those of Panel B. We can frame this decision as how to minimize total relevant costs. To buy MP3s and use the capacity to make HD converters, is to lower total relevant costs by $2,500,000. We have an extra contribution of $2,500,000 under this alternative to pay off our remaining total fixed costs.

such as the supplier's reputation for quality and timely delivery. This is a supply-chain management skill. Other factors include process improvements and strategic factors such as agility, product differentiation, and cost leadership.

CARRYING COSTS OF INVENTORY

What if Windsor-Essex will pay cash for the MP3 players it buys? Assume that the purchases of inventory will be used uniformly each month and that all inventory is used prior to the next payment for a new purchase when calculating the average cost of inventory. Based on the information below, which of the two purchasing alternatives is more economical?

Annual estimated MP3 player requirements for next year	1,000,000 units
Cost per unit when each purchase is equal to 10,000 units	$ 16.00
Cost per unit when each purchase is equal to or greater than 500,000 units; $16 minus 1% discount	$ 15.84
Cost of a purchase order	$ 500.00

Alternatives under consideration:

  A. Make 100 purchases of 10,000 units each during the next year
  B. Make 2 purchases of 500,000 units each during the next year

Average investment in inventory:

A. *(10,000 units × $16.00 per unit)/2	$ 80,000
B. *(500,000 units × $15.84 per unit)/2	$3,960,000
Annual rate of return if the cash is invested elsewhere (e.g., bonds or shares) at the same level of risk as the investment in inventory	9.0%

*The example assumes that MP3 player purchases will be used up uniformly throughout the year. The average investment in inventory during the year is the cost of inventory when a purchase is received plus the cost of inventory just prior to the delivery of the next purchase (in this example zero) divided by 2.

The following table presents two alternatives:

	Alternative A: Make 100 Purchases of 10,000 Units Each During the Year (1)	Alternative B: Make 2 Purchases of 500,000 Units Each During the Year (2)	Difference (3) = (1) − (2)
Annual purchase-order costs (100 purchase orders × $500/purchase order; 2 purchase orders × $500/ purchase order	$ 50,000	$ 1,000	$ 49,000
Annual purchase costs (1,000,000 units × $16.00/unit; 1,000,000 × $15.84/unit)	16,000,000	15,840,000	160,000
Annual rate of return that could be earned if investment in inventory were invested elsewhere at the same level of risk (opportunity cost) (0.09 × $80,000; 0.09 × $3,960,000)	7,200	356,400	(349,200)
Relevant costs	$16,057,200	$16,197,400	$(140,200)

The opportunity cost of holding inventory is the income forgone by tying up money in inventory and not investing it elsewhere. The opportunity cost would not be recorded in the accounting system because, once the alternative of investing money elsewhere is rejected, there are no transactions related to this alternative to record. On the basis of the costs recorded in the accounting system (purchase-order costs and purchase costs), Windsor-Essex would erroneously conclude that making two purchases of 500,000 units each is the least costly alternative.

Column 3, however, indicates that, consistent with the trends toward holding smaller inventories, purchasing smaller quantities of 10,000 units 100 times a year is preferred to purchasing 500,000 units twice during the year. The lower opportunity cost of holding smaller inventory exceeds the higher purchase and ordering costs. If the opportunity cost of money tied up in inventory were greater than 9% per year, or if other incremental benefits of holding lower inventory were considered—such as lower insurance, materials-handling, storage, obsolescence, and breakage costs—making 100 purchases would be even more economical.

STRATEGIC AND QUALITATIVE FACTORS

Strategic and qualitative factors also affect outsourcing decisions. For example, Windsor-Essex may prefer to manufacture MP3 players in-house to retain control over the design, quality, reliability, and delivery schedules of the MP3 players it uses in its television systems. Conversely, despite the cost advantages of insourcing, Windsor-Essex may prefer to outsource, become a smaller and leaner organization, and focus on areas of its core competencies—the manufacture and sale of IID components. Advertising companies, such as J. Walter Thompson, do only the creative and planning aspects of advertising (their core competencies), and they outsource production activities, such as film, photography, and illustration.

Of course, offshoring and outsourcing are not without risk.[1] As a company's dependence on its suppliers increases, suppliers could increase prices and let quality and delivery performance slip. For example, raw materials outsourced for manufacturing of pet food was found to be contaminated with melamine. This chemical is toxic to humans and animals because it causes kidney failure if consumed in large enough doses. It was the autopsies of deceased pets in North America that revealed the contamination. These suppliers subsequently were found to have exported contaminated powdered raw milk. The problem was discovered when infants fell ill and some died in the exporting country.

[1]Outsourcing is usually only one business function in the value chain, while offshoring can refer to the entire set of business functions in the value chain.

To minimize risks, companies generally enter into long-term contracts with their suppliers that specify costs, quality, and delivery schedules. Intelligent managers will build close partnerships or alliances with a few key suppliers, teaming with suppliers on design and manufacturing decisions, and building a culture of and commitment to quality and timely delivery. Toyota goes so far as to send its own engineers to improve suppliers' processes.

Offshoring and outsourcing decisions invariably have a long-run horizon in which the financial costs and benefits of outsourcing become more uncertain. Almost always, strategic and qualitative factors such as those described here become important determinants of the outsourcing decision. Weighing all these factors requires the exercise of considerable management judgment and care.

IRRELEVANCE OF BOOK VALUE IN EQUIPMENT REPLACEMENT DECISIONS

The illustrations in this chapter have shown that expected future costs that do not differ among alternatives are irrelevant. Now we return to the idea that all past costs are irrelevant. Consider an example of equipment replacement. The irrelevant cost illustrated here is the **book value** (original cost minus accumulated amortization) of the existing equipment. Assume that the Tormart Company is considering replacing a metal-cutting machine for aircraft parts with a more technically advanced model. The new machine has an automatic quality-testing capability and is more efficient than the old machine. The new machine, however, has a shorter life. The Tormart Company uses the straight-line amortization method. Sales of aircraft parts ($1.1 million per year) will be unaffected by the replacement decision. Summary data on the existing machine and the replacement machine are as follows:

	Existing Machine	Replacement Machine
Original cost	$1,000,000	$600,000
Useful life	5 years	2 years
Current age	3 years	0 years
Remaining useful life	2 years	2 years
Accumulated amortization	$600,000	Not acquired yet
Book value	$400,000	Not acquired yet
Current disposal value (in cash)	$40,000	Not acquired yet
Terminal disposal value (in cash 2 years from now)	$0	$0
Annual operating costs (maintenance, energy, repairs, coolants, and so on)	$800,000	$460,000

To focus on the main concept of relevance, we ignore the time value of money in this illustration.

Exhibit 11-7 presents a cost comparison of the two machines. Some managers would not replace the old machine because it would entail recognizing a $360,000 "loss on disposal" ($400,000 book value minus $40,000 current disposal price); retention would allow spreading the $400,000 book value over the next two years in the form of "amortization expense" (a term more appealing than "loss on disposal").

We can apply our definition of relevance to four commonly encountered items in equipment replacement decisions such as the one facing the Tormart Company:

1. *Book value of old machine.* Irrelevant—it is a past (historical) cost. All past costs are "down the drain." Nothing can change what has already been spent or what has already happened.

2. *Current disposal price of old machine.* Relevant—it is an expected future cash inflow that differs between alternatives.

3. *Gain or loss on disposal.* This is the algebraic difference between items 1 and 2. It is a meaningless combination blurring the distinction between the irrelevant book value and the relevant disposal price. Each item should be considered separately.

4. *Cost of new machine.* Relevant—it is an expected future cash outflow that will differ between alternatives.

EXHIBIT 11-7

Cost Comparison—Replacement of Machinery, Including Relevant and Irrelevant Items for the Tormart Company

	Two Years Together		
	Keep	Replace	Difference
Sales	$2,200,000	$2,200,000	—
Operating costs:			
Cash operating costs	1,600,000	920,000	$680,000
Old machine book value:			
Periodic writeoff as amortization	400,000	—	—
or Lump sum writeoff	—	400,000*	
Current disposal price of old machine	—	(40,000)*	40,000
New machine cost, written off periodically as amortization	—	600,000	(600,000)
Total operating costs	2,000,000	1,880,000	120,000
Operating income	$ 200,000	$ 320,000	$120,000

*In a formal income statement, these two items would be combined as "loss on disposal of machine" of $360,000.

The difference column in Exhibit 11-7 shows that the book value of the old machine is not an element of difference between alternatives and could be completely ignored for decision-making purposes. No matter what the timing of the charge against revenue, the amount charged is still $400,000 regardless of the alternative chosen because it is a past (historical) cost. The advantage of replacing is $120,000 for the two years together.

In either event, the unamortized cost will be written off with the same ultimate effect on operating income. The $400,000 enters into the income statement either as a $400,000 offset against the $40,000 proceeds to obtain the $360,000 loss on disposal in the current year, or as $200,000 amortization in each of the next two years. But how it appears in the income statement is irrelevant to the replacement decision. In contrast, the $600,000 cost of the new machine is relevant because it can be avoided by deciding not to replace.

In our example, old equipment has a book value of $400,000 and a current disposal price of $40,000. What are the sunk costs in this case? The entire $400,000 is sunk because it represents an outlay made in the past that cannot be changed. Past costs and sunk costs are synonyms.

Exhibit 11-8 concentrates on relevant items only. Note that the same answer (the $120,000 net difference) will be obtained even though the book value is completely omitted from the calculations. The only relevant items are the cash operating costs, the disposal price of the old machine, and the cost of the new machine (represented as amortization in Exhibit 11-8).

EXHIBIT 11-8

Cost Comparison—Replacement of Machinery, Relevant Items Only for the Tormart Company

	Two Years Together		
	Keep	Replace	Difference
Cash operating costs	$1,600,000	$ 920,000	$680,000
Current disposal price of old machine	—	(40,000)	40,000
New machine, written off periodically as amortization	—	600,000	(600,000)
Total relevant costs	$1,600,000	$1,480,000	$120,000

Decision makers vary in their preference between the formats presented in Exhibits 11-7 and 11-8. Some prefer the format used in Exhibit 11-7 because it illustrates why some items are irrelevant to the decision. Other managers prefer the format used in Exhibit 11-8, because it is concise.

PRODUCT MIX DECISIONS

Companies with capacity constraints, such as Windsor-Essex, must decide which products to make and in what quantities to maximize operating profit. When a multiple-product plant operates at full capacity, managers must choose how to use the available capacity and which products to emphasize. These decisions frequently have a short-run focus. How to minimize cost is a different objective that may dominate the product mix decision. For example, General Mills must continually adapt the mix of its different products to short-run fluctuations in materials costs, selling prices, and demand. Throughout this section, we assume that as short-run changes in product mix occur, the only costs that change are those that are variable with respect to the number of units produced (and sold).

Analysis of individual product contribution margins provides insight into the product mix that maximizes operating income. This is the same approach taken in Chapter 3. Consider Power Engines, a company that manufactures engines for a broad range of commercial and consumer products. At its Calgary, Alberta, plant, it assembles two engines—a snowmobile engine and a boat engine. Information about these products is as follows:

	Snowmobile Engine	Boat Engine
Selling price	$800	$1,000
Variable costs per unit	560	625
Contribution margin per unit	$240	$ 375

At first glance, boat engines appear more profitable than snowmobile engines. The product to be emphasized, however, is not necessarily the product with the higher individual contribution margin per unit. Rather, managers should aim for the *highest contribution margin per unit of the constraining factor*—that is, the scarce, limiting, or critical factor. The constraining factor restricts or limits the production or sale of a given product. (See also Chapter 19 on the theory of constraints.)

Assume that only 600 machine hours are available daily for assembling engines. Additional capacity cannot be obtained in the short run. Power Engines can sell as many engines as it produces. The constraining factor, then, is machine-hours. It takes two machine-hours to produce one snowmobile engine and five machine-hours to produce one boat engine.

	Snowmobile Engine	Boat Engine
Contribution margin per engine	$240	$375
Machine-hours required to produce one engine	2 machine-hours	5 machine-hours
Contribution margin per machine-hour (240 ÷ 2; 375 ÷ 5)	$120	$75
Total contribution margin for 600 machine-hours ($120 × 600; $75 × 600)	$72,000	$45,000

Producing snowmobile engines contributes more contribution margin per machine-hour, which is the constraining factor in this example. Therefore, choosing to emphasize snowmobile engines is the correct decision. Other considerations could include the availability of direct materials, components, or skilled labour, as well as financial and sales considerations. In a retail department store, the constraining factor may be linear metres of display space. The greatest possible contribution margin per unit of the constraining factor yields the maximum operating income.

As you can imagine, in many cases a manufacturer or retailer must meet the challenge of trying to maximize total operating income for a variety of products, each with more than one constraining factor. The problem of formulating the most profitable production schedules and the most profitable product mix is essentially that of maximizing the total contribution margin in the face of many constraints. Optimization techniques, such as the linear programming technique discussed below, help solve these complicated problems.

Finally, there is the question of managing the bottleneck constraint to increase output and, therefore, contribution margin:

♦ Can the available machine-hours for assembling engines be increased beyond 600—for example, by reducing idle time?
♦ Can the time needed to assemble each snowmobile engine (two machine-hours) and each boat engine (five machine-hours) be reduced—for example, by reducing setup time and processing time of assembly?
♦ Can quality be improved so that constrained capacity is used to produce only good units rather than some good and some defective units? Can some of the assembly operations be outsourced to allow more engines to be built?

Implementing any of these options will likely require Power Engines to incur incremental costs. Power Engines will implement only those options whose benefits of higher contribution margins exceed the costs. Instructors and students who, at this point, want to explore these issues in more detail can go to the section in Chapter 19 titled "Theory of Constraints and Throughput Contribution Analysis" (pp. 776–781) and then return to this chapter without any loss of continuity.

LINEAR PROGRAMMING

Linear programming (LP) is an optimization technique used to maximize total contribution margin (the objective function) given multiple constraints. **Optimization techniques** are ways to find the best answer using a mathematical model. LP models typically assume that all costs can be classified as either variable or fixed with respect to a single driver (units of output). LP models also require particular assumptions to hold. When these assumptions fail, other decision models should be considered.[2]

Consider again the example of Power Engines. Suppose that both the snowmobile and boat engines must be tested on a very expensive machine before they are shipped to customers. The available testing machine time is limited. Production data are as follows:

Department	Available Daily Capacity in Hours	Use of Capacity in Hours per Unit of Product		Daily Maximum Production in Units	
		Snowmobile Engine	Boat Engine	Snowmobile Engine	Boat Engine
Assembly	600 machine-hours	2.0	5.0	300*	120
Testing	120 testing-hours	1.0	0.5	120	240

*For example, 600 machine-hours ÷ 2.0 machine-hours per snowmobile engine = 300, the maximum number of snowmobile engines that the assembly department can make if it works exclusively on snowmobile engines.

Exhibit 11-9 summarizes these and other relevant data. Note that snowmobile engines have a contribution margin of $240 and that boat engines have a contribution margin of $375. Material shortages for boat engines will limit production to 110 boat engines per day. How many engines of each type should be produced daily to maximize operating income?

Steps in Solving an LP Problem   We use the data in Exhibit 11-9 to illustrate the three steps in solving an LP problem. Throughout this discussion, S equals the number of units of snowmobiles produced, and B equals the number of units of boat engines produced.

[2]Other decision models are described in G. Eppen, F. Gould, and C. Schmidt, *Quantitative Concepts for Management* (Englewood Cliffs, N.J.: Prentice-Hall, 1991) and S. Nahmias, *Production and Operations Analysis* (Homewood, Ill.: Irwin, 1993).

EXHIBIT 11-9
Operating Data for Power Engines

| | Department Capacity (per Day) in Product Units | | | Variable Cost per Unit | Contribution Margin per Unit |
Product	Assembly	Testing	Selling Price		
Only snowmobile engines	300	120	$ 800	$560	$240
Only boat engines	120	240	$1,000	$625	$375

◆ **Step 1: Determine the objective.** The **objective function** of a linear program expresses the objective or goal to be maximized (for example, operating income) or minimized (for example, operating costs). In our example, the objective is to find the combination of products that maximizes total contribution margin in the short run. Fixed costs remain the same regardless of the product mix chosen and are therefore irrelevant. The linear function expressing the objective for the total contribution margin (TCM) is:

$$TCM = \$240S + \$375B$$

◆ **Step 2: Specify the constraints.** A **constraint** is a mathematical inequality or equality that must be satisfied by the variables in a mathematical model. The following linear inequalities depict the relationships in our example:

Assembly department constraint	$2S + 5B \le 600$
Testing department constraint	$1S + 0.5B \le 120$
Material shortage constraint for boat engines	$B \le 110$
Negative production is impossible	$S \ge 0$ and $B \ge 0$

The three solid lines on the graph in Exhibit 11-10 show the existing constraints for assembly and testing and the material shortage constraint.[3] A line means the constraint never appears with an exponent or square root. If it did, then the line would curve and the relationship would be curvilinear. In Exhibit 11-10,

EXHIBIT 11-10
Linear Programming—Graphic Solution for Power Engines

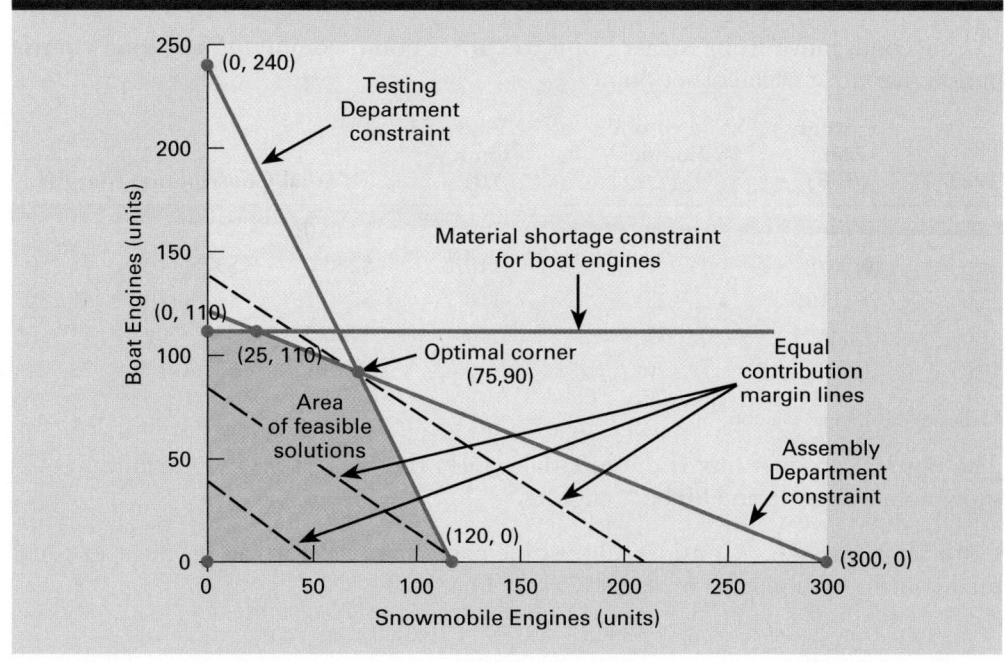

[3]For an example of how the lines are plotted in Exhibit 11-10, use equal signs instead of inequality signs and assume for the assembly department that $B = 0$; then $S = 300$ (600 machine-hours ÷ 2 machine-hours per snowmobile engine). Assume that $S = 0$; then $B = 120$ (600 machine-hours ÷ 5 machine-hours per boat engine). Connect those two points with a straight line.

all the constraints are labelled and appear as straight lines. The coefficients of the constraints are often called *technical coefficients*. For example, in the assembly department, the technical coefficient is two machine-hours for snowmobile engines and five machine-hours for boat engines.

The feasible alternatives are those combinations of quantities of snowmobile engines and boat engines that satisfy all the constraining factors. The shaded "Area of feasible solutions" in Exhibit 11-10 shows the boundaries of those product combinations that are feasible, or technically possible.

◆ **Step 3: Compute the optimal solution.** We present two approaches for finding the optimal solution: the trial-and-error approach and the graphic approach. These approaches are easy to use in our example, because there are only two variables in the objective function and a small number of constraints. An understanding of these two approaches provides insight into LP modelling. In most real-world LP applications, however, managers use computer software packages to calculate the optimal solution.[4]

Trial-and-Error Approach   The optimal solution can be found by working with the coordinates of the corners of the area of feasible solutions. The approach is simple. First, select any set of corner points and compute the total contribution margin. Five corner points appear in Exhibit 11-10. It is helpful to use simultaneous equations to obtain the exact graph coordinates. To illustrate, the point ($S = 75$, $B = 90$) can be derived by solving the two pertinent constraint inequalities as simultaneous equations:

$$2S + 5B = 600 \tag{1}$$
$$1S + 0.5B = 120 \tag{2}$$

Multiplying (2) by 2.0, we get $\quad\quad 2S + 1B = 240 \tag{3}$

Subtracting (3) from (1) $\quad\quad\quad\quad 4B = 360$

Therefore $\quad\quad\quad\quad\quad\quad\quad\quad B = 360 \div 4 = 90$

Substituting B in (2) $\quad\quad 1S + 0.5(90) = 120$

$$S = 120 - 45 = 75$$

Given $S = 75$ and $B = 90$, TCM = $\$240(75) + \$375(90) = \$51,750$.

Second, move from corner point to corner point, computing the total contribution margin at each corner point:

Trial	Corner Point (S, B)	Snowmobile Engines (S)	Boat Engines (B)	Total Contribution Margin
1	(0, 0)	0	0	$\$240(0)\quad + \$375(0)\quad = \$\quad\quad 0$
2	(0, 110)	0	110	$\$240(0)\quad + \$375(110) = \quad 41,250$
3	(25, 110)	25	110	$\$240(25) + \$375(110) = \quad 47,250$
4	(75, 90)	75	90	$\$240(75) + \$375(90)\quad = \quad 51,750*$
5	(120, 0)	120	0	$\$240(120) + \$375(0)\quad = \quad 28,800$

*Indicates the optimal solution

The optimal product mix is the mix that yields the highest total contribution—75 snowmobile engines and 90 boat engines.

Graphic Approach   Consider all possible combinations that will produce an equal total contribution margin of, say, $\$12,000$. That is,

$$\$240S + \$375B = \$12,000$$

[4]Although the trial-and-error and graphic approaches can be useful for two or possibly three variables, they are impractical when many variables exist. One alternative is to use the Solver function in Excel. Please refer to the online tutorial for a full presentation of how to input data into the Solver menus to minimize cost.

This set of $12,000 contribution margins is a straight dashed line in Exhibit 11-10 through ($S = 50, B = 0$) and ($S = 0, B = 32$). Other equal total contribution margins can be represented by lines parallel to this one. In Exhibit 11-10, we show three dashed lines. The equal total contribution margins increase as the lines get farther from the origin because lines drawn farther from the origin represent more sales of both snowmobile and boat engines.

The optimal line is the one farthest from the origin but still passing through a point in the area of feasible solutions. This line represents the highest contribution margin. The optimal solution is the point at the corner ($S = 75, B = 90$). This solution will become apparent if you put a ruler on the graph and move it outward from the origin and parallel with the $12,000 line. The idea is to move the ruler as far away from the origin as possible (that is, to increase the total contribution margin) without leaving the area of feasible solutions. In general, the optimal solution in a maximization problem lies at the corner where the dashed line intersects an extreme point of the area of feasible solutions. Moving the ruler out any farther puts it outside the feasible region.

The key to the optimal solution is exchanging a given contribution margin per unit of scarce resource for some other contribution margin per unit of scarce resource. Examine Exhibit 11-10 and consider moving from corner ($S = 25, B = 110$) to corner ($S = 75, B = 90$). In the assembly department, each machine-hour devoted to 1 unit of boat engines (B) may be given up (sacrificed or traded) for 2.5 units of snowmobile engines (S) (5 hours required for 1 boat engine, 2 hours required for 1 snowmobile engine). Will this exchange add to profitability? Yes, as shown here:

Total contribution margin at ($S = 25, B = 110$): $240 × 25 + $375 × 110		$47,250
Added contribution margin from product S by moving to corner ($S = 75, B = 90$): (75 − 25) × $240	$12,000	
Lost contribution margin from product B by moving to corner ($S = 75, B = 90$): (110 − 90) × $375	(7,500)	
Net additional contribution margin		4,500
Total contribution margin at ($S = 75, B = 90$): $240 × 75 + $375 × 90		$51,750

As we move from corner ($S = 25, B = 110$) to corner ($S = 75, B = 90$), we are contending with the assembly department constraint. In this department, there is a net advantage of trading 1 unit of B for 2.5 units of S. At corner ($S = 25, B = 110$), the testing department constraint comes into effect. Should we move to corner ($S = 120, B = 0$) along the testing department constraint? No. An analysis (not presented) similar to the one here will show that such a move is not worthwhile.

SENSITIVITY ANALYSIS

Sensitivity analysis was discussed in Chapter 3 in a different context. In the Power Engines example, large changes in the contribution margin per unit may not affect the optimal product mix if there are no nearby corner points. What are the implications of uncertainty about the accounting or technical coefficients used in the LP model? Changes in coefficients affect the slope of the objective function (the equal contribution margin lines) or the area of feasible solutions. Consider how a change in the contribution margin of snowmobile engines from $240 to $300 per unit might affect the optimal solution. Assume the contribution margin for boat engines remains unchanged at $375 per unit. The revised objective function will be:

$$\text{TCM} = \$300S + \$375B$$

Using the trial-and-error approach, calculate the total contribution margin for each of the five corner points described in the table on page 446. The optimal solution is still ($S = 75, B = 90$).

Now suppose the contribution margin of snowmobile engines is lower than $240 per unit. By repeating the preceding steps, you will find that the optimal solution will not change so long as the contribution margin of the snowmobile engine does not fall below $150. *Big changes in the contribution margin per unit of snowmobile engines have no effect on the optimal solution.*

What happens if the contribution margin falls below $150? The optimal solution will then shift to the corner ($S = 25$, $B = 110$). Snowmobile engines now generate so little contribution margin per unit that Power Engines will choose to shift its mix in favour of boat engines.

USING EXCEL SOLVER

One of the benefits of technology is that far more complex profit maximization and cost minimization problems can be readily solved. Understanding the technique of linear programming is fundamental to implementing the technology available in Excel called Solver. This program is typically found in newer editions of Excel by clicking on the MS Office logo in the top left corner of the spreadsheet, selecting Excel options from the bottom of the dropdown menu and then the Add-Ins from the pop-up menu. Solver appears on the list just under the Analysis ToolPak. Click on Solver and the installation usually takes seconds.

Campbell and Juryn Ltd. (CJL) operate two paper mills: Mill 1 (M1) with a maximum capacity of 20,000 tonnes and Mill 2 (M2) with a maximum capacity of 30,000 tonnes. Their three customers, Newspaper A (NA), Newspaper B (NB), and Newspaper C (NC) demand 12,000, 20,000, and 16,000 tonnes of newsprint respectively. At any point in this highly competitive market, should CJL either fail to deliver or boost its price, the Newspapers A, B, and C will simply switch suppliers.

To ship from Mill 1 to Newspaper A costs $20/tonne, to Newspaper B costs $28/tonne, and to Newspaper C costs $40/tonne. In comparison, it costs $40/tonne to ship from Mill 2 to NA, $36/tonne to ship to NB, and $32/tonne to ship to NC. Until now CJL simply shipped newsprint to customers from either mill that could supply it.

Mr. Janz, the controller of CJL, identified a problem. In the last month the cost of shipping newsprint to customers was $1,512,000. CJL could not continue to be profitable unless the company either increased the cost per tonne or reduced the total monthly costs of shipping. If CJL tried to increase the cost per tonne, the newspapers would simply find a new supplier, so the executive team's problem is how to reduce the cost of transportation. Mr. Janz could use a manual method of linear programming or enter the linear program into an Excel spreadsheet and use Solver. He must use the data he has gathered from the MIS and set up a spreadsheet in Excel in a way suitable to use Solver to predict the least-cost solution. Either way, Mr. Janz is trying to determine how much should be shipped from each mill to each newspaper customer to minimize the total cost of shipments.

Assume M1NA is the tonnes of newsprint shipped from Mill 1 to Newspaper A, so the cost will be $20(M1NA). From M1 to NB the costs will be $28(M1NB), and from M1 to NC will be $40(M1NC). Similarly the costs to ship from Mill 2 to Newspaper A will be $40(M2NA). From M2 to NB the costs will be $36(M2NB), and from M2 to NC the costs will be $32(M2NC). Mr. Janz has created a total cost equation and will use Solver to minimize C, the cost:

C(M1NA, M1NB, M1NC, M2NA, M2NB, M2NC)

This statement represents the sum of the tonnes shipped from each of M1 and M2 to each Newspaper A, B, C multiplied by the costs of shipment to each. In Excel, Mr. Janz programs the target cell with this objective function using the Excel command =SUMPRODUCT (and then highlights two sets of cells).

Objective Function | - | =SUMPRODUCT(B16:D17, B25:D26)

The minimized cost will appear in this cell when Solver completes the calculation of the unknowns M1NA, M1NB, etc. that will minimize the total cost of shipment. The second set of cells B25:D26 are already filled in with the cost per tonne shipped from each mill to each newspaper. On the spreadsheet in Exhibit 11-11, Mr. Janz has specified all

EXHIBIT 11-11
Shipments between Locations Matrix for CJL

	A	B	C	D	E	F
13	**Shipments between Locations Matrix:**					
14			**To Location:**			
15	**From Location:**	**Newspaper A**	**Newspaper B**	**Newspaper C**	**Total**	**Supply**
16	Mill 1	–	–	–	–	<=	20,000
17	Mill 2	–	–	–	–	<=	30,000
18	Total	–	–	–			
19		‖	‖	‖		
20	Demand	12,000	20,000	16,000		

the formulae in B16:D17 coloured blue. The purple cells are the given inputs entered with a set of cells that specify the relationship of supply and demand constraints. This is not required for Solver, but it does help Mr. Janz interpret the solution.

The blue coloured cells in Exhibit 11-11 are called a matrix, which is simply a set of rows and columns of related data, formulae, or both. Matrices are identified first by the number of rows of inputs and then by the number of columns. The matrix in Exhibit 11-11 has 2 rows indicating the mills and 3 columns indicating the customers, and is therefore a 2×3 matrix. Mr. Janz's constraints are in the first matrix in the final three columns. The last column is the maximum output of M1 of 20,000 tonnes and 30,000 tonnes for M2. The column to the left of it shows what the constraint means. The column beside that is programmed as the =SUM(B16:D16) and =SUM(B17:D17).

Below is a Cost Matrix that is also 2×3, but all the input has been given. To use Solver it must be true that the two matrices indicated in the parentheses are of the same dimensions. This is the case for Mr. Janz as both matrices are 2×3.

	A	B	C	D	E	F
22	**Cost Matrix**					
23			**To Location:**			
24	**From Location:**	**Newspaper A**	**Newspaper B**	**Newspaper C**		
25	Mill 1	20	28	40		
26	Mill 2	40	36	32		

In text form, this is:

$$M1NA + M1NB + M1NC \leq 20,000$$

to recognize the maximum output of M1, and

$$M2NA + M2NB + M1NC \leq 30,000$$

to recognize the maximum output of M2. Moreover, neither mill can ship negative tonnes of newsprint; therefore:

$$M1NA, M1NB, M1NC, M2NA, M2NB, M2NC \geq \text{(non-zero constraint)}$$

Mr. Janz now must click on Solver to access the dialogue box shown on the next page and, using a series of mouse clicks, inputs the defaults, the action required (minimization), the target cell where the total cost will appear, and the constraints. There is no typing required; he simply has to make sure the correct cells and symbols for the constraints are clicked accurately in turn.[5]

After all the constraints are input, instead of clicking on "Add" Mr. Janz clicks on "Solve." Exhibit 11-12 shows the calculations that appear in the previously empty cells.

[5]Mr. S. Janz formulated this problem and Mr. A. Campbell produced the Excel format and Solver screen captures with narrative to explain the CJL Solver programming and solution.

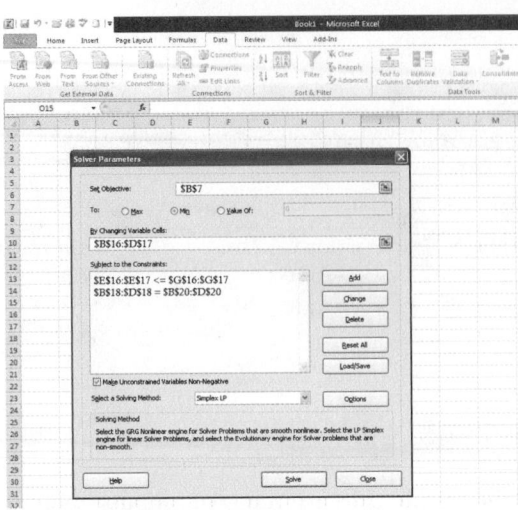

Setup Solver in this manner. To add constraints, simply click on the "Add" button, and input the necessary constraints.

Mr. Janz knows from the programming of the Objective function that the total cost will be $1,408,000, which is lower than last month's total cost of $1,512,000. Through correct scheduling of shipments from the right mill to the right customer, Mr. Janz has shown the owners of CJL how to reduce their costs and improve their operating profit. The Solver results box shown below will also appear, giving Mr. Janz the option to save the solution, run a sensitivity analysis, or restore the original values and start again with a different set of inputs and constraints. When there is no solution, the dialogue box will give Mr. Janz an error message, which is one reason why he might choose to restore the original values. In other words, an error message tells Mr. Janz that had he created a graphic similar to Exhibit 11-10, there is no feasible set of solutions (the area coloured in blue) for the constraints and inputs.

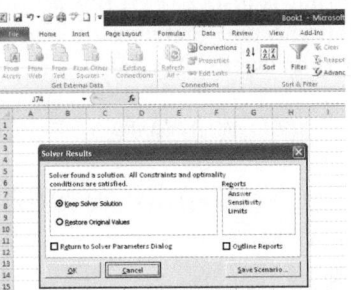

EXHIBIT 11-12
Solved Matrices for CJL

	A	B	C	D	E	F
12	**Objective Function**		1,408,000			
13	**Shipments between Locations:**					
14			**To Location:**			
15	**From Location:**	**Newspaper A**	**Newspaper B**	**Newspaper C**	**Total**	**Supply**
16	Mill 1	12,000	8,000	–	20,000 <=	20,000
17	Mill 2	–	12,000	16,000	28,000 <=	30,000
18	Total	12,000	20,000	16,000		
19		||	||	||		
20	Demand	12,000	20,000	16,000		
21						
22	**Cost Matrix**					
23			**To Location:**			
24	**From Location:**	**Newspaper A**	**Newspaper B**	**Newspaper C**		
25	Mill 1	20	28	40		
26	Mill 2	40	36	32		

REDUCE NEGATIVE EFFECTS AND CONFLICT

UNIT COSTS CAN MISLEAD

Explain how to reduce the negative effects and conflicts arising in relevant-cost analyses.

Unit-cost data can often help in a cost analysis. Nevertheless, they can also mislead decision makers in two important ways:

1. *When irrelevant costs are included.* Consider the $5.00 per unit allocation of fixed direct manufacturing labour and manufacturing overhead costs in the one-time-only special-order decision for Surf Gear (see Exhibit 11-3). This $5.00 per unit cost is irrelevant given the assumptions of our example and therefore should be excluded.

2. *When unit costs at different output levels are compared.* Generally, managers use total fixed costs rather than unit costs. Then, if desired, the total fixed costs can be unitized. Machinery sales personnel, for example, may brag about the low unit costs of using their new machines. However, they sometimes neglect to mention that the unit costs are based on outputs far in excess of their prospective customers' current or anticipated production levels.

Consider, for example, a new machine that costs $100,000, is capable of producing 100,000 units over its useful life, and has a zero terminal disposal price. The salesperson may represent the machine-related costs per unit to be $1. This amount is incorrect if the company anticipates a total demand of, say, only 50,000 units over the useful life of the machine (unit cost would be $100,000 ÷ 50,000 = $2). Unitized fixed costs over different production levels can be particularly misleading.

PITFALLS IN RELEVANT-COST ANALYSIS

One pitfall in relevant-cost analysis is to assume that all variable costs are relevant. In the Surf Gear example, the marketing costs of $5 per unit are variable but not relevant because Surf Gear incurs no incremental marketing costs for the special order—the business "walked in the door."

A second pitfall is to assume that all fixed costs are irrelevant. Consider fixed manufacturing costs. In our example, we assume that the extra production of 5,000 towels per month does not affect fixed manufacturing costs. That is, we assume that the relevant range is at least from 30,000 to 35,000 towels per month. In some cases, however, the extra 5,000 towels might increase fixed manufacturing costs.

Assume that Surf Gear would have to run three shifts of 16,000 towels per shift to achieve full capacity of 48,000 towels per month. Increasing the monthly production from 30,000 to 35,000 would require a partial third shift, because two shifts alone could produce only 32,000 towels. This extra shift would probably increase fixed manufacturing costs, making them relevant for this decision.

The best way to avoid these two pitfalls is to focus first and foremost on the relevance concept. Always require each item included in the analysis to be

◆ an expected future revenue or cost, and
◆ different between the alternatives.

CONFUSING TERMINOLOGY

Many different terms are used to describe the costs of specific products and services. Exhibit 11-13 presents several different unit-cost numbers using the data from column 1 of Exhibit 11-3. **Business function costs** are the sum of all the costs (variable costs and fixed costs) in a particular business function in the value chain. For example, manufacturing costs are $12.00 per unit, and marketing costs are $7 per unit. For inventory costing purposes, absorption costs are used as a synonym for manufacturing costs. **Full product costs** refer to the sum of all the costs in all the business functions in the value chain (R&D, design, production, marketing, distribution, and customer service). Full product costs in Exhibit 11-13 are $19.00 per unit.

Managers use terms such as *business function costs* and *full product costs* differently. To avoid being confused, you must understand their exact meanings in a given situation.

EXHIBIT 11-13
Variety of Cost Terms for Surf Gear* Using Unit-Cost Data from Exhibit 11-3

	A	B	C	D	E	F
1		Variable	Fixed	Manufacturing		Full
2		Product	Product	(Absorption)	Marketing	Product
3		Costs	Costs	Costs**	Costs**	Costs
4	Variable manufacturing costs	$ 7.50		$ 7.50		$ 7.50
5	Variable marketing costs	5.00			$5.00	5.00
6	Fixed manufacturing costs		$4.50	4.50		4.50
7	Fixed marketing costs	—	2.00	—	2.00	2.00
8		$12.50	$6.50	$12.00	$7.00	$19.00
9						
10	*In this example, marketing costs include distribution and customer-service costs, and there are no R&D or product design costs.					
11	**Business function costs					

DECISIONS AND PERFORMANCE EVALUATION

Consider our equipment replacement example for the Tormart Company discussed earlier. If the decision model demands choosing the alternative that will minimize total costs over the life span of the equipment, then the analysis in Exhibits 11-7 and 11-8 dictates replacing rather than keeping. In the real world, however, would the manager replace? The answer depends on the manager's perceptions of whether the decision model is consistent with the performance evaluation model, which describes the basis on which the manager's performance is judged. If the performance evaluation model conflicts with the decision model, the performance evaluation model often prevails in influencing a manager's behaviour.

For example, the decision model in Exhibit 11-7, based on a relevant-cost analysis over the life of the two machines, favours replacing the machine. But if the manager's promotion or bonus hinges on the first year's operating income performance under accrual accounting, the manager's temptation not to replace will be overwhelming. The reason is that accrual accounting models for measuring performance will show a higher first-year operating income if the old machine is kept than if it is replaced (as the following table shows):

	First-Year Results: Accrual Accounting	
	Keep	**Replace**
Revenue	$1,100,000	$1,100,000
Operating costs		
Cash operating costs	$800,000	$460,000
Amortization	200,000	300,000
Loss on disposal	—	360,000
Total operating costs	1,000,000	1,120,000
Operating income (loss)	$ 100,000	$ (20,000)

Even if top management's goals are long term (and consistent with the decision model), the subordinate manager's concern is more likely to be short term if his or her evaluation is based on short-run measures such as operating income.

Resolving the conflict between the decision model and the performance evaluation model is frequently a baffling problem in practice. In theory, resolving the difficulty seems obvious—simply design consistent models. For instance, in our replacement example, year-by-year effects on operating income of replacement can be budgeted over the planning horizon of two years. The manager would be evaluated on the understanding that the first year would be expected to be poor, the next year much better.

Many companies—such as Cisco Systems, General Electric, and Novartis—design systems that seek to align decision-making models and performance-evaluation models by integrating strategy with performance evaluation. Accountants who understand opportunity cost can implement this type of solution too. In a profit centre, for example, the manager is evaluated on operating income less the imputed interest cost of holding assets such as accounts receivable and inventory, and the opportunity cost of not collecting the cash or not selling the finished goods. This is one way to remove the incentive to produce into inventory to make short-term operating income look good. Even though the financial accounting system cannot record opportunity costs, they are nevertheless calculated for performance evaluation. This removes conflicting incentives when managers make decisions.

In practice, accounting systems rarely track each decision separately. Performance evaluation focuses on responsibility centres for a specific time period, not on projects or individual items of equipment for their entire useful lives. Therefore, the impacts of many different decisions are combined in a single performance report. Top management, through the reporting system, is rarely aware of particular desirable alternatives that were not chosen by subordinate managers. One solution, with the inexpensive technology now available, is to add project performance to the MIS.

Consider another conflict between the decision model and the performance evaluation model. Suppose a manager buys a particular machine only to discover that a better machine could have been purchased in its place. The decision model clearly indicates that replacing the existing machine with the better machine will improve operating income. The manager is reluctant to take action because replacing the machine so soon after its purchase may reflect badly on the manager's capabilities and performance. If the manager's superiors have no knowledge of the better machine, the manager may prefer to keep, rather than replace, the existing machine. Of course, one reason why decisions of this type are made by a team of top managers is to make it more difficult to hide mistakes. The objective is to learn from mistakes, not blame individuals.

PULLING IT ALL TOGETHER—PROBLEM FOR SELF-STUDY

(Try to solve this problem before examining the solution that follows.)

PROBLEM

Wally Lewis is manager of the engineering development division of Mainland Products. Lewis has just received a proposal signed by all 10 of his engineers to replace the office computers (PCs) with newer models. Lewis is not enthusiastic about the proposal.

	Old PCs	New PCs
Original cost	$300,000	$135,000
Useful life	5 years	3 years
Current age	2 years	0 years
Remaining useful life	3 years	3 years
Accumulated amortization	$120,000	Not acquired yet
Current book value	$180,000	Not acquired yet
Current disposal value (in cash)	$95,000	Not acquired yet
Terminal disposal value (in cash 3 years from now)	$0	$0
Annual computer-related cash operating costs	$40,000	$10,000
Annual revenue	$1,000,000	$1,000,000
Annual non-computer-related operating costs	$880,000	$880,000

Lewis's annual bonus includes a component based on division operating income. He has a promotion possibility next year that would make him a group vice-president of Mainland Products.

REQUIRED

1. Compare the costs of the old PCs and new PCs options. Consider the cumulative results for the three years together, ignoring the time value of money. What is the best alternative?
2. What are some important interdependencies that should be considered?
3. Explain how this is either a short-term or a long-term decision.
4. Explain how the table indicates how book value should be considered in this replacement decision.
5. Why might Lewis be reluctant to purchase the 10 new computers?

SOLUTION

1. The following table considers all cost items when comparing future costs of the old and new PCs options:

All Items	Three Years Together		
	Old PCs	New PCs	Difference
Revenues	$3,000,000	$3,000,000	—
Operating costs:			
Non-computer-related operating costs	2,640,000	2,640,000	—
Computer-related cash operating costs	120,000	30,000	$ 90,000
Old PC book value:			
Periodic writeoff as amortization	180,000	—	
or Lump sum writeoff	—	180,000	
Current disposal price of PCs	—	(95,000)	95,000
New PCs, written off periodically			
as amortization		135,000	(135,000)
Total operating costs	2,940,000	2,890,000	50,000
Operating income	$ 60,000	$ 110,000	$ 50,000

Alternatively, the analysis could focus on only those items in the preceding table that differ across the alternatives.

Relevant Items	Three Years Together		
	Old PCs	New PCs	Difference
Computer-related cash operating costs	$120,000	$ 30,000	$ 90,000
Current disposal price of old PCs	—	(95,000)	95,000
New PCs, written off periodically			
as amortization	—	135,000	(135,000)
Total relevant costs	$120,000	$ 70,000	$ 50,000

The conclusion from this analysis is that operating income would be strengthened by $50,000 if the old PCs were replaced with new PCs.

2. This is a system management decision about how engineers can best gather and communicate various types of engineering nonfinancial data. Systems management affects areas of capacity management, process improvement, and overall financial performance. This manager should not be making this decision on his own, but as part of a team that includes the managers of these other areas.
3. One reason this is a long-term decision is that the useful life of the PCs is longer than one year, although likely less than three years for an engineer whose productivity improves when the best equipment and software is available.
4. In the table, the old PC book value appears as $180,000 in both alternatives; one is a line below the other. Book value is irrelevant because the acquisition cost of

the old PCs is a historical cost and will remain unchanged irrespective of this decision. The book value of the old machines is not an element of difference between alternatives and could be completely ignored for decision-making purposes.

5. The accrual accounting operating incomes for the first year under the "keep old PCs" versus the "buy new PCs" alternatives are as follows:

	Keep Old PCs	Buy New PCs
Revenue	$1,000,000	$1,000,000
Operating costs:		
Non-computer-related operating costs	$880,000	$880,000
Computer-related operating costs	40,000	10,000
Amortization	60,000	45,000
Loss on disposal of old PCs	—	85,000*
Total operating costs	980,000	1,020,000
Operating income	$ 20,000	$ (20,000)

*$85,000 = book value of old PCs, $180,000 − current disposal price, $95,000.

Lewis would probably react negatively to the expected operating loss of $20,000 if the old PCs are replaced as compared to an operating income of $20,000 if the old PCs are kept. The decision would eliminate the component of his bonus based on operating income. He might also perceive the $20,000 operating loss as reducing his chances of being promoted to a group vice-president. This, however, is not in the best interests of Mainland Products because the obsolete PCs are slowing down the production of his engineers.

Engineers represent capacity—labour capacity—and their time is constrained. The extra time they spend on projects because they have no access to modern equipment is also a waste of money for Mainland. Fewer projects can be undertaken and completed, which affects the top line, incoming revenue, of the company. If engineering salaries are fixed, then any incremental revenue that could be gained if the engineers could work more effectively would go straight to operating income. Wally needs an accountant to point out important relevant information that remains unconsidered in this decision.

SUMMARY POINTS

The following question-and-answer format summarizes the chapter's learning outcomes. Each point presents a key question, and the guidelines are the answer to that question.

LEARNING OUTCOMES	GUIDELINES
1. How do decision processes unfold?	Both quantitative and qualitative information is relevant. Relevant information changes a decision, differs among the alternatives, and is information about the future. Historical information about the past is useful but not relevant.
2. How does relevance differ for short- and long-term decisions about production output level?	In the short term, fixed costs cannot change between alternatives, while long-term decisions are almost always capacity decisions that will change fixed costs. In the short term, there must be idle capacity to ensure existing production is not changed or interrupted by any added commitment to new production.
3. Why is opportunity cost relevant and book value irrelevant?	Opportunity cost is the contribution to income that is forgone or rejected by not using a limited resource in its next-best alternative use. Opportunity cost is included in decision making because it represents the best alternative way in which an organization could have used its resources had it not made the decision it did. Book value is a historical cost that cannot be changed irrespective of any decision; therefore, it is irrelevant.

4. What are the key concepts when making product and customer mix decisions?	The product, branch, segment, or customer group yielding the highest contribution margin per *constrained* resource should be selected. Managers should ignore allocated overhead costs when making decisions about discontinuing and adding customers, branches, and segments. They should focus instead on how total costs differ among alternatives.
5. What potential problems should be avoided in relevant-cost analysis?	Two potential problems to avoid in relevant-cost analysis are (a) making incorrect general assumptions—such as all variable costs are relevant and all fixed costs are irrelevant— and (b) losing sight of grand totals, focusing instead on unit amounts. Top management also faces a persistent challenge—that is, making sure that the performance evaluation model of subordinate managers is consistent with the decision model. A common inconsistency is to tell subordinate managers to take a multiple-year view in their decision making but then judge their performance only on the basis of the current year's operating income.

TERMS TO LEARN

This chapter and the Glossary at the end of the book contain definitions of the following important terms:

book value (p. 441)
business function costs (p. 451)
constraint (p. 445)
differential cost (p. 430)
differential revenue (p. 430)
expected value (p. 429)
full product costs (p. 451)
incremental costs (p. 430)
incremental revenue (p. 430)
insource (p. 434)

linear programming (LP) (p. 444)
make/buy decisions (p. 434)
net relevant cost (p. 430)
objective function (p. 445)
opportunity cost (p. 438)
optimization technique (p. 444)
out-of-pocket costs (p. 430)
outlay costs (p. 430)
outsource (p. 434)
paralysis by analysis (p. 429)

qualitative factors (p. 431)
quantitative factors (p. 428)
relevant costs (p. 430)
relevant revenue (p. 430)
risk-weights (p. 429)
sunk costs (p. 433)
vertical integration (p. 434)

ASSIGNMENT MATERIAL

MyAccountingLab Make the grade with MyAccountingLab: The questions, exercises, and problems marked in red can be found on MyAccountingLab at **www.myaccountinglab.com**. You can practise them as often as you want, and most feature step-by-step guided instructions to help you find the right answer. Exercises and problems with an Excel icon in the margin have an accompanying Excel template on MyAccountingLab.

SHORT-ANSWER QUESTIONS

11-1 Provide examples of interdependencies and relate them to the decision framework.

11-2 Define *relevant cost*. Why are historical costs irrelevant?

11-3 Distinguish between *quantitative* and *qualitative* factors in decision making.

11-4 Describe two potential problems that should be avoided in relevant-cost analysis.

11-5 Define *opportunity cost*.

11-6 "A component part should be purchased whenever the purchase price is less than its total manufacturing cost per unit." Do you agree? Explain briefly.

11-7 "Management should always maximize sales of the product with the highest contribution margin per unit." Do you agree? Explain briefly.

11-8 "Managers should always buy inventory in quantities that result in the lowest purchase cost per unit." Do you agree? Explain briefly.

11-9 "A branch office or business segment that shows negative operating income should be shut down." Do you agree? Explain briefly.

11-10 "Cost written off as depreciation on equipment already purchased is always irrelevant." Do you agree? Explain briefly?

11-11 "Managers will always choose the alternative that maximizes operating income or minimizes costs in the decision model." Do you agree? Explain briefly.

11-12 "All future costs are relevant." Do you agree? Explain briefly.

EXERCISES

11-13 Terminology. A number of terms are listed below:

cost minimization	optimization technique
differential cost	out-of-pocket costs
full product costs	outlay cost
incremental costs	paralysis by analysis
incremental revenue	sunk costs
objective function	profit maximization
opportunity cost	

REQUIRED
Select the terms from the above list to complete the following sentences.

A full absorption cost refers to all manufacturing costs including all MOH, whereas a _____ refers to all period or non-manufacturing costs as well as all manufacturing costs to bring the product to point of sale. The _____ is the value lost because a different alternative was not chosen. The _____ and _____ are the unique inflows and outflows arising from a specific alternative, should it be chosen. Similarly an _____ arises from implementation of a specific alternative. In comparison, a differential cost is the savings or added costs that arise when comparing alternatives to the current state. At some point the choice must be made and frequently a management team can suffer _____ because they seek more and more information. There are some costs that are always irrelevant and one category is _____ that have already been spent and cannot be recovered by making a different decision. One way to select an alternative is to use an _____ called linear programming. Optimization under specific constraints on resources may target either in _____ or _____. The technical name to calculate what will be optimized is the _____.

11-14 Disposal of assets. Answer the following questions.

1. Difference in favour of remachining, $3,300

1. A company has an inventory of 1,000 assorted parts for a line of missiles that has been discontinued. The inventory cost is $88,000. The parts can be either (a) remachined at total additional costs of $33,000 and then sold for $38,500 or (b) sold as scrap for $2,200. Which action is more profitable? Show your calculations.
2. A truck, costing $110,000 and uninsured, is wrecked on its first day in use. It can be either (a) disposed of for $11,000 cash and replaced with a similar truck costing $112,200 or (b) rebuilt for $93,500, and thus be brand-new as far as operating characteristics and looks are concerned. Which action is less costly? Show your calculations.

11-15 Inventory decision, opportunity costs. Lawnox, a manufacturer of lawn mowers, predicts that it will purchase 240,000 spark plugs next year. Lawnox estimates that 20,000 spark plugs will be required each month. A supplier quotes a price of $9 per spark plug. The supplier also offers a special discount option: If all 240,000 spark plugs are purchased at the start of the year, a discount of 4% off the $9 price will be given. Lawnox can invest its cash at 10% per year. It costs Lawnox $200 to place each purchase order.

1. Opportunity cost of interest forgone, $94,680

REQUIRED

1. What is the opportunity cost of interest forgone from purchasing all 240,000 units at the start of the year instead of in 12 monthly purchases of 20,000 units per order?
2. Would this opportunity cost be recorded in the accounting system? Why?
3. Should Lawnox purchase 240,000 units at the start of the year or 20,000 units each month? Show your calculations.

11-16 Relevant and irrelevant costs. Answer the following questions.

REQUIRED

1. Dalton Computers makes 5,000 units of a circuit board, CB76, at a cost of $230 each. Variable cost per unit is $180 and fixed cost per unit is $50. Peach Electronics offers to supply 5,000 units of CB76 for $210. If Dalton buys from Peach it will be able to save $20 per unit of fixed costs but continues to incur the remaining $30 per unit. Should Dalton accept Peach's offer? Explain.

2. AP Manufacturing is deciding whether to keep or replace an old machine. It obtains the following information:

	Old Machine	New Machine
Original cost	$10,000	$8,000
Useful life	10 years	4 years
Current age	6 years	0 years
Remaining useful life	4 years	4 years
Accumulated amortization	$6,000	Not acquired yet
Book value	$4,000	Not acquired yet
Current disposal value (in cash)	$2,500	Not acquired yet
Terminal disposal value (4 years from now)	$0	$0
Annual cash operating costs	$20,000	$12,000

AP Manufacturing uses straight-line amortization. Ignore the time value of money and income taxes. Should AP replace the old machine? Explain.

11-17 The careening personal computer. (W. A. Paton) An employee in the accounting department of a certain business was moving a personal computer from one room to another. As he came alongside an open stairway, he slipped and let the computer get away from him. It went careening down the stairs with a great racket and wound up at the bottom, completely wrecked. Hearing the crash, the office manager came rushing out and turned rather pale when he saw what had happened. "Someone tell me quickly," the manager yelled, "if that is one of our fully amortized items." A check of the accounting records showed that the smashed computer was, indeed, one of those items that had been written off. "Thank God!" said the manager.

REQUIRED
Explain and comment on the point of this anecdote.

11-18 Closing and opening stores. Sanchez Corporation runs two convenience stores, one in Vancouver and one in Surrey. Operating income for each store in 2013 is as follows:

	Vancouver Store	Surrey Store
Revenues	$1,070,000	$860,000
Operating costs		
Cost of goods sold	750,000	660,000
Lease rent (renewable each year)	90,000	75,000
Labour costs (paid on an hourly basis)	42,000	42,000
Depreciation of equipment	25,000	22,000
Utilities (electricity, heating)	43,000	46,000
Allocated corporate overhead	50,000	40,000
Total operating costs	1,000,000	885,000
Operating income (loss)	$ 70,000	$ (25,000)

The equipment has a zero disposal value. In a senior management meeting, Maria Lopez, the management accountant at Sanchez Corporation, makes the following comment, "Sanchez can increase its profitability by closing down the Surrey store or by adding another store like it."

REQUIRED

1. By closing down the Surrey store, Sanchez can reduce overall corporate overhead costs by $44,000. Calculate Sanchez's operating income if it closes the Surrey store. Is Maria Lopez's statement about the effect of closing the Surrey store correct? Explain.

2. Calculate Sanchez's operating income if it keeps the Surrey store open and opens another store with Revenue and costs identical to the Surrey store (including a cost of $22,000 to

acquire equipment with a one-year useful life and zero disposal value). Opening this store will increase corporate overhead costs by $4,000. Is Maria Lopez's statement about the effect of adding another store like the Surrey store correct? Explain.

11-19 Relevance of equipment costs. The Auto Wash Company has just today paid for and installed a special machine for polishing cars at one of its several outlets. It is the first day of the company's fiscal year. The machine costs $20,000. Its annual cash operating costs total $15,000. The machine will have a four-year useful life and a zero terminal disposal value.

1 5
1. a. The difference is $8,000 for four years taken together

After the machine has been used for only one day, a salesperson offers a different machine that promises to do the same job at annual cash operating costs of $9,000. The new machine will cost $24,000 cash, installed. The "old" machine is unique and can be sold outright for only $10,000, minus $2,000 removal cost. The new machine, like the old one, will have a four-year useful life and zero terminal disposal value.

Revenue, all in cash, will be $150,000 annually, and other cash costs will be $110,000 annually, regardless of this decision.

For simplicity, ignore income taxes and the time value of money.

REQUIRED

1. a. Prepare a statement of cash receipts and disbursements for each of the four years under each alternative. What is the cumulative difference in cash flow for the four years taken together?

   b. Prepare income statements for each of the four years under each alternative. Assume straight-line depreciation. What is the cumulative difference in operating income for the four years taken together?

   c. What are the irrelevant items in your presentations in requirements a and b? Why are they irrelevant?

2. Suppose the cost of the "old" machine was $1 million rather than $20,000. Nevertheless, the old machine can be sold outright for only $10,000, minus $2,000 removal cost. Would the net differences in requirements 1a and 1b change? Explain.

3. Is there any conflict between the decision model and the incentives of the manager who has just purchased the "old" machine and is considering replacing it a day later?

11-20 Product mix, constrained resource. Taylor Furniture produces and sells specialty mattresses. Production is a machine-intensive process. Taylor's variable costs are direct material costs, variable machining costs, and sales commissions. Marion Taylor, the owner, is planning production for the coming year and collects the following data:

4
1. Machine-hours required, 55,650

	Estimated Demand (units)	Selling Price	Direct Material Cost per Unit	Variable Machining Cost per Unit
Nealy	1,800	$3,000	$750	$600
Tersa	4,500	2,100	500	500
Pelta	39,000	800	100	200

◆ Salespeople are paid a 5% commission on each Nealy or Tersa sold, and a 10% commission on each Pelta sold. All other marketing and administrative costs are fixed and, along with the fixed manufacturing costs, total $8,750,000.

◆ Annual capacity is 50,000 machine-hours, which is limited by the availability of machines. Variable machining costs are $200 per hour.

◆ Taylor Furniture holds negligible inventories to minimize business risk.

REQUIRED

1. Calculate the machine-hours required to satisfy the estimated demand for each type of mattress.

2. What is the contribution margin per unit earned from each type of mattress?

3. Advise Marion Taylor about the most profitable production levels of the three products.

4. Suppose Taylor Furniture can lease additional machining capacity on an as-needed basis. What is the maximum amount that Marion Taylor would be willing to pay for each hour of additional machining capacity in the coming year?

11-21 Sell or process further. (J. Watson) Xylon Processing Limited is a chemical manufacturer. Two chemicals, Aardyn and Gargaton, are produced from the common chemical xylon. The joint process requires 15,000 litres of xylon to be processed at a cost of $21,500 (including the cost of the chemical itself). From these 15,000 litres, the company produces 9,600 litres of Aardyn and 5,400 litres of Gargaton. The joint costs of $21,500 are allocated $13,760 to Aardyn and $7,740 to Gargaton. The company can sell the Aardyn and the Gargaton at the

2
Incremental revenue from further processing, $22,848

split-off point for $15,360 and $8,748, respectively. Alternatively, the company can process the Aardyn further to produce 9,600 litres of Anardyn. The Anardyn sells for $2.38 per litre and additional processing costs are $6,945.

REQUIRED
Should Xylon sell Aardyn, or should it process it further to produce Anardyn?

11-22 **Special order, activity-based costing.** (CMA, adapted) The Award Plus Company manufactures medals for winners of athletic events and other contests. Its manufacturing plant has the capacity to produce 10,000 medals each month. Current production and sales are 7,500 medals per month. The company normally charges $150 per medal. Cost information for the current activity level is as follows:

Variable costs that vary with number of units produced	
Direct materials	$ 262,500
Direct manufacturing labour	300,000
Variable costs (for setups, materials handling, quality control, and so on)	
that vary with number of batches, 150 batches × $500 per batch	75,000
Fixed manufacturing costs	275,000
Fixed marketing costs	175,000
Total costs	$1,087,500

Award Plus has just received a special one-time-only order for 2,500 medals at $100 per medal. Accepting the special order would not affect the company's regular business. Award Plus makes medals for its existing customers in batch sizes of 50 medals (150 batches × 50 medals per batch = 7,500 medals). The special order requires Award Plus to make the medals in 25 batches of 100 each.

REQUIRED
1. Should Award Plus accept this special order? Show your calculations.
2. Suppose plant capacity were only 9,000 medals instead of 10,000 medals each month. The special order must either be taken in full or be rejected completely. Should Award Plus accept the special order? Show your calculations.
3. As in requirement 1, assume that monthly capacity is 10,000 medals. Award Plus is concerned that if it accepts the special order, its existing customers will immediately demand a price discount of $10 in the month in which the special order is being filled. They would argue that Award Plus's capacity costs are now being spread over more units and that existing customers should get the benefit of these lower costs. Should Award Plus accept the special order under these conditions? Show your calculations.

11-23 **Make versus buy, activity-based costing.** The Svenson Corporation manufactures cellular modems. It manufactures its own cellular modem circuit boards (CMCB), an important part of the cellular modem. It reports the following cost information about the costs of making CMCBs in 2012 and the expected costs in 2013:

	Current Costs in 2012	Expected Costs in 2013
Variable manufacturing costs		
Direct material cost per CMCB	$ 180	$ 170
Direct manufacturing labour cost per CMCB	50	45
Variable manufacturing costs per batch for		
setups, materials handling, and quality control	1,600	1,500
Fixed manufacturing costs		
Fixed manufacturing overhead costs that can be		
avoided if CMCBs are not made	320,000	320,000
Fixed manufacturing overhead costs of plant		
depreciation, insurance, and administration that		
cannot be avoided even if CMCBs are not made	800,000	800,000

Svenson manufactured 8,000 CMCBs in 2012 in 40 batches of 200 each. In 2013, Svenson anticipates needing 10,000 CMCBs. The CMCBs would be produced in 80 batches of 125 each.

The Minton Corporation has approached Svenson about supplying CMCBs to Svenson in 2013 at $300 per CMCB on whatever delivery schedule Svenson wants.

11-22 (margin note) 1. Incremental operating income, $50,000

11-23 (margin note) 1. Manufacturing cost per unit, $339

1. Calculate the total expected manufacturing cost per unit of making CMCBs in 2013.
2. Suppose the capacity currently used to make CMCBs will become idle if Svenson purchases CMCBs from Minton. On the basis of financial considerations alone, should Svenson make CMCBs or buy them from Minton? Show your calculations.
3. Now suppose that if Svenson purchases CMCBs from Minton, its best alternative use of the capacity currently used for CMCBs is to make and sell special circuit boards (CB3s) to the Essex Corporation. Svenson estimates the following incremental revenue and costs from CB3s:

Total expected incremental future revenues	$2,000,000
Total expected incremental future costs	$2,150,000

On the basis of financial considerations alone, should Svenson make CMCBs or buy them from Minton? Show your calculations.

11-24 Product mix, constrained resource. Westford Company produces three products, A110, B382, and C657. Unit data for the three products follow:

1. B382 contribution margin per unit, $14

	Product		
	A110	**B382**	**C657**
Selling price	$84	$56	$70
Variable costs:			
Direct materials	24	15	9
Other variable costs	28	27	40

All three products use the same direct material, Bistide. The demand for the products far exceeds the direct material available to produce the products. Bistide costs $3 per kilogram and a maximum of 5,000 kilograms is available each month. Westford must produce a minimum of 200 units of each product.

1. How many units of product A110, B382, and C657 should Westford produce?
2. What is the maximum amount Westford would be willing to pay for another 1,000 kilograms of Bistide?

11-25 Selection of most profitable product. Body-Builders, Inc., produces two basic types of weight-lifting equipment, Model 9 and Model 14. Pertinent data are as follows:

Contribution margin per unit of machine time, Model 9, $19.80

	Per Unit	
	Model 9	**Model 14**
Sales price	$110.00	$77.00
Costs:		
Direct materials	30.80	14.30
Direct manufacturing labour	16.50	27.50
Variable manufacturing overhead*	27.50	13.75
Fixed manufacturing overhead*	11.00	5.50
Marketing costs (all variable)	15.40	11.00
Total costs	$101.20	$72.05
Operating Income	$ 8.80	$ 4.95

*Allocated on the basis of machine-hours.

The weight-lifting craze is such that enough of either Model 9 or Model 14 can be sold to keep the plant operating at full capacity. Both products are processed through the same production departments.

Which products should be produced? Briefly explain your answer.

Excel Application:

Step-by-Step

1. Open the spreadsheet. At the top, create an "Original Data" section for the data provided by Body-Builders Inc. Reproduce the matrix of given information in the spreadsheet. Be sure to program any arithmetic calculations. For example, the total cost is programmed as =SUM(Cell address first: Cell address last).

2. Skip two rows and create a "Product Mix Analysis" section. Create columns for Model 9 and Model 14 and rows for "Selling Price per Unit," "Variable Cost per Unit," "Contribution Margin per Unit," "Relative Use of Machine-Hours per Unit of Product," and "Contribution Margin per Unit of Machine Time." Use the data from the Original Data matrix to calculate selling price per unit, variable cost per unit, and contribution margin per unit.

3. On the "Relative Use of Machine-Hours per Unit of Product" row, enter the *relative* output of units of product per machine-hour for Models 9 and 14, respectively. (*Hint*: Variable and fixed manufacturing overhead are allocated on the basis of machine-hours, and the variable and fixed manufacturing overhead costs per unit for Model 9 are twice as high as for Model 14.)

4. Enter calculations for contribution margin per unit of machine time for Models 9 and 14 by multiplying contribution margin per unit by the relative use of machine-hours per unit.

5. Check the accuracy of your spreadsheet. Go to the Original Data section and change the selling price of Model 14 from $77 to $75.90 per unit. If you programmed your spreadsheet correctly, contribution margin per unit of machine time for Model 14 should change to $18.70.

PROBLEMS

1. Full product cost per unit, $5.90

11-26 Multiple choice, comprehensive problem on relevant costs. The following are the Class Company's unit costs of manufacturing and marketing a high-style pen at an output level of 20,000 units per month:

Manufacturing cost	
Direct materials	$1.00
Direct manufacturing labour	1.20
Variable manufacturing overhead cost	0.80
Fixed manufacturing overhead cost	0.50
Marketing cost	
Variable	1.50
Fixed	0.90

REQUIRED

The following situations refer only to the preceding data; there is *no connection* between the situations. Unless stated otherwise, assume a regular selling price of $6 per unit. Choose the best answer to each question. Show your calculations.

1. For an inventory of 10,000 units of the high-style pen presented in the balance sheet, the appropriate unit cost to use is (a) $3.00, (b) $3.50, (c) $5.00, (d) $2.20, or (e) $5.90.

2. The pen is usually produced and sold at the rate of 240,000 units per year (an average of 20,000 per month). The selling price is $6 per unit, which yields total annual revenue of $1,440,000. Total costs are $1,416,000, and operating income is $24,000, or $0.10 per unit. Market research estimates that unit sales could be increased by 10% if prices were cut to $5.80. Assuming the implied cost-behaviour patterns continue, this action, if taken, would:

   a. Decrease operating income by $7,200.
   b. Decrease operating income by $0.20 per unit ($48,000) but increase operating income by 10% of revenue ($144,000), for a net increase of $96,000.
   c. Decrease fixed cost per unit by 10%, or $0.14, per unit, and thus decrease operating income by $0.06 ($0.20 – $0.14) per unit.
   d. Increase unit sales to 264,000 units, which at the $5.80 price would give total revenue of $1,531,200 and lead to costs of $5.90 per unit for 264,000 units, which would equal $1,557,600, and result in an operating loss of $26,400.
   e. None of these.

3. A contract with the government for 5,000 units of the pens calls for the reimbursement of all manufacturing costs plus a fixed fee of $1,000. No variable marketing costs are incurred on the government contract. You are asked to compare the following two alternatives:

Sales Each Month to	Alternative A	Alternative B
Regular customers	15,000 units	15,000 units
Government	0 units	5,000 units

Operating income under alternative B is greater than that under alternative A by (a) $1,000, (b) $2,500, (c) $3,500, (d) $300, or (e) none of these.

4. Assume the same data with respect to the government contract as in requirement 3 except that the two alternatives to be compared are

Sales Each Month to	Alternative A	Alternative B
Regular customers	20,000 units	15,000 units
Government	0 units	5,000 units

Operating income under alternative B relative to that under alternative A is (a) $4,000 less, (b) $3,000 greater, (c) $6,500 less, (d) $500 greater, or (e) none of these.

5. The company wants to enter a foreign market in which price competition is keen. The company seeks a one-time-only special order for 10,000 units on a minimum-unit-price basis. It expects that shipping costs for this order will amount to only $0.75 per unit, but the fixed costs of obtaining the contract will be $4,000. The company incurs no variable marketing costs other than shipping costs. Domestic business will be unaffected. The selling price to break even is (a) $3.50, (b) $4.15, (c) $4.25, (d) $3.00, or (e) $5.00.

11-27 Multiple choice, comprehensive problem on relevant costs (continuation of 11-26).

6. The company has an inventory of 1,000 units of pens that must be sold immediately at reduced prices. Otherwise, the inventory will become worthless. The unit cost that is relevant for establishing the minimum selling price is (a) $4.50, (b) $4.00, (c) $3.00, (d) $5.90, or (e) $1.50.

6. Variable marketing costs are $1.50

7. A proposal is received from an outside supplier who will make and ship the high-style pens directly to the Class Company's customers as sales orders are forwarded from Class's sales staff. Class's fixed marketing costs will be unaffected, but its variable marketing costs will be slashed by 20%. Class's plant will be idle, but its fixed manufacturing overhead will continue at 50% of present levels. How much per unit would the company be able to pay the supplier without decreasing operating income? (a) $4.75, (b) $3.95, (c) $2.95, (d) $5.35, or (e) none of these.

11-28 Relevant costs, contribution margin, product emphasis. The Beach Comber is a take-out food store at a popular beach resort. Susan Sexton, owner of the Beach Comber, is deciding how much refrigerator space to devote to four different drinks. Pertinent data on these four drinks are as follows:

1. Contribution margin per case of orange juice, $9.00

	Cola	Lemonade	Punch	Natural Orange Juice
Selling price per case	$18.80	$20.00	$27.10	$39.20
Variable cost per case	$14.20	$16.10	$20.70	$30.20
Cases sold per foot of shelf space per day	25	24	4	5

Sexton has a maximum front shelf space of 12 feet to devote to the four drinks. She wants a minimum of 1 foot and a maximum of 6 feet of front shelf space for each drink.

REQUIRED
1. Compute the contribution margin per case of each type of drink.
2. A co-worker of Sexton's recommends that she maximize the shelf space devoted to those drinks with the highest contribution margin per case. Evaluate this recommendation.
3. What shelf-space allocation for the four drinks would you recommend for the Beach Comber? Show your calculations.

11-29 Opportunity cost. (H. Schaefer) Wolverine Corporation is working at full production capacity producing 10,000 units of a unique product, Rosebo. Manufacturing costs per unit for Rosebo are as follows:

1. Variable costs per unit, $11

Direct materials	$ 2.00
Direct manufacturing labour	$ 3.00
Manufacturing overhead	$ 5.00
Total manufacturing cost	$10.00

The unit manufacturing overhead cost is based on a variable cost per unit of $2.00 and fixed costs of $30,000 (at full capacity of 10,000 units). The selling costs, all variable, are $4.00 per unit, and the selling price is $20 per unit.

A customer, the Miami Company, has asked Wolverine to produce 2,000 units of Orangebo, a modification of Rosebo. Orangebo would require the same manufacturing processes as Rosebo. Miami Company has offered to pay Wolverine $15.00 for a unit of Orangebo and half the selling costs per unit.

REQUIRED

1. What is the opportunity cost to Wolverine of producing the 2,000 units of Orangebo? (Assume that no overtime is worked.)
2. Buckeye Corporation has offered to produce 2,000 units of Rosebo for Wolverine so that Wolverine may accept the Miami offer. That is, if Wolverine accepts the Buckeye offer, Wolverine would manufacture 8,000 units of Rosebo and 2,000 units of Orangebo and purchase 2,000 units of Rosebo from Buckeye. Buckeye would charge Wolverine $14.00 per unit to manufacture Rosebo. Should Wolverine accept the Buckeye offer? (Support your conclusions with specific analysis.)
3. Suppose Wolverine had been working at less than full capacity, producing 8,000 units of Rosebo at the time the Orangebo offer was made. What is the minimum price Wolverine should accept for Orangebo under these conditions? (Ignore the previous $15.00 selling price.)

(4) **11-30 Optimal production plan, computer manufacturer.** Information Technology, Inc. assembles and sells two products: printers and desktop computers. Customers can purchase either (a) a computer or (b) a computer plus a printer. The printers are *not* sold without the computer. The result is that the quantity of printers sold is equal to or less than the quantity of desktop computers sold. The contribution margins are $240 per printer and $120 per computer.

Each printer requires 7.2 hours' assembly time on production line 1 and 12 hours' assembly time on production line 2. Each computer requires 4.8 hours' assembly time on production line 1 only. (Many of the components of each computer are preassembled by external vendors.) Production line 1 has 28.8* hours of available time per day. Production line 2 has 24 hours of available time per day.

Let X represent units of printers and Y represent units of desktop computers. The production manager must decide on the optimal mix of printers and computers to manufacture.

*Line 1 is actually two parallel lines, each used 14.4 hours per day. To simplify calculations, count as one line with 28.8 hours.

REQUIRED

1. Express the production manager's problem in an LP format.
2. Which combination of printers and computers will maximize the operating income of Information Technology? Use both the trial-and-error and the graphic approach.

(4) **11-31 Optimal production mix.** (CMA, adapted) Della Simpson Inc. sells two popular brands of cookies, Della's Delight and Bonny's Bourbon. Della's Delight goes through the Mixing and Baking Departments and Bonny's Bourbon, a filled cookie, goes through the Mixing, Filling, and Baking departments.

Michael Shirra, vice-president of sales, believes that at the current price, Della Simpson can sell all of its daily production of Della's Delight and Bonny's Bourbon. Both cookies are made in batches of 3,000 cookies. The batch times (in minutes) for producing each type of cookie and the minutes available per day are as follows:

Maximize $300D + $250 B
where D = Della's Delight
and B = Bonny's Burbon

	Department Minutes		
	Mixing	**Filling**	**Baking**
Della's Delight	30	0	10
Bonny's Bourbon	15	15	15
Minutes available per day	660	270	300

Revenue and cost data for each type of cookie are:

	Della's Delight	Bonny's Bourbon
Revenue per batch	$ 475	$ 375
Variable cost per batch	$ 175	$ 125
Contribution margin per batch	$ 300	$ 250
Monthly fixed costs (allocated to each product)	$18,650	$22,350

REQUIRED

1. Using D to represent the batches of Della's Delight and B to represent the batches of Bonny's Bourbon made and sold each day, formulate Shirra's decision as a linear programming model.
2. Compute the optimal number of batches of each type of cookie that Della Simpson Inc. should make and sell each day to maximize operating income.

11-32 **Opportunity costs, book value.** Larry Miller, the general manager of Basil Software, scheduled a meeting on June 2, 2014 with Nicole Nguyen, sales manager, Andy Ayim, accountant, and Ellen Eisner, software operations manager, to discuss the development and release of Basil Software's new version of its spreadsheet package, Easyspread 2.0. It is only a question of time before other software firms have a package that matches Easyspread 2.0. Nicole Nguyen, the sales manager, could hardly control her enthusiasm for the new product.

3

1. Net relevant OI on Easyspread 1.0, $165

Nicole Nguyen: This product is exactly what the market has been waiting for. We should not delay, by even a single day, the introduction of this product. Let's make July 1, 2014, the sales release date.

Ellen Eisner: I don't disagree with Nicole's assessment of the market potential for this product, but I have a problem. The threatened strike by our printers caused us to purchase large quantities of user's manuals for Easyspread 1.0. We don't like to store the manuals separately, so we also got extra disks duplicated. The manuals and diskettes were then packaged and shrink-wrapped. We are currently holding 60,000 completed packages, which equals the expected sales for July, August, and September 2014 of Easyspread 1.0. I think we should make October 1, 2014, the expected release date of Easyspread 2.0. This date would enable us to sell all of our inventory of Easyspread 1.0.

Larry Miller: Nicole, do you see any problem with Ellen's suggestion? Our inventory of Easyspread 1.0 seems rather large for us to ignore. If we introduce Easyspread 2.0 on July 1, what would we do with the inventory of Easyspread 1.0 that we currently hold?

Nicole Nguyen: We currently sell Easyspread 1.0 to our wholesalers and distributors for $165.00 each. The additional optimization features in Easyspread 2.0 mean that we should be able to sell Easyspread 2.0 to our distributors for about $203.50. We should not ignore the higher profit margins from Easyspread 2.0. It is true, though, that each time we sell one unit of Easyspread 2.0, we forgo the sale of one unit of Easyspread 1.0. Since the expected demand for Easyspread 2.0 is at least as large as the demand for Easyspread 1.0, we may have to throw away the existing inventory of Easyspread 1.0 once we introduce Easyspread 2.0.

Larry Miller: Andy, you've heard what Nicole and Ellen have to say. I would like you to do a detailed analysis of the alternatives, and let me know within a week what you come up with. We need to make a decision on this one way or another, and we need to do so soon.

When Andy Ayim returned to his office, he pulled out the cost records he had developed for Easyspread 1.0 and Easyspread 2.0. The unit costs for the two products could be summarized as follows:

	Easyspread 1.0	Easyspread 2.0
Manuals, disks	$ 22.00	$ 27.50
Development costs	82.50	115.50
Marketing and administration costs	27.50	33.00
Total cost per unit	$132.00	$176.00

The following additional facts are available:

a. Basil contracts with outside vendors to print manuals and duplicate disks.

b. Development costs are allocated on the basis of the total costs of developing the software and the anticipated unit sales over the life of the software.

c. Marketing and administration costs are fixed costs in 2014, incurred to support all activities of Basil Software. Marketing and administration costs are allocated to products on the basis of the budgeted Revenue from each of the products. The preceding unit costs assume Easyspread 2.0 will be introduced on July 1, 2014.

REQUIRED

1. Based on financial considerations only, is Basil Software better off introducing Easyspread 2.0 immediately or waiting? Explain your conclusion, clearly identifying relevant and irrelevant costs.

2. What other factors might Nicole Nguyen and Ellen Eisner raise? What factors might Larry Miller consider important?

Contribution margin per machine-hour, Taylor $52

11-33 Choosing customers. Broadway Printers operates a printing press with a monthly capacity of 2,000 machine-hours. Broadway has two main customers: Taylor Corporation and Kelly Corporation. Data on each customer for January follows:

	Taylor Corporation	Kelly Corporation	Total
Revenues	$120,000	$80,000	$200,000
Variable costs	42,000	48,000	90,000
Contribution margin	78,000	32,000	110,000
Fixed costs (allocated)	60,000	40,000	100,000
Operating income	$ 18,000	$ (8,000)	$ 10,000
Machine-hours required	1,500 hours	500 hours	2,000 hours

Kelly Corporation indicates that it wants Broadway to do an *additional* $80,000 worth of printing jobs during February. These jobs are identical to the existing business Broadway did for Kelly in January in terms of variable costs and machine-hours required. Broadway anticipates that the business from Taylor Corporation in February will be the same as that in January. Broadway can choose to accept as much of the Taylor and Kelly business for February as its capacity allows. Assume that total machine-hours and fixed costs for February will be the same as in January.

REQUIRED

What action should Broadway take to maximize its operating income? Show your calculations.

11-34 Contribution approach, relevant costs. Air Pacific has leased a single jet aircraft that it operates between Vancouver and the Fijian Islands. Only tourist-class seats are available on its planes. An analyst has collected the following information:

1. Total contribution margin from passengers per flight, $88,000

Seating capacity per plane	360 passengers
Average number of passengers per flight	200 passengers
Average one-way fare	$500
Variable fuel costs	$14,000 per flight
Food and beverage service costs (no charge to passenger)	$20 per passenger
Commission to travel agents paid by Air Frisco (all tickets are booked by travel agents)	8% of fare
Fixed annual lease costs allocated to each flight	$53,000 per flight
Fixed ground-services (maintenance, check in, baggage handling) costs allocated to each flight	$7,000 per flight
Fixed flight-crew salaries allocated to each flight	$4,000 per flight

Assume that fuel costs are unaffected by the actual number of passengers on a flight.

REQUIRED

1. Calculate the total contribution margin from passengers that Air Pacific earns on each one-way flight between Vancouver and Fiji.

2. The Market Research Department of Air Pacific indicates that lowering the average one-way fare to $480 will increase the average number of passengers per flight to 212. On the basis of financial considerations alone, should Air Pacific lower its fare? Show your calculations.

3. Travel International, a tour operator, approaches Air Pacific with the possibility of chartering its aircraft. The terms of charter are as follows: (a) For each one-way flight, Travel International will pay Air Pacific $74,500 to charter the plane and to use its flight crew and ground-service staff; (b) Travel International will pay for fuel costs; and (c) Travel International will pay for all food costs. On the basis of financial considerations alone, should Air Pacific accept Travel International's offer? Show your calculations. What other factors should Air Pacific consider in deciding whether to charter its plane to Travel International?

11-35 Reduce conflict. The Pastel Company must reach a make/buy decision with respect to a high-volume, easily made metal tool, RG1. Sean Gray, the cost analyst, estimates the following costs and production information for the 50,000 units of RG1 that are expected to be put into production.

⑤

1. Net benefit of outsourcing, $219,450

Total direct materials costs	$660,000
Direct manufacturing labour costs (all variable)	$220,000
Manufacturing overhead costs (all fixed)	$440,000
Good units of RG1 manufactured and sold	40,000 units
Units of RG1 scrapped for zero revenue	10,000 units

York Corporation has offered to supply as many units of RG1 as Pastel needs for $23.10 per unit. If Pastel buys RG1 from York instead of manufacturing it in-house, Pastel would be able to save $263,450 of the $440,000 fixed manufacturing overhead costs. (There is no alternative use for the capacity currently used to make RG1.)

Gray shows his analysis to Jim Berry, the controller. Berry does not like what he sees. He asks Gray to review all his assumptions and calculations, commenting, "The yield assumptions you made are very low. I think this plant can achieve much better quality than we have in the past. Better quality will reduce our costs and make them competitive with the outside purchase price." Gray knows that Berry is very concerned about purchasing RG1 from an outside supplier because it will mean that some of his close friends who work on the RG1 line will be laid off. Berry had played a key role in convincing management to produce RG1 in-house.

Gray rechecks his calculations. He believes it is unlikely that the plant can achieve the quality levels it would take for the make alternative to be superior to the buy alternative.

REQUIRED
1. Based on the information Gray obtains, should Pastel make or buy RG1?
2. For what levels of scrap would the make alternative be preferred to purchasing from outside?
3. Evaluate whether Jim Berry's suggestion to Gray to review his estimates is unethical. Will it be unethical for Gray to change his analysis to support the make alternative? What steps should Gray take next?

11-36 Equipment upgrade versus replacement. (A. Spero, adapted) The TechMech Company produces and sells 6,000 modular computer desks per year at a selling price of $500 each. Its current production equipment, purchased for $1,500,000 and with a five-year useful life, is only two years old. It has a terminal disposal value of $0 and is depreciated on a straight-line basis. The equipment has a current disposal price of $600,000. However, the emergence of a new molding technology has led TechMech to consider either upgrading or replacing the production equipment. The following table presents data for the two alternatives:

②

1. Total relevant cost to replace, $5,040,000

	File Edit View Insert Format Tools Data Window Help		
	A	B	C
1		**Upgrade**	**Replace**
2	One-time equipment costs	$2,700,000	$4,200,000
3	Variable manufacturing cost per desk	$ 140	$ 80
4	Remaining useful life of equipment (years)	3	3
5	Terminal disposal value of equipment	$ 0	$ 0

All equipment costs will continue to be depreciated on a straight-line basis. For simplicity, ignore income taxes and the time value of money.

1. Should TechMech upgrade its production line or replace it? Show your calculations.
2. Now suppose the one-time equipment cost to replace the production equipment is somewhat negotiable. All other data are as given previously. What is the maximum one-time equipment cost that TechMech would be willing to pay to replace the old equipment rather than upgrade it?
3. Assume that the capital expenditures to replace and upgrade the production equipment are as given in the original exercise, but that the production and sales quantity is not known. For what production and sales quantity would TechMech (a) upgrade the equipment or (b) replace the equipment?
4. Assume that all data are as given in the original exercise. Dan Doria is TechMech's manager, and his bonus is based on operating income. Because he is likely to relocate after about a year, his current bonus is his primary concern. Which alternative would Doria choose? Explain.

11-37 Optimal product mix. (CMA, adapted) OmniSport's Plastics Department is currently manufacturing 5,000 pairs of skates annually, making full use of its machine capacity. Presented below are the selling price and costs associated with OmniSport's skates.

Contribution per machine-hour, $46.80 ÷ 1.5 = $31.20; $28.40 ÷ 0.5 = $56.80

Sales price		$117.60
Costs:		
Direct materials	$ 9.60	
Direct manufacturing labour	14.40	
Variable manufacturing overhead	28.80	
Fixed manufacturing overhead	21.60	
Marketing costs (all variable)	18.00[a]	92.40
Operating income		$25.20

Note: 5,000 pairs of skates × 1.5 hr/pair = 7,500 hours to complete

[a]$18.00 − $7.20 = $10.80 selling and administrative costs.

OmniSport believes it could sell 8,000 pairs of skates annually if it had sufficient manufacturing capacity. Colcott Inc., a steady supplier of quality products, has agreed to provide 6,000 pairs of skates per year at a price of $90 per pair delivered to OmniSport's facility.

Jack Petrone, OmniSport's product manager, has suggested that the company can make better use of its Plastics Department by manufacturing snowboard bindings. Petrone believes that OmniSport could expect to sell 12,000 snowboard bindings annually at a price of $72 per binding. Petrone's estimate of the costs to manufacture the bindings is presented next.

Selling price per snowboard binding		$72.00
Costs per snowboard binding		
Moulded plastic	19.20	
Other direct materials	4.80	
Variable machine operating costs ($19.20/hour)	7.60[b]	
Manufacturing overhead costs	7.20	
Marketing and administrative costs	16.80[c]	55.60
Operating income per snowboard binding		16.40

[b]12,000 snowboard bindings × 0.5 hr/snowboard binding = 6,000 hours, leaving 7,500 − 6,000 = 1,500 hours to complete skates at 1.5 hr/pair of skates = 1,000 pairs of skates completed.
[c]$16.80 − $7.20 = $9.60 Selling and administrative costs.

Other information pertinent to OmniSport's operations is presented below.

◆ An allocated $7.20 fixed overhead cost per unit is included in the marketing and administrative cost for all the purchased and manufactured products. Total fixed and variable marketing and administrative costs for the purchased skates would be $12 per pair ($12 − $7.20 = $4.80 selling and administrative costs).
◆ In the Plastics Department, OmniSport uses machine-hours as the allocation base for other manufacturing overhead costs. The fixed manufacturing overhead component of these costs for the current year is the $36,000 of fixed plantwide manufacturing overhead that has been allocated to the Plastics Department.

Which product or products should OmniSport manufacture and/or purchase to maximize operating income? Show all calculations.

11-38 Relevance, quantitative and qualitative. Louisville Corporation produces baseball bats for kids that it sells for $32 each. At capacity, the company can produce 50,000 bats a year. The costs of producing and selling 50,000 bats are as follows:

1. Increase in operating income if Ripkin order accepted, $90,000

	Cost per Bat	Total Costs
Direct materials	$12	$ 600,000
Direct manufacturing labour	3	150,000
Variable manufacturing overhead	1	50,000
Fixed manufacturing overhead	5	250,000
Variable selling expenses	2	100,000
Fixed selling expenses	4	200,000
Total costs	$27	$1,350,000

REQUIRED

1. Suppose Louisville is currently producing and selling 40,000 bats. At this level of production and sales, its fixed costs are the same as given in the table above. Ripkin Corporation wants to place a one-time special order for 10,000 bats at $25 each. Louisville will incur no variable selling costs for this special order. Should Louisville accept this one-time special order? Show your calculations.
2. Now suppose Louisville is currently producing and selling 50,000 bats. If Louisville accepts Ripkin's offer it will have to sell 10,000 fewer bats to its regular customers.
   a. On financial considerations alone, should Louisville accept this one-time special order? Show your calculations.
   b. On financial considerations alone, at what price would Louisville be indifferent between accepting the special order and continuing to sell to its regular customers at $32 per bat?
   c. What other factors should Louisville consider in deciding whether to accept the one-time special order?

11-39 Product mix. (N. Melumad, adapted) Pendleton Engineering makes cutting tools for metal-working operations. It makes two types of tools: R3, a regular cutting tool, and HP6, a high-precision cutting tool. R3 is manufactured on a regular machine but HP6 must be worked on both the regular machine and a high-precision machine. The following information is available:

1. Net relevant benefit R3 and HP6 respectively, $1,550,000, $1,500,000

	R3	HP6
Selling price	$ 121	$ 180
Variable manufacturing cost per unit	$ 72	$ 120
Variable marketing cost per unit	$ 18	$ 42
Budgeted total fixed overhead costs	$350,000	$550,000
Hours required to produce 1 unit on the regular machine	1	.5

The following additional information is available:
a. Pendleton faces a capacity constraint on the regular machine of 50,000 hours per year.
b. Pendleton has no capacity constraint on the high-precision machine.
c. Of the $550,000 budgeted fixed overhead costs of HP6, $300,000 is for lease payments for the high-precision machine. This cost is charged entirely to HP6 because Pendleton uses the machine exclusively to produce HP6. The leasing agreement for the high-precision machine can be cancelled at any time without penalties.
d. All other fixed overhead costs cannot be changed.

REQUIRED

1. What product mix—that is, how many units of R3 and HP6—will maximize Pendleton's operating income? Show your calculations.
2. Suppose Pendleton can increase the annual capacity of the regular machine by 15,000 hours at a cost of $180,000. Should Pendleton increase the capacity of the regular machine

by 15,000 machine-hours? By how much will Pendleton's operating income increase? Show your calculations.

3. Suppose that the capacity of the regular machine has been increased to 65,000 hours. Pendleton has been approached by Carter Corporation to supply 20,000 units of another cutting tool, S3, for $120 per unit. S3 is exactly like R3 except that its variable marketing costs are $15 per unit. What product mix should Pendleton choose to maximize operating income?

1. Total relevant data alternative 1, make, $190,000 + $3.3X

11-40 Relevance, short-term. (A. Atkinson) Oxford Engineering manufactures small engines. The engines are sold to manufacturers who install them in such products as lawn mowers. The company currently manufactures all the parts used in these engines but is considering a proposal from an external supplier who wants to supply the starter assembly used in these engines. The starter assembly is currently manufactured in Division 3 of Oxford Engineering. The costs relating to Division 3 for the past 12 months were as follows:

Direct materials	$220,000
Direct manufacturing labour	165,000
Manufacturing overhead	440,000
Total	$825,000

Over the past year, Division 3 manufactured 150,000 starter assemblies; the average cost for the starter assembly is computed as $5.50 ($825,000 ÷ 150,000).

Further analysis of manufacturing overhead revealed the following information. Of the total manufacturing overhead reported, only 25% is considered variable. Of the fixed portion, $150,000 is an allocation of general overhead that would remain unchanged for the company as a whole if production of the starter assembly is discontinued. A further $100,000 of the fixed overhead is avoidable if self-manufacture of the starter assembly is discontinued. The balance of the current fixed overhead, $80,000, is the division manager's salary. If self-manufacture of the starter assembly is discontinued, the manager of Division 3 will be transferred to Division 2 at the same salary. This move will allow the company to save the $40,000 salary that would otherwise be paid to attract an outsider to this position.

REQUIRED

1. Tidnish Electronics, a reliable supplier, has offered to supply starter assembly units at $4 per unit. Since this price is less than the current average cost of $5.50 per unit, the vice-president of manufacturing is eager to accept this offer. Should the outside offer be accepted? (*Hint:* Production output in the coming year may be different from production output in the last year.)

2. How, if at all, would your response to requirement 1 change if the company could use the vacated plant space for storage and, in so doing, avoid $50,000 of outside storage charges currently incurred? Why is this information relevant or irrelevant?

COLLABORATIVE LEARNING CASE

1. Hardt forecast to make 32,000 units, $714,840

11-41 Make versus buy, governance. (CMA, adapted) Lynn Hardt, a management accountant with the Paibec Corporation, is evaluating whether a component, MTR-2000, should continue to be manufactured by Paibec or purchased from Marley Company, an outside supplier. Marley has submitted a bid to manufacture and supply the 32,000 units of MTR-2000 that Paibec will need for 2014 at a unit price of $17.30, to be delivered according to Paibec's production specifications and needs. While the contract price of $17.30 is only applicable in 2014, Marley is interested in entering into a long-term arrangement beyond 2014.

From plant records and interviews with John Porter, the plant manager, Hardt gathered the following information regarding Paibec's costs to manufacture 30,000 units of MTR-2000 in 2013:

	File Edit View Insert Format Tools Data Window
	A	B
1		**Costs for**
2		**30,000**
3		**Units in 2013**
4	Direct materials	$195,000
5	Direct manufacturing labour	120,000
6	Plant space rental	84,000
7	Equipment leasing	36,000
8	Other manufacturing overhead	225,000
9	Total manufacturing costs	$660,000
10		

Hardt has collected the following additional information related to manufacturing MTR-2000:

◆ Variable costs per unit in 2014 for the MTR-2000 are expected to be the same as variable costs per unit in 2013.
◆ Plant rental and equipment lease are annual contracts that are going to be expensive to wiggle out of. Porter estimates it will cost $10,000 to terminate the plant rental contract and $5,000 to terminate the equipment-lease contract.
◆ 40% of the other manufacturing overhead is variable, proportionate to the direct manufacturing labour costs. The fixed component of other manufacturing overhead is expected to remain the same whether MTR-2000 is manufactured by Paibec or outsourced to Marley.
◆ Paibec's just-in-time policy means inventory is negligible.

Hardt is aware that cost studies can be threatening to current employees because the findings may lead to reorganizations and layoffs. She knows that Porter is concerned that outsourcing MTR-2000 will result in some of her close friends being laid off. Therefore, she performs her own independent analysis of competitive and other economic data which reveals that:

◆ Prices of direct materials are likely to increase by 8% in 2014 compared to 2013.
◆ Direct manufacturing labour rates are likely to be higher by 5% in 2014 compared to 2013.
◆ The plant rental contract can, in fact be terminated by paying $10,000. Paibec will not have any need for this space if MTR-2000 is outsourced.
◆ The equipment lease can be terminated by paying $3,000.

Hardt shows Porter her analysis. Porter argues that Hardt is ignoring the amazing continuous improvement that is occurring at the plant and that the increases in direct material prices and direct manufacturing labour rates assumed by Hardt will not occur. But Hardt is very confident about the accuracy of the information she has collected.

REQUIRED
1. Based on the information Hardt has obtained, should Paibec make MTR-2000 or buy it? Show all calculations.
2. What other factors should Paibec consider before making a decision?
3. What should Lynn Hardt do in response to John Porter's comments?

11-42 Relevance, short-term. Hernandez Corporation is bidding on a new construction contract, here called Contract No. 1. If the bid is accepted, work will begin in a few days, on January 1, 2014. Contract No. 1 requires a special cement. Hernandez has already purchased 10,000 kilograms of the special cement for $20,000. The current purchase cost of the cement is $2.40 per kilogram. The company could sell the cement now for $1.60 per kilogram after all selling costs. Hernandez will also bid on Contract No. 2 one month from now. If Contract No. 1 is not landed, the special cement will be available for Contract No. 2. If Contract No. 1 is landed, Hernandez will need to buy 10,000 kilograms of another grade of cement for $2.50 per kilogram to fulfill Contract No. 2.

1. Relevant cost, $25,000

If it is not used in either of these two ways, the special cement would be of no use to the company and would be sold a little more than a month from now for $1.50 per kilogram after all selling costs.

The president of Hernandez, Julio Gomez, is puzzled about the appropriate total cost of the special cement to be used in bidding on Contract No. 1. Competition is intense and markups are very thin, so determining the relevant material costs when bidding on Contract No. 1 is crucial.

REQUIRED
1. Suppose Gomez is certain that Hernandez will land Contract No. 2; what (relevant) cost figure should Gomez use for the special cement when bidding on Contract No. 1?
2. This part requires knowledge of the material on decision making under uncertainty, which was covered in Chapter 3. Suppose Gomez estimates a probability of 0.7 that Hernandez will land Contract No. 2. What (relevant) cost figure should Gomez use for the special cement when bidding on Contract No. 1?
3. Suppose Hernandez could sell the special cement now for $2.30 per kilogram after all selling costs (instead of $1.60 per kilogram as described in paragraph 1). Suppose Gomez is certain that Hernandez will land Contract No. 2. What (relevant) cost figure should Gomez use for the special cement when preparing a bid on Contract No. 1?

Pricing Decisions, Product Profitability Decisions, and Cost Management

12

BUSINESS MATTERS

Relevant Costs Inform Pricing Decisions

Parker Hannifin, a global industrial parts maker, priced its 800,000 different products at total cost plus 30% for years. In 2001 the new CEO changed this strategy to target pricing after touring its 221 facilities. The CEO focused on the customer's willingness to pay (similar to the retail industry) and found 28% of the products were priced too low. Overnight Parker raised its prices within the range of 3% to as high as 60% (the average price increase was 5%). Knowing the price premiums, the company focused on selling those products with the highest premium and added $200 million to operating income by 2006 on revenue of $9.4 billion.

LEARNING OUTCOMES

After studying this chapter, you should be able to

1. Discuss the major influences on both short- and long-run pricing decisions.

2. Evaluate existing information to decide on a competitive price for a special order.

3. Apply two of three pricing methods: target pricing to set target costs and cost-plus pricing.

4. Explain how target pricing and cost-plus pricing help achieve long-term operating income profitability.

5. Describe life-cycle pricing and discuss some non-cost factors in pricing decisions, including fair business practices and environmental sustainability.

This chapter describes how managers integrate relevant information about consumer demand at different prices to manage their costs, influence supply, and earn a predicted profit. Managers make pricing decisions about the products and services their companies deliver in a highly competitive environment. There is no universal principle of relevant cost selection for product pricing when different customers demand different value propositions from different products.

Influences of costs vary among products and services, and pricing decisions differ greatly in both their time horizons and their contexts. Identifying and filtering facts that are relevant will lead to improved pricing decisions. In practice, the key to profitability is that companies sell units at the price a customer is willing to pay.

MAJOR INFLUENCES ON PRICING

1 Discuss the major influences on both short- and long-run pricing decisions.

Three pricing strategies are discussed in this chapter:

1. **Target pricing**, where the price is based on what customers are willing to pay.
2. **Cost-plus pricing**, where a flat rate target profit percentage is added to the full product cost.
3. **Life-cycle pricing** (cradle to grave), which includes the environmental costs of production, reclamation, recycling, and reuse of materials.

None of these strategies is the best choice for all products. Customers, costs, and competitors all influence which of the three strategies is most appropriate. Legislation and ability to pay also play important parts in the decision of a pricing strategy. Pricing decisions also depend on the time horizon—relevant information in the short run will differ from relevant information for the long-run pricing decision. Some factors can be controlled by managers of a company, while others, such as the nature of the competition, are uncontrollable. In Chapter 12 it becomes apparent that pricing decisions are as complex as the capacity management decisions considered in Chapter 11. Three major influences on pricing decisions are as follows:

◆ *Customers*. Managers must always examine pricing problems through the eyes of their customers. A price increase may cause customers to reject a company's product and choose a competing or substitute product because they perceive that the substitute provides more value or benefit in use for the price they are willing to pay. Availability, customization, and quality all affect willingness to pay.

◆ *Costs*. Companies price products to exceed the costs of making them. In Chapter 9, throughput, variable, and full absorption costing models were discussed, but these are only manufacturing costs. Generally, a company must not only cover full product costs, which include operating expenses (period costs), but also be able to price higher than full product cost to turn a profit. ABC systems provide superior information upon which to base pricing decisions.

◆ *Competitors*. Competitors' reactions influence pricing decisions. At one extreme, a business without a rival can set higher prices. This is called a monopoly. Even where there are only a few rivals, high prices can also be charged, as in the oil industry. This is called an oligopoly. At the other extreme, where there are many rivals, no single company can affect a price increase and must take the price the customers are willing to pay. This is called competition and one rival can spark a price war. Lowering prices to capture more volume can drive weaker rivals out of business.

Corporations weigh customers, competitors, and costs differently. Companies selling commodity products such as steel, wheat, and rice have many competitors, each offering identical products. The customers in the market set the price, but cost data can help sellers decide on the output levels that best meet a company's particular profit objective. In less competitive markets where products can be distinguished or differentiated by their desirable features (e.g., luxury automobiles), the pricing decision depends on three factors:

1. How much customers value and will pay for the attributes of the product.
2. The costs of producing, selling, distributing, and after-sale service of a product.
3. The pricing strategies of any competitors.

Managers of a company who know about its rival's technology, plant capacity, and operating policies can estimate a rival's costs, which is valuable information in setting competitive prices. For multinational corporations with excess production capacity, there are opportunities to sell the same product at different prices in different countries.

PRODUCT COST CATEGORIES AND TIME HORIZON

Chapter 1 described customer satisfaction, continuous improvement, and the dual internal/external focus as increasingly important themes in management. Pricing is an area where these themes converge. For example, charging lower prices for high-quality products is important for customer satisfaction, an external focus. But when prices are lower, costs must be reduced as well to maintain constant profitability. Continuous improvement, an internal focus, is one way to match the rate of cost decrease to the rate of price decrease.

Cost reduction includes all six value-chain business functions, from R&D to customer service. *Upstream costs* refer to pre-production costs of R&D and product or process design, or both. *Downstream costs* are post-production costs incurred to make a sale and keep customers satisfied (marketing, distribution, after-sales service). Full product costing will recover all upstream, production, and downstream costs plus some profit.

In computing the costs within the six business functions, relevance is an important concept because it answers the question "What difference does the cost make among the available alternatives?" The answer depends on the capacity available, the alternative uses of capacity, and the time horizon. Most pricing decisions are either short run or long run. Short-run decisions include both pricing for a one-time-only special order with no long-term implications and adjusting product mix and output volume in a competitive market. The time horizon for short-run decisions is typically six months or less, but sometimes as long as a year. Long-run decisions include pricing a product in a major market where price setting has considerable leeway. A time horizon of a year or longer is used when computing relevant costs for these long-run decisions. Many pricing decisions have both short-run and long-run implications. The next section examines some short-run pricing decisions.

THE DECISION FRAMEWORK: RELEVANT COSTS IN SHORT-RUN PRICING

There are times when even short-run decisions on how to allocate capacity require consideration of incremental fixed costs. Consider a one-time-only special order from a customer to supply products for the next few months. Acceptance or rejection of the order will not affect the revenue (units sold or the selling price per unit) from existing sales outlets, and the customer is unlikely to place any future sales orders. Below we illustrate how to include incremental fixed costs, a one-time startup cost, in just such a short-run pricing decision. Central to this pricing decision is understanding the difference in capacity use by a special order relative to ordinary capacity use.

Step 1: Identify the Problem   Astel Computers has been invited by Datatech Corporation to bid competitively for a 5,000-unit special order of Astel's Provalue notebook computer. If Astel is successful it will take three months to complete this project. Datatech will sell Provalue computers under its own brand name in

> Evaluate existing information to decide on a competitive price for a special order.
>
> ②

regions and markets where Astel does not sell Provalue. Assume that whether Astel bids successfully for the job or not will have no effect on Astel's ordinary revenue—neither the units sold nor the selling price—from existing sales channels.

Step 2: Gather Information   Before Astel can bid on Datatech's offer, Astel's managers must first estimate how much it will cost to supply the 5,000 notebooks. Similar to the Surf Gear example in Chapter 11, the relevant costs Astel's managers must focus on include all direct and indirect costs throughout the value chain that will change by accepting the one-time-only special order from Datatech. Astel's managers outline the relevant costs in the following table:

Direct materials ($460 × 5,000 computers)	$2,300,000
Direct manufacturing labour ($64 per computer × 5,000 computers)	320,000
Fixed costs of additional capacity to manufacture Provalue	250,000
Total costs	$2,870,000*

*No additional costs will be required for R&D, design, marketing, distribution, or customer service.

Astel has some fully depreciated equipment used to generate additional capacity from time to time. If their bid is successful, this additional production would exceed Astel's current operating capacity. Astel plans to start up the fully depreciated equipment and operate a dedicated production line for three months only. Astel will incur one-time fixed startup costs of $250,000. This fixed cost is relevant to the decision of what price Astel will quote in its competitive bid. In contrast, the special order for Surf Gear in Chapter 11 required no additional capacity and therefore no relevant fixed costs.

The manufacturing costs of Provalue are calculated using the activity-based costing (ABC) approach described in Chapter 5. Astel has three direct manufacturing cost categories (direct materials, direct manufacturing labour, and direct machining costs). Astel's management views direct materials costs and direct manufacturing labour costs as variable with respect to the units of Provalue produced. Astel's information system reports the quantities of batches of components (kits) purchased and used as direct materials. The cost of kits per finished Provalue computer is $460. The direct manufacturing labour hours of 3.2 DMLH per Provalue are also reported and costed at the rate of $20/DMLH. This direct cost is $64 per finished Provalue notebook.

Direct machining costs do not vary over the relevant range of production—they are fixed long-run costs based on practical capacity (see Chapter 9). The fixed cost of capacity is $11,400,000. Assuming no significant difference between practical capacity and master budget demand of 150,000, the capacity cost recoverable per Provalue will be $76/notebook ($11.4 million ÷ 150,000 notebooks). At two direct machine-hours per notebook, the rate is $38/DMH ($76/notebook ÷ 2 DMH). Provalue's direct manufacturing costs in total are $600 per unit. The indirect MOH data are also available from Astel's ABC system.

Direct Manufacturing Costs	Cost Driver	Rate	Cost Driver Q/Notebook	Cost per Notebook
Direct materials cost (throughput cost)*	notebook	$460	1.0	$460
Direct manufacturing labour costs*	DMLH	$ 20	3.2	64
Total variable direct manufacturing cost per notebook				524
Fixed direct machine cost (unitized, master budget)				76
Total direct fixed and variable costs				$600

*Astel's managers have calculated these rates.

For the Datatech bid, however, there is one key difference in direct costs. Direct materials and manufacturing costs will remain at $524/Provalue, but the direct fixed cost of capacity will be only $50/Provalue. This is because the equipment required to produce the 5,000 units, should Astel win the bid, will only cost $250,000 on the dedicated production line. The total direct manufacturing costs for the Datatech bid will be only $574/Provalue rather than $600/Provalue. Once the job is complete the line will be shut down. The indirect manufacturing overhead (MOH) is also relevant.

INDIRECT MOH AND ABC COSTING AT ASTEL

With an ABC system in place, indirect manufacturing overhead costs (MOH) are variable directly with respect to their appropriate cost drivers. For example, the purchasing activities result in purchase orders. The purchasing cost pool comprises ordering and receiving activities. Staff members responsible for placing orders can be reassigned or laid off in the long run if fewer orders are required to support production of the Provalue notebook. There are two additional indirect MOH cost pools (testing and inspection, and rework) in Astel's accounting ABC system. The following table summarizes the activity cost pools, the cost driver for each activity, and the cost per unit of the cost driver that Astel uses to allocate manufacturing overhead costs to products:

Manufacturing Activity	Description of Activity	Cost Driver	Cost per Unit of Cost Driver
1. Ordering and receiving	Placing orders, receiving, and paying for components	Number of orders	$80 per order
2. Testing and inspection	Testing components and final product	Testing hours	$2 per testing-hour
3. Rework	Correcting and fixing errors and defects	Units reworked	$40 per unit reworked

The ABC system does depict a real relationship between orderly changes in cost drivers and orderly changes in their respective cost pools. These relationships are one-to-one and direct. At the batch level (several components ordered at one time), order and receiving costs are driven by quantity of orders, not the quantity of components per order (input unit level). If Astel wins the bid, minimizing the number of orders by increasing the components per order will reduce the costs of ordering and receiving for the additional 5,000 units of Provalue produced. There are 22,500 orders placed to purchase the components required, and we assume that the Provalue has 450 components supplied by different suppliers. For each component, 50 orders are placed to match the just-in-time (JIT) production schedule (see Chapter 20).

Rework is quite high. The defect rate is 12,000 on normal production of 150,000, or 8%. Each defective Provalue takes 2.5 hours of rework for a total of 30,000 DMLH (12,000 defective Provalues × 2.5 DMLH). The budgeted cost per rework hour is $40/DMLH, in part because of the seniority of these workers, to generate a rework cost per unit of $100 ($40 × 2.5 DMLH). The total annual rework cost of $1,200,000 (12,000 Provalue defects × $100/defect) recovered from the sale of all 150,000 is $8 ($1,200,000 ÷ 150,000 finished Provalues). Reducing the defect rate would reduce production costs per unit.

This defect rate means Astel has a very tight and time-consuming quality control function, taking 20 hours of testing per finished Provalue computer for a total of 4.5 million testing-hours (30 testing-hours × 150,000 Provalue). The rate per quality control hour used is $2. The total cost of quality control for one finished Provalue is $60 (30 hours × $2). Simplifying the production process would reduce opportunities for assembly error and the time required for inspecting and testing.

Step 3: Forecast Future Outcomes on the Basis of Available Information   This is a relatively straightforward task because Astel has an ABC system in place. Astel's managers have their budget in place and have made their assumptions about growth explicit. Astel uses a long-run time horizon to price forecast. Because of its JIT production schedule, Astel's 2012 budget has no beginning or ending inventory of Provalue in 2012. Normal annual demand is for 150,000 units. Using the available information, Astel's decision team calculates Provalue's variable manufacturing costs on ordinary production, both direct and indirect, as $604 and its full absorption costs as $680 per Provalue notebook ready for sale, as shown in the following table, which reports all the costs per saleable unit, all of which must be recovered. Currently at $1,000 per notebook, Astel's predicted gross margin is $320 per notebook ($1,000 − $680), or 32%.

Total direct fixed and variable costs				600
Variable Manufacturing Overhead Costs				
Ordering and receiving activity*	orders	$6	2.0	12
Testing and inspecting activity direct labour cost rate*	DLH	2	30.0	60
Rework direct manufacturing labour cost rate*	DMLH	40		8
Total variable manufacturing overhead cost per notebook				80
Total variable manufacturing cost per notebook (variable cost)				604
Total manufacturing cost (full absorption)				680

*Astel's managers have calculated these rates: 2.5 DMLH/defect × $40/DMLH × 12,000 defects/year = $1,200,000; rework cost per notebook = $1,200,000 ÷ 150,000 notebooks = $8/notebook.

For the Datatech job, the recoverable direct fixed cost per notebook will be only $50, not $76/Provalue. For this particular job the relevant full absorption cost is $654/notebook ($680 − $76 + $50). The price that provides the same gross margin of 32% would be roughly $962/Provalue [Price = $654 ÷ (1 − 0.32)].

Fortunately, Astel has additional, reliable competitive information. One competitor has excess capacity and may be able to bid on a contribution margin basis rather than a full absorption cost basis. This bid could be as low as $665/notebook. Astel believes the highest bid from other competitors with older and less efficient equipment and no excess capacity could be $720. These competitors may not be invited to bid by Datatech. The highest bid is expected to be $765.

At $665, Astel's gross margin for this job would decrease to $11 per notebook, or approximately 1.65%. This is a very slim margin for error and Astel's managers need to carefully assess the risk that they will undercost this job given the startup of unfamiliar equipment. Implicitly Astel's pricing policy has defaulted to a cost-plus basis. The discussion will revolve around just what the appropriate "plus" amount should be to win the bid and most likely provide additional gross margin to contribute toward paying the $33 million of non-manufacturing costs incurred from the predicted ordinary production for the year. Exhibit 12-1 summarizes all of the information Astel's decision team has gathered.

The non-manufacturing costs of $33 million will remain, regardless of whether Astel wins this bid or not. They are irrelevant and therefore Astel should not use full product cost. Nor should Astel use simple throughput or total variable manufacturing cost because neither the $524 nor the $604 cover the additional direct fixed cost of this job (see Chapter 9).

Astel's managers also need to carefully reconsider the probability that Datatech will decide to undercut Astel's selling price in the current markets. If Astel's managers believe this is a significant risk, the relevant costs of the bidding decision should include the contribution margin lost on sales to existing customers. If Astel's managers view the threat to its existing business from accepting the Datatech order to be serious enough, they may decide not to bid for the Datatech business, or they may quote Datatech a price close to the price Astel charges its other customers. After carefully evaluating the situation, Astel's managers conclude that Datatech will not undercut prices to Astel's customers.

Step 4: Decide among Alternatives Astel has a variety of alternatives between two extreme anticipated bids. The company may bid at the low value of $665/Provalue or the high value of $765/Provalue. Before making a decision Astel must undertake more analysis, which is described in the next section.

	Values	Per Month	Operating Costs	Per Year
Production = Sales volume Q notebooks*	150,000	12,500	R&D	$ 5,400,000
Rework rate as a percent of total Q produced* 8%	12,000	1,000	Design	6,000,000
Orders of components*	300,000	25,000	Marketing	15,000,000
Direct machine hours per year (master budget capacity)*	300,000		Distribution	3,600,000
Unitized direct machine hours per notebook*	2		Customer service	3,000,000
Direct machine cost/hour	$ 38.00		Total	$33,000,000
Direct machine costs—fixed*	$11,400,000	$950,000	Per unit	$ 220
Unitized direct machine hour cost/notebook	$ 76.00	$950,000		
Total ordering and receiving costs per year*	$ 1,800,000	$150,000		

	Cost Driver	Rate	Cost Driver Q/Notebook	Cost per Notebook
Direct Manufacturing Costs				
Direct materials cost (throughput cost)*	notebook	$460	1.0	$460
Direct manufacturing labour costs*	DMLH	$ 20	3.2	64
Total variable direct manufacturing cost per notebook				524
Fixed direct machine cost (unitized, master budget)				76
Total direct fixed and variable costs				600
Variable Manufacturing Overhead Costs				
Ordering and receiving activity*	orders	$ 6	2.0	12
Testing and inspecting activity direct labour cost rate*	DLH	$ 2	30.0	60
Rework direct manufactuing labour cost rate*	DMLH	$ 40		8
Total variable manufacturing overhead cost per notebook**				80
Total manufacturing cost (full absorption)				680
Non-manufacturing costs*	notebook	$220	1	220
Total product cost per unit (full cost)				$900

*Astel's managers have calculated these rates (see p. 478 for calculations).

**Total variable manufacturing cost per notebook (variable cost): $604

Step 5: Evaluate Performance If Astel does submit a winning bid, then the company needs to gather performance data over the next three months to assess the actual compared to predicted profitability.

TARGET PRICING USING TARGET COSTING

The starting point for pricing decisions can be

Apply two of three pricing methods: target pricing to set target costs and cost-plus pricing.

◆ Market-based (target pricing)
◆ Cost-based (cost-plus pricing)
◆ Life-cycle (cradle to grave costs, including reclamation, recycling, reusing)

The market-based approach to pricing starts by asking: Given what our customers want and how our competitors will react to what we do, what price should we charge? The cost-based approach to pricing starts by asking: What does it cost us to make this product, and hence what price should we charge that will recoup our costs and produce a desired profit? Both approaches consider customers, competitors, and costs. Only their starting points differ. The third pricing strategy, life-cycle pricing, will be discussed later in this chapter.

Companies may take one of two approaches. Some companies start by anticipating customer and competitor reactions and then examine costs—the market-based approach. In very competitive markets (for example, steel, petroleum products, wheat, and rice) the market-based approach is logical. The items produced or services provided by one company are almost identical to those produced or provided by others, so companies have no influence over the prices customers are willing to pay.

In contrast, other companies first look at costs and then consider customers or competitors—the cost-based approach. Companies in noncompetitive markets favour this approach because they do not need to respond either to competitors' prices or consumers' reactions. In industries where there is more product differentiation (for example, automobiles, consumer electronics, management consulting, and professional services) firms have more discretion over prices, products, and services. Notice that all companies consider all three factors, but their starting points differ. A final decision on price, product, and service is made after evaluating these external influences on pricing along with the costs to produce and sell the product. We will begin by considering the market-based approach.

TARGET PRICING AND TARGET COSTING

Market-based pricing starts with a target price. A **target price per unit** is the estimated price for a product or service that potential customers will pay. This estimate is based on an understanding of customers' perceived value for a product or service and how competitors will price competing products or services. A **target margin percentage** the company sets will depend on the pricing policy. If the policy is full absorption cost, then the target may well be a target gross margin percentage. If the pricing is full product cost, then the target will be operating margin or operating profit percentage. If the pricing is full variable cost recovery, then the target margin will be contribution margin or profit percentage. If the pricing is full cost recovery, then the target will be net margin or net profit percentage.

All margin percentages are calculated by dividing the dollar value of the target margin by total revenue (see Chapter 3). In the long run, the corporation will not survive unless it has a policy of full cost recovery. In the short-run—for example, a special order—less than full cost recovery can be the best pricing policy.

In the Surf Gear case in Chapter 11, the contribution margin and full variable cost recovery was most rational. In the Astel example, the gross margin and full absorption cost recovery is most rational. But both cases are outside the ordinary course of business. Should Astel implement a target pricing policy for the Datatech job, it can accept the $665/notebook as a target price and then determine how to drive its current cost of $654 per notebook down to achieve a target 32% gross margin. If Astel wants to achieve its current 32% gross margin percentage, it must increase its existing full absorption cost by enough to generate this target in a cost-plus policy. Exhibit 12-2 indicates the different arithmetic methods that result in very different prices.

Given the competitive intelligence available, the cost-plus price is well above what any competing bid is likely to be. Under this policy, Astel should not bid at all. Under the target pricing policy, Astel should only bid the lowball price if it is likely that the company can drive down its existing full absorption costs by $218.80 per finished Provalue. This is an approximately 33% cost reduction to earn a target gross margin percentage of 32%. It will be up to the managers of Astel to decide if this is possible or whether to set a less aggressive gross margin percentage target and enter a bid higher than $665. Clearly, however, they cannot bid cost plus at $961.76 when the highest anticipated bid is $765.

When a company chooses the target pricing approach, it has to rely on its sales and marketing organization, through close contact and interaction with customers, to identify customers' needs and their perceived value for a product or service. Market research studies about product features that customers want and the prices they are willing to pay for those features are often needed. Increasingly, through statistical analyses of data (often referred to as data mining) provided by swiping loyalty cards such as Air Miles, and accessing personal profiles on social networking services such as Facebook, companies identify the characteristics of their typical customers and how well these match with their intended customer base.

Target Pricing: Astel's Managers Assume the Lowball Bid as the Target Price per Unit $665			Cost Plus: Astel's Managers Assume the Gross Margin Percentage = 32% = $654 per Unit		
Revenue − COGS	= GM	Revenue = $665	Revenue		X
Revenue ÷ Revenue	= 1.00		− COGS		$654
COGS ÷ Revenue	= COGS %	= X ÷ $665	GM	= X − 654	= GM
GM ÷ Revenue (given)	= GM %	= 32.0%	GM %	= GM/X	= 32.0%
1.00 − GM %	= COGS %	= 68.0%	COGS % + GM %	= 1.00	
Target cost is COGS	= $665 × 68%	= $452.20	GM %	= 32.0%	
			COGS %	= 68.0%	= $654
			Target price	X − $654	= 32%X
				X − 32%X	= $654
				X(1 − 0.32)	= 654
			Revenue per unit	X	= $654 ÷ 0.68
			Revenue per unit		= $961.76
			Gross margin		= $307.76
			Gross margin %		= $307.76 ÷ $961.76
					= 32.0%

The target pricing approach is particularly difficult when products are highly differentiated and have a very short consumer life cycle. Personal electronic devices are one example where innovation in technology drives the introduction of audio-visual playback devices such as the iPad, cell phones, BlackBerrys, and products combining attributes of all three. The life cycle prior to the introduction of a new product is approximately six months. The process of target pricing requires a lot of retracing between relevant customer preference data and value engineering. The process re-engineering approach is discussed in Chapter 13.

THE HIGHBALL BID TARGET PRICING ALTERNATIVE

Assume that Astel's managers decide that a target price of $765 instead of $665 per unit might be successful. Then, implementing the identical arithmetic illustrated in Exhibit 12-2, the target cost becomes approximately $520 ($765 × 68%). This requires an immediate reduction of approximately $134. In the short term, Astel is more likely to achieve a 20% savings on COGS than to achieve 33% savings. The weakness of this approach is the assumption that a high bid will be successful against Astel's competitors.

If Astel can afford to have its bid rejected, then $765 is a better bid than the lowball bid. If Astel, for strategic reasons, cannot afford to have its bid rejected by Datatech, then this is a very risky alternative. Possible strategic considerations would include the possibility of building a long-term relationship with Datatech and obtaining higher normal sales to Datatech that would recover some of the non-manufacturing costs to design and market the Provalue notebook.

THE DECISION FRAMEWORK AND LONG-TERM PRICING

In the long term, a **target cost per unit** is more appropriately based on full product costs instead of full absorption costs. The **full product cost** is the estimated long-run cost per unit of a product (or service) that, when sold at the target price, enables the company to achieve the **target operating income per unit**. A full product cost includes all manufacturing and non-manufacturing costs (period costs). The appropriate profit target margin is now the operating income (margin) in dollars or the operating income (margin) percentage calculated as the operating income ÷ revenue

Explain how target pricing and cost-plus pricing help achieve long-term operating income profitability.

(see Chapter 2). Companies can use the decision framework to determine long-term pricing decisions.

Step 1 For Astel, the problem is how to sustain long-term competitiveness for the Provalue product, given the short product life cycle. Astel's managers know they have at most six months to sell production of Provalue notebooks at $1,000 per unit. They set a target full product cost at $720 per unit. This is the price that a competitor with excess capacity could have submitted for the Datatech opportunity. Astel will face this price relatively soon in its normal market. Notice that the current full product cost is $900/Provalue notebook (Exhibit 12-1). The managers do not want to change their assumed operating margin percentage, now at 10%. Finally, the managers assume all the COGS and non-manufacturing costs per unit at the budgeted 2012 levels. Manufacturing savings arise because of reduced complexity.

Step 2 Before Astel can decide how to achieve its target cost, it requires high-quality data. These data have already been gathered for the Datatech bid and are shown in Exhibit 12-1.

Step 3 Astel is forecasting two changes in the production of Provalue notebooks. First is a decrease in the defect rate from 8% to 6.5% achieved through simplification of the current design of Provalue. The second is that with a reduced price, Astel will sell 200,000 rather than 150,000 units in 2012.

Astel managers also anticipate that the direct materials cost for the kits will decrease to $385 because they require fewer components. The anticipated decrease in components, despite an increase in units produced, is from 22,500 to 21,250 with no change in the number of orders. The quantity of direct manufacturing hours required per unit is also forecast to decrease from 3.2 DMLH/Provalue to 2 DMLH/Provalue.

Accompanying these changes will be a reduction in testing and inspection hours from 30 to 15 hours per unit. In combination with the increased units inspected, the decrease in testing-hours will be 1,500,000—from 4,500,000 to 3,000,000. These will all generate savings to achieve the lower target total product cost. On a net basis, however, the increased units produced with the reduced defect rate will result in an increase from 30,000 to 32,500 rework hours. The original and revised manufacturing cost budget is shown in Exhibit 12-3.

If Astel's managers can achieve their new targets, then the full absorption costs will decrease from $680/Provalue notebook to $540/Provalue notebook. Additional non-manufacturing cost savings reduce unit non-manufacturing cost to $180/Provalue notebook. Total product costs become $720/Provalue notebook. The target price becomes $800 based on the desired 10% operating margin percentage.

Exhibit 12-4 illustrates the total effect of the changes in the forecast summarized in the right side of Exhibit 12-3. Notice that the gross margin percent (GM%) $\approx 18.8\%$ (GM ÷ COGS). This is almost half of the original GM% of 32%.

Exhibit 12-5 illustrates the total effect of all budgeted changes to the manufacturing and non-manufacturing costs for 2012. The operating margin percentage does achieve the 10% target, which has remained unchanged from the original target.

Step 4 Having this understanding of customers and competitors has become important for three reasons:

1. Competition from lower-cost producers has meant that prices cannot be increased.

2. Products are on the market for shorter periods of time, leaving less time and opportunity to recover from pricing mistakes.

3. Customers have become more knowledgeable and demand quality products at reasonable prices.

EXHIBIT 12-3
Target Costing for Provalue

	A	B	C	D	E	F	G	H	I	J	K	L	M	N	O	P
1	ORIGINAL BUDGETED PROVALUE MANUFACTURING COSTS 2012								REVISED BUDGETED PROVALUE MANUFACTURING COSTS 2012							
2	Output Level: 150,000								Output Level: 200,000							
3							Total	Input							Total	Input
4		Cost					Quantity of	Cost							Quantity of	Cost
5		Driver	Quantity	Unit of	Quantity	Unit of	Cost Driver	Driver		Cost Driver	Quantity	Unit of	Quantity	Unit of	Cost Driver	Driver
6		(1)	(2)	Measure	(3)	Measure	(4) = (2) × (3)	Rate		(1)	(2)	Measure	(3)	Measure	(4) = (2) × (3)	Rate
7	**Direct Costs**								**Direct Costs**							
8	Direct materials	No. of kits	1.0	kit per output unit	150,000	output units	150,000	$460	Direct materials	No. of kits	1.0	kit per output unit	200,000	output units	200,000	$385
9	Direct manufacturing labour (DMLH)	DMLH	3.2	DMLH per output unit	150,000	output units	480,000	$ 20	Direct manufacturing labour (DMLH)	DMLH	2.65	DMLH per output unit	200,000	output units	530,000	$ 20
10	Direct machining-fixed (DMH)	DMH hours	2.0	DMH per output unit	150,000	output units	300,000	$ 38	Direct machining - fixed (DMH)	DMH hours	1.5	DMH per output unit	200,000	output units	300,000	$ 38
11	**Overhead Costs**								**Overhead Costs**							
12	Ordering and receiving	No. of orders	50.0	orders per component	450	components	22,500	$ 80	Ordering and receiving	No. of orders	50.0	orders per component	425	components	21,250	$ 80
13	Testing and inspection (TH)	Testing hours	30.0	TH per output unit	150,000	output units	4,500,000	$ 2	Testing and inspection (TH)	Testing hours	15.0	TH per output unit	200,000	output units	3,000,000	$ 2
14	Rework (RMH)	Rework hours	2.5	RMH per defective unit*	12,000	defective units	30,000	$ 40	Rework (RMH)	Rework hours	2.5	RMH per defective unit†	13,000	defective units	32,500	$ 40
15	Defect rate				8.0%	defect rate			Defect rate				6.5%	defect rate		
16																
17	*8% defect rate × 150,000 output units = 12,000 defective units								†6.5% defect rate × 200,000 output units = 13,000 defective units							

EXHIBIT 12-4
Total Target Costs Budgeted for 2012

	A	B	C	D
1		PROVALUE II		PROVALUE
2		Estimated	Estimated	Manufacturing
3		Manufacturing Costs	Manufacturing	Cost per Unit
4		for 200,000 Units	Cost per Unit	(Exhibit 12-1)
5		(1)	(2) = (1) ÷ 200,000	(3)
6	Direct manufacturing costs:			
7	Direct material costs (200,000 units × $385 per unit)	$ 77,000,000	$385.00	$460.00
8	Direct manufacturing labour costs (300,000 hours × $20 per hour)	10,600,000	$ 53.00	64.00
9	Direct machining costs (fixed) (530,000 machine-hours × $38 per machine-hour)	11,400,000	57.00	76.00
10	Direct manufacturing costs	99,000,000	495.00	600.00
11	Manufacturing overhead costs:			
12	Ordering and receiving costs (21,250 orders × $80 per order)	1,700,000	8.50	12.00
13	Testing and inspection costs (3,000,000 hours × $2 per hour)	6,000,000	30.00	60.00
14	Rework costs (32,500 rework hours × $40 per hour)	1,300,000	6.50	8.00
15	Manufacturing overhead costs	9,000,000	45.00	80.00
16	Total manufacturing costs	$108,000,000	$540.00	$680.00

EXHIBIT 12-5
Budgeted Income Statement for Astel Corporation for 2012

	A	B	C
1		Estimated	Estimated
2		Total Amounts	Total Amount
3		for 200,000 Units	per Unit
4		(1)	(2) = (1) ÷ 200,000
5	Revenue	$160,000,000	$800
6	Cost of goods sold[a] (from Exhibit 12-4)	108,000,000	540
7	Operating costs[b]		
8	R&D costs	4,000,000	20
9	Design costs of product and process	6,000,000	30
10	Marketing costs	18,000,000	90
11	Distribution costs	4,400,000	22
12	Customer-service costs	3,600,000	18
13	Total operating costs	36,000,000	180
14	Full cost of the product	144,000,000	720
15	Operating income	$ 16,000,000	$ 80
16			
17	[a]Cost of goods sold = Total manufacturing costs because there is no beginning or inventory for Provalue II in 2012.		
18	[b]Numbers of operating-cost line items are assumed without supporting calculations.		

The current design must be changed and the customers have supplied information that will help with a redesign that might also reduce costs. A thorough value analysis will help the team pinpoint how to eliminate superfluous design features, but this is an absorption costing challenge involving all business functions. **Value analysis** focuses on the product design stage where there is the greatest opportunity to change design, materials, and manufacturing processes to reduce costs. For example, the reliability of the computer can be enhanced by using a simpler motherboard. However, the newly designed computer will not support the top-of-the-line video card, but this is of little concern to Astel because video quality is not important to Astel's targeted customers. The decisions made at the design stage will lock in some costs—for example, the lower cost of the simpler motherboard. This is an example of how a decision will affect a future outcome, the target cost.

So now Astel is considering a new design, which is a long-term decision. Exhibit 12-5 gives the estimated full product cost per unit as $720—the target cost per unit for Provalue. Astel's goal is to sell the redesigned Provalue in 2012 to replace the current model at the target price, achieve target cost, and earn the target operating income. The new design may require different capacity and labour skills or, at the very least, changes in existing capacity management. New suppliers may be needed as well as new information added to the MIS. All costs, both variable and fixed, are relevant because the company must recover all the costs of the project. If Astel has no alternative but to succeed in this project and its best estimates indicate it cannot compete, then the company's best alternative is to shut down. For the shutting-down alternative, all costs, whether fixed or variable, are relevant.

VALUE-ANALYSIS AND CROSS-FUNCTIONAL TEAMS

Usually a value-analysis team consists of top management experts in marketing, product design and engineering, process improvement, supply-chain management, distribution, customer service, and management accounting. The team evaluates the impact of design innovations and modifications on all business functions of the value chain. They choose modifications that have the greatest value to their customers relative to the costs required to provide those features. Here are some of the team's ideas:

◆ Use a simpler, more reliable motherboard without complex features.
◆ Design Provalue so that various parts snap-fit together rather than solder together to decrease direct manufacturing labour-hours and the related costs.
◆ Simplify the Provalue design and use fewer components to decrease ordering and receiving costs and also decrease testing and inspection costs.
◆ Design Provalue to be lighter and smaller to reduce distribution and packaging costs.
◆ Design Provalue to reduce repair costs at customer sites to lower customer-service costs.

Another source of information is reverse engineering—that is, disassembling and analyzing competitors' products to determine product designs and materials and to become acquainted with the technologies competitors use.

Key concepts in value analysis are cost incurrence and locked-in costs. **Cost incurrence** arises when a resource is sacrificed or consumed. Financial reporting systems recognize and record costs only when costs are incurred and this transactions logic assures reliability. Astel's costing system, for example, recognizes the direct materials costs of Provalue as each unit of Provalue is assembled and sold. But Provalue's direct materials costs per unit are determined much earlier when designers finalize the components that will go into Provalue. Direct materials costs per unit of Provalue are locked in (or designed in) at the product design stage. **Locked-in costs** (or **designed-in costs**) are those costs that have not yet been incurred but that will be incurred in the future on the basis of decisions that have already been made.

Locked-in costs become unavoidable. For example, rework costs incurred during manufacturing could be locked in by a faulty design. Similarly, in the software industry, costs of producing software are often locked in at the design and analysis stage. Costly and difficult-to-fix errors that appear during coding and testing are frequently locked in by bad designs.

Costs are not always locked in at the design stage. In some industries (such as bulk chemical manufacturing, legal, and consulting) costs are locked in and incurred at about the same time. If costs are not locked in early, cost reduction can be achieved right up to the time when costs are incurred. In these cases, costs are lowered through improved operating efficiency and productivity (for example, reducing the time it takes to do a task) rather than better design. Many companies combine value engineering with *kaizen* or continuous improvement methods that seek to improve productivity and eliminate waste during production and delivery of products.

Management accountants use their understanding of the technical and business aspects of the entire value chain to quickly estimate cost savings and to explain the cost implications of alternative design choices to the team. These cost estimates are based on the parts and processes required by the new design.

Having finished the value analysis, Astel's management team feels it has two alternatives: respond less aggressively to its competitors or replace Provalue with a newly designed computer that has fewer complex features and is therefore less costly to make. Astel decides to go with the second alternative.

Exhibit 12-6 illustrates how the locked-in cost curve and the cost-incurrence curve might appear in the case of Provalue. (The numbers underlying the graph are assumed.) The bottom curve plots the cumulative costs per unit incurred in different business functions. The top curve plots the cumulative costs locked in. Both curves deal with the same total cumulative costs per unit. The graph emphasizes the wide divergence between the time when costs are locked in and the time when those costs are incurred. In our example, once the product and processes are designed, nearly 87% (say, $780 ÷ $900) of the unit costs of Provalue are locked in when only about 8% (say, $76 ÷ $900) of the unit costs are actually incurred. For example, at the end of the design stage, costs such as direct materials, direct manufacturing labour, direct machining, and many manufacturing, marketing, distribution, and customer-service overheads are all locked in. To reduce total costs, Astel must act to modify the design before costs get locked in.

EXHIBIT 12-6
Pattern of Cost Incurrence and Locked-in Costs for Provalue

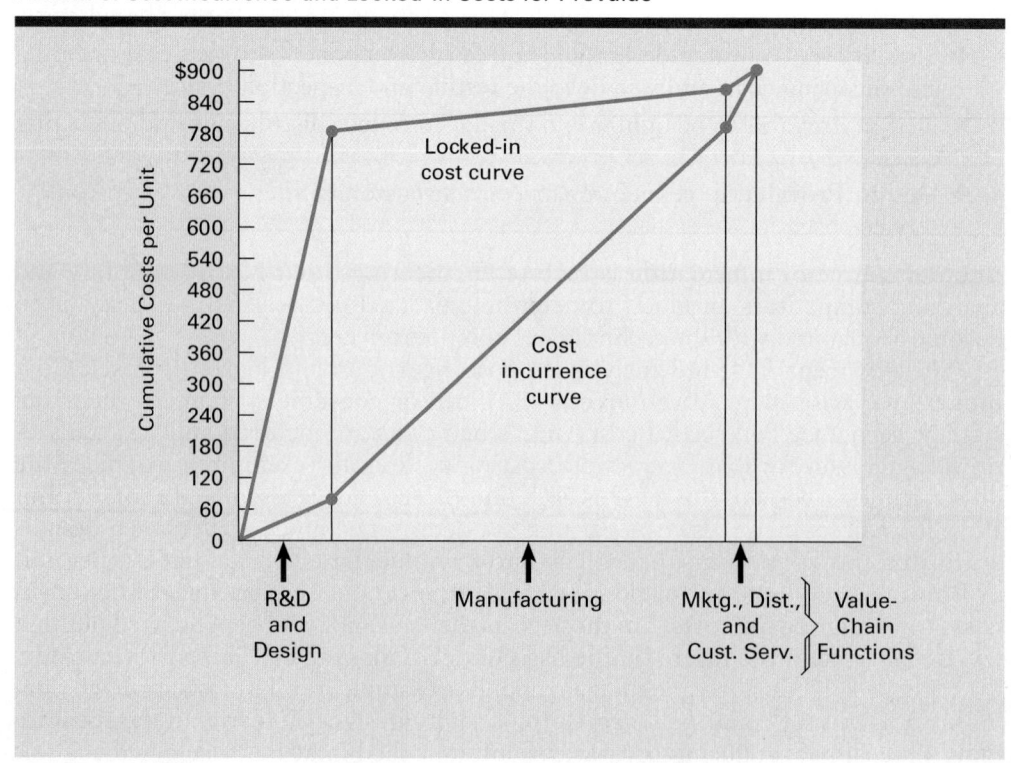

In the Provalue example, direct materials, direct manufacturing labour, and machining costs are value-added costs; ordering and testing costs fall in the grey area (customers perceive some portion of but not all of these costs as necessary for adding value); and rework costs are non-value-added costs. Astel's goal is to reduce and if possible eliminate non-value-added costs such as ordering, quality control, and rework costs by reducing the defect rate.

Eliminating or reducing the defect rate may entail process improvements, but another reason to re-examine the production process is the anticipated volume of production. The higher the volume produced and sold, the lower Astel's fixed cost allocation rate per unit will be and the more readily it will achieve its target cost. But this brings with it the temptation to produce to inventory, especially under absorption costing. Changing performance evaluation can reduce or eliminate this incentive. It may also be possible to design Provalue in a way that reduces the proportion of fixed costs.[1] This illustrates the interdependence among value-chain functions where the interdependence is caused by conflicting policies.

Reducing variable costs requires reducing unit input costs, which may be achieved by good negotiation or changing suppliers, or quantity of the input consumed. Other factors such as appropriate training, production scheduling, and maintenance also contribute to reduced direct labour costs. The variable direct and indirect costs throughout the value chain are interdependent. For example, replacing the motherboard with a simpler, less expensive component will reduce direct material costs per unit but may require a more complex assembly which will increase variable manufacturing labour costs. In itself the more complex assembly may cause an increase in defects. This is an example of how one outcome, driven externally by customer preference, affects two other outcomes driven internally by the consumption of labour in a more complex process.

Value engineering is a systematic evaluation of all aspects of the value chain. The purpose is to reduce costs but retain both product attributes and quality the customer desires and will pay for. Both value engineering and target costing have some undesirable effects if these processes are mismanaged:

◆ Decreased morale if employees fail to attain performance targets.
◆ A poorly designed product as the cross-functional team compromises on the various customer attributes.
◆ A protracted development cycle causing a missed market opportunity.
◆ Conflict among business functions, as the goal is to remove non-value-added costs wherever they arise, but the burden of cost reduction will be unequal.

Strong employee participation in the new project and realistic expectations regarding the difficulties of full manufacturing of new products using new processes will encourage employees. Keeping the focus on the customer's priorities among the attributes will reduce the problem of compromises within the pricing team. Disciplined progress toward the goal of a timely introduction of a new product will reduce the problem of paralysis by analysis. Nourishing a co-operating corporate culture of cost reduction and providing incentives to celebrate each improvement will reduce conflict.

Step 5   Astel will, of course, gather information throughout this change to a different design process and compare the actual outcomes achieved to those which were budgeted. This feedback will provide managers with the data they need not only to control change, but also to learn.

COST-PLUS PRICING

In the previous section, Astel used an external market-based approach in its long-run pricing decisions. One alternative strategy has an internal focus to determine a cost-based price. This is the cost-plus pricing strategy. Managers can turn to numerous pricing formulas based on cost. The starting point is relevant information about

---

[1]P. Woodlock, "Does It Matter How Targeted Costs Are Achieved?" *The Journal of Corporate Accounting & Finance*, 11.3, (2000): 43–52.

Extreme Target Pricing at IKEA

IKEA is the world's largest furniture retailer with 186 stores in 31 countries. Products are known for unpronounceable names, flat packaging, and do-it-yourself assembly instructions. IKEA uses aggressive target pricing and relentless cost management to keep their prices about 30% to 50% below the competition. IKEA identifies gaps in the current product portfolio, surveys competitors to discover the market price, then sets a target price that is 30% to 50% less than the market. A brief describing the new target cost and basic product specifications is submitted for bidding among IKEA's 1,800 suppliers in 55 countries that compete to present the lowest bid. Finally, internal and freelance designers compete to determine the product's final design based on price, function, and materials to be used.

This value-engineering process promotes volume-based cost efficiencies throughout the design and production process. All IKEA products can be shipped unassembled in flat packages, which reduces shipping costs to one-sixth that of competitors. In-store customer service is sparse with few salespeople and there is no free product delivery. Founder Ingvar Kamprad once noted, "Waste of resources is a mortal sin at IKEA. Expensive solutions are often a sign of mediocrity, and an idea without a price tag is never acceptable."

Sources: L. Margonelli, "How IKEA Designs Its Sexy Price Tags," *Business 2.0* (October 2002); R. Cooper and W. Chew, "Control Tomorrow's Costs Through Today's Designs," *Harvard Business Review* (January–February 1996); Ingvar Kamprad and IKEA, Harvard Business School case number 9–390–132; O. Burkeman, "The Miracle of Älmhult," *The Guardian* (June 17, 2004).

costs, not relevant information about attributes and price. The general formula for setting a price adds a markup to the cost base:

Cost base	$ X
Markup component	Y
Prospective selling price	$X + Y

Consider a cost-based pricing formula that Astel could use for the redesigned Provalue. Assume that Astel's engineers have successfully redesigned the Provalue—the Provalue II—and that Astel uses a 12% markup on the full product cost per unit in developing the prospective selling price.

Cost base (full product cost per unit, from Exhibit 12-5)	$720.00
Markup component (12% × $720)	86.40
Prospective selling price	$806.40

The markup was obtained by first estimating the **target rate of return on investment (ROI)**. The target ROI is the target operating income that an organization must earn divided by **invested capital**. Invested capital to redesign the Provalue is defined as total assets (long-term or fixed assets plus current assets), in total $96 million. Companies usually specify their target ROI. Suppose Astel's (pretax) target ROI is 18%. The target operating income that Astel must earn from Provalue II can then be calculated as follows:

Invested capital	$96,000,000
Target rate of return on investment	18%
Total target operating income (18% × $96,000,000)	$17,280,000
Target operating income per unit of Provalue II ($17,280,000 ÷ 200,000 units)	$ 86.40

The calculation indicates that Astel needs to earn a target operating income of $86.40 on each unit of Provalue II. The $86.40 expressed as a percentage of the full product cost per unit of $720 equals 12% ($86.40 ÷ $720).

The ROI cost-plus pricing method is often used when prices are regulated. In Canada, examples include milk, hydro-electric power, and telecommunications. The government regulators examine the full product costs of the supplier and negotiate a target ROI. The new price is established on this cost-plus basis for a specified time period with periodic, regulated increases. Suppliers may not charge consumers a rate higher than the contracted rate.

Do not confuse the 18% target ROI with the 12% operating income markup percentage. The 18% target rate of return on investment expresses Astel's expected operating income as a percentage of investment. The 12% markup expresses operating income per unit as a percentage *of the full product cost* per unit. Notice this is not the operating margin percentage either, which is defined as the operating margin (income) divided by total revenue. Astel establishes the target ROI and calculates its dollar value for the Provalue project, then determines the markup percentage on the cost base required to obtain the dollar value of ROI.

Companies sometimes find it difficult to determine the capital invested to support a product. Computing invested capital requires allocations of investments in equipment and buildings (used for design, production, marketing, distribution, and customer service) to individual products—a difficult and sometimes arbitrary task. Some companies therefore prefer to use alternative cost bases and markup percentages that do not require calculations of invested capital to set price.

ALTERNATIVE COST-PLUS METHODS

We illustrate these alternatives using the Astel example. Exhibit 12-7 separates the cost per unit for each value-chain business function into its variable and fixed components (without providing details of the calculations). The following table illustrates some alternative cost bases and markup percentages:

Cost Base	Estimated Cost per Unit of Provalue II (1)	Markup Percentage (2)	Markup Component for Provalue II (3) = (1) × (2)	Forecast Selling Price For Provalue II (4) = (1) + (3)
Variable manufacturing cost	$483.00	65%	$313.95	$796.95
Variable product cost	547.00	45	246.15	793.15
Manufacturing cost (COGS)	540.00	50	270.00	810.00
Absorption cost	720.00	12	86.40	806.40

To illustrate the markup calculations, we have assumed (but not derived) the markup percentages in the table. The different cost bases and markup percentages that we use in the table give prospective selling prices that are relatively close to one another. In practice, a company will choose a cost base that it regards as reliable, and a markup percentage on the basis of its experience in pricing products and to recover its costs and earn a desired return on investment. For example, a company may choose a full product cost base if it is unsure about variable and fixed cost distinctions.

The markup percentages in the table vary a great deal, from a high of 65% on variable manufacturing costs to a low of 12% on absorption costs. The reason is that the company must still cover all costs even though it is using variable COGS as its cost base. The higher the operating leverage (see Chapter 3) the higher are fixed costs, both COGS and period, as a percentage of total costs. To set a price high enough to cover both total period costs and COGS requires a higher percentage of variable costs be added. The markup percentage on full product costs is much lower because this cost already includes all period costs and COGS. The desired markup percentage may need to be adjusted depending on the competitiveness of the product market. Markups and profit margins tend to be lower in more competitive markets.

EXHIBIT 12-7
Estimated Cost Structure of Provalue II for 2012

Business Function	Estimated Variable Cost per Unit	Estimated Fixed Cost per Unit[a]	Business-Function Cost per Unit
R&D	$ 8	$ 12	$ 20
Design of product/process	10	20	30
Manufacturing	483	57	540
Marketing	25	65	90
Distribution	13	9	22
Customer service	8	10	18
Total	$547	$173	$720
	↑	↑	↑
	Per-unit variable cost of the product	Per-unit fixed cost of the product	Per-unit full cost of the product

[a]Based on budgeted annual capacity of 200,000 units.

Surveys indicate that most managers use full product costing and include unitized fixed costs from COGS and period costs per unit as well as variable costs per unit from both COGS and period costs in the cost base when making their pricing decisions. The advantages cited for including unitized fixed costs for pricing decisions include the following:

◆ *Full product cost recovery.* For long-run pricing decisions, absorption costing informs managers of the bare minimum costs they need to recover to continue in business rather than shut down. Using variable costs as a base does not give managers this information. There is then a temptation to engage in excessive long-run price cutting as long as prices give a positive contribution margin. Long-run price cutting, however, may result in long-run revenue being less than long-run full product costs, resulting in the company going out of business.

◆ *Price stability.* Managers believe that a full product cost policy for pricing promotes price stability, because it limits the ability of managers to cut prices. Managers prefer price stability because it facilitates planning.

◆ *Simplicity.* A full product cost policy does not require a detailed analysis of cost behaviour patterns to separate costs into fixed and variable components for each product. Calculating variable costs for each product is expensive and prone to errors. For these reasons, many managers believe that full product cost pricing meets the cost-benefit test.

Including unit fixed costs when pricing is not without its problems. Allocating fixed costs to products can be somewhat arbitrary. Calculating fixed cost per unit requires an estimate of expected future sales quantities. If actual sales fall short of this estimate, the actual full product cost per unit could exceed price.

COST-PLUS PRICING CONTRASTED AGAINST TARGET PRICING

The selling prices calculated under cost-plus pricing are prospective or forecast prices. For example, suppose Astel's initial product design results in a $750 cost for the redesigned Provalue. Assuming a 12% markup, Astel sets a prospective price of $840 [$750 + (12% × $750)]. Since the notebook market is extremely competitive, customer and competitor reactions to this price may force Astel to reduce the markup percentage and reduce the price to $800. Alternatively, Astel may redesign Provalue again to reduce cost to $720 per unit, as in our example, and achieve a markup of $80 per unit. The eventual design and cost-plus price balance the conflicting tensions among costs, markup, and customer reactions.

The target-pricing approach eliminates the need to go back and forth among cost-plus prospective prices, customer reactions, and design and cost modifications. Instead, the target-pricing approach first determines product characteristics and price on the basis of customer preferences and competitor responses. The target price then serves to focus and motivate managers to achieve the target cost to earn the target operating income. Sometimes the target cost is not achieved. Managers must then redesign the product, adjust the price, or work with a smaller margin.

Suppliers who provide relatively unique products and services—accountants and management consultants, for example—frequently use cost-plus pricing. Professional service firms set prices on the basis of hourly cost-plus billing rates of partners, managers, and support staff. These prices are, however, reduced in competitive situations. Professional service firms also consider a multiyear client perspective when choosing prices. Chartered accountants, for example, may charge a client a low price initially and higher prices later, a practice called lowballing.

Refined cost driver identification and cost information play an important role in both cost-plus pricing and target costing and pricing. The identification of cost drivers is critical as managers do value engineering to cost down their products—to reduce the cost of a product while still satisfying customer expectations. Service companies such as home repairs, automobile repairs, and architectural firms use a cost-plus pricing method called the time and materials method. Individual jobs are priced based on materials and labour time. The price charged for materials equals the cost of materials plus a markup. The price charged for labour represents the cost of labour, allocated overhead, and a markup. Therefore, the price charged for each cost item includes its own markup.

Assume that the full cost of a product is $50, of which $20 is fixed and avoidable if the product is discontinued and $30 is a variable cost per unit. Also assume that the fixed cost rate is based on sales of 1,000 units. Avoidable costs are those that will not be incurred if a company stops the activity that causes the cost. At a unit sales price of $35 there will still be a positive contribution margin of $5 per unit ($35 unit sales price − $30 unit variable cost = $5 unit contribution margin). The total contribution margin will be $5,000 if the sales volume is 1,000 units ($5 unit contribution margin × 1,000 units = $5,000 total contribution margin). The remaining avoidable costs are incurred and total $20,000 ($20 avoidable per unit × 1,000 units = $20,000) because the product has not been discontinued. There will be an unrecovered cost of $15,000 using full product costing ($20,000 − $5,000 = $15,000). This company will have to sell a minimum of 4,000 units to cover the fixed cost of $20,000 ($5 unit contribution margin × 4,000 units sold = $20,000) and be profitable in the long-run.

LIFE-CYCLE PRICING AND RELEVANT QUALITATIVE FACTORS IN PRICING

The meaning of a **product life cycle** is viewed differently by different stakeholders. From the internal view of the company, the product life cycle spans the time from initial R&D to the time at which support to customers is withdrawn. If the company is purchasing an asset, then its life cycle begins with the acquisition through maintenance to disposal. **Life-cycle budgeting** requires that managers estimate full product costs across the entire value chain of business functions. This view is evolving, however, to include recycling, reuse, and reclamation costs of disposing of obsolete finished products.

Customer life-cycle costing focuses on the external customer's costs to acquire, maintain, and dispose of the product or services. In a highly competitive environment, the customer will determine the target price of a product based on this assessment. Recently Chrysler offered a guaranteed price of $2.50 per U.S. gallon of gasoline (or the equivalent of $0.66 per litre) for two years with the purchase of any

Describe life-cycle pricing and discuss some non-cost factors in pricing decisions, including fair business practices and environmental sustainability.

Chrysler vehicle. This pricing strategy will reduce the operating costs and thus the life-cycle costs of Chrysler's vehicles.

Life-cycle costing tracks and accumulates the actual costs attributable to each product from start to finish. The terms *cradle-to-grave costing* and *womb-to-tomb costing* convey the sense of fully capturing all costs associated with the product. Clearly, in this long-term approach the past, current, and expected cost behaviour for a specific product will change as technology and other factors affect the product's usefulness. Throughout its life cycle, improvements need to be made to the product simply to keep costs and price within a competitive range. This is particularly important if the company has focused on a strategy of agility and customization to differentiate their product.

Life-cycle budgeted costs can provide important information for pricing decisions. For some products, the development period is relatively long and many costs are incurred before manufacturing. Consider Insight, Inc., a computer software company developing a new accounting package, General Ledger. Assume the following budgeted amounts for General Ledger over a six-year product life cycle:

	Years 1 and 2
R&D costs	$240,000
Design costs	160,000

	Years 3 to 6	
	Total Fixed Costs	**Variable Unit Costs**
Production costs	$100,000	$25
Marketing costs	70,000	24
Distribution costs	50,000	16
Customer-service costs	80,000	30

To be profitable, Insight must generate revenue to cover costs in all six business functions. A product life-cycle budget highlights the importance of setting prices and budgeting revenue to recover costs in all the value-chain business functions rather than costs in only some of the functions (such as production). The life-cycle budget also indicates the costs to be incurred over the life of the product. Exhibit 12-8 presents the life-cycle budget for General Ledger. The sensitivity analysis reports on three sets of assumptions about selling price and sales quantity combinations. These alternatives reflect the general economic principle that, in a competitive market, as the price of a commodity increases the demand or quantity sold decreases.

A sensitivity analysis (see Chapter 3) of three combinations of both prospective selling price per package and demand are shown. The high nonproduction costs at Insight are readily apparent in Exhibit 12-8. For example, R&D and product design costs constitute more than 30% of total costs for each of the three combinations of selling price and predicted sales quantity. At 5,000 in sales, the costs in years 1 and 2 are 34% of total life cycle costs ($400,000 ÷ $1,175,000 = 0.34 or 34%) and at 2,500 in sales, this increases to 42.7%. Insight should put a premium on having as accurate a set of revenue and cost predictions for General Ledger as possible, given the high percentage of total life-cycle costs incurred before any production begins and before any revenue is received.

Exhibit 12-8 assumes that the selling price per package is the same over the entire life cycle. For strategic reasons, however, Insight may choose to "skim the market" by charging higher prices to customers eager to try General Ledger when it first comes out and lower prices to customers who are willing to wait. The life-cycle budget will then express this strategy.

EXHIBIT 12-8
Budgeted Life-Cycle Revenue and Costs for the General Ledger Software Package*

| | Alternative Selling Price/ Sales Quantity Combinations | | |
	1	2	3
Selling price per package	$ 400	$ 480	$ 600
Sales quantity in units	5,000	4,000	2,500
Life-cycle revenues ($400 × 5,000; $480 × 4,000; $600 × 2,500)	$2,000,000	$1,920,000	$1,500,000
Life-cycle costs:			
R&D costs	240,000	240,000	240,000
Design costs of product/process	160,000	160,000	160,000
Production costs:			
$100,000 + ($25 × 5,000); $100,000 + ($25 × 4,000); $100,000 + ($25 × 2,500)	225,000	200,000	162,500
Marketing costs:			
$70,000 + ($24 × 5,000); $70,000 + ($24 × 4,000); $70,000 + ($24 × 2,500)	190,000	166,000	130,000
Distribution costs:			
$50,000 + ($16 × 5,000); $50,000 + ($16 × 4,000); $50,000 + ($16 × 2,500)	130,000	114,000	90,000
Customer-service costs:			
$80,000 + ($30 × 5,000); $80,000 + ($30 × 4,000); $80,000 + ($30 × 2,500)	230,000	200,000	155,000
Total life cycle costs	1,175,000	1,080,000	937,500
Life-cycle operating income	$ 825,000	$ 840,000	$ 562,500

*This exhibit does not take into consideration the time value of money when computing life-cycle revenues or life-cycle costs. Chapters 22 and 23 outline how this important factor can be incorporated into such calculations.

DEVELOPING LIFE-CYCLE REPORTS

Most accounting systems emphasize reporting on a calendar basis—monthly, quarterly, and annually. In contrast, product life-cycle reporting does not have this calendar-based focus. Consider the life spans of four Insight products shown below, where each product spans more than one calendar year:

	Year 1	Year 2	Year 3	Year 4	Year 5	Year 6
General Ledger package						
Law package						
Payroll package						
Engineering package						

Developing life-cycle reports for each product requires tracking costs and revenue on a product-by-product basis over several calendar periods. For example, the R&D costs included in a product life-cycle cost report are often incurred in different calendar years. When R&D costs are tracked over the entire life cycle, the total magnitude of these costs for each individual product can be computed and analyzed.

A product life-cycle reporting format offers at least three important benefits:

1. The full set of revenue and costs associated with each product becomes visible. Manufacturing costs are highly visible in most accounting systems, but the costs associated with upstream areas (for example, R&D) and downstream areas (for example, customer service) are frequently less visible on a product-by-product basis.

2. Differences between products in the percentage of their total costs incurred at early stages in the life cycle are highlighted. The higher this percentage, the more important it is for managers to develop, as early as possible, accurate predictions of the revenue for that product.

3. Interrelationships among business function cost categories are highlighted. For example, companies that cut back their R&D and product design costs may experience major increases in customer-service costs in subsequent years. Those costs arise because products fail to meet promised quality-performance levels. A life-cycle revenue and cost report prevents such causally related changes among business function costs from being hidden (buried) as they are in annual income statements.

Life-cycle costs further reinforce the importance of locked-in costs, target costing, and value engineering in pricing and cost management. For products with long life cycles, a very small fraction of the total life-cycle costs are actually incurred at the time when costs are locked in. But locked-in costs will determine how actual costs will be incurred later. For example, poor product design can lock in very costly rework and quality-control activities at the production stage.

CONDUCTING FAIR BUSINESS AND PRICING DECISIONS

The *Competition Act* in Canada is the legislation enacted to "protect the specific public interest in free competition."[2] Each of the pricing practices discussed below is a criminal offence for contravening the Act.[3] For example, under section 50(1) of the Act, companies cannot engage in **price discrimination** between two customers with the intent to reduce or obstruct competition among customers. There are four key elements of the price discrimination laws:

1. They apply to manufacturers, not service providers.
2. Different pricing to different customers is not an offence unless there is intent to obstruct competition among the customers.
3. Different pricing to different customers on the basis of different costs of production is not an offence.
4. Illegality hinges on the intent to obstruct or destroy competition when a manufacturer engages in price discrimination.[4]

Consider the prices airlines charged for a round-trip flight from Toronto to Beijing during the 2008 Summer Olympics. Booking prior to the opening day of the Olympics, a direct Air Canada one-week return flight in economy-class was listed on Expedia.ca as $1,772. Booking the opening day of the Olympics and returning one week later cost $2,809, and during the last week of the Olympics the flight would have cost you $2,799. Can the price differences be explained by the difference in the cost to Air Canada of these round-trip flights? No, it cost the airline the same amount of money to transport the passenger from Toronto to Beijing and back regardless of whether the passenger flew August 1, 8, or 18, 2008.

In the airline example, the demand for airline tickets comes from two main sources: business travellers and pleasure travellers. Business travellers generally travel to their destinations and return home within the same week. These aspects make business travellers' demand for air travel relatively insensitive to prices. The insensitivity of demand to price changes is called demand inelasticity. Airlines can charge business travellers higher fares because the higher fares have little effect on demand and earn higher operating income for the airlines.

Beijing National Stadium

[2]See *Weidman v. Schragge* (1912), 20 C.C.C. 177 at 147 where the Supreme Court of Canada first considered the rationale to regulate trades and industries.
[3]Although a "practice" is not specifically defined, more than one sale is likely required to establish this is a corporate practice. The practice of price discrimination does not actually have to result in any observable adverse effect on competition for companies to contravene the Act.
[4]This section is provided with assistance from Russell Hoffman, LLB., MBA.

Pleasure travellers, on the other hand, have a less pressing need to return home during the week—in fact, they generally prefer to spend weekends at their destinations. Since they pay for their tickets themselves, they are much more sensitive to price than the business traveller (demand is more price-elastic). For pleasure travellers, it is profitable for the airlines to keep fares low to stimulate demand. Requiring a Saturday-night stay distinguishes between the two customer segments. The airline company price-discriminates between the two market segments to take advantage of the different sensitivities to prices exhibited by the business and pleasure travellers. Price differences exist even though there is no cost difference in serving the two segments.

It is also illegal under section 50(1)(c) of the Act to engage in **predatory pricing**, which occurs when manufacturers sell products at lower than cost with the intent to reduce competition. It is difficult to say with any certainty what the legal thresholds are because few cases have been tried.[5] To clarify matters, the Director of Investigation and Research at Consumer and Corporate Affairs Canada released the *Predatory Pricing and Enforcement Guidelines* (the *Guidelines*) on May 21, 1992. In these *Guidelines* the Director defined predatory pricing as a "situation where a dominant firm charges low prices over a long enough period of time so as to drive a competitor from the market or deter others from entering and raises prices to recoup its losses."[6] According to these *Guidelines*, the predator must account for more than 35% of the market and be able to sustain a pricing increase for more than two years after the period of low pricing for its actions to be considered predatory pricing.

In determining whether pricing is "unreasonably low," the courts draw a distinction between pricing a product above average variable cost and below. It is likely that as long as a product is sold above average cost (even when the price is below average total product cost), and it cannot be established that the accused would have made a greater total contribution to overhead by raising prices, a court will not find the price "unreasonably low." In economic terms, the court is aware of the effect of price inelasticity of demand.

In a 1981 case, *R. v. Consumers Glass Co.*,[7] the accused, which sold small plastic lids prior to 1975, had faced reduced demand for its products. The competition cut prices by 2% to 3% and Consumers responded by cutting prices 16%, and then a further 5% while still recovering all variable costs. The Court held that "it is better for a manufacturer to produce and sell at a loss, than to cease production and suffer the loss of having to bear all fixed overhead."[8]

There are only limited circumstances when pricing below average variable costs will be tolerated by the courts. In *R. v. Hoffmann-La Roche Ltd.*[9] the Ontario Court of Appeal affirmed the trial judge's decision of an "unreasonably low" price. In this trial, it was held that the pharmaceutical firm that chose to combat new competition in the hospital market by giving away Valium was "selling" its products at an unreasonably low price. The year-long Valium giveaways were in response to a new competitor's price reductions of 25% to 50% of the Hoffmann-La Roche Ltd. price.

The Court stated that in determining the reasonableness or unreasonableness of a particular price it will "take into account all the economic costs, which include the direct production costs as well as any potential future savings or benefits."[10] This includes looking at benefits that derive to related markets or future markets. The trial judge continued, stating that the Court should look into four general considerations to determine if the price was unreasonably low:

1. The magnitude of difference between the average variable cost and the sales price is important, and the greater the unrecovered average variable cost, the greater the probability the price will be seen as unreasonable.

[5]Although the Supreme Court of Canada has never considered a case under this section, *R. v. Hoffmann-La Roche Ltd.* (1980), 28 O.R. (2d) 164, was affirmed by the Ontario Court of Appeal in 1981, 125 D.L.R. (3d) 607 (C.A.).

[6]Director of Investigation and Research, "Executive Summary," *Predatory Pricing Enforcement Guidelines* (Ottawa: Consumer and Corporate Affairs Canada, 1992).

[7](1981), 33 O.R. (2d) 228 (H.C.)

[8]Ibid. at 238.

[9]See n. 5 *supra*.

[10]*R. v. Hoffmann-La Roche Ltd.*, p. 199.

2. The greater the duration of sales at less than average variable cost, the more likely the price will be declared unreasonable.

3. The circumstances of the situation need to be taken into account, because a price cut to defend against a competitor may be justifiable.

4. Any accrual of external or long-term benefits to the seller arising from selling at a price below average variable cost is considered, and the higher the estimated long-term benefit, the more likely the price will be seen as unreasonable.[11]

Managers and accountants who are responsible for compliance must design an internal control system that collects cost data in a way that transparently discloses all variable costs. They must also record both non-manufacturing and manufacturing variable costs to ensure managers know the threshold below which they may be accused of predatory pricing. Documenting the decision process can provide a defence against the accusation that the intent of the price cut was to obstruct or destroy competition.

Dumping is closely related to predatory pricing and occurs when a non-Canadian company:

1. sells goods in Canada at a price below the market value in the home country,

2. receives a government subsidy, and

3. the action materially injures or threatens to materially injure an industry in Canada.

If dumping is proven under section 42(1)(c)(ii) of the *Special Import Measures Act* (SIMA), the Canadian International Trade Tribunal has the power to impose a countervailing duty on the goods to prevent the recurrence of the material injury. Cases related to dumping have occurred in the agricultural and automotive industries and more recently in the softwood lumber industry.[12]

Collusive pricing is also a violation of the *Competition Act*. Collusive pricing occurs when companies in an industry conspire in their pricing and output decisions to achieve a price above the competitive price. Section 45 of the Act makes it a criminal offence to conspire, agree, or combine with another person to prevent, lessen, or unduly restrain competition. Collusive pricing violates the Act because an agreement on pricing and output levels prevents competition among the companies in an industry. Recently, suspicions have been voiced regarding alleged collusive pricing among retail gasoline companies, but no one has filed a lawsuit.

In addition to price discrimination, pricing decisions also consider other non-cost considerations such as capacity constraints. **Peak-load pricing** is the practice of charging a higher price for the same product or service when demand approaches physical capacity limits. That is, the prices charged during busy periods (when loads on the system are high) are greater than the prices charged when slack or excess capacity is available. Peak-load pricing can be found in the telephone, telecommunication, hotel, car rental, and electric utility industries. The following are the daily rental rates charged by Discount Car Rental for compact cars rented at their Yonge and Bloor Toronto location at 8 a.m. and returned by noon the next day:

Weekdays (Monday – Thursday)	$39 per day
Weekends (Friday – Sunday)	$32 per day

Discount's incremental costs of renting a car are the same whether the car is rented on a weekday or a weekend. So what explains the difference in prices? We offer two separate but related explanations. One explanation is that there is a greater demand for cars during weekdays because of business activity. Faced with capacity limits, Discount raises rental rates to levels that the market will bear. A second explanation is that the rental rates are a form of price discrimination. During weekdays,

[11]*R. v. Hoffmann-La Roche Ltd.*, pp. 200–204.
[12]See *American Farm Bureau Federation v. Canadian Import Tribunal* (1990), 74 D.L.R. (4th) 449.

the demand for cars comes largely from business travellers who need to rent cars to conduct their business and who are relatively insensitive to prices. Charging higher rental rates during weekdays is profitable because it has little effect on demand. In contrast, the demand for weekend rentals comes largely from nonbusiness or pleasure travellers who are more price-sensitive. Lower rates stimulate demand from these individuals and increase Discount's operating income. Under either explanation, the pricing decision is not driven by cost considerations.

ENVIRONMENTAL SUSTAINABILITY

Environmental sustainability and *life-cycle costing* touch on the increasing social concern about what constitutes the end of a product's life cycle. The internal view of companies begins with the research, development, and design of a product and ends with its full production, but concerns about environmental sustainability are extending that view. Costs of anti-pollution measures, responsible waste disposal during production, and disposal of obsolete products now must be included in the life-cycle costs. Decisions about materials also affect environmental sustainability, as illustrated in Chapter 7. Formerly, these choices did not lock in disposal and recycling costs, but now in Germany, for example, new legislation requires manufacturers to pay for recycling of products and reclamation of materials from their obsolete products.

To achieve high yields, the mixed input must be separated from the disassembled products before the reprocessing process begins.[13] Benefits to producers from reusing and remoulding the reprocessed plastic casings arise not only from reduced direct materials cost but also reduced impact on the environment as the demand for newly produced high-value plastics decreases. The reclamation of mixed input—for example, obsolete laptop computers—requires careful separation. Both the plastic and metal must be reclaimed using different processes. The high price of some metals makes reclamation not only central in environmental sustainability but also profitable.

Manufacturers can reclaim the 1.36 billion kilograms of high-value plastic used in casings for laptops, smartphones, and HDTV converters by recycling the casings back into a high-value plastic supply chain. Telus recycled 17,024 tonnes of materials of which 6% arose from electronic products. At a disposal cost of $70 per tonne, Telus estimated it avoided approximately $2 million in landfill fees. Used, recycled, and surplus equipment produced $4.8 million revenue that would not have otherwise been realized.[14]

Companies are developing a better understanding of how to design products, processes, and procedures to prevent and reduce pollution over the product's life cycle and eliminate avoidable environmental costs. Still, currently less than 1% of the high-value plastic consumed in manufacture of electronic products is recovered. A new industry will not evolve on its own until profitable yields of appropriate high-value plastic can be reasonably anticipated from a low- or negative-value mixed input of reclaimable and recyclable plastics. One straightforward value-added solution is to design a recycling process that begins with disassembly and sorting of the high- from low-value plastics.

The enactment of strict environmental laws for resource extraction and refining industries has introduced tougher environmental standards and increased the penalties and fines for polluting the air and contaminating subsurface soil and groundwater. The goal is to include ecological responsibility as a *value-added cost* engineered in at the design phase.[15] It is difficult to forget watching millions of litres of oil gushing into the

---

[13]P. Rios, J. A. Stuart, and E. Grant, "Plastics Disassembly versus Bulk Recycling: Engineering Design for End-of-Life Electronics Resource Recovery," *Environmental Science & Technology*, 37 (2003): 5463–5470.

[14]TELUS, *Leading the Telecommunications Sector in CSR* at www.nrcan-rncan.gc.ca/sd-dd/pubs/csr-rse/pdf/cas/telus_e.pdf.

[15]E. Westkämper, J. Niemann, and A. Dauensteiner, "Economic and Ecological Aspects in Product Life Cycle Evaluation," *Proceedings of the Institute of Mechanical Engineers* 215. B (2001): 673–681.

Gulf of Mexico from a BP offshore deep water well in 2010. Environmental costs are often locked in at the product and process design phase, but some arise from negligence.

One example is gold. Over 90% of gold production is direct material for the jewellery industry. Reclamation of even very small amounts of gold from obsolete finished products carries with it a far smaller potential environmental cost than refining. The demand for gold, however, exceeds the supply available from recycled gold. As little as approximately 22 grams of gold per tonne of ore can be profitable at September 2011's price of $1,849 per ounce (28.3 grams).

Refining raw ore involves the use of sulphuric acid, cyanide, and heavy metals such as arsenic, lead, cadmium, and mercury that can leak into groundwater from the residue (tailings) left after refining the ore. Cyanide is instantly lethal to humans in a solution of 2 parts per million (ppm). Canada has adopted the World Health Organization (WHO) standard permitting 0.2 ppm. The US Environmental Protection Agency (EPA) has estimated over 40% of the western US watersheds are already affected by water pollution from mining, and the remediation costs will be in the hundreds of millions of dollars.

Responsible companies such as Barrick continue to develop refining techniques to avoid environmental pollution. But not all mining companies are like Barrick. Some use an extraction method called heap leaching. Minute amounts of gold are extracted from the ore that is dumped in a pit lined with plastic (either polyvinyl chloride (PVC) or polyethylene) or clay and sprayed with sodium cyanide of 250–500 ppm. Today in the United States over 1 billion tonnes of tailings per year are produced from heap leaching. Tailings can reach a height exceeding 90 metres.

During the decade ending in 1992, at one site close to the Alamosa River–Rio Grande watershed in Colorado, at least nine leakages of cyanide from the same mine into the groundwater were detected. The U.S. EPA demanded penalties of US$40 million in fines from the mine. The Canadian owner, Cambior, declared bankruptcy and was sued by the U.S. government for US$150 million and, in a plea bargain settled in 1996, Cambior paid a maximum fine of US$20 million. Reclamation costs paid by U.S. taxpayers to date have exceeded US$100 million. The same company also controlled a heap leach operation in Guyana on the Omai River. In 1995 over 3.17 billion litres of liquid at 25 ppm flushed into the river and flowed to the Essequibo, a principal river in South America. The company abandoned the mine, which the government closed in 2008.

Leakage and spills continue. In 2000, a spill of 100 million litres into the Tisza River from the Baia Mara mine in Romania flowed to the Danube. The spill polluted the river waters of Romania, Hungary, and the former Yugoslavia. Under legislation in place at the time, the Australian company Arul operating the mine could not be held liable for damages outside of Romania. New European legislation now holds companies responsible for transborder pollution in Europe. For example, a spill of 80 tonnes of cyanide would incur a fine of US$50 million.

Most of the technologies to prevent leakage and failure are far younger than heap leaching. While some companies are bearing the full cost of research to make the refining of gold more ecologically sound for all, others leave behind chemicals and heavy metals that eventually contaminate the land and water and all the organisms dependent upon them. A key question is the extent to which consumers, who demand environmental sustainability, will pay for the real life-cycle costs of gold jewellery. With few exceptions, remediation of abandoned mine pits is paid from tax revenue collected from the general population, not from either the producers or consumers of the product.

Some companies such as Barrick and Apple adopt proactive strategies to remedy the environmental effects of production. Others adopt a reactive strategy of minimal compliance with health, safety, and environmental regulations. Still others ignore the problems they create until confronted with them in court. Their legal costs, including fines, comprise part of the life-cycle costing of the risks of environmental degradation, being caught, and being successfully prosecuted. For yet other

Environmental Sustainability, Ecological Friendliness—Who Cares?

A survey of 167 U.K. companies indicated that 58% expressed concern with reducing consumption of non-renewable energy, 57% with appropriate waste disposal, and 41% with reducing or eliminating emissions and pollution. These percentages, however, varied widely from one industry to the next. For example, 83% in the food industry expressed concern about energy consumption, in contrast to 36% of those in retail, of which 64% were concerned with waste. Taxes on landfill use and energy costs have increased. Only half the companies, however, had adopted formal environmental policies—only 16% had explicit environmental targets, and 48% had decided upon systematic certification such as the EU's Eco-Management and Audit Scheme (EMAS) or the Responsible Care system in the chemical industry.

Management accountants, with their specific expertise in applying sound costing methods, can improve life-cycle costing techniques by providing reliable estimates of relevant environmental costs.

Source: F. Dahlmann, S. Brammer, and A. Millington, "Environmental Management in the United Kingdom: New Survey Evidence," *Management Decision,* 46.2 (2008): 264–283.

companies, excellent environmental practices can generate revenue through the sale of emissions credits on global exchanges in Chicago and Montreal. Those unable or unwilling to adopt benchmark practices can incorporate the purchase of emissions credits into their environmental sustainability strategy.[16]

[16]Much of this section was based on information from S. Fields, "Tarnishing the Earth: Gold Mining's Dirty Secret," *Environmental Health Perspectives* 109.10 (2001): A474–481 at www.jstor.org/sici?sici=0091-6765(200110)109:10%3CA474:TTEGMD%3E2.0.CO;2-4; I. M. Kiss, "The Bond Is Dead," *Central Europe Review* 2.7 (2000) at www.ce-review.org/00/7/kiss7.html; S. G. Vick, "Failure of the Omai Tailings Dam," *Geotechnical News*, September (1996): 34–40 at www.infomine.com/publications/docs/Vick1996.pdf; N. Langerman, "Cyanide Spill," *Chemical Health and Safety*, 7.3 May–June (2000): 41–42 at www.sciencedirect.com/science?_ob=HomePageURL&_method=userHomePage&_btn=Y&_acct=C000050221&_version=1&_urlVersion=0&_userid=10&md5=6b8f8a0bb11c4ebe676f09e6d7da52c8; and L. Loopnarine, "Wounding Guyana: Gold Mining and Environmental Degradation," *Revista Europea de Estudios Latinoamericanos y del Caribe*, 73 October (2002): 83–90 at ww.cedla.uva.nl/60_publications/PDF_files_publications/73RevistaEuropea/73Loopnarine.pdf.

PULLING IT ALL TOGETHER—PROBLEM FOR SELF-STUDY

(Try to solve this problem before examining the solution that follows.)

PROBLEM

Reconsider the Astel Computer example (pp. 475–490). Astel's marketing manager realizes that a further reduction in prices is necessary to sell 200,000 units of the redesigned Provalue. To maintain a target profitability of $16 million, or $80 per unit (the same amounts shown in Exhibit 12-5, p. 484), Astel will need to reduce costs of Provalue by $6 million, or $30 per unit. Astel targets a reduction of $4 million, or $20 per unit, in manufacturing costs, and $2 million, or $10 per unit, in

PROVALUE II MANUFACTURING COST DATA

Output Level: 200,000

	Cost Driver (1)	Quantity (2)	Unit of Measure	Quantity (3)	Unit of Measure	Total Quantity of Cost Driver (4) = (2) × (3)	Input Cost Driver Rate
Direct Costs							
Direct materials	No. of kits	1.0	kit per output unit	200,000	output units	200,000	$385
Direct manufacturing labour (DMLH)	DMLH	2.65	DMLH per output unit	200,000	output units	530,000	$ 20
Direct machining - fixed (DMH)	DMH hours	1.5	DMH per output unit	200,000	output units	300,000	$ 38
Overhead Costs							
Ordering and receiving	No. of orders	50.0	orders per component	425	components	21,250	$ 80
Testing and inspection (TH)	Testing hours	15.0	TH per output unit	200,000	output units	3,000,000	$ 2
Rework (RMH)	Rework hours	2.5	RMH per defective unit*	13,000	defective units	32,500	$ 40
Defect rate				6.5%	defect rate		

*6.5% defect rate × 200,000 output units = 13,000 defective units

PROVALUE III MANUFACTURING COST DATA

Output Level: 200,000

	Cost Driver (1)	Quantity (2)	Unit of Measure	Quantity (3)	Unit of Measure	Total Quantity of Cost Driver (4) = (2) × (3)	Input Cost Driver Rate
Direct Costs							
Direct materials	No. of kits	1.0	kit per output unit	200,000	output units	200,000	$ 375
Direct manufacturing labour (DMLH)	DMLH	2.65	DMLH per output unit	200,000	output units	530,000	$ 20
Direct machining - fixed (DMH)	DMH hours	1.5	DMH per output unit	200,000	output units	300,000	$ 38
Overhead Costs							
Ordering and receiving	No. of orders	50.0	orders per component	400	components	20,000	$ 60
Testing and inspection (TH)	Testing hours	14.0	TH per output unit	200,000	output units	2,800,000	$1.70
Rework (RMH)	Rework hours	2.5	RMH per defective unit*	13,000	defective units	32,500	$ 32
Defect rate				6.5%	defect rate		

marketing, distribution, and customer-service costs. The cross-functional team assigned to this task proposes the following changes to manufacture a different version of Provalue, called Provalue II:

1. Reduce direct materials and ordering costs by purchasing subassembled components rather than individual components.
2. Reengineer ordering and receiving. Reduce ordering and receiving costs per order.
3. Reduce testing time and the labour and power required per hour of testing.
4. Develop new rework procedures to reduce rework costs per hour.

No changes are proposed in direct manufacturing labour costs per unit and in total machining costs. The spreadsheet on page 500 summarizes the cost-driver quantities and the cost per unit of each cost driver for Provalue III compared with initially redesigned notebook now referred to as the Provalue II.

REQUIRED
1. What long-term factors are relevant in target pricing?
2. Will the proposed changes achieve the target cost of $20 per output unit and for a total cost reduction of $4 million to manufacture Provalue III? Show your calculations using Exhibit 12-5 as an example.
3. As a producer of electronics, what environmental factors should Astel consider?
4. Explain the importance of locked-in costs.
5. If Astel decided upon life-cycle pricing, justify a management choice between the value-chain focus and the customer life-cycle focus.

SOLUTION
1. Astel must consider fixed as well as variable costs and use absorption costing to ensure the target price will cover all costs of production including period costs.
2. Exhibit 12-9 presents the manufacturing costs for Provalue III based on the proposed changes. Manufacturing costs will decline from $108 million, or $540 per unit (Exhibit 12-4), to $104 million, or $522 per unit (Exhibit 12-9), and will achieve the target reduction of $4 million, or $20 per unit.
3. Electronics producers can recycle the high-value plastic covers and other components for recycling. Recycling is more environmentally sustainable than new plastics production, can avoid disposal costs, and can improve revenue. These recycling costs and benefits can be locked in at the design stage of Provalue III.

EXHIBIT 12-9
Target Manufacturing Costs of Provalue III for 2011 Based on Proposed Changes

Output Level: 200,000 Output Units	PROVALUE III	
	Total Manufacturing Costs (1)	Manufacturing Cost per Output Unit (2) = (1) ÷ 200,000
Direct manufacturing costs:		
Direct materials costs	$ 75,000,000	$375.00
Direct manufacturing labour costs	10,600,000	20.00
Direct machining costs (fixed)	11,400,000	38.00
Direct manufacturing costs	$ 97,000,000	$433.00
Manufacturing overhead costs:		
Ordering and receiving	1,200,000	60.00
Testing and inspection	4,760,000	23.80
Rework	1,040,000	5.20
Manufacturing overhead costs	$7,000,000	$89.00
Total manufacturing costs	$104,000,000	$522.00

In addition, Astel could consider price discrimination if it has a global customer base. The ability to pay could determine that a lower price would be charged to customers in developing countries than in developed. Astel views its product life cycle from an internal perspective without considering the needs of groups other than its customers. In fact, if Astel were producing in Europe, the life cycle of Provalue III would extend to disposal of the obsolete product.

4. Locked-in costs become unavoidable. Astel is planning to invest $96 million in the redesign and wants to avoid a situation where rework costs incurred during manufacturing are locked in by a faulty design. Design decisions influence direct materials costs through the choices of printed circuit boards and add-on features used in Provalue. Better designs also reduce both product failures in the plant and the time it takes to rework defective products. Ease in assembly decreases direct manufacturing labour costs. Fewer components reduces ordering and materials-handling costs and decreases the time required for testing and inspection. Finally, designing Provalue to reduce the need for repairs as well as the time it takes to service and repair Provalue at customer sites reduces customer service costs.

5. This is a highly competitive environment with a short product life cycle. These two factors justify a customer life-cycle pricing policy wherein the customer sets the price target. Astel must then determine the full product costs such that the operating income meets a targeted percentage of full product costs.

SUMMARY POINTS

The following question-and-answer format summarizes the chapter's learning outcomes. Each point presents a key question, and the guidelines are the answer to that question.

LEARNING OUTCOMES	GUIDELINES
1. What are the three major influences on pricing decisions?	Customers, competitors, and costs influence prices through their effects on demand and supply—customers and competitors affect demand, and costs affect supply. These factors will differ depending on the time horizon of the pricing decision. The time horizon affects the set of costs that are relevant to assure profitability.
2. How do companies implement either target pricing or cost-plus pricing to achieve short-term profitability?	Target pricing is one response to a decision with a long-term time horizon. Target price is driven by the customer in the marketplace. It is the estimated price that potential customers are willing to pay for a product or service. Given the GM%, the target cost is [(1 − GM%) × Target price]. In comparison, the cost-plus approach to pricing adds a markup component to a cost base, usually the full product cost, as the starting point for pricing decisions. Prices are then modified on the basis of customers' reactions and competitors' responses. Therefore, the size of the "plus" is determined by the market.
3. How do companies price products using target costing?	Target cost per unit is the estimated long-run cost of a product or service that, when sold, enables the company to achieve target operating income per unit. The challenge for the organization is to make the necessary cost improvements through value analysis and value-engineering methods to achieve the target cost.
4. How do companies implement target and cost-plus pricing for long-term profitability?	Over the long term, the target ROI determines the target of operating income divided by total product costs required. In a competitive environment, the customer determines the target price. Given the target price, the target ROI will determine the full product target cost that is divided into the operating income.
5. How do companies choose between customer life-cycle and life-cycle pricing?	In a highly competitive environment, companies must respond to the value-in-use for which customers will pay throughout their acquisition, maintenance, and disposal of the product. Failure to do so will impair profit because customers can purchase a substitute. This is customer life-cycle costing. The corporation must then set its target costs to achieve a long-term return on their investment in the product. Life-cycle pricing is an internal focus on ensuring all the corporation's value-chain costs for all business functions, including recycling, reuse, and reclamation of the product on disposal are included.

This chapter and the Glossary at the end of the book contain definitions of the following important terms:

collusive pricing (p. 496)
cost incurrence (p. 485)
cost-plus pricing (p. 474)
customer life-cycle costing (p. 491)
designed-in costs (p. 485)
dumping (p. 496)
full-product costs (p. 481)
invested capital (p. 488)
life-cycle budgeting (p. 491)

life-cycle costing (p. 492)
life-cycle pricing (p. 474)
locked-in costs (p. 485)
peak-load pricing (p. 496)
predatory pricing (p. 495)
price discrimination (p. 494)
product life cycle (p. 491)
target cost per unit (p. 481)
target margin percentage (p. 480)

target operating income
    per unit (p. 481)
target price per unit (p. 480)
target pricing (p. 474)
target rate of return on investment
    (ROI) (p. 488)
value analysis (p. 485)
value engineering (p. 487)

ASSIGNMENT MATERIAL

MyAccountingLab   Make the grade with MyAccountingLab: The questions, exercises, and problems marked in red can be found on MyAccountingLab at **www.myaccountinglab.com**. You can practise them as often as you want, and most feature step-by-step guided instructions to help you find the right answer. Exercises and problems with an Excel icon in the margin have an accompanying Excel template on MyAccountingLab.

SHORT-ANSWER QUESTIONS

12-1 What are the three major influences on pricing decisions?

12-2 "The relevant costs for pricing decisions are full product costs." Comment.

12-3 Give two examples of pricing decisions with a short-run focus.

12-4 How is activity-based costing useful for pricing decisions?

12-5 Describe two alternative approaches to long-run pricing decisions.

12-6 What does *product life cycle* mean?

12-7 How does collusive pricing differ from predatory pricing?

12-8 What is life-cycle budgeting?

12-9 "It is not important for a firm to distinguish between cost incurrence and locked-in costs." Do you agree? Explain.

12-10 What are three benefits of using a product life-cycle reporting format?

12-11 Describe three alternative cost-plus methods.

12-12 Give two examples where the difference in the costs of two products or services is much smaller than the difference in their prices.

EXERCISES

12-13 Terminology. A number of terms are listed below:

target pricing   target cost per unit
value engineering   value analysis
price discrimination   peak-load pricing
life-cycle pricing   customer life-cycle pricing
invested capital   target return on investment

REQUIRED
Select the terms from the above list to complete the following sentences.

_____ is a policy well suited to a highly competitive environment where many substitutes are available and may provide customers with the same valuable attributes at lower cost.
_____ is set after the price and target margin are determined. This target margin may be in percent or dollars at either the gross or operating margin level.

In a highly competitive environment, _____ refers to the total cost of ownership of a product including purchase, operating costs, maintenance, and disposal. In comparison, _____ refers to the total cost to the seller of the product from cradle to grave.

The _____ refers in this chapter to total assets. The _____ is the target operating income divided by the invested capital.

_____ is illegal because the manufacturer's intent is to obstruct or destroy competition. In contrast, _____ is the practice of charging the highest rate to provide a service when demand for the service is highest. It is common practice and not illegal.

_____ is the evaluation by a top management team of any innovations and modifications to any business function that customers would value most highly. In comparison, _____ is a process to retain both quality and all attributes that customers value while reducing costs.

⑤ **12-14 Non-cost factors.** Examples of prices charged by Phones-R-Us for long-distance telephone calls within Canada at different times of the day and week are as follows:

Peak period (8 a.m. to 6 p.m., Monday through Friday)	Basic rate
Evenings (6 p.m. to 11 p.m., Monday through Friday)	35% savings
Nights and weekends	60% savings

REQUIRED

Are there differences in incremental or outlay costs per minute for Phones-R-Us for telephone calls made during peak hours compared with telephone calls made at other times of the day?

④ ⑤ **12-15 Cost-plus, target pricing, working backward.** (S. Sridhar, adapted) Waterbury, Inc., manufactures and sells RF17, a specialty raft used for whitewater rafting. In 2013, it reported the following:

1. Variable costs per unit of RF17, $216

	A	B
	File Edit View Insert Format Tools Data Window	
	A	B
1		**2013**
2	Units produced and sold	20,000
3	Investment	$2,400,000
4	Full cost per unit	$ 300
5	Rate of return on investment	20% (expected profit)
6	Markup percentage on variable cost	50%

REQUIRED

1. What was the selling price in 2013? What was the percentage markup on full cost? What was the variable cost per unit?
2. Waterbury is considering raising its selling price to $348. However, at this price, its sales volume is predicted to fall by 10%. If Waterbury's cost structure (variable cost per unit and total fixed costs) remains unchanged and if its demand forecast is accurate, should it raise the selling price to $348?
3. In 2014, due to increased competition, Waterbury must reduce its selling price to $315 in order to sell 20,000 units. The manager of the rafts division reduces annual investment to $2,100,000 but still demands a 20% target rate of return on investment. If fixed costs cannot be changed in this time frame, what is the target variable cost per unit?

② **12-16 Cost-plus target return on investment pricing.** John Beck is the managing partner of a business that has just finished building a 60-room motel. Beck anticipates that he will rent these rooms for 16,000 nights next year (or 16,000 room-nights). All rooms are similar and will rent for the same price. Beck estimates the following operating costs for next year:

1. Target contribution per room-night, $38

Variable operating costs	$4 per room-night
Fixed costs	
Salaries and wages	$177,000
Maintenance of building and pool	40,000
Other operating and administration costs	141,000
Total fixed costs	$358,000

The capital invested in the motel is $1,000,000. The partnership's target return on investment is 25%. Beck expects demand for rooms to be uniform throughout the year. He plans to price the rooms at full cost plus a markup on full cost to earn the target return on investment.

REQUIRED

1. What price should Beck charge for a room-night? What is the markup as a percentage of the full cost of a room-night?
2. Beck's market research indicates that if the price of a room-night determined in requirement 1 is reduced by 10%, the expected number of room-nights Beck could rent would increase by 10%. Should Beck reduce prices by 10%? Show your calculations.

12-17 **Short-run pricing, capacity constraints.** Manitoba Dairy, maker of specialty cheeses, produces a soft cheese from the milk of Holstein cows raised on a special corn-based diet. One kilogram of soft cheese, which has a contribution margin of $8, requires 4 litres of milk. A well-known gourmet restaurant has asked Manitoba Dairy to produce 2,000 kilograms of a hard cheese from the same milk of Holstein cows. Knowing that the dairy has sufficient unused capacity, Elise Princiotti, owner of Manitoba Dairy, calculates the costs of making one kilogram of the desired hard cheese:

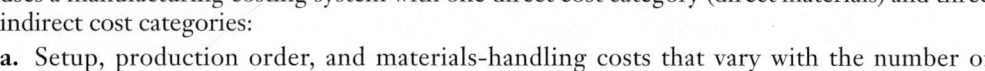
1. Variable cost per kg, $15 + 5 + 3 = $23

Milk (10 litres × $1.50 per litre)	$15
Variable direct manufacturing labour	5
Variable manufacturing overhead	3
Fixed manufacturing cost allocated	6
Total manufacturing cost	$29

REQUIRED

1. Suppose Manitoba Dairy can acquire all the Holstein milk that it needs. What is the minimum price per kilogram it should charge for the hard cheese?
2. Now suppose that the Holstein milk is in short supply. Every kilogram of hard cheese produced by Manitoba Dairy will reduce the quantity of soft cheese that it can make and sell. What is the minimum price per kilogram it should charge to produce the hard cheese?

12-18 **Target costs, effect of product-design changes on product costs.** Medical Instruments uses a manufacturing costing system with one direct cost category (direct materials) and three indirect cost categories:

1. Total manufacturing cost per unit HJ6 in 2012, $1,738

a. Setup, production order, and materials-handling costs that vary with the number of batches.

b. Manufacturing operations costs that vary with machine-hours.

c. Costs of engineering changes that vary with the number of engineering changes made.

In response to competitive pressures at the end of 2012, Medical Instruments used value-engineering techniques to reduce manufacturing costs. Actual information for 2012 and 2013 is:

	2012	2013
Setup, production order, and materials-handling costs per batch	$ 8,000	$ 7,500
Total manufacturing-operations cost per machine-hour	$ 55	$ 50
Cost per engineering change	$12,000	$10,000

The management of Medical Instruments wants to evaluate whether value engineering has succeeded in reducing the target manufacturing cost per unit of one of its products, HJ6, by 10%.

Actual results for 2012 and 2013 for HJ6 are:

	Actual Results for 2012	Actual Results for 2013
Units of HJ6 produced	3,500	4,000
Direct material cost per unit of HJ6	$1,200	$1,100
Total number of batches required to produce HJ6	70	80
Total machine-hours required to produce HJ6	21,000	22,000
Number of engineering changes made	14	10

1. Calculate the manufacturing cost per unit of HJ6 in 2012.
2. Calculate the manufacturing cost per unit of HJ6 in 2013.
3. Did Medical Instruments achieve the target manufacturing cost per unit for HJ6 in 2013? Explain.
4. Explain how Medical Instruments reduced the manufacturing cost per unit of HJ6 in 2013.

 12-19 Value-added, non-value-added costs. The Marino Repair Shop repairs and services machine tools. A summary of its costs (by activity) for 2012 is as follows:

1. Grey area total, $100,000

a. Materials and labour for servicing machine tools	$800,000
b. Rework costs	75,000
c. Expediting costs caused by work delays	60,000
d. Materials-handling costs	50,000
e. Materials-procurement and inspection costs	35,000
f. Preventive maintenance of equipment	15,000
g. Breakdown maintenance of equipment	55,000

REQUIRED

1. Classify each cost as value-added, non-value-added, or in the grey area in between.
2. For any cost classified in the grey area, assume 65% is value-added and 35% is non-value-added. How much of the total of all seven costs is value-added and how much is non-value-added?
3. Marino is considering the following changes: (a) introducing quality-improvement programs whose net effect will be to reduce rework and expediting costs by 75% and materials and labour costs for servicing machine tools by 5%; (b) working with suppliers to reduce materials-procurement and inspection costs by 20% and materials-handling costs by 25%; and (c) increasing preventive-maintenance costs by 50% to reduce breakdown-maintenance costs by 40%. Calculate the effect of programs (a), (b), and (c) on value-added costs, non-value-added costs, and total costs. Comment briefly.

 12-20 Life-cycle product costing. Intentical Inc. manufactures game systems. Intentical has decided to create and market a new system with wireless controls and excellent video graphics. Intentical's managers are thinking of calling this system the Yew. Based on past experience they expect the total life cycle of the Yew to be four years, with the design phase taking about a year. They budget the following costs for the Yew:

1. BEP in units, 714,840

		Total Fixed Costs over Four Years	Variable Cost per Unit
Year 1	R&D costs	$6,590,000	—
	Design costs	1,450,000	—
Years 2–4	Production	19,560,000	$50 per unit
	Marketing and distribution	5,242,000	10 per unit
	Customer service	2,900,000	—

REQUIRED

1. Suppose the managers at Intentical price the Yew game system at $110 per unit. How many units do they need to sell to break even?
2. The managers at Intentical are thinking of two alternative pricing strategies.
   a. Sell the Yew at $110 each from the outset. At this price, they expect to sell 1,500,000 units over its life cycle.
   b. Boost the selling price of the yew in year 2 when it first comes out to $240 per unit. At this price they expect to sell 100,000 units in year 2. In years 3 and 4 drop the price to $110 per unit. The managers expect to sell 1,200,000 units in years 3 and 4.
   Which pricing strategy would you recommend? Explain.
3. What other factors should Intentical consider in choosing its pricing strategy?

12-21 Target prices, target costs, activity-based costing. Snappy Tiles is a small distributor of marble tiles. Snappy identifies its three major activities and cost pools as ordering, receiving and storage, and shipping, and it reports the following details for 2012:

②
1. Operating income for 2012, $45,000

Activity	Cost Driver	Quantity of Cost Driver	Cost per Unit of Cost Driver
1. Placing and paying for orders of marble tiles	Number of orders	500	$50 per order
2. Receiving and storage	Loads moved	4,000	$30 per load
3. Shipping of marble tiles to retailers	Number of shipments	1,500	$40 per shipment

For 2012, Snappy buys 250,000 marble tiles at an average cost of $3 per tile and sells them to retailers at an average price of $4 per tile. Assume Snappy has no fixed costs and no inventories.

REQUIRED
1. Calculate Snappy's operating income for 2012.
2. For 2013, retailers are demanding a 5% discount off the 2012 price. Snappy's suppliers are only willing to give a 4% discount. Snappy expects to sell the same quantity of marble tiles in 2013 as in 2012. If all other costs and cost-driver information remain the same, calculate Snappy's operating income for 2013.
3. Suppose further that Snappy decides to make changes in its ordering and receiving-and-storing practices. By placing long-run orders with its key suppliers, Snappy expects to reduce the number of orders to 200 and the cost per order to $25 per order. By redesigning the layout of the warehouse and reconfiguring the crates in which the marble tiles are moved, Snappy expects to reduce the number of loads moved to 3,125 and the cost per load moved to $28. Will Snappy achieve its target operating income of $0.30 per tile in 2013? Show your calculations.

12-22 Product costs, activity-based costing systems. Executive Power (EP) manufactures and sells computers and computer peripherals to several nationwide retail chains. Johan Farnham is the manager of the printer division. Its two largest selling printers are P-41 and P-63.

①
1. Total full absorption product costs P-63, $604.80

The manufacturing cost of each printer is calculated using EP's activity-based costing system. EP has one direct manufacturing cost category (direct materials) and the following five indirect manufacturing cost pools:

Indirect Manufacturing Cost Pool	Allocation Base	Allocation Rate	Measure of Value-Added
1. Materials handling	Number of parts	$ 1.44	per part
2. Assembly management	Hours of assembly time	$48.00	per hour of assembly time
3. Machine insertion of parts	Number of machine-inserted parts	$ 0.84	per machine-inserted part
4. Manual insertion of parts	Number of manually inserted parts	$ 2.52	per manually inserted part
5. Quality testing	Hours of quality testing time	$30.00	testing-hour

Product characteristics of P-41 and P-63 are as follows:

	P-41	P-63
Direct-materials costs	$489.00	$350.52
Number of parts	85 parts	46 parts
Hours of assembly time	3.2 hours	1.9 hours
Number of machine-inserted parts	49 parts	31 parts
Number of manually inserted parts	36 parts	15 parts
Hours of quality testing	1.4 hours	1.1 hours

REQUIRED
What is the manufacturing cost of P-41? of P-63?

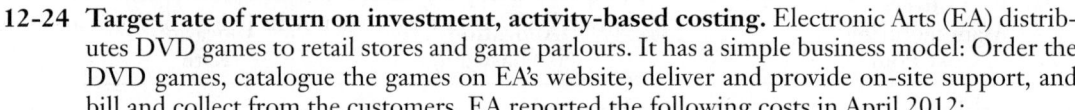

12-23 Relevant-cost approach to short-run pricing decisions. The Montreal Company is an electronics business with eight product lines. Income data for one of the products (XT-107) for June 2012 are:

Revenue		
200,000 units at average price of $100 each		$20,000,000
Variable costs		
Direct materials at $35 per unit	$7,000,000	
Direct manufacturing labour at $10 per unit	2,000,000	
Variable manufacturing overhead at $6 per unit	1,200,000	
Sales commissions at 15% of revenue	3,000,000	
Other variable costs at $5 per unit	1,000,000	
Total variable costs		14,200,000
Contribution margin		5,800,000
Fixed costs		5,000,000
Operating income		$ 800,000

Dorval Ltd., an instruments company, has a problem with its preferred supplier of XT-107 components. This supplier has had a three-week labour strike. Dorval approaches the Montreal sales representative, Elise Marcotte, about providing 3,000 units of XT-107 at a price of $75 per unit. Marcotte informs the XT-107 product manager, Jim McMahon, that she would accept a flat commission of $8,000 rather than the usual 15% of revenue if this special order were accepted. Montreal has the capacity to produce 300,000 units of XT-107 each month, but demand has not exceeded 200,000 units in any month in the past year.

REQUIRED
1. If the 3,000-unit order from Dorval is accepted, how much will operating income increase or decrease? (Assume the same cost structure as in June 2012.)
2. McMahon ponders whether to accept the 3,000-unit special order. He is afraid of the precedent that might be set by cutting the price. He says, "The price is below our full cost of $96 per unit. I think we should quote a full price, or Dorval will expect favoured treatment again and again if we continue to do business with it." Do you agree with McMahon? Explain.

12-24 Target rate of return on investment, activity-based costing. Electronic Arts (EA) distributes DVD games to retail stores and game parlours. It has a simple business model: Order the DVD games, catalogue the games on EA's website, deliver and provide on-site support, and bill and collect from the customers. EA reported the following costs in April 2012:

Activity	Cost Driver	Quantity	Cost per Unit of Cost Driver
Ordering	Number of game vendors	40	$250 per vendor
Cataloguing	Number of new titles	20	$100 per title
Delivery and support	Number of deliveries	400	$ 15 per delivery
Billing and collection	Number of customers	300	$ 50 per customer

In April 2012, EA purchased 12,000 game DVDs at an average cost of $15 per DVD, and it sold them at an average price of $22 per DVD. The catalogue on the website and the customer interactions that occur during delivery are EA's main marketing inputs. EA incurs no other costs.

REQUIRED
1. Calculate EA's operating income for April 2012. If the monthly investment in EA is $300,000, what rate of return on investment does the business earn?
2. The current crop of game systems is maturing, and prices for games are beginning to decline. EA anticipates that from May onward, it will be able to sell 12,000 game DVDs each month for an average of $18 per DVD, and it will have to pay vendors an average of $12 per DVD. Assuming other costs are the same as in April, will EA be able to earn its 15% target rate of return on investment?
3. EA's small workforce gathers as a team and considers process improvements. They recommend "firing" the marginal vendors—those who need a lot of "hand holding" but whose titles are not very popular.

They agree that they should shift some of their resources from vendor relationships and cataloguing to delivery and customer relationships. In May 2012, EA reports the following support costs:

Activity	Cost Driver	Quantity	Cost per Unit of Cost Driver
Ordering	Number of game vendors	30	$200 per vendor
Cataloguing	Number of new titles	15	$100 per title
Delivery and support	Number of deliveries	450	$ 20 per delivery
Billing and collection	Number of customers	300	$ 50 per customer

At a selling price of $18 and a cost of $12 per DVD, how many game DVDs must EA sell in May 2012 to earn its 15% target rate of return on investment?

12-25 Relevant-cost approach to pricing decisions, special order. The following financial data apply to the DVD production plant of the Dill Company for October 2012:

1. Increase in operating income, $600

	Budgeted Manufacturing Cost per DVD
Direct materials	$1.60
Direct manufacturing labour	0.90
Variable manufacturing overhead	0.70
Fixed manufacturing overhead	1.00
Total manufacturing cost	$4.20

Variable manufacturing overhead varies with the number of units produced. Fixed manufacturing overhead of $1 per DVD is based on budgeted fixed manufacturing overhead of $150,000 per month and budgeted production of 150,000 DVDs per month. The Dill Company sells each DVD for $5.

Marketing costs have two components:

◆ Variable marketing costs (sales commissions) of 5% of revenue.
◆ Fixed monthly costs of $65,000.

During October 2012, Lyn Randell, a Dill Company salesperson, asked the president for permission to sell 1,000 DVDs at $4 per DVD to a customer not in Dill's normal marketing channels. The president refused this special order because the selling price was below the total budgeted manufacturing cost.

REQUIRED
1. What would have been the effect on monthly operating income of accepting the special order?
2. Comment on the president's "below manufacturing costs" reasoning for rejecting the special order.
3. What other factors should the president consider before accepting or rejecting the special order?

12-26 Target operating income, value-added costs, service company. Carasco Associates prepares architectural drawings to conform to local structural-safety codes. Its income statement for 2012 is:

1. Total value-added costs, $471,600

Revenue	$680,000
Salaries of professional staff (8,000 hours × $50 per hour)	400,000
Travel	18,000
Administrative and support costs	160,000
Total costs	578,000
Operating income	$102,000

Following is the percentage of time spent by professional staff on various activities:

Making calculations and preparing drawings for clients	75%
Checking calculations and drawings	4
Correcting errors found in drawings (not billed to clients)	7
Making changes in response to client requests (billed to clients)	6
Correcting own errors regarding building codes (not billed to clients)	8
Total	100%

Assume administrative and support costs vary with professional-labour costs.

Pricing Decisions, Product Profitability Decisions, and Cost Management **509**

Consider each requirement independently.

1. How much of the total costs in 2012 are value-added, non-value-added, or in the grey area in between? Explain your answers briefly. What actions can Carasco take to reduce its costs?
2. Suppose Carasco could eliminate all errors so that it did not need to spend any time making corrections and, as a result, could proportionately reduce professional-labour costs. Calculate Carasco's operating income for 2012.
3. Now suppose Carasco could take on as much business as it could complete, but it could not add more professional staff. Assume Carasco could eliminate all errors so that it does not need to spend any time correcting errors. Assume Carasco could use the time saved to increase revenue proportionately. Assume travel costs will remain at $18,000. Calculate Carasco's operating income for 2012.

PROBLEMS

1. Total cost of repair option, $145

12-27 Cost-plus, time and materials. Mazzoli Brothers is an auto repair shop. Mazzoli's cost accounting system tracks two cost categories: direct labour (working on the cars) and direct materials (parts). Mazzoli uses a time-and-materials pricing system, with direct labour marked up 100% and direct materials marked up 50% to recover indirect costs of support staff, support materials, and shared machines and tools, and to earn a profit.

Johanna White brings her car to the shop. The head mechanic, Luke Bariess, concludes her car's problem is with the clutch plate. He considers two options: replace the clutch plate or repair it. The cost information available to Bariess follows:

File Edit View Insert Format Tools Data			
	A	B	C	D
1		**Labour**		**Materials**
2	Repair option	3.5 hours		$ 40
3	Replace option	1.5 hours		$200
4	Markup	100%		50%
5				
6	Labour rate	$30	per labour-hour	

REQUIRED

1. Why might Mazzoli use different markup rates for direct materials and for direct labour?
2. If Bariess presents White with the replace or repair options, what price would he quote for each?
3. If the two options were equally safe and effective for the three years that White intends to use the car before junking it, which option would she choose?
4. If Bariess's objective is to maximize profits, which option would Bariess recommend to White? Is this the option chosen by White in requirement 3? Comment on your answers in requirements 3 and 4.

1. a. Total sales revenue, $4,725,000

12-28 Cost-plus, target pricing, working backward. The new CEO of Roile Manufacturing has asked for a variety of information about the operations of the firm from last year. The CEO is given the following information, but with some data missing:

Total sales revenue	?
Number of units produced and sold	500,000 units
Selling price	?
Operating income	$225,000
Total investment in assets	$2,500,000
Variable cost per unit	$2.50
Fixed costs for the year	$3,250,000

REQUIRED

1. Find (a) total sales revenue, (b) selling price, (c) rate of return on investment, and (d) markup percentage on full cost for this product.

2. The new CEO has a plan to reduce fixed costs by $250,000 and variable costs by $0.50 per unit. Using the same markup percentage as in requirement 1, calculate the new selling price.

3. Assume the CEO institutes the changes in requirement 2 including the new selling price, expecting to sell more units of product because of the lower price. However, the reduction in variable cost has resulted in lower product quality leading to 10% fewer units being sold compared to before the change. Calculate operating income (loss).

12-29 Target prices, target costs, value engineering, cost incurrence, locked-in costs, activity-based costing. Cutler Electronics makes a Blu-ray player, CE100, which has 80 components. Cutler sells 7,000 units each month for $70 each. The costs of manufacturing CE100 are $45 per unit, or $315,000 per month. Monthly manufacturing costs incurred are:

②
1. Manufacturing cost per unit of New CE100, $39.92

Direct material costs	$182,000
Direct manufacturing labour costs	28,000
Machining costs (fixed)	31,500
Testing costs	35,000
Rework costs	14,000
Ordering costs	3,360
Engineering costs (fixed)	21,140
Total manufacturing costs	$315,000

Cutler's management identifies the activity cost pools, the cost driver for each activity, and the cost per unit of the cost driver for each overhead cost pool as follows:

Manufacturing Activity	Description of Activity	Cost Driver	Cost per Unit of Cost Driver
1. Machining costs	Machining components	Machine-hour capacity	$4.50 per machine-hour
2. Testing costs	Testing components and final product (Each unit of CE100 is tested individually.)	Testing-hours	$2 per testing-hour
3. Rework costs	Correcting and fixing errors and defects	Units of CE100 reworked	$20 per unit
4. Ordering costs	Ordering of components	Number of orders	$21 per order
5. Engineering costs	Designing and managing of products and processes	Engineering-hour capacity	$35 per engineering-hour

Cutler's management views direct material costs and direct manufacturing labour costs as variable with respect to the units of CE100 manufactured. Over a long-run horizon, each of the overhead costs described in the preceding table varies, as described, with the chosen cost drivers.

The following additional information describes the existing design:

a. Testing and inspection time per unit is 2.5 hours.

b. 10% of the CE100s manufactured are reworked.

c. Cutler places two orders with each component supplier each month. Each component is supplied by a different supplier.

d. It currently takes 1 hour to manufacture each unit of CE100.

In response to competitive pressures, Cutler must reduce its price to $62 per unit and its costs by $8 per unit. No additional sales are anticipated at this lower price. However, Cutler stands to lose significant sales if it does not reduce its price. Manufacturing has been asked to reduce its costs by $6 per unit. Improvements in manufacturing efficiency are expected to yield a net savings of $1.50 per Blu-ray player, but that is not enough. The chief engineer has proposed a new modular design that reduces the number of components to 50 and also simplifies testing. The newly designed Blu-ray player, called "New CE100," will replace CE100.

The expected effects of the new design are as follows:

a. Direct material cost for the New CE100 is expected to be lower by $2.20 per unit.

b. Direct manufacturing labour cost for the New CE100 is expected to be lower by $0.50 per unit.

c. Machining time required to manufacture the New CE100 is expected to be 20% less, but machine-hour capacity will not be reduced.

d. Time required for testing the New CE100 is expected to be lower by 20%.

e. Rework is expected to decline to 4% of New CE100s manufactured.

f. Engineering-hours capacity will remain the same.

Pricing Decisions, Product Profitability Decisions, and Cost Management **511**

Assume that the cost per unit of each cost driver for CE100 continues to apply to New CE100.

REQUIRED

1. Calculate Cutler's manufacturing cost per unit of New CE100.
2. Will the new design achieve the per-unit cost-reduction targets that have been set for the manufacturing costs of New CE100? Show your calculations.
3. The problem describes two strategies to reduce costs: (a) improving manufacturing efficiency and (b) modifying product design. Which strategy has more impact on Cutler's costs? Why? Explain briefly.

1. Normal markup, 85.19%

12-30 Relevant-cost approach to pricing decisions. Stardom, Inc. cans peaches for sale to food distributors. All costs are classified as either manufacturing or marketing. Stardom prepares monthly budgets. The March 2012 budgeted absorption-costing income statement is as follows:

Revenue (1,000 crates × $100 a crate)	$100,000
Cost of goods sold	60,000
Gross margin	40,000
Marketing costs	30,000
Operating income	$ 10,000
Normal markup percentage: $40,000 ÷ $60,000 = 66.7% of absorption cost	

Monthly costs are classified as fixed or variable (with respect to the number of crates produced for manufacturing costs and with respect to the number of crates sold for marketing costs):

	Fixed	Variable
Manufacturing	$20,000	$40,000
Marketing	16,000	14,000

Stardom has the capacity to can 1,500 crates per month. The relevant range in which monthly fixed manufacturing costs will be "fixed" is from 500 to 1,500 crates per month.

REQUIRED

1. Calculate the markup percentage based on total variable costs.
2. Assume that a new customer approaches Stardom to buy 200 crates at $55 per crate for cash. The customer does not require any marketing effort. Additional manufacturing costs of $2,000 (for special packaging) will be required. Stardom believes that this is a one-time-only special order because the customer is discontinuing business in six weeks' time. Stardom is reluctant to accept this 200-crate special order because the $55-per-crate price is below the $60-per-crate absorption cost. Do you agree with this reasoning? Explain.
3. Assume that the new customer decides to remain in business. How would this longevity affect your willingness to accept the $55-per-crate offer? Explain.

1. Billing rate, $17.27 per hour

12-31 Cost-plus and market-based pricing. (CMA, adapted) Best Test Laboratories evaluates the reaction of materials to extreme increases in temperature. Much of the company's early growth was attributable to government contracts, but recent growth has come from expansion into commercial markets. Two types of testing at Best Test are Heat Testing (HTT) and Arctic-Condition Testing (ACT). Currently, all of the budgeted operating costs are collected in a single overhead pool. All of the estimated testing-hours are also collected in a single pool. One rate per test-hour is used for both types of testing. This hourly rate is marked up by 45% to recover administrative costs and taxes, and to earn a profit.

Rick Shaw, Best Test's controller, believes that there is enough variation in the test procedures and cost structure to establish separate costing rates and billing rates at a 45% markup. He also believes that the inflexible rate structure currently being used is inadequate in today's competitive environment. After analyzing the company data, he has divided operating costs into the following three cost pools:

Labour and supervision	$ 491,840
Setup and facility costs	402,620
Utilities	368,000
Total budgeted costs for the period	$1,262,460

Rick Shaw budgets 106,000 total testing-hours for the coming period. This is also the cost driver for labour and supervision. The budgeted quantity of cost driver for setup and facility costs is 800 setup-hours. The budgeted quantity of cost driver for utilities is 10,000 machine-hours.

Rick has estimated that HTT uses 60% of the testing-hours, 25% of the setup-hours, and half the machine-hours.

REQUIRED

1. Find the single rate for operating costs based on testing-hours and the hourly billing rate for HTT and ACT.
2. Find the three activity-based rates for operating costs.
3. What will the billing rate for HTT and ACT be based on the activity-based costing structure? State the rates in terms of testing-hours. Referring to both requirements 1 and 2, which rates make more sense for Best Test?
4. If Best Test's competition all charge $20 per hour for arctic testing, what can Best Test do to stay competitive?

12-32 **Cost-plus and market-based pricing.** St. John's Temps, a large labour contractor, supplies contract labour to building-construction companies. For 2012, St. John's Temps has budgeted to supply 80,000 hours of contract labour. Its variable costs are $12 per hour, and its fixed costs are $240,000. Roger Mason, the general manager, has proposed a cost-plus approach for pricing labour at full cost plus 20%.

1. Price per hour at full cost plus 20%, $15 × 1.20 = $18 per hour

REQUIRED

1. Calculate the price per hour that St. John's Temps should charge based on Mason's proposal.
2. The marketing manager supplies the following information on demand levels at different prices:

Price per Hour	Demand (Hours)
$16	120,000
17	100,000
18	80,000
19	70,000
20	60,000

St. John's Temps can meet any of these demand levels. Fixed costs will remain unchanged for all the demand levels. On the basis of this additional information, calculate the price per hour that St. John's Temps should charge to maximize operating income.
3. Comment on your answers to requirements 1 and 2. Why are they the same or different?

12-33 **Pricing of a special order.** Fane Industries Ltd. has been approached by a customer who wishes to purchase 50,000 units of its product at $52 per unit. The customer requires delivery within one month. The company has capacity to produce 350,000 units per month and has 5,000 units currently in stock. Sales to Fane's regular customers are forecast at 325,000 units for the upcoming month. The sales manager has indicated that if the company accepts the special order, it would be able to recover 30% of the sales lost to regular customers. Units sold through normal distribution channels have a selling price of $70 per unit and the gross margin earned on each unit is $24. Selling and administration costs total $16 per unit.

1. Net benefit, $128,000

A further analysis determined that the variable manufacturing costs of the regular units are $35 per unit with variable selling costs of $12 per unit. Because of the nature of the special order, the selling costs will be reduced to $8.00 per unit.

REQUIRED

1. Should Fane accept the offer from the customer?
2. What is the minimum price Fane should charge for this order?
3. What factors should be considered in pricing special orders?

12-34 **Life-cycle costing.** Fearless Furniture Manufacturing (FFM) has been manufacturing furniture for the home for over 30 years. George Fearless, the owner, has decided he would like to manufacture an executive desk that contains space for not only a laptop dock but also an MP3 player dock. Based on his experience with furniture, he believes the desk will be a popular item for four years, and then will be obsolete because technology will have changed again.

1. Budgeted life-cycle operating income per desk, $3,970,400

FFM expects the design phase to be very short; maybe four months. There is no R&D cost because the idea came from George, without any real research. Also, fixed production costs will not be high because FFM has excess capacity in the factory. The FFM accountants have developed the following budget for the new executive desk:

		Fixed	Variable
Months 1–4	Design costs	$700,000	—
Months 5–36	Production	$ 9,000	$225 per desk
	Marketing	3,000	—
	Distribution	2,000	$ 20 per desk
Months 37–52	Production	$ 9,000	$225 per desk
	Marketing	1,000	—
	Distribution	1,000	$ 22 per desk

The design cost is for the total period of four months. The fixed costs of production, marketing, and distribution are the expected costs per month. Ignore time value of money.

REQUIRED
1. Assume FFM expects to make and sell 16,000 units in the first 32 months (months 5–36) of production (500 units per month), and 4,800 units (300 per month) in the last 16 months (months 37–52) of production. If FFM prices the desks at $500 each, how much profit will FFM make in total and on average per desk?
2. Suppose FFM is wrong about the demand for these executive desks, and after the first 36 months it stops making them altogether. It sells 16,000 desks for $400 each with the costs described for months 5–36, and then incurs no additional costs and generates no additional revenue. Will this have been a profitable venture for FFM?
3. Will your answer to requirement 2 change if FFM still must incur the estimated fixed production costs for the whole period through month 52, even if FFM stops making executive desks at the end of 36 months?

2 5

1. Contribution margin at a price of $500, $420 × 100 passengers = $42,000

12-35 Airline pricing, considerations other than cost in pricing. Snowbound Air is about to introduce a daily round-trip flight from Edmonton to Winnipeg and is determining how it should price its round-trip tickets.

The market research group at Snowbound Air segments the market into business and pleasure travellers. It provides the following information on the effects of two different prices on the number of seats expected to be sold and the variable cost per ticket, including the commission paid to travel agents:

Price Charged	Variable Cost per Ticket	Number of Seats Expected to Be Sold	
		Business	Pleasure
$ 500	$ 80	200	100
2,000	180	190	20

Pleasure travellers start their travel during one week, spend at least one weekend at their destination, and return the following week or thereafter. Business travellers usually start and complete their travel within the same work week. They do not stay over weekends.

Assume that round-trip fuel costs are fixed costs of $24,000 and that fixed costs allocated to the round-trip flight for airplane-lease costs, ground services, and flight-crew salaries total $188,000.

REQUIRED
1. If you could charge different prices to business travellers and pleasure travellers, would you? Show your computations.
2. Explain the key factor (or factors) for your answer in requirement 1.
3. How might Snowbound Air implement price discrimination? That is, what plan could the airline formulate so that business travellers and pleasure travellers each pay the price desired by the airline?

4 5

1. Bid amount, $88,000

12-36 Governance and pricing. Baker, Inc. is preparing to submit a bid for a ball-bearings order. Greg Lazarus, controller of the Bearings Division of Baker, has asked John Decker, the cost analyst, to prepare the bid. To determine the amount of the bid, Baker's policy is to mark up the full costs of the order by 10%. Lazarus tells Decker that he is keen on winning the bid and that the bid amount he calculates should be competitive.

Direct materials		$40,000
Direct manufacturing labour		10,000
Overhead costs		
Design and parts administration	$4,000	
Production order	5,000	
Setup	5,500	
Materials handling	6,500	
General and administration	9,000	
Total overhead costs		30,000
Full product costs		$80,000

All direct costs and 30% of overhead costs are incremental costs of the order.

Lazarus reviews the numbers and says, "Your costs are way too high. You have allocated too many overhead costs to this order. You know our fixed overhead is not going to change if we win this order and manufacture the bearings. Rework your numbers. You have got to make the costs lower."

Decker verifies that his numbers are correct. He knows that Lazarus wants this order because the additional revenue from the order would lead to a big bonus for Lazarus and the senior division managers. Decker knows that if he does not come up with a lower bid, Lazarus will be very upset.

REQUIRED

1. Using Baker's pricing policy and based on Decker's estimates, calculate the total amount Baker should bid for the ball-bearings order.
2. Calculate the incremental costs of the ball-bearing order. Why do you think Baker uses full costs of the order rather than incremental costs in its bidding decisions?
3. Evaluate whether Lazarus' suggestion to Decker to use lower cost numbers is unethical. Would it be unethical for Decker to change his analysis so that a lower cost can be calculated? What steps should Decker take to resolve this situation?

COLLABORATIVE LEARNING CASE

12-37 **Target prices, target costs, value engineering.** Avery, Inc., manufactures two component parts for the television industry:

1. Tvez total ABC overhead allocation, $545,000

◆ Tvez. Annual production and sales of 50,000 units at a selling price of $48.72 per unit.
◆ Premia. Annual production and sales of 25,000 units at a selling price of $72 per unit.

Avery includes all R&D and design costs in engineering costs. Assume that Avery has no marketing, distribution, or customer-service costs.

The direct and overhead costs incurred by Avery on Tvez and Premia are described as follows:

	Tvez	Premia	Total
Direct materials costs (variable)	$1,020,000	$720,000	$1,740,000
Direct manufacturing labour costs (variable)	360,000	240,000	600,000
Direct machining costs (fixed)	180,000	120,000	300,000
Manufacturing overhead costs:			
Machine setup costs			112,500
Testing costs			600,000
Engineering costs			480,000
Manufacturing overhead costs			1,192,500
Total costs			$3,832,500

Avery's management identifies the following activity cost pools, cost drivers for each activity, and the costs per unit of cost driver for each overhead cost pool:

Activity	Description	Cost Driver	Cost per Unit of Cost Driver
Setup	Preparing machine to manufacture a new batch of products	Setup hours	$30 per setup-hour
Testing	Testing components and final product (each unit is tested individually)	Testing hours	$2.40 per testing-hour
Engineering	Designing products and processes and ensuring their smooth functioning	Complexity of product and process	Costs assigned to products by special study

Over a long-run time horizon, Avery's management views direct materials costs and direct manufacturing labour costs as variable with respect to the units of Tvez and Premia produced. Direct machining costs for each product do not vary over this time horizon and are fixed long-run costs. Overhead costs vary with respect to their chosen cost drivers. For example, setup costs vary with the number of setup-hours. Additional information is as follows:

	Tvez	Premia
Production batch size	500 units	200 units
Setup time per batch	15 hours	18 hours
Testing and inspection time per unit of product produced	2.5 hours	5 hours
Engineering costs incurred on each product	$200,000	$280,000

Avery is facing competitive pressure to reduce the price of Tvez and has set a target price of $48.00, well below its current price of $52.50. The challenge for Avery is to reduce the cost of Tvez. Avery's engineers have proposed a new product design and process improvements for the "New Tvez" to replace Tvez. The new design would improve product quality, and reduce scrap and waste. The reduction in prices will not enable Avery to increase its current sales. (However, if Avery does not reduce prices, it will lose sales.)

The expected effects of the new design relative to Tvez are as follows:
1. Direct materials costs for New Tvez are expected to decrease by $2.50 per unit.
2. Direct manufacturing labour costs for New Tvez are expected to decrease by $0.70 per unit.
3. Time required for testing each unit of New Tvez is expected to be reduced by 0.5 hours.
4. Machining time required to make New Tvez is expected to decrease by 20 minutes. It currently takes one hour to manufacture one unit of Tvez. The machines are dedicated to the production of New Tvez.
5. New Tvez will take 7 setup-hours for each setup.
6. Engineering costs are unchanged.

Assume that the batch sizes are the same for New Tvez as for Tvez. If Avery requires additional resources to implement the new design, it can acquire these additional resources in the quantities needed. Further assume the costs per unit of cost driver for the New Tvez are the same as those described for Tvez.

INSTRUCTIONS
Form groups of two students to complete the following requirements.

REQUIRED
1. Develop full product costs per unit for Tvez and Premia, using an activity-based product costing approach.
2. What is the markup on the full product cost per unit for Tvez?
3. What is Avery's target cost per unit for New Tvez if it is to maintain the same markup percentage on the full product cost per unit as it had for Tvez?
4. Will the New Tvez design achieve the cost reduction targets that Avery has set?
5. What price would Avery charge for New Tvez if it used the same markup percentage on the full product cost per unit for New Tvez as it did for Tvez?
6. What price should Avery charge for New Tvez, and what next steps should Avery take regarding New Tvez?

Strategy, Balanced Scorecard, and Profitability Analysis

BUSINESS MATTERS

Balanced Performance Measures of Social and Financial Results

Pearson PLC is a global media company with a 2010 net profit of £743 million, of which 60% was generated by textbook sales. Pearson PLC has won recognition for environmental achievements, including recycling and reuse of 95% of its textbooks. Pearson PLC disburses funds for the Pearson Peacekeeping Centre (PPC), operating as the Lester B. Pearson Canadian International Peacekeeping Training Centre. The late Lester B. Pearson was a Canadian Prime Minister who won the Nobel Peace Prize in 1957 after organizing a U.N. Emergency Force to avoid war over control of the Suez Canal. In 2009, the Pearson Peacekeeping Centre focused on training African policewomen in Darfur to protect the civilian population against gender-based violence.

Marjorie Scardino, Pearson's CEO, said in the 2010 Annual Report that strategy is a manifesto for disruption and radical reinvention of the corporation, not a placid restatement of business as usual. In reflecting on the recent turbulence from the financial and political changes worldwide, she emphasized the need to keep learning and changing before it is unavoidable at Pearson PLC. Her overall approach is to buck the tide, not ride it into a profitable future that more often than not emerges before we can perceive the change.

Source: http://www.pearson.com/media/files/annual-reports/Pearson_AR10.pdf p. 4 and 14.

LEARNING OUTCOMES

After studying this chapter, you should be able to

1. Explain how the relative strength of five competitive forces help managers identify two types of strategy.

2. Identify Porter's five factors and apply the decision framework to a strategic choice.

3. Identify balanced scorecard measures appropriate to a cost leadership strategy.

4. Evaluate strategic success at implementing a cost leadership strategy using balanced scorecard measures.

5. Analyze the results from specific productivity and capacity control strategies to achieve balanced scorecard expectations.

Strategy specifies how an organization can create value for its customers while differentiating itself from its competitors. Strategy is both open and flexible, but strategic outcomes arise from a deliberate, rational, reflective process. This chapter discusses an important tool to measure the success of competitive corporate strategy—the balanced scorecard (BSC).[1] The BSC translates a corporation's strategy into a comprehensive set of performance measures to assess how well the strategy is implemented through changes to how a corporation operates.

Application of the BSC will be explored using Chipset Inc., a manufacturer of linear integrated circuit devices (LICDs) used in communication networks. Chipset has one specialized model, LCX1. Chipset consulted extensively with its customers and designed this chip to meet their needs. Important features of the LCX1 are its versatility in many integrated circuits used in different devices, and the scaleability of the chips. **Scaleability** means one chip can be added to another in a single circuit to increase the speed and power of the device.

Chipset currently has 10 customers demanding approximately equal volumes of the LCX1, and has the practical capacity to meet normal demand growth. The efficiency and yield from the production process is due to the engineering talent of Chipset's product and process designers. The company follows a target pricing policy because similar products are readily available to its customers. The company has set its return on investment (ROI) and operating income margin percentage, which will determine the target cost of the LCX1.

Industry analysts anticipate an annual growth rate of 10% in market size from which Chipset will benefit because it already has the capacity to match this growth. Chipset can increase production readily because it has some older and fully depreciated production equipment that can provide excess capacity when required. Managers continue to consider the pros and cons of retention or disposal of this equipment to replace it with newer equipment. Chipset's current production capacity enables it to convert 3,750,000 cm^2 of silicon each year. A disposal decision depends on any streamlining in the current production process to improve yields (see Chapter 7). Additional equipment purchases are only available in increments to process 250,000 cm^2 of silicon wafers.

FIVE FORCES ANALYSIS TO DEFINE STRATEGIC ALTERNATIVES

① Explain how the relative strength of five competitive forces help managers identify two types of strategy.

In formulating its strategy for long-term success, a corporation needs to understand its own strengths and weaknesses, as well as the opportunities and threats of the economic environment. Overlap between corporate strengths to counter threats and maximize opportunities as well as identifying remedies for weaknesses describe a corporation's **distinctive** or **core competence**. Distinctive competence is a unique combination of human and capital resources that enables a company to outperform competitors.

Michael Porter, a Harvard University business professor and leading expert on strategy, has identified five competitive forces that all corporations face. A competent analysis of Porter's five forces is key to a successful strategic decision. The corporate team must examine (1) competitors, (2) potential entrants into the market, (3) equivalent products, (4) the price-setting power of customers, and (5) the price-setting power of suppliers.[2] A rigorous and disciplined analysis will enable the corporate team to identify the level of competitive rivalry in its business environment and how to best exploit its own core competence to outperform its rivals. Porter's five forces are illustrated in Exhibit 13-1, and we look at each in detail below.

[1]See R. S. Kaplan and D. P. Norton, *The Balanced Scorecard* (Cambridge: Harvard Business School Press, 1996); R. S. Kaplan and D. P. Norton, *The Strategy-Focused Organization: How Balanced Scorecard Companies Thrive in the New Business Environment* (Boston: Harvard Business School Press, 2001); and R. S. Kaplan and D. P. Norton, *Strategy Maps: Converting Intangible Assets into Tangible Outcomes* (Boston: Harvard Business School Press, 2004).

[2]M. Porter, *Competitive Strategy* (New York: Free Press, 1980); M. Porter, *Competitive Advantage* (New York: Free Press, 1985); and M. Porter, "What Is Strategy?" *Harvard Business Review* (November–December 1996): 61–78.

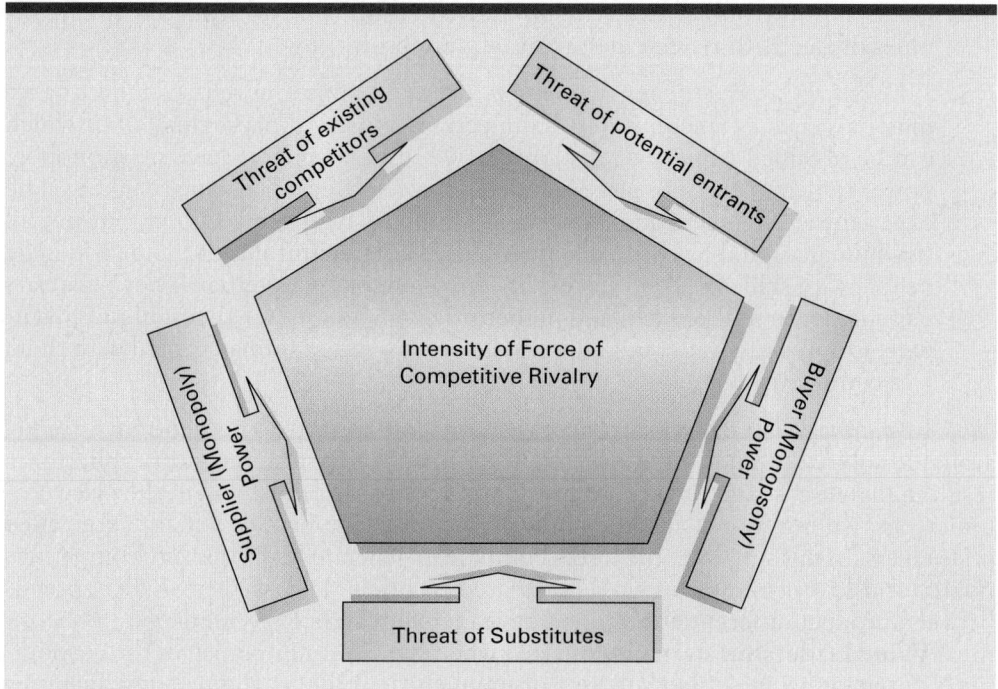

1. *Competitors.* Chipset's LCX1 model has superior features relative to its competitors in the LICD market. Competition, however, is high, and Chipset is a price taker with price set by customers who want quick delivery of reliable, customized chips. The return on investment (ROI) increases as the quantity produced increases because the fixed cost per chip goes down. This is called **economies of scale** and is central to reducing costs for mass-produced items. The less unused capacity, the lower Chipset can reduce its price per unit and retain the same operating margin.

2. *Potential new entrants.* There are few new entrants because existing competition keeps the profit margins low. Capital investment is also high because it is costly to purchase new equipment and plants, and to train workers to produce LCIDs. Chipset's operating profit will bear less burden of amortization expense because some productive machinery is fully depreciated. Chipset has already recovered this capacity cost through sales of chips in the past and can choose to exclude it from their current prices to compete on low price. Mature manufacturers like Chipset have experienced workers who can produce more product with fewer mistakes than a new entrant. This improves yield and reduces the labour cost per saleable chip below what could be achieved by a new entrant. The strength and maturity of Chipset's equipment and human capital both create barriers to entry for new competitors.

3. *Substitute products.* Chipset's engineers developed the LCX1 to be versatile and flexible, which, along with the price and speed of delivery, reduces the risk a rival can develop a substitute chip with the same desirable performance attributes. Through close work with its key customers, Chipset practices continuous quality improvement to customize chips and improve scaleability to please its customers, without jeopardizing the mass market. The talent of its product and process design engineers who developed the scaleable LCX1 is one element of Chipset's core competence, which cannot be imitated as long as the engineers remain.

4. *Price-setting power of customers (monopsony).* Telecommunications providers such as BCE, Telus, and Rogers would purchase chips like Chipset's LCX1. Because they purchase such large quantities, customers can bargain aggressively for lower prices. They have price-setting or monopsony power. This threat can be

particularly acute for customized products with few customers: If the dominant customer walks away and there is not another to take its place, then the manufacturer is in trouble. Chipset supplies 10 customers with roughly equal volumes of LXC1 to reduce the threat of monopsony power.

5. *Price-setting power of input suppliers (monopoly).* Chipset purchases high quality materials such as silicon wafers, connectivity pins, and packaging, all of which can be obtained from several suppliers. Chipset's suppliers have no monopoly power to demand a high price and, like Chipset, they are also price takers. The experienced engineers and workers at Chipset have been retained, but not all this human capital has been documented. **Human capital** is the value added by people with skill and experience gained from working together. They have bargaining power and can demand higher prices and wages for their unique advantage. Or they can walk out Chipset's door, taking their human capital with them to a competitor.

In summary, large numbers of competitors, low barriers to new entrants, readily available substitutes, and high price-setting power of customers and suppliers can result in higher cost and lower revenue. Corporations that must accept the price customers are willing to pay and the costs monopsony suppliers can charge are called price takers. In this situation, the forces combine to generate high-intensity competitive rivalry and low profit margins. The strategic choice discussed in this chapter is between product differentiation (or value leadership) and cost leadership.

Value leadership strategies succeed when the customer perceives the corporation's output as having either superior or uniquely desirable attributes for which they will pay a higher price. The ability for a corporation to offer desirable products is called **product differentiation**. Value leadership can help assure long-term profitability when a company can differentiate its product successfully.

Corporations can implement a value leadership strategy by closely investigating and analyzing the preferences of their consumers. As competitors develop substitutes and patents expire, corporations can sustain their competitive advantage by developing new products. The result may be that more scarce financial resources are devoted to R&D and market research than to the purchase of machine capacity. Profit arises from a higher unit price rather than from lowering costs to increase the volume of sales.

Cost leadership strategies succeed when a corporation can produce products that are at least equal to others in the market at the lowest cost. Highly intense competitive rivalry characterizes industries that mass produce outputs with many substitutes available from many suppliers. Producers cannot raise prices to cover costs of innovation when customers do not value innovation. Customers will simply purchase an equivalent product at a lower price from a competitor. Competition will drive profit to the thinnest of margins.

A cost leadership strategy often leads to highly automated processes to mass produce large volumes of products. Given a specific fixed cost of capacity, the greater the volume of output produced and sold in the relevant range, the more advantageous are the economies of scale. Corporations may choose to grow by expanding existing capacity. Or they can design different products that can be produced using the same equipment and plant. This is called **economies of scope**. For example, a decision to introduce different product lines of hair shampoo for oily, dry, and normal hair will exploit economies of scope.

PORTER'S FIVE FORCES AND RETURN ON INVESTMENT (ROI)

Dividing the estimated returns or earnings of investments by the total investment costs gives the return on investment (ROI). Porter's five forces model links an appropriate strategic decision to the improved opportunities for economic return on investment. Over its lifetime, an investment is supposed to earn (or return) at least as much as the investment cost. This is consistent with the target pricing approach in Chapter 12, which linked the financial effects of short-term pricing decisions with long-term ROI.

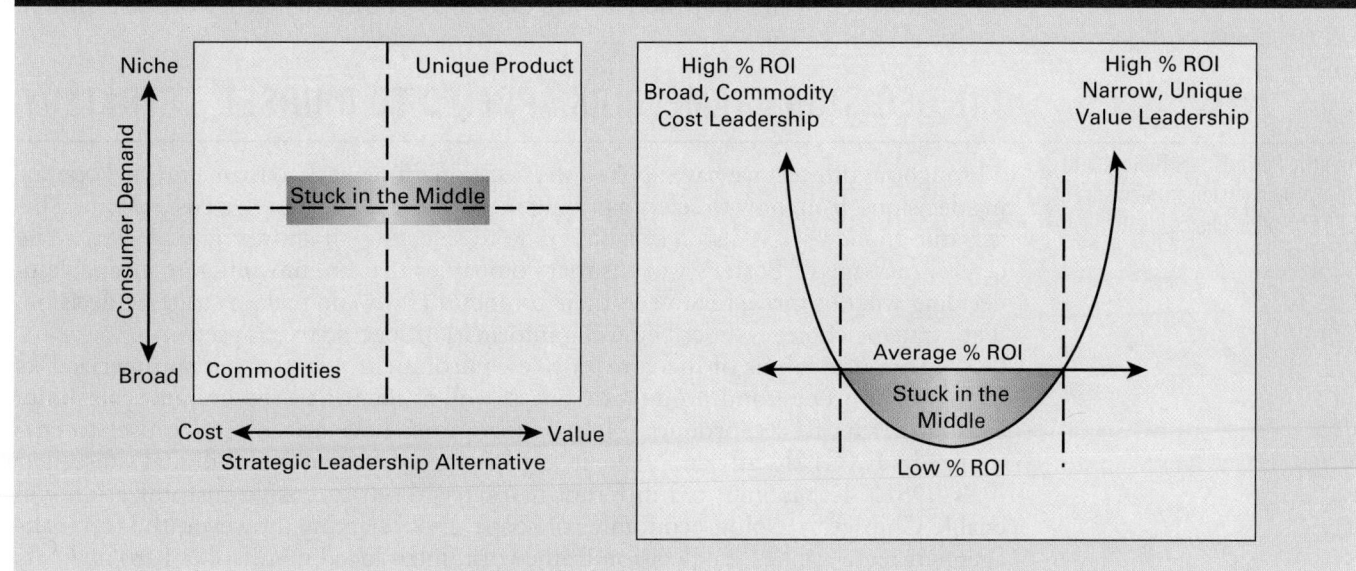

But pricing cannot be done independently of competitive context where the seller is a price taker. Porter's framework demonstrates the economics of why this is true. The strategic decision to pursue profit through either value or cost leadership affects not only potential ROI but also choices among increasingly refined methods of cost identification and control. The decision to pursue cost leadership leads logically to more sophisticated cost measurement and control methods.

The left side of Exhibit 13-2 shows a diagram that illustrates the two opposed strategies most appropriate to the intensity of competitive rivalry, defined by the supply of and demand for a product. In the upper right is the value leadership strategy with a unique or differentiated product, and in the bottom left is the cost leadership strategy for mass-produced outputs. On the right, the U-shape emphasizes that there are two focused cost or value leadership strategies that will potentially provide an above average ROI relative to an unfocused strategy of "stuck in the middle." As you move up vertically on the U-shaped curve, the ROI improves. The ROI actually enjoyed depends on how well the company executes either cost or value leadership. If stuck in the middle, then the average ROI is the *best* possible. The space above the horizontal arrow indicating an average ROI is the increasing opportunity cost of being stuck in the middle.[3]

In Chapter 12 we made the link between pricing and achieving a planned ROI. The improvement in ROI obtained from making a strategic choice to best match the corporate strengths and weaknesses to the threats and opportunities does not arise simply by choosing either value or cost leadership, however. For example, cost leadership requires an excellent costing system. This strategy, appropriate in a context of mass production, requires close attention to fixed cost management (see Chapters 8 and 9). Without a cost system separating fixed from variable overhead cost pools, the company will be lost when actually doing cost management at the level required to succeed at cost leadership.

In addition to an excellent costing system, companies like Chipset will need timely Level 4 variance reports to keep close track of yield and mix variances (see Chapter 7). Tracking these variances is a way to measure the ongoing effectiveness of the engineers who have designed the production processes that are the distinctive competence of Chipset. But engineering benefits the entire corporate effort and is not merely a product-level cost. Understanding this will help Chipset's management

---

[3]A tremendous amount of research indicates a lagged relationship between strategic implementation and magnitude of operating margin that is indeed U-shaped. But the winning strategy differs among industries (e.g., Thornhill and R.E. White, *Strategic Management Journal* 28 (2007): 553–561).

team select appropriate nonfinancial measures of benefit that apply not only to distinct outputs but also to other business functions. The selection and application of these measures of interdependency are discussed in the balanced scorecard (BSC).

THE DECISION FRAMEWORK APPLIED TO CHIPSET'S STRATEGY

2 Identify Porter's five factors and apply the decision framework to a strategic choice.

Throughout this text we have applied the decision framework to many internal operating decisions, from how to select a pricing method to how to design a cost system. This versatile framework is also a reliable guide to selecting an appropriate strategy. The central message of Porter's work is that companies that are unwilling or incapable of deciding will not thrive relative to their competitors who do make a strategic decision. The strategic choice is described using information specific to Chipset.

From its analysis of the competitive environment, Chipset has summarized its strengths in process and product design as well as identified the unique scaleability attribute of its LCX1 product. New opportunities have arisen for Chipset to customize its LXC1 slightly and make it suitable for a different use in digital subscriber lines (DSL). Expanding to a different market without extensive customization will enable Chipset to exploit economies of scope. Before acting, however, the top management team applies the decision framework, introduced in Chapter 1, to make its decision between the value or cost leadership strategy to pursue.

Step 1: Identify the problem Chipset's managers understand they must choose one of two basic strategies—*value* or *cost leadership*. There are elements of customization at Chipset, but the important attribute designed into its product is that the chips can be linked in arrays to boost performance and power of different devices. Chipset's competitors also provide customized designs and unique product features for their customers, but their products lack scaleability. To fuel future growth, Chipset must decide between either their current core competence or committing to development of innovative highly customized products for which customers will pay more.

Step 2: Gather and analyze relevant information Chipset gathers intelligence data about its competitor, Visilog, and market data from customers to improve Chipset's understanding of the environment. Top management analyzes the new data and produces the **customer preference map** shown in Exhibit 13-3. The *y*-axis describes various desirable attributes of the LCX1, which customers perceive as adding value. The *x*-axis compares the ratings of important attributes from (1) poor to (5) very good for both Chipset and Visilog. The collected data indicates that Visilog has chosen value (product) leadership. The map highlights the trade-offs for each company.

EXHIBIT 13-3
Customer Preference Map for LICDs

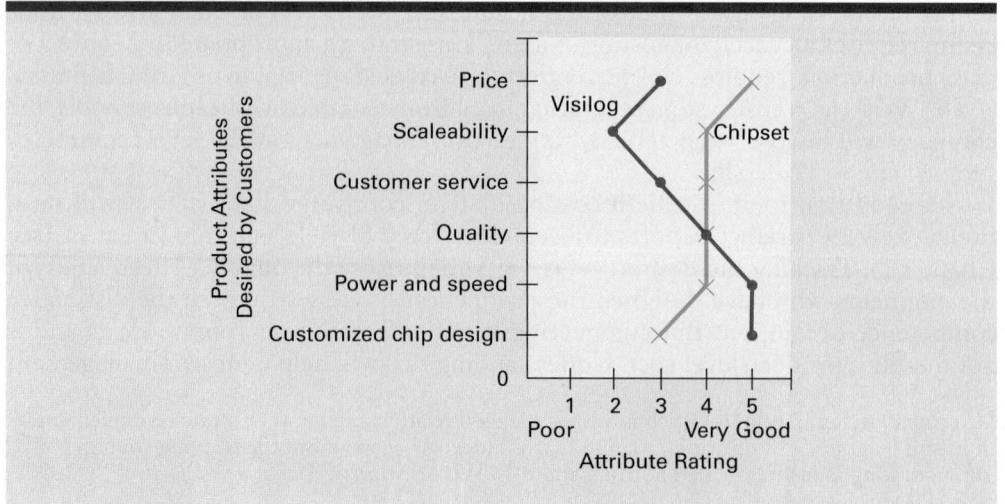

Chipset's LCX1 chip has an advantage in terms of price, customer service, and scaleability. In terms of scaleability, Chipset's LCX1 technology allows Chipset's customer to achieve different performance levels by simply altering the number of LCX1 units in their product. Visilog's customized chips, though not scaleable, are individually faster and more powerful.

Step 3: Make predictions about the future LCX1 is somewhat differentiated from competing products, but it is not unique. If Chipset were to pursue unique product development, it would be competing against giants in the microchip industry such as Intel and AMD who already possess a competitive advantage in R&D. Differentiating LCX1 further is costly, but profitable if the life cycle for the product would result in satisfactory ROI and Chipset's customers would pay. But product life cycles are as short as 90 days. Chips are obsolete almost as soon as they are marketed, and customers know they can wait only a short time for a superior product. They will not pay a premium price adequate to reach an above average ROI. The alternative strategy is cost leadership.

Step 4: Make the decision between the two strategies In a highly automated manufacturing process, Chipset can enjoy cost reduction from economies of scale and scope. Chipset's current engineering staff is more skilled at making product and process improvements than at creatively designing new products and technologies. Their talent, however, has enabled Chipset to exploit its equipment capacity more effectively and keep costs lower than competitors. In addition, Chipset scores "very good" on pricing, while Visilog ranks only average. Chipset concludes it will retain the scaleable design of LCX1 but lower its price and improve quality and customer service. Chipset concludes it should follow a *cost leadership* strategy. Chipset will not purchase more capacity, but instead will increase its yield.

Step 5: Implement the decision, evaluate performance, and learn To achieve its cost leadership strategy, Chipset must improve its own internal production process and increase yield. Producing more chips is one way this company will drive down its full absorption cost. But strategy requires some integration of product and process development. Chipset can rely on its core competence, the process engineers, and the skill of its workers, but as change is implemented Chipset must ensure it retains this human capital. There are other important value functions where operations will change in a coordinated way to focus on implementing the strategy smoothly and cost-effectively. As the company reengineers and simplifies both product and processes to reduce opportunities for error, improve quality, and speed up the production cycle, some retraining of Chipset's labour will be needed.

Chipset's engineering changes will be driven by customer's requirements, sustaining scaleability, and cost reduction through reengineering and retraining. There are choices to be made as to how to implement the decision. Chipset decides it would be sensible to avoid the loss of morale from downsizing. Instead, to retain its human capital, Chipset will pay to retrain experienced workers in quality control. Retraining will be consistent with Chipset's history of placing a high value on its people and giving them new opportunities.

Exhibit 13-4 presents a strategy map for Chipset illustrating how the company can implement their cost leadership strategy to coordinate corporate resources and control change. Executing the activities on the strategy map effectively will make it more likely that Chipset will meet its financial targets. The changes to operations are interdependent and the four tiers and the interdependence among them are illustrated by arrows. There are a limited number of activities in each tier of the strategy map, and these activities are often referred to as **key success factors (KSF)** or **key performance factors (KPF)**.

The arrows on the strategy map can be read in a straightforward way. Each one indicates how the strategy aligns different business functions, listed vertically. Measures of the indicators in each oval will keep Chipset's management team focused on how well the strategy is being implemented. The strategy map is a way to succinctly illustrate the key success factors that are interdependent at Chipset.

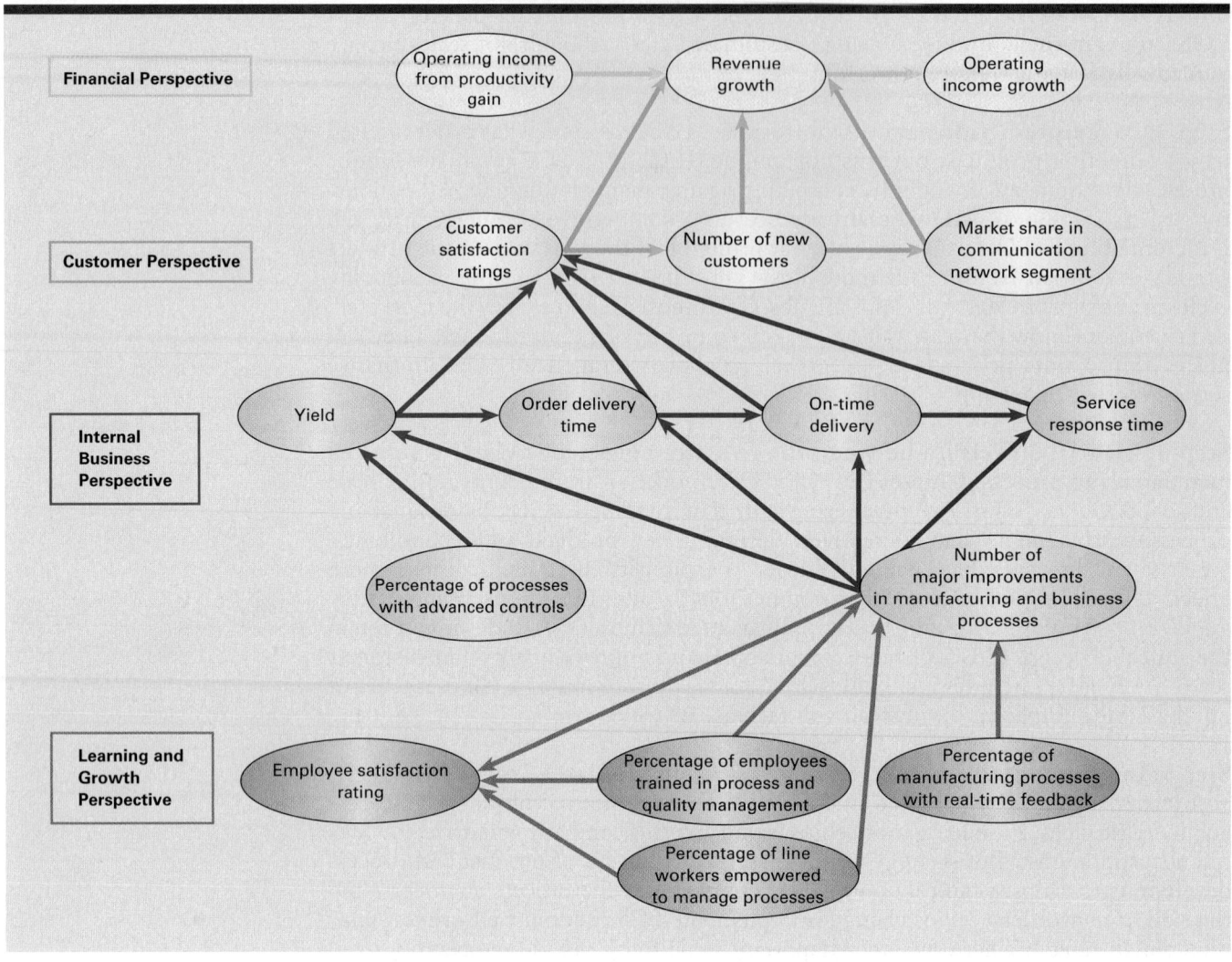

Successful achievement of one critical success factor depends on successful achievement in others.

Notice that the arrows leading from Learning and Strategy to the large circle "Number of major improvements in manufacturing and business processes" lead to Chipset's core competence in internal business process design. It is continuous improvements that result in improved performance in the other factors measuring performance. Each of the measures of internal business factors link to expected increases in customer satisfaction. The concentration of arrows leading to this oval identify it as a KPF. Increasing the quantity and quality of chips in a specific time period will improve the order-to-delivery cycle and, of course, on-time delivery. Chipset is also targeting a more effective and efficient customer-service time, although the quantity of after-sales service should decrease as the quality of LCX1 increases.

This is sensible in a commodity market where there are many substitutes for a product. Dissatisfied customers can easily move to another supplier. Finally, notice that most of the arrows from the customer perspective factors are pointing to improved revenue through sales growth. Chipset expects its market share to grow because of LCX1's versatility and improved customer satisfaction. Successful implementation should also improve operating income as economies of scale and scope reduce costs.

Chipset's most important change to implement will be to reengineer business processes. **Reengineering** (or **redesigning**) is the fundamental rethinking and redesign of business processes to achieve improvements in critical measures such as cost, quality, speed, and customer satisfaction.[4] Over the next several periods of implementation, Chipset will want to obtain feedback to measure the success or failure of their redesigning efforts. One approach, the balanced scorecard, will produce required feedback to assess the success of the strategy.

BALANCED SCORECARD: MEASURES OF PERFORMANCE

The **balanced scorecard (BSC)** is a way to assess how coherently corporate strategy has been implemented in day-to-day operations. It provides a reliable and multi-dimensional measure of how effectively and efficiently managers have controlled corporate resources—an evaluation of the quality of stewardship. First introduced in 1996 by R.S. Kaplan and D.P. Norton, the BSC links short-term operating outcomes to long-run goals. Exhibit 13-5 illustrates measures that Chipset chose, consistent with both the measures and the four perspectives presented in Exhibit 13-4.

Identify balanced scorecard measures appropriate to a cost leadership strategy. ③

The essence of a good BSC is that it represents the interdependencies among KPFs using financial and nonfinancial performance measures of cost and benefit. It is consistent with Porter's perspective on competitive strategy and the importance of making a decision about strategy. The BSC justifies the benefit of nonfinancial measures of corporate success in areas where no financial measures are available, but which actually enhance profits. For example, one study reported how an antenna installation company used customer satisfaction surveys to identify an important KPF: a shortened installation cycle time.[5] By improving its internal process, the company also shortened its cash-to-cash cycle between taking the customer's order and receiving payment. In principle, the same applies to Chipset's redesign efforts. By shortening the cycle between order-taking, producing, shipping, invoicing, and collection, Chipset will shorten its cash-to-cash cycle as well as please its customers. With more time to complete more orders, there is also more time to increase the volume of Chipset's customers and increase market share.

Chipset will realize economies of scale by producing more product in a shorter time. While the product is customized, Chipset has decided to compete on a cost rather than value leadership strategy. This means spending the money on improved processes and perhaps new equipment, rather than differentiating its products by paying more for R&D. BSC measures that Chipset will use to obtain feedback are summarized in the following sections.

FINANCIAL PERSPECTIVE—RELIABILITY AND FINANCIAL ACCOUNTING

The **financial perspective** highlights achievement of financially strategic goals. The maximization of shareholder value is a strategic goal shared by all for-profit businesses. Chipset's financial targets include increasing revenues and generating capacity costs savings.

Improving order-delivery and customer response time will help maintain existing customers, generate sales to new customers, and increase revenues. Increasing the volume of LCX1 manufactured will produce capacity cost savings through economies of scale.

CUSTOMER PERSPECTIVE—FINANCIAL AND NONFINANCIAL MEASURES

The **customer perspective** identifies the targeted market segments and measures the company's success in these segments. Chipset's measures of customer satisfaction include shortening the order cycle, improving quality, and ensuring the LCX1 has value-added attributes.

[4]See M. Hammer and J. Champy, *Reengineering the Corporation: A Manifesto for Business Revolution* (New York: Harper, 1993); Ruhli, Treichler, and Schmidt, "From Business Reengineering to Management Reengineering—A European Study," *Management International Review* (1995): pp. 361–371; and K. Sandberg, "Reengineering Tries a Comeback—This Time for Growth, Not Just for Cost Savings," *Harvard Management Update* (November 2001).
[5]R.E. Paladino, "Balanced Forecasts Drive Value," *Strategic Finance* (January, 2005): 37–42.

EXHIBIT 13-5
Specific BSC Measures Consistent with Chipset's Strategy

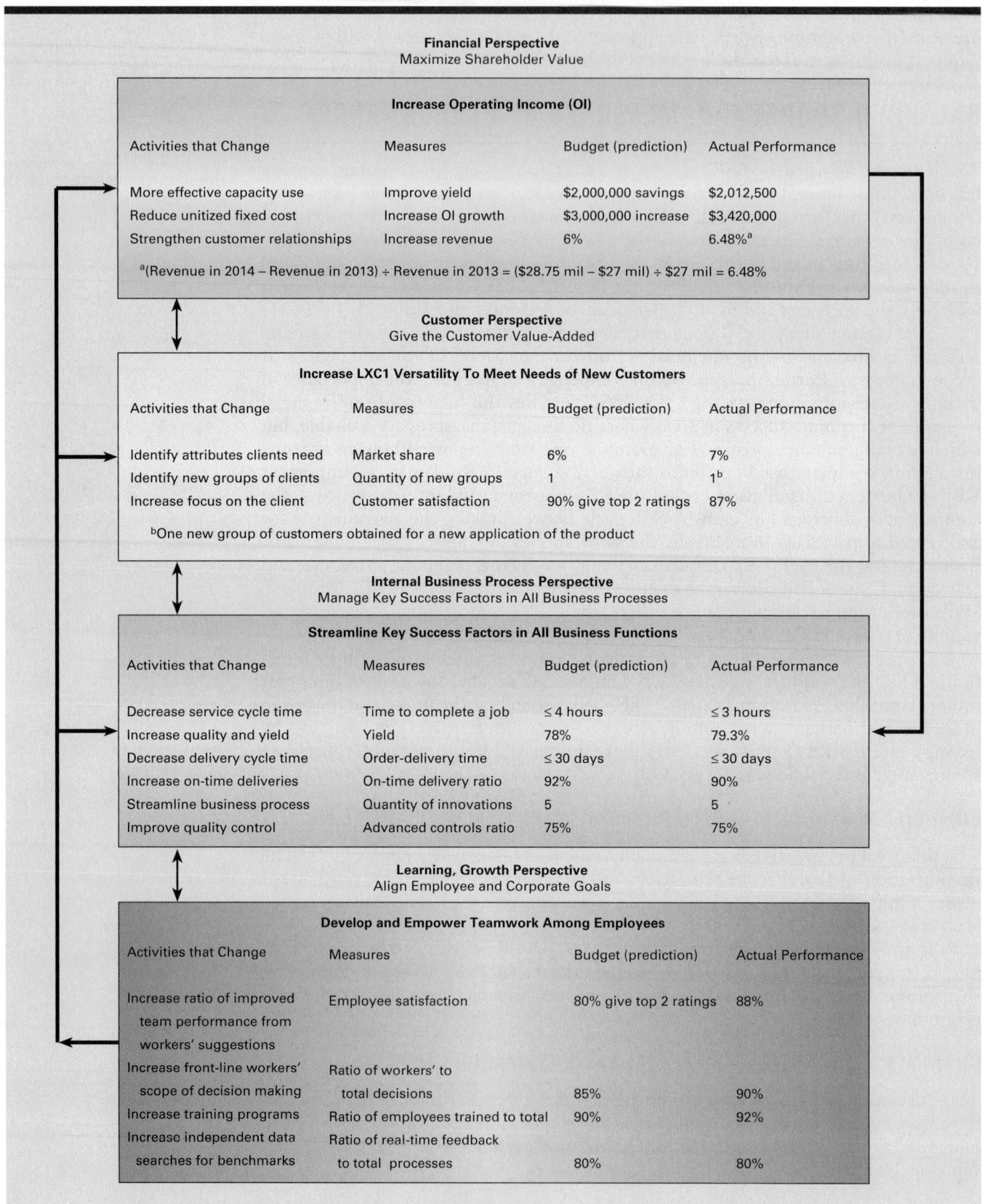

Financial Perspective
Maximize Shareholder Value

Increase Operating Income (OI)

Activities that Change	Measures	Budget (prediction)	Actual Performance
More effective capacity use	Improve yield	$2,000,000 savings	$2,012,500
Reduce unitized fixed cost	Increase OI growth	$3,000,000 increase	$3,420,000
Strengthen customer relationships	Increase revenue	6%	6.48%[a]

[a](Revenue in 2014 – Revenue in 2013) ÷ Revenue in 2013 = ($28.75 mil – $27 mil) ÷ $27 mil = 6.48%

Customer Perspective
Give the Customer Value-Added

Increase LXC1 Versatility To Meet Needs of New Customers

Activities that Change	Measures	Budget (prediction)	Actual Performance
Identify attributes clients need	Market share	6%	7%
Identify new groups of clients	Quantity of new groups	1	1[b]
Increase focus on the client	Customer satisfaction	90% give top 2 ratings	87%

[b]One new group of customers obtained for a new application of the product

Internal Business Process Perspective
Manage Key Success Factors in All Business Processes

Streamline Key Success Factors in All Business Functions

Activities that Change	Measures	Budget (prediction)	Actual Performance
Decrease service cycle time	Time to complete a job	≤ 4 hours	≤ 3 hours
Increase quality and yield	Yield	78%	79.3%
Decrease delivery cycle time	Order-delivery time	≤ 30 days	≤ 30 days
Increase on-time deliveries	On-time delivery ratio	92%	90%
Streamline business process	Quantity of innovations	5	5
Improve quality control	Advanced controls ratio	75%	75%

Learning, Growth Perspective
Align Employee and Corporate Goals

Develop and Empower Teamwork Among Employees

Activities that Change	Measures	Budget (prediction)	Actual Performance
Increase ratio of improved team performance from workers' suggestions	Employee satisfaction	80% give top 2 ratings	88%
Increase front-line workers' scope of decision making	Ratio of workers' to total decisions	85%	90%
Increase training programs	Ratio of employees trained to total	90%	92%
Increase independent data searches for benchmarks	Ratio of real-time feedback to total processes	80%	80%

Chipset will continue to improve value-added attributes to the customer by increasing the versatility of its existing product rather than using R&D to create a highly differentiated product. In this way, Chipset plans to increase the groups of customers who will purchase the LCX1. This is why Chipset will measure both increases in its existing market share and increases in its market size from growth in customers with new uses for the LCX1.

The power of customers in a market where competitive rivalry is high, such as Chipset's, is to impose a target pricing strategy on the company (see Chapter 12). As a price taker, Chipset will either meet a target cost to preserve ROI and operating profit margin, or incur excessive cost and sacrifice ROI and profit margin. Chipset's plan to achieve higher yield from the same capacity means achieving cost savings from internal **organic revenue growth** in similar products. This will exploit economies of scope, consistent with its cost leadership strategy. Growth by acquiring similar products from other companies is called growth in **adjacencies**, which is another way to exploit economies of scope.

A year-to-year percentage improvement in revenue compared to a target percentage transforms a short-term operating performance measure into a measure of how well a long-term growth strategy has been executed in the past 12 months. This is why Chipset set a target revenue growth rate at 6%, to align short-term performance measure with its long-term ROI measure.

INTERNAL BUSINESS PROCESS PERSPECTIVE—RELEVANCE OF CUSTOMERS

The **internal business process perspective** requires analysis of how to improve internal operations, which implicates the entire value chain of business functions. Chipset's core competence is in process innovation. Chipset's talented engineers have gathered information on similar processes used within all industries. Using this information, Chipset has determined a number of performance targets related to the effectiveness and efficiency of their processes versus the most effective and efficient processes used. Chipset benchmarked their performance to learn from others, striving to become the best, achieving high yield at low cost.

Chipset can find this benchmarking information through public disclosure of financial data, industry reports, and physically disassembling (reverse engineering) competitor's products to compare them to Chipset's design and production processes. A *benchmark* is the best process and performance attainable. Generally, fewer components and simpler product design lead to lower costs of assembly. Fewer components also mean fewer opportunities to make errors in production and increase opportunities to use more advanced quality control systems.

Chipset will measure the implementation of advanced controls as a percentage of the total of all stages in the production process. To make sure the advances are improving customer satisfaction, Chipset will also create cross-functional teams of sales, purchasing, and production workers to make sure the improvements meet the customers' needs. The success of these teams will be measured by percentage of on-time total deliveries and days to deliver on an order.

Chipset's goal is to improve its yield, or the inverse, productivity. **Productivity** is measured as the ratio of inputs divided by outputs. The lower the quantity of inputs needed per output, the higher the productivity. *Yield* is the ratio of volume of output divided by quantity of input. As yield increases, the cost per LCX1 will decrease. Careful control of costs will require frequent and reliable reports of various input costs and variance analyses. Level 4 variance analyses of yield and substitutable input mix from various suppliers will help Chipset assess its success at cost control and increased yield (see Chapter 7).

Changes in other business functions, in particular the customer after-sales service cycle, are also a key success factor, according to Chipset's information. Chipset has determined that the industry's current benchmark is three hours in after-sales customer service cycle time. As it increases volume of customers, the total customer response time must decrease and productivity improve from the existing resources. Provided the improvement in quality is realized in the product and process redesign, there should be fewer after-sales service requests from customers.

LEARNING AND GROWTH PERSPECTIVE—MANAGING INTELLECTUAL CAPITAL

The **learning and growth perspective** has expanded to become a field of study of its own on the identification, development, retention, and valuation of **intellectual capital**. Intellectual capital is hard to identify, let alone measure and relate to competitive advantage,[6] which makes this the most intangible target of management. The goal of intellectual capital management is to apply, retain, and expand knowledge and improve long-term competitive success.

Chipset's BSC emphasizes retention of experienced workers and provides incentives to increase teamwork. Chipset will reward effective suggestions for improvement in its key business processes and measure success through increased employee satisfaction. To improve the quality of working life for the workers, Chipset intends to push down decision making to front-line working teams. Those who can first observe a problem can diagnose and remedy the problem.

NONFINANCIAL BSC MEASURES AT CHIPSET

The balanced scorecard takes into account not only financial targets, but also targets based on social, legal, and environmental perspectives. Today, companies must respond to increasingly complex arrays of customer demands for social, legal, and environmental as well as financial sustainability. This multidimensional demand for corporate sustainability has led companies like Pearson PLC to product three annual reports. One is the familiar financial report, the second is their social responsibility report, and the third is their environmental sustainability report. Global companies take the triple bottom line seriously. Recent research provides evidence that investors recognize and reward companies that implement best practices. The shareholders are rewarded because the market value of these firms is higher than firms that ignore social and environmental sustainability practices.[7]

For example, Pearson PLC pursues an environmental strategy to achieve climate neutrality with respect to carbon emissions. The company will measure its unavoidable CO_2 emissions and has pledged to generate outputs that absorb as many tonnes of CO_2 as Pearson emits. Since 2007, the company has reduced its emissions from 1.62 to 1.04 tonnes per full-time employee on a like-for-like basis that excludes acquisitions. In 2007 Pearson set a target of 95% recycling and reuse of unsold product, but by 2009 Pearson had exceeded this and achieved 99%. Pearson has also reduced its use of plastic in packaging by 85% since implementing its strategy.

From the legal compliance, or corporate governance, perspective, companies have for a long time taken for granted that bribes are an acceptable way of doing business. But new legislation in the U.K. requires that companies operating there put internal controls in place to prevent bribes.[8] The United States and Germany have aggressively prosecuted multinational companies that indulge in bribery and kickbacks to obtain business. For example, Siemens paid $1.3 billion in fines to settle fraud charges in Germany and the United States, despite signing the International Convention on Combating Bribery of Foreign Officials in 1999.

Canada has been criticized by the watchdog agency that audits compliance with the treaty for only convicting one company of bribery. From research on 104 international companies, there is evidence that good corporate governance or stewardship strengthens global competitiveness. Improved productivity, cost leadership,

[6]T. Sällebrant, J. Hansen, N. Bontis, and P. Hofman-Bang, "Managing Risk with Intellectual Capital Statements," *Management Decision* 45.9 (2007): 1470–1483.

[7]S-F. Lo, H-J. Sheu, "Is Corporate Sustainability a Value-Increasing Strategy for Business?" *Corporate Governance* 15.2 (March 2007): 345–358.

[8]http://www.allenovery.com/AOWEB/Knowledge/Editorial.aspx?contentTypeID=1&itemID=55579&prefLangID=410, http://www.canada.com/business/Significant+concerns+over+Canada+anti+bribery+laws+OECD/4514132/story.html, http://www.fasken.com/en/the-bribery-act-2010-and-the-pharmaceutical-and-medical-device-sectors-11-17-2010/, all accessed May 4, 2011.

capacity utilization, and measures of value creation all contribute to competitive advantage.[9]

More than legal compliance, however, customers have successfully gained corporate attention using social media to expose companies such as Nike and IKEA, which have employed child labour in offshore factories. Tyson Foods, a global food processor, found its unhygienic slaughtering and processing practices posted on YouTube by People for the Ethical Treatment of Animals (PETA). PETA continues its Internet campaign against YUM!, the owner of Kentucky Fried Chicken, to replace Tyson Foods as its supplier.

The BSC has changed how management teams understand the way to improve profits and requires careful understanding of the interdependence between the firm and its competitive environment. When companies offshore and source their materials, labour, and merchandise globally, they are held accountable for the practices of all their business partners. **Enterprise risk management (ERM)** expands triple bottom line responsibility beyond the firm itself. The purpose of ERM is to identify risk and align the firm's strategy and measures of success using many different measures. This is the power of the BSC.

FEATURES OF A GOOD BALANCED SCORECARD

A good BSC design has several features:

◆ It tells the story of a company's strategy by clarifying a limited sequence of orderly relationships among key success factors. People have cognitive limits; therefore, a good BSC focuses on a limited set of linked measures that, if improved in an orderly way, will increase profitability.

◆ The BSC communicates the strategy to all members of the organization by translating the strategy into a coherent and linked set of understandable and measurable operational targets. Guided by the BSC, managers and employees take actions and make decisions that aim to achieve the company's strategy. To focus these actions, some companies, such as Mobil and Bank of Montreal, have developed BSCs at the division and department levels.

◆ Improvements in nonfinancial performance measures usually lead to improvements in financial performance measures. In not-for-profit enterprises, nonfinancial factors measure the achievement of almost all key objectives.

◆ The BSC limits the number of measures used by identifying only the most critical key success factors (KSF). Avoiding a proliferation of measures focuses management's attention on those that are central to strengthening the corporation's core competence. Although strategy is stable in the long term, KSFs may change over time and so too must the BSC measures.

◆ The BSC highlights suboptimal tradeoffs that managers may make when they fail to consider operational and financial measures together. For example, a company for which innovation is central to product differentiation could achieve superior short-run financial performance by reducing money spent on R&D. A good BSC would signal that the short-run financial performance may have been achieved by taking actions that hurt future financial performance because a leading indicator of that performance, R&D spending and R&D output, has declined.

PITFALLS WHEN IMPLEMENTING A BALANCED SCORECARD

Pitfalls to avoid when implementing a balanced scorecard include the following:

◆ Strategy requires knowledge of how orderly changes in a corporation can better assure success in a changing competitive environment. Orderly change focuses on shoring up the weak KSFs and nourishing the strong KSFs that sustain core competence. A critical challenge is to identify the strength and speed

---

[9]Chi-Kun Ho, "Corporate Governance and Corporate Competitiveness: An International Analysis," *Corporate Governance and Corporate Competitiveness*, 13.2 (March 2005): 211–253.

of the orderly changes among the nonfinancial and financial measures. Management must gather evidence of these linkages over time. Evolving the BSC over time avoids the paralysis by analysis associated with trying to design the "perfect" scorecard at the outset.

♦ Scarce corporate resources means tradeoffs or priority-setting must occur among various strategic goals. For example, emphasizing quality and on-time performance beyond a point may not be worthwhile—improving these objectives may be inconsistent with profit maximization.

♦ The BSC includes the intangible achievement of good management of intellectual capital. Qualitative or subjective measures such as interviews and surveys to assess intellectual and corporate sustainability achievements provide a rich basis upon which to assess progress.

♦ Intangible costs are extremely difficult to estimate, but intangible benefits even more so. Nonfinancial measures of the benefits of improved information technology, advocacy of human rights, and reduction of carbon emissions are not standardized. Management accountants play a large liaison role in translating qualitative measures made by technical experts into financial measures of benefit.

♦ Managers tend to focus on what their performance is measured by rather than corporate success. Excluding nonfinancial measures when evaluating performance will reduce the significance and importance given to managing nonfinancial BSC measures. Many of the nonfinancial measures serve as leading indicators of future financial performance. The Chipset example will show how improvements in nonfinancial factors lead to improvements in financial factors.

EVALUATION USING THE BSC

4 Evaluate strategic success at implementing a cost leadership strategy using balanced scorecard measures.

Having implemented some changes, Chipset can measure its actual achievement against benchmarks in the BSC budget targets shown in Exhibit 13-5. The comparisons in this section are important to strategic cost management. Strategic cost management identifies the use of cost information to measure the successful implementation of a strategy. Performance indicators isolate and measure contributions to favourable operating income change arising from the choice of a cost leadership strategy apart from those arising from industry change and product customization.

Chipset has focused on comparing actual operating performance over two different time periods and explicitly linking the performance to strategic choices. Improvements in performance measures will be interpreted as successful implementation of strategy. While Chipset has chosen cost leadership, more complex companies with portfolios of product and service bundles may select more complex strategies. When value leadership is selected, these types of companies cannot simply ignore cost—cost leadership is important to profitability for any company. The difference will lie in the BSC measures of success when implementing the selected strategy.

The following simplified example illustrates how operating-income changes between two years can be divided into components that can describe how successful a company has been with regard to cost leadership, product differentiation, and growth.[10] From the first two tables, notice that Chipset has reduced its unit sales price from $27 to $25, but increased its operating income.

---

[10]For other details, see R. Banker, S. Datar, and R. Kaplan, "Productivity Measurement and Management Accounting," *Journal of Accounting, Auditing and Finance* (1989): 528–554; and A. Hayzen and J. Reeve, "Examining the Relationships in Productivity Accounting," *Management Accounting Quarterly* (2000).

	2013	2014
1. Units of LCX1 produced and sold	1,000,000	1,150,000
2. Selling price	$27	$25
3. Direct materials (square centimetres of silicon wafers)	3,000,000	2,900,000
4. Direct material cost per square centimetre	$1.40	$1.50
5. Manufacturing processing capacity (in square centimetres of silicon wafer)	3,750,000	3,500,000
6. Conversion costs (all manufacturing costs other than direct material costs)	$16,050,000	$15,225,000
7. Conversion cost per unit of capacity (Row 6 ÷ Row 5)	$4.28	$4.35
8. R&D employees	40	39
9. R&D costs	$4,000,000	$3,900,000
10. R&D cost per employee (Row 9 ÷ Row 8)	$100,000	$100,000

Chipset implemented key elements of its strategy late in 2013 and early 2014, expecting financial improvement by late 2014. If the improvements were not expected until 2015, Chipset could still compare 2013 to 2015. In a more complex analysis, Chipset could evaluate its progress across all three years. This emphasizes that implementation of a strategic plan occurs over several years, and immediate improvement is inconsistent with the long-term strategic perspective. Chipset provides the following additional information:

◆ Annual conversion costs depend on the total capacity (measured as cm² of silicon wafers, or practical capacity of the LCX1, that *can* be produced). This capacity cost is fixed. The direct manufacturing labour costs are relatively small compared to capacity costs and are based on time worked, not output quantity produced. Capacity costs can *only* be reduced by selling equipment, laying off workers, or reassigning them to non-manufacturing tasks.

◆ The amount spent on R&D is discretionary. Chipset's managers decide on this at the beginning of each year. The R&D work does not depend on the quantity of LCX1 produced. Engineers earn approximately $100,000 annually.

◆ Marketing and sales non-manufacturing costs are small relative to other costs. The company has 10 customers who purchase roughly the same quantity of LCX1 in a year. Engineers work closely with customers to provide continuous improvements that meet the customers' needs. The customer relationship manager works with the engineers and the production department to ensure Chipset can fill the order according to the requirements of the customer. This cross-functional approach recognizes the interdependence of design, sales, and production and assures customer satisfaction. It costs approximately $80,000 to support each customer.

◆ The investment base and asset structure are not materially different in the years 2013 and 2014. Operating income for each year is as follows:

	2013	2014
Revenue		
($27 per unit × 1,000,000 units; $25 per unit × 1,150,000 units)	$27,000,000	$28,750,000
Costs		
Direct material costs		
($1.40/sq. cm. × 3,000,000 sq. cm.; $1.50/sq. cm. × 2,900,000 sq. cm.)	4,200,000	4,350,000
Conversion costs		
($4.28/sq. cm. × 3,750,000 sq. cm.; $4.35/sq. cm. × 3,500,000 sq. cm.)	16,050,000	15,225,000
R&D costs ($100,000 × 40 employees; $100,000 × 39 employees)	4,000,000	3,900,000
Total costs	24,250,000	23,475,000
Operating income	$ 2,750,000	$ 5,275,000
Change in operating income		↑ $2,525,000 F ↑

Chipset now wants to evaluate how much of this $2,525,000 increase in operating income can be attributed to successful implementation of the company's strategy.[11] To do so, they must examine three main analysis components: growth, price recovery, and productivity. Each component will be isolated from the favourable or unfavourable variance generated by the others.

THE GROWTH COMPONENT

The growth component measures the increase in revenues minus the increase in costs from selling more units of LCX1 in 2014 (1,150,000 units) than in 2013 (1,000,000 units). That is, the output prices, input prices, efficiencies, and capacities of 2013 are assumed to continue into 2014. This isolates the effect of increased sales volume from all other revenue effects.

Revenue Effect of Growth

$$\text{Revenue effect of growth} = \left(\begin{array}{c} \text{Actual units of} \\ \text{output sold} \\ \text{in 2014} \end{array} - \begin{array}{c} \text{Actual units of} \\ \text{output sold} \\ \text{in 2013} \end{array} \right) \times \begin{array}{c} \text{Selling} \\ \text{price} \\ \text{in 2013} \end{array}$$

$$= (1{,}150{,}000 \text{ units} - 1{,}000{,}000 \text{ units}) \times \$27 \text{ per unit}$$

$$= \$4{,}050{,}000 \text{ F}$$

This component is favourable (F) because it increases operating income, all other things held equal. Decreases in operating income are unfavourable (U). The analysis assumes that in this highly competitive environment the 2013 selling price continued into 2014.

Cost Effect of Growth   Of course, to produce the higher output sold in 2014, more inputs would be needed. The cost increase from growth measures the amount by which costs in 2014 would have increased (1) if the relationship between inputs and outputs that existed in 2013 had continued in 2014, and (2) if prices of inputs in 2013 had continued in 2014. We use 2013 input–output relationships and 2013 input prices because the goal is to isolate the increase in costs caused solely by the growth in units sold of 150,000 units of LCX1 between 2013 and 2014.

$$\text{Cost effect of growth for variable costs} = \left(\begin{array}{c} \text{Units of input} \\ \text{required to} \\ \text{produce 2014} \\ \text{output in 2013} \end{array} - \begin{array}{c} \text{Actual units of} \\ \text{input used} \\ \text{to produce} \\ \text{2013 output} \end{array} \right) \times \begin{array}{c} \text{Input} \\ \text{price} \\ \text{in 2013} \end{array}$$

$$\text{Cost effect of growth for direct materials} = \left(3{,}000{,}000 \text{ sq.cm.} \times \frac{1{,}150{,}000 \text{ units}}{1{,}000{,}000 \text{ units}} - 3{,}000{,}000 \text{ sq.cm.} \right) \times \$1.40 \text{ per sq.cm.}$$

$$= (3{,}450{,}000 \text{ sq.cm.} - 3{,}000{,}000 \text{ sq.cm.}) \times \$1.40 \text{ per sq.cm.} = \$630{,}000 \text{ U}$$

$$\text{Cost effect of growth for fixed costs} = \left(\begin{array}{c} \text{Actual units of capacity in} \\ \text{2013 if adequate to produce} \\ \text{2014 output in 2013} \\ \text{OR} \\ \text{If 2013 capacity inadequate} \\ \text{to produce 2014 output in 2013,} \\ \text{units of capacity required} \\ \text{to produce 2014 output in 2013} \end{array} - \begin{array}{c} \text{Actual units} \\ \text{of capacity} \\ \text{in 2013} \end{array} \right) \times \begin{array}{c} \text{Price per} \\ \text{unit of} \\ \text{capacity} \\ \text{in 2013} \end{array}$$

$$\text{Cost effect of growth for conversion costs} = (3{,}750{,}000 \text{ sq.cm.} - 3{,}750{,}000 \text{ sq.cm.}) \times \$4.28 \text{ per sq.cm.} = \$0$$

[11]The manufacturing conversion cost pool is almost 100% fixed cost. Chipset's strategy is cost leadership. It will improve profit by increasing the quantity of saleable LCX1. It will redesign the production process without spending more money to increase capacity.

All conversion costs are fixed at practical capacity of 3,750,000 cm² of silicon wafers at a total cost of $16,050,000, or $4.28/cm² (rows 5, 6, 7 of data on p. 531). In 2013, Chipset would have needed 3,450,000 cm² of direct materials to produce 3,450,000 LCX1. The actual quantity produced is within the relevant range with no additional capacity cost or conversion cost.

The R&D costs, however, are discretionary but would not change in 2013 even if Chipset had produced and sold a larger quantity of LCX1:

Cost effect of
growth for = (40 employees − 40 employees) × $100,000 per employee = $0
R&D costs

In summary, the net increase in operating income as a result of growth equals:

Revenue effect of growth		$4,050,000 F
Cost effect of growth		
Direct material costs	$630,000 U	
Conversion costs	0	
R&D costs	0	630,000 U
Change in operating income due to growth		$3,420,000 F

THE PRICE-RECOVERY COMPONENT

The price-recovery component of operating income measures the change in revenues and the change in costs to produce the 1,150,000 units of LCX1 manufactured in 2014 as a result of the change in the prices of LCX1.

Revenue Effect of Price Recovery Note that this calculation focuses on the decrease in the price of LCX1 between 2013 and 2014. The objective of the revenue effect of price recovery is to isolate the change in revenue between 2013 and 2014 due solely to the change in selling prices.

$$
\begin{array}{c}
\text{Revenue effect} \\
\text{of product differentiation} \\
\text{component}
\end{array}
=
\left(
\begin{array}{c}
\text{Selling price} \\
\text{in 2014}
\end{array}
-
\begin{array}{c}
\text{Selling price} \\
\text{in 2013}
\end{array}
\right)
\times
\begin{array}{c}
\text{Actual units of} \\
\text{output sold} \\
\text{in 2014}
\end{array}
$$

$$= (\$25 - \$27) \times 1,150,000 = \$2,300,000 \text{ U}$$

Cost Effect of Price Recovery This calculation focuses on the effect of changes in the prices of inputs. Because of the anticipated change in manufacturing conversion costs, these fixed costs must be considered to capture the full cost effect of price recovery. The cost of direct materials required to produce 3,450,000 cm² has already been considered when calculating the cost effect of growth (p. 532).

$$
\begin{array}{c}
\text{Cost effect of} \\
\text{price recovery for} \\
\text{variable costs}
\end{array}
=
\left(
\begin{array}{c}
\text{Input price} \\
\text{in 2014}
\end{array}
-
\begin{array}{c}
\text{Input price} \\
\text{in 2013}
\end{array}
\right)
\times
\begin{array}{c}
\text{Units of input} \\
\text{required to} \\
\text{produce 2014} \\
\text{output in 2013}
\end{array}
$$

Cost effect of
price recovery for = ($1.50 per sq.cm. − $1.40 per sq.cm.) × 3,450,000 sq.cm. = $345,000 U
direct materials

The cost effect of price recovery for fixed costs is:

$$
\begin{array}{c}
\text{Cost effect of} \\
\text{price recovery for} \\
\text{fixed costs}
\end{array}
=
\left(
\begin{array}{c}
\text{Price per} \\
\text{unit of} \\
\text{capacity} \\
\text{in 2014}
\end{array}
-
\begin{array}{c}
\text{Price per} \\
\text{unit of} \\
\text{capacity} \\
\text{in 2013}
\end{array}
\right)
\times
\begin{array}{c}
\text{Actual units of capacity in} \\
\text{2013, if adequate to produce} \\
\text{2014 output in 2013} \\
\text{OR} \\
\text{If 2013 capacity inadequate to} \\
\text{produce 2014 output in 2013,} \\
\text{units of capacity required to} \\
\text{produce 2014 output in 2013}
\end{array}
$$

The cost effects of price recovery conversion and R&D fixed costs are:

Conversion costs: ($4.35 per cm^2 − $4.28 per cm^2) × 3,750,000 cm^2 = $262,500 U
R&D costs: ($100,000 per employee − $100,000 per employee) × 40 employees = $0

In summary, the net decrease in operating income attributable to price recovery when there is adequate capacity and R&D employees are constant (cost effect of growth, pp. 532–533) is:

Revenue effect of price recovery		$2,300,000 U
Cost effect of price recovery		
Direct material costs	$345,000 U	
Conversion costs	262,500 U	
R&D costs	0	607,500 U
Change in operating income due to price recovery		$2,907,500 U

THE PRODUCTIVITY COMPONENT

Productivity is the ratio of finished output units divided by input quantity. The contribution of productivity to the change in operating income uses current input costs in 2014. There is no revenue effect because the focus is on cost. The first calculation isolates the decrease in variable costs arising from use of fewer inputs, improved input mix, and less capacity compared to those used in 2013.[12]

$$\text{Cost effect of productivity for variable costs} = \left(\begin{array}{c} \text{Actual units of input used to produce 2014 output} \end{array} - \begin{array}{c} \text{Units of input required to produce 2014 output in 2013} \end{array} \right) \times \begin{array}{c} \text{Input price in 2014} \end{array}$$

Chipset's quality and yield improvements reduced the quantity of direct materials (inputs) required to generate higher productivity in 2014 relative to 2013:

$$\text{Cost effect of productivity for fixed costs} = \left(\begin{array}{c} \text{Actual units of capacity in 2014} \end{array} - \begin{array}{c} \text{Actual units of capacity in 2013, if adequate to produce 2014 output in 2013} \\ \text{OR} \\ \text{If 2013 capacity inadequate to produce 2014 output in 2013, units of capacity required to produce 2014 output in 2013} \end{array} \right) \times \begin{array}{c} \text{Price per unit of capacity in 2014} \end{array}$$

Based on the 2013 data given on page 531 and these analyses, the cost effects of fixed conversion costs on productivity are:

Conversion costs: (3,500,000 sq. cm. − 3,750,000 sq. cm.) × $4.35 per sq. cm. = $1,087,500 F
R&D costs: (39 employees − 40 employees) × $100,000 per employee = $100,000 F

Chipset's managers decreased manufacturing capacity in 2014 to 3,500,000 cm^2. They accomplished this by selling off old equipment and retraining manufacturing workers to perform non-manufacturing tasks. One R&D manager voluntarily left

---

[12]The productivity-component calculation uses actual 2014 input prices, whereas its counterpart, the efficiency variance in Chapters 7 and 8, uses budgeted prices for 2014. This chapter assumes the forecast year is unfolding as this analysis occurs. Year 2014 prices are used in the productivity calculation because it is real-time information and not a forecast. Chipset wants managers to choose input quantities to minimize costs in 2014 based on currently prevailing prices. If the forecast prices were used, they would have been outdated and irrelevant. In Chapters 7 and 8 the goal was to assess plan against actual. Now that managers are in 2014 and actual prices are known, they can be substituted for the forecast made a year ago.

Chipset and was not replaced, which reduced R&D expense. In summary, the net increase in operating income attributable to productivity is:

Cost effect of productivity	
Direct material costs	$ 825,000 F
Conversion costs	1,087,500 F
R&D costs	100,000 F
Change in operating income due to productivity	2,012,500 F

The productivity component reveals that Chipset increased its operating income in several ways consistent with the strategy of cost leadership. Chipset improved quality and yield, and reduced capacity costs. The company can conduct a more detailed analysis of partial and total factor productivity changes to obtain a deeper understanding of the effectiveness of Chipset's cost leadership strategy.

FURTHER ANALYSIS OF GROWTH, PRICE-RECOVERY, AND PRODUCTIVITY COMPONENTS

Exhibit 13-6 summarizes the growth, price-recovery, and productivity components that contributed to a total favourable variance in operating income in 2014. Consistent with its strategic choice and orderly implementation of change, productivity contributed $2,012,500 and growth contributed $3,420,000. Price recovery decreased operating income by $2,907,500 because the unit sales price declined simultaneously with cost increases for inputs. With no further product differentiation, Chipset could not offset this decrease by charging a higher price. Managers are planning to evaluate what modest improvements in the LCX1 customers would pay for relative to the costs to further customize its product. But at the same time, Chipset cannot jeopardize the versatility and economies of scale benefits of producing a standardized product.

As in all variance and profit analysis, the thoughtful analyst will want to look at the sources of operating income more closely. For instance, in the Chipset example growth may have been helped by an increase in industry market size. Therefore, at least a part of the increase in operating income may be attributable to favourable economic conditions in the industry rather than to any successful implementation of strategy. Some of the growth may also have come as a result of a management decision at Chipset to take advantage of its productivity gains by cutting prices. In this case, the increase in operating income from cost leadership equals the productivity gain, plus any increase in operating income from growth in market share attributable to productivity improvements, minus any decrease in operating income from a strategic decision to lower prices.

EXHIBIT 13-6
Strategic Analysis of Profitability

	Income Statement Amounts in 2013 (1)	Revenue and Cost Effects of Growth Component in 2014 (2)	Revenue and Cost Effects of Price-Recovery Component in 2014 (3)	Cost Effect of Productivity Component in 2014 (4)	Income Statement Amounts in 2014 (5) = (1) + (2) + (3) − (4)
Revenue	$27,000,000	$4,050,000 F	$2,300,000 U	—	$28,750,000
Costs	24,250,000	630,000 U	607,500 U	$2,012,500 F	23,475,000
Operating income	$ 2,750,000	$3,420,000 F	$2,907,500 U	$2,012,500 F	$ 5,275,000
			$2,525,000 F		

Change in operating income

To illustrate these ideas, consider again the Chipset example and the following additional information:

◆ The market growth rate in the industry is 10%. That is, of the 150,000 (1,150,000 − 1,000,000) units of increased sales of LCX1 between 2013 and 2014, 100,000 (10% × 1,000,000) units are due to an increase in industry market size (which Chipset would have benefited from regardless of its productivity gains), and the remaining 50,000 units are due to an increase in market share.

◆ There was a $1.35 or 5% decrease in the target price of LCX1 (0.05 × $27 = $1.35). The remaining decrease of $0.65 arose from taking advantage of Chipset's productivity gain. As a result Chipset's total reduction in unit sales price was $2.00 ($1.35 + $0.65).

Clearly, some of the improvement came from a growth in market size rather than any action by Chipset. This effect can be calculated as follows:

$$\$3,420,000 \text{ (Exhibit 13-6, column 2)} \times \frac{100,000 \text{ units}}{150,000 \text{ units}} = \underline{\$2,280,000} \text{ F}$$

Lacking a differentiated product, Chipset is unable to pass along increases in input prices to its customers. The effect of product differentiation on operating income is:

Change in operating income due to a decline in the selling price of LCX1 (other than the strategic reduction in price included as part of the cost-leadership component) $1.35/unit × 1,150,000 units	$1,552,500 U
Change in prices of inputs (cost effect of price recovery)	607,500 U
Change in operating income due to product differentiation	$2,160,000 U

The change in operating income between 2013 and 2014 due to implementing the cost leadership strategy is:

Productivity component	$2,012,500 F
Effect of strategic decision to reduce price ($0.65/unit × 1,150,000 units)	747,500 U
Growth in market share due to productivity improvement and strategic decision to reduce prices $3,420,000 (Exhibit 13-6, column 2) × $\frac{50,000 \text{ units}}{150,000 \text{ units}}$	1,140,000 F
Change in operating income due to cost leadership	$2,405,000 F

In summary, the change in operating income between 2013 and 2014 is:

Change due to industry market size	$2,280,000 F
Change due to product differentiation	2,160,000 U
Change due to cost leadership	2,405,000 F
Change in operating income	$2,525,000 F

Under different assumptions of how changes in prices affect the quantity of LCX1 sold, the analyst will attribute different amounts to the different measures. The important point, though, is that the productivity gains of $2,012,500 Chipset made in 2014 were key to the operating income increases in 2014.

SPECIFIC PRODUCTIVITY IMPROVEMENT MEASURES

Productivity measures the relationship between actual outputs produced and actual inputs used (both quantities and costs). The lower the quantity of inputs for a given quantity of outputs (or the higher the outputs for a given quantity of inputs), the higher the level of productivity. Measuring productivity improvements over time highlights the specific output–input relationships that contribute to cost leadership.

Partial productivity, the most frequently used productivity measure, compares the quantity of output produced with the quantity of an individual input used. The higher the ratio, the greater the productivity. In its most common form, partial productivity is expressed as a ratio:

$$\text{Partial productivity} = \frac{\text{Quantity of output produced}}{\text{Quantity of input used}}$$

Analyze the results from specific productivity and capacity control strategies to achieve balanced scorecard expectations.

Consider only direct materials productivity at Chipset in the year 2014.

$$\begin{aligned}\frac{\text{Direct materials}}{\text{partial productivity}} &= \frac{\text{Quantity of LCX1 units produced during 2014}}{\text{Quantity of direct materials used to produce LCX1 in 2014}} \\[6pt] &= \frac{1{,}150{,}000 \text{ units of LCX1}}{2{,}900{,}000 \text{ sq. cm. of direct materials}} \\[6pt] &= 0.397 \text{ units of LCX1 per sq. cm. of direct materials}\end{aligned}$$

Direct materials partial productivity ignores Chipset's other inputs, manufacturing conversion costs, and R&D. Partial productivity measures become meaningful when comparisons are made that examine productivity changes over time, either across several facilities or relative to a benchmark. Exhibit 13-7 presents partial productivity measures for Chipset's various inputs for 2013 and 2014 using information from the productivity calculations on page 531. These measures compare the actual inputs used in the year 2014 to produce 1,150,000 units of LCX1 with the inputs that would have been used in 2014 had the input-output relationship from 2013 continued in 2014.

Partial productivity measures differ between fixed and variable costs of inputs. For fixed-cost inputs such as manufacturing conversion capacity, partial productivity will measure the reduction in overall capacity from 2013 to 2014 (3,750,000 cm^2 of silicon wafers to 3,500,000 cm^2) regardless of the actual capacity used in each year. A major advantage of partial productivity measures is that they focus on a single input. As a result, they are simple to calculate and easily understood by operations personnel.

EXHIBIT 13-7
Comparing Chipset's Partial Productivities in 2013 and 2014

Input (1)	Partial Productivity in 2014 (2)	Comparable Partial Productivity Based on 2013 Input-Output Relationships (3)	Percentage Change from 2013 to 2014 (4)
Direct materials	$\dfrac{1{,}150{,}000}{2{,}900{,}000} = 0.397$	$\dfrac{1{,}150{,}000}{3{,}450{,}000} = 0.333$	$\dfrac{0.397 - 0.333}{0.333} = 19.2\%$
Manufacturing conversion capacity	$\dfrac{1{,}150{,}000}{3{,}500{,}000} = 0.329$	$\dfrac{1{,}150{,}000}{3{,}750{,}000} = 0.307$	$\dfrac{0.329 - 0.307}{0.307} = 7.2\%$
R&D	$\dfrac{1{,}150{,}000}{39} = 29{,}487$	$\dfrac{1{,}150{,}000}{40} = 28{,}750$	$\dfrac{29{,}487 - 28{,}750}{28{,}750} = 2.6\%$

Managers and supervisors examine these numbers to understand the reasons underlying productivity changes from one period to the next. Various possibilities are improved training and lower turnover (learning and growth), increased incentives to suggest productivity improvements, changes in the production process, higher quality inputs, substitution of machine- for labour-hours, and advanced quality control (internal business process). One drawback, of course, is the interdependencies illustrated in Exhibit 13-4, whereby improvement in one measure will lead to improvements in other related measures. This is why a different approach is needed to ensure that an isolated change in fact improved total productivity (see Chapter 7, yield variance).

Total factor productivity (TFP), or total productivity, considers the result of changing all inputs simultaneously. TFP is the ratio of the quantity of output produced to the costs of all inputs used, where the inputs are combined on the basis of current period prices.

$$\text{Total factor productivity} = \frac{\text{Quantity of output produced}}{\text{Costs of all inputs used}}$$

TFP considers all inputs simultaneously and also considers the tradeoffs across inputs based on current input prices. Do not be tempted to think of all productivity measures as physical measures lacking financial content—how many units of output are produced per unit of input. Total factor productivity is intricately tied to minimizing total cost—a financial objective. We next measure changes in TFP at Chipset from 2013 to 2014.

CALCULATING AND COMPARING TOTAL FACTOR PRODUCTIVITY

We first calculate Chipset's TFP in 2014 using 2014 prices and 1,150,000 units of output produced (using information from the first column of the productivity component calculations on p. 531).

$$\begin{aligned}
\frac{\text{Total factor productivity}}{\text{for 2014 using 2014 prices}} &= \frac{\text{Quantity of output produced in 2014}}{\text{Costs of inputs used in 2014 based on 2014 prices}} \\
&= \frac{1{,}150{,}000}{(2{,}900{,}000 \times \$1.50) + (3{,}500{,}000 \times \$4.35) + (39 \times \$100{,}000)} \\
&= \frac{1{,}150{,}000}{\$23{,}475{,}000} \\
&= 0.048988 \text{ units of output per dollar of input cost}
\end{aligned}$$

By itself, the 2014 TFP of 0.048988 units of LCX1 per dollar of input is not particularly helpful. We need something to compare it against. One alternative is to compare TFPs of other similar companies in 2014. However, finding similar companies and obtaining accurate comparable data is often difficult. Companies therefore usually compare their own TFP over time.

In the Chipset example, we use as a benchmark TFP the inputs that Chipset would have used in 2013 to produce 1,150,000 units of LCX1 at 2014 prices (that is, we use the costs calculated from the second column in the productivity component calculations on p. 531). The 2014 prices are used because using the current year's (2014) prices in both calculations controls for input price differences and focuses the analysis on the adjustments the manager made in the quantities of inputs in response to changes in prices.

$$\begin{aligned}
\frac{\text{Benchmark}}{\text{TFP}} &= \frac{\text{Quantity of output produced in 2014}}{\substack{\text{Costs of inputs that would have been used in 2013} \\ \text{to produce 2014 output}}} \\
&= \frac{1{,}150{,}000}{(3{,}450{,}000 \times \$1.50) + (3{,}750{,}000 \times \$4.35) + (40 \times \$100{,}000)} \\
&= \frac{1{,}150{,}000}{\$25{,}487{,}500} \\
&= 0.045120 \text{ units of output per dollar of input cost}
\end{aligned}$$

Using 2014 prices, total factor productivity increased 8.6% [(0.048988 − 0.045120) ÷ 0.045120] from 2013 to 2014. Note that the 8.6% increase in TFP equals the $2,012,500 gain (Exhibit 13-6, column 4, p. 535) divided by the $23,475,000 of actual costs incurred in 2014 (Exhibit 13-6, column 5). TFP increased because Chipset produced more output per dollar of input in 2014 relative to 2013, measured in both years using 2014 prices.

The gain in TFP occurs because Chipset increases the partial productivities of individual inputs and, consistent with its strategy, seeks the least expensive combination of inputs to produce LCX1. Note that TFP increases cannot be due to differences in input prices because we used year 2014 prices to evaluate both the inputs that Chipset would have used in 2013 to produce 1,150,000 units of LCX1 and the inputs actually used in 2014.

A major advantage of TFP is that it measures the combined productivity of all inputs used to produce output. Therefore, it explicitly considers gains from using fewer physical inputs as well as substitution among inputs. Managers can analyze these numbers to understand the reasons for changes in TFP. For example, Chipset's managers will try to evaluate whether the increase in TFP from 2013 to 2014 was due to better human resource management practices, higher quality of materials, or improved manufacturing methods. Chipset will adopt the most successful practices and use TFP measures to implement and evaluate strategy by setting targets and monitoring trends.

Many companies, such as Monsanto, a manufacturer of fibres, and Motorola, a microchip manufacturer, use both partial productivity and total factor productivity to evaluate performance. *Partial productivity and TFP measures work best together because the strengths of one are the weaknesses of the other.*

Although TFP measures are comprehensive, operations personnel find financial TFP measures more difficult to understand and less useful than physical partial productivity measures in performing their tasks. Physical measures of manufacturing labour partial productivity, for example, provide direct feedback to workers about output produced per labour-hour worked by focusing on factors within the workers' control. Manufacturing labour partial productivity also has the advantage that it can be easily compared across time periods because it uses physical inputs rather than inputs that are weighted by the prices prevailing in different periods. Workers, therefore, often prefer to tie productivity-based bonuses to gains in manufacturing labour partial productivity.

Unfortunately, this situation creates incentives for workers to substitute materials (and capital) for labour, which improves their own productivity measure while possibly decreasing overall productivity of the company as measured by TFP. To overcome the possible incentive problems of partial productivity measures, some companies—for example, TRW and Whirlpool—explicitly adjust bonuses based on manufacturing labour partial productivity for the effects of other factors such as investments in new equipment and higher levels of scrap. That is, they combine partial productivity with TFP-like measures.

CAPACITY CONTROL MEASURES

How, then, can managers reduce capacity-based fixed costs? The key is in understanding and managing unused capacity. To understand unused capacity, managers find it useful to classify costs into *engineered* and *discretionary* categories. Exhibit 13-8 show differences between the two types of costs.

Engineered costs arise specifically from a clear cause-and-effect relationship between output (or cost driver) and the (direct or indirect) resources used to produce that output. In the Chipset example, direct materials costs are an example of direct engineered costs. Manufacturing conversion costs are an example of indirect engineered costs. Consider the year 2014. The output of 1,150,000 units of LCX1 results in 2,900,000 cm^2 of silicon wafers used in work-in-process and finished goods inventories. Manufacturing conversion resources needed and used to process 1,150,000 units of LCX1 equal $12,615,000 ($4.35/cm^2 × 2,900,000 cm^2), assuming that the cost of resources used increases proportionately with the number of units started.

	Engineered Costs (Examples: Manufacturing, Distribution)	Discretionary Costs (Examples: R&D, Advertising, Public Relations)
Type of process or activity	**a.** Detailed and physically observable **b.** Repetitive	**a.** Black box (knowledge of process is sketchy or unavailable) **b.** Nonrepetitive or nonroutine
Level of uncertainty (the possibility that actual costs will deviate from expected costs)	Moderate or small	Large

Source: This exhibit is a modification of one suggested by H. Itami.

Total manufacturing conversion costs are higher ($15,225,000) because they are related to the manufacturing capacity required to process 3,500,000 cm^2 of silicon wafer ($4.35/cm^2 × 3,500,000 cm^2). These costs are fixed in the short run, but, over time, there is a clear cause-and-effect relationship among output, manufacturing capacity required, and manufacturing conversion costs needed. Thus, engineered costs can be either variable or fixed in the short run.

Discretionary costs have two important features: (1) they arise from periodic (usually yearly) decisions regarding the maximum amount to be incurred, and (2) they have no clearly measurable cause-and-effect relationship between output and resources used. Examples of discretionary costs include advertising, executive training, R&D, healthcare, and corporate staff department costs such as legal, human resources, and public relations. The most noteworthy aspect of discretionary costs is that managers are seldom confident that the "correct" amounts are being spent. The founder of Lever Brothers, an international consumer-products company, once noted, "Half the money I spend on advertising is wasted; the trouble is, I don't know which half." In the Chipset example, R&D costs are discretionary costs because there is no measurable cause-and-effect relationship between output of 1,150,000 LCX1 produced and R&D resources needed or used.

Infrastructure costs arise from having property, plant, equipment, and a functioning organization. Examples are amortization, long-run lease rental, and the acquisition of long-run technical capabilities (e.g., software). These costs are generally fixed costs because they are committed to and acquired before they are used to full capacity. Infrastructure costs can be engineered or discretionary.

For instance, manufacturing overhead costs incurred at Chipset to acquire manufacturing capacity are an infrastructure cost that is an example of an engineered cost. In the long run, there is a clear cause-and-effect relationship between output and lease rental costs needed to produce that output. R&D costs incurred to acquire technical capability are an infrastructure cost that is an example of a discretionary cost. There is no clear cause-and-effect relationship between output and R&D costs incurred.

Engineered costs differ from discretionary costs along two key dimensions:

◆ The type of process.
◆ The level of uncertainty.

Engineered costs pertain to processes that are detailed, physically observable, and repetitive, such as manufacturing or customer-service activities. In contrast, discretionary costs are associated with processes that are sometimes called *black boxes*, because they are less precise and not well understood.

Uncertainty refers to the possibility that an actual amount will deviate from an expected amount. The higher the level of uncertainty about the relationship between resources used and outputs, the less likely a cause-and-effect relationship will exist, leading the cost to be classified as a discretionary cost.

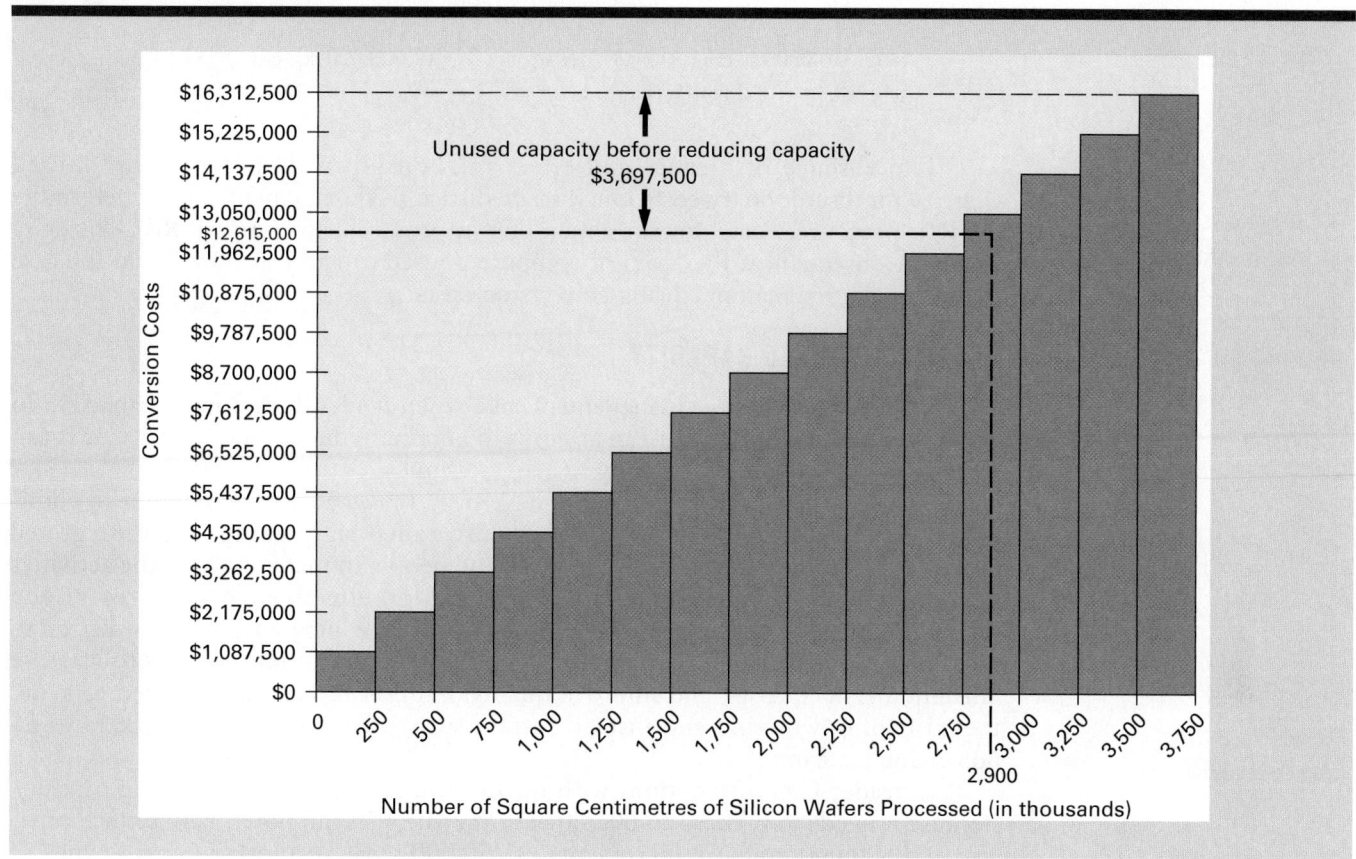

In contrast, there is a low level of uncertainty about the effect of output on manufacturing conversion resources used because other factors do not affect this relationship. Uncertainty is greater in the case of discretionary costs such as R&D because, in most cases, R&D resources are committed well before any output is produced.

How does the distinction between engineered and discretionary costs help a manager to understand and manage unused capacity? Actually, the different types of costs have very different relationships to capacity. Consider first the engineered manufacturing conversion costs. Chipset management indicates that manufacturing capacity can be added or reduced in increments of 250,000 cm². Manufacturing conversion costs are a discontinuous step function, as shown in Exhibit 13-9.

Each step represents increments of 250,000 cm² units of capacity at a cost of $1,087,500. At each step, manufacturing conversion costs are fixed. For example, manufacturing conversion costs are fixed at $13,050,000 if Chipset wants enough capacity to process between 2,750,001 and 3,000,000 units. If the company wants to convert 3,100,000 cm² of silicon wafers, then it must increase capacity to 3,250,000 cm² at an additional cost of $1,087,500 ($4.35/cm² × 250,000 cm²).

At the start of the year 2013, Chipset has the capacity to process 3,750,000 cm² of silicon. Quality and productivity improvements made during 2013 enabled Chipset to produce 1,150,000 units of LCX1 by processing 2,900,000 cm² of silicon wafers. Chipset calculates its unused manufacturing capacity as 850,000 cm² (3,750,000 − 2,900,000) units for 2014. As shown in Exhibit 13-9, at a conversion cost of $4.35/cm², the total cost of unused capacity is $3,697,500. But recall from Chapter 9 that the cost of unused capacity is non-value added to the customer. In a highly competitive market where cost leadership is the successful strategy, Chipset must be as certain as possible that most of its newly purchased capacity will be used or endure a decrease in its operating income margin percent.

$$\begin{array}{l}\text{Cost of} \\ \text{unused capacity}\end{array} = \begin{array}{l}\text{Cost of capacity} \\ \text{at the beginning} \\ \text{of the year}\end{array} - \begin{array}{l}\text{Manufacturing resources} \\ \text{used during the year}\end{array}$$

$$= (3{,}750{,}000 \text{ sq. cm.} \times \$4.35 \text{ per sq. cm.}) - (2{,}900{,}000 \text{ sq. cm.} \times \$4.35 \text{ per sq. cm.})$$

$$= \$16{,}312{,}500 - \$12{,}615{,}000 = \$3{,}697{,}500$$

The absence of a cause-and-effect relationship makes identifying unused capacity for discretionary costs much more difficult. Management cannot determine the R&D resources used for the actual output produced to compare R&D capacity against. Consequently, they cannot compute unused capacity as they did in the case of the engineered manufacturing conversion costs.

MANAGING UNUSED CAPACITY

What actions can Chipset management take when it identifies unused capacity? In general, it has two options. It can attempt to eliminate the unused capacity or it can attempt to use the unused capacity to grow revenues.

In recent years, many companies have tried to *downsize* in an attempt to eliminate their unused capacity. **Downsizing** (also called **rightsizing**) is an integrated approach to configure processes, products, and people to match costs to the activities needed to be performed to operate efficiently and effectively in the present and future. Companies such as General Motors and Sunlife Financial have downsized to focus on their core businesses and have instituted organizational changes to increase efficiency, reduce costs, and improve quality. Chipset has already decided to avoid the costs of downsizing and instead retrain surplus manufacturing workers to do non-manufacturing tasks.

Consider Chipset's options with respect to its unused manufacturing capacity. Because it needs to process 2,900,000 cm^2 in 2014, it could potentially reduce capacity to 3,000,000 units (in increments of 250,000 cm^2), resulting in cost savings of $3,262,500 [(3,750,000 cm^2 − 3,000,000 cm^2) × $4.35/cm^2]. Chipset's strategy, however, is not only to cut costs but also to grow its business at least 10%. Chipset only reduces its manufacturing capacity by 250,000 cm^2, from 3,750,000 units to 3,500,000 units, saving $1,087,500 ($4.35/cm^2 × 250,000). It retains some unused capacity for future growth. By avoiding deep cuts in capacity, it also maintains the morale of its skilled and capable workforce. The success of this strategy will depend on Chipset achieving the future growth it has projected.

Chipset makes similar decisions with respect to the engineered selling and customer-service costs. At the start of 2014, Chipset had the capacity to serve 60 customers. Chipset currently has served 46 customers, resulting in unused service capacity of 14 customers, which corresponds to $1,120,000 ($80,000 × 14) in selling and customer-service costs. (Recall that it costs $80,000 to support each customer.) Chipset could potentially reduce selling and customer-service capacity by 10 customers. However, because the company anticipates adding 10 more customers in the near future, it decides to only reduce its selling and customer-service capability from 60 to 55 customers, realizing savings of $400,000 ($80,000 × 5). Chipset's goal is to align its selling and customer-service capabilities of 55 customers with its manufacturing capacity of 1,150,000 LCX1 units.

Because identifying unused capacity for discretionary costs is difficult, downsizing or otherwise managing this unused capacity is also difficult. Chipset's management used judgment and discretion and did not replace an engineer who voluntarily left. This reduced R&D costs by $100,000 in 2014. Deeper cuts in R&D costs, however, could harm the business by slowing down critically needed product and process improvements. The key is to balance the need for cost reductions without compromising quality, continuous improvement, and future growth.

As we saw in our discussion of the productivity component, fixed costs are tied to capacity. Unlike variable costs, fixed costs do not change automatically with changes in the level of the cost driver (such as units started into production, in the case of manufacturing overhead costs). Productivity improvements never occur automatically when costs are fixed. The only way to reduce these costs is to reduce capacity (plant, equipment, or the balance in the use of human and machine-intensive conversion processes). This analysis begins with control strategies for variable costs.

(Try to solve this problem before examining the solution that follows.)

PROBLEM

Following a strategy of product differentiation, Westwood Corporation makes a high-end kitchen range hood, KE8. Westwood presents the following data for the years 2011 and 2012.

	2011	2012
1. Units of KE8 produced	40,000	42,000
2. Selling price	$100	$110
3. Direct materials (m^2)	120,000	123,000
4. Direct materials costs per m^2	$10	$11
5. Manufacturing capacity for KE8	50,000 units	50,000 units
6. Total manufacturing conversion costs	$1,000,000	$1,100,000
7. Manufacturing conversion costs per unit of capacity (Row 6 ÷ Row 5)	$20	$22
8. Selling and customer-service capacity	30 customers	29 customers
9. Total selling and customer-service costs	$720,000	$725,000
10. Cost per customer of selling and customer-service capacity (Row 9 ÷ Row 8)	$24,000	$25,000

Westwood produces no defective units, but it wants to reduce direct materials usage per unit of KE8 in 2012. Manufacturing conversion costs in each year depend on production capacity defined in terms of KE8 units that can be produced. Selling and customer-service costs depend on the number of customers that the customer and service functions are designed to support. Westwood has 23 customers in 2011 and 25 customers in 2012. The industry market size for high-end kitchen range hoods increased 5% from 2011 to 2012.

REQUIRED

1. Describe briefly key elements that you would include in Westwood's balanced scorecard.
2. How would improved corporate governance improve Westwood's corporate competitiveness?
3. How would BSC measures of environmental sustainability contribute to Westwood's enterprise risk management?
4. Calculate the growth, price-recovery, and productivity components of changes in operating income between 2011 and 2012.
5. Without doing any more calculations, explain in a few sentences whether Westwood was successful in implementing its strategy.

SOLUTION

1. Key elements that Westwood should include in its balanced scorecard are:

   ◆ *Financial perspective.* Operating income growth from charging higher prices on KE8.
   ◆ *Customer perspective.* Market share in high-end kitchen range market and customer satisfaction.
   ◆ *Internal business perspective.* Manufacturing quality, order-delivery time, on-time delivery, and new product features added.

- *Learning and growth perspective.* Development time for designing new products and improving manufacturing processes.

2. Improving any one of the five dimensions of corporate governance improves the others. Improved corporate governance also improves competitiveness because all the factors affect customer, financial, and intellectual capital management.

3. Increasingly countries are enacting legislation that requires reclamation, recycling, and remediation activities be paid for by companies causing the need for these activities. The risk to the enterprise is that their current life-cycle pricing practices fail to include reasonable estimates of environmental life-cycle costs. Global companies need to measure their performance in a BSC format to provide relevant information to improve their strategy to respond to mandatory compliance with new legislation—good corporate governance.

4. Operating income for each year is as follows:

	2011	2012
Revenue ($100 × 40,000; $110 × 42,000)	$4,000,000	$4,620,000
Costs		
Direct materials costs ($10 × 120,000; $11 × 123,000)	1,200,000	1,353,000
Manufacturing conversion costs ($20 × 50,000; $22 × 50,000)	1,000,000	1,100,000
Selling and customer-service costs ($24,000 × 30; $25,000 × 29)	720,000	725,000
Total costs	2,920,000	3,178,000
Operating income	$1,080,000	$1,442,000
Change in operating income		↓ $362,000 F ↓

The Growth Component

$$\begin{pmatrix} \text{Revenue effect} \\ \text{of growth} \\ \text{component} \end{pmatrix} = \begin{pmatrix} \text{Actual units} \\ \text{of output sold} \\ \text{in 2012} \end{pmatrix} - \begin{pmatrix} \text{Actual units of} \\ \text{output sold in} \\ 2011 \end{pmatrix} \times \begin{pmatrix} 2011 \\ \text{output} \\ \text{price} \end{pmatrix}$$

$$= (42,000 - 40,000) \times \$100 = \$200,000 \text{ F}$$

$$\begin{pmatrix} \text{Cost effect} \\ \text{of growth} \\ \text{component} \end{pmatrix} = \begin{pmatrix} \text{Actual units of input/capacity that} \\ \text{would have been used to produce} \\ \text{year 2012 output assuming the} \\ \text{same input-output relationship} \\ \text{that existed in 2011} \end{pmatrix} - \begin{pmatrix} \text{Actual units of} \\ \text{input/capacity to} \\ \text{produce 2011} \\ \text{output} \end{pmatrix} \times \begin{pmatrix} \text{Year} \\ 2011 \\ \text{prices} \end{pmatrix}$$

Direct materials costs that would be required in 2011 to produce 42,000 units instead of the 40,000 units produced in 2011, assuming the 2011 input-output relationship continued into 2012, equal 126,000 m^2 (120,000/40,000 × 42,000). Manufacturing conversion costs and selling and customer-service costs will not change since adequate capacity exists in 2011 to support year 2012 output and customers.

The cost effects of growth component are:

Direct materials costs	(126,000 − 120,000) × $10	=	$60,000 U
Manufacturing conversion costs	(50,000 − 50,000) × $20	=	0
Selling and customer-service costs	(30 − 30) × $24,000	=	0
Cost effect of growth component			$60,000 U

In summary, the net increase in operating income as a result of the growth component equals:

Revenue effect of growth component	$200,000 F
Cost effect of growth component	60,000 U
Increase in operating income due to growth component	$140,000 F

The Price-Recovery Component

$$\begin{array}{c}\text{Revenue effect of} \\ \text{product differentiation} \\ \text{component}\end{array} = \left(\begin{array}{c}\text{Output price} \\ \text{in 2012}\end{array} - \begin{array}{c}\text{Output price} \\ \text{in 2011}\end{array}\right) \times \begin{array}{c}\text{Actual units of} \\ \text{output sold} \\ \text{in 2012}\end{array}$$

$$= (\$110 - \$100) \times 42{,}000 = \$420{,}000 \text{ F}$$

$$\begin{array}{c}\text{Cost effect} \\ \text{of product} \\ \text{differentiation}\end{array} = \left(\begin{array}{c}\text{Input price} \\ \text{in 2012}\end{array} - \begin{array}{c}\text{Input price} \\ \text{in 2011}\end{array}\right) \times \begin{array}{c}\text{Actual units of input/capacity that} \\ \text{would have been used to produce} \\ \text{year 2012 output assuming the} \\ \text{same input-output relationship} \\ \text{that existed in 2011}\end{array}$$

Direct materials costs	($11 − $10) × 126,000 =	$126,000 U
Manufacturing conversion costs	($22 − $20) × 50,000 =	100,000 U
Selling and customer-service costs	($25,000 − $24,000) × 30 =	30,000 U
Total cost effect of price-recovery component		$256,000 U

In summary, the net increase in operating income as a result of the price-recovery component equals:

Revenue effect of price-recovery component	$420,000 F
Cost effect of price-recovery component	256,000 U
Increase in operating income due to price-recovery component	$164,000 F

The Productivity Component

$$\begin{array}{c}\text{Productivity/} \\ \text{cost leadership} \\ \text{component}\end{array} = \left(\begin{array}{c}\text{Actual units of} \\ \text{input/capacity to} \\ \text{produce year} \\ \text{2012 input}\end{array} - \begin{array}{c}\text{Actual units of input/capacity} \\ \text{that would have been used to} \\ \text{produce year 2012 output} \\ \text{assuming the same input-} \\ \text{output relationship that} \\ \text{existed in 2011}\end{array}\right) \times \begin{array}{c}\text{Year} \\ \text{2012} \\ \text{prices}\end{array}$$

The productivity component of cost changes are:

Direct materials costs	(123,000 − 126,000) × $11 =	$33,000 F
Manufacturing conversion costs	(50,000 − 50,000) × $20 =	0
Selling and customer-service costs	(29 − 30) × $25,000 =	25,000 F
Increase in operating income due to productivity component		$58,000 F

The change in operating income between 2011 and 2012 can be analyzed as follows:

	Income Statement Amounts in 2011 (1)	Revenue and Cost Effects of Growth Component in 2012 (2)	Revenue and Cost Effects of Price-Recovery Component in 2012 (3)	Cost Effect of Productivity Component in 2012 (4)	Income Statement Amounts in 2012 (5) = (1) + (2) + (3) + (4)
Revenue	$4,000,000	$200,000 F	$420,000 F	—	$4,620,000
Costs	2,920,000	60,000 U	256,000 U	$58,000 F	3,178,000
Operating income	$1,080,000	$140,000 F	$164,000 F	$58,000 F	$1,442,000

$362,000 F

Change in operating income

5. The analysis of operating income indicates that Westwood was successful in implementing its product differentiation strategy. The company was able to continue to charge a premium price for KE8. Westwood was also able to earn additional operating income from improving its productivity. The growth in units (from 40,000 to 42,000) was attributable entirely to the 5% increase in market size rather than Westwood's product differentiation strategy.

The following question-and-answer format summarizes the chapter's learning outcomes. Each point presents a key question, and the guidelines are the answer to that question.

LEARNING OUTCOMES	GUIDELINES
1. What are two generic strategies a company can use?	Porter's five forces analysis indicates two potential strategies. One is value leadership, appropriate when customers will pay a premium price for unique or highly differentiated products. The second is cost leadership, appropriate when there are plenty of substitutes for a commodity product and many competitors. Corporations selecting the strategy appropriate to the customer's willingness to pay will open an opportunity for superior ROI. Target pricing begins with a target ROI, given the customer's target price. This drives the calculation of the target operating income margin percentage from which are derived the target costs. In a commodity market where cost leadership is the appropriate strategy, improving the operating income margin percentage depends on avoiding the "stuck in the middle" situation.
2. How can an organization translate its strategy into a set of performance measures?	Strategy requires choice, but the best strategic choice must be implemented well. Using the interdependencies highlighted by BSC measures reveals the alignment of actual with specified distinctive competence. Distinctive competence is the key internal strength that will sustain successful achievement of a strategy.
3. What are the four interdependent financial and nonfinancial corporate performance measures in the BSC?	These four measures include the customer-service perspective, which relates to design and selection of products. The second is the internal process perspective or design of products and production processes to meet customer expectations. The third is the learning and growth perspective, which influences the rate of innovation and successful implementation of products and processes to meet customer expectations. Aligning these three will result in improvement in the fourth perspective, financial results.
4. How can companies evaluate their success?	Strategic success can be measured by growth, price-recovery, and productivity components of improved operating income. A company is considered successful in implementing its strategy when changes in operating income align closely with that strategy.
5. What cost control strategies are important?	Productivity improvement and capacity utilization are two key cost control strategies.

This chapter and the Glossary at the end of the book contain definitions of the following important terms:

adjacencies (p. 527)
balanced scorecard (BSC) (p. 525)
core competence (p. 518)
cost leadership (p. 520)
customer perspective (p. 525)
customer preference map (p. 522)
discretionary costs (p. 540)
distinctive competence (p. 518)
downsizing (p. 542)
economies of scale (p. 519)
economies of scope (p. 520)
engineered costs (p. 539)

enterprise risk management (ERM) (p. 529)
financial perspective (p. 525)
infrastructure costs (p. 540)
intellectual capital (p. 528)
internal business process perspective (p. 527)
human capital (p. 520)
key performance factors (p. 523)
key success factors (p. 523)
learning and growth perspective (p. 528)
organic revenue growth (p. 527)

partial productivity (p. 537)
product differentiation (p. 520)
productivity (p. 527)
redesigning (p. 524)
reengineering (p. 524)
rightsizing (p. 542)
scaleability (p. 518)
strategy (p. 518)
total factor productivity (TFP) (p. 538)
value leadership (p. 520)

SHORT-ANSWER QUESTIONS

13-1 Define *strategy*.

13-2 Describe the five key forces to consider when analyzing an industry.

13-3 Describe two generic strategies.

13-4 What is a customer preference map and why is it useful?

13-5 What is reengineering?

13-6 What are four key perspectives in the balanced scorecard?

13-7 What is a strategy map?

13-8 Describe three features of a good balanced scorecard.

13-9 What are three important pitfalls to avoid when implementing a balanced scorecard?

13-10 Describe three key components of a strategic analysis of operating income.

13-11 What is the difference between a stakeholder and a shareholder?

13-12 How does an engineered cost differ from a discretionary cost?

13-13 What is downsizing?

13-14 "We are already measuring total factor productivity. Measuring partial productivity would be of no value." Do you agree? Comment briefly.

EXERCISES

13-15 Terminology. A number of terms are listed below:

adjacencies	balanced scorecard (BSC)	competitive advantage
core competence	cost leadership	customer perspective
distinctive competence	economies of scale	economies of scope
engineered costs	enterprise risk management	financial perspective
key success factors (KSF)	internal process perspective	learning and growth perspective
organic revenue	product differentiation	reengineering
strategy	value leadership	

REQUIRED

Select the terms from the above list to complete the following sentences.

Any management team must understand how it created value for its customers and decide how to accomplish this goal better than all its competitors. This is a decision about _____. For exciting new products and products with no substitutes, consumers are willing to pay a premium price. Focusing on inventing and commercializing products with unique attributes is a _____ _____ (or _____ _____) strategy. For most mass-produced products sold by many competitors, consumers readily find substitutes. ____ _____ is the alternative strategy that improves profitability and ROI through _____ __ _____ and _____ __ _____. Usually this means the management team will work on increasing the quantity of output using the same capacity. The fixed cost per unit produced will decrease and, if price is fixed, then profit will increase. Often cost leadership (or reduction) is achieved by _____ the production process. Growth can also be achieved by producing similar but not identical products and this is _____ _____ growth that provides economies of scope. This type of growth can also be achieved through merger and acquisition or growth through _____.

Implementing strategy successfully depends in part on correct identification of the _____ _____ of a company. This is also called the company's _____ _____. _____ _____ is identified by a resource or set of resources available to a company that enable it to execute its business activities more profitably than other competitors. Management teams must align the choice of strategy with the competitive advantage to implement a strategy well. The resource or set of resources that provide competitive advantage are called ___ _____ _____ (___).

To obtain feedback on how successful the implementation of strategy is, a _____ _____ (___) is often used. The BSC is the foundation of more technologically intensive _____ ___ _____ (___) systems. The BSC and ERM require refined cost reporting systems. The BSC measures success from four perspectives, _____ _____, _____ _____, _____/_____ and of course _____ _____. The BSC approach provides a more detailed basis upon which to evaluate the success of implementation of strategy.

① 13-16 **Balanced scorecard.** La Flamme Corporation manufactures corrugated cardboard boxes. It competes and plans to grow by producing high-quality boxes at a low price that are delivered to customers in a timely manner. Many other manufacturers produce similar boxes. La Flamme believes that continuously improving its manufacturing processes and having satisfied employees are critical to implementing its strategy in 2013.

REQUIRED

1. Is La Flamme's 2013 strategy one of product differentiation or cost leadership? Explain briefly.
2. Portage Corporation, a competitor of La Flamme, manufactures corrugated boxes with more designs and colour combinations than La Flamme at a higher price. Portage's boxes are of high quality but require more time to produce and so have longer delivery times. Draw a simple customer preference map as in Exhibit 13-3 (p. 522) for La Flamme and Portage using the attributes of price, delivery time, quality, and design.
3. Indicate two measures you would expect to see under each perspective in La Flamme's balanced scorecard for 2013. Use a strategy map as in Exhibit 13-4 (p. 524) to explain your answer.

① 13-17 **Analysis of growth, price-recovery, and productivity components** (continuation of Exercise 13-16). An analysis of La Flamme's operating income changes between 2013 and 2014 shows the following:

Operating income for 2014	$1,700,000
Add growth component	70,000
Deduct price-recovery component	(60,000)
Add productivity component	140,000
Operating income for 2013	$1,850,000

The industry market size for corrugated boxes did not grow in 2014, input prices did not change, and La Flamme reduced the price of its boxes in line with the market.

REQUIRED

1. Was La Flamme's gain in operating income in 2014 consistent with the strategy you identified in requirement 1 of Exercise 13-16?
2. Explain the productivity component. In general, does it represent savings in only variable costs, only fixed costs, or both variable and fixed costs?

④ 13-18 **Strategy, balanced scorecard.** Meredith Corporation makes a special-purpose D4H machine used in the textile industry. Meredith has designed the D4H machine for 2013 to be distinct from its competitors. It has been generally regarded as a superior machine. Meredith presents the following data for the years 2012 and 2013.

	2012	2013
1. Units of D4H produced and sold	200	210
2. Selling price	$40,000	$42,000
3. Direct materials (kilograms)	300,000	310,000
4. Direct material cost per kilogram	$8.00	$8.50
5. Manufacturing capacity (units of D4H)	250	250
6. Total conversion costs	$2,000,000	$2,025,000
7. Conversion cost per unit of capacity	$8,000	$8,100
8. Selling and customer-service capacity	100 customers	95 customers
9. Total selling and customer-service costs	$1,000,000	$940,500
10. Selling and customer-service capacity cost per customer	$10,000	$9,900
11. Design staff	12	12
12. Total design costs	$1,200,000	$1,212,000
13. Design cost per employee	$100,000	$101,000

Meredith produces no defective machines, but it wants to reduce direct materials usage per D4H machine in 2013. Manufacturing conversion costs in each year depend on production capacity defined in terms of D4H units that can be produced, not the actual units of D4H produced. Selling and customer-service costs depend on the number of customers that Meredith can support, not the actual number of customers Meredith serves. Meredith has 75 customers in 2012 and 80 customers in 2013. At the start of each year, management uses its discretion to determine the number of design staff for the year. The design staff and costs have no direct relationship with the quantity of D4H produced or the number of customers to whom D4H is sold.

REQUIRED

1. Is Meredith's strategy one of product differentiation or cost leadership? Explain briefly.
2. Describe briefly key elements that you would include in Meredith's balanced scorecard and the reasons for doing so.

13-19 Strategic analysis of operating income. Refer to the information in Exercise 13-18.

1. Change in operating income, $607,500 F

REQUIRED

1. Calculate the change in operating income of Meredith Corporation in 2012 and 2013.
2. Calculate the growth, price-recovery, and productivity components of changes in operating income between 2012 and 2013.
3. Comment on your answer in requirement 2. What do these components indicate?

13-20 Analysis of growth, price-recovery, and productivity components (continuation of Exercise 13-19). Suppose that between 2012 and 2013 the market for Meredith's special-purpose machines grew at 3%. All increases in market share (that is, sales increases greater than 3%) are the result of Meredith's strategic actions.

Change in operating income from industry market-size factor, $168,000 F

REQUIRED

Calculate how much of the change in operating income between 2012 and 2013 is due to industry market-size factors, cost leadership, and product differentiation. How successful has Meredith been in implementing its strategy? Explain.

13-21 Identifying and managing unused capacity. Refer to the Meredith Corporation information in Exercise 13-18.

1. a. Amount of unused manufacturing capacity, 40 units

REQUIRED

1. Where possible, calculate the amount and cost of unused capacity for (a) manufacturing, (b) selling and customer service, and (c) design at the beginning of 2013 based on 2013 production. If you could not calculate the amount and cost of unused capacity, indicate why not.
2. Suppose Meredith can add or reduce its manufacturing capacity in increments of 30 units. What is the maximum amount of costs that Meredith could save by downsizing manufacturing capacity?
3. Meredith, in fact, does not eliminate any of its unused manufacturing capacity. Why might Meredith not downsize?

13-22 Balanced scorecard. Following is a random-order listing of perspectives, strategic objectives, and performance measures for the balanced scorecard.

Pg. 526

Perspectives /Categories	Performance Measures
Internal business process	Percentage of defective product units
Customer	Return on assets
Learning and growth	Number of patents
Financial	Employee turnover rate
	Net income
Strategic Objectives	Customer profitability
Acquire new customers	Percentage of processes with real-time feedback
Increase shareholder value	Return on sales
Retain customers	Average job-related training hours per employee
Improve manufacturing quality	Return on equity
Develop profitable customers	Percentage of on-time deliveries by suppliers
Increase proprietary products	Product cost per unit
Increase information-system capabilities	Profit per salesperson
Enhance employee skills	Percentage of error-free invoices
On-time delivery by suppliers	Customer cost per unit
Increase profit generated by each salesperson	Earnings per share
Introduce new product	Number of new customers
Minimize invoice error rate	Percentage of customers retained

REQUIRED

For each perspective, select those strategic objectives from the list that best relate to it. For each strategic objective, select the most appropriate performance measure(s) from the list.

④ **13-23 Strategy, balanced scorecard, service company.** Snyder Corporation is a small information systems consulting firm that specializes in helping companies implement sales management software. The market for Snyder's products is very competitive. To compete, Snyder must deliver quality service at a low cost. Snyder bills clients in terms of units of work performed, which depends on the size and complexity of the sales management system. Snyder presents the following data for the years 2012 and 2013.

	2012	2013
1. Units of work performed	60	70
2. Selling price	$ 50,000	$ 48,200
3. Software implementation labour-hours	30,000	32,000
4. Cost per software implementation labour-hour	$ 60	$ 63
5. Software implementation support capacity (units of work)	90	90
6. Total cost of software implementation support	$360,000	$369,000
7. Software implementation support capacity cost per unit of work	$ 4,000	$ 4,100
8. Number of employees doing software development	3	3
9. Total software development costs	$375,000	$390,000
10. Software development cost per employee	$125,000	$130,000

Software implementation labour-hour costs are variable costs. Software implementation support costs for each year depend on the software implementation support capacity (defined in terms of units of work) that Snyder chooses to maintain each year. It does not vary with the actual units of work performed each year. At the start of each year, management uses its discretion to determine the number of software-development employees. The software-development staff and costs have no direct relationship with the number of units of work performed.

REQUIRED

1. Is Snyder Corporation's strategy one of product differentiation or cost leadership?
2. Describe briefly key elements that you would include in Snyder's balanced scorecard and your reasons for doing so.

④ **13-24 Strategic analysis of operating income.** Refer to the information in Exercise 13-23.

1. Change in operating income, $134,000 F

REQUIRED

1. Calculate the change in operating income of Snyder Corporation in 2012 and 2013.
2. Calculate the growth, price-recovery, and productivity components of changes in operating income between 2012 and 2013.
3. Comment on your answer in requirement 2. What do these components indicate?

⑤ **13-25 Analysis of growth, price-recovery, and productivity components** (continuation of Exercise 13-24). Suppose that during 2013 the market for implementing sales management software increased by 5%, and that Snyder experiences a 1% decline in prices. Assume that any further decreases in selling prices and increases in market share are strategic choices by Snyder's management to implement Snyder's cost leadership strategy.

Change in operating income from industry market-size factor, $ 60,000 F

REQUIRED

Calculate how much of the change in operating income between 2012 and 2013 is due to industry market-size factors, cost leadership, and product differentiation. How successful has Snyder been in implementing its strategy?

⑤ **13-26 Identifying and managing unused capacity.** Refer to the Snyder Corporation information in Exercise 13-23.

1. a. Amount of unused software implementation support capacity, 20

REQUIRED

1. Where possible, calculate the amount and cost of unused capacity for (a) software implementation support and (b) software development at the beginning of 2013, based on units of work to be performed in 2013. If you could not calculate the amount and cost of unused capacity, indicate why not.
2. Suppose Snyder can add or reduce its software implementation support capacity in increments of 5 units. What is the maximum amount of costs that Snyder could save by downsizing software implementation support capacity?
3. Snyder, in fact, does not eliminate any of its unused software implementation support capacity. Why might Snyder not downsize?

13-27 **Growth, price-recovery, and productivity components.** Oceano T-Shirt Company sells a variety of T-shirts. Oceano presents the following data for its first two years of operations, 2012 and 2013. For simplicity, assume that all purchasing and selling costs are included in the average cost per T-shirt and that each customer buys one T-shirt.

	2012	2013
Number of T-shirts purchased	200,000	250,000
Number of T-shirts lost	2,000	3,300
Number of T-shirts sold	198,000	246,700
Average selling price	$25.00	$26.00
Average cost per T-shirt	$10.00	$8.50
Administrative capacity in terms of number of customers that can be served	4,000	3,750
Administrative costs	$1,200,000	$1,162,500
Administrative cost per customer	$300	$310
Design staff	5	5
Total design costs	$250,000	$275,000
Design cost per employee	$50,000	$55,000

REQUIRED
1. Is Oceano's strategy one of value or cost leadership? Explain briefly.
2. Describe briefly the key elements Oceano should include in its balanced scorecard and the reasons it should do so.

13-28 **Strategic analysis of operating income** (continuation of 13-27). Refer to Exercise 13-27.

REQUIRED
1. Calculate Oceano's operating income in both 2012 and 2013.
2. Calculate the growth, price-recovery, and productivity components that explain the change in operating income from 2012 to 2013.
3. Comment on your answers in requirement 2. What do each of these components indicate?

1. Change in operating income, $1,351,700 F

PROBLEMS

13-29 **Balanced scorecard, non-profit, governance.** Sunset Heights Animal Rescue & Protection Society (SHARP) is a non-profit organization dedicated to the rescue and protection of domestic animals. It operates several animal shelters in the Sunset Heights area (including animal adoption services), rescues injured or abused domestic animals, and educates volunteers, pet owners, and potential pet owners on animal guardianship.

As with all charitable organizations, it is facing increased competition in raising funds and recruiting volunteers. It is also experiencing greater demands for accountability from its donors. Recently it was unable to respond to its board of directors on the costs of running each of its programs and its allocation of funds received to various programs. Although SHARP is expected to operate with a balanced budget, it reported an operating deficit last year.

REQUIRED
1. Create a balanced scorecard for SHARP. In your answer, consider the various programs/services SHARP provides.
2. What are the corporate governance issues raised, and how might they be addressed?

13-30 **Balanced scorecard and strategy.** Dransfield Company manufactures an electronic component, ZP98. This component is significantly less expensive than similar products sold by Dransfield's competitors. Order-processing time is very short; however, approximately 10% of products are defective and returned by the customer. Returns and refunds are handled promptly. Yorunt Manufacturing, Dransfield's main competitor, has a higher priced product with almost no defects, but a longer order-processing time.

REQUIRED
1. Draw a simple customer preference map for Dransfield and Yorunt using the attributes of price, quality, and delivery time. Use the format of Exhibit 13-3 (p. 522).
2. Is Dransfield's current strategy that of product differentiation or cost leadership?

3. Dransfield would like to improve quality without significantly increasing costs or order-processing time. Dransfield's managers believe the increased quality will increase sales. What elements should Dransfield include in its balanced scorecard?

4. Draw a strategy map like the one in Exhibit 13-4 (p. 524) to explain cause-and-effect relationships in Dransfield's balanced scorecard.

13-31 Strategic analysis of operating income (continuation of 13-30). Refer to Problem 13-30. Assume that in 2013, Dransfield has changed its processes and trained workers to recognize quality problems and fix them before products are finished and shipped to customers. Quality is now at an acceptable level. Cost per pound of materials is about the same as before, but conversion costs are higher, and Dransfield has raised its selling price in line with the market. Sales have increased and returns have decreased. Dransfield's managers attribute this to higher quality and a price that is still less than Yorunt's. Information about the current period (2013) and last period (2012) follows.

1. Change in operating income, $36,820

		2012	2013
1a.	Units of ZP98 produced and sold	5,000	6,250
1b.	Units of ZP98 returned	500	225
1c.	Net sales in units	4,500	6,025
2.	Selling price	$44	$50
3.	Direct materials (pounds) used	2,500	3,125
4.	Direct materials cost per pound	$10	$10
5.	Manufacturing capacity in units of ZP98	8,000	8,000
6.	Total conversion costs	$128,000	$184,000
7.	Conversion cost per unit of capacity	$16	$23
8.	Selling and customer-service capacity	60 customers	60 customers
9.	Total selling and customer-service costs	$4,000	$4,180
10.	Selling and customer-service capacity cost per customer	$66.67	$69.67
11.	Advertising staff	1	1
12.	Total advertising costs	$20,000	$24,000
13.	Advertising cost per employee	$20,000	$24,000

Conversion costs in each year depend on production capacity defined in terms of ZP98 units that can be produced, not the actual units produced. Selling and customer-service costs depend on the number of customers that Dransfield can support, not the actual number of customers it serves. Dransfield has 50 customers in 2012 and 60 customers in 2013. At the start of each year, management uses its discretion to determine the number of advertising staff for the year. Advertising staff and its costs have no direct relationship with the quantity of ZP98 units produced and sold or the number of customers who buy ZP98.

REQUIRED

1. Calculate the change in operating income of Dransfield Company for 2012 and 2013.
2. Calculate the growth, price-recovery, and productivity components that explain the change in operating income from 2012 to 2013.
3. Comment on your answer in requirement 2. What do these components indicate?

13-32 Analysis of growth, price-recovery, and productivity components (continuation of 13-31). Suppose that during 2013, the market for ZP98 grew 8%. All increases in market share (that is, sales increases greater than 8%) are the result of Dransfield's strategic actions.

Unit increase due to market share, 1,165

REQUIRED

Calculate how much of the change in operating income from 2012 to 2013 is due to the industry market-size factor, product differentiation, and cost leadership. How does this relate to Dransfield's strategy and its success in implementation? Explain.

13-33 Identifying and managing unused capacity (continuation of 13-31). Refer to the information for Dransfield Company in 13-31.

1. a. Amount of unused capacity, 1,750 units

REQUIRED

1. Calculate the amount and cost of unused capacity for:
   a. Manufacturing
   b. Sales and customer service
   c. Advertising
   If you are unable to calculate the amount and cost of unused capacity, explain why.
2. State two reasons Dransfield might downsize and two reasons they might not downsize.

3. Assume Dransfield has several product lines, of which ZP98 is only one. The manager for the ZP98 product line is evaluated on the basis of manufacturing and customer sales and service costs, but not advertising costs. The manager wants to increase capacity for customers because he thinks the market is growing, and this will cost an additional $1,098. However, the manager is not going to use this extra capacity immediately, so he classifies it as advertising cost rather than customer sales and service cost. How will the deliberate misclassification of this cost affect:

a. The operating income overall?

b. The growth, price-recovery, and productivity components?

c. The evaluation of the ZP98 manager?

You are not required to calculate any numbers when answering requirement 3. Only discuss whether it will have a positive, negative, or no effect; and comment on the ethics of the manager's actions.

13-34 Balanced scorecard. (R. Kaplan, adapted) Caltex, Inc., refines gasoline and sells it through its own Caltex Gas Stations. On the basis of market research, Caltex determines that 60% of the overall gasoline market consists of "service-oriented customers," medium- to high-income individuals who are willing to pay a higher price for gas if the gas stations can provide excellent customer service, such as a clean facility, a convenience store, friendly employees, a quick turnaround, the ability to pay by credit card, and high-octane premium gasoline. The remaining 40% of the overall market are "price shoppers" who look to buy the cheapest gasoline available. Caltex's strategy is to focus on the 60% of service-oriented customers. Caltex's balanced scorecard for 2013 follows. For brevity, the initiatives taken under each objective are omitted.

Objectives	Measures	Target Performance	Actual Performance
Financial Perspective			
Increase shareholder value	Operating-income changes from price recovery	$90,000,000	$95,000,000
	Operating-income changes from growth	$65,000,000	$67,000,000
Customer Perspective			
Increase market share	Market share of overall gasoline market	10%	9.8%
Internal-Business-Process Perspective			
Improve gasoline quality	Quality index	94 points	95 points
Improve refinery performance	Refinery-reliability index (%)	91%	91%
Ensure gasoline availability	Product-availability index (%)	99%	100%
Learning-and-Growth Perspective			
Increase refinery process capability	Percentage of refinery processes with advanced controls	88%	90%

REQUIRED

1. Was Caltex successful in implementing its strategy in 2013? Explain your answer.

2. Would you have included some measure of employee satisfaction and employee training in the learning-and-growth perspective? Are these objectives critical to Caltex for implementing its strategy? Why or why not? Explain briefly.

3. Explain how Caltex did not achieve its target market share in the total gasoline market but still exceeded its financial targets. Is "market share of overall gasoline market" the correct measure of market share? Explain briefly.

4. Is there a cause-and-effect linkage between improvements in the measures in the internal business-process perspective and the measure in the customer perspective? That is, would you add other measures to the internal-business-process perspective or the customer perspective? Why or why not? Explain briefly.

5. Do you agree with Caltex's decision not to include measures of changes in operating income from productivity improvements under the financial perspective of the balanced scorecard? Explain briefly.

13-35 Engineered and discretionary overhead costs, unused capacity, customer help-desk. BrightStar, a cable television operator, had 900,000 subscribers in 2012. The company employs eight customer help-desk representatives to respond to customer questions and problems. During 2012, each customer help-desk representative worked eight hours per day for 250 days at a fixed annual salary of $48,000. The company received 72,000 telephone calls from its customers in 2012. Each call took an average of 10 minutes.

2. a. Available customer help-desk capacity, 16,000 hours

1. Do you think customer help-desk costs at BrightStar are engineered costs or discretionary costs? Explain your answer.
2. Calculate the cost of unused customer help-desk capacity in 2012 under each of the following two assumptions: (a) customer help-desk costs are engineered costs and (b) customer help-desk costs are discretionary costs.
3. Assume that BrightStar had 1,020,000 subscribers in 2013 and that the 2012 percentage of telephone calls received to total subscribers continued into 2013. Customer help-desk capacity in 2013 was the same as it was in 2012. Calculate the cost of unused customer help-desk capacity in 2013 under each of the following two assumptions: (a) customer-service costs are engineered costs and (b) customer-service costs are discretionary costs.

13-36 Balanced scorecard. Lee Corporation manufactures various types of colour laser printers in a highly automated facility with high fixed costs. The market for laser printers is competitive. The various colour laser printers on the market are comparable in terms of features and price. Lee believes that satisfying customers with products of high quality at low costs is key to achieving its target profitability. For 2012, Lee plans to achieve higher quality and lower costs by improving yields and reducing defects in its manufacturing operations. Lee will train workers and encourage and empower them to take the necessary actions. Currently, a significant amount of Lee's capacity is used to produce products that are defective and cannot be sold. Lee expects that higher yields will reduce the capacity that Lee needs to manufacture products. Lee does not anticipate that improving manufacturing will automatically lead to lower costs because Lee has high fixed costs. To reduce fixed costs per unit, Lee could lay off employees and sell equipment, or it could use the capacity to produce and sell more of its current products or improved models of its current products.

Lee's balanced scorecard (initiatives omitted) for the just-completed fiscal year 2012 follows:

Objectives	Measures	Target Performance	Actual Performance
Financial Perspective			
Increase shareholder value	Operating-income changes from productivity improvements	$1,000,000	$400,000
	Operating-income changes from growth	$1,500,000	$600,000
Customer Perspective			
Increase market share	Market share in colour laser printers	5%	4.6%
Internal-Business-Process Perspective			
Improve manufacturing quality	Yield	82%	85%
Reduce delivery time to customers	Order-delivery time	25 days	22 days
Learning-and-Growth Perspective			
Develop process skills	Percentage of employees trained in process and quality management	90%	92%
Enhance information-system capabilities	Percentage of manufacturing processes with real-time feedback	85%	87%

REQUIRED

1. Was Lee successful in implementing its strategy in 2013? Explain.
2. Is Lee's balanced scorecard useful in helping the company understand why it did not reach its target market share in 2013? If it is, explain why. If it is not, explain what other measures you might want to add under the customer perspective and why.
3. Would you have included some measure of employee satisfaction in the learning-and-growth perspective and new-product development in the internal-business-process perspective? That is, do you think employee satisfaction and development of new products are critical for Lee to implement its strategy? Why or why not? Explain briefly.
4. What problems, if any, do you see in Lee improving quality and significantly downsizing to eliminate unused capacity?

13-37 Partial productivity measurement. Guble Company manufactures wallets from fabric. In 2012, Guble made 2,500,000 wallets using 1,875,000 metres of fabric. In 2013, Guble plans to make 2,650,000 wallets and wants to make fabric use more efficient. At the same time, Guble wants to reduce capacity; capacity in 2012 was 3,000,000 wallets at a total cost of $9,000,000. Guble wants to reduce capacity to 2,800,000 wallets, at a total cost of $8,680,000 in 2013.

Suppose that in 2013 Guble makes 2,650,000 wallets, uses 1,669,500 metres of fabric, and reduces capacity to 2,800,000 units and costs to $8,680,000.

REQUIRED

1. Calculate the partial-productivity ratios for materials and conversion (capacity costs) for 2013, and compare them to a benchmark for 2012 calculated based on 2013 output.
2. How can Guble Company use the information from the partial-productivity calculations?

13-38 Total factor productivity (continuation of 13-37). Refer to the data for problem 13-37. Assume the fabric costs $4 per metre in 2013 and $4.10 per metre in 2012.

1. Total factor productivity for 2013 using 2013 prices, 0.1725 units of output/$1.00 of input

REQUIRED

1. Compute Guble Company's total factor productivity (TFP) for 2013.
2. Compare TFP for 2013 with a benchmark TFP for 2012 inputs based on 2013 output.
3. What additional information does TFP provide that partial productivity measures do not?

13-39 Downsizing. (CMA, adapted) Mayfair Corporation currently subsidizes cafeteria services for its 250 employees. Mayfair is in the process of reviewing the cafeteria services as cost-cutting measures are needed throughout the organization to keep the prices of its products competitive. Two alternatives are being evaluated: downsize the cafeteria staff and offer a reduced menu or contract with an outside vendor.

1. Downsizing plan subsidy, $25,231

The current cafeteria operation has five employees with a combined annual salary of $155,000 plus additional employee benefits at 25% of salary. The cafeteria operates 260 days each year, and the costs for utilities and equipment maintenance average $52,000 annually. The daily sales include 100 entrées at $7.20 each, 90 sandwiches or salads at an average price of $4.50 each, plus an additional $300 for beverages and desserts. The cost of all cafeteria supplies is 62% of revenues.

The plan for downsizing the current operation envisions retaining two of the current employees whose combined base annual salaries total $94,000. An entrée would no longer be offered, and prices of the remaining items would be increased slightly. Under this arrangement, Mayfair expects daily sales of 160 sandwiches or salads at a higher average price of $5.10. The revenue for beverages and desserts is expected to increase to $340 each day. Because of the elimination of the entrée, the cost of all cafeteria supplies is expected to drop to 52% of revenues. All other conditions of operation would remain the same. Mayfair is willing to continue to subsidize this reduced operation but will not spend more than 20% of the current subsidy.

A proposal has been received from Wilco Foods, an outside vendor that is willing to supply cafeteria services. Wilco has proposed to pay Mayfair $1,300 per month for use of the cafeteria and utilities. Mayfair would be expected to cover equipment repair costs. In addition, Wilco would pay Mayfair 8% of all revenues received above the breakeven point; this payment would be made at the end of the year. All other costs incurred by Wilco to supply the cafeteria services are variable and equal 75% of revenues. Wilco plans to charge $7.80 for an entrée, and the average price for the sandwich or salad would be $5.50. All other daily sales are expected to average $370. Wilco expects daily sales of 70 entrées and 98 sandwiches or salads.

REQUIRED

1. Determine whether the plan for downsizing the current cafeteria operation would be acceptable to Mayfair Corporation. Show all calculations.
2. Is the Wilco Foods proposal more advantageous to Mayfair Corporation than the downsizing plan? Show all calculations.

COLLABORATIVE LEARNING CASE

13-40 Strategic analysis of operating income. Halsey Company sells women's clothing. Halsey's strategy is to offer a wide selection of clothes and excellent customer service and to charge a premium price. Halsey presents the following data for 2012 and 2013. For simplicity, assume that each customer purchases one piece of clothing.

2. Change in operating income, $21,300 F

	2012	2013
1. Pieces of clothing purchased and sold	40,000	40,000
2. Average selling price	$60	$59
3. Average cost per piece of clothing	$40	$41
4. Selling and customer-service capacity	51,000 customers	43,000 customers
5. Selling and customer-service costs	$357,000	$296,700
6. Selling and customer-service capacity cost per customer (Line 5 ÷ Line 4)	$7 per customer	$6.90 per customer
7. Purchasing and administrative capacity	980 designs	850 designs
8. Purchasing and administrative costs	$245,000	$204,000
9. Purchasing and administrative capacity cost per distinct design (Line 8 ÷ Line 7)	$250 per design	$240 per design

Total selling and customer-service costs depend on the number of customers that Halsey has created capacity to support, not the actual number of customers that Halsey serves. Total purchasing and administrative costs depend on purchasing and administrative capacity that Halsey has created (defined in terms of the number of distinct clothing designs that Halsey can purchase and administer). Purchasing and administrative costs do not depend on the actual number of distinct clothing designs purchased. Halsey purchased 930 distinct designs in 2012 and 820 distinct designs in 2013.

At the start of 2013, Halsey planned to increase operating income by 10% over operating income in 2012.

REQUIRED

1. Is Halsey's strategy one of product differentiation or cost leadership? Explain.
2. Calculate the change in Halsey's operating income in 2012 and 2013.
3. Calculate the growth, price-recovery, and productivity components of changes in operating income between 2012 and 2013.
4. Does the strategic analysis of operating income indicate Halsey was successful in implementing its strategy in 2013? Explain.

13-41 Balanced scorecard, sustainability. Okanagan Orchard Products Ltd. is a manufacturer of jams and jellies. It distributes its products to food retailers across Canada. Okanagan's objective is to be the number one distributor of its product lines in Canada. Okanagan competes against a limited number of Canadian companies, but also must compete against several large American food manufacturers. It seeks to increase market share through the delivery of quality products. It believes it can achieve its objectives through high quality control in its manufacturing processes, improved efficiency (particularly relating to yields), and innovation of its products.

Okanagan has had problems with employee turnover, both in production and administration. It pays competitive wages but still has struggled managing employee turnover. Employee surveys have determined that employees do not believe the company provides adequate training or support and that employees are unaware of opportunities for advancement.

REQUIRED

1. Create a balanced scorecard for Okanagan Orchard Products Ltd. using the traditional four perspectives.
2. What types of sustainability measures would you recommend for Okanagan?
3. What specific measures could Okanagan take to address its employee turnover issues?

Period Cost Application

14

BUSINESS MATTERS

Good Period Overhead Cost-Application Methods Improve Management Decisions

Cogeco provides bundled telephone, television, and Internet access services to its customers. With the pending deregulation of digital telecommunications provision in Canada, Cogeco will face more competitors. Careful target pricing will assure Cogeco's continued profitability. Target prices determine Cogeco's target ROI and operating margin percent as well as the constraints on target costing. In the long run, Cogeco's decisions about cost application will signal how costs actually flow to core divisions in proportion to the benefits each division receives. The application of indirect costs will affect the total costs assigned to finished goods or services from core divisions. Decisions at Cogeco about cost-application methods will reflect trade-offs among cost-benefit, simplicity, and economic plausibility.

LEARNING OUTCOMES

After studying this chapter, you should be able to

1. Apply relevance as a criterion to decide how to allocate non-manufacturing (period) costs.

2. Evaluate and select between a single- and dual-rate cost method to apply period costs of IT services.

3. Analyze how the selection of the simple or dual-cost allocation rate affects the calculation of efficiency variance.

4. Evaluate and select among three cost allocation methods for a product-sustaining inventoriable period cost and a facilities-sustaining period cost.

5. Analyze cost allocation procedures to apply common costs and justify contractual reimbursement terms.

6. Appendix. Use matrix algebra to apply the reciprocal method to allocating costs of support divisions.

The purpose of this chapter and Chapter 15 is to explain and apply techniques to allocate support department, or period overhead, costs. Support department cost allocation is treated separately in part because most period costs are excluded from inventoriable costs by accounting standards. But prices of the finished output must recover *all* manufacturing and non-manufacturing costs for corporations to remain profitable. Period costs, such as R&D and IT services arising from business functions other than production, are essential to management of an entire corporation. The non-manufacturing costs (period costs) are facilities-sustaining. Financial accountants refer to period costs as operating expenses (see Chapters 2, 3). These costs must somehow be assigned to outputs in a way that reflects the truth about economic activities. If there is more than one distinct output and if the non-manufacturing costs of IT services provide different levels of value added to each distinct output, as judged by the customer, then the customer should be willing to pay for that value added. The task of the management team is to select the best method of cost assignment that most accurately includes the value added.

THE RELEVANCE CRITERION

<table>
<tr><td>① Apply relevance as a criterion to decide how to allocate non-manufacturing (period) costs.</td></tr>
</table>

Cost allocation is the alternative used when tracing is economically infeasible (see Chapter 4). Often it is not economically plausible to try to determine how an orderly change in a direct cost driver simultaneously occurs with and explains some proportion of an orderly change in a period cost. As explained in Chapter 5, the benefits of most facilities-sustaining costs are not observable and therefore cannot be readily measured. The management team must select an observable and countable input to signal different levels of value added. For example, even if the pages of hardcopy advertising could be counted and costed, it makes no sense to answer the question "How many pages of advertising does it take to manufacture a smartphone?" This makes the logic of cost allocation for many period costs different from the logic behind allocating indirect MOH (see Chapters 4, 5, and 10). The goal is to allocate period costs of non-manufacturing activities proportional to the different levels of benefit provided to each of the users. The users may be non-manufacturing business functions as well.

The activities of upstream and downstream business functions are often interdependent. As illustrated in Exhibit 14-1, upstream business activities incur pre-production costs, and downstream business activities incur post-production costs. The activities in customer service, a downstream business function, can sometimes be reduced by spending more on product and process design in R&D, an upstream business function. Period cost allocation methods exist to account for this reciprocity. Regardless of the method chosen, however, the sales price of the product or service needs to be high enough to recover all costs. **Full product costing** requires the recovery of all costs generated by all business functions in the value chain.

EXHIBIT 14-1
Period Cost Allocation—One Part of the Big Picture

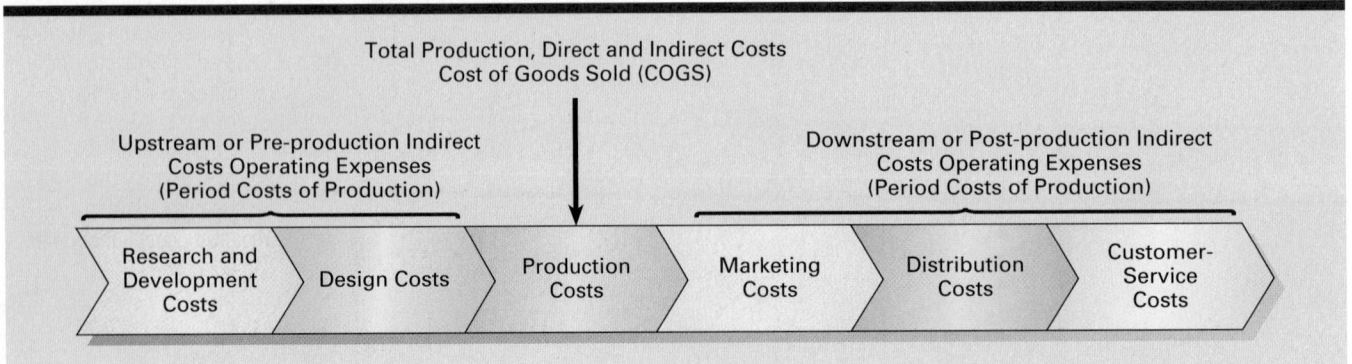

There is no universal rule to tell accountants how to allocate either manufacturing or non-manufacturing costs. But throughout the text we have consistently noted that, if outputs are identical, a simple average will be an appropriate way to calculate a cost allocation rate. If, however, the outputs (jobs) are not using resources identically, then using a simple average runs the risk of inadvertent over- or undercosting of the product. The threat posed by overcosting and overpricing in a highly competitive market is that customers will not pay a higher price when lower-priced substitutes are readily available. In highly competitive markets most sellers are price takers, because consumers set the acceptable price above which they will not purchase a product or service. Often this is referred to as the discipline of the market—consumers rule when competition is intense. The threat posed by undercosting is that you cannot identify why your profits are dropping even as sales volume increases.

ABC relied on an economically plausible relationship between the contributors to the MOH cost pool and the activities of production (see Chapter 5). As mentioned above, this logic does not readily apply for non-manufacturing or period cost pools. When products and services are bundled together in different combinations, as they are for telecommunications providers, the choice of allocation methods for non-manufacturing costs becomes particularly important. A **product bundle** can be a combination of two or more different products, two or more different services, or products combined with services. Clearly, non-manufacturing resource consumption and the accompanying period costs differ between production of goods and production of services (see Chapter 4).

Careful costing of combinations of quantities of products and services in each bundle provides three important benefits. First, more accurate costing will result in more accurate full product pricing. In a highly competitive market this protects market share. Second, refined costing systems improve the budgeting process. When companies are price takers there is no option to simply raise the price to cover excess cost. A good budget can signal when it is time to exit an unprofitable market as well as how to sustain or improve profit. Third, feedback in the form of periodic variance analyses indicates when business functions are consuming more resources than budgeted (see Chapters 7 and 8). Regaining control of resources actually used is essential to controlling costs. Finally, understanding which product bundles are more or less profitable enables managers to select the most profitable among existing opportunities. When resources are constrained, this capability reduces opportunity costs (see Chapters 11 and 12).

RELEVANCE

Managers face a wide variety of business decisions. They can improve the decisions they make by improving how they allocate non-manufacturing costs. Ultimately full product costing requires all period costs be allocated to the product on some reasonable basis. Selecting the most appropriate method of allocation will generate higher quality information. The higher the quality of information, the better able the management team will be to select only the costs relevant to different types of decisions. Four possible decisions requiring appropriate allocation of period costs are to:

◆ Provide information for economic decisions.
◆ Motivate managers and employees.
◆ Justify either costs or reimbursement internally or externally.
◆ Measure GAAP-compliant income and assets for reports to external parties.

The same combination of costs in the six business functions do not often satisfy each of the four purposes listed. For economic decision purposes, the costs in all six functions should be included. For motivation purposes, costs from more than one function are often included. Non-manufacturing support costs are common to many business functions. For example, some Japanese companies require product designers to incorporate production and downstream business function costs (e.g., distribution, customer service, and manufacturing) into their project cost estimates. The aim is to focus attention on how different product design options affect the total costs of all business functions in the value chain.

For cost reimbursement purposes, contracts will often state any business function costs that must be excluded from reimbursement. Cost reimbursement rules governing government contracts may, for example, explicitly exclude marketing costs. For purposes of income and asset measurement, inventoriable costs under GAAP include only manufacturing costs. In Canada, R&D and design costs are expensed to the accounting period in which they are incurred unless they can be directly associated solely with a product or service currently generating revenue. Different external parties require the use of different costing rules.

Before undertaking any refinements to the existing costing system, it is important to consider both costs and benefits of the project. The time, aggravation, and money in changing the costing system are all too evident. The benefits are less evident. If the decision has been made to proceed, then many choices of contributors to significant period cost pools and cost drivers can be contentious. But rapid advances in technology have reduced the financial costs of collecting and processing timely cost information. Even small companies have either adopted or developed costing systems that use multiple cost allocation bases to improve the quality of information to make decisions.

JUSTIFICATION OF RELEVANCE

Justification gives the costing system validity and relevance. The purpose of a costing system is to reveal facts about actual performance. Without this economic substance, costing systems provide no benefit. Managers may incorporate one or more of the following justifications for their decisions about the design of a costing system.

Causality When there is a direct cause-and-effect relationship of one business function cost driver to the quantities consumed by user business functions, then causality is a credible justification. Non-manufacturing upstream and downstream costs are, by definition, indirect period costs; therefore, causality cannot be a justification for a cost driver. However, cost benefit does justify the selection of a cost driver.

Benefit Received The internal users of the upstream or downstream service are identified as the beneficiaries. The broader the scope of service provided by, for example, R&D, the more important it is to allocate these costs proportionately to the benefits received by the internal users. Ultimately the period cost pool must be allocated in proportion to the unequal benefits received by each distinct product, not business function.

If there is only one product, then there is one complication to simply using an average period cost allocation rate. The complication is that, like a manufacturing overhead cost pool, the support cost pool comprises both variable and fixed costs. The fixed cost of a period cost pool never varies with the quantity of output in the production function of the value chain. The period fixed cost depends on the long-term capacity purchased for the support activities of, for example, IT services. In the situation where there is more than one distinct product manufactured by the company, it is highly probable the production divisions will use the IT services unequally. In this situation, a single average rate will underallocate the period cost to one product and overallocate the period cost to another. This distorts the full product cost and therefore will result in inadvertent over- and underpricing and a loss of profitability.

It is not an easy task to choose the cost driver that is the best measure of the unequal benefits received by each user sharing the service. For example, the costs of IT payroll service provision divided by total employess results in a cost allocation rate per employee. Assume it costs more to process wage earners than those receiving salary. Also assume that one distinct product is produced primarily by wage earners and the other primarily by salaried employees. Then the cost assignment will not reflect the economic fact of how IT service costs arise. The objective is to allocate the cost in a way that reflects the different level of benefit received by each distinct type of product. The product using the most wage earners in the production process will be undercosted using an average rate per employee.

A more appropriate cost driver would be number of IT hours used to process payroll. The benefit to each distinct product will vary as the number of IT hours varies. Using IT hours means the distinct type of product using the highest IT hours will be allocated the highest proportion of total service department costs. To justify cost assignment using cost-benefit requires careful analysis of how the period costs are actually consumed. The cost driver chosen must reflect the actual and unequal distribution of benefit to each distinct type of product.

Fairness   Most often, fairness is defined as equality, but equality often depends on the perspective of the affected parties.[1] There is no standardized procedure to negotiate fairness. If the parties believe the process is undertaken in good faith among all who may be affected and they have equal access to relevant information, the outcome will be perceived as fair. If fairness is defined as equality of outcome, then a simple average should be sufficient to determine a cost allocation rate.

Ability to Bear   The ability to bear the burden of cost depends on the various stakeholders' agreement about fairness. Bundled products often result in difficult negotiations about ability to bear. The bundle may generate large volume because one element of the bundle is a loss leader. This strategy can increase both market share and size disproportionately to the ability to bear. Thus the bundle can be highly profitable when the loss leader is sold based on a variable costing policy. But remember that it is illegal to price below total variable costs (see Chapter 12). The loss leader has no ability to bear any further burden of costs of non-manufacturing support services. Selling prices for other products, services, or bundles will subsidize the element of the product bundle that is losing money.

DECIDING BETWEEN SINGLE- AND DUAL-RATE COST METHODS

The management team at Computer Horizons Inc. (CHI) must decide how to cost their two products, notebooks and peripherals. CHI's **core (operating, production) divisions** produce each product. A core division adds value to output for which the customer will pay. In Exhibit 14-2, IT services, a non-manufacturing cost, is allocated between the two core divisions, Notebook and Peripherals. To simplify the illustration, only the Notebook allocation path is shown in full as the solid blue line. The decision framework is used by Computer Horizons to come to a decision.

> Evaluate and select between a single- and dual-rate cost method to apply period costs of IT services.
> **2**

Step 1: Identify the Problem   CHI has defined their problem as a long-term economic problem. How should the managers establish what its full product costs are for each of the notebook and peripherals products? They have focused on IT services, a non-manufacturing or period cost incurred to support other divisions at CHI. In a highly competitive environment where many substitute products are readily available, CHI wants to avoid any inadvertent over- or undercosting of its two products. The company has a target pricing and costing policy.

The company could simply use an average cost allocation rate to allocate its non-manufacturing cost pool, IT services. This is the **single-rate method**. The cost driver will be IT hours used. This approach will reflect the different consumption of the service by the two core production divisions for the notebook computer and the peripherals. Alternatively, CHI could choose a **dual-rate method** whereby the fixed and variable cost contributors to the IT services cost pools are allocated based on different cost drivers.

---

[1]Kaplow and Shavell review legal literature and observe that "notions of fairness are many and varied. They are analyzed and rationalized by different writers in different ways, and they also typically depend upon the circumstances under consideration. Accordingly, it is not possible to identify a consensus view on these notions. . . ." See L. Kaplow and S. Shavell, "Fairness versus Welfare," *Harvard Law Review*, February 2001.

EXHIBIT 14-2
Full Product Costing at the Edmonton Production Plant of Computer Horizons

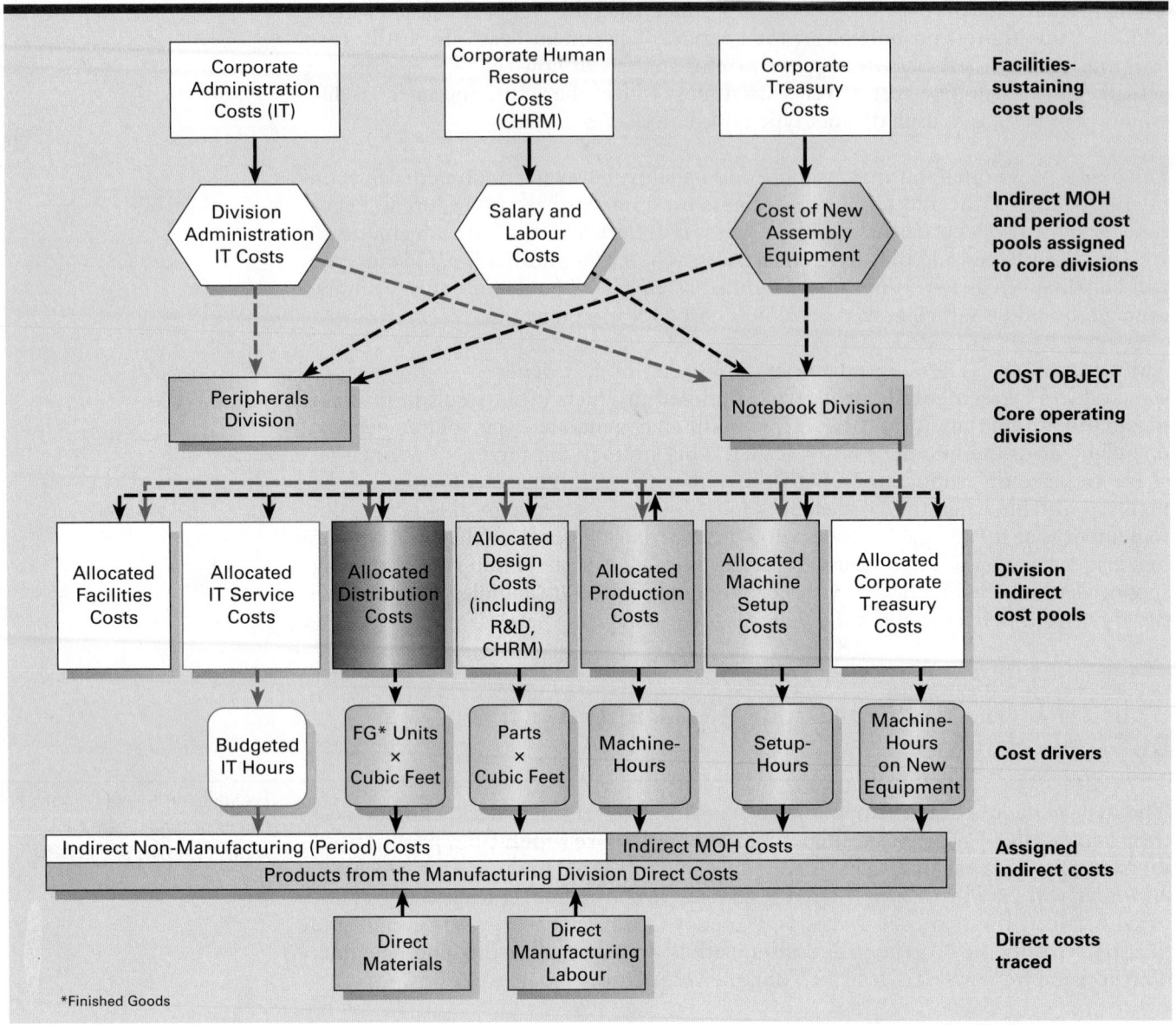

Step 2: Gather Relevant Information   CHI's manufacturing plants are located in Canada, the United States, Mexico, Singapore, and the United Kingdom, and it has marketing operations in more than 20 countries. Every month it consolidates accounting information from each of its operations to use in its planning and control decisions.

At the top of Exhibit 14-2 are the facilities-sustaining non-manufacturing costs of corporate treasury, corporate human resources (CHRM), and corporate administration (IT). The overhead cost pools are on the second level and must be appropriately allocated to the cost objects, the two core divisions in the third tier. The cost of new equipment will be a fixed MOH cost pool and is blue-coloured. This cost will be allocated to production cost objects (in this case, the core divisions). Non-manufacturing cost drivers are not blue and will also be allocated to the core divisions.

One important core production cost is the purchase of new assembly equipment to ensure efficient and effective production of peripherals and notebooks. Through training, hiring, and reimbursement programs, CHRM performs these functions centrally through Corporate Treasury, not decentrally in each production division. Corporate IT costs enable effective JIT planning in both core divisions and support the divisions of CHRM and investment undertaken to sustain the two core divisions.

The various costs and potential cost drivers for IT services will be the basis for a typical revision of a costing system. The *budgeted* costs, available capacity, and use of IT hours (the cost driver) are shown in the following table:

	Budget	Actual
Fixed costs of IT infrastructure	$300,000 per year	
Total capacity available	1,500 IT hours	
Master budget long-term usage (quantity) in hours		
Notebook division budget	800 IT hours	900
Peripherals division budget	400 IT hours	300
Total	1,200 IT hours	1200
Unitized fixed cost/IT hour (used in dual rate)	$ 250	
Budgeted variable costs per hour in the 1,000 to 1,500-hour relevant range (used in dual rate)	$ 200/IT hour	
Total IT average hourly cost allocation rate (used in single rate)	$ 450	

Under the dual-rate method, the allocation method for the Notebook division indicates the following cost application:

Fixed-cost function (800 hours ÷ 1,200 hours) × $300,000	$200,000 per year
Variable-cost function	$ 200 per hour used

The cost application to the Peripherals division would be:

Fixed-cost function (400 hours ÷ 1,200 hours) × $300,000	$100,000 per hour used
Variable-cost function	$ 200 per hour used

Step 3: Make Predictions about the Future CHI's core division managers can now readily produce a forecast from each alternative method of allocating the IT services period cost pool. Based on *budgeted* use as the quantity of the cost driver and *budgeted* cost-driver rates, under the single-rate method, the costs of IT services would be $540,000 ($450 × 1,200 IT hours). This way of determining a cost allocation rate is called the *standard* or *budget method* (see Chapter 4). Fixed costs at the rate of $250/IT hour will be incurred whether the computer runs its 1,500-hour practical capacity, its 1,200-hour master budgeted usage (see Chapter 9), or even only 600 IT hours' usage.

Under the dual-rate method, the fixed cost pool is separated from the variable cost pool to reflect a proportional benefit to the user. Based on the budgeted use for each division of the 1,200 master budget IT hours, the ratio of divisional to total fixed cost pool of $300,000 can be calculated. The Notebook division consumes 800 of 1,200 IT hours, or two-thirds (800 IT hours ÷ 1,200 IT hours) of total IT master budgeted capacity. This ratio results in $200,000 of total IT services fixed costs that will be applied to the Notebook division ($300,000 × ⅔). The remaining one-third (400 IT hours ÷ 1,200 IT hours), or $100,000, is applied to the fixed cost pool for the Peripherals division. Total cost of IT services remains at $540,000.

		Dual Rate		
	Single Rate	Fixed	Variable	Total
Budgeted IT Allocation				
Notebook division 800 × $450	$360,000			$360,000
Peripherals division 400 × $450	180,000			180,000
Budgeted IT Allocation				
Notebook division (800 × $250) + (800 × $200)		$200,000	$160,000	$360,000
Peripherals division (400 × $250) + (400 × $200)		100,000	80,000	180,000

Step 4: Decide on and Implement an Alternative Management at Computer Horizons now need to choose a costing system to apply the period costs of IT services to the two core production divisions. Cost-benefit of implementing this costing

system is an important factor. The single-rate method is simple, but costing software (that would make the dual-rate method easier) is inexpensive and for small businesses even an Excel spreadsheet will be adequate. Most small businesses own Microsoft Office already and there is no incremental software acquisition cost. It will take minimal time to create a monthly flexible budget spreadsheet for the two divisions, including variance analyses (see Chapter 8). Larger corporations can readily acquire or apply existing budgeting software to accommodate either a single- or dual-rate cost system.

But using the budgeted $450 per hour single-rate method transforms what is a fixed cost to IT Services (and to CHI) into a variable cost to users of IT hours. The greater the number of IT hours budgeted, the lower should be the fixed-cost rate to the user. There is an incentive when using the master budget approach to overestimate the quantity of IT hours budgeted to build slack into the budgeted period cost pool for each division. When the division then actually consumes a higher number of IT hours, if there is no adjustment to the unitized fixed-cost rate, then the unfavourable variance will be smaller than an honest estimate of the unitized cost rate would product.

This presents two problems in a highly competitive environment. First, the master budget quantity of IT hours used is the wrong denominator. In theory, the practical capacity of 1,500 IT hours should determine the unitized fixed cost rate, not the master budget 1,200 IT hours (see Chapter 9). The appropriate rate should be $200 ($300,000 ÷ 1,500 IT hours), not $250/IT hour. Customers will not pay for poor capacity utilization policies, nor underwrite the future growth of market share from the short-term master budget level of 1,200 to the long-term normal demand level, usually close to the practical capacity level of 1,500 IT hours used. Unused capacity cost is non-value added to the customer.

In theory, CHI cannot expect to recover $15,000 of unused IT hours in its full product costs (see Chapters 9 and 12). To fully exploit its cost leadership strategy, implementing a cost system can reveal these opportunity costs (see Chapters 11 and 13). Knowing these costs provides an incentive to CHI to lower its target cost threshold through reengineering or other cost reduction policies (see Chapter 13). Alternatively, it provides an incentive to IT services to seek special projects that contribute more than $200/IT hour and pay some of the $15,000 that cannot be recovered through sales of either notebooks or peripherals.

In practice, $50/IT hour has only affected the cost per IT hour allocated to divisions, not outputs. Full product costing has not yet been undertaken and the effect on the target cost may be trivial. In principle, however, this $50 per IT hour is only one of many potential fixed-cost discrepancies that could arise throughout the entire value chain. CHI managers are foolish to ignore small differences like this, because these discrepancies can accumulate to a significant unrecoverable amount. Using a single-rate method could result in a significant over estimation of the full product cost. In the long term, CHI could eliminate a profitable product.

The second problem with the single-rate method is that internal users will not pay $450/IT hour if they have the option to outsource their IT services at a lower cost. This is the reason for a downward demand spiral (see Chapter 9). As the total actual capacity used decreases, the internal unitized fixed cost increases. Customers still will not pay any unitized fixed cost above $200/IT hour. The unrecoverable fixed cost per unit will increase for CHI, although the actual cost for the user divisions could decrease dramatically. Profits will be eroded if CHI selects a single rate allocation method, unless it can find an alternate use for excess IT capacity.

Implementing the dual rate method, CHI's executives can provide an incentive for honest capacity-use estimates by its managers. Further, by using the practical capacity, managers will have no incentive to underestimate the quantity of IT hours they expect to consume. The use of practical capacity sets a standard unitized rate for fixed costs per IT hour. The dual-rate method also informs the IT services, Notebook, and Peripherals division leaders of the capacity available and the opportunity cost to

CHI when IT services within capacity available is outsourced. The dual rate method indicates that full practical capacity use will reduce the unrecoverable cost to CHI and improve corporate profitability. This will not lead to overuse of capacity because there is also a variable cost of $200/IT hour that far outweighs any decrease in unitized fixed cost.

Step 5: Implement the Decision and Evaluate Performance   After implementation, CHI should generate feedback on actual compared to budgeted performance for its IT services, Notebook, and Peripherals division managers. Under the single-rate method, variance analysis will not indicate losses to CHI as a corporation when managers choose to outsource IT services costing less than $450/IT hour to a third party charging above $200/IT hour in a fully variable cost.

ANALYSIS OF FAVOURABLE AND UNFAVOURABLE EFFICIENCY VARIANCES

In the example illustrated in Exhibit 14-3, the effects of a zero, unfavourable, and favourable efficiency variance on costs applied using the single-rate method are shown for three cases.

Analyze how the selection of the simple or dual cost allocation rate affects the calculation of efficiency variance.

The budget of $300,000 fixed costs for IT services has been applied based on the master budgeted quantity of IT service hours of 800 for Notebook and 400 for Peripherals. Assume that a zero efficiency variance for the Notebook division (actual = budgeted use) exists in all three cases. Case 1 reports the effect on allocating the $300,000 in total fixed costs when there is also zero efficiency variance in Peripherals. In case 2, Peripherals incurs an unfavourable efficiency variance (actual > budgeted use), and in case 3, Peripherals incurs a favourable efficiency variance (actual < budgeted use).

EXHIBIT 14-3
Effect of Variations in Actual Usage on Costs Applied to Core Divisions

	Actual Usage (Hours)		Budgeted Usage as the Allocation Base		Actual Usage as the Allocation Base	
	Notebook Division	Peripherals Division	Notebook Division	Peripherals Division	Notebook Division	Peripherals Division
Case 1	800	400	$200,000*	$100,000ᵃ	$200,000*	$100,000ᵃ
Case 2	800	700	200,000*	100,000ᵃ	160,000ᵇ	140,000
Case 3	800	200	200,000*	100,000ᵃ	240,000ᶜ	60,000ᵈ

$$* \quad \frac{800}{(800 + 400)} \times \$300,000$$

$$a \quad \frac{400}{(800 + 400)} \times \$300,000 \qquad\qquad c \quad \frac{800}{(800 + 200)} \times \$300,000$$

$$b \quad \frac{800}{(800 + 700)} \times \$300,000 \qquad\qquad d \quad \frac{200}{(800 + 200)} \times \$300,000$$

In case 1, fixed costs applied equal the expected amount for both fixed and variable costs in both divisions. In case 2, the fixed cost applied is $40,000 less to the Notebook division than expected ($160,000 versus $200,000). But this does not reflect economic reality. In fact, the fixed cost should remain at $200,000 because there has been a zero efficiency variance in IT hours used in the Notebook division. The Peripherals division reports an increase from $100,000 to $140,000 in fixed costs that might be attributed to the unfavourable overconsumption of IT service hours. However, only the $200/IT hour increases total cost to Peripherals because it is a variable cost. Fixed cost should remain constant.

Under the single-rate cost system, feedback is uninformative. It suggests that a bonus for coming in under budget is due to the Notebook division manager and a penalty for coming in over budget is due to the Peripherals manager. Neither conclusion reflects the economic facts. The Notebook manager should receive no reward for meeting budget. If there is a penalty for an unfavourable variance, then the Peripherals manager will not be penalized in proportion to the excess variable cost incurred of $80,000 (700 IT hours − 300 IT hours × $200/IT hour), but only the false signal of $40,000 sent in the report of fixed costs ($140,000 − $100,000). This cannot be considered fair by any party.

In case 3, the fixed-cost allocation is $40,000 more than expected ($240,000 versus $200,000). The increase of $40,000 even though the Notebook division's actual and budgeted usage are equal arises because of a higher unitized rate. The fixed costs are spread over actual use of 1,000 (800 + 200) rather than 1,200 IT hours. The unitized rate increases to $300/IT hour and the $240,000 in fixed costs applies to the Notebook division ($300/IT hour × 800 IT hours). Again, it is perverse that the manager of the Notebook division should be penalized for being on target. On a variable cost basis, the Peripherals manager has saved only $20,000 (100 IT hours × $200/IT hour), not $40,000 for CHI.

Using a single rate is almost guaranteed to set up conflict between the managers of Notebook and Peripherals. The needs of both divisions are in economic fact independent of one another, not dependent upon one another. When costs are applied based on actual use, and the unitized rate adjusted, this transforms what should be an independent feedback measure into an interdependent measure. It will not take long for both managers to outsource more and more of their IT service hours. Motivated by either retaliation or survival, neither manager will act in the best interests of CHI as a corporation.

This will be acute for a division in which an unfavourable efficiency variance recurs (see Chapter 8). The division continually uses more IT hours than it honestly budgeted. Increased honest use of IT hours up to 300 in excess capacity will reduce the unitized fixed cost rate that must be recovered through sale of CHI's products. It will improve the level of total recoverable costs. This should not penalize any other divisional manager and will provide an incentive for efficient capacity use because an incremental $200/IT hour will flow to CHI's internal provider rather than out to a third party. Operating profit will increase, all other things being equal.

For motivation and reimbursement, the feedback from variance analyses should distinguish between controllable and uncontrollable costs. Capacity decisions cannot be readily changed in the short run—they are not controllable by the production managers in each core division. What these managers can control is the use of the variable component of both the inventoriable and period cost pools in a way that maximizes profit for the company as a whole. It may be from time to time that non-manufacturing overhead, such as IT, has been dedicated asymmetrically to product development, and recovery of this investment should be tracked.

MANUFACTURING OVERHEAD COST ALLOCATION METHODS ARE IRRELEVANT

Cost assignment choices were first described in Chapter 4 in the context of manufacturing overhead and GAAP compliance. For GAAP-compliant external reporting,

Wrong Choice! Bad Judgment! Lesson Learned!

Value added from proper cost allocation comes not from the arithmetic, but from guidance to other managers. Contractual compliance is an exceptional motivator when deciding on allocation methods. The corporation is held accountable by either government or other contracting parties to be honest when reporting costs incurred on a project.

At Boeing in October 2002, Darleen Druyun, a senior U.S. Air Force acquisition officer, negotiated a multi-million-dollar contract for NATO's lease and purchase of 100 KC 767 Boeing tankers for aerial refuelling. NATO's total cost was estimated at $25 billion. In November 2002, as Druyun prepared to retire from the Air Force, she removed herself from discussions involving Boeing. In January 2003 she joined Boeing as an executive in its defence business operations. Boeing had previously hired Druyun's son and daughter.

In December 2003, *The Wall Street Journal* reported, "Actions related to Ms. Druyun's hiring in January 2003 are now the subject of Pentagon and Justice Department probes as well as Congressional scrutiny." Senator John McCain had raised the alarm and demanded Congress to investigate. Druyun was fired from Boeing. She pleaded guilty, paid a $5,000 fine, served 9 months in jail, and completed 150 hours of community service and 7 months of community confinement after her release from jail. Boeing CFO Michael Sears, who offered Druyun a job at Boeing while negotiations were underway with the US Air Force, was also fired. Convicted of malfeasance, he paid a fine of $250,000, served 4 months in jail, and completed 200 hours of community service. Phil Condit, CEO of Boeing, resigned. Boeing paid a fine of $615 million in a plea bargain deal with the government and retained its status as number one contractor.

In the years since the Sears–Druyun situation, Boeing redoubled its ethics and compliance efforts. In addition to ongoing oversight and training, all employees annually sign a code of conduct certification and participate in ethics discussions with both senior executives and managers. In 2011, the U.S. Air Force selected Boeing to build its new KC-46A air refuelling tanker.

Sources: Todd Blecher, Boeing; A. M. Squeo and J. L. Lunsford, "How Two Officials Got Caught by Pentagon's Revolving Door," *The Wall Street Journal*, December 18, 2003, p. A1. http://www.aviationweek.com/aw/blogs/defense/index.jsp?plckController=Blog&plckScript=blogScript&plckElementId=blogDest&plckBlogPage=BlogViewPost&plckPostId=Blog%3A27ec4a53-dcc8-42d0-bd3a-01329aef79a7Post%3A658155a6-8b08-41b7-8947-7-3715b239d23, accessed February 21, 2011; http://topics.nytimes.com/topics/reference/timestopics/people/d/darleen_a_druyun/index.html, accessed February 21, 2011; http://www.airforce-magazine.com/MagazineArchive/Pages/2004/February%202004/0204tanker.aspx, accessed February 21, 2011.

there is rarely an issue of cost assignment. There may arise issues, however, in reporting costs for purposes of contract reimbursement. It is the responsibility of the management accountant to point out options to top managers as they negotiate contract terms. This will avoid ambiguity in defining reimbursable costs and expensive litigation. For internal reporting purposes, the cost assignment that best motivates employees may conflict with the highest quality of information for use in economic decisions.

GAAP usually requires the exclusion of all non-manufacturing costs from inventoriable costs. The management team at CHI need not be concerned about actual, budget, or normal methods of assigning period costs to obtain a full product cost. These three methods are only relevant to the assignment of manufacturing overhead costs. For external reporting purposes, all non-manufacturing overhead is expensed in the period in which it occurs and does not accumulate in any inventory. Similarly for contract purposes, it is rare that any customer would pay for period costs. These costs were not incurred primarily to serve a customer and are non-value-added to that customer. In fact, the customer is more likely to demand transparent internal controls be in place to reduce the difficulty of auditing the costs for which the customer was invoiced.

DECIDING AMONG DIRECT, STEP-DOWN, AND RECIPROCAL COST ALLOCATION METHODS

In many cases, the costs of a division will include costs allocated from other divisions. Rather than use an inappropriate actual unitized fixed cost rate based on actual results, there are three alternatives: *direct*, *step-down*, and *reciprocal* cost allocation. To simplify, the corporation in the following example contains only two support divisions, maintenance and IT services, and two core or operating divisions in production, machining and assembly.

RELEVANCE

A strong caution here is to remember that there is no standardized corporate structure. Neither GAAP nor the demand for economic plausibility requires identical value chains, identical business functions in each component of the value chain, or identical classification of costs in each component. In centralized corporate structures, most facilities-sustaining activities are undertaken at corporate headquarters. The period cost application methods selected would differ from a decentralized structure.

In decentralized corporate structures, business functions such as R&D will be undertaken at a divisional level. Practically, in the example, R&D incurs significant IT costs as it provides services to each core division. Each corporate situation differs. It takes an alert management accountant to exercise professional judgment when making decisions in costing system design. The decisions must be appropriate to the individual corporation as well as the specific purpose of costing.

Step 1 Top management at Castleford Engineering Ltd. (CEL) has witnessed profit erosion and suspects its method of allocating product-sustaining MOH and facilities-sustaining IT services is inappropriate. If true, then the costing system itself is failing to reveal the distortions in cost that are undermining CEL's attempts at cost leadership.

Step 2 Gathering information reveals that at CEL maintenance services are provided to two different activity centres in the production area, machining and assembly. But maintenance services also repairs and maintains the computers in IT services, which also supports maintenance services, machining, and assembly, as shown in Exhibit 14-4.

Costs are accumulated in each division for planning and control purposes. For inventory costing, however, the support division costs of CEL must be allocated to the core divisions. Only the period costs contributing to the production of its units can be allocated to inventory and COGS, according to GAAP. For internal purposes, however, CEL can apply the proportion of cost pools relevant to achieving the purpose for the cost allocation in the first place.

In looking at the percentages in the table in Exhibit 14-4 for Plant Maintenance (PM), we can see that this support division provides a total of 8,000 hours of support work: 20% (1,600 ÷ 8,000) goes to the Information Technology (IT) support division; 30% (2,400 ÷ 8,000) to the core Machining Division (M); and 50% (4,000 ÷ 8,000) to the core Assembly Division (A). Under GAAP, these costs are classified as inventoriable manufacturing overhead (MOH) costs.

Step 3 As CEL studies its three alternatives, the forecast outcomes will be compared to the economic reality of CEL's production and support activities. The goal for CEL is to adopt the method that best reflects full product costs to assist in more accurate target costing, given their target price, ROI, and operating margin percentage.

Step 4 The budgeted or predicted data generated by CEL are illustrated in the table at the bottom of Exhibit 14-4. This forecast provides the data required to evaluate the three alternative allocation methods—direct, step-down, and reciprocal allocation.

EXHIBIT 14-4

Budget Data and Relationships Among Support and Core Functions at Castleford Engineering Ltd., 2013

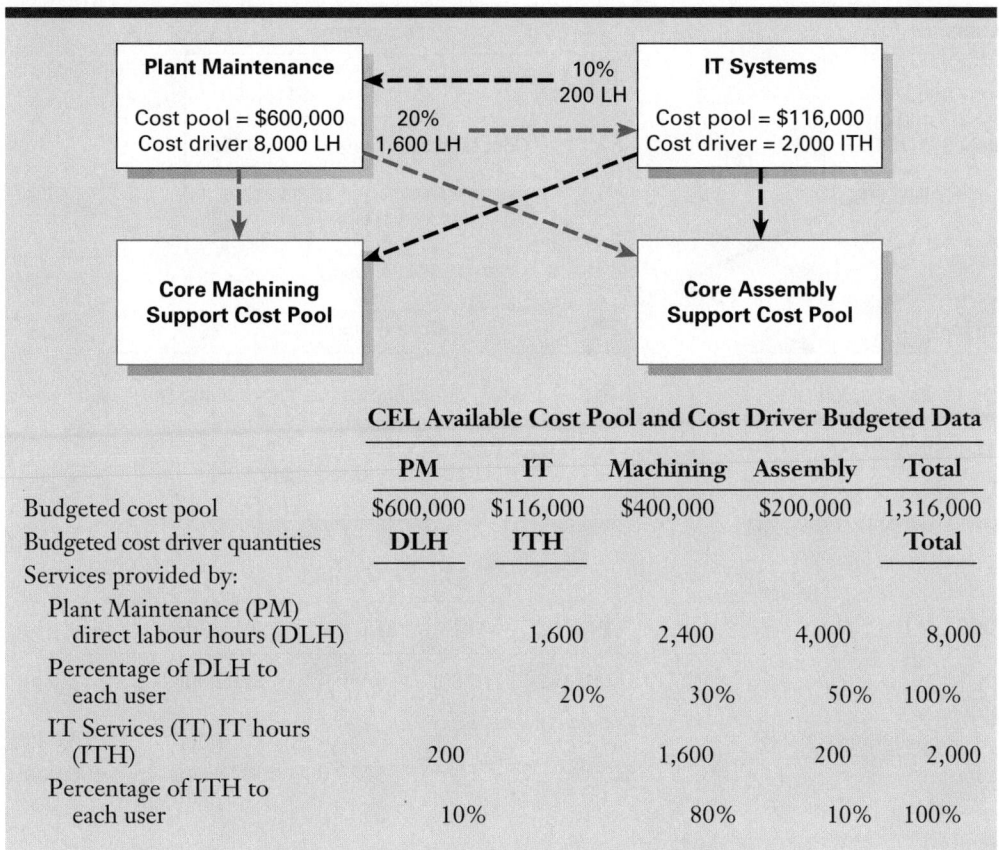

	PM	IT	Machining	Assembly	Total
Budgeted cost pool	$600,000	$116,000	$400,000	$200,000	1,316,000
Budgeted cost driver quantities	**DLH**	**ITH**			Total
Services provided by:					
Plant Maintenance (PM) direct labour hours (DLH)		1,600	2,400	4,000	8,000
Percentage of DLH to each user		20%	30%	50%	100%
IT Services (IT) IT hours (ITH)	200		1,600	200	2,000
Percentage of ITH to each user	10%		80%	10%	100%

CEL Available Cost Pool and Cost Driver Budgeted Data

DIRECT METHOD

The **direct allocation method** (often called the **direct method**) is simple and intuitive. It is readily explained and inexpensive to implement because little training is required. Any service rendered by one support division to another support division is ignored. The relationship illustrated in the top line of Exhibit 14-5, wherein $11,600 of the IT cost pool is spent to support PM and $120,000 ($600,000 × 20%) of the PM cost pool that supports IT, is ignored. This is a straightforward average costing method but, in total, the Machining and Assembly core production functions will bear $131,600 higher than the reality of how the burden should be distributed. This represents approximately 18% of the PM and IT support cost pools ($131,600 ÷ $716,000).

The budgeted total values of the PM and IT cost pools are constant. The denominators are not the total hours provided by PM and IT, but rather only those hours provided to the core production activities. The denominator is understated and the cost allocation rate is overstated. This leads to either a write-off or proration of overallocated MOH to the operating divisions Machining and Assembly. Of course, for tax purposes, this overallocated overhead must be prorated (see Chapter 4).

As illustrated, by ignoring the use of the DLH and ITH (IT hours) by the two service divisions, the total cost drivers decrease from 8,000 DLH to 6,400 DLH for PM and from 2,000 ITH to 1,800 ITH for IT services. The total budgeted cost pools remain constant. The cost driver rate for PM becomes $93.75/DLH ($600,000 ÷ 6,400 DLH) and for IT services, approximately $64.44/ITH. The costs applied to Machining and Assembly on this basis will, of course, include the burden that should be borne by PM and IT services for the costs of each other's support services. This is summarized in Exhibit 14-5.

Although this simple approach is readily explained, it is not readily justified. There are no activities for the row entitled IT Services (IT) IT Hours (ITH) in either

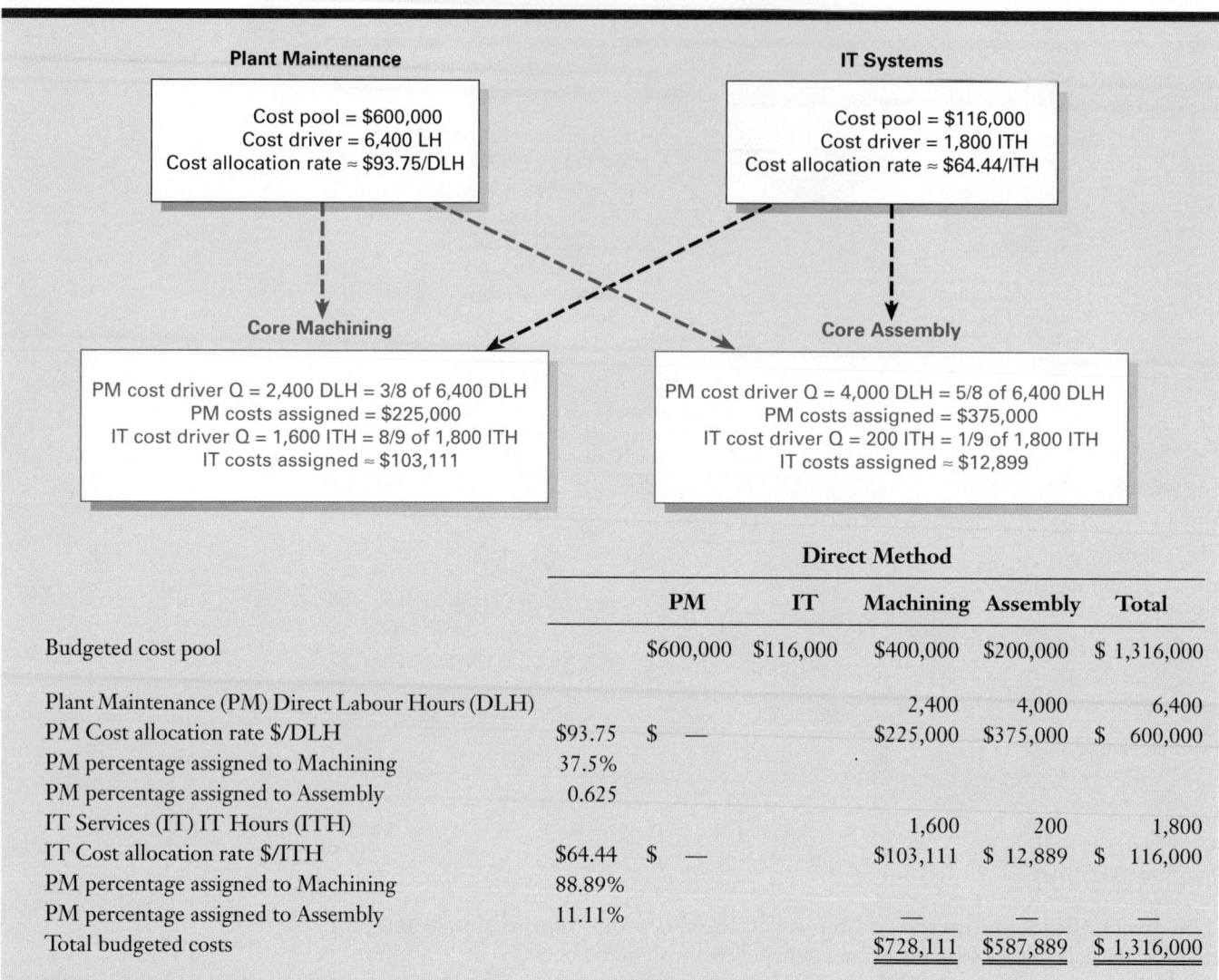

Plant Maintenance

Cost pool = $600,000
Cost driver = 6,400 LH
Cost allocation rate ≈ $93.75/DLH

IT Systems

Cost pool = $116,000
Cost driver = 1,800 ITH
Cost allocation rate ≈ $64.44/ITH

Core Machining

PM cost driver Q = 2,400 DLH = 3/8 of 6,400 DLH
PM costs assigned = $225,000
IT cost driver Q = 1,600 ITH = 8/9 of 1,800 ITH
IT costs assigned ≈ $103,111

Core Assembly

PM cost driver Q = 4,000 DLH = 5/8 of 6,400 DLH
PM costs assigned = $375,000
IT cost driver Q = 200 ITH = 1/9 of 1,800 ITH
IT costs assigned ≈ $12,899

		PM	IT	Machining	Assembly	Total
			Direct Method			
Budgeted cost pool		$600,000	$116,000	$400,000	$200,000	$ 1,316,000
Plant Maintenance (PM) Direct Labour Hours (DLH)				2,400	4,000	6,400
PM Cost allocation rate $/DLH	$93.75	$ —		$225,000	$375,000	$ 600,000
PM percentage assigned to Machining	37.5%					
PM percentage assigned to Assembly	0.625					
IT Services (IT) IT Hours (ITH)				1,600	200	1,800
IT Cost allocation rate $/ITH	$64.44	$ —		$103,111	$ 12,899	$ 116,000
PM percentage assigned to Machining	88.89%					
PM percentage assigned to Assembly	11.11%			—	—	—
Total budgeted costs				$728,111	$587,889	$ 1,316,000

The percentage of PM assigned to Machining is based on 6,400 DLH in the denominator and budgeted use in the numerator.
The percentage of IT assigned to Machining is based on 1,800 ITH in the denominator and budgeted use in the numerator.

Machining or Assembly that cause the 200 DLH of PM, which is listed in the column entitled Assembly, or the 1,600 ITH of IT, which is listed under the column entitled Machining that justify an added burden on the hours budgeted in the two core production activities. Based on totals, an apples to apples calculation, the rate for PM should be only $75/DLH and the rate for IT services should be $58/ITH. Neither causality nor fairness will provide a justification for this method. The cost paid by these core divisions is not proportional to the benefits received from the support services.

Prior to any audit and adjustments to the costs allocated to COGS and inventory, the gross margin will be understated because COGS will be overstated. This will make it difficult for CEL to achieve realistic target costs in the production divisions, but easier on the support providers to achieve their target costs. The distortion could lead CEL to reduce resources, perhaps direct machine or direct manufacturing hours in production, when it should be reducing IT services or PM hours. The link between COGS and gross margin is obscured by implementing this method. It may be the case at CEL, however, that neither PM nor IT services can bear these respective burdens and the method is justified not on ability to pay.

STEP-DOWN METHOD

The **step-down method** (sometimes called the **step allocation method**, or **sequential method**) recognizes the cost of services provided by one support division to the other before allocating the remaining services cost pool to the core divisions. The method does not recognize the cost of services provided by each cost pool to the other, though. Once the PM service costs have been deducted and added to IT services, there is no subsequent inflow of costs of IT services to PM. The smaller PM cost pool and the larger IT services cost pool will then be allocated to Machining and Assembly.

A decision on how to rank the two service providers must be made on some justifiable basis. Usually the highest percentage of service provided to other services is ranked first, followed in order by the others. An alternative would be to rank on the basis of highest to lowest cost of services provided to other divisions. The costs of service provision are removed from the original budgeted total cost pools of each service provider.

If CEL implemented the step-down method based on hours of service, then the cost of 20% of DLH provided to IT would be deducted before allocating the remainder in the PM cost pool to Machining and Assembly. The reason is that the IT percentage is only 10% of ITH provided to PM. The total cost to provide 1,600 DLH to IT is $120,000 ($600,000 × 20%) and the total cost to provide 200 ITH to PM is only $11,600 ($116,000 × 10%), as shown in Exhibit 14-6. For CEL, both alternatives lead to the same sequencing. In the first line of the table, the predicted cost pools are reported. The percentage of ITH to PM is reported as 20% and the dollar value reported in the IT column.

Now the total cost pool of IT more than doubles to $236,000 as shown, but the total cost driver has also decreased slightly to 1,800 ITH. Of course the result is a large increase in the cost allocation rate to approximately $131.11/ITH ($236,000 ÷ 1,800 ITH). The PM cost pool has decreased by the amount allocated to IT systems and is now $480,000 as shown in the top box on the left of Exhibit 14-6 and the DLH measuring the benefit of PM to core divisions is 6,400 DLH. The cost allocation rate is $75/DLH ($480,000 ÷ 6,400 DLH).

Following through from PM to Machining, the 20% of DLH to serve IT services has been given, leaving 80% of the total PM cost pool, or $480,000, to be applied. The 1,600 DLH have been applied to IT and what remains is 6,400 DLH. The PM cost allocation rate will be $75/DLH ($480,000 ÷ 6,400 DLH). Machining is budgeted to consume 2,400 DLH, or 30%, of available hours (2,400 DLH ÷ 8,000 DLH) and costs. The cost applied to Machining will be $180,000 (either $75/DLH × 2,400 DLH or 30% × $600,000). The remaining cost of 4,000 DLH is applied to Assembly. Exhibit 14-6 summarizes this approach; notice that the percentages are determined by the DLH, not the size of the cost pool.

The IT services cost pool has increased by 20% of PM, or $120,000, applied using the step-down method. The IT services cost pool of $236,000 is not adjusted for the 200 ITH of service provided to PM. This means the total cost driver is not 2,000 ITH but rather, consistent with the direct method, it is 1,800 ITH. The cost driver rate is approximately $131.11/ITH ($236,000 ÷ 1,800 ITH). Of the 1,800 ITH, the Assembly activities will consume 200 ITH, or 1/9 of the budgeted hours and costs (200 ITH ÷ 1,800 ITH), or $26,222. The same amount can be calculated using the cost driver rate ($131.11 × 200 ≈ $26,222). The remaining 8/9 of the budgeted ITH and costs (1,600 ITH ÷ 1,800 ITH) will be $209,778 and can be obtained by simple subtraction.

This method lacks the simplicity of the direct method, and it also lacks the economic plausibility of the reciprocal method where the use of support services by each division is applied to one another first. The step-down method is neither readily explained nor readily justified. There is, however, an improvement obtained by using a method that reflects the reality of the application of the largest support services cost pool rather than none. A significant misstatement in costs would be remedied for CEL should it implement this method. The difference in cost application between the direct and the step-down methods will be:

	IT	Machining	Assembly
Direct method	$ —	$728,111	$587,889
Step-down method, PM sequenced first	120,000	789,778	526,222
Difference	$(120,000)	$ (61,667)	$ 61,667

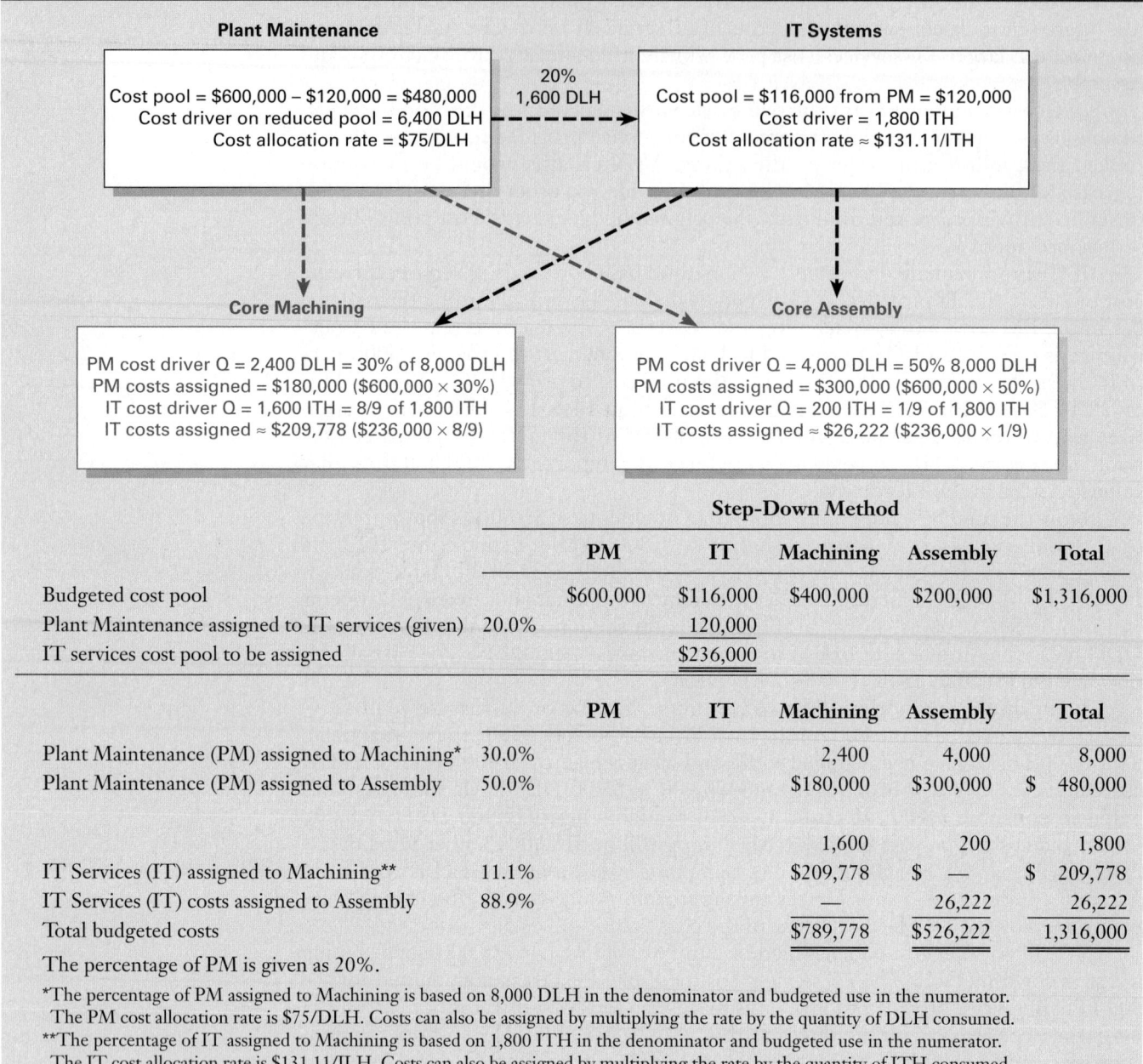

Step-Down Method	PM	IT	Machining	Assembly	Total
Budgeted cost pool	$600,000	$116,000	$400,000	$200,000	$1,316,000
Plant Maintenance assigned to IT services (given) 20.0%		120,000			
IT services cost pool to be assigned		$236,000			

	PM	IT	Machining	Assembly	Total
Plant Maintenance (PM) assigned to Machining* 30.0%			2,400	4,000	8,000
Plant Maintenance (PM) assigned to Assembly 50.0%			$180,000	$300,000	$ 480,000
			1,600	200	1,800
IT Services (IT) assigned to Machining** 11.1%			$209,778	$ —	$ 209,778
IT Services (IT) costs assigned to Assembly 88.9%			—	26,222	26,222
Total budgeted costs			$789,778	$526,222	1,316,000

The percentage of PM is given as 20%.

*The percentage of PM assigned to Machining is based on 8,000 DLH in the denominator and budgeted use in the numerator. The PM cost allocation rate is $75/DLH. Costs can also be assigned by multiplying the rate by the quantity of DLH consumed.
**The percentage of IT assigned to Machining is based on 1,800 ITH in the denominator and budgeted use in the numerator. The IT cost allocation rate is $131.11/ILH. Costs can also be assigned by multiplying the rate by the quantity of ITH consumed.

If CEL has been using the direct method, then the core production in Machining has been underapplied to the costs of PM. From a purely qualitative perspective, it is going to be difficult to convince Machining to accept an increased burden that was borne by Assembly in the past. It would be unusual for Assembly to object, because its applied total budgeted costs decrease. The inconsistency between the treatment of PM and IT service support costs will be one basis upon which implementation of the step-down method could falter. It is relatively straightforward for Machining to "cry poor" and claim that Assembly is better able to bear these costs.

RECIPROCAL METHOD—LINEAR EQUATION, SOLVER, AND MATRIX ALGEBRA[2]

The **reciprocal allocation method** adjusts budgeted costs to explicitly include costs of mutual services rendered among support areas in each other's cost pools. The

[2]David Gowing (PEng, MSc Finance) developed the matrix algebra functions and examples. D. Franz, "Using Matrix Algebra Functions in Spreadsheet Modifications," AAA Western Regional Conference, May 2, 2008 and online at http://papers.ssrn.com/sol3/papers.cfm?abstract_id=1001542.

result is a budgeted complete **reciprocated cost** pool for each support services division. Another term often used is **artificial cost**. This approach is another application of linear programming undertaken in Chapter 11. Either the Solver or Matrix functions in Excel can also be used. The drawback for the linear equation method is that it becomes unwieldy beyond problems that are more complex than simple two support services and two core production divisions. Both Solver and Matrix extend computational competence to any number of support services and core production divisions.

Using matrix algebra in Excel, it is only the reciprocal support division allocations that require this treatment and the goal is to obtain the complete reciprocated or artificial costs in a more efficient manner than using simultaneous equations. No matrix algebra is required to calculate the allocations of support division costs to the two operating divisions.

Linear Equation Method   The simultaneous linear equation method requires three steps:[3]

1. *Express support division costs and reciprocal relationships in linear equation form.* Let PM be the complete reciprocated costs of PM, and IS be the complete reciprocated costs of IS. The relationships are:

$$PM = \$600{,}000 + 0.1IS \qquad (1)$$

$$IS = \$116{,}000 + 0.2PM \qquad (2)$$

The 0.1IS term in equation (1) is the percentage of the IS resources consumed by PM. But the IS reciprocated cost pool includes 20% of the PM cost pool. In equation (1) the 10% IS term must be adjusted to include the additional PM costs before solving.

2. *Substitute equation (2) for the term IS in equation (1).* The resulting equation is shown in the first line:

$$PM = \$600{,}000 + [0.1(\$116{,}000 + 0.2PM)]$$
$$PM = \$600{,}000 + \$11{,}600 + 0.02PM$$
$$0.98PM = \$611{,}600$$
$$PM = \$624{,}082$$

In the second line, the known quantities, $600,000 in the PM cost pool and the $11,600 or 10% of the IS cost pool, replace the terms of the equation in the first line. Be careful to notice in line 1 that the 10% is outside an expression containing two terms, of which one is 0.2PM. Multiplying 0.2PM by 0.1 gives 0.02PM, as shown in the second line. The second line can be understood as 100%PM = $600,000 + $11,600 + 2%PM. Collecting similar terms and subtracting 2%PM from both sides of the equation gives the third line. Only one unknown remains. Dividing both sides of the equation by 0.98 provides the result in the final line of PM = $624,082 ($611,600 ÷ 0.98).

Next we need to *substitute known values into equation (2)*. The first value is provided by CEL's budget and the second from the artificial cost pool calculated for PM:

$$IS = \$116{,}000 + 0.2(\$624{,}082) = \$240{,}816$$

Where more than two support divisions have reciprocal relationships, either Solver or the Matrix function in Excel can be used to calculate the artificial costs of each support division.

---

[3]The reciprocal allocation method requires iteration. Iteration is a mathematical approach to solving a problem that requires an estimate of the answer to begin solving a system of linear equations. By repeatedly substituting improved estimates, the error term in the equations converges to zero, or the best answer. Undertaking reciprocal allocation in Excel, the iteration is automatic.

3. *Apply the complete artificial costs of each support division to all other divisions (both support and operating divisions) on the basis of the usage proportions (based on total units of service provided to all divisions).* Consider the IT Division, which has a complete reciprocated cost of $240,816. This amount would be applied is as follows:

To Plant Maintenance ($\frac{1}{10} \times$ $240,816)	=	$ 24,082	
To Machining ($\frac{8}{10} \times$ $240,816), rounded	=	192,652	
To Assembly ($\frac{1}{10} \times$ $240,816)	=	24,082	
Total		$240,816	

The artificial cost pool used to download the PM service support costs to Machining and Assembly is $624,082, and for the IT service support costs is $240,816. Both have expanded to include the costs of PM and IT services reciprocally provided to each other.

One source of confusion to some managers using the reciprocal cost allocation method is why the complete reciprocated (artificial) costs of the support divisions of $864,898 ($624,082 and $240,816 in Exhibit 14-7) exceed their budgeted amount of $716,000 ($600,000 and $116,000). The excess of $148,898 ($24,082 for PM and $124,816 for IT) is the total of costs that are reciprocally allocated between support divisions. The total costs allocated to the operating divisions under the reciprocal allocation method remain only $716,000.

Under the reciprocal method, the cost allocation rates rounded to the nearest dollar are $78/DLH for the PM services and $120/ITH for the IT services. The table below summarizes the total costs applied to each division based on the three different methods.

	PM	IT	Machining	Assembly
Direct method	$ —	$ —	$728,111	$587,889
Step-down method, PM sequenced first	—	120,000	789,778	526,222
Reciprocal method	$24,082	124,816	779,878	536,122

The reciprocal method is a more economically plausible method. It treats all support division costs equally, but there remain two important issues before implementation. First, the method is more complex and CEL may incur considerable training costs. This method may be too costly for CEL's needs, given the benefits in improved forecasting and full product costing accuracy.

Second, Machining will bear more overhead burden than it has in the past. The increase is slightly lower under this method ($51,767) than under the step-down method ($61,667) relative to the direct method. Nevertheless, an increase of $51,767 over $728,111 is still approximately a 7% increase in total overhead applied to Machining. It is likely there will be resistance to the new method from Machining, but the improved accuracy in costing may also benefit this user division. For example, the hourly rate for ITH may focus Machining on reducing its ITH consumption.

Step 5 CEL obtains feedback on the practical implications of adopting one of the three cost allocation methods. The company conducts a quick "what if" analysis of how each method would generate a different full product cost in a competitive bid situation.

CEL still has not progressed to assign the fully allocated Machining and Assembly cost pools to complete full job (or product) costing. The burden of overhead costs now reside in core divisions, not on the units of finished jobs (goods). Assume that CEL uses machine-hours (DMH) as the Machining cost driver and the total budgeted hours is 4,000. In Assembly the cost driver is direct manufacturing labour-hours (DMLH) and the total budgeted hours is 3,000. Under the three different overhead cost application methods, the total Machining and Assembly cost pools assigned to units of finished jobs (goods) differ somewhat. The denominator or

EXHIBIT 14-7
Reciprocal Method of Allocating Support Division Costs Using Linear Equations at Castleford Engineering for 2013

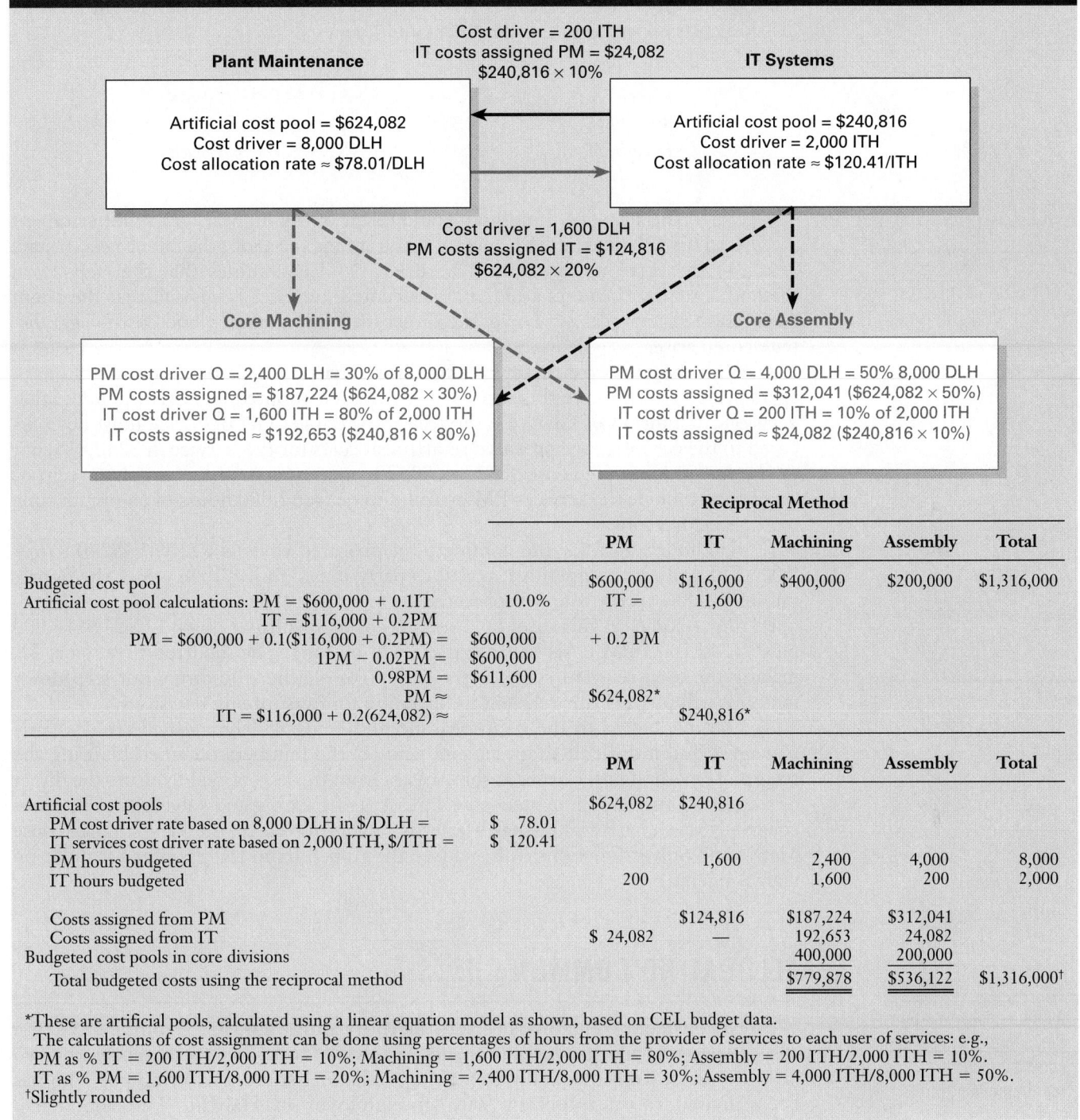

		PM	IT	Machining	Assembly	Total
Budgeted cost pool		$600,000	$116,000	$400,000	$200,000	$1,316,000
Artificial cost pool calculations: PM = $600,000 + 0.1IT	10.0%	IT =	11,600			
IT = $116,000 + 0.2PM						
PM = $600,000 + 0.1($116,000 + 0.2PM) =	$600,000	+ 0.2 PM				
1PM − 0.02PM =	$600,000					
0.98PM =	$611,600					
PM ≈		$624,082*				
IT = $116,000 + 0.2(624,082) ≈			$240,816*			

		PM	IT	Machining	Assembly	Total
Artificial cost pools		$624,082	$240,816			
PM cost driver rate based on 8,000 DLH in $/DLH =	$ 78.01					
IT services cost driver rate based on 2,000 ITH, $/ITH =	$ 120.41					
PM hours budgeted			1,600	2,400	4,000	8,000
IT hours budgeted		200		1,600	200	2,000
Costs assigned from PM			$124,816	$187,224	$312,041	
Costs assigned from IT		$ 24,082	—	192,653	24,082	
Budgeted cost pools in core divisions				400,000	200,000	
Total budgeted costs using the reciprocal method				$779,878	$536,122	$1,316,000†

*These are artificial pools, calculated using a linear equation model as shown, based on CEL budget data.
The calculations of cost assignment can be done using percentages of hours from the provider of services to each user of services: e.g.,
PM as % IT = 200 ITH/2,000 ITH = 10%; Machining = 1,600 ITH/2,000 ITH = 80%; Assembly = 200 ITH/2,000 ITH = 10%.
IT as % PM = 1,600 ITH/8,000 ITH = 20%; Machining = 2,400 ITH/8,000 ITH = 30%; Assembly = 4,000 ITH/8,000 ITH = 50%.
†Slightly rounded

cost driver remains constant while the cost pools vary and so, too, do the cost driver rates, as shown:

Support Division Cost Allocation Method	Total Budgeted Costs after Support Overhead Allocation of All Division Costs		Budgeted Overhead Rate per Hour for Product Costing Purposes	
	Machining	Assembly	Machining 4,000 DMH	Assembly 3,000 DMLH
Direct	$728,111	$587,889	$182	$196
Step-down	789,778	526,222	197	175
Reciprocal	779,877	536,123	195	179

These differences in budgeted overhead rates with alternative support division cost allocation methods can be important to managers. For example, consider a cost reimbursement contract that uses 100 DMH and 15 assembly DMLH. The support division costs allocated to this contract would be:

Direct	$21,140	$182 × 100 + $196 × 15
Step-down	22,325	$197 × 100 + $175 × 15
Reciprocal	22,185	$195 × 100 + $179 × 15

Use of the step-down method would result in the highest cost reimbursement to CEL. This will benefit CEL only if, when it bids for a job, the client fails to state which of the three methods must be used. If CEL assumes that the step-down method is required, enters a bid and is accepted but later is advised that the client required the reciprocal or, worse, the direct method, a lengthy and costly legal dispute could arise.

With the high cost driver rate for IT services, should the core division managers decide to outsource this service? The method adopted by CEL will affect that decision. Assume all of CEL's IT services are variable. The bid price must be compared to the complete reciprocated or artificial costs for this service of $240,816, not the budgeted IT service cost of $116,000. The reason is that the complete reciprocated costs include the services PM provides to deliver 2,000 hours of computer time to *all* three divisions.

The hourly rate for the complete reciprocated costs is $120.41 ($240,816 ÷ 2,000 ITH). To be competitive, the third party must bid less than either the hourly rate of $120.41 or the total reciprocated cost of $240,816 to improve the company's operating income. In this case, the relevant costs of shutting down IT are $116,000 plus $124,816 of PM costs because these will no longer be incurred to support IT, making the total relevant cost savings $240,816. Neither the direct nor step-down methods will provide this relevant information for outsourcing decisions.[4]

The roadblocks to the reciprocal method being widely adopted are (1) many managers find it difficult to understand and (2) the numbers obtained by using the reciprocal method differ little, in some cases, from those obtained by using the direct or step-down method. The mechanical process of creating and solving simultaneous equations was a barrier, but that barrier is now removed by the very simple-to-use Matrix and Solver functions in Excel (see the Appendix to this chapter for more on matrix algebra).

ALLOCATING COMMON COSTS

5 Analyze cost allocation procedures to apply common costs and justify contractual reimbursement terms.

We next consider two methods used to allocate **common costs**. A common cost is a cost of operating a facility, operation, activity, or like cost object that is shared by two or more users. Consider Jason Stevens, a graduating student in Winnipeg who has been invited to an interview with an employer in Halifax. The round-trip Winnipeg–Halifax airfare is $1,200. A week before leaving, Stevens is also invited to an interview with an employer in Montreal. The round-trip Winnipeg–Montreal fare is $800. Stevens decides to combine the two recruiting stops into a Winnipeg–Montreal–Halifax trip that will cost $1,500 in airfare. The $1,500 is a common cost that benefits both employers. There are two methods for allocating this common cost between the two potential employers: the stand-alone method and the incremental method.

---

[4]Technical issues when using the reciprocal method in outsourcing decisions are discussed in R. S. Kaplan and A. A. Atkinson, *Advanced Management Accounting*, 3rd ed. (Upper Saddle River, N.J.: Prentice Hall, 1998), pp. 73–81.

STAND-ALONE COST ALLOCATION METHOD

The **stand-alone cost allocation method** uses information pertaining to each cost object as a separate operating entity to determine the cost allocation weights. For the airfare common cost of $1,500, information about the separate (stand-alone) return airfares ($1,200 and $800) is used to determine the allocation weights:

Halifax employer: $\dfrac{\$1,200}{\$1,200 + \$800} \times \$1,500 = 0.60 \times \$1,500 = \$900$

Montreal employer: $\dfrac{\$800}{\$800 + \$1,200} \times \$1,500 = 0.40 \times \$1,500 = \$600$

Advocates of this method often emphasize an equity or fairness rationale. That is, fairness occurs because each employer bears a proportionate share of total costs in relation to its individual stand-alone costs.

INCREMENTAL COST ALLOCATION METHOD

The **incremental cost allocation method** ranks the individual cost objects and then uses this ranking to allocate costs among those cost objects. The first-ranked cost object is termed the *primary party* and is allocated costs up to its cost as a stand-alone entity. The second-ranked cost object is termed the *incremental party* and is allocated the additional cost that arises from there being two users instead of only the primary user. If there are more than two parties, the nonprimary parties will also need to be ranked.

Consider Jason Stevens and his $1,500 airfare cost. Assume that the Halifax employer is viewed as the primary party. Stevens's rationale was that he had already committed to go to Halifax. The cost allocations would then be:

Party	Cost Allocated	Costs Remaining to Be Allocated to Other Parties
Halifax (primary)	$1,200	$300 = $1,500 − $1,200
Montreal (incremental)	300	0

The Halifax employer is allocated the full Winnipeg–Halifax airfare. The non-allocated part of the total airfare is allocated to the Montreal employer. Had the Montreal employer been chosen as the primary party, the cost allocations would have been Montreal, $800 (the stand-alone Winnipeg–Montreal return airfare), and Halifax, $700 ($1,500 – $800). Where there are more than two parties, this method requires them to be ranked and the common costs allocated to those parties in the ranked sequence.

Under the incremental method, the primary party typically receives the highest allocation of the common costs. Not surprisingly, most users in common cost situations propose themselves as the incremental party. In some cases, the incremental party is a newly formed "organization" such as a new product line or a new sales territory. Chances for its short-term survival may be enhanced if it bears a relatively low allocation of common costs.

A caution is appropriate here regarding Stevens's cost allocation options. His chosen method must be acceptable to each prospective employer. Indeed, some prospective employers may have guidelines that recruiting candidates must follow. For example, the Montreal employer may have a policy that the maximum reimbursable airfare is a seven-day advance booking price in economy class. If this amount is less than the amount that Stevens would receive under (say) the stand-alone method, then the employer's upper-limit guideline would govern how much could be allocated to that interviewer. Stevens should obtain approval before he purchases his ticket as to what cost allocation method(s) each potential employer views as acceptable.

Disputes over how to allocate common costs are often encountered. The final section of this chapter discusses the role of cost data in contracting. This is also an area where disputes about cost allocation frequently arise.

JUSTIFYING REIMBURSEMENT COSTS

Many commercial contracts include clauses that require the use of cost accounting information. Examples include:

1. A contract between the Department of National Defence and a company designing and assembling a new fighter plane. The price paid for the plane is based on the contractor's costs plus a preset fixed fee.

2. A research contract between a university and a government agency. The university is reimbursed its direct costs plus an overhead rate that is a percentage of direct costs.

3. A contract between an energy-consulting firm and a hospital. The consulting firm receives a fixed fee plus a share of the energy-cost savings arising from the consulting firm's recommendations.

Contract disputes arise with some regularity, often with respect to cost allocation. The areas of dispute between the contracting parties can be reduced by making the "rules of the game" explicit in writing at the time the contract is signed. Such rules of the game include the definition of cost items allowed, the permissible cost-allocation bases, and how differences between budgeted and actual costs are to be handled.

CONTRACTING

There are two main approaches to reimbursing costs as determined by a contract:

1. The *contractor is paid a set price without analysis of actual contract cost data.* This approach is used, for example, where there is competitive bidding, where there is adequate price competition, or where there is an established catalogue with prices quoted for items sold in substantial quantities to the general public.

2. The *contractor is paid after analysis of actual contract cost data.* In some cases, the contract will explicitly state that reimbursement is based on actual allowable costs plus a set fee. This arrangement is a cost-plus contract.

FAIRNESS OF PRICING

When uncertainty is high, as in many defence contracts involving new weapons and equipment, contracts are rarely subject to competitive bidding. Why? Because no contractor is willing to assume all the risk. Hence, market-based fixed-price setting fails to attract a contractor, or the resulting price is too outrageously high for the government. So the government assumes a major share of the risks. It negotiates contracts by using costs as a substitute for selling prices as ordinarily set by suppliers in open markets. In this contracting arena, a cost allocation may be difficult to defend on the basis of any cause-and-effect reasoning. Nonetheless, the contracting parties may still view it as a "reasonable" or "fair" means to help establish a selling price. Some costs become "allowable," but others are "unallowable." An **allowable cost** is a cost that the contract parties agree to include in the costs to be reimbursed. Some contracts specify how allowable costs are to be determined. For example, only economy-class airfares may be allowable in a contract. Other contracts identify cost categories that are nonallowable. For example, the costs of lobbying activities and the costs of alcoholic beverages are not allowable costs on some contracts.

(Try to solve this problem before examining the solution that follows.)

PROBLEM

This problem illustrates how the costs of two corporate support divisions are allocated to operating divisions.

Computer Horizons budgets the following amounts for its two central corporate support divisions (Legal and Human Resources) in supporting each other and the two manufacturing divisions, the Laptop Division (LTD) and the Work Station Division (WSD):

	A	B	C	D	E	F
		SUPPORT		**OPERATING**		
		Legal	**Human Resources**			
		Division	**Division**	**LTD**	**WSD**	**Total**
4	**BUDGETED USAGE**					
5	Legal (hours)	—	250	1,500	750	2,500
6	(Percentages)	—	10%	60%	30%	100%
7	Human Resources (hours)	2,500	—	22,500	25,000	50,000
8	(Percentages)	5%	—	45%	50%	100%
9						
10	**ACTUAL USAGE**					
11	Legal (hours)	—	400	400	1,200	2,000
12	(Percentages)	—	20%	20%	60%	100%
13	Human Resources (hours)	2,000	—	26,600	11,400	40,000
14	(Percentages)	5%	—	66.5%	28.5%	100%
15	Budgeted fixed overhead costs before any interdivision cost allocations	$360,000	$475,000	—	—	$835,000
16	Actual variable overhead costs before any interdivision cost allocations	$200,000	$600,000	—	—	$800,000

The company needs to improve the accuracy of its cost allocations to improve the competitiveness of its prices.

REQUIRED

1. What are other possible reasons a company would undertake improved cost allocation? ①
2. What are the possible cost drivers of the Legal Division? ②
3. Why might Computer Horizons choose budgeted rather than actual cost allocation rates for this project? ③
4. What amount of support division costs for Legal and Human Resources will be allocated to LTD and WSD using (a) the direct method, (b) the step-down method (allocating the Legal Division costs first), and (c) the reciprocal method using linear equations? ④
5. If Computer Horizons were justifying reimbursement from a contract, how would this project improve its position? ⑤

SOLUTION

1. One objective may be to motivate employees through challenging performance targets accompanied by substantial compensation if they are achieved. The effectiveness of using period cost allocation to accomplish this depends on what is perceived as fair by those affected. Generally speaking, if people
   ◆ believe the decision makers and the decision process is undertaken in good faith,
   ◆ are given the opportunity to participate in distributive decision making,

◆ have access to relevant information about the consequences, and

◆ are treated with respect and sensitivity when they are not beneficiaries, but bear burdens,

then they will accept that the distribution was fair although it was burdensome for them but not others.

A second reason is legal, to verify and justify that particular period cost is allowable per specific contract terms. The methods of cost allocation in this chapter can be used to justify beyond reasonable doubt a cost is allowable. Nevertheless, the same principles of fairness apply and the preferable approach is that the parties of the contract negotiate the allocation method and the specifics of its implementation.

A third reason is to measure income and assets. An additional burden is imposed, however, that the allocation method chosen be justifiable within GAAP if the values of income and assets are publicized. Different methods will impose different costs on different divisions and this in turn will be reported in segmented statements of income.

2. Cost drivers should be chosen on the basis of their capacity to explain a reasonable proportion of total change in the cost pool (see Chapter 13). Choices include sales, assets employed, estimated duration of legal activity. Notice that these choices include an output measure of activity (sales), a capacity input measure (assets employed), and a measure of time (duration of legal activity).

3. The choice of rates can affect managers' behaviour. When budgeted rates are used, the consumers of support resources will know in advance what the pro forma costs will be and this improves their planning.

4. Exhibits 14-5 (p. 570), 14-6 (p. 572), and 14-7 (p. 575) present the computations for allocating the fixed and variable support division costs. A summary of these costs follows:

	Laptop Division (LTD)	Work Station Division (WSD)
(a) Direct Method		
Fixed costs	$465,000	$370,000
Variable costs	470,000	330,000
	$935,000	$700,000
(b) Step-Down Method		
Fixed costs	$458,053	$376,947
Variable costs	488,000	312,000
	$946,053	$688,947
(c) Reciprocal Method		
Fixed costs	$462,513	$372,487
Variable costs	476,364	323,636
	$938,877	$696,123

5. Contractors may price their job prior to it being undertaken and they establish what costs are allowable. An accurate cost allocation project will enable Computer Horizons to understand and separate allowable from other costs. The company will be better able to justify its claim for reimbursement is fair and within the terms of the contract.

APPENDIX: MATRIX ALGEBRA

6 Use matrix algebra to apply the reciprocal method to allocating costs of support divisions.

This appendix will explain how to use matrix algebra to compute cost allocation for support divisions using the reciprocal allocation method. With only a bit of technical input on matrix algebra, management accountants can readily input a coefficient matrix, provided they can create the linear equation of each of the cost functions. There are normal mathematics functions available on any Excel spreadsheet, =minverse(and =mmult(, that are used to quickly determine the artificial cost matrix. Once the raw data are entered, a simple click of the mouse will produce the results as the Excel program completes all the calculations necessary. This method enables management accountants to almost instantaneously provide the reciprocal cost allocations for complex systems such as the one illustrated in Exhibit 14-7 (p. 575).

The **vector of constants** is simply the list of cost pools of each support and operating division. These data are entered in a single row in Exhibit 14-7 instead of in a single column. The name of the cost pool is not used, only the dollar values expressed in thousands of dollars to simplify the inputs. The method of entering these data is shown below:

Cost Pool	Vector of Constants
PM	600
IT	116
Machining	400
Assembly	200

You will recall from Chapter 11 that any orderly array of data can be called a **matrix**. A matrix is identified first by the number of rows and second by the number of columns. A matrix that is only one column of numbers is called a **vector**. A vector can have many rows, but Excel sets a limit of 52 rows. The vector of constants shown is also a 4×1 matrix. We will only use the support cost pool numbers highlighted in purple under the title "Vector of Constants" when solving the reciprocal allocation problem.

The support divisions are highlighted because reciprocal cost allocation applies only to PM and IT, listed as the first two cost pools. The use of the matrix function in Excel automates the calculation of the artificial cost pools. As a matter of interest, the vector of constants we will use to solve for the artificial cost matrix is the 2×1 matrix highlighted in purple. The analysis requires use of the allocation percentages, but recall the focus is on only the support cost pools PM and IT as outlined in the table. These cost percentage data for PM and IT form a 2×4 matrix (2 rows, 4 columns). We focus on only these percentages because they refer only to the support divisions to which reciprocal allocation applies. This is called the **coefficient matrix**, which summarizes the cost allocation percentages used to calculate the complete reciprocated costs.

It is important to notice the dimensions of the vector of constants in this support division matrix because the number of rows determines the order in which the two matrices are multiplied. More importantly, the number of columns (2) in the first matrix *must* equal the number of rows (2) in the second. If this is not true, then the multiplication cannot be done.[5]

	% Costs Used By			
	PM	**IT**	**Machining**	**Assembly**
PM	0	0.2	0.3	0.5
IT	0.1	0	0.8	0.1
M	0	0	1	0
A	0	0	0	1

The raw data for the cost allocation percentages provided in CEL's budget are summarized in the table below. These percentages are calculated using the total cost driver of 8,000 DLH for PM and 2,000 IT Hours for IT services as denominators. The numerators for different user divisions are the budgeted DLH and IT hours provided in CEL's budget. The percentage data is entered in the identical manner and order as the percentages in Exhibit 14-4 on page 569, but decimals instead of percentage format are used.

The final set of artificial costs will be a matrix of 2×1 as indicated by the first number in the identification of the matrix of cost percentages, and the last number identifying the vector of constants matrix. This is important because it tells you how to highlight the cells in Excel to successfully multiply the matrices.

---

[5]The 2×4 matrix of percentages must be multiplied by the 4×1 vector of constants and the notation is $(2 \times 4) \cdot (4 \times 1)$. Notice the last number in the first set of parentheses is identical to the first number in the last set of parentheses—both are 4s, indicating that matrix multiplication can occur. This implies, for example, that you can multiply a (3×2) matrix by a (2×1) matrix and the solution matrix will be (3×1), a list of dollar amounts.

MATRIX MULTIPLICATION

The coefficient matrix is a 2×2 matrix where the entries are the coefficients of the equations (1) and (2) (p. 573), for each of the support division costs allocated reciprocally to one another. This matrix is simply a restatement of the coefficients in the linear equations defining your problem.[6] The matrix comprises the numbers opposite the rows labelled PM and IT and the columns labelled PM and IT, which is why the dimensions are 2×2.[7] The equations shown in the first two lines of the Consumption of Support table below are a restatement of equations 1 and 2, which you have already produced on p. 573. You must manually input the coefficient matrix based on the information in the two transposed equations.

Consumption of Support

Supplier of Support Service	PM	IT	Cost Pool	
PM	0	0.2	$600	PM = \$600 + (0 × PM) + (0.1 × IT) (1)
IT	0.1	0	$116	IT = \$116 + (0.2 × PM) + (0 × IT) (2)

Artificial Costs > Cost Pool

Transpose the allocated costs for PM in 1:	1.0 × PM − 0.1 × IT = \$600
Transpose the allocated costs for IT in 2:	−0.2 × PM + 1.0 × IT = \$116

The coefficient matrix in Excel is called the *source matrix*. The vector of constants has no special Excel reference. When you use Excel, highlight only the quantities; never highlight the row or column titles. To summarize, the two matrices you will use to solve for the amounts reciprocally allocated are:

	Coefficient Matrix		Vector of Constants
	PM	IT	Cost Pools
PM	1	−0.1	$600
IT	−0.2	1	$116

The first matrix algebra function to calculate the artificial costs will create the inverse of the coefficient matrix, which is also a 2×2 matrix. Now you are ready to use Excel to manipulate the data and solve the problem. First you must highlight an empty set of destination cells, a 2×2 matrix of 2 columns and 2 rows. With the matrix still highlighted, move the cursor in the f_x dialogue box[8] at the top of the spreadsheet and type =minverse(.

Type =minverse(without any spaces or period. At this point the words MINVERSE(**array**) will appear just under the f_x dialogue box. Now you simply move the cursor to the coefficient matrix and highlight the four numerical entries:

1	−0.1
−0.2	1

Finally, press Ctrl + Shift + Enter; hold the three keys down simultaneously, then release them simultaneously. The inverse matrix will appear with the values shown:

1.020408	0.102041
0.204082	1.020408

[6]A coefficient is the known quantity by which you multiply an unknown, such as 0.2PM where 0.2 is the coefficient.

[7]The transpose of the matrix is equivalent to any algebraic transposition. In a single equation, *transpose* means to take elements of the equation from one to the other side of the equal sign. This means the sign of any coefficient will change. Assume the coefficient matrix is A and the vector of constants is B. We are trying to find the multipliers X, such that A × X = B; therefore, if we transpose A then X = [A × (−1)] × B. The matrix A × (−1) is called the inverse of matrix A. This inverse can be calculated by hand readily but Excel is more efficient. For those interested, one excellent text on matrix algebra is *Modern Matrix Algebra* by David R. Hill and Bernard Kolman.

[8]If you do not have an f_x dialogue box on your toolbar you can add it in by customizing your toolbar options.

This matrix will now be multiplied by the vector of constants, the original two cost pools for PM and IT. First you must highlight an empty set of destination cells, a 1×2 matrix of 1 column and 2 rows. With the matrix still highlighted, move the cursor in the f_x dialogue box at the top of the spreadsheet and type: = mmult(. Please note there is a space after the = sign but not after the word *mmult*. At this point the words MMULT(**array1**, array2) will appear just under the f_x dialogue box. The first **array1** is what you're going to multiply, which is the inverse matrix. Highlight the four numerical quantities in the inverse matrix and type a comma,

1.0204082	0.1020408
0.2040816	1.0204082

then move the cursor to highlight the two amounts in the vector of constants (highlighted originally in purple on p. 581):

600
116

To complete the matrix multiplication, press Ctrl + Shift + Enter and hold simultaneously, then release all three simultaneously. The solution, the artificial costs, will appear in the destination cells as shown:

624.08163
240.81633

As with the linear equation method, no more is required than the artificial cost pools be allocated to the operating divisions as shown:

	Operating Departments		
Supplier	M	A	Artificial Costs > Cost Pool
PM	0.3	0.5	$642.082 PM = (0.3 × PM) + (0.8 × IT) + $400
IT	0.8	0.1	$240.816 IT = (0.5 × PM) + (0.1 × IT) + $200

In this situation, the PM and IT costs are the artificial costs.

	Artificial Costs > Cost Pool
Transpose the allocated costs for PM:	−0.3 × PM − 0.8 × IT = $400
Transpose the allocated costs for IT:	−0.5 × PM − 0.1 × IT = $200

Therefore, the final cost allocations must be:

Artificial Cost Pools		**Original Cost Pools**	
M	$ 779.878	PM	$ 600
A	536.122	IT	116
	$1,316.000	M	400
		A	200
		Total	$1,316

Notice that the costs allocated to the operating divisions using the artificial cost pools sum to the original cost pool total. The allocation dollar values are identical to those calculated using the linear equation method. The benefit of knowing how to use the matrix algebra function for reciprocal allocation of support division costs is that far more complex (and realistic) cost allocations can be readily done among more than two support divisions and more than two operating divisions.

The following question-and-answer format summarizes the chapter's learning outcomes. Each point presents a key question, and the guidelines are the answer to that question.

LEARNING OUTCOMES	GUIDELINES
1. What use is it to allocate period costs?	There are four reasons to calculate the full product, job, or process cost: (a) to provide information for economic decisions, (b) to motivate managers and employees, (c) to justify costs or compute reimbursement, and (d) to measure income and assets for reporting to external parties.
2. Should a manager use the single-rate or the dual-rate cost allocation method?	The single-rate system allocates all support costs based on an average rate. In a highly competitive environment where corporations are price takers, this system overallocates all fixed costs. The dual-rate method separates variable from fixed cost pools. This method reveals the costs of unused capacity, which are not recoverable from customers because this is a non-value-added cost. The dual-rate method enables more accurate target costing.
3. Should actual, normal, or standard costing be applied?	*Normal costing* is a term used when assigning manufacturing overhead costs. The methods are irrelevant to assigning non-manufacturing costs. GAAP requires period costs be expensed, not accumulated in inventory as value-added to finished goods. The use of either budgeted or actual use of the resource supplied by the support service will affect the assignment of period costs. Allocation of period costs is done for internal purposes.
4. What methods can a manager use to allocate costs of support divisions to one another and to core production divisions?	The three methods are direct, step-down, and reciprocal. The direct method is simple but fails to represent the economic reality of cost flows between support divisions. The step-down method represents support cost flow from one to the other support division in sequence. The economic reality of cost flows is not represented. Both methods will misapply support division costs. Ultimately costs assigned to products, jobs, processes will be too high or too low. The reciprocal method fully represents the economic reality of cost flows but is arithmetically more challenging to explain. It is superior to the other two methods because it is consistent, fair, and more accurately assigns full costs, recoverable when output is sold.
5. What methods can a manager use to allocate common costs to two or more users?	Common costs are the costs of operating a facility, of an activity, or of a cost object that are shared by two or more users. The stand-alone cost allocation method uses information pertaining to each user of the cost object to determine cost allocation weights. The incremental cost allocation method ranks individual users of the cost object and allocates common costs first to the primary user and then to the other incremental users.
6. What is one benefit of using Matrix or Solver functions in Excel?	One benefit is that more realistic reciprocal cost allocation problems can be almost instantly solved where several period cost pools can be reciprocally allocated to each other and then to several operating departments. These situations are more realistic.

This chapter and the Glossary at the end of the book contain definitions of the following important terms:

allowable cost (p. 578)
artificial cost (p. 573)
coefficient matrix (p. 581)
common cost (p. 576)
core division (p. 561)
direct allocation method (p. 569)
direct method (p. 569)
dual-rate method (p. 561)
full product costing (p. 558)

incremental cost allocation
   method (p. 577)
matrix (p. 581)
operating division (p. 561)
product bundle (p. 559)
production division (p. 561)
reciprocal allocation method (p. 572)
reciprocated cost (p. 573)
sequential method (p. 570)

single-rate method (p. 561)
stand-alone cost allocation
   method (p. 577)
step allocation method (p. 570)
step-down method (p. 570)
vector (p. 581)
vector of constants (p. 581)

SHORT-ANSWER QUESTIONS

14-1 "I am going to focus on the customers of my business and leave cost allocation issues to my accountant." Do you agree with this comment by a division president?

14-2 Describe how the dual-rate method is useful to division managers in decision making.

14-3 What are four purposes of cost allocation?

14-4 What criteria might be used to justify cost allocation decisions? Which are the dominant criteria?

14-5 What are two basic reasons for a management team to select one period cost allocation method over another?

14-6 How do cost-benefit considerations affect choices by a company about the allocation of indirect criteria?

14-7 Name three decisions managers face when designing the cost allocation component of an accounting system.

14-8 Give examples of bases used to allocate corporate cost pools to the operating divisions of an organization.

14-9 Why might a manager prefer that budgeted rather than actual indirect cost allocation rates be used for costs being allocated to her division from another division?

14-10 "To ensure unbiased cost allocations, fixed indirect costs should be allocated on the basis of estimated long-run use by user division managers." Do you agree? Why?

14-11 Specify the strengths and weaknesses among the three methods of allocating the costs of service divisions to production divisions.

14-12 What is theoretically the most defensible method for allocating service division costs?

14-13 Distinguish between two methods of allocating common costs.

14-14 What is one key method to avoid disputes over allocation of support costs with respect to government contracts?

EXERCISES

14-15 **Terminology.** A number of terms are listed below:

artificial cost pools	common cost
core operating division	direct method
dual-rate	incremental cost allocation method
sequential method	stand-alone cost allocation method
price taker	Reciprocal method
	common cost pool

REQUIRED
Select the terms from the above list to complete the following sentences.

Target pricing is a policy well suited to a highly competitive environment where the corporation is a _____ because customers set the price. Depending on the proportion of fixed costs in the pool, the management team must choose between a _____ or a single-rate cost pool. Cost leadership is an appropriate policy and the _____ most accurately reflects cost flows from support divisions back and forth among one another and to _____. To implement the reciprocal method, the support cost pools must be arithmetically adjusted to create _____, which are then the basis for all cost allocation.

The _____ is an improvement over the _____ of applying support costs, but only reports the flow of support departments to one another in one direction. The support divisions are first ranked on some basis from highest to lowest flow of either costs or resources then step down from the largest to smallest support division. Then the adjusted support cost pools are allocated to core operating divisions.

A _____ arises when two or more users share benefits from consuming a corporate resource. There are two ways to recognize proportional cost and benefit. The _____ defines each cost object as if it were the only output. The _____ ranks those who share in benefits from incurring the total common cost pool from high to low. The highest ranked is the primary party who bears most of the total shared cost. The remaining incremental parties share the difference between the total common cost pool minus the costs allocated to the primary party. Disputes over the primary party often arise.

1. Overhead rate, 361.7%

14-16 Criteria of cost allocation decisions—Intermediate. Dave Meltzer went to Lake Tahoe for his annual winter vacation. Unfortunately, he broke his ankle severely while skiing and had to spend two days at the Tahoe General Hospital. Meltzer's insurance company received a $4,800 bill for his two-day stay. One item that caught Meltzer's eye was a $10.62 charge for a roll of cotton. Meltzer was a salesman for Johnson & Johnson and knew that the cost to the hospital of the roll of cotton would be in the $2.20 to $3 range. He asked for a breakdown of how the $10.62 charge was derived. The accounting office of the hospital sent him the following information:

a. Invoiced cost of cotton roll	$ 2.30
b. Processing of paperwork for purchase	0.50
c. Supplies room management fee	0.60
d. Operating-room and patient-room handling charge	1.50
e. Administrative hospital costs	1.00
f. Research-related recoupment	0.50
g. Malpractice insurance costs	1.10
h. Cost of treating uninsured patients	2.62
i. Profit component	0.50
Total	$10.62

Meltzer believes the overhead charge is obscene. He comments, "There was nothing I could do about it. When they come in and dab your stitches, it's not as if you can say, 'Keep your cotton roll. I brought my own.'"

REQUIRED
1. Compute the overhead rate Tahoe General Hospital charged on the cotton roll.
2. What criteria might Tahoe General use to justify allocation of each of the overhead items (b) through (i) in the preceding list? Examine each item separately, and use the allocation justifications in your answer.
3. What should Meltzer do about the $10.62 charge for the cotton roll?

1. a. Costs allocated to Mississauga under single-rate method based on practical capacity, $3,000

14-17 Single-rate versus dual-rate methods, support division. The Ontario power plant that services all manufacturing divisions of Ontario Engineering has a budget for the coming year. This budget has been expressed in the following monthly terms:

Manufacturing Department	Needed at Practical Capacity Production Level (kilowatt-hours)	Average Expected Monthly Usage (kilowatt-hours)
Mississauga	10,000	8,000
Cambridge	20,000	9,000
Burlington	12,000	7,000
Brantford	8,000	6,000
Total	50,000	30,000

The expected monthly costs for operating the power plant during the budget year are $15,000: $6,000 variable and $9,000 fixed.
1. Assume that a single cost pool is used for the power plant costs. What budgeted amounts will be allocated to each manufacturing division if (a) the rate is calculated based on practical capacity and costs are allocated based on practical capacity and (b) the rate is calculated based on expected monthly usage and costs are allocated based on expected monthly usage?
2. Assume the dual-rate method is used with separate cost pools for the variable and fixed costs. Variable costs are allocated on the basis of expected monthly usage. Fixed costs are allocated on the basis of practical capacity. What budgeted amounts will be allocated to each manufacturing division? Why might you prefer the dual-rate method?

14-18 Single-rate method, budgeted versus actual costs and quantities. Chocolat Inc. is a producer of premium chocolate based in Owen Sound. The company has a separate division for each of its two products: dark chocolate and milk chocolate. Chocolat purchases ingredients from Toronto for its Dark Chocolate Division and from Barrie for its Milk Chocolate Division. Both locations are the same distance from Chocolat's Owen Sound plant.

Chocolat Inc. operates a fleet of trucks as a cost centre that charges the divisions for variable costs (drivers and fuel) and fixed costs (vehicle amortization, insurance, and registration fees) of operating the fleet. Each division is evaluated on the basis of its operating income. For 2013, the trucking fleet had a practical capacity of 50 round trips between the Owen Sound plant and the two suppliers. It recorded the following information:

	Budgeted	Actual
Costs of truck fleet	$115,000	$96,750
Number of round trips for Dark Chocolate Division (Owen Sound plant–Toronto)	30	30
Number of round trips for Milk Chocolate Division (Owen Sound plant–Barrie)	20	15

REQUIRED
1. Using the single-rate method, allocate costs to the Dark Chocolate Division and the Milk Chocolate Division in these three ways:
   a. Calculate the budgeted rate per round trip and allocate costs based on round trips budgeted for each division.
   b. Calculate the budgeted rate per round trip and allocate costs based on actual round trips used by each division.
   c. Calculate the actual rate per round trip and allocate costs based on actual round trips used by each division.
2. Describe the advantages and disadvantages of using each of the three methods in requirement 1. Would you encourage Chocolat Inc. to use one of these methods? Explain and indicate any assumptions you made.

14-19 Dual-rate method, budgeted versus actual costs, and practical capacity versus actual quantities (continuation of 14-18). Chocolat Inc. decides to examine the effect of using the dual-rate method for allocating truck costs to each round trip. At the start of 2013, the budgeted costs were:

Variable cost per round trip	$ 1,500
Fixed costs	$40,000

The actual results for the 45 round trips made in 2013 were:

Variable costs	$60,750
Fixed costs	$36,000
	$96,750

Assume all other information to be the same as in Exercise 14-18.

REQUIRED
1. Using the dual-rate method, what are the costs allocated to the Dark Chocolate Division and the Milk Chocolate Division when (a) variable costs are allocated using the budgeted rate per round trip and actual round trips used by each division, and when (b) fixed costs are allocated based on the budgeted rate per round trip and round trips budgeted for each division?
2. From the viewpoint of the Dark Chocolate Division, what are the effects of using the dual-rate method rather than the single-rate method?

1. a. Costs allocated to Govt.,
$1,120,000

14-20 Support division cost allocation, direct and step-down methods. Phoenix Partners provides management consulting services to government and corporate clients. Phoenix has two support divisions—Administrative Services (AS) and Information Systems (IS)—and two operating divisions—Government Consulting (Govt.) and Corporate Consulting (Corp.). For the first quarter of 2013, Phoenix's cost records indicate the following:

	Support		Operating		
	AS	IS	Govt.	Corp.	Total
Budgeted overhead costs before any interdepartment cost allocations	$600,000	$2,400,000	$8,756,000	$12,452,000	$24,208,000
Support work supplied by AS (budgeted head count)	—	25%	40%	35%	100%
Support work supplied by IS (budgeted computer time)	10%	—	30%	60%	100%

REQUIRED
1. Allocate the two support divisions' costs to the two operating divisions using the following methods:
   a. Direct method
   b. Step-down method (allocate AS first)
   c. Step-down method (allocate IS first)
2. Compare and explain differences in the support division costs allocated to each operating division.
3. What approaches might be used to decide the sequence in which to allocate support divisions when using the step-down method?

14-21 Support division cost allocation, reciprocal method (continuation of 14-20). Refer to the data given in Exercise 14-20.

1. a. Allocation of AS costs,
$600,000 + 0.10 ($2,615,385)

REQUIRED
1. Allocate the two support divisions' costs to the two operating divisions using the reciprocal method. Use (a) linear equations and (b) repeated iterations.
2. Compare and explain differences in requirement 1 with those in requirement 1 of Exercise 14-20. Which method do you prefer? Why?

14-22 Allocating costs of support divisions, step-down and direct methods. The Central Valley Company has prepared division overhead budgets for budgeted-volume levels before allocations as follows:

1. Allocate building and grounds expenses at $0.10/sq. m.

Support departments:		
Building and grounds	$10,000	
Personnel	1,000	
General plant administration	26,090	
Cafeteria: operating loss	1,640	
Storeroom	2,670	$ 41,400
Operating departments:		
Machining	34,700	
Assembly	48,900	83,600
Total for support and operating departments		$125,000

Management has decided that the most appropriate inventory costs are achieved by using individual division overhead rates. These rates are developed after support division costs are allocated to operating divisions.

Bases for allocation are to be selected from the following:

Department	Direct Manufacturing Labour-Hours	Number of Employees	Square Metres of Floor Space Occupied	Manufacturing Labour-Hours	Number of Requisitions
Building and grounds	0	0	0	0	0
Personnel[a]	0	0	2,000	0	0
General plant administration	0	35	7,000	0	0
Cafeteria: operating loss	0	10	4,000	1,000	0
Storeroom	0	5	7,000	1,000	0
Machining	5,000	50	30,000	8,000	2,000
Assembly	15,000	100	50,000	17,000	1,000
Total	20,000	200	100,000	27,000	3,000

[a]Basis used is number of employees.

REQUIRED
1. Using the step-down method, allocate support division costs. Develop overhead rates per direct manufacturing labour-hour for machining and assembly. Allocate the costs of the support divisions in the order given in this problem. Use the allocation base for each support division you think is most appropriate.
2. Using the direct method, rework requirement 1.
3. Based on the following information about two jobs, determine the total overhead costs for each job by using rates developed in (a) requirement 1 and (b) requirement 2.

	Direct Manufacturing Labour-Hours	
	Machining	Assembly
Job 88	18	2
Job 89	3	17

4. The company evaluates the performance of the operating division managers on the basis of how well they managed their total costs, including allocated costs. As the manager of the MachiningDivision, which allocation method would you prefer from the results obtained in requirements 1 and 2? Explain.

14-23 Fixed cost allocation. Three restaurants in a downtown area of a large city have decided to share a valet service and parking lot for their customers. The cost of the service and lot is $10,000 per month. The owners of the restaurants need to decide how to divide the $10,000 cost. The actual usage, planned usage, and practical capacity in the month of May was:

Restaurant	Actual Parking Spots Used	Planned Parking Spots	Practical Capacity Parking Spots
A	1,500	1,600	2,000
B	1,400	1,300	1,500
C	1,300	1,100	1,500

REQUIRED
1. Allocate the fixed cost to each restaurant using actual, planned, and capacity usage measures.
2. In this situation, which method of allocation makes the most sense?

14-24 Direct and step-down allocation. E-books, an online book retailer, has two operating divisions—Corporate Sales and Consumer Sales—and two support divisions—Human Resources and Information Systems. Each sales division conducts merchandising and marketing operations independently. E-books uses number of employees to allocate Human Resources costs and processing time to allocate Information Systems costs. The following data are available for September 2014:

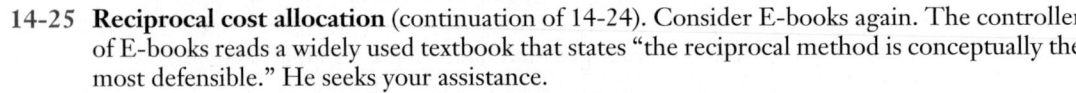

	Support Divisions		Operating Divisions	
	Human Resources	Information Systems	Corporate Sales	Consumer Sales
Budgeted costs incurred before any interdivision cost allocations	$72,700	$234,400	$998,270	$489,860
Support work supplied by Human Resources Division				
Budgeted number of employees	—	21	42	28
Support work supplied by Information Systems Division				
Budgeted processing time (in minutes)	320	—	1,920	1,600

REQUIRED
1. Allocate the support divisions' costs to the operating divisions using the direct method.
2. Rank the support divisions based on the percentage of their services provided to other support divisions. Use this ranking to allocate the support divisions' costs to the operating divisions based on the step-down method.
3. How could you have ranked the support divisions differently?

14-25 Reciprocal cost allocation (continuation of 14-24). Consider E-books again. The controller of E-books reads a widely used textbook that states "the reciprocal method is conceptually the most defensible." He seeks your assistance.

REQUIRED
1. Describe the key features of the reciprocal method.
2. Allocate the support divisions' costs (Human Resources and Information Systems) to the two operating divisions using the reciprocal method.
3. In the case presented in this exercise, which method (direct, step-down, or reciprocal) would you recommend? Why?

PROBLEMS

14-26 Single-rate, dual-rate, and practical capacity allocation. Beauty Division Store has a new promotional program that offers a free gift-wrapping service for its customers. Beauty's customer-service division has practical capacity to wrap 7,500 gifts at a budgeted fixed cost of $6,750 each month. The budgeted variable cost to gift wrap an item is $0.50. Although the service is free to customers, a gift-wrapping service cost allocation is made to the division where the item was purchased. The customer-service division reported the following for the most recent month:

Department	Actual Number of Gifts Wrapped	Budgeted Number of Gifts to Be Wrapped	Practical Capacity Available for Gift-Wrapping
Women's face wash	2,100	2,475	2,625
Men's face wash	750	825	938
Fragrances	1,575	1,800	1,969
Body wash	525	450	656
Hair products	1,050	1,200	1,312
Total	6,000	6,750	7,500

REQUIRED
1. Using the single-rate method, allocate gift-wrapping costs to different divisions in these three ways:
   a. Calculate the budgeted rate based on the budgeted number of gifts to be wrapped and allocate costs based on the budgeted use (of gift-wrapping services).

b. Calculate the budgeted rate based on the budgeted number of gifts to be wrapped and allocate costs based on actual usage.

c. Calculate the budgeted rate based on the practical gift-wrapping capacity available and allocate costs based on actual usage.

2. Using the dual-rate method, compute the amount allocated to each division when (a) the fixed-cost rate is calculated using budgeted costs and the practical gift-wrapping capacity, (b) fixed costs are allocated based on budgeted usage of gift-wrapping services, and (c) variable costs are allocated using the budgeted variable cost rate and actual usage.

3. Comment on your results in requirements 1 and 2. Discuss the advantages of the dual-rate method.

14-27 Allocating costs to divisions. Gether Corporation manufactures appliances. It has four divisions: Refrigerator, Stove, Dishwasher, and Microwave Oven. Each division is located in a different city and the headquarters is located in Mississauga, Ontario. Headquarters incurs a total of $14,255,000 in costs, none of which are direct costs of any of the divisions. Revenues, costs, and facility space for each division are as follows:

1. Allocation to Stove based on square metres, $3,207,375

	Refrigerator	Stove	Dishwasher	Microwave Oven
Revenue	$10,900,000	$18,800,000	$11,500,000	$6,780,000
Direct costs	5,700,000	10,400,000	6,200,000	3,220,000
Segment margin	5,200,000	8,400,000	5,300,000	3,560,000
Square metres of floor space occupied	130,000	90,000	80,000	100,000

Gether wants to allocate the indirect costs of headquarters on the basis of either square metres or segment margin for each division.

REQUIRED

1. Allocate the indirect headquarters costs to each division, first using square metres of space and then using segment margin as the allocation base. Calculate the division operating margins after each allocation in dollars and as a percentage of revenue.

2. Which allocation base do you prefer? Why?

3. Should any of the divisions be dropped based on your calculations? Why or why not?

14-28 Support division cost allocations; single-division cost pools; direct, step-down, and reciprocal methods. The Manes Company has two products. Product 1 is manufactured entirely in Division X. Product 2 is manufactured entirely in Division Y. To produce these two products, the Manes Company has two support divisions: A (a materials-handling division) and B (a power-generating division).

1. Allocation of A to X using direct method, $62,500

An analysis of the work done by divisions A and B in a typical period follows:

		Used By		
Supplied By	**A**	**B**	**X**	**Y**
A	—	100	250	150
B	500	—	100	400

The work done in Division A is measured by the direct labour-hours of materials-handling time. The work done in Division B is measured by the kilowatt-hours of power. The budgeted costs of the support divisions for the coming year are:

	Division A (Materials Handling)	Division B (Power Generation)
Variable indirect labour and indirect materials costs	$ 70,000	$10,000
Supervision	10,000	10,000
Amortization	20,000	20,000
	$100,000	$40,000
	+ Power costs	+ Materials-handling costs

The budgeted costs of the operating divisions for the coming year are $1,500,000 for Division X and $800,000 for Division Y.

Supervision costs are salary costs. Amortization in Division B is the straight-line amortization of power-generation equipment in its nineteenth year of an estimated 25-year useful life; the equipment is old but well maintained.

REQUIRED

1. What are the allocations of costs of support divisions A and B to operating divisions X and Y using (a) the direct method, (b) the step-down method (allocate Division A first), (c) the step-down method (allocate Division B first), and (d) the reciprocal method?
2. An outside company has offered to supply all the power needed by the Manes Company and to provide all the services of the present power division. The cost of this service will be $40 per kilowatt-hour of power. Should Manes accept? Explain.

⑤

1. Allocation to Wright Inc. under stand-alone cost allocation method, $28,800

14-29 Common costs. Wright Inc. and Brown Inc. are two small clothing companies that are considering leasing a dyeing machine together. The companies estimated that in order to meet production, Wright needs the machine for 900 hours and Brown needs it for 600 hours. If each company rents the machine on its own, the fee will be $40 per hour of usage. If they rent the machine together, the fee will decrease to $32 per hour of usage.

REQUIRED

1. Calculate Wright's and Brown's respective share of fees under the stand-alone cost allocation method.
2. Calculate Wright's and Brown's respective share of fees using the incremental cost allocation method. Assume Wright to be the primary party.
3. Which method would you recommend Wright and Brown use to share the fees?

1. Home Security Systems allocation using the direct method, $4,282

14-30 Support cost allocation to support and operations. Magnum T.A. Inc. specializes in the assembly and installation of high-quality security systems for the home and business segments of the market. The four departments at its highly automated state-of-the-art assembly plant are as follows:

Service Departments	Assembly Departments
Engineering Support	Home Security Systems
Information Systems Support	Business Security Systems

The budgeted level of service relationships at the start of the year was:

		Used by		
Supplied by	**Engineering Support**	**Information Systems Support**	**Home Security Systems**	**Business Security Systems**
Engineering Support	—	0.10	0.40	0.50
Information Systems Support	0.20	—	0.30	0.50

The actual level of service relationships for the year was:

		Used by		
Supplied by	**Engineering Support**	**Information Systems Support**	**Home Security Systems**	**Business Security Systems**
Engineering Support	—	0.15	0.30	0.55
Information Systems Support	0.25	—	0.15	0.60

Magnum collects fixed costs and variable costs of each department in separate cost pools. The actual costs (in thousands) in each pool for the year were:

	Fixed-Cost Pool	Variable-Cost Pool
Engineering Support	$2,800	$8,500
Information Systems Support	8,100	3,750

Fixed costs are allocated on the basis of the budgeted level of service. Variable costs are allocated on the basis of the actual level of service.

The support department costs allocated to each assembly department are allocated to products on the basis of units assembled. The units assembled in each department during the year were:

Home Security Systems	7,950 units
Business Security Systems	3,750 units

REQUIRED

1. Allocate the support department costs to the assembly departments using a dual-rate system and (a) the direct method, (b) the step-down method (allocate Information Systems Support first), (c) the step-down method (allocate Engineering Support first), and (d) the reciprocal method.
2. Compare the support department costs allocated to each Home Security Systems unit assembled and each Business Security Systems unit assembled under (a), (b), (c), and (d) in requirement 1.
3. What factors might explain the very limited adoption of the reciprocal method by many organizations?

14-31 Support cost allocation processes. Environ Petroleum Company is engaged in all phases of exploring, refining, and marketing of oil and petrochemical products. To ensure full compliance with all applicable laws, the company has a legal department staffed by lawyers who have expertise in a variety of legal areas. The top management of Environ wants to motivate all operating managers to seek legal counsel from the in-house lawyers whenever necessary to avoid violation of any laws during the course of its operations.

Currently, users of the Legal Department are allocated cost at a $400 standard hourly rate based on actual usage. The chief financial officer has suggested that department managers would make more use of the Legal Department's services, and thus avoid potential legal pitfalls, if services were provided free of cost to their departments.

REQUIRED

Comment on the proposal of the chief financial officer. Do you have any alternative suggestion(s)?

14-32 Cost allocation to divisions. Forber Bakery makes baked goods for grocery stores, and has three divisions: Bread, Cake, and Doughnuts. Each division is run and evaluated separately, but the main headquarters incurs costs that are indirect costs for the divisions. Costs incurred in the main headquarters are:

1. Bread operating income, $4,700,000

Human resources (HR) costs	$1,900,000
Accounting department costs	1,400,000
Rent and amortization	1,200,000
Other	600,000
Total costs	$5,100,000

The Forber upper management currently allocates this cost to the divisions equally. One of the division managers has done some research on activity-based costing and proposes the use of different allocation bases for the different indirect costs—number of employees for HR costs, total revenues for accounting division costs, square metres of space for rent and amortization costs, and equal allocation among the divisions of "other" costs. Information about the three divisions follows:

	Bread	Cake	Doughnuts
Total revenues	$20,900,000	$4,500,000	$13,400,000
Direct costs	14,500,000	3,200,000	7,250,000
Segment margin	$ 6,400,000	$1,300,000	$ 6,150,000
Number of employees	400	100	300
Square metres of space	10,000	4,000	6,000

1. Allocate the indirect costs of Forber to each division equally. Calculate division operating income after allocation of headquarters costs.
2. Allocate headquarters costs to the individual divisions using the proposed allocation bases. Calculate the division operating income after allocation. Comment on the allocation bases used to allocate headquarters costs.
3. Which division manager do you think suggested this new allocation? Explain briefly. Which allocation do you think is "better"?

14-33 Matrix algebra. A firm that manufactures specialized scientific equipment, Nominal Engineering Inc. (NEI), has decided to implement a new costing system to more accurately allocate its support costs. The company anticipates this will improve the competitiveness of its bids for design contracts and provide solid justification when it claims reimbursement for contracted costs. NEI has four support divisions: Engineering (design), Accounting, Information Systems (IS), and Human Resources Administration (HR). NEI's two operating divisions are geographically separate. One is national and the other international. The table summarizes the five cost pools and the percentage of costs allocated to each division. The four support divisions are interdependent and each uses the resources of the others. Because the goal of NEI is improved accuracy of cost allocation, the top management team decides to use the reciprocal cost allocation method for the support division costs. The table summarizes the cost pools and the percentage of each cost pool to be allocated to each division. The cost pools are reported in millions of dollars.

Supplier of Support Service	Vector of Constants	Consumption of Support: Support Divisions				Operating Divisions		Check
	Cost Pools	Engineering	Accounting	IS	HR	National	International	
Engineering	$ 36	0	0.1	0.2	0.05	0.35	0.3	1
Accounting	20	0.1	0	0.1	0.05	0.45	0.3	1
IS	20	0.2	0.1	0	0.05	0.4	0.25	1
HR	10	0.1	0.1	0.1	0	0.4	0.3	1

Operating Divisions

National	30
International	22
	$138

REQUIRED

1. Use the matrix algebra function in Excel to calculate the inverse of the coefficient matrix for support divisions.
2. Multiply the inverse of the coefficient matrix by the vector of constants to obtain the artificial costs.
3. Calculate the allocation of costs to the support divisions and the two operating divisions.

14-34 Matrix algebra. Computer retailer Lowest Price Bargains Ltd. (LPBL) sells computers of all models and sizes at low prices. The company can keep its costs down with very careful cost allocation of both its three operating divisions and its three support divisions, which are interdependent and consume one another's resources. The three support divisions are Corporate Treasury, Corporate Human Resource Management (CHRM), and Information Technology (IT). The three core operating divisions are Sales & Marketing, Purchasing, and Consumer Services & Returns. LPBL uses reciprocal cost allocation for its support divisions. A table summarizes the cost pools and the cost allocations among all six divisions:

2. Engineering artificial costs, $47.32112

2. Corporate Treasury artificial costs, $162.30043

Supplier of Support Service	Cost Pools	Corporate Treasury	CHRM	IS	Sales & Mktg.	Purchasing	Consumer Services & Returns	Check
	Vector of Constants	**Consumption of Support: Support Divisions**			**Operating Divisions**			
Corporate Treasury	$ 96	0	0.2	0.25	0.15	0.2	0.2	1
CHRM	49	0.1	0	0.2	0.25	0.25	0.2	1
IT	156	0.25	0.15	0	0.2	0.2	0.2	1

Operating Divisions	
Sales & Marketing	84
Purchasing	203
Consumer Services & Returns	36
	$624

REQUIRED

1. Use the matrix algebra function in Excel to calculate the inverse of the coefficient matrix for support divisions.
2. Multiply the inverse of the coefficient matrix by the vector of constants to obtain the artificial costs.
3. Calculate the allocation of costs all divisions.

14-35 Support cost allocation processes. (CMA, adapted) Bulldog Inc. is a large manufacturing company that runs its own electrical power plant from the excess steam produced in its manufacturing process. Power is provided to two production departments—Department A and Department B. The capacity of the power plant was originally determined by the expected peak demands of the two production departments. The expected average usage and peak demands are, respectively, 60 percent and 66,000,000 kilowatt-hours (kwh) for Department A and 40 percent and 44,000,000 kWh for Department B.

The budgeted monthly costs of producing power, based on normal usage of 100,000,000 kWh, are $30,500,000 in fixed costs and $8,000,000 in variable costs. For November, the actual kWh used was 60,000,000 by Department A and 20,000,000 by Department B. Actual fixed costs were $30,500,000, and actual variable costs were $8,000,000.

Terry Lamb, the controller, prepared the following monthly report:

1. Based on Budgeted Rate × Actual Usage Allocation of variable costs to Department B = $1,600,000

Bulldog Inc.
Monthly Allocation Report
November 2014

Power plant usage	80,000,000 kWh
Actual costs:	
Fixed	$30,500,000
Variable	8,000,000
Total	$38,500,000
Rate per kWh	($38,500,000 ÷ 80,000,000 kWh) $ 0.48125
Allocations	
To Department A	(60,000,000 kWh × $0.48125) $28,875,000
To Department B	(20,000,000 kWh × $0.48125) 9,625,000
Total allocated	$38,500,000

Lamb fully allocated all power plant costs on the basis of actual kilowatt-hours used by each production department. This report will be submitted to the two production department operating managers.

1. Discuss at least two problems with the monthly allocation report prepared by Lamb for November 2014 at Bulldog Inc.
2. Prepare a revised monthly allocation report for November 2014 using a flexible-budget approach.
3. Discuss the behavioural implications of Lamb's monthly allocation report for November 2014 on the production managers of Department B at Bulldog Inc.

14-36 Common cost allocation and contracts. Jason Miller and Eric Jackson would like to lease an office building to open their separate law offices. The building has a total of 1,700 square metres of office space. Miller and Jackson need 1,000 square metres and 700 square metres, respectively. If each rents the space on his own, the rent will be $1 per square metre. If they rent the space together, the rent will decrease to $0.80 per square metre.

REQUIRED

1. Calculate Miller's and Jackson's respective share of the rent under the stand-alone cost-allocation method.
2. Do requirement 1 using the incremental cost allocation method. Assume Miller to be the primary party.
3. What method would you recommend Miller and Jackson use to share the rent?

COLLABORATIVE LEARNING CASE

1. Lodging stand-alone revenue, $582

14-37 Revenue allocation, bundled products. Heavenly Resorts operates a five-star hotel with a world-recognized championship golf course. Heavenly has a decentralized management structure with three divisions:

◆ Lodging (rooms, conference facilities)
◆ Food (restaurants and in-room service)
◆ Recreation (golf course, tennis courts, and so on)

Starting next month, Heavenly Resorts will offer a two-day, two-person "getaway package" for $1,000. This deal includes:

◆ Two nights' stay for two in an ocean-view room—separately priced at $800 ($400 per night for two).
◆ Two rounds of golf—separately priced at $375 ($187.50 per round). One person can do two rounds, or two people can do one round each.
◆ Candlelight dinner for two at the exclusive Heavenly Resorts Restaurant—separately priced at $200 ($100 per person).

Jenny Lee, president of the Recreation Division, recently asked the CEO of Heavenly Resorts how her division would share in the $1,000 revenue from the package. The golf course was operating at 100% capacity. Under the getaway-package rules, participants who booked one week in advance were guaranteed access to the golf course. Lee noted that every "getaway" booking would displace $375 of golf bookings. She emphasized that the high demand reflected the devotion of her team to keeping the golf course rated one of the "Best 10 Courses in the World" by *Golf Monthly*. As an aside, she also noted that the Lodging and Food divisions had to turn away customers only during "peak-season events such as the New Year's period."

REQUIRED

1. Using selling prices, allocate the $1,000 getaway-package revenue to the three divisions using:
   a. The stand-alone revenue-allocation method
   b. The incremental revenue-allocation method (with Recreation first, then Lodging, and then Food)
2. What are the pros and cons of the two methods in requirement 1?

Cost Allocation: Joint Products and Byproducts

Challenges of Joint Cost Allocation

The Hibernia offshore oil field project off the coast of Newfoundland is a joint venture among many companies, including ExxonMobil Canada. The costs of lifting oil from the ocean's floor are shared among the companies investing in this project. The crude oil pumped will be refined into a variety of petroleum products. The lifting costs common to all produced products will be recovered by allocating or sharing these joint costs in some reasonable way. The partners will evaluate two market-based cost allocation methods to identify the more appropriate method that best reflects the facts of the actual proportion of joint resources (and costs) shared among them.

After studying this chapter, you should be able to

1. Distinguish among different types of saleable products, scrap, and toxic waste.

2. Analyze the physical measure and sales value at splitoff methods to allocate joint costs.

3. Evaluate two different market-based cost allocation methods to identify which is most appropriate to decide whether to sell at splitoff or process further.

4. Identify the strategic implications of a decision to implement one joint cost allocation method.

5. Account for byproducts using two different methods.

Costing for the more complex case in which two or more products are simultaneously produced involves joint costs. A variety of products share core activities of production up to a point in the production process. After this point, processing the products further involves separate production activities and separate costs. The goal is to choose the cost allocation method that best reflects how the costs actually flow throughout a real economic process. The choice is not often straightforward because corporations allocate costs in ways most appropriate to the business decisions they must make.

JOINT-COST BASICS

1 Distinguish among different types of saleable products, scrap, and toxic waste.

Joint costs are the costs of a production process that yields multiple **main products** simultaneously. A **product** is any output that can be sold at full product cost plus profit, or enables the company to avoid purchasing direct materials. When a process yields many products, the main product is the one with the highest sales value. If two or more products have high sales value, they are called **joint products**. Products of relatively low sales value are called **byproducts**. During production, **scrap**, which has minimal to zero sales value, may also be produced. These relationships are illustrated in Exhibit 15-1.

The processing of poultry, for example, yields feathers, giblets, wings, thighs, and entire birds. Often heads, feet, skin, and internal organs are processed differently and ground as byproducts for use in animal meal. White breast meat, the highest revenue-generating product, is obtained from the front end of the bird; dark meat from the back end. Other edible products include chicken wings and giblets. There are many inedible products that have a diverse set of uses. For example, poultry feathers are used in bedding and sporting goods. Poultry companies use individual product cost information for different customers (e.g., supermarkets, fast food outlets) and the sales mix differs for these customers. A subset of products is placed into frozen storage, which creates demand for individual product cost information for the purpose of inventory valuation.

Byproducts often used to be waste product for which a use has now been found. Scrap may be referred to as waste. Processes in some extractive industries generate toxic waste, such as cyanide, lead, toluene, sulphuric acid, or dioxin. Toxic waste has negative revenue when the costs of reclamation and remediation are considered. Costs of recovering or disposing of toxic emissions is a life-cycle cost that should be added to joint production costs prior to allocating this cost pool to main, joint, or byproducts. Exhibit 15-2 lists a variety of industries in which joint costs are incurred in their production processes.

In joint cost processes, the **splitoff point** is the juncture in a production process where two or more main products become separately identifiable. **Separable costs** are the full product costs of processing incurred by each identifiable product beyond the splitoff point. Decisions about whether to sell work in process or process further can be made at or beyond the splitoff point. In practice, the classification of products from byproducts is not straightforward and changes over time, especially when prices are volatile.

EXHIBIT 15-1
Classification of Products of a Joint Production Process

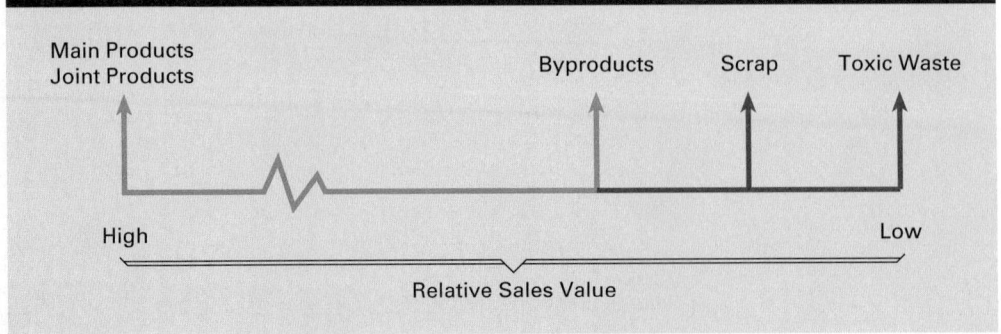

EXHIBIT 15-2
Industries Incurring Joint Costs

Industry	Separable Products at the Splitoff Point
Agriculture and Food Processing	
Cocoa beans	Cocoa butter, cocoa powder, cocoa drink mix, tanning cream
Lambs	Lamb cuts, tripe, hides, bones, fat
Hogs	Bacon, ham, spare ribs, pork roast
Raw milk	Cream, liquid skim
Lumber	Lumber of varying grades and shapes
Turkeys	Breasts, wings, thighs, drumsticks, internal organs, feather meal, poultry meal
Extractive Industries	
Coal	Coke, gas, benzol, tar, ammonia
Copper ore	Copper, silver, lead, zinc
Petroleum	Crude oil, natural gas, raw LPG
Salt	Hydrogen, chlorine, caustic soda
Chemical Industries	
Raw LPG (liquefied petroleum gas)	Butane, ethane, propane
Crude oil	Gasoline, kerosene, benzene, naphtha
Semiconductor Industry	
Fabrication of silicon-wafer chips	Memory chips of different quality (as to capacity), speed, life expectancy, and temperature tolerance

In offshore processing of hydrocarbons to yield oil and gas, water is also an output. The water is recycled back into the ocean. The actual outputs exceed the number of products because water is not sold. The processing of ores often requires the removal of overburden or soil, and the ore is then finely crushed to extract coal, silver, iron, or gold. Both the crushed ore and soil are outputs stored rather than sold. Later, as part of the environmental remediation plan, the crushed ore is used as landfill in the pits and the soil is replaced over the filled-in pits. Corporations then replant in the soil to return the site to its fully remediated state. The storage and transportation of these outputs will generate costs, but there is no cost of the outputs themselves. These outputs are not products because they are not sold.

Different reasons to allocate joint costs include:

◆ Calculation of inventoriable costs and cost of goods sold for external financial statements and reports for income tax authorities.

◆ Calculation of inventoriable costs and cost of goods sold for internal financial reporting. Such reports are used in division profitability analysis when determining compensation for division managers.

◆ Cost reimbursement under contracts when only a portion of a business's products or services is sold or delivered to a single customer (such as a government agency).

◆ Customer profitability analysis where individual customers purchase varying combinations of joint products or byproducts as well as other products of the company.

◆ Insurance settlement calculations when damage claims made by businesses with joint products, main products, or byproducts are based on cost information.

◆ Rate regulation when one or more of the jointly produced products or services is subject to price regulation.

◆ Contract litigation in which costs of joint products are key inputs.

There are four joint cost allocation methods from which managers may choose. The **physical measure method** allocates joint costs on the basis of their relative proportions at the splitoff point, using a common physical measure such as weight or volume of the total production of each product. The **sales value at splitoff method** allocates joint costs on the basis of the relative sales value at the splitoff point of the total production in the accounting period for each product.

These two methods may be appropriate when the products can be sold at splitoff, but often the joint product is processed further at splitoff. In these cases, two slightly more complex market methods are more appropriate, the estimated NRV method and the constant gross margin percentage NRV method. The estimated NRV method allocates joint costs on the basis of the *relative estimated net realizable value* (expected final sales value in the ordinary course of business minus the expected separable costs of production and marketing of the total production of the period). The constant gross margin percentage NRV method works in reverse. For each product, the gross margin (based on the overall gross margin percentage) and separable costs are deducted from the final sales value of units produced. The residual amount for each product is its allocation of joint costs.

As with virtually all cost accounting problems, the decision framework introduced in Chapter 1 can be used to decide on an appropriate cost allocation method.

Step 1: Identify the Problem   Farmers' Dairy is a producer of dairy products in Canada. There is no competition for Farmers' Dairy because the industry is fully regulated in Canada. The Dairy Farmers of Canada sets and announces monthly support prices and quotas for raw milk and milk outputs. The government sets and enforces standards of quality and safety as well as butterfat content that defines the type of output and therefore the price of various milk products.

There are two markets: fluid milks, which account for about 33% of total dairy production, and industrial products such as butter, cheese, and ice cream. One-third of milk output is a commodity, such as 2% partly skimmed milk. People purchase such products on price. There is no shortage of outlets from which milk can be purchased, from retailers such as Shoppers Drug Mart to gas stations. For producers, cost leadership is the appropriate strategy to assure profitability of these finished goods. Milk manufacturers compete on target, fully regulated price while retailers such as Shoppers Drug Mart sell milk as a loss leader and, in a highly competitive retail market, count on volume and other higher margin products to turn a profit.

Some of the remaining outputs from raw milk processing may be highly differentiated through the addition of nutritional supplements, flavourings, the extraction of allergens such as lactose, and so on. A unique or differentiated product is price inelastic for consumers and value leadership is an appropriate strategy to expand market share and profitability through growth. Consumers are willing to absorb additional costs of processing provided the attributes of the milk product are seen as desirable attributes.

Dairy cows each produce about 9,462 kg of raw milk, and there are about 978,400 dairy cows in Canada, most in Ontario and Quebec. Almost 25 million hecto litres (hL) were produced in 2010.[1] The physical fact is that the initial process of pasteurization cannot be observed without compromising the pasteurized milk's safety. It is not possible until after pasteurization to measure quantities that will flow into further separable joint processes, so pasteurization gives rise to joint costs when milk is manufactured.

Step 2: Gather Information   Gathering information from Farmers' Dairy's information system for a specific time period, the $345,000 joint costs produced 1,000 hL of cream and 3,000 hL of liquid skim (see Exhibit 15-3).

[1]Source: *Milk*, Dairy Farmers of Ontario Annual Report 2010.

EXHIBIT 15-3
Farmer's Dairy Overview

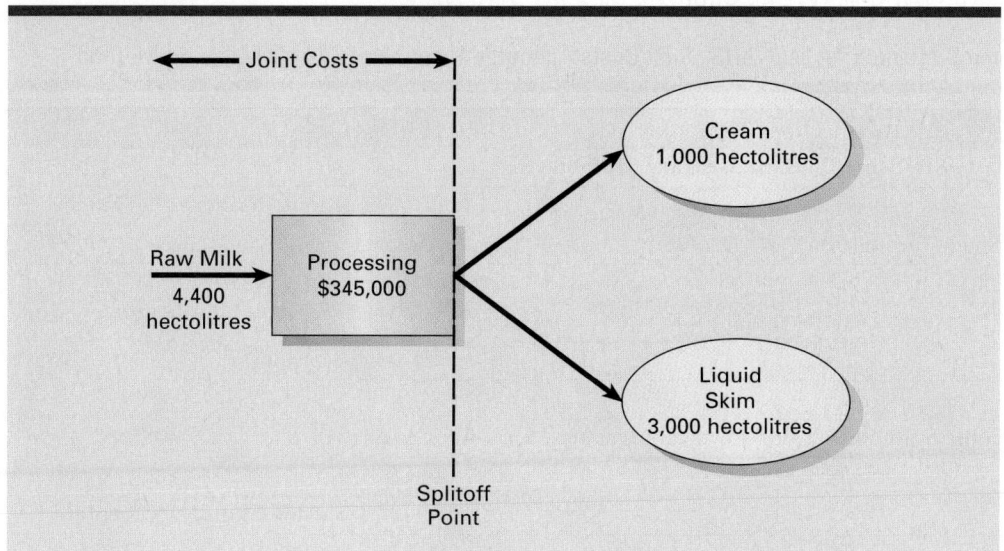

Farmers' Dairy purchases raw milk from individual farms and processes it up to the splitoff point, where two products (cream and liquid skim) are obtained. These two products are sold to an independent company that markets and distributes them to supermarkets and other retail outlets. The first two joint cost allocation methods will be compared under this simple assumption. But, in fact, Farmers' Dairy could process further and can use cost allocation to decide whether or not it is profitable to process the joint product further.

Below is some summary data for Farmers' Dairy for the month of May 2013:

◆ Raw milk processed: 4,400 hL of fluid raw milk with a 10% shrinkage of 400 hL due to evaporation and spillage, to net 4,000 hL of cream and liquid skim for sale. One hectolitre equals 100 litres. After the raw milk is received at the Farmers' Dairy processing plant it is separated in machines.

◆ Inventories: The inventory amounts are shown in the table below.

A	B	C
1		**Joint Costs**	
2 Joint costs (costs of 4,400 hL of raw milk and processing to splitoff point)		$345,000
3	**Cream**	**Liquid Skim**
4 Beginning inventory (hectolitres)	0	0
5 Production (hectolitres)	1,000	3,000
6 Sales (hectolitres)	800	900
7 Ending inventory (hectolitres)	200	2,100
8 Selling price per hectolitre	$155.00	$ 75.00

◆ Cost of processing 4,400 hL of fluid raw milk and processing it up to the splitoff point to yield 1,000 hL of cream and 3,000 hL of liquid skim: $345,000.

Step 3: Forecast Future Outcomes   Farmers' Dairy now needs to identify, analyze, and evaluate the three joint cost allocation alternatives, beginning with the two simplest: physical measure and sales value at splitoff. Both joint cost allocation methods can be used for costing the inventory of cream and liquid skim as well as determining cost of goods sold.

PHYSICAL MEASURE METHOD

Exhibit 15-4 presents summary data for May 2013:

EXHIBIT 15-4
Farmers' Dairy Product-Line Income Statement for May 2013: Joint Costs Allocated Using the Physical Measure Method

	A	B	C	D
1	**PANEL A: Allocation of Joint Costs Using Physical Measure Method**			
2		Cream	Liquid Skim	Total
3	Physical measure of total production (hectolitres)	1,000	3,000	4,000
4	Weighting (1,000 ÷ 4,000; 3,000 ÷ 4,000)	0.25	0.75	
5	Joint costs allocated (0.25 × $345,000; 0.75 × $345,000)	$ 86,250	$258,750	$345,000
6	Joint production cost per hectolitre	$ 86.25	$ 86.25	
7				
8	**PANEL B: Product-Line Income Statement Using Physical Measure Method for May 2013**			
9				
10		Cream	Liquid Skim	Total
11	Revenues (800 hL × $155/hL; 900 hL × $75/hL)	$124,000	$ 67,500	$191,500
12	Cost of goods sold (joint costs)			
13	Production costs (0.25 × $345,000; 0.75 × $345,000)	86,250	258,750	345,000
14	Deduct ending inventory (200 hL × $86.25/hL; 2,100 hL × $86.25/hL)	(17,250)	(181,125)	(198,375)
15	Cost of goods sold (joint costs)	69,000	77,625	146,625
16	Gross margin	$ 55,000	$ (10,125)	$ 44,875
17	Gross margin percentage (Gross margin ÷ Revenue)	44.4%	−15.0%	23.4%

Panel A illustrates the allocation of joint costs to individual products to calculate cost per hectolitre of cream and liquid skim for ending inventory valuation. This method allocates joint costs on the basis of total hectolitres; therefore, the cost per hectolitre is the same for both products. Panel B presents the product-line income statement using the physical measure method. The gross margin percentages are 44.4% for cream and a *loss* of 15% for liquid skim.

The advantages of this method are that it is observable, readily verifiable, and economically plausible. Economic plausibility arises from the actual physical process of production. The different quantities were actually split off during a specific time period. The cost flow reflects the economic fact of production. The average cost allocation rate is applied equally to each unit of input of WIP used in each separable product after splitoff.

It may be, however, that the separable costs of the product with the lower quantity at splitoff are far lower and the sales price per unit of the finished product is far higher than for the high quantity WIP product at splitoff. Strategically, it may also be that the lower quantity cost and higher unit sales price product is differentiated. Value leadership is the appropriate strategy in this case to expand market share. Customers will be willing to pay more for the unique attributes of this product. The corporation has the opportunity to recover costs of unused capacity, particularly if the joint cost pool has a high fixed cost component.

The high quantity product may be a commodity for which customers set the price. Cost leadership is the appropriate strategy here and customers will not pay for the costs of unused capacity (see Chapter 13). Using an average cost allocation rate will impair the corporation's opportunity to recover full product costs of including unused capacity. The differentiated product has a more robust ability to bear fixed unused capacity costs than the commodity product.

SALES VALUE AT SPLITOFF METHOD

In Exhibit 15-5, Panel A, the sales value at splitoff of the May 2013 production is $155,000 for cream and $225,000 for liquid skim.

EXHIBIT 15-5

Farmers' Dairy Product-Line Income Statement for May 2013: Joint Costs Allocated Using the Sales Value at Splitoff Method

	A	B	C	D
1	**PANEL A: Allocation of Joint Costs Using Sales Value at Splitoff Method**			
2		**Cream**	**Liquid Skim**	**Total**
3	Sales value of total production at splitoff point (1,000 hL × $155/hL; 3,000 hL × $75/hL)	$155,000	$225,000	$380,000
4	Weighting ($155,000 ÷ $380,000; $225,000 ÷ $380,000)	40.789%	59.211%	
5	Joint costs allocated (0.40789 × $345,000; 0.59211 × $345,000, rounded)	$140,722	$204,278	$345,000
6	Joint production cost per hectolitre	$140.722	$ 68.093	
7				
8	**PANEL B: Product-Line Income Statement Using Sales Value at Splitoff Method for May 2013**			
9		**Cream**	**Liquid Skim**	**Total**
10	Revenue (800 hL × $155/hL; 900 hL × $75.00/hL)	$124,000	$ 67,500	$191,500
11	Cost of goods available for sale (joint costs) Production costs (0.40789 × $345,000; 0.59211 × $345,000, rounded)	140,722	204,278	345,000
12	Deduct ending inventory (200 hL × $140.722/hL; 2,100 hL × $68.093/hL, rounded)	(28,144)	(142,995)	(171,139)
13	Cost of goods sold (joint costs)	112,578	61,283	173,861
14	Gross margin	$ 11,422	$ 6,217	$ 17,639
15	Gross margin percentage (Gross margin ÷ Revenue, rounded)	9.2%	9.2%	9.2%
16				
17	*Note:* Suppose Farmers' Dairy has beginning inventory of cream and liquid skim milk in May 2013. Suppose further that when this inventory is sold, Farmers' earns a gross margin different from 9.2%. Then the gross margin percentage for cream and liquid skim milk will be different from the figures shown. The actual value of the gross margin percentage depends on the proportion of sales of each product from beginning inventory and the proportion from current period production.			

Simple division of the joint cost pool (the numerator) by total revenue (the denominator) provides an average cost allocation rate. The cost pool is assigned on the basis of each product's percentage of total revenue. This approach uses the sales value of the *entire production of the accounting period* (1,000 hL of cream and 3,000 hL of liquid skim). The reason is that joint costs were incurred on all the units produced, not simply the units sold during the current sales period. Panel B presents the product-line income statement using the sales value at splitoff method.

Both cream and liquid skim have gross margin percentages of 9.2% (the gross margin percentages are always equal under this method). There are no beginning and ending inventories because all products are sold at the splitoff. The total revenue includes consideration of both sales price per unit and quantity of inputs physically used to produce each separable product. Revenue recognized during a specific accounting period, however, must be reported product by product. This method is verifiable and economically plausible, but it assumes all products are sold at splitoff.

Note how the sales value at splitoff method follows the benefits-received criterion of cost allocation: Costs are allocated to products in proportion to their revenue-generating power (expected revenue). This method is both straightforward and intuitive. The difficulty with assuming all products are sold at splitoff is that there must actually be a market for the joint product separate from finished goods or there is no economic plausibility. Regulated markets provide shadow prices for these intermediate outputs, but competitive markets do not.

Under the benefits-received criterion, the physical measures method is less desirable than the sales value at splitoff method. The main reason is that the physical weights used for allocating joint costs may have no relationship to the revenue-producing power of the individual products. Consider a mine that extracts ore containing gold, silver, and lead. Use of a common physical measure (tonnes) would result in almost all the costs being allocated to the product that weighs the most—lead, which has the lowest revenue-producing power. This costing method is not only inconsistent with the revenue objective, which is to earn revenue from sales of gold and silver, but also distorts the profit per tonne of the three products—the profit per tonne of gold and silver will be overstated while that of lead will show a sizeable loss.

Another issue arises if the physical measures of output are not straightforward. For example, oil, a liquid, and natural gas, a vapour, are both outputs from production. The physical measure for oil is barrels, but gas is not measured in barrels; therefore, a common measure of equivalent units, such as British thermal units (BTU), must be calculated. Most accountants will have to rely on outside technical expertise to complete this calculation. Finally, byproducts and outputs with zero sales value (such as dirt in gold mining) will be excluded from the physical measure used in the denominator.

DECIDING WHETHER TO SELL AT SPLITOFF OR PROCESS FURTHER

3 Evaluate two different market-based cost allocation methods to identify which is most appropriate to decide whether to sell at splitoff or process further.

In this section we'll look at the remaining two cost allocation methods for joint costs. Let's assume the same situation for Farmers' Dairy as above except that both the cream and liquid skim can be processed further. Using the decision framework, Farmers' Dairy can decide whether it is a good idea to sell at splitoff or process further.

Step 1   Farmers' Dairy is deciding whether to sell at splitoff or process further.

Step 2   From Farmers' Dairy, the following information is known:

◆ *Cream → buttercream:* 1,000 hL of cream are further processed to yield 800 hL of buttercream at additional processing (separable) costs of $135,000. Buttercream is sold for $420 per hL.

◆ *Liquid skim → condensed milk:* 3,000 hL of liquid skim are further processed to yield 2,000 hL of condensed milk at additional processing costs of $270,000. Condensed milk is sold for $305 per hL.

Sales during the accounting period, May 2013, were 750 hL of buttercream and 1,930 hL of condensed milk. Exhibit 15-6 presents an overview of the basic relationships. Panel A illustrates both the basic relationships in the conversion process from raw milk into cream and liquid skim in a joint production process and the separate processing of cream into buttercream as well as liquid skim into condensed milk. Panel B provides the data for this decision.

Step 3   As Farmers' Dairy studies two alternatives to sales value at splitoff, it will compare the gross margins forecast by each method. The decision will have long-term effects on the company's profitability. The goal is to implement the method that best reflects cost flows of the actual physical process. The sell or process further decision requires no reporting to external parties of the cost of goods sold, but the economic plausibility of this forecast value is central to the future economic health of Farmers' Dairy.

Step 4   The actual data for May 2013 are the basis for forecasting how the two alternative cost allocation methods would affect the estimates of gross margin. As reported in Exhibit 15-6, Farmers' Dairy sold 750 hL, not 800 hL, of cream, leaving 50 hL in inventory. Only 1,930 hL of condensed milk was sold with 70 hL remaining in finished goods inventory at the end of May. This method provides a way to cost ending inventory, unlike either the physical measure or sales value as splitoff methods.

ESTIMATED NET REALIZABLE VALUE (NRV) METHOD

The **estimated net realizable value (NRV) method** allocates joint costs on the basis of the *relative estimated net realizable value* (expected final sales value in the ordinary course of business minus the total expected *separable* costs of production and

EXHIBIT 15-6
Farmers' Dairy: Actual Data for May 2013

PANEL A: Graphical Presentation of Processing

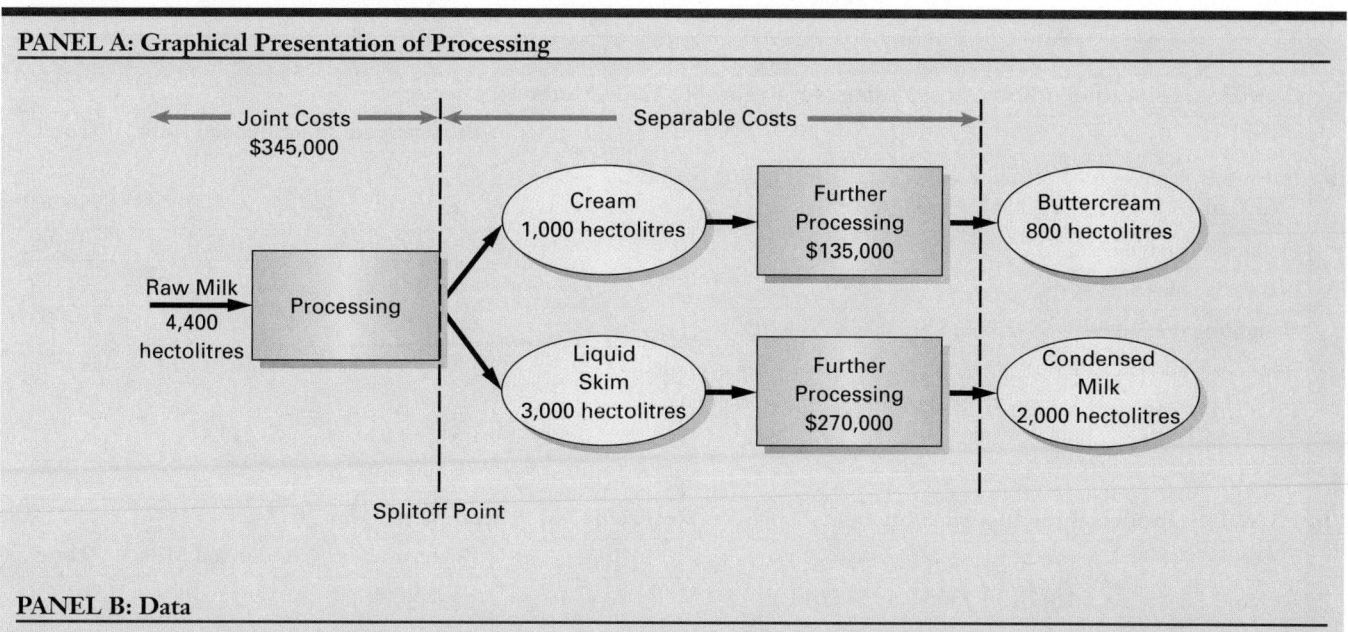

PANEL B: Data

	A	B	C	D	E
1		**Joint Costs**		**Buttercream**	**Condensed Milk**
2	Joint costs (costs of 4,400 hL fluid milk and processing to splitoff point)	$345,000			
3	Separable cost of processing 1,000 hL cream into 800 hL of buttercream			$135,000	
4	Separable cost of processing 3,000 hL liquid skim into 2,000 hL condensed milk				$270,000
5					
6		**Cream**	**Liquid Skim**	**Buttercream**	**Condensed Milk**
7	Beginning inventory (hectolitres)	0	0	0	0
8	Production (hectolitres)	1,000	3,000	800	2,000
9	Transfer for further processing (hectolitres)	1,000	3,000		
10	Sales (hectolitres)			750	1,930
11	Ending inventory (hectolitres)	0	0	50	70
12	Selling price per hectolitre	$ 155.00	$75.00	$ 420.00	$ 305.00

marketing of the total production of the period). This method is an alternative when selling prices for one or more products at splitoff do not exist. Its strength and weakness is that all upstream, production, and downstream separable costs are included in cost of goods sold. While this produces a full product cost, it is also contrary to GAAP and cannot be used for external reporting.

Exhibit 15-7 illustrates the forecast gross margins for both products. Panel A illustrates how joint costs are allocated to individual products to calculate the cost per hectolitre of buttercream and condensed milk for ending inventory valuation. Panel B presents the product-line income statement using the NRV method. Gross margin percentages are 24.8% for buttercream and 17.7% for condensed milk. The reason is that the total costs are allocated proportionally to the total estimated NRV, as shown in line 6 of the exhibit. A change in one cost element will affect both estimated proportions and be spread equally over the cost of both products.

	A	B	C	D
1	**PANEL A: Allocation of Joint Costs Using Net Realizable Value Method**			
2		**Buttercream**	**Condensed Milk**	**Total**
3	Final sales value of total production during the accounting period (800 hL × $420/hL; 2,000 hL × $305/hL)	$336,000	$610,000	$946,000
4	Deduct separable costs	135,000	270,000	405,000
5	Net realizable value at splitoff point	$201,000	$340,000	$541,000
6	Weighting ($201,000 ÷ $541,000; $340,000 ÷ $541,000)	0.37	0.63	
7	Joint costs allocated (0.37 × $345,000; 0.63 × $345,000, rounded)	$128,179	$216,821	$345,000
8	Production cost per hectolitre ([$128,179 + $135,000] ÷ 800 hL; [$216,821 + $270,000] ÷ 2,000 hL)	$ 328.97	$ 243.41	
9				
10	**PANEL B: Product-Line Income Statement Using Net Realizable Value Method for May 2013**			
11		**Buttercream**	**Condensed Milk**	**Total**
12	Revenue (750 hL × $420/hL; 1,930 hL × $305/hL)	$315,000	$588,650	$903,650
13	Cost of goods sold Joint costs (0.37 × $345,000; 0.63 × $345,000, rounded)	128,179	216,821	345,000
14	Separable costs	135,000	270,000	405,000
15	Production costs	263,179	486,821	750,000
16	Deduct ending inventory (50 hL × $328.97; 70 hL × $243.41)	(16,449)	(17,039)	(33,406)
17	Cost of goods sold	246,730	469,782	716,594
18	Gross margin	$ 68,270	$118,868	$187,056
19	Gross margin percentage (Gross margin ÷ Revenue)	21.7%	20.2%	20.7%

CONSTANT GROSS MARGIN PERCENTAGE OF NRV METHOD

The **constant gross margin percentage of NRV method** works in reverse to the estimated NRV method. For each product, the gross margin (based on the overall gross margin percentage) and total separable costs are deducted from the final sales value of units produced. The residual amount for each product is its allocation of joint costs.

This method allocates joint costs in such a way that the overall gross margin percentage is identical for all the individual products. This method entails three steps:

1. Compute the overall gross margin percentage.

2. Use the overall gross margin percentage and deduct the gross margin from the final sales values to obtain the total costs that each product should bear.

3. Deduct the expected separable costs from the total costs to obtain the joint cost allocation.

Exhibit 15-8, Panel A, illustrates these three steps for allocating the $345,000 joint costs between buttercream and condensed milk in the Farmer's Dairy example to calculate the cost per hectolitre of buttercream and condensed milk for valuation of ending inventory. Panel B presents the product-line income statement for the constant gross margin percentage NRV method. The tenuous assumption underlying this method is that all the products have the same ratio of cost to sales value. A constant ratio of cost to sales value across products is rarely seen in companies that produce multiple products but have no joint costs.

This variation on the NRV method means the gross margin percentage will be identical for each product, regardless of its separable costs. In effect, products

EXHIBIT 15-8
Farmers' Dairy Joint Costs Constant Gross Margin Percentage of NRV Allocation, May 2013

	A	B	C	D
1	**PANEL A: Allocation of Joint Costs Using Constant Gross Margin Percentage NRV Method**			
2	**Step 1**			
3	Final sales value of total production during the accounting period (800 hL × $420/hL; 2,000 hL × $305)	$946,000		
4	Deduct joint and separable costs ($345,000 + $135,000 + $270,000)	750,000		
5	Gross margin	$196,000		
6	Gross margin percentage (Gross margin ÷ Revenue)	20.719%		
7				
8	**Step 2**	**Buttercream**	**Condensed Milk**	**Total**
9	Final sales value of total production during accounting period (800 hL × $420/hL; 2,000 hL × $305)	$336,000	$610,000	$946,000
10	Deduct gross margin, using constant gross margin percentage (20.719% × $336,000; 20.719% × $610,000)	69,615	126,385	196,000
11	Total production costs	266,385	483,615	750,000
12	**Step 3**			
13	Deduct separable costs	(135,000)	(270,000)	(405,000)
14	Joint costs allocated	$131,385	$213,615	$345,000
15				
16	**PANEL B: Product-Line Income Statement Using Constant Gross Margin Percentage NRV Method for May 2013**			
17		**Buttercream**	**Condensed Milk**	**Total**
18	Revenue (750 hL × $420/hL; 1,930 hL × $305/hL)	$315,000	$588,650	$903,650
19	Cost of goods sold Joint costs (from Panel A, Step 3)	131,385	213,615	345,000
20	Separable costs	135,000	270,000	405,000
21	Production costs	266,385	483,615	750,000
22	*Deduct ending inventory (50 hL × $332.981/hL; 70 hL × $241.808)	(16,649)	(16,927)	(33,576)
23	Cost of goods sold	249,736	466,688	716,424
24	Gross margin	$ 65,264	$121,962	$187,226
25	Gross margin percentage (Gross margin ÷ Revenue)	20.7%	20.7%	20.7%
26				
27	*Total production cost of buttercream ÷ Total production of buttercream	$332.981 per hL		
28	Total production cost of condensed milk ÷ Total production of condensed milk		$241.808 per hL	

with relatively high separable costs are subsidized because they are assigned a lower proportion of joint costs. This seems counter-intuitive if the purpose of cost allocation is to avoid cross-subsidization.

COMPARISON OF METHODS

Because the costs are joint in nature, managers cannot use the cause-and-effect criterion in making this choice. Managers cannot be sure what causes what cost when examining joint costs. The purpose of the joint cost allocation is important. Consider rate regulation. Market-based measures are difficult to use in this context. It is circular to use selling prices as a basis for setting prices (rates) and at the same time use selling prices to allocate the costs on which prices (rates) are based. Physical measures represent one joint cost allocation approach appropriate for rate regulation.

In competitive markets, the benefits-received criterion leads to a preference for the sales value at splitoff point method (or other related revenue or market-based methods). Additional benefits of this method include the following:

♦ *No anticipation of subsequent management decisions.* The sales value at splitoff method does not presuppose an exact number of subsequent steps undertaken for further processing.

♦ *Availability of a meaningful common denominator to compute the weighting factors.* The denominator of the sales value at splitoff method (revenue) is an economically meaningful one. In contrast, there may be no common denominator to implement the physical measure method for all the separable products (for example, when some products are liquids and other products are solids).

♦ *Simplicity.* The sales value at splitoff method is simple. In contrast, the estimated NRV method can be very complex in operations with multiple products and multiple splitoff points. The total sales value at splitoff is unaffected by any change in the production process after the splitoff point.

However, it is not always feasible to use the sales value at splitoff method because in unregulated markets, market prices may not appear until after processing beyond the splitoff point has occurred. In fact, there may be no market for the product at splitoff and thus no sales are possible.

The NRV value method is the predominant choice. But both NRV methods can be used for joint products that have no market value at splitoff. These methods always require assumptions about the quantities or volume of product produced, the unit selling price for each product, the quantity sold, and the dollar value of total separable costs. This is not straightforward because, for example, in petrochemical plants there are alternatives among possible subsequent steps in processing after splitoff. Companies will frequently change further processing to exploit fluctuations in the separable costs of each processing stage or in the selling prices of individual products.

Under the estimated NRV method, each such change in separable costs would affect the joint cost allocation percentages symmetrically. The decrease in one product's separable cost will decrease the NRV cost allocation rate for both products. Any decrease in estimated NRV percentage for the more efficiently processed product will reflect only a portion of the cost savings. Of course, as one NRV percentage decreases, the other increases in the same amount.

Consider two chicken processing companies: Northern and West Coast. Northern classifies white breast meat as the only main product and all others are byproducts. The revenue from byproducts will reduce the main product chicken processing costs. White breast meat is often further processed into many individual products (such as trimmed chicken and marinated chicken). The separable cost of this further processing is added to the cost per kilogram of deboned white breast meat to obtain the cost of further-processed products.

West Coast classifies any product sold to a retail outlet as a joint product. Such products include breast fillets, half-breasts, thighs, whole legs, and wings. Products not sold to a retail outlet are classified as byproducts. Revenue that will be earned from byproducts is offset against the chicken-processing cost before that cost is allocated among the joint products. Average selling prices of products sold to retail outlets are used to allocate net chicken processing cost to the individual joint products. Distribution costs of transporting the chicken products from the processing plants to retail outlets are not taken into account when determining weights for joint cost allocation.[2]

Step 5: Farmers' Dairy, following common practice, would evaluate the benefits of the cost allocation system they implemented. The implementation of NRV influences the quality of information Farmers' Dairy would use to evaluate the alternatives of selling or processing further. None of the methods is GAAP-compliant and

[2]Adapted from conversations with executives of poultry firms.

there is no usefulness other than internal planning and control. The best method is the one that provides the best estimate of gross margin percentage and best helps Farmers' Dairy realize a targeted level of profitability. If using the most predominant market-based allocation method provides data inappropriate to the decision situation, then Farmers' Dairy is only impairing the quality of data used internally by selecting the simplest method, sales value at splitoff. But, if sales values do exist and Farmers' Dairy produces many types of milk product, then it may be best off using the simplest market-based method.

All the preceding joint cost allocation methods can be criticized as arbitrary and incomplete simply because they are estimates. As a result, some companies refrain from joint cost allocation entirely. Instead, they carry all inventories at estimated NRV per GAAP standards. Revenue on each product is recognized when production is completed. Accountants ordinarily criticize carrying inventories at estimated NRV because this practice contradicts the revenue recognition standard. For large numbers of rapidly changing items, the inventory value is based on a reduction to sales value minus an expected gross margin to estimate NRV (see Exhibit 15-8). This avoids treating cost of goods available for sale as if finished goods were already sold.

IRRELEVANCE OF JOINT COSTS FOR DECISION MAKING

No technique for allocating joint product costs should guide management decisions regarding whether a product should be sold at the splitoff point or processed beyond splitoff. When a product is an inevitable result of a joint process, the decision to further process should not be influenced either by the size of the total joint costs or by the portion of the joint costs allocated to particular products. The amount of joint costs incurred up to splitoff ($345,000)—and how it is allocated—is irrelevant in deciding whether to process further. The economic reality is that the joint costs of $345,000 are the same whether or not further processing is done. They do not differ between the two alternatives; therefore, they cannot influence the decision and are irrelevant.

Incremental costs are those costs that differ between the alternatives being considered (such as sell or process further). It is not always the case that all upstream, production, and downstream separable costs always differ among products. Some separable costs may also be joint—for example, the costs of distribution of pallets with combinations of products on them. In contrast, some distribution centres may choose to bear the cost of transportation for one product but not others.

SELL OR FURTHER PROCESS?

Exhibit 15-9 presents the product-line income statement with no allocation of joint costs for the sell or process further decision. The separable costs are assigned first,

EXHIBIT 15-9
Farmers' Dairy Product-Line Income Statement for May 2013: No Allocation of Joint Costs

	A	B	C	D
1		Buttercream	Condensed Milk	Total
2	Produced and sold (buttercream, 750 hL × $420/hL; 1,930 hL × $305/hL)	$315,000	$588,650	$903,650
3	Produced but not sold (buttercream 50 hL × $420/hL; 70 hL × $305/hL)	21,000	21,350	42,350
4	Total sales value of production	336,000	610,000	946,000
5	Separable costs (given)	135,000	270,000	405,000
6	Contribution to joint costs and operating income	$201,000	$340,000	541,000
7	Joint costs (given)			375,000
8	Gross margin			$166,000
9	Gross margin percentage (Gross margin ÷ Revenue)			18.4%

which highlights for managers the cause-and-effect relationship between individual products and the costs incurred to process them. The joint costs are not allocated to buttercream and condensed milk as individual products. The decision to incur additional costs beyond splitoff should be based on the incremental operating income attainable beyond the splitoff point (see Chapter 11).

The incremental analysis for these decisions to further process is as follows:[3]

	Buttercream	Condensed Milk	Total
Incremental revenue (buttercream–cream; liquid skim–condensed milk)	$191,000	$507,650	$698,650
Incremental costs (buttercream–cream; liquid skim–condensed milk)	135,000	270,000	405,000
Incremental gross margin	$56,000	$237,650	$293,650
	29.32%	46.81%	

The relevant information for Farmers' Dairy is reported in the first column of the table below. If Farmers' had incorrectly included allocated joint costs under the NRV method, and if only one product were to be processed further, then the choice would be buttercream because its gross margin is higher than condensed milk. If the correct incremental data were used, then the choice would be condensed milk, not buttercream, and the potential incremental gross margin would be far higher. By considering irrelevant costs, Farmers' Dairy would forgo a very lucrative opportunity to exploit the less lucrative one.

	Joint Cost Allocation Is Irrelevant		
	No Allocation	NRV	Constant GM
Gross margin percentage (Gross margin ÷ Revenue)	18.4%		20.7%
Buttercream		24.8%	
Condensed milk		17.7%	
Total gross margin percentage	18.4%	42.5%	20.7%

CHALLENGES FOR MANAGEMENT ACCOUNTANTS

4 Identify the strategic implications of a decision to implement one joint cost allocation method.

There is potential conflict between the cost concepts used for decision making and those used for evaluating the performance of managers. If managers make process-further or sell decisions using an incremental revenue/incremental cost approach, the resulting budgeted product-line income statement using any of the three market methods will all show each individual product budgeted to have a positive (or zero) operating income (as long as the incremental costs do not exceed the incremental revenues). In contrast, allocating joint costs using a physical measure can show a manager being responsible for one or more products budgeted to have losses, even though the company has higher operating income by producing those products in a joint-product setting.

Consider again Farmers' Dairy and the cost allocation decision between physical measure and sales value at splitoff, with the following change: The selling price per hL of liquid skim increases by 20%. This change would not affect the joint costs allocated and the cost of goods computed using the physical measure method (see Exhibit 15-4, p. 602), but it would affect the revenues of the liquid skim product. The revised product-line income statement for May 2013 using the physical measure method is shown on the next page:

---

[3]Buttercream is a further processing of cream. Cream revenue was $124,000 (Exhibit 15-4) for 500 hL at $155/hL. The NRV unit price after further processing is $420/hL and the new quantity is 750 hL, resulting in Buttercream revenue of $315,000. The difference between the Buttercream and Cream revenue is $191,000.

Overcoming the Challenges of Joint Cost Allocation

When you think of companies such as the Ganong Bros. Ltd., Maple Leaf Foods, or Petro-Canada, perhaps the first thing that comes to mind is chocolate truffles, a hot dog at a hockey game, or the high cost of gasoline. You don't think about the management accounting challenges faced daily at these companies. Unfortunately, any allocation process is arbitrary. This gives production managers, who are evaluated on process cost control, the opportunity to lobby for joint cost allocations that assign the lowest joint costs to their division. However, allocating joint costs to please one production division is rarely in the best interests of the company as a whole.

Challenges with joint cost allocations can also arise when two separate companies, such as ExxonMobil Canada and Suncor, enter into a joint venture to extract crude oil and natural gas, with one company processing primarily the crude oil and the other processing primarily the natural gas. The contract terms will spell out how joint costs of refining are to be allocated. Management accountants ensure that both parties agree to an understandable and economically plausible method. They are also licensed to audit reports to ensure adherence to the contract terms.

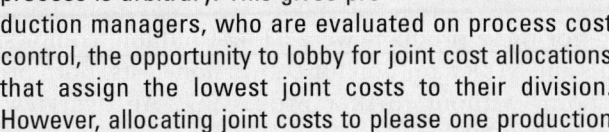

A	B	C	D
1 PANEL B: Product-Line Income Statement Using Physical Measure Method for May 2013			
2	**Cream**	**Liquid Skim**	**Total**
3 Revenues (800 hL × $155/hL; 900 hL × $90/hL)	$124,000	$81,000	$205,000
4 Cost of goods sold (joint costs)			
5 Production costs (0.25 × $345,000; 0.75 × $345,000)	86,250	258,750	345,000
6 Deduct ending inventory (200 hL × $86.25/hL; 2,100 hL × $86.25/hL)	(17,250)	(181,125)	(198,375)
7 Cost of goods sold (joint costs)	69,000	77,625	146,625
8 Gross margin	$ 55,000	$ 3,375	$ 58,375
9 Gross margin percentage (Gross margin ÷ Revenue)	44.4%	4.2%	28.5%

Under these assumptions, the budgeted profit margin for liquid skim product changes dramatically from a loss of −15.0% to a positive 4.2%. On the basis of the initial loss reported using the physical measure method, a manager who is evaluated on product-by-product gross margin information will be reluctant to process the raw milk into cream and liquid skim to avoid having to explain why liquid skim is being produced at a negative gross margin. This also obscures the opportunity to exploit added profitability from processing further into buttercream and condensed milk. Under this method, a price change, which is beyond the processing manager's control, is crucial to improving profitability. Use of a market-based joint cost allocation method avoids this situation.

ACCOUNTING FOR BYPRODUCTS

Processes that yield joint products often also yield byproducts—products that have relatively low sales value compared with the sales value of the main or joint product(s). To simplify the discussion of accounting for byproducts, consider a two-product example consisting of a main product and a byproduct.

The Westlake Corporation processes timber into fine-grade lumber and wood chips that are used as mulch in gardens and lawns. Information about these products follows:

◆ Fine-grade lumber (the main product)—sells for $505 per thousand board feet (MBF), or $0.505 per board foot
◆ Wood chips (the byproduct)—sell for $86 per oven-dried tonne

> Account for byproducts using two different methods.

Data for 2013 are as follows:

	Beginning Inventory	Production	Sales	Ending Inventory
1				
2 Fine-grade lumber, million board feet (MMBF)	0	4,000	3,950	50
3 Wood chips, thousands of oven-dried tonnes	0	700	450	250
4	**Softwood**	**Chips**		
5 Prices (per MBF, lumber, per tonne, chips)	$505	$ 86		
6	**Direct Materials**	**Conversion**	**Total**	
7 Joint manufacturing costs ($ millions)	$356	$1,068	$1,424	
8 *Note:* MBF = thousand board feet; MMBF = million board feet				

Joint manufacturing costs for these products were $1,424 million, comprising $356 million for direct materials and $1,068 million for conversion costs. Both products are sold at the splitoff point without further processing. An overview of Westlake Corporation is shown in Exhibit 15-10.

Two byproduct accounting methods will be presented. Method A (the production byproduct method) recognizes byproducts in the financial statements at the time their production is completed. Method B (the sale byproduct method) delays recognition of byproducts until the time of their sale.[4] Recognition of byproducts at the time of production is conceptually correct. Where recognition at the time of sales occurs in practice, it is usually rationalized on the grounds that the dollar amounts of byproducts are immaterial. Exhibit 15-11 presents the income statement of Westlake Corporation under both methods.

METHOD A: BYPRODUCTS ARE RECOGNIZED WHEN PRODUCTION IS COMPLETED

This method recognizes in the financial statements the byproduct—700 tonnes of wood chips—as it is produced in 2013. The estimated net realizable value from the

EXHIBIT 15-10
Overview of Westlake Corporation

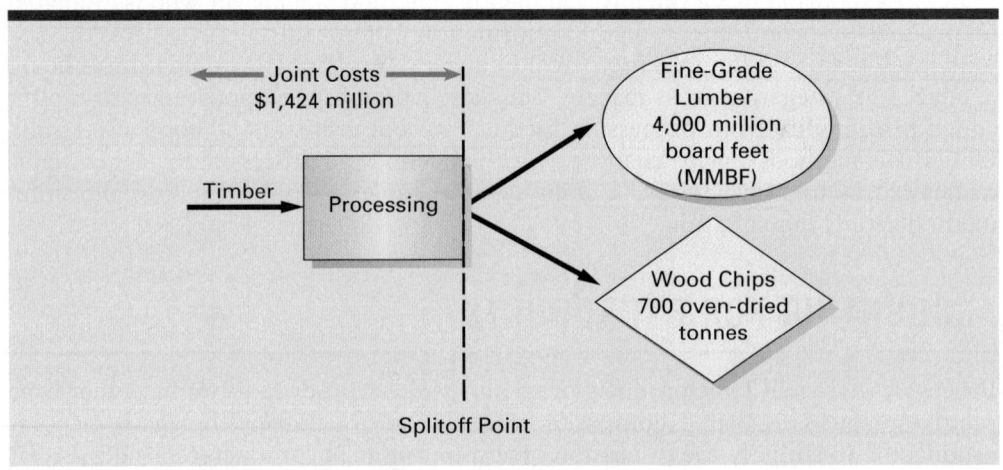

[4]Further discussion on byproduct accounting methods is in C. Cheatham and M. Green, "Teaching Accounting for Byproducts," *Management Accounting News & Views* (Spring 1988): 14–15; and D. Stout and D. Wygal, "Making Byproducts a Main Product of Discussion: A Challenge to Accounting Educators," *Journal of Accounting Education* (1989): 219–233. See also P. D. Marshall and R. F. Dombrowski, "A Small Business Review of Accounting for Primary Products, Byproducts and Scrap," *The National Public Accountant* (February/March 2003): 10–13.

EXHIBIT 15-11
Income Statements of Westlake Corporation for July 2013 Using the Production and Sales
Methods for Byproduct Accounting

	Production Method	Sales Method
Revenue (in millions)		
Main product fine-grade lumber (3,950 MMBF × $505/MBF)	$1,995	$1,995
Byproduct pulp-quality wood chips (450 tonnes × $86/tonne)	—	39
Total revenue	1,995	2,034
Cost of goods sold		
Total manufacturing costs	1,424	1,424
Deduct byproduct sales value (700 tonnes × $86/tonne)	(60)	$ —
Net manufacturing costs	1,364	1,424
Deduct main product ending inventory	(17)	(18)
Cost of goods sold	1,347	1,406
Gross margin	$ 649	$ 628
Gross margin percentage	32.5%	30.9%
Inventoriable costs (end of the period)		
Main product fine-grade lumber	$17.05[a]	$ 17.80[b]
Byproduct pulp-quality wood chips	$86.00[c]	$ 0[d]

[a]$1,364 × 50 ÷ 4,000 = $17.05
[b]$1,424 × 50 ÷ 4,000 = $17.80
[c]$86 × 250 = $21,500 total for remaining tonnes in inventory.
[d]Zero inventory value carried in books for byproduct not sold under sales method.

byproduct is offset against the costs of the main (or joint) products. The following
journal entries illustrate this method (all amounts in millions):

1. Work in Process ... $ 356
   Accounts Payable ... $ 356
   To record direct materials purchased and used in production.
2. Work in Process ... $1,068
   Various accounts ... $1,068
   To record conversion costs in the joint process during 2013; examples include energy, manufacturing supplies, all manufacturing labour, and plant amortization.
3. Byproduct Inventory: Chips ... $ 60
   Finished goods: Softwood ($1,424 − $60) ... $1,364
   Work in Process ($356 + 1,068) ... $1,424
   To record cost of goods completed during 2013.
4a. Cost of Goods Sold ... $1,347
    Finished Goods: Softwood ... $1,347
    To record the cost of the main product sold during 2013.
4b. Cash or Accounts Receivable (3,950/MMBF × $505/MBF) ... $1,995
    Revenue: Softwood ... $1,995
    To record the sale of the main product during 2013.
5. Cash or Accounts Receivable (450 × $86) ... $ 39
   Byproduct Inventory: Chips ... $ 39
   To record the sale of the byproduct during 2013.

This method reports the byproduct inventories of oven-dried wood chips on the balance sheet at their per-tonne selling price.

One variant of this method would be to report byproduct inventory at its estimated net realizable value reduced by a normal profit margin. When the byproduct inventory is sold in a subsequent period, the income statement would match the selling price with the "net" selling price reported for the byproduct inventory.

METHOD B: BYPRODUCTS ARE RECOGNIZED AT TIME OF SALE

This method makes no journal entries until sale of the byproduct occurs. Revenues of the byproduct are reported as a revenue item in the income statement at the time of sale. In the Westlake Corporation example, byproduct revenue in 2013 would be $39 million because only 450,000 tonnes of chips are sold in 2013.

All amounts in millions:

1. Work in Process	$ 356	
Accounts Payable		$ 356
To record direct materials purchased and used in production.		
2. Work in Process	$1,068	
Various accounts		$1,068
To record conversion costs in the joint process during 2013; examples include energy, manufacturing supplies, all manufacturing labour, and plant amortization.		
3. Finished Goods: Softwood	$1,424	
Work in Process ($356 + $1,068)		$1,424
To record cost of goods completed during 2013.		
4a. Cost of Goods Sold	$1,406	
Finished Goods: Softwood		$1,406
To record the cost of the main product sold during 2013.		
4b. Cash or Accounts Receivable (3,950/MMBF × $505/MBF)	$1,995	
Revenue: Softwood		$1,995
To record the sale of the main product during 2013.		
5. Cash or Accounts Receivable (450 × $86)	$ 39	
Revenue: Chips		$ 39
To record the sale of the byproduct during 2013.		

Method B is rationalized in practice primarily on the grounds that the dollar amounts of byproducts are immaterial. However, this method permits managers to "manage" reported earnings by timing when they sell byproducts. Managers may stockpile byproducts so that they have the flexibility to give revenues a "boost" at opportune times.

PULLING IT ALL TOGETHER—PROBLEM FOR SELF-STUDY

(Try to solve this problem before examining the solution that follows.)

PROBLEM

Inorganic Chemicals (IC) processes salt into various industrial products. In July 2013, IC incurred joint costs of $100,000 to purchase salt and convert it into two saleable products: caustic soda and chlorine. Although there is an active outside market for chlorine, IC processes all 800 tonnes of chlorine it produces into 500 tonnes of PVC (polyvinyl chloride), which is then sold. There were no beginning or ending inventories of salt, caustic soda, chlorine, or PVC in July. Information for July 2013 production and sales follows:

	A	B	C	D
1		**Joint Costs**		**PVC**
2	Joint costs (costs of salt and processing to splitoff point)	$100,000		
3	Separable cost of processing 800 tonnes chlorine into 500 tonnes PVC			$20,000
4				
5		**Caustic Soda**	**Chlorine**	**PVC**
6	Beginning inventory (tonnes)	0	0	0
7	Production (tonnes)	1,200	800	500
8	Transfer for further processing (tonnes)		800	
9	Sales (tonnes)	1,200	—	500
10	Ending inventory (tonnes)	0	0	0
11	Selling price per tonne in active outside market (for products not actually sold)		$ 75	
12	Selling price per tonne for products sold	$ 50		$ 200

REQUIRED

1. Allocate the joint costs of $100,000 between caustic soda and chlorine under (a) the sales value at splitoff method and (b) the physical measure method. ②
2. Allocate the joint costs of $100,000 between caustic soda and PVC under the estimated NRV method. ②
3. What is the gross margin percentage of (a) caustic soda and (b) PVC under the estimated three allocation methods? ②
4. Lifetime Swimming Pool Products offers to purchase 800 tonnes of chlorine in August 2013 at $75 per tonne. Assume all other production and sales data are the same for August as they were for July. This sale of chlorine to Lifetime would mean that no PVC would be produced by IC in August. How would accepting this offer affect IC's August 2013 operating income? ③

SOLUTION

1a. Sales value at splitoff method

	A	B	C	D
1	**Allocation of Joint Costs Using Sales Value at Splitoff Method**	**Caustic Soda**	**Chlorine**	**Total**
2	Sales value of total production at splitoff point (1,200 tonnes × $50 per tonne; 800 tonnes × $75 per tonne)	$60,000	$60,000	$120,000
3	Weighting ($60,000 ÷ $120,000; $60,000 ÷ $120,000)	0.50	0.50	
4	Joint costs allocated (0.50 × $100,000; 0.50 × $100,000)	$50,000	$50,000	$100,000

1b. Physical measures method

	A	B	C	D
1	**Allocation of Joint Costs Using Physical Measure Method**	**Caustic Soda**	**Chlorine**	**Total**
2	Physical measure of total production (tonnes)	1,200	800	2,000
3	Weighting (1,200 tonnes ÷ 2,000 tonnes; 800 tonnes ÷ 2,000 tonnes)	0.60	0.40	
4	Joint costs allocated (0.60 × $100,000; 0.40 × $100,000)	$60,000	$40,000	$100,000

2. Estimated net realizable value method

	A	B	C	D
1	**Allocation of Joint Costs Using Estimated Net Realizable Value Method**	**Caustic Soda**	**PVC**	**Total**
2	Final sales value of total production during accounting period (1,200 tonnes × $50 per tonne; 500 tonnes × $200 per tonne)	$60,000	$100,000	$160,000
3	Deduct separable costs to complete and sell	0	20,000	20,000
4	Net realizable value at splitoff point	$60,000	$ 80,000	$140,000
5	Weighting ($60,000 ÷ $140,000; $80,000 ÷ $140,000)	$\frac{3}{7}$	$\frac{4}{7}$	
6	Joint costs allocated (caustic, $\frac{3}{7}$ × $100,000; chlorine, $\frac{4}{7}$ × $100,000)	$42,857	$ 57,143	$100,000

3a. Caustic soda

	A	B	C	D
1				Estimated
2		**Sales Value**	**Physical**	**Net Realizable**
3		**at Splitoff**	**Measure**	**Value**
4	Sales	$60,000	$60,000	$60,000
5	Joint costs	50,000	60,000	42,857
6	Gross margin	$10,000	$ 0	$17,143
7	Gross margin percentage	16.67%	0%	28.57%

3b. PVC

	A	B	C	D
1				Estimated
2		**Sales Value**	**Physical**	**Net Realizable**
3		**at Splitoff**	**Measure**	**Value**
4	Sales	$100,000	$100,000	$100,000
5	Joint costs	50,000	40,000	57,143
6	Separable costs	20,000	20,000	20,000
7	Gross margin	$ 30,000	$ 40,000	$ 22,857
8	Gross margin percentage	30.00%	40.00%	22.86%

4. Incremental revenue from further processing of chlorine into PVC:

(500 tonnes × $200 per tonne) − (800 tonnes × $75 per tonne)	$40,000
Incremental costs of further processing chlorine into PVC	20,000
Incremental operating income from further processing	$20,000

The operating income of Inorganic Chemicals would be reduced by $20,000 if it sold 800 tonnes of chlorine to Lifetime Swimming Pool Products instead of further processing the chlorine into PVC for sale.

The following question-and-answer format summarizes the chapter's learning outcomes. Each point presents a key question, and the guidelines are the answer to that question.

LEARNING OUTCOMES	GUIDELINES
1. How can products be distinguished?	Products have positive sales value. Main and joint products have high total sales value at the splitoff point. A byproduct has a comparatively low total sales value at the splitoff point Products can change from byproducts to joint products when their total sales values significantly increase; they can change from joint products to byproducts when their total sales values significantly decrease. Scrap has no sales value and toxic waste has negative value. Outputs such as dirt and water from extraction industries have no sales value but are used to reclaim land.
2. What methods can be used to allocate joint costs to individual products?	The methods available to allocate joint costs to products are physical measure and sales value at splitoff. There may be no common physical measure upon which to allocate joint costs of products. There may be no market at splitoff and therefore the joint products are not saleable, although revenue would otherwise be a common measure upon which to allocate joint costs.
3. What other market-based methods can replace sales value at splitoff?	Both estimated net realizable value and constant margin percentage of net realizable value can provide a cost allocation base upon which to allocate total product costs when no market exists for joint products at splitoff. Neither method is GAAP-compliant because separable non-manufacturing costs are included in cost of goods available for sale.
4. What strategic implications arise when basing sell or process-further decisions on allocated joint costs?	Allocated joint costs are irrelevant to any sell or process-further decision. The joint costs, by definition, will not change under either alternative. Including these costs impairs the quality of information upon which this decision will be based. No internal feedback will indicate the managers have incorrectly included an irrelevant cost. In the long term, companies will miss the opportunity to process beyond splitoff and improve operating margin.
5. What methods can be used to account for byproducts?	Byproduct accounting methods differ on whether byproducts are recognized in financial statements at the time of production or at the time of sale. Recognition at the time of production is conceptually correct. Recognition at the time of sale is often used in practice because dollar amounts of byproducts are immaterial.

TERMS TO LEARN

This chapter and the Glossary at the end of the book contain definitions of the following important terms:

byproduct (p. 598)
constant gross margin percentage of
    NRV method (p. 606)
estimated net realizable value
    (NRV) method (p. 604)

joint costs (p. 598)
joint products (p. 598)
main product (p. 598)
physical measure method (p. 600)
product (p. 598)

sales value at splitoff method (p. 600)
scrap (p. 598)
separable costs (p. 598)
splitoff point (p. 598)

ASSIGNMENT MATERIAL

MyAccountingLab Make the grade with MyAccountingLab: The questions, exercises, and problems marked in red can be found on MyAccountingLab at **www.myaccountinglab.com**. You can practise them as often as you want, and most feature step-by-step guided instructions to help you find the right answer. Exercises and problems with an Excel icon in the margin have an accompanying Excel template on MyAccountingLab.

SHORT-ANSWER QUESTIONS

15-1 Give two examples of industries in which joint costs are found. For each example, what are the individual products at or beyond the splitoff point?

15-2 What is a joint cost? What is a separable cost?

15-3 Distinguish between a joint product and a byproduct.

15-4 Why might the number of products in a joint cost setting differ from the number of outputs? Give an example.

15-5 Provide three reasons for allocating joint costs to individual products or services.

15-6 Why does the sales value at splitoff method use the sales value of the total production in the accounting period and not just the sales value of the products sold?

15-7 Describe a situation in which the sales value at splitoff method cannot be used but the estimated NRV method can be used for joint cost allocation.

15-8 Distinguish between the sales value at splitoff method and the estimated NRV method.

15-9 Give two limitations of the physical measure method of joint cost allocation.

15-10 How might a company simplify its use of the estimated NRV method when the final selling prices can vary sizably in an accounting period and management makes frequent changes to the point at which it sells individual products?

15-11 Why is the constant gross margin percentage NRV method sometimes called a "joint cost and a profit allocation" method?

15-12 "Managers must decide whether a product should be sold at splitoff or processed further. The sales value at splitoff method of joint cost allocation is the best method for generating the information managers need." Do you agree? Why?

15-13 "Managers should consider only additional revenues and separable costs when making decisions about selling now or processing further." Do you agree? Why?

15-14 Describe two major methods to account for byproducts.

EXERCISES

15-15 **Terminology.** A number of terms are listed below:

byproduct	constant gross margin percentage
estimated net realizable value	joint products
main product	physical measure
product	sales value at splitoff
scrap	separable costs
splitoff point	

REQUIRED
Select the terms from the above list to complete the following sentences.

Companies provide value-added to their customers through the sale of more than one _____. A product is any output or service that can be sold for a price that recovers the total costs to bring the product to the customer plus some reasonable profit. Some products yield both a _____ with the highest sales price, a _____ that requires little if any further processing but is sold for a far lower price, and _____, which is usually unused direct materials recovered and sold for almost nothing. Two or more products of sold at a high price are called joint products. The costs of producing more than one product can be common or _____ plus _____ to complete each product. The _____ determines what pool comprises the joint costs that must be allocated on a reasonable basis. The allocation methods are _____, _____, _____, _____. The task of the management team is to select the method of joint cost allocation that best represents what actually happened in the physical production process.

15-16 **Joint cost allocation, insurance settlement.** Quality Chicken grows and processes chickens. Each chicken is disassembled into five main parts. Information pertaining to production in July 2012 is:

Parts	Kilograms of Product	Wholesale Selling Price per Kilogram When Production Is Complete
Breasts	100	$0.55
Wings	20	0.20
Thighs	40	0.35
Bones	80	0.10
Feathers	10	0.05

Joint cost of production in July 2012 was $50.

A special shipment of 40 kilograms of breasts and 15 kilograms of wings has been destroyed in a fire. Quality Chicken's insurance policy provides reimbursement for the cost of the items destroyed. The insurance company permits Quality Chicken to use a joint cost allocation method. The splitoff point is assumed to be at the end of the production process.

REQUIRED

1. Compute the cost of the special shipment destroyed using:
   a. Sales value at splitoff method.
   b. Physical measure method (kilograms of finished product).
2. What joint cost allocation method would you recommend Quality Chicken use? Explain.

15-17 Joint products and byproducts (continuation of 15-16). Quality Chicken is computing the ending inventory values for its July 31, 2012, balance sheet. Ending inventory amounts on July 31 are 15 kilograms of breasts, 4 kilograms of wings, 6 kilograms of thighs, 5 kilograms of bones, and 2 kilograms of feathers.

⑤

1. Wings ending inventory, $0.49

Quality Chicken's management wants to use the sales value at splitoff method. However, they want you to explore the effect on ending inventory values of classifying one or more products as a byproduct rather than a joint product.

REQUIRED

1. Assume Quality Chicken classifies all five products as joint products. What are the ending inventory values of each product on July 31, 2012?
2. Assume Quality Chicken uses the production method of accounting for byproducts. What are the ending inventory values for each joint product on July 31, 2012, assuming breasts and thighs are the joint products and wings, bones, and feathers are byproducts?
3. Comment on differences in the results in requirements 1 and 2.

15-18 Usefulness of joint cost allocation. Roundtree Chocolates manufactures and distributes chocolate products. It purchases cocoa beans and processes them into two intermediate products:
◆ Chocolate powder liquor base.
◆ Milk chocolate liquor base.

②

1. Chocolate-powder liquor base weighting, 0.35

These two intermediary products become separately identifiable at a single splitoff point. Every 500 kilograms of cocoa beans yields 20 four-litre containers of chocolate powder liquor base and 30 four-litre containers of milk chocolate liquor base.

The chocolate powder liquor base is further processed into chocolate powder. Every 20 containers of chocolate powder liquor base yields 200 kilograms of chocolate powder. The milk chocolate liquor base is further processed into milk chocolate. Every 30 containers of milk chocolate liquor base yields 340 kilograms of milk chocolate.

The following is an overview of the manufacturing operations at Roundtree Chocolates:

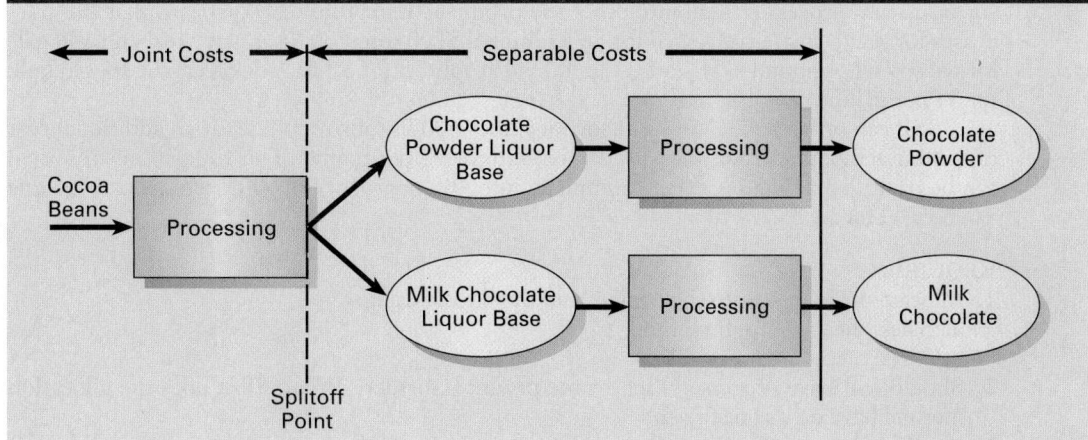

Production and sales data for August 2013 are as follows:

◆ Cocoa beans processed, 5,000 kilograms.
◆ Costs of processing cocoa beans to splitoff point (including purchase of beans) = $12,000.

	Production	Sales	Unit Selling Price
Chocolate powder	2,000 kilograms	2,000 kilograms	$4.80 per kilogram
Milk chocolate	3,400 kilograms	3,400 kilograms	$6.00 per kilogram

The August 2013 separable costs of processing chocolate powder liquor base into chocolate powder are $5,100. The August 2013 separable costs of processing milk chocolate liquor base into milk chocolate are $10,500.

Roundtree fully processes both of its intermediate products into chocolate powder or milk chocolate. There is an active market for these intermediate products. In August 2013, Roundtree could have sold chocolate powder liquor base for $25.20 a container and milk chocolate liquor base for $31.20 a container.

REQUIRED

1. Calculate how the joint costs of $12,000 would be allocated between chocolate powder liquor base and milk chocolate liquor base under each of the following methods: (a) sales value at splitoff, (b) physical measure (containers), (c) estimated NRV, and (d) constant gross margin percentage NRV.
2. What is the gross margin percentage of chocolate powder and milk chocolate under methods (a), (b), (c), and (d) in requirement 1?
3. Could Roundtree Chocolates have increased its operating income by a change in its decision to fully process both of its intermediate products?

1. Weighting for
turpentine, 0.75

15-19 Irrelevance of joint costs. The Wood Spirits Company produces two products, turpentine and methanol (wood alcohol), by a joint process. Joint costs amount to $144,000 per batch of output. Each batch totals 40,000 litres: 25% methanol and 75% turpentine. Both products are processed further without gain or loss in volume. Separable processing costs are methanol, $0.90 per litre; turpentine, $0.60 per litre. Methanol sells for $6.30 per litre. Turpentine sells for $4.20 per litre.

REQUIRED

1. How much joint cost per batch should be allocated to turpentine and to methanol, assuming that joint costs are allocated on a physical measure (number of litres at splitoff point) basis?
2. If joint costs are to be assigned on an NRV basis, how much joint cost should be assigned to turpentine and to methanol?
3. Prepare product-line income statements per batch for requirements 1 and 2. Assume no beginning or ending inventories.
4. The company has discovered an additional process by which the methanol (wood alcohol) can be made into laboratory ethanol. The selling price of this product would be $18 a litre. Additional processing would increase separate costs $2.70 per litre (in addition to the $0.90 per litre separable cost required to yield methanol). The company would have to pay excise taxes of 20% on the selling price of the product. Assuming no other changes in cost, what is the joint cost applicable to the ethanol (using the NRV method)? Should the company produce the ethanol? Show your computations.

1. Weighting, cookies,
soymeal, 0.556

15-20 Joint cost allocation: sell immediately or process further. Iowa Soy Products (ISP) buys soy beans and processes them into other soy products. Each tonne of soy beans that ISP purchases for $300 can be converted for an additional $200 into 500 lbs of soy meal and 100 gallons of soy oil. A pound of soy meal can be sold at splitoff for $1 and soy oil can be sold in bulk for $4 per gallon.

ISP can process the 500 lbs of soy meal into 600 lbs of soy cookies at an additional cost of $300. Each pound of soy cookies can be sold for $2 per pound. The 100 gallons of soy oil can be packaged at a cost of $200 and made into 400 quarts of Soyola. Each quart of Soyola can be sold for $1.25.

REQUIRED

1. Allocate the joint cost to the cookies and the Soyola using:
   a. Sales value at splitoff method.
   b. NRV method.
2. Should ISP have processed each of the products further? What effect does the allocation method have on this decision?

15-21 Net realizable value method. Convad Company is one of the world's leading corn refiners. It produces two joint products, corn syrup and corn starch, using a common production process.

In July 2013, Convad reported the following production and selling price information:

	Corn Syrup	Corn Starch	Joint Costs
Joint costs (costs of processing corn to splitoff point)			$325,000
Separable cost of processing beyond splitoff point	$375,000	$93,750	
Beginning inventory (cases)	0	0	
Production and sales (cases)	12,500	6,250	
Ending inventory (cases)	0	0	
Selling price per case	$50	$25	

REQUIRED
Allocate the $325,000 joint costs using the NRV method.

Joint costs allocated to corn starch, $65,000

15-22 Joint cost allocation, sales value, physical measure, NRV methods. Instant Foods produces two types of microwavable products—beef-flavoured ramen and shrimp-flavoured ramen. The two products share common inputs such as noodles and spices. The production of ramen results in a waste product referred to as stock, which Instant dumps at negligible costs in a local drainage area. In June 2013, the following data were reported for the production and sales of beef-flavoured and shrimp-flavoured ramen:

1. Special B joint costs allocated, $60,000

	Joint Costs
Joint costs (costs of noodles, spices, and other inputs and processing to splitoff point)	$240,000

	Beef Ramen	Shrimp Ramen
Beginning inventory (tonnes)	0	0
Production (tonnes)	10,000	20,000
Sales (tonnes)	10,000	20,000
Selling price per tonne	$10	$15

Due to the popularity of its microwavable products, Instant decides to add a new line of products that targets dieters. These new products are produced by adding a special ingredient to dilute the original ramen and are to be sold under the names Special B and Special S, respectively. The monthly data for all the products follow:

	Joint Costs	Special B	Special S
Joint costs (costs of noodles, spices, and other inputs and processing to splitoff point)	$240,000		
Separable costs of processing 10,000 tonnes of beef ramen into 12,000 tonnes of Special B		$48,000	
Separable cost of processing 20,000 tonnes of shrimp ramen into 24,000 tonnes of Special S			$168,000

	Beef Ramen	Shrimp Ramen	Special B	Special S
Beginning inventory (tonnes)	0	0	0	0
Production (tonnes)	10,000	20,000	12,000	24,000
Transfer for further processing (tonnes)	10,000	20,000		
Sales (tonnes)			12,000	24,000
Selling price per tonne	$10	$15	$18	$25

REQUIRED
1. Calculate Instant's gross margin percentage for Special B and Special S when joint costs are allocated using:
   a. Sales value at splitoff method.
   b. Physical measure method.
   c. Net realizable value method.

2. Recently, Instant discovered that the stock it is dumping can be sold to cattle ranchers at $5 per tonne. In a typical month with the production levels shown above, 4,000 tonnes of stock are produced and can be sold by incurring marketing costs of $10,800. Sherrie Dong, a management accountant, points out that in treating the stock as a joint product and using the sales value at splitoff method the stock product would lose about $2,228 each month, so it should not be sold. How did Dong arrive at that final number, and what do you think of her analysis? Should Instant sell the stock?

1. a. Crude oil joint costs
allocated, $270

15-23 Joint cost allocation, process further. Sinclair Oil & Gas, a large energy conglomerate, jointly processes purchased hydrocarbons to generate three nonsaleable intermediate products: ICR8, ING4, and XGE3. These intermediate products are further processed separately to produce Crude Oil, Natural Gas Liquids (NGL), and Natural Gas (measured in liquid equivalents). An overview of the process and results for August 2013 is shown here. (*Note:* The numbers are small to keep the focus on key concepts.)

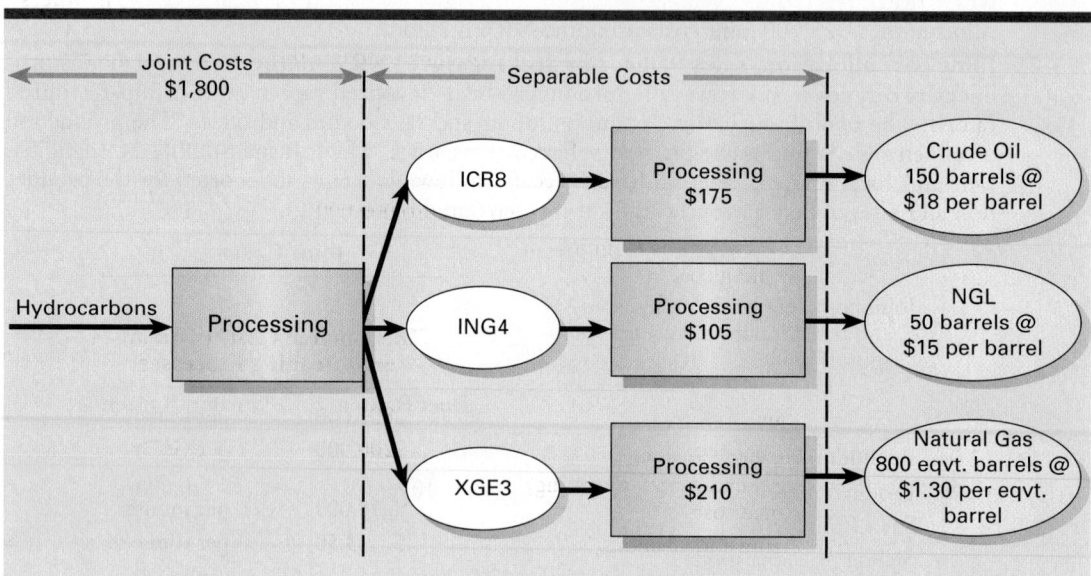

A federal law has recently been passed that taxes crude oil at 30% of operating income. No new tax is to be paid on natural gas liquid or natural gas. Starting August 2013, Sinclair Oil & Gas must report a separate product-line income statement for crude oil. One challenge facing Sinclair Oil & Gas is how to allocate the joint cost of producing the three separate saleable outputs. Assume no beginning or ending inventory.

REQUIRED
1. Allocate the August 2013 joint cost among the three products using:
   a. Physical measure method.
   b. NRV method.
2. Show the operating income for each product using the methods in requirement 1.
3. Which, if any, method would you use for product emphasis? Explain.
4. Draft a letter to the taxation authorities on behalf of Sinclair Oil & Gas that justifies the joint cost allocation method you recommend Sinclair use.

1. Weight for Z, 0.15

15-24 Alternative methods of joint cost allocation, ending inventories. The Darl Company operates a simple chemical process to convert a single material into three separate items, referred to here as X, Y, and Z. All three end products are separated simultaneously at a single splitoff point.

Products X and Y are ready for sale immediately upon splitoff without further processing or any other additional costs. Product Z, however, is processed further before being sold. There is no available market price for Z at the splitoff point.

The selling prices quoted here are expected to remain the same in the coming year. During 2013, the selling prices of the items and the total amounts sold were:

◆ X—120 tonnes sold for $1,500 per tonne.
◆ Y—340 tonnes sold for $1,000 per tonne.
◆ Z—475 tonnes sold for $700 per tonne.

The total joint manufacturing costs for the year were $400,000. Darl spent an additional $200,000 to finish product Z.

There were no beginning inventories of X, Y, or Z. At the end of the year, the following inventories of completed units were on hand: X, 180 tonnes; Y, 60 tonnes; Z, 25 tonnes. There was no beginning or ending work in process.

1. Compute the cost of inventories of X, Y, and Z for balance sheet purposes and the cost of goods sold for income statement purposes as of December 31, 2013, using the following joint cost allocation methods:
   a. NRV method.
   b. Constant gross margin percentage NRV method.
2. Compare the gross margin percentages for X, Y, and Z using the two methods given in requirement 1.

15-25 **Process further or sell, byproduct.** (CMA, adapted) Newcastle Mining Company (NMC) mines coal, puts it through a one-step crushing process, and loads the bulk raw coal onto river barges for shipment to customers.

1. Incremental costs, $73,900,000

   NMC's management is currently evaluating the possibility of further processing the raw coal by sizing and cleaning it and selling it to an expanded set of customers at higher prices. The option of building a new sizing and cleaning plant is ruled out as being financially infeasible. Instead, Amy Kimbell, a mining engineer, is asked to explore outside contracting arrangements for the cleaning and sizing process. Kimbell puts together the following summary:

Selling price of raw coal	$27	per tonne
Cost of producing raw coal	$22	per tonne
Selling price of sized and cleaned coal	$36	per tonne
Annual raw coal output	10,000,000	tonnes
Percentage of material weight loss in sizing/cleaning coal	6%	

	Incremental Costs of Sizing and Cleaning Processes	
Direct labour	$800,000	per year
Supervisory personnel	$200,000	per year
Heavy equipment: rental, operating, maintenance costs	$ 25,000	per month
Contract sizing and cleaning	$ 3.50	per tonne of raw coal
Outbound rail freight	$ 240	per 60-tonne rail car

   Kimbell also learns that 75% of the material loss that occurs in the cleaning and sizing process can be salvaged as coal fines, which can be sold to steel manufacturers for their furnaces. The sale of coal fines is erratic and NMC may need to stockpile it in a protected area for up to one year. The selling price of coal fines ranges from $15 to $24 per tonne and costs of preparing coal fines for sale range from $2 to $4 per tonne.

1. Prepare an analysis to show whether it is more profitable for NMC to continue selling raw bulk coal or to process it further through sizing and cleaning. (Ignore coal fines in your analysis.)
2. How would your analysis be affected if the cost of producing raw coal could be held down to $20 per tonne?
3. Now consider the potential value of the coal fines and prepare an addendum that shows how their value affects the results of your analysis prepared in requirement 1.

15-26 **Accounting for a main product and a byproduct.** (Cheatham and Green, adapted) Yum Inc. is a producer of potato chips. A single production process at Yum Inc. yields potato chips as the main product and a byproduct that can also be sold as a snack. Both products are fully processed by the splitoff point, and there are no separable costs.

1. Total revenues under sales method, $668,000

   For September 2013, the cost of operations is $480,000. Production and sales data are as follows:

	Production (in kg)	Sales (in kg)	Selling Price per kg
Main product: Potato chips	40,000	32,000	$20
Byproduct	8,000	5,600	$ 5

There were no beginning inventories on September 1, 2013.

1. What is the gross margin for Yum Inc. under the production method and the sales method of byproduct accounting?
2. What are the inventory costs reported in the balance sheet on September 30, 2013, for the main product and byproduct under the two methods of byproduct accounting in requirement 1?

15-27 Joint costs and byproducts. (W. Crum) Royston Inc. is a large food processing company. It processes 120,000 kilograms of peanuts in the Peanuts Department at a cost of $160,000 to yield 10,000 kilograms of product A, 60,000 kilograms of product B, and 20,000 kilograms of product C.

♦ Product A is processed further in the Salting Department to yield 10,000 kilograms of salted peanuts at a cost of $20,000 and sold for $10 per kilogram.
♦ Product B (Raw Peanuts) is sold without further processing at $2 per kilogram.
♦ Product C is considered a byproduct and is processed further in the Paste Department to yield 20,000 kilograms of peanut butter at a cost of $10,000 and sold for $3 per kilogram.

The company wants to make a gross margin of 10% of revenues on product C and needs to allow 25% of revenues for marketing costs on product C. An overview of operations follows:

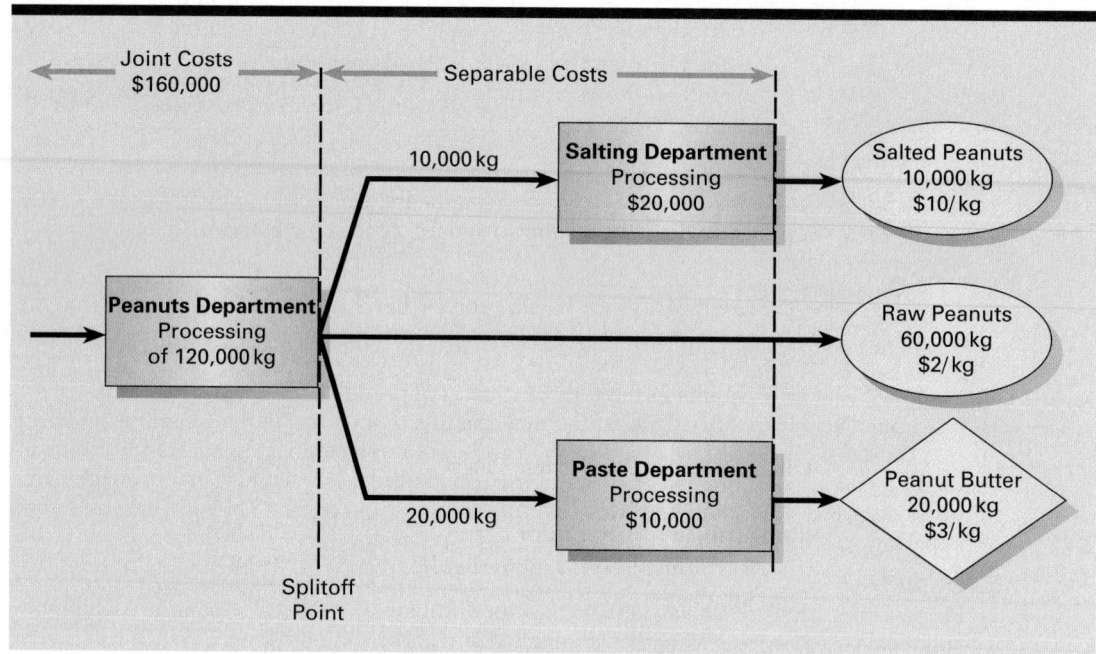

REQUIRED
1. Compute unit costs per kilogram for products A, B, and C, treating C as a byproduct. Use the NRV method for allocating joint costs. Deduct the NRV of the byproduct produced from the joint cost of products A and B.
2. Compute unit costs per kilogram for products A, B, and C, treating all three as joint products and allocating joint costs by the NRV method.

15-28 Byproduct, disposal costs, governance. Chemtech Chemicals, a multinational company, has a subsidiary located in a small East European country. The country has only a few environmental protection laws, and even those that exist are not strictly enforced. The subsidiary's three major products emerge at splitoff point from a common input. The joint costs are allocated to each product using the sales values at splitoff method. In addition to the three joint products, another product that emerges at splitoff point is a hazardous material. The hazardous material can be dumped into the Gulf at zero cost to the company. Alternatively, it can be processed further and sold as a cleaning liquid.

The cost accountant responsible for joint cost allocation presented the following comparative analysis to you, the controller:

	Alternatives	
	Dump in the Gulf	**Process Further**
Revenue	$0	$ 600,000
Costs:		
Further processing	0	360,000
Allocated joint costs	0	300,000
Marketing and distribution	0	60,000
Total costs	0	720,000
Net realizable value	$0	$(120,000)

REQUIRED

1. Comment on the comparative analysis prepared by the cost accountant purely from a financial perspective. Show any supporting computations.
2. Assume, regardless of your conclusion in requirement 1, that adopting the process-further alternative would lead to a decrease in the company's operating income. Disposal of the hazardous waste in a manner different than dumping it into the Gulf would also be costly. Discuss the legal and ethical implications of dumping the hazardous material into the Gulf.

15-29 **Joint cost allocation, process further or sell.** (CMA, adapted) Sonimad Sawmill Inc. (SSI) purchases logs from independent timber contractors and processes the logs into three types of lumber products:

1. a. Joint costs allocated to posts, $307,692

◆ Studs for residential buildings (walls, ceilings).
◆ Decorative pieces (fireplace mantels, beams for cathedral ceilings).
◆ Posts used as support braces (mine support braces, braces for exterior fences on ranch properties).

These products are the result of a joint sawmill process that involves removal of bark from the logs, cutting the logs into a workable size, and then cutting the individual products from the logs.

The joint process results in the following costs of products for a typical month:

Direct materials (rough timber logs)	$ 500,000
Debarking (labour and overhead)	50,000
Sizing (labour and overhead)	200,000
Product cutting (labour and overhead)	250,000
Total joint costs	$1,000,000

Product yields and average sales values on a per-unit basis from the joint process are as follows:

Product	Monthly Output of Materials at Splitoff Point	Fully Processed Selling Price
Studs	75,000 units	$ 8
Decorative pieces	5,000 units	100
Posts	20,000 units	20

The studs are sold as rough-cut lumber after emerging from the sawmill operation without further processing by SSI. Also, the posts require no further processing beyond the splitoff point. The decorative pieces must be planed and further sized after emerging from the sawmill. This additional processing costs $100,000 per month and normally results in a loss of 10% of the units entering the process. Without this planing and sizing process, there is still an active intermediate market for the unfinished decorative pieces in which the selling price averages $60 per unit.

1. Based on the information given for Sonimad Sawmill, allocate the joint processing costs of $1,000,000 to the three products using:
   a. Sales value at splitoff method
   b. Physical measure method (volume in units)
   c. NRV method
2. Prepare an analysis for Sonimad Sawmill that compares processing the decorative pieces further, as they currently do, with selling them as a rough-cut product immediately at splitoff.
3. Assume Sonimad Sawmill announced that in six months it will sell the unfinished decorative pieces at splitoff due to increasing competitive pressure. Identify at least three types of likely behaviour that will be demonstrated by the skilled labour in the planing-and-sizing process as a result of this announcement. Include in your discussion how this behaviour could be influenced by management.

PROBLEMS

1. Gross margin percentage method A, 41.4%

15-30 Accounting for byproducts—Advanced. (Cheatham and Green, adapted) Bill Dundee is the owner and operator of Western Bottling, a bulk soft-drink producer. A single production process yields two bulk soft drinks, Rainbow Dew (the main product) and Resi-Dew (the byproduct). Both products are fully processed at the splitoff point, and there are no separable costs.

Summary data for September 2013 are as follows:

◆ Cost of soft-drink operations = $144,000
◆ Production and sales data:

	Production (in Litres)	Sales (in Litres)	Selling Price per Litre
Main product (Rainbow Dew)	10,000	8,000	$24.00
Byproduct (Resi-Dew)	2,000	1,400	2.40

There were no beginning inventories on September 1, 2013. The following is an overview of operations:

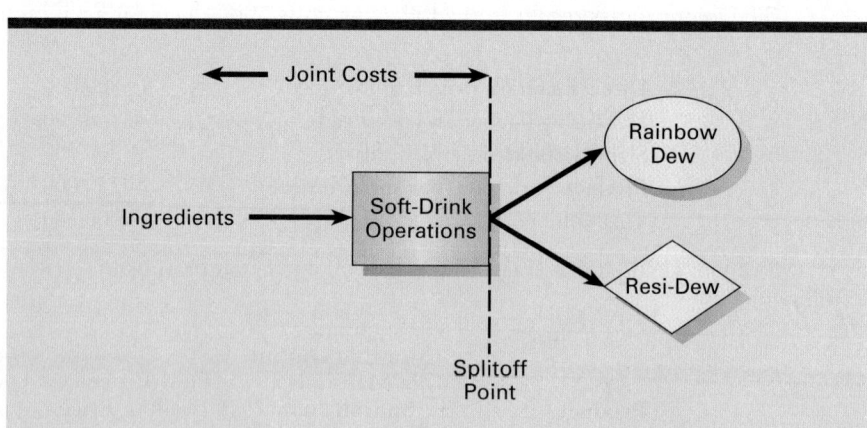

REQUIRED

1. What is the gross margin for Western Bottling under methods A and B of byproduct accounting?
2. What are the inventory amounts reported in the balance sheet on September 30, 2010, for Rainbow Dew and Resi-Dew under each of the two methods of byproduct accounting cited in requirement 1?
3. Which method would you recommend Western Bottling use? Explain.

2

1. Joint cost allocation for product C, 0.25

15-31 Alternative methods of joint cost allocation, product-mix decisions. The Sunshine Oil Company buys crude vegetable oil. Refining this oil results in four products at the splitoff point: A, B, C, and D. Product C is fully processed by the splitoff point. Products A, B, and D can individually be further refined into Super A, Super B, and Super D. In the most recent month (December), the output at the splitoff point was:

◆ Product A, 300,000 litres.
◆ Product B, 100,000 litres.
◆ Product C, 50,000 litres.
◆ Product D, 50,000 litres.

The joint costs of purchasing and processing the crude vegetable oil were $100,000. Sunshine had no beginning or ending inventories. Sales of product C in December were $50,000. Products A, B, and D were further refined and then sold. Data related to December are:

	Separable Processing Costs to Make Super Products	Sales
Super A	$200,000	$300,000
Super B	80,000	100,000
Super D	90,000	120,000

Sunshine had the option of selling products A, B, and D at the splitoff point. This alternative would have yielded the following revenues for the December production:

◆ Product A, $50,000.
◆ Product B, $30,000.
◆ Product D, $70,000.

REQUIRED
1. Compute the gross margin percentage for each product sold in December, using the following methods for allocating the $100,000 joint costs:
   a. Sales value at splitoff.
   b. Physical measure.
   c. NRV.
2. Could Sunshine have increased its December operating income by making different decisions about the further processing of products A, B, or D? Show the effect on operating income of any changes you recommend.

15-32 **Joint cost allocation, relevant costs.** (R. Capettini, adapted) Consider the following scenario. Each day, a butcher buys a 200-kilogram pig for $360. The pig can be processed to yield the following three products:

2. Joint costs allocated to Ham, $130.43

	Selling Price per kg	Weight (kg)
Pork chops	$4.80	30
Ham	$3.60	50
Bacon	$1.44	120
		200

Day 1 The butcher buys a pig. The $360 joint cost of the pig is allocated to individual products based on the relative weights of the products.

	Selling Price	Weight (kg)	Revenues	−	Joint Costs Allocated	=	Operating Income
Pork chops	$4.80	30	$144.00	−	$ 54.00	=	$ 90.00
Ham	3.60	50	180.00	−	90.00	=	90.00
Bacon	1.44	120	172.80	−	216.00	=	(43.20)
			$496.80	−	$360.00	=	$136.80

Day 2   The butcher buys an identical pig and throws out the bacon because it has been shown to lose money. She now has 80 kilograms of "good output."

	Selling Price	Weight (kg)	Revenues	−	Joint Costs Allocated	=	Operating Income
Pork chops	$4.80	30	$144.00	−	$135.00	=	$ 9.00
Ham	3.60	50	180.00	−	225.00	=	(45.00)
			$324.00	−	$360.00	=	$(36.00)

Day 3 The butcher buys an identical pig and throws out the ham and the bacon because they have been shown to lose money. She now has 30 kilograms of "good output."

	Selling Price	Weight (kg)	Revenues	−	Joint Costs Allocated	=	Operating Income
Pork chops	$4.80	30	$144.00	−	$360.00	=	$(216.00)
			$144.00	−	$360.00	=	$(216.00)

Day 4 The butcher buys an identical pig and throws out the whole pig because each product has been shown to lose money. Therefore, she loses $360.

REQUIRED

1. Comment on the preceding series of decisions.
2. How would the joint costs be allocated to all three products using the sales value at splitoff method?
3. Should the operating income numbers from requirement 2 be used to determine whether the butcher is better off by selling or not selling individual products? Explain briefly.

15-33 Accounting for a byproduct. West-Coast Oceanic Water (WOW) desalinates and bottles sea water. The desalinated water is in high demand from a large group of environmentally conscious people on the west coast of Canada. During March, WOW processes 1,000 litres of sea water and obtains 800 litres of drinking water and 50 kilograms of sea salt (the rest of the sea water evaporates in the desalinization process). Processing the 1,000 litres of water costs WOW $1,500. WOW sells 600 litres of the desalinated water in 2-litre containers for $8 per container. In addition, WOW sells 40 kilograms of sea salt for $1.20 per kilogram. Due to the relatively small proportion of sea salt, WOW has decided to treat it as a byproduct.

1. Inventoriable cost of main product, $3.60 per container

REQUIRED

1. Assuming WOW accounts for the byproduct using the production method, what is the inventoriable cost for each product and WOW's gross margin?
2. Assuming WOW accounts for the byproduct using the sales method, what is the inventoriable cost for each product and WOW's gross margin?
3. Discuss the difference between the two methods of accounting for byproducts.

15-34 Joint cost allocation. Elsie Dairy Products Corp buys one input, full-cream milk, and refines it in a churning process. From each gallon of milk, Elsie produces two cups (one pound) of butter and two quarts (eight cups) of buttermilk. During May 2012, Elsie bought 10,000 gallons of milk for $15,000. Elsie spent another $5,000 on the churning process to separate the milk into butter and buttermilk. Butter could be sold immediately for $2 per pound and buttermilk could be sold immediately for $1.50 per quart.

1. a. Joint costs allocated to butter, $4,000

Elsie chooses to process the butter further into spreadable butter by mixing it with canola oil, incurring an additional cost of $0.50 per pound. This process results in two tubs of spreadable butter for each pound of butter processed. Each tub of spreadable butter sells for $2.50.

REQUIRED

1. Allocate the $20,000 joint cost to the spreadable butter and the buttermilk using:
   a. Physical measure method (using cups) of joint cost allocation.
   b. Sales value at splitoff method of joint cost allocation.
   c. NRV method of joint cost allocation.
   d. Constant gross margin percentage NRV method of joint cost allocation.
2. Each of these measures has advantages and disadvantages; what are they?
3. Some claim that the sales value at splitoff method is the best method to use. Discuss the logic behind this claim.

15-35 Further-processing decision (continuation of 15-34). Elsie has decided that buttermilk may sell better if it were marketed for baking and sold in pints. This would involve additional packaging at an incremental cost of $0.25 per pint. Each pint could be sold for $0.90. (*Note:* 1 quart = 2 pints.)

1. Process further NRV—butter, $45,000

1. If Elsie uses the sales value at splitoff method, what combination of products should Elsie sell to maximize profits?
2. If Elsie uses the physical measure method, what combination of products should Elsie sell to maximize profits?
3. Explain the effect that the different cost allocation methods have on the decision to sell the products at splitoff or to process them further.

15-36 Joint cost allocation with a byproduct. The Cumberland Mine is a small mine that extracts coal in central Alberta. Each tonne of coal mined is 40% Grade A coal, 40% Grade B coal, and 20% coal tar. All output is sold immediately to a local utility. In May, Cumberland mined 1,000 tonnes of coal. It spent $10,000 on the mining process. Grade A coal sells for $100 per tonne. Grade B coal sells for $60 per tonne. Cumberland gets one-quarter of a vat of coal tar from each tonne of coal tar processed. The coal tar sells for $60 per vat. Cumberland treats Grade A and Grade B coal as joint products, and treats coal tar as a byproduct.

⑤

1. Joint costs to be charged to joint products, $7,000

REQUIRED

1. Assume that Cumberland allocates the joint costs to Grade A and Grade B coal using the sales value at splitoff method and accounts for the byproduct using the production method. What is the inventoriable cost for each product and Cumberland's gross margin?
2. Assume that Cumberland allocates the joint costs to Grade A and Grade B coal using the sales value at splitoff method and accounts for the byproduct using the sales method. What is the inventoriable cost for each product and Cumberland's gross margin?
3. Discuss the difference between the two methods of accounting for byproducts, focusing on what conditions are necessary to use each method.

15-37 Byproduct-costing journal entries (continuation of 15-36). Cumberland's accountant needs to record the information about the joint products and byproducts in the general journal, but is not sure what the entries should be. Cumberland Mines has hired you as a consultant to help its accountant.

⑤

1. DR WIP inventory, 10,000; CR A/P, etc., 10,000

REQUIRED

1. Show journal entries at the time of production and at the time of sale assuming Cumberland accounts for the byproduct using the production method.
2. Show journal entries at the time of production and at the time of sale assuming Cumberland accounts for the byproduct using the sales method.

15-38 Accounting for a byproduct. Sanjana's Silk Shirts (SSS) hand-makes blouses and sells them to high-end department stores. SSS buys bolts of silk for $300 each. Out of each bolt it gets 30 blouses, which it sells for $90 each. SSS's new manager has suggested taking the scraps left after cutting out the blouses and using them to make scarves. By carefully cutting the blouses, SSS can produce 6 scarves from each bolt, which it can sell for $25 each. During September, SSS buys 50 bolts of silk and spends an additional $10,000 on the cutting and sewing process. By the end of the month, SSS sells 1200 blouses and 260 scarves made from these bolts. Because the scarves are lower in value than the blouses, SSS decides to treat the scarves as a byproduct.

⑤

1. Inventoriable cost of main product, $11.67 per blouse

REQUIRED

1. Assuming SSS accounts for the byproduct using the production method, what is the inventoriable cost of each product and SSS's gross margin?
2. Assuming SSS accounts for the byproduct using the sales method, what is the inventoriable cost of each product and SSS's gross margin?
3. Show all journal entries for the month of September assuming SSS accounts for the byproduct using (a) the production method and (b) the sales method.

15-39 Estimated net realizable value method, byproducts. (CMA, adapted) The Princess Corporation grows, processes, packages, and sells three joint apple products: (a) sliced apples that are used in frozen pies, (b) applesauce, and (c) apple juice. The skin of the apple, processed as animal feed, is treated as a byproduct. Princess uses the estimated NRV method to allocate costs of the joint process to its joint products. The byproduct is inventoried at its selling price when produced; the net realizable value of the byproduct is used to reduce the joint production costs before the splitoff point. Details of Princess's production process are presented here:

①

1. a. Net kilograms of juice, 67,500 kg

◆ The apples are washed and the skin is removed in the Cutting Department. The apples are then cored and trimmed for slicing. The three joint products and the byproduct are recognizable after processing in the Cutting Department. Each product is then transferred to a separate department for final processing.

- The trimmed apples are forwarded to the Slicing Department, where they are sliced and frozen. Any juice generated during the slicing operation is frozen with the slices.
- The pieces of apple trimmed from the fruit are processed into applesauce in the Crushing Department. The juice generated during this operation is used in the applesauce.
- The core and any surplus apple pieces generated from the Cutting Department are pulverized into a liquid in the Juicing Department. There is a loss equal to 8% of the weight of the good output produced in this department.
- The outside skin is chopped into animal feed and packaged in the Feed Department. It can be kept in cold storage until needed.

A total of 270,000 kilograms of apples entered the Cutting Department during November. The following schedule shows the costs incurred in each department, the proportion by weight transferred to the four final processing departments, and the selling price of each end product.

Processing Data and Costs, November 2013

Departments	Costs Incurred	Proportion Transferred to Department	Selling Price per Kilogram of Final Product
Cutting	$ 72,000		
Slicing	13,536	33%	$0.96
Crushing	10,260	30	0.66
Juicing	3,600	27	0.48
Feed	840	10	0.12
Total	$100,236	100%	$2.22

REQUIRED

1. The Princess Corporation uses the estimated NRV method to determine inventory cost of its joint products; byproducts are reported on the balance sheet at their selling price when produced. For the month of November 2013, calculate the following:
   a. The output for apple slices, applesauce, apple juice, and animal feed, in kilograms.
   b. The estimated NRV at the splitoff point for each of the three joint products.
   c. The amount of the cost of the Cutting Department assigned to each of the three joint products and the amount assigned to the byproduct in accordance with corporate policy.
   d. The gross margins in dollars for each of the three joint products.
2. Comment on the significance to management of the gross margin dollar information by joint product for planning and control purposes, as opposed to inventory costing purposes.

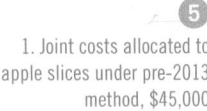

1. Joint costs allocated to apple slices under pre-2013 method, $45,000

15-40 Joint product/byproduct distinctions, governance (continuation of 15-39). The Princess Corporation classifies animal feed as a byproduct. The byproduct is inventoried at its selling price when produced; the net realizable value of the product is used to reduce the joint production costs before the splitoff point. Before 2013, Princess classified both apple juice and animal feed as byproducts. These byproducts were not recognized in the accounting system until sold. Revenues from their sale were treated as a revenue item at the time of sale.

The Princess Corporation uses a "management by objectives" basis to compensate its managers. Every six months, managers are given "stretch" operating-income-to-revenue ratio targets. They receive no bonus if the target is not met and a fixed amount if the target is met or exceeded.

REQUIRED

1. Assume that Princess managers aim to maximize their bonuses over time. What byproduct method (the pre-2013 method or the 2013 method) would the manager prefer?
2. How might a controller gain insight into whether the manager of the Apple Products division is "abusing" the accounting system in an effort to maximize his or her bonus?
3. Describe an accounting system for the Princess Corporation that would reduce "gaming" behaviour by managers with respect to accounting rules for byproducts.

COLLABORATIVE LEARNING CASES

15-41 Usefulness of joint cost allocation. In the United States, organ procurement organizations (OPOs), transplant centres, and the medical professions coordinate the organ donation process. The U.S. government pays for this treatment through its Medicare program.

What price should the U.S. government pay for these organs from the taxes it collects from all citizens? Often multiple organs are removed from a single donor, meaning that there are joint costs such as operating room time, surgeons' fees, and medications to preserve the organs. The OPOs insist all costs be allocated to each organ, irrespective of whether the organ is actually collected for transplant. For example, lung and kidney donations may be planned, but the surgeon discovers post-mortem that the lungs are not viable. A portion of joint costs will still be assigned to the lungs; otherwise, total costs of the donation would be assigned to the kidneys.

The payer, the U.S. government, does not want to pay the joint costs assigned to the lungs. The Medicare program pays only for transplanted organs. Over 62% of all kidney transplants are paid for by Medicare. Six years ago, a government audit revealed that, of the total of $80 million in organ acquisition costs, $47 million were unallowable and unsupported.*

Some organs, such as one kidney, part of a liver, part of a lung, bone marrow, and stem cells, can be recovered from live donors. The recovery of these organs requires major surgery and patients are anaesthetized. The surgeon ensures the donor's organs are suffused with a protective chemical and removes the organ. The donated organ is preserved in a chemical and placed in a refrigerated container for immediate transport. The donor often recovers after two to five days in hospital.

In contrast, stem cells are recovered from live donors who receive medication to increase the number of stem cells in the blood for four to five days prior to the transplant. The process is similar to a blood donation. The stem cells are extracted from whole blood removed intravenously from the donor's arm. The rest of the blood is returned to the donor while the stem cells are sealed in plastic packs, placed in a special container, and transported to the recipient. The donor usually returns home to rest for the remainder of the day before resuming normal life. The stem cells are injected intravenously into the recipient's arm.

REQUIRED

Form groups of two or more students to complete the following requirements.
1. Of the reasons to use acceptable methods to allocate joint costs, which ones are relevant in this case?
2. What costs are incurred beyond the splitoff point that differ between these two types of donations?
3. What would the separable costs be?
4. In Canada, where all medically necessary care is paid for from tax revenue, of what relevance is joint cost allocation?

15-42 **Joint cost allocation.** Memory Manufacturing Company (MMC) produces memory modules in a two-step process: chip fabrication and module assembly.

1. a. Total production costs of deluxe model, $19,694

In chip fabrication, each batch of raw silicon wafers yields 500 standard chips and 500 deluxe chips. Chips are classified as standard or deluxe on the basis of their density (the number of memory bits on each chip). Standard chips have 500 memory bits per chip, and deluxe chips have 1,000 memory bits per chip. Joint costs to process each batch are $24,000.

In module assembly, each batch of standard chips is converted into standard memory modules at a separately identified cost of $1,000 and then sold for $8,500. Each batch of deluxe chips is converted into deluxe memory modules at a separately identified cost of $1,500 and then sold for $25,000.

REQUIRED

1. Allocate joint costs of each batch to deluxe modules and standard modules using (a) the NRV method, (b) the constant gross margin percentage NRV method, and (c) the physical measure method, based on the number of memory bits. Which method should MMC use?
2. MMC can process each batch of 500 standard memory modules to yield 400 DRAM modules at an additional cost of $1,600. The selling price per DRAM module would be $26. Assume MMC uses the physical measure method. Should MMC sell the standard memory modules or the DRAM modules?

*Sources: Department of Health and Human Services Centers for Medicare & Medicaid Services, "Ruling No.: CMS-1543-R," December 21, 2006; Department of Health and Human Services, Office of Inspector General, "Review of Organ Acquisition Costs Claimed by Certified Transplant Centers (A-09-05-00034)," September 28, 2006; and Jim Warren, "CMS Enforcement of Rule Covering Organ Acquisition Fees Could Shut Down Some OPOs, Transplant Centers," Transplant News, April 28, 2003.

Revenue and Customer Profitability Analysis

BUSINESS MATTERS

Revenue

Royalty contracts are by and large revenue-sharing contracts. Oil companies pay a percentage of revenue to governments from whom they lease mineral development rights. Publishers pay royalties to their authors. Recording companies pay royalties to recording artists. The creative content of $2.8 billion blockbusters like *Avatar* rewards their creators with a percentage of that revenue, a royalty. Profitable authors are retained to create more products; others are not.

Government, too, allocates tax revenue to different ministries. In specific cases, such as gambling revenue, the government allocates contracted amounts to non-profit service organizations. The achievements of these non-profits are then measured by government relative to commitments the organizations have made. The government will continue to fund those which are effective and meet their commitments.

LEARNING OUTCOMES

After studying this chapter, you should be able to

1. Select a method and allocate revenue from a product bundle to its distinct components.

2. Apply an ABC system to allocate costs when the customer is the cost object.

3. Calculate and interpret four levels of revenue variance analyses.

4. Generate a customer profitability profile.

5. Analyze relevant profitability data and decide whether to drop or add customers or branches.

1 Select a method and allocate revenue from a product bundle to its distinct components.

Revenues are inflows of assets (almost always cash or accounts receivable) received for products or services provided to customers. Just as costs can be allocated to specific products, services, customers, or some other more relevant cost object, so too can revenues. **Revenue allocation** occurs when revenues must be assigned to distinct types of sales, but it is not economically feasible to trace the revenue (which would result in a more accurate assignment of revenues to products). The more accurate the assignment of revenue, the more reliable and relevant is the information on which many new product introductions and product-mix decisions are made.

Revenue allocation is a way to reflect the economic reality that revenue is a pool generated by the sale of distinct product and service bundles in a corporate portfolio. Companies combine or create bundles of outputs to generate more value-added for customers without incurring added costs. In this way, the bundle responds to the desire for a customized product and at the same time provides the supplier with economies of scale.

Governments also use revenue-allocation formulas to distribute tax revenue to various social welfare programs such as university education and health care. Government determination of how revenue is allocated will make a significant difference to people who require those services. For example, the allocation of casino

CONCEPTS IN ACTION — GOVERNANCE

Revenue Allocation by the Government and First Nations

First Nations casinos on reserves in Alberta are regulated under the Alberta Gaming and Liquor Commission (AGLC). Gaming licence fees pay for the commission's operating costs. Net of winnings paid, commissions, and a percentage paid to the federal government, the Alberta Lottery Fund (ALF) and the First Nations Development Fund Grant Program (FNDF) share the proceeds from slot machines. In 2009–2010, total proceeds from casinos was $234 million, of which some were First Nations casinos (see the first pie chart).

The government transfers responsibility and control of 30% of revenue distribution back to the FNDF. The AGLC retains the other 70%. The revenue flowing from gaming to First Nations groups is considered charitable gaming proceeds. The government regulates how these proceeds

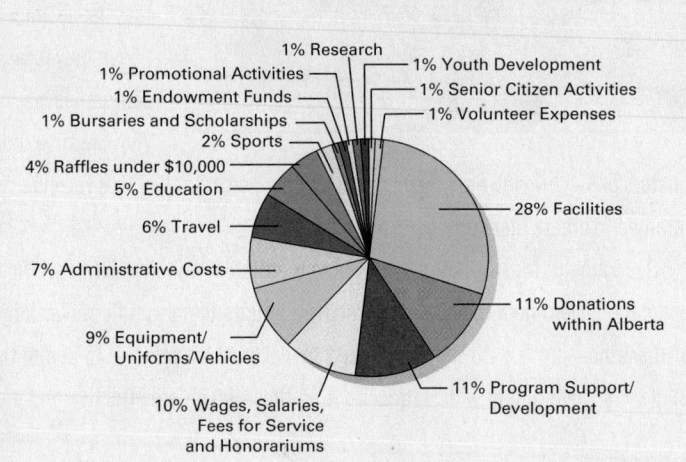

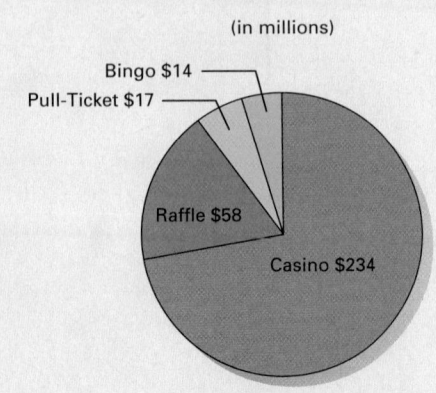

should be allocated by the First Nations groups. The second pie-chart illustrates the distribution by First Nations groups to safety, addiction treatment, subsidized housing and services, seniors and elder support, cultural events, and life skills training.

Source: Alberta Gaming Research Institute, "Revenue Allocation," May 1, 2007, www.abgaminginstitute.ualberta.ca/Alberta_casinos_ revenue_ allocation.cfm, accessed March 23, 2009; Alberta Gaming Research Institute, "Quick Facts — Gaming," www.gaming.gov.ab.ca/pdf/ quickfacts/quickfacts_gaming.pdf, accessed March 23, 2009; http://www. aglc.ca/pdf/charitable_gaming/2008_2009_charitable_gaming_report.pdf, accessed October 19, 2010; http://www.aglc.ca/pdf/charitable_gaming/ 2009_2010_charitable_gaming_report.pdf, accessed May 4, 2011, pp. 1, 14.

revenue retained by one First Nations band in Alberta illustrates how allocation can affect individuals in a group. The band retains about 30% of total casino revenue net of prizes paid out. This band then makes quarterly payments to its eligible beneficiaries, those social welfare agencies approved for funding by the government.

Internal revenue allocation arises when companies sell product bundles. A **product bundle** is a combination of two or more products or services sold together for a single price. For example, Cogeco bundles its high-speed Internet access with its HD converter and land-line telephone service at a price lower than that for which each service is sold separately (refer to the opening of Chapter 14). The price is set to meet the customer's expectation of value-added, especially when competition is intense and companies are price takers.

The single price for the bundled product is typically less than the sum of the prices of the products in the bundle, should they be purchased separately. The company can be very profitable when a lower price drives higher consumer demand that requires a higher volume of production. Economies of scale mean that the increased production gives rise to a lower unitized cost per output, which improves the company's gross margin percentage.

DECIDING ON A REVENUE-ALLOCATION METHOD

Where individual department or division managers have revenue or profit responsibilities for individual products, the issue is how to *fairly* allocate the bundled revenue amount among the individual products in the bundle. Let's look at an example. SG Company develops, sells, and supports three software packages both individually and as bundled products:

1. *WordMaster.* Current version is WordMaster 5.0, which was released 36 months ago. WordMaster was the company's initial product.

2. *SpreadMaster.* Current version is SpreadMaster 3.0, which was released 18 months ago.

3. *FinanceMaster.* Current version is FinanceMaster 2.0. This product, the company's most recent addition, has been its most successful. The 2.0 version was released 2 months ago.

SG's management team must decide how to allocate revenue from its bundled product ("suite") sales. The team will decide between the stand-alone and incremental revenue allocation methods. The team should choose the method that best reflects the economic reality of how much revenue each component generates. For internal purposes, the more representationally faithful the method, the higher the quality of information SG will have to make other operating decisions. SG's reliable MIS provides ready access to data for both unit prices and costs:

Product	Sales Price	Manufacturing Cost per Unit
Stand-alone		
WordMaster	$125	$18
SpreadMaster	150	20
FinanceMaster	225	25
Suite		
Word + Spread	$220	
Word + Finance	280	
Finance + Spread	305	
Word + Finance + Spread	380	

The managers are keenly interested in individual-product profitability figures because they operate separate profit centres for each product. Their performance evaluation and remuneration depend on profits at or larger than predicted (budgeted). SG's Software Department engineers are also organized on an individual product basis and receive a bonus based on percentage of product profitability. It is straightforward for managers to predict that if the revenue per unit decreases when their products are sold in a bundle, with no other change, their profit will decrease along with their remuneration. Strategically, bundling products can increase overall corporate profitability, but that is only one decision criterion.

As we learned in Chapter 13, the balanced scorecard indicates that retention of knowledgeable and competent managers directly reduces recruitment and training costs. If managers believe the method is unfair, they can simply walk out SGs door. Their knowledge of effective and efficient sales practices as well as software development could benefit some competitor. In addition, good managers encourage and nourish loyalty among customers and often software engineers are needed to troubleshoot customer service issues. Customers' loyalty can often be to a sales manager or to an engineer. In a competitive environment where there are many substitutes, the customer could follow the person and simply purchase the competitor's product.

Taking nonfinancial factors like these into account makes the revenue-allocation decision difficult. We will explain the stand-alone and incremental methods, which are the two alternatives from which SG's management team can choose. Each method is analogous to cost allocation methods discussed in Chapter 14. After choosing, SG will obtain feedback on how well actual performance met expectations. In this way, they can learn how to improve performance and align incentives in more appropriately.

STAND-ALONE REVENUE-ALLOCATION METHODS

The **stand-alone revenue-allocation method** is a weighted-average method. SG will use *product*-specific information about products in the bundle to determine the weights used to allocate the bundled revenues to each distinct product. The term *stand-alone* refers to the product as a separate (nonsuite) item. There are alternative ways to calculate the weights, unit sales price, unit manufacturing costs, physical units, and total revenue per product in the bundle. Consider the Word and Finance suite, which sells for $280:

1. *Selling prices.* The unit sales prices are $125 for WordMaster and $225 for FinanceMaster. The individual price of the component is calculated as a percentage of product bundle revenue. Then the percentage is multiplied by the product bundle price of $280 to assign the product-bundle revenue to each component:

$$\text{Word:} \quad \frac{\$125}{\$125 + \$225} \times \$280 = 0.357 \times \$280 = \$100$$

$$\text{Finance:} \quad \frac{\$225}{\$125 + \$225} \times \$280 = 0.643 \times \$280 = \$180$$

This method recognizes the different contribution to revenue made by each unit, but fails to recognize any difference in pricing policies or strategic classification of each product. One may be a commodity while the other may be a differentiated product. One may be the result of target pricing while the other may be the result of cost-plus.

2. *Unit manufacturing costs.* The individual *costs* are $18 for Word and $25 for Finance. The individual cost of the component is calculated as a percentage of product-bundle cost. Then the percentage is multiplied by the product bundle price of $280 to assign the product bundle revenue to each component:

$$\text{Word:} \quad \frac{\$18}{\$18 + \$25} \times \$280 = 0.419 \times \$280 = \$117$$

$$\text{Finance:} \quad \frac{\$25}{\$18 + \$25} \times \$280 = 0.581 \times \$280 = \$163$$

This method will only be as reliable as the costing system used at SG; otherwise, SG runs the risk of unintentional cross-subsidization. Traditional single overhead cost pool systems fail to reliably assign shared costs when there is unequal benefit to distinct products. One product will be overcosted and the other undercosted.

3. *Physical units.* This method gives each product unit in the suite the same weight when allocating suite revenue to individual products. The SG bundle of Word plus Finance suite will weight each product 50% to allocate revenue of $280:

$$\text{Word:} \quad \frac{1}{1+1} \times \$280 = 0.50 \times \$280 = \$140$$

$$\text{Finance:} \quad \frac{1}{1+1} \times \$280 = 0.50 \times \$280 = \$140$$

This method has the benefit of simplicity, but it is not sensible if the products in a bundle have wildly different unit sales prices. For example, selling a bundle comprising a dishwasher plus a box of detergent and then allocating the revenue per bundle 50/50 overprices the allocated detergent revenue and underallocates the dishwasher revenue. The disproportionate amount of cost compared to the revenue generated by the sale of a box of detergent is what makes this method inappropriate for this product bundle. This method would also be inappropriate when the retailer bundles special insurance with the product because the components of the bundle are not both physical units.

4. *Stand-alone product revenues.* Stand-alone total product revenues will capture the quantity of each product sold as well as their selling prices. Assume that the stand-alone revenues are WordMaster, $28 million; SpreadMaster, $15 million; and FinanceMaster, $7 million. The weights for the Word and Finance suites would be:

$$\text{Word:} \quad \frac{\$28 \text{ million}}{\$28 \text{ million} + \$7 \text{ million}} \times \$280 = 0.80 \times \$280 = \$224$$

$$\text{Finance:} \quad \frac{\$7 \text{ million}}{\$28 \text{ million} + \$7 \text{ million}} \times \$280 = 0.20 \times \$280 = \$56$$

Assume the lower revenue allocation to FinanceMaster is, in part, due to it being released in mid-year. The unit selling price weights are the best available external indicator distinguishing different benefit received from selling each distinct product. Market-based weighting places the distinct products in their external competitive context, which is consistent with a cost leadership strategy.

These four approaches to determining weights with the stand-alone method yield the following revenue allocations to individual products:

Revenue-Allocation Weights	WordMaster	FinanceMaster
Selling prices	$100	$180
Unit manufacturing costs	117	163
Physical units	140	140
Stand-alone product revenues	224	56

If SG has a cost-plus pricing policy, then unit manufacturing costs may be the best choice. If SG has a target pricing policy, then stand-alone product revenues may be the best choice. Each choice will be consistent with internal pricing policies. The method that honestly reflects the economic reality of what each product contributes to SG's profitability, consistent with the competitive intensity and SG's strategy, will guide the management decision.

INCREMENTAL REVENUE-ALLOCATION METHOD

The **incremental revenue-allocation method** ranks the individual products in a bundle and then uses this ranking to allocate the bundled revenues to these individual products. The first-ranked product is termed the *primary product* in the bundle, the second-ranked product is termed the *first incremental product*, the third-ranked product is the *second incremental product*, and so on.

How is the ranking of products in the incremental revenue-allocation method determined? One approach is to survey customers on the relative importance of individual products in their decision to purchase the bundled products. A second approach is to use internal data on recent stand-alone performance of the individual products in the bundle. A third approach is for top management to decide the rankings based on their knowledge or intuition.

Consider again the pricing of the Word and Finance suite. Assume WordMaster is designated as the primary product. If the suite revenue exceeds the stand-alone revenue of the primary product, the primary product is allocated 100% of its stand-alone revenue. This is the case for the Word and Finance suite. The suite revenue of $280 exceeds the stand-alone revenue of $125 for WordMaster; WordMaster is allocated revenues of $125, with the remaining or residual revenue of $155 ($280 – $125) allocated to FinanceMaster:

Product	Revenue Allocated	Cumulative Revenue Allocated
WordMaster	$125	$125
FinanceMaster ($280 – $125)	155	$280
Total	$280	

Clearly, the ranking of the individual products in the suite is a key factor in determining the revenues allocated to individual products. Under the incremental revenue-allocation method, all users of the revenue object want to be the first-ranked user, because the first-ranked user will be allocated a larger portion of the revenues. If FinanceMaster were the primary product, the revenue allocated would be $225 (stand-alone sales price), not $155, and WordMaster would be allocated $55, not $125. The differences between these two allocations are material for managers who may be paid on the basis of new revenue generated or total revenue generated. This is called a **zero-sum game**, which is where what one gains the other loses. This is another example where the purpose of allocation must be clear and one allocation method is not satisfactory to achieve all purposes.

If SG sells equal quantities of WordMaster and FinanceMaster, then the *Shapley value* method allocates the average of the revenues allocated as the primary and first incremental products:

$$\text{WordMaster:} \quad \frac{\$125 + \$55}{2} = \$180 \div 2 = \$90$$

$$\text{FinanceMaster:} \quad \frac{(\$225 + \$155)}{2} = \$380 \div 2 = \$190$$

$$\text{Total} \qquad\qquad\qquad = \$280$$

But what if, in the most recent quarter, SG sells 80,000 units of WordMaster and 20,000 units of FinanceMaster? Because SG sells four times as many units of WordMaster, its managers believe that the sales of the Word + Finance suite are four times more likely to be driven by WordMaster as the primary product. The *weighted Shapley value* method takes this into account by weighting the revenue allocations when WordMaster is the primary product four times as much as when FinanceMaster is the primary product:

$$\text{WordMaster:} \quad \frac{(\$125 \times 4 + \$55 \times 1)}{(4 + 1)} = \frac{\$555}{5} = \$111$$

$$\text{FinanceMaster:} \quad \frac{(\$225 \times 1 + \$155 \times 4)}{(4 + 1)} = \frac{\$845}{5} = \$169$$

$$\text{Total} \qquad\qquad\qquad\qquad = \$280$$

When there are more than two products in the suite, the incremental revenue-allocation method allocates suite revenues sequentially. Assume WordMaster is the primary product in SG's three-product suite (Word + Finance + Spread). FinanceMaster is the first incremental product, and SpreadMaster is the second incremental product. This suite sells for $380. The allocation of the $380 suite revenues proceeds as follows:

Product	Revenue Allocated	Cumulative Revenue Allocated
WordMaster	$125	$125
FinanceMaster ($280 − $125)	155	$280 (price of Word + Finance suite)
SpreadMaster ($380 − $280)	100	$380 (price of Word + Finance + Spread suite)
Total	$380	

Now suppose WordMaster is the primary product, SpreadMaster is the first incremental product, and FinanceMaster is the second incremental product:

Product	Revenue Allocated	Cumulative Revenue Allocated
WordMaster	$125	$125
SpreadMaster ($220 − $125)	95	$220 (price of Word + Spread suite)
FinanceMaster ($380 − $220)	160	$380 (price of Word + Spread + Finance suite)
Total	$380	

The ranking of the individual products in the suite determines the revenues allocated to them. Product managers at SG would likely differ on how they believe their individual products contribute to sales of the suite products. It is possible that each product manager would claim to be responsible for the primary product in the Word + Finance + Spread suite!

Calculating the *Shapley value* mitigates this problem because each product is considered as a primary, first-incremental, and second-incremental product. Assuming equal weights on all products, the revenue allocated to each product is an average of the revenues calculated for each product under these different assumptions: FinanceMaster, $180; WordMaster, $87.50; and SpreadMaster, $112.50:

Order			Revenues Allocated to Each Product		
Primary	**First Incremental**	**Second Incremental**	**FinanceMaster**	**WordMaster**	**SpreadMaster**
FinanceMaster	WordMaster	SpreadMaster	$225	$ 55 ($280 − $225)	$100 ($380 − $225 − $55)
FinanceMaster	SpreadMaster	WordMaster	$225	$ 75 ($380 − $225 − $80)	$ 80 ($305 − $225)
WordMaster	FinanceMaster	SpreadMaster	$155 ($280 − $125)	$125	$100 ($380 − $125 − $155)
WordMaster	SpreadMaster	FinanceMaster	$160 ($380 − $125 − $95)	$125	$ 95 ($220 − $125)
SpreadMaster	FinanceMaster	WordMaster	$155 ($305 − $150)	$ 75 ($380 − $150 − $155)	$150
SpreadMaster	WordMaster	FinanceMaster	$160 ($380 − $150 − $70)	$ 70 ($220 − $150)	$150
Total:			$1,080	$525	$675
Average Revenue Allocated:			$1,080 ÷ 6 = $180	$525 ÷ 6 = $87.50	$675 ÷ 6 = $112.50

Because the stand-alone revenue-allocation method does not require rankings of individual products in the suite, this method is less likely to cause debates among product managers. An inappropriate method will bias and degrade the usefulness of internal information for decision making. In the design of a defensible internal control system, it is essential to assess allocation method choices to ensure good corporate governance.

None of the methods, however, changes the economic reality that any bundled suite of products will generate a lower unit sales price per product than the revenue generated when products are sold individually. The techniques of revenue allocation fail to resolve the incentives problem. SG must encourage managers to accept and willingly promote sales of the suite, which aligns with corporate profitability even at the expense of maximizing their personal remuneration. Otherwise, the gain in corporate profit will be very short-term as the best managers and software engineers leave SG to work for its competitors.

OTHER REVENUE-ALLOCATION METHODS

Management's judgment is an alternative method of revenue allocation. The difficulty is ensuring the method is defensible by the CEO and CFO, who must provide written assurance of the quality of internal control. The president of one software company decided to issue a set of revenue-allocation weights because the managers of the three products in the bundle could not agree.

The factors the president considered included stand-alone selling prices (all three were very similar), stand-alone unit sales (A and B were over 10 times more than C), product ratings by independent experts, and consumer awareness. The Product C manager complained that his 10% weighting dramatically short-changed the contribution of Product C to suite revenues. The president responded that its inclusion in the suite greatly increased consumer exposure to Product C, with the result that Product C's total revenues would be far larger (even with only 10% of suite revenues) than had it not been included in the suite at all.

ABC: THE COST OBJECT IS THE CUSTOMER

2 Apply an ABC system to allocate costs when the customer is the cost object.

Managers solve problems—where there are no problems there is no need to manage anything. We have assumed for our next example that the company Spring Distribution, which sells bottled water, has decided upon a cost leadership strategy. The management team at Spring Distribution makes decisions as they receive feedback on how successfully they have implemented their cost leadership strategy. Managing profit requires the management team to make decisions on an ongoing basis to implement strategy in response to important internal and external changes in an intensely competitive context.

Spring Distribution has two distinct distribution channels: (1) a wholesale distribution channel, in which the wholesaler sells to supermarkets, drugstores, and other stores, and (2) a retail distribution channel for a small number of business customers. Consistent with its cost leadership strategy, the company has an ABC system. The system has improved the management team's understanding of how the overhead costs of shared resources can be assigned proportionally to benefits provided to each distinct customer service.

The MIS can also provide data that enables Spring Distribution to assign the overhead cost pools proportionally to the benefits received by its customers. By selecting the customer as a cost object, the management team can rank their customers in order of total costs to provide services to each. We begin by analyzing ABC customer cost assignment, then proceed to revenue analysis to determine customer profitability. The cost object is neither an output nor an activity but rather a customer. The desired outcome is profit maximization, and ultimately the management team will have the data required to rank the profitability of each customer.

CUSTOMER ABC ANALYSIS

Chapters 5 and 14 discussed the *cost hierarchy* concept, in which costs are categorized into different cost pools. Each cost pool arises from shared use of common resources (overhead). The beneficiaries sharing the resources can be distinguished because they do not share equally. The cost allocation base or cost driver for each cost pool measures the amount of benefit received. An ABC system where the customer is the cost object classifies shared costs into five categories:

◆ *Customer output unit-level costs*—costs of activities to sell each output unit to a customer. An example for Spring is product-handling costs of each case sold.
◆ *Customer batch-level costs*—costs of activities that are related to a group of units (cases) sold to a customer. Examples are costs incurred to process orders or to make Spring's two types of deliveries.
◆ *Customer-sustaining costs*—costs of activities to support individual customers, regardless of the number of units or batches of product delivered to the customer. Examples are the downstream costs of visits to customers or costs of displays at customer sites after Spring's distribution activity.
◆ *Distribution-channel costs*—costs of activities related to a particular distribution channel rather than to each unit of product, each batch of product, or specific customers. An example is the salary of the manager of Spring's retail distribution channel.
◆ *Corporate-sustaining costs*—costs of activities that cannot be traced to individual customers or distribution channels. Examples are top-management and general-administration costs.

Spring uses its customer-cost hierarchy to assist managers in decisions made at different levels in this hierarchy. We will now consider decisions made at the individual customer level. Note from these descriptions that four of the five levels of Spring's cost hierarchy closely parallel the cost hierarchy described in Chapter 5, except that Spring focuses on *customers*, whereas the cost hierarchy in Chapter 5 focused on *products*. Spring has one additional cost hierarchy category—distribution-channel costs, for the costs it incurs to support its wholesale and retail distribution channels.

First consider customer revenues. Data from Spring Distribution's MIS for four customers are reported for June 2013 in Exhibit 16-1. These data suggest that Spring Distribution should track future sales to customer G to confirm that the $1.20-per-case discount translates into higher future sales. Managers find customer profitability analysis useful for several reasons. First, it frequently highlights how vital a small set of customers is to total profitability. Managers need to ensure that the interests of these customers receive high priority. Microsoft uses the phrase "not all revenue dollars are endowed equally in profitability" to stress this key point. Second, when a customer is ranked in the "loss category," managers can focus on ways to make future business with this customer more profitable.

Spring is particularly interested in analyzing customer-level indirect costs that are incurred in the first three categories of the customer-cost hierarchy: customer output unit-level costs, customer batch-level costs, and customer-sustaining costs. Spring believes that it can work with customers to reduce these costs. It believes that customer actions will have less impact on distribution-channel and corporate-sustaining costs.

EXHIBIT 16-1
Customer Profitability Analysis for Four Customers of Spring Distribution for June 2013

	A	B	C	D	E
1		CUSTOMER			
2		A	B	G	J
3	Units sold	42,000	33,000	2,900	2,500
4	List selling price	$ 14.40	$ 14.40	$ 14.40	$ 14.40
5	Price discount	$ 0.96	$ 0.24	$ 1.20	$ —
6	Invoice price	$ 13.44	$ 14.16	$ 13.20	$ 14.40
7	Revenues (Row 3 × Row 6)	$564,480	$467,280	$38,280	$36,000

The five activity areas used to collect costs for selling-related costs, cost drivers, and rates are as follows:

Activity Area	Cost Rate and Driver	Cost Hierarchy Category
Product handling	$0.50 per case sold	Customer output-unit-level costs
Order taking	$ 100 per purchase order	Customer batch-level costs
Delivery vehicles	$ 2 per delivery kilometre travelled	Customer batch-level costs
Rush deliveries	$ 300 per expedited delivery	Customer batch-level costs
Visits to customers	$ 80 per sales visit	Customer-sustaining costs

The table below provides information on the quantity of cost driver consumed or used by each customer:

	Customer			
	A	B	G	J
Number of purchase orders	30	25	15	10
Number of deliveries	60	30	20	15
Kilometres travelled per delivery	5	12	20	6
Number of rush deliveries	1	—	2	—
Number of visits to customers	6	5	4	3

Spring Distribution can use the information on ABC in Exhibit 16-2 to assist its customers in reducing their consumption of the cost drivers. Consider a comparison of Customer G with Customer A: Customer G's total purchases (2,900 cases) is only 7% the size of Customer A's total purchases (42,000 cases). Customer G, however, requires one-half the number of purchase orders, two-thirds the number of visits, one-third the number of deliveries, and double the number of rush deliveries. To improve the profitability of Customer G, Spring must encourage this customer to request fewer customer visits and rush deliveries as well as larger but fewer purchases.

EXHIBIT 16-2
Customer Profitability Analysis for Four Customers of Spring Distribution for June 2013

	A	B	C	D	E
1			CUSTOMER		
2		A	B	G	J
3	Revenues at list price: $14.40 × 42,000; 33,000; 2,900; 2,500	$604,800	$475,200	$41,760	$36,000
4	Price discount: $0.96 × 42,000; $0.24 × 33,000; $1.20 × 2,900; $0 × 2,500	40,320	7,920	3,480	—
5	Revenues at actual price	564,480	467,280	38,280	36,000
6	Cost of goods sold: $12 × 42,000; 33,000; 2,900; 2,500	504,000	396,000	34,800	30,000
7	Gross margin	60,480	71,280	3,480	6,000
8	Customer-level operating costs				
9	Product handling: $0.50 × 42,000; 33,000; 2,900; 2,500	21,000	16,500	1,450	1,250
10	Order taking: $100 × 30; 25; 15; 10	3,000	2,500	1,500	1,000
11	Delivery vehicles: $2 × (5 × 60); (12 × 30); (20 × 20); (6 × 15)	600	720	800	180
12	Rush deliveries: $300 × 1; 0; 2; 0	300	—	600	—
13	Visits to customers: $80 × 6; 5; 4; 3	480	400	320	240
14	Total customer-level operating costs	25,380	20,120	4,670	2,670
15	Customer-level operating income	$ 35,100	$ 51,160	$(1,190)	$ 3,330

EXHIBIT 16-3

Income Statement for Spring Distribution in 2013

	A	B	C	D	E	F	G	H	I	J	K	L	M	N
1		CUSTOMER DISTRIBUTION CHANNELS												
2		Wholesale Customers						Retail Customers						
3		Total	Total	A1	A2	A3	•	Total	A[a]		B[a]		G[a]	J[a]
4		(1) = (2) + (7)	(2)	(3)	(4)	(5)	(6)	(7)	(8)		(9)		(10)	(11)
5	Revenues (at actual prices)	$12,138,120	$10,107,720	$1,946,000	$1,476,000	•	•	$2,030,400	$564,480		$467,280		•	•
6	Customer-level costs	11,633,760	9,737,280	1,868,000	1,416,000	•	•	1,896,480	529,380 [b]		416,120 [b]		•	•
7	Customer-level operating income	504,360	370,440	78,000	60,000	•	•	133,920	$35,100		$51,160		•	•
8	Distribution-channel costs	160,500	102,500					58,000						
9	Distribution-channel operating income	343,860	$267,940					$ 75,920						
10	Corporate-sustaining costs	263,000												
11	Operating income	$80,860												
12														
13	[a]Full details are presented in Exhibit 16-2													
14	[b]Cost of goods sold + Total customer-level operating costs from Exhibit 16-2													

The ABC system underlying Exhibit 16-2 provides a road map to facilitate less use of cost drivers by a customer to promote cost reduction. Another advantage of ABC is that it highlights a second way cost reduction can be promoted by Spring Distribution—Spring can take actions to reduce the costs in each of its own activity areas. For example, order taking currently is estimated to cost $100 per purchase order. By making its own ordering process more efficient (such as having its customers order electronically), Spring can reduce its costs even if its customers make the same number of orders.

Exhibit 16-3 reports Spring Distribution's monthly operating income. The hierarchical format in Exhibit 16-3 distinguishes among various degrees of objectivity when allocating costs, and it dovetails with the different levels at which decisions are made and performance is evaluated. The issue of when and what costs to allocate is another example of the "different costs to match the economic facts" idea emphasized throughout the text.

The customer-level operating income of customers A and B in Exhibit 16-2 are shown in columns 8 and 9 of Exhibit 16-3. Some managers and management accountants advocate fully allocating all costs to customers and distribution channels so that:

◆ The sum of operating incomes of all customers in a distribution channel (segment) equals the operating income of the distribution channel.

◆ The sum of the distribution-channel operating incomes equals companywide operating income.

The justification is that customers and products must eventually be profitable on a full-product (or service) cost basis. For some decisions, such as pricing, allocating all costs ensures that long-run prices are set at a level to cover the cost of all resources used to produce and sell products. In an intensely competitive environment, Spring Distribution's management team would likely choose a target pricing policy. As a price taker, this would ensure Spring would not lose profitable customers because it mispriced its distribution service.

Consider corporate-sustaining costs such as top-management and general-administration costs. Spring's managers have concluded that there is neither a cause-and-effect nor a benefits-received relationship between any cost-allocation base and corporate-sustaining costs. Consequently, allocation of corporate-sustaining costs serves no useful purpose in decision making, performance evaluation, or motivation. For example, suppose Spring allocated the $263,000 of corporate-sustaining costs to its distribution channels: $173,000 to the wholesale channel and $90,000 to the retail channel. Using information from Exhibit 16-3, the retail channel would then show a loss of $14,080 ($75,920 – $90,000).

If this same situation persisted in subsequent months, should Spring shut down the retail distribution channel? No, because if retail distribution were discontinued, corporate-sustaining costs would be unaffected. Allocating corporate-sustaining costs to distribution channels could give the misleading impression that the potential cost savings from discontinuing a distribution channel would be greater than the likely amount.

REVENUE VARIANCE ANALYSES

③ Calculate and interpret four levels of revenue variance analyses.

In this section we will calculate variances that use revenue information as a key input. Profitability analysis requires thorough understanding of the causes of both revenue and costs. The finer or more detailed the analyses of what caused unexpected outcomes, the more relevant the information available to managers who must remedy the situation. Feedback is essential in complex and ongoing decision making where new information changes the likelihood of future outcomes.

Spring's MIS separates all variable customer-level costs from distribution-channel and corporate-sustaining costs, which are classified as fixed costs. To simplify the sales-variance analysis and calculations, we assume that all Spring's variable costs are variable with respect to units (cases) sold. One consequence is that average batch sizes remain the same as the total cases sold vary. Without this assumption, the analysis would become more complex and would have to be done using the ABC-variance analysis approach described in Chapter 8.

Customer revenue analysis is enhanced by tracking as much detail as possible to explain why customers differ in their revenues. Two variables explain revenue differences across the four customers presented in Exhibits 16-1 and 16-2: (1) the volume of bottles purchased and (2) the magnitude of price discounting.

Price discounting is the reduction of selling prices below listed levels to encourage an increase in purchases by customers. It is important to remember that the management team has selected a cost leadership strategy that requires minimizing cost. When customers set price, the company that delivers on the value proposition at the least cost will have a higher profit. Spring Distribution's management team could engage in a price war to capture volume, but this is extremely risky in a competitive market. Assuming that this company is a cost leader, price discounting can only hurt profit as its competitors retaliate by lowering their price to match or beat that of Spring Distribution.

Price discounts are a function of multiple factors, including the volume of product purchased (higher-volume customers receive higher discounts) and the desire to sell to a customer who might help promote sales to other customers. Discounts could also be due to poor negotiating by a salesperson or the unwanted effect of an incentive plan based only on revenues. At no time should price discounts run afoul of the law by way of price discrimination, predatory pricing, or collusive pricing. Price discounts can also be unethical—for example, when discounts are given by pharmaceutical representatives to doctors to encourage them to prescribe a particular drug.

Companies that record only the invoice price in their information system would not be able to readily track the magnitude of their price discounting (except in the extreme case of a single-product company with a constant list price in the accounting period).[1] Tracking discounts by customer, and by salesperson, can provide valuable

[1] Further analysis of customer revenues could distinguish between gross revenues and net revenues. This approach would highlight differences across customers in sales returns. Additional discussion of ways to analyze revenue differences across customers is in R. S. Kaplan and R. Cooper, *Cost and Effect* (Boston, Mass.: Harvard Business School Press, 1998), Chapter 10.

information about ways to improve customer profitability. For example, companies may institute a corporate policy to ensure that any volume-based price discounting policy is enforced for customers with decreasing volume as well as those with increasing volume. It may also require its salespeople to obtain approval before giving large discounts to customers not normally qualifying for them. In addition, it could track the future sales of customers that its salespeople argue warrant a sizable price discount due to their predicted "high growth potential." Salespeople who have a poor track record in predicting the future growth of customers may be given additional training in sales forecasting (or may even be encouraged to seek employment elsewhere).

The following information, from Spring Distribution's MIS, will be used to calculate several variances for the company. Budget and actual data for June 2013 are shown in the table below:

Budget Data for June 2013

	Selling Price per Unit (1)	Variable Cost per Unit (2)	Contribution Margin per Unit (3) = (1) − (2)	Sales Volume in Units (4)	Sales Mix (Based on Units) (5)	Contribution Margin (6) = (3) × (4)
Wholesale channel	$13.37	$12.88	$0.49	712,000	80%[a]	$348,880
Retail channel	14.10	13.12	0.98	178,000	20%	174,440
Total				890,000	100%	$523,320

"Unit" in the column headings refers to a case of 24 bottles
[a]Percentage of unit sales to wholesale channel = 712,000 units ÷ 890,000 total units = 80%.

Actual Data for June 2013

	Selling Price per Unit (1)	Variable Cost per Unit (2)	Contribution Margin per Unit (3) = (1) − (2)	Sales Volume in Units (4)	Sales Mix (Based on Units) (5)	Contribution Margin (6) = (3) × (4)
Wholesale channel	$13.37	$12.88	$0.49	756,000	84%	$370,440
Retail channel	14.10	13.17	0.93	144,000	16%	133,920
Total				900,000	100%	$504,360

The budgeted and actual fixed distribution-channel costs and corporate-sustaining costs are $160,500 and $263,000, respectively.

STATIC-BUDGET VARIANCE

The *static-budget variance* is calculated as:

Static-budget variance = Actual results − Static budget amount

Our analysis focuses on the difference between actual and budgeted contribution margins (column 6 in the preceding tables). The total static-budget variance is $18,960 U (actual contribution margin of $504,360 − budgeted contribution margin of $523,320). Managers can gain more insight about the static-budget variance by subdividing it into the flexible-budget variance and the sales-volume variance.

FLEXIBLE-BUDGET AND SALES-VOLUME VARIANCES

Flexible-budget Variance   The *flexible-budget variance* is a Level 2 variance calculated as:

Flexible-budget variance = Actual results − Flexible-budget amount

The flexible-budget variance is the difference between an actual result and the corresponding flexible-budget amount based on actual output level in the budget period. The flexible-budget contribution margin is equal to budgeted contribution margin per unit (case) times actual units (cases) sold of each product. Exhibit 16-4, column 2, shows the flexible-budget calculations. The flexible budget measures the contribution margin that Spring would have budgeted for the actual quantities of

EXHIBIT 16-4
Flexible-Budget and Sales-Volume Variance Analysis of Spring Distribution for June 2013

	A	B	C	D	E	F	G
1		**Actual Results:**		**Flexible Budget:**		**Static Budget:**	
2		**Actual Units of**		**Actual Units of**		**Budgeted Units of**	
3		**All Products Sold ✕**		**All Products Sold ✕**		**All Products Sold ✕**	
4		**Actual Sales Mix ✕**		**Actual Sales Mix ✕**		**Budgeted Sales Mix ✕**	
5		**Actual Contribution**		**Budgeted Contribution**		**Budgeted Contribution**	
6		**Margin per Unit**		**Margin per Unit**		**Margin per Unit**	
7		**(1)**		**(2)**		**(3)**	
8	Wholesale	900,000 ✕ 0.84 ✕ $0.49 =	$370,440	900,000 ✕ 0.84 ✕ $0.49 =	$370,440	890,000 ✕ 0.80 ✕ $0.49 =	$348,880
9	Retail	900,000 ✕ 0.16 ✕ $0.93 =	133,920	900,000 ✕ 0.16 ✕ $0.98 =	141,120	890,000 ✕ 0.20 ✕ $0.98 =	174,440
10			$504,360		$511,560		$523,320
11			⬆	$7,200 U	⬆	$11,760 U	⬆
12	Level 2			Flexible-budget variance		Sales-volume variance	
13			⬆		$ 18,960 U		⬆
14	Level 1			Static-budget variance			
15							
16							

cases sold. The flexible-budget variance is the difference between columns 1 and 2 in Exhibit 16-4.

Recall that the levels of detail introduced in Chapter 7 included the static-budget variance (level 1), the flexible-budget variance (level 2), and the sales-volume variance (level 2). The sales-quantity and sales-mix variances are level 3 variances that subdivide the sales-volume variance.[2] Exhibit 16-4 illustrates how to reconcile Levels 1 and 2 revenue variance analyses for the current sales mix of products sold through the two distribution channels.

The key difference between columns 1 and 2 is that actual units sold of each product is multiplied by actual contribution margin per unit in column 1 and budgeted contribution margin per unit in column 2. The $7,200 U flexible-budget variance arises because actual contribution margin on retail sales of $0.93 per case is lower than the budgeted amount of $0.98 per case. Spring's management is aware that this difference of $0.05 per case resulted from excessive price discounts, and they have put in place controls to reduce discounts in the future.

Special attention is paid to companies with multiple products or services and to companies selling the same product or service in multiple distribution channels. Companies such as Cisco, GE, and Hewlett-Packard perform similar analyses because they sell their products through multiple distribution channels—for example, via the Internet, over the telephone, and in retail stores.

Sales-Volume Variance   The *sales-volume variance* is calculated as:

$$\text{Sales-volume variance} = \left(\begin{array}{c} \text{Actual sales} \\ \text{quantity in units} \end{array} - \begin{array}{c} \text{Static-budget sales} \\ \text{quantity in units} \end{array} \right) \times \begin{array}{c} \text{Budgeted contribution} \\ \text{margin per unit} \end{array}$$

The sales-volume variance shows the effect of the difference between the actual and budgeted quantity of the variable used to "flex" the flexible budget. The sales-volume variance of $11,760 U is the difference between columns 2 and 3 in Exhibit 16-4. Exhibit 16-5 presents these calculations in graphic format.

[2]The presentation of the variances in this chapter draws on teaching notes prepared by J. K. Harris.

EXHIBIT 16-5
Overview of Levels 1 and 2 Revenue Variances for June 2013

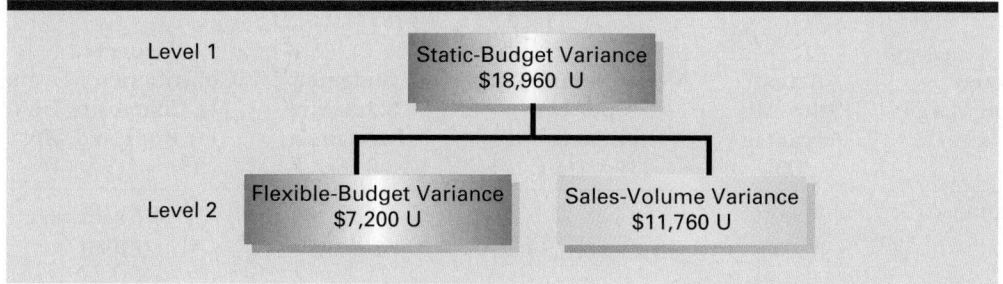

Interpretation of Levels 1 and 2 Revenue Variance The flexible-budget variance of \$7,200 U arose because the actual Q produced and sold cost more than it should have. Of course, the flexible-budget costs should be lower than the static, especially for variable costs. That makes this unfavourable variance particularly worrying for Spring's management team. The sales-volume variance arises for the same reason. All other things being equal, the actual revenue should decrease when the actual Q produced is lower than the static-budget amount. But the sales-volume variance comprises the sum of the sales-mix and sales-quantity variance. Spring's management team can gain more insight by analyzing these two components separately.

SALES-MIX VARIANCE AND SALES-QUANTITY VARIANCE

The **sales-mix variance** is one of the Level 3 variances calculated as the difference between two amounts: (1) the budgeted amount for the actual sales mix and (2) the budgeted amount for the budgeted sales mix. This level of analysis is based on the same principle as the input mix variances discussed in Chapter 7. In the case of revenue variances, however, the managers of each product would have some discretion in how their individual and product bundles were sold. The formula for computing the sales-mix variance in terms of the contribution margin for Spring is:

$$\begin{array}{c}\text{Sales-mix} \\ \text{variance}\end{array} = \begin{array}{c}\text{Actual units of} \\ \text{all products sold}\end{array} \times \left(\begin{array}{c}\text{Actual sales-} \\ \text{mix percentage}\end{array} - \begin{array}{c}\text{Budgeted sales-} \\ \text{mix percentage}\end{array}\right) \times \begin{array}{c}\text{Budgeted} \\ \text{contribution} \\ \text{margin per unit}\end{array}$$

	Actual Units of All Products Sold	×	(Actual Sales-Mix Percentage	−	Budgeted Sales-Mix Percentage)	×	Budgeted Contribution Margin per Unit	=	Sales-Mix Variance
Wholesale	900,000 units	×	(84.00%	−	80.00%)	×	\$0.49 per unit	=	\$ 17,640 F
Retail	900,000 units	×	(16.00%	−	20.00%)	×	\$0.98 per unit	=	\$(35,280) U
Total sales-mix variance									\$(17,640) U

A favourable sales-mix variance arises for the wholesale channel because the 84% actual sales-mix percentage exceeds the 80% budgeted sales-mix percentage. In contrast, the retail channel has an unfavourable variance because the 16% actual sales-mix percentage is less than the 20% budgeted sales-mix percentage. The sales-mix variance is unfavourable because actual sales mix shifted toward the less-profitable wholesale channel relative to budgeted sales mix.

The concept underlying the sales-mix variance is best explained in terms of budgeted contribution margin per composite unit of the sales mix. A **composite unit** is a hypothetical unit with weights based on the mix of individual units. For actual sales mix, the composite unit consists of 0.84 units of sales to the wholesale channel and 0.16 units of sales to the retail channel. For budgeted sales mix, the composite unit consists of 0.80 units of sales to the wholesale channel and 0.20 units of sales to the retail channel. The table below reports budgeted contribution margin per composite unit, computed in columns 3 and 5, for actual and budgeted mix:

	Budgeted Contribution Margin per Unit (1)	Actual Sales-Mix Percentage (2)	Budgeted Contribution Margin per Unit for Actual Mix (3) = (1) × (2)	Budgeted Sales-Mix Percentage (4)	Budgeted Contribution Margin per Composite Unit for Budgeted Mix (5) = (1) × (4)
Wholesale	$0.49	84.00%	$0.4116	80.00%	$0.3920
Retail	0.98	16.00%	0.1568	20.00%	0.1960
			$0.5684		$0.5880

Actual sales mix has a budgeted contribution margin per composite unit of $0.5684. Budgeted sales mix has a budgeted contribution margin per composite unit of $0.5880. Budgeted contribution margin per composite unit can be computed in another way by dividing total budgeted contribution margin of $523,320 by total budgeted units of 890,000: $523,320 ÷ 890,000 units = $0.5880 per unit. The effect of the sales-mix shift for Spring is to decrease budgeted contribution margin per composite unit by $0.0196 ($0.5880 – $0.5684). For the 900,000 units actually sold, this decrease translates to a $17,640 U sales-mix variance ($0.0196 per unit × 900,000 units).

The **sales-quantity variance** is the difference between two amounts: (1) the budgeted contribution margin based on actual units sold of all products and the budgeted mix, and (2) the contribution margin in the static budget (which is based on the budgeted units to be sold of all products and the budgeted mix). The formula for calculating the sales-quantity variance in terms of contribution margin is:

$$\text{Sales-quantity variance} = \left(\begin{array}{c}\text{Actual units of} \\ \text{all products sold}\end{array} - \begin{array}{c}\text{Budgeted units of} \\ \text{all products sold}\end{array}\right) \times \begin{array}{c}\text{Budgeted sales-} \\ \text{mix percentage}\end{array} \times \begin{array}{c}\text{Budgeted} \\ \text{contribution} \\ \text{margin per unit}\end{array}$$

	(Actual Units of All Products Sold	−	Budgeted Units of All Products Sold)	×	Budgeted Sales-Mix Percentage	×	Budgeted Contribution Margin per Unit	=	Quantity Variance
Wholesale	(900,000	−	890,000)	×	80.00%	×	$0.49 per unit	=	$ 3,920 F
Retail	(900,000	−	890,000)	×	20.00%	×	$0.98 per unit	=	1,960 F
Total sales-quantity variance									$ 5,880 F

Exhibit 16-6 reports the results of the Levels 2 and 3 variance analyses in columnar format.

The sales-quantity variance is favourable when actual units of all products sold exceed budgeted units of all products sold. Spring sold 10,000 more cases than were budgeted, resulting in a $5,880 F sales-quantity variance (also equal to budgeted contribution margin per composite unit for the budgeted sales mix times the additional cases sold, $0.5880 × 10,000). Exhibit 16-7 illustrates graphically how to reconcile Level 3 and Level 2 variances.

Interpretation of Level 3 Revenue Variances Managers should probe why the $17,640 U sales-mix variance occurred in June 2013. Is the shift in sales mix because, as the analysis in the previous section showed, profitable retail customers proved to be more difficult to find? Is it because a competitor in the retail channel provided better service at a lower price? Or is it because the initial sales-volume estimates were made without adequate analysis of the potential market?

Sales depend on overall demand for the industry's products as well as the company's share of the market for bottled water. Assume that Spring derived its total unit sales budget for 2013 from a management estimate of a 25% market share and a total industry sales forecast of 3,560,000 units (0.25 × 3,560,000 units = 890,000 units). For June 2013, actual industry sales were 4,000,000 and Spring's actual market share was 22.5% (900,000 ÷ 4,000,000 = 0.225 or 22.5%).

EXHIBIT 16-6
Sales-Mix and Sales-Quantity Variance Analysis of Spring Distribution for June 2013

	A	B	C	D	E	F	G
1		**Flexible Budget:**				**Static Budget:**	
2		**Actual Units of**		**Actual Units of**		**Budgeted Units of**	
3		**All Products Sold ×**		**All Products Sold ×**		**All Products Sold ×**	
4		**Actual Sales Mix ×**		**Budgeted Sales Mix ×**		**Budgeted Sales Mix ×**	
5		**Budgeted Contribution**		**Budgeted Contribution**		**Budgeted Contribution**	
6		**Margin per Unit**		**Margin per Unit**		**Margin per Unit**	
7		**(1)**		**(2)**		**(3)**	
8	Wholesale	900,000 × 0.84 × $0.49 =	$370,440	900,000 × 0.80 × $0.49 =	$352,800	890,000 × 0.80 × $0.49 =	$348,880
9	Retail	900,000 × 0.16 × $0.98 =	141,120	900,000 × 0.20 × $0.98 =	176,400	890,000 × 0.20 × $0.98 =	174,440
10			$511,560		$529,200		$523,320
11			↑	$17,640 U	↑	$5,880 F	↑
12	Level 3			Sales-mix variance		Sales-quantity variance	
13			↑		$ 11,760 U		↑
14	Level 2				Sales-volume variance		

EXHIBIT 16-7
Overview of Levels 1, 2 and 3 Revenue Variances for Spring Distribution for June 2013

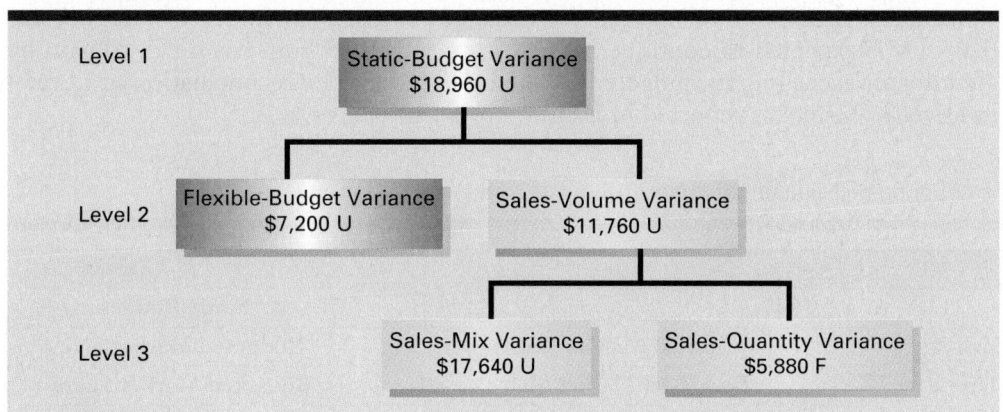

Managers would want to determine the reasons for the increase in sales. Did higher sales come as a result of a competitor's distribution problems? Better customer service? Or growth in the overall market? Further insight into the causes of the sales-quantity variance can be gained by analyzing changes in Spring's share of the total market available relative to any change in the size of the entire market.

MARKET-SHARE VARIANCE

The **market-share variance** is one of the Level 4 variances calculated as the difference between two amounts: (1) the budgeted amount based on actual market size in units, *actual market share*, calculated using the budgeted contribution margin per composite unit for the budgeted mix, and (2) the budgeted market size in units, *budgeted market share*, calculated using the budgeted contribution margin per composite unit for the budgeted mix. The formula for computing the market-share variance in terms of contribution margin for Spring is:

$$\text{Market-share variance} = \text{Actual market size in units} \times \left(\text{Actual market share} - \text{Budgeted market share} \right) \times \text{Budgeted contribution margin per composite unit for budgeted mix}$$

= 4,000,000 units (cases) × (0.225 − 0.25) × $0.5880 per unit (case)
= $58,800 U

The budgeted contribution margin per composite unit for the budgeted mix (also known as budgeted average contribution margin per unit) can be calculated using the approach outlined earlier in this chapter.

MARKET-SIZE VARIANCE

The **market-size variance** is the difference between two amounts: (1) the budgeted amount based on *actual market size in units*, budgeted market share, and budgeted contribution margin per composite unit for budgeted mix, and (2) the static-budget amount based on the *budgeted market size in units*, budgeted market share, and budgeted contribution margin per composite unit for budgeted mix. The formula for computing the market-size variance in terms of contribution margin for Spring is:

$$\begin{array}{l}\text{Market-size} \\ \text{variance}\end{array} = \left(\begin{array}{l}\text{Actual market} \\ \text{size in units}\end{array} - \begin{array}{l}\text{Budgeted market} \\ \text{size in units}\end{array}\right) \times \begin{array}{l}\text{Budgeted} \\ \text{market share}\end{array} \times \begin{array}{l}\text{Budgeted contribution} \\ \text{margin per composite} \\ \text{unit for budgeted mix}\end{array}$$

$$= (4,000,000 \text{ units (cases)} - 3,560,000) \times 0.25 \times \$0.5880$$
$$= \$64,680 \text{ F}$$

The market-size variance is favourable because actual market size, or total consumer demand, increased 440,000 cases, or 12.4%[3], compared to budgeted market size. Managers should probe the reasons for the market-share and market-size variances for June 2013. Was the $58,800 unfavourable market-share variance because of competitors providing better service and offering a lower price? Did Spring's products experience quality-control problems that were the subject of negative media coverage? Is the $64,680 F market-size variance because of an increase in market size that can be expected to continue in the future? If yes, Spring has much to gain by attaining or exceeding its budgeted 25% market share. The reconciliation of Level 4 to Level 3 variance is reported in Exhibit 16-8.

EXHIBIT 16-8
Level 4 Revenue Variance Analysis of Spring Distribution for June 2013

	A	B	C	D	E	F
1						**Static Budget:**
2		**Actual Market Size ×**		**Actual Market Size ×**		**Budgeted Market Size ×**
3		**Actual Market Share ×**		**Budgeted Market Share ×**		**Budgeted Market Share ×**
4		**Budgeted Average**		**Budgeted Average**		**Budgeted Average**
5		**Contribution Margin**		**Contribution Margin**		**Contribution Margin**
6		**per Unit**		**per Unit**		**per Unit**
7		$4,000,000 \times 0.225^a \times \$0.5880^b$		$4,000,000 \times 0.25^c \times \$0.5880^b$		$3,560,000 \times 0.25^c \times \$0.5880^b$
8		$529,200		$588,000		$523,320
9						
10			$58,800 U		$64,680 F	
11	Level 4		Market-share variance		Market-size variance	
12						
13				$5,880 F		
14	Level 3			Sales-quantity variance		
15						
16	F = favourable effect on operating income U = unfavourable effect on operating income					
17	ªActual market share: 900,000 units ÷ 4,000,000 units = 0.225 or 22.5%					
18	bBudgeted average contribution margin per unit: $523,320 ÷ 890,000 units = $0.5880 per unit					
19	cBudgeted market share: 890,000 ÷ 3,560,000 units = 0.25 or 25%					

[3] $(4,000,000 - 3,560,000) \div 3,560,000 = 0.124 \text{ or } 12.4\%$

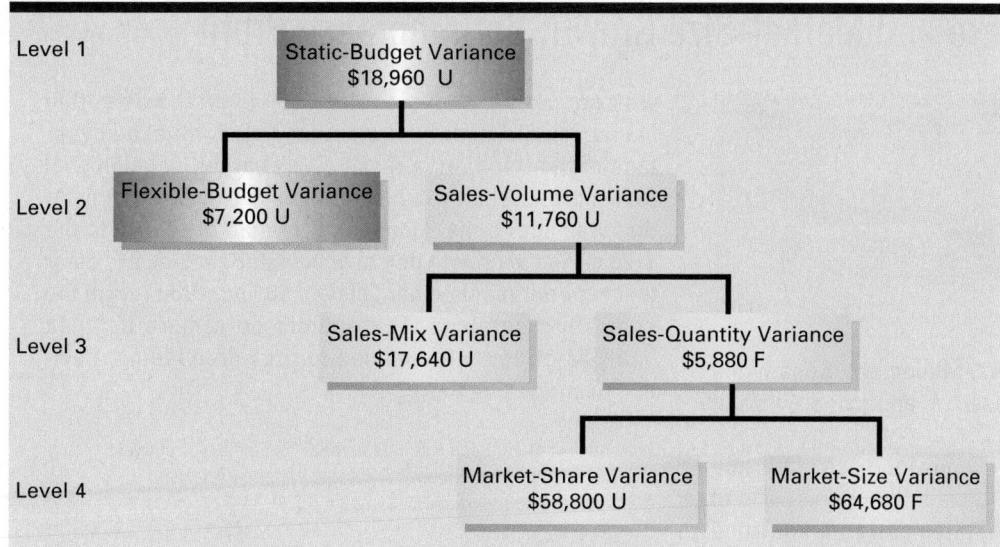

Spring Distribution's management team is now in a position to use its four-level revenue variance analysis, along with its ABC customer cost analyses, to produce a customer profitability profile. Exhibit 16-9 presents an overview of the Level 1 to Level 4 variances and how each level of variance reconciles to each other.

Interpretation of Level 4 Revenue Variances Some companies place more emphasis on the market-share variance than the market-size variance when evaluating their managers. That's because they believe the market-size variance is influenced by economy-wide factors and shifts in consumer preferences that are outside the managers' control, whereas the market-share variance measures how well managers performed relative to their peers. Be cautious when computing the market-size variance and the market-share variance. Reliable information on market size and market share is available for some but not all industries. The automobile, computer, and television industries are cases in which market-size and market-share statistics are widely available. In other industries, such as management consulting and personal financial planning, information about market size and market share is far less reliable.

The sales-mix variance, sales-quantity variance, market-share variance, and market-size variance can also be calculated in a multiproduct company, in which each individual product has a different contribution margin per unit. Managers do understand that there will be random events that cause actual performance to vary from expected. Timely feedback alerts them when a variance may have a non-random cause. The sales-mix variance helps direct attention to a non-random change in variable costs or unit price that has reduced the contribution margin. The sales-quantity variance isolates and directs attention toward a non-random change in quantities produced and sold. Recall that using the contribution margin approach implies zero ending inventory of finished goods (Chapter 3). Knowing actual demand did not meet the pro forma will also alert managers to expect an unfavourable production volume variance.

The managerial task, based on this feedback, is to decide upon the best response. The unfavourable variances have only revealed what occurred, not how it occurred. If there is a controllable cause, then the team will find an operating remedy. If there is an uncontrollable cause, then the best decision may be to change the budget and deal with a new set of expectations, as unfavourable as they may be.

The realized outcome has caused managers to reassess their prior assessments about the likelihood of achieving some targeted quantity of sales. Based on their reassessment, a new decision is made about the utilization of capacity. After this decision is made, a new denominator is chosen for the fixed overhead allocations.

Market-share and market-size variances reveal generally what variances are controllable and uncontrollable. In a competitive market it is rare that a single company

can control market size. The demand for a product or a service depends on consumer preference. In classical economic models, preferences are formed prior to and independently of specific consumption decisions. Once consumers express their preference, demand or market size is known and suppliers attempt to influence the proportion of that market they serve, or market share.

Thus, an unfavourable market size variance has strategic implications. For example, the reduced demand for SUVs implies a long-term decision to change capacity. The cause of the reduced market size, high fuel prices, is beyond the control of vehicle manufacturers. Another potential remedy is innovative use of alternative, less expensive fuels, which requires redesign of the internal combustion engine. A third alternative would be to expand using adjacencies and simply harvest the benefits of the capacity already in place.

In contrast, an unfavourable market-share variance has operating implications. The reduced demand for products made by a specific company with no accompanying reduction in market size provides different relevant information. Remedies include improved understanding of the value proposition, improved product attributes, or improved timeliness. In some cases, a strategic remedy is required. This was true for the reduction in demand for KFC products as a result of a candid video on YouTube of slaughtering practices by the supplier of chicken. There is increasing influence of corporate and environmental sustainability issues on the operations of for-profit companies.

CUSTOMER PROFITABLITY ANALYSIS

4 Generate a customer profitability profile.

Once a company such as Spring Distribution decides to measure customer profitability, management accountants are responsible for articulating the benefits of such measurements. This can be problematic because the sales organizations in most companies are compensated on the basis of revenues, not customer profits. Therefore, the sales force may be reluctant to follow a strategy of serving only profitable customers and taking actions to change the behaviour and buying patterns of those that are unprofitable.

When it comes to customer profitability analysis, the sales force is not the only part of an organization that may pose challenges for management accountants. Line managers are sometimes surprised by which customers are profitable and which are not, because they may assume a company's largest customer is profitable.

However, this customer may consume high levels of customer support and actually be unprofitable.

Management accountants need to communicate to the sales force why measuring customer profits is critical to the organization. For example, they need to explain what might happen if change does not occur and how customer profitability analysis can help the company reallocate resources to increase both revenues and profits. Management accountants must make it a point to team up with line managers when designing the system to calculate customer profitability. Customer profitability analysis should always be based on a thorough understanding of business processes so that it correctly represents the costs incurred to support different customers.

Consider a distributor of medical supplies to hospitals. It strategically prices each of its services separately. For example, if a hospital wants a rush delivery or special packaging, the distributor charges the hospital an additional price for each particular service. Hospitals that value these services continue to demand them and pay for them while hospitals that do not value these services drop them, saving the distributor some costs. This is how the distributor's pricing strategy influences customer behaviour in a way that increases the distributor's revenues or decreases its costs. Spring Distribution follows a similar policy.

We will focus mainly on **customer profitability analysis** in Spring's retail distribution channel. The list selling price in this channel is $14.40 per case (unit), while the purchase cost to Spring is $12 per case. If every bottle were sold at its list price in this distribution channel, Spring would earn a gross margin of $2.40 per case. This high-percentage contribution by a small number of customers is a common finding in many studies. It highlights the importance of Spring Distribution maintaining good relations with this pivotal set of customers.

The data on all customers, retrieved from Spring's MIS, is reported in Exhibit 16-10. Wholesale customers comprise new data, as do the distribution-channel costs and corporate-sustaining costs. The format of Exhibit 16-10 is based on Spring's cost hierarchy. All costs incurred to serve customers are not included in customer-level

EXHIBIT 16-10
Customer Profitability Analysis for Retail Channel Customers: Spring Distribution, June 2013

	A	B	C	D	E	F
1						Cumulative
2						Customer-Level
3		Customer-				Operating Income
4		Level		Customer-Level	Cumulative	as a % of Total
5		Operating	Customer	Operating Income	Customer-Level	Customer-Level
6	Customer	Income	Revenue	Divided by Revenue	Operating Income	Operating Income
7	Code	(1)	(2)	(3) = (1) ÷ (2)	(4)	(5) = (4) ÷ $133,920
8	B	$ 51,160	$ 467,280	10.95%	$ 51,160	38.20%
9	A	35,100	564,480	6.22	86,260	64.41
10	C	21,070	255,640	8.24	107,330	80.14
11	D	17,580	277,000	6.35	124,910	93.27
12	F	7,504	123,500	6.08	132,414	98.88
13	J	3,330	36,000	9.25	135,744	101.36
14	E	3,176	193,000	1.65	138,920	103.73
15	G	(1,190)	38,280	−3.11	137,730	102.84
16	H	(1,690)	38,220	−4.42	136,040	101.58
17	I	(2,120)	37,000	−5.73	133,920	100.00
18		$133,920	$2,030,400			

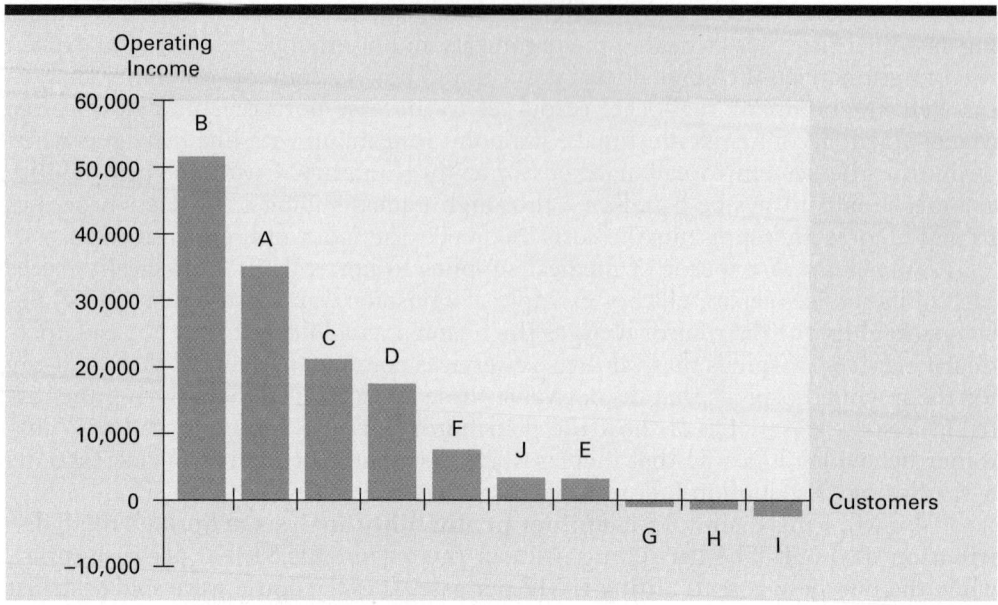

costs and therefore are not allocated to customers in Exhibit 16-10. Distribution-channel costs such as the salary for the manager of the retail distribution channel are not included in customer-level costs and are not allocated to customers. Instead, these costs are identified as costs of the distribution channel as a whole. That is because Spring's management believes that changes in the retail channel manager's salary will not affect the behaviour of a specific customer.

Distribution-channel costs will be affected only by decisions pertaining to the whole channel, such as a decision to discontinue retail distribution. Another reason Spring does not allocate distribution-channel costs to customers is motivation. Spring's managers contend that salespersons responsible for managing individual customer accounts would lose motivation if their bonuses were affected by the allocation to customers of distribution-channel costs over which they have almost no influence.

Exhibit 16-11 ranks customers on revenue (after price discounts). Three of the four smallest customers (based on revenue) are unprofitable. Moreover, customer E, with revenues of $193,000, is only marginally profitable. Further analysis revealed that a former sales representative gave customer E excessive discounts in an attempt to meet a monthly sales-volume target.

Managers often find the bar chart presentation to be the most intuitive way to visualize customer profitability. The highly profitable customers clearly stand out. Moreover, the number of loss-customers and the magnitude of their losses are apparent and focus management attention on how to improve the profitability of these loss-customers.

ASSESSING CUSTOMER VALUE

The "80–20" rule also prevails among customers. Of total profit, 80% will come from 20% of the customers. Customer profitability analysis is attention-getting and directs management attention on maintaining the best possible retention ratio of these customers and transforming the remainder into more profitable customers. The information in Exhibits 16-3 (p. 643) and 16-10 (p. 653) relates to customer profitability in a single accounting period. This is one of several factors that managers should consider in deciding how to allocate resources across customers. Other factors include the following:

◆ *Short-run and long-run customer profitability.* This factor will be influenced by factors 2 and 3 below, as well as by the level of resources likely to be required to retain the accounts.

- ◆ *Customer retention likelihood.* The more likely a customer is to continue doing business with a company, the more valuable the customer. Customers can differ in their loyalty and their willingness to "shop their business" on a frequent basis.

- ◆ *Customer growth potential.* This factor will be influenced by the likely growth of the industry of the customer and the likely growth of the customer (due to, say, the customer's ability to develop new products). This factor will also be influenced by cross-selling opportunities—that is, when a customer of one of the company's products becomes a customer of one or more of the company's other products.

- ◆ *Increases in overall demand from having well-known customers.* Some customers are highly valuable because they have established reputations that make them very useful to mention in sales visits. Other customers are valuable because of their willingness to provide product endorsements.

- ◆ *Ability to learn from a customer.* Customers can be an important source of ideas about new products or ways to improve existing products. Customers willing to provide such input can be especially valuable.

Managers should be particularly cautious when deciding to drop customers. Short-run profitability reports may provide misleading signals about their long-run profitability. Moreover, not all costs assigned to a customer may be variable with respect to short-run reductions in purchases by customers. It is typically *not* the case that a policy of dropping any currently unprofitable customer (sometimes called "revenue shedding") will eliminate in the short run all the costs assigned to that customer.

CUSTOMER MIX ANALYSIS

The goal of customer profitability analysis is to use high quality data to make decisions that will improve the profitability of a company. In addition to making choices among products, companies must often decide whether they should add some customers and drop others. This section illustrates relevant-revenue and relevant-cost analysis when different cost drivers are identified for different activities in activity-based costing. The cost object in our example is customers. The analysis focuses on customer profitability at Allied West, the west coast sales office of Allied Furniture, a wholesaler of specialized furniture.

The MIS at Allied West provides detailed cost information on three customers for the year 2013, as reported in Exhibit 16-12.

Analyze relevant profitability data and decide whether to drop or add customers or branches. ⑤

EXHIBIT 16-12
Customer Profitability Analysis for Allied West

	Vogel	Brenner	Wisk	Total
Sales	$500,000	$300,000	$ 400,000	$1,200,000
Cost of goods sold	370,000	220,000	330,000	920,000
Materials-handling labour	41,000	18,000	33,000	92,000
Materials-handling equipment cost written off as amortization	10,000	6,000	8,000	24,000
Rent	14,000	8,000	14,000	36,000
Marketing support	11,000	9,000	10,000	30,000
Purchase orders and delivery processing	13,000	7,000	12,000	32,000
General administration	20,000	12,000	16,000	48,000
Total operating costs	479,000	280,000	423,000	1,182,000
Operating income	$ 21,000	$ 20,000	$ (23,000)	$ 18,000
Allocated corporate costs				24,000
				$ (6,000)

Allied West wholesales furniture to three local retailers: Vogel, Brenner, and Wisk. Additional information on Allied West's costs for different activities at various levels of the cost hierarchy is as follows:

- Materials-handling labour costs vary with the number of units of furniture shipped to customers.

- Different areas of the warehouse stock furniture for different customers. Materials-handling equipment in an area and amortization costs on the equipment are identified with individual customer accounts. Any equipment not used remains idle. The equipment has a one-year useful life and zero disposal price.

- Allied West allocates rent to each customer account based on the amount of warehouse space occupied by the products to be shipped to that customer.

- Marketing costs vary with the number of sales visits made to customers.

- Purchase order costs vary with the number of purchase orders received; delivery processing costs vary with the number of shipments made.

- Allied West allocates fixed general administration costs to customers based on dollar sales made to each customer.

The management team's task is to analyze these data, assuming they are faithful to the economic facts of what each customer costs. From the analysis, Allied West can predict the effects of dropping any customer on their profitability. The final step will be to track actual against budgeted improvements in profit.

DROP A CUSTOMER

Exhibit 16-12 indicates a loss of $23,000 on sales to Wisk. Allied West's manager believes this loss occurred because Wisk places many low-volume orders with Allied, resulting in high purchase order, delivery processing, materials-handling, and marketing activity. Allied West is considering several possible actions with respect to the Wisk account: reducing its own costs of supporting Wisk by becoming more efficient, cutting back on some of the services it offers Wisk, charging Wisk higher prices, or dropping the Wisk account. The following analysis focuses on the operating income effect of dropping the Wisk account. The following financial facts are from the ABC system about the effect of reducing various upstream, core, and downstream activities related to the Wisk account:

1. Dropping the Wisk account will save cost of goods sold, materials-handling labour, marketing support, purchase order, and delivery processing costs incurred on the Wisk account.

2. Dropping the Wisk account will mean that the warehouse space currently occupied by products for Wisk and the materials-handling equipment used to move them will become idle.

3. Dropping the Wisk account will have no effect on fixed general administration costs.

Exhibit 16-13 is in full rather than differential cost format (see Chapter 11). The analysis predicts that Allied West's operating income will be $15,000 lower if it drops the Wisk account, so Allied decides to keep the Wisk account. The last column in Exhibit 16-13 indicates in detail why the cost savings from dropping the Wisk account, $385,000, is not enough to offset the loss of $400,000 in revenue. The full cost format provides the explanation. Amortization, rent, and general administration costs will not change if the Wisk account is dropped.

Assume that there is an alternative use for the warehouse capacity freed up if Wisk is dropped as a customer. Allied has the alternative to lease the extra warehouse space to the Sanchez Corporation, which has offered $20,000 per year for it. Then the $20,000 that Allied would receive would be the opportunity cost of continuing to use the warehouse to service Wisk. Allied would gain $5,000 by dropping the Wisk account ($20,000 from lease revenue minus lost operating income of $15,000).

EXHIBIT 16-13
Relevant-Cost Analysis for Allied West Dropping the Wisk Account

	Amount of Total Revenues and Total Costs		Difference: Incremental (Loss in Revenue and Savings in Costs from Dropping Wisk Account)
	Keep Wisk Account	Drop Wisk Account	
Sales	$1,200,000	$800,000	$(400,000)
Cost of goods sold	920,000	590,000	330,000
Materials-handling labour	92,000	59,000	33,000
Materials-handling equipment cost written off as amortization	24,000	24,000	—
Rent	36,000	36,000	—
Marketing support	30,000	20,000	10,000
Purchase orders and delivery processing	32,000	20,000	12,000
General administration	48,000	48,000	—
Total operating costs	1,182,000	797,000	385,000
Operating income	$ 18,000	$ 3,000	$ (15,000)

Before reaching a final decision, however, the management team must examine whether Wisk can be made more profitable. Activities use might be changed such that services supplied to Wisk earn more than the $20,000 from leasing to Sanchez. Allied must also consider qualitative factors such as the effect of the decision on Allied's reputation for developing stable, long-run business relationships.

ADD A CUSTOMER

Suppose that in addition to dropping the Wisk account, Allied is evaluating the profitability of substituting a customer, Loral. Allied is already paying rent of $36,000 for the warehouse and is incurring general administration costs of $48,000. These costs will not change if Loral is added as a customer. Loral is a customer with a profile much like Wisk's. Suppose Allied predicts other revenues and costs of doing business with Loral to be the same as those described under the Wisk column of Exhibit 16-13. Should Allied substitute Loral as a customer?

Exhibit 16-14 predicts that incremental revenues will not exceed incremental costs by $7,000. Allied would not prefer to substitute Loral as a customer for Wisk.

One key point is that the cost of acquiring new equipment to support the Loral order (written off as amortization of $8,000 in Exhibit 16-14) is included as a relevant cost. It is relevant because this cost can be avoided if Allied decides not to do business with Loral. Note the critical distinction here. Amortization cost is irrelevant in deciding whether to drop Wisk as a customer (because it is a past cost), but the purchase cost of the new equipment that will then be written off as amortization in the future is relevant in deciding whether to add Loral as a new customer.

DROP OR ADD BRANCHES

Companies periodically confront decisions about discontinuing or adding branches or business segments. For example, given Allied West's expected loss of $6,000 (see Exhibit 16-12), should it be closed? Assume that closing Allied West will have no effect on total corporate-office costs. Exhibit 16-15 reports the relevant revenue and cost analyses (in column 1) using the data from the final column in Exhibit 16-12. The revenue losses of $1,200,000 will exceed the cost savings of $1,158,000, leading to a decrease in operating income of $42,000. Allied West should not be closed down.

The key reasons are that closing Allied West will neither save amortization costs of $24,000, which is a past or sunk cost (see above), nor actual total corporate

EXHIBIT 16-14
Relevant-Cost Analysis for Dropping the Wisk Account and Adding the Loral Account

	(Loss in Revenue) and Savings in Costs from Dropping Wisk Account (1)	Incremental Revenue and (Incremental Costs) from Adding Loral Account (2)
Revenue	$(400,000)	$400,000
Cost of goods sold	330,000	(330,000)
Furniture-handling labour	33,000	(33,000)
Furniture-handling equipment cost written off as amortization	0	(8,000)
Rent	0	0
Marketing support	10,000	(10,000)
Purchase-order and delivery processing	12,000	(12,000)
General administration	0	0
Corporate-office costs	0	0
Total costs	385,000	(393,000)
Effect on operating income (loss)	$ (15,000)	$ 7,000

EXHIBIT 16-15
Relevant-Revenue and Relevant-Cost Analyses for Closing Allied West and Opening Allied South

	(Loss in Revenue) and Savings in Costs from Closing Allied West (1)	Incremental Revenue and (Incremental Costs) from Opening Allied South (2)
Revenue	$(1,200,000)	$1,200,000
Cost of goods sold	920,000	(920,000)
Furniture-handling labour	92,000	(92,000)
Furniture-handling equipment cost written off as amortization	0	(25,000)
Rent	36,000	(36,000)
Marketing support	30,000	(30,000)
Purchase-order and delivery processing	32,000	(32,000)
General administration	48,000	(48,000)
Corporate-office costs	0	0
Total costs	1,158,000	(1,183,000)
Effect on operating income (loss)	$ (42,000)	$ 17,000

costs. Corporate costs allocated to various sales offices will change but not decline in total. The $24,000 no longer allocated to Allied West will be allocated to other sales offices. Therefore, the $24,000 of allocated corporate costs should not be included as expected cost savings from closing Allied West.

Now suppose Allied Furniture has the opportunity to open another sales office, Allied South, whose revenues and costs would be identical to Allied West's, including a cost of $25,000 to acquire materials-handling equipment with a one-year useful life and zero disposal value.

Opening this office will have no effect on total corporate costs. Should Allied Furniture open Allied South? Exhibit 16-15, column 2, indicates that it should do so because opening Allied South will increase operating income by $17,000. As before, the cost of new equipment (written off as amortization) is relevant. But the point here is to ignore allocated corporate costs and focus on actual total corporate-office costs. Total corporate costs will not change if Allied South is opened and, hence, these costs are irrelevant.

(Try to solve this problem before examining the solution that follows.)

PROBLEM

The Payne Company manufactures two types of vinyl flooring. Budgeted and actual operating data for 2013 are:

	Static Budget			Actual Results		
	Commercial	Residential	Total	Commercial	Residential	Total
Unit sales in rolls	20,000	60,000	80,000	25,200	58,800	84,000
Contribution margin	$10,000,000	$24,000,000	$34,000,000	$11,970,000	$24,696,000	$36,666,000

In late 2012, a marketing research firm estimated industry volume for commercial and residential vinyl flooring for 2013 at 800,000 rolls. Actual industry volume for 2013 was 700,000 rolls.

REQUIRED

1. Compute the sales-mix variance and the sales-quantity variance by type of vinyl flooring and in total. (Compute all variances in terms of contribution margins.)
2. Compute the market-share variance and the market-size variance.
3. What insights do the variances calculated in requirements 1 and 2 provide about Payne Company's performance in 2013?

SOLUTION

1. Actual sales-mix percentage:

$$\text{Commercial} = 25,200 \div 84,000 = 0.30, \text{ or } 30\%$$

$$\text{Residential} = 58,800 \div 84,000 = 0.70, \text{ or } 70\%$$

Budgeted sales-mix percentage:

$$\text{Commercial} = 20,000 \div 80,000 = 0.25, \text{ or } 25\%$$

$$\text{Residential} = 60,000 \div 80,000 = 0.75, \text{ or } 75\%$$

Budgeted contribution margin per unit:

$$\text{Commercial} = \$10,000,000 \div 20,000 \text{ units} = \$500 \text{ per unit}$$

$$\text{Residential} = \$24,000,000 \div 60,000 \text{ units} = \$400 \text{ per unit}$$

	Actual Units of All Products Sold	×	(Actual Sales-Mix Percentage − Budgeted Sales-Mix Percentage)	×	Budgeted Contribution Margin per Unit	=	Sales-Mix Variance
Commercial	84,000 units	×	(0.30 − 0.25)	×	$500 per unit	=	$2,100,000 F
Residential	84,000 units	×	(0.70 − 0.75)	×	$400 per unit	=	1,680,000 U
Total sales-mix variance							$ 420,000 F

	(Actual Units of All Products Sold − Budgeted Units of All Products Sold)	×	Budgeted Sales-Mix Percentage	×	Budgeted Contribution Margin per Unit	=	Sales-Quantity Variance
Commercial	(84,000 units − 80,000 units)	×	0.25	×	$500 per unit	=	$ 500,000 F
Residential	(84,000 units − 80,000 units)	×	0.75	×	$400 per unit	=	1,200,000 F
Total sales-quantity variance							$1,700,000 F

2. Actual market share = 84,000 ÷ 700,000 = 0.12, or 12%

Budgeted market share = 80,000 ÷ 800,000 units = 0.10, or 10%

Budgeted contribution margin

per composite unit = $34,000,000 ÷ 80,000 units = $425 per unit

of budgeted mix

Budgeted contribution margin per composite unit of budgeted mix can also be calculated as:

Commercial: $500 per unit × 0.25 = $125

Residential: $400 per unit × 0.75 = 300

Budgeted contribution margin per

composite unit $425

$$\begin{array}{c}\text{Market-share}\\\text{variance}\end{array} = \begin{array}{c}\text{Actual}\\\text{market size}\\\text{in units}\end{array} \times \left(\begin{array}{ccc}\text{Actual}&&\text{Budgeted}\\\text{market}&-&\text{market}\\\text{share}&&\text{share}\end{array}\right) \times \begin{array}{c}\text{Budgeted}\\\text{contribution margin}\\\text{per composite unit}\\\text{for budgeted mix}\end{array}$$

= 700,000 units × (0.12 − 0.10) × $425 per unit

= $5,950,000 F

$$\begin{array}{c}\text{Market-size}\\\text{variance}\end{array} = \left(\begin{array}{c}\text{Actual}\\\text{market size}-\\\text{in units}\end{array}\begin{array}{c}\text{Budgeted}\\\text{market size}\\\text{in units}\end{array}\right) \times \begin{array}{c}\text{Budgeted}\\\text{market}\\\text{share}\end{array} \times \begin{array}{c}\text{Budgeted}\\\text{contribution margin}\\\text{per composite unit}\\\text{for budgeted mix}\end{array}$$

= (700,000 units − 800,000 units) × 0.10 × $425 per unit

= $4,250,000 U

Note that the algebraic sum of the market-share variance and the market-size variance is equal to the sales-quantity variance: $5,950,000 F + $4,250,000 U = $1,700,000 F.

3. Both the sales-mix variance and the sales-quantity variance are favourable. The favourable sales-mix variance occurred because the actual mix comprised more of the higher-margin commercial vinyl flooring. The favourable sales-quantity variance occurred because the actual total quantity of rolls sold exceeded the budgeted amount.

The company's large favourable market-share variance is due to a 12% actual market share compared with a 10% budgeted market share. The market-size variance is unfavourable because the actual market size was 100,000 rolls less than the budgeted market size. Payne's performance in 2013 appears to be very good.

Although overall market size declined, the company sold more units than budgeted by gaining market share.

SUMMARY POINTS

The following question-and-answer format summarizes the chapter's learning outcomes. Each point presents a key question, and the guidelines are the answer to that question.

LEARNING OUTCOMES	GUIDELINES
1. What is product bundling and why does it give rise to revenue-allocation issues?	Bundling occurs when two or more products (or services) sell together for a single price. There are three methods of revenue allocation, and management teams should choose the method that most closely represents economic reality. Good judgment is needed because the method selected affects remuneration of managers of individual products in the bundle who are often evaluated on product revenues or product operating incomes.
2. Of what relevance is an ABC system to evaluating the relative profitability of customers?	The data provided by an ABC system more readily distinguishes among more and less expensive customer value propositions. Particularly for price takers in an intensely competitive environment, when product/service mix pricing differs among customers, management teams must select those customers who are most profitable to the company.

3. How can Level 3 and 4 revenue variances be helpful to a management team?	Calculating Level 3 and 4 revenue variances directs attention to what has actually happened relative to what was expected. Revenue variances are best explained by marketing, which is responsible for sales volume forecasts and pricing of individual and bundled units. Revenue variance analyses are essential to evaluating and ranking product/service profitability.
4. How can a customer profitability profile be used?	The profile enables management teams to more readily select costs relevant to ranking the profitability of individual customers and entire groups of customers. The alternatives of negotiating new prices or reducing customer sustaining costs are clearer. The customer or group yielding the highest contribution margin per constrained resource should be retained.
5. What are the key concepts when making product and customer mix decisions?	The product, branch, segment, or customer group yielding the highest contribution margin per *constrained* resource should be selected. Managers should ignore allocated overhead costs when making decisions about discontinuing and adding customers, branches, and segments. They should focus instead on how total costs differ among alternatives.

TERMS TO LEARN

This chapter and the Glossary at the end of the book contain definitions of the following important terms:

composite unit (p. 647)
customer profitability analysis (p. 653)
incremental revenue-allocation method (p. 637)
market-share variance (p. 649)

market-size variance (p. 650)
price discounting (p. 644)
product bundle (p. 635)
revenue allocation (p. 634)
sales-mix variance (p. 647)

sales-quantity variance (p. 648)
stand-alone revenue-allocation method (p. 636)
zero-sum game (p. 638)

ASSIGNMENT MATERIAL

SHORT-ANSWER QUESTIONS

16-1   Describe how companies are increasingly facing revenue-allocation decisions.

16-2   Distinguish between the stand-alone revenue-allocation method and the incremental revenue-allocation method.

16-3   Identify and discuss arguments that individual product managers may put forward to support their preferred revenue-allocation method.

16-4   How might a dispute over the allocation of revenues of a bundled product be resolved?

16-5   Show how managers can gain insight into the causes of a sales-volume variance by drilling down into the components of this variance.

16-6   How can the concept of a composite unit be used to explain why an unfavourable total sales-mix variance of contribution margin occurs?

16-7   Explain why a favourable sales-quantity variance occurs.

16-8   Distinguish between a market-size variance and a market-share variance.

16-9   Why might some companies choose not to compute market-size and market-share variances?

16-10   Why is customer profitability analysis a vitally important topic to managers?

16-11   Are for-profit businesses the only users of revenue allocation? Explain.

16-12   "A customer profitability profile highlights those customers that should be dropped to improve profitability." Do you agree? Explain.

16-13   Give an example of three types of different levels of costs in a customer cost hierarchy.

16-14   How can the extent of price discounting be tracked on a customer-by-customer basis?

EXERCISES

16-15 Terminology. A number of terms are listed below:

composite unit	customer profitability analysis	incremental
market-share	market size	sales-mix
sales quantity	standalone	product bundles

REQUIRED

Select the terms from the above list to complete the following sentences.

To satisfy their customers' value proposition and benefit from economies of scale, companies often create customized _____ from individual products. This is also called a _____. The decision the management team needs to make is how to allocate the bundled revenue to each component of the bundle. There are two methods: _____ and _____ revenue allocation. In combination with ABC systems, the management team can examine detailed variance reports of _____, _____, _____, and _____ variance. This informs the team how well they are implementing their strategy. The team can also use the customer as cost object in an ABC system and conduct a _____ to determine whether to drop or add customers, stores, or branches to improve profit.

1. a. Allocation to St. Anne, $1,500,000

16-16 Allocation of common costs. The cities of St. Anne, St. Teresa, and St. Steven are considering the implementation of a new program to handle disposal of hazardous waste to comply with a new, more stringent provincial law. Because of the close proximity of the three cities, a joint program has been suggested. The annual cost of separate programs and a joint program are:

City	Capacity	Cost
St. Anne	100,000 tonnes	$2,100,000
St. Teresa	25,000 tonnes	$1,400,000
St. Steven	175,000 tonnes	$3,500,000
Joint Program	300,000 tonnes	$5,000,000

REQUIRED

1. Allocate the $5,000,000 cost of the joint program to each of the three cities using:
   a. The stand-alone method.
   b. The incremental-allocation method (in the order of the most waste to the least waste).
2. How do you think the citizens of each community would feel about each of the two methods of allocation?

1. a. Allocated to *RCC*, $36

16-17 Revenue allocation. Lee Shu-yu Inc. produces and sells DVDs to business people and students who are planning extended stays in China. It has been very successful with two DVDs: *Beginning Mandarin* and *Conversational Mandarin*. It is introducing a third DVD, *Reading Chinese Characters*. It has decided to market its new DVD in two different packages grouping the *Reading Chinese Characters* DVD with each of the other two language DVDs. Information about the separate DVDs and the packages follows.

DVD	Selling Price
Beginning Mandarin (BegM)	$60
Conversational Mandarin (ConM)	$50
Reading Chinese Characters (RCC)	$40
BegM + RCC	$90
ConM + RCC	$72

REQUIRED

1. Using the selling prices, allocate revenues from the *BegM + RCC* package to each DVD in that package using (a) the stand-alone method, (b) the incremental method, and (c) the Shapley value method.
2. Using the selling prices, allocate revenues from the *ConM + RCC* package to each DVD in that package using (a) the stand-alone method, (b) the incremental method, in either order, and (c) the Shapley value method.
3. Which method is most appropriate for allocating revenues among the DVDs? Why?

1. Laower-tier tickets, $14,000 U

16-18 Variance analysis, multiple products. The Penguins play in the North American Ice Hockey League. The Penguins play in the Downtown Arena (owned and managed by the City of Downtown), which has a capacity of 15,000 seats (5,000 lower-tier seats and 10,000 upper-tier seats). The Downtown Arena charges the Penguins a per-ticket charge for use of the facility. All tickets are sold by the Reservation Network, which charges the Penguins a reservation fee per ticket. The Penguins' budgeted contribution margin for each type of ticket in 2013 is computed as follows:

	Lower-Tier Tickets	Upper-Tier Tickets
Selling price	$35	$14
Downtown Arena fee	10	6
Reservation Network fee	5	3
Contribution margin per ticket	$20	$ 5

The budgeted and actual average attendance figures per game in the 2013 season are:

	Budgeted Seats Sold	Actual Seats Sold
Lower tier	4,000	3,300
Upper tier	6,000	7,700
Total	10,000	11,000

There was no difference between the budgeted and actual contribution margin for lower-tier or upper-tier seats.

The manager of the Penguins was delighted that actual attendance was 10% above budgeted attendance per game, especially given the depressed state of the local economy in the past six months.

REQUIRED

1. Compute the sales-volume variance for each type of ticket and in total for the Penguins in 2013. (Calculate all variances in terms of contribution margins.)
2. Compute the sales-quantity and sales-mix variances for each type of ticket and in total in 2013.
3. Present a summary of the variances in requirements 1 and 2. Comment on the results.

16-19 Variance analysis, working backward. The Jinwa Corporation sells two brands of wine glasses, Plain and Chic. Jinwa provides the following information for sales in the month of June 2013:

1. Sales mix, 80% Plain, 20% Chic

Static-budget total contribution margin	$5,600
Budgeted units to be sold of all glasses	2,000 units
Budgeted contribution margin per unit of Plain	$2 per unit
Budgeted contribution margin per unit of Chic	$6 per unit
Total sales-quantity variance	$1,400 U
Actual sales-mix percentage of Plain	60%

All variances are to be computed in contribution-margin terms.

REQUIRED

1. Calculate the sales-quantity variances for each product for June 2013.
2. Calculate the individual-product and total sales-mix variances for June 2013. Calculate the individual-product and total sales-volume variances for June 2013.
3. Briefly describe the conclusions you can draw from the variances.

16-20 Variance analysis, multiple products. SodaKing manufactures and sells three soft drinks: Kola, Limor, and Orlem. Budgeted and actual results for 2013 are as follows:

1. Sales mix, 16% Kola, 24% Limor, 60% Orlem

	Budget for 2013			Actual for 2013		
Product	Selling Price	Variable Cost per Carton	Cartons Sold	Selling Price	Variable Cost per Carton	Cartons Sold
Kola	$6.00	$4.00	400,000	$6.20	$4.50	480,000
Limor	$4.00	$2.80	600,000	$4.25	$2.75	900,000
Orlem	$7.00	$4.50	1,500,000	$6.80	$4.60	1,620,000

REQUIRED

1. Compute the total sales-volume variance, the total sales-mix variance, and the total sales-quantity variance. (Calculate all variances in terms of contribution margin.) Show results for each product in your computations.
2. What inferences can you draw from the variances computed in requirement 1?

16-21 Market-share and market-size variances (continuation of 16-20). SodaKing prepared the budget for 2013 assuming a 10% market share based on total sales in the western region of Canada. The total soft-drinks market was estimated to reach sales of 25 million cases in the region. However, actual total sales volume in the western region was 24 million cases.

Actual market share, 12.5%

Calculate the market-share and market-size variances for SodaKing in 2013. (Calculate all variances in terms of contribution margin.) Comment on the results.

16-22 Customer profitability, service company. Instant Service (IS) repairs printers and photocopiers for five multisite companies in a tri-city area. IS's costs consist of the cost of technicians and equipment that are directly traceable to the customer site and a pool of office overhead. Until recently, IS estimated customer profitability by allocating the office overhead to each customer based on share of revenues. For 2013, IS reported the following results:

	Avery	Okie	Wizard	Grainger	Duran	Total
Revenues	$260,000	$200,000	$322,000	$122,000	$212,000	$1,116,000
Technician and equipment cost	182,000	175,000	225,000	107,000	178,000	867,000
Office overhead allocated	31,859	24,507	39,457	14,949	25,978	136,750
Operating income	$ 46,141	$ 493	$ 57,543	$ 51	$ 8,022	$ 112,250

Tina Sherman, IS's new controller, notes that office overhead is more than 10% of total costs, so she spends a couple of weeks analyzing the consumption of office overhead resources by customers. She collects the following information:

Activity Area	Cost Driver Rate
Service-call handling	$75 per service call
Parts ordering	$80 per web-based parts order
Billing and collection	$50 per bill (or reminder)
Customer database maintenance	$10 per service call

	Avery	Okie	Wizard	Grainger	Duran
Number of service calls	150	240	40	120	180
Number of web-based parts orders	120	210	60	150	150
Number of bills (or reminders)	30	90	90	60	120

1. Compute customer-level operating income using the new information that Sherman has gathered.
2. Prepare exhibits for IS similar to Exhibits 16-10 and 16-12. Comment on the results.
3. What options should IS consider, with regard to individual customers, in light of the new data and analysis of office overhead?

16-23 Customer profitability, distribution. Figure Four is a distributor of pharmaceutical products. Its ABC system has five activities:

Activity Area	Cost Driver Rate in 2013
1. Order processing	$40 per order
2. Line-item ordering	$ 3 per line item
3. Store deliveries	$50 per store delivery
4. Carton deliveries	$ 1 per carton
5. Shelf-stocking	$16 per stocking-hour

Rick Flair, the controller of Figure Four, wants to use this ABC system to examine individual customer profitability within each distribution market. He focuses first on the mom-and-pop single-store distribution market. Two customers are used to exemplify the insights available with the ABC approach. Data pertaining to these two customers in August 2013 are as follows:

	Charlesville Pharmacy	Chapelville Pharmacy
Total orders	13	10
Average line items per order	9	18
Total store deliveries	7	10
Average cartons shipped per store delivery	22	20
Average hours of shelf-stocking per store delivery	0	0.5
Average revenue per delivery	$2,400	$1,800
Average cost of goods sold per delivery	$2,100	$1,650

1. Use the ABC information to compute the operating income of each customer in August 2013. Comment on the results and what, if anything, Flair should do.
2. Flair ranks the individual customers in the mom-and-pop single-store distribution market on the basis of monthly operating income. The cumulative operating income of the top 20% of customers is $55,680. Figure Four reports operating losses of $21,247 for the bottom 40% of its customers. Make four recommendations that you think Figure Four should consider in light of this new customer profitability information.

PROBLEMS

16-24 Customer profitability, responsibility for environmental cleanup, governance. ① ④ Industrial Fluids, Ltd. (IFL) manufactures and sells fluids used by metal-cutting plants. These fluids enable metal-cutting to be done more accurately and more safely.

IFL has more than 1,000 customers. It is currently undertaking a customer profitability analysis. Arian Papandopolis, a newly hired accountant and MBA, is put in charge of the project. One cost relevant to her analysis is IFL's liability for its customers' fluid disposal.

Papandopolis discovers that IFL may have responsibility under Canadian environmental legislation for the disposal of toxic waste by its customers. Moreover, she visits ten customer sites and finds dramatic differences in their toxic-waste handling procedures. She describes one site owned by Acme Metal as an "environmental nightmare about to become a reality." She tells the IFL controller that even if they have only one-half of the responsibility for the cleanup at Acme's site, they will still be facing very high damages. He is displeased at the news. Acme Metal has not paid its account to IFL for the past three months and has formally filed for bankruptcy. The controller cautions Papandopolis to be careful in her written report. He notes that "IFL does not want any smoking guns in its files in case of subsequent litigation."

REQUIRED

1. As Papandopolis prepares IFL's customer profitability analysis, how should she handle any estimates of litigation and cleanup costs that IFL may be held responsible for?
2. How should Papandopolis handle the Acme Metal situation when she prepares a profitability report for this customer?

16-25 Revenue allocation, bundled products, customer profitability. Athletic Programs (AP) ① sells exercise DVDs through television infomercials. It uses a well-known sports celebrity in each DVD. Each celebrity receives a share (typically varying between 10% and 25%) of the revenue from the sale of their DVD. In recent months, AP has started selling its exercise DVDs in bundled form as well as in individual form. Typically, the bundled products are offered to people who telephone for a specific DVD after watching an infomercial. Each infomercial is for a specific exercise DVD. As a marketing experiment, AP has begun to advertise the bundled product at the end of some infomercials in a select set of markets. Sales in 2013 of three DVDs that have been sold individually, as well as in bundled form, are as follows:

1. Royalties for SuperAbs, $170,100

	Average Retail Price	Net Units Sold	Royalty Paid to Celebrity
Individual sales:			
SuperAbs	$42	27,000	15%
SuperArms	$37	53,000	25%
SuperLegs	$27	20,000	18%
Bundled product sales			
SuperAbs + SuperArms	$62	18,000	?
SuperAbs + SuperLegs	$54	6,000	?
SuperArms + SuperLegs	$44	11,000	?
SuperAbs + SuperArms + SuperLegs	$67	22,000	?

REQUIRED

1. What royalty would be paid to the celebrity on each DVD for the individual sales in 2013?
2. What royalty would be paid to each celebrity for the bundled product sales in 2013 using:
   a. The stand-alone revenue-allocation method (with average retail price as the weight)?
   b. The incremental revenue-allocation method (with SuperArms ranked 1, SuperAbs ranked 2, and SuperLegs ranked 3)?

3. Discuss the relative merits of the two revenue-allocation methods in requirement 2.

4. Assume the incremental revenue-allocation method is used. What alternative approaches could be used to determine the sequence in which the bundled revenue could be allocated to individual products?

16-26 Customer profitability, distribution. Spring Distribution has decided to analyze the profitability of five new customers. It buys bottled water at $12 per case and sells to retail customers at a list price of $14.40 per case. Data pertaining to the five customers are:

	Customer				
	P	**Q**	**R**	**S**	**T**
Cases sold	2,080	8,750	60,800	31,800	3,900
List selling price	$14.40	$14.40	$14.40	$14.40	$14.40
Actual selling price	$14.40	$14.16	$13.20	$13.92	$12.96
Number of purchase orders	15	25	30	25	30
Number of customer visits	2	3	6	2	3
Number of deliveries	10	30	60	40	20
Miles travelled per delivery	14	4	3	8	40
Number of expedited deliveries	0	0	0	0	1

Activity	Cost Driver Rate
Order taking	$100 per purchase order
Customer visits	$80 per customer visit
Deliveries	$2 per delivery mile travelled
Product handling	$0.50 per case sold
Expedited deliveries	$300 per expedited delivery

REQUIRED

1. Compute the customer-level operating income of each of the five retail customers now being examined (P, Q, R, S, and T). Comment on the results.

2. What insights are gained by reporting both the list selling price and the actual selling price for each customer?

3. What factors should Spring Distribution consider in deciding whether to drop one or more of the five customers?

16-27 Variance analysis, sales-mix, and sales-quantity variances. Aussie Infonautics Inc. produces handheld Windows CE–compatible organizers. Aussie Infonautics markets three different handheld models. PalmPro is a souped-up version for the executive on the go; PalmCE is a consumer-oriented version; and PalmKid is a stripped-down version for the young adult market. You are Aussie Infonautics' senior vice-president of marketing. The CEO has discovered that the total contribution margin came in lower than budgeted, and it is your responsibility to explain to him why actual results are different from the budget. Budgeted and actual operating data for the company's third quarter of 2013 are as follows:

Budgeted Operating Data, Third Quarter 2013

	Selling Price	Variable Cost per Unit	Contribution Margin per Unit	Sales Volume in Units
PalmPro	$379	$182	$197	12,500
PalmCE	269	98	171	37,500
PalmKid	149	65	84	50,000
				100,000

Actual Operating Data, Third Quarter 2013

	Selling Price	Variable Cost per Unit	Contribution Margin per Unit	Sales Volume in Units
PalmPro	$349	$178	$171	11,000
PalmCE	285	92	193	44,000
PalmKid	102	73	29	55,000
				110,000

REQUIRED

1. Compute the actual and budgeted contribution margins in dollars for each product and in total for the third quarter of 2013.
2. Calculate the actual and budgeted sales mixes for the three products for the third quarter of 2013.
3. Calculate total sales-volume, sales-mix, and sales-quantity variances for the third quarter of 2013. (Calculate all variances in terms of contribution margins.)
4. Given that your CEO is known to have temper tantrums, you want to be well prepared for this meeting. In order to prepare, write a paragraph or two comparing actual results to budgeted amounts.

16-28 Market-share and market-size variances (continuation of 16-27). Aussie Infonautics' senior vice president of marketing prepared his budget at the beginning of the third quarter assuming a 25% market share based on total sales. The total handheld-organizer market was estimated by Foolinstead Research to reach sales of 400,000 units worldwide in the third quarter. However, actual sales in the third quarter were 500,000 units.

② 1. Budgeted average contribution margin per unit, $130.75

REQUIRED

1. Calculate the market-share and market-size variances for Aussie Infonautics in the third quarter of 2013 (calculate all variances in terms of contribution margins).
2. Explain what happened based on the market-share and market-size variances.
3. Calculate the actual market size, in units, that would have led to no market-size variance (again using budgeted contribution margin per unit). Use this market-size figure to calculate the actual market share that would have led to a zero market-share variance.

16-29 Variance analysis, multiple products. Debbie's Delight Inc. operates a chain of cookie stores. Budgeted and actual operating data for its three Calgary stores for August 2013 are as follows:

② ③ 1. Chocolate chip sales-volume variance, $25,200 F

Budget for August 2013

	Selling Price per kg	Variable Cost per kg	Contribution Margin per kg	Sales Volume in kg
Chocolate chip	$4.50	$2.50	$2.00	45,000
Oatmeal raisin	5.00	2.70	2.30	25,000
Coconut	5.50	2.90	2.60	10,000
White chocolate	6.00	3.00	3.00	5,000
Macadamia nut	6.50	3.40	3.10	15,000
				100,000

Actual for August 2013

	Selling Price per kg	Variable Cost per kg	Contribution Margin per kg	Sales Volume in kg
Chocolate chip	$4.50	$2.60	$1.90	57,600
Oatmeal raisin	5.20	2.90	2.30	18,000
Coconut	5.50	2.80	2.70	9,600
White chocolate	6.00	3.40	2.60	13,200
Macadamia nut	7.00	4.00	3.00	21,600
				120,000

Debbie's Delight focuses on contribution margin in its variance analysis.

1. Compute the total sales-volume variance for August 2013.
2. Compute the total sales-mix variance for August 2013.
3. Compute the total sales-quantity variance for August 2013.
4. Comment on your results in requirements 1, 2, and 3.

16-30 Market-share and market-size variances (continuation of 16-29). Debbie's Delight attains a 10% market share based on total sales of the Calgary market. The total Calgary market is expected to be 1,000,000 kilograms in sales volume for August 2013. The actual total Calgary market for August 2013 was 960,000 kilograms in sales volume.

Budgeted average contribution margin per unit, $2.35

REQUIRED

Compute the market-share and market-size variances for Debbie's Delight in August 2013. Calculate all variances in contribution-margin terms. Comment on the results.

16-31 Relevance, quantitative and qualitative. The Department of National Defence has the difficult decision of deciding which military bases to close down. Military and political factors obviously matter, but cost savings are also an important factor. Consider two naval bases—one in Vancouver, British Columbia, and one in Halifax, Nova Scotia. National Defence has decided that it needs only one of those two bases permanently, so one must be shut down. The decision regarding which base to shut down will be made on cost considerations alone. The following information is available:

a. The Vancouver base was built at a cost of $100 million. The operating costs of the base are $400 million per year. The base is built on land owned by National Defence, so it pays nothing for the use of the property. If the base is closed, the land will be sold to developers for $500 million.

b. The Halifax base was built at a cost of $150 million on land leased by National Defence from private citizens. National Defence can choose to lease the land permanently for an annual lease payment of $3 million per year. If it decides to keep the Halifax base open, National Defence plans to invest $60 million in a fixed income note, which at 5% interest will earn the $3 million the government needs for the lease payments. The land and buildings will immediately revert to the owner if the base is closed. The operating costs of the base, excluding lease payments, are $300 million per year.

c. If the Vancouver base is closed down, National Defence will have to transfer some personnel to the Halifax facility. As a result, the yearly operating costs at Halifax will increase by $100 million per year. If the Halifax facility is closed down, no extra costs will be incurred to operate the Vancouver facility.

REQUIRED

The British Columbia delegation argues that it is cheaper to close down the Halifax base, for two reasons: (1) it would save $100 million per year in additional costs required to operate the Halifax base, and (2) it would save $3 million per year in lease payments. (Recall that the Vancouver base requires no cash payments for use of the land because the land is owned by National Defence.) Do you agree with the British Columbia delegation's arguments and conclusions? In your answer, identify and explain all costs that you consider relevant and all costs that you consider irrelevant for the base-closing decision.

16-32 Customer profitability and ABC hierarchy. The Sherriton Hotels chain embarked on a new customer loyalty program in 2013. The 2013 year-end data have been collected, and it is now time for you to determine whether the loyalty program should be continued, discontinued, or perhaps altered to improve loyalty and profitability levels at Sherriton.

1. Gold Program contribution margin, $12,295,800

Sherriton's loyalty program consists of three different customer loyalty levels. All new customers can sign up for the Sherriton Bronze Card—this card provides guests with a complimentary bottle of wine (cost to the chain is $5 per bottle) and $20 in restaurant coupons each night (cost to the chain is $10). Bronze customers also receive a 10% discount off the nightly rate. The program enables the chain to track a member's stays and activities. Once a customer has stayed and paid for 20 nights at any of the chain's locations worldwide, he or she is upgraded to Silver Customer status. Silver benefits include the bottle of wine (cost to the chain is $5 per bottle), $30 in restaurant coupons (cost to the chain is $15), and 20% off every night from the twenty-first night on. A customer who reaches the 50-night level is upgraded to Gold Customer status. Gold status increases the nightly discount to 30% and replaces the $5 bottle of wine with a bottle of champagne (cost to the chain is $20 per bottle). As well, $40 in restaurant coupons are granted (cost to the chain is $20).

The average full price for one night's stay is $200. The chain incurs variable costs of $65 per night, exclusive of loyalty program costs. Total fixed costs for the chain are $140,580,000. Sherriton operates ten hotels with, on average, 500 rooms each. All hotels are open for business 365 days a year, and approximate average occupancy rates are around 80%. Following are some loyalty program characteristics:

Loyalty Program	Number of Customers	Average Number of Nights per Customer
Gold	2,673	60
Silver	9,174	35
Bronze	88,330	10
No program	240,900	1

Note that an average Gold Customer would have received the 10% discount for his or her first 20 stays, received the 20% discount for the next 30 stays, and the 30% discount only for the last ten nights. Assume that all program members signed on to the program the first time they stayed with one of the chain's hotels. Also, assume the restaurants are managed by a 100%-owned subsidiary of Sherriton.

REQUIRED
1. Calculate the program contribution margin for each of the three programs, as well as for the group of customers not subscribing to the loyalty program. Which program is the most profitable? Which is the least profitable? Do not allocate fixed costs to individual rooms or specific loyalty programs.
2. Develop an income statement for Sherriton for the year ended December 31, 2013.
3. What is the average room rate per night? What are average variable costs per night inclusive of the loyalty program?
4. Explain what drives the profitability (or lack thereof) of the most and least profitable loyalty programs (again, one of these may be the "no program" option).

16-33 Customer profitability, customer-cost hierarchy. Ramish Electronics has only two retail and two wholesale customers. Information relating to each customer for 2013 follows (in thousands):

1. North America wholesaler customer-level operating income, $58,150

	Wholesale Customers		Retail Customers	
	North America Wholesaler	South America Wholesaler	Big Sam Stereo	World Market
Revenues at list price	$420,000	$580,000	$130,000	$100,000
Discounts from list prices	30,000	40,000	7,000	500
Cost of goods sold	325,000	455,000	118,000	90,000
Delivery costs	450	650	200	125
Order processing costs	800	1,000	200	130
Costs of sales visits	5,600	5,500	2,300	1,350

Ramish's annual distribution-channel costs are $38 million for wholesale customers and $7 million for retail customers. Its annual corporate-sustaining costs, such as salary for top management and general administration costs, are $65 million. There is no cause-and-effect or benefits-received relationship between any cost allocation base and corporate-sustaining costs. That is, corporate-sustaining costs could be saved only if Ramish Electronics were to completely shut down.

REQUIRED
1. Calculate customer-level operating income using the format in Exhibit 16-2.
2. Prepare a customer-cost hierarchy report, using the format in Exhibit 16-13.
3. Ramish's management decides to allocate all corporate-sustaining costs to distribution channels: $51 million to the wholesale channel and $14 million to the retail channel. As a result, distribution-channel costs are now $89 million ($38 million + $51 million) for the wholesale channel and $21 million ($7 million + $14 million) for the retail channel. Calculate the distribution-channel-level operating income. On the basis of these calculations, what actions, if any, should Ramish's managers take? Explain.

16-34 Customer profitability in a manufacturing firm. Bizzan Manufacturing makes a component they call P14-31. This component is manufactured only when ordered by a customer, so Bizzan keeps no inventory of P14-31. The list price is $100 per unit, but customers who place "large" orders receive a 10% discount on price. Currently, the salespeople decide whether an order is large enough to qualify for the discount. When the product is finished, it is packed in cases of ten. When a customer order is not a multiple of ten, Bizzan uses a full case to pack the partial amount left over (e.g., if Customer C orders 25 units, three cases will be required). Customers pick up the order so Bizzan incurs costs of holding the product in the warehouse until customer pickup. The customers are manufacturing firms; if the component needs to be exchanged or repaired, customers can come back within ten days for free exchange or repair.

The full cost of manufacturing a unit of P14-31 is $80. In addition, Bizzan incurs customer-level costs.

Customer-level cost-driver rates are:

Order taking	$380 per order
Product handling	$ 10 per case
Warehousing (holding finished product)	$ 55 per day
Rush order processing	$520 per rush order
Exchange and repair costs	$ 40 per unit

Information about Bizzan's five biggest customers follows:

	A	B	C	D	E
Number of units purchased	5,000	2,400	1,200	4,000	8,000
Discounts given	10%	0	10%	0	10% on half the units
Number of orders	10	12	48	16	12
Number of cases	500	240	144	400	812
Days in warehouse (total for all orders)	13	16	0	12	120
Number of rush orders	0	2	0	0	5
Number of units exchanged/repaired	0	30	5	20	95

The salesperson gave customer C a price discount because, although Customer C ordered only 1,200 units in total, 12 orders (one per month) were placed. The salesperson wanted to reward customer C for repeat business. All customers except E ordered units in the same order size. Customer E's order quantity varied, so E got a discount some of the time but not all the time.

REQUIRED
1. Calculate the customer-level operating income for these five customers. Use the format in Exhibit 16-2. Prepare a customer profitability analysis by ranking the customers from most to least profitable, as in Exhibit 16-2.
2. Discuss the results of your customer profitability analysis. Does Bizzan have unprofitable customers? Is there anything Bizzan should do differently with its five customers?

② ④ ⑤
1. Customer 02 customer-level operating income, $900

16-35 Customer profitability. Ring Delights is a new company that manufactures custom jewellery. Ring Delights currently has six customers referenced by customer number: 01, 02, 03, 04, 05, and 06. Besides the costs of making the jewellery, the company has the following activities:

1. Customer orders. The salespeople, designers, and jewellery makers spend time with the customer. The cost driver rate is $40 per hour spent with a customer.
2. Customer fittings. Before the jewellery piece is completed the customer may come in to make sure it looks right and fits properly. Cost driver rate is $25 per hour.
3. Rush orders. Some customers want their jewellery quickly. The cost driver rate is $100 per rush order.
4. Number of customer return visits. Customers may return jewellery up to 30 days after the pickup of the jewellery to have something refitted or repaired at no charge. The cost driver rate is $30 per return visit.

Information about the six customers follows. Some customers purchased multiple items. The cost of the jewellery is 70% of the selling price.

Customer number	01	02	03	04	05	06
Sales revenue	$600	$4,200	$300	$2,500	$4,900	$700
Cost of item(s)	$420	$2,940	$210	$1,750	$3,430	$490
Hours spent on customer order	2	7	1	5	20	3
Hours on fittings	1	2	0	0	4	1
Number of rush orders	0	0	1	1	3	0
Number of return visits	0	1	0	1	5	1

1. Calculate the customer-level operating income for each customer. Rank the customers in order of most to least profitable and prepare a customer profitability analysis, as in Exhibit 16-12.
2. Are any customers unprofitable? What is causing this? What should Ring Delights do with respect to these customers?

16-36 Open a store. (CMA, adapted) Voltaire, a renowned pastry chef employed at a four-star hotel, has decided to open his own exclusive pastry shop. He has $100,000 to invest and the information he has obtained is as follows:

◆ There is a 55% probability the market size in the area will be 600,000 pastries per year and a 45% chance it will be 450,000 pastries per year.
◆ Price per pastry is assumed to be $4.00 and this is the basis for predicting Voltaire's market share.
◆ Variable costs are $2.60 per pastry.

The market share Voltaire will capture depends on where he locates. There are two possibilities:

◆ Location A costs $38,000 annual rent, where Voltaire will capture 30% of the pastry market (his market share). Fixed costs excluding rent are estimated at $90,000 per year.
◆ Location B costs $12,000 annual rent, where Voltaire will capture 22% of the pastry market (his market share). Fixed costs excluding rent are estimated at $54,000 per year.

REQUIRED

1. Based on your quantitative analysis, what is the best choice of location for Voltaire?
2. There is a consultant who sells industry market information. How much should Voltaire be willing to pay to know with certainty what the total market size is?

16-37 Customer profitability and governance. Glat Corporation manufactures a product called the glat, which it sells to merchandising firms such as International House of Glats (IHoG), Glats-R-Us (GRU), Glat Marcus (GM), Glat City (GC), Good Glats (GG), and Glat-mart (Gmart). The list price of a glat is $40, and the full manufacturing costs are $30. Salespeople receive a commission on sales, but the commission is based on number of orders taken, not on sales revenue generated or number of units sold. Salespeople receive a commission of $20 per order (in addition to regular salary).

Glat Corporation makes products based on anticipated demand. Glat Corporation carries an inventory of glats, so rush orders do not result in any extra manufacturing costs over and above the $30 per glat. Glat Corporation ships finished product to the customer at no additional charge to the customer for either regular or expedited delivery. Glat incurs significantly higher costs for expedited deliveries than for regular deliveries.

Expected and actual customer-level cost driver rates are:

Order taking (excluding sales commission)	$28 per order
Product handling	$1 per unit
Delivery	$1 per km driven
Expedited (rush) delivery	$300 per shipment

Because salespeople are paid $20 per order, they break up large orders into multiple smaller orders. This practice reduces the actual order-taking cost by $16 per smaller order (from $28 per order to $12 per order) because the smaller orders are all written at the same time. This lower cost rate is not included in budgeted rates because salespeople create smaller orders without telling management or the accounting department. Also, salespeople offer customers discounts to entice them to place more orders; GRU and Gmart each receive a 5% discount off the list price of $40.

5

1. If Voltaire opens location B, Expected operating income = $98,010

4

GM customer-level operating incomes, $2,340

Information about Glat's clients follows:

	IHG	GRU	GM	GC	GG	Gmart
Total number of units purchased	200	540	300	100	400	1,000
Number of actual orders	2	12	2	2	4	10
Number of written orders per actual order	2	1*	3	2	4	2
Total number of km driven to deliver all products	80	120	72	28	304	100
Number of expedited deliveries	0	4	0	0	1	3

*Because GRU places 12 separate orders, its order costs are $28 per order. All other orders are multiple smaller orders and so have actual order costs of $12 each.

REQUIRED

1. Using the information above, calculate the expected customer-level operating income for the six customers of Glat Corporation. Use the number of written orders at $28 each to calculate expected order costs.
2. Recalculate the customer-level operating income using the number of written orders but at their actual $12 cost per order instead of $28 (except for GRU, whose actual cost is $28 per order). How will Glat Corporation evaluate customer-level operating cost performance this period?
3. Recalculate the customer-level operating income if salespeople had not broken up actual orders into multiple smaller orders. Don't forget to also adjust sales commissions.
4. How is the behaviour of the salespeople affecting the profit of Glat Corporation? Is their behaviour ethical? What could Glat Corporation do to change the behaviour of the salespeople?

② ④ ⑤
1. Division A variable cost of goods sold, $416,500

16-38 Closing down divisions. Patterson Corporation has four operating divisions. During the first quarter of 2014, the company reported total income from operations of $55,000 and the following results for each division:

	Division			
	A	**B**	**C**	**D**
Sales	$550,000	$780,000	$970,000	$460,000
Cost of goods sold	490,000	520,000	575,000	390,000
Selling and admin. expenses	140,000	230,000	240,000	120,000
Operating income (loss)	$ (80,000)	$ 30,000	$155,000	$ (50,000)

Further analysis of costs reveals the following percentages of variable costs in each division:

	Division			
	A	**B**	**C**	**D**
Cost of goods sold	85%	84%	94%	96%
Selling and admin. expenses	64%	64%	70%	78%

Closing down any division would result in savings of 50% of the fixed costs of that division. Top management is very concerned about the unprofitable divisions (A and D) and is considering shutting them down.

REQUIRED

1. Calculate the contribution margin for the two unprofitable divisions (A and D).
2. On the basis of financial considerations alone, should the top management of Patterson shut down Division A? Division D?
3. What other factors should the top management of Patterson consider before making a decision?

16-39 Revenue allocation for bundled products. Pebble Resorts operates a five-star hotel with a world-recognized championship golf course. It has a decentralized management structure. There are three divisions:

1. Revenue stand-alone allocation for Lodging, $447

◆ Lodging (rooms, conference facilities)
◆ Food (restaurants and in-room service)
◆ Recreation (golf course, tennis courts, and so on)

Starting next month, Pebble will offer a two-day, two-person "getaway package" deal for $770. This deal includes:

◆ Two nights' stay for two in an ocean-view room—separately priced at $704 ($352 per night for two).
◆ Two rounds of golf separately priced at $330 ($165 per round). One person can do two rounds, or two can do one round each.
◆ Candlelight dinner for two at the exclusive Pebble Pacific Restaurant—separately priced at $88 per person.

Samantha Lee, president of the Recreation Division, recently asked the CEO of Pebble Resorts how her division would share in the $770 revenue from the package. The golf course was operating at 100% capacity (and then some). Under the "getaway package" rules, participants who booked one week in advance were guaranteed access to the golf course. Lee noted that every "getaway" booking would displace a $165 booking. She stressed that the high demand reflected the devotion of her team to keeping the golf course rated in the "Best 10 Courses in the World" listings in Golf Monthly magazine. As an aside, she also noted that the Lodging and Food divisions only had to turn away customers on "peak-season events such as the New Year's period."

REQUIRED
1. Allocate the $770 "getaway package" revenue to the three divisions using:
   a. The stand-alone revenue-allocation method.
   b. The incremental revenue-allocation method (with Recreation first, then Lodging, and then Food).
   Use unit selling prices as the weights in (a) and (b).
2. What are the pros and cons of (a) and (b) in requirement 1?

16-40 Revenue allocation for bundled products. Pétale Parfum (PP) manufactures and sells upscale perfumes. In recent months, PP has started selling its products in bundled form, as well as in individual form. Sales in 2013 of three products that have been sold individually are as follows:

1. The weight for Innocence, $220

	Retail Price	Units Sold
Stand-alone		
Fraîche	$110	20,000
Désarmer	88	37,500
Innocence	275	20,000
Suite		
Fraîche + Désarmer	165	
Fraîche + Innocence	308	

REQUIRED
1. Compute the weights for allocating revenues to each division for each of the bundled products using:
   a. The stand-alone revenue-allocation method based on total revenues of individual products.
   b. The incremental revenue-allocation method, with Innocence ranked 1; Désarmer, 2; and Fraîche, 3, based on retail prices of individual products. According to this ranking, the primary product in a suite has the highest rank, and so on.
2. Recalculate the allocation using the Shapley and the weighted Shapley value methods. What method would you recommend and why?

5

1. If the Surrey store is closed, Sundry's operating income = $ 7,000

16-41 Closing and opening stores. Sundry Corporation runs two convenience stores, one in Vancouver and one in Surrey. Operating income for each store in 2014 follows:

	Vancouver	Surrey
Revenues	$1,070,000	$860,000
Operating costs:		
Cost of goods sold	750,000	660,000
Lease rent (renewable each year)	90,000	75,000
Labour (paid on an hourly basis)	42,000	42,000
Amortization of equipment	25,000	22,000
Utilities (electricity, heating)	43,000	46,000
Allocated corporate overhead	50,000	40,000
Total operating costs	1,000,000	885,000
Operating income (loss)	70,000	(25,000)

The equipment has a remaining useful life of one year and zero disposal price. In a senior management meeting, Maria Lopez, the management accountant at Sundry Corporation, makes the following comment: "Sundry can increase its profitability by closing down the Surrey store or by adding more stores like it."

REQUIRED

Answer the following questions referring to the preceding data.

1. Calculate Sundry's operating income if it closes down the Surrey store. By closing down the store, Sundry can reduce overall corporate overhead costs by $44,000. Is Maria Lopez correct? Explain.
2. Calculate Sundry's operating income if it opens another store with revenues and costs identical to the Surrey store (including a cost of $22,000 to acquire equipment with a one-year useful life and zero disposal price). Opening this store will increase corporate overhead costs by $4,000. Is Maria Lopez correct? Explain.

2 3

1. Ontario operating margin after allocating headquarter costs, $940,000

16-42 Cost allocation and decision making. Greenbold Manufacturing has four divisions named after its locations: Ontario, Alberta, Yukon, and Saskatchewan. Corporate headquarters is in Manitoba. Greenbold corporate headquarters incurs $5,600,000 per period, which is an indirect cost of the divisions. Corporate headquarters currently allocates this cost to the divisions based on the revenues of each division. The CEO has asked each division manager to suggest an allocation base for the indirect headquarters costs from among revenues, segment margin, direct costs, and number of employees. Below is relevant information about each division:

	Ontario	Alberta	Yukon	Saskatchewan
Revenues	$7,800,000	$8,500,000	$6,200,000	$5,500,000
Direct costs	$5,300,000	$4,100,000	$4,300,000	$4,600,000
Segment margin	$2,500,000	$4,400,000	$1,900,000	$900,000
Number of employees	2,000	4,000	1,500	500

REQUIRED

1. Allocate the indirect headquarters costs of Greenbold Manufacturing to each of the four divisions using revenues, direct costs, segment margin, and number of employees as the allocation bases. Calculate operating margins for each division after allocating headquarters costs.
2. Which allocation base do you think the manager of the Saskatchewan division would prefer? Explain.
3. What factors would you consider in deciding which allocation base Greenbold should use?
4. Suppose the Greenbold CEO decides to use direct costs as the allocation base. Should the Saskatchewan division be closed? Why or why not?

1

1. Stand-alone revenue allocation for *Negotiating*, $1,400,000

16-43 Revenue allocation, bundled products. Business Horizons (BH) produces and markets DVDs for sale to the business community. It hires well-known business speakers to present new developments in their area of expertise in DVD format. The compensation paid to each speaker is individually negotiated. It always has a component based on the percentage of revenues from the sale of the DVD, but that percentage is not uniform across speakers. Moreover, some speakers negotiate separate fixed-dollar payments or multiple-DVD deals.

BH sells most DVDs as separate items. However, there is a growing trend for DVDs also to be sold as part of bundled packages. BH offered bundled packages of its three best-selling DVDs in 2013. Individual and bundled sales of these three DVDs for 2013 are:

Individual Sales

Speaker	Title	Units Sold	Selling Price	Speaker Royalty
Jeannett Smith	Negotiating for Win–Win	25,000	$150	24%
Mark Coyne	Marketing for the Internet	17,000	$120	16%
Laurie Daley	Electronic Commerce	8,000	$130	19%

Bundled Product Sales

Titles in Bundle	Units Sold	Selling Price
Negotiating for Win–Win + Marketing for the Internet	12,000	$210
Negotiating for Win–Win + Electronic Commerce	5,000	$220
Marketing for the Internet + Electronic Commerce	4,000	$190
Negotiating + Marketing + Electronic Commerce	11,000	$280

REQUIRED
1. Allocate the bundled product revenues to the individual DVDs using the stand-alone revenue-allocation method (using selling prices as the weights).
2. Describe (without computations) an alternative method of allocating the bundled product revenue to that in requirement 1.

COLLABORATIVE LEARNING CASE

16-44 Relevance of variance analyses. As a producer of wine in the Niagara region, you have the opportunity to either lease vineyards from local grape-growers or to purchase grapes from other farmers. In the past you have purchased grapes from the Okanagan Valley in British Columbia, and from the Sonoma Valley in California.

The quality of wine depends in part on the quality of grapes input to the fermenting process, but your fermenting machinery has a fixed capacity. Any unused capacity in one year cannot be applied to a different use. To obtain the best return, your preference is to operate at practical capacity even if projected demand or normal capacity is higher. An interesting opportunity in the industry is the ability to enter into a contract in the spring to pay a specific dollar value for grapes harvested in the fall.

Financial experts call this a hedging contract because you are protecting yourself against the risk that actual prices in the fall (the spot price) will be higher than your spring contracted price (the strike price). The quantity and quality of grapes harvested each year depend largely on a single uncontrollable factor—the weather. In spring you must decide on the input mix of harvested and purchased grapes that you believe is most likely to make the best use of available practical capacity—but you have no idea what the weather will be in the months before harvest.

A supplier approaches you in the spring with a proposition to sell you grapes and specifies the strike price. This supplier from the Okanagan provides you with a historical trend chart that summarizes the association between weather and yield from the vineyard for the last eight years.

REQUIRED
1. Explain your reasons for your contracting decision.
2. Of what use would similar information on your own market share be?

Process Costing

BUSINESS MATTERS

Allocation Affects Net Income—Reliable Estimates Are Important

Royal Dutch Shell is a global explorer and developer of energy sources. It is important to the Shell managers to plan, control, and report their year-to-year profitability. To accomplish this, they must allocate more closely the costs of Royal Dutch Shell's activities to reflect the timing, amount, and costs of those activities. Doing so means that managers can be confident that the profits will be realized. The goal of allocation is to match the quantity of actual activities and their timing to the flow of costs incurred from them. However, it is not feasible to trace every single cost to a single activity. Nor is every single activity uniquely linked to a single unit of output. What should the Shell managers do?

Fortunately for the Shell managers, process-costing techniques have been developed that will provide a suitably close and reliable approximation of the timing and flow of costs for a number of Shell's processes.

LEARNING OUTCOMES

After studying this chapter, you should be able to

1. Distinguish process- from job-costing allocation methods within the decision framework, and apply the weighted-average method of inventory valuation when the beginning work-in-process inventory is zero.

2. Contrast the journal entries for a process-costing system when there is and when there is not ending work-in-process inventory using the weighted-average method of inventory valuation.

3. Apply the weighted-average method of process costing to calculate the cost of goods manufactured and transferred out when there is both beginning and ending work-in-process inventory.

4. Analyze weighted-average, FIFO, and standard-costing methods of inventory valuation of cost of goods manufactured and transferred out.

5. Apply process-costing methods to report transferred-in costs and operations costing.

This chapter introduces the procedure of process cost allocation. In a process-costing system, the unit cost of a product or service is obtained by assigning total costs to many identical or similar units. In a manufacturing process-costing setting, each unit receives the same or similar amounts of direct material costs, direct manufacturing labour costs, and indirect manufacturing costs (manufacturing overhead).

One simplifying characteristic of continuous processes is that the output is homogeneous. One output unit is essentially identical to another, such as a litre of milk, a barrel of oil, a printed circuit for a smartphone, T-shirts, or a TV satellite dish. Allocation is a way to assign costs to units of output when it is infeasible to trace costs directly to output. As you know already, direct costs are traced, but indirect costs are allocated.

PROCESS-COSTING CALCULATIONS

1 Distinguish process- from job-costing allocation methods within the decision framework, and apply the weighted-average method of inventory valuation when the beginning work-in-process inventory is zero.

Deciding upon a process-costing system is, in many ways, easier than making other cost allocation decisions. In the simplest system there are only two cost pools. One is the prime cost pool comprising all direct material (DM) costs. The second is the conversion cost pool comprising all direct manufacturing labour and other indirect MOH costs. The cost driver for the prime cost pool is straightforward—the quantity of direct materials used during the accounting period. The cost driver for the conversion cost pool is predetermined as well. The resulting conversion cost rate is a straightforward weighted average cost of all identical units begun in the time period.

Step 1: Identify the Problem and Uncertainties The accounting problem is to design a cost assignment system that best matches the flow of costs to the flow of physical production of *identical* outputs. The physical processes cannot be directly observed often because it would be unsafe and unprofitable to do so. Moreover, direct observation would fail to reveal how complete each conversion process is for each unit of input remaining in the process. The purpose is to estimate full absorption cost per unit for both work in process (WIP) and finished goods inventory undertaken during a specific time period.

The stages of the conversion process are largely mechanized and continue 24/7/365, but accounts must be reported periodically—at least once a month. The method of reporting cost flows needs to meet the periodic reporting requirements without interrupting what is an unending conversion process. Similar to many costing situations, there is no perfect method to match the cost flow precisely to the physical fact of product conversion. There are variations, however, on the process-costing method from which the management team can make a choice.

Step 2: Gather Relevant Information Assume, first, that both the quantity of direct material (DM) and the time that direct material is input can be observed and reported. Second, assume that conversion is a joint costing activity throughout this physical transformation. Third, the exit of identical units of finished goods can be observed and measured. Fourth, assume measures of quantities of inputs of DM and of conversion activities are reliably measured and reported in the month they are consumed. Finally, assume costs of DM and conversion activities are reliably reported in the month the DM is used.

The task of accountants is to design a costing process to reflect as efficiently and effectively as possible the timing and accumulated costs of physical conversion. It is difficult because all units entering the process at the beginning of a time period accumulate costs until the finished goods can be sold. The costs will only be recovered fully (plus a reasonable profit) through the sale of finished goods available for sale each time period.

Step 3: Forecast Future Outcomes Input quantities of DM can be reliably measured in physical units as well as the DM cost pool. The cost driver rate is readily calculated as the total DM cost pool divided by the total physical units of input. The direct materials cost pool is called a *prime cost pool*.

Now the rate per unit of input is calculated and the costs must be assigned to output units. Accountants use engineering reports of actual yield. The yield ratio (see Chapter 7) multiplied by the cost driver rate assigns DM costs to each fully complete output unit. Provided the process is under control and purchase prices are stable, the direct materials' cost assigned should be relatively constant from one time period to the next. A third and fourth level variance analysis will confirm whether or not this is the case. The management team will forecast this cost based on the assumption that DM are 100% consumed at the moment they are added to the conversion process.

The remaining costs to transform raw materials into finished goods, including any direct manufacturing labour costs, comprise a second indirect cost pool called the conversion cost pool. There may be one conversion cost pool for all stages in a process or a conversion cost pool for each stage. Because the process is highly mechanized, a large part of the cost pool will be fixed MOH costs of equipment, insurance, taxes, and so on in addition to the variable operating costs of production that are not direct materials costs.

The cost driver used to calculate a conversion cost pool rate is called the **equivalent unit (EU)**. An EU expresses a 100% completed unit, weighted by the percentage of completion of actual partially completed WIP. For example, two identical inputs that are 50% complete are equivalent to one physical output unit if it was 100% complete, or 1 EU = 2 × 50% EU. This measures all units at all stages of completion using a common denominator of EU.

At the end of a month, a process engineer estimates or forecasts that all units that remain in WIP are 35% complete. The management team can forecast that it will take approximately 2.8571 EU partially complete to equal one 100% complete physical unit (1 ÷ 0.35 = 2.85714 EU and 1 EU = 2.85714 × 35%). A unit 35% complete has incurred 35% of total full absorption costs as well. Of course, one EU 100% complete is 1 EU = 1 × 100% and 100% of total full absorption process costs have been incurred to produce the finished good.

The conversion cost pool is reported monthly in the information system. The percentage complete is also reported and the expected yield on the DM is also known. This enables the management team to calculate both the DM cost rate and use the weighted average EU to calculate the conversion cost rate. To calculate the conversion cost rate, divide the total conversion cost pool by the total output measured as EU. Notice that this method assigns conversion costs directly to the equivalent of finished products at a simple weighted average cost rate.

The corporation then subtracts the estimated full absorption cost of finished goods sold to calculate gross margin, the value of all WIP and the value of all finished goods for the time period. Estimated gross margin and cost of goods sold can be compared to budgeted performance to assess if the process and profit are both under control.

From an engineering perspective, many continuous processes flow through readily identifiable, separate stages of production. For example, raw milk must be pasteurized, homogenized, and fortified with vitamins before it is ready for packaging, transportation, and sale. Each stage of production can be identified by the machine in which the milk is located, although just how complete the conversion is can't be observed for a single litre of milk.

One litre of milk that is 98% homogenized looks identical to one litre that is 42% homogenized. What is necessary is that engineers measure and report the percentages reliably and in a timely way and the cost pools are reported in the accounting system in the same quality. The goal is to measure cost flows in the way that best reflects the production activities that actually occurred during a specific time period.

Step 4: Make Decisions by Choosing Among Alternatives Engineers and accountants alike know that only finished goods can be sold to recover the production costs plus profit. This means not only the dollar value of assigned costs but also the timing of their assignment will affect forecasts of gross margin.

The alternative methods of assigning the conversion cost pool to either WIP or finished goods are weighted average; first in, first out (FIFO); and standard costing. The criterion to focus on when making a decision is what method best tells managers the costs incurred from the physical activities of continuous production in a particular time period. The choice of method affects both the calculation of the conversion cost pool allocation rates and the multiplier used to assign costs to work-in-process and finished goods inventories.

Managers must be able to depend on the separation of costs of finished goods available for sale, because these costs can be fully recovered if demand and pricing are appropriate. The inputs remaining in WIP cannot be sold and the costs will remain unrecovered until such time as these inputs are 100% converted and sold. In fact, WIP is an opportunity cost that delays the realization of revenue until the inputs are finally available for sale. Clearly, inventory management is one important path to realizing the maximum profit in any specific time period. This is best achieved when the estimates of conversion costs allocated to direct materials, WIP, and finished goods inventories are reliable.

Step 5: Implement the Decision, Evaluate Performance, and Learn If accountants have selected the best of the three GAAP alternatives available to measure the joint costs of continuous production processes, then the managers can assess actual to forecast performance with some confidence. Forecasts predict reasonable measures of future costs. Budgeted costs are a commitment to the future consumption of resources. When actual reports are compared to predicted, some level of difference will indicate when a process is within or out of control.

In many industries, processes are continuous and production managers are paid bonuses when they perform at or better than their cost targets. The more accurately the process costing system reflects the physical reality of production, or its economic substance, the fairer will be the remuneration from one time period to the next. The best process cost allocation system will be a reliable basis upon which to price outputs in order to recover all costs. Finally, when finished goods inventory quantities increase beyond a target, this can alert managers to decreased demand issues that will affect longer-term profitability and capacity decisions.

PROCESS COSTING: ALTERNATIVE METHODS

Imagine a multi-stage conversion process for milk products. As the raw milk proceeds through pasteurization and homogenization, so too must the costs of these activities. There are three methods to calculate the cost driver rates for the direct materials used in a specific time period, say one month, and for the pasteurization process.

The **weighted-average process-costing method** calculates the average equivalent unit (EU) cost of the pasteurization done to date (regardless of the period in which it was done) and assigns it to units completed and transferred out for homogenizing, and to EU in ending WIP inventory (EI WIP) for the pasteurizing process. In a continuous process there will always be WIP at each stage of conversion. The quantity of WIP will always be measured in EU based on an estimate of percentage of completion.

The **first-in, first-out (FIFO) process-costing method** assigns the cost of the prior accounting period's EUs in beginning work-in-process inventory (BI WIP) to the *first* EUs completed and transferred out in the current time period. The method then assigns the remaining costs of the time period to the EU added to and converted during the current period. The costs of EU complete and transferred out are kept separate from those remaining in EI WIP. Of course, these EU and costs become the beginning quantities and value of BI WIP in the subsequent time period. Both the weighted-average and FIFO alternatives are GAAP-compliant for external reporting purposes.

The **standard-costing method** relies on the estimation of yield, the standard input quantity required to produce one standard output unit. Engineers in the production department provide this information. The purchasing department provides information on standard costs per input unit. The standard cost is then multiplied by the percentage of completion to determine the cost allocation rate per EU. This method is GAAP-compliant and when all things are equal may be the most effective and efficient method for internal reporting and cost control purposes.

WEIGHTED-AVERAGE METHOD OF ASSIGNING CONVERSION COSTS

The purpose is to select the best method of assigning prime and conversion costs of milk pasteurization (the process) in one month. Appropriate information is available about the physical process and the flow of costs. To simplify, calculations will be illustrated for the physical flow of raw milk from direct materials through the process in one month. Costs of completely and incompletely pasteurized raw milk will be assigned to the appropriate inventories at month-end.

Assume there are no inputs in beginning inventories for either direct materials (DM) or the conversion cost pool. Therefore, there is a beginning balance of 0 physical units and $0 in both the prime and conversion inventories and cost pools. Assume 100% of the raw milk used is either fully or partially converted in one month. Note that there is a difference between 100% using the DM and 100% converting the DM. Assume all WIP of raw milk remaining in the conversion process is 50% converted, while the rest is 100% converted and physically flows on to the homogenization process; at this point the costs transfer out of pasteurization to homogenization. Of 250 hectolitres (hL) of raw milk used, 150 hL was fully converted and 100 hL was only 50% converted and remained as EI WIP at month-end in the process.[1]

The costs of DM and 100% conversion transfer to match the physical flow of milk. Assume the DM, or prime, cost pool is $2,000 for the month and the total (conversion) cost pool is $2,500 for a total cost of goods manufactured of $4,500. The task now is to assign costs to the 150 hL fully pasteurized and transferred out, and the 100 hL 50% pasteurized, which remains in EI WIP pasteurization. Exhibit 17-1 summarizes this information.

◆ **Step 1**: Report the physical units in hectolitres (hL) of raw milk 100% used and convert to EU. This is straightforward. The 250 hL of raw milk input to the process during the month is 100% used. Thus, the DM used in one month is also 250 EU (250 hL × 1.00 = 250 EU).

EXHIBIT 17-1

Summarizing the Physical and Cost Flow of Production Using the Weighted-Average Method to Calculate Cost Driver Rates

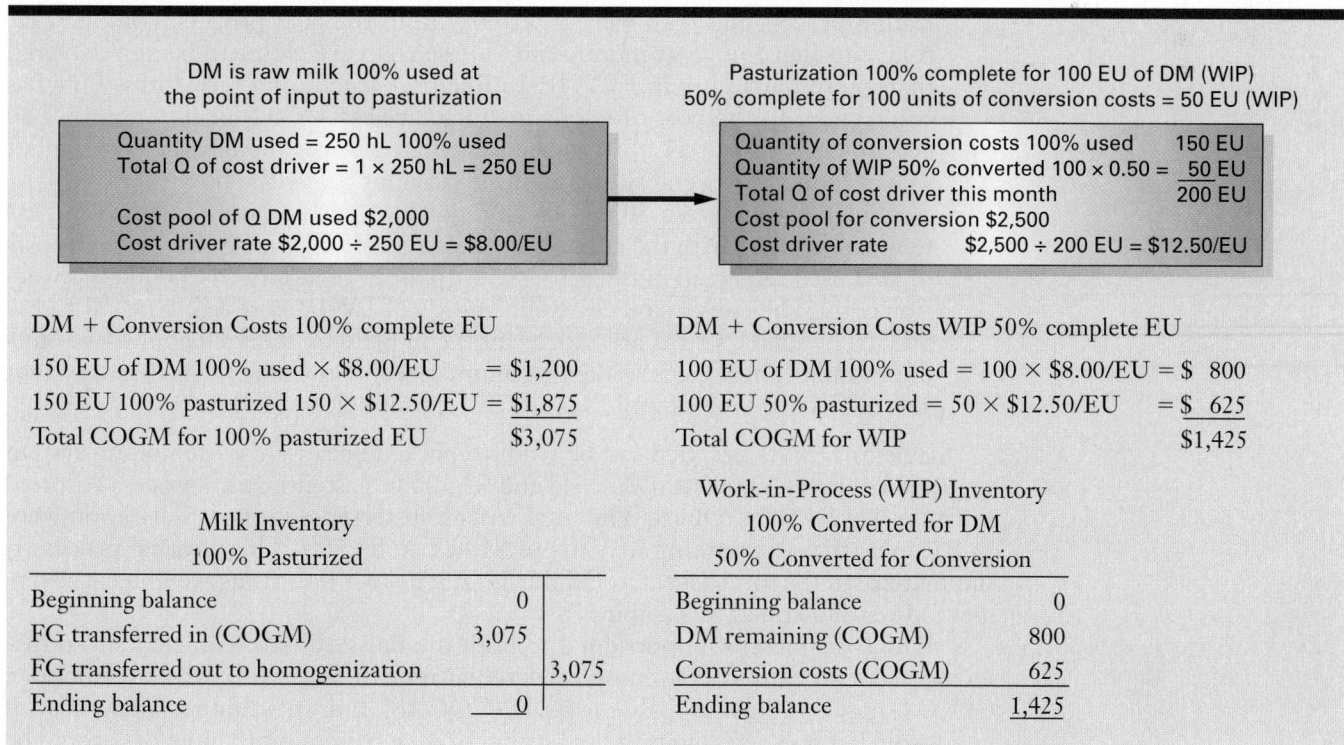

Now the calculation of raw milk both fully and partially converted in one month must be calculated to establish the physical flow of hectolitres through pasteurization and separate it from the hectolitres remaining in the process at month-end. Again, the calculation of raw milk fully pasteurized and flowing on to homogenization is straightforward and is 150 EU (150 hL × 1.00 = 150 EU). This is the first calculation inside the blue box on the right side of Exhibit 17-1. This box represents the calculation of the DM cost driver rate per EU for the month. Below are the calculations of DM and process costs for each 100% completed EU.

The information system also reports that the 100 hL (250 hL − 150 hL) of raw milk that did not flow to homogenization was 50% complete. Thus 100 hL × 0.50 = 50 EU of raw milk remaining in WIP at month-end. This calculation is in the second line in the blue box on the right in Exhibit 17-1. In total the EU that flowed into the process was 200 EU (150 EU + 50 EU = 200 EU). This is the total cost driver measured in EU and is the third line in the blue box on the right side of Exhibit 17-1. It is the sum of the first and second lines to calculate the cost driver rate of pasteurization. Now we have one common measure of the relevant flows of milk from DM to pasteurization, then out to homogenization. These EU will be used to assign costs.

◆ **Step 2:** Calculate the cost driver rates for direct materials fully processed. Inside the left box of Exhibit 17-1 the calculations are summarized. The direct materials used rate is straightforward because the information system reports that the total direct materials used cost pool for the month was $2,000. The cost driver rate is simply $2,000 ÷ 250 EU = $8.00/EU.

The pasteurization cost pool (conversion costs) was $2,500 in total for the month. The total EU fully and partly processed has been calculated in step 1 as 200 EU. The cost driver rate for the conversion cost pool is $2,500 ÷ 200 EU = $12.50/EU.

◆ **Step 3:** Assign costs of DM used and conversion to the two relevant inventory accounts, WIP and 100% pasteurized EU (Finished Goods). Only 150 EU of DM flowed both into and out of the pasteurization cost pool. The prime cost (DM used) was $8.00/EU × 150 EU = $1,200. The process cost rate was $12.50/EU × 150 EU = $1,875. The total costs that flowed into the pasteurization process and then were transferred into the next process, homogenization, equalled $3,075 at month-end. These costs are closer to being recovered than those remaining in EI WIP. In financial accounting terms, this flow has contributed to the cost of goods manufactured (COGM) in the month. The accumulated cost of $3,075 has been calculated below the blue box on the left side of Exhibit 17-1 and shown in the T-account below the box.

Finally, there were 50 EU of DM that flowed into and remained in pasteurization along with the costs. This means $8.00/EU × 100 EU = $800 costs of DM used remained in the process cost pool WIP at month-end plus conversion costs. The conversion costs remaining as EI WIP were $12.50 × 50 EU = $625. The total COGM are $1,425 for incomplete pasteurized equivalent units of raw milk. These calculations are summarized below the blue box on the right side of Exhibit 17-1 as well as in the T-account below the box.

The total costs assigned can be readily checked because the accounting system reported a total of $2,000 in DM used and $2,500 in pasteurization process costs for the month = $4,500 COGM. The total costs transferred out of pasteurization were $3,075 plus those remaining in WIP of $1,425 = $4,500. The physical process is summarized in the spreadsheet in Exhibit 17-2. The cost flow using weighted-average method was illustrated in Exhibit 17-1.

The costs must be apportioned to both the units 100% completed and transferred out and those 50% completed remaining in WIP to correctly calculate COGM, cost of goods available for sale (COGAS) and, most importantly, cost of goods sold (COGS). Amounts at the bottom of each column of Exhibit 17-2 could be used to report the financial results on a statement of cost of goods manufactured for the pasteurization process for the month for this milk manufacturing company.

EXHIBIT 17-2
Calculating Equivalent Unit Costs and Assigning Costs to Completed Units and Ending WIP
Inventory for Pasteurization of Raw Milk for a Particular Month

	A	B	C	D
		Total		
		Production	Direct	Conversion
3	CALCULATE COST ALLOCATION RATES	Costs	Materials	Costs
4	Cost added during the month (cost pools)	$4,500	$2,000	$2,500
5	Divide by equivalent units of work done in current period (Exhibit 17-1 final line, cost allocation base EU)		÷ 250	÷ 200
6	Cost per equivalent unit (cost allocation rate)		$ 8.00	$ 12.50
7	Total costs to account for	$4,500		
8	ASSIGNMENT OF COSTS:			
9	Completed and transferred out			
10	Direct materials (150 EU from Exhibit 17-1 × $8.00)	$1,200		
11	Conversion costs (150 EU from Exhibit 17-1 × $12.50)	1,875		
12	Total units completed and transferred out	3,075		
13	Work-in-process ending inventory (100 of DM consumed; 50 converted EU in WIP)	1,425		
14	Total costs accounted for	$4,500		
15				

The requirements of GAAP include not only an initial inventory valuation but also impairment testing. The inventory values must be at the lower of cost or net realizable value. Obsolete or unusable inventories of partially completed raw milk must be deducted from inventory balances. Milk is a perishable good and from time to time the supply of completely processed milk has far outpaced demand. Any financial reduction in inventory value will affect the profitability of an industrial milk processing company. An appropriate process costing system to assign costs ensures adequate internal control of not only the physical process but also the cost reporting process.

WEIGHTED-AVERAGE METHOD WITH NO BEGINNING WIP INVENTORY

2 Contrast the journal entries for a process-costing system when there is and when there is not ending work-in-process inventory using the weighted-average method of inventory valuation.

The easiest way to learn process costing is by example. Consider the following illustration, which is somewhat different from the first. In this continuous process, the outputs are identical circuit boards. Global Defence Inc. manufactures thousands of components for missiles and military equipment. We will focus on the production of one of these components, DG-19. The DG-19 is a critical part in a military defence system to control drones. Global Defence assembles and tests the DG-19.

The Assembly process is manual. Completed subassemblies arrive for robot testing and final addition of an expensive printed circuit. Prior to adding the last circuit to the DG-19, thorough quality control and inspection must be done as part of the conversion. These are processes that incur an indirect cost of MOH and are done by robots in a clean room. Either the final component is inserted into the tested subassembly or the subassembly is discarded for rework.

Only those subassemblies that pass the Testing process will have the final circuit board added by a robot. The completed DG-19 is immediately transferred to Finished Goods. All DM form one cost pool and all conversion costs, including direct manufacturing labour, form the second cost pool, which includes both the Assembly and Testing process costs. Only those circuit boards completely converted use 100% of the direct materials.

The process costing system for DG-19 has a single direct cost category (direct materials) and a single indirect process cost category (conversion costs). Every effort is made to ensure that all completed DG-19 units are identical and meet a set of demanding performance specifications. Direct materials are added at the end of the testing process and are 100% consumed.

Conversion costs are added evenly during both hand assembly and robotic testing processes. Conversion costs include manufacturing labour, indirect materials, security, plant amortization, insurance, and so on. Basically, conversion costs include all manufacturing costs except direct material costs. Exhibit 17-3 summarizes these facts.

EXHIBIT 17-3
The Illustrated Process at Global Defence Inc.

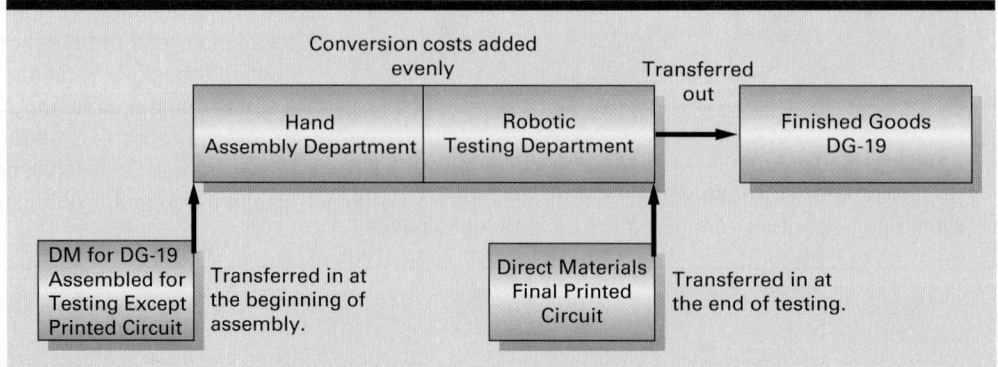

The manufacture of the DG-19 component will illustrate three cases:

◆ **Case 1:** Process costing with no beginning inventory (BI) or ending inventory (EI) WIP of DG-19—that is, all units are started and fully completed by the end of the accounting period. This case illustrates the basic averaging-of-costs idea that is a key feature of process-costing systems.

◆ **Case 2:** Process costing with no BI WIP but an EI WIP of DG-19—that is, some units of DG-19 started during the accounting period are incomplete at the end of the period. This means that no direct materials have been added to the incomplete circuit boards at the end of Hand Assembly.

◆ **Case 3:** Process costing with both BI WIP and EI WIP of DG-19.

For *Case 1*, on January 1, 2012, the value is $0 for BI WIP of DG-19 circuit boards and all direct materials. In January 2012, Global Defence started, completed hand assembly of, and transferred out to the robotic testing phase 400 DG-19 units. All the DM costs of $32,000 were added and all completed units and costs were transferred out to Finished Goods. The total costs for January 2012 were:

Direct materials costs added during January	$32,000
Conversion costs added during January	24,000
Total Assembly department costs added during January	$56,000

With zero BI and EI WIP, no inventory valuation is necessary. By averaging, the hand assembly cost per unit of DG-19 would simply be $56,000, 400 units = $140, itemized as follows:

Direct materials ($32,000 ÷ 400) cost per unit	$ 80
Conversion costs ($24,000 ÷ 400) cost per unit	60
Assembly department cost per unit	$140

This case shows that in a process-costing system, unit costs can be averaged by dividing total cost in a given accounting period by total units produced in the period. The facts of the specific situation permit a simple average cost per physical unit calculation for both the direct and indirect cost pools. Because each unit is identical, there is no reason to believe any single unit would cost more to produce than the other units. All units receive the identical amount of direct materials and conversion costs. If organizations mass-produce standard units, then they can use this simple average-costing approach when there are no incomplete units at the end of each accounting period. Here is another way to summarize this information:

Global Defence Inc., January 2012—Case 1 (No Beginning and No Ending WIP Inventory, Hand Assembly)

	Physical Units	Conversion Rate	Equivalent Units (EU)	Direct Materials	Conversion	Total
BI WIP	0			$ 0	$ 0	
Started (added) this month	400			32,000	24,000	
Units to account for	400					
Good units completed and transferred out this month	400	100%	400			
EI WIP this month	0	0%	0			
Units accounted for	400		400			
Total costs to date				$32,000	$24,000	$56,000
Cost per EU (cost allocation rate $/EU)				$ 80.00	$60.00	$140.00
				($32,000 ÷ 400 EU)	($24,000 ÷ 400 EU)	

GLOBAL DEFENCE—ENDING WIP INVENTORY VALUATION USING THE WEIGHTED-AVERAGE METHOD

Case 2. In February 2012, Global Defence places another 400 units of DG-19 into production. Recall there is no beginning inventory of partially completed units in the Assembly department on February 1, 2012, because all units placed into production in January were fully completed by February 1. During February, however, customer delays in placing orders for DG-19 prevented the complete assembly of all units started in February. Only 175 units were completed and transferred out to the Testing department. This means that 225 units remained in the Assembly department's EI WIP and no final circuit boards were added to these units as at the end of February. The production engineers estimated that the conversion of the 225 units in EI WIP was 60% complete. The total costs for the Assembly department for February 2012 were:

Direct materials costs added during February	$32,000
Conversion costs added during February	18,600
Total Assembly department costs added during February	$50,600

Exhibit 17-4 records flow of production in units. The Physical Units column records the units in beginning WIP inventory (which was 0) and the quantity started in February (which was 400), giving the 400 total units to account for. The quantity completed and transferred out of the Assembly department (175 physical units) and the EI WIP (225 physical units) are then recorded, giving the 400 total quantity accounted for. The Equivalent Units columns report the EU for both the direct materials and indirect conversion cost pools for the EU completed and transferred out and the units remaining in EI WIP. Multiplying the percentage of completion by the physical units in the first column results in the EU. The total EU to divide into the conversion cost pool will be 310 EU (175 EU 100% complete plus 225 EU 60% complete). In February there will be 400 EU used to calculate the DM cost rate. Exhibit 17-4 shows in detail the calculation of the EU for both the DM and conversion cost pools.

Direct materials ($32,000 ÷ 400) cost per unit	$80.00
Conversion costs ($18,600 ÷ 310) cost per EU	$60.00

Exhibit 17-5 shows the cost pools and calculation of cost allocation rates per EU. It then shows the assignment of costs to units completed and transferred out, and to partially completed units remaining in ending WIP inventory.

EXHIBIT 17-4
Summarizing the Flow of Production in Physical Units and Equivalent Units for the Hand Assembly Department of Global Defence Inc. for February 2012—Case 2 (Ending WIP Inventory but No Beginning WIP Inventory)

	A	B	C	D
1				Equivalent Units
2		Physical	Direct	Conversion
3	Flow of Production	Units	Materials	Costs
4	Work in process, beginning	0		
5	Started during February	400		
6	To account for	400		
7	Completed and transferred out during February	175	175	175
8	Work in process, ending inventory, Hand Assembly[a]	225		
9	(225 × 100%; 225 × 60%)		225	135
10	Accounted for	400		
11	Work done in February only		400	310
12				
13	[a]Degree of completion in this department: direct materials, 100%; conversion costs, 60%.			

EXHIBIT 17-5
Calculating Equivalent Unit Costs and Assigning Costs to Completed Units and Ending
WIP, Hand Assembly

	A	B	C	D
		Total		
1				
2		**Production**	**Direct**	**Conversion**
3		**Costs**	**Materials**	**Costs**
4	Cost added during February	$50,600	$32,000	$18,600
5	Divide by equivalent units of work done in current period (Exhibit 17-4)		÷ 400	÷ 310
6	Cost per equivalent unit		$ 80	$ 60
7	Total costs to account for	$50,600		
8	Assignment of costs:			
9	Work in process ending inventory, Hand Assembly (225 units)			
10	Direct materials	$18,000	(225 × $80)	
11	Conversion costs	8,100	(135 EU from Exhibit 17-4 × $60)	
12	Total work in process	26,100		
13	Completed and transferred out (175 units from Exhibit 17-4)	24,500	(175 × ($80 + $60))	
14	Total costs accounted for	$50,600		
15				

At the top of Exhibit 17-5, the Direct Materials column shows that $32,000 of direct materials was purchased and should have been added to the 400 units started during February. There were no direct materials BI WIP. Thus the cost rate of direct materials was $80/EU ($32,000 ÷ 400 EU from Exhibit 17-4 = $80/EU). The Conversion Costs column shows the conversion cost pool for the Assembly department for February was $18,600. Thus the cost per EU for conversion costs was $60 ($18,600 ÷ 310 EU from Exhibit 17-4 = $60/EU). The total production costs to be accounted for during the month are the sum of the direct materials and conversion costs, $50,600.

The bottom section of Exhibit 17-5 multiplies the cost rates by EU both remaining in EI WIP and assigned and transferred out to EI finished goods. The costs are assigned using the weighted-average method. Recall that the weighted average is very straightforward because the weights have already been provided in transforming the physical units into EU. The cost allocation rates are already weighted. In the case of the DM cost pool, the weight for both complete and incomplete physical units is 100% or 1. The weight for the conversion cost pool for units transferred out is 1 or 100% and 0.60 or 60% for incomplete units in EI WIP.

Exhibit 17-5 shows that the COGM assigned for the 175 completed units is $24,500 (175 × $80/EU for direct materials + 175 × $60/EU for conversion costs). The value of EI WIP is not quite as straightforward to calculate. The direct materials remain 100% used for the 225 units in EI WIP; therefore, this cost is $18,000 (225 EU × $80/EU = $18,000). The conversion cost for the 135 EU in EI WIP is $8,100 (135 EU × $60/EU = $8,100). The total value of EI WIP at the end of February is $26,100 ($18,000 + $8,100 = $26,100). The completed and transferred-out amount of $24,500 and the EI WIP amount of $26,100 sum to $50,600, the total costs of the Assembly department to account for in February.

Process-costing systems separate costs into cost categories according to the timing of when costs are introduced into the process. Only two cost pools are required in the Global Defence example because all conversion costs are assumed to be added to the process at an even rate over time. If, however, direct manufacturing labour were added to the process at different times than all other conversion costs, then a third cost pool would be necessary. In this situation, we could no longer assume all conversion activities occur at a uniform rate; therefore, separate estimates of equivalent units would be required for the manufacturing labour and the quality-control assembly processes.

The costs transferred out as reported in the bottom section of Exhibit 17-5 is an accounting process wherein the costs follow the EU through conversion. The methods to value EI WIP are constrained for external reporting purposes by GAAP to either the weighted-average or the FIFO (first-in, first-out) method. At this point in the Global Defence example, no decision need be made because the BI WIP was $0 in both January and February. The choice of methods will make a difference in *Case 3*, however, because there is BI WIP to be converted and transferred out in March.

JOURNAL ENTRIES

Process-costing journal entries are basically like those made in the job-costing system. That is, DM and conversion costs are accounted for in a similar way as in job-costing systems. The main difference is that, in process costing, there is often more than one EI WIP—in our Global Defence example, there is Work in Process—Assembly and Work in Process—Testing. Global Defence purchases DM as needed. These materials are delivered directly to the Assembly department. Using dollar amounts from Exhibit 17-5, summary journal entries for the month of February at Global Defence Inc. are as follows:

1. Work in Process—Assembly $32,000
       Accounts Payable $32,000
    To record direct materials purchased and used in
        production during February.
2. Work in Process—Assembly $18,600
       [Various accounts] $18,600
    To record Assembly department conversion costs for
        February; examples include energy, manufacturing supplies,
        all manufacturing labour, and plant amortization.
3. Work in Process—Testing $24,500
       Work in Process—Assembly $24,500
    To record cost of goods completed and transferred
        from Assembly to Testing during February.

Exhibit 17-6 shows a general sketch of the flow of costs through the T-accounts. The key T-account, Work in Process—Assembly, shows an ending balance of $26,100.

EXHIBIT 17-6
Flow of Costs in a Process-Costing System, Hand Assembly Department of Global Defence Inc. for February 2012

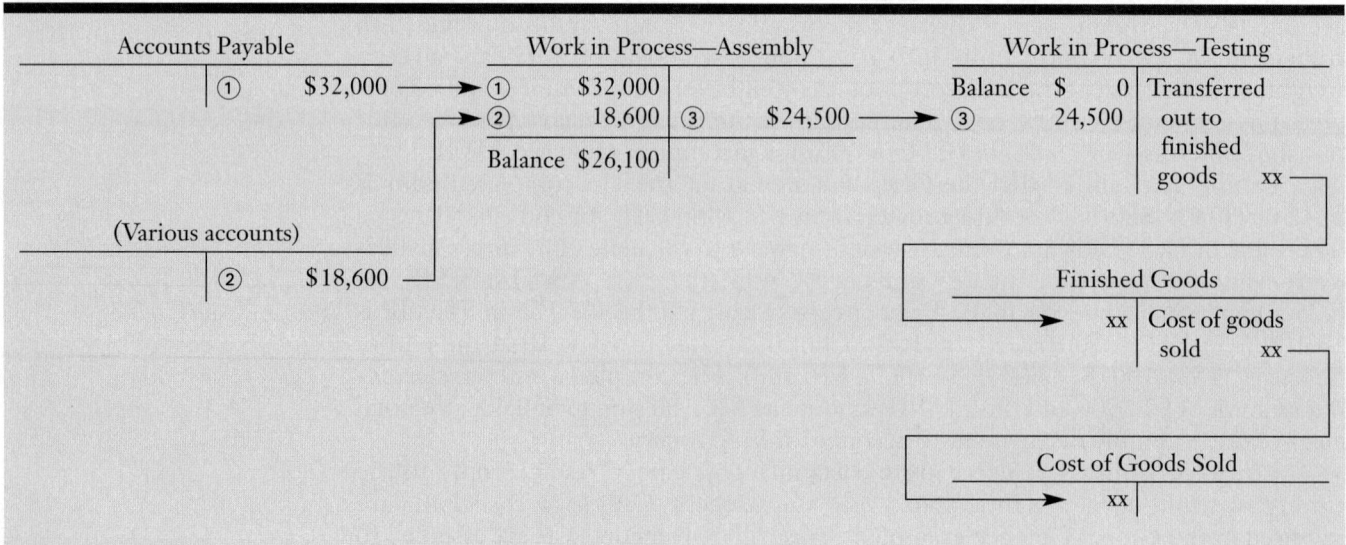

For presentation in correct financial-reporting format, the dollar values presented in Exhibit 17-5 (and the journal entries) for the Assembly department are reported below:

Global Defence Inc. Schedule of Cost of Goods Manufactured, Hand Assembly Department for the Month Ended:	January 31, 2012 (Case 1) Weighted Average		February 29, 2012 (Case 2) Weighted Average	
Direct Materials				
Beginning inventory of direct materials	$ 0		$ 0	
Purchases of direct materials during the month	32,000		32,000	
Cost of direct materials available for use	32,000		32,000	
Ending inventory of direct materials for the month	0		0	
Direct materials used during the month		$32,000		$ 32,000
All conversion costs	24,000		18,600	
Total conversion costs		24,000		18,600
Manufacturing costs incurred during the month		56,000		50,600
Beginning work-in-process inventory		0		0
Total manufacturing costs to account for		56,000		50,600
Ending work-in-process inventory		0		(26,100)
Cost of goods manufactured—transferred out to Testing department		$56,000		$ 24,500

In double-entry bookkeeping, this report from the Assembly department represents only half the transaction. The other half is the receipt into inventory of both the physical units and the COGM by the Testing department. The physical units received by the Testing department from the Assembly department are subcomponents, which are direct materials. The dollar value of the monthly COGM represents the direct materials transferred in or added to the Testing department's purchases for the month. Strictly speaking, these direct materials were not purchased from an external party but nevertheless are treated as internal purchases. Ascertaining the correct transfer price is less straightforward than presented in this chapter and is fully discussed in Chapter 23.

WEIGHTED-AVERAGE METHOD WITH BEGINNING AND ENDING WIP INVENTORY

Case 3. At the beginning of March 2012, Global Defence had 225 partially assembled DG-19 physical units in the Assembly department. During March 2012, Global Defence placed another 275 physical units into production. The total physical units in various stages of production during March was 500 (225 beginning physical units + 275 physical units = 500 physical units), of which 400 were completed and transferred out to the Testing department.

At the end of March 2012, there were 100 physical units remaining in Assembly that were 50% complete. During March, DM costs of $19,800 and conversion costs of $16,380 were added in the Assembly department, for total costs of $36,180 added during March. With a non-zero BI WIP, a choice must be made with respect to the timing of when either BI WIP or the new units DM are converted fully and transferred out to the Testing department—weighted average or FIFO.

The EU calculation in the weighted-average method is only concerned with total EU of work done. The work to complete the EU remaining from last month in March's BI WIP is not distinguished from those units added and converted this month. All EU fully converted are assumed to be converted at an equal rate in March. The weighted-average method is not fine enough to reflect the physical timing of conversion of BI WIP in which conversion and DM costs have already been accumulated from new EU. Thus, the stage of completion of the current-period BI WIP is irrelevant and not used in the computation. The flow of physical units and the calculation of EU for the Assembly department for March 2012 are shown in Exhibit 17-7.

Apply the weighted-average method of process costing to calculate the cost of goods manufactured and transferred out when there is both beginning and ending work-in-process inventory.

EXHIBIT 17-7

Summarizing the Flow of Production in Physical Units and Equivalent Units for the Hand Assembly Department of Global Defence Inc. for March 2012—Case 3, Weighted-Average Method with Beginning and Ending WIP Inventory

	A	B	C	D
1				Equivalent Units
2		Physical	Direct	Conversion
3	Flow of Production	Units	Materials	Costs
4	Work in process, beginning inventory, Hand Assembly (February EI WIP, Exhibit 17-4)	225		
5	Started during current period (given, p. 689)	275		
6	To account for	500		
7	Completed and transferred out during March	400	400	400
8	Work in process, ending inventory, Hand Assembly[a] (given, p. 689)	100		
9	(100 × 100%; 100 × 50%)		100	50
10	Accounted for	500		
11	Work done to date		500	450
12				
13	[a]Degree of completion in this department: direct materials, 100%; conversion costs, 50%.			

The weighted-average cost is the total of all costs entering the WIP account (regardless of whether it is from beginning work in process or from work started during the period) divided by total equivalent units of work done to date in Hand Assembly:

$$\text{EU in BI WIP} + \begin{array}{c}\text{EU of work done}\\\text{in current period}\end{array} = \begin{array}{c}\text{EU completed and transferred}\\\text{out in current period}\end{array} + \text{EU in EI WIP}$$
$$225 + 275 = 400 + 100$$

Exhibit 17-8 shows the calculation of the direct materials and conversion cost per EU, and the assignment of costs to units either completed and transferred out or remaining in EI WIP. The dollars follow the EU, which are either 100% converted and transferred out to the Testing department, or remain 50% complete in the EI WIP of the Assembly department, allocated on a weighted-average cost per EU. In column C are the EU used to calculate the cost allocation rate for the DM cost pool. In column D are the EU used to calculate the cost allocation rate for the March conversion cost pool. The total costs of March EI WIP are calculated in Exhibit 17-8 as follows:

Direct materials:
 100 equivalent units × weighted-average
  cost per equivalent unit of $75.60 $ 7,560
Conversion costs:
 50 equivalent units × weighted-average
  cost per equivalent unit of $54.40   2,720
Total costs of ending work in process $10,280

As shown in Exhibit 17-8, for cost assignment, the completed and transferred-out amount of $52,000 and the EI WIP amount of $10,280 in March, $62,280, are the total costs of the Assembly department to account for in March. It is important to note that the factor for direct materials EU is 100%, or 1, but that is not always the case. It is entirely possible to encounter a conversion process wherein the direct materials of partially converted units are also only partially used. The factor for DM used is unique and unrelated to the conversion factor. Thus it is possible for partially converted units to have consumed 20% of DM and 75% of conversion inputs, for example.

The following table summarizes the total costs to account for and the $62,280 accounted for in Exhibit 17-8. The arrows indicate that costs of units completed and

EXHIBIT 17-8
Calculating Equivalent Unit Costs and Assigning Costs to Completed Units and Ending WIP Inventory for the Hand Assembly Department of Global Defence Inc. for March 2012—Case 3, Weighted-Average Method with Beginning and Ending WIP Inventory

	A	B	C	D
1		**Total**		
2		**Production**	**Direct**	**Conversion**
3		**Costs**	**Materials**	**Costs**
4	Work in process, beginning (February EI WIP, Exhibit 17-5)	$26,100	$18,000	$ 8,100
5	Costs added in current period (given, p. 689)	36,180	19,800	16,380
6	Costs incurred to date		$37,800	$24,480
7	Divide by equivalent units of work done to date (Exhibit 17-7)		÷ 500	÷ 450
8	Cost per equivalent unit of work done to date		$ 75.60	$ 54.40
9	Total costs to account for	$62,280		
10	Assignment of costs:			
11	Completed and transferred out (400 units)	$52,000	$(400^a \times \$75.60) + (400^a \times \$54.40)$	
12	Work in process, ending (100 units)	10,280	$(100^b \times \$75.60) + (50^b \times \$54.40)$	
13	Total costs accounted for	$62,280		
14				
15	[a]Equivalent units completed and transferred out from Exhibit 17-7.			
16	[b]Equivalent units in ending work in process from Exhibit 17-7.			

transferred out and costs of units in ending work in process are calculated using average total costs obtained after merging costs of BI WIP added in the current period.

Costs to Account for		Costs Accounted for Calculated at Weighted-Average Cost	
Beginning work in process	$26,100	Completed and transferred out	$52,000
Costs added in current period	36,180	Ending work in process	10,280
Total costs to account for	$62,280	Total costs accounted for	$62,280

The information Global Defence has calculated for the month of March based on the weighted-average method of inventory valuation is summarized below in the accounting format illustrated in Exhibit 2-10 (p. 42):

Global Defence Inc.
Schedule of Cost of Goods Manufactured,
Hand Assembly Department
for the Month Ended:

March 31, 2012
Weighted Average

Direct materials		
Beginning inventory of direct materials	$ 0	
Purchases of direct materials during the month	19,800	
Cost of direct materials available for use	19,800	
Ending inventory of direct materials for the month	0	
Direct materials used during the month		$19,800
All conversion costs	16,380	
Total conversion costs		16,380
Manufacturing costs incurred during the month		36,180
Beginning work-in-process inventory		26,100
Total manufacturing costs to account for		62,280
Ending work-in-process inventory		(10,280)
Costs of goods manufactured—transferred out to Testing department		$52,000

Using dollar amounts from Exhibit 17-8, summary journal entries for the month of March at Global Defence Inc. are:

1. Work in Process—Hand Assembly	$19,800	
Accounts Payable		$19,800
To record direct materials purchased and used in production during March.		
2. Work in Process—Hand Assembly	$16,380	
[Various accounts]		$16,380
To record Hand Assembly department conversion costs for March; examples include energy, manufacturing supplies, all manufacturing labour, and plant amortization.		
3. Work in Process—Testing	$52,000	
Work in Process—Hand Assembly		$52,000
To record cost of units completed and transferred from Hand Assembly to Testing during March.		

The key T-account, Work in Process—Hand Assembly, would show the following:

Work in Process—Assembly			
Beginning inventory, March 1	$26,100	③ Transferred out to Work in	
① Direct materials	19,800	Process—Testing	$52,000
② Conversion costs	16,380		
Ending inventory, March 31	$10,280		

FIRST-IN, FIRST-OUT AND STANDARD-COST METHODS

4 Analyze weighted-average, FIFO, and standard-costing methods of inventory valuation of cost of goods manufactured and transferred out.

In contrast to the weighted-average method, the first-in, first-out (FIFO) process-costing method assigns the cost of the prior accounting period's equivalent units in BI WIP inventory to the first units completed and transferred out. It assigns the cost of equivalent units worked on during the current period first to complete beginning inventory, then to start and complete new units, and finally to units in ending work-in-process inventory. This method assumes that the earliest EU in the WIP—Assembly account are completed first.

A distinctive feature of the FIFO process-costing method is that the costs of work done on BI WIP before the current period are kept separate from work done in the current period. Costs incurred in the *current period* and units produced in the *current period* are used to calculate costs per EU of work done in the current period. In contrast, EU and cost-per-EU calculations in the weighted-average method merge the units and costs in BI WIP with units and costs of work done in the current period, and make no distinction between the units.

The following observations help explain the physical units calculations in Exhibit 17-9:

◆ From the March data given on page 689, 400 physical units were completed during March. The FIFO method assumes that the first 225 of these units were from BI WIP; thus 175 physical units (400 physical units – 225 physical units) must have been started and completed during March.

◆ EI WIP consists of 100 physical units (275 physical units – 175 physical units) partially converted in March.

◆ Note that the physical units "to account for" equal the physical units "accounted for" (500 units).

Under the FIFO method, the EU calculations focus on only what has been converted in March. Under the FIFO method, the work done in the current period is assumed to first complete the 225 units in beginning work in process. The EU of

EXHIBIT 17-9

Summarizing the Flow of Production in Physical Units and Equivalent Units for the Assembly Department of Global Defence Inc. for March 2012—Case 3, FIFO Method with Beginning and Ending WIP Inventory

	A	B	C	D
			Equivalent Units	
		Physical	**Direct**	**Conversion**
	Flow of Production	**Units**	**Materials**	**Costs**
4	Work in process, beginning (February EI WIP, Exhibit 17-4)	225	(work done before current period)	
5	Started during current period (given, p. 689)	275		
6	To account for	500		
7	Completed and transferred out during current period:			
8	From beginning work in process[a]	225		
9	[225 × (100% − 100%); 225 × (100% − 60%)]		0	90
10	Started and completed	175[b]		
11	(175 × 100%; 175 × 100%)		175	175
12	Work in process, ending[c] (given, p. 689)	100		
13	(100 × 100%; 100 × 50%)		100	50
14	Accounted for	500		
15	Work done in March only		275	315
16				
17	[a]Degree of completion in this department: direct materials, 100%; conversion costs, 60%.			
18	[b]400 physical units completed and transferred out minus 225 physical units completed and transferred out from beginning work-in-process inventory.			
19	[c]Degree of completion in this department: direct materials, 100%; conversion costs, 50%.			

work done in March on the BI WIP are computed by multiplying the 225 physical units by the percentage of work remaining to be done to complete these units: 0% for direct materials because the beginning work in process is 100% complete with respect to direct materials, and 40% for conversion costs, because the beginning work in process is 60% complete with respect to conversion costs. The results are 0 EU (225 physical units × 0.0 = 0) of work for direct materials and 90 EU (225 physical units × 0.40 = 90 EU) for conversion costs.

Next, the work done in the current period is assumed to start and complete the next 175 units. The EU of work done on the 175 physical units started and completed are computed by multiplying 175 units by 100% for both direct materials and conversion costs, because all work on these units is done in the current period. Therefore, there are 175 EU (175 physical units × 1.0 = 175 EU) started and completed in March.

Finally, the work done in the current period is assumed to start but leave incomplete the final 100 physical units as EI WIP. The EU of work done on the 100 physical units of EI WIP are calculated by multiplying 100 physical units by 100% for direct materials (because all direct materials have been added for these units in the current period) and 50% for conversion costs (because 50% of conversion and corresponding costs have been undertaken and consumed in the current period). The flow of production in physical units and EU is summarized in Exhibit 17-9.

In FIFO, the logic of the flow of costs is that all of February's costs must be transferred out first. The EI WIP from February is 60% converted, which means the remaining 40% conversion must be paid from the conversion cost pool for March. The total conversion cost for March is given as $16,380. The actual conversion EU comprise the 90 (225 physical units × 0.40 = 90 EU) remaining from February, the 175 (175 physical units × 1.0 = 175 EU) begun and completed in March, and the 50 (100 physical units × 0.50 = 50 EU) remaining in Assembly. The actual cost allocation rate for March, based on only those conversion costs incurred in March, is $52.00 [$16,380 ÷ (90 + 175 + 50) = $52.00].

Finally, the work done in the current period is assumed to start but leave incomplete the final 100 units as ending work in process. The EU of work done on the 100 units of ending work in process are calculated by multiplying 100 physical units by 100% for DM (because all direct materials have been added for these units in the current period) and 50% for conversion costs (because 50% of conversion work has been done on these units in the current period). Under FIFO, the EI WIP comes from physical units that were started but not fully completed during the current period. The total cost of the 100 partially assembled physical units in ending work in process consists of:

Direct materials:	
100 equivalent units × cost per equivalent unit in March of $72	$7,200
Conversion costs:	
50 equivalent units × cost per equivalent unit in March of $52	2,600
Total costs of work in process on March 31	$9,800

The diagram below summarizes the flows of each element of total costs to account for and the costs already accounted for of $62,280 in Exhibit 17-10. Notice how under the FIFO method the layers of beginning work in process and costs added in the current period are kept separate. The arrows indicate where the costs in each layer go (that is, to units completed and transferred out, or to ending work in process). Be sure to include the costs of beginning work in process ($26,100) when calculating the costs of units completed from beginning inventory.

Costs to Account for		Costs Accounted for Calculated on a FIFO Basis	
		Completed and transferred out:	
Beginning work in process	$26,100	Beginning work in process	$26,100
Costs added in current period	36,180	Used to complete beginning work in process	4,680
		Started and completed	21,700
		Completed and transferred out	52,480
		Ending work in process	9,800
Total costs to account for	$62,280	Total costs accounted for	$62,280

Exhibit 17-10 shows the calculation of the direct materials and conversion cost per equivalent unit, and the assignment of costs to units completed and transferred out and to EI WIP using the FIFO method of process costing. The completed and transferred out amount of $52,480 and the EI WIP amount of $9,800 sum to $62,280, the total costs the Assembly department needs to account for in March.

The information Global Defence calculated for the month of March based on the FIFO method of valuation of inventory is summarized below and compared to the amounts obtained using the weighted-average method:

Global Defence Inc. Schedule of Cost of Goods Manufactured, Assembly Department for the Month Ended:	March 31, 2012 Weighted Average		March 31, 2012 FIFO	
Direct materials				
Beginning inventory of direct materials	$ 0		$ 0	
Purchases of direct materials during the month	19,800		19,800	
Cost of direct materials available for use	19,800		19,800	
Ending inventory of direct materials for the month	0		0	
Direct materials used during the month		$19,800		$ 19,800
All conversion costs	16,380		16,380	
Total conversion costs		16,380		16,380
Manufacturing costs incurred during the month		36,180		36,180
Beginning work-in-process inventory		26,100		26,100
Total manufacturing costs to account for		62,280		62,280
Ending work-in-process inventory		(10,280)		(9,800)
Cost of goods manufactured—transferred out to Testing department		$52,000		$ 52,480

EXHIBIT 17-10

Calculating Equivalent Unit Costs and Assigning Costs to Completed Units and Ending WIP Inventory for the Assembly Department of Global Defence Inc. for March 2012—Case 3, FIFO Method with Beginning and Ending WIP Inventory

	A	B	C	D
1		Total		
2		Production	Direct	Conversion
3		Costs	Materials	Costs
4	Work in process, beginning (February EI WIP, Exhibit 17-5)	$26,100	(work done before current period)	
5	Costs added in current period (given, p. 689)	36,180	$19,800	$16,380
6	Divide by equivalent units of work done in current period (Exhibit 17-9)		÷ 275	÷ 315
7	Cost per equivalent unit of work done in current period		$ 72	$ 52
8	Total costs to account for	$62,280		
9	Assignment of costs:			
10	Completed and transferred out (400 units):			
11	Work in process, beginning (225 units)	$26,100		
12	Costs added to beginning work in process in current period	4,680	$(0^a \times \$72) + (90^a \times \$52)$	
13	Total from beginning inventory	30,780		
14	Started and completed (175 units)	21,700	$(175^b \times \$72) + (175^b \times \$52)$	
15	Total costs of units completed and transferred out	52,480		
16	Work in process, ending (100 units)	9,800	$(100^c \times \$72) + (50^c \times \$52)$	
17	Total costs accounted for	$62,280		
18				
19	ᵃEquivalent units used to complete beginning work in process from Exhibit 17-9.			
20	ᵇEquivalent units started and completed from Exhibit 17-9.			
21	ᶜEquivalent units in ending work in process from Exhibit 17-9.			

The journal entries under the FIFO method parallel the journal entries under the weighted-average method. The only difference is that the entry to record the cost of goods completed and transferred out would be for $52,480 under the FIFO method instead of $52,000 under the weighted-average method.

Only rarely is an application of pure FIFO ever encountered in process costing. As a result, this method should really be called a modified or departmental FIFO method because FIFO is applied within a department to compile the cost of units transferred out, but the units transferred in during a given period are usually carried at a single average unit cost as a matter of convenience. For example, the average cost of units transferred out of the Assembly department is $52,480 ÷ 400 units = $131.20 per DG-19 unit. The Assembly department uses FIFO to distinguish between monthly batches of production. The succeeding department, Testing, however, costs these units (that consist of costs incurred in February and March) at one average unit cost ($131.20 in this illustration). If this averaging were not done, the attempt to track costs on a pure FIFO basis throughout a series of processes would be unduly cumbersome, if not impossible.

COMPARING WEIGHTED-AVERAGE AND FIFO METHODS

The following table summarizes the costs assigned to units completed and those still in process under the weighted-average and FIFO process-costing methods for our example:

	Weighted Average (from Exhibit 17-8)	FIFO (from Exhibit 17-10)	Difference
Cost of units completed and transferred out	$52,000	$52,480	+$480
Work in process, ending	10,280	9,800	−$480
Total costs accounted for	$62,280	$62,280	

The weighted-average ending inventory is higher than the FIFO ending inventory by $480, or 4.9% ($480 ÷ $9,800). This is a significant difference when aggregated over the many thousands of components that Global Defence makes. The weighted-average method in our example also results in lower COGS and hence higher operating income and higher tax payments than the FIFO method. Differences in EU costs of BI WIP and work done during the current period account for the differences in weighted-average and FIFO costs. Recall that the cost per EU of BI WIP was greater than the cost per EU of work done during the period.

For the Assembly department, FIFO assumes that all the higher-cost prior-period units in BI WIP are the first to be completed and transferred out while EI WIP consists of only the lower-cost current-period units. The weighted-average method, however, smooths out cost per EU by assuming that more of the lower-cost units are completed and transferred out, while some of the higher-cost units are placed in EI WIP. Hence, in this example, the weighted-average method results in a lower cost of units completed and transferred out and a higher EI WIP relative to FIFO.

Unit costs can differ materially between the weighted-average and FIFO methods when (1) the direct materials or conversion costs per unit vary from period to period and (2) the physical inventory levels of work in process are large in relation to the total number of units transferred out. This means that both gross margin and operating income will differ materially between the two approaches. As companies move toward long-term procurement contracts that smooth out the unit cost differences from one time period to another, and toward eliminating inventory, the difference between these two cost estimates will decrease.

Managers need feedback about their most recent performance (March in this illustration) to plan and improve their future performance. A major advantage of FIFO is that it gives managers actual information from which they can judge their performance in the current period independently from that in the preceding period.

Work done during the current period is vital information for these planning and control purposes.

Managers in operations often receive cash bonuses based on minimizing costs. The weighted-average method reports the lowest COGM transferred out for the Assembly department. Notice that regardless of the GAAP method chosen, for purposes of deducting COGM to arrive at taxable income, the total cost is identical. What is added to EI WIP is deducted from COGM completed and transferred out. There is no tax benefit to either choice. The manager, however, would prefer to report lower rather than higher COGM, and without accounting training could choose FIFO over the weighted-average method. However, as those trained in financial accounting know, this benefit will most likely reverse out in the next accounting time period—the iron law of accruals. Managers who know this should be indifferent between the two GAAP methods of process costing.

COMPUTATIONS UNDER STANDARD COSTING

This section assumes that you have already studied Chapters 7 and 8.

As we have mentioned, companies that use process-costing systems produce numerous like or similar units of output. Setting standard quantities for inputs is often relatively straightforward in such companies. Standard costs per input unit may then be assigned to the physical standards to develop standard costs.

One weakness of standard costing, however, is that the standard must be updated when significant changes occur in process, quantity, and/or unit input cost. The overallocation or underallocation of process costs must be prorated prior to the calculation of taxable income.

Weighted-average and FIFO methods become very complicated when used in industries that produce a variety of products. For example, a steel rolling mill uses various steel alloys and produces sheets of various sizes and of various finishes. The items of direct materials are not numerous, nor are the operations performed. But used in various combinations, they yield so great a variety of products that inaccurate costs for each product result if the broad averaging procedure of historical process costing is used. Similarly, complex conditions are frequently found in plants that manufacture rubber products, textiles, ceramics, paints, and packaged food products. As we shall see, standard costing is especially useful in these situations.

The intricacies of weighted-average and FIFO historical costing methods and the conflicts between them are also eliminated by using standard costs. We again use the Assembly department of Global Defence Inc. as an example, except this time we assign standard costs to the process. The same standard costs apply in February and March of 2012.

We have incomplete units in both BI and EI WIP. Exhibit 17-9 presented the results of the FIFO method. Exhibit 17-11 summarizes the flow of production in both physical units and EU for the standard-costing method of process costing. Notice in Exhibit 17-11 that the standard-costing method also assumes that the earliest EU in BI WIP are completed first. Work done in the current period for direct materials is 275 EU. Work done in the current period for conversion costs is 315 EU.

Exhibit 17-12 shows the standard cost per EU, and the assignment of costs to units completed and transferred out and to EI WIP using the standard-costing method of process costing, ending with a summary of variances. The standard-costing method requires no calculation of the cost allocation rates for either direct materials purchases or conversion costs. Cost rate per EU are already given as standard costs: direct materials, $74, and conversion costs, $54. These rates have been decided upon using one of the approaches described in Chapter 4. The bookkeeping to adjust the COGM and EI WIP for overallocation or underallocation is straightforward, and this method has the added advantage of drawing a manager's attention to unfavourable cost variances. This method provides an opportunity to apply management-accounting analyses of variances to ascertain where the costs of a process require explanation and perhaps remedy.

EXHIBIT 17-11
Summarizing the Flow of Production in Physical Units and Equivalent Units for the Assembly Department of Global Defence Inc. for March 2012—Standard Costing with Beginning and Ending WIP Inventory

	A	B	C	D
1				**Equivalent Units**
2		**Physical**	**Direct**	**Conversion**
3	**Flow of Production**	**Units**	**Materials**	**Costs**
4	Work in process, beginning (February EI WIP, Exhibit 17-4)	225		
5	Started during current period (given, p. 689)	275		
6	To account for	500		
7	Completed and transferred out during current period:			
8	From beginning work in process[a]	225		
9	[225 × (100% − 100%); 225 × (100% − 60%)]		0	90
10	Started and completed	175[b]		
11	(175 × 100%; 175 × 100%)		175	175
12	Work in process, ending[c] (given, p. 689)	100		
13	(100 × 100%; 100 × 50%)		100	50
14	Accounted for	500		
15	Work done in March only		275	315
16				
17	[a]Degree of completion in this department: direct materials, 100%; conversion costs, 60%.			
18	[b]400 physical units completed and transferred out minus 225 physical units completed and transferred out from beginning work-in-process inventory.			
19	[c]Degree of completion in this department: direct materials, 100%; conversion costs, 50%.			

The total debits to WIP—Assembly differ from total debits to WIP—Assembly under the actual-cost-based weighted-average and FIFO methods. That's because, as in all standard-costing systems, the debits to the WIP account are at standard costs rather than actual costs. Notice that in comparing Exhibit 17-10 to Exhibit 17-12, all the quantities are identical; it is the rates that change. In Exhibit 17-10 the direct materials cost allocation rate is $72/EU and the conversion cost allocation rate is $52/EU, while the direct materials standard cost rate is $74/EU in Exhibit 17-12 and the standard conversion cost rate is $54/EU. The standard costs total $61,300 in Exhibit 17-12. Using T-accounts, the flow of costs of Global Defence Inc. transformation process is illustrated in Exhibit 17-13. Any variance between the standard and actual costs incurred also transfers into and out of the various process accounts.

ACCOUNTING FOR VARIANCES

Process-costing systems using standard costs usually accumulate actual costs separately from the inventory accounts. For example, the actual data are recorded in the first two entries shown below. Recall that Global Defence purchases direct materials as needed and that these materials are delivered directly to the Assembly department. The total variances are recorded in the next two entries. The final entry transfers out the completed goods at standard costs.

1.	Assembly Department Direct Materials Control (at actual)	$19,800	
	Accounts Payable		$19,800
	To record direct materials purchased and used in production during March.		

EXHIBIT 17-12

Standard Costs per Equivalent Unit and Assigning Costs to Completed Units and Ending WIP Inventory for the Assembly Department of Global Defence Inc. for March 2012—Standard-Costing Method with Beginning and Ending WIP Inventory

	A	B	C	D
1		Total		
2		Production	Direct	Conversion
3		Costs	Materials	Costs
5	Standard cost per equivalent unit (given, p. 697)		$ 74	$ 54
6	Work in process, beginning (given, Exhibit 17-11)			
7	Direct materials, 225 × $74; Conversion costs, 135 × $54	$23,940	$16,650	$ 7,290
9	Costs added in current period at standard costs			
10	Direct materials, 275 × $74; Conversion costs, 315 × $54	37,360	$20,350	$17,010
11	Total costs to account for	$61,300		
12	Assignment of costs at standard costs:			
13	Completed and transferred out (400 units):			
14	Work in process, beginning (225 units)	$23,940		
15	Costs added to beginning work in process in current period	4,860	$(0^a \times \$74) + (90^a \times \$54)$	
16	Total from beginning inventory	28,800		
17	Started and completed (175 units)	22,400	$(175^b \times \$74) + (175^b \times \$54)$	
18	Total costs of units completed and transferred out	51,200		
19	Work in process, ending (100 units)	10,100	$(100^c \times \$74) + (50^c \times \$54)$	
20	Total costs to account for	$61,300		
21	Summary of variances for current performance:			
22	Costs added in current period at standard costs (see above)		$20,350	$17,010
23	Actual costs incurred (given, p. 689)		$19,800	$16,380
24	Variance		$ 550 F	$ 630 F
25				
26	[a]Equivalent units used to complete beginning work in process from Exhibit 17-11.			
27	[b]Equivalent units started and completed from Exhibit 17-11.			
28	[c]Equivalent units in ending work in process from Exhibit 17-11.			

This cost control account is debited with actual costs and credited later with standard costs assigned to the units worked on.

2. Assembly Department Conversion Costs Control (at actual) $16,380
  [Various accounts] $16,380
  To record Assembly department conversion costs for March.

(Entries 3, 4, and 5 use standard-cost dollar amounts from Exhibit 17-12)

3. Work in Process—Assembly (at standard costs) $20,350
  Direct Materials Variances $ 550
  Assembly Department Direct Materials Control 19,800
  To record actual direct materials used and total direct materials variances.

4. Work in Process—Assembly (at standard costs) $17,010
  Conversion Costs Variances $ 630
  Assembly Department Conversion Costs Control 16,380
  To record actual conversion costs and total conversion costs variances.

5. Work in Process—Testing (at standard costs) $51,200
  Work in Process—Assembly (at standard costs) $51,200
  To record cost of units completed and transferred at standard cost from Assembly to Testing.

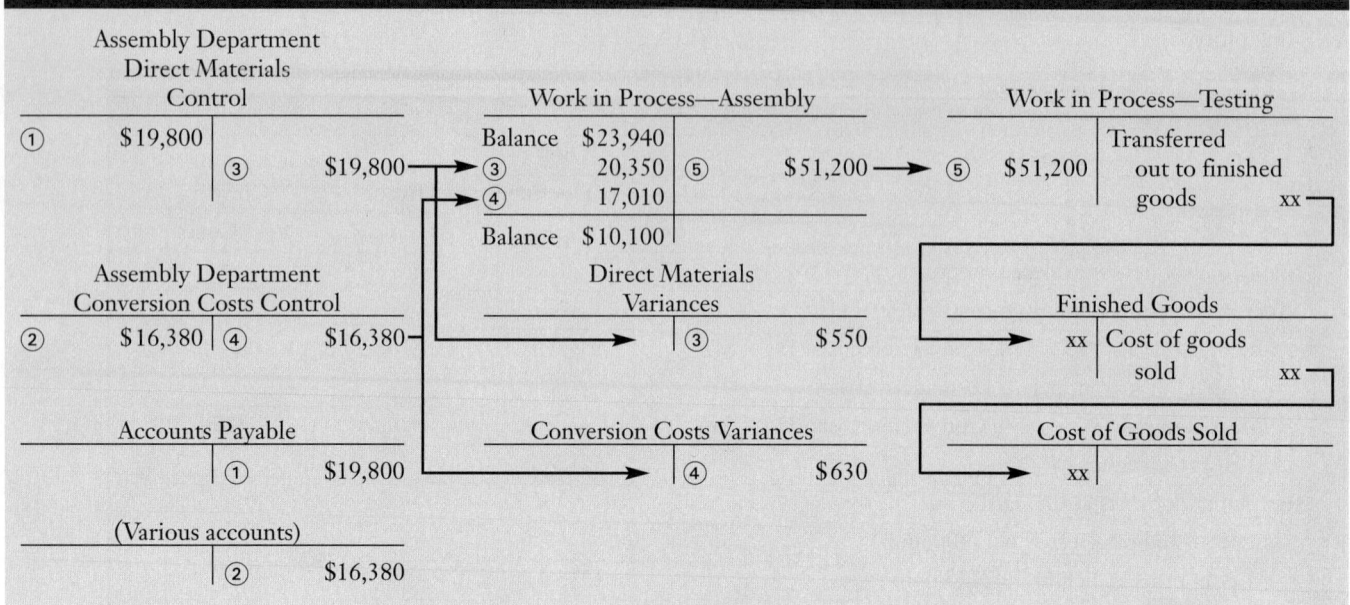

Variances arise under the standard-costing method, as in entries 3 and 4, because the standard costs assigned to products on the basis of work done in the current period do not usually equal the actual costs incurred in the current period. Variances can be measured and analyzed in little or great detail for feedback, control, and decision-making purposes. Exhibit 17-13 illustrates how the costs flow using T-accounts.

HYBRID-COSTING SYSTEMS

Product-costing systems must often be designed to fit the particular characteristics of different production systems. Many production systems are a hybrid—they have some features of custom-order manufacturing and other features of mass-production manufacturing. Manufacturers of a relatively wide variety of closely related standardized products tend to use a hybrid system. Consider Ford Motor Company. Automobiles may be manufactured in a continuous flow, but each may be customized with a special combination of engine size, transmission, music system, and so on. Companies develop **hybrid-costing systems** to meet these individual needs.

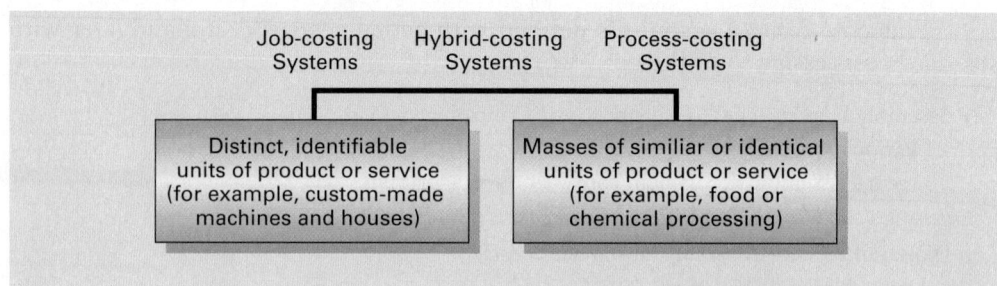

TRANSFERRED-IN COSTS IN PROCESS COSTING

5 · Apply process-costing methods to report transferred-in costs and operations costing.

Many process-costing systems have two or more processes in the conversion cycle, as does Global Defence Inc. Ordinarily, as units move from one process to the next, related costs are also transferred by monthly journal entries. The first example of pasteurization of raw milk illustrated this matching of cost flow to physical conversion. The fully pasteurized milk, along with estimated costs, transferred out of the pasteurization process into the homogenization process and then into the fortification processes until conversion of raw milk into the final product was complete. If standard costs are used, the accounting for such transfers is relatively simple. However, if weighted average or FIFO is used, the accounting can become more complex.

To illustrate, we now extend our Global Defence Inc. example to include the process of testing that is undertaken in the Testing department. The process is one of testing and inspection. Once the DG-19 subassemblies pass inspection, additional direct materials, such as the housing for the closed circuit, complete the unit in readiness for shipment to the customer.

Assume conversion costs are added evenly during the Testing process. As units complete the Testing process, they are immediately transferred to Finished Goods. The COGM become cost of goods available for sale (COGAS) and upon sale will become cost of goods sold (COGS). Subcomponents are transferred into Testing after they complete the Assembly process. But whereas the Assembly department received subcomponents from an external supplier for conversion, the Testing process receives subcomponents from an internal supplier—the Assembly process. Conceptually, however, the units transferred into Testing are direct materials. The costs of all the transferred-in physical units from the Assembly process are, however, called transferred-in costs, not direct materials costs, for the Testing process. These costs will differ depending upon the choice of weighted average ($52,000) or FIFO ($52,480) used to estimate the Assembly process' COGM and EI WIP.

With respect to the physical units of transferred-in costs, they are 100% complete as BI WIP for the Testing department. They are not complete with respect to any conversion or any direct materials added by the Testing department. Unless the transferred-in physical units are 100% converted, no direct materials will be added by the Testing department. That is, no unfinished circuits will be placed in their housing unless they successfully pass all tests and quality inspections. Direct materials costs for Testing will consist of only those costs incurred to acquire direct materials from external third parties. These additional direct materials are added at the end of the Testing process. These data for the process of Testing in March 2012 have been reported in the information system:

	A	B	C	D	E
		Physical Units (DG-19s)	Transferred-in Costs	Direct Materials	Conversion Costs
3	Work in process, beginning inventory (March 1)	240	$33,600	$ 0	$18,000
4	Degree of completion, beginning work in process		100%	0%	62.5%
5	Transferred-in during March	400			
6	Completed and transferred out during March	440			
7	Work in process, ending inventory (March 31)	200			
8	Degree of completion, ending work in process		100%	0%	80%
9	Total costs added during March				
10	Direct materials and conversion costs			$13,200	$48,600
11	Transferred-in (Weighted-average from Exhibit 17-8)[a]		$52,000		
12	Transferred-in (FIFO from Exhibit 17-10)[a]		$52,480		
13					
14	[a] The transferred-in costs during March are different under the weighted-average method (Exhibit 17-8) and the FIFO method (Exhibit 17-10). In our example, beginning work-in-process inventory of $51,600 ($33,600 + $0 + $18,000) is the same under both the weighted-average and FIFO inventory methods because we assume costs per equivalent unit to be the same in both January and February. If costs per equivalent unit had been different in the two months, work-in-process inventory at the end of February (beginning of March) would be costed differently under the weighted-average and FIFO methods. The basic approach to process costing with transferred-in costs, however, would still be the same as what we describe in this section.				

Transferred-in costs (or **previous department costs**) are costs incurred in a previous department that are carried forward as part of the product's cost as it moves to a subsequent department for processing. That is, as the physical units move from one department to the next, their costs per EU move with them. Thus, costs accumulate and those of the Testing process include transferred-in costs as well as any additional direct materials costs and conversion costs added in Testing.

TRANSFERRED-IN COSTS AND THE WEIGHTED-AVERAGE METHOD

To examine the weighted-average process-costing method with transferred-in costs, we need to add calculations to the process illustrated in Exhibits 17-7 and 17-8 for the weighted-average method in the Assembly department.

EXHIBIT 17-14

Summarizing the Flow of Production in Physical Units and Equivalent Units Using the Weighted-Average Method of Process Costing for the Testing Department of Global Defence Inc. for March 2012

	A	B	C	D	E
1				Equivalent Units	
2		Physical	Transferred-in	Direct	Conversion
3	**Flow of Production**	**Units**	**Costs**	**Materials**	**Costs**
4	Work in process, beginning (given, p. 701)	240	(work done before current period)		
5	Transferred-in during current period (given, p. 701)	400			
6	To account for	640			
7	Completed and transferred out during current period	440	440	440	440
8	Work in process, ending[a] (given, p. 701)	200			
9	(200 × 100%; 200 × 0%; 200 × 80%)		200	0	160
10	Accounted for	640			
11	Work done to date		640	440	600
12					
13	[a]Degree of completion in this department: transferred-in costs, 100%; direct materials, 0%; conversion costs, 80%				

Exhibit 17-14 shows the flow of production in both physical units and EU. The computations are basically the same as the calculations of EU under the weighted-average method for the Assembly department in Exhibit 17-7, except for the addition of transferred-in costs.

Exhibit 17-15 has been expanded to illustrate the allocation of the Direct Materials cost pool using the conversion rates appropriate to the BI WIP of the Testing department and the good units completed and transferred out this month. The addition of this calculation of the quantity in the cost allocation base for this cost pool is quite straightforward in an all-or-nothing process and was excluded in the Assembly department analysis for this reason. It is more frequently the case that

EXHIBIT 17-15

Calculating Equivalent Unit Costs and Assigning Costs to Completed Units and Ending WIP Inventory for the Testing Department of Global Defence Inc. for March 2012—Weighted-Average Method with Beginning and Ending WIP Inventory

	A	B	C	D	E
1		**Total**			
2		**Production**	**Transferred-in**	**Direct**	**Conversion**
3		**Costs**	**Costs**	**Materials**	**Costs**
4	Work in process, beginning (given, p. 701)	$ 51,600	$33,600	$ 0	$18,000
5	Costs added in current period (given, p. 701)	113,800	52,000	13,200	48,600
6	Costs incurred to date		$85,600	$13,200	$66,600
7	Divide by equivalent units of work done to date (Exhibit 17-14)		÷ 640	÷ 440	÷ 600
8	Cost per equivalent unit of work done to date		$133.75	$ 30	$ 111
9	Total costs to account for	$165,400			
10	Assignment of costs:				
11	Completed and transferred out (440 units)	$120,890	(440* × $133.75) + (440* × $30) + (440* × $111)		
12	Work in process, ending (200 units)	44,510	(200[†] × $133.75) + (0[†] × $30) + (160[†] × $111)		
13	Total costs accounted for	$165,400			
14					
15	*Equivalent units completed and transferred out from Exhibit 17-14.				
16	[†]Equivalent units in ending work in process from Exhibit 17-14.				

direct materials are assumed to be added evenly throughout a process. The cost allocation base is always the EU, not the physical units.

Exhibit 17-15 also reports the new cost pool to be considered, the costs transferred in to the Testing department from physical units transferred out by the Assembly department. The transferred-in cost pool consists of two cost elements. The first is the EI WIP of the Testing department, which was 62.5% converted, and 0% of direct materials had been added to these 240 physical units. These units were all transferred into the Testing department from the Assembly department during the month of February. The transferred-in costs remaining in BI WIP of the Testing department at the beginning of March equal $33,600. No direct materials were added; therefore, there is $0 reported in the first line of Exhibit 17-15 for direct materials. The dollar value of conversion costs for the EI WIP in February and therefore BI WIP of March for the Testing department is also given as $18,000, and this is reported in the final column of cost pools in Exhibit 17-15.

The information in Exhibit 17-8 illustrating the March weighted-average costs for the Assembly department reported the total COGM transferred out for the 400 completed physical units was $52,000, which appears as the dollar value of physical units transferred in to the Testing department on the second line of Exhibit 17-15 in the Transferred-in Costs column. The total transferred-in, direct materials, and conversion costs in the Testing department for those 440 fully completed units are $165,400 for the month of March. The dollar amounts in the Testing direct materials and Testing conversion cost pools are given as shown.

In Exhibit 17-15, the cost assignment is based on the cost allocation rates shown in the top section of the Exhibit. The first line refers to the EU completed and transferred out to Finished Goods and the second refers to the EU remaining in EI WIP. Notice that 0 EU remaining in EI WIP consumed any direct materials, the housing for the circuit boards, during March. Using the dollar amount from Exhibit 17-15, the journal entry for the transfer out of the Testing department to Finished Goods inventory is:

Finished Goods	$120,890	
Work in Process—Testing		$120,890
To transfer units to Finished Goods inventory.		

Entries to the key T-account, Work in Process—Testing, follow, using information from Exhibit 17-15:

Work in Process—Testing

Beginning inventory, March 1	$51,600	Transferred out	$120,890
Transferred-in costs	52,000		
Direct materials	13,200		
Conversion costs	48,600		
Ending inventory, March 31	$44,510		

TRANSFERRED-IN COSTS AND THE FIFO METHOD

To examine the FIFO process-costing method with transferred-in costs, we must refer back to Exhibit 17-10 on page 695 for both the transferred-out COGM from the Assembly department and the physical units completed and transferred out. It is important to understand that in a series of interdepartmental transfers, each department is regarded as being separate and distinct for accounting purposes. All costs transferred in during a given accounting period are carried at one unit cost figure regardless of whether previous departments used the weighted-average or the FIFO method.

Exhibit 17-16 shows the flow of production in both physical units and EU under the FIFO method of process costing. Other than considering transferred-in costs, the computations of equivalent units are basically the same as those under the FIFO method for the Assembly department shown in Exhibit 17-9 on page 693.

Exhibit 17-17 shows the calculation of the transferred-in direct materials, and conversion cost per equivalent unit, and the assignment of costs to units completed and transferred out and to EI WIP using the FIFO method of process costing. Although under FIFO the transferred-in cost allocation rate is calculated as a simple

EXHIBIT 17-16

Summarizing the Flow of Production in Physical Units and Equivalent Units Using the FIFO Method of Process Costing for the Testing Department of Global Defence Inc. for March 2012

	A	B	C	D	E
1				Equivalent Units	
2		Physical	Transferred-in	Direct	Conversion
3	**Flow of Production**	**Units**	**Costs**	**Materials**	**Costs**
4	Work in process, beginning (given, p. 702)	240	(work done before current period)		
5	Transferred-in during current period (given, p. 702)	400			
6	To account for	640			
7	Completed and transferred out during current period:				
8	From beginning work in process[a]	240			
9	[240×(100% − 100%); 240×(100% − 0%); 240×(100% − 62.5%)]		0	240	90
10	Started and completed	200[b]			
11	(200 × 100%; 200 × 100%; 200 × 100%)		200	200	200
12	Work in process, ending[c] (given, p. 702)	200			
13	(200 × 100%; 200 × 0%; 200 × 80%)		200	0	160
14	Accounted for	640			
15	Work done in current period only		400	440	450
16					
17	[a]Degree of completion in this department: transferred-in costs, 100%; direct materials, 0%; conversion costs, 62.5%.				
18	[b]440 physical units completed and transferred out minus 240 physical units completed and transferred out from beginning work-in-process inventory.				
19	[c]Degree of completion in this department: transferred-in costs, 100%; direct materials, 0%; conversion costs, 80%.				

EXHIBIT 17-17

Calculating Equivalent Unit Costs and Assigning Costs to Completed Units and Ending WIP Inventory for the Testing Department of Global Defence Inc. for March 2012—FIFO Method with Beginning and Ending WIP Inventory

	A	B	C	D	E
1		**Total**			
2		**Production**	**Transferred-in**	**Direct**	**Conversion**
3		**Costs**	**Costs**	**Materials**	**Costs**
4	Work in process, beginning (given, p. 702)	$ 51,600	(work done before current period)		
5	Costs added in current period (given, p. 702)	114,280	$52,480	$13,200	$48,600
6	Divide by equivalent units of work done in current period (Exhibit 17-16)		÷ 400	÷ 440	÷ 450
7	Cost per equivalent unit of work done in current period		$131.20	$ 30	$ 108
8	Total costs to account for	$165,880			
9	Assignment of costs:				
10	Completed and transferred out (440 units)				
11	Work in process, beginning (240 units)	$ 51,600			
12	Costs added to beginning work in process in current period	16,920	(0[a] × $131.20) + (240[a] × $30) + (90[a] × $108)		
13	Total from beginning inventory	68,520			
14	Started and completed (200 units)	53,840	(200[b] × $131.20) + (200[b] × $30) + (200[b] × $108)		
15	Total costs of units completed and transferred out	122,360			
16	Work in process, ending (200 units)	43,520	(200[c] × $131.20) + (0[c] × $30) + (160[c] × $108)		
17	Total costs accounted for	$165,880			
18					
19	[a]Equivalent units used to complete beginning work in process from Exhibit 17-16.				
20	[b]Equivalent units started and completed from Exhibit 17-16.				
21	[c]Equivalent units in ending work in process from Exhibit 17-16.				

average of the cost pool of transferred-in costs for the month of March divided by the total of 400 physical units, this is not the case for the remaining two cost pools. The direct materials costs added in the Testing department are calculated based on the 440 EU completed and transferred out this month. Conversion costs of Testing are divided by the total equivalent units finished in the current time period, which have been calculated in Exhibit 17-16 as 450 EU.

The reasoning for using only $52,480 in the Transferred-in, $13,200 in the Direct Materials, and $48,600 in the Conversion cost pools is that these are the only relevant costs for the month of March in the Testing department using FIFO. Based on the appropriate cost allocation rates, the costs are assigned using the appropriate EU beginning with the 90 EU to be converted from BI WIP first (240 physical units multiplied by (1 - 62.5%) = 90 EU). Notice that direct materials are added to 240 EU because these 240 physical units must be 100% converted before the Testing department adds any direct materials at all.

In Exhibit 17-17, the total costs to account for and accounted for of $165,880 under the FIFO method differ from the corresponding amounts under the weighted-average method of $165,400 because of the different costs of completed units transferred in from the Assembly department under the two methods ($52,480 under FIFO and $52,000 under weighted average).

Using the dollar amount from Exhibit 17-17, the journal entry for the transfer out to Finished Goods inventory is:

Finished Goods	$122,360	
Work in Process—Testing		$122,360
To transfer units to Finished Goods inventory.		

Entries to the key T-account, Work in Process—Testing, follow, using information from Exhibit 17-17:

Work in Process—Testing

Beginning inventory, March 1	$51,600	Transferred out	$122,360
Transferred-in costs	52,480		
Direct materials	13,200		
Conversion costs	48,600		
Ending inventory, March 31	$43,520		

The dollar values using the weighted-average and FIFO methods reported in Exhibits 17-16 and 17-17 for the Testing department are summarized and compared for the month of March.

Global Defence Inc. **Schedule of Cost of Goods Manufactured,** **Testing Department** **for the Month Ended:**	**March 31, 2012** **Weighted Average**		**March 31, 2012** **FIFO**	
Direct Materials				
Beginning inventory of direct materials	$ 0		$ 0	
Purchases of direct materials during the month	13,200		13,200	
Cost of direct materials available for use	13,200		13,200	
Ending inventory of direct materials for the month	0		0	
Direct materials used during the month		$13,200		$ 13,200
All conversion costs	48,600		48,600	
Total conversion costs		48,600		48,600
Manufacturing costs incurred during the month		61,800		61,800
Beginning work-in-process inventory	33,600		33,600	
Transferred-in cost of goods manufactured from Assembly	52,000		52,480	
Total manufacturing costs to account for		85,600		86,080
Ending work-in-process inventory		(44,510)		(43,520)
Cost of goods manufactured—transferred out to Finished Goods		$130,110		$129,600

COMMON MISTAKES WITH TRANSFERRED-IN COSTS

Here are some common pitfalls to avoid when accounting for transferred-in costs:

1. Remember that transferred-in costs from previous departments are cost pools that must be added into your calculations.

2. In calculating costs to be transferred on a FIFO basis, do not overlook the costs assigned at the beginning of the period to units that were in process but are now included in the units transferred out. For example, do not overlook the $51,600 in Exhibit 17-17.

3. The cost allocation rates most likely will fluctuate from month to month because they are based on actual costs incurred. Therefore, transferred units may contain batches accumulated at different unit costs. For example, the 400 units transferred in at $52,480 in Exhibit 17-17 using the FIFO method consist of units that have different unit costs for direct materials and conversion costs when these units were worked on in the Assembly department (see Exhibit 17-10, p. 695). Remember, however, that when these units are transferred in to the Testing department, they are at one average unit cost of $131.20 ($52,480 ÷ 400), as in Exhibit 17-17.

4. Units may be measured in different terms in different departments. Consider each department separately. Unit costs could be based on kilograms in the first department and litres in the second; therefore, as units are received by the second department, their measurements must be converted to litres to ensure comparable cost allocation bases and rates.

PULLING IT ALL TOGETHER—PROBLEM FOR SELF-STUDY

(Try to solve this problem before examining the solution that follows.)

PROBLEM

Allied Chemicals operates a thermo-assembly process as the second of three processes at its plastics plant. Direct materials in thermo-assembly are added at the end of the process. Conversion costs are added evenly during the process. The following data pertain to the Thermo-Assembly department for 2012.

	A	B	C	D	E
1		Physical	Transferred-in	Direct	Conversion
2		Units	Costs	Materials	Costs
3	Work in process, beginning inventory	50,000			
4	Degree of completion, beginning work in process		100%	0%	80%
5	Transferred in during current period	200,000			
6	Completed and transferred out during current period	210,000			
7	Work in process, ending inventory	?			
8	Degree of completion, ending work in process		100%	0%	40%

REQUIRED

Compute equivalent units under (1) the weighted-average method and (2) the FIFO method.

SOLUTION

1. The weighted-average method uses equivalent units of work done to date to compute cost per equivalent unit. The calculation of equivalent units follows:

	A	B	C	D	E
1			Equivalent Units		
2		Physical	Transferred-in	Direct	Conversion
3	Flow of Production	Units	Costs	Materials	Costs
4	Work in process, beginning (given)	50,000			
5	Transferred in during current period (given)	200,000			
6	To account for	250,000			
7	Completed and transferred out during current period	210,000	210,000	210,000	210,000
8	Work in process, ending[a]	40,000[b]			
9	(40,000 × 100%; 40,000 × 0%; 40,000 × 40%)		40,000	0	16,000
10	Accounted for	250,000			
11	Work done to date		250,000	210,000	226,000
12					
13	[a]Degree of completion in this department: transferred-in costs, 100%; direct materials, 0%; conversion costs, 40%.				
14	[b]250,000 physical units to account for minus 210,000 physical units completed and transferred out.				

2. The FIFO method uses equivalent units of work done in the current period only to compute cost per equivalent unit. The calculations of equivalent units follows:

	A	B	C	D	E
1			Equivalent Units		
2		Physical	Transferred-in	Direct	Conversion
3	Flow of Production	Units	Costs	Materials	Costs
4	Work in process, beginning (given)	50,000			
5	Transferred in during current period (given)	200,000			
6	To account for	250,000			
7	Completed and transferred out during current period:				
8	From beginning work in process[a]	50,000			
9	[50,000 × (100% − 100%); 50,000 × (100% − 0%); 50,000 × (100% − 80%)]		0	50,000	10,000
10	Started and completed	160,000[b]			
11	(160,000 × 100%; 160,000 × 100%; 160,000 × 100%)		160,000	160,000	160,000
12	Work in process, ending[c]	40,000[d]			
13	(40,000 × 100%; 40,000 × 0%; 40,000 × 40%)		40,000	0	16,000
14	Accounted for	250,000			
15	Work done in current period only		200,000	210,000	186,000
16					
17	[a]Degree of completion in this department: transferred-in costs, 100%; direct materials, 0%; conversion costs, 80%.				
18	[b]210,000 physical units completed and transferred out minus 50,000 physical units completed and transferred out from beginning work-in-process inventory.				
19	[c]Degree of completion in this department: transferred-in costs, 100%; direct materials, 0%; conversion costs, 40%.				
20	[d]250,000 physical units to account for minus 210,000 physical units completed and transferred out.				

SUMMARY POINTS

The following question-and-answer format summarizes the chapter's learning outcomes. Each point presents a key question, and the guidelines are the answer to that question.

LEARNING OUTCOMES

1. What are the key differences that distinguish job from process costing?

GUIDELINES

The motivation to use job costing is that different jobs consume different resources at different rates; therefore, their costs differ. Indirect cost assignment systems are designed to report these differences in an economic, effective, and efficient way. The cost object is the job. The motivation to use process costing is that all outputs consume virtually identical resources at constant rates; therefore, the costs of outputs are identical. Indirect cost assignment systems are designed to accumulate and match the costs of each process to the physical conversion occurring during the process. The cost object is the process.

2. How are costs assigned to units completed and units in ending WIP using the weighted-average method?	The weighted-average method is one of three methods used to assign costs to either completed units that have moved on to the next process (finished) or to work-in-process (WIP) inventory. The cost driver is equivalent units, and all cost allocation rates are calculated on a cost per equivalent unit. Each cost pool (finished or WIP) is assigned on the basis of the equivalent units either completed or remaining in ending WIP inventory. The main difference in journal entries is that, in a process-costing system, there is a separate WIP account for each process.
3. What is a transferred-out cost?	The physical flow of raw materials through different processes of conversion is matched by the transfer of accumulated costs out of one process for 100% completed conversion of the inputs, and into the account for the next process. No cost disappears but rather accumulates and is transferred to COGAS, and then, after sale, to COGS. A sale is the only point at which costs can be recovered, plus reasonable profit.
4. What are the first-in, first-out method and standard-costing method of process costing?	The first-in, first-out (FIFO) method computes unit costs based on costs incurred during the period and equivalent units of work done in the current period. FIFO assigns the costs of the beginning work-in-process inventory to the first units completed and assigns the costs of the equivalent units worked on during the current period first to complete beginning inventory, next to started and completed new units, and finally to units in ending work-in-process inventory. Under the standard-costing method, cost allocation rates are already in place as standard costs per unit when assigning cost to units completed and to units in ending work-in-process inventory. Standard costing is not a GAAP-compliant method to value inventories or costs.
5. What is a transferred-in cost?	The costs of goods manufactured, those physical units completed in a prior conversion process, are transferred out of the prior department at the end of a specified time period. These become the beginning balance of transferred-in costs for the next department in the conversion process.

TERMS TO LEARN

This chapter and the Glossary at the end of the book contain definitions of the following important terms:

equivalent unit (EU) (p. 679)
first-in, first-out (FIFO) process-
   costing method (p. 680)

hybrid-costing system (p. 700)
previous department costs (p. 701)
standard-costing method (p. 680)

transferred-in costs (p. 701)
weighted-average process-costing
   method (p. 680)

ASSIGNMENT MATERIAL

MyAccountingLab   Make the grade with MyAccountingLab: The questions, exercises, and problems marked in red can be found on MyAccountingLab at **www.myaccountinglab.com**. You can practise them as often as you want, and most feature step-by-step guided instructions to help you find the right answer. Exercises and problems with an Excel icon in the margin have an accompanying Excel template on MyAccountingLab.

SHORT-ANSWER QUESTIONS

17-1 Give three examples of industries that often use process-costing systems.

17-2 In process costing, why are costs often divided into two main classifications?

17-3 Explain equivalent units. Why are equivalent-unit calculations necessary in process costing?

17-4 State two conditions under which computing equivalent units will make a material difference to reported inventory amounts.

17-5 Describe the distinctive characteristic of weighted-average computations in assigning costs to units completed and ending work in process.

17-6 Describe the distinctive characteristic of FIFO computations in assigning costs to units completed and ending work in process.

17-7 Identify the main difference between journal entries in process costing and the ones in job costing.

17-8 "Standard-cost procedures are particularly applicable to process-costing situations." Do you agree? Why?

17-9 Why should the accountant distinguish between transferred-in costs and additional direct material costs for each subsequent department in a process-costing system?

17-10 "Transferred-in costs are those incurred in the preceding accounting period." Do you agree? Explain.

17-11 "There's no reason for me to get excited about the choice between the weighted-average and FIFO methods in my process-costing system. I have long-term contracts with my materials suppliers at fixed prices." State the conditions under which you would (a) agree and (b) disagree with this statement, made by a plant controller. Explain.

EXERCISES

17-12 **Terminology.** A number of terms are listed below:

equivalent unit (EU)   first-in, first-out (FIFO)
weighted-average process-costing method   standard-costing method

REQUIRED
Select the terms from the above list to complete the following sentences.

In process costing, the cost object is the entire production process. The method is used for mass-produced items that are identical. That is why a weighted average can be used to calculate the ratio of work in process to finished goods. A common denominator must be found because a physical unit 100% converted has cost more to produce than one that is only 50% converted and remains in work-in-process inventory. The benefits of the conversion process are unequally shared between the items in each type of inventory. The average conversion rate is calculated using a denominator called an _____ ( ). There are three methods to assign conversion costs to finished goods and work in process. The choice of method should be made by the management team such that the method is economically plausible. The method reflects the facts of the economic outcome of the production process in a specified time period. The three methods are _____(____) method, the _____, and the _____.

17-13 **Equivalent units, zero beginning inventory.** A&A Inc. is a manufacturer of digital cameras. It has two departments: Assembly and Testing. In January 2012, the company incurred $750,000 on direct materials and $798,000 on conversion costs, for a total manufacturing cost of $1,548,000.

1

1. Unit cost, $154.80

REQUIRED
1. Assume there was no beginning inventory of any kind on January 1, 2012. During January, 10,000 cameras were placed into production and all 10,000 were fully completed at the end of the month. What is the unit cost of an assembled camera in January 2012?
2. Assume that during February 10,000 cameras were placed into production. Further assume the same total assembly costs for January are also incurred in February 2012, but only 9,000 cameras are fully completed at the end of February. All direct materials have been added to the remaining 1,000 cameras. However, on average, these remaining 1,000 cameras are only 50% complete as to conversion costs. (a) What are the equivalent units for direct materials and conversion costs and their respective costs per equivalent unit for February? (b) What is the unit cost of an assembled camera in February 2012?
3. Explain the difference in your answers to requirements 1 and 2.

17-14 **Journal entries** (continuation of 17-13). Refer to requirement 2 of Exercise 17-13.

2

1. Work-in-process Assembly DR, $750,000

REQUIRED
Prepare summary journal entries for the use of direct materials and incurrence of conversion costs. Also prepare a journal entry to transfer out the cost of goods completed. Show the postings to the Work-in-Process account.

17-15 **Zero beginning inventory, materials introduced in middle of process.** Roary Chemicals has a Mixing department and a Refining department. Its process-costing system in the Mixing department has two direct materials cost categories (Chemical P and Chemical Q)

1

1. Equivalent units, conversion costs, 45,000

and one conversion costs pool. The following data pertain to the Mixing department for July 2012:

Physical Units:	
Work in process, July 1	0
Units started	50,000
Completed and transferred to Refining department	35,000
Costs:	
Chemical P	$250,000
Chemical Q	70,000
Conversion costs	135,000

Chemical P is introduced at the start of operations in the Mixing department, and Chemical Q is added when the product is three-quarters completed in the Mixing department. Conversion costs are added evenly during the process. The ending work in process in the Mixing department is two-thirds completed.

REQUIRED
1. Compute the equivalent units in the Mixing department for July 2012 for each cost category.
2. Compute (a) the cost of goods completed and transferred to the Refining department during July and (b) the cost of work in process as of July 31, 2012.

1. Equivalent unit conversion costs, 52,500

17-16 Weighted-average method, assigning costs. Bio Doc Corporation is a biotech company based in Milpita. It makes a cancer-treatment drug in a single processing department. Direct materials are added at the start of the process. Conversion costs are added evenly during the process. Bio Doc uses the weighted-average method of process costing. The following information for July 2012 is available:

	Equivalent Units		
	Physical Units	Direct Materials	Conversion Costs
Work in process, July 1*	12,500	12,500	8,750
Started during July	50,000		
Completed and transferred out during July	42,500	42,500	42,500
Work in process, July 31†	20,000	20,000	10,000

*Degree of completion: direct materials, 100%; conversion costs, 70%.
†Degree of completion: direct materials, 100%; conversion costs, 50%.

Total Costs for July 2012

Work in process, beginning		
Direct materials	$75,000	
Conversion costs	87,500	$162,500
Direct materials added during July		350,000
Conversion costs added during July		463,750
Total costs to account for		$976,250

REQUIRED
1. Calculate the cost per equivalent unit for direct materials and conversion costs.
2. Summarize total costs to account for, and assign total costs to units completed (and transferred out) and to units in ending work in process.

1. Direct materials cost per equivalent unit, $7.00

17-17 FIFO method, assigning costs. Refer to the information in Exercise 17-16.

REQUIRED
Do Exercise 17-16 using the FIFO method. Note that you first need to calculate the equivalent units of work done in the current period (for direct materials and conversion costs) to complete beginning work in process, to start and complete new units, and to produce ending work in process.

17-18 Standard-costing method, assigning costs. Refer to the information in Exercise 17-16.
Suppose Bio Doc determines standard costs of $6.60 per equivalent unit for direct materials
and $10.40 per equivalent unit for conversion costs for both beginning work in process and
work done in the current period.

2. Total direct materials cost
variance, $20,000 U

REQUIRED
1. Do Exercise 17-16 using the standard-costing method. Note that you first need to calculate
   the equivalent units of work done in the current period (for direct materials and conversion
   costs) to complete beginning work in process, to start and complete new units, and to produce ending work in process.
2. Compute the total direct materials and conversion costs variances for July 2012.

17-19 Weighted-average method, equivalent units and unit costs. Consider the following data
for the Assembly Division of a satellite manufacturer:

2. Direct materials cost per
equivalent unit, $701,837.80

	Physical Units (satellites)	Direct Materials	Conversion Costs
Beginning work in process (May 1)*	8	$ 5,426,960	$ 1,001,440
Started in May 2012	55		
Completed during May 2012	51		
Ending work in process (May 31)†	12		
Costs added during May 2012		$35,420,000	$15,312,000

*Degree of completion: direct materials, 90%; conversion costs, 40%.
†Degree of completion: direct materials, 60%; conversion costs, 30%.

The Assembly Division uses the weighted-average method of process costing.

REQUIRED
1. Compute equivalent units for direct materials and conversion costs. Show physical units in
   the first column of your schedule.
2. Calculate cost per equivalent unit for direct materials and conversion costs.

17-20 Weighted-average method, assigning costs (continuation of 17-19).

Conversion cost per equivalent unit of work done to date,
$298,780.95

REQUIRED
For the data in Exercise 17-19, summarize total costs to account for, and assign these costs to
units completed (and transferred out) and to units in ending work in process.

17-21 FIFO method, equivalent units and unit costs. Refer to the information in Exercise 17-19.
Suppose the Assembly Division uses the FIFO method of process costing instead of the
weighted-average method.

2. Direct materials cost per
equivalent unit, $694,510

REQUIRED
1. Compute equivalent units for direct materials and conversion costs. Show physical units in
   the first column of your schedule.
2. Calculate cost per equivalent unit for direct materials and conversion costs.

17-22 FIFO method, assigning costs (continuation of 17-21).

Total cost of work in process,
$6,072,908

REQUIRED
For the data in Exercise 17-19, use the FIFO method to summarize total costs to account for,
and assign these costs to units completed and transferred out, and to units in ending work in
process.

17-23 Standard-costing method, assigning costs. Refer to the information in Exercise 17-19.
Suppose the Assembly Division uses the standard-costing method of process costing. Suppose
further that the Assembly Division determines standard costs of $700,000 per equivalent unit
for direct materials and $300,000 per equivalent unit for conversion costs for both beginning
work in process and work done in the current period.

3. Total direct materials cost
variance, $280,000 F

REQUIRED
1. Compute equivalent units for direct materials and conversion costs. Show physical units in
   the first column of your schedule.
2. Summarize total costs to account for, and assign these costs to units completed and transferred out, and to units in ending work in process.
3. Compute the total direct material and conversion cost variances for May 2012.

17-24 Transferred-in costs, weighted-average method. Asaya Clothing Inc. is a manufacturer of winter clothes. It has a Knitting department and a Finishing department. This exercise focuses on the Finishing department. Direct materials are added at the end of the process. Conversion costs are added evenly during the process. Asaya uses the weighted-average method of process costing. The information for June 2012 is shown below.

	Physical Units (tonnes)	Transferred-in Costs	Direct Materials	Conversion Costs
Work in process, beginning inventory (June 1)	75	$75,000	$ 0	$30,000
Degree of completion, beginning work in process		100%	0%	60%
Transferred in during June	135			
Completed and transferred out during June	150			
Work in process, ending inventory (June 30)	60			
Degree of completion, ending work in process		100%	0%	75%
Total costs added during June		$142,500	$37,500	$78,000

REQUIRED

1. Calculate equivalent units (tonnes) of transferred-in costs, direct materials, and conversion costs.
2. Summarize total costs to account for, and calculate the cost per equivalent unit for transferred-in costs, direct materials, and conversion costs.
3. Assign total costs to units completed (and transferred out) and to units in ending work in process.

17-25 Transferred-in costs, FIFO method. Refer to the information in Exercise 17-24. Suppose that Asaya uses the FIFO method instead of the weighted-average method in all of its departments. The only changes to Exercise 17-24 under the FIFO method are that the total transferred-in costs of beginning work in process on June 1 are $60,000 (instead of $75,000) and total transferred-in costs added during June are $130,800 (instead of $142,500).

REQUIRED

Do Exercise 17-24 using the FIFO method. Note that you first need to calculate the equivalent units of work done in the current period (for transferred-in costs, direct materials, and conversion costs) to complete beginning work in process, to start and complete new units, and to produce ending work in process.

17-26 Weighted-average method, equivalent units and unit costs. Consider the following data for the Assembly Division of Fenton Watches Inc.:

	Physical Units	Direct Materials	Conversion Costs
Beginning work in process (May 1)*	80	$ 493,360	$ 91,040
Started in May 2012	500		
Completed during May 2012	460		
Ending work in process (May 31)†	120		
Costs added during May 2012		$3,220,000	$1,392,000

*Degree of completion: direct materials, 90%; conversion costs, 40%.
†Degree of completion: direct materials, 60%; conversion costs, 30%.

The Assembly Division uses the weighted-average method of process costing.

REQUIRED

Compute equivalent units for direct materials and conversion costs. Show physical units in the first column of your schedule.

17-27 Weighted-average method, assigning costs (continuation of 17-26).

REQUIRED

For the data in Exercise 17-26, summarize total costs to account for, calculate cost per equivalent unit for direct materials and conversion costs, and assign total costs to units completed (and transferred out) and to units in ending work in process.

17-28 FIFO method, equivalent units. Refer to the information in Exercise 17-26. Suppose the Assembly Division at Fenton Watches Inc. uses the FIFO method of process costing instead of the weighted-average method.

4
Direct materials equivalent units, 460

REQUIRED
Compute equivalent units for direct materials and conversion costs. Show physical units in the first column of your schedule.

17-29 FIFO method, assigning costs (continuation of 17-28).

4
Total cost of work in process, ending, $612,000

REQUIRED
For the data in Exercise 17-26, use the FIFO method to summarize total costs to account for, calculate cost per equivalent unit for direct materials and conversion costs, and assign total costs to units completed (and transferred out) and to units in ending work in process.

17-30 Standard-costing method, assigning costs. Bucky's Boxes makes boxes for moving. It sells its boxes to major national moving companies. Because of the simple nature of the production process, Bucky's uses standard costing. The following information for July 2012 is available.

4
2. Total cost of work in process, ending, $411,240

	Physical Units	Direct Materials	Conversion Costs
Standard cost per equivalent unit		$ 1.30	$ 2.10
Work in process, beginning inventory (July 1)	185,000	$240,500	$ 97,125
Degree of completion of beginning work in process		100%	25%
Started during July	465,000		
Completed and transferred out	512,000		
Work in process, ending inventory (July 31)	138,000		
Degree of completion of ending work in process		100%	80%
Actual total costs added during July		$607,500	$1,207,415

REQUIRED
1. Compute equivalent units for each cost category.
2. Summarize total costs to account for, and assign total costs to units completed and transferred out and to units in ending work in process.

PROBLEMS

17-31 Weighted-average method. Larsen Corp. manufactures car seats in its Sarnia plant. Each car seat passes through the Assembly department and the Testing department. This problem focuses on the Assembly department. The process-costing system at Larsen Corp. has a single direct cost category (direct materials) and a single indirect cost category (conversion costs). Direct materials are added at the beginning of the process. Conversion costs are added evenly during the process. When the Assembly department finishes work on each car seat, it is immediately transferred to Testing.

2
3. Total cost of work in process, ending, $772,750

Larsen Corp. uses the weighted-average method of process costing. Data for the Assembly department for October 2012 are:

	Physical Units (car seats)	Direct Materials	Conversion Costs
Work in process, October 1*	5,000	$1,250,000	$ 402,750
Started during October 2012	20,000		
Completed during October 2012	22,500		
Work in process, October 31†	2,500		
Total costs added during October 2012		$4,500,000	$2,337,500

*Degree of completion: direct materials, ?%; conversion costs, 60%.
†Degree of completion: direct materials, ?%; conversion costs, 70%.

1. For each cost category, compute equivalent units of work done in October 2012 in the Assembly department. Show physical units in the first column of your schedule.
2. For each cost category, summarize total Assembly department costs for October 2012 and calculate the cost per equivalent unit.
3. Assign total costs to units completed and transferred out and to units in ending work in process.

17-32 Journal entries (continuation of 17-31).

REQUIRED

Prepare a set of summarized journal entries for all October 2012 transactions affecting Work in Process—Assembly. Set up a T-account for Work in Process—Assembly, and post the entries to it.

17-33 FIFO method (continuation of 17-31).

REQUIRED

Do Problem 17-31 using the FIFO method of process costing. Explain any difference between the cost per equivalent unit in the Assembly department under the weighted-average method and the FIFO method.

17-34 Transferred-in costs, weighted-average method (related to 17-31 to 17-33). Larsen Corp., as you know, is a manufacturer of car seats. Each car seat passes through the Assembly department and Testing department. This problem focuses on the Testing department. Direct materials are added when the Testing department process is 90% complete. Conversion costs are added evenly during the Testing department's process. As work in Assembly is completed, each unit is immediately transferred to Testing. As each unit is completed in Testing, it is immediately transferred to Finished Goods.

Larsen Corp. uses the weighted-average method of process costing. Data for the Testing department for October 2012 are:

	Physical Units (car seats)	Transferred-in Costs	Direct Materials	Conversion Costs
Work in process, October 1*	7,500	$2,932,500	$ 0	$ 835,460
Transferred in during October 2012	?			
Completed during October 2012	26,300			
Work in process, October 31†	3,700			
Costs added during October 2012		$7,717,500	$9,704,700	$3,955,900

*Degree of completion: transferred-in costs, ?%; direct materials, ?%; conversion costs, 70%.
†Degree of completion: transferred-in costs, ?%; direct materials, ?%; conversion costs, 60%.

REQUIRED

1. What is the percentage of completion for (a) transferred-in costs and direct materials in beginning work-in-process inventory and (b) transferred-in costs and direct materials in ending work-in-process inventory?
2. For each cost category, compute equivalent units in the Testing department. Show physical units in the first column of your schedule.
3. For each cost category, summarize total Testing department costs for October 2012, calculate the cost per equivalent unit, and assign total costs to units completed (and transferred out) and to units in ending work in process.
4. Prepare journal entries for October transfers from the Assembly department to the Testing department, and from the Testing department to Finished Goods.

17-35 Transferred-in costs, FIFO process-costing method (continuation of 17-34). Refer to the information in Problem 17-34. Suppose that Larsen Corp. uses the FIFO method instead of the weighted-average method in all of its departments. The only changes to Problem 17-34 under the FIFO method are that total transferred-in costs of beginning work in process on October 1 are $2,881,875 (instead of $2,932,500) and that total transferred-in costs added during October are $7,735,250 (instead of $7,717,500).

REQUIRED

Using the FIFO process-costing method, address the requirements of Problem 17-34.

(Margin notes)

② Cost of goods completed and transferred out to Testing, CR $7,717,500

④ 3. Total cost of work in process, ending for FIFO, $755,000

⑤ 2. Work in process ending, conversion costs, 2,220 equivalent units

⑤ 4. Work in Process—Testing Department, DR $7,735,250

17-36 Weighted-average method. Porter Handcraft is a manufacturer of picture frames for large retailers. Every picture frame passes through two departments: the Assembly department and the Finishing department. This problem focuses on the Assembly department. The process-costing system at Porter has a single direct cost category (direct materials) and a single indirect cost category (conversion costs). Direct materials are added when the Assembly department process is 10% complete. Conversion costs are added evenly during the Assembly department's process.

3 Total cost of work in process, ending, $4,400

Porter uses the weighted-average method of process costing. Consider the following data for the Assembly department in April 2012:

	Physical Units (frames)	Direct Materials	Conversion Costs
Work in process, April 1*	75	$ 1,775	$ 135
Started during April 2012	550		
Completed during April 2012	500		
Work in process, April 30†	125		
Costs added during April 2012		$17,600	$10,890

*Degree of completion: direct materials, 100%; conversion costs, 40%.
†Degree of completion: direct materials, 100%; conversion costs, 20%.

REQUIRED

Summarize the total Assembly department costs for April 2012, and assign total costs to units completed (and transferred out) and to units in ending work in process.

17-37 Journal entries (continuation of 17-36).

3 Work in Process—Assembly Department, DR $17,600

REQUIRED

Prepare a set of summarized journal entries for all April transactions affecting Work in Process—Assembly. Set up a T-account for Work in Process—Assembly, and post the entries to it.

17-38 FIFO method (continuation of 17-36).

4 FIFO Work-in-process, ending, $4,550

REQUIRED

Do Problem 17-36 using the FIFO method of process costing. If you did Problem 17-36, explain any difference between the cost of work completed and transferred out and the cost of ending work in process in the Assembly department under the weighted-average method and the FIFO method.

17-39 Transferred-in costs, weighted-average method. Publish Inc. has two departments: Printing and Binding. Each department has one direct cost category (direct materials) and one indirect cost category (conversion costs). This problem focuses on the Binding department. Books that have undergone the printing process are immediately transferred to the Binding department. Direct material is added when the binding process is 80% complete. Conversion costs are added evenly during binding operations. When those operations are done, the books are immediately transferred to Finished Goods. Publish Inc. uses the weighted-average method of process costing. The following is a summary of the April 2012 operations of the Binding department.

5 1. Total cost of work in process, ending, $38,463

	Physical Units (books)	Transferred-in Costs	Direct Materials	Conversion Costs
Beginning work in process	900	$ 32,775	$ 0	$15,000
Degree of completion, beginning work in process		100%	0%	40%
Transferred in during April 2012	2,700			
Completed and transferred out during April	3,000			
Ending work in process (April 30)	600			
Degree of completion, ending work in process		100%	0%	60%
Total costs added during April		$144,000	$26,700	$69,000

1. Summarize the total Binding department costs for April 2012, and assign these costs to units completed (and transferred out) and to units in ending work in process.
2. Prepare journal entries for April transfers from the Printing department to the Binding department and from the Binding department to Finished Goods.

17-40 Transferred-in costs, FIFO costing (continuation of 17-39). Refer to the information in Problem 17-39. Suppose that Publish Inc. uses the FIFO method instead of the weighted-average method in all of its departments. The only changes to Problem 17-39 under the FIFO method are that total transferred-in costs of beginning work in process on April 1 are $27,855 (instead of $32,775) and that total transferred-in costs added during April are $141,750 (instead of $144,000).

1. Total FIFO cost of work in process, $39,780

REQUIRED

1. Using the FIFO process-costing method, do Problem 17-39.
2. If you did Problem 17-39, explain any difference between the cost of work completed and transferred out and the cost of ending work in process in the Binding department under the weighted-average method and the FIFO method.

1. Total cost of work in process, ending, $23,360

17-41 Transferred-in costs, weighted-average and FIFO. Frito-Lay Inc. manufactures convenience foods, including potato chips and corn chips. Production of corn chips occurs in four departments: Cleaning, Mixing, Cooking, and Drying and Packaging. Consider the Drying and Packaging department, where direct materials (packaging) is added at the end of the process. Conversion costs are added evenly during the process. Suppose the accounting records of a Frito-Lay plant provided the following information for corn chips in its Drying and Packaging department during a weekly period (week 37):

	Physical Units (cases)	Transferred-in Costs	Direct Materials	Conversion Costs
Beginning work in process, week 37*	1,250	$29,000	$ 0	$ 9,060
Transferred in during week 37 from Cooking department	5,000			
Completed during week 37	5,250			
Ending work in process, week 37†	1,000			
Costs added during week 37		$96,000	$25,200	$38,400

*Degree of completion: transferred-in costs, 100%; direct materials, ?%; conversion costs, 80%.
†Degree of completion: transferred-in costs, ?%; direct materials, ?%; conversion costs, 40%.

REQUIRED

1. Using the weighted-average method, summarize the total Drying and Packaging department costs for week 37, and assign total costs to units completed (and transferred out) and to units in ending work in process.
2. Assume that the FIFO method is used for the Drying and Packaging department. Under FIFO, the transferred-in costs for work-in-process beginning inventory in week 37 are $28,920 (instead of $29,000 under the weighted-average method), and the transferred-in costs during the week from the Cooking department are $94,000 (instead of $96,000 under the weighted-average method). All other data are unchanged. Summarize the total Drying and Packaging department costs for week 37 and assign total costs to units completed and transferred out and to units in ending work in process using the FIFO method.

3. Total variance for direct materials, $11,875 U

17-42 Standard costing with beginning and ending work in process. Paquita's Pearls Company (PPC) is a manufacturer of knock-off jewellery. Paquita attends Fashion Week in New York City every September and February to gauge the latest fashion trends in jewellery. She then makes trendy jewellery at a fraction of the cost of those designers who participate in Fashion Week. This fall's biggest item is triple-stranded pearl necklaces. Because of her large volume, Paquita uses process costing to account for her production. In October, she had started some of the triple strands. She continued to work on those in November. Costs and output figures are as follows:

Paquita's Pearls Company Process Costing
for the Month Ended November 30, 2012

	Units	Direct Materials	Conversion Costs
Standard cost per unit		$2.50	$10.00
Work in process, beginning inventory (November 1)	25,000	$62,500	$ 187,500
Degree of completion of beginning work in process	100%	100%	75%
Started during October	126,250		
Completed and transferred out	125,000		
Work in process, ending inventory (November 30)	26,250		
Degree of completion of ending work in process		100%	50%
Actual total costs added during November		$327,500	$1,207,415

REQUIRED

1. Compute equivalent units for direct materials and conversion costs. Show physical units in the first column of your schedule.
2. Compute the total standard costs of pearls transferred out in November and the total standard costs of the November 30 inventory of work in process.
3. Compute the total November variances for direct materials and conversion costs.

17-43 Operation costing. Two styles of men's shoes are manufactured by the Comfort Fit Shoe Company: Designer and Regular. Designer style is made from leather, and Regular style uses synthetic materials. Three operations—cutting, sewing, and packing—are common to both styles, but only Designer style passes through a lining operation. The conversion cost rates for 2012 are:

Total costs of work order 815, $69,000

	Cutting	Sewing	Lining	Packing
Rate per unit (pair)	$11	$16	$9	$3

Details of two work orders processed in August are:

	Work Order 815	Work Order 831
Style	Designer	Regular
Number of units (pairs)	1,000	5,000
Direct materials costs	$30,000	$50,000

REQUIRED

Calculate the total costs and the total cost per unit of work order 815 and work order 831.

17-44 Operation costing, equivalent units. (CMA, adapted) Plastco Industries manufactures a variety of plastic products, including a series of moulded chairs. The three models of moulded chairs, which are all variations of the same design, are Standard (can be stacked), Deluxe (with arms), and Executive (with arms and padding). The company uses batch manufacturing and has an operation-costing system.

1. b. Total unit cost of Executive model, $82.13

Plastco has an extrusion operation and subsequent operations to form, trim, and finish the chairs. Plastic sheets are produced by the extrusion operation, some of which are sold directly to other manufacturers. During the forming operation, the remaining plastic sheets are moulded into chair seats and the legs are added. The Standard model is sold after this operation. During the trim operation, the arms are added to the Deluxe and Executive models and the chair edges are smoothed. Only the Executive model enters the finish operation, where the padding is added. All of the units produced receive the same steps within each operation.

The May production run had a total manufacturing cost of $898,000. The units of production and direct materials costs incurred are as follows:

	Units Produced	Extrusion Materials	Form Materials	Trim Materials	Finish Materials
Plastic sheets	5,500	$ 60,000	$ 0	$ 0	$ 0
Standard model	6,500	72,000	24,000	0	0
Deluxe model	3,500	36,000	12,000	9,000	0
Executive model	2,500	24,000	8,000	6,000	12,000
	18,000	$192,000	$44,000	$15,000	$12,000

Manufacturing costs of production assigned during the month of May were:

	Extrusion Operation	Form Operation	Trim Operation	Finish Operation
Direct manufacturing labour	$152,000	$60,000	$30,000	$18,000
Manufacturing overhead	240,000	72,000	39,000	24,000

REQUIRED

1. For each product produced by Plastco Industries during May, determine (a) the unit cost and (b) the total cost. Be sure to account for all costs incurred during the month, and support your answer with appropriate calculations.
2. Without considering your answer in requirement 1, assume that 1,500 units of the Deluxe model produced during May remained in work in process at the end of the month. These units were 100% complete as to materials costs and 60% complete in the trim operation. Determine the cost of the 1,500 units of the Deluxe model in the work-in-process inventory at the end of May.

COLLABORATIVE LEARNING CASES

17-45 Equivalent-unit computations, benchmarking, governance. Margaret Major is the corporate controller of Leisure Suits. Leisure Suits has 20 plants worldwide that manufacture basic suits for retail stores. Each plant uses a process-costing system. At the end of each month, each plant manager submits a production report and a production cost report. The production report includes the plant manager's estimate of the percentage of completion of the ending work in process as to direct materials and conversion costs. Major uses these estimates to compute the equivalent units of work done in each plant and the cost per equivalent unit of work done for both direct materials and conversion costs in each month. Plants are ranked from 1 to 20 in terms of (a) cost per equivalent unit of direct materials and (b) cost per equivalent unit of conversion costs. Each month, Major publishes a report that she calls "Benchmarking for Efficiency Gains at Leisure Suits." The three top-ranked plants on each category receive a bonus and are written up as the best in their class in the company newsletter.

Major has been pleased with the success of her benchmarking program. However, she has heard some disturbing news. She has received some unsigned letters stating that two plant managers have been manipulating their monthly estimates of percentage of completion in an attempt to obtain "best in class" status.

REQUIRED

1. How and why might plant managers "manipulate" their monthly estimates of percentage of completion?
2. Major's first instinct is to contact each plant controller and discuss the problem raised by the unsigned letters. Is that a good idea?
3. Assume that the plant controller's primary reporting responsibility is to the plant manager and that each plant controller receives the phone call from Major mentioned in requirement 2. What is the ethical responsibility of each plant controller (a) to Margaret Major and (b) to Leisure Suits in relation to the equivalent unit information each plant provides for the "Benchmarking for Efficiency" report?
4. How might Major gain some insight into whether the equivalent-unit figures provided by particular plants are being manipulated?

17-46 Operation costing. Farkas Shoes, a high-end shoe manufacturer, produces two lines of shoes for women. The shoes are identical in design, but differ in the materials used and the trim added to the shoes. The basic shoes are made from a synthetic leather, have a synthetic insole, and have plain buttons decorating the upper. The elaborate shoes are made from genuine leather, have a special insole, and have creative buttons applied to the upper. Each shoe is assumed to use an identical amount of conversion costs for a given operation. Work orders 10399 and 10400 are representative work orders for the two types of shoes.

⑤
1. Budgeted conversion cost per pair of shoes, operation 4, $2.10 per pair

Farkas Shoes
Selected Work Orders
for the Month Ended February 28, 2012

	Work Order 10399	Work Order 10400
Quantity (pairs of shoes)	1,000	150
Direct materials	Synthetic leather	Genuine leather
	Synthetic insole	FitDry insole
	Plain buttons	Creative buttons
Operations		
1. Cut leather	Use	Use
2. Shape leather	Use	Use
3. Treat leather	Do not use	Use
4. Sew shoes	Use	Use
5. Machine application of buttons	Use	Do not use
6. Hand application of buttons	Do not use	Use

Selected budget information for February follows:

	Basic	Elaborate	Total
Units	30,000	2,250	32,250
Direct material costs	$390,000	63,000	$453,000

Budgeted conversion costs for each operation for February follow:

Operation 1	$145,125	Operation 4	$67,725
Operation 2	58,050	Operation 5	13,500
Operation 3	4,275	Operation 6	2,025

REQUIRED

1. Using budgeted pairs of shoes as the denominator, calculate the budgeted conversion cost rates for each of the six operations.
2. Using the information in requirement 1, calculate the budgeted cost of goods manufactured for the two February work orders.
3. Based on the two representative work orders for February, calculate the budgeted cost of each pair of shoes.

Spoilage, Rework, and Scrap

18

Allocation of Spoilage, Rework, and Scrap— Profit Means Revenue Exceeds All Costs

Undelivered planes cannot earn revenue. During the manufacture of the new A380, Airbus minimized the environmental impact of this aircraft for its entire life cycle. From contractual agreements to transportation of parts and finished product to decommissioning the A380, Airbus has insisted on implementation of best environmental practices. The jetliner exceeds the minimum required by international environmental standards set out in ISO 14001. The cargo planes can carry 150 tonnes over 5,600 kilometres with 21% lower operating costs.

But manufacturing problems in wiring the aircraft plagued production on this $14 billion project. Poorly fitted wiring on 20 finished aircraft had to be ripped out and scrapped and new wiring installed. This caused a huge delay in delivery, and FedEx cancelled a $3 billion order for 10 planes as a result.[1]

After studying this chapter, you should be able to

1 Distinguish among spoilage, rework, and scrap, and apply the appropriate methods to account for normal and abnormal spoilage.

2 Apply process-costing methods to account for spoilage using weighted-average and first-in, first-out (FIFO) methods.

3 Apply the standard-costing method to account for spoilage, and allocate costs of normal spoilage.

4 Apply job cost allocation procedures to account for spoilage in job costing.

5 Apply cost allocation procedures to account for reworked units and scrap.

[1] Nelson D. Schwartz, "Big Plane, Big Problems," *Fortune*, March 1, 2007; Michelle Dunlop, "Airbus Delivers First A380 Today, More Than a Year Late," *HeraldNet*, October 15, 2007, available at www.heraldnet.com/article/20071015NEWS0/710150041&news01ad51; Airbus website: www.airbus.com/en/aircraftfamilies/a380/freight.html accessed July 4, 2008.

This chapter examines three costs that arise as a result of defects—spoilage, rework, and scrap—and ways to account for them. Chapter 19 discusses aspects of quality management and control to prevent spoilage. Managing spoilage, rework, and scrap is a challenge for many companies, regardless of capacity or the products they manufacture. Inputs paid for that cannot be converted into a saleable product represent costs that cannot be fully recovered by a company. Minimizing costs may require redesign of production processes, increased frequency of quality inspection, retraining of workers, or purchase of new types of materials. The timely and accurate recording of these unrecoverable costs will direct prompt attention toward eliminating the causes and their costs. Reduced spoilage lowers non-value-added costs that will not be recovered from customers in the sales price.

DEFINING AND ACCOUNTING FOR SPOILAGE, REWORK, AND SCRAP

> **1** Distinguish among spoilage, rework, and scrap, and apply the appropriate methods to account for the costs of normal and abnormal spoilage.

The terms *spoilage*, *rework*, and *scrap* are not interchangeable. For a financial accountant, the costs must be classified differently because under GAAP different transactions give rise to each type of cost. Some amount of spoilage, rework, or scrap is an inherent part of many production processes. One example is semiconductor manufacturing, in which the products are so complex and delicate that some spoiled units are invariably produced and cannot be reworked.

Spoilage refers to output that fails to attain either a specified performance level or standard of composition. For example, in fermenting beer, hops (shown) are added to wort[2] for flavour. Hops also inhibit the growth of spoilage bacteria that would ruin the taste of the final product. Other examples are broken silicon wafers, T-shirts sold as "seconds" at outlet malls, and defective aluminum cans.

Rework is the conversion of production rejects into reusable products of the same or lower quality.[3] For example, cooked sausage ends can be reprocessed into pizza topping. Leftover ground raw poultry can be cooked and processed into chili. Damaged motherboards can also be reworked (shown).

Scrap is a residual material that results from manufacturing a product. Scrap such as hard candy chips (shown) can be reheated and reused in new batches.[4] Scrap such as silicon templates that remain after parts are stamped can also be reused. Scrap has low total sales value to scrap collectors compared with the total sales value of the product.

Exhibit 18-1 illustrates these differences graphically. Often these costs are locked in during the design of a product (see Chapter 12). Processes with a few simple steps are less prone to spoilage and defects than those with many complex steps. To minimize cost, managers want to determine the costs of spoilage and distinguish between the costs of normal and abnormal spoilage (illustrated under Spoilage in Exhibit 18-1). Eliminating the unrecoverable spoilage costs can result from improving the efficiency and effectiveness of production processes.

Normal spoilage arises under efficient operating conditions as a result of predictable rates of failure in a production process. Normal spoilage may be a locked-in

---

[2]*Wort* refers to the mixture of malt and other grains with water that is ready for fermentation. http://www.microbiologyprocedure.com/industrial-microbiology/beer-manufacturing.htm, accessed August 8, 2011.

[3]http://www.gov.mb.ca/agriculture/foodsafety/processor/cfs02s112.html, accessed August 8, 2011; S.D.P. Flapper and R.H. Teunter, "Logistic planning of rework with deteriorating work-in-process," *International Journal of Production Economics*, 88.11 (2004): 51–19.

[4]http://www.allbusiness.com/wholesale-trade/merchant-wholesalers-nondurable/550143-1.html, accessed August 8, 2011.

EXHIBIT 18-1
Classification of Spoilage, Rework, and Scrap

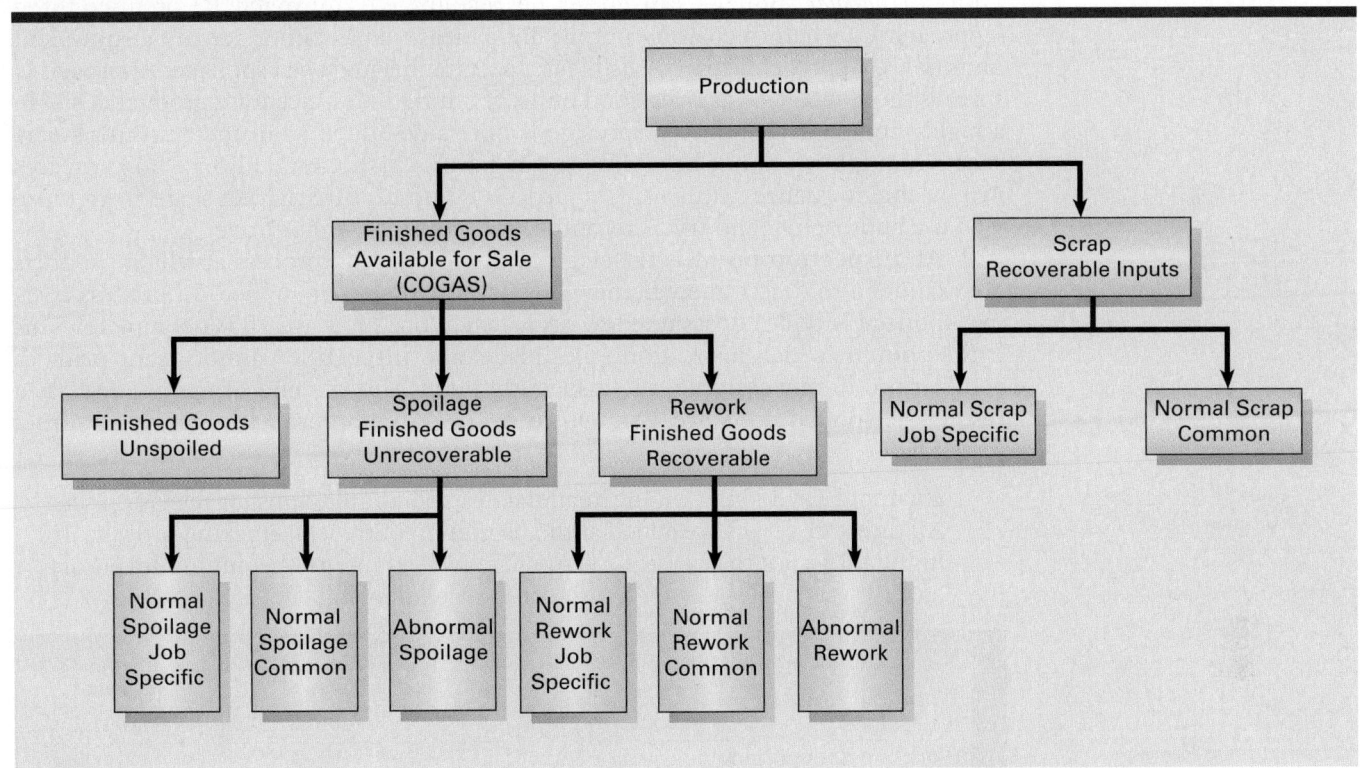

cost, which managers accept when they invest in equipment with a specific failure rate. These costs are not considered controllable or avoidable. GAAP permits including the costs of normal but not abnormal spoilage in the costs of goods manufactured (COGM). The cost is transferred to cost of goods sold when the good units are sold. Normal spoilage rates should be calculated using the total *unspoiled* units completed as the base, not the total *actual* units because total actual units will include both abnormal and normal spoilage.

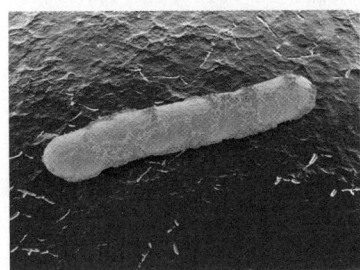

Abnormal spoilage is spoilage that is unexpected under efficient operating conditions but is regarded as controllable and avoidable. Food contamination from salmonella (shown), listeria, or e-coli bacteria are an example of abnormal spoilage. Automobile recalls are a second example. Diligent hygiene and machine maintenance can prevent unexpected outbreaks and breakdowns. Safe procedures can prevent contamination and accidents. Skillful procurement can prevent the purchase of substandard direct materials. Storing perishables at appropriate temperatures can prevent mould and fungal growth. Abnormal spoilage costs are written off as losses of the accounting period in which detection of the spoiled units occurs. For the most informative internal feedback, the Loss from Abnormal Spoilage account should appear in a detailed income statement as a separate line item and not be buried as an indistinguishable part of the COGM.

Many companies, such as Toyota Motor Corporation, adhere to a perfection standard as a part of their emphasis on total quality control. Their ideal goal is zero defects. Hence, all spoilage would be treated as abnormal. Issues about accounting for spoilage arise in both process-costing and job-costing systems. We first present the accounting for spoilage in process-costing systems because it is an extension of the discussion of process costing introduced in Chapter 17.

Units of *normal* spoilage can either be recognized (approach R) or uncounted (approach U) when calculating output units measured as either actual or equivalent units (EU). Approach R makes visible the costs associated with spoilage. Approach U spreads the spoilage costs over good units, resulting in less accurate product costs. In a highly competitive industry, spoilage is not value-added from the customer's perspective and they will not be willing to pay for this cost. Competitors who know this will be able to reduce prices using approach R and capture market share from those who use approach U and try to recapture this cost in a higher price.

An **inspection point** is the stage of the production process at which products are examined to determine whether they are acceptable or spoiled. In process costing, spoilage is typically assumed to occur when products are 100% complete. This is the point at which inspection takes place, and inspection cannot occur prior to completion. In our example, the inspection point is at the end of the process. As a result, the spoiled units are assumed to be 100% complete with respect to direct materials.[5]

Example 1: Chipmakers Inc. manufactures computer chips for television sets. All direct materials are added at the beginning of the chip-making process. To highlight issues that arise with spoilage, we assume no beginning inventory and 10% normal spoilage. In May 2013, the following data are available:

	A	B	C
1		**Physical**	**Direct**
2		**Units**	**Material**
3	Work in process, beginning inventory (May 1)	0	
4	Started during May	10,000	
5	Good units completed and transferred out during May	5,000	
6	Units spoiled (all normal spoilage)	1,000	
7	Work in process, ending inventory (May 31)	4,000	
8	Degree of completion of ending work in process		100%
9	Direct materials costs added in May		$270,000

Exhibit 18-2 calculates and assigns cost per unit of direct materials using approach R and approach U. Approach R shows 10,000 equivalent units (EU) of output: 5,000 EU in good units completed, 4,000 units in ending work in process (EI WIP), and 1,000 EU in normal spoilage (all 100% complete and permitted in COGM).

Approach U shows 9,000 EU of output: 5,000 EU in good units completed and 4,000 EU in EI WIP. Not counting the EU for normal spoilage in approach U decreases the total in the denominator resulting in a higher cost rate/EU. A $30 EU cost in approach U (by not measuring actual spoiled units), instead of a $27 EU cost in approach R (by measuring spoiled units), is assigned to 4,000 EI WIP that have not reached the inspection point. Chipmakers Inc. does not know if these units are spoiled or not, but nonetheless assigns costs as if there were spoilage.

Under approach U, when these 4,000 units are inspected, the normal spoilage will be 400 units assigned a cost of $30/EU. These 400 units, however, already bear the burden of spoilage cost from the costs assigned at $30/EU in the previous time period when they were not yet inspected. These 400 units are bearing a double burden of spoilage cost while the finished goods of May are underburdened with spoilage cost of the time period. The financial flow of costs is not matched to actual economic events.

Approach R has a further advantage. It highlights the cost of normal spoilage to management so that no time will be wasted investigating expected unfavourable production cost variances. Therefore, we will use approach R to present process costing with spoilage.

[5] The allocation issue arises because the quantity of spoilage in May is assumed as 1,000 while the quantity past the inspection point is an actual quantity.

EXHIBIT 18-2
Effect of Recognizing Equivalent Units in Spoilage for Direct Materials Costs for Chipmakers Inc. for May 2013

A	B	C
	Approach R:	**Approach U:**
	Counting Spoiled	**Not Counting Spoiled**
	Units When Computing	**Units When Computing**
	Output in Equivalent	**Output in Equivalent**
	Units	**Units**
6 Costs to account for	$270,000	$270,000
7 Divide by equivalent units of output	÷ 10,000	÷ 9,000
8 Cost per equivalent units of output	$ 27	$ 30
9 Assignment of costs:		
10 Good units completed (5,000 units × $27 per unit; 5,000 units × $30 per unit)	$135,000	$150,000
11 Add normal spoilage (1,000 units × $27 per unit)	27,000	0
12 Total costs of good units completed and transferred out	162,000	150,000
13 Work in process, ending (4,000 units × $27 per unit; 4,000 units × $30 per unit)	108,000	120,000
14 Cost accounted for	$270,000	$270,000

PROCESS COSTING WITH SPOILAGE UNDER THE WEIGHTED-AVERAGE AND FIFO METHODS

We illustrate process costing with spoilage using the following example:

> **Example 2:** Anzio Company manufactures a wooden recycling container in its Processing department. Direct materials for this product are introduced at the beginning of the production cycle. At the start of production, all direct materials required to make one output unit are bundled together in a single kit. Conversion costs are added evenly during the cycle. Some units of this product are spoiled as a result of defects only detectable at inspection of finished units. Normally, the spoiled units are 10% of the good output. Summary data for July 2013 are as follows:

Apply process-costing methods to account for spoilage using weighted-average and first-in, first-out (FIFO) methods.

A	B	C	D	E
	Physical	Direct	Conversion	Total
	Units	Materials	Costs	Costs
	(1)	(2)	(3)	(4) = (2) + (3)
4 Work in process, beginning inventory (July 1)	1,500	$12,000	$ 9,000	$ 21,000
5 Degree of completion of ending work in process		100%	60%	
6 Started during July	8,500			
7 Good units completed and transferred out during July	7,000			
8 Work in process, ending inventory (July 31)	2,000			
9 Degree of completion of ending work in process		100%	50%	
10 Total costs added during July		$76,500	$89,100	$165,600
11 Normal spoilage as a percentage of good units	10%			
12 Degree of completion of normal spoilage		100%	100%	
13 Degree of completion of abnormal spoilage		100%	100%	

The approach used in Chapter 17 needs only slight modification to accommodate spoilage. The key change is in calculating the number of spoiled units as you organize the data for the flow of physical units of output. The conversion and direct material costs must be given, and we assume direct materials are converted 100%. The calculation of conversion costs is based on equivalent units (EU), not physical units, and the total EU converted is the conversion cost allocation base. The cost allocation rate is simply the total conversion cost pool divided by the total EU. Then the direct materials and conversion costs must be assigned to ending inventory Work in Process (EI WIP) and transferred out to Finished Goods, which will provide a statement of COGM for July.

♦ *Summarize the flow of physical units of output.* Identify both normal and abnormal spoilage. The number of total units is 10,000 for the month and the total spoiled units for the month is calculated as follows:

$$\text{Total spoilage} = \left(\begin{array}{c}\text{Units in beginning} \\ \text{work-in-process} \\ \text{inventory}\end{array} + \text{Units started}\right) - \left(\begin{array}{c}\text{Good units} \\ \text{completed and} \\ \text{transferred out}\end{array} + \begin{array}{c}\text{Units in ending} \\ \text{work-in-process} \\ \text{inventory}\end{array}\right)$$

$$= (1,500 + 8,500) - (7,000 + 2,000)$$

$$= 10,000 - 9,000$$

$$= 1,000 \text{ units}$$

Normal spoilage at Anzio's Processing department is 10% of the 7,000 units of good output that is 100% completed, or 700 units. Thus the formula for abnormal spoilage will be:

$$\text{Abnormal spoilage} = \text{Total spoilage} - \text{Normal spoilage}$$

$$= 1,000 - 700$$

$$= 300 \text{ units}$$

♦ *Compute the conversion cost allocation base in equivalent units (EU).* Compute EU for spoilage in the same way as for good units. Because Anzio inspects at the completion point, the same amount of work will be done on each spoiled unit and each 100% completed good unit.

♦ *Compute the direct materials (DM) cost allocation rate per equivalent unit ($/EU).* The details of this step do not differ from those in Chapter 17. We assume that spoiled units are included in the computation of output units. The total DM cost pool for July is $88,500 for 10,000 EU 10% used, giving a rate of $8.85/EU during July.

♦ *Compute the conversion cost allocation rate per equivalent unit ($/EU).* The details of this step do not differ from those in Chapter 17. We assume that spoiled units are included in the computation of output units. The total conversion cost pool for July is $98,100 for 9,000 EU, giving a rate of $10.90/EU during July.

♦ *Summarize total costs to account for.* These are all the costs of production for the month of July, or $186,600.

♦ *Assign these costs to units completed, spoiled units, and units in ending work in process (EI WIP).* This step now includes calculation of the cost of spoiled units and the cost of good units.

But Anzio has the choice of three inventory costing methods—weighted-average, FIFO, or standard costing. Process costing under each of these inventory methods incorporates the timing of cost recognition slightly differently.

WEIGHTED-AVERAGE METHOD AND SPOILAGE

Exhibit 18-3 summarizes the flow of production data and includes calculations of equivalent units (EU) of normal and abnormal spoilage based on the information provided for Anzio Company. All good and spoiled units are considered 100% completed. The physical flow of units through the process is illustrated in the blue boxes and the accompanying cost flows in the silver boxes.

In Exhibit 18-4, the details of the calculations are illustrated. Panel A summarizes the flow of production in physical units and equivalent units, and includes

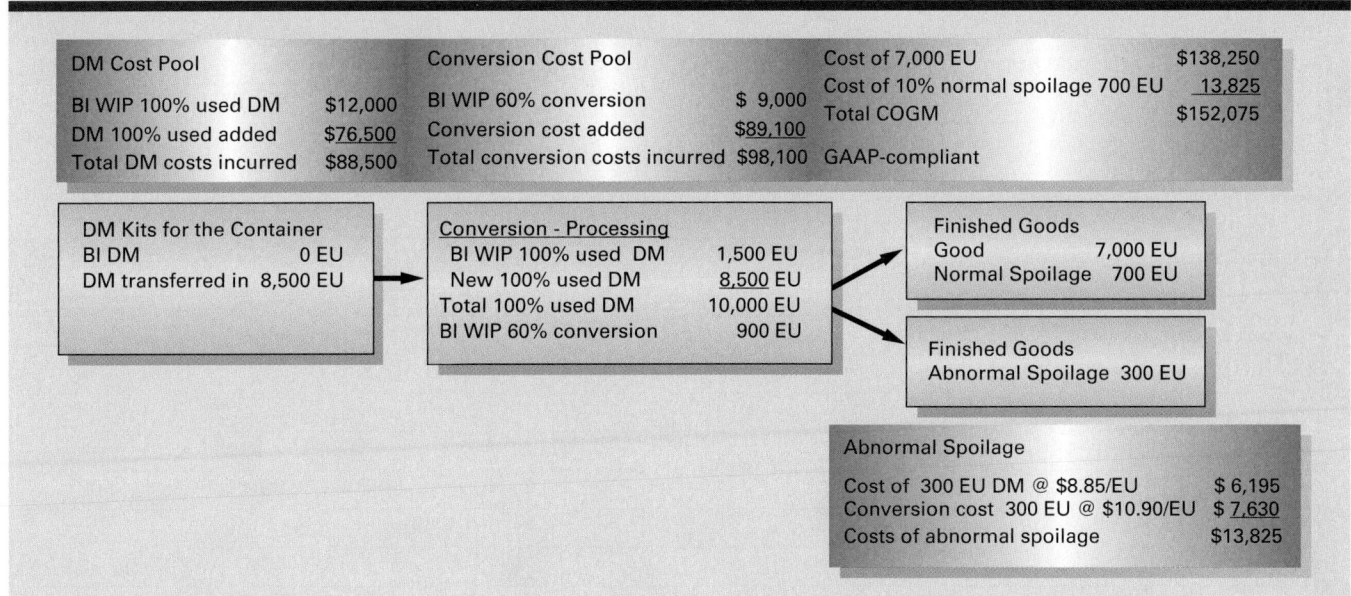

calculations of equivalent units of normal and abnormal spoilage. These are the data represented in the blue boxes in Exhibit 18-3. The data in the silver boxes are represented in Panel B, which begins with the calculation of the cost per equivalent unit, then applies the costs to the units completed and transferred out, including normal spoilage, abnormal spoilage, and EI WIP. In Panel B, notice how, for each cost pool, the costs of BI WIP of unfinished units remaining from last month and finished in the current period are totalled and divided by the EU of all work done to date to calculate the weighted-average cost. These unit costs are multiplied by the EU calculated in Panel A to assign costs to the completed units, spoiled units, and EI WIP.

The costs of normal spoilage of $13,825 are added to the DM (700 units × $8.85 = $6,195) and added to the conversion costs (700 × $10.90 = $7,630) of the good units [7,000 units × ($8.85 + $10.90) = $138,250]. Hence, the cost per good unit completed and transferred out equals the total costs transferred out (including the costs of normal spoilage) divided by the number of good units produced, $152,075 ÷ 7,000 = $21.725. It is *not* equal to $19.75, the sum of the costs per EU of direct materials, $8.85, and conversion costs, $10.90. Instead, the cost per good unit is equal to the total cost of DM and conversion costs per EU, $19.75, *plus* a share of the normal spoilage, $1.975 ($13,825 ÷ 7,000 = $1.975), for a total of $21.725 per good unit. The $5,925 costs of abnormal spoilage are assigned to the Loss from Abnormal Spoilage account and do not appear in the good-unit costs.[6]

The total costs to account for of $186,600 are recorded in a journal entry as a debit to the Work-in-Process (WIP) Inventory account. This account must also be credited with the costs of abnormal spoilage of $5,925 and the cost of good units converted and transferred out of $152,075, which includes costs of normal spoilage of $13,825. The total EI WIP will be $28,600.

FIFO METHOD AND SPOILAGE

Exhibit 18-5 uses the FIFO method: Panel A focuses on EU of work done in the current period and Panel B keeps the costs of the beginning work-in-process inventory (BI WIP) separate and distinct from the costs of work done in the current period when assigning costs.

Panel A of Exhibit 18-5 summarizes the flow of production in physical units and EU, including calculations of EU of normal and abnormal spoilage. Panel B

---

[6]The actual costs of spoilage (and rework) are often greater than the costs recorded in the accounting system because opportunity costs of disruption of the production line, storage, and lost contribution margins are not recorded in accounting systems. Chapter 19 discusses these opportunity costs from a management viewpoint.

EXHIBIT 18-4
Weighted-Average Method of Process Costing with Spoilage—Forming Department of Anzio Company for July 2013

	A	B	C	D
1	**PANEL A: Summarize Output in Physical Units and Compute Equivalent Units**			
2				**Equivalent Units**
3		**Physical**	**Direct**	**Conversion**
4	**Flow of Production**	**Units**	**Materials**	**Costs**
5	Work in process, beginning (given, p. 725)	1,500		
6	Started during current period (given, p. 725)	8,500		
7	To account for	10,000		
8	Good units completed and transferred out during the current period	7,000	7,000	7,000
9	Normal spoilage[a]	700		
10	(700 × 100%; 700 × 100%)		700	700
11	Abnormal spoilage[b]	300		
12	(300 × 100%; 300 × 100%)		300	300
13	Work in process, ending[c] (given, p. 725)	2,000		
14	(2,000 × 100%; 2,000 × 50%)		2,000	1,000
15	Accounted for	10,000		
16	Work done to date		10,000	9,000
17				
18	[a]Normal spoilage is 10% of good units transferred out: 10% × 7,000 = 700 units. Degree of completion of normal spoilage in this			
19	department: direct materials, 100%; conversion costs, 100%.			
20	[b]Abnormal spoilage = Total spoilage − Normal spoilage = 1,000 − 700 = 300 units. Degree of completion of abnormal spoilage			
21	in this department: direct materials, 100%; conversion costs, 100%.			
22	[c]Degree of completion in this department: direct materials, 100%; conversion costs, 50%.			
23				
24	**PANEL B: Compute Cost per Equivalent Unit, Summarize Total Costs to Account For, and Assign**			
25	**Total Costs to Units Completed, to Spoiled Units, and to Units in Ending Work in Process**			
26		**Total**		
27		**Production**	**Direct**	**Conversion**
28		**Costs**	**Materials**	**Costs**
29	Work in process, beginning (given, p. 725)	$ 21,000	$12,000	$ 9,000
30	Costs added in the current period (given, p. 725)	165,600	76,500	89,100
31	Costs incurred to date		$88,500	$98,100
32	Divide by equivalent units of work done to date		÷10,000	÷9,000
33	Cost per equivalent unit		$ 8.85	$ 10.90
34	Total costs to account for	$186,600		
35	Assignment of costs:			
36	Good units completed and transferred out (7,000 units):			
37	Costs before adding normal spoilage	$138,250	(7,000[d] × $8.85) + (7,000[d] × $10.90)	
38	Normal spoilage (700 units)	13,825	(700[d] × $8.85) + (700[d] × $10.90)	
39 (A)	Total costs of good units completed and transferred out	152,075		
40 (B)	Abnormal spoilage (300 units)	5,925	(300[d] × $8.85) + (300[d] × $10.90)	
41 (C)	Work in process, ending (2,000 units)	28,600	(2,000[d] × $8.85) + (1,000[d] × $10.90)	
42 (A+B+C)	Total costs accounted for	$186,600		
43				
44	[d]Equivalent units of direct materials and conversion costs calculated in Panel A.			

EXHIBIT 18-5

First-In, First-Out (FIFO) Method of Process Costing with Spoilage—Forming Department of Anzio Company for July 2013

	A	B	C	D
			Equivalent Units	
		Physical	**Direct**	**Conversion**
	Flow of Production	**Units**	**Materials**	**Costs**
1	**PANEL A: Summarize Output in Physical Units and Compute Equivalent Units**			
5	Work in process, beginning balance (given)	1,500		
6	Started during current period (given)	8,500		
7	To account for	10,000		
8	Good units completed and transferred out during the current period			
9	From beginning work in process inventory[a]	1,500		
10	$1,500 \times (100\% - 100\%); 1,500 \times (100\% - 60\%)$		—	600
11	Started and completed[b]	5,500		
12	$5,500 \times 100\%; 5,500 \times 100\%$		5,500	5,500
13	Normal spoilage[c]	700		
14	$700 \times 100\%; 700 \times 100\%$		700	700
15	Abnormal spoilage[d]	300		
16	$300 \times 100\%; 300 \times 100\%$		300	300
17	Work in process, ending balance[e] (given)	2,000		
18	$2,000 \times 100\%; 2,000 \times 50\%$		2,000	1,000
19	Accounted for	10,000		
20	Work done in current period only		8,500	8,100

[a] Degree of completion in this department: direct materials, 100%; conversion costs, 60%.

[b] 7,000 physical units completed and transferred out minus 1,500 physical units completed and transferred from BI WIP.

[c] Normal spoilage is 10% of good units transferred out: 10% × 7,000 = 700 units. Degree of completion of normal spoilage in this department: direct materials, 100%; conversion costs, 100%.

[d] Abnormal spoilage = Actual spoilage − Normal spoilage = 1,000 − 700 = 300 units. Degree of completion of abnormal spoilage in this department: direct materials, 100%; conversion costs, 100%.

[e] Degree of completion in this department: direct materials, 100%; conversion costs, 50%.

PANEL B: Compute Cost per Equivalent Unit, Summarize Total Costs to Account For, and Assign Total Costs to Units Completed, to Spoiled Units, and to Units in Ending Work in Process

			Total		**Direct**	**Conversion**
			Production		**Materials**	**Costs**
			Costs			
34		Work in process, beginning balance (given)	$ 21,000			
35		Costs added in the current period (given)	165,600		$76,500	$89,100
36		Divide by equivalent units of work done in the current period			÷8,500	÷8,100
37		Cost per equivalent unit			$ 9	$ 11
38		Total costs to account for	$186,600			
39		Assignment of costs:				
40		Good units completed and transferred out (7,000 units):				
41		Work in process beginning balance (1,500 units)	$ 21,000			
42		Costs added in current period[f]	6,600	=	$(0^f \times \$9) + (600^f \times \$11)$	
43		Total from beginning inventory before normal spoilage	27,600			
44		Started and completed before normal spoilage (5,500 units)	110,000	=	$(5,500^f \times \$9) + (5,500^f \times \$11)$	
45		Normal spoilage (700 units)	14,000	=	$(700^f \times \$9) + (700^f \times \$11)$	
46 A		Total costs of good units completed and transferred out	151,600			
47 B		Abnormal spoilage (300 units)	6,000	=	$(300^f \times \$9) + (300^f \times \$11)$	
48 C		Work in process, ending balance (2,000 units)	29,000	=	$(2,000^f \times \$9) + (1,000^f \times \$11)$	
49 A + B + C		Total costs accounted for	$186,600			

[f] Equivalent units of direct materials and conversion costs calculated in Panel A.

begins with the calculation of the cost per EU, then applies the costs to the units completed and transferred out, including normal spoilage, as well as the abnormal spoilage and EI WIP. All spoilage costs are assumed to be related to units completed during this period, using the unit costs of the current period.

In Exhibit 18-5, there are several items that are different from what was shown for the weighted-average method in Exhibit 18-4. First, the BI WIP for the FIFO method includes good units that were 60% completed in the previous month. This means they must be 40% converted in the current month. These BI WIP units must be the first to be accounted for with respect to costs transferred out each month. Because DM is 100% consumed at the beginning of conversion, the current month's DM costs assigned to BI WIP of 600 EU (1,500 physical units × 0.4 = 600 EU) already 60% converted last month will be zero.

The added DM costs for the current month will be assigned to only the 8,500 physical units started; hence, the DM cost per unit is \$9.00/EU (\$76,500 ÷ 8,500 EU = \$9.00/EU). The added conversion costs for this month will be assigned to only the 8,100 EU, including the 1,000 EU in EI WIP (2,000 physical units × 0.5 = 1,000 EU). The cost allocation rate for the conversion cost pool is \$11.00/EU (\$89,100 ÷ 8,100 EU = \$11.00/EU). All the spoilage for this month will be calculated at these two rates and spoiled units are 100% converted.

If the FIFO method were used in its purest form, normal spoilage costs would be split between the goods started and completed during the current period and those completed from BI WIP—using the appropriate unit costs of the period in which the units were worked on. The simpler, modified FIFO method, as illustrated in Exhibit 18-5, in effect uses the unit costs of the current period for assigning normal spoilage costs to the goods completed from BI WIP. This modified FIFO method assumes that all normal spoilage traceable to the BI WIP was started and completed during the current period.

PROCESS COSTING STANDARD COSTS

③ Apply the standard-costing method to account for spoilage, and allocate costs of normal spoilage.

This section assumes you have studied Chapters 7 and 8 and the standard costs method in Chapter 17. Otherwise, omit this section.

Standard-costing methods can also be used to account for normal and abnormal spoilage. We illustrate how much simpler the calculations of conversion costs become by continuing our Anzio Company example; however, journal entries must be made to account for the variances between standard and actual costs.

Suppose Anzio Company develops standard costs for the Forming department. Assume the same standard costs apply to the beginning inventory and to work done in July 2013:

Standard Costs for Forming Department

Direct materials	\$ 8.50
Conversion costs	10.50
Total manufacturing cost	\$19.00

Assume the same standard costs per unit also apply to the beginning inventory: 1,500 (1,500 × 100%) EU of DM and 900 (1,500 × 60%) EU of conversion costs. Hence, the beginning inventory at standard costs is:

Direct materials: 1,500 × \$8.50/unit	\$12,750
Conversion costs: 900 × \$10.50/unit	9,450
Total manufacturing cost	\$22,200

Exhibit 18-6, Panel A, shows the flow of production in physical units and EU, including normal spoilage and abnormal spoilage. The FIFO calculation is unchanged. Panel B shows the cost per EU and the assignment of costs to units completed and transferred out (including normal spoilage) to abnormal spoilage and to EI WIP. Panel B contains no calculation of a cost allocation rate because this rate is already given as a standard cost. The actual costs were provided in the initial table on

EXHIBIT 18-6

Use of Standard Cost in Process Costing with Spoilage—Forming Department of Anzio Company for July 2013

	A	B	C	D
1	**PANEL A: Summarize Output in Physical Units and Compute Equivalent Units**			
2			**Equivalent Units**	
3		**Physical**	**Direct**	**Conversion**
4	**Flow of Production**	**Units**	**Materials**	**Costs**
5	Work in process, beginning balance (given)	1,500		
6	Started during current period (given)	8,500		
7	To account for	10,000		
8	Good units completed and transferred out during the current period			
9	From beginning work in process inventory[a]	1,500		
10	1,500 × (100% − 100%); 1,500 × (100% − 60%)		—	600
11	Started and completed[b]	5,500		
12	5,500 × 100%; 5,500 × 100%		5,500	5,500
13	Normal spoilage[c]	700		
14	700 × 100%; 700 × 100%		700	700
15	Abnormal spoilage[d]	300		
16	300 × 100%; 300 × 100%		300	300
17	Work in process, ending balance[e] (given)	2,000		
18	2,000 × 100%; 2,200 × 50%		2,000	1,000
19	Accounted for	10,000		
20	Work done in current period only		8,500	8,100
21				
22	[a]Degree of completion in this department: direct materials, 100%; conversion costs, 60%.			
23	[b]7,000 physical units completed and transferred out minus 1,500 physical units completed and transferred from BI WIP.			
24	[c]Normal spoilage is 10% of good units transferred out: 10% × 7,000 = 700 units. Degree of completion of			
25	normal spoilage in this department: direct materials 100%; conversion costs 100%.			
26	[d]Abnormal spoilage = Actual spoilage − Normal spoilage = 1,000 − 700 = 300 units. Degree of completion			
27	of abnormal spoilage in this department: direct materials 100%; conversion costs, 100%.			
28	[e]Degree of completion in this department: direct materials 100%; conversion costs, 50%.			
29	**PANEL B: Standard Cost per Equivalent Unit, Summarize Total Costs to Account For,**			
30	**and Assign Total Costs to Units Completed, to Spoiled Units, and to Units in Ending Work in Process**			
31		**Total**		
32		**Production**	**Direct**	**Conversion**
33		**Costs**	**Materials**	**Costs**
34	Standard cost per equivalent unit (given)	$ 19.00	$ 8.50	$ 10.50
35	Work in process, beginning balance (given)	$ 22,200		
36	Costs added in the current period (at standard)	157,300 =	72,250[g] +	85,050[h]
37	Total costs to account for	$179,500		
38	Cost per equivalent unit (at standard)		$ 8.50	$ 10.50
39	Assignment of costs:			
40	Good units completed and transferred out (7,000 units):			
41	Work in process beginning balance (1,500 units)	$ 22,200		
42	Costs added in current period[f] (0 × $8.50; 600 × $10.50)	6,300 =	$ — +	$ 6,300
43	Total from beginning inventory before normal spoilage	28,500		
44	Started and completed before normal spoilage (5,500 units)	104,500 =	46,750 +	57,750
45	Normal spoilage (700 units)	13,300 =	5,950 +	7,350
46 A	Total costs of good units completed and transferred out	146,300		
47 B	Abnormal spoilage (300 units)	5,700 =	2,550 +	3,150
48 C	Work in process, ending balance (2,000 × $8.50; 1,000 × $10.50)	27,500 =	17,000 +	10,500
49 A + B + C	Total costs accounted for	$179,500	$ 72,250	$85,050
50	Summary of variances for current performance:			
51	Costs added in current period at standard costs (see above)		$ 72,250	$85,050
52	Actual costs incurred (given, p. 725)		76,500	89,100
53	Variance		$ (4,250) U	$ (4,050) U
54				
55	[f]Equivalent units of direct materials and conversion costs calculated in Panel A.			
56	[g]8,500 equivalent units × $8.50			
57	[h]8,100 equivalent units × $10.50			

Managing Waste and Environmental Costs at Toyota

Toyota's president defined waste as "anything other than the minimum amount of equipment, materials, parts, space, and workers' time which are absolutely essential to add value to the product."

Currently, Toyota has reduced its landfill waste to approximately 59,000 tonnes per year, down over 50% from 160,000 tonnes per year in 1995, excluding recycled material. The volume of waste remaining in landfill after incineration and recycling was 8,900 tonnes. Yield improvements (reduction of scrap and waste of inputs) and the use of returnable and recyclable packaging have helped Toyota achieve this reduction. Currently the company has a vehicle recovery rate of 98% through design changes to create easy-to-remove components. Toyota has also eliminated the use of cadmium and chromium, reduced the use of PVC, and eliminated the use of asbestos in its vehicles.

Sources: J. Newberry, "A Goal of Zero," *Cincinnati Post* (June 30, 2003); Toyota Sustainability Report, 2006, http://www.toyota.co.jp/en/environmental_rep/06/download/index.html, accessed July 11, 2008.

page 725, but the total standard, or pro forma, costs must be assigned. Using the methods presented in Chapters 7 and 8, variances have been calculated and indicate unfavourable variances for both DM and conversion. This approach directs management's attention to the decrease in gross margin, and, all other things being equal, operating income this month. There is, as yet, no explanation for these variances.

Regardless of the method managers choose to assign conversion costs, the COGM, COGAS, and COGS must conform to GAAP for valuation of inventory. The three methods presented are in conformance, and all three methods arrive at the identical actual costs added during the month of July.

JOURNAL ENTRIES

The information from Panel B in Exhibits 18-4, 18-5, and 18-6 supports the following journal entries:

	Weighted Average		FIFO		Standard	
1. Finished Goods	$152,075		$151,600		$146,300	
Work in Process—Forming		$152,075		$151,600		$146,300
To transfer good units completed in July.						
2. Loss from Abnormal Spoilage	$ 5,925		$ 6,000		$ 5,700	
Work in Process—Forming		$ 5,925		$ 6,000		$ 5,700
To recognize abnormal spoilage detected in July.						
3. Work in Process—Forming (at standard costs)					$ 72,250	
Direct Materials Variances					4,250	
Forming Department Direct Materials Control						$ 76,500
To record actual direct materials used and total direct materials variances.						
4. Work in Process—Forming (at standard costs)					$ 85,050	
Conversion Costs Variance					4,050	
Forming Department Conversion Costs Control						$ 89,100
To record actual conversion costs and total conversion cost variances.						

ALLOCATING COSTS OF NORMAL SPOILAGE

Spoilage might actually occur at various points or stages of the production cycle, but spoilage is typically not detected until one or more specific points of inspection. The cost of spoiled units is assumed to be all costs incurred by spoiled units before inspection. When spoiled goods have a disposal value, the net cost of spoilage is computed by deducting disposal value from the costs of the spoiled goods accumulated to the point of inspection.

The unit costs of abnormal and normal spoilage are the same when the two are detected simultaneously. However, situations might arise when abnormal spoilage is detected at a different point from normal spoilage. In such cases, the unit cost of abnormal spoilage would differ from the unit cost of normal spoilage. Costs of abnormal spoilage are separately accounted for as losses for the period. Recall, however, that normal spoilage costs are added to costs of good units.

Accounting for normal spoilage, therefore, raises an additional issue: Should normal spoilage costs be allocated between completed units and ending WIP inventory? One approach is to presume that normal spoilage occurs at the inspection point in the production cycle and to allocate its cost over all units that have passed that point. In the Anzio Company example, spoilage is assumed to occur when finished units are inspected, so no cost of normal spoilage is allocated to EI WIP.

Whether the cost of normal spoilage is allocated to the units in EI WIP in addition to completed units depends strictly on whether they have passed the point of inspection. For example, if the inspection point is presumed to be the halfway stage of the production cycle, work in process that is more than 50% completed is allocated a full measure of normal spoilage costs, calculated on the basis of all costs incurred before the point of inspection. But work in process that is less than 50% completed is not allocated any normal spoilage costs. Additional discussion concerning various assumptions about spoilage appears in the next section.

INSPECTION AND SPOILAGE AT INTERMEDIATE STAGES OF COMPLETION

Consider how the timing of inspection at various stages of completion affects the amount of normal and abnormal spoilage. Assume that normal spoilage is 10% of the good units passing inspection in the Forging department of Dana Corporation, a manufacturer of automobile parts. Direct materials are added at the start of production in the Forging department. Conversion costs are allocated evenly during the process.

Suppose inspection had occurred at the 20%, 50%, or 100% completion stage. Spoilage totals 8,000 units in all cases. Note how the number of units of normal spoilage and abnormal spoilage change. Normal spoilage is computed on the number of *good units* that pass the inspection point *in the current period*. The following data are for October 2013:

Flow of Production	Physical Units Inspection at Stage of Completion		
	at 20%	at 50%	at 100%
Work in process, beginning (25%)[a]	11,000	11,000	11,000
Started during October	74,000	74,000	74,000
To account for	85,000	85,000	85,000
Good units completed and transferred out (85,000 − 8,000 spoiled − 16,000 ending)	61,000	61,000	61,000
Normal spoilage	6,600[b]	7,700[c]	6,100[d]
Abnormal spoilage (8,000 − normal spoilage)	1,400	300	1,900
Work in process, ending balance[a]	16,000	16,000	16,000
Accounted for	85,000	85,000	85,000

[a]Degree of completion for conversion costs of this department at the dates of the work-in-process inventories is 25%.
[b]10% × (74,000 units started − 8,000 units spoiled), since only the units started passed the 20% completion inspection point in the current period. Beginning work in process is excluded from this calculation because it is already 25% complete.
[c]10% × (85,000 units − 8,000 units spoiled), since *all* units passed the 50% completion inspection point in the current period.
[d]10% × 61,000 since 61,000 units were fully completed and inspected in the current period.

To see the number of units passing each inspection point, focus on the vertical lines at the 20%, 50%, and 100% inspection points in the diagram below. Note that the vertical line at 20% cuts two horizontal lines: 50,000 good units started and completed and 16,000 units in ending work in process, for a total of 66,000 good units. (It does not cut the line representing work done on the 11,000 good units completed from beginning work in process because these units were already 25% complete at the start of the period and hence were not inspected this period.) Normal spoilage equals 10% × 66,000 = 6,600 units. Similarly, the vertical line at the 50% point cuts all three horizontal lines, indicating that 11,000 + 50,000 + 16,000 = 77,000 good units pass this point. Normal spoilage in this case is 10% × 77,000 = 7,700 units. At the 100% point, normal spoilage = 10% × (11,000 + 50,000) = 6,100 units.

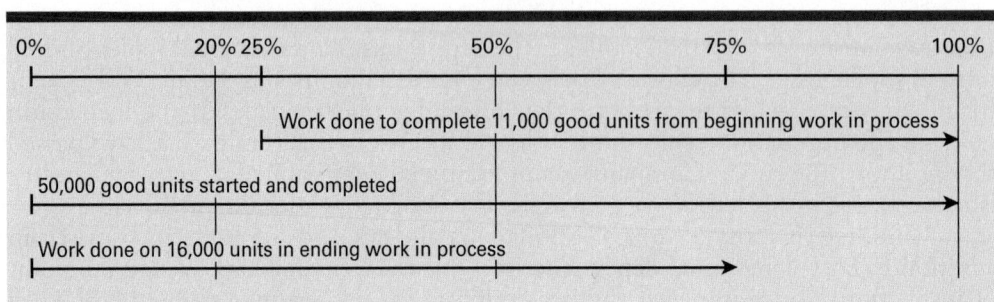

Exhibit 18-7 illustrates the computation of equivalent units assuming inspection at the 50% completion stage. The calculations depend on how much of the direct materials and conversion costs were incurred to get the units to the point of inspection. The spoiled units, in this case, have a full measure of direct materials and a 50% measure of conversion costs. The computations of equivalent-unit costs and the assignments of total costs to units completed and in ending work in process would be similar to those in previous illustrations. Since ending work in process has passed the inspection point in this example, these units would bear normal spoilage costs, just like the units that have been completed and transferred out.

EXHIBIT 18-7

Computing Equivalent Units with Spoilage Using Weighted-Average Method of Process Costing with Inspection at 50% of Completion for the Forging Department of Dana Corporation for October 2013

| | | Equivalent Units | |
Flow of Production	Physical Units	Direct Materials	Conversion Costs
Work in process, beginning[a]	11,000		
Started during current period	74,000		
To account for	85,000		
Good units completed and transferred out	61,000	61,000	61,000
Normal spoilage (7,700 × 100%; 7,700 × 50%)	7,700	7,700	3,850
Abnormal spoilage (300 × 100%; 300 × 50%)	300	300	150
Work in process, ending[b] (16,000 × 100%; 16,000 × 75%)	16,000	16,000	12,000
Accounted for	85,000		
Total work done to date		85,000	77,000

[a]Degree of completion: direct materials, 100%; conversion costs, 25%.
[b]Degree of completion: direct materials, 100%; conversion costs, 75%.

JOB COSTING AND SPOILAGE

The concepts of normal and abnormal spoilage also apply to job-costing systems. Abnormal spoilage is usually regarded as controllable by the manager. It is separately identified with the goal of eliminating it altogether. Costs of abnormal spoilage are not considered to be product manufacturing costs and are written off as costs of the period in which detection occurs. Normal or planned spoilage in job-costing systems, however, is considered part of normal manufacturing costs, although increasingly managers are tolerating only small amounts of spoilage as normal. The costs are then assigned to individually distinct jobs, a step unnecessary in process costing since masses of similar units are manufactured.

Apply job cost allocation procedures to account for spoilage in job costing.

4

We illustrate the accounting for spoilage in job costing using the following example:

Example 3: In Hull Machine Shop, five aircraft parts out of a job lot of 50 aircraft parts are spoiled. Costs assigned up to the point of inspection are $100 per unit. Hull calculates these costs on the basis of its inventory costing assumptions—weighted average, FIFO, or standard costs. We do not, however, emphasize cost-flow assumptions in our presentation here or in subsequent sections. The current disposal price of the spoiled parts is estimated to be $30 per part. When the spoilage is detected, the spoiled goods are inventoried at $30 per unit.

Normal Spoilage Common to All Jobs In some cases, spoilage may be considered a normal characteristic of a given production cycle. The spoilage inherent in the process only coincidentally occurs when a specific job is being worked on. The spoilage then is not attributable, and hence is not charged, to the specific job. Instead, it is costed as manufacturing overhead. The budgeted manufacturing overhead allocation rate includes a provision for normal spoilage cost. Therefore, normal spoilage cost is spread, through overhead allocation, over all jobs rather than loaded on specific jobs only.[7]

Materials Control (spoiled goods at current disposal value): 5 × $30	$150	
Manufacturing Department Overhead Control (normal spoilage): 5 × $70	350	
Work-in-Process Control (specific job): 5 × $100		$500

Normal Spoilage Attributable to a Specific Job When normal spoilage occurs because of the specifications of a specific job, that job bears the cost of the spoilage reduced by the current disposal value of that spoilage. The journal entry to recognize the disposal value of the salvage (items in parentheses indicate subsidiary postings) is as follows:

Materials Control (spoiled goods at current disposal value): 5 × $30	$150	
Work-in-Process Control (specific job): 5 × $30		$150

The effect of this accounting is that the net cost of the normal spoilage, $350 ($500 − $150), becomes a direct cost of the 45 (50 − 5) good units produced.

Abnormal Spoilage If the spoilage is abnormal, the net loss is highlighted to management by charging the loss to an abnormal loss account:

Materials Control (spoiled goods at current disposal value): 5 × $30	$150	
Loss from Abnormal Spoilage: 5 × $70	350	
Work-in-Process Control (specific job): 5 × $100		$500

---

[7]Note that costs *already assigned to products* are being charged back to Manufacturing Overhead Control, which generally accumulates only costs incurred, not both costs incurred and costs already assigned.

Reworked units are unacceptable units of production that are subsequently reworked into good units and sold. The cost of rework is frequently material and therefore included in COGM.

Consider the Hull Machine Shop data (Example 3). Assume that the five spoiled parts used in our Hull Machine Shop illustration are reworked. The journal entry for the $500 of total costs (details of costs assumed) assigned to the five spoiled units before considering rework costs is as follows:

Work-in-Process Control	$500	
Materials Control		$200
Wages Payable		200
Manufacturing Overhead Allocated		100

Assume that rework costs equal $190 (direct materials, $40; direct labour, $100; manufacturing overhead, $50).

Normal Rework Common to All Jobs When rework is normal and not attributable to any specific job, the costs of rework are charged to manufacturing overhead and spread, through overhead allocation, over all jobs.

Manufacturing Department Overhead Control (rework)	$190	
Materials Control		$ 40
Wages Payable		100
Manufacturing Overhead Allocated		50

Notice that the Manufacturing Overhead Control (MOH Control) and Manufacturing Overhead (MOH) are allocated in the same journal entry. MOH Control is debited because the normal rework is common to all jobs and is not attributable to a specific job. In this case, the additional MOH costs incurred to rework the units (for example, utilities, materials handling, inspection) are spread over all jobs by including an allowance for estimated rework in the pro forma MOH. This allowance is credited to MOH allocated.

Normal Rework Attributable to a Specific Job If the rework is normal but occurs because of the requirements of a specific job, the rework costs are charged to that job. The journal entry is as follows:

Work-in-Process Control (specific job)	$190	
Materials Control		$ 40
Wages Payable		100
Manufacturing Overhead Allocated		50

Abnormal Rework If the rework is abnormal, it is highlighted to management by charging abnormal rework to a separate loss account.

Loss from Abnormal Rework	$190	
Materials Control		$ 40
Wages Payable		100
Manufacturing Overhead Allocated		50

Accounting for rework in process costing only requires abnormal rework to be distinguished from normal rework. Abnormal rework is accounted for as in job costing. Since masses of similar units are manufactured, accounting for normal rework follows the accounting described for normal rework common to all jobs.

Costing rework highlights the resources wasted on activities that would not have to be undertaken if the product were made correctly. It prompts management to seek ways to reduce rework—for example, by designing new products or processes, training workers, or investing in new machines. Calculating rework costs helps management perform cost-benefit analyses for various alternatives. To emphasize the importance of eliminating rework and to simplify the accounting, some companies expense all rework, including the costs of normal rework, as an expense of the current period.

ACCOUNTING FOR SCRAP

Scrap is a product that has minimal (frequently zero) sales value compared with the sales value of the main or joint product(s).

There are two major aspects of accounting for scrap:

◆ Planning and control, including physical tracking.
◆ Inventory costing, including when and how to affect operating income.

Initial entries to scrap records are most often in physical or nonfinancial terms such as in kilograms or units. In various industries, items such as stamped-out metal sheets are quantified by weighing, counting, or some other expedient means. Scrap records not only help measure efficiency, but also often focus on a tempting source for theft. Scrap reports are prepared as source documents for periodic summaries of the amount of actual scrap compared with budgeted norms or standards. Scrap is either sold or disposed of quickly, or stored in some routine way for later sale, disposal, or reuse.

The tracking of scrap often extends into the financial records. Most companies maintain a distinct cost for scrap somewhere in their cost accounting system. The issues here are similar to those discussed in Chapter 15 regarding the accounting for byproducts:

◆ When should any value of scrap be recognized in the accounting records: at the time of production of scrap or at the time of sale of scrap?
◆ How should revenue from scrap be accounted for?

To illustrate, we extend our Hull Machine Shop example by assuming that the manufacture of aircraft parts generates scrap. We further assume that the normal scrap from a job lot has a total sales value of $45.

RECOGNIZING SCRAP AT THE TIME OF SALE

When scrap is sold, the simplest accounting is to regard scrap sales as a separate line item of other revenues. The journal entry is

| Sale of scrap: | Cash or Accounts Receivable | $45 | |
| | Sales of Scrap | | $45 |

Rework costs are recorded when incurred because they tend to be material in their amount. Scrap has minimal salvage value and is not material. Scrap may not be recorded and included in COGM but rather may be recorded at the time of sale as COGS.

Scrap Attributable to a Specific Job Job-costing systems sometimes trace the sales of scrap to the jobs that yielded the scrap. This method is used only when the tracing can be done in an economically feasible way. For example, Hull Machine Shop and particular customers may reach an agreement that provides for charging specific jobs with all rework or spoilage costs, and for crediting these jobs with all scrap sales that arise from them. The journal entry is:

Scrap returned to storeroom:	[No journal entry. Memo of quantity received and related job is entered in the inventory record.]		
Sale of scrap:	Cash or Accounts Receivable	$45	
	Work-in-Process Control		$45
	Posting made to specific job record.		

Managing Toxic Waste and Environmental and Corporate Sustainability

The DuPont Corporation manufactures a wide range of chemicals and chemical products, and calls the spoilage and scrap it generates *waste*. Chemical waste, often toxic, impacts the environment, and legislation requires environmentally safe disposal. Special disposal costs increase the cost of generating waste. DuPont calculates the full costs of waste to include (1) the costs of materials lost in the chemical process minus their disposal value; (2) the full costs of semi-finished and finished products spoiled; (3) the full costs of disposal of or treating the waste, such as site charges for hazardous waste or costs of scrubbers and biotreatment plants to treat the waste; and (4) the costs of any solvents used to clean plant and equipment as a result of generating waste.

The company focuses on avoidance of waste altogether as the best way to achieve profitability and environmental performance, and it rewards managers for reducing waste. The company's new process for Terathane® significantly reduces environmental emissions and energy use. Relative to the old technology, the new technology reduced air emissions by 91,000 kilograms, solid waste by 11 million kilograms, aqueous waste by 11 million kilograms, and steam use by more than 68 million kilograms, while generating cost savings of more than US$5 million a year.

Sources: Adapted from Environmental Respect Awards, DuPont Corporation, and based on discussions with Dale Martin, manager, Environmental Effectiveness; C. Holliday, "Sustainable Growth, the DuPont Way," *Harvard Business Review,* September 2001, pp. 129–134.

Unlike spoilage and rework, there is no cost attached to the scrap, and hence no normal or abnormal scrap. All scrap sales, whatever the amount, are credited to the specific job. Scrap sales reduce the costs of the job. In job costing, the cost of scrap is already in the WIP account for each job generating the scrap. These costs are already accounted for, and therefore no journal entry is necessary. When the scrap is sold, however, the WIP account must be decreased (credited) to reduce the cost of the job by the amount of the scrap's disposal value.

RECOGNIZING SCRAP AT THE TIME OF PRODUCTION

Our preceding illustrations assume that scrap returned to the storeroom is sold or disposed of quickly and hence not assigned an inventory cost figure. Scrap, however, sometimes has a significant market value, and the time between storing it and selling or reusing it can be quite long. Under these conditions, the company is justified in inventorying scrap at a conservative estimate of net realizable value so that production costs and related scrap recovery may be recognized in the same accounting period. Some companies tend to delay sales of scrap until the market price is most attractive. Volatile price fluctuations are typical for scrap metal. If scrap inventory becomes significant, it should be inventoried at some "reasonable value"—a difficult task in the face of volatile market prices.

Scrap Attributable to a Specific Job   The journal entry in the Hull Machine Shop example is:

Scrap returned to storeroom:	Materials Control	$45
	Work-in-Process Control	$45

Scrap Common to All Jobs   The journal entry in this case is:

Scrap returned to storeroom: Materials Control $45
                                             Manufacturing Department Overhead
                                             Control $45

Observe that the Materials Control account is debited in place of Cash or Accounts Receivable.

When this scrap is sold, the journal entry is:

Sale of scrap: Cash or Accounts Receivable $45
                                             Materials Control $45

Scrap is sometimes reused as direct materials rather than sold as scrap. Then it should be debited to Materials Control as a class of direct materials and carried at its estimated net realizable value. For example, the entries when the scrap generated is common to all jobs are:

Scrap returned to storeroom: Materials Control $45
                                             Manufacturing Department
                                             Overhead Control $45
Reuse of scrap: Work-in-Process Control $45
                                             Materials Control $45

The accounting for scrap under process costing follows the accounting for jobs when scrap is common to all jobs since process costing is used to cost the mass manufacture of similar units. The high cost of scrap focuses management's attention on ways to reduce scrap and to use it more profitably. For example, General Motors has redesigned its plastic injection moulding processes to reduce the scrap plastic that must be broken away from its moulded parts. General Motors also regrinds and reuses the plastic scrap as direct materials, saving substantial input costs.

PULLING IT ALL TOGETHER—PROBLEM FOR SELF-STUDY

(Try to solve this problem before examining the solution that follows.)

PROBLEM
Burlington Textiles has some spoiled goods that had an assigned cost of $40,000 and zero net disposal value.

REQUIRED
Prepare a journal entry for each of the following conditions under (a) process costing (Department A) and (b) job costing:
1. Abnormal spoilage of $40,000
2. Normal spoilage of $40,000 regarded as common to all operations
3. Normal spoilage of $40,000 regarded as attributable to specifications of a particular job

SOLUTION

(a) Process Costing			**(b) Job Costing**		
1. Loss from Abnormal Spoilage	$40,000		Loss from Abnormal Spoilage	$40,000	
Work in Process—Dept. A		$40,000	Work-in-Process Control (specific job)		$40,000
2. No entry until units are complete and transferred out; then the normal spoilage costs are transferred as part of the cost of good units.			Manufacturing Overhead Control	$40,000	
			Work-in-Process Control (specific job)		$40,000
Work in Process—Dept. A	$40,000				
Work in Process—Dept. A		$40,000			
3. Not applicable			No entry. Normal spoilage cost remains in Work-in-Process Control (specific job)		

SUMMARY POINTS

The following question-and-answer format summarizes the chapter's learning outcomes. Each point presents a key question, and the guidelines are the answer to that question.

LEARNING OUTCOMES	GUIDELINES
1. What are spoilage, rework, and scrap?	Spoilage refers to units of production that do not meet the standards required by customers for good units and that are discarded or sold for reduced prices. Rework is unacceptable units that are subsequently repaired and sold as acceptable finished goods. Scrap is material left over when making a product; it has low sales value compared with the sales value of the main product. Normal spoilage is uncontrollable and unavoidable. Abnormal spoilage is both controllable and avoidable. GAAP permits costs of normal spoilage in the cost of goods manufactured but abnormal spoilage must be recorded as a loss for the accounting period in which it is detected.
2. How do the weighted-average method and FIFO method of process costing differ in calculating the costs of good units and spoilage?	The weighted-average method combines costs in beginning inventory with costs of the current period when determining the costs of good units (which include a normal spoilage amount) and the costs of abnormal spoilage. The FIFO method keeps separate the costs in beginning inventory from the costs of the current period when determining the costs of good units (which include a normal spoilage amount) and the costs of abnormal spoilage.
3. How does the standard-costing method of process costing calculate the costs of good units and spoilage?	The standard-costing method uses standard costs to determine the costs of good units (which include a normal spoilage amount) and the costs of abnormal spoilage.
4. How do job-costing systems account for spoilage and rework?	Normal spoilage specific to a job is assigned to that job or, if common to all jobs, it is allocated as part of manufacturing overhead. Loss from abnormal spoilage is recorded as a cost of the accounting period in which it is detected. Completed reworked units should be indistinguishable from nonreworked good units. Normal rework can be assigned to a specific job, or, if common to all jobs, as part of manufacturing overhead. Abnormal rework is written off as a cost of the accounting period in which it is detected.
5. How is scrap accounted for?	Scrap is recognized in the accounting records either at the time of its sale or at the time of its production. Sale of scrap, if immaterial, is often recognized as other revenue. If material, the sale of scrap or its net realizable value reduces the cost of a specific job, or, if common to all jobs, reduces manufacturing overhead.

This chapter and the Glossary at the end of the book contain definitions of the following important terms:

abnormal spoilage (p. 723)   normal spoilage (p. 722)   scrap (p. 722)
inspection point (p. 724)   rework (p. 722)   spoilage (p. 722)

MyAccountingLab   Make the grade with MyAccountingLab: The questions, exercises, and problems marked in red can be found on MyAccountingLab at **www.myaccountinglab.com.** You can practise them as often as you want, and most feature step-by-step guided instructions to help you find the right answer. Exercises and problems with an Excel icon in the margin have an accompanying Excel template on MyAccountingLab.

SHORT-ANSWER QUESTIONS

18-1 Why is there an unmistakable trend in manufacturing to improve quality?

18-2 Distinguish among spoilage, reworked units, and scrap.

18-3 "Normal spoilage is planned spoilage." Discuss.

18-4 "Costs of abnormal spoilage are losses." Explain.

18-5 "What has been regarded as normal spoilage in the past is not necessarily acceptable as normal spoilage in the present or future." Explain.

18-6 "Units of abnormal spoilage are inferred rather than identified." Explain.

18-7 "In accounting for spoiled goods, we are dealing with cost assignment rather than cost incurrence." Explain.

18-8 "Total input includes abnormal as well as normal spoilage and is, therefore, inappropriate as a basis for computing normal spoilage." Do you agree? Explain.

18-9 "The point of inspection is the key to the allocation of spoilage costs." Do you agree? Explain.

18-10 "The unit cost of normal spoilage is the same as the unit cost of abnormal spoilage." Do you agree? Explain.

18-11 "In job costing, the costs of normal spoilage that occur while a specific job is being done are charged to the specific job." Do you agree? Explain.

18-12 "The costs of reworking defective units are always charged to the specific jobs where the defects were originally discovered." Do you agree? Explain.

18-13 "Abnormal rework costs should be charged to a loss account, not to manufacturing overhead." Do you agree? Explain.

18-14 When is a company justified in inventorying scrap?

EXERCISES

18-15 Terminology. A number of terms are listed below:

abnormal spoilage   inspection point
normal spoilage   rework
scrap

REQUIRED

Select the terms from the above list to complete the following sentences.

There is no perfect machine, nor is there a perfect manufacturing process. That is why each process has at least one _____ to assess the output quality and send the units back for _____ and ultimately on for sale, or _____ them. Costs of reworked units are non-value-added for the customer who will, therefore, not pay for them. The company bears this cost. The difference between _____ and _____ is in accounting for the costs. _____ is predictable but unavoidable; therefore, GAAP allows this cost in cost of goods manufactured. _____ is avoidable but unpredictable and GAAP requires this cost be expensed. These costs did not produce an asset from which future revenue will be recovered and therefore are not part of cost of goods manufactured.

①

1. Normal spoilage,
6,600 units

18-16 Normal and abnormal spoilage in units. The following data, in physical units, describe a grinding process for January:

Work in process, beginning	19,000
Started during current period	150,000
To account for	169,000
Spoiled units	12,000
Good units completed and transferred out	132,000
Work in process, ending	25,000
Accounted for	169,000

Inspection occurs at the 100% completion stage. Normal spoilage is 5% of the good units passing inspection.

REQUIRED
1. Compute the normal and abnormal spoilage in units.
2. Assume that the equivalent-unit cost of a spoiled unit is $10. Compute the amount of potential savings if all spoilage were eliminated, assuming that all other costs would be unaffected. Comment on your answer.

②

Total equivalent units for
conversion costs, 9,750 units

18-17 Weighted-average method, spoilage, equivalent units. (CMA, adapted) Consider the following data for November 2013 from Grey Manufacturing Company, which makes silk pennants and uses a process-costing system. All direct materials are added at the beginning of the process, and conversion costs are added evenly during the process. Spoilage is detected upon inspection at the completion of the process. Spoiled units are disposed of at zero net disposal price. Grey Manufacturing Company uses the weighted-average method of process costing.

	Physical Units (pennants)	Direct Materials	Conversion Costs
Work in process, November 1*	1,000	$ 1,423	$ 1,110
Started during November 2013	?		
Good units completed and transferred out during November 2013	9,000		
Normal spoilage	100		
Abnormal spoilage	50		
Work in process, November 30†	2,000		
Total costs added during November 2013		$12,180	$27,750

*Degree of completion: direct materials, 100%; conversion costs, 50%.
†Degree of completion: direct materials, 100%; conversion costs, 30%.

REQUIRED
Compute the equivalent units of work done in the current period for direct materials and conversion costs. Show physical units in the first column of your schedule.

②

Conversion cost per
equivalent unit, $2.96

18-18 Weighted-average method, assigning costs (continuation of 18-17).

REQUIRED
For the data in Exercise 18-17, summarize total costs to account for, calculate the cost per equivalent unit for direct materials and conversion costs, and assign total costs to units completed and transferred out (including normal spoilage), to abnormal spoilage, and to units in ending work in process.

②

Total equivalent units for
conversion costs in current
period only, 9,250 units

18-19 FIFO method, spoilage, equivalent units. Refer to the information in Exercise 18-17. Suppose Grey Manufacturing Company uses the FIFO method of process costing instead of the weighted-average method.

Compute equivalent units for direct materials and conversion costs. Show physical units in the first column of your schedule.

18-20 FIFO method, assigning costs (continuation of 18-19).

REQUIRED

For the data in Exercise 18-19, use the FIFO method to summarize total costs to account for, calculate the cost per equivalent unit for direct materials and conversion costs, and assign total costs to units completed and transferred out (including normal spoilage), to abnormal spoilage, and to units in ending work in process.

18-21 Weighted-average method, spoilage. Appleton Company makes wooden toys in its Forming department, and it uses the weighted-average method of process costing. All direct materials are added at the beginning of the process, and conversion costs are added evenly during the process. Spoiled units are detected upon inspection at the end of the process and are disposed of at zero net disposal value. Summary data for August 2013 are as follows:

	A	B Physical Units	C Direct Materials	D Conversion Costs
1				
2	Work in process, beginning inventory (August 1)	2,000	$17,700	$10,900
3	Degree of completion of beginning work in process		100%	50%
4	Started during August	10,000		
5	Good units completed and transferred out during August	9,000		
6	Work in process, ending inventory (August 31)	1,800		
7	Degree of completion of ending work in process		100%	75%
8	Total costs added during August		$81,300	$93,000
9	Normal spoilage as a percentage of good units	10%		
10	Degree of completion of normal spoilage		100%	100%
11	Degree of completion of abnormal spoilage		100%	100%

REQUIRED

1. For each cost category, calculate equivalent units. Show physical units in the first column of your schedule.

2. Summarize total costs to account for, calculate cost per equivalent unit for each cost category, and assign total costs to units completed and transferred out (including normal spoilage), to abnormal spoilage, and to units in ending work in process.

18-22 Standard-costing method, spoilage, and journal entries. Aaron Inc. is a manufacturer of vents for water heaters. The company uses a process-costing system to account for its work-in-process inventories. When Job 512 was being processed in the machining department, a piece of sheet metal was off-centre in the bending machine and two vents were spoiled. Because this problem occurs periodically, it is considered normal spoilage and is consequently recorded as an overhead cost. Because this step comes first in the procedure for making the vents, the only costs incurred were $250 for direct materials. Assume the sheet metal cannot be sold, and its cost has been recorded in work-in-process inventory.

REQUIRED

Prepare the journal entries to record the spoilage incurred.

18-23 Recognition of loss from spoilage—Elementary. Arokia Electronics manufactures cell phone models in its Saskatoon plant. Suppose the company provides you with the following information regarding operations for September 2013:

Total cell phones manufactured	10,000
Phones rejected as spoiled units	500
Total manufacturing cost	$209,000

Assume the spoiled units have no disposal value.

1. What is the unit cost of making the 10,000 cell phones?

2. What is the total cost of the 500 spoiled units?

3. If the spoilage is considered normal, what is the increase in the unit cost of good phones manufactured as a result of the spoilage?

18-24 Weighted-average method, spoilage. Chipcity Inc. is a fast-growing manufacturer of computer chips. Direct materials are added at the start of the production process. Conversion costs are added evenly during the process. Some units of this product are spoiled as a result of defects not detectable before inspection of finished goods. Spoiled units are disposed of at zero net disposal value. Chipcity uses the weighted-average method of process costing.

Summary data for September 2013 are:

1. Total equivalent units for conversion costs, 2,880 units

	Physical Units (computer chips)	Direct Materials	Conversion Costs
Work in process, beginning inventory (Sept. 1)	600	$ 96,000	$ 15,300
Degree of completion of beginning WIP		100%	30%
Started during September	2,550		
Good units completed and transferred out during September	2,100		
Work in process, ending inventory (Sept. 30)	450		
Degree of completion of ending WIP		100%	40%
Total costs added during September		$567,000	$230,400
Normal spoilage as a percentage of good units	15%		
Degree of completion of normal spoilage		100%	100%
Degree of completion of abnormal spoilage		100%	100%

REQUIRED

1. For each cost category, compute equivalent units. Show physical units in the first column of your schedule.

2. Summarize total costs to account for, calculate cost per equivalent unit for each cost category, and assign total costs to units completed and transferred out (including normal spoilage), to abnormal spoilage, and to units in ending work in process.

1. Equivalent units for conversion costs for the current period, 2,700 units

18-25 FIFO method, spoilage. Refer to the information in Exercise 18-24.

REQUIRED

Do Exercise 18-24 using the FIFO method of process costing.

18-26 Standard-costing method, spoilage. Refer to the information in Exercise 18-23. Suppose Chipcity determines standard costs of $200 per equivalent unit for direct materials and $75 per equivalent unit for conversion costs for both beginning work in process and work done in the current period.

2. Total costs to account for, $846,000

REQUIRED

Do Exercise 18-24 using the standard-costing method.

18-27 Spoilage and job costing. (L. Bamber) Bamber Kitchens produces a variety of items in accordance with special job orders from hospitals, plant cafeterias, and university dormitories. An order for 2,500 cases of mixed vegetables costs $6.00 per case: direct materials, $3.00; direct manufacturing labour, $2.00; and manufacturing overhead allocated, $1.00. The manufacturing overhead rate includes a provision for normal spoilage. Consider each requirement independently.

1. Unit cost of remaining cases, $6.00

REQUIRED

1. Assume that a labourer dropped 200 cases. Suppose that part of the 200 cases could be sold to a nearby prison for $200 cash. Prepare a journal entry to record this event. Calculate and explain briefly the unit cost of the remaining 2,300 cases.

2. Refer to the original data. Tasters at the company reject 200 of the 2,500 cases. The 200 cases are disposed of for $400. Assume that this rejection rate is considered normal. Prepare a journal entry to record this event, and:

   a. Calculate the unit cost if the rejection is attributable to exacting specifications of this particular job.

   b. Calculate the unit cost if the rejection is characteristic of the production process and is not attributable to this specific job.

   c. Are unit costs the same in requirements 2a and 2b? Explain your reasoning briefly.

3. Refer to the original data. Tasters rejected 200 cases that had insufficient salt. The product can be placed in a vat, salted, and reprocessed into jars. This operation, which is considered normal, will cost $200. Prepare a journal entry to record this event, and:

   a. Calculate the unit cost of all the cases if this additional cost was incurred because of the exacting specifications of this particular job.

   b. Calculate the unit cost of all the cases if this additional cost occurs regularly because of difficulty in seasoning.

   c. Are unit costs the same in requirements 3a and 3b? Explain your reasoning briefly.

18-28 Reworked units, costs of rework. Grey Goods assembles washing machines at its Cambridge plant. In February 2013, 60 tumbler units that cost $44 each from a new supplier were defective and had to be disposed of at zero disposal price. That new supplier is now bankrupt. Grey Goods was able to rework all 60 washing machines by substituting new tumbler units purchased from one of its existing suppliers. Each replacement tumbler cost $50.

REQUIRED

1. What alternative approaches are there to account for the materials costs of reworked units?

2. Should Grey Goods use the $44 or $50 amount as the costs of materials reworked? Explain.

3. What other costs might Grey Goods include in its analysis of the total costs of rework due to the tumbler units purchased from the (now) bankrupt supplier?

18-29 Scrap, job-order costing. Mendola Corp. has an extensive job-costing facility that uses a variety of metals. Consider each requirement independently.

1. Job 372 Work-in-Process Control, CR $490

REQUIRED

1. Job 372 uses a particular metal alloy that is not used for any other job. Assume that scrap is material in amount and sold for $490 quickly after it is produced. Prepare the journal entry.

2. The scrap from Job 372 consists of a metal used by many other jobs. No record is maintained of the scrap generated by individual jobs. Assume that scrap is accounted for at the time of its sale. Scrap totalling $4,000 is sold. Prepare two alternative journal entries that could be used to account for the sale of scrap.

3. Suppose the scrap generated in requirement 2 is returned to the storeroom for future use, and a journal entry is made to record the scrap. A month later, the scrap is reused as direct material on a subsequent job. Prepare the journal entries to record these transactions.

PROBLEMS

18-30 Weighted-average method, spoilage. The Red Deer Company is a food-processing com- pany based in Alberta. It operates under the weighted-average method of process costing and has two departments: Cleaning and Packaging. For the Cleaning department, conversion costs are added evenly during the process, and direct materials are added at the beginning of the process. Spoiled units are detected upon inspection at the end of the process and are

1. Normal spoilage equivalent units, conversion costs, 1,850 units

disposed of at zero net disposal value. All completed work is transferred to the Packaging department. Summary data for May follow:

	A	B	C	D
		Physical Units	Direct Materials	Conversion Costs
1	**The Red Deer Company: Cleaning Department**			
2	Work in process, beginning inventory (May 1)	2,500	$ 2,500	$ 2,000
3	Degree of completion of beginning work in process		100%	80%
4	Started during May	22,500		
5	Good units completed and transferred out during May	18,500		
6	Work in process, ending inventory (May 31)	4,000		
7	Degree of completion of ending work in process		100%	25%
8	Total costs added during May		$22,500	$20,000
9	Normal spoilage as a percentage of good units	10%		
10	Degree of completion of normal spoilage		100%	100%
11	Degree of completion of abnormal spoilage		100%	100%

REQUIRED

For the Cleaning department, summarize total costs to account for, and assign total costs to units completed and transferred out (including normal spoilage), to abnormal spoilage, and to units in ending work in process. Carry unit-cost calculations to four decimal places when necessary. Calculate final totals to the nearest dollar. (Problem 18-32 explores additional facets of this problem.)

18-31 FIFO method, spoilage. Refer to the information in Problem 18-30.

EU of direct materials, 22,500

REQUIRED

Do Problem 18-30 using the FIFO method of process costing. (Problem 18-33 explores additional facets of this problem.)

18-32 Weighted-average method, Packaging department (continuation of 18-30). In Red Deer Company's Packaging department, conversion costs are added evenly during the process, and direct materials are added at the end of the process. Spoiled units are detected upon inspection at the end of the process and are disposed of at zero net disposal value. All completed work is transferred to the next department. The transferred-in costs for May equal the total cost of good units completed and transferred out in May from the Cleaning department, which were calculated in Problem 18-30 using the weighted-average method of process costing. Summary data for May follow:

EU of direct materials, work done to date, 16,000

	A	B	C	D	E
		Physical Units	Transferred-in Costs	Direct Materials	Conversion Costs
1	**The Red Deer Company: Packaging Department**				
2	Work in process, beginning inventory (May 1)	7,500	$16,125	$ 0	$ 6,125
3	Degree of completion of beginning work in process		100%	0%	80%
4	Started during May	18,500			
5	Good units completed and transferred out during May	15,000			
6	Work in process, ending inventory (May 31)	10,000			
7	Degree of completion of ending work in process		100%	0%	25%
8	Total costs added during May		?	$1,600	$12,375
9	Normal spoilage as a percentage of good units	5%			
10	Degree of completion of normal spoilage			100%	100%
11	Degree of completion of abnormal spoilage			100%	100%

REQUIRED

For the Packaging department, use the weighted-average method to summarize total costs to account for and assign total costs to units completed and transferred out (including normal spoilage), to abnormal spoilage, and to units in ending work in process.

18-33 FIFO method, Packaging department (continuation of 18-31). Refer to the information in Problem 18-32 except for the transferred-in costs for May, which equal the total cost of good units completed and transferred out in May from the Cleaning department, which were calculated in Problem 18-31 using the FIFO method of process costing.

Transferred-in costs EU in
current period only, 18,500

REQUIRED

For the Packaging department, use the FIFO method to summarize total costs to account for, and assign total costs to units completed and transferred out (including normal spoilage), to abnormal spoilage, and to units in ending work in process.

18-34 Job-costing spoilage and scrap. (F. Mayne) Hamilton Metal Fabricators, Inc., has a large job, No. 2734, that calls for producing various ore bins, chutes, and metal boxes for enlarging a copper concentrator. The following charges were made to the job in November 2013:

1. b. Accounts receivable or
cash, DR 1,995

Direct materials	$40,400
Direct manufacturing labour	22,600
Manufacturing overhead	11,300

The contract with the customer called for the total price to be based on a cost-plus approach. The contract defined cost to include direct materials, direct manufacturing labour costs, and manufacturing overhead to be allocated at 50% of direct manufacturing labour costs. The contract also provided that the total costs of all work spoiled was to be removed from the billable cost of the job and that the benefits from scrap sales were to reduce the billable cost of the job.

1. In accordance with the stated terms of the contract, prepare journal entries for the following two items:
   a. A cutting error was made in production. The up-to-date job cost record for this batch of work showed materials of $975, direct manufacturing labour of $600, and allocated overhead of $300. Because fairly large pieces of metal were recoverable, the company believed their value was $800 and that the materials recovered could be used on other jobs. The spoiled work was sent to the warehouse.
   b. Small pieces of metal cuttings and scrap in November 2013 amounted to $1,995, which was the price quoted by a scrap dealer. No journal entries were made with regard to the scrap until the price was quoted by the scrap dealer. The scrap dealer's offer was immediately accepted.
2. Consider normal and abnormal spoilage. Suppose the contract described above had contained the clause "a normal spoilage allowance of 1% of the job costs will be included in the billable costs of the job."
   a. Is this clause specific enough to define exactly how much spoilage is normal and how much is abnormal? Explain.
   b. Repeat requirement 1a with this "normal spoilage of 1%" clause in mind. You should be able to provide two slightly different journal entries.

18-35 Weighted-average method, spoilage. Superchip specializes in the manufacture of microchips for aircraft. Direct materials are added at the start of the production process. Conversion costs are added evenly during the process. Some units of this product are spoiled as a result of defects not detectable before inspection of finished goods. Normally, the spoiled units are 15% of the good units transferred out. Spoiled units are disposed of at zero net disposal price.

1. Normally spoiled
units, 210

Superchip uses the weighted-average method of process costing. Summary data for September 2013 are:

	Physical Units (microchips)	Direct Materials	Conversion Costs
Work in process, September 1*	400	$ 76,800	$ 12,240
Started during September 2013	1,700		
Good units completed and transferred out during September 2013	1,400		
Work in process, September 30†	300		
Costs added during September 2013		$453,600	$184,320

*Degree of completion: direct materials, 100%; conversion costs, 30%.
†Degree of completion: direct materials, 100%; conversion costs, 40%.

REQUIRED

1. For each cost element, compute the equivalent units. Show physical units in the first column.

2. For each cost element, calculate the cost per equivalent unit.

3. Summarize the total costs to account for, and assign these costs to units completed and transferred out (to normal spoilage), to abnormal spoilage, and to units in ending work in process.

②

Direct materials total costs to be accounted for, $530,400

③

Direct materials total costs to be accounted for, $516,600

③

Normal spoilage at 40%, 7,440 units

③

Abnormal spoilage, 3,750 units

18-36 FIFO method, spoilage. Refer to the information in 18-35.

REQUIRED

Repeat question 1 from Problem 18-35 using the FIFO method of process costing.

18-37 Standard-costing method, spoilage—Elementary. Refer to the information in Problem 18-35. Suppose Superchip determines standard costs of $246 per (equivalent) unit for direct materials and $96 per (equivalent) unit for conversion costs for both beginning work in process and work done in the current period.

REQUIRED

Repeat question 2 from Problem 18-35 using standard costs.

18-38 Physical units, inspection at various stages of completion. Normal spoilage is 6% of the good units passing inspection in a forging process. In March, a total of 10,000 units were spoiled. Other data include units started during March, 120,000; work in process, beginning, 14,000 units (20% completed for conversion costs); work in process, ending, 11,000 units (70% completed for conversion costs).

REQUIRED

In columnar form, compute the normal and abnormal spoilage in units, assuming the inspection point is at (a) the 15% stage of completion, (b) the 40% stage of completion, and (c) the 100% stage of completion.

18-39 Weighted-average method, inspection at 80% completion. (A. Atkinson) Ottawa Manufacturing is a furniture manufacturer with two departments: Moulding and Finishing. The company uses the weighted-average method of process costing. In August, the following data were recorded for the Finishing department:

Units of beginning work-in-process inventory	12,500
Percentage completion of beginning work-in-process units	25%
Cost of direct materials in beginning work in process	$ 0
Units started	87,500
Units completed	62,500
Units in ending inventory	25,000
Percentage completion of ending work-in-process units	95%
Spoiled units	12,500
Total costs added during current period:	
Direct materials	$819,000
Direct manufacturing labour	$794,500
Manufacturing overhead	$770,000
Work in process, beginning:	
Transferred-in costs	$103,625
Conversion costs	$ 52,500
Cost of units transferred in during current period	$809,375

Conversion costs are added evenly during the process. Direct materials costs are added when production is 90% complete. The inspection point is at the 80% stage of production. Normal spoilage is 10% of all good units that pass inspection. Spoiled units are disposed of at zero net disposal value.

REQUIRED

For August, summarize total costs to account for, and assign these costs to units completed and transferred out (including normal spoilage), to abnormal spoilage, and to units in ending work in process.

18-40 Spoilage in job costing. Whitefish Machine Shop is a manufacturer of motorized carts for vacation resorts. Pat Cruz, the plant manager of Whitefish, obtains the following information for Job #10 in August 2013. A total of 40 units were started, and 5 spoiled units were detected and rejected at final inspection, yielding 35 good units. The spoiled units were considered to be normal spoilage. Costs assigned prior to the inspection point are $1,000 per unit. The current disposal price of the spoiled units is $200 per unit. When the spoilage is detected, the spoiled goods are inventoried at $200 per unit.

4 5
1. Normal spoilage, 14.3%

REQUIRED
1. What is the normal spoilage rate?
2. Prepare the journal entries to record the normal spoilage, assuming:
   a. The spoilage is related to a specific job.
   b. The spoilage is common to all jobs.
   c. The spoilage is considered to be abnormal spoilage.

18-41 Rework in job costing, journal entry (continuation of 18-40). Assume that the five spoiled units of Whitefish Machine Shop's Job #10 can be reworked for a total cost of $1,800. A total cost of $5,000 associated with these units has already been assigned to Job #10 before the rework.

5
1. Journal entry CR Various Accounts, $1,800

REQUIRED
Prepare the journal entries for the rework, assuming:
1. a. The rework is related to a specific job.
   b. The rework is common to all jobs.
   c. The rework is considered to be abnormal.

18-42 Scrap at time of sale or at time of production, journal entries (continuation of 18-41). Assume that Job #10 of Whitefish Machine Shop generates normal scrap with a total sales value of $300 (it is assumed that the scrap returned to the storeroom is sold quickly).

5
1. Journal entry CR Scrap Revenue, $300

REQUIRED
Prepare the journal entries for the recognition of scrap, assuming:
1. a. The value of scrap is immaterial and scrap is recognized at the time of sale.
   b. The value of scrap is material, is related to a specific job, and is recognized at the time of sale.
   c. The value of scrap is material, is common to all jobs, and is recognized at the time of sale.
   d. The value of scrap is material, scrap is recognized as inventory at the time of production, and is recorded at its net realizable value.

18-43 Job costing, rework. Solutions Corporation is a manufacturer of computer chips based in Nepean. It manufactures two types of computer chips, CS1 and CS2. The costs of manufacturing each CS1 chip, excluding rework costs, are direct materials, $60; direct manufacturing labour, $12; and manufacturing overhead, $38. Defective units are sent to a separate rework area. Rework costs per CS1 chip are direct materials, $12; direct manufacturing labour, $9; and manufacturing overhead, $15.

5
1. Journal entry CR Manufacturing Overhead Allocated, $3,040

In August 2013, Solutions manufactured 1,000 CS1 chips and 500 CS2 chips; 80 of the CS1 chips and none of the CS2 chips required rework. Solutions classifies 50 of the CS1 chips reworked as normal rework caused by inherent problems in its production process that coincidentally occurred only during the production of CS1. Hence the rework costs for these 50 CS1 chips are normal rework costs not specifically attributable to the CS1 product. Solutions classifies the remaining 30 units of CS1 chips reworked as abnormal rework. Solutions allocates manufacturing overhead on the basis of machine-hours required to manufacture CS1 and CS2. Each CS1 and CS2 chip requires the same number of machine-hours.

REQUIRED
1. Prepare journal entries to record the accounting for the cost of the spoiled chips and for rework.
2. What were the total rework costs of CS1 chips in August 2013?

18-44 Job costing, spoilage, governance. (CMA, adapted) Richmond Company manufactures products that often require specification changes or modifications to meet customers' needs. Still, Richmond has been able to establish a normal spoilage rate of 2.5% of normal input. Normal spoilage is recognized during the budgeting process and classified as a component of manufacturing overhead when determining the overhead rate.

4
1. Normal spoilage, 3,000 units

Rose Drummond, one of Richmond's inspection managers, obtains the following information for Job No. R1192-122 that was recently completed. A total of 122,000 units were started, and 5,000 units were rejected at final inspection yielding 117,000 good units.

Drummond noted that 900 of the first units produced were rejected because of a design defect that was considered very unusual; this defect was corrected immediately, and no further units were rejected for this reason. These units were disposed of after incurring an additional cost of $1,440. Drummond was unable to identify a rejection pattern for the remaining 4,100 rejected units. These units can be sold at $8.40 per unit.

Direct materials	$2,635,200
Direct manufacturing labour	2,196,000
Manufacturing overhead	3,513,600
Total manufacturing costs	$8,344,800

The total costs for all 122,000 units of Job No. R1192-122 are presented here. The job has been completed, but the costs have yet to be transferred to Finished Goods.

REQUIRED
1. Calculate the unit quantities of normal and abnormal spoilage.
2. Prepare the appropriate journal entry (or entries) to properly account for Job No. R1192-122, including spoilage, disposal, and transfer of costs to Finished Goods Control.
3. Richmond Company has small profit margins and is anticipating very low operating income for the year. The controller, Thomas Rutherford, tells Martha Perez, the management accountant responsible for Job No. R1192-122, the following: "This was an unusual job. I think all 5,000 spoiled units should be considered normal." Martha knows that similar jobs had been done in the past and that the spoilage levels for Job R1192-122 were much greater than in the past. She feels Thomas made these comments because he wants to show higher operating income for the year.
   a. Prepare the journal entry (or entries), similar to the journal entry (or entries) prepared in requirement 2, to account for Job No. R1192-122 if all spoilage were considered normal. By how much will Richmond's operating income be affected if all spoilage is considered normal?
   b. What should Martha Perez do?

18-45 Physical units, inspection at various stages of completion. Normal spoilage is 7% of the good units passing inspection in a forging process. In March, a total of 12,000 units were spoiled. Other data include units started during March, 129,000; work in process, beginning, 16,000 units (20% completed for conversion costs); work in process, ending, 13,000 units (70% completed for conversion costs).

REQUIRED
In columnar form, compute the normal and abnormal spoilage in units, assuming inspection at 15%, 40%, and 100% stages of completion.

18-46 Job costing, scrap. Wheels Corporation makes two different types of hubcaps for cars—models HM3 and JB4. Circular pieces of metal are stamped out of steel sheets (leaving the edges as scrap), formed, and finished. The stamping operation is identical for both types of hubcaps. During May, Wheels manufactured 20,000 units of HM3 and 10,000 units of JB4. In May, manufacturing costs per unit of HM3 and JB4 before accounting for the scrap are as follows:

	HM3	JB4
Direct materials	$12.00	$18.00
Direct manufacturing labour	3.60	4.80
Materials-related manufacturing overhead (materials handling, storage, etc.)	2.40	3.60
Other manufacturing overhead	7.20	9.60
Unit manufacturing costs	$25.20	$36.00

Materials-related manufacturing costs are allocated to products at 20% of direct materials costs. Other manufacturing overhead is allocated to products at 200% of direct manufacturing labour costs. Since the same metal sheets are used to make both types of hubcaps, Wheels maintains no records of the scrap generated by the individual products. Scrap generated during manufacturing is accounted for at the time it is returned to the storeroom as an offset to materials-related manufacturing overhead. The value of scrap generated during May and returned to the storeroom was $8,400.

REQUIRED

1. Prepare a journal entry to summarize the accounting for scrap during May.
2. Suppose the scrap generated in May was sold in June for $8,400. Prepare a journal entry to account for this transaction.
3. What adjustments, if any, would you make for scrap when calculating the manufacturing cost per unit for HM3 and JB4 in May? Explain.

COLLABORATIVE LEARNING CASE

18-47 FIFO method, spoilage, working backward. The Cooking Department of Spicier Inc. uses a process-costing system. Direct materials are added at the beginning of the cooking process. Conversion costs are added evenly during the cooking process. Consider the following data for the Cooking department of Spicier Inc. for January:

1. Total equivalent units for conversion costs, 78,500 units

	Physical Units	Direct Materials	Conversion Costs
Work in process, January 1*	10,000	$ 264,000	$ 36,000
Started during January	74,000		
Good units completed and transferred out during January	61,000		
Spoiled units	8,000		
Work in process, January 31	15,000		
Costs added during January		$1,776,000	$1,130,400
Cost per equivalent unit of work done in January		$ 24	$ 14.40

*Degree of completion: direct materials, 100%; conversion costs, 25%.

Spicier uses the FIFO method of process costing. Inspection occurs when production is 100% completed. Normal spoilage is 11% of good units completed and transferred out during the current period.

INSTRUCTION

Form pairs of students to complete the following requirements.

REQUIRED

1. For each cost category, compute equivalent units of work done in the current period (January).
2. For each cost category, compute equivalent units of work done to complete beginning work-in-process inventory, to start and complete new units, for normal and abnormal spoilage units, and to produce ending work-in-process inventory.
3. For each cost category, calculate the percentage of completion of ending work-in-process inventory.
4. Summarize total costs to account for, and assign these costs to units completed (and transferred out), normal spoilage, abnormal spoilage, and ending work in process.

Cost Management: Quality, Time, and the Theory of Constraints

BUSINESS MATTERS

Improve Poor Quality

Defective components can cause dramatic consequences. One flawed component used in computers that control space shuttle engines caused a space shuttle engine to shut down 1.5 seconds into its ignition sequence. The defect, discovered during a firing test with an empty shuttle, did not threaten any lives, but testing revealed an undisclosed flaw. After an extensive investigation, approximately 1,600 components were purged from the controllers.

LEARNING OBJECTIVES

After studying this chapter, you should be able to

1. Apply balanced scorecard (BSC) concepts to the analysis of quality.

2. Analyze quality-control problems using three methods.

3. Analyze the benefits of using both financial and nonfinancial measures of quality.

4. Evaluate methods using time as a competitive tool.

5. Evaluate the strengths and weaknesses of the theory of constraints (TOC) and activity-based costing (ABC) for managing bottlenecks.

This chapter expands on the concepts of the balanced scorecard (BSC; Chapter 13) to illustrate how managers can improve quality. Global competition and increasing customer intolerance for both long wait times and poor quality mean managers must remove obstructions to achieving on-time deliveries of outputs at the quality customers expect to receive. Quality improvements support both a cost- and value-leadership strategy.

The BSC requires integration of customer long-term demand for desirable attributes with the achievement of performance standards in the strategic management of internal business processes. In the transformation to a knowledge-based economy, the contribution of intelligent policies to improve the rate of learning and growth can be a competitive advantage, especially in labour-intensive processes. The focus in this chapter will be on those measures that illustrate links among improved quality, timeliness, and increased throughput to satisfy customers and gain competitive advantage. Ultimately, successful strategic performance results will achieve the financial results of targeted earnings and ROI.

QUALITY AS A COMPETITIVE TOOL

1 Apply balanced scorecard (BSC) concepts to the analysis of quality.

In a challenging world of global competition, most companies view quality management as a key success factor. Quality on the production line (conformance to technical specifications) reduces costs and supports a cost leadership strategy. Quality may also differentiate one product from what might otherwise be a selection of substitutes and in this way supports a value-leadership strategy. Several prestigious, high-profile awards—for example, the Malcolm Baldrige Quality Award in North America, the Deming Prize in Japan, and the Premio Nacional de Calidad in Mexico—have been instituted to recognize exceptional quality.

Global companies can readily access international standards on management quality measurement, ranging from easily interpreted graphic symbols to safety in nuclear power plants. The International Standards Organization (ISO) certification registers companies that conform to a specific level of quality. ISO 9004 is the international benchmark for global quality systems management, and ISO 14001 is the benchmark for environmental management. New ISO 26000 standards for corporate social responsibility and ISO 31000 standards for risk management emphasize the growing importance of quality control in all dimensions of corporate performance.

The Standards Council of Canada issues accreditation to companies meeting the ISO 14001 standards of environmental management. Canada also has formal domestic environmental legislation. Corporate governance failures to comply can result in multi-million-dollar fines. ISO 14064 standards for greenhouse gas (GHG) accounting, reporting, and emissions trading are actively promoted by the World Resources Institute (WRI) and the World Business Council for Sustainable Development (WBCSD).

ISO 22000 sets standards on food safety management, ISO 22005 on traceability, and ISO/TS 22003 on auditing and certification of these standards. The ISO 28000 standards on supply-chain security management address security issues at all stages of the supply process to manage threats such as terrorism, fraud, and piracy. ISO 26000 on corporate social responsibility (CSR) covers a range of topics as illustrated in Exhibit 19-1. Notice that standards of quality for environmental protection are one dimension of the seven interdependent core dimensions of CSR.

ISO 31000 sets standards for high-quality performance in enterprise risk management (ERM). It is the most recent set of ISO standards encompassing human, financial, and process safety. ISO 31000, 26000, 14001, and 9004 are integrated with one another. In February 2010, the Canadian Standards Association adopted the principles and guidelines illustrated in the graphic for ISO 31000, shown in Exhibit 19-2. The standards can be integrated with Canadian and provincial risk standards. ISO 31000 is now a National Standard of Canada.[1]

[1] http://www.csa.ca/cm/ca/en/search/article/csa-announces-canadian-adoption-of-iso31000-standard. Accessed June 20, 2011.

EXHIBIT 19-1
ISO 26000 Standards for Corporate Social Responsibility

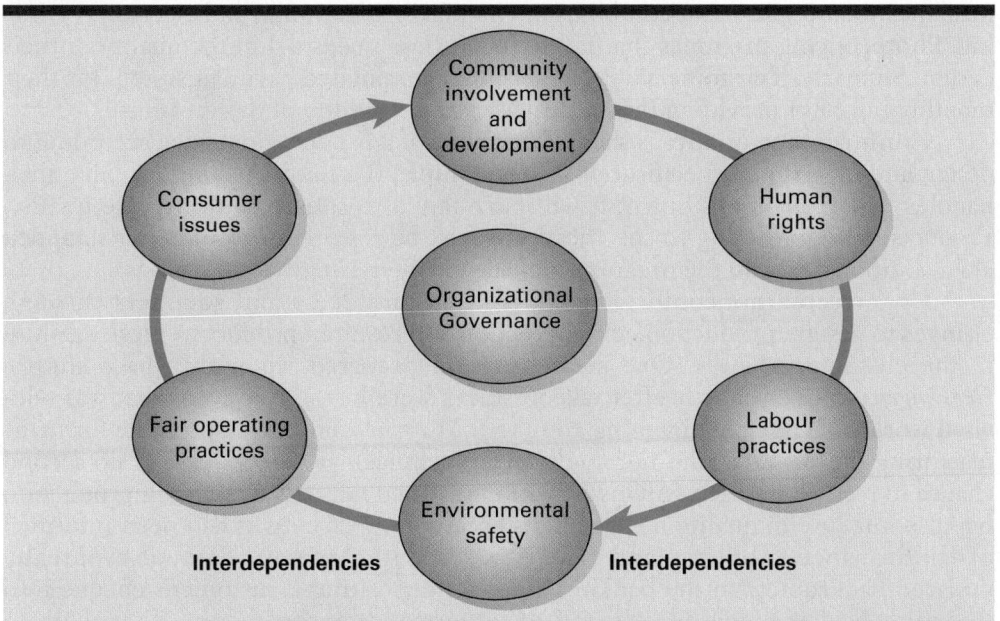

EXHIBIT 19-2
ISO 31000 Standards for Enterprise Risk Management

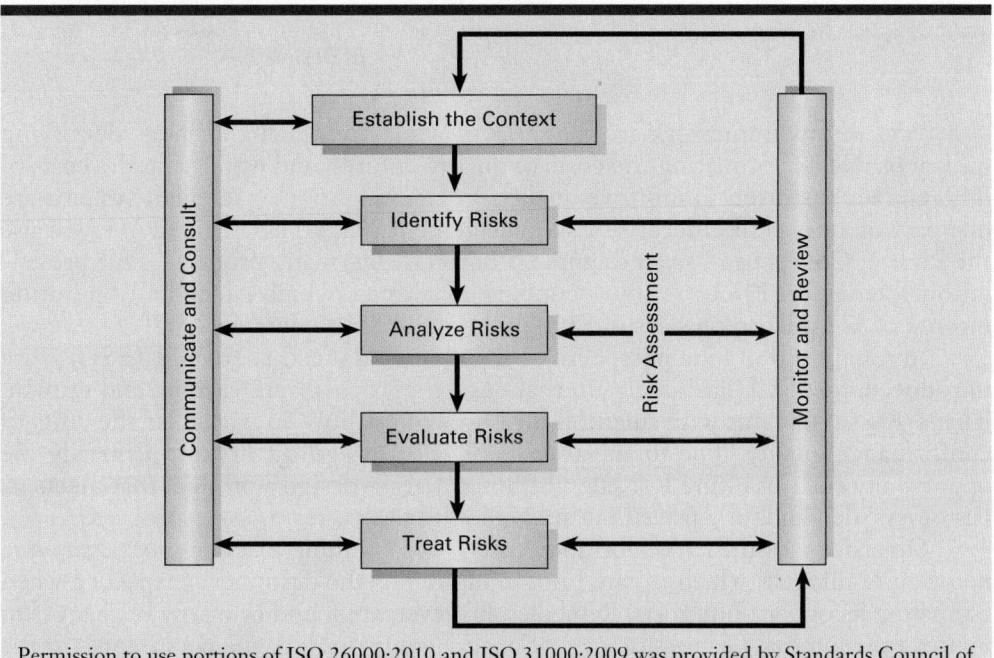

THE BSC—FOUR PERSPECTIVES TO MEASURE THE COSTS OF QUALITY

The term *quality* refers to a wide variety of factors—fitness for use, the degree to which a product satisfies the needs of a customer, or the degree to which a product conforms to design specification and engineering requirements. We discuss two basic aspects of quality—quality of design and conformance quality. The first may arise in any of the business functions of the value chain. The second arises in the production process.

Quality of design measures how closely the characteristics of products or services match the needs and wants of customers. Suppose customers of photocopying machines want copiers that combine copying, faxing, scanning, and electronic printing. Photocopying machines that fail to meet these needs fail in the quality of their design. Similarly, if customers of a bank want an automated payment system for their monthly bills, not providing this facility would be a quality of design failure.

Conformance quality is the performance of a product or service according to design and production specifications. For example, if a photocopying machine mishandles paper or breaks down, it will have failed to satisfy conformance quality. Products not conforming to specifications must be repaired, reworked, or scrapped at an additional cost to the organization (see Chapter 18).

Uncorrected nonconformance errors by producers and suppliers through changes to design, production, and inspection will result in product or service failure in the customer's hands. One such situation occurred when the space shuttle *Challenger* exploded shortly after takeoff. Lives were lost in this event that was televised worldwide. The engineering company, Morton Thiokol, responsible for manufacturing the part that did not conform to technical specifications had no second chance to recover business. An investigation revealed not only a failure in production but also a failure in quality management because top executives had been informed of conformance problems and failed to respond. Morton Thiokol eventually declared bankruptcy. In the banking industry, depositing a customer's cheque into the wrong bank account is an example of conformance quality failure. The following diagram illustrates our framework for quality of conformance and design:

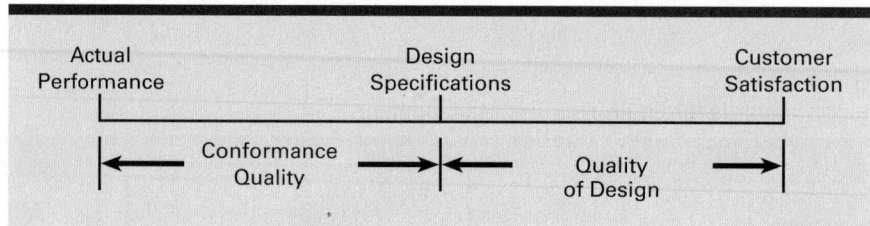

Within this framework are the tasks of managing quality such as identifying quality problems, estimating the costs of quality failures, and estimating the costs of different actions taken to improve quality. In fact, quality-management systems are one part of an overall enterprise risk management (ERM) assessment. We will use the Photon Corporation as an example. Photon makes many products. Our presentation focuses on Photon's photocopying machines, which earned an operating income of $24 million on sales of $300 million (20,000 copiers) in 2012.

In Chapter 13, four perspectives from the balanced scorecard (BSC) were introduced: financial, customer, internal business process, and learning and growth. This discussion begins with financial measures of quality—in particular the costs of conformance quality. The financial costs of poor design quality are primarily the opportunity costs of future lost sales if Photon fails to design a product that meets its customers' demands at a price they are willing to pay.

Objective measures of opportunity costs—of something that does not occur—are notoriously difficult, which is why Photon highlights the customer perspective when estimating its opportunity costs. Remedies, however, are found primarily in changes to improve the internal business process of quality control. Thus, the perspectives of the BSC are interdependent for successful execution of a quality-management strategy.

FINANCIAL PERSPECTIVE

The financial perspective of Photon's balanced scorecard includes measures such as revenue growth and operating income—financial measures that are likely to be affected by quality-improvement programs. Photon measures **costs of quality (COQ)**, which are costs incurred to prevent or rectify the production of a low-quality product. Management accountants who apply various techniques to measure these costs are producing a means to an end. The costs are important relevant information to managers who must decide on what action to take to achieve conformance targets.

EXHIBIT 19-3
Items Pertaining to Cost-of-Quality Reports

Prevention Costs	Appraisal Costs	Internal Failure Costs	External Failure Costs
Design engineering	Inspection	Spoilage	Customer support
Process engineering	Online product manufacturing and process inspection	Rework	Manufacturing/process engineering for external failures
Supplier evaluations		Scrap	
Preventive equipment maintenance		Machine repairs	
Quality training	Product testing	Manufacturing/process engineering on internal failures	Warranty repair costs
Testing of new materials			Liability claims

These costs focus on conformance quality and are incurred in all areas of the value chain. They are classified into four categories:

1. **Prevention costs.** Costs incurred to preclude the production of products that do not conform to specifications.

2. **Appraisal costs.** Costs incurred to detect which of the individual units of products do not conform to specifications.

3. **Internal failure costs.** Costs incurred to detect a nonconforming product before it is shipped to customers.

4. **External failure costs.** Costs incurred to detect a nonconforming product after it is shipped to customers.

Exhibit 19-3 presents examples of individual cost-of-quality items in each of these four categories reported on COQ reports.

The items in Exhibit 19-3 are all derived from the business functions comprising the value chain and expand on the internal failure costs of spoilage, rework, and scrap described in Chapters 15 and 18. Photon determines the costs of quality of its photocopying machines using the costing process illustrated in Exhibit 4-2 on page 108.

The top management team will be implementing ABC, and for this overhead cost has selected the photocopying machines as the cost object. There are 20,000 photocopiers and the goal is to calculate the total costs of quality for these machines. There are no direct costs of quality. To implement a full quality-management system, the indirect costs of quality will pertain to prevention, appraisal, internal failure, and external failure. Failure costs in the form of spoilage and rework (Chapter 18) are only a part of total internal failure costs of the photocopier manufacturing process. The costs incurred in the internal system of production are summarized in Exhibit 19-4.

Costs include either cost driver or allocation rates, the quantity of either the cost driver or the cost allocation base, the total costs, and the performance measure of cost as a percentage of revenue. Photon uses the ABC method. For example, Photon's team chose as the cost driver the inspection hours rather than number of inspections for the inspection activity. Inspection hours has a better cause-and-effect relationship with inspection costs, which means change in the quantity of inspection hours can explain most of the change in the value of this cost pool.

The team must also decide what costs, both fixed and variable, constitute a homogeneous cost pool (see Chapter 14) for each activity throughout all the business functions of the value chain. This is one reason why the ABC strategy fits well with BSC. Both ABC and BSC require an understanding of the interdependence among business functions in the value chain. A quality-management strategy includes all internal business functions, not merely production.

Having established the activities, cost drivers, and cost pools, it is straightforward to calculate each cost driver rate and assign costs to the photocopying

EXHIBIT 19-4
Analysis of Activity-Based Costs of Quality (COQ) for Photocopying Machines at Photon Corporation

	A	B	C	D	E	F	G
1	**PANEL A: COQ REPORT**						**Percentage of**
2		**Cost Allocation**		**Quantity of Cost**		**Total**	**Revenues**
3	**Cost of Quality and Value-Chain Category**	**Rate[a]**		**Allocation Base**		**Costs**	**(5) = (4) ÷**
4	(1)	(2)		(3)		(4) = (2) × (3)	**$300,000,000**
5	*Prevention costs*						
6	Design engineering (R & D/Design)	$ 80	per hour	40,000	hours	$ 3,200,000	1.1%
7	Process engineering (R & D/Design)	$ 60	per hour	45,000	hours	2,700,000	0.9
8	Total prevention costs					5,900,000	2.0
9	*Appraisal costs*						
10	Inspection (Manufacturing)	$ 40	per hour	240,000	hours	9,600,000	3.2
11	Total appraisal costs					9,600,000	3.2
12	*Internal failure costs*						
13	Rework (Manufacturing)	$100	per hour	100,000	hours	10,000,000	3.3
14	Total internal failure costs					10,000,000	3.3
15	*External failure costs*						
16	Customer support (Marketing)	$ 50	per hour	12,000	hours	600,000	0.2
17	Transportation (Distribution)	$240	per load	3,000	loads	720,000	0.2
18	Warranty repair (Customer service)	$110	per hour	120,000	hours	13,200,000	4.4
19	Total external failure costs					14,520,000	4.8
20	Total costs of quality					$40,020,000	13.3
21							
22	[a]Amounts assumed.						
23							
24	**PANEL B: OPPORTUNITY COST ANALYSIS**						
25						**Total Estimated**	**Percentage**
26						**Contribution**	**of Revenues**
27	**Cost of Quality Category**					**Margin Lost**	**(3) = (2) ÷**
28	(1)					(2)	**$300,000,000**
29	*External failure costs*						
30	Estimated forgone contribution margin						
31	and income on lost sales					$12,000,000[b]	4.0%
32	Total external failure costs					$12,000,000	4.0
33							
34	[b]Calculated as total revenues minus all variable costs (whether output-unit, batch, product-sustaining, or facility-sustaining) on lost sales in 2012. If poor quality causes Photon to lose sales in subsequent years as well, the opportunity costs will be even greater.						

machines. The quantities of each activity consumed are in column 3 of Exhibit 19-4. For example, photocopying machines use 240,000 inspection-hours. Column 4 of Exhibit 19-4, Panel A, shows the indirect costs of quality of the photocopying machines, which equals the total quantity of the cost allocation base used by the photocopying machines for each activity (column 3) multiplied by the cost allocation rate (column 2).

Photon's total cost of quality in the COQ report for photocopying machines is $40.02 million (bottom of column 4, Panel A), or 13.3% of current revenues (bottom of column 5). Costs reported on this COQ do not represent the total costs of quality for a company's photocopying process. COQ reports typically exclude opportunity costs, such as forgone contribution margins and income from lost sales, lost production, or lower prices, that result from poor quality. Opportunity costs (potential cost savings) are difficult to estimate and are generally not recorded in financial accounting systems. Nevertheless, opportunity costs can be substantial. Managerial accountants should provide information about opportunity costs to direct management's attention toward key items to remedy with quality-improvement programs. Neglecting such change will probably cause financial loss.

CUSTOMER-SERVICE PERSPECTIVE

Using data from the market research department, Photon Corporation's management team estimates the financial value of probable lost sales of 2,000 photocopying machines because of external failures. The forgone contribution and operating income of $12 million measures the financial costs from dissatisfied customers who have returned machines to Photon and from sales lost because potential new customers become aware of quality problems. Total costs of quality (including opportunity costs) equal $52.02 million (Exhibit 19-4, Panel A, $40.02 million + Panel B, $12 million), or 17.34% of current sales. Opportunity costs account for 23% ($12 million ÷ $52.02 million) of Photon's total costs of quality.

The COQ report and the opportunity cost analysis highlight Photon's high internal and external failure costs. The advantage of the balanced scorecard framework is that Photon does not have to wait for this opportunity cost to arise nor to analyze its financial results to estimate the costs of quality failure. The nonfinancial measures of the customer perspective in the balanced scorecard provide advance warning of the potential costs of internal and external failure.

Even if products and services are defect-free and fully satisfy conformance quality, they will not be effective or sell well unless they also have design quality—that is, unless they satisfy customer needs. Usually management accountants are responsible for maintaining and reporting nonfinancial measures. Like many companies, Photon measures customer satisfaction trends over time. Measures include:

- Market research information on customer preferences and satisfaction with specific attributes and the overall value proposition.
- Market share.
- Percentage of customers giving high customer satisfaction ratings.
- Number of customer complaints (companies estimate that for every customer who actually complains, there are 10 to 20 others who have had bad experiences with the product but have not complained).
- Percentage of products that fail soon after delivery.
- Customer-response time (the difference between scheduled delivery date and date requested by the customer).
- On-time delivery rate (percentage of shipments made on or before the scheduled delivery date).

Often customer complaints arise because of technical nonconformance, an internal production process failure frequently measured as defect rate or mean time between failures (MTBF). FedEx, for example, tracks measures of customer satisfaction similar to those listed above in its overnight delivery business. Management steps in and investigates if, over time, these numbers deteriorate below standard performance thresholds.

In addition to these routine nonfinancial measures, many companies like Procter & Gamble conduct surveys to measure customer satisfaction. Surveys serve two objectives. First, they provide a deeper perspective into customer experiences and preferences. Second, they provide a glimpse into features that customers would like future products to have.

LEARNING AND GROWTH PERSPECTIVE

The **learning curve** reflects the common intuition that practice makes perfect. People take less time to do familiar tasks than unfamiliar ones. The nonlinear or curvilinear relationship of total output produced relative to quantity of labour input reflects progress in producing outputs. With good training and supervision, over time people learn from their experience. They will make fewer mistakes when conforming with product, service, and process specifications. Both rework production activities and materials costs should decrease along with costs of processing customer returns. The output will be more reliable, and the people doing the labour will be able to produce more outputs faster as they gain experience. The company will begin to benefit fully from both reengineering and economies of scale.

The plot of this time series of quality and quantity of output over time illustrates the effect of the learning curve. The learning curve is a curvilinear mathematical production function that shows how the ratio of quantity produced increases at a faster rate than the rate at which the time spent in activities of production decreases (Q_t output ÷ Q_t DMLH).

Management accountants whose task is to analyze costs, however, would be more interested in the experience curve. The **experience curve** is a cost function that shows how full product costs per unit (including manufacturing, marketing, distribution, and so on) decrease as total quantity produced increases. The experience curve illustrates that part of learning comes from doing. Whereas Boeing first documented the learning-curve effect, the Boston Consulting Group first popularized the experience-curve effect. The relationship is roughly stated that at each point when cumulative production doubles, costs decrease by a predictable percentage, ranging from 10% to 30% depending on the industry.

With respect to capacity, information systems have shifted from in-house to widely distributed systems such as cloud computing. Companies such as Amazon, with huge database capacity and exceptionally experienced database designers, are leasing capacity to smaller companies at approximately $72/hour. This is well below the cost of in-house development of the 5,000 servers (minimum) required to generate this type of economy of scale in IT infrastructure.[2]

Understanding the experience curve explains in part what is meant by the first-mover advantage. The first company to market with a successful output will grow as demand grows. As the volume of output grows, the unit cost will decrease because people have learned how to avoid and resolve errors and simply complete tasks more quickly.

To fully understand and successfully implement the economies of scale implied by the experience curve, however, management accountants need to understand the mechanics of the learning curve. The strategic benefits of the learning curve only arise if the learning stays within the company and the company passes on cost reductions to its customers to stimulate growth in demand.

In a broader perspective, the learning-curve effect illustrates how important good training and low turnover are to the long-term profitability of a company. The quantitative effects of the learning- and experience-curve effects can be reliably modelled and provide objective evidence of future cost savings based on past data. Better cost forecasts that are free of bias improve both budgeting and pricing outcomes in organizations. In not-for-profit organizations where the goal is to break even, as learning- and experience-curve effects are realized, the breakeven amount decreases and reliable plans can be made to expand the benefits provided on the same revenue base.

The underlying assumption of the learning-curve relationship is that direct manufacturing labour-hours (DMLH) necessary to complete a unit of production will decrease by a constant percentage each time the production quantity is doubled. This is a long-term accumulation of quantity produced from the inception of production. It is a strategy that requires long-term data to implement; a single year or even two years of data is inadequate. The reason is that quantity must double for the learning-curve effect to be observable, and as the cumulative quantity increases, the time to double also increases. A single year of data often is not a long enough time horizon to observe the doubling and, therefore, the constant rate of cost reduction.

This concept was defined mathematically years ago by an engineer at Boeing. We begin with Exhibit 19-5, which graphs the comparison of two types of nonlinear or learning-curve relationships. An incremental unit time learning model is illustrated on the left. A cumulative average time learning model is illustrated on the right. In both panels, the top line illustrates how incremental learning affects the nonlinear relationship between quantity produced and quantity of DMLH input. The lower line illustrates how cumulative learning affects the nonlinear relationship between quantity produced and quantity of DMLH input. In both examples, we assume that there is a constant rate of decrease in DMLH of 20% each time quantity of output doubles.

To model the nonlinear relationship between a faster rate of change in output (the outcome variable y) relative to input (the cause or predictor variable X) requires

[2]http://www.cloudcomputingeconomics.com/2009/01/experience-curves-for-data-center.html, accessed June 20, 2011.

EXHIBIT 19-5
Plots for the Incremental Unit-Time Learning Model

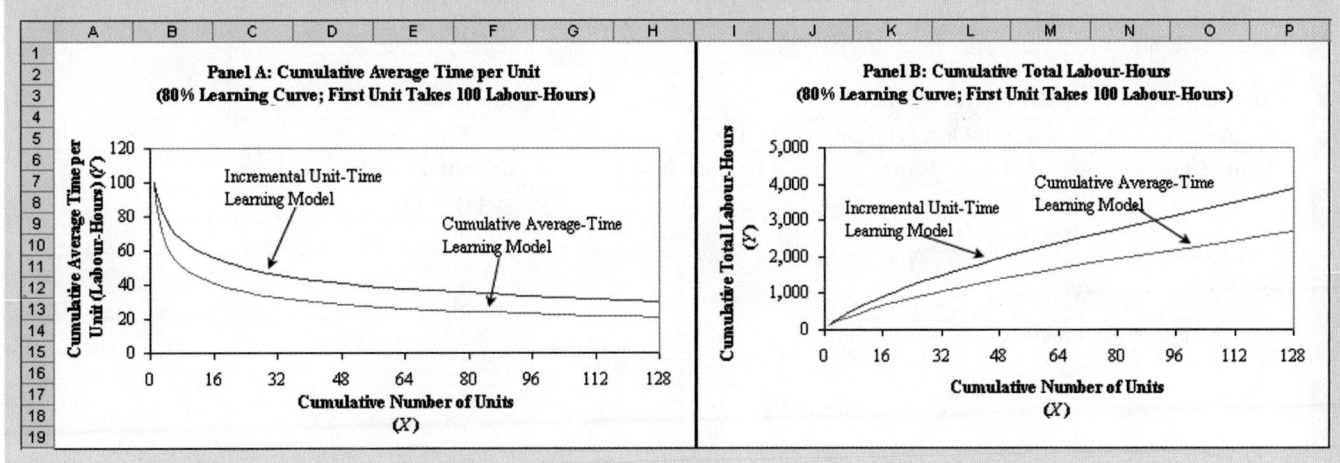

Panel A: Cumulative Average Time per Unit (80% Learning Curve; First Unit Takes 100 Labour-Hours)

Panel B: Cumulative Total Labour-Hours (80% Learning Curve; First Unit Takes 100 Labour-Hours)

the use of natural logarithms, -ln(x), one of the two common types of logarithms. The natural logarithm uses a base e = 2.71828 . . . when modelling a relationship. The other common logarithm uses the more familiar base of 10.[3]

Incremental Unit-Time Learning Model In the **incremental unit-time learning model**, the incremental unit-time (the time needed to produce the last unit) declines by a constant percentage each time the cumulative quantity of units produced

CONCEPTS IN ACTION—STRATEGY

Knowledge Reduces Production Costs!

Gamers, those who play computer games frequently, will be well aware of the benefits arising from the experience curve. Management accountants, however, exploit the cost reduction from increasing yield that arises in all the business functions of the value chain.

Cost leadership can be a very successful strategy for the first mover (the first entrant or pioneer into a market). The benefits of the experience curve protect first movers in new industries such as renewable energy. As competitors attempt to enter the market, pioneers can take the initiative to lower prices and lure buyers to the same quality of product at a lower price and further increase their volumes. As demand doubles, volumes double and costs decrease at a predictable and constant rate.

Many companies incorporate learning-curve effects when evaluating performance. For example, the Nissan Motor Company sets assembly labour efficiency standards for new models of cars after taking into account the learning that will occur as more units are produced. Organizing people into specialized groups or training people in several phases of the production process and rotating them periodically to perform different tasks has been shown to help improve the quality of products. Management accountants who understand the experience-curve effect can gather and use data to implement human resource training policies to achieve cost leadership.

[3]Logarithm is the inverse of exponentiation, e.g., let $x = 100$: $10^2 = 100$

$$2 = \log_{10} 100$$

when using the logarithm of base 10. When using the ln or natural logarithmic function, the basis of the calculation of the exponent is e = 2.71828. . . . If you raise 2.71828 to the exponent 4.605170 . . . ($2.71828^{4.605170}$) the answer is 99.99996 . . . rounded to 100, e.g., let $x = 100$ then ln(x) is:

$$e^{4.605170} = 100$$

$$4.605170 = \ln(100)$$

Most mathematics texts provide tables of logarithmic and natural logarithmic values.

EXHIBIT 19-6
The Incremental Unit-Time Learning Model

	A	B	C	D	E	F
1		80% Learning Curve				
2						
3	Cumulative	Individual Unit-Time		Cumulative	Cumulative	
4	Number of	for Xth Unit $(y)^{-b}$:		Total Time:	Average Time per	
5	Units (X)	Labour-Hours		Labour-Hours	Unit: Labour-Hours	
6	(1)	(2)		(3)	(4) = (3) ÷ (1)	
7	1	100.00		100.00	100.00	E9 = D9 ÷ A9
8	2	80.00	= (100 × 0.8)	180.00	90.00	
9	3	70.21		250.21	83.40	
10	4	64.00	= (80 × 0.8)	314.21	78.55	
11	5	59.56		373.77	74.75	
12	6	56.17		429.94	71.66	
13	7	53.45		483.39	69.06	
14	8	51.20	= (64 × 0.8)	534.59	66.82	
15	9	49.29		583.88	64.88	
16	10	47.65		631.53	63.15	
17	11	46.21		677.74	61.61	
18	12	44.93		722.67	60.22	
19	13	43.79		766.46	58.96	
20	14	42.76		809.22	57.80	
21	15	41.82		851.04	56.74	
22	16	40.96	= (51.2 × 0.8)	892.00	55.75	
23						
24	Note: The mathematical relationship underlying the incremental unit-time learning model is:					
25		$y = aX^{-b}$				
26	where y = Time (labour-hours) taken to produce the last single unit					
27	X = Cumulative number of units produced					
28	a = Time (labour-hours) required to produce the first unit					
29	b = Factor used to calculate incremental unit-time to produce units					
30	$= \dfrac{\text{ln (learning-curve \% in decimal form)}}{\text{ln } 2}$					
31	For an 80% learning curve, $b = \ln 0.8 \div \ln 2 = -0.2231 \div 0.6931 = -0.3219$					
32	When $X = 3$, $a = 100$, $b = -0.3219$					
33	$y = 100 \times 3^{-0.3219} = 70.21$ labour-hours					
34	The cumulative total time when $X = 3$ is $100 + 80 + 70.21 = 250.21$ labour-hours.					
35	Numbers in the table may not be exact because of rounding.					

doubles. Exhibit 19-6 illustrates the incremental unit-time learning model with an 80% learning curve. To the left, in Exhibit 19-5, is the cumulative average time per unit when the first unit requires 100 DMLH to produce but each subsequent unit takes only 80% of the time required for its predecessor. The mathematical function and calculations are shown in Exhibit 19-6.

We assume that there is a constant rate of decrease in DMLH of 20% each time quantity of output doubles. It is counterintuitive, but a higher percentage learning rate (e.g., 90% rather than 80%) indicates a slower rate of learning. Consider in Exhibit 19-6 the row for two cumulative units. Under this 80% learning curve, the cumulative average time per unit is 80 labour-hours. If the rate of learning had been 90%, the cumulative average time per unit would have been 90 labour-hours (100 × 0.90). The incremental unit-time model forecasts that when quantity of output doubles from 2 to 4 units it will take on average 80 DMLH (80% × 100 DMLH) to produce the second unit. When output doubles again from 4 to 8 units it will take on average 64 DMLH (80% × 80 DMLH) to produce the fourth unit, and so on. This model forecasts that it will take 180 DMLH to produce a total of 2 units, 250.21 DMLH to produce a total of 3 units, and 314.21 DMLH to produce a total of 4 units.

EXHIBIT 19-7
The Cumulative Average-Time Learning Model

	A	B	C	D	E	F
1		80% Learning Curve				
2						
3	Cumulative	Cumulative		Cumulative	Individual Unit	
4	Number	Average Time		Total Time:	Time for Xth	
5	of Units (X)	per Unit (y)*: Labour-Hours		Labour-Hours	Unit: Labour-Hours	
6	(1)	(2)		(3) = (1) × (2)	(4)	
7	1	100.00		100.00	100.00	E9=D9−D8=210.63−160.00
8	2	80.00	= (100 × 0.8)	160.00	60.00	
9	3	70.21		210.63	50.63	
10	4	64.00	= (80 × 0.8)	256.00	45.37	
11	5	59.56		297.80	41.80	
12	6	56.17		337.02	39.22	
13	7	53.45		374.15	37.13	
14	8	51.20	= (64 × 0.8)	409.60	35.45	
15	9	49.29		443.61	34.01	
16	10	47.65		476.50	32.89	
17	11	46.21		508.31	31.81	
18	12	44.93		539.16	30.85	
19	13	43.79		569.27	30.11	
20	14	42.76		598.64	29.37	
21	15	41.82		627.30	28.66	
22	16	40.96	= (51.2 × 0.8)	655.36	28.06	
23						
24	*The mathematical relationship underlying the cumulative average time learning model is:					
25	$y = aX^b$					
26	where y = Cumulative average time (labour-hours) per unit					
27	X = Cumulative number of units produced					
28	a = Time (labour-hours) required to produce the first unit					
29	b = Factor used to calculate cumulative average time to produce units					
30	1. The value of b is calculated as					
31	$\dfrac{\text{ln (learning-curve \% in decimal form)}}{\text{ln 2}}$					
32	For an 80% learning curve, $b = \ln 0.8 \div \ln 2 = -0.2231 \div 0.6931 = -0.3219$.					
33	When $X = 3$, $a = 100$, $b = -0.3219$,					
34	$y = 100 \times 3^{-0.3219} = 70.21$ labour-hours					
35	2. The cumulative total time when $X = 3$ is $70.21 \times 3 = 210.63$ labour-hours.					
36	3. The individual unit-times in column E are calculated using the data in column D. For example, the individual unit-time for the third unit is 50.63 labour-hours (210.63 − 160.00). Numbers in the table may not be exact because of rounding.					

Cumulative Average-Time Learning Model The **cumulative average-time learning model** depicts a relationship such that the cumulative average time per unit declines by a constant percentage each time the cumulative quantity of units produced doubles. To the right in Exhibit 19-5 is the cumulative total DMLH to produce total quantities of outputs when learning has an incremental effect on DMLH required. Exhibit 19-7 illustrates the cumulative average-time learning model with an 80% learning curve.

The 80% means that when the quantity of units produced is doubled from X to $2X$, the cumulative average time per unit for the $2X$ units is 80% of the cumulative average time per unit for the X units. In other words, average time per unit drops by 20%. Panel A in Exhibit 19-5 shows the cumulative average time per unit for this model of the effect of learning on DMLH required in the lower curved line. Notice that the total labour time is accumulating at a slower rate (column D in Exhibit 19-7). This is because the effect of learning is modelled differently for the cumulative than for the incremental model.

The cumulative model uses the average time per unit based on the most recent quantity of units produced. While the first unit took 100 DMLH, the first two took on average only 80 DMLH to produce each one. Therefore, the total time to produce two units is only 160 DMLH (2 × 80 DMLH). When three units were produced, it took on average 70.21 DMLH to produce each one. The total time to produce three units was 210.63 DMLH (3 × 70.21 DMLH). It took, on average, 64 DMLH to produce each of four units for a total of 256 DMLH (4 × 64 DMLH), and so on. Panel B of Exhibit 19-5 illustrates the cumulative total DMLH to produce total quantities of outputs when learning has a cumulative effect on DMLH required (100 + 80 + 70.21 + 64 + 51.20). Simply put, people are learning faster using this model than under the incremental unit-time model.

The more preferable model is the one that more accurately approximates the real physical process of manufacturing DMLH consumption as production levels increase. The choice can be decided only on a case-by-case basis. Engineers, plant managers, and workers are good sources of information on the amount and type of learning actually occurring as production increases. Plotting this information is helpful in selecting the appropriate model.

Setting Prices, Budgets, and Standards Forecasts of costs should allow for learning. Consider the data in Exhibit 19-7 for the cumulative average time learning model. Suppose the variable costs subject to learning effects consist of direct manufacturing labour ($20 per DMLH) and related overhead ($30 per DMLH). Management should forecast the costs shown in Exhibit 19-8.

These data show that the effects of the learning curve could have a major influence on decisions. For example, a company might set an extremely low selling price on its product to generate high demand. As the company's production increases to meet this growing demand, costs per unit drop. The company rides the product costs down the learning curve as it establishes a higher market share. Although the company may have earned little on its first unit sold—it may actually have lost money—the company earns more profit per unit as output increases.

EXHIBIT 19-8
Forecasting Costs Using Learning Curves

	A	B	C	D	E	F
1		Cumulative				
2	Cumulative	Average Time	Cumulative	Cumulative Costs		Additions to
3	Number of	per Unit:	Total Time:	at $50 per		Cumulative
4	Units	Labour-Hours[a]	Labour-Hours[a]	Labour-Hour		Costs
5	1	100.00	100.00	$ 5,000	(100.00 × $50)	$ 5,000
6	2	80.00	160.00	8,000	(160.00 × $50)	3,000
7	4	64.00	256.00	12,800	(256.00 × $50)	4,800
8	8	51.20	409.60	20,480	(409.60 × $50)	7,680
9	16	40.96	655.36	32,768	(655.36 × $50)	12,288
10						
11	[a]Based on the cumulative average-time learning model. See Exhibit 19-7 for the computation of these amounts.					

Alternatively, subject to legal and other considerations, the company might set a low price on just the final eight units. After all, the labour and related overhead costs per unit are forecast to be only $12,288 for these final eight units ($32,768 − $20,480). The per-unit costs of $1,536 on these final eight units ($12,288 ÷ 8) are much lower than the $5,000 costs of the first unit produced.

Routine processes provide the best opportunities for exploiting the experience curve to implement a cost leadership strategy. In contrast, value leadership often depends on quick commercialization of R&D innovations. But innovative products are unlikely to provide economies of scope and internal business processes must be reengineered. The temporary lack of experience will increase costs of production, for which purchasers must be willing to pay if the company is to retain or improve profit. The experience curve will, however, predictably reduce costs.

A 2011 example of RIM and its introduction of a substitute product, the Playbook, after months of delay, is an example of difficulties faced by new entrants into a market. Apple's product, the iPad, had already been on the market for over a year, and the recall of Playbook shook the confidence of RIM's loyal customer base and its investors alike. RIM downsized and continues to struggle for market share.

ANALYZE QUALITY-CONTROL PROBLEMS—INTERNAL BUSINESS PROCESSES

Analyze quality-control problems using three methods. ②

Tools such as statistical quality control (SQC) or statistical process control (SPC) provide relevant nonfinancial quantitative information. These data are a formal means of distinguishing between random variation and nonrandom variation in an operating process. A key method of reporting SQC results is a **control chart**, which illustrates in a graph a time series of successive observations of a particular step, procedure, or operation taken at regular time intervals. In addition to actual results, the expected range of specified results is also presented. Only **outliers**, those observations outside the specified limits, are ordinarily regarded as nonrandom and worth investigating.

Exhibit 19-9 presents control charts for the daily defect rates observed at Photon's three production lines. Defect rates in the prior 60 days for each plant were assumed to provide a good basis from which to calculate the distribution of daily defect rates. The arithmetic mean (μ, read "mu") and standard deviation (σ, read "sigma") are the two parameters of the distribution that are used in the control charts in Exhibit 19-9. On the basis of experience, the company decides that any observation outside the $\mu \pm 2\sigma$ range should be investigated[4].

In a standard normal distribution, the arithmetic mean of the population, or μ, is simply the sum of all observed values divided by the number of observations made. The standard deviation measures how much each actual observation deviates from the mean. If the deviation is caused by random factors, then 68.27% of all observed values will fall within one standard deviation (either + or −) from the mean.

Approximately 95.45% will fall within two, 99.73% within three, 99.994% within four, 99.9994% within five, and 99.9999998% within six standard deviations of the mean. Companies with a reputation for the highest quality achieve what is known as sigma6 quality. That is to say their failure rate is less than or equal to 1 in 10 million. Photon's goal is to achieve less than or equal to 4.55 or approximately 5 failures out of every 100 photocopiers produced. While this may be a measure of high quality for a photocopier, for a heart valve used to replace a damaged human valve this is not a satisfactory failure rate.

In Exhibit 19-9 all observations for production line A are within the range of $\pm 2\sigma$ from the mean. The report signals that no investigation is necessary. The last

---

[4]In Chapter 10 the discussion of a range of expected values around μ or the average predicted value of the MOH cost pool each time period, was discussed. The basic assumption was that the distribution of error or residual values would be random and form a bell-shaped curve. The shape of the distribution for the learning curve discussed in this chapter is called exponential. The type of distribution influences a knowledgeable management team when it decides the range of values within which actual output can differ from predicted output and still signal a process in control.

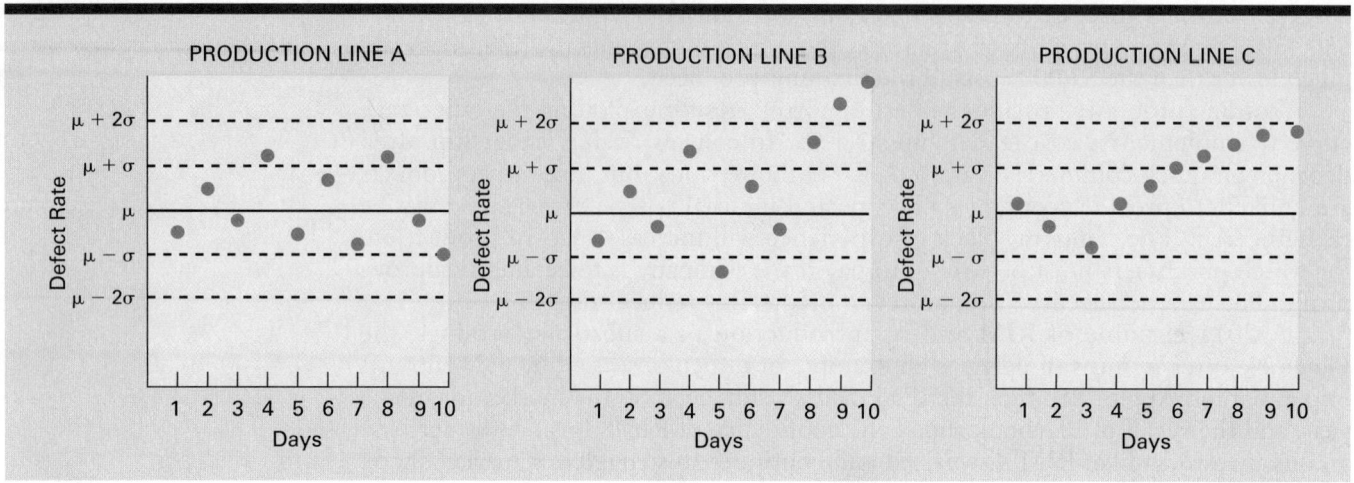

two observations for production line B signal that an out-of-control occurrence is highly probable. This may be due to random events or may be a signal of an ongoing issue that will not be resolved by doing nothing. Given the $\pm 2\sigma$ rule, this would lead to an investigation. Production line C illustrates a process that would not prompt an investigation under the $\pm 2\sigma$ rule but may well be out of control. Note that the last eight observations show a clear direction and that the direction by day 5 is away from the mean. Statistical procedures have been developed using the trend as well as the level of the variable in question to evaluate whether a process is out of control.

PARETO DIAGRAMS

Observations outside control limits serve as inputs to *Pareto diagrams*. A **Pareto diagram** or frequency chart indicates how frequently each type of failure (defect) occurs. Exhibit 19-10 presents a Pareto diagram for Photon's quality problems. Fuzzy and unclear copies are the most frequently recurring problem.

The fuzzy-copy problem results in high rework costs because, in many cases, Photon discovers the fuzzy-image problem only after the copier has been built. Sometimes fuzzy images occur at customer sites, resulting in high warranty and repair costs. This Pareto diagram is another attention-directing report, but the real value added arises from determining the cause(s) of the defect rate.

EXHIBIT 19-10
Pareto Diagram for the Photon Corporation

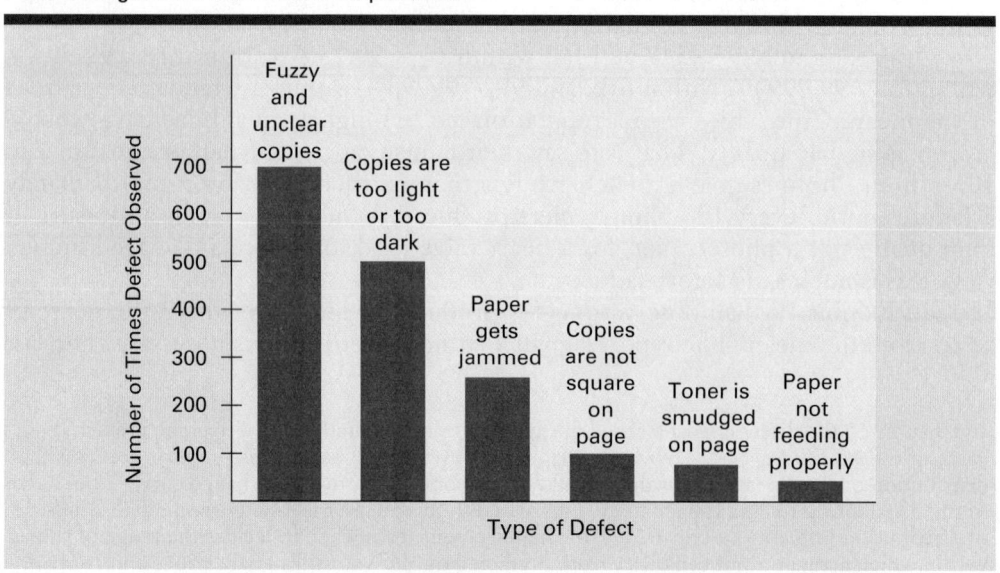

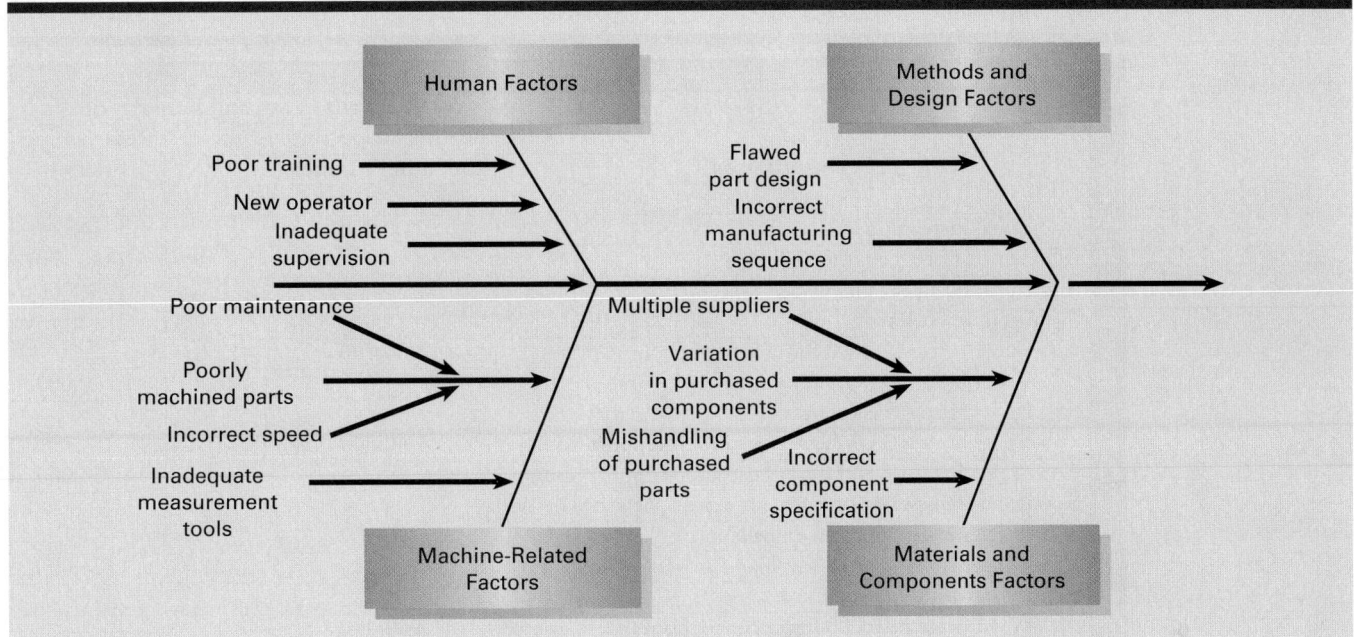

The SQC signalled where the quality problem is most likely to arise: Production lines B and C. The Pareto diagram signalled what the most probable quality problem is because, of the total possible quality problems, "fuzzy and unclear copies" occurs most frequently. These two reports indicate where managers should investigate further to ascertain what is causing the quality problem.

CAUSE-AND-EFFECT DIAGRAMS

The most frequently occurring problems identified by the Pareto diagram are analyzed using cause-and-effect diagrams. A **cause-and-effect diagram** identifies potential causes of failures or defects. As a first step, Photon analyzes the causes of the most frequently occurring failure—fuzzy and unclear copies. Exhibit 19-11 presents the cause-and-effect diagram for this problem.

The exhibit identifies four major categories of potential causes of failure: human factors, methods and design factors, machine-related factors, and materials and components factors. As additional arrows are added for each cause, the general appearance of the diagram begins to resemble a fishbone (hence, cause-and-effect diagrams are also called *fishbone diagrams*).[5]

The analysis of quality problems is aided by automated equipment and computers that record the number and types of defects and the operating conditions that existed at the time the defects occurred. Using these inputs, computer programs simultaneously prepare control charts, Pareto diagrams, and cause-and-effect diagrams.

RELEVANT COSTS AND BENEFITS OF QUALITY IMPROVEMENT

Careful analysis of the cause-and-effect diagram reveals that the steel frame (or chassis) of the copier is often mishandled as it travels from the suppliers' warehouses to Photon's plant. The frame must satisfy very precise specifications and tolerances; otherwise, various copier components (such as drums, mirrors, and lenses) attached to the frame will be improperly aligned. Mishandling causes the dimensions of the frame to vary from specifications, resulting in fuzzy images.

Analyze the benefits of using both financial and nonfinancial measures of quality.

[5]See P. Clark, "Getting the Most from Cause-and-Effect Diagrams," *Quality Progress* (June 2000).

EXHIBIT 19-12

Estimated Effect of Quality-Improvement Actions on Costs of Quality for Photocopying Machines at Photon Corporation

	A	B	C	D
1		**Relevant Costs and Benefits of**		
2		**Further Inspecting**		**Redesigning**
3	**Relevant Items**	**Incoming Frames**		**Frames**
4	**(1)**	**(2)**		**(3)**
5	Additional inspection and testing costs	$(400,000)		—
6	Additional process engineering costs	—		$ (300,000)
7	Additional design engineering costs	—		(160,000)
8	Savings in rework costs			
9	($40 per hour × 24,000 fewer rework-hours)	960,000		
10	($40 per hour × 32,000 fewer rework-hours)			1,280,000
11	Savings in customer-support costs			
12	($20 per hour × 2,000 fewer customer-support hours)	40,000		
13	($20 per hour × 2,800 fewer customer-support hours)			56,000
14	Savings in transportation costs for repair parts			
15	($180 per load × 500 fewer loads moved)	90,000		
16	($180 per hour × 700 fewer loads moved)			126,000
17	Savings in warranty repair costs			
18	($45 per hour × 20,000 fewer repair-hours)	900,000		
19	($45 per hour × 28,000 fewer repair-hours)			1,260,000
20	Total contribution margin from additional sales			
21	(250 additional copiers × $6,000 per copier)	1,500,000		
22	(300 additional copiers × $6,000 per copier)			1,800,000
23	Net cost savings and additional contribution margin	$3,090,000		$4,062,000
24	Difference in favour of redesigning frame	↑	$972,000	↑

The team of engineers working to solve the fuzzy-image problem offers two alternative solutions: (1) to improve the inspection of the frame immediately upon delivery or (2) to redesign and strengthen the frame and the containers used to transport them to better withstand mishandling during transportation.

Should Photon inspect incoming frames more carefully or redesign them and their containers? Exhibit 19-12 shows the costs and benefits of each option.

1. *Estimated incremental costs:* $400,000 for the inspection alternative; $460,000 for the redesign alternative, including $300,000 process engineering and $160,000 design engineering.

2. *Cost savings from less rework, customer support, and repairs:* Exhibit 19-12, lines 9 and 10, show that reducing rework results in savings of $40 per hour. Exhibit 19-4, Panel A, column 2, line 13 (see page 758), shows total rework cost per hour of $100. Why the difference? Because Photon concludes that as it improves quality, it will save only the $40 variable cost per rework-hour, not the $60 fixed cost per rework-hour.

   Exhibit 19-12, line 9, shows the inspection alternative is expected to eliminate 24,000 rework-hours and therefore save variable costs of $960,000 ($40 per hour × 24,000 rework-hours). The redesign alternative (Exhibit 19-12, line 10) is expected to eliminate 32,000 rework-hours and therefore save variable costs of $1,280,000 ($40 per rework-hour × 32,000 rework-hours). Exhibit 19-12 also shows expected variable-cost savings in customer support, transportation, and warranty repair for the two alternatives.

3. *Increased contribution margin from higher sales as a result of building a reputation for quality and performance* (Exhibit 19-12, lines 21 and 22): $1,500,000 for 250 copiers under the inspection alternative and $1,800,000 for 300 copiers under the redesign alternative. This benefit is important because quality improvements cannot always be translated into lower costs. For example, laying off workers (as a result of quality improvements) to reduce costs can adversely

affect the morale of employees and limit future quality initiatives. Management should always look for opportunities to generate higher revenues from quality improvements.

Exhibit 19-12 shows that both the inspection and the redesign alternatives yield net benefits relative to the status quo. However, the net benefits from the redesign alternative are expected to be $972,000 greater. The costs of a poorly designed frame appear in the form of higher manufacturing, marketing, distribution, and customer-service costs, as internal and external failures begin to mount. But these costs are locked in when the frame is designed. Thus, it is not surprising that redesign will yield significant savings.

In the Photon example, lost contribution margin occurs because Photon's repeated external failures damage its reputation for quality, resulting in lost sales. Lost contribution margin can also occur as a result of internal failures. Suppose Photon's manufacturing capacity is fully used. In this case, rework uses up valuable manufacturing capacity and causes the company to forgo contribution margin from producing and selling additional copiers. Suppose Photon could produce and (subsequently) sell an additional 600 copiers by improving quality and reducing rework. The costs of internal failure would then include lost contribution margin of $3,600,000 ($6,000 contribution margin per copier, 600 copiers). This $3,600,000 is the opportunity cost of poor quality.

Photon can use its COQ report to examine interdependencies across the four categories of quality-related costs. In our example, redesigning the frame increases costs of prevention activities (design and process engineering), decreases costs of internal failure (rework), and decreases costs of external failure (warranty repairs).

Costs of quality give more insight when managers compare trends over time. In successful quality programs, the costs of quality as a percentage of sales and the costs of internal and external failure as a percentage of total costs of quality should decrease over time. Many companies—for example, Digital Equipment Corporation, Solectron, and Toyota—believe they should eliminate all failure costs and have zero defects.

COSTS OF DESIGN QUALITY

Our discussion so far has focused on measuring the cost of conformance quality and the methods that companies use to reduce these costs. In addition to conformance quality, companies must also pay attention to quality of design by designing products that satisfy customer needs. The costs of design quality refer to costs incurred to prevent, or costs arising from, low quality of design. These costs include the costs of designing a product and the production, marketing, distribution, and customer-service costs wasted on supporting a poorly designed product. A significant component of these costs is the opportunity cost of sales lost from not producing a product that customers want. Many of these costs are very difficult to measure precisely. For this reason, most companies do not measure the financial costs of design quality.

BSC—NONFINANCIAL MEASURES OF INTERNAL-BUSINESS-PROCESS QUALITY

Prevention costs, appraisal costs, and internal failure costs are examples of financial measures of quality performance inside the company. Most companies monitor both financial and nonfinancial measures of internal quality.

Photon measures internal-business-process quality using the following nonfinancial measures:

- ◆ Defect rate—the percentage of defective to total units.
- ◆ Average repair time to fix machines at the customer's site.
- ◆ Rework rate—the percentage of reworked to total units.
- ◆ Number of different types of defects analyzed using control charts, Pareto diagrams, and cause-and effect diagrams.
- ◆ Number of design and process changes made.

By themselves, nonfinancial measures of quality have limited meaning. They are more informative when management examines trends over time. To prepare this report, the management accountant must review the numbers to ensure that non-financial measures are calculated accurately and consistently, and must then present the information to help management evaluate internal quality performance. Management accountants help companies improve quality in multiple ways—they compute the costs of quality, assist in developing cost-effective solutions to quality problems, and provide feedback about quality improvement.

BSC—LEARNING AND GROWTH NONFINANCIAL MEASURES OF QUALITY

Photon's managers have analyzed performance to determine the drivers of internal-business-process quality. Photon measures the following factors in the learning and growth perspective in the balanced scorecard:

- Employee turnover ratio (number of employees who leave compared with the average total number of employees).
- Employee empowerment ratio (number of processes in which employees have the right to make decisions without consulting supervisors compared with the total number of processes).
- Employee satisfaction ratio (employees indicating high satisfaction ratings compared with the total employees surveyed).
- Employee training rate (percentage of employees trained in different quality-enhancing methods).

These quality-related balanced scorecard measures provide the best information when managers examine trends and relationships (across the learning and growth, the internal business process, the customer, and the financial perspectives) over time as they seek to improve performance. To provide information on trends, management accountants must review the nonfinancial measures for accuracy and consistency.

BSC—EVALUATING QUALITY—FINANCIAL AND NONFINANCIAL MEASURES

Measuring the financial costs of quality and measuring the nonfinancial aspects of quality have distinctly different advantages. The advantages of the costs of quality (COQ) measures are as follows:

- COQ focuses attention on how costly poor quality can be throughout all business functions of a value chain, including communication.
- Financial COQ measures are a useful way of comparing different quality-improvement programs and setting priorities for achieving maximum cost reduction.
- Financial COQ measures serve as a common denominator for evaluating trade-offs among prevention and failure costs. COQ provides a single, summary measure of quality performance.

The advantages of nonfinancial measures of quality are that they:

- Are often easy to quantify and easy to understand.
- Direct attention to physical processes and hence focus attention on the precise problem areas that need improvement.
- Provide immediate short-run feedback on whether quality-improvement efforts have, in fact, succeeded in improving quality.
- Are useful indicators of long-run performance.

Most organizations use both financial and nonfinancial quality measures to measure quality performance.

The Cost of Quality Failure at Firestone

Company and division managers feel pressure to meet quarterly and annual financial performance targets. Quality-control and assurance activities carry significant costs, but quality failures can cost far more. As Bridgestone/Firestone, Inc., makers of Firestone tires, learned during a widely publicized recall of 6.5 million tires in 2000, the financial, public-relations, and legal effects of quality failure can be disastrous. Firestone received thousands of unfavourable news stories, more than 200 lawsuits from angry customers, and high-profile congressional inquiries about the failures.

On May 22, 2001, Ford announced the further recall of 13 million tires. Ford ended its relationship with Firestone. Firestone suffered 40% revenue declines in key segments and a US$510 million loss in 2000. It also paid out over US$1 billion in recall-related costs (including new tires, claim settlements, and lawsuits), lost US$10 billion in stock market capitalization, and dismissed most Bridgestone/Firestone corporate executives in the United States and Japan. The production quality-control issue was made worse because top management was fully aware of the problem and failed to remedy it.

Ford Motor Company—Firestone's largest US customer for a century—conducted an analysis that indicated that tires from Firestone's Decatur, Illinois, plant exhibited tendencies to come apart at high speeds, which caused vehicles, especially Ford's popular Explorer sports utility vehicle, to roll over. In the United States, the National Highway Traffic Safety Administration (NHSTA) requires companies and suppliers to report unusual vehicle failures. The investigation revealed that neither Ford nor Firestone conformed to this legislation. It was the NHSTA that informed Ford of an unusual frequency of rollover accidents involving its Ford Explorer.

At this point, Firestone had failed to prevent failure prior to the product reaching the customer's hands. Although both companies displayed public remorse and

began working together in handling the recall, Firestone responded to Ford's study by stating:

> We are confident in the quality of our tires and in the effectiveness of our inspection processes at the Decatur, Illinois, plant and at all of our plants. . . . Like all Bridgestone/Firestone production facilities, the Decatur plant adheres to stringent standards of quality control where every tire is subject to strict inspection by both people and machines at every step of the manufacturing process, from raw material through finished tire. And, every production employee, at each of our plants, receives substantial training before they work on the line. . . . The plant also has received quality awards from our customers, including Ford, General Motors, and Nissan.

Scrutiny of quality practices at Firestone told a different story. In late 1999, it was found that tread separation among light-truck tires had risen 18.6% during the previous year. This change led Firestone engineers to investigate tread separation, and they identified tread separation as a critical performance issue at their October 2000 quarterly quality meeting. Another investigation at Firestone reported that the number of warranty claims for ATX and ATXII tires made at the Decatur facility between 1994 and 1996 were three to six times higher than claims for tires made at all other US Firestone plants. Although quality improved after 1996, claim rates remained significantly higher for the Decatur plant than at all other facilities.

These findings—coupled with news that tread separation caused Ford to replace the same, or similar, tires on nearly 50,000 of its vehicles in 16 South American and Asian countries starting in 1999—led most observers to conclude that the rollovers were being caused by Firestone tire defects. A Harvard Business School case notes:

> Although the rising cost of claims and lawsuits regarding the Firestone ATX tire was apparently discussed at some quarterly financial meetings beginning in 1997, the matter did not go beyond the finance area which maintained information on claims costs. As [Vice President Gary] Crigger explained: "Claims and lawsuits are not considered to be representative throughout a line . . . [but] individual cases that occur for a variety of reasons. So they have never been part of [tire] performance evaluation."

Both companies had the relevant nonfinancial and financial information indicating quality failure. Neither company calculated cost-of-quality failure and implemented remedies. Firestone failed to incorporate both the

(continued)

opportunity cost of legal proceedings and the loss of Ford as their customer. With an ERP strategy, and using the process described in this chapter, Firestone's executives could have recognized the interdependence of legal, financial, and production nonfinancial information and made decisions to better protect the company's most valuable asset—its customers.

Sources: L. S. Payne, "Recall 2000: Bridgestone Corp. (A)," HBS Case No. 9-302-013 (Boston: Harvard Business School Publishing, 2003); S. Govindaraj and B. Jaggi, "Market Overreaction to Product Recall Revisited—The Case of Firestone Tires and the Ford Explorer," *Review of Quantitative Finance and Accounting* (July 2004); D. Welch, "Firestone: Is This Brand Beyond Repair?" *BusinessWeek*, June 11, 2001; "Firestone Decatur Tire Plant Inspection—Defective Tires," Bridgestone America Holdings press release (Nashville, TN: August 13, 2001).

TIME AS A COMPETITIVE TOOL

4 Evaluate methods using time as a competitive tool.

Companies increasingly view time as a key variable in competition.[6] Doing things faster helps to increase revenues and decrease costs. For example, a moving company such as United Van Lines will be able to generate more revenues if it can move goods from one place to another faster and on time. Companies such as Wal-Mart also report lower costs from their emphasis on time. They cite, for example, the need to carry less inventory because of their ability to respond rapidly to customer demands.

In this section we will focus on *operational measures of time*, which reveal how quickly companies respond to customers' demands for their products and services and the reliability with which these companies meet scheduled delivery dates. Two common operational measures of time are customer-response time and on-time performance.

CUSTOMER-RESPONSE TIME

Customer-response time is the amount of time between when a customer places an order for a product or requests a service and when the product or service is delivered to the customer. A timely response to customer requests is a key competitive factor in many industries. Exhibit 19-13 illustrates components of customer-response time that can be measured. Consider the example of Airbus, first introduced in the opening vignette to this chapter. In the case of Airbus, **order receipt time** is the time it takes the marketing department to send engineering and other specifications to the manufacturing department. One remedy implemented by Airbus was to install a new software system enabling engineers in Toulouse to communicate directly with those in Hamburg. This improved conformance.

EXHIBIT 19-13
Components of Customer-Response Time

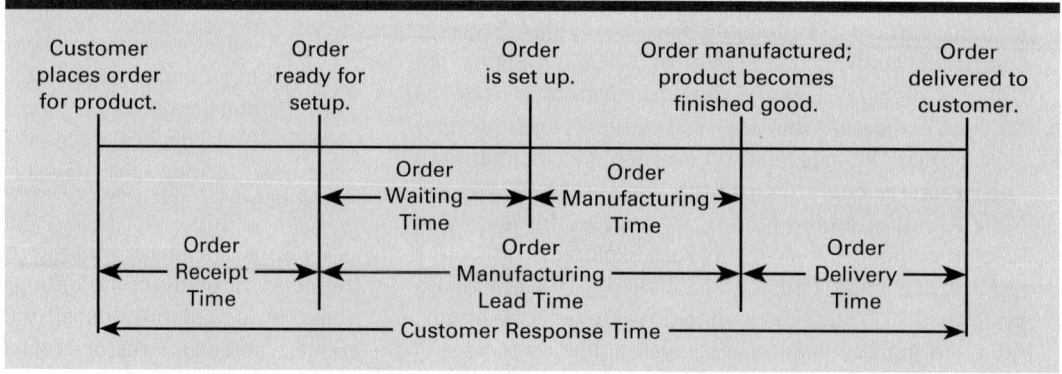

[6]See G. Stalk and T. Hout, *Competing Against Time* (New York: Free Press, 1990); K. Eisenhardt and S. Brown, "Time Pacing: Competing in Strategic Markets That Won't Stand Still," *Harvard Business Review* (March–April 1998); T. Willis and A. Jurkus, "Product Development: An Essential Ingredient of Time-Based Competition," *Review of Business* (2001).

Manufacturing lead time is the time between when the order is ready to start on the production line (ready to be set up) and when it becomes a finished good. Manufacturing lead time includes waiting time plus manufacturing time for the order. An order may be delayed because the equipment the order requires is busy processing orders that arrived earlier. **Manufacturing cycle time** refers to the sum of waiting time plus production cycle time. Some companies evaluate their response time improvement using a measure called **manufacturing cycle efficiency (MCE)**. MCE is the ratio of value-added manufacturing cycle time divided by the total manufacturing cycle time:

$$MCE = (\text{Value-added manufacturing time} \div \text{Manufacturing cycle time})$$

As discussed in Chapter 12, wait time is not value-added; therefore, this measure is a time yield measure of value-added time divided by total time of manufacture. Wait time or non-value-added time includes that spent by the manufacturer waiting for parts, inspection time, rework and repair time, and materials-handling time.

Order delivery time is the time it takes distribution to pick up the order from manufacturing and deliver it to the customer. The new software system at Airbus also avoided delays caused by rewiring and shortened the order delivery time to meet the customer's requirements. For retail catalogue companies, the time from the placement of the order to the customer's receipt of the product is often shorter than the 7- to 10-day delivery delay of retail stores such as The Brick and The Bay. Retail catalogue companies delivering in less than 7 days use time as a competitive advantage for their service.

On-time performance refers to situations in which the product or service is actually delivered at the time it is scheduled to be delivered. Consider FedEx, which specifies a price per package and a next-day delivery time of 10:30 a.m. for its overnight courier service. FedEx measures on-time performance by how often it meets its stated delivery time of 10:30 a.m. On-time performance is an important element of customer satisfaction because customers want and expect on-time deliveries.

Commercial airlines gain loyal passengers from consistent on-time service. Note that there is a tradeoff between customer-response time and on-time performance. Simply scheduling longer customer-response times, such as FedEx scheduling deliveries at 1 p.m. instead of 10:30 a.m., or airlines lengthening scheduled arrival times, makes it easier to achieve on-time performance (although this tactic could displease customers).

UNCERTAINTY AND BOTTLENECKS AS DRIVERS OF TIME

A **time driver** is any factor where change in the factor causes a change in the speed with which an activity is undertaken. What are the drivers of time? We consider two of the most important: (1) *Uncertainty about when customers will order products or services.* For example, the more randomly a company receives orders for its machine tools, the more likely that queues will form and delays will occur. (2) *Limited capacity and bottlenecks.* A **bottleneck** is an operation in which the work required to be performed approaches or exceeds the available capacity. For example, a bottleneck is created when products that need to be processed at a particular machine arrive while the machine is busy processing other products.

Consider the example of Falcon Works (FW), which uses one turning machine to convert steel bars into one specialty component, A22. FW makes this component only after FW's customers order the component. To focus on manufacturing lead time, we assume that FW's order receipt time and order delivery time are minimal. FW acquires direct materials when it receives an order, rather than waiting until just before manufacturing is scheduled to start, because of uncertainty about (1) how long it will take to obtain materials from suppliers and (2) when manufacturing will start.

FW expects it will receive 30 orders, but it could actually receive 10, 20, or 50 orders of A22. Each order is for 1,000 units. Each order will take 100 hours of manufacturing time (8 hours of setup time to clean and prepare the machine, and 92 hours of processing time). The annual capacity of the machine is 4,000 hours. If FW receives the number of orders it expects, the total amount of manufacturing time required on the machine will be 3,000 (100×30) hours, which is within the available machine capacity of 4,000 hours. Even though expected capacity utilization is not strained, queues and delays will still occur because uncertainty about when FW's customers will place an order may cause the order to be received while the machine is processing another order.

In the single-product case, under certain assumptions about the pattern of customer orders and how orders will be processed, the **average waiting time**, the average amount of time that an order will wait in line before it is set up and processed, equals:

$$\frac{\text{Average number of orders of A22} \times \left(\text{Manufacturing time for A22}\right)^2}{2 \times \left[\text{Annual machine capacity} - \left(\text{Average number of orders of A22} \times \text{Manufacturing time for A22}\right)\right]}$$

$$= \frac{30 \times (100)^2}{2 \times [4{,}000 - (30 \times 100)]} = \frac{30 \times 10{,}000}{2 \times (4{,}000 - 3{,}000)} = \frac{300{,}000}{2 \times 1{,}000} = \frac{300{,}000}{2{,}000} = 150 \text{ hours}$$

The precise technical assumptions are (1) that customer orders for the product follow a Poisson distribution[7] with a mean equal to the expected number of orders (30 in our example) and (2) that orders are processed on a first-in, first-out (FIFO) basis. The Poisson arrival pattern for customer orders has been found to be reasonable in many real-world settings. The FIFO assumption can be modified. Under the modified assumptions, the basic queuing and delay effects will still occur, but the precise formulas will be different.

Our formula describes only the average waiting time. A particular order may happen to arrive when the machine is free, in which case manufacturing will start immediately. In other situations, FW may receive an order while two other orders are waiting to be processed. In this case, the delay will be longer than 150 hours. The average manufacturing lead time for an order of A22 is 250 hours (150 hours of average waiting time + 100 hours of manufacturing time). Note that manufacturing time per order is a squared term in the numerator. It indicates the disproportionately large impact manufacturing time has on waiting time. (See Concepts in Action, page 780.)

The longer the manufacturing time, the greater the probability that the machine will be in use when an order arrives. This leads to longer delays. The denominator in this formula measures excess capacity or **cushion**. The smaller the cushion, the greater the probability of delay because the higher is the probability the machine will be processing an earlier order. Throughout this section, we use manufacturing lead time to refer to manufacturing lead time for an order.

FW is considering whether to introduce a new product, C33. FW expects to receive 10 orders of C33 (each order for 800 units) in the coming year. Each order will take 50 hours of manufacturing time (3 hours of setup time and 47 hours of processing time). The expected demand for A22 will be unaffected whether or not FW introduces C33.

The average waiting time before an order is set up and processed is given by the following formula, which is an extension of the formula described earlier for the single-product case:

$$\frac{\left[\text{Average number of orders of A22} \times \left(\text{Manufacturing time for A22}\right)^2\right] + \left[\text{Average number of orders of C33} \times \left(\text{Manufacturing time for C33}\right)^2\right]}{2 \times \left[\text{Annual machine capacity} - \left(\text{Average number of orders of A22} \times \text{Manufacturing time for A22}\right) - \left(\text{Average number of orders of C33} \times \text{Manufacturing time for C33}\right)\right]}$$

$$= \frac{[30 \times (100)^2] + [10 \times (50)^2]}{2 \times [4{,}000 - (30 \times 100) - (10 \times 50)]} = \frac{(30 \times 10{,}000) + (10 \times 2{,}500)}{2 \times (4{,}000 - 3{,}000 - 500)}$$

$$= \frac{300{,}000 + 25{,}000}{2 \times 500} = \frac{325{,}000}{1{,}000} = 325 \text{ hours}$$

Introducing C33 causes average waiting time to more than double, from 150 hours to 325 hours. To understand why, think of excess capacity as a cushion for absorbing the shocks of variability and uncertainty in the arrival of customer orders. Introducing C33 causes excess capacity to shrink, increasing the chance that at any point in time, new orders will arrive while existing orders are being manufactured.

[7]A Poisson distribution is a statistical distribution that is almost bell-shaped but is mathematically defined in a different way than a Normal distribution.

The cushion is cut in half from 1,000 to 500 hours, doubling the average wait time by halving the denominator. The product introduction also increases demand on capacity by 25,000 hours, which increases the numerator but at a slower rate than the increase in the denominator. The total effect of introducing the C33 is to increase average waiting time by 117% [(325 − 150) ÷ 150].

With the addition of another product, average manufacturing lead time for A22 is 425 hours (325 hours of average waiting time + 100 hours of manufacturing time), and for C33 it is 375 hours (325 hours of average waiting time + 50 hours of manufacturing time). Note that C33 spends 86.67% (325 ÷ 375) of its manufacturing lead time just waiting for manufacturing to start!

RELEVANT REVENUES AND COSTS OF TIME

Should FW introduce product C33? Consider the following information:

Product	Annual Average Number of Orders	Average Selling Price per Order If Average Manufacturing Lead Time per Order Is		Direct Material Cost per Order	Inventory Carrying Cost per Order per Hour
		Less than 300 Hours	More than 300 Hours		
A22	30	$22,000	$21,500	$16,000	$1.00
C33	10	10,000	9,600	8,000	0.50

Note that manufacturing lead times affect both revenues and costs in our example. Revenues are affected because customers are willing to pay a slightly higher price for faster delivery. Direct materials costs and inventory carrying costs are the only costs affected by the decision to introduce C33. Inventory carrying costs usually consist of the opportunity costs of investment tied up in inventory (see Chapter 11) and the relevant costs of storage such as space rental, spoilage, deterioration, and materials handling. Companies usually calculate inventory carrying costs on a per-order-per-year basis. To simplify computations, we express inventory carrying costs on a per-order-per-hour basis. FW incurs inventory carrying costs for the duration of the wait time and manufacturing time. Exhibit 19-14 presents relevant revenues and relevant costs that the management accountant would calculate for this decision.

EXHIBIT 19-14
Determining Expected Relevant Revenues and Relevant Costs for Falcon Works' Decision to Introduce C33

Relevant Items	Alternative 1: Introduce C33 (1)	Alternative 2: Do Not Introduce C33 (2)	Difference (3) = (1) − (2)
Expected revenues	$741,000ᵃ	$660,000ᵇ	$ 81,000
Expected variable costs	560,000ᶜ	480,000ᵈ	(80,000)
Expected inventory carrying costs	14,625ᵉ	7,500ᶠ	(7,125)
Expected total costs	574,625	487,500	(87,125)
Expected revenues minus expected costs	$166,375	$172,500	$ (6,125)

ᵃ($21,500 × 30) + ($9,600 × 10) = $741,000; average manufacturing lead time will be more than 300 hours.
ᵇ($22,000 × 30) = $660,000; average manufacturing lead time will be less than 300 hours.
ᶜ($16,000 × 30) + ($8,000 × 10) = $560,000.
ᵈ$16,000 × 30 = $480,000.
ᵉ(Average manufacturing lead time for A22 × Inventory carrying cost per order for A22 × Expected number of orders for A22) + (Average manufacturing lead time for C33 × Inventory carrying cost per order for C33 × Expected number of orders for C33) = (425 × $1.00 × 30) + (375 × $0.50 × 10) = $12,750 + $1,875 = $14,625.
ᶠAverage manufacturing lead time for A22 × Inventory carrying cost per order for A22 × Expected number of orders for A22 = 250 × $1.00 × 30 = $7,500.

The preferred alternative is not to introduce C33. Note that C33 is rejected despite having a positive contribution margin of at least $1,600 ($9,600 − $8,000) per order. Recall, too, that FW's machine has the capacity to process C33 because the machine will, on average, use only 3,500 of the available 4,000 hours. *The key to the decision is to recognize the relevant negative effects of C33 on the existing product A22.* The following table presents the expected loss in revenues and expected increase in costs of using up extra capacity on the turning machine to manufacture C33:

Effect of Increasing Average Manufacturing Lead Time

Product	Expected Loss in Revenues for A22 (1)	Expected Increase in Carrying Costs for All Products (2)	Expected Increase in Carrying Costs of Introducing C33 (3) = (1) + (2)
A22	$15,000[a]	$5,250[b]	$20,250
C33	—	1,875[c]	1,875
Total	$15,000	$7,125	$22,125

[a]($22,000 − $21,500) per order × 30 expected orders = $15,000.
[b](425 − 250) hours per order × $1.00 per hour × 30 expected orders = $5,250.
[c](375 − 0) hours per order × $0.50 per hour × 10 expected orders = $1,875.

Introducing C33 causes the average manufacturing lead time of A22 to increase from 250 hours to 425 hours. This increases inventory carrying costs. Introducing C33 also causes A22's revenues to decrease because it would, on average, take more than 300 hours to manufacture A22. The expected costs of introducing C33 equals $22,125, which exceeds C33's expected contribution margin of $16,000 ($1,600 per order × 10 expected orders). FW should choose not to produce C33.

We have described a simple setting to explain the effects of uncertainty and capacity constraints and the relevant revenues and relevant costs of time.[8] Delays can be reduced by increasing the capacity at the bottleneck to reduce queues, delays, and inventories. When demand uncertainty is high, *some* cushion is desirable. Companies can increase capacity in several ways. One is to reduce setup time by improving the efficiency of the setup process. Another is to invest in new equipment. Many companies are investing in flexible manufacturing systems that can be programmed to quickly switch from producing one product to producing another. Delays can also be reduced through careful scheduling of orders on machines—for example, by batching similar jobs together for processing.

THEORY OF CONSTRAINTS AND THROUGHPUT CONTRIBUTION ANALYSIS

5 Evaluate the strengths and weaknesses of the theory of constraints (TOC) and activity-based costing (ABC) for managing bottlenecks.

The **theory of constraints (TOC)** describes methods to maximize operating income when faced with some bottleneck and some non-bottleneck operations. It defines three measurements:[9]

◆ *Throughput contribution* equals sales revenue minus direct materials costs (see Chapter 9).

---

[8]Other complexities such as analyzing a network of machines, priority scheduling, and allowing for uncertainty in processing times are beyond the scope of this book. In these cases, the basic queuing and delay effects persist, but the precise formulas are more complex.
[9]See E. Goldratt and J. Cox, *The Goal* (New York: North River Press, 1986); E. Goldratt, *The Theory of Constraints* (New York: North River Press, 1990); E. Noreen, D. Smith, and J. Mackey, *The Theory of Constraints and Its Implications for Management Accounting* (New York: North River Press, 1995); and M. Woeppel, *Manufacturers' Guide to Implementing the Theory of Constraints* (Boca Raton, FL: Lewis Publishing, 2000).

◆ *Investments (inventory)* equals the sum of materials costs of direct materials inventory, work-in-process inventory, and finished goods inventory; R&D costs; and costs of equipment and buildings.

◆ *Operating costs* equals all operating costs (other than direct materials) incurred to earn throughput contribution; includes salaries and wages, rent, utilities, and amortization.

The objective of TOC is to increase throughput contribution while decreasing investments and operating costs. *The theory of constraints considers short-run time horizons and assumes other current operating costs to be fixed.* The management process is illustrated in Exhibit 19-15. The bottleneck must be located because this capacity constraint will determine the entire plant's throughput contribution. The general manager can enlist the line managers to reveal where large quantities of direct or WIP inventory await further processing. The immediate remedy is to maximize the capacity of the bottleneck. This means the flow of all non-bottlenecked resources will be determined by the bottleneck capacity.

Maximizing the bottleneck is an important example of the concept presented in Chapter 11: To maximize overall contribution margin, the plant must maximize contribution margin (in this case, throughput contribution) of the constrained or bottlenecked resource. For this reason, the bottleneck machine must always be kept running, not waiting for jobs. To achieve this, companies often maintain a small buffer inventory of jobs waiting for the bottleneck machine. The bottleneck machine sets the pace for all non-bottleneck machines. That is, the output at the non-bottleneck operations is tied or linked to the needs of the bottleneck machine. For example, workers at non-bottleneck machines are not motivated to improve their productivity if the additional output cannot be processed by the bottleneck machine. Producing more non-bottleneck output only creates excess inventory; it does not increase throughput contribution.

In the longer term, top management must take actions to increase bottleneck efficiency and capacity—the objective is to increase throughput contribution minus the incremental costs of taking such actions. The management accountant plays a key role by calculating throughput contribution, identifying relevant and irrelevant costs, and doing a cost-benefit analysis of alternative actions to increase bottleneck efficiency and capacity.

EXHIBIT 19-15
The Debottleneck Management Process

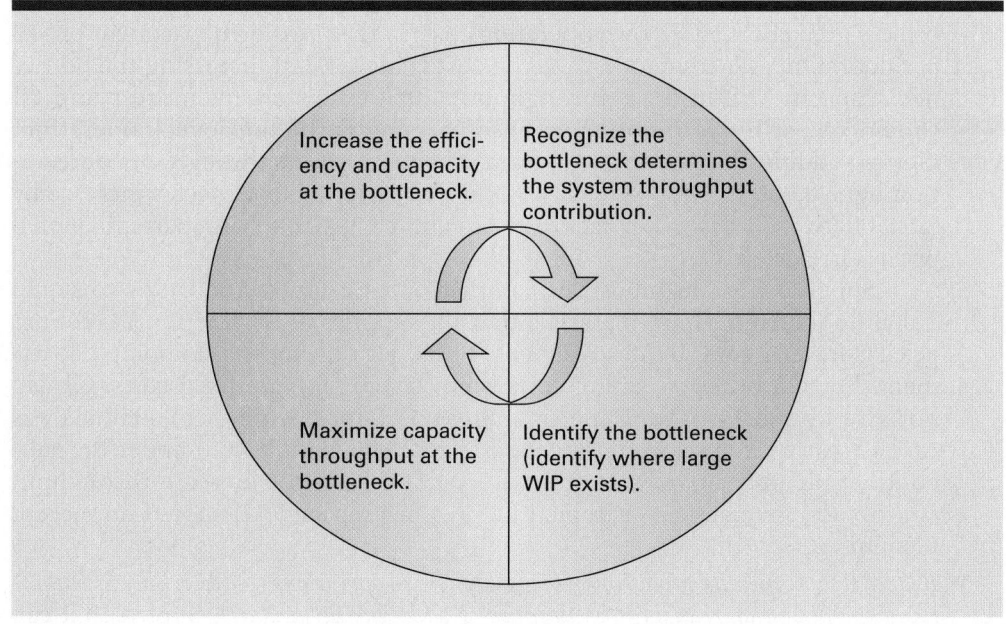

We illustrate debottlenecking with the example of Cardinal Industries (CI). CI manufactures car doors in two operations—stamping and pressing. Additional information is as follows:

	Stamping	Pressing
Capacity per hour	20 units	15 units
Annual capacity (6,000 hours of capacity available in each operation; 6,000 hours × 20 units/hour; 15 units/hour)	120,000 units	90,000 units
Annual production and sales	90,000 units	90,000 units
Other fixed operating costs (excluding direct materials)	$720,000	$1,080,000
Other fixed operating costs per unit produced ($720,000 ÷ 90,000 units; $1,080,000 ÷ 90,000 units)	$8 per unit	$12 per unit

Each door sells for $100 and has direct materials costs of $40. Variable costs in other functions of the value chain—R&D, design of products and processes, marketing, distribution, and customer service—are negligible. CI's output is constrained by the capacity of 90,000 units at the pressing operation. The actions taken to maximize the bottleneck capacity include the following:

♦ *Eliminate idle time (time when the pressing machine is neither being set up to process products nor actually processing products) at the bottleneck operation.* CI is considering permanently positioning two workers at the pressing operation. The sole responsibility of additional direct manufacturing labourers would be to unload finished units as soon as one batch of units is processed and to set up the machine to process the next batch. Suppose the annual cost of this action is $48,000 and the effect of this action is to increase bottleneck output by 1,000 units per year. CI should incur this additional cost because, based on incremental cost and revenue analysis, CI's relevant throughput contribution increases by $60,000 [1,000 units × (selling price, $100 – direct materials costs, $40)], which exceeds the additional cost of $48,000. All other costs are irrelevant.

♦ *Process only those parts or products that increase sales and throughput contribution, not parts or products that remain in finished goods or spare parts inventory.* Manufacturing products that sit in inventory do not increase throughput contribution.

♦ *Shift products that do not have to be made on the bottleneck machine to non-bottleneck machines or to outside facilities.* Suppose the Spartan Corporation, an outside contractor, offers to press 1,500 doors at $15 per door from direct materials that CI supplies. This is a standard make/buy decision for CI. Spartan's quoted price is greater than CI's own operating costs in the pressing department of $12 per door. On an incremental basis the cost is higher, but increasing the bottleneck capacity will increase throughput contribution for the entire plant. CI should accept Spartan's offer because pressing is the bottleneck operation. Getting additional doors pressed from outside increases throughput contribution by $90,000 [($100 – $40) × 1,500 doors], while relevant costs increase by $22,500 ($15 × 1,500). The fact that CI's unit cost is less than Spartan's quoted price is irrelevant.

Suppose Gemini Industries, another outside contractor, offers to stamp 2,000 doors from direct materials that CI supplies at $6 per door. Gemini's price is lower than CI's operating cost of $8 per door in the stamping department. For CI, other operating costs such as stamping are fixed costs. CI will not save by subcontracting the stamping operations. An incremental analysis reveals that total costs would increase by $12,000 ($6 × 2,000) under the subcontracting alternative. Stamping more doors will not increase throughput contribution, which is constrained by pressing capacity. CI should not accept Gemini's offer.

♦ *Reduce setup time and processing time at bottleneck operations (for example, by simplifying the design or reducing the number of parts in the product).* Suppose CI can reduce setup time at the pressing operation by incurring additional costs of

$55,000 a year. Suppose further that reducing setup time enables CI to press 2,500 more doors a year. CI should incur the costs to reduce setup time because throughput contribution increases by $150,000 [($100 − $40) × 2,500], which exceeds the additional costs incurred of $55,000. It would not be worthwhile for CI to incur any incremental costs to reduce machining time consumed at the stamping operation. Other operating costs will increase, but throughput contribution will remain unaffected. Throughput contribution increases only by increasing bottleneck output. Machine time is not bottlenecked and increasing non-bottleneck output has no effect.

◆ *Improve the quality of parts or products manufactured at the bottleneck operation.* Poor quality is often more costly at a bottleneck operation than it is at a non-bottleneck operation. The cost of poor quality at a non-bottleneck operation is the cost of materials wasted. If CI produces 1,000 defective doors at the stamping operation, the cost of poor quality is $40,000 (direct materials cost per unit, $40 × 1,000 doors). No throughput contribution is forgone because stamping has excess capacity. Despite the defective production, stamping can produce and transfer 90,000 doors to the pressing operation. At a bottleneck operation, the cost of poor quality is the cost of materials wasted plus the opportunity cost of lost throughput contribution.

Bottleneck capacity not wasted in producing defective units could be used to generate additional sales and throughput contribution. If CI produces 1,000 defective units at the pressing operation, the cost of poor quality is $100,000: direct materials cost of $40,000 (direct materials cost per unit, $40 × 1,000 units) plus forgone throughput contribution of $60,000 [($100 − $40) × 1,000 doors].

The high costs of poor quality at the bottleneck operation mean that bottleneck time should not be wasted processing units that are defective. That is, inspection should be done before processing parts at the bottleneck to ensure that only good-quality units are transferred to the bottleneck operation. Also, quality-improvement programs should focus on ensuring that bottlenecks produce minimal defects.

If the remedies are successful, the capacity of the pressing operation will increase and eventually exceed the capacity of the stamping operation. The bottleneck will then shift to the stamping operation. CI should then focus continuous-improvement actions on increasing stamping efficiency and capacity. For example, the contract with Gemini Industries to stamp 2,000 doors at $6 per door from direct materials supplied by CI becomes attractive now because throughput contribution increases by ($100 − $40) × 2,000 − $120,000, while costs increase by $12,000 ($6 × 2,000). TOC emphasizes the management of bottlenecks as the key to improving the performance of the system as a whole. It focuses on the short-run maximization of throughput contribution—revenues minus materials costs.

TOC is less useful for the long-run management of costs, because it does not model the behaviour of costs or identify individual activities and cost drivers. Instead, it regards operating costs as given and fixed. ABC is an alternative strategy that takes a longer-run perspective when more costs can be managed; the focus is on improving processes by eliminating non-value-added activities and reducing the costs of performing value-added activities. ABC systems, therefore, are more useful for long-run pricing, long-run cost control and profit planning, and capacity management. The short-run TOC emphasis on maximizing throughput contribution by managing bottlenecks complements the long-run strategic-cost-management focus of ABC.[10]

BSC AND TIME-RELATED MEASURES

In this section, we use the balanced scorecard to summarize how financial and non-financial measures of time relate to one another. We classify these measures under the four perspectives of the balanced scorecard—financial, customer, internal business

---

[10]For an excellent evaluation of TOC, operations management, cost accounting, and the relationship between TOC and activity-based costing, see A. Atkinson, "Cost Accounting, the Theory of Constraints, and Costing" (Issue Paper, CMA Canada, December 2000).

Debottlenecking on the Internet!

In 2004, Intel's chief technology officer, Patrick Gelsinger, warned that the World Wide Web was becoming so overloaded with traffic that it might eventually collapse. In 2007 Deloitte & Touche confirmed that exponential[11] growth in web use was creating online bottlenecks as too many people were trying to simultaneously access the same information on the same server. This is a particularly serious problem for companies that take orders online because more than 40% of online shoppers abandon a transaction if response time is too slow. In 2006, Wal-Mart, Disney, and Amazon.com lost millions in sales because their sites crashed during the busiest shopping day of the year in the US, Thanksgiving. In 2007, a two-day crash in voice-over IP (VoIP) telephone service company Skype reduced the market value of shares of its parent company, e-Bay, by over $1 billion. Debottlenecking is an activity that will reduce the costs of quality failures and support either a cost or value leadership strategy.

Debottlenecking remedies include remote caching (storing duplicated data) and remote mirroring. Social networking site MySpace stores its seldom-updated content on Akamai's third-party global network of over 15,000 servers. Each MySpace user's request for content is routed to the Akamai's server that is geographically closest and results in the fastest data transmission or cycle time between request for content and its delivery. Remote mirroring is the storage of huge databases in different geographically remote locations. Using redundant arrays of inexpensive disks (RAID), each extra copy is not only a backup in the event of system crashes but relieves traffic congestion by enabling rerouting around bottlenecks to data RAID sites with lower traffic and faster response times. Both remedies relieve bottleneck constraints, increase capacity, and reduce customer-response time to improve the profitability of the Internet's most popular sites.

Sources: *Risk Management* (May 2001); *The Wall Street Journal* (March 20, 2001); *Business Wire* (October 4, 1999); and a poll conducted by http://www.esearch.com in 1999; "'Beware of the End of the World (Wide Web),' Says Intel," Fortune.com, September 10, 2004, http://www.forbes.com/execpicks/feeds/general/2004/09/10/generalcomtex_2004_09_10_ir_0000-5884-KEYWORD.Missing.html, accessed September 13, 2004; "Downtime and Lost Revenue," NetSource America, http://www.netsourceamerica.com/welcome.html, accessed June 5, 2006; D. Shand, "Banish Bottlenecks," *Computer World,* April 10, 2000, http://www.computerworld.com/news/2000/story/0,11280,44371,00.html, accessed September 17, 2004; T. Wilson, "The Cost of Downtime," http://internetweek.cmp.com/lead/lead073099.htm, accessed June 5, 2006; D. Riley, "EBay Sees $1 billion Knocked Off Market Cap; Skype Outages Continue," Techcrunch.com (August 16, 2007), http://www.techcrunch.com/2007/08/15/ebay-sees-1-billion=knocked-off=market-cap-as-skype-outages-continue, accessed September 10, 2007; *Telecommunications Predictions: TMT Trends 2007.* Deloitte Touche Tohmatsu (January 2007); E. Schuman, "Black Friday Turns Servers Dark at Wal-Mart, Macy's" eWeek.com, http://www.eweek.com/article2/0,1759,206354,00.asp?kc=EWRSS03119TX1K0000.594, accessed September 12, 2007; "If You're Going to Plan Online Doorbusters, Shouldn't You Plan Ahead for the Traffic?" Techdirt.com, http://www.techdirt.com/articles/20061127/003210.shtml, accessed September 12, 2007.

processes, and learning and growth. Managers use the balanced scorecard measures to reduce delays and to increase throughput of their bottleneck operations.

Financial measures

Revenue losses or price discounts attributable to delays

Carrying cost of inventories

Throughput contribution minus operating costs

Customer measures

Customer-response time (the time it takes to fulfill a customer order)

On-time performance (delivering a product or service by the scheduled time)

[11]A pattern for an exponential function is curvilinear $f(x) = ax^b$ and results from raising a fixed base x to a variable power b = 1, 2, 3 . . . for example.

Internal-business-process measures

Average manufacturing time for key products

Idle time at bottleneck operations

Defective units produced at bottleneck operations

Average reduction in setup time and processing time at bottleneck operations

Learning and growth measures

Employee satisfaction

Number of employees trained in managing bottleneck operations

Note the cause-and-effect linkages across these measures. For example, better employee training leads to better management of bottleneck operations, which in turn leads to better customer-response times and higher revenues and throughput contributions. Managers use time-related measures in the balanced scorecard to help them identify actions that improve customer-response times and create long-run competitive advantage.

PULLING IT ALL TOGETHER—PROBLEM FOR SELF-STUDY

(Try to solve this problem before examining the solution that follows.)

PROBLEM

The Sloan Corporation is a moving company that transports household goods from one city to another within North America. It measures quality of service in terms of (a) time required to transport goods, (b) on-time delivery (within two days of agreed-upon delivery date), and (c) number of lost or damaged shipments. Sloan is considering investing in a new scheduling and tracking system costing $160,000 per year, which should help it improve performance with respect to items (b) and (c). The following information describes Sloan's current performance and the expected performance if the new system is implemented:

	Current Performance	Expected Future Performance
On-time delivery performance	85%	95%
Variable costs per carton lost or damaged	$60	$60
Fixed cost per carton lost or damaged	$40	$40
Number of cartons lost or damaged per year	3,000 cartons	1,000 cartons

Sloan expects that each percentage point increase in on-time performance will result in revenue increases of $20,000 per year. Sloan's contribution margin percentage is 45%.

REQUIRED

1. Should Sloan acquire the new system?
2. What is the minimum amount of revenue increase that needs to occur for the benefits from the new system to exceed the costs?
3. What nonfinancial measures may be important?
4. What other nonfinancial benefits may be obtained?

SOLUTION

1. Additional costs of the new scheduling and tracking system are $160,000 per year.

Additional annual sales from improving on-time performance $20,000 (95% − 85% or 10 percentage points)	$200,000
Contribution margin from additional annual revenues 45% × $200,000	$ 90,000
Reduction in costs per year from fewer cartons lost or damaged (only variable costs are relevant) $60 × (3,000 − 1,000)	120,000
Total additional benefits	$210,000

Therefore, since benefits outweigh costs, Sloan should acquire the new system.

2. As long as Sloan earns a contribution margin of $40,000 (to cover incremental costs of $160,000—relevant variable cost savings of $120,000) from additional annual sales, investing in the new system is beneficial. This contribution margin corresponds to additional sales of $40,000 ÷ 0.45 = $88,889.

3. The new system performance provides Sloan with the time to serve more customers without expanding its fleet. This nonfinancial measure will help assess whether the anticipated benefits were realized. It also affords Sloan a new opportunity, perhaps, to tell its customers where in the transportation system the product is. This nonfinancial measure of effectiveness may also help Sloan identify opportunities to improve its internal business process. It enables Sloan to identify bottlenecks and devise remedies.

4. The longer-term benefits to Sloan include opportunities such as providing tracking services for others in the supply chain as a new source of revenue. This new service may require some additional infrastructure such as a website, but the cost is low relative to the cost of increasing the fleet. The tracking service to customers could reduce the number of customer complaints in two ways. First, tracking enables Sloan to debottleneck and actually reduce transportation time. Second, customers observing the transport process improve their own understanding of where unavoidable delays can occur. By using nonfinancial measures, Sloan can more carefully target its service to meet or exceed the value proposition of its customers and improve its competitiveness.

SUMMARY POINTS

The following question-and-answer format summarizes the chapter's learning outcomes. Each point presents a key question, and the guidelines are the answer to that question.

LEARNING OUTCOMES	GUIDELINES
1. What are the four categories of a cost-of-quality program and how does BSC help identify and reduce the costs of quality failure?	Four cost categories in a cost-of-quality program are prevention, appraisal, internal failure, and external failure costs. The financial perspective from the BSC enables a management team to identify the costs of quality failure. These are the costs of detection and prevention, appraisal, and internal and external failure. The cost of external failure is highest because there is a risk of losing customers. ISO 31000 standards assist teams in identifying and controlling enterprise-wide risks such as the cost of quality-control failures after external detection. Learning and experience contribute to cost reduction from rework and product recalls, repairs, and replacements.
2. What methods can managers use to identify quality problems and improve quality?	Three methods to identify quality problems and improve quality are (a) control charts, which distinguish random from nonrandom variations in an operating process; (b) Pareto diagrams, which indicate how frequently each type of failure occurs; and (c) cause-and-effect diagrams, which identify potential causes of failure.

3. How do managers augment the relevant costs and benefits of quality improvements?	The relevant costs of quality improvements are the incremental costs to implement the quality program. The relevant benefits are the cost savings and the estimated increase in contribution margin from the higher sales due to quality improvements. Nonfinancial measures of customer satisfaction include number of customer complaints and on-time delivery rate. Nonfinancial measures of internal quality performance include product defect levels and process yields. Financial data help managers decide on tradeoffs among prevention, appraisal, and failure costs where nonfinancial measures direct attention to problems.
4. What is customer-response time? What are the reasons for and the costs of delays?	Customer-response time is the duration between the time a customer places an order for a product or service and the time the product or service is delivered to the customer. Delays occur because of (a) uncertainty about when customers will order products or services and (b) bottlenecks due to limited capacity. Bottlenecks are operations at which the work to be performed approaches or exceeds the available capacity. The costs of delays include lower revenues and increased inventory carrying costs.
5. What three measures do managers need to implement the theory of constraints?	The three measures in the theory of constraints are (a) throughput contribution (equal to revenues minus direct materials cost of the goods sold); (b) investments (equal to the sum of materials costs in direct materials, and work-in-process and finished goods inventories, R&D costs, and costs of equipment and buildings); and (c) operating costs (equal to all operating costs, other than direct materials costs, incurred to earn throughput contribution).

TERMS TO LEARN

This chapter and the Glossary at the end of the book contain definitions of the following important terms:

appraisal costs (p. 757)
average waiting time (p. 774)
bottleneck (p. 773)
cause-and-effect diagram (p. 767)
conformance quality (p. 756)
control chart (p. 765)
costs of quality (COQ) (p. 756)
cumulative average time learning
    model (p. 763)
cushion (p. 774)

customer-response time (p. 772)
experience curve (p. 760)
external failure costs (p. 757)
incremental unit time learning
    model (p. 761)
internal failure costs (p. 757)
learning curve (p. 759)
manufacturing cycle efficiency (p. 773)
manufacturing cycle time (p. 773)
manufacturing lead time (p. 773)

on-time performance (p. 773)
order delivery time (p. 773)
order receipt time (p. 772)
outliers (p. 765)
Pareto diagram (p. 766)
prevention costs (p. 757)
quality of design (p. 756)
theory of constraints (TOC)
    (p. 776)
time driver (p. 773)

ASSIGNMENT MATERIAL

MyAccountingLab   Make the grade with MyAccountingLab: The questions, exercises, and problems marked in red can be found on MyAccountingLab at **www.myaccountinglab.com.** You can practise them as often as you want, and most feature step-by-step guided instructions to help you find the right answer. Exercises and problems with an Excel icon in the margin have an accompanying Excel template on MyAccountingLab.

SHORT-ANSWER QUESTIONS

19-1   Describe two benefits of improving quality.

19-2   How does conformance quality differ from quality of design? Explain.

19-3   Name two items classified as prevention costs.

19-4   Distinguish between internal failure costs and external failure costs.

19-5 "Companies should focus on financial measures of quality because these are the only measures of quality that can be linked to bottom-line performance." Do you agree? Explain.

19-6 Give two examples of nonfinancial measures of customer satisfaction.

19-7 "There is no tradeoff between customer-response time and on-time performance." Do you agree? Explain.

19-8 Give two reasons why delays occur.

19-9 "Companies should always make and sell all products whose selling prices exceed variable costs." Do you agree? Explain.

19-10 Describe the three main measures used in the theory of constraints.

19-11 Describe the four key steps in managing bottleneck resources.

19-12 Of what strategic importance is it to management accountants to understand the learning-curve effect on costs?

EXERCISES

19-13 Terminology. A number of terms are listed below:

appraisal costs	cause-and-effect diagram
conformance quality	control chart
costs of quality (COQ)	cumulative average-time learning model
design costs	experience curve
external failure costs	incremental unit-time learning model
internal failure costs	learning curve
Pareto diagram	prevention costs
quality of design	

REQUIRED

Select the terms from the above list to complete the following sentences.

The cost of quality failures include those of _____, _____, _____, and _____. The costs may arise from poor _____, and the output will fail to meet customer expectations. They may also arise from poor _____ or failure during production to conform to design specifications. The total ____ __ _____ (___) failure in the customer's hand are not merely financial but can be nonfinancial, including fatalities. A high-quality process quality management system will track all four COQ types to detect and prevent quality failures. Successful quality control can be measured using a BSC. From the perspective of customers, market share and size can increase. From the learning and growth perspective, analysis and tracking of the both the _____ and _____ _____ improves the reliability of predictions of orderly cost decreases. Both the _____ ____ _____ _____ and _____ _____ _____ ____ _____ will improve the management and control of quality. From the perspective of internal business control, quality can be tracked using a _____ _____, _____ _____, and _____ _____ or fishbone diagrams.

19-14 Learning curve, cumulative average-time learning model. Global Defence manufactures radar systems. It has just completed the manufacture of its first newly designed system, RS-32. Manufacturing data for the RS-32 follow:

At 4 units the total variable MOH = $145,800

	A	B	C
1	Direct material cost	$80,000	per unit of RS-32
2	Direct manufacturing labour time for first unit	3,000	direct manufacturing labour-hours
3	Learning curve for manufacturing labour time per radar system	90%	cumulative average time[a]
4	Direct manufacturing labour cost	$ 25	per direct manufacturing labour-hour
5	Variable manufacturing overhead cost	$ 15	per direct manufacturing labour-hour
6			
7	[a]Using the formula (p. 762), for a 90% learning curve, $b = \dfrac{\ln 0.90}{\ln 2} = \dfrac{-0.105361}{0.693147} = -0.152004$		
8			

Calculate the total variable costs of producing 2, 4, and 8 units.

19-15 Learning curve, incremental unit-time learning model. Assume the same information for Global Defence as in Exercise 19-14, except that Global Defence uses a 90% incremental unit-time learning model as a basis for predicting direct manufacturing labor-hours. (A 90% learning curve means $b = 0.152004$.)

1. At 2 units the total DMLH cost = $142,500

REQUIRED

1. Calculate the total variable costs of producing 2, 3, and 4 units.
2. If you solved Exercise 19-14, compare your cost predictions in the two exercises for 2 and 4 units. Why are the predictions different? How should Global Defence decide which model it should use?

19-16 Costs of quality. (CMA, adapted) Costen Inc. produces cell phone equipment. Jessica Tolmy, Costen's president, decided to devote more resources to the improvement of product quality after learning that her company had been ranked fourth in product quality in a 2010 survey of cell phone users. Costen's quality-improvement program has now been in operation for two years, and the cost report shown below has recently been issued.

1. 6/30/2011 total quality costs % of revenues, 24.7%

Semi-Annual COQ Report, Costen Inc.
(in thousands)

	6/30/2011	12/31/2011	6/30/2012	12/31/2012
Prevention costs				
Machine maintenance	$ 440	$ 440	$ 390	$ 330
Supplier training	20	100	50	40
Design reviews	50	214	210	200
Total prevention costs	510	754	650	570
Appraisal costs				
Incoming inspections	108	123	90	63
Final testing	332	332	293	203
Total appraisal costs	440	455	383	266
Internal failure costs				
Rework	231	202	165	112
Scrap	124	116	71	67
Total internal failure costs	355	318	236	179
External failure costs				
Warranty repairs	165	85	72	68
Customer returns	570	547	264	188
Total external failure costs	735	632	336	256
Total quality costs	$2,040	2,159	$1,605	$1,271
Total revenues	$8,240	$9,080	$9,300	$9,020

REQUIRED

1. For each period, calculate the ratio of each COQ category to revenues and to total quality costs.
2. Based on the results of requirement 1, would you conclude that Costen's quality program has been successful? Prepare a short report to present your case.
3. Based on the 2013 survey, Jessica Tolmy believed that Costen had to improve product quality. In making her case to Costen management, how might Tolmy have estimated the opportunity cost of not implementing the quality-improvement program?

19-17 Costs of quality analysis. Safe Rider produces car seats for children from newborn to two years old. The company is worried because one of its competitors has recently come under public scrutiny because of product failure. Historically, Safe Rider's only problem with its car seats was stitching in the straps. The problem can usually be detected and repaired during an internal inspection. The cost of the inspection is $5, and the repair cost is $1. All 100,000 car seats were inspected last year and 5% were found to have problems with the stitching in the straps during the internal inspection. Another 2% of the 100,000 car seats had problems with the stitching, but the internal inspection did not discover them.

1. Appraisal cost, $500,000

Defective units that were sold and shipped to customers needed to be shipped back to Safe Rider and repaired. Shipping costs are $10, and repair costs are $1. However, the out-of-pocket costs (shipping and repair) are not the only costs of defects not discovered in the internal inspection. For 20% of the external failures, negative word of mouth will result in a loss of sales, lowering the following year's contribution margin by $500 for each of the 20% of units with external failures.

REQUIRED

1. Calculate appraisal cost.
2. Calculate internal failure cost.
3. Calculate out-of-pocket external failure cost.
4. Determine the opportunity cost associated with the external failures.
5. What are the total costs of quality?
6. Safe Rider is concerned with the high up-front cost of inspecting all 100,000 units. It is considering an alternative internal inspection plan that will cost only $1.50 per car seat inspected. During the internal inspection, the alternative technique will detect only 2.5% of the 100,000 car seats that have stitching problems. The other 4.5% will be detected after the car seats are sold and shipped. What are the total costs of quality for the alternative technique?
7. What factors other than cost should Safe Rider consider before changing inspection techniques?

1. a. Cost of improving quality of plastic, $2,500,000

19-18 Costs of quality analysis, ethical considerations. Refer to information in Exercise 19-17 in answering this question. Safe Rider has discovered a more serious problem with the plastic core of its car seats. An accident can cause the plastic in some of the seats to crack and break, resulting in serious injuries to the occupant. It is estimated that this problem will affect about 200 car seats in the next year. This problem could be corrected by using a higher quality of plastic that would increase the cost of every car seat produced by $25. If this problem is not corrected, Safe Rider estimates that out of the 200 accidents, customers will realize that the problem is due to a defect in the seats in only two cases. Safe Rider's legal team has estimated that each of these two accidents would result in a lawsuit that could be settled for about $750,000. All lawsuits settled would include a confidentiality clause, so Safe Rider's reputation would not be affected.

REQUIRED

1. Assuming that Safe Rider expects to sell 100,000 car seats next year, what would be the cost of increasing the quality of all 100,000 car seats?
2. What will be the total cost of the lawsuits next year if the problem is not corrected?
3. Safe Rider has decided not to increase the quality of the plastic because the cost of increasing the quality exceeds the benefits (saving the cost of lawsuits). What do you think of this decision? (*Note:* Because of the confidentiality clause, the decision will have no effect on Safe Rider's reputation.)
4. Are there any other costs or benefits that Safe Rider should consider?

1. a. 2012 percentage of defective units shipped, 5%

19-19 Nonfinancial measures of quality and time. Worldwide Cell Phones (WCP) has developed a cell phone that can be used anywhere in the world (even in countries like Japan that have a relatively unique cell phone system). WCP has been receiving complaints about the phone. For the past two years, WCP has been test marketing the phones and gathering nonfinancial information related to actual and perceived aspects of the phone's quality. They expect that, given the lack of competition in this market, increasing the quality of the phone will result in higher sales and thereby higher profits.

Quality data for 2012 and 2013 include the following:

	2012	2013
Cell phones produced and shipped	2,000	10,000
Number of defective units shipped	100	400
Number of customer complaints	150	250
Units reworked before shipping	120	700
Manufacturing lead time	15 days	16 days
Average customer-response time	30 days	28 days

REQUIRED

1. For each year, 2012 and 2013, calculate:
   a. Percentage of defective units shipped.
   b. Customer complaints as a percentage of units shipped.
   c. Percentage of units reworked during production.
   d. Manufacturing lead time as a percentage of total time from order to delivery.
2. Referring to the information computed in requirement 1, explain whether WCP's quality and timeliness have improved.
3. Why would manufacturing lead time have increased while customer-response time decreased? (It may be useful to first describe what is included in each time measurement—see Exhibit 19-11 on p. 767.)

19-20 Quality improvement, relevant costs, relevant revenues. TechnoPrint manufactures and sells 20,000 high-technology printing presses each year. The variable and fixed costs of rework and repair are as follows:

	Variable Costs	**Fixed Cost**	**Total Cost**
Rework cost per hour	$ 80	$120	$200
Repair costs			
Customer support cost per hour	40	60	100
Transportation cost per load	360	120	480
Warranty repair cost per hour	90	130	220

TechnoPrint's current presses have a quality problem that causes variations in the shade of some colours. Its engineers suggest changing a key component in each press. The new component will cost $55 more than the old one. In the next year, however, TechnoPrint expects that with the new component it will (1) save 12,875 hours of rework, (2) save 900 hours of customer support, (3) move 200 fewer loads, (4) save 7,000 hours of warranty repairs, and (5) sell an additional 150 printing presses, for a total contribution margin of $1,800,000. TechnoPrint believes that even as it improves quality, it will not be able to save any of the fixed costs of rework or repair. TechnoPrint uses a one-year time horizon for this decision, because it plans to introduce a new press at the end of the year.

REQUIRED

1. Should TechnoPrint change to the new component? Show your calculations.
2. Suppose the estimate of 150 additional printing presses sold is uncertain. What is the minimum number of additional printing presses that TechnoPrint needs to sell to justify adopting the new component?

19-21 Nonfinancial quality measures, on-time delivery. Checkers Pizza promises to deliver pizzas in 25 minutes or less. If pizzas are not delivered on time, then the customer receives $5 off the price of the order. Some store managers, who receive bonuses based on store profits, believe that the guarantee is a win-win situation for Checkers. Because the average pizza sells for $9 but has a marginal cost of $2.25, the store makes a profit no matter what the delivery time. If a pizza is delivered on time, then the store earns $6.75 ($9 − $2.25) per pizza. If a pizza is delivered late, then the store still earns $1.75 ($9 − $5 − $2.25) per pizza. If more than one pizza is ordered, then Checkers makes even more money because it gives only one $5 discount per order.

The head of the Checkers chain is worried that this perceived win-win situation may encourage a complacent attitude in store managers with respect to on-time deliveries. While short-run profits are still earned with late deliveries, repeated late deliveries could lead to annoyance on the part of customers and eventually to a loss of customers. Therefore, the Checkers corporate headquarters has decided to gather information about late deliveries and customer satisfaction. It has developed a survey that asks delivery customers to rate their satisfaction based on three attributes: delivery service, value for money, and overall satisfaction with Checkers. Responses can range from 1 to 5, where 1 is "Awful" and 5 is "Excellent." The following responses were gathered from stores in a single city:

	Store 1	**Store 2**	**Store 3**	**Store 4**
Percentage of deliveries that were late	10%	5%	12%	25%
Average rating of delivery service	4	4.5	3.8	2
Average rating of value received	3.5	4.1	3.5	1.5
Average overall satisfaction with Checkers	3.6	4	3	2

4

1. Waiting time, 9 minutes

REQUIRED

1. Examine the relationship between the percentage of deliveries that were late and average responses to the three survey questions. Do the data provide any support for Checkers headquarters' concerns?
2. Estimate the effect of changes in the late-delivery percentage on average overall satisfaction with Checkers. Use the customer satisfaction score as the dependent variable. Based on this analysis, compute the impact of a change from 5% late deliveries to 7% late deliveries on overall customer satisfaction.
3. What factors would Checkers need to consider when determining whether the delivery guarantee is actually beneficial for the company?

19-22 Waiting time, service industry. The registration advisers at a small university (SU) help 4,000 students develop each of their class schedules and register for classes each semester. Each adviser works for 10 hours a day during the registration period. SU currently has 10 advisers. While advising an individual student can take anywhere from 2 to 30 minutes, it takes an average of 12 minutes per student. During the registration period, the 10 advisers see an average of 300 students a day.

REQUIRED

1. Using the formula on p. 774, calculate how long the average student will have to wait in the adviser's office before being advised.
2. The head of the registration advisers would like to increase the number of students seen each day, because at 300 students a day it would take 14 working days to see all of the students. This is a problem because the registration period lasts for only two weeks (10 working days). If the advisers could advise 400 students a day, it would take only two weeks (about 10 days). However, they want to make sure that the waiting time is not excessive. What would be the average waiting time if 400 students were seen each day?
3. SU wants to know the effect of reducing the average advising time on the average wait time. If SU can reduce the average advising time to 10 minutes, what would be the average waiting time if 400 students were seen each day?

4

1. a. Wait time, 12 minutes

19-23 Waiting time, cost considerations, customer satisfaction. Refer to the information presented in Exercise 19-22. The head of the registration advisers at SU has decided that the advisers must finish their advising in two weeks and therefore must advise 400 students a day. However, the average waiting time given a 12-minute advising period will result in student complaints, as will reducing the average advising time to 10 minutes. SU is considering two alternatives:

a. Hire two more advisers for the two-week (10-working-day) advising period. This will increase the available number of advisers to 12 and therefore lower the average waiting time.
b. Increase the number of days that the advisers will work during the two-week registration period to 6 days a week. If SU increases the number of days worked to six per week, then the 10 advisers need only see 350 students a day to advise all the students in two weeks.

REQUIRED

1. What would the average wait time be under each alternative described above?
2. If advisers earn $100 per day, which alternative would be cheaper for SU (assume that if advisers work 6 days in a given work week, they will be paid time and a half for the sixth day)?
3. From a student satisfaction point of view, which of the two alternatives would be preferred? Why?

4

2. Total manufacturing time, 22 days

19-24 Manufacturing cycle time, manufacturing cycle efficiency. (CMA, adapted) Torrance Manufacturing evaluates the performance of its production managers based on a variety of factors, including cost, quality, and cycle time. The following information relates to the average amount of time needed to complete an order for its one product:

Wait time:	
From order being placed to start of production	8 days
From start of production to completion	6 days
Inspection time	2 days
Process time	4 days
Move time	2 days

REQUIRED

1. Compute the manufacturing cycle efficiency for an order.
2. Compute the manufacturing cycle time (or lead time) for an order.

19-25 Theory of constraints, throughput contribution, relevant costs. The Mayfield Corporation manufactures filing cabinets in two operations: machining and finishing. It provides the following information:

5

1. Increase in throughput contribution, $40,000

	Machining	Finishing
Annual capacity	100,000 units	80,000 units
Annual production	80,000 units	80,000 units
Fixed operating costs (excluding direct materials)	$640,000	$400,000
Fixed operating costs per unit produced ($640,000 ÷ 80,000; $400,000 ÷ 80,000)	$8 per unit	$5 per unit

Each cabinet sells for $72 and has direct material costs of $32 incurred at the start of the machining operation. Mayfield has no other variable costs. Mayfield can sell whatever output it produces. The following requirements refer only to the preceding data. There is no connection between the requirements.

REQUIRED

1. Mayfield is considering using some modern jigs and tools in the finishing operation that would increase annual finishing output by 1,000 units. The annual cost of these jigs and tools is $30,000. Should Mayfield acquire these tools? Show your calculations.
2. The production manager of the Machining department has submitted a proposal to do faster setups that would increase the annual capacity of the Machining department by 10,000 units and would cost $5,000 per year. Should Mayfield implement the change? Show your calculations.
3. An outside contractor offers to do the finishing operation for 12,000 units at $10 per unit, double the $5 per unit that it costs Mayfield to do the finishing in-house. Should Mayfield accept the subcontractor's offer? Show your calculations.
4. The Hunt Corporation offers to machine 4,000 units at $4 per unit, half the $8 per unit that it costs Mayfield to do the machining in-house. Should Mayfield accept Hunt's offer? Show your calculations.

19-26 Theory of constraints, throughput contribution, quality. Refer to the information in Exercise 19-25 in answering the following requirements. There is no connection between the requirements.

5

2. Forgone throughput contribution, $80,000

REQUIRED

1. Mayfield produces 2,000 defective units at the machining operation. What is the cost to Mayfield of the defective items produced? Explain your answer briefly.
2. Mayfield produces 2,000 defective units at the finishing operation. What is the cost to Mayfield of the defective items produced? Explain your answer briefly.

PROBLEMS

19-27 Quality improvement, relevant costs, and relevant revenues. The Thomas Corporation sells 300,000 V262 valves to the automobile and truck industry. Thomas has a capacity of 110,000 machine-hours and can produce 3 valves per machine-hour. V262's contribution margin per unit is $8. Thomas sells only 300,000 valves because 30,000 valves (10% of the good valves) need to be reworked. It takes 1 machine-hour to rework 3 valves, so 10,000 hours of capacity are used in the rework process. Thomas's rework costs are $210,000. Rework costs consist of:

2

1. Contribution margin per machine-hour for V262, $24

♦ Direct materials and direct rework labour (variable costs): $3 per unit
♦ Fixed costs of equipment, rent, and overhead allocation: $4 per unit

Thomas's process designers have developed a modification that would maintain the speed of the process and ensure 100% quality and no rework. The new process would cost $315,000 per year. The following additional information is available:

♦ The demand for Thomas's V262 valves is 370,000 per year.
♦ The Jackson Corporation has asked Thomas to supply 22,000 T971 valves (another product) if Thomas implements the new design. The contribution margin per T971 valve is $10. Thomas can make two T971 valves per machine-hour with 100% quality and no rework.

1. Suppose Thomas's designers implement the new design. Should Thomas accept Jackson's order for 22,000 T971 valves? Show your calculations.
2. Should Thomas implement the new design? Show your calculations.
3. What nonfinancial and qualitative factors should Thomas consider in deciding whether to implement the new design?

19-28 Quality improvement, relevant costs, and relevant revenues. The Tan Corporation uses multicolour moulding to make plastic lamps. The moulding operation has a capacity of 200,000 units per year. The demand for lamps is very strong. Tan will be able to sell whatever output quantities it can produce at $40 per lamp.

Tan can start only 200,000 units into production in the Moulding department because of capacity constraints on the moulding machines. If a defective unit is produced at the moulding operation, it must be scrapped at a net disposal value of zero. Of the 200,000 units started at the moulding operation, 30,000 defective units (15%) are produced. The cost of a defective unit, based on total (fixed and variable) manufacturing costs incurred up to the moulding operation, equals $25 per unit, as follows:

Direct materials (variable)	$16 per unit
Direct manufacturing labour, setup labour, and materials-handling labour (variable)	3 per unit
Equipment, rent, and other allocated overhead, including inspection and testing costs on scrapped parts (fixed)	6 per unit
Total	$25 per unit

Tan's designers have determined that adding a different type of material to the existing direct materials would result in no defective units being produced, but it would increase the variable costs by $4 per lamp in the Moulding department.

REQUIRED

1. Should Tan use the new material? Show your calculations.
2. What nonfinancial and qualitative factors should Tan consider in making the decision?

19-29 Statistical quality control, airline operations. Jetrans Airlines operates daily round-trip flights on the London–Vancouver route using a fleet of three 747s: the Spirit of Birmingham, the Spirit of Glasgow, and the Spirit of Manchester. The budgeted quantity of fuel for each round-trip flight is the 12-month mean (average) round-trip fuel consumption of 757,082 litres, with a standard deviation of 75,708 litres. A litre-unit is 3,785.4 litres. Therefore the round-trip fuel consumption average is 200 litre-units, with a standard deviation of 20 litre-units. This is an example of the conference method of estimating costs using complex, but industry-appropriate, units.

Using a statistical quality control (SQC) approach, Shirley Watson, the Jetrans operations manager, investigates any round-trip with fuel consumption that is greater than two standard deviations from the mean. In October, Watson receives the following report for round-trip fuel consumption for the three planes on the London–Vancouver route:

Flight	Spirit of Birmingham (Litre-Units)	Spirit of Glasgow (Litre-Units)	Spirit of Manchester (Litre-Units)
1	208	206	194
2	187	188	208
3	194	192	221
4	202	214	208
5	211	184	242
6	215	226	234
7	216	198	249
8	218	212	227
9	221	202	232
10	232	186	244

Side margin notes:
1. Additional direct materials cost, $800,000
1. Control limit, 160 to 240 litre-units

REQUIRED

1. Using the $\pm 2\sigma$ rule, what variance-investigation decisions would be made?
2. Present SQC charts for round-trip fuel usage for each of the three 747s in October. What inferences can you draw from the charts?
3. Some managers propose that Jetrans Airlines present its SQC charts in monetary terms rather than in physical-quantity terms (litre-units). What are the advantages and disadvantages of using monetary fuel costs rather than litre-units in the SQC charts?

19-30 Compensation linked with profitability, waiting time, and quality measures. Mid-Atlantic Healthcare USA operates two medical groups, one in Philadelphia and one in Baltimore. The semi-annual bonus plan for each medical group's president has three components:

1. Philadelphia January–June bonus paid, $156,500

a. *Profitability performance.* Add 1% of operating income.
b. *Average patient waiting time.* Add $50,000 if the average waiting time for a patient to see a doctor after the scheduled appointment time is less than 15 minutes. If average patient waiting time is more than 15 minutes, add nothing.
c. *Patient satisfaction performance.* Deduct $50,000 if patient satisfaction (measured using a survey asking patients about their satisfaction with their doctor and their overall satisfaction with Mid-Atlantic Healthcare) falls below 70 on a scale from 0 (lowest) to 100 (highest). No additional bonus is awarded for satisfaction scores of 70 or more.

Semi-annual data for 2013 for the Philadelphia and Baltimore groups are as follows:

	January–June	July–December
Philadelphia		
Operating income	$10,650,000	$10,600,000
Average waiting time	14 minutes	16 minutes
Patient satisfaction	79	82
Baltimore		
Operating income	$9,000,000	$950,000
Average waiting time	17 minutes	14.5 minutes
Patient satisfaction	66	70

REQUIRED

1. Compute the bonuses paid in each half year of 2013 to the Philadelphia and Baltimore medical group presidents.
2. Discuss the validity of the components of the bonus plan as measures of profitability, waiting-time performance, and patient satisfaction. Suggest one shortcoming of each measure and how it might be overcome (by redesign of the plan or by another measure).
3. Why do you think Mid-Atlantic Healthcare USA includes measures of both operating income and waiting time in its bonus plan for group presidents? Give one example of what might happen if waiting time were dropped as a performance measure.

19-31 Waiting times, manufacturing lead times. The SRG Corporation uses an injection moulding machine to make a plastic product, Z39. SRG makes products only after receiving firm orders from its customers. SRG estimates that it will receive 50 orders for Z39 (each order is for 1,000 units) during the coming year. Each order of Z39 will take 80 hours of machine time. The annual capacity of the machine is 5,000 hours.

1. a. Average order waiting time for Z39, 160 hours

REQUIRED

1. Calculate (a) the average amount of time that an order for Z39 will wait in line before it is processed and (b) the average manufacturing lead time per order for Z39.
2. SRG is considering introducing a new product, Y28. SRG expects it will receive 25 orders of Y28 (each order for 200 units) in the coming year. Each order of Y28 will take 20 hours of machine time. The average demand for Z39 will be unaffected by the introduction of Y28. Calculate (a) the average waiting time for an order received and (b) the average manufacturing lead time per order for each product, if SRG introduces Y28.

19-32 Waiting times, relevant revenues, and relevant costs (continuation of 19-31). SRG is still deciding whether it should introduce Y28. The following table provides information on selling prices, variable costs, and inventory carrying costs for Z39 and Y28. SRG will incur additional variable costs and inventory carrying costs for Y28 only if it introduces Y28. Fixed costs equal to 40% of variable costs are allocated to all products produced and sold during the year.

| Product | Annual Average Number of Orders | Selling Price per Order If Average Manufacturing Lead Time per Order Is | | Variable Cost per Order | Inventory Carrying Cost per Order per Hour |
		Less than 320 Hours	More than 320 Hours		
Z39	50	$27,000	$26,500	$15,000	$0.75
Y28	25	8,400	8,000	5,000	0.25

REQUIRED

1. Should SRG manufacture and sell Y28? Show your calculations.
2. Should SRG manufacture and sell Y28 if the data are changed as follows: Selling price per order is $6,400, instead of $8,400, if average manufacturing lead time per order is less than 320 hours; and $6,000, instead of $8,000, if average manufacturing lead time per order is more than 320 hours. All other data for Y28 are the same.

19-33 Manufacturing lead times, relevant revenues, and relevant costs. The Brandt Corporation makes wire harnesses for the aircraft industry. Brandt is uncertain about when and how many customer orders will be received. The company makes harnesses only after receiving firm orders from its customers. Brandt has recently purchased a new machine to make two types of wire harnesses, one for Boeing airplanes (B7) and the other for Airbus Industries airplanes (A3). The annual capacity of the new machine is 6,000 hours. The following information is available for next year:

| Customer | Annual Average Number of Orders | Manufacturing Time Required | Selling Price per Order If Average Manufacturing Lead Time per Order Is | | Variable Cost per Order | Inventory Carrying Cost per Order per Hour |
			Less than 200 Hours	More than 200 Hours		
B7	125	40 hours	$15,000	$14,400	$10,000	$0.50
A3	10	50 hours	13,500	12,960	9,000	0.45

REQUIRED

1. Calculate the average manufacturing lead times per order (a) if Brandt manufactures only B7 and (b) if Brandt manufactures both B7 and A3.
2. Even though A3 has a positive contribution margin, Brandt's managers are evaluating whether Brandt should (a) make and sell only B7 or (b) make and sell both B7 and A3. Which alternative will maximize Brandt's operating income? Show your calculations.
3. What other factors should Brandt consider in choosing between the alternatives in requirement 2?

19-34 Theory of constraints, throughput contribution, relevant costs. Cabano Industries manufactures electronic testing equipment. Cabano also installs the equipment at customers' sites and ensures that it functions smoothly. Additional information on the Manufacturing and Installation departments is as follows (capacities are expressed in terms of the number of units of electronic testing equipment):

	Equipment Manufactured	Equipment Installed
Annual capacity	400 units per year	300 units per year
Equipment manufactured and installed	300 units per year	300 units per year

Cabano manufactures only 300 units per year because the Installation department has only enough capacity to install 300 units. The equipment sells for $40,000 per unit (installed) and has direct material costs of $15,000. All costs other than direct material costs are fixed. The following requirements refer only to the preceding data. There is no connection between the requirements.

REQUIRED

1. Cabano's engineers have found a way to reduce equipment manufacturing time. The new method would cost an additional $50 per unit and would allow Cabano to manufacture 20 additional units a year. Should Cabano implement the new method? Show your calculations.
2. Cabano's designers have proposed a change in direct materials that would increase direct material costs by $2,000 per unit. This change would enable Cabano to install 320 units of equipment each year. If Cabano makes the change, it will implement the new design on all equipment sold. Should Cabano use the new design? Show your calculations.
3. A new installation technique has been developed that will enable Cabano's engineers to install 10 additional units of equipment a year. The new method will increase installation costs by $50,000 each year. Should Cabano implement the new technique? Show your calculations.
4. Cabano is considering how to motivate workers to improve their productivity (output per hour). One proposal is to evaluate and compensate workers in the Manufacturing and Installation departments on the basis of their productivities. Do you think the new proposal is a good idea? Explain briefly.

19-35 Theory of constraints, throughput contribution, quality, relevant costs. Aardee Industries manufactures pharmaceutical products in two departments: Mixing and Tablet-Making. Additional information on the two departments follows. Each tablet contains 0.5 grams of direct materials.

5. Direct materials costs per tablet, $0.40

	Mixing	Tablet Making
Capacity per hour	150 grams	200 tablets
Monthly capacity		
(2,000 hours available in each department)	300,000 grams	400,000 tablets
Monthly production	200,000 grams	390,000 tablets
Fixed operating costs (excluding direct materials)	$ 16,000	$ 39,000
Fixed operating cost per tablet		
($16,000 ÷ 200,000 grams; $39,000 ÷ 390,000 tablets)	$ 0.08 per gram	$ 0.10 per tablet

The Mixing department makes 200,000 grams of direct materials mixture (enough to make 400,000 tablets) because the Tablet-Making department has only enough capacity to process 400,000 tablets. All direct material costs are incurred in the Mixing department. Aardee incurs $156,000 in direct material costs. The Tablet-Making department manufactures only 390,000 tablets from the 200,000 grams of mixture processed; 2.5% of the direct materials mixture is lost in the tablet-making process. Each tablet sells for $1. All costs other than direct material costs are fixed costs. The following requirements refer only to the preceding data. There is no connection between the requirements.

REQUIRED

1. An outside contractor makes the following offer: If Aardee will supply the contractor with 10,000 grams of mixture, the contractor will manufacture 19,500 tablets for Aardee (allowing for the normal 2.5% loss of the mixture during the tablet-making process) at $0.12 per tablet. Should Aardee accept the contractor's offer? Show your calculations.
2. Another company offers to prepare 20,000 grams of mixture a month from direct materials Aardee supplies. The company will charge $0.07 per gram of mixture. Should Aardee accept the company's offer? Show your calculations.
3. Aardee's engineers have devised a method that would improve quality in the Tablet-Making department. They estimate that the 10,000 tablets currently being lost would be saved. The modification would cost $7,000 a month. Should Aardee implement the new method? Show your calculations.
4. Suppose that Aardee also loses 10,000 grams of mixture in its Mixing department. These losses can be reduced to zero if the company is willing to spend $9,000 per month in quality-improvement methods. Should Aardee adopt the quality-improvement method? Show your calculations.

Cost Management: Quality, Time, and the Theory of Constraints **793**

5. What are the benefits of improving quality in the Mixing Department compared with improving quality in the Tablet-Making Department?

1. Appraisal costs, $300,000

19-36 Governance and quality. Information from a quality report for 2012 prepared by Lindsey Williams, assistant controller of Citocell, a manufacturer of electric motors, is as follows:

Revenue	$10,000,000
Inspection of production	$ 90,000
Warranty liability	$ 260,000
Product testing	$ 210,000
Scrap	$ 230,000
Design engineering	$ 200,000
Percentage of customer complaints	5%
On-time delivery rate	93%

Davey Evans, the plant manager of Citocell, is eligible for a bonus if the total costs of quality as a percentage of revenue are less than 10%, the percentage of customer complaints is less than 4%, and the on-time delivery rate exceeds 92%. Evans is unhappy about the customer complaints of 5% because, when preparing her report, Williams actually surveyed customers regarding customer satisfaction. Evans expected Williams to be less proactive and to wait for customers to complain. Evans's concern with Williams's approach is that it introduces subjectivity into the results and also fails to capture the seriousness of customers' concerns. "When you wait for a customer to complain, you know he is complaining because it is something important. When you do customer surveys, customers mention whatever is on their mind, even if it is not terribly important."

John Roche, the controller, asks Williams to see him. He tells her about Evans's concerns. "I think Davey has a point. See what you can do." Williams is confident that the customer complaints are genuine and that customers are concerned about quality and service. She believes it is important for Citocell to be proactive and obtain systematic and timely customer feedback, and then to use this information to make improvements. She is also well aware that Citocell has not done customer surveys in the past, and that, except for her surveys, Evans would probably be eligible for the bonus. She is confused about how to handle Roche's request.

REQUIRED
1. Calculate the ratio of each cost-of-quality category (prevention, appraisal, internal failure, and external failure) to revenue in 2012. Are the total costs of quality as a percentage of revenue less than 10%?
2. Would it be unethical for Williams to modify her analysis? What steps should Williams take to resolve this situation?

1. Chatty Chelsey contribution margin per unit, $16

19-37 Theory of constraints, contribution margin, sensitivity analysis. Low Tech Toys (LTT) produces dolls in two processes: moulding and assembly. LTT is currently producing two models: Chatty Chelsey and Talking Tanya. Production in the Moulding department is limited by the amount of materials available. Production in the Assembly department is limited by the amount of trained labour available. The only variable costs are materials in the Moulding department and labour in the Assembly department. Following are the requirements and limitations by doll model and department:

	Moulding Materials	Assembly Time	Selling Price
Chatty Chelsey	1.5 kg per doll	20 minutes per doll	$35 per doll
Talking Tanya	2 kg per doll	30 minutes per doll	$45 per doll
Materials/labour available	30,000 kg	8,400 hours	
Cost	$10 per kg	$12 per hour	

REQUIRED
1. If LTT sold only one type of doll, which doll would it produce? How many of these dolls would it make and sell?
2. If LTT sells two Chatty Chelseys for each Talking Tanya, how many dolls of each type would it produce and sell? What would be the total contribution margin?

3. If LTT sells two Chatty Chelseys for each Talking Tanya, how much would production and contribution margin increase if the Moulding department could buy 10 more kilograms of materials for $10 per kilogram?
4. If LTT sells two Chatty Chelseys for each Talking Tanya, how much would production and contribution margin increase if the Assembly department could get 10 more labour-hours at $12 per hour?

19-38 Methods of analyzing quality-control problems. The Murray Corporation manufactures, sells, and installs photocopying machines. Murray has placed heavy emphasis on reducing defects and failures in its production operations. Murray wants to apply the same total quality management (TQM) principles to managing its accounts receivables.

2
1. One example is long delay in receiving payment.

REQUIRED
1. On the basis of your knowledge and experience, what would you classify as failures in accounts receivables?
2. Give examples of prevention activities that could reduce failures in accounts receivables.
3. Draw a Pareto diagram of the types of failures in accounts receivables and a fishbone diagram of possible causes of one type of failure in accounts receivables.

19-39 BSC analysis of quality. (CMA, adapted) Bergen Inc. produces cell phones at its London plant. In recent years, the company's market share has been eroded by stiff competition from Asian and European competitors. Price and product quality are the two key areas in which companies compete in this market.

1
1. One fact is that total quality costs as a percentage of total revenue have declined from 23.4% to 13.1%.

Jerry Holman, Bergen's president, decided to devote more resources to the improvement of product quality after learning that his company's products had been ranked fourth in product quality in a 2011 survey of telephone equipment users. He believed that Bergen could no longer afford to ignore the importance of product quality. Bergen's quality improvement program has now been in operation for two years, and the cost report shown below has recently been issued.

As they were reviewing the report, Sheila Haynes, manager of sales, asked Tony Reese, production manager, what he thought of the quality program. "The work is really moving through the Production Department," replied Reese. "We used to spend time helping the Customer Service Department solve their problems, but they are leaving us alone these days."

Semi-Annual Costs of Quality Report, Bergen Inc.
(in thousands)

	6/30/2012	12/31/2012	6/30/2013	12/31/2013
Prevention costs				
Machine maintenance	$ 258	$ 258	$ 228	$ 192
Training suppliers	6	54	24	18
Design reviews	24	122	120	114
Total prevention costs	288	434	372	324
Appraisal costs				
Incoming inspection	54	64	43	26
Final testing	192	192	168	113
Total appraisal costs	246	256	211	139
Internal failure costs				
Rework	144	127	106	74
Scrap	82	77	50	48
Total internal failure costs	226	204	156	122
External failure costs				
Warranty repairs	83	37	30	28
Customer returns	314	301	139	96
Total external failure costs	397	338	169	124
Total quality costs	$1,157	$1,232	$ 908	$ 709
Total production and sales	$4,944	$5,448	$5,580	$5,412

1. By analyzing the Cost-of-Quality Report presented, determine whether Bergen Inc.'s quality-improvement program has been successful. List specific evidence to support your answer.
2. Jerry Holman believed that the quality-improvement program was essential and that Bergen Inc. could no longer afford to ignore the importance of product quality. Discuss how Bergen could measure the opportunity cost of not implementing the quality-improvement program.

19-40 BSC analysis of quality. Ontario Industries manufactures two types of refrigerators, Olivia and Solta. Information on each refrigerator is as follows:

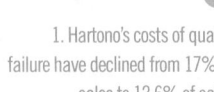

1. Olivia Prevention costs, 2.25% of revenue

	Olivia	Solta
Units manufactured and sold	10,000 units	5,000 units
Selling price	$2,400	$1,800
Variable costs per unit	$1,440	$ 960
Hours spent on design	6,000	1,000
Testing and inspection hours per unit	1	0.5
Percentage of units reworked in plant	5%	10%
Rework costs per refrigerator	$ 600	$ 480
Percentage of units repaired at customer site	4%	8%
Repair costs per refrigerator	$ 720	$ 540
Estimated lost sales from poor quality	—	300 units

The labour rates per hour for various activities are as follows:

Design	$90 per hour
Testing and inspection	$48 per hour

REQUIRED

1. Calculate the costs of quality for Olivia and Solta classified into prevention, appraisal, internal failure, and external failure categories.
2. For each type of refrigerator, calculate the ratio of each COQ item as a percentage of sales. Compare and comment on the costs of quality for Olivia and Solta.
3. Give two examples of nonfinancial quality measures that Ontario Industries could monitor as part of a total quality-control effort.

19-41 Financial and nonfinancial analysis of quality. The Hartono Corporation manufactures and sells industrial grinders. The following table presents financial information pertaining to quality in 2013 and 2012 (in thousands):

1. Hartono's costs of quality failure have declined from 17% of sales to 12.6% of sales

	2012	2013
Sales	$10,000	$12,500
Line inspection	110	85
Scrap	250	175
Design engineering	100	240
Cost of returned goods	60	145
Product-testing equipment	50	50
Customer support	40	30
Rework costs	160	135
Preventive equipment inspection	35	90
Product liability claims	200	100
Incoming materials inspection	20	40
Breakdown maintenance	90	40
Product-testing labour	220	75
Training	45	120
Warranty repair	300	200
Supplier evaluations	20	50

1. Classify the cost items in the table into prevention, appraisal, internal failure, or external failure categories.
2. Calculate the ratio of each COQ category to sales in 2012 and 2013. Comment on the trends in costs of quality between 2012 and 2013.
3. Give two examples of nonfinancial quality measures that Hartono Corporation could monitor as part of a total quality-control effort.

19-42 Financial and nonfinancial analysis of quality. Pacific-Dunlop supplies tires to major automotive companies. It has two tire plants in Ontario, in Kitchener and Napanee. The quarterly bonus plan for each plant manager has three components:

a. **Profitability performance.** Add 2% of operating income.
b. **On-time delivery performance.** Add $12,000 if on-time delivery performance to the ten most important customers is 98% or better. If on-time performance is below 98%, add nothing.
c. **Product quality performance.** Deduct 50% of cost of sales returns from the ten most important customers.

Quarterly data for 2012 on the Kitchener and Napanee plants are as follows:

1. Total bonus paid April–June, Kitchener, $15,600

	January–March	April–June	July–September	October–December
Kitchener				
Operating income	$ 960,000	$1,020,000	$ 840,000	$1,080,000
On-time delivery*	98.4%	98.6%	97.1%	97.9%
Cost of sales returns*	$ 21,600	$ 31,200	$ 12,000	$ 30,000
Napanee				
Operating income	$1,920,000	$1,800,000	$2,160,000	$2,280,000
On-time delivery*	95.6%	97.1%	97.9%	98.4%
Cost of sales returns*	$ 42,000	$ 40,800	$ 33,600	$ 26,400

*For the ten most important customers.

REQUIRED

1. Compute the bonuses paid in each quarter of 2012 to the plant managers of the Kitchener and Napanee plants.
2. Discuss the three components of the bonus plan as measures of profitability, on-time delivery, and product quality.
3. Why would you want to evaluate plant managers on the basis of both operating income and on-time delivery?
4. Give one example of what might happen if on-time delivery were dropped as a performance evaluation measure.

19-43 Customer-response time, on-time delivery. Pizzafest Inc. makes and delivers pizzas to homes and offices in the Vancouver area. Fast, on-time delivery is one of Pizzafest's key strategies. Pizzafest provides the following information for the year 2012 about its customer-response time—the amount of time between when a customer calls to place an order and when the pizza is delivered to the customer:

1. Pizzas delivered in 30 minutes or less January–June, 2012, 25%

	January–June	July–December
1. Pizzas delivered in 30 minutes or less	120,000	180,000
2. Pizzas delivered in between 31 and 45 minutes	240,000	312,000
3. Pizzas delivered in between 46 and 60 minutes	96,000	84,000
4. Pizzas delivered in between 61 and 75 minutes	24,000	24,000
Total pizzas delivered	480,000	600,000

REQUIRED

1. For January–June 2012 and July–December 2012, calculate the percentage of pizzas delivered in each of the four time intervals (30 minutes or less, 31 to 45 minutes, 46 to 60 minutes, and 61 to 75 minutes). On the basis of these calculations, has customer-response time improved in July–December 2012 compared with January–June 2012?

2. When customers call Pizzafest, they often ask how long it will take for the pizza to be delivered to their home or office. If Pizzafest quotes a long time interval, customers will often not place the order. If Pizzafest quotes too short a time interval and the pizza is not delivered on time, customers get upset and Pizzafest will lose repeat business. Based on the January–June 2012 data, what maximum customer-response time should Pizzafest quote to its customers if (a) it wants to have an on-time delivery performance of at least 75%, and (b) it wants to have an on-time delivery performance of at least 95%?

3. If Pizzafest had quoted the maximum customer-response times you calculated in requirements 2a and 2b, would it have met its on-time delivery performance targets of 75% and 95% respectively for the period July–December 2012?

COLLABORATIVE LEARNING CASE

1. Incremental revenues,
$5,625,000

19-44 Quality improvement, theory of constraints. The Wellesley Corporation makes printed cloth in two departments: Weaving and Printing. Direct material costs are Wellesley's only variable costs. The demand for Wellesley's cloth is very strong. Wellesley can sell whatever output quantities it produces at $1,250 per roll to a distributor who markets, distributes, and provides customer service for the product. Wellesley provides the following information:

	Weaving	Printing
Monthly capacity	10,000 rolls	15,000 rolls
Monthly production	9,500 rolls	8,550 rolls
Direct material cost per roll of cloth processed at each operation	$ 500	$ 100
Fixed operating costs	$2,850,000	$427,500
Fixed operating cost per roll ($2,850,000, 9,500 rolls; $427,500, 8,550 rolls)	$ 300 per roll	$ 50 per roll

Wellesley can start only 10,000 rolls of cloth in the Weaving department because of capacity constraints of the weaving machines. If the Weaving department produces defective cloth, the cloth must be scrapped and yields zero net disposal value. Of the 10,000 rolls of cloth started in the Weaving department, 500 (5%) defective rolls are produced. The cost of a defective roll, based on total (fixed and variable) manufacturing cost per roll incurred up to the end of the weaving operation, equals $785 per roll, as follows:

Direct material cost per roll (variable)	$500
Fixed operating cost per roll ($2,850,000 ÷ 10,000 rolls)	285
Total manufacturing cost per roll in Weaving department	$785

The good rolls from the Weaving department (called grey cloth) are sent to the Printing department. Of the 9,500 good rolls started at the printing operation, 950 (10%) defective rolls are produced and scrapped at zero net disposal value. The cost of a defective roll based on total (fixed and variable) manufacturing cost per unit incurred up to the end of the printing operation, equals $930 per roll, calculated as follows:

Total manufacturing cost per roll in Weaving department		$785
Printing department manufacturing cost per roll		
Direct material cost per roll (variable)	$100	
Fixed operating cost per roll ($427,500 ÷ 9,500 rolls)	45	
Total manufacturing cost per roll in Printing department		145
Total manufacturing cost per roll		$930

The Wellesley Corporation's total monthly sales of printed cloth equal the Printing department's output. Each requirement refers only to the preceding data. There is no connection between the requirements.

REQUIRED

1. The Printing department is considering buying 5,000 additional rolls of grey cloth from an outside supplier at $900 per roll. The Printing department manager is concerned that the cost of purchasing the grey cloth is much higher than Wellesley's cost of manufacturing it. The quality of the grey cloth acquired from the outside supplier is very similar to that manufactured in-house. The Printing department expects that 10% of the rolls obtained from the outside supplier will result in defective products. Should the Printing department buy the grey cloth from the outside supplier? Show your calculations.

2. Wellesley's engineers have developed a method that would lower the Printing department's rate of defective products to 6% at the printing operation. Implementing the new method would cost $350,000 per month. Should Wellesley implement the change? Show your calculations.

3. The design engineering team has proposed a modification that would lower the Weaving department's rate of defective products to 3%. The modification would cost the company $175,000 per month. Should Wellesley implement the change? Show your calculations.

19-45 Curvilinear cost functions. Below are the data and some results of an OLS linear regression. The explanatory power of the quantity produced and sold (the predictor variable) to explain changes in the size of the indirect manufacturing cost pool is approximately 38%. This exceeds the threshold value for r^2 for a reliable relationship of 30%. As a management accountant who is familiar with OLS linear regression modelling, you are, however, uneasy with the results.

1. The scatter of actual (X,Y) data points around the (X,y) predicted regression line shows a pattern.

Observation	Cumulative Q of Sales & Production	Quantity Q Sold & Produced	Indirect Manufacturing Cost Pool	Average Cost per Unit
1	198	198	$277.200	$1.400
2	398	200	196.000	0.980
3	792	592	406.112	0.686
4	1153	561	384.846	0.686
5	1317	164	112.504	0.686
6	1584	267	128.213	0.480
7	2296	712	341.902	0.480
8	2816	520	249.704	0.480
9	2933	117	56.183	0.480
10	3168	235	78.993	0.336
11	3852	684	229.920	0.336
12	4348	496	166.725	0.336
13	4551	203	68.236	0.336
14	4812	261	87.733	0.336
15	5515	703	236.306	0.336
16	6091	576	193.617	0.336
17	6336	245	57.648	0.235
18	6587	251	59.060	0.235
19	7274	687	161.650	0.235
20	7846	572	134.590	0.235
21	8102	256	60.236	0.235
22	8303	201	47.295	0.235
23	9026	723	170.120	0.235
24	9709	683	160.709	0.235
25	10001	292	68.707	0.235
26	10255	254	59.766	0.235

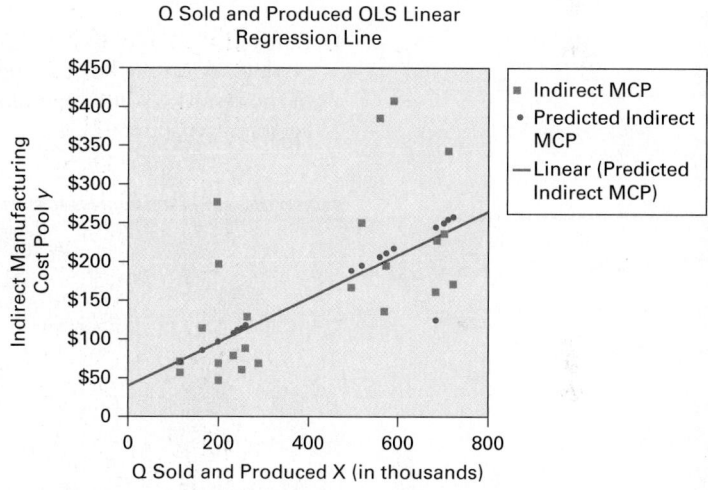

Q Sold and Produced OLS Linear Regression Line

Regression Statistics	DMH	Std Error	t-Stat	P-value
R Square	0.3837			
Observations	26.0			
df	25.0			
Intercept a	$36.4844	36.2683	1.0060	0.3245
Slope b	$0.3046	0.0788	3.8651	0.0007
Confidence	95.0%		95.0%	
Critical Value df = 25	2.060		2.060	

In groups of two or three, complete the following requirements.

1. What output causes your unease?
2. What step did you miss, and what should you do at this point?
3. Examine the plot of the residuals. How would the management team interpret this result? What is the next step?

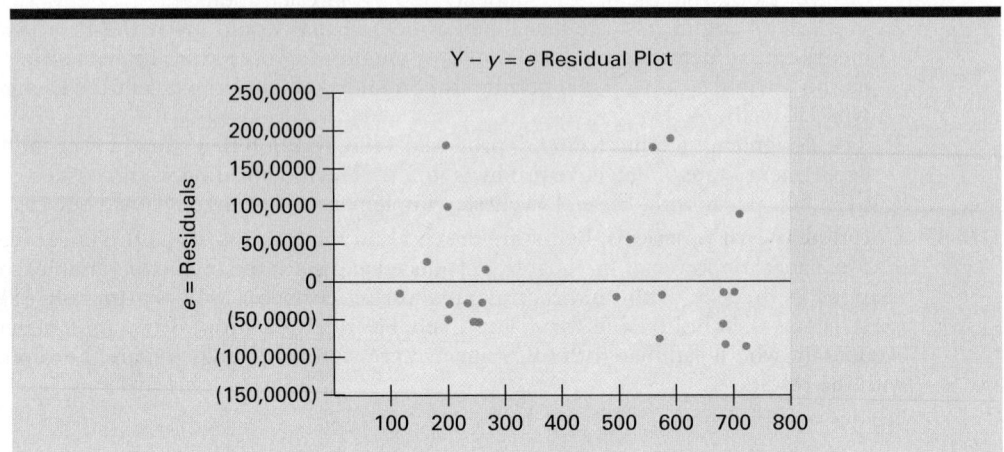

4. Refer to the table of data. Using Excel, plot the actual values of the quarterly MOH cost pool. Click on the box to report R^2 and add a logarithmic trendline. Below is an illustration of the result of your Excel plot. What does this step of the specification analysis tell a management accountant?

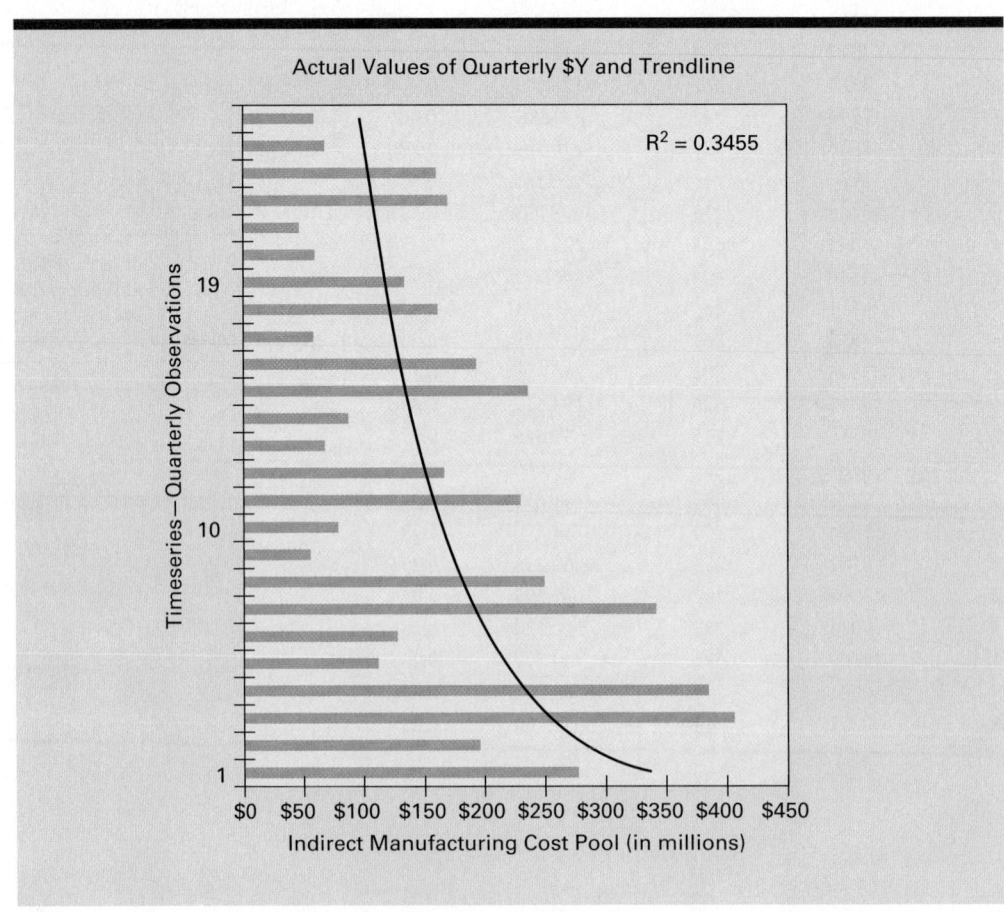

5. Using Excel, plot the average-cost-per-unit curve including a trendline. Of what use is this information to the management team?

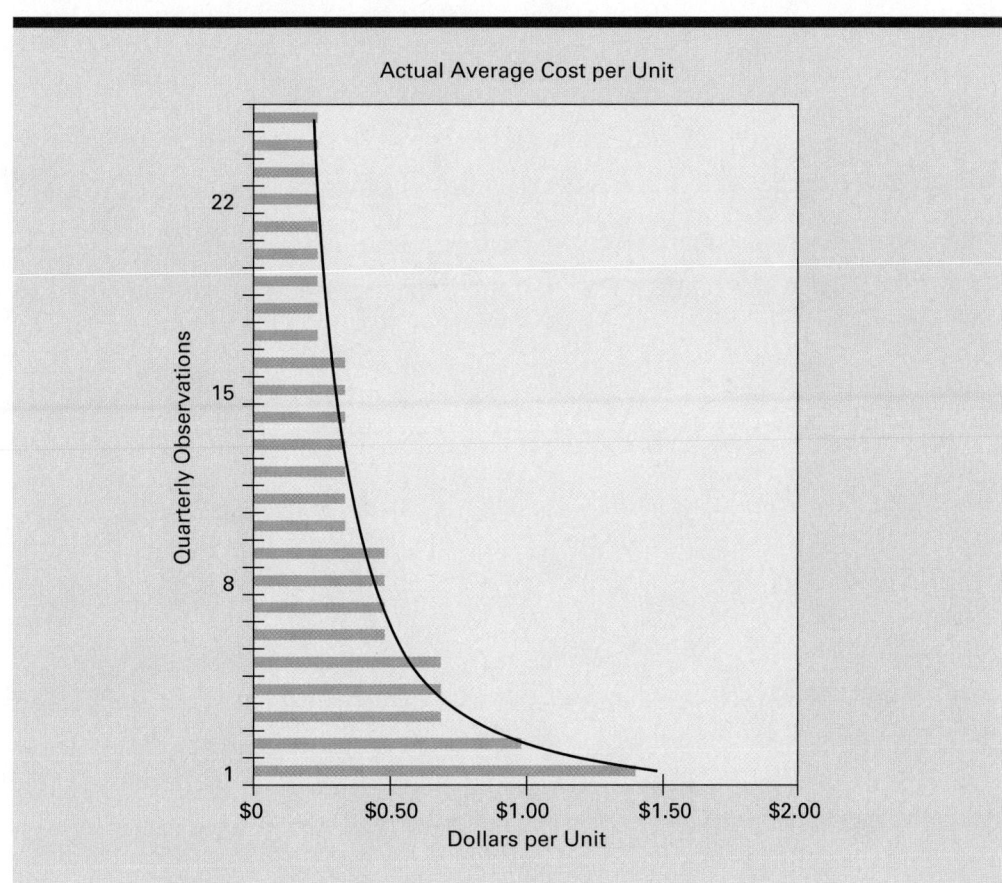

Inventory Cost Management Strategies

BUSINESS MATTERS

Inventory Cost Management Strategies

Customers require much shorter order-to-delivery cycles. Manufacturers respond by demanding more frequent and exceptionally reliable, fast delivery of components from their suppliers. Transportation companies such as Challenger Freight have invested in MIS to improve response times and deliver materials quickly on a just-in-time (JIT) basis. For manufacturers, this reduces inventory levels and costs. The manufacturer's agile response allows customer demand to pull products through the production cycle rather than the manufacturing-push of products through the production cycle to await a customer's order.

At the extreme, companies such as Dell do not even begin assembly until the order has been placed and paid for. In an intensely competitive environment where the product life cycle may be as short as 90 days before substitutes are available, Dell customizes its product to customer specifications yet adheres to a cost leadership strategy. It manages its supply chain so that materials are not ordered until required. The JIT system and the demand pull of Dell means the company carries little if any inventory. An alternative cost accounting system, backflush costing, simplifies the inventory accounting cycle as well.

LEARNING OUTCOMES

After studying this chapter, you should be able to

1. Evaluate relevant data and decide on the economic order quantity (EOQ).

2. Resolve conflicts that can arise from results of EOQ and performance models.

3. Analyze the relevant benefits and costs of JIT alternatives.

4. Differentiate a materials requirements planning (MRP) strategy from an enterprise resource planning (ERP) strategy of supply-chain management.

5. Evaluate and decide upon an appropriate backflush costing method.

In this chapter, three supply-chain strategies are presented, compared, and contrasted. Supply-chain management is a strategy. The buyer and suppliers act in partnership, sharing otherwise sensitive and confidential information to reduce partnership costs below what could be achieved separately (see Chapter 13). There are several alternatives and the goal is to manage and control the cost of inventory yet ensure a smooth flow of production. Retail and manufacturing companies alike need to manage their COGS as well as revenue as they meet the demand of customers and maximize revenue. Under just-in-time materials requirement planning, and back-flush costing methods of accounting for inventory, the tradeoffs among various costs differ but the goals remain constant.

Inventory management is a pivotal part of profit planning for manufacturing and merchandising companies. Materials costs can account for more than 50% of total costs in some manufacturing companies and more than 70% of total costs in retail companies. Unused material is unsold product, and the carrying costs to retain material in various inventories can represent up to 35% of annual manufacturing costs. Accounting information has a key role in inventory valuation and cost control strategies.

INVENTORY MANAGEMENT

1 Evaluate relevant data and decide on the economic order quantity (EOQ).

Inventory management is the planning, coordinating, and control activities related to the flow of inventory into, through, and from the organization. Costs associated with goods for resale include opportunity costs of which the management accountant is aware but which are not recorded in the financial accounting management information system (MIS). Consider retailers where the cost of goods sold constitutes the largest single cost item. The following breakdown of operations for two major retailers is illustrative:

	Loblaw Companies	Sobeys Inc.
Sales	100.0%	100.0%
Cost of sales and other expenses	91.9%	95.9%
Depreciation and amortization	1.8%	1.4%
Interest and taxes	2.6%	1.1%
Net income	3.7%	1.6%

With a high level of perishable inventory and low net income percentage, managers in the grocery retail industry must make accurate decisions regarding the purchasing and managing of goods for sale or incur avoidable costs of spoilage. Dry good inventories also require a cash outflow to suppliers, and the shorter the cash-to-cash cycle, the higher will be the revenue for these retailers.

COSTS ASSOCIATED WITH GOODS FOR SALE

The descriptions of the cost categories indicate that some of the relevant costs for making inventory decisions and managing goods for sale are not available in existing accounting systems. The following cost categories are important when managing inventories and goods for sale:

◆ **Purchasing costs** consist of the acquisition costs of goods acquired from suppliers including freight in, the transportation costs. These direct costs usually make up the largest single cost category of goods for sale. Supplier credit terms, discounts for different purchase order sizes, and frequency of ordering affect purchasing costs.

◆ **Ordering costs** consist of the costs to prepare and issue a purchase order. These support department overhead costs vary with the number of purchase orders processed, special processing, receiving, inspection, and payment costs.

- **Carrying costs** arise when a business holds inventories of goods for sale. These manufacturing overhead costs include the costs associated with storage, such as storage space rental and insurance, obsolescence, and spoilage, which are reported by the financial accounting management information system (MIS). Also relevant for managers are the opportunity costs of the investment tied up in inventory (see Chapter 11), assessed by applying managerial accounting techniques.

- **Stockout costs** occur when a company runs out of an item for which there is customer demand. A company may respond to the shortfall or stockout by expediting an order from a supplier. Expediting costs of a stockout include the additional ordering costs plus any associated transportation costs. Alternatively, the company may lose a sale due to the stockout. In this case, stockout costs include the opportunity cost of the lost contribution margin on the sale plus any contribution margin lost on future sales hurt by customer ill-will caused by the stockout.

- *Costs of quality (COQ)* were defined and discussed in Chapter 19. Four categories of costs of quality are often distinguished: (a) prevention costs, (b) appraisal costs, (c) internal failure costs, and (d) external failure costs.

- **Shrinkage costs** arise from theft, embezzlement, misclassifications, and clerical errors. This cost is measured by the difference between the cost of inventory recorded without theft or other incidents and the cost of inventory physically counted. Shrinkage is often an important performance measure by which management effectiveness is evaluated. In grocery retail the operating margin is very small—approximately 2%. Control of inventory shrinkage is one of a store manager's prime responsibilities. To make up for a loss of $1,000 due to shrinkage, a store would have to earn an additional $50,000 in revenue ($1,000 ÷ 0.02 = $50,000).

Information technology, such as the scheduling, inventory control, and costing system software provided by Seradex, and bar code and radio-frequency identification (RFID) on items, increases reliability and timeliness of inventory data. For example, bar-coding technology is a low-cost way to capture purchases and sales of individual units. This creates an instantaneous record of inventory movements and helps in the management of purchasing, carrying, and stockout costs. In the sections that follow, we consider how to calculate relevant costs for different inventory-related decisions.

ECONOMIC ORDER QUANTITY PROCUREMENT MODEL

For manufacturers, procurement is basically the placement of a purchase order in enough time to ensure continuous processing. The first major decision in managing goods for sale is deciding how much of a given product to order. The management team can use an **economic order quantity (EOQ)** procurement model to calculate the optimal quantity of inventory to order. The simplest version of this model incorporates only ordering costs and carrying costs into the calculation. Assume:

- The same fixed quantity is ordered at each reorder point.
- Demand, ordering costs, and carrying costs are certain. The **purchase order lead time**—the time between the placement of an order and its delivery—is also certain.
- Purchasing costs per unit are unaffected by the quantity ordered. This assumption makes purchasing costs irrelevant to determining EOQ, because purchasing costs of all units acquired will be the same, whatever the order size in which the units are ordered.
- No stockouts occur. One justification for this assumption is that the costs of a stockout are prohibitively high. We assume that to avoid these potential costs, management always maintains adequate inventory so that no stockout can occur.

♦ In deciding the size of the purchase order, management considers the COQ and shrinkage only to the extent that these costs affect ordering costs or carrying costs.

Given these assumptions, EOQ analysis ignores purchasing costs, stockout costs, and quality costs. To determine EOQ, we minimize the relevant ordering and carrying costs (those ordering and carrying costs that are affected by the quantity of inventory ordered):

Total relevant costs = Total relevant order costs + Total relevant carrying costs

Within the decision framework, the following example of DVDWorld assumes that the management team understands its procurement process and its intensely competitive environment. Second, the company is capital intensive and mass produces commodity output with minimal customization. Third, there are substitute outputs readily available so the management team has adopted a cost leadership strategy. Finally, assume that the required data are available from the MIS to design and implement an effective procurement process.

In this case, as a result of high investment in equipment, profit will improve if the manufacturing process is continuous. More will be produced by the equipment than if the process were interrupted and the company will maximize yield and benefit from economies of scale. Managers want to eliminate controllable interruption to the manufacturing cycle arising from lack of access to materials, labour, and overhead support. In manufacturing a commodity, standardized production means that the procurement process can also be standardized. On the one hand, excess inventory is a non-value-added cost from the customer's perspective but, on the other hand, stockouts will interrupt the continuous process.

Example: DVDWorld, a retailer, sells packages of blank DVDs to its customers. It purchases packages of DVDs from Sontek at $14 a package. Sontek pays all incoming freight. No incoming inspection is necessary, as Sontek has a superb reputation for delivering quality merchandise. Annual demand is 13,000 packages, at a rate of 250 packages per week. DVDWorld requires a 15% annual return on investment. The purchase order lead time is two weeks. The following cost data are available:

Relevant ordering costs per purchase order		$200.00
Relevant carrying costs per package per year:		
Required annual return on investment, 15% × $14	$2.10	
Relevant insurance, materials handling, breakage, etc., per year	3.10	$ 5.20

Carrying costs are higher than you may think. In many companies, average annual carrying costs exceed 30% of purchasing costs. In the DVDWorld example, annual carrying costs are 37% ($5.20 ÷ $14.00) of purchasing costs. What is the economic order quantity of packages of DVDs? The formula underlying the EOQ model is:

$$EOQ = \sqrt{\frac{2DP}{C}}$$

Where:

EOQ = Economic order quantity

D = Demand in units for a specified time period (one year in this example)

P = Relevant ordering costs per purchase order

C = Relevant carrying costs of one unit in stock for the time period used for D (one year in this example)

The formula indicates that EOQ increases with demand and ordering costs and decreases with carrying costs. Notice the square root in this equation. Either an exponent or a square root signals that the relationship is nonlinear—it is a curve, as illustrated in Exhibit 20-1. You may be familiar with calculating EOQ, reorder point, and safety stock from finance or production courses. In those courses, costs for the

EXHIBIT 20-1
Ordering Costs and Carrying Costs for DVDWorld

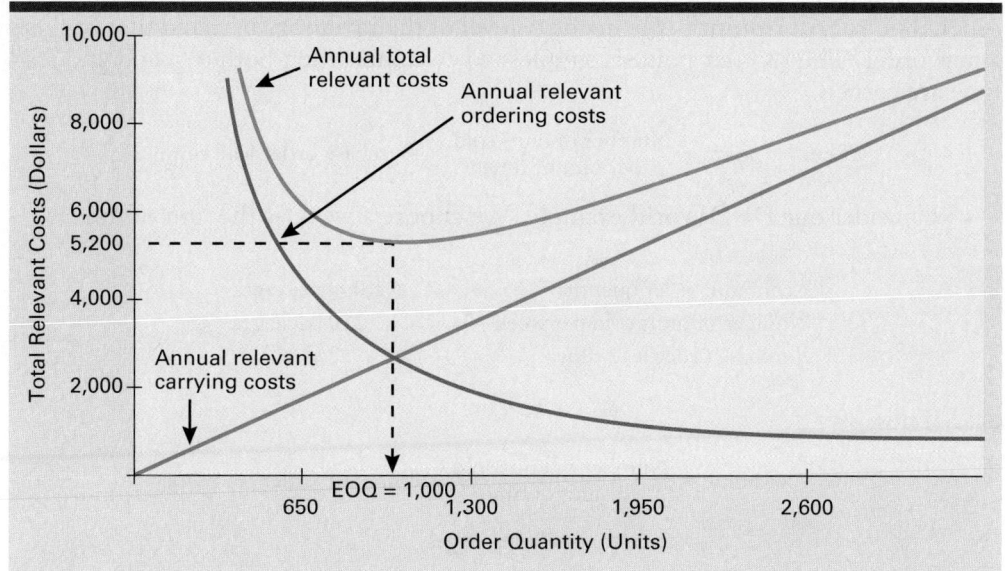

formulas are assumed. Here you will see that management accountants help (1) decide what costs to include in the formulas and (2) estimate the dollar value of the costs. We can use this formula to determine the EOQ for DVDWorld as follows:

$$EOQ = \sqrt{\frac{2 \times 13,000 \times \$200}{\$5.20}} = \sqrt{1,000,000} = 1,000 \text{ packages}$$

Therefore, DVDWorld should order 1,000 DVD packages each time to minimize total ordering and carrying costs. The total annual relevant costs (TRC) for any order quantity Q can be calculated using the following formula:

$$TRC = \begin{array}{c} \text{Total annual relevant} \\ \text{ordering costs} \end{array} + \begin{array}{c} \text{Total annual relevant} \\ \text{carrying costs} \end{array}$$

$$= \begin{array}{c} \text{Number of} \\ \text{purchase orders} \\ \text{per year} \end{array} \times \begin{array}{c} \text{Relevant} \\ \text{ordering costs per} \\ \text{purchase order} \end{array} + \begin{array}{c} \text{Average inventory} \\ \text{in units} \end{array} \times \begin{array}{c} \text{Annual relevant} \\ \text{carrying costs of} \\ \text{1 unit for a year} \end{array}$$

$$= \left(\frac{D}{Q}\right) \times P + \left(\frac{Q}{2}\right) \times C = \frac{DP}{Q} + \frac{QC}{2}$$

(Note that in this formula, Q can be any order quantity, not just the EOQ.) When $Q = 1,000$ units,

$$TRC = \frac{13,000 \times \$200}{1,000} + \frac{1,000 \times \$5.20}{2}$$

$$= \$2,600 + \$2,600 = \$5,200$$

The number of deliveries each time period (in our example, one year) is:

$$\frac{D}{EOQ} = \frac{13,000}{1,000} = 13 \text{ deliveries}$$

Exhibit 20-1 shows a graph analysis of the total annual relevant costs of ordering (DP/Q) and carrying inventory $(QC/2)$ under various order sizes (Q), and illustrates the tradeoff between the two types of costs. The larger the order quantity, the higher the annual relevant carrying costs, but the lower the annual relevant ordering costs. *The total annual relevant costs are at a minimum where total relevant ordering costs and total relevant carrying costs are equal* (in the DVDWorld example, each equals $2,600).

WHEN TO ORDER, ASSUMING CERTAINTY

The second major decision in dealing with cost of goods available for sale is when to order. The **reorder point** is the quantity level of the inventory on hand that triggers a new order. The reorder point is simplest to compute when both demand and lead time are certain:

$$\text{Reorder point} = \frac{\text{Number of units sold}}{\text{per unit of time}} \times \text{Purchase order lead time}$$

Consider our DVDWorld example. We choose a week as the unit of time:

Economic order quantity	1,000 packages
Number of units sold per week	250 packages
Purchase order lead time	2 weeks

Thus:

$$\text{Reorder point} = \frac{\text{Number of units sold}}{\text{per unit of time}} \times \text{Purchase order lead time}$$

$$= 250 \times 2 = 500 \text{ packages}$$

DVDWorld will order 1,000 packages of DVDs each time its inventory stock falls to 500 packages. The intuition for the reorder point is that DVDWorld must reorder when inventory on hand falls to the level at which it equals the amount needed for sales that will occur during the purchase order lead time.

The graph in Exhibit 20-2 presents the behaviour of the inventory level of DVD packages, assuming demand occurs uniformly throughout each week.[1] If the purchase order lead time is two weeks, a new order will be placed when the inventory level reaches 500 DVD packages so that the 1,000 packages ordered are received at the time inventory reaches zero.

EXHIBIT 20-2
Inventory Level of DVD Packages for DVDWorld*

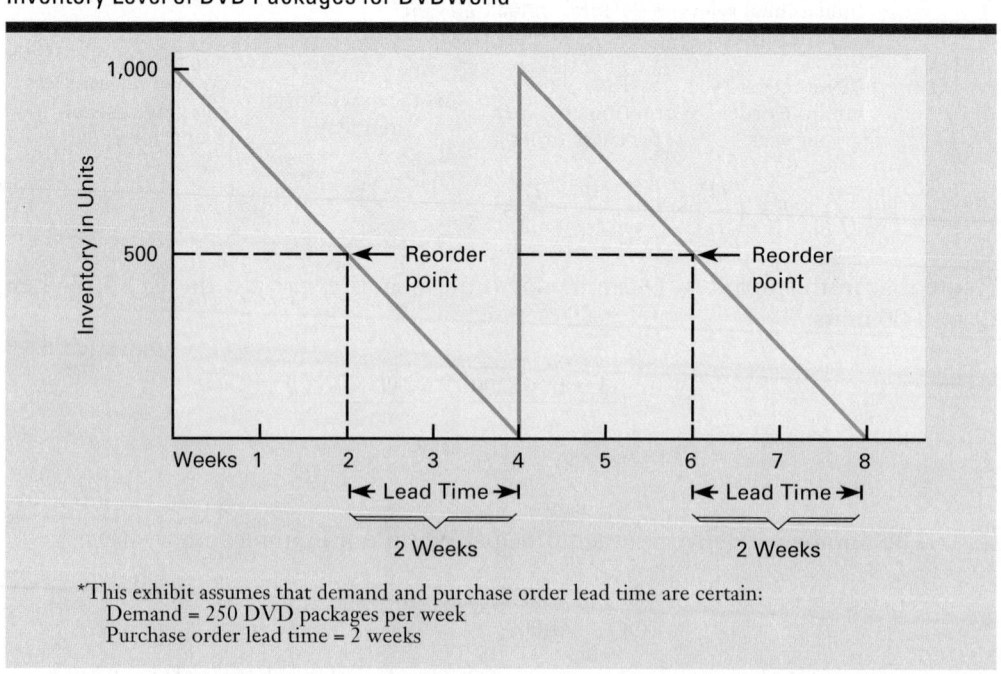

*This exhibit assumes that demand and purchase order lead time are certain:
Demand = 250 DVD packages per week
Purchase order lead time = 2 weeks

[1]This handy but special formula does not apply when the receipt of the order fails to increase inventory to the reorder-point quantity (for example, when the lead time is three weeks and the order is a one-week supply). In these cases, orders will overlap.

SAFETY STOCK

So far, we have assumed that demand and purchase order lead time are certain. When retailers are uncertain about the demand, the lead time, or the quantity that suppliers can provide, they often hold safety stock. **Safety stock** is inventory held at all times regardless of inventory ordered using EOQ. Like a capacity cushion, safety stock is a buffer against unexpected increases in demand or lead time and unavailability of stock from suppliers.

In the DVDWorld example, stockout costs include only the cost of rush orders, because rush orders are assumed to fully satisfy customer demand. However, stockouts can result in opportunity costs—lost contribution margin on lost current sales and lost future sales—and some companies adopt a safety stock policy. Safety stock, like unused capacity cushions, also creates opportunity costs.

In our example, expected demand is 250 packages per week, but the company's managers feel that a maximum demand of 400 packages per week may occur. If the managers decide that the costs of stockout are prohibitive, they may decide to hold safety stock of 300 packages. The opportunity cost of stockouts must also exceed the opportunity cost of holding safety stock. This amount is the maximum excess demand of 150 packages per week for the two weeks of purchase order lead time. The computation of safety stock hinges on demand forecasts. Managers will have some notion—usually based on experience—of the range of weekly demand. When calculating safety stock, the tradeoff is between stockout costs and carrying costs. Columns G and H in Exhibit 20-3 illustrate this tradeoff.

A frequency distribution based on prior daily or weekly levels of demand provides data for computing the associated costs of maintaining safety stock. Assume

EXHIBIT 20-3
Computation of Safety Stock for DVDWorld When Reorder Point Is 500 Units

	A	B	C	D	E	F	G	H	I
1	Safety	Demand							
2	Stock	Levels			Relevant	Number	Expected	Relevant	Relevant
3	Level	Resulting	Stockout	Probability	Stockout	of Orders	Stockout	Carrying	Total
4	in Units	in Stockouts	in Units[a]	of Stockout	Costs[b]	per Year[c]	Costs[d]	Costs[e]	Costs
5	(1)	(2)	(3) = (2) − 500 − (1)	(4)	(5) = (3) × \$4	(6)	(7) = (4) × (5) × (6)	(8) = (1) × \$5.20	(9) = (7) + (8)
6	0	600	100	0.20	\$ 400	13	\$1,040		
7		700	200	0.09	800	13	936		
8		800	300	0.06	1,200	13	936		
9							\$2,912	\$ 0	\$2,912
10	100	700	100	0.09	400	13	\$ 468		
11		800	200	0.06	800	13	624		
12							\$1,092	\$ 520	\$1,612
13	200	800	100	0.06	400	13	\$ 312	\$1,040	\$1,352
14	300	—	—	—	—	—	\$ 0[f]	\$1,560	\$1,560
15									
16	[a]Demand level resulting in stockouts − Inventory available during lead time (excluding safety stock); 500 units − safety stock.								
17	[b]Stockout in units × Relevant stockout costs of \$4 per unit.								
18	[c]Annual demand, 13,000 ÷ 1,000 EOQ = 13 orders per year.								
19	[d]Probability of stockout × Relevant stockout costs × Number of orders per year.								
20	[e]Safety stock × Annual relevant carrying costs of \$5.20 per unit (assumes that safety stock is on hand at all times and that there is no overstocking caused by decreases in expected usage).								
22	[f]At a safety stock level of 300 units, no stockouts will occur and, hence, expected stockout costs = \$0.								

that one of seven different levels of demand will occur over the two-week purchase order lead time at DVDWorld.

Total Demand for Two Weeks	Units						
	200	300	400	500	600	700	800
Probability (sums to 1.00)	0.06	0.09	0.20	0.30	0.20	0.09	0.06

We see that 500 is the most likely level of demand for two weeks, because it is assigned the highest probability of occurrence. We also see that there is a 0.35 probability that demand will be between 600, 700, and 800 packages (0.20 + 0.09 + 0.06 = 0.35).

If a customer calls DVDWorld to buy DVDs, and the store has none in stock, it can rush order them to the customer at a cost to DVDWorld of $4 per package. The relevant stockout costs in this case are $4 per package. The optimal safety stock level is the quantity of safety stock that minimizes the sum of the relevant annual stockout and carrying costs. Recall that the relevant carrying costs for DVDWorld are $5.20 per unit per year.

Exhibit 20-3 presents the total annual relevant stockout and carrying costs when the reorder point is 500 units. We need only consider safety stock levels of 0, 100, 200, and 300 units, since demand will exceed the 500 units of stock available at reordering by 0 if demand is 500, by 100 if demand is 600, by 200 if demand is 700, and by 300 if demand is 800. The total annual relevant stockout and carrying costs would be minimized at $1,352 when a safety stock of 200 packages is maintained. Think of the 200 units of safety stock as extra stock that DVDWorld maintains. For example, DVDWorld's total inventory of DVDs at the time of reordering its EOQ of 1,000 units would be 700 units (the reorder point of 500 units plus the safety stock of 200 units).

JUST-IN-TIME (JIT) PROCUREMENT AND EOQ MODEL PARAMETERS

Just-in-time (JIT) purchasing is a strategy to purchase goods or materials such that a delivery immediately precedes demand or use. JIT is a different inventory management model to minimize the cost of inventories. Ideally, the manufacturer waits for the customer to order and pay for the finished goods, then initiates manufacturing. It is a customer demand-pull strategy rather than a supply-push strategy of production. JIT requires organizations to restructure their relationships with suppliers and place smaller, more frequent purchase orders. JIT can be implemented in both the retail and manufacturing sectors of the economy.

Companies moving toward JIT procurement argue that the cost of carrying inventories (parameter C in the EOQ model) has been dramatically underestimated in the past. This cost includes storage costs, spoilage, obsolescence, and opportunity costs such as investment tied up in inventory. The cost of placing a purchase order (parameter P in the EOQ model) has also been reevaluated. Three factors are causing sizable reductions in P:

◆ Companies are increasingly establishing long-run purchasing arrangements in which price and quality dimensions that apply over an extended period are agreed to by both parties. Individual purchase orders occur without any additional negotiation over price or quality in this period.

◆ Companies have increased their use of electronic links, such as the Internet, to place purchase orders. Electronic commerce (e-commerce) is one of the fastest growing areas of the Internet. The cost of placing some orders on the Internet is estimated at as much as one one-hundredth the cost of placing orders by telephone or by mail.

◆ Companies are increasing the use of purchase cards (similar to consumer credit cards like VISA and MasterCard). Purchasing personnel are given total dollar limits or individual transaction dollar limits. As long as personnel stay within these limits, the traditional labour-intensive procurement approval mechanisms are not required.

Both increases in the carrying cost (C) and decreases in the ordering cost per purchase order (P) result in smaller EOQ amounts. Exhibit 20-4 analyzes the sensitivity of

EXHIBIT 20-4
Sensitivity of EOQ to Variations in Relevant Ordering and Carrying Costs for DVDWorld

	A	B	C	D	E
1	**Relevant Carrying**	**Annual Demand (D) = 13,000 units**			
2	**Costs per Package**	**Relevant Ordering Costs per Purchase Order (P)**			
3	**per Year (C)**	**$200**	**$150**	**$100**	**$30**
4	$ 5.20	EOQ = 1,000	EOQ = 866	EOQ = 707	EOQ = 387
5	7.00	862	746	609	334
6	10.00	721	624	510	279
7	15.00	589	510	416	228

DVDWorld's EOQ to illustrate the economics of smaller and more frequent purchase orders. The analysis presented in Exhibit 20-4 supports JIT procurement—that is, having a smaller EOQ and placing more frequent orders—as relevant carrying costs increase and relevant ordering costs per purchase order decrease.

JIT STRATEGY AND LEAN MANUFACTURING

Consider JIT purchasing by Chrysler, which has 10 assembly plants in North America. Parts and supplies are flown in from 2,000 locations with each plant off-loading up to 600 truckloads per day. Physical inventory count in the plants is measured in "a couple of hours." The company's central tracking group monitors and responds 24/7 to automated alerts signalling glitches in the supply chain. Supply analysts use a production control portal that extends into the software systems of suppliers and shippers as well as those of Chrysler itself.

The production control portal provides access to information on the status of parts and the likelihood of a stockout well in advance. Suppliers failing to ship according to an agreed-upon schedule are alerted that a shipment should have been made but was not. Suppliers who fail to deliver components on time, or components that fail to meet agreed-upon quality standards, can cause a failure in Chrysler's assembly plant to meet its own scheduled deliveries for vehicles.

JIT strategy means companies do not have large amounts of material inventories on hand to provide a cushion to the production line if deliveries are late or parts are defective. JIT requires a high level of information sharing with suppliers who commit to deliver components in narrow time windows. We now explore the relationship between JIT purchasing and the EOQ decision model already discussed in this chapter.

The risk for JIT procurement arises in any interruption in transportation of materials. Delays at border crossings between the United States and Canada have caused some suppliers to rethink whether JIT remains a viable strategy. The costs of stockouts are reaching the point of exceeding the carrying costs for holding inventory. The 2011 earthquake in Japan resulted in the shut-down of the Canadian Toyota automobile manufacturing plant in Cambridge and stockouts of electronic components for the mobile communications industry.

Just-in-time (JIT) production (also called **lean production**) is a response within a manufacturing process to implement an internal demand-pull system. Each element in an assembly process is completed just as it is required in the next step of the process. In a JIT production line, manufacturing activity at any particular workstation is prompted by the need for that station's output at the following station. Production space is redesigned to minimize the materials handling time from one assembly cell to the next. Teams providing direct labour are also situated to eliminate delay in progress toward completing the finished goods. The goals of lean manufacturing systems are to eliminate non-value-added spoilage and scrap, reduce carrying costs, and improve customer satisfaction.

Demand triggers each step of the production process, starting with customer demand for a finished product at the end of the process and working all the way back to the demand for direct materials at the beginning of the process. In this way, demand pulls an order through the production line. The demand-pull feature of JIT production systems requires close coordination among workstations. By implementing a lean

Lean Manufacturing

Each year, hundreds of thousands of rock music fans flock to Dave Matthews Band concerts. Although many of them stop by the merchandise stand to pick up a T-shirt or poster after the show ends, soon they will have another option . . . buying a multiple-CD set that contains a professional recording of the entire concert they just saw! A JIT strategy, enabled by recent advances in digital audio and CD-burning technology, now allows fans to relive the live concert experience as soon as ten minutes after the final chord is played.

Clear Channel Entertainment uses an army of high-speed CD burners to produce concert recordings. As soon as each song is complete, Instant Live's engineers burn the track onto hundreds of CDs using the digital signals heard live through the audio mixing hardware and software and broadcast live to fans at the concert—of course, no editing or remastering can be done.

At the end of the show one last song is burned and the CDs packaged. In smaller venues the logistics of distribution to merchandisers are less difficult than in large amphitheatres. During Instant Live's initial testing, up to 20% of concert-goers bought these CDs, to the tune of US$15 to US$30 each. The artists got US$6 to US$8 from each CD sold, with the remaining money split among the record label, the concert venue, and the recording company.

Digital technology assures better sound quality, near-immediate production turnaround, and low finished-goods carrying costs. Further, these recordings can also be distributed through retailers and artist websites.

Sources: S. Chartland, "How to Take the Concert Home," *The New York Times,* May 3, 2004; S. Humphries, "Get Your Official 'Bootleg' Here," *Christian Science Monitor,* November 21, 2003; S. Knopper, "Live Discs a Hit with Fans," *Rolling Stone,* November 7, 2003; S. Galupo, "Death of the Live Concert Album?" *Washington Times,* July 9, 2004.

production system model, managers aim to simultaneously meet customer demand in a timely way, with high-quality products, and at the lowest possible total cost. Lean manufacturing is most financially feasible when availability and prices of inputs are relatively constant and production cycles are well controlled.

Companies implementing lean production systems manage inventories by eliminating (or at least minimizing) them. The main features in a lean production system are as follows:

◆ Production is organized in **manufacturing cells**, a grouping of all the different types of equipment used to make a given product. Materials move from one machine to another where various operations are performed in sequence. Materials-handling costs are minimized.

◆ Workers are hired and trained to be multiskilled and capable of performing a variety of operations and tasks including minor repairs and routine maintenance of equipment. This training adds greatly to the flexibility of the plant.

◆ Defects are aggressively eliminated (TQM). Because of the tight links between stages in the production line, and the minimal inventories at each stage, defects arising at one stage quickly affect other stages in the line. JIT creates an urgency for solving problems immediately and eliminating the root causes of defects as quickly as possible. TQM is an essential component of any JIT production system.

◆ *Setup time*, which is the time required to get equipment, tools, and materials ready to start the production of a component or product, is reduced. Simultaneously *manufacturing lead time*, which is the amount of time from when an order is ready to start on the production line (ready to be set up) to when it becomes a finished good, is reduced. Reducing setup time makes production in smaller batches economical, which in turn reduces inventory levels. Reducing manufacturing lead time enables a company to respond faster to changes in customer demand (see the Concepts in Action box).

- Suppliers are selected on the basis of their ability to deliver quality materials in a timely manner. Most companies implementing JIT production also implement the JIT purchasing methods described earlier in this chapter. JIT plants expect JIT suppliers to provide high-quality goods and make frequent deliveries of the exact quantities specified on a timely basis. Suppliers often deliver materials directly to the plant floor to be immediately placed into production.

CHALLENGES IN SUPPLY-CHAIN COST MANAGEMENT

Resolve conflicts that can arise from results of EOQ and performance models. ❷

The level of inventories held by retailers is influenced by demand patterns of their customers and supply relationships with their distributors, manufacturers, suppliers, and so on. The term *supply chain* describes the flow of goods, services, and information from cradle to grave (womb to tomb), regardless of whether those activities occur in the same organization or among other organizations. Chapter 1 introduced this concept using the example of a supply chain in the smartphone industry. One point well documented in supply-chain analysis is that there are significant total gains to companies in this supply chain from coordinating their activities and sharing information.

Procter & Gamble's (P&G) experience with their Pampers product illustrates the gains from supply-chain coordination. Retailers selling Pampers encounter some variability in weekly demand, despite babies consuming diapers at a relatively steady rate. However, there was pronounced variability in retailers' orders to the manufacturer (P&G), and even more variability in orders by P&G to its own suppliers. Trade promotions worsened the situation because retailers took advantage of lower prices to increase their inventory for future sales. One result was that high levels of inventory were often held at various stages in the supply chain.

P&G responded by sharing information as well as planning and coordinating activities throughout its supply chain. The retailers shared their daily sales information about Pampers with P&G, their distributors, and their suppliers. This updated sales information reduced the level of uncertainty that manufacturers and the manufacturers' suppliers had about retail demand for Pampers.

The reduction in demand uncertainty led to fewer stockouts at the retail level, reduced inventory of unsold Pampers at P&G, reduced expedited manufacturing orders, and lower inventories being held by each company in the supply chain. The benefits of supply-chain coordination at P&G have been so great that retailers such as Wal-Mart have contracted with P&G to manage Wal-Mart's retail inventories on a just-in-time basis. This practice is called *supplier- or vendor-managed inventory*. Supply-chain management, however, is not without its challenges.

A supply chain is one way for manufacturers to start better managing their own inventory. Of course, the need to produce high-quality products at competitive cost levels leads managers at manufacturing companies to also seek additional ways to manage their inventories. Numerous systems have been developed to help managers plan and implement production and inventory activities.

ESTIMATING RELEVANT COSTS OF A SUPPLY CHAIN

Obtaining accurate estimates of the cost parameters used in the EOQ decision model is a challenging task. For example, the relevant annual carrying costs of inventory consist of *incremental or outlay costs plus the opportunity cost of capital*. Calculating the cost of capital is taught in finance.

What are the relevant incremental costs of carrying inventory? Only those costs that vary with the quantity of inventory held—for example, insurance, property taxes, costs of obsolescence, costs of breakage, shrinkage, warehouse rent, and salaries paid to warehouse workers. Salaries paid to clerks, storekeepers, and materials handlers, however, are irrelevant if they are unaffected by changes in inventory levels. If these salary costs decrease as inventories decrease, however, such as if the clerks, storekeepers, and materials handlers are transferred to other activities or laid off, then these salaries are relevant incremental costs of carrying inventory. Similarly, the costs of storage space owned that cannot be used for other profitable purposes as inventories decrease are irrelevant. But if the space has other profitable uses, or if rental cost is tied to the amount of space occupied, storage costs are relevant incremental costs of carrying inventory.

What is the relevant opportunity cost of capital? It is the return forgone by investing capital in inventory rather than elsewhere. It is calculated as the required rate of return multiplied by those costs per unit that vary with the number of units purchased and that are incurred at the time the units are received. Examples of these costs per unit are purchase price, incoming freight, and incoming inspection.

Opportunity costs are not calculated on investments, say, in buildings, if these investments are unaffected by changes in inventory levels. In the case of stockouts, calculating the relevant opportunity costs requires an estimate of the lost contribution margin on that sale as well as on future sales hurt by customer ill-will resulting from the stockout. Relevant ordering costs are only those ordering costs that change with the number of orders placed (for example, costs of preparing and issuing purchase orders and receiving and inspecting materials).

COST OF A PREDICTION ERROR

Our discussion suggests that predicting relevant costs is difficult and requires care. Managers understand that their projections will seldom be flawless. This leads to the question: What is the cost of an incorrect prediction when actual relevant costs are different from the relevant predicted costs used for decision making?

Continuing our earlier example, suppose DVDWorld's relevant ordering costs per purchase order are $100 instead of the predicted $200. We can calculate the cost of this prediction error in a logical manner, as follows:

◆ *Compute the monetary outcome from the best action that could have been taken, given the actual amount of the cost input.* The appropriate inputs are $D = 13,000$ units, $P = \$100$, and $C = \$5.20$. The economic order quantity size is:

$$\text{EOQ} = \sqrt{\frac{2DP}{C}}$$

$$= \sqrt{\frac{2 \times 13,000 \times \$100}{\$5.20}} = \sqrt{500,000}$$

$$= 707 \text{ packages (rounded)}$$

The total annual relevant cost when EOQ = 707 is

$$\text{TRC} = \frac{DP}{Q} + \frac{QC}{2}$$

$$= \frac{13,000 \times \$100}{707} + \frac{707 \times \$5.20}{2}$$

$$= \$1,839 + \$1,838 = \$3,677$$

◆ *Compute the monetary outcome from the best action on the basis of the incorrect amount of the predicted cost input.* The planned action when the relevant ordering costs per purchase order are predicted to be $200 is to purchase 1,000 packages in each order. The total annual relevant costs using this order quantity when $D = 13,000$ units, $P = \$100$, and $C = \$5.20$ are:

$$\text{TRC} = \frac{13,000 \times \$100}{1,000} + \frac{1,000 \times \$5.20}{2}$$

$$= \$1,300 + \$2,600 = \$3,900$$

◆ *Compute the difference between the monetary outcomes.*

	Monetary Outcome
Step 1	$3,677
Step 2	3,900
Difference	$ (223)

The cost of the prediction error is only $223, or just over 6% of the relevant total costs of $3,677 because the total annual relevant costs curve in Exhibit 20-1 (p. 807) is relatively flat over the range of order quantities from 650 to 1,300. *An important feature of the EOQ model is that the total relevant costs are rarely sensitive to minor variations in cost predictions. The square root in the EOQ model reduces the sensitivity of the decision to errors in predicting its inputs.*

In the following section we consider a planning-and-control and performance-evaluation issue that frequently arises when managing inventory.

GOAL-CONGRUENCE ISSUES

Goal-congruence issues can arise when there is an inconsistency between the decision model and the model used to evaluate the performance of the person implementing the decision. For example, the absence of recorded opportunity costs in conventional accounting systems raises the possibility of a conflict between the EOQ model's optimal order quantity and the order quantity that the purchasing manager, evaluated on conventional accounting numbers, regards as optimal.

If annual carrying costs are excluded when evaluating the performance of managers, the managers may favour purchasing a larger order quantity than the EOQ decision model indicates is optimal. Companies such as Coca-Cola and Wal-Mart resolve this conflict by designing the performance evaluation system so that the carrying costs, including a required return on investment, are charged to the appropriate manager.

The opportunity cost of the investment tied up in inventory can be reduced by reducing inventory levels. We now discuss just-in-time purchasing, an approach that has led to dramatic reductions in inventories being held by some companies.

RELEVANCE AND THE JIT STRATEGY OF SUPPLY-CHAIN MANAGEMENT

Analyze the relevant benefits and costs of JIT alternatives. ③

The JIT purchasing model is not guided solely by the EOQ model. As discussed earlier (pp. 805–807), the EOQ model is designed to emphasize only the tradeoff between carrying and ordering costs. Inventory management extends beyond ordering and carrying costs to include purchasing costs, stockout costs, and quality costs. The quality of materials and goods and timely deliveries are important motivations for using JIT purchasing, and stockout costs are an important concern. We add these features as we move from the EOQ decision model to present the JIT purchasing model.

DVDWorld has recently established an Internet business-to-business (B2B) purchase-order link with Sontek. DVDWorld triggers a purchase order for DVDs by a single computer entry. Payments are made electronically for batches of deliveries, rather than for each individual delivery. These changes reduce the ordering cost from $200 to only $2 per purchase order! DVDWorld will use the Internet purchase-order link whether or not it shifts to a JIT strategy. DVDWorld is negotiating to have Sontek deliver 100 packages of DVDs 130 times per year (5 times every 2 weeks), instead of delivering 1,000 packages 13 times per year, as shown in Exhibit 20-3 (p. 809). Sontek is willing to make these frequent deliveries, but it would add $0.02 to the price per DVD package. DVDWorld's required rate of return on investment remains at 15%. Assume the annual relevant carrying cost of insurance, materials handling, shrinkage, breakage, and the like remains at $3.10 per package per year.

Suppose that DVDWorld incurs no stockout costs under its current purchasing policy because demand and purchase order lead times over each four-week period are certain. DVDWorld's major concern is that lower inventory levels from implementing JIT purchasing will lead to more stockouts because demand variations and delays in supplying DVDs are more likely to occur in the short time intervals between supplies under JIT purchasing. Sontek assures DVDWorld that its new manufacturing processes enable it to respond rapidly to changing demand patterns. Consequently, stockouts may not be a serious problem. DVDWorld expects to incur stockout costs on 150 DVD packages each year under a JIT purchasing policy. In the event of a stockout, DVDWorld will have to rush-order DVD packages at a cost of $4 per package. Should DVDWorld implement JIT purchasing?

Exhibit 20-5 compares (1) the incremental costs DVDWorld incurs when it purchases DVDs from Sontek under its current purchasing policy with (2) the incremental costs DVDWorld would incur if Sontek supplied DVDs under a JIT policy. The difference in the two incremental costs is the relevant savings of JIT purchasing. In other methods of comparing the two purchasing policies, the analysis would include only the relevant costs—those costs that differ between the two alternatives. Exhibit 20-5 shows a net cost savings of $1,789 per year from shifting to a JIT purchasing policy.

EXHIBIT 20-5
Annual Relevant Costs of Current Purchasing Policy and JIT Purchasing Policy for DVDWorld

A	B	C
	Relevant Costs Under	
	Current Purchasing Policy	**JIT Purchasing Policy**
Relevant Item		
Purchasing costs		
$14 per unit × 13,000 units per year	$182,000	
$14.02 per unit × 13,000 units per year		$182,260
Ordering costs		
$200 per order × 13 orders per year	2,600	
$2 per order × 130 orders per year		260
Opportunity carrying costs, required return on investment		
0.15 per year × $14 cost per unit × 250[a] units of average inventory per year	525	
0.15 per year × $14.02 cost per unit × 250[b] units of average inventory per year		526
Other carrying costs (insurance, materials handling, breakage, and so on)		
$3.10 per unit per year × 250[a] units of average inventory per year	775	
$3.10 per unit per year × 150[c] units of average inventory per year		465
Stockout costs		
$4 per unit × 0 units per year	—	
$4 per unit × 150 units per year		600
Total annual relevant costs	$185,900	$ 184,111
Annual difference in favour of JIT purchasing	$1,789	
[a]Average inventory = 1,000 ÷ 52/13 = 250		
[b]Average inventory = 100/week × 2.5 orders/week = 250		
[c]Maximum demand 400/week − average inventory 250/week = 150		

RELEVANT COSTS OF QUALITY AND TIMELY DELIVERIES

The timely delivery of quality products is particularly crucial in JIT purchasing environments. Defective materials and late deliveries often bring the whole plant to a halt, resulting in forgone contribution margin on lost sales. Companies that implement JIT purchasing choose their suppliers carefully and pay special attention to developing long-run supplier partnerships. Some suppliers are very cooperative with a business's attempts to adopt JIT purchasing. For example, Frito-Lay, which has a large market share in potato chips and other snack foods, makes more frequent deliveries to retail outlets than many of its competitors. The company's corporate strategy emphasizes service to retailers and consistency, freshness, and quality of the delivered product.

What are the relevant costs when choosing suppliers? Consider again our DVDWorld example. The Denton Corporation also supplies DVDs. It offers to supply all of DVDWorld's DVD needs at a price of $13.80 per package (less than Sontek's price of $14.02) under the same JIT delivery terms that Sontek offers. Denton proposes an electronic hookup identical to Sontek's that would make DVDWorld's ordering costs $2.00 per purchase order. DVDWorld's relevant outlay carrying costs of insurance, materials handling, breakage, and so on per package per year is $3.10 if it purchases DVDs from Sontek and $3.00 if it purchases from Denton. Should DVDWorld buy from Denton? Not before considering the relevant costs of quality and also the relevant costs of failing to deliver on time.

DVDWorld has used Sontek in the past and knows that Sontek fully deserves its reputation for delivering quality merchandise on time. In fact, DVDWorld does not even inspect the DVD packages that Sontek supplies, therefore incurring zero inspection costs. Denton, however, does not enjoy as sterling a reputation for quality. When evaluating and choosing suppliers, quality and on-time delivery become increasingly important as the emphasis shifts away from minimizing purchasing costs toward minimizing costs across the entire value chain of business functions. DVDWorld anticipates the following negative aspects of using Denton:

- DVDWorld would incur additional inspection costs of $0.05 per package.
- Average stockouts of 360 DVD packages each year would occur, largely resulting from late deliveries. Denton cannot rush-order DVD packages to DVDWorld on short notice, causing an additional cost of $4 per package.
- Customers would likely return 2.5% of all packages sold owing to poor quality of the DVDs. DVDWorld estimates its additional costs to handle each returned package at $10.

Exhibit 20-6 presents the relevant costs of purchasing from Sontek and from Denton. Even though Denton is offering a lower price per package, the total relevant costs of purchasing goods from Sontek are lower by $1,847 per year. Selling high-quality merchandise also has nonfinancial and qualitative benefits. For example, offering Sontek's high-quality DVDs enhances DVDWorld's reputation and increases customer goodwill, which may lead to higher future profitability.

JIT'S EFFECT ON COSTING SYSTEMS

In reducing the need for materials handling, warehousing, and incoming inspection, JIT systems reduce overhead costs. JIT systems also facilitate the direct tracing of some costs that were formerly classified as overhead. For example, the use of manufacturing cells makes it easy to trace materials handling and machine operating costs to specific products or product families made in specific cells. These costs then become direct costs of those products. Also, the use of multiskilled workers in these cells allows the costs of setup, minor maintenance, and quality inspection to become easily traced direct costs.

FINANCIAL BENEFITS OF JIT AND RELEVANT COSTS

Early advocates say the benefit of JIT production is lower carrying costs of inventory. But there are other benefits to lower inventories, such as intensifying emphasis

EXHIBIT 20-6
Annual Relevant Costs of Purchasing from Sontek and Denton

	A	B	C
		Relevant Costs of Purchasing from	
	Relevant Item	**Sontek**	**Denton**
3	Purchasing costs		
4	$14.02 per unit × 13,000 units per year	$182,260	
5	$13.80 per unit × 13,000 units per year		$179,400
6	Ordering costs		
7	$2.00 per order × 130 orders per year	260	
8	$2.00 per order × 130 orders per year		260
9	Inspection costs		
10	No inspection necessary	—	
11	$0.05 per unit × 13,000 units per year		650
12	Opportunity carrying costs, required return on investment		
13	0.15 per year × $14.02 × 250[a] units of average inventory per year	526	
14	0.15 per year × $13.80 × 250[a] units of average inventory per year		518
15	Other carrying costs (insurance, materials handling, breakage, etc.)		
16	$3.10 per unit per year × 250[a] units of average inventory per year	775	
17	$3.00 per unit per year × 250[a] units of average inventory per year		750
18	Stockout costs		
19	$4 per unit × 150 units per year	600	
20	$4 per unit × 360 units per year		1,440
21	Customer returns costs		
22	No customer returns	—	
23	$10 per unit returned × 2.5% units returned × 13,000 units		3,250
24	Total annual relevant costs	$184,421	$186,268
25	Annual difference in favour (disfavour) of Sontek	$1,847	
26	[a]Average inventory = 100/week × 2.5 orders per week = 250		

on improved quality (by eliminating scrap, rework, and spoilage), and reduced manufacturing lead times. Management accounting provides the information required for managers to calculate the relevant benefits and costs of reduced inventories in JIT systems.

Consider the Emco Corporation, a manufacturer of brass fittings. Emco is considering implementing a JIT production system. Suppose that to implement JIT production, Emco must incur $100,000 in annual tooling costs to reduce setup times. Suppose further that JIT will reduce average inventory by $500,000. Also, relevant costs of insurance, space, materials-handling, and setup will decline by $30,000 per year. The company's required rate of return on inventory investments is 10% per year. Should Emco implement JIT? On the basis of the numbers provided, we would be tempted to say no because annual relevant cost savings in carrying costs amount to $80,000 [($500,000 × 0.10) + $30,000], which is less than the additional annual tooling costs of $100,000.

Our analysis, however, has not considered other benefits of lower inventories in JIT production. For example, Emco estimates that implementing JIT will reduce rework on 500 units each year, resulting in savings of $50 per unit. Also, better quality and faster delivery will allow Emco to charge $2 more per unit on the 20,000 units that it sells each year. The annual relevant quality and delivery benefits from JIT and lower inventory levels equal $65,000 (rework savings, $50 × 500 + additional contribution margin, $2 × 20,000). Total annual relevant benefits and cost savings equal

$145,000 ($80,000 + $65,000), which exceeds annual JIT implementation costs of $100,000. Therefore, Emco should implement a JIT production system. Management accountants face challenges like this when valuing inventory and implementing JIT.

PERFORMANCE MEASURES AND CONTROL

To manage and reduce inventories, the management accountant must also design performance measures to evaluate and control JIT production. Examples of information the management accountant may use are as follows:

◆ Personal observation by production line workers and team leaders.

◆ Financial performance measures such as the inventory turnover ratio (cost of goods sold ÷ average inventory), which is expected to increase.

◆ Nonfinancial performance measures of time, inventory, and quality, such as manufacturing lead time, units produced per hour, and days inventory is on hand.

◆ Manufacturing lead time, expected to decrease.

◆ Units produced per hour, expected to increase.

◆ Total setup time for machines, expected to decrease total manufacturing time.

◆ Number of units requiring rework or scrap, expected to decrease total number of units started and completed.

Personal observation and nonfinancial performance measures are the dominant methods of control. These methods are the most timely, intuitive, and easy-to-comprehend measures of plant performance. Rapid, meaningful feedback is critical because the lack of buffer inventories in a demand-pull system creates added urgency to detect and solve problems quickly.

INVENTORY MANAGEMENT: MRP AND ERP

We now consider another widely used type of inventory system—**materials requirements planning (MRP)**. A key feature of MRP is its push-through approach, whereas JIT is a demand-pull approach. MRP manufactures finished goods for inventory on the basis of demand forecasts. MRP uses (1) demand forecasts for the final products; (2) a bill of materials outlining the materials, components, and subassemblies for each final product; and (3) the quantities of materials, components, finished products, and product inventories to predetermine the necessary outputs at each stage of production.

Panasonic Corporation of North America is a supply-chain partner with Best Buy. Panasonic used to wait for orders from Best Buy and then initiate the process of filling the order. Now Best Buy collects information on sales of all Panasonic items at its stores' point-of-sale (POS) checkout stations. Best Buy's computers transmit this information to a unit of i2 Technologies Inc. in India. i2 Technologies provides forecasting and other supply-chain analytics to Panasonic. The forecast of demand, modelled on Best Buy's actual sales of Panasonic products, is now transmitted electronically from i2 to Panasonic. i2 Technologies' forecasts are the basis for Panasonic's production schedule. This illustrates how forecast demand pushes production.

Taking into account the lead time required to purchase materials and to manufacture components and finished products, a master production schedule specifies the quantity and timing of each item to be produced. Once scheduled production starts, the output of each department is pushed through the production line whether it is needed or not. The result is often an accumulation of inventory at workstations that receive work they are not yet ready to process.

Inventory management is a key challenge in an MRP system. The management accountant can play several important roles in meeting this challenge. A key role is maintaining accurate and timely information pertaining to materials, work in

Differentiate a materials requirements planning (MRP) strategy from an enterprise resource planning (ERP) strategy of supply-chain management.

④

process, and finished goods inventories. A major cause of unsuccessful attempts to implement MRP systems has been the problem of collecting and updating inventory records. Calculating the full cost of carrying finished goods inventory motivates other actions. For example, instead of storing product at multiple (and geographically dispersed) warehouses, National Semiconductor contracted with FedEx to airfreight its microchips from a central location in Singapore to customer sites worldwide. The change enabled National to move products from plant to customer in 4 days rather than 45, and to reduce distribution costs from 2.6% to 1.9% of revenues. These benefits subsequently led National to outsource all its logistics to FedEx, including shipments among its own plants in the United States, Scotland, and Malaysia.

A second role of the management accountant is providing estimates of the setup costs for each production run at a plant, the downtime costs, and carrying costs of inventory. Costs of setting up a production run are analogous to ordering costs in the EOQ model. When the costs of setting up machines or sections of the production line are high (for example, as with a blast furnace in an integrated steel mill), processing larger batches of materials and incurring larger inventory carrying costs is the optimal approach because it reduces the number of setups that must be made. When setup costs are small, processing smaller batches is optimal because it reduces carrying costs. Similarly, when the costs of downtime are high, there can be sizable benefits from maintaining continuous production.

ENTERPRISE RESOURCE PLANNING (ERP) SYSTEMS[2]

For both MRP and JIT supply-chain strategies, the most important resource is effective and efficient communication of relevant information. The speed of information flow from buyers to suppliers is a problem for large companies with fragmented information systems. Systems to program and control manufacturing do not communicate with those tracking inventory, for example. These incompatible systems are spread across the business functions of the value chain.

Enterprise resource planning (ERP) systems improve internal business process flows of information enabling effective inventory cost control. An ERP system is an integrated set of software modules including accounting, distribution, manufacturing, purchasing, human resources, and other functions. An ERP system integrates all the information from a company into a single database that collects data and feeds it into applications supporting all of a company's business activities. All internal software operations receive data in real time, heightening the visibility of the interdependencies and bottlenecks in the entire business process. With an ERP system, companies can choose a supply-chain strategy that demands accurate and timely sharing of information to parties external to the company.

For example, using an ERP system, a salesperson can generate a contract for a customer in Germany, verify the customer's credit limits, and place a production order. The system schedules manufacturing in, say, Brazil, requisitions materials from inventory, orders components from suppliers, and schedules shipment. It also credits sales commissions to the salesperson and records all the costing and financial accounting information.

ERP systems give low-level managers, workers, customers, and suppliers access to operating information. This benefit, coupled with tight coordination across business functions, enables ERP systems to rapidly shift manufacturing and distribution plans in response to changes in supply and demand. Companies believe that an ERP system is essential to support JIT and MRP initiatives because of the effect it has on lead times. Using an ERP system, Autodesk, a maker of computer-aided design software, reduced order lead times from 2 weeks to 1 day; Fujitsu reduced lead times from 18 to 1.5 days. ERP systems are the basis for demand forecasts and MRP as part of a company's operations and logistics modules.

---

[2]For an excellent discussion, see T. H. Davenport, "Putting the Enterprise into the Enterprise System," *Harvard Business Review*, July–August 1998; also see A. Cagilo, "Enterprise Resource Planning Systems and Accountants: Towards Hybridization?" *European Accounting Review*, May 2003.

Although the tight coupling of systems throughout a business streamlines administrative and financial processes and saves costs, it can also make the system large and unwieldy. Because of their complexity, suppliers of ERP systems[3] such as SAP, Baan, Peoplesoft, and Oracle provide software packages that are standard but that can be customized, although at considerable cost. Without some customization, unique and distinctive features that confer strategic advantage will not be available. The challenge when implementing ERP systems is to strike the right balance between systems that are common across all of a company's business and geographical locations and systems that for strategic reasons are designed to be unique.

Adopting an MRP or JIT supply-chain approach requires diverse organizations to cooperate and communicate on a broad set of issues. This challenge is not always successfully met. Not surprisingly, not all supply-chain initiatives have delivered the initially projected financial and operating benefits. The next section discusses *backflush costing*, which is a job-costing system that dovetails with JIT production and is less costly to operate than most traditional costing systems described in Chapters 4, 7, 8, and 9.

BACKFLUSH COSTING

Evaluate and decide upon an appropriate backflush costing method. ⑤

A lean, demand-pull manufacturing system reduces or eliminates inventory in excess of what customers want. The continuous mass-production system reduces to a process costing system. The absence of inventories makes choices about equivalent units and cost flow assumptions (such as weighted average or first-in, first-out) or inventory costing methods (such as absorption or variable costing) unimportant. There is no beginning and ending inventory; therefore, almost all manufacturing costs of a period flow directly into cost of goods sold. The rapid conversion of direct materials to finished goods that are either immediately or have already been sold simplifies the traditional costing described in Chapter 2.

SIMPLIFIED NORMAL OR STANDARD COSTING

Traditional and standard costing systems use **sequential tracking** (also called **synchronous tracking**), which is any product costing method in which the accounting system entries occur in the same order as actual purchases and production. The traditional methods of accounting for manufacturing costs using either weighted average or FIFO are GAAP-compliant. One accounting report for a specified time period can serve two purposes—external reporting and internal planning and control. But the traditional system is accrual- rather than cash-based. Internally, for control purposes, management teams often need to make adjustments to match the financial to the production cycle.

These traditional systems track costs sequentially as products pass from direct materials, to work in process, to finished goods, and finally to sales, as shown here. Some have called this the "just in case" system.

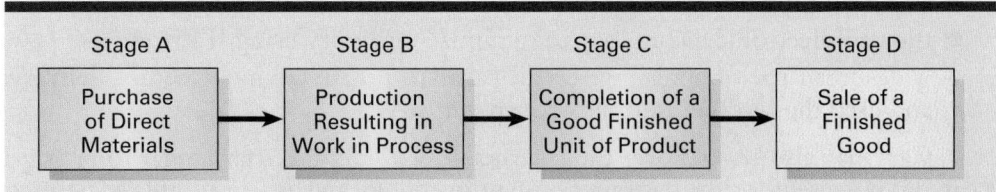

A sequential tracking costing system would have four trigger points, corresponding to separate journal entries being made at Stages A, B, C, and D. The term **trigger point** refers to a stage in the cycle, beginning with purchase of direct materials (Stage A) to sale of finished goods (Stage D), at which journal entries are made in the accounting system. This is a routine type of sequential accounting system to track costs. Revenue will not be realized until Stage D, although production costs will be incurred at Stage A when the order is placed.

[3]Even the smallest business can afford an ERP system. At Internet sites like SourceForge (http://sourceforge.net), free ERP and other open-source software can be downloaded.

The accumulation of costs of direct materials and the use of resources to transform them into finished goods are reported as current assets, such as inventory. The costs plus some profit will be recovered within 12 months when a sale is made.[4] Where competition is intense and substitutes are readily available, the goods are standard outputs. A sequential process costing system is adequate and GAAP-compliant, but overhead cost assignment can be complicated.

Through the Internet, though, an enormous variety of goods can be ordered, but the customer must pay in full in advance of receiving the goods. When the sale and payment is processed first, as happens with an Internet order, there is no cost of goods sold until the production process begins. The company must record the receipt of revenue to recognize it, but this revenue will not be realized until the finished goods are shipped to the customer. The costs of production begin to be incurred *after* Stage D and the short production cycle usually means there is no work in process of any significant value. Delivery times of less than two weeks mean the costs of direct materials and transformation into finished goods is almost immediate with little or no work-in-process inventory.

The shorter the production cycle, the less likely any adjustments will be required to match the cash to cash and to the production cycle. If the production does not begin until the customer has ordered and paid online by credit card (Stage D), and it takes only days to assemble and ship the finished good, then there is almost no lead or lag in turning direct materials and WIP inventory into finished goods. The shorter the production cycle, the less probable it is that there will be any WIP or FG inventory of significant value (Stages B, C). Once finished, the good is shipped to the customer and the producer's obligation is complete; therefore, revenue can be recognized. With the ease of online order-taking accompanied by a required credit card payment, there is rarely any accounts receivable. This means that all the laborious allocation of manufacturing costs required in Chapter 2 is no longer necessary.

Dell has used this model and achieved high profit in a very competitive industry. Moreover, it serves knowledgeable customers who specify from an available selection precisely what brands of parts they require in the computer. The ouput is customized but sold at a low cost. Because customers know how to obtain the performance they want and because demand for attributes in computers has become standardized, Dell can satisfy a large market share.

Parts are also mass produced, but Dell does not have to inventory the parts because it can order them online from suppliers who then ship the parts by air, usually out of Hong Kong, to North America and other production plant locations. Parts, while expensive, do not weigh much and the suppliers' market is so competitive the suppliers are willing to ship small quantities frequently to large buyers such as Dell. These factors created an opportunity for Dell's profitable adoption of the strategy of agility. Dell took advantage of

◆ the increased knowledgeability of consumers about technical specifications,
◆ standardization of customer demand for attributes of computers,
◆ the new electronic technology to minimize inventory using JIT, and
◆ widespread use of consumer credit cards to obtain payment before delivery, and used the Internet to transform an industry.

Cars may also be sold over the Internet; however, it takes far longer to produce a car and prepare it for the customer's use prior to sale, and as a result the accounting issues are different. Many assembly plants are located offshore, where labour is very inexpensive. The weight of the individual car means it is often shipped by sea or rail to avoid prohibitively expensive air transportation costs to consumers living in North America and Europe. This prolongs the delay in handing the keys to the customer,

---

[4]In GAAP-compliant financial reporting, any current or short-term asset such as inventory informs the reader the intent is to sell the inventory and recognize revenue within 12 months. If this is not true, then the inventory must be revalued to lower of cost or net realizable value (see Chapter 2).

who is unlikely to have paid using a consumer credit card. The production cycle triggers payment when the car is delivered, not when it is ordered.

For Dell, with its short production cycle, there will be no WIP inventory and no excess of finished goods over demand. The sale and payment initiates production. In this approach, cost of goods available for sale is zero because there will be no unsold inventory. Risk arises when the product or service does not match the customer's requirements. In that case, the cost of any unsold finished goods is potentially an unrecoverable cost. For customized products, it is highly unlikely two knowledgeable customers will require, for example, a notebook computer with identical specifications for the parts. Inventory will also arise when completed goods are packaged but not yet shipped to the customer who, in Dell's model, has already paid.

Outputs incompletely assembled and waiting to be moved to the next stage or cell in the production process will give rise to WIP inventory. Overhead cost assignment issues almost disappear. All waste and scrap costs are both expected and direct costs. But the detailed data required for multi-level variance analyses of overhead costs are no longer available with backflush costing. Any variance between actual and standard costs at the end of the time period, theoretically, will be zero. Any actual inventory costs will be treated as a variance and written off rather than prorated because they will be insignificant.

Backflush costing reflects the economic reality of production. It is an economically plausible method that reports on the reality of the flow of costs in the cash to cash cycle. It reduces the accounting cycle to a single step from Stage D back to Stage A, initiated by the immediate payment for a finished good. There is no inventory to value and report on the balance sheet because the costs flow with little delay to the cost of goods sold for which payment has already been made.

A good cost estimate is required for a company such as Dell to insure a reasonable profit. When costs of production are relatively stable, most companies use the standard costing method to estimate cost of goods sold, and then make adjusting entries at the end of each time period to be GAAP- and CRA-compliant. The adjusting entries will capture any change between the standard or predetermined costs and the actual costs.[5] Unfortunately, although standard costing is GAAP-compliant, it is *not* permitted by CRA to report taxable income (see Chapters 2, 4). Companies such as Dell can use backflush costing for internal purposes to report cash costs of sale and advance customer payments, which most accurately reflects the economic facts of production. But companies cannot use this method for financial and tax reporting to external parties.

In lean manufacturing, the design of the process eliminates variance. This method of production is an internal JIT delivery system. The steps in transforming direct materials, and of course the flow of costs, do not begin until the previous step has been completed. In the jargon of lean manufacturing, each step is called a cell. In a process of this type, there is little or no work in process remaining at each stage of transformation. With no work-in-process inventory, backflush costing may be the best way to reflect the economic facts of the actual production process. Again, however, production cycle times at each step must be short and the process itself cannot have bottlenecks.

Of course one can immediately ask, without feedback on the actual cost flow throughout the process, how can the management team know if the internal process design is optimal? Moreover, backflush costing is inappropriate if the production cycle is longer than the accounting period. When this happens there will inevitably be inventory. This negates the justification for using backflush costing even if there is a lean, demand-pull manufacturing system in place.

Relatively inexpensive software is available to fully automate backflush accounting. The manufacturer simply labels the finished product with either a bar code or RFID and scans the unit. This initiates a computer program that attributes quantities of direct materials to appropriate inventories, based on standard quantities

---

[5]As you may recall from Chapter 4, normal and actual costing are GAAP-compliant reporting methods when calculating and reporting Cost of Goods Sold for the income statement and when valuing inventory for the balance sheet.

and unit costs. Using either standard or normal costs, the program assigns material and conversion costs and indirect costs to the finished unit. Of course, if the bar code is inaccurate, then the backflush costing will be inaccurate.

Some programs both inform the distributor that the product is ready for pickup and delivery to the customer and inform the customer of the status of their order(s) as well as calculate variances using data from other information systems such as payroll and purchasing. Scrap, rework, and spoilage costs can be entered as standard, direct costs of finished goods. Where journal entries for one or more stages in the cycle are omitted, the journal entries for a subsequent stage use normal or standard costs to work backward to flush out the costs in the cycle for which journal entries were not made.

BACKFLUSH COSTING METHODS

The following three examples illustrate backflush costing. To underscore basic concepts, we assume no direct materials variances in any of the examples. The management team should choose the method that best reflects the economic facts of its business. The three examples differ in the number and placement of trigger points at which journal entries are made in the accounting system:

	Number of Journal Entry Trigger Points	Location in Cycle Where Journal Entries Made
Example 1	3	Stage A. Purchase of direct materials (called "raw materials").
		Stage C. Completion of unspoiled good finished units of product.
		Stage D. Sale of finished goods.
Example 2	2	Stage A. Purchase of direct materials (called "raw materials").
		Stage D. Sale of finished goods.
Example 3	2	Stage C. Completion of unspoiled good finished units of product.
		Stage D. Sale of finished goods.

In all three examples, there are no journal entries in the accounting system for work in process (Stage B). These three examples of backflush costing are typically used where the amounts of work in process are small. With just-in-time production, sizable reductions in work in process have occurred.

Example 1: Trigger Points are Stages A, C, and D   This example uses three trigger points to illustrate how backflushing can eliminate the need for a separate Work-in-Process account. A hypothetical company, Silicon Valley Computer (SVC), produces keyboards for personal computers. For April, there were no beginning inventories of raw materials. Moreover, there is zero beginning and ending work in process.

SVC has only one direct manufacturing cost category (direct or raw materials) and one indirect manufacturing cost category (conversion costs). All labour costs at the manufacturing facility are included in conversion costs. From its bill of materials (description of the types and quantities of materials) and an operations list (description of operations to be undergone), SVC determines the April standard direct materials costs per keyboard unit of $19 and the standard conversion costs of $12. SVC has two inventory accounts:

Type	Account Title
Combined direct materials and any direct material in work in process	Inventory: Raw and In-Process Control
Finished goods	Finished Goods Control

Trigger point 1 occurs when materials are purchased. These costs are charged to Inventory: Raw and In-Process Control.

Actual conversion costs are recorded as incurred under backflush costing, just as in other costing systems, and charged to Conversion Costs Control. Conversion costs are allocated to products at trigger point 2—the transfer of units to Finished

Goods. This example assumes that under- or overallocated conversion costs are written off to cost of goods sold monthly. This flow of costs is analogous to job costing in Chapter 4, except backflush costing bypasses the WIP Control account.

SVC undertakes the following analysis and journal entries of the costs to units sold and to inventories:

1. Record the direct materials purchased during the accounting period. Assume April purchases of $1,950,000:

   Entry (a) Inventory: Raw and In-Process Control $1,950,000
                  Accounts Payable Control $1,950,000

2. Record the incurrence of conversion costs during the accounting period. Assume that conversion costs are $1,260,000:

   Entry (b) Conversion Costs Control $1,260,000
                  [Various accounts (such as Accounts
                      Payable Control and Wages Payable)] $1,260,000

3. Determine the number of finished units manufactured during the accounting period. Assume that 100,000 keyboard units were manufactured in April.

4. Compute the budgeted or standard costs of each finished unit. The standard cost is $31 ($19 direct materials + $12 conversion costs) per unit.

5. Record the cost of finished goods completed during the accounting period. In this case, 100,000 units × $31 = $3,100,000. This step gives backflush costing its name.

   Up to this point in the operations, the costs have not been recorded sequentially with the flow of product along its production route. Instead, the output trigger reaches back and pulls the standard costs of direct materials from Inventory: Raw and WIP and the standard conversion costs for manufacturing the finished goods.

   Entry (c) Finished Goods Control $3,100,000
                  Inventory: Raw and In-Process Control $1,900,000
                  Conversion Costs Allocated   1,200,000

6. Record the cost of goods sold during the accounting period. Assume that 99,000 units were sold in April (99,000 units × $31 = $3,069,000).

   Entry (d) Cost of Goods Sold $3,069,000
                  Finished Goods Control $3,069,000

7. Record under- or overallocated conversion costs. Actual conversion costs may be under- or overallocated in any given accounting period. Chapter 4 discussed various ways to account for under- or overallocated manufacturing overhead costs. Many companies write off underallocations or overallocations to cost of goods sold only at year-end; other companies, like SVC, do so monthly.

   Companies that use backflush costing typically have low inventories, so proration of under- or overallocated costs between finished goods and cost of goods sold is less often necessary. The journal entry for the $60,000 difference between actual conversion costs incurred and standard conversion costs allocated would be:

   Entry (e) Conversion Costs Allocated $1,200,000
                  Cost of Goods Sold   60,000
                  Conversion Costs Control $1,260,000

The April ending inventory balances are:

   Inventory: Raw and In-Process $50,000
   Finished Goods, 1,000 units × $31   31,000
   Total inventories $81,000

EXHIBIT 20-7
Journal Entries in Backflush Costing

PANEL A, EXAMPLE 1: THREE TRIGGER POINTS—PURCHASE OF DIRECT MATERIALS, COMPLETION OF UNSPOILED GOOD FINISHED UNITS, AND SALE OF FINISHED GOODS

Transactions

(a) Purchase of direct materials[a]	Inventory: Raw and In-Process Control	$1,950,000	
	Accounts Payable Control		$1,950,000
(b) Incur conversion costs	Conversion Costs Control	1,260,000	
	Various Accounts		1,260,000
(c) Completion of good finished units[a]	Finished Goods Control	3,100,000	
	Inventory: Raw and In-Process Control		1,900,000
	Conversion Costs Allocated		1,200,000
(d) Sale of finished goods[a]	Cost of Goods Sold	3,069,000	
	Finished Goods Control		3,069,000
(e) Underallocated or overallocated conversion costs	Conversion Costs Allocated	1,200,000	
	Cost of Goods Sold	60,000	
	Conversion Costs Control		1,260,000

PANEL B, EXAMPLE 2: TWO TRIGGER POINTS—PURCHASE OF DIRECT MATERIALS AND SALE OF FINISHED GOODS

Transactions

(a) Purchase of direct materials[a]	Inventory Control	$1,950,000	
	Accounts Payable Control		$1,950,000
(b) Incur conversion costs	Conversion Costs Control	1,260,000	
	Various Accounts		1,260,000
(c) Completion of good finished units	No entry		
(d) Sale of finished goods[a]	Cost of Goods Sold	3,069,000	
	Inventory Control		1,881,000
	Conversion Costs Allocated		1,188,000
(e) Underallocated or overallocated conversion costs	Conversion Costs Allocated	1,188,000	
	Cost of Goods Sold	72,000	
	Conversion Costs Control		1,260,000

PANEL C, EXAMPLE 3: TWO TRIGGER POINTS—COMPLETION OF UNSPOILED GOOD FINISHED UNITS AND SALE OF FINISHED GOODS

Transactions

(a) Purchase of direct materials	No entry		
(b) Incur conversion costs	Conversion Costs Control	$1,260,000	
	Various Accounts		$1,260,000
(c) Completion of good finished units[a]	Finished Goods Control	3,100,000	
	Accounts Payable Control		1,900,000
	Conversion Costs Allocated		1,200,000
(d) Sale of finished goods[a]	Cost of Goods Sold	3,069,000	
	Finished Goods Control		3,069,000
(e) Underallocated or overallocated conversion costs	Conversion Costs Allocated	1,200,000	
	Cost of Goods Sold	60,000	
	Conversion Costs Control		1,260,000

[a]A trigger point.

Exhibit 20-7, Panel A, summarizes the journal entries for this example. Exhibit 20-8 provides an overview of this version of backflush costing. The elimination of the typical WIP account reduces the amount of detail in the accounting system.

Units on the production line may still be tracked in physical terms, but there is "no attaching of costs" to specific work orders as they flow along the production cycle. In fact, there are no work orders or labour time tickets in the accounting system.

The use of three triggers to make journal entries in Example 1 will result in SVC's backflush costing system reporting costs similar to sequential tracking when SVC has minimal work-in-process inventory. In Example 1, any inventories

EXHIBIT 20-8
General Ledger Overview of Backflush Costing

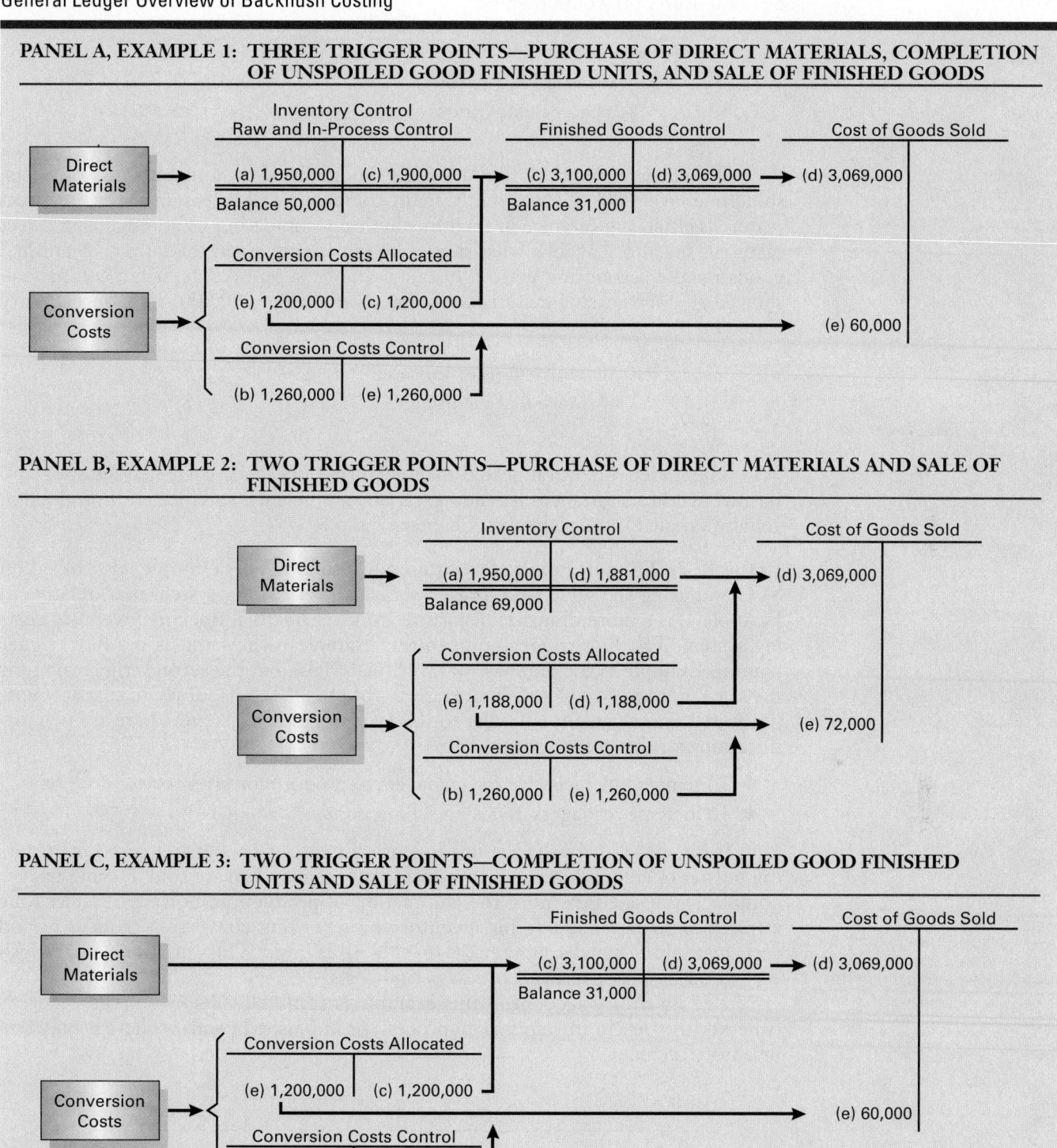

PANEL A, EXAMPLE 1: THREE TRIGGER POINTS—PURCHASE OF DIRECT MATERIALS, COMPLETION OF UNSPOILED GOOD FINISHED UNITS, AND SALE OF FINISHED GOODS

PANEL B, EXAMPLE 2: TWO TRIGGER POINTS—PURCHASE OF DIRECT MATERIALS AND SALE OF FINISHED GOODS

PANEL C, EXAMPLE 3: TWO TRIGGER POINTS—COMPLETION OF UNSPOILED GOOD FINISHED UNITS AND SALE OF FINISHED GOODS

of raw materials or finished goods are recognized in SVC's backflush costing system when they first appear (as would be done in a costing system using sequential tracking).

The accounting for variances between actual costs incurred and standard costs allowed and the disposition of variances is basically the same under all standard costing systems. The procedures are described in Chapters 7 and 8. In Example 1, suppose the direct materials purchased had an unfavourable price variance of $42,000. Entry (a) would then be:

Inventory: Raw and In-Process Control	$1,950,000	
Raw Materials Price Variance	42,000	
Accounts Payable Control		$1,992,000

Direct materials are often a large proportion of total manufacturing costs, sometimes over 60%. Consequently, many companies will at least measure the direct materials efficiency variance in total by physically comparing what remains in direct materials inventory against what should be remaining, given the output of finished goods for the accounting period. In our example, suppose that such a comparison showed an unfavourable materials efficiency variance of $90,000. The journal entry would be:

Raw Materials Efficiency Variance	$90,000	
Inventory: Raw and In-Process Control		$90,000

The under- or overallocated manufacturing overhead costs may be split into various overhead variances (spending variance, efficiency variance, and production volume variance) as explained in Chapters 7 and 8.

Example 2: Trigger Points Are Stages A and D
This example, also based on SVC and using the same data, presents a backflush costing system that, relative to Example 1, is a more dramatic departure from a sequential tracking inventory costing system. The first trigger point in this example is the same as the first trigger point in Example 1 (the purchase of direct materials), but the second trigger point is the sale—not the completed manufacture—of finished units. Toyota's cost accounting at its Kentucky plant is similar to this type of costing system. There are two justifications for this accounting system:

◆ To remove the incentive for managers to produce for inventory.
◆ To increase managers' focus on selling units.

If the value of finished goods inventory includes conversion costs, managers can bolster operating income by producing more units than are sold. Having trigger point 2 as the sale instead of the completion of production, however, reduces the attractiveness of producing for inventory by recording conversion costs as period costs instead of capitalizing them as inventoriable costs. This variation of backflush costing treats all conversion costs as period costs.

The inventory account in this example is confined solely to direct materials (whether they are in storerooms, in process, or in finished goods). There is only one inventory account:

Type	Account Title
Combined direct materials inventory and any direct materials in work in process and finished goods	Inventory Control

Exhibit 20-7, Panel B, presents the journal entries in this case. Entry (a) is prompted by the same trigger point 1 as in Example 1, the purchase of direct materials. Entry (b) for the conversion costs incurred is recorded in an identical manner as in Example 1. Trigger point 2 is the sale of good finished units (not their production, as in Example 1), so there is no entry corresponding to entry (c) of Example 1. The cost of finished units is computed only when finished units are sold (which corresponds to entry (d) of Example 1): 99,000 units sold × $31 = $3,069,000, consisting of direct materials (99,000 × $19 = $1,881,000) and conversion costs allocated (99,000 × $12 = $1,188,000).

No conversion costs are inventoried. That is, compared to Example 1, Example 2 does not attach $12,000 ($12 per unit $\times$ 1,000 units) of conversion costs to finished goods inventory. Hence, Example 2 allocates $12,000 less in conversion costs than Example 1. Of the $1,260,000 in conversion costs, $1,188,000 is allocated at standard cost to the units sold. The remaining $72,000 ($1,260,000 – $1,188,000) of conversion costs is underallocated. Entry (e) in Exhibit 20-7, Panel B, presents the journal entry if SVC, like many companies, writes off these underallocated costs monthly as additions to cost of goods sold.

The April ending balance of Inventory Control is $69,000 ($50,000 direct materials still on hand + $19,000 direct materials embodied in the 1,000 units manufactured but not sold during the period). Exhibit 20-8 provides an overview of this version of backflush costing. Entries are keyed to Exhibit 20-7, Panel B. The approach described in Example 2 closely approximates the costs computed using sequential tracking when a company holds minimal work in process and finished goods inventories.

Example 3: Trigger Points Are Stages C and D   This example presents an extreme and simpler version of backflush costing. It has only one trigger point for making journal entries to inventory—SVC's completion of finished units. Exhibit 20-7, Panel C, presents the journal entries in this case, using the same data as in Examples 1 and 2. Note that since the purchase of direct materials is not a trigger point, there is no entry corresponding to entry (a)—purchases of direct materials. Exhibit 20-8 provides an overview of this version of backflush costing. Entries are keyed to Exhibit 20-7, Panel C.

Compare entry (c) in Exhibit 20-7, Panel C, with entries (a) and (c) in Exhibit 20-7, Panel A. The simpler version in Example 3 ignores the $1,950,000 purchases of direct materials (entry (a) of Example 1). At the end of April, $50,000 of direct materials purchased has not yet been placed into production ($1,950,000 – $1,900,000 = $50,000), nor has it been entered into the inventory costing system.

Example 3 does not record accounts payable for direct materials until the products being manufactured are completely through the production process! As a result, this version of backflush costing is feasible only if there is a very short lag between receipt of direct materials and completion of the finished goods. Other journal entries must be made in addition to the trigger-point entries. Journal entries must be made for conversion costs incurred and for disposing of underallocated or overallocated conversion costs.

Extending Example 3, backflush costing systems could also use the sale of finished goods (instead of the production of finished goods) as the only trigger point. This version of backflush costing would be most suitable for a JIT production system with minimal direct materials, work-in-process, and finished goods inventories because this backflush costing system would maintain no inventory accounts.

SPECIAL CONSIDERATIONS IN BACKFLUSH COSTING

The accounting illustrated in Examples 1, 2, and 3 above does not strictly adhere to the GAAP of external reporting. For example, WIP (an asset) exists but is not recognized in the accounting system. Advocates of backflush costing, however, cite the materiality concept in support of these versions of backflushing. They claim that if inventories are low or their total costs are not subject to significant change from one accounting period to the next, operating income and inventory costs developed in a backflush costing system will not differ materially from the results generated by a system that adheres to generally accepted accounting principles.

Suppose material differences in operating income and inventories do exist between the results of a backflush costing system and those of a conventional standard costing system. An adjustment can be recorded to make the backflush numbers satisfy external reporting requirements. For example, the backflush entries in Example 2 would result in expensing all conversion costs as a part of COGS ($1,188,000 at standard costs + $72,000 writeoff of underallocated conversion costs = $1,260,000). But suppose conversion costs were regarded as sufficiently material in

Inventory Valuation, Cost of Goods Sold, GAAP

Trouble erupts when companies seeking increases in income overstate inventory value. Aware of this perverse incentive to managers, management accountants must pay careful attention to and correctly record both the physical quantity of inventories and values ascribed to them. A recent survey by *CFO Magazine* found that since 2001, one-fifth of financial executives said they felt more pressure to use accounting methods to "make results appear more favourable" and that 47% have felt pressure from superiors to use aggressive accounting techniques.

Many management accountants, as internal auditors, have the authority and expertise to either prevent or curtail this abuse. One remedy is to adopt a JIT strategy. Inventory overstatement is not a danger with a JIT strategy because the value of inventory is immaterial. But a JIT system brings on different challenges for management accountants. To successfully implement JIT, management accountants must be comfortable working in a changing and ambiguous environment and balance the demands of different managers.

Marketing managers may seek greater levels of customization and customer responsiveness that production and purchasing managers find burdensome. Several of the rewards of moving to a JIT system—more reliable deliveries to customers and greater customer responsiveness—may be difficult to quantify in the short run. Management accountants must therefore motivate their teams to focus on long-term successes. At Cessna, for example, it wasn't until its third year of using lean manufacturing for its single-engine aircraft and business jets that the company began to see productivity gains in the 40% to 60% range.

Sources: T. Damos, "CFO Pressure Cooker," *Fortune,* June 28, 2004. H. Timmons, "El Paso Says Reserves May Have Been Falsified," *The New York Times,* May 4, 2004, p. C14.

amount to be included in Inventory Control. Then entry (e), closing the Conversion Costs accounts, would change as shown:

Original entry (e)	Conversion Costs Allocated	$1,188,000	
	Cost of Goods Sold	72,000	
	Conversion Costs Control		$1,260,000
Revised entry (e)	Conversion Costs Allocated	$1,188,000	
	Inventory Control (1,000 units × $12)	12,000	
	Cost of Goods Sold	60,000	
	Conversion Costs Control		$1,260,000

Criticisms of backflush costing focus mainly on the absence of audit trails—the ability of the accounting system to pinpoint the uses of resources at each step of the production process. The absence of large amounts of materials and WIP inventory means that managers can keep track of operations by personal observations, computer monitoring, and nonfinancial measures.

What are the implications of JIT and backflush costing systems for ABC systems? Simplifying the production process, as in a JIT system, makes more of the costs direct and so reduces the extent of overhead cost allocations. Simplified ABC systems are often adequate for companies implementing JIT. But even these simpler ABC systems can enhance backflush costing. Costs from ABC systems give relatively more accurate budgeted conversion costs per unit for different products, which are then used in the backflush costing system. The activity-based cost data are also useful for product costing, decision making, and cost management.

(Try to solve this problem before examining the solution that follows.)

PROBLEM 1

Lee Company has a Singapore plant that manufactures MP3 players. One component is an XT chip. Expected demand is for 5,200 of these chips in March 2013. Lee estimates the ordering cost per purchase order to be $250. The monthly carrying cost for one unit of XT in stock is $5.

REQUIRED

1. Compute the EOQ for the XT chip.
2. Compute the number of deliveries of XT in March 2013.
3. What are some conflicts that can arise from the use of an EOQ model?
4. Identify relevant costs and benefits of a JIT strategy.
5. What is the key difference between MRP and JIT supply-chain management strategies?
6. What resource is essential to successful implementation of either MRP or JIT strategies?

SOLUTION

1.
$$EOQ = \sqrt{\frac{2 \times 5,200 \times \$250}{\$5}}$$

$$= 721 \text{ chips (rounded)}$$

2. Number of deliveries $= 5,200 \div 721 = 8$ (rounded up)
3. The EOQ model focuses on the tradeoff between carrying and ordering costs but ignores purchasing, stockout, and quality costs. A performance measure for the purchasing manager could be a purely financial accounting measure which excludes the opportunity cost of misstating the EOQ. The EOQ optimal solution and the optimal performance threshold will not match because opportunity cost is included in considering the best EOQ. A similar problem arises if annual carrying costs of excess inventory are excluded from the performance measure for purchasing managers.
4. Relevant costs include purchasing, ordering, carrying, stockout, and opportunity costs. Financial accounting standards determine the methods of accounting for all but opportunity costs for purposes of external reporting. COGS and inventory valuation methods are standardized. For internal purposes, however, tradeoffs are required between incurring one type versus another of opportunity costs. Management accountants have the expertise required to provide this relevant information.
5. A JIT supply-chain management strategy is based on demand pull. The demand, an order for goods, initiates the system to supply goods. An MRP supply-chain management strategy is based on demand push, wherein a forecast of demand is sent directly to the supplier rather than an order. The demand forecast initiates the system to supply goods.
6. Both the JIT and MRP supply-chain strategies require effective information sharing. Often the information stored by one business function software in a company cannot be readily transmitted to another, which incurs delay. An ERP information system collects information from different computer systems into a single database and removes delay.

PROBLEM 2

Littlefield Company uses a backflush costing system with three trigger points:

◆ Purchase of direct materials
◆ Completion of good finished units of product
◆ Sale of finished goods

There are no beginning inventories. Information for April 2013 is:

Direct materials purchased	$ 880,000
Direct materials used	$ 850,000
Conversion costs incurred	$ 422,000
Conversion costs allocated	$ 400,000
Costs transferred to finished goods	$1,250,000
Cost of goods sold	$1,190,000

REQUIRED

1. Prepare journal entries for April (without disposing of underallocated or over-allocated conversion costs). Assume there are no direct materials variances.
2. Under an ideal JIT production system, how would the amounts in your journal entries differ from the journal entries in requirement 1?

SOLUTION

1. Journal entries for April are:

Entry (a)	Inventory: Materials and In-Process Control	$ 880,000	
	Accounts Payable Control		$ 880,000
	(direct materials purchased)		
Entry (b)	Conversion Costs Control	$ 422,000	
	Various accounts (such as		
	Wages Payable Control)		$ 422,000
	(conversion costs incurred)		
Entry (c)	Finished Goods Control	$1,250,000	
	Inventory: Materials and In-Process Control		$ 850,000
	Conversion Costs Allocated		400,000
	(standard cost of finished goods completed)		
Entry (d)	Cost of Goods Sold	$1,190,000	
	Finished Goods Control		$1,190,000
	(standard costs of finished goods sold)		

2. Under an ideal JIT production system, if the manufacturing lead time per unit is very short, there could be zero inventories at the end of each day. Entry (c) would be $1,190,000 finished goods production (to match finished goods sold in entry (d)), not $1,250,000. If the Marketing department could only sell goods costing $1,190,000, the JIT production system would call for direct materials purchases and conversion costs of lower than $880,000 and $422,000, respectively, in entries (a) and (b).

SUMMARY POINTS

The following question-and-answer format summarizes the chapter's learning outcomes. Each point presents a key question, and the guidelines are the answer to that question.

LEARNING OUTCOMES	GUIDELINES
1. How do managers use the EOQ model?	The economic order quantity (EOQ) decision model calculates the optimal quantity of inventory to order by balancing ordering and carrying costs. The larger the order quantity, the higher the annual carrying costs and the lower the annual ordering costs. The EOQ model includes both costs recorded in the financial accounting system and opportunity costs not recorded in the financial accounting system.

2. How can companies reduce the conflict between the EOQ decision model and the models used for performance evaluation?	The opportunity cost of investment tied up in inventory is a key input in the EOQ decision model. Some companies include opportunity costs when evaluating managers so that the EOQ decision model is consistent with the performance evaluation model.
3. What are the features of a JIT strategy of supply-chain management?	A JIT strategy is based on demand-pull. Five features of a JIT production system are (a) organizing production in manufacturing cells, (b) hiring and training multiskilled workers, (c) emphasizing total quality management, (d) reducing manufacturing lead time and setup time, and (e) building strong supplier relationships.
4. How do materials requirement planning (MRP) systems differ from enterprise resource planning (ERP) systems?	Materials requirement planning (MRP) systems use a "push-through" approach that manufactures finished goods for inventory on the basis of demand forecasts. ERP systems are information management systems that consolidate data from different computer systems into a single database.
5. How does backflush costing simplify job costing?	Backflush costing delays recording some of the journal entries relating to the cycle from purchase of direct materials to the sale of finished goods. Traditional job-costing systems use sequential tracking, in which recording of the journal entries occurs in the same order as actual purchases and progress in production. Most backflush costing systems do not record journal entries for the work-in-process stage of production. Some backflush costing systems also do not record entries for either the purchase of direct materials or the completion of finished goods.

TERMS TO LEARN

This chapter and the Glossary at the end of the book contain definitions of the following important terms:

backflush costing (p. 823)
carrying costs (p. 805)
economic order quantity
    (EOQ) (p. 805)
enterprise resource planning
    (ERP) (p. 820)
inventory management (p. 804)
just-in-time (JIT) production (p. 811)

just-in-time (JIT) purchasing (p. 810)
lean production (p. 811)
manufacturing cells (p. 812)
materials requirements planning
    (MRP) (p. 819)
ordering costs (p. 804)
purchase order lead time (p. 805)
purchasing costs (p. 804)

reorder point (p. 808)
safety stock (p. 809)
sequential tracking (p. 821)
shrinkage costs (p. 805)
stockout costs (p. 805)
synchronous tracking (p. 821)
trigger point (p. 821)

ASSIGNMENT MATERIAL

MyAccountingLab Make the grade with MyAccountingLab: The questions, exercises, and problems marked in red can be found on MyAccountingLab at **www.myaccountinglab.com.** You can practise them as often as you want, and most feature step-by-step guided instructions to help you find the right answer. Exercises and problems with an Excel icon in the margin have an accompanying Excel template on MyAccountingLab.

SHORT-ANSWER QUESTIONS

20-1 Why do better decisions regarding the purchasing and managing of goods for sale frequently cause dramatic percentage increases in net income?

20-2 Name five cost categories that are important in managing goods for sale in a retail organization.

20-3 What assumptions are made when using the simplest version of the economic order quantity (EOQ) decision model?

20-4 Give examples of costs included in annual carrying costs of inventory when using the EOQ decision model.

20-5 Give three examples of opportunity costs that typically are not recorded in accounting systems, although they are relevant to the EOQ model.

20-6 What are the steps in computing the cost of a prediction error when using the EOQ decision model?

20-7 Why might goal-congruence issues arise when an EOQ model is used to guide decisions on how much to order?

20-8 Describe just-in-time (JIT) purchasing and its benefits.

20-9 What are three factors causing reductions in the cost to place purchase orders of materials?

20-10 What is supply-chain analysis and how can it benefit manufacturers and retailers?

20-11 What are some obstacles to companies adopting a supply-chain approach?

20-12 What are the main features in a JIT production system?

20-13 Distinguish job-costing systems using sequential tracking from backflush costing.

20-14 Describe three different versions of backflush costing.

EXERCISES

20-15 **Terminology.** A number of terms are listed below:

backflush costing	carrying costs
economic order quantity	enterprise resource planning (ERP)
inventory management	just-in-time (JIT) production
just-in-time (JIT) purchasing	lean production
ordering costs	purchasing costs
reorder point safety stock	shrinkage costs
stockout costs	synchronous tracking
trigger point	

REQUIRED

Select the terms from the above list to complete the following sentences.

Supply-chain strategy decisions determine _____ activities. Managing inventory involves the identification of three relevant costs, _____, _____ and _____. One strategy of _____ will match to a production decision of _____ or _____ production. This JIT purchasing strategy will minimize _____ of inventory and reduce or eliminate both _____ and _____ but may increase _____ costs. The goal of the management team is to minimize the overall combination of costs associated with inventory management. Any inventory management model requires careful analysis to identify the _____ _____, the economic _____ _____ _____ and the _____ _____. The management team requires high-quality information in a database of the type found in _____ _____ _____ systems. ERP systems are demand-pull systems. Implementing a good demand-pull system requires a highly coordinated information flow that supports lean production. Lean production (JIT) can eliminate inventory and therefore _____ _____ is appropriate. With no WIP or materials inventories, the need for sequential or _____ _____ of costs of production through the inventories is no longer necessary. Instead _____ _____ are identified such as materials purchase and completion of unspoiled finished goods. Costs transfer at only these two trigger points from the Direct Materials to the Finished Goods inventory.

20-16 **Economic order quantity for retailer.** Fan Base (FB) operates a megastore featuring sports merchandise. It uses an EOQ decision model to make inventory decisions. It is now considering inventory decisions for its Los Angeles Galaxy soccer jerseys product line. This is a highly popular item. Data for 2013 are:

Expected annual demand for Galaxy jerseys	10,000
Ordering cost per purchase order	$200
Carrying cost per year	$ 7 per jersey

Each jersey costs FB $40 and sells for $80. The $7 carrying cost per jersey per year comprises the required return on investment of $4.80 (12% $40 purchase price) plus $2.20 in relevant insurance, handling, and theft-related costs. The purchasing lead time is 7 days. FB is open 365 days a year.

REQUIRED

1. Calculate the EOQ.
2. Calculate the number of orders that will be placed each year.
3. Calculate the reorder point.

1. EOQ ≈ 756 jerseys

20-17 Economic order quantity, effect of parameter changes (continuation of 20-16). Athletic Textiles (AT) manufactures the Galaxy jerseys that Fan Base (FB) sells to its customers. AT has recently installed computer software that enables its customers to conduct "one-stop" purchasing using state-of-the-art website technology. FB's ordering cost per purchase order will be $30 using this new technology.

1
1. EOQ ≈ 293 jerseys

REQUIRED

1. Calculate the EOQ for the Galaxy jerseys using the revised ordering cost of $30 per purchase order. Assume all other data from Exercise 20-16 are the same. Comment on the result.
2. Suppose AT proposes to "assist" FB. AT will allow FB customers to order directly from the AT website. AT would ship directly to these customers. AT would pay $10 to FB for every Galaxy jersey purchased by one of FB's customers. Comment qualitatively on how this offer would affect inventory management at FB. What factors should FB consider in deciding whether to accept AT's proposal?

20-18 EOQ for a retailer. The Cloth Centre sells fabrics to a wide range of industrial and consumer users. One of the products it carries is denim cloth, used in the manufacture of jeans and carrying bags. The supplier for the denim cloth pays all incoming freight. No incoming inspection of the denim is necessary because the supplier has a track record of delivering high-quality merchandise. The purchasing officer of the Cloth Centre has collected the following information:

1
1. EOQ ≈ 2,000 metres

Annual demand for denim cloth	20,000 metres
Ordering cost per purchase order	$160
Carrying cost per year	20% of purchase costs
Safety-stock requirements	None
Cost of denim cloth	$8 per metre

The purchasing lead time is 2 weeks. The Cloth Centre is open 250 days a year (50 weeks for 5 days a week).

REQUIRED

1. Calculate the EOQ for denim cloth.
2. Calculate the number of orders that will be placed each year.
3. Calculate the reorder point for denim cloth.

20-19 EOQ for manufacturer. Lakeland Company, which produces lawn mowers, purchases 18,000 units of a rotor blade part each year at a cost of $60 per unit. Lakeland requires a 15% annual rate of return on investment. In addition, the relevant carrying cost (for insurance, materials handling, breakage, and so on) is $6 per unit per year. The relevant ordering cost per purchase order is $150.

1
1. EOQ ≈ 600 units

REQUIRED

1. Calculate Lakeland's EOQ for the rotor blade part.
2. Calculate Lakeland's annual relevant ordering costs for the EOQ calculated in requirement 1.
3. Calculate Lakeland's annual relevant carrying costs for the EOQ calculated in requirement 1.
4. Assume that demand is uniform throughout the year and known with certainty so that there is no need for safety stocks. The purchase-order lead time is half a month. Calculate Lakeland's reorder point for the rotor blade part.

20-20 Sensitivity of EOQ to changes in relevant ordering and carrying costs. Alyia Company's annual demand for Model X253 is 10,000 units. Alyia is unsure about the relevant carrying cost per unit per year and the relevant ordering cost per purchase order. This table presents six possible combinations of carrying and ordering costs.

1
1. EOQ (D = $10, C $300), 775

Relevant Carrying Cost per Unit per Year	Relevant Ordering Cost per Purchase Order
$10	$300
$10	$200
$15	$300
$15	$200
$20	$300
$20	$200

1. Determine EOQ for Alyia for each of the relevant ordering and carrying-cost alternatives.
2. How does your answer to requirement 1 give insight into the impact on EOQ of changes in relevant ordering and carrying costs?

1. Increased operating profit, $600,000

20-21 Inventory management and the balanced scorecard. Devin Sports Cars (DSC) has implemented a balanced scorecard to measure and support its just-in-time production system. In the learning and growth category, DSC measures the percentage of employees who are cross-trained to perform a wide variety of production tasks. Internal business process measures are inventory turns and on-time delivery. The customer perspective is measured using a customer satisfaction measure, and financial performance using operating income. DSC estimates that if it can increase the percentage of cross-trained employees by 5%, the resulting increase in labour productivity will reduce inventory-related costs by $100,000 per year and shorten delivery times by 10%. The 10% reduction in delivery times, in turn, is expected to increase customer satisfaction by 5%, and each 1% increase in customer satisfaction is expected to increase revenues by 2% due to higher prices.

REQUIRED

1. Assume that budgeted revenues in the coming year are $5,000,000. Ignoring the costs of training, what is the expected increase in operating income in the coming year if the number of cross-trained employees is increased by 5%?
2. What is the most DSC would be willing to pay to increase the percentage of cross-trained employees if it is only interested in maximizing operating income in the coming year?
3. What factors other than short-term profits should DSC consider when assessing the benefits from employee cross-training?

1. Total net incremental costs, current system, $650,000

20-22 JIT production, relevant benefits, relevant costs. The Champion Hardware Company manufactures specialty brass door handles at its Kitchener plant. Champion is considering implementing a JIT production system. The following are the estimated costs and benefits of JIT production:

a. Annual additional tooling costs would be $100,000.
b. Average inventory would decline by 80% from the current level of $1,000,000.
c. Insurance, space, materials handling, and setup costs, which currently total $300,000 annually, would decline by 25%.
d. The emphasis on quality inherent in JIT production would reduce rework costs by 30%. Champion currently incurs $200,000 in annual rework costs.
e. Improved product quality under JIT production would enable Champion to raise the price of its product by $4 per unit. Champion sells 40,000 units each year.

  Champion's required rate of return on inventory investment is 15% per year.

REQUIRED

1. Calculate the net benefit or cost to Champion if it adopts JIT production at the Kitchener plant.
2. What nonfinancial and qualitative factors should Champion consider when making the decision to adopt JIT production?
3. Suppose Champion implements JIT production at its Kitchener plant. Give examples of performance measures Champion could use to evaluate and control JIT production. What would be the benefit of Champion implementing an enterprise resource planning (ERP) system?

1. Finished Goods Control DR, $3,484,000

20-23 Backflush costing and JIT production. Road Warrior Corporation assembles handheld computers that have scaled-down capabilities of laptop computers. Each handheld computer takes 6 hours to assemble. Road Warrior uses a JIT production system and a backflush costing system with three trigger points:

◆ Purchase of direct materials.
◆ Completion of good finished units of product.
◆ Sale of finished goods.

  There are no beginning inventories of materials or finished goods. The following data are for August 2013:

Direct materials purchased	$2,754,000
Direct materials used	$2,733,600
Conversion costs incurred	$ 723,600
Conversion costs allocated	$ 750,400

Road Warrior records direct materials purchased and conversion costs incurred at actual costs. When finished goods are sold, the backflush costing system "pulls through" standard direct material cost ($102 per unit) and standard conversion cost ($28 per unit). Road Warrior produced 26,800 finished units in August 2013 and sold 26,400 units. The actual direct material cost per unit in August 2013 was $102, and the actual conversion cost per unit was $27.

REQUIRED

1. Prepare summary journal entries for August 2013 (without disposing of under- or overallocated conversion costs).
2. Post the entries in requirement 1 to T-accounts for applicable Inventory: Materials and In-Process Control, Finished Goods Control, Conversion Costs Control, Conversion Costs Allocated, and Cost of Goods Sold.
3. Under an ideal JIT production system, how would the amounts in your journal entries differ from those in requirement 1?

20-24 **Backflush costing, two trigger points, materials purchase and sale** (continuation of 20-23). Assume the same facts as in Exercise 20-23, except that Road Warrior now uses a backflush costing system with the following two trigger points:

◆ Purchase of direct materials.
◆ Sale of finished goods.

⑤

1. Cost of Goods Sold DR, $3,432,000

The Inventory Control account will include direct materials purchased but not yet in production, materials in work in process, and materials in finished goods but not sold. No conversion costs are inventoried. Any under- or overallocated conversion costs are written off monthly to Cost of Goods Sold.

REQUIRED

1. Prepare summary journal entries for August, including the disposition of under- or overallocated conversion costs.
2. Post the entries in requirement 1 to T-accounts for Inventory Control, Conversion Costs Control, Conversion Costs Allocated, and Cost of Goods Sold.

20-25 **Backflush costing, two trigger points, completion of production and sale** (continuation of 20-24). Assume the same facts as in Exercise 20-24, except now Road Warrior uses only two trigger points, the completion of good finished units of product and the sale of finished goods. Any under- or overallocated conversion costs are written off monthly to Cost of Goods Sold.

⑤

1. Conversion Costs Allocated $750,400

REQUIRED

1. Prepare summary journal entries for August, including the disposition of under- or overallocated conversion costs.
2. Post the entries in requirement 1 to T-accounts for Finished Goods Control, Conversion Costs Control, Conversion Costs Allocated, and Cost of Goods Sold.

PROBLEMS

20-26 **Effect of different order quantities on ordering costs and carrying costs, EOQ.** Koala Blue, a retailer of bed and bath linen, sells 234,000 packages of Mona Lisa designer sheets each year. Koala Blue incurs an ordering cost of $81 per purchase order placed with Mona Lisa Enterprises and an annual carrying cost of $11.70 per package. Liv Carrol, purchasing manager at Koala Blue, seeks your help: She wants to understand how ordering and carrying costs vary with order quantity.

①

1. Total relevant costs, scenario 1, $26,325

	Scenario				
	1	**2**	**3**	**4**	**5**
Annual demand (packages)	234,000	234,000	234,000	234,000	234,000
Cost per purchase order	$ 81	$ 81	$ 81	$ 81	$ 81
Carrying cost per package per year	$ 11.70	$ 11.70	$ 11.70	$ 11.70	$ 11.70
Quantity (packages) per purchase order	900	1,500	1,800	2,100	2,700
Number of purchase orders per year					
Annual relevant ordering costs					
Annual relevant carrying costs					
Annual total relevant costs of ordering and carrying inventory					

1. Complete the preceding table for Liv Carrol. What is the EOQ? Comment on your results.
2. Mona Lisa is about to introduce a Web-based ordering system for its customers. Liv Carrol estimates that Koala Blue's ordering costs will be reduced to $49 per purchase order. Calculate the new EOQ and the new annual relevant costs of ordering and carrying inventory.
3. Liv Carrol estimates that Koala Blue will incur a cost of $2,000 to train its two purchasing assistants to use the new Mona Lisa system. Help Liv Carrol present a case to upper management showing that Koala Blue will be able to recoup its training costs within the first year of adoption.

2. Weekly demand, 2,500 pairs of shoes

20-27 EOQ, uncertainty, safety stock, reorder point. Clarkson Shoe Co. produces and sells excellent quality walking shoes. After production, the shoes are distributed to 20 warehouses around the country. Each Warehouse services approximately 100 stores in its region. Clarkson uses an EOQ model to determine the number of pairs of shoes to order for each warehouse from the factory. Annual demand for Warehouse OR2 is approximately 120,000 pairs of shoes. The ordering cost is $250 per order. The annual carrying cost of a pair of shoes is $2.40 per pair.

REQUIRED
1. Use the EOQ model to determine the optimal number of pairs of shoes per order.
2. Assume each month consists of approximately 4 weeks. If it takes 1 week to receive an order, at what point should Warehouse OR2 reorder shoes?
3. Although OR2's average monthly demand is 10,000 pairs of shoes (120,000 ÷ 12 months), demand each month may vary from the average by up to 20%. To handle the variation in demand Clarkson has decided that OR2 should maintain enough safety stock to cover any demand level. How much safety stock should Warehouse OR2 hold? How will this affect the reorder point and reorder quantity?
4. What is the total relevant ordering and carrying costs with safety stock and without safety stock?

1. Annual cost of producing and carrying J-Pods in inventory, $3,040,000

20-28 MRP and ERP. MacroHard Corp. produces J-Pods, music players that can download thousands of songs. MacroHard forecasts that demand in 2013 will be 48,000 J-Pods. The variable production cost of each J-Pod is $50. Due to the large $50,000 cost per setup, MacroHard plans to produce J-Pods once a month in batches of 4,000 each. The carrying cost of a unit in inventory is $20 per year.

REQUIRED
1. Using an MRP system, what is the annual cost of producing and carrying J-Pods in inventory? (Assume that, on average, half of the units produced in a month are in inventory.)
2. A new manager at MacroHard has suggested that the company use the EOQ model to determine the optimal batch size to produce. (To use the EOQ model, MacroHard needs to treat the setup cost in the same way it would treat ordering cost in a traditional EOQ model.) Determine the optimal batch size and number of batches. Round up the number of batches to the nearest whole number. What would be the annual cost of producing and carrying J-Pods in inventory if it uses the optimal batch size?
3. MacroHard is also considering switching from an MRP system to a JIT system. This will result in producing to demand in batch sizes of 500 J-Pods. The frequency of production batches will force MacroHard to reduce setup time and will result in a reduction in setup cost. The new setup cost will be $5,000 per setup. What is the annual cost of producing and carrying J-Pods in inventory under the JIT system?
4. Compare the models analyzed in the previous parts of the problem. What are the advantages and disadvantages of each?

1. EOQ ≈ 4,000 computers

20-29 Effect of management evaluation criteria on EOQ model. Computers 4 U is an online company that sells computers to individual consumers. The annual demand for one model that will be shipped from the northeast distribution centre is estimated to be 500,000 computers. The ordering cost is $800 per order. The cost of carrying a computer in inventory is $50 per year, which includes $20 in opportunity cost of investment. The average purchase cost of a computer is $200.

REQUIRED
1. Compute the optimal order quantity using the EOQ model.
2. Compute the number of orders per year and the annual relevant total cost of ordering and holding inventory.
3. Assume that the benchmark that is used to evaluate distribution centre managers includes only the out-of-pocket costs incurred (that is, managers' evaluations do not include the opportunity cost of investment tied up in holding inventory). If the manager makes the EOQ decision based upon the benchmark, the order quantity would be calculated using a

carrying cost of $30, not $50. How would this affect the EOQ amount and the actual annual relevant cost of ordering and carrying inventory?

4. What will the inconsistency between the actual carrying cost and the benchmark used to evaluate managers cost the company? Why do you think the company currently excludes the opportunity costs from the calculation of the benchmark? What could the company do to encourage the manager to make decisions more congruent with the goal of reducing total inventory costs?

20-30 **Effect of EOQ ordering on supplier costs** (continuation of Problem 20-29). IMBest Computers supplies computers to Computers 4 U. Terry Moore, the president of IMBest, is pleased to hear that Computers 4 U will be ordering 500,000 computers. Moore has asked his accounting and production departments to team up and determine the best production schedule to meet Computers 4 U's desired delivery schedule. Assume that the computers would be ordered in batches of 2,000 and that there would be 250 orders annually. Because Computers 4 U's employees work a 5-day work week for 50 weeks a year, they would expect to receive an order every day. They have developed the following two production alternatives:

1. Setup cost, Alternative A, $50,000

A. IMBest could produce the 10,000 units demanded per week (2,000 × 5) in one large run on Mondays. Shipments would be made each day. If this option is chosen then IMBest would only have to set up the machines once a week, but would incur carrying costs to hold the computers in inventory until Computers 4 U's desired delivery date.

B. IMBest could rearrange its production schedule during the week and produce 2,000 computers each day of the week, totalling 10,000 computers per week. Shipments would be made at the end of each production day. If it chooses this alternative, then it will incur setup costs every day, but carrying costs would be negligible and are assumed to be zero.

REQUIRED

1. If setup costs are $1,000 per setup and carrying costs are $50 per computer per year, what would be the annual cost of each alternative?
2. How much would carrying costs have to increase before the preferred alternative would change?

20-31 **JIT purchasing, relevant benefits, relevant costs.** (CMA, adapted) The Margro Corporation is an automotive supplier that uses automatic turning machines to manufacture precision parts from steel bars. Margro's inventory of raw steel averages $600,000. John Oates, president of Margro, and Helen Gorman, Margro's controller, are concerned about the costs of carrying inventory. The steel supplier is willing to supply steel in smaller lots at no additional charge. Gorman identifies the following effects of adopting a JIT inventory program to virtually eliminate steel inventory:

1. Total incremental costs, JIT purchasing policy, $156,500

◆ Without scheduling any overtime, lost sales due to stockouts would increase by 35,000 units per year. However, by incurring overtime premiums of $40,000 per year, the increase in lost sales could be reduced to 20,000 units per year. This would be the maximum amount of overtime that would be feasible for Margro.

◆ Two warehouses currently used for steel bar storage would no longer be needed. Margro rents one warehouse from another company under a cancellable leasing arrangement at an annual cost of $60,000. The other warehouse is owned by Margro and contains 12,000 square metres. Three-quarters of the space in the owned warehouse could be rented for $1.50 per square metre per year. Insurance and property tax costs totalling $14,000 per year would be eliminated.

Margro's required rate of return on investment is 20% per year. Margro's budgeted income statement for the year ending December 31, 2013 (in thousands) is as follows:

Margro Corporation Budgeted Income Statement
For the Year Ending December 31, 2013
(in thousands)

Revenue (900,000 units)		$10,800
Cost of goods sold		
Variable costs	$4,050	
Fixed costs	1,450	
Total costs of goods sold		5,500
Gross margin		5,300
Marketing and distribution costs		
Variable costs	$ 900	
Fixed costs	1,500	
Total marketing and distribution costs		2,400
Operating income		$ 2,900

1. Calculate the estimated dollar savings (loss) for the Margro Corporation that would result in 2013 from the adoption of JIT purchasing.
2. Identify and explain other factors that Margro should consider before deciding whether to adopt JIT purchasing.

③

1. Total costs Maji, $935,930

20-32 Supply-chain effects on total relevant inventory cost. Cow Spot Computer Co. outsources the production of motherboards for its computers. It has narrowed down its choice of suppliers to two companies: Maji and Induk. Maji is an older company with a good reputation, while Induk is a newer company with cheaper prices. Given the difference in reputation, 5% of the motherboards will be inspected if they are purchased from Maji, but 25% of the motherboards will be inspected if they are purchased from Induk. The following data refers to costs associated with Maji and Induk.

	Maji	Induk
Number of orders per year	50	50
Annual motherboards demanded	10,000	10,000
Price per motherboard	$93	$90
Ordering cost per order	$10	$8
Inspection cost per unit	$5	$5
Average inventory level	100 units	100 units
Expected number of stockouts	100	300
Stockout cost (cost of rush order) per stockout	$5	$8
Units returned by customers for replacing motherboards	50	500
Cost of replacing each motherboard	$25	$25
Required annual return on investment	10%	10%
Other carrying cost per unit per year	$2.50	$2.50

REQUIRED

1. What is the relevant cost of purchasing from Maji and Induk?
2. What factors other than cost should Cow Spot consider?

⑤

1. Finished Goods Control DR, $945,000

20-33 Backflush costing and JIT production. The Acton Corporation manufactures electrical meters. For August, there were no beginning inventories of direct materials and no beginning or ending work in process. Acton uses a JIT production system and backflush costing with three trigger points for making entries in the accounting system:

◆ Purchase of direct materials—debited to Inventory: Materials and In-Process Control
◆ Completion of good finished units of product—debited to Finished Goods Control
◆ Sale of finished goods

Acton's August standard cost per meter is direct material, $25; and conversion cost, $20. The following data apply to August manufacturing:

Direct materials purchased	$550,000
Conversion costs incurred	$440,000
Number of finished units manufactured	21,000
Number of finished units sold	20,000

REQUIRED

1. Prepare summary journal entries for August (without disposing of under- or overallocated conversion costs). Assume no direct materials variances.
2. Post the entries in requirement 1 to T-accounts for Inventory: Materials and In-Process Control, Finished Goods Control, Conversion Costs Control, Conversion Costs Allocated, and Cost of Goods Sold.

⑤

1. Cost of Goods Sold DR, $900,000

20-34 Backflush, two trigger points, materials purchase and sale (continuation of 20-33). Assume that the second trigger point for Acton Corporation is the sale—rather than the completion—of finished goods. Also, the inventory account is confined solely to direct materials, whether these materials are in a storeroom, in work in process, or in finished goods. No conversion costs are inventoried. They are allocated to the units sold at standard costs. Any under- or overallocated conversion costs are written off monthly to Cost of Goods Sold.

1. Prepare summary journal entries for August, including the disposition of under- or overallo-cated conversion costs. Assume no direct materials variances.

2. Post the entries in requirement 1 to T-accounts for Inventory Control, Conversion Costs Control, Conversion Costs Allocated, and Cost of Goods Sold.

20-35 Backflush, two trigger points, completion of production and sale (continuation of 20-33). Assume the same facts as in Problem 20-33 except now there are only two trigger points: the completion of good finished units of product and the sale of finished goods.

1. Conversion Costs Allocated
$420,000

REQUIRED

1. Prepare summary journal entries for August, including the disposition of under- or overallo-cated conversion costs. Assume no direct materials variances.

2. Post the entries in requirement 1 to T-accounts for Finished Goods Control, Conversion Costs Control, Conversion Costs Allocated, and Cost of Goods Sold.

20-36 Lean accounting. Flexible Security Devices (FSD) has introduced a just-in-time production process and is considering the adoption of lean accounting principles to support its new pro-duction philosophy. The company has two product lines: Mechanical Devices and Electronic Devices. Two individual products are made in each line. The company's traditional cost accounting system allocates all plant-level overhead costs to individual products. Product-line overhead costs are traced directly to product lines, and then allocated to the two individual products in each line. Equipment costs are directly traced to products. The latest accounting report using traditional cost accounting methods included the following information (in thousands of dollars).

2. Value stream operating income, Mechanical Devices, $227

	Mechanical Devices		Electronic Devices	
	Product A	Product B	Product C	Product D
Sales	$700	$500	$900	$450
Direct materials (based on quantity used)	200	100	250	75
Direct manufacturing labour	150	75	200	60
Equipment costs	90	125	200	100
Allocated product-line overhead	110	60	125	50
Allocated plant-level overhead	50	35	80	25
Operating income	$100	$105	$ 45	$140

FSD has determined that each of the two product lines represents a distinct value stream. It has also determined that $120,000 of the allocated plant-level overhead costs repre-sents occupancy costs. Product A occupies 20% of the plant's square footage, Product B occu-pies 20%, Product C occupies 30%, and Product D occupies 15%. The remaining square footage is occupied by plant administrative functions or is not being used. Finally, FSD has decided that direct material should be expensed in the period it is purchased, rather than when the material is used. According to purchasing records, direct material purchase costs during the period were:

	Mechanical Devices		Electronic Devices	
	Product A	Product B	Product C	Product D
Direct materials (purchases)	$190	$125	$250	$90

REQUIRED

1. What are the cost objects in FSD's lean accounting system? Which of FSD's costs would be excluded when computing operating income for these cost objects?

2. Compute operating income for the cost objects identified in requirement 1 using lean accounting principles. Why does operating income differ from the operating income com-puted using traditional cost accounting methods?

20-37 EOQ conflicts. Ralph Menard is the owner of a truck repair shop. He uses an EOQ model for each of his truck parts. He initially predicts the annual demand for heavy-duty tires to be 2,000. Each tire has a purchase price of $60. The incremental ordering costs per purchase order are $48. The incremental carrying costs per year are $4.80 per unit plus 10% of the supplier's purchase price.

1. Annual relevant ordering and carrying costs, $1,440

1. Calculate the EOQ for heavy-duty tires, along with the sum of annual relevant ordering costs and carrying costs.
2. Suppose Menard is correct in all his predictions except the purchase price. (He ignored a new law that abolished tariff duties on imported heavy-duty tires, which led to lower prices from foreign competitors.) If he had been a faultless predictor, he would have foreseen that the purchase price would drop to $36 at the beginning of the year and would be unchanged throughout the year. What is the cost of the prediction error?

20-38 Backflush costing. The Ronowski Company produces telephones. For June, there were no beginning inventories of raw materials and no beginning and ending work in process. Ronowski uses a JIT production system and backflush costing with three trigger points for making entries in its accounting system:

1. Conversion Costs Control DR, $3,696,000

◆ Purchase of direct (raw) materials
◆ Completion of good finished units of product
◆ Sale of finished goods

   Ronowski's June standard cost per unit of telephone product is direct materials, $31.20; conversion costs, $18. There are three inventory accounts:

◆ Inventory: Raw
◆ Inventory: In-Process Control
◆ Finished Goods Control

   The following data apply to June manufacturing:

Raw materials purchased	$6,360,000
Conversion costs incurred	$3,696,000
Number of finished units manufactured	200,000
Number of finished units sold	192,000

REQUIRED

1. Prepare summary journal entries for June (without disposing of under- or overallocated conversion costs). Assume no direct materials variances.
2. Post the entries in requirement 1 to T-accounts for applicable Inventory Control, Conversion Costs Control, Conversion Costs Allocated, and Cost of Goods Sold.

20-39 Supplier evaluation and relevant costs of quality and timely deliveries. Copeland Sporting Goods is evaluating two suppliers of footballs, Big Red and Quality Sports. Pertinent information about each potential supplier follows:

Total annual relevant costs, Big Red, $738,940

Relevant Item	Big Red	Quality Sports
Purchase price per unit (case)	$ 60.00	$ 61.20
Ordering costs per order	$ 7.20	$ 7.20
Inspection costs per unit	$ 0.02	$ 0.00
Insurance, material handling, and so on per unit per year	$ 4.00	$ 4.50
Annual demand	12,000 units	12,000 units
Average quantity of inventory held during the year	100 units	100 units
Required return on investment	15%	15%
Stockout costs per unit	$ 24	$ 12
Stockout units per year	350 units	60 units
Customer returns	300 units	25 units
Customer-return costs per unit	$ 30	$ 30

REQUIRED

Calculate the relevant costs of purchasing (1) from Big Red and (2) from Quality Sports using the format of Exhibit 20-6 (p. 818). From whom should Copeland buy footballs?

20-40 Supply-chain analysis, company viewpoints. Manufacturing companies participating in a supply-chain initiative linking manufacturers and retailers recently made the following comments on the benefits of the initiative:

◆ "Receiving better information has allowed us to forecast and reduce inventory levels . . ."
◆ "You produce only what you need and that keeps the product and floor cost down."

- "There is more accuracy with the retailer's needs so that we can fine-tune our production scheduling."
- "The inventory levels are lower and we have less waste by not overstocking the warehouses."

Manufacturing companies highlighted the following information from retailers as most valuable to them:

- "We would like to see [the retailers] forward planning expectations of their sales."
- "We could use retail store level data on a daily basis and better scanner information."
- "Better forecasts, decisions about shelving and shelf allocations by retailers would help."
- "I wish we had access to each retailer's sales forecasts and the advertisements that they will be running next."

REQUIRED

1. What are the major benefits from adopting a supply-chain approach? Use the comments above as a prompt to a more detailed discussion. Explain how these benefits can lead to increased operating income.
2. What are the key obstacles to a manufacturer adopting a supply-chain approach?

20-41 Backflush costing, income manipulation, governance. Shira Honig, the chief financial officer of Silicon Valley Computer, is an enthusiastic advocate of just-in-time production. The SVC Keyboard Division that produces keyboards for personal computers has made dramatic improvements in its operations by a highly successful JIT implementation. The Keyboard Division president now wants to adopt backflush costing.

Honig discusses the backflush costing proposal with Ralph Strong, the controller of SVC. Strong is totally opposed to backflush costing. He argues that it will open up "Pandora's box" as regards allowing division managers to manipulate reported division operating income. A member of Strong's group outlines the three possible variations of backflush costing shown in Exhibits 20-7 and 20-8 (pp. 826–827). Strong notes that none of these three methods track work in process. He asserts that this omission would allow managers to "artificially change" reported operating income by manipulating work-in-process levels. He is especially scathing about the backflush costing where no entries are made until a sale occurs. He comments:

> Suppose the Division has already met its target operating income and wants to shift some of this year's income to next year. Under backflush costing with sale of finished goods as the trigger point, the Division will have an incentive to not make sales this year of goods produced this year. This is a bizarre incentive. I rest my case about why we should stay with a job-costing system using sequential tracking.

Strong concludes that as long as reported accounting numbers are central to SVC's performance and bonus reviews, backflush costing should never be adopted.

REQUIRED

1. What factors should SVC consider in deciding whether to adopt a version of backflush costing?
2. Are Strong's concerns about income manipulation sufficiently important for SVC to not adopt backflush costing?
3. What other ways has SVC to motivate managers to not "artificially change" reported income?

20-42 Purchase order size for retailer, EOQ, just-in-time purchasing. The 24-Hour Mart operates a chain of supermarkets. Its best-selling soft drink is Fruitslice. Demand (D) in April for Fruitslice at its Regina supermarket is estimated to be 7,200 cases (24 cans in each case). In March, the Regina supermarket estimated the ordering costs per purchase order (P) for Fruitslice to be $36. The carrying costs (C) of each case of Fruitslice in inventory for a month were estimated to be $1.20. At the end of March, the Regina 24-Hour Mart reestimated its carrying costs to be $1.80 per case per month to take into account an increase in warehouse-related costs.

During March, 24-Hour Mart restructured its relationship with suppliers. It reduced the number of suppliers from 600 to 180. Long-term contracts were signed only with those suppliers that agreed to make product quality checks before shipping. Each purchase order would be made by linking into the suppliers' computer network. The Regina 24-Hour Mart estimated that these changes would reduce the ordering costs per purchase order to $6. The 24-Hour Mart is open 30 days in April.

1. a. EOQ, 658 cases (always round up)

1. Calculate the economic order quantity in April for Fruitslice. Use the EOQ model, and assume in turn that
   a. $D = 7,200$; $P = \$36$; $C = \$1.20$
   b. $D = 7,200$; $P = \$36$; $C = \$1.80$
   c. $D = 7,200$; $P = \$6$; $C = \$1.80$
2. How does your answer to requirement 1 give insight into the retailer's movement toward JIT purchasing policies?

COLLABORATIVE LEARNING CASE

20-43 Backflushing. The following conversation occurred between Brian Richardson, plant manager at Glendale Engineering, and Charles Cheng, plant controller. Glendale manufactures automotive component parts, such as gears and crankshafts, for automobile manufacturers. Richardson has been very enthusiastic about implementing JIT and about simplifying and streamlining production and other business processes.

"Charles," Richardson began, "I would like to substantially simplify our accounting in the new JIT environment. Can't we just record one journal entry at the time we ship products to our customers? I don't want to have our staff spending time tracking inventory from one stage to the next, when we have as little inventory as we do."

"Brian," Cheng said, "I think you are right about simplifying the accounting, but we still have a fair amount of direct materials and finished goods inventory that varies from period to period, depending on the demand for specific products. Doing away with all inventory accounting may be a problem."

"Well," Richardson replied, "you know my desire to simplify, simplify, simplify. I know that there are some costs of oversimplifying, but I believe that, in the long run, simplification pays dividends. Why don't you and your staff study the issues involved, and I will put it on the agenda for our next management meeting."

REQUIRED

1. What version of backflush costing would you recommend that Cheng adopt? Remember Richardson's desire to simplify the accounting as much as possible. Develop support for your recommendation.
2. Think about the three versions of backflush costing shown in this chapter. These versions differ with respect to the number and types of trigger points used. Suppose your goal of implementing backflush costing is to simplify the accounting, but only if it closely matches the sequential-tracking approach. Which version of backflush costing would you propose if:
   a. Glendale had no direct materials and no work-in-process inventories but did have finished goods inventory?
   b. Glendale had no work-in-process and no finished goods inventories but did have direct materials inventory?
   c. Glendale had no direct materials, no work-in-process, and no finished goods inventories?
3. Backflush costing has its critics. In an article in the magazine *Management Accounting* titled "Beware of the New Accounting Myths," R. Calvasina, E. Calvasina, and G. Calvasina state:

   > The periodic (backflush) system has never been reflective of the reporting needs of a manufacturing system. In the highly standardized operating environments of the present JIT era, the appropriate system to be used is a perpetual accounting system based on an up-to-date, realistic set of standard costs. For management accountants to backflush on an actual cost basis is to return to the days of the outdoor privy (toilet).

   Comment on this statement.

PART SIX

Capital Budgeting: Methods of Investment Analysis

BUSINESS MATTERS

Investment Decisions and Relevant Costs

Capital budgeting for projects such as the Confederation Bridge linking Prince Edward Island to New Brunswick reflects a company's long-term strategic plans. Construction of the bridge took almost four years at a cost of $1 billion. The bridge has been designed for a 100-year lifetime. Tolls paid to cross the bridge vary with the number of axles and the type of vehicle. For example, an automobile with 2 axles costs $43.25, motorcycle $17.25, and pedestrians $4 each one-way trip, which escalates every year at a rate of 75% of the annual consumer price index (CPI). The subsidy was calculated based on the annual 1992 costs of $41.9 million to the government to operate a ferry service, which ceased the day the bridge opened. This subsidy is paid to Strait Crossing Bridge Ltd. (SCBL) in return for building, financing, operating, and maintaining the bridge until 2032, when the operating rights revert to the federal government. The bridge fulfills the government's constitutional obligation to provide PEI and the mainland with mutual, affordable, and reliable access.

LEARNING OUTCOMES

After studying this chapter, you should be able to

1. Apply the concept of the time value of money to capital budgeting decisions.

2. Evaluate discounted cash flow (DCF) and non-DCF methods to calculate rate of return (ROR).

3. Apply the concept of relevance to DCF methods of capital budgeting.

4. Assess the complexities in capital budgeting within an interdependent set of value-chain business functions.

5. Apply the concept of defensive strategic investment to the capital budgeting process.

This chapter introduces long-term **investment decisions** and internal cost control methods. An investment is a long-term cash allocation decision. Payments are made for years, perhaps decades. Comparisons of expected and actual outcomes from long-term investments (also called **investment programs** or **projects**) affect the balance sheet, income statement, and cash flow statement of companies.

Whereas operating costs such as the $41.9 million paid to SCBL by the federal government are short-term and performance-based, the contract ending in 2032 is long-term. When ownership transfers back to Ottawa, the federal government can then operate and maintain the bridge for its remaining 65-year life. SCBL will have received payment for their services, but prior to entering into the contract, they needed to carefully estimate what the relevant costs would be for the duration of the project as well as the revenues. The tolls and the escalation clause were negotiated to assure an agreed-upon rate of return for SCBL and the government throughout the project's entire lifetime.

Multi-year projects of this type require careful planning and control over several years, and the capital budget is one means to direct attention toward potential problems that may require remedy. **Capital budgeting** is the process of collating information in a familiar pro forma financial accounting format.

To fully grasp the importance of capital budgeting, the differences between the capital and operating budgets, each of which has its particular section on the cash flow statement, must be well understood. The outflow of cash from new investment or inflow from liquidating investments is reported in the cash flow statement as cash flow to (from) investments. The outflow of cash to repay long-term financing or inflow from new long-term financing is reported on the cash flow statement as cash flow to (from) financing. Both of these are separate from the operating cash flow on the cash flow statement.

The capital budget provides a basis for evaluating how appropriate the strategic choices made by top management have been. Strategies are usually long-term plans for future growth, although in sunset industries such as DVD movie rentals, the best strategy may be to simply harvest the rewards of past investment without making new investments for the future.

If a corporation is implementing a value-leadership strategy to receive premium prices for its outputs, it must make careful investment choices. Strategy will be implemented by paying today for research, patents, new equipment, and new employees to acquire higher revenue in the future. It is rare that corporations can pay for all desirable investments. The top management team often needs to postpone investments in one area to favour another. Investment decisions are the greatest challenge to a management team's strategic competence and commitment to the long-term benefit of the corporation.

A cost leadership strategy also requires investment for long-term growth, made more difficult when product or service lifecycles are short. Especially in electronics and telecommunications, products and services are obsolete within months of their introduction. But the people, equipment, and knowledge are much longer-lived. It could be more cost-effective to retrain labour to produce new products on depreciated equipment than to purchase new equipment and lay off labour.

Projects often require long-term financing, although corporate financing decisions are beyond the scope of this text. The Confederation Bridge project, for both providers and investors, produced a capital asset with an estimated useful life of at least a century. For the providers, this long-term asset is the contract; for the investors it is the bridge itself. The investors expect that they will earn more over the estimated useful life of the bridge than what they paid for their investment. Each service provider and investor in the project took risk and will earn a return. This is their return on investment (ROI).

SCBL took price and scheduling risk during the 44 months it took to construct the bridge. This is because the government would pay SCBL no annual subsidy until the bridge opened for use. The government and SCBL together took traffic or demand risk that enough traffic would cross the bridge to provide an expected annual profit that would accumulate to generate the long-term ROI. Investors took financing risk, providing funds to pay for construction that they could have invested elsewhere. In contrast to operating decisions, it is the balancing of risk and return that is the central consideration for investment decisions.

APPLYING THE CONCEPT OF THE TIME VALUE OF MONEY TO CAPITAL BUDGETING

Apply the concept of the time value of money to capital budgeting decisions.

Capacity management to sustain or accelerate growth of profit is the focus of capital budgeting decisions. Notice the unbreakable link between annual profit and its accumulation over the life of the investment, which sums to the ROI. Capacity is purchased to service the long-term growth in demand for outputs. Long-term or normal demand, rather than master-budget demand, relative to practical capacity is a key determinant of investment decisions (see Chapter 9).

But the longer a time horizon, the higher the uncertainty associated with future outcomes. In practical terms, the longer it takes to realize long-term demand the less probable it will actually be realized. It is unwise for a management team to base long-term capital budgeting decisions on the income statement of the current period. Investment in a long-term project almost always will decrease the reported operating income in the near term, but it is expected to increase both operating cash flow and operating income over the longer term. The current period's income does not report any effects of future investment projects or programs.

ACCRUALS ARE NOT CASH

It is important to understand that accrual accounting estimates of value are reported on the income statement and balance sheet. Theoretically, income is the residual from changes to assets and liabilities. The financial estimates of value for these long-term accounts are accruals made according to GAAP and reported on the balance sheet. Specific GAAP applies to the recognition and reporting of long-term contracted inflows of revenue. Neither long-term assets, long-term liabilities, nor equity are debits or credits to the cash account of any company.

As the current asset and liability sections of the balance sheet makes clear, revenue and expenses do not equal cash paid to or by the company. The cash account, a current asset, is reported on the balance sheet as the sum of all cash and cash equivalents. Cash flow will not equal either operating or net income for the current period. Accounts receivable reports cash payments owing to the company within the following 12 months, while accounts payable reports cash payments owed by the company within the following 12 months. Companies cannot pay their obligations with accounts receivable; they must pay in cash. Companies without cash to fulfill their contractual obligations are either insolvent or bankrupt. Therefore, the management team must focus on predicted cash flow when creating a capital budget. The predicted timing and amount of cash inflow and outflow is especially important.

The cash flow statement reconciles the prior year's ending cash balance reported on the balance sheet with the current year's ending cash balance. The realized cash inflow of revenue and cash outflow of expense payments is reported in the operating cash flow portion of the cash flow statement using either the direct or indirect method.[1] A quick glance at any set of financial statements will quickly confirm that neither operating income nor net income equals operating cash flow.

The GAAP-compliant statement of cash flow, however, also reports long-term sources of cash such as new debt issued by the company in the form of bonds and debentures or incurred by the company in the form of long-term loans and mortgages. Payments against old debt obligations are cash flow out within the reporting

---

[1]To review these financial accounting concepts, refer to any introductory financial accounting textbook.

time period. This cash outflow repays principal and interest amounts due on the financing incurred in the past. Investments also generate cash inflows from long-term assets put to use to provide value added to customers for which they will pay. Indeed, this is the definition of an asset—that which generates future benefits—and those benefits are conventionally measured as cash inflow. In this chapter, methods of measuring the cash flows of different alternative future investments will be presented with their strengths and weaknesses in different situations.

The sum of the operating cash flow, the cash flow from or to financing, and the cash flow from or to investments comprises a full cash flow statement reporting the realized net cash flow for the reporting time period. The realized net cash flow reconciles the cash balance on the prior period's balance sheet to the cash balance reported on the current period's balance sheet.

THE DECISION FRAMEWORK AND CAPITAL BUDGETING

Our focus is on the decision process leading to changes in the long-term asset and liability accounts intended to affect core operations of a company. Identification of the relevant costs and benefits of investing in or divesting long-term assets (or projects) begins with a discussion of cost analysis. The capital budgeting decision process model illustrated in Exhibit 21-1 illustrates a series of interdependent decisions. The team needs to be confident in the data quality, but the most important data is often either unreliable or missing. No analysis can remedy this characteristic of long-term investment risk.

The management team must establish whether its goal is to sustain a cost or a value leadership strategy for its investment decisions. The consensus within the team is central to the choice of the most appropriate investments. Analyzing information in light of the selected strategy requires explicit discussion and agreement on the assumptions that will be used to assess all the current investment alternatives. With a plan of assessment in place and good data, the team can identify and evaluate the relative strengths and weaknesses of the current alternatives, including the alternative of doing nothing. The evaluation comprises predictions of future performance outcomes.

There are several techniques available to analyze and predict future outcomes from investment data. Some are more imprecise but are nevertheless best at reflecting the actual economic reality of the company. The mathematics of more precise analyses may obscure some simple realities of a company instead of revealing them.

EXHIBIT 21-1
Capital Budgeting Decision Process Model

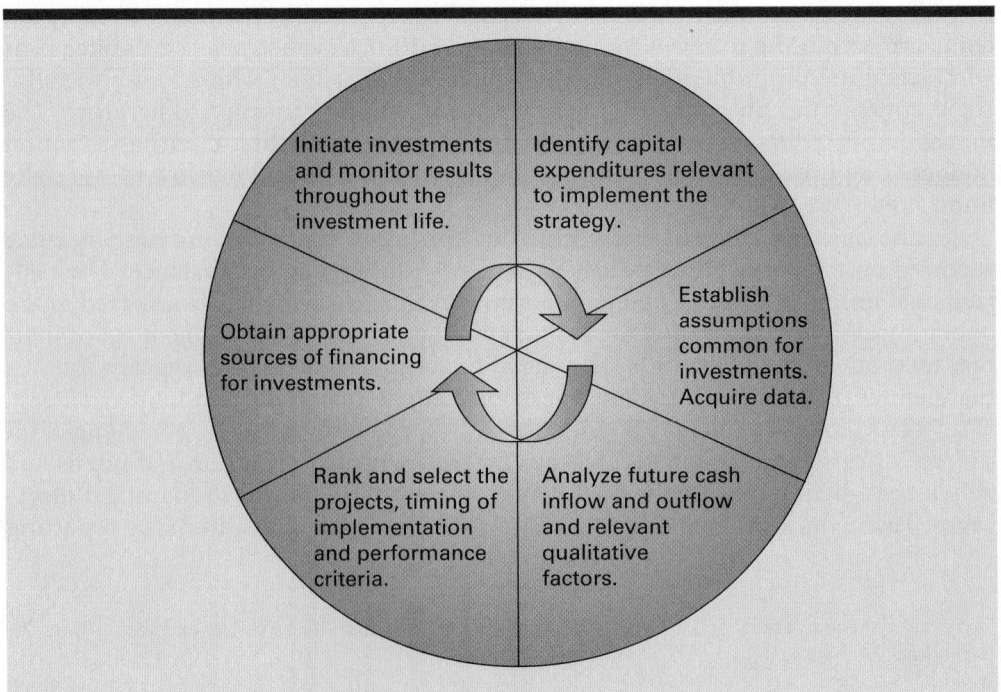

With the convenience and speed of current technology, however, the lack of mathematical skill is no longer an excuse to choose an inferior analytical technique. Nevertheless, the management team must be able to justify its recommendations. Their explanations need to highlight the different effects of each alternative on the company's key success factors.

The measures of investment performance differ from those of operating success; however, accurate feedback is essential to a company. The reports of investment performance should be made in the context of how well the strategy is being implemented rather than on a month-to-month or even year-to-year contribution to profitability basis. In some cases this contribution is the result of bad luck rather than bad management decisions, and the best performance measures will isolate to some extent the effects due to good management from those due to bad luck. Capital budgeting is a decision process wherein feedback is central. Feedback provides relevant information that will change prior expectations about likely long-term outcomes. As prior expectations change, so too could decisions made in earlier time periods in order to reduce a company's unexpected losses or to enhance prospects of future gains.

CAPITAL BUDGETING

The process is called capital budgeting in large part because there are insufficient corporate resources, including access to financing, to pursue all attractive investments. The capital budget represents a selection of long-term investments that fall within a specified budget constraint.

We have assumed that the corporate strategy is in place, but what must be decided is the best investment or investments to make that will implement the strategy. Strategic investments include those made for ERP systems, supply-chain management, or agility to incorporate both cost leadership and product customization. A revenue growth strategy could be achieved by expanding core business or expanding into adjacencies. Investments would differ depending on the strategy chosen.

Many alternatives could be chosen to implement a growth strategy, and each will draw upon and contribute to corporate resources in different ways. What will be constant among the alternative investments is the large capital expenditures that must be made to provide capacity to implement a strategy. The top management team must demonstrate due diligence in exploring the risk and return associated with each expenditure.

Risk and return analysis is presented fully in introductory finance courses. One widely taught model is called the capital asset pricing model (CAPM), which depicts an investing universe where the risk-return relationship is linear. The risk is the predictor and the return is the outcome variable in this regression (see Chapter 10). Risk models themselves are complex, and our focus here is on estimating return. To estimate the return over time on an investment, using discounted cash flow (DCF) models, information on the most likely relevant cash outflows and inflows as well as their timing must be gathered.

Capital budgeting emphasizes the role of financial information in investment decisions; however, nonfinancial and qualitative factors must also be considered. Nonfinancial factors include the effect of an investment on market share, revenue mix, productivity, yield, and environmental sustainability. Qualitative factors could include the effect of an investment on corporate governance and perceived corporate social responsibility.

Organizations choose those projects whose likely (predicted) long-term benefits exceed costs by the greatest amount. Formal analyses under any method include only predicted outcomes quantified in financial terms. Management teams use managerial judgment to take into account nonfinancial and qualitative considerations. Evaluating costs and benefits is often the responsibility of the management accountant. This means the measures of performance need to be associated with the value added from incurring the costs of the investment.

The ratio of the predicted cost inflow minus outflow divided by the total outflow for the investment is one measure of the **rate of return (ROR)**. It is similar to calculating an operating margin percentage, but total expected cash flows replace accruals as the basis for the calculation. It is worthwhile to recall that expected value is a specific mathematical term that multiplies a measure of outcome by its probability. The probabilities must add to 1.00 for each predicted outcome. The sum of these products is the expected value across all predicted outcomes (Chapter 3).

Long-term investments are appropriately financed by long-term debt to avoid the opportunity costs of spending too much cash immediately and jeopardizing the solvency of the corporation. Good long-term debt contracts match the timing of cash outflows to pay obligations somewhat closely to the timing of predicted cash inflows. For example, an investment with a useful life of 25 years would be financed by a 25-year long-term debt contract. At a minimum, when a company spends cash too early on a risky investment, the opportunity cost includes interest forgone on risk-free investments. Sources of financing include internally generated cash flow from operations and externally generated cash flow from capital markets (equity and debt instruments). Notice the relevance of operating cash flow, a short-term performance indicator, to the financing decision.

Internally generated cash flow must be adequate to cover any working capital outlays in the first year of a long-term investment because rarely do long-term investments generate cash inflow in their early years. Working capital outflow could include cash paid for supplies and employee training, increase in ongoing maintenance, and so on. Working capital outflow may occur throughout the project's lifetime. In the terminal year, however, this outflow will be zero and constitute a savings realized when the project ends. In capital budgeting, working capital is recovered at the end of the project's life cycle.[2]

Financing is most often the treasury function of an organization. Once the investment decision is made, then the financing must be acquired. Again this is an information-gathering process, and if financing is unavailable at a reasonable cost it will change the rank of the investment decision. In reality, financing opportunities are often investigated simultaneously with the formal analyses of the costs and benefits of various investments. One reason is that interest expense is a cash cost of any investment financed by debt.

As the project is implemented, the company must evaluate whether capital investments are being made as scheduled and within the budget. Integral to the selection of investments is the selection of appropriate performance criteria such as ROR. As the project generates cash inflows, monitoring and control may include a post-investment audit in which the predictions made at the time the project was selected are compared with the actual results.

This chapter emphasizes the information acquisition, selection, implementation, and control stages of capital budgeting because these are the stages in which the management accountant is most involved. Beyond the numbers, however, the ability of individual managers to "sell" their own projects to senior management is often pivotal in the acceptance or rejection of projects.

Exhibit 21-2 illustrates two different dimensions of cost analysis:

◆ The project dimension, for which life-cycle costing should be used (Chapter 12).
◆ The time dimension, for which the time value of money must be considered.

Each project is represented in Exhibit 21-2 as a distinct horizontal rectangle. The life of each project is longer than one accounting period. Capital budgeting focuses on the entire useful life of the project to consider all cash inflows or cash savings from the investment. The transparent vertical rectangle in Exhibit 21-2 illustrates the accounting-period focus on income determination and routine planning and control. This cross-section emphasizes the company's performance for the 2012 accounting period.

---

[2]Net working capital is an accrual concept and is the difference between short-term or current assets and short-term or current liabilities. The current assets are cash inflows forgone and current liabilities are cash outflows conserved. But the realization of both must occur within 12 months. This is an example of the lag between the accounting reporting cycle and the cash-to-cash cycle.

EXHIBIT 21-2
The Project and Time Dimensions of Capital Budgeting

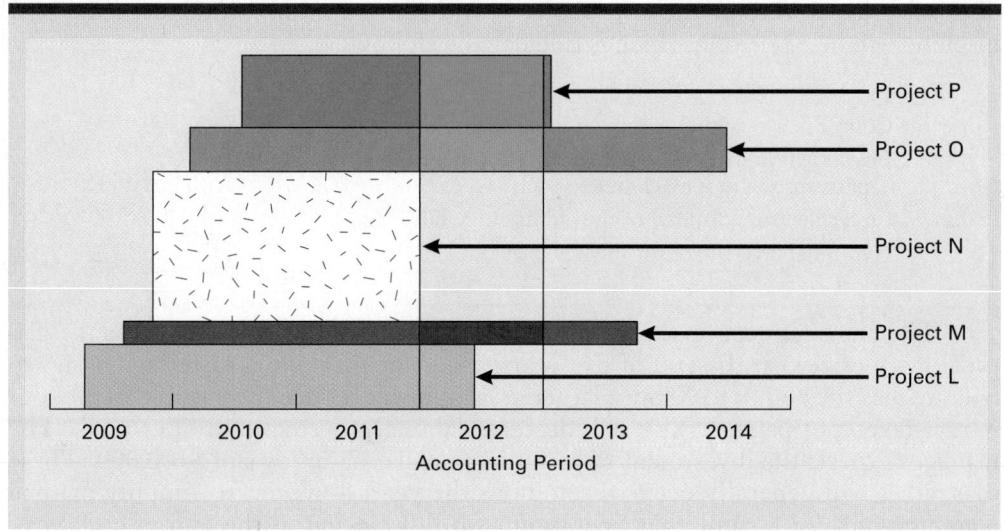

Accounting operating income is of particular interest to the manager because bonuses are frequently based on this value. Both operating cash flow and net income reported in an accounting period are important because they affect a public company's share price. Excessive focus on short-run income and operating cash flow, however, can cause a company to forgo long-term profitability. Successful management teams will balance short-term accounting-period considerations against longer-term project considerations in their decision process.

The accounting system that corresponds to the project dimension in Exhibit 21-2 is termed *life-cycle costing*. This system, described in Chapter 12, accumulates revenues and costs on a project-by-project basis. For example, a life-cycle costing statement for a new car project at Toyota could encompass a four-year period during which the costs of business activities throughout the value chain would be accumulated for the project. This accumulation is a management, *not* a financial, accounting effort to measure income on a period-by-period basis for internal management purposes. External reporting must conform to GAAP.

Any system that focuses on the life span of a project must cover several years and thus must consider the time value of money. The *time value of money* takes into account the fact that a dollar (or any other monetary unit) received today is worth more than a dollar received tomorrow. The reason is that $1 received today can be invested to start earning a risk-free return of perhaps 3.55% per year so that it grows to $1.0355 at the end of the year. The time value of money is the opportunity cost (the return of $0.0355 forgone) from not having the money today to invest. Capital budgeting focuses on projects that can be accounted for using life-cycle costing and that must be evaluated taking into consideration the time value of money.

We use information from Lifetime Care Hospital to illustrate capital budgeting. Lifetime Care is a not-for-profit organization that is not subject to taxes. Chapter 22 introduces tax considerations in capital budgeting.

One of Lifetime Care's goals is to improve the productivity of its X-ray department. To achieve this goal, the manager of Lifetime Care identifies a need to purchase a new state-of-the-art X-ray machine to replace an existing machine. The search stage yields several alternative models, but the hospital's technical staff focuses on one machine, XCAM8, as being particularly suitable. They next begin to acquire information for a more detailed evaluation. Quantitative financial information for the formal analysis follows.

Revenue will remain unchanged regardless of whether the new X-ray machine is acquired. Lifetime Care charges a fixed rate for a particular diagnosis, regardless of the number of X-rays taken. The only relevant financial benefit in evaluating

Lifetime's decision to purchase the X-ray machine is the cash savings in operating costs. The existing X-ray machine can operate for another five years and will have a disposal price of zero at the end of five years. The initial investment for the new machine will be $379,100, which is calculated as follows:

Cost of new machine	$372,890
Investment in working capital (supplies and spare parts for the new machine)	10,000
Cash flow from disposal of the old machine (after tax)	(3,790)
Net initial investment for the new machine	$379,100

The manager expects the new machine to have a five-year useful life and a disposal price of zero at the end of five years. The new machine is faster and easier to operate, has the ability to X-ray a larger area, and will reduce the average number of X-rays taken per patient. This will decrease labour, power, and utilities costs. The manager expects the investment to result in annual cash inflows of $100,000. These cash flows will generally occur throughout the year; however, to simplify manual computations, we assume that operating cash flows occur at the end of each year. The cash inflows are expected to come from cash savings in operating costs of $100,000 for each of the first four years and $90,000 in year 5 plus recovery of working capital investment of $10,000 in year five.

Managers at Lifetime Care also identify the following nonfinancial quantitative and qualitative benefits of investing in the new X-ray equipment:

1. *Quality:* Higher-quality X-rays will lead to improved diagnoses and better patient treatment.

2. *Safety:* The greater efficiency of the new machine would mean that X-ray technicians and patients are exposed to fewer of the possibly harmful effects of X-ray radiation.

These nonfinancial benefits are not considered in the formal financial analysis.

In the *selection* stage, managers must decide whether Lifetime Care should purchase the new X-ray machine.

DISCOUNTED CASH FLOW (DCF) METHODS

There are two **discounted cash flow (DCF)** methods: net present value (NPV) and internal rate of return (IRR). The payback method and the accrual accounting rate of return method, which are both non-DCF methods and are discussed later in this chapter, fail to consider the time value of money. DCF measures the cash inflows and outflows of a project as if they occurred at a single point in time so that they can be compared in an appropriate way. Both DCF methods recognize that the use of money has an opportunity cost—return forgone. The intuition of DCF is that a dollar in the treasury today is certain and therefore worth more than a dollar collected in the future because the future is uncertain. Because the DCF methods explicitly and routinely weight cash flows by the time value of money, they are usually the best (most comprehensive) methods to use for long-run decisions.

DCF focuses on *cash* inflows and outflows rather than on *operating income* as used in conventional accrual accounting. Cash is invested now with the expectation of receiving a greater amount of cash in the future. Avoid injecting accrual concepts of accounting into DCF analysis. For example, amortization is deducted as an accrual expense when calculating operating income under accrual accounting. It is never deducted in DCF analysis because this expense entails no cash outflow. Instead, the capital cost allowance (CCA) is the appropriate cash flow deduction (see Chapter 22).

The compound interest tables and formulas used in DCF analysis are included in Appendix A of this textbook. (Appendix A will be used frequently in Chapters 21 and 22). These tables are not essential because all the values can be readily calculated in Excel or by using a programmable calculator. The tables, however, only present the various factors rounded to three decimals while calculators and Excel carry up to eleven decimals or more. You may obtain slightly different results arising from trivial rounding errors.

Net present value (NPV) is calculated using the **required rate of return (RRR)**, which is the minimum acceptable rate of return on an investment. It is the return that the organization could expect to receive elsewhere for an investment of comparable risk. This rate is also called the **discount rate, hurdle rate,** or **(opportunity) cost of capital**. When working with internal rate of return (IRR), the RRR is used as a point of comparison. Chapter 22 discusses issues encountered in estimating this rate. The top management team would take time to decide on the acceptable ROR *before* calculating the NPV. Assume that the required rate of return, or discount rate, for the Lifetime Care X-ray machine project is 8%.[3]

NET PRESENT VALUE (NPV) METHOD

The **net present value (NPV)** method calculates the expected net monetary gain or loss from a project by discounting all expected future cash inflows and outflows to the present point in time, using the required rate of return. Assume that initial cash outflow occurs at the beginning of the year designated at t = 0, but that any cash inflow is realized at year-end, designated as t = 1, 2, 3, which designates the lifetime of the investment. This reflects economic plausibility because the asset must be purchased and on-site ready to generate cash. This takes time. To simplify, the model assumes that, while the cash outflow to purchase the asset is immediate at t = 0, there is a 365-day lag before any cash inflow is realized at t = 1. After t = 1, the time periods are assumed to be equal and one year long.

Only projects with a positive net present value are acceptable because the return from these projects exceeds the cost of capital (the return available by investing the capital elsewhere). Managers prefer projects with higher NPVs to projects with lower NPVs, if all other things are equal. Using the NPV method entails the following:

◆ *Sketch the relevant cash inflows and outflows.* The right side of Exhibit 21-3 shows how these cash flows are portrayed. Outflows appear in parentheses. Exhibit 21-3 can help the decision makers organize the data in a systematic way. Note that Exhibit 21-3 includes the outflow for the new machine at year 0, the time of the acquisition. The NPV method focuses only on cash flows. NPV analysis is indifferent to where the cash flows come from (operations, purchase or sale of equipment, or investment or recovery of working capital) and to the accrual accounting treatments of individual cash flow items (for example, amortization costs on equipment purchases).

◆ *Choose the correct compound interest table from Appendix A.* In our example, we can discount each year's cash flow separately using Table 2 (Appendix A). If the annual cash flow is uniform, then we can compute the present value of an annuity using Table 4 (Appendix A).

If we use Table 2, we find the discount factors for periods 1–5 under the 8% column. Approach 1 in Exhibit 21-3 presents the five discount factors. Because the investment produces an annuity, a series of equal cash flows at equal intervals, we may use Table 4. We find the discount factor for five periods under the 8% column. Approach 2 in Exhibit 21-3 shows that this discount factor is 3.993 (3.993 is the sum of the five discount factors used in approach 1). To obtain the present value figures, multiply the discount factors by the appropriate cash amounts in the sketch in Exhibit 21-3.

---

[3]From a finance point of view the correct discount rate is the weighted average cost of capital (WACC). In practice, investments rarely have the same risk and almost never cost the same, which is why the discount rate is weighted. As a practical matter, however, it is extremely difficult to calculate the cost of equity capital (the equity risk premium) reliably. If the management team believes the future risk of a specific project will resemble past risks in all significant ways, then the WACC is as reliable as a subjective decision. Nevertheless, the choice of a discount rate is a very complex strategic management decision beyond the scope of this text.

EXHIBIT 21-3
Net Present Value Method: Lifetime Care Hospital's New X-Ray Machine

	A	B	C	D	E	F	G	H	I
1			Net initial investment	$379,100					
2			Useful life	5 years					
3			Annual cash inflow	$100,000					
4			Required rate of return	8%					
5									
6		**Present Value**	**Present Value of**	**Sketch of Relevant Cash Flows at End of Each Time Period**					
7		**of Cash Flow**	**$1 Discounted at 8%**	**0**	**1**	**2**	**3**	**4**	**5**
8	**Approach 1: Discounting Each Year's Cash Flow Separately**[a]								
9	Net initial investment	$(379,100) ◄	1.000 ◄	$(379,100)					
10		92,600 ◄	0.926 ◄		$100,000				
11		85,700 ◄	0.857 ◄			$100,000			
12	Annual cash inflow {	79,400 ◄	0.794 ◄				$100,000		
13		73,500 ◄	0.735 ◄					$100,000	
14		68,100 ◄	0.681 ◄						$100,000
15	NPV if new machine purchased	$ 20,200							
16									
17	**Approach 2: Using Annuity Table**[b]								
18	Net initial investment	$(379,100) ◄	1.000 ◄	$(379,100)					
19					$100,000	$100,000	$100,000	$100,000	$100,000
20									
21	Annual cash inflow	399,300 ◄	3.993 ◄						
22	NPV if new machine purchased	$ 20,200							
23									
24	*Note:* Parentheses denote relevant cash outflows throughout all exhibits in Chapter 21.								
25	[a]Present values from Table 2, Appendix A at the end of the book. For example, $0.857 = 1 \div (1.08)^2$.								
26	[b]Annuity present value from Table 4, Appendix A. The annuity table value of 3.993 is the sum of the individual discount rates 0.926 + 0.857 + 0.794 + 0.735 + 0.681, subject to rounding.								

◆ *Sum the present value figures to determine the net present value.* If the sum is zero or positive, the NPV model indicates that the project should be accepted. That is, its expected rate of return equals or exceeds the required rate of return. If the total is negative, the project is undesirable. Its expected rate of return is below the required rate of return.

Assumptions about the timing and amount of cash flows are extremely important. If you use a programmable calculator or a popular spreadsheet program to calculate NPV, you may obtain a slightly different answer than if you use a compound interest table. The reason is that the compound interest table in Appendix A assumes the cash inflow all occurs at the *end* of each year, whereas many programs default to assume the inflow occurs at the beginning of each year. Most programs include an option to choose your assumption about the timing of cash inflows and the number of decimal places.

Exhibit 21-3 indicates an NPV of $20,200 at the required rate of return of 8%; the expected return from the project exceeds the 8% required rate of return. Therefore, the project is desirable. The 0 signifies the net initial investment flowed out at the beginning of the first year of the investment's lifetime. The 1, 2, . . . 5 signify the cash inflow at the *end* of years 1, 2, . . . 5. The lifetime of this investment is five years. The cash flows from the project are adequate to (1) recover the net initial investment in the project and (2) earn a return greater than 8% on the investment tied up in the project from period to period. Had the NPV been negative, the project would have been undesirable on the basis of financial considerations.

Of course, the manager of the hospital must also weigh nonfinancial factors. Consider the reduction in the average number of individual X-rays taken per patient with the new machine. This reduction is a qualitative benefit of the new machine given the health risks to patients and technicians. Other qualitative benefits of the new machine are the better diagnoses and treatments that patients receive. Had the NPV been negative, the manager would need to judge whether the nonfinancial benefits outweigh the negative NPV.

It is important that you not proceed until you thoroughly understand Exhibit 21-3. Compare approach 1 with approach 2 to see how Table 4 in Appendix A merely aggregates the present value factors of Table 2. That is, the fundamental table is Table 2; Table 4 reduces calculations when there is an annuity—a series of equal cash flows at equal intervals. The DCF approach answers the question of whether a project will break even or generate positive cash flow over its lifetime, but does not answer the question of what the return on the investment will be. This question is answered by using the internal rate of return method.

EVALUATE TWO DCF AND TWO NON-DCF METHODS TO CALCULATE THE ROR

Evaluate discounted cash flow (DCF) and non-DCF methods to calculate rate of return (ROR).

The **internal rate of return (IRR)** is the discount rate at which the present value of expected cash inflows from a project equals the present value of expected cash outflows of the project. It is the operational equivalent of breakeven. That is, the IRR is the discount rate that makes NPV = $0. IRR is sometimes called the **time-adjusted rate of return**. Where the NPV requires the management team to select a discount rate, with the IRR method the discount rate is determined by the data. The IRR is the discount rate at which the investment will break even over its lifetime. The cash outflow will exactly equal the discounted cash inflows.

As in the NPV method, the sources of cash flows and the accrual accounting treatment of individual cash flows are irrelevant to the IRR calculations. We illustrate the computation of the IRR using the X-ray machine project of Lifetime Care. Exhibit 21-4 presents the cash flows and shows the calculation of the NPV using a 10% discount rate. At a 10% discount rate, the NPV of the project is zero. Therefore, the IRR for the project is 10%. All qualitative and nonfinancial considerations being equal, managers will choose projects with an IRR exceeding the required rate of return by the greatest amount.

How do we determine the 10% discount rate that yields NPV = $0? In most cases, analysts solving capital budgeting problems have a calculator or software application programmed to provide the internal rate of return. Without a calculator or software program, a trial-and-error approach can provide the answer:

◆ Try a discount rate and calculate the NPV of the project using that discount rate.

◆ If the NPV is less than zero, try a lower discount rate. (A lower discount rate will increase the NPV; remember, we are trying to find a discount rate for which NPV = $0.) If the NPV is greater than zero, try a higher discount rate to lower the NPV.

Keep adjusting the discount rate until NPV = $0. In the Lifetime Care example, a discount rate of 8% yields NPV of +$20,200 (see Exhibit 21-4). A discount rate of 12% yields NPV of –$18,600 (3.605, the present value annuity factor from Table 4, × $100,000 – $379,100). Therefore, the discount rate that makes NPV = $0 must lie between 8% and 12%. We happen to try 10% and get NPV = $0. Hence, the IRR is 10%.

The step-by-step computations of an internal rate of return are easier when the cash inflows are equal, as in our example. Information from Exhibit 21-4 can be expressed in the following equation:

$$\$379,100 = \text{Present value of annuity of } \$100,000 \text{ at } x\% \text{ for 5 years}$$

EXHIBIT 21-4

Internal Rate-of-Return Method: Lifetime Care Hospital's New X-Ray Machine[a]

	A	B	C	D	E	F	G	H	I
1			Net initial investment	$379,100					
2			Useful life	5 years					
3			Annual cash inflow	$100,000					
4			Annual Discount rate	10%					
5									
6		**Present Value**	**Present Value of**	**Sketch of Relevant Cash Flows at End of Each Time Period**					
7		**of Cash Flow**	**$1 Discounted at 10%**	**0**	**1**	**2**	**3**	**4**	**5**
8	**Approach 1: Discounting Each Year's Cash Flow Separately[b]**								
9	Net initial investment	$(379,100) ◄—	1.000 ◄—	$(379,100)					
10		90,900 ◄—	0.909 ◄—		$100,000				
11		82,600 ◄—	0.826 ◄—			$100,000			
12	Annual cash inflow	75,100 ◄—	0.751 ◄—				$100,000		
13		68,300 ◄—	0.683 ◄—					$100,000	
14		62,100 ◄—	0.621 ◄—						$100,000
15	NPV if new machine purchased[c] (the zero difference proves that the internal rate of return is 10%)	$ 0							
16									
17	**Approach 2: Using Annuity Table**								
18	Net initial investment	$(379,100) ◄—	1.000 ◄—	$(379,100)					
19					$100,000	$100,000	$100,000	$100,000	$100,000
20									
21	Annual cash inflow	379,100 ◄—	3.791[d] ◄—						
22	NPV if new machine purchased	$ 0							
23									
24	*Note:* Parentheses denote relevant cash outflows throughout all exhibits in Chapter 21.								
25	[a]The internal rate of return is computed by methods explained on pp. 854–855.								
26	[b]Present values from Table 2, Appendix A at the end of the book.								
27	[c]Sum is $(100) due to rounding. We round to $0.								
28	[d]Annuity present value from Table 4, Appendix A. The annuity table value of 3.791 is the sum of the individual discount rates 0.909 + 0.826 + 0.751 + 0.683 + 0.621, subject to rounding.								

Or, using Table 4 (Appendix A), what factor F will satisfy the following equation?

$$\$379,100 = \$100,000F$$

$$F = 3.791$$

On the five-period line of Table 4, find the percentage column that is closest to 3.791. It is exactly 10%. If the factor F falls between the factors in two columns, straight-line interpolation is used to approximate the IRR. (For an illustration of interpolation, see requirement 1 of the Problem for Self-Study on page 870 at the end of this chapter.)

A project is accepted only if the internal rate of return exceeds the required rate of return (the opportunity cost of capital). In the Lifetime Care example, the X-ray machine has an IRR of 10%, which is greater than the required rate of return of 8%. On the basis of financial factors, Lifetime Care should invest in the new machine. If the IRR exceeds the RRR, then the project has a positive NPV when project cash flows are discounted at the RRR. If the IRR equals the RRR, NPV = $0. If the IRR is less than the RRR, NPV is negative. Obviously, managers prefer projects with higher IRRs to projects with lower IRRs, if all other things are equal. The IRR of 10% means that the cash inflows from the project are adequate to:

◆ Recover the net initial investment in the project.
◆ Earn a return of exactly 10% on investment tied up in the project over its useful life.

Despite the limitations of the IRR method, surveys report its widespread use, probably not only because managers find the IRR method easy to understand, but also because in most instances their decisions would be unaffected by using IRR or NPV. In some cases, however, as when comparing two projects with unequal lives or unequal investments, the two methods will not indicate the same decision.

This text emphasizes the NPV method, which has the important advantage that the end result of the computations is dollars, not a percentage. We can therefore add the NPVs of individual independent projects to estimate the effect of accepting a combination of projects. In contrast, the IRRs of individual projects cannot be added or averaged to derive the IRR of a combination of projects.

A second advantage of the NPV method is that we can use it in situations where the required rate of return varies over the life of the project. For example, suppose in the X-ray machine example Lifetime Care has a required rate of return of 8% in years 1, 2, and 3 and 12% in years 4 and 5. The total present value of the cash inflows is as follows:

Year (1)	Cash Inflows (2)	Required Rate of Return (3)	Present Value of $1 Discounted at Required Rate (4)	Total Present Value of Cash Inflows (5) = (4) × (2)
1	$100,000	8%	0.926	$ 92,600
2	100,000	8	0.857	85,700
3	100,000	8	0.794	79,400
4	100,000	12	0.636	63,600
5	100,000	12	0.567	56,700
				$378,000

Given the net initial investment of $379,100, NPV calculations indicate that the project is unattractive: it has a negative NPV of –$1,100 ($378,000 – $379,100). However, it is not possible to use the IRR method to infer that the project should be rejected. The existence of different required rates of return in different years (8% for years 1, 2, and 3 versus 12% for years 4 and 5) means there is not a single RRR that the IRR (a single figure) must exceed for the project to be acceptable.

SENSITIVITY ANALYSIS

To highlight the basic differences between the NPV and IRR methods, we have assumed that the expected values of cash flows will occur for certain. Obviously, in reality managers know that their predictions are imperfect and thus uncertain. To examine how a result will change if the predicted financial outcomes are not achieved or if an underlying assumption changes, managers can use sensitivity analysis, a what-if technique first introduced in Chapter 3.

Sensitivity analysis can take various forms. For example, suppose Lifetime Care management believes forecast savings are uncertain and difficult to predict. Management could then ask: What is the minimum annual cash savings that will cause us to invest in the new X-ray machine (that is, for NPV = $0)? For the data in Exhibit 21-4, let ACI = annual cash inflows and let NPV = $0. The net initial

EXHIBIT 21-5

Net Present Value Calculations for Lifetime Care Hospital Under Different Assumptions of Annual Cash Flows and Required Rates of Return[a]

	A	B	C	D	E	F
1	**Required**	**Annual Cash Flow**				
2	**Rate of Return**	**$80,000**	**$90,000**	**$100,000**	**$110,000**	**$120,000**
3	6%	$(42,140)	$ (20)	$42,100	$84,220	$126,340
4	8%	$(59,660)	$(19,730)	$20,200	$60,130	$100,060
5	10%	$(75,820)	$(37,910)	$ 0	$37,910	$ 75,820
6						
7	[a]All calculated amounts assume the project's useful life is five years.					

investment is $379,100, and the present-value factor at the 8% required rate of return for a five-year annuity of $1 is 3.993. Then:

$$NPV = \$0$$
$$3.993A - \$379,100 = \$0$$
$$3.993A = \$379,100$$
$$A = \$94,941$$

Thus, at the discount rate of 8%, annual cash inflows can decrease to $94,941 (a decline of $100,000 − $94,941 = $5,059) before NPV falls below zero. If management believes it can attain annual cash savings of at least $94,941, it could justify investing in the new X-ray machine on financial grounds alone.

Computer spreadsheets enable managers to conduct systematic, efficient sensitivity analyses. Exhibit 21-5 shows how the net present value of the X-ray machine project is affected by variations in (1) the annual cash inflows and (2) the required rate of return. NPVs can also vary with the useful life of a project. Sensitivity analysis helps a manager focus on those decisions that are most sensitive, and it eases the manager's mind about those decisions that are not so sensitive. For the X-ray machine project, Exhibit 21-5 shows that variations in either the annual cash inflows or the required rate of return have sizable effects on NPV.

NON-DCF CAPITAL BUDGETING METHODS

We now consider two methods for capital budgeting, neither of which accounts for the time value of money. The methods are payback and accounting rate of return. If forgone interest in a risk-free investment is immaterial, then the time value of money can be ignored. This is also appropriate if cash inflow will begin within a short time and repay the initial investment quickly. These are short-term projects in a managerial, not financial, accounting context. If the project life cycle is less than three to five years, risk is low, and the risk-free rate of return also low and stable, then a non-DCF method may be most appropriate. One non-DCF method assumes uniform cash flow throughout the project life cycle; the other method assumes non-uniform cash flows.

PAYBACK METHOD: UNIFORM CASH FLOWS

The **payback method** measures the time it will take to recoup, in the form of net cash inflows, the net initial investment in a project. Like NPV and IRR, the payback method does not distinguish the sources of cash inflows (operations, disposal of equipment, or recovery of working capital). It does, however, assume *uniform cash flows* through the expected life cycle. In the Lifetime Care example, the X-ray machine costs $379,100, has a five-year expected useful life, and generates a \$100,000 uniform cash inflow each year. The payback calculations[4] are as follows:

$$\text{Payback} = \frac{\text{Net initial investment}}{\text{Uniform increase in annual cash flows}}$$

$$= \frac{\$379,100}{100,000} = 3.791 \text{ years}$$

Under the payback method, organizations often choose a cutoff period for a project. The greater the risks of a project, the shorter the cutoff period. The reason is that when faced with higher risks, managers would like to more quickly recover the investments they have made. For example, a software development company may use a payback period of one to two years for investment decisions. The company's top management team may only consider blockbuster products or services because the life cycle is so short. Projects with a payback period less than the cutoff period are acceptable. Those with a payback period greater than the cutoff period are rejected. If Lifetime's cutoff period under the payback method is three years, Lifetime will reject the new machine. If Lifetime uses a cutoff period of four years, Lifetime will consider the new machine to be acceptable.

The payback method highlights liquidity, which is often an important factor in capital budgeting decisions. Managers prefer projects with shorter paybacks (more liquid) to projects with longer paybacks, if all other things are equal. Projects with shorter payback periods give the organization more flexibility because funds for other projects become available sooner. Also, managers are less confident about cash flow predictions that stretch far into the future.

The shorter the payback, the more confident managers can feel that their forecasts are on target. Behaviourally, most managers of investment centres receive bonuses and promotions based on actual rates of return on investment relative to the industry average. The shorter time it takes, the more likely the manager will personally benefit from a high ROR investment decision and be promoted. Of course the link of high risk to high ROR may mean that after promotion, the successor is left to rescue a risky project gone wrong.

The major strength of the payback method is that it is easy to understand. Like the DCF methods described previously, the payback method is not affected by accrual accounting conventions like amortization. Advocates of the payback method argue that it is a handy measure when (1) estimates of profitability are not crucial and preliminary screening of many proposals is necessary and (2) the predicted cash flows in later years of the project are highly uncertain.

Two major weaknesses of the payback method are (1) it neglects the time value of money and (2) it neglects to consider project cash flows after the net initial investment is recovered. Consider an alternative to the \$379,100 X-ray machine mentioned earlier. Assume that another X-ray machine, with a three-year useful life and zero terminal disposal price, requires only a \$300,000 net initial investment and will also result in cash inflows of \$100,000 per year. First, compare the two payback periods:

$$\text{Payback period for machine 1:} = \frac{\$379,100}{\$100,000} = 3.791 \text{ years}$$

$$\text{Payback period for machine 2:} = \frac{\$300,000}{\$100,000} = 3.000 \text{ years}$$

The payback criterion would favour buying the \$300,000 machine, because it has a shorter payback. In fact, if the cutoff period is three years, then Lifetime Care would not acquire machine 1 because it fails to meet the payback criterion. Consider next the NPV of the two investment options using Lifetime Care's 8% required rate

[4]Cash savings from the new X-ray machine occur *throughout* the year, but for simplicity in calculating NPV and IRR, we assume they occur at the *end* of each year. A literal interpretation of this assumption would imply a payback of four years because Lifetime Care will only recover its investment when cash inflows occur at the end of the fourth year. The calculations shown in this chapter, however, better approximate Lifetime Care's payback on the basis of uniform cash flows throughout the year.

of return for the X-ray machine investment. At a discount rate of 8%, the NPV of machine 2 is $12,300 (2.577, the present value annuity factor for three years at 8% from Table 4 × $100,000 = $257,700, the net initial investment of $300,000). Machine 1, as we know, has a positive NPV of $20,200 (from Exhibit 21-3). The NPV criterion suggests that Lifetime Care should acquire machine 1. Machine 2, with a negative NPV, would fail to meet the NPV criterion. The payback method gives a different answer from the NPV method because the payback method (1) does not consider cash flows after the payback period and (2) does not discount cash flows.

An added problem with the payback method is that choosing too short a cutoff period for project acceptance may promote the selection of only short-lived projects; the organization will tend to reject long-term, positive-NPV projects. Companies often use both the payback and DCF method to select positive NPV projects with an acceptably short payback period.

The payback formula is designed for uniform annual cash inflows. When payback is short term, the opportunity cost of money, interest forgone, is immaterial. This is why the time value of money is ignored. When annual cash inflows are *not uniform*, the payback computation takes a cumulative form. The years' net cash inflows are accumulated until the amount of the net initial investment has been recovered. Assume that Venture Law Group is considering the purchase of video-conferencing equipment for $150,000. The equipment is expected to provide total cash savings of $380,000 over the next five years, due to reduced travel costs and more effective use of associates' time. The cash savings occur uniformly throughout each year, but non-uniformly across years. Payback occurs during the third year:

Year	Cash Savings	Cumulative Cash Savings	Net Initial Investment Yet to Be Recovered at the End of the Year
0	—	—	$150,000
1	$ 50,000	$ 50,000	100,000
2	60,000	110,000	40,000
3	80,000	190,000	—
4	90,000	280,000	—
5	100,000	380,000	—

Straight-line interpolation within the third year, which has cash savings of $80,000, reveals that the final $40,000 needed to recover the $150,000 investment (that is, $150,000 − $110,000 recovered by the end of year 2) will be achieved halfway through year 3 (in which $80,000 of cash savings occur):

$$\text{Payback} = 2 \text{ years} + \left(\frac{\$40,000}{\$80,000} \times 1 \text{ year} \right) = 2.5 \text{ years}$$

The videoconferencing example has a single cash outflow of $150,000 at year 0. Where a project has multiple cash outflows occurring at different points in time, these outflows are added to derive a total cash outflow figure for the project. No adjustment is made for the time value of money when adding these cash outflows in computing the payback period.

ACCRUALS IN INVESTMENT EVALUATION

The **accrual accounting rate of return (AARR)** is an accounting measure of income divided by an accounting measure of investment. It is also called **accounting rate of return** or **return on investment (ROI)**. Note that NPV, IRR, and payback are all based on cash flows, whereas AARR is based on accrual accounting. We illustrate AARR for the Lifetime Care example using the project's net initial investment as the denominator:

$$\text{AARR} = \frac{\text{Increase in expected average annual operating income}}{\text{Net initial investment}}$$

If Lifetime Care purchases the new X-ray machine, the increase in expected average annual savings in operating costs will be $98,000. This amount is the total operating savings of $490,000 ($100,000 for four years and $90,000 in year 5) ÷ 5.

The new machine has a zero terminal disposal price. Straight-line amortization on the new machine is $372,890 ÷ 5 = $74,578. The net initial investment is $379,100. The accrual accounting rate of return is equal to:

$$\text{AARR} = \frac{\$98,000 - \$74,578}{\$379,100} = \frac{\$23,422}{\$379,100} = 6.18\%$$

In practice, there are variations on this formula. Some companies use "increase in expected average annual operating income" in the numerator and/or "average investment per year" in the denominator. The AARR method focuses on how investment decisions affect operating income numbers routinely reported by organizations. The AARR of 6.18% indicates the rate at which a dollar of investment generates operating income.

Timing affects both total cash inflow and total cash outflow under DCF analyses and payback. As the years advance from the point at which the investment was made, the multiplier to calculate the present value decreases. The result of the arithmetic is that the farther out in time a cash outflow is, the less its discounted value will be, whereas the closer in time to the initial investment a cash inflow is, the greater its discounted value will be. Knowing this simple manipulation can occur, a management accountant must exercise professional judgment because advancing a cash inflow as little as one year or delaying a cash outflow can make the difference in attaining a hurdle rate. The same tactics will shorten the payback.

ASSESSING RELEVANCE IN DCF ANALYSES

The key point of discounted cash flow methods is to focus exclusively on differences in expected future cash flows that result from implementing a project. All cash flows are treated the same, whether they arise from operations, purchase or sale of equipment, or investment in or recovery of working capital. The opportunity cost and the time value of money are tied to the cash flowing in to or out of the organization, not to the source of the cash.

One of the biggest challenges in DCF analysis is determining those cash flows that are relevant to making the decision. One reason is that rapid technological change can dramatically shorten the predicted lifetime of an investment after the investment has been made. Estimating a reasonable useful life is one of the biggest challenges in capital budgeting.

Relevant cash flows are expected future cash flows that differ between the alternatives. At Lifetime Care, the alternatives are either to continue to use the old X-ray machine or to replace it with the new machine. The relevant cash flows are the differences in cash flows between continuing to use the old machine and purchasing the new one. *When reading this section, focus on identifying future expected cash flows of each alternative and differences in cash flows between alternatives.*

Capital investment projects (for example, purchasing a new machine) typically have five major categories of cash flows: (1) initial investment in machine and working capital, (2) cash flow from current disposal of the old machine, (3) recurring operating cash flows, (4) cash flow from terminal disposal of the machine and recovery of working capital, and (5) income tax impacts on cash flows. We discuss the first four categories here, using Lifetime Care's purchase decision of the X-ray machine as an illustration. Income tax effects are described in Chapter 22.

1. **Initial investment.** Two components of investment cash flows are (a) the cash outflow to purchase the machine and (b) the working capital cash outflows.
    a. *Initial machine investment.* These outflows, made for purchasing plant, equipment, and machines, occur in the early periods of the project's life and include cash outflows for transporting and installing the item. In the Lifetime Care example, the $372,890 cost (including transportation and

Apply the concept of relevance to DCF methods of capital budgeting.

3

installation costs) of the X-ray machine is an outflow in year 0. These cash flows are relevant to the capital budgeting decision because they will be incurred only if Lifetime decides to purchase the new machine.

b. *Initial working capital investment.* Investments in plant, equipment, machines, and in the sales promotions for product lines are invariably accompanied by incremental investments in working capital. These investments take the form of current assets, such as receivables and inventories (supplies and spare parts for the new machine in the Lifetime Care example) minus current liabilities, such as accounts payable. Working capital investments are similar to machine investments. In each case, available cash is tied up.

The Lifetime Care example assumes a $10,000 incremental investment in working capital (supplies and spare parts inventory) if the new machine is acquired. The incremental working capital investment is the difference between the working capital required to operate the new machine (say, $15,000) and the working capital required to operate the old machine (say, $5,000). The $10,000 additional investment in working capital is a cash outflow in year 0.

2. **Current disposal price of old machine.** Any cash received from disposal of the old machine is a relevant cash inflow (in year 0) because it is an expected future cash flow that differs between the alternatives of investing and not investing in the new machine. If Lifetime Care invests in the new X-ray machine, it will be able to dispose of its old machine for $3,790. These proceeds are included as cash inflow in year 0.

Recall from Chapter 11 that the book value (original cost minus accumulated amortization) of the old equipment is irrelevant. It is a sunk cost. Nothing can change what has already been spent or what has already happened.

The net initial investment for the new X-ray machine, $379,100, is the initial machine investment plus the initial working capital investment minus current disposal price of the old machine: $372,890 + $10,000 − $3,790 = $379,100.

3. **Recurring operating cash flows.** This category includes all recurring operating cash flows that differ among the alternatives. Organizations make capital investments to generate cash inflows in the future. These inflows may result from producing and selling additional goods or services, or, as in the Lifetime Care example, from savings in operating cash costs. Recurring operating cash flows can be net outflows in some periods. For example, oil production may require large expenditures every five years (say) to improve oil extraction rates. Focus on operating cash flows, not on accrued revenues and costs.

To underscore this point, consider the following additional facts about the Lifetime Care X-ray machine example:

◆ Total X-Ray department overhead costs will not change whether the new machine is purchased or the old machine is kept. The X-Ray department overhead costs are allocated to individual X-ray machines—Lifetime has several—on the basis of the labour costs for operating each machine. Because the new X-ray machine will have lower labour costs, overhead allocated to it will be $30,000 less than the amount allocated to the machine it is replacing.

◆ Amortization on the new X-ray machine using the straight-line method is $74,578 [(original cost, $372,890 − expected terminal disposal price, $0) ÷ useful life, 5 years].

The savings in operating cash flows (labour and materials) of $100,000 in each of the first four years and $90,000 in the fifth year are clearly relevant because they are expected future cash flows that will differ between the alternatives of investing and not investing in the new machine. But what about the decrease in allocated overhead costs of $30,000? What about amortization of $74,578?

a. *Overhead costs.* The key question is do total overhead cash flows decrease as a result of acquiring the new machine? In our example, they do not. Total

X-Ray department overhead costs remain the same whether or not the new machine is acquired. They are fixed costs such as insurance. What changes is the overhead allocated to individual machines. The overhead costs allocated to the new machine are $30,000 less, but this additional $30,000 will simply be assigned to *other* machines in the department. No cash flow savings in total overhead occur. Therefore, the $30,000 should not be included as part of recurring operating cash inflows.

b. *Amortization.* Amortization is irrelevant because it is a noncash allocation of costs, whereas DCF is based on inflows and outflows of cash. In DCF methods, the initial cost of equipment is regarded as a *lump sum* outflow of cash at year 0. Deducting amortization from operating cash inflows would be counting the lump sum amount twice. What we will examine in the following chapter is the cash flow effect of tax regulations on capital budgeting.

4. **Terminal disposal price of investment.** The disposal of the investment at the date of termination of a project generally increases cash inflow in the year of disposal. Errors in forecasting the terminal disposal price are seldom critical on long-duration projects, because the present value of amounts to be received in the distant future is usually small. Two components of the terminal disposal price of an investment are (a) the terminal disposal price of the machine and (b) the recovery of working capital.

a. *Terminal disposal price of machine.* At the end of the useful life of the project, the initial machine investment may not be recovered at all, or it may be only partially recovered in the amount of the terminal disposal price.

The relevant cash inflow is the difference in expected terminal disposal prices at the end of five years under the two alternatives—the terminal disposal price of the new machine (zero in the case of Lifetime Care) minus the terminal disposal price of the old machine (also zero in the Lifetime Care example).[5]

b. *Recovery of working capital.* The initial investment in working capital is usually fully recouped when the project is terminated. At that time, inventories and receivables necessary to support the project are no longer needed.

The relevant cash inflow is the difference in the expected working capital recovered under the two alternatives. If the new X-ray machine is purchased, Lifetime Care will recover $15,000 of working capital in year 5. If the new machine is not acquired, Lifetime will recover $5,000 of working capital in year 5, at the end of the useful life of the old machine. The relevant cash inflow in year 5 if Lifetime invests in the new machine is $10,000 ($15,000 − $5,000).

Some capital investments *reduce* working capital. Assume that a computer-integrated manufacturing (CIM) project with a seven-year life will reduce inventories and hence working capital by $20 million from, say, $50 million to $30 million. This reduction will be represented as a $20-million cash inflow for the project at year 0. At the end of seven years, the recovery of working capital will show a relevant cash outflow of $20 million because the company recovers only $30 million of working capital under CIM rather than the $50 million of working capital it would have recovered had it not implemented CIM.

Exhibit 21-6 presents the relevant cash inflows and outflows for Lifetime Care's decision to purchase the new machine as described in the items in the preceding list. The total relevant cash flows for each year are the same as the relevant cash flows used in Exhibits 21-3 and 21-4 to illustrate the NPV and IRR methods.

---

[5]The Lifetime Care example assumes that both the new and the old machine have a future useful life of five years. If instead the old machine had a useful life of only four years, management could choose to evaluate the investment decision over a four-year horizon. In this case, Lifetime's management would need to predict the terminal disposal price of the new machine at the end of four years.

	A	B	C	D	E	F	G	H
1						Sketch of Relevant Cash Flows		
2								
3		End of Time Period:	0	1	2	3	4	5
4	1a	Initial machine investment	$(372,890)					
5	b	Initial working capital investment	(10,000)					
6	2	Current disposal price of old machine	3,790					
7		Net initial investment	$(379,100)					
8	3	Recurring operating cash flows		$100,000	$100,000	$100,000	$100,000	$ 90,000
9	4a	Terminal disposal price of new machine						—
10	b	Recovery of working capital						10,000
11		Total relevant cash inflows and outflows						
12		as shown in Exhibits 21-3 and 21-4	$(379,100)	$100,000	$100,000	$100,000	$100,000	$100,000

While there is no uniform method of calculating AARR, the interpretation in any situation is that the greater the positive difference between the AARR of a project and the AARR hurdle rate, the more preferable the project is. This method is similar to the IRR method because it provides the answer to the question "What is the rate of return on this project?", but the AARR uses operating income rather than cash flow. Because cash flow and time value of money are central to investment project decisions, both the IRR and NPV methods are preferred over the AARR method.[6] On the other hand, AARR calculations use numbers reported in the financial statements and provide managers with forecasts of operating income on the statement of earnings if a project is accepted. In contrast to the payback method, AARR includes income earned throughout the lifetime of a project, whereas the payback method includes cash flows only up to the point of payback. Many companies worldwide use more than one capital budgeting method to analyze alternatives.

COMPLEXITIES IN CAPITAL BUDGETING APPLICATIONS

④ Assess the complexities in capital budgeting within an interdependent set of value-chain business functions.

In this section, we consider some challenging aspects of predicting outcomes in the information acquisition stage and of choosing projects.

PREDICTING THE FULL SET OF BENEFITS AND COSTS

Consider an example of introducing computer-integrated manufacturing (CIM) technology into the production process. The factors that companies consider for this type of decision are far broader than costs alone. For example, the reasons for introducing CIM technology—faster response time, higher product quality, and greater flexibility in meeting changes in customer preferences—are often to increase revenues and contribution margins. Ignoring the revenue effects underestimates the financial benefits of CIM investments. As we describe below, however, the revenue benefits of technology investments are often difficult to quantify in financial terms. Nevertheless, competitive and revenue advantages are important managerial considerations when introducing CIM.

---

[6]Note that if amortization is calculated as economic amortization (the decline in the present value of future cash flows) under the AARR method, and if operating income and investment are adjusted each year for this amortization, the AARR each year will equal the project's IRR. In practice, however, the book amortization and investment value used in AARR computations are not calculated in this way.

EXHIBIT 21-7
Factors Considered in Making Capital Budgeting Decisions for CIM Projects

Examples of Financial Outcomes	Examples of Nonfinancial and Qualitative Outcomes
Lower direct labour costs	Reduction in manufacturing cycle time
Lower hourly support labour costs	Increase in manufacturing flexibility
Less scrap and rework	Increase in business risk due to higher fixed cost structure
Lower inventory costs	Improved product delivery and service
Increase in software and related costs	Reduction in product development time
Costs of retraining personnel	Faster response to market changes
	Increased learning by workers about automation
	Improved competitive position in the industry

Exhibit 21-7 presents examples of the broader set of factors that companies in the United States, Australia, Japan, and the United Kingdom weigh in evaluating CIM technology. The benefits include:

1. *Faster response to market changes.* An automated plant can, for example, make major design modifications (such as switching from a two-door to a four-door car) relatively quickly. To quantify this benefit requires some notion of consumer demand changes that may occur many years in the future and of the manufacturing technology choices made by competitors (defensive investment).

2. *Increased worker knowledge of automation.* If workers have a positive experience with CIM, the company can implement other automation projects more quickly and more successfully. Quantifying this benefit requires a prediction of the company's subsequent automation plans. Survey evidence emphasizes the importance of linking CIM decisions to a company's overall competitive strategies (intellectual capital management).

Predicting the full set of costs also presents problems. Three classes of costs are difficult to measure and are often underestimated:

1. Costs associated with a reduced competitive position in the industry. If other companies in the industry are investing in CIM, a company not investing in CIM will probably suffer a decline in market share because of its inferior quality and slower delivery performance. Several companies in the machine tool industry that continued to use a conventional manufacturing approach experienced rapid drops in market share after their competitors introduced CIM.

2. Costs of retraining the operating and maintenance personnel to handle the automated facilities.

3. Costs of developing and maintaining the software and maintenance programs to operate the automated manufacturing activities.

RECOGNIZING THE FULL TIME HORIZON OF THE PROJECT

The time horizon of CIM projects can stretch well beyond ten years. Many of the costs are incurred and are highly visible in the early years of adopting CIM; in contrast, important benefits may not be realized until many years after the adoption of CIM. A long time horizon should be considered when evaluating CIM investments.

Difficulties in predicting the full set of benefits and costs and long time horizons also arise in other investment decisions—for example, R&D projects and oil exploration.

PERFORMANCE EVALUATION AND THE SELECTION OF PROJECTS

The use of the accrual accounting rate of return for evaluating performance can often deter a manager from using DCF methods for capital budgeting decisions.

Long-Term Contracts and Performance Evaluation at Enron

Publicly listed companies often announce their long-term projects to investors. If people who may buy or already own the shares believe the projects are of high quality and the anticipated return is commensurate with risk, then it is likely the share price will increase as more people choose to purchase shares than sell them. Enron was a publicly listed company that went spectacularly bankrupt.

When Enron entered into a long-term contract to sell gas to the Chicago-based Peoples Gas, Light & Coke Co., Enron's share price rose to represent the financial market's assessment of the deal. The share-price increase was a signal that share purchasers believed future cash inflows would exceed past rates of return on Enron's contracts. But there was a problem.

Enron's performance management system ranked all employees within a business group from the best to the worst performers. Employees in the bottom 20% were warned about their performance and were terminated if they showed no significant improvement. Enron recorded the total NPV of all future cash flows for long-term contracts as revenue in the year the contract was signed, and compensated managers on this basis. With no post-investment audit process in place, when anticipated future cash flow failed to materialize, there was no attention-directing report. This pressure to perform, coupled with the opportunity to report higher operating income based on optimistic assumptions about future natural gas prices, created a strong temptation to inflate estimates of future cash flows—and managers did so. Among other duties, accountants are expected to detect and remedy internal control-system weaknesses of this nature.

Source: M. Salter, L. Levesque, and M. Ciampa, "The Rise and Fall of Enron," Harvard Business School working paper, 2002.

Consider Peter Costner, the manager of the X-Ray department at Lifetime Care Hospital. The NPV method for capital budgeting indicates that Peter should purchase the new X-ray machine, since it has a positive NPV of $20,200.

Suppose top management of Lifetime Care uses the AARR for judging the X-Ray department's performance. Peter may consider not purchasing the new X-ray machine if the AARR of 6.18% on the investment reduces his overall AARR and so negatively affects his department's performance. The AARR on the new X-ray machine is low because the investment increases the denominator and, as a result of amortization, also reduces the numerator (operating income) in the AARR computation.

Obviously, there is an inconsistency between citing DCF methods as being best for capital budgeting decisions and then using a different method to evaluate subsequent performance. As long as such practice continues, managers will be tempted to make capital budgeting choices on the basis of accrual accounting rates of return, even though such choices are not in the best interests of the organization. Such temptations become more pronounced if managers are frequently transferred (or promoted), or if annual operating income is important in their evaluations and their compensation plans. The reason is that the manager's performance is being evaluated over short time horizons. The manager has no motivation to use a DCF model to take into account cash flows that will occur in the distant future. Those cash flows will not influence the manager's performance evaluation.

MANAGEMENT CONTROL OF THE INVESTMENT ACTIVITY

Some initial investments, such as purchasing X-ray or videoconferencing equipment, are relatively easy to implement. Other initial investments, such as building shopping malls or new manufacturing plants, are more complex and take more time. In the latter case, monitoring and controlling the investment schedules and budgets are critical to the success of the overall project.

Assumptions made by managers of a company drive the evaluation of alternative investments. A company may develop a simple DCF analysis using, for example, a 12% discount rate for all projects. As a company grows globally, risks of otherwise identical projects can vary widely and the issue of currency repatriation (reporting foreign revenue and cost in domestic currency) and political instability affect many countries. Expansion by a Canadian energy producer into Argentina or Somalia, for example, carries higher risk than expansion into the Gulf of Mexico.

Failing to adjust assumptions about the required rate of return to account for higher risk, such as regulatory and currency risk, produces a biased valuation of investment alternatives. Another factor that creates fundamental difficulties for applying analytic models of domestic investments to overseas expansion is the increasing complexity of international financing. Global expansion strategies require a capital budgeting process that evaluates each proposed investment as a distinct opportunity with unique risks. A single discount rate does not fit all alternatives.

An approach could begin by considering representatives from various countries and deriving a weighted average cost of capital (WACC) for each project. WACC is covered in introductory finance courses. Briefly, WACC calculations require measuring all of the constituent parts of financing for projects: the cost of debt, the target capital structure, the local-country tax rates, and an appropriate cost of equity.[7]

To capture the country-specific risks in foreign markets, one approach is to calculate a cost of debt and a cost of equity for each representative project using domestic data. The risk-free investment is assessed using the difference between the yield on local government bonds and the yield on corresponding domestic government Treasury bonds to both the cost of debt and the cost of equity. The difference, or *sovereign spread*, can approximate the incremental borrowing costs (and market risk) in the local country. This approach is a more sophisticated way to think about capital budgeting risk and its cost of capital around the world.

MANAGEMENT CONTROL OF THE PROJECT—POST-INVESTMENT AUDIT

A post-investment audit compares the predictions of investment costs and outcomes made at the time a project was selected to the actual results. It provides management with feedback about the investment's performance. Suppose, for example, that actual outcomes (operating cash savings from the new X-ray machine in the Lifetime Care example) are much lower than predicted outcomes. Management must then investigate whether this occurred because the original estimates were overly optimistic or because there were problems in implementing the project. Both types of problems are a concern.

Optimistic estimates are a concern because they may result in the acceptance of a project that would otherwise have been rejected. To discourage optimistic estimates, companies like DuPont maintain records comparing actual performance to the estimates made by individual managers when seeking approval for capital investments. DuPont believes that post-investment audits discourage managers from making unrealistic forecasts. Problems in implementing a project are an obvious concern because the returns from the project will not meet expectations. Post-investment audits can point to areas requiring corrective action.

Care should be exercised when performing a post-investment audit. It should be done only after project outcomes have stabilized. Doing the audit early may give a misleading picture. Obtaining actual data to compare against estimates is often not easy. For example, actual labour cost savings from the new X-ray machine may not be comparable to the estimated savings, because the actual number and types of X-rays taken may be different from the quantities assumed during the capital budgeting process. Post-investment audits of capital projects require information about project-specific costs and benefits. It can be extremely costly, however, to disentangle these actual outcomes as if they were independent from, instead of interdependent with, overall corporate outcomes.

[7]Based on "Globalizing the Cost of Capital and Capital Budgeting at AES," Harvard Business School Case No. 9-204-109.

The absence of post-investment audits can lead managers to overstate project cash inflows and to accept projects that should never have been undertaken. Implementation problems, such as not achieving budgeted revenues or exceeding budgeted costs, are a concern because the returns from the project will then be inadequate. Post-investment audits can point to areas of implementation that need improvement (such as better quality-control processes). Other benefits, such as the impact on patient treatment, may be difficult to quantify.

It is interesting that the convergence to new international accounting board (IAB) regulations in both Canada and the Unites States require an annual post-investment review. Upon review, if the carrying value (acquisition cost less accumulated amortization) materially misstates the long-term investment or liability values, then an impairment must be reported. The reported values must also be adjusted along with explanatory notes informing investors of the key changes in assumptions that explain the impairment. Should a reversal happen in subsequent years to the impairment, then the values must be readjusted to reflect their higher value. This change to financial accounting standards will lead to a new demand for the skills in applying management accounting methods long used in capital budgeting and forecasts to retrospective reporting of performance on the balance sheet.

DEFENSIVE STRATEGY IN CAPITAL BUDGETING

5 | Apply the concept of defensive strategic investment to the capital budgeting process.

A company's strategy is the source of its strategic capital budgeting decisions. Strategic investments may be undertaken offensively to grow market share and profitability or defensively to avoid impairing a company's competitive advantage. A defensive strategy will mean that quantitative factors, while somewhat important, are secondary to the qualitative choice to defend market share.

Offensive strategies have been exhibited in many industries. Strategic decisions by WestJet, such as expansion to fly to US and European destinations, required capital investments be made in several countries. The strategic decision by Chapters Indigo to support book sales over the Internet required capital investments creating chapters.indigo.ca and an Internet infrastructure. Bell Canada Enterprises' decision to enter the media industry resulted in a big investment to acquire both *The Globe and Mail* and CTV.

Defensive strategies include cell phone companies such as Motorola, Nokia, and Samsung adding features that provide Internet access, email, and text-messaging to their phone capabilities. Companies that fail to provide these product attributes will suffer a decline in market share. The capital investment may be higher than the benefit, but it prevents a long-term decline in revenue and profit. This type of investment is extremely difficult to quantify because the opportunity cost and likelihood of lost market share are very difficult to predict.

Capital investment decisions that are strategic in nature require managers to consider a broad range of factors that may be difficult to estimate. Consider some of the difficulties of justifying investments in computer-integrated manufacturing (CIM) technology made by companies such as Mitsubishi, Sony, and Audi. In CIM, computers give instructions that quickly and automatically set up and run equipment to manufacture many different products. Quantifying these benefits requires some notion of consumer-demand changes that may occur many years in the future because limitations of the machinery lock in limitations to designs flexible enough to respond to changing consumer preferences.

Initially, the first investors in CIM took an offensive strategy to improve the quality and the market share of their products. Very quickly, however, the investment for subsequent companies became a defensive strategy to stop erosion of their existing market share to higher-quality, lower-cost products. CIM technology also increases worker knowledge of and experience with automation; however, the benefit of this knowledge and experience is difficult to measure. Managers need to develop judgment and intuition to make these decisions.

CUSTOMER VALUE AND CAPITAL BUDGETING

To remain viable, companies must keep their profitable customers and gain new ones. Consider Potato Supreme, which makes potato products for sale to retail outlets. It is currently analyzing two of its customers: Shine Stores and Always Open. Potato Supreme predicts the following cash flow from operations, net of income taxes (in thousands), from each customer account for the next five years:

	2012	2013	2014	2015	2016
Shine Stores	$1,450	$1,305	$1,175	$1,058	$ 950
Always Open	690	1,160	1,900	2,950	4,160

Which customer is more valuable to Potato Supreme? Looking at only the first year, 2012, Shine Stores provides more than double the cash flow compared to Always Open ($1,450 versus $690). A different picture emerges, however, when looking over the entire five-year horizon. Using Potato Supreme's 10% RRR, the NPV of the Always Open customer is $7,610, compared to $4,591 for Shine Stores (computations not shown). These NPV amounts are calculated using the 10% NPV of $1,318 ($1,450 × 0.909) for Shine Stores and $627 ($690 × 0.909) for Always Open.

Note how NPV captures in its estimate of customer value the future growth of Always Open. Potato Supreme uses this information to allocate more resources and salespersons to service the Always Open account. Potato Supreme can also use NPV calculations to examine the effects of alternative ways of increasing customer loyalty and retention, such as introducing frequent-purchaser cards.

A comparison of year-to-year changes in customer NPV estimates highlights whether managers have been successful in maintaining long-run profitable relationships with their customers. Suppose the NPV of Potato Supreme's customer base declines 15% in one year. Management can then examine the reasons for the decline, such as aggressive pricing by competitors, and devise new product development and marketing strategies for the future.

Capital One, a financial-services company, uses NPV to estimate the value of different credit-card customers. Cellular telephone companies such as Rogers and Telus attempt to sign up customers for multiple years of service. The objective is to prevent "customer churn," customers switching frequently from one company to another. The higher the probability of customer churn, the lower the NPV of the customer to the telecommunications company.

INVESTMENT IN RESEARCH AND DEVELOPMENT

Companies such as Research In Motion (RIM), a global leader in designing, manufacturing, and marketing innovative wireless mobile communications like the BlackBerry, regard R&D projects as important strategic investments. R&D payoffs are not only more uncertain than other investment projects, but also will often occur far into the future. Most companies engaged in these types of investment projects stage their R&D so they have the choice to increase or decrease their investment at different points in time based on its success. This option feature of R&D investments—called *real options*—is an important aspect of R&D investments and increases the NPV of these investments. That's because a company can limit its losses when things are going badly and take advantage of new opportunities when things are going well.

(Try to solve this problem before examining the solution that follows.)

PROBLEM
Let's revisit the Lifetime Care X-ray machine project. Assume that the expected annual cash inflows are $130,000 instead of $100,000. All other facts are unchanged: a $379,100 net initial investment, a five-year useful life, a zero terminal disposal price, and an 8% required rate of return. Year 5 cash inflows include a $10,000 recovery of working capital. When calculating breakeven time, assume that the investment in the X-ray machine will occur immediately after management approves the project.

REQUIRED
Compute the following:
1. Discounted cash flow
   a. Net present value
   b. Internal rate of return
2. Payback period
3. Accrual accounting rate of return on net initial investment
4. Calculate the payback period using discounted cash flows. Assume (for calculation purposes) that cash outflows and cash inflows occur at the end of each period.
5. To what five areas would you direct your attention when assessing relevant from irrelevant cash flows for two alternative long-term investments?
6. What prominent change in financial accounting standards has contributed to the importance of the interconnection of management accounting and financial reporting processes?
7. Aside from a growth strategy, for what other reason might managers undertake new investment?

SOLUTION
1. a. NPV = ($130,000 × 3.993) − $379,100
      = $519,090 − $379,100 = $139,990
   b. There are several approaches to computing the IRR. One is to use a calculator with an IRR function; this gives an IRR of 21.16%. An alternative approach is to use Table 4 in Appendix A:

$$\$379,100 = \$130,000\,F$$

$$F = \frac{\$379,100}{\$130,000} = 2.916$$

On the five-period line of Table 4, the column closest to 2.916 is 22%. To obtain a more accurate number, straight-line interpolation can be used:

	Present Value	Factors
20%	2.991	2.991
IRR	—	2.916
22%	2.864	—
Difference	0.127	0.075

$$\text{IRR} = 20\% + \frac{0.075}{0.127}(2\%) = 21.18\%$$ (difference due to rounding of PV factor to 3 decimals)

2. $$\text{Payback} = \frac{\text{Net initial investment}}{\text{Uniform increase in annual cash flows}}$$

$$= \$379,100 \div \$130,000 = 2.92 \text{ years}$$

3.

$$\text{AARR} = \frac{\text{Increase in expected average annual operating income}}{\text{Net initial investment}}$$

$$\begin{aligned}\text{Increase in expected average annual operating savings} &= [(\$130{,}000 \times 4) + \$120{,}000] \div 5 \\ &= \$128{,}000\end{aligned}$$

$$\text{Average annual amortization} = \$372{,}890 \div 5 = \$74{,}578$$

$$\begin{aligned}\text{Increase in expected average annual operating income} &= \$128{,}000 - \$74{,}578 \\ &= \$53{,}422\end{aligned}$$

$$\text{AARR} = \frac{\$53{,}422}{\$379{,}100} = 14.09\%$$

4. Payback using discounted cash flow computations is as follows:

Year	PV Discount Factor at 8% (1)	Investment Cash Outflows (2)	PV of Investment Cash Outflows* (3) = (1) × (2)	Cumulative PV of Investment Cash Outflows* (4)	Cash Inflows (5)	PV of Cash Inflows* (6) = (1) × (5)	Cumulative PV of Cash Inflows* (7)
0	1.000	$379,100	$379,100	$379,100			
1	0.926				$130,000	$120,380	$120,380
2	0.857				130,000	111,410	231,790
3	0.794				130,000	103,220	335,010
4	0.735				130,000	95,550	430,560
5	0.681				130,000	88,530	519,090

*At year 0.

$$\begin{aligned}\text{BET} &= 3 \text{ years} + \frac{(\$379{,}100 - \$335{,}010)}{95{,}550} \\ &= 3 \text{ years} + \frac{44{,}090}{95{,}550} \\ &= 3.46 \text{ years}\end{aligned}$$

5. The five areas where cash flows may differ are the cost of initial investment, including working capital requirements; liquidation values of any old investments; recurring cash flows; overhead costs, including amortization (or CCA); and the terminal disposal price.

6. The convergence from national to international financial accounting and reporting standards now requires an annual post-investment audit. In addition, new standards for long-term liabilities require an annual review of their carrying value as well as an annual impairment test for long-term assets. The methods of capital budgeting are now recommended for use in valuation for financial reporting purposes.

7. Strategically, if competitors are undertaking specific types of long-term investments, failing to do so is highly likely to put a firm at a competitive disadvantage. An example is upgrading management information and control systems. A defensive strategy is to upgrade if all competitors are doing so. Thus, investments may be for growth or defence.

The following question-and-answer format summarizes the chapter's learning outcomes. Each point presents a key question, and the guidelines are the answer to that question.

LEARNING OUTCOMES	GUIDELINES
1. What does the term *time value of money* recognize?	The term recognizes that money received earlier is worth more because of the returns that can be generated sooner.
2. What are the disadvantages of DCF and non-DCF (payback and AARR) methods of capital budgeting?	The NPV method computes a result in dollars not percentages and can be used where the required rates of return vary over the life of the project. The payback method neglects any cash flow after the payback period and the time value of money. The AARR is an after-tax operating income divided by a measure of the investment. The AARR does not consider the time value of money. The payback and AARR methods are nondiscounted cash flow methods whereas the NPV and IRR are discounted cash flow methods.
3. What does *relevance* mean in DCF analyses?	*Relevance* in this context means cash flow. No accruals, sunk cost, or cash flows unchanged by alternatives are relevant when these capital budgeting methods are applied. All cash flow is treated identically irrespective of its source from operations, financing, or disinvestment.
4. What conflicts can arise between using discounted cash flow methods for capital budgeting decisions and accrual accounting for performance evaluation? How can these conflicts be reduced?	Frequently, the decision made using a DCF method will not report good "operating income" results in the project's early years under accrual accounting. For this reason, managers are tempted not to use DCF methods even though the decisions based on them would be the best for the company over the long run. This conflict can be reduced by evaluating managers on a project-by-project basis, looking at their ability to achieve the amounts and timing of forecast cash flows.
5. What are the implications of a defensive long-term investment?	A defensive strategic or long-term investment is made for purposes of defending market-share. The quantitative and non-quantitative factors are secondary to this purpose. One very great difficulty is properly identifying and assessing the long-term opportunity cost of lost market-share.

This chapter and the Glossary at the end of the book contain definitions of the following important terms:

accounting rate of return (p. 860)
accrual accounting rate of return (AARR) (p. 860)
capital budgeting (p. 846)
discount rate (p. 853)
discounted cash flow (DCF) (p. 852)

hurdle rate (p. 853)
internal rate of return (IRR) (p. 855)
investment decision (p. 846)
investment program (p. 846)
investment project (p. 846)
net present value (NPV) (p. 853)

(opportunity) cost of capital (p. 853)
payback method (p. 858)
rate of return (ROR) (p. 849)
required rate of return (RRR) (p. 853)
return on investment (ROI) (p. 860)
time-adjusted rate of return (p. 855)

MyAccountingLab Make the grade with MyAccountingLab: The questions, exercises, and problems marked in red can be found on MyAccountingLab at **www.myaccountinglab.com.** You can practise them as often as you want, and most feature step-by-step guided instructions to help you find the right answer. Exercises and problems with an Excel icon in the margin have an accompanying Excel template on MyAccountingLab.

SHORT-ANSWER QUESTIONS

21-1 "Capital budgeting has the same focus as accrual accounting." Do you agree? Explain.

21-2 List and briefly describe each of the six parts in the capital budgeting decision process.

21-3 What is the essence of the discounted cash flow method?

21-4 "Only quantitative outcomes are relevant in capital budgeting analyses." Do you agree? Explain.

21-5 How can sensitivity analysis be incorporated in DCF analysis?

21-6 What is the payback method? What are its main strengths and weaknesses?

21-7 Describe the accrual accounting rate-of-return method. What are its main strengths and weaknesses?

21-8 "The trouble with discounted cash flow techniques is that they ignore amortization costs." Do you agree? Explain.

21-9 "Let's be more practical. DCF is not the gospel. Managers should not become so enchanted with DCF that strategic considerations are overlooked." Do you agree? Explain.

21-10 "The net present value method is the preferred method for capital budgeting decisions. Therefore, managers will always use it." Do you agree? Explain.

21-11 "All overhead costs are relevant in NPV analysis." Do you agree? Explain.

21-12 List and briefly describe the five major categories of cash flows included in capital investment projects.

21-13 "Managers' control of job projects generally focuses on four critical success factors." Identify those factors.

21-14 Bill Watts, president of Western Publications, accepts a capital-budgeting project advocated by Division X. This is the division in which the president spent his first ten years with the company. On the same day, the president rejects a capital-budgeting project proposal from Division Y. The manager of Division Y is incensed. She believes that the Division Y project has an internal rate of return at least ten percentage points above that of the Division X project. She comments, "What is the point of all our detailed DCF analysis? If Watts is panting over a project, he can arrange to have the proponents of that project massage the numbers so that it looks like a winner." What advice would you give the manager of Division Y?

EXERCISES

21-15 **Terminology.** A number of terms are listed below:

accounting rate of return	accrual accounting rate of return (AARR)
adjusted rate of return	capital budgeting
discount rate	discounted cash flow (DCF)
hurdle rate	internal rate of return (IRR)
investment decision	investment programs
investment projects	investments
net present value (NPV) method	payback method
(opportunity) cost of capital	required rate of return (RRR)
rate of return (ROR)	time-adjusted rate of return
return on investment (ROI)	

REQUIRED

Select the terms from the above list to complete the following sentences.

The goal of _____ _____ is to provide capacity in a planned and orderly manner that will match the predicted demand growth of the company and achieve a targeted _____ ____ __ _____ on these investments. The determination of the ROR links closely to the operating income or profit on sales (Chapter 12). That is why _____, (_____ _____) affect the balance sheet, the income statement and the statement of cash flow. Capital budgeting requires a careful analysis the amount and timing of cash outflows and cash inflows. There are four methods from which a management team can choose, ___ _____ __(___), _____ ____ __ _____, _____, _____ _____ ____ __ _____ (or _____ __ _____(___)). The first two methods require the calculation of discounted cash flow. The NPVmethod requires that the management team determine what its _____ ____ _____(___) must be (also called the discount rate, hurdle rate, or opportunity cost of capital). This discount rate is the return the team could expect from investing in a different project of similar risk. In contrast the IRR (sometimes called the _____ ____ __ _____) is fully determined by cash inflow and outflow. It is the rate at which the discounted net cash flow is zero. The _____ method is based on nominal, not discounted, cash flow. It is simply the total investment divided by cash inflow to determine the time it takes to recover the cost of the investment. The ____ is calculated by dividing the increase in an accrual, expected average operating income, by the cost of the initial investment.

21-16 Exercises in compound interest, no income taxes. To be sure that you understand how to use the tables in Appendix A at the end of this book, solve the following exercises. Ignore income tax considerations. The correct answers, rounded to the nearest dollar, appear on pages 883–884.

REQUIRED

1. You have just won $5,000. How much money will you accumulate at the end of ten years if you invest it at 6% compounded annually? At 14%?
2. Ten years from now, the unpaid principal of the mortgage on your house will be $89,550. How much do you need to invest today at 6% interest compounded annually to accumulate the $89,550 in ten years?
3. If the unpaid mortgage on your house in ten years will be $89,550, how much money do you need to invest at the end of each year at 6% to accumulate exactly this amount at the end of the tenth year?
4. You plan to save $5,000 of your earnings at the end of each year for the next ten years. How much money will you accumulate at the end of the tenth year if you invest your savings compounded at 12% per year?
5. You have just turned 65 and an endowment insurance policy has paid you a lump sum of $200,000. If you invest the sum at 6%, how much money can you withdraw from your account in equal amounts at the end of each year so that at the end of ten years (age 75) there will be nothing left?
6. You have estimated that for the first ten years after you retire you will need a cash inflow of $50,000 at the end of each year. How much money do you need to invest at 6% at your retirement age to obtain this annual cash inflow? At 20%?
7. The following table shows two schedules of prospective operating cash inflows, each of which requires the same net initial investment of $10,000 now:

	Annual Cash Inflows	
Year	Plan A	Plan B
1	$ 1,000	$ 5,000
2	2,000	4,000
3	3,000	3,000
4	4,000	2,000
5	5,000	1,000
Total	$15,000	$15,000

The required rate of return is 6% compounded annually. All cash inflows occur at the end of each year. In terms of net present value, which plan is more desirable? Show your computations.

21-17 Capital budgeting methods, no income taxes. Guelph Company runs hardware stores in Ontario's Golden Triangle area. Guelph's management estimates that if it invests $160,000 in a new computer system, it can save $60,000 in annual cash operating costs. The system has an expected useful life of five years and no terminal disposal value. The required rate of return is 12%. Ignore income tax issues in your answers. Assume all cash flows occur at year-end except for initial investment amounts.

1. a. Discount factor for 12% over 5 years, 3.605

REQUIRED

1. Calculate the following for the new computer system:
   a. Net present value.
   b. Payback period.
   c. Internal rate of return.
   d. Accrual accounting rate of return based on the net initial investment (assume straight-line depreciation).
2. What other factors should Guelph Company consider in deciding whether to purchase the new computer system?

21-18 New assets: comparison of approaches in capital budgeting. Panayiotis, the owner and manager of Micos Ltd., is evaluating the acquisition of new equipment needed to attend a new line of business. He has two alternatives: either buy two small machines or one large and more automatic machine:

2. Discount factor, 2 small machines, 3.5460

	Buy 2 Small Machines	Buy 1 Large Machine
Net initial investment to acquire the asset	$100,000 per machine	$250,000
Useful life of the acquired asset	4 years both machines	5 years
Recurring cash inflow per year	$ 70,000	$ 70,000
Recurring cash outflow per year	$ 5,000 per machine	$ 15,000
Required rate of return for both projects	5%	

REQUIRED

1. Determine the payback period in years.
2. Determine the present value of total recurring cash flows.
3. Determine the net present value of the project.
4. Do you estimate that the IRR of the project is higher or lower than 5%?
5. If both projects were independent, would you accept them?

21-19 New equipment purchase. Norberto Garcia, general manager of the Argentinean sub-sidiary of Innovation Inc., is considering the purchase of new industrial equipment to improve efficiency at its Cordoba plant. The equipment has an estimated useful life of five years. The estimated cash flows for the equipment are shown in the table that follows, with no antici-pated change in working capital. Innovation has a 12% required rate of return. Assume amor-tization is calculated on a straight-line basis. Assume all cash flows occur at year-end except for initial investment amounts.

1. a. Present value of 5-year annuity, $112,656

Initial investment	$80,000
Annual cash flow from operations (excluding the amortization effect)	$31,250
Cash flow from terminal disposal of equipment	$ 0

REQUIRED

1. Calculate (a) net present value, (b) payback period, and (c) internal rate of return.
2. Compare and contrast the capital budgeting methods in requirement 1.
3. The controller of Innovation Inc. received Garcia's estimates but adjusted them to capture the added risk of doing the project in Argentina. Recalculate item 1 with a required rate of return of 20% and explain if the project will be approved by Innovation Inc. for its Argentinean subsidiary.

21-20 Capital budgeting with uneven cash flows, no income taxes. Southern Cola is consider-ing the purchase of a special-purpose bottling machine for $23,000. It is expected to have a useful life of four years with no terminal disposal value. The plant manager estimates the fol-lowing savings in cash operating costs:

1. Present value of savings of cash operating costs, $21,170

Year	Amount
1	$10,000
2	8,000
3	6,000
4	5,000
Total	$29,000

Southern Cola uses a required rate of return of 16% in its capital budgeting decisions. Ignore income taxes in your analysis. Assume all cash flows occur at year-end except for initial invest-ment amounts.

REQUIRED

Calculate the following for the special-purpose bottling machine:

1. Net present value.
2. Payback period.
3. Internal rate of return.
4. Accrual accounting rate of return based on net initial investment. (Assume straight-line depreciation. Use the average annual savings in cash operating costs when computing the numerator of the accrual accounting rate of return.)

1. Plan 1 NPV, ($3,901,725)

21-21 Comparison of projects, no income taxes. (CMA, adapted) New Bio Corporation is a rapidly growing biotech company that has a required rate of return of 12%. It plans to build a new facility in Mississauga, Ontario. The building will take two years to complete. The building contractor offered New Bio a choice of three payment plans, as follows:

◆ **Plan I** Payment of $375,000 at the time of signing the contract and $4,425,000 upon completion of the building. The end of the second year is the completion date.

◆ **Plan II** Payment of $1,500,000 at the time of signing the contract and $1,500,000 at the end of each of the two succeeding years.

◆ **Plan III** Payment of $150,000 at the time of signing the contract and $1,500,000 at the end of each of the three succeeding years.

REQUIRED

1. Using the net present value method, calculate the comparative cost of each of the three payment plans being considered by New Bio.
2. Which payment plan should New Bio choose? Explain.
3. Discuss the financial factors, other than the cost of the plan and the nonfinancial factors that should be considered in selecting an appropriate payment plan.

1. A Payback, 3 years

21-22 Payback and NPV methods, no income taxes. (CMA, adapted) Andrews Construction is analyzing its capital expenditure proposals for the purchase of equipment in the coming year. The capital budget is limited to $6,000,000 for the year. Lori Bart, staff analyst at Andrews, is preparing an analysis of the three projects under consideration by Corey Andrews, the company's owner.

	File Edit View Insert Format Tools Data Window Help			
	A	B	C	D
1		**Project A**	**Project B**	**Project C**
2	**Projected cash outflow**			
3	Net initial investment	$3,000,000	$1,500,000	$4,000,000
4				
5	**Projected cash inflows**			
6	Year 1	$1,000,000	$ 400,000	$2,000,000
7	Year 2	1,000,000	900,000	2,000,000
8	Year 3	1,000,000	800,000	200,000
9	Year 4	1,000,000		100,000
10				
11	Required rate of return	10%	10%	10%

REQUIRED

1. Because the company's cash is limited, Andrews thinks the payback method should be used to choose between the capital budgeting projects.
   a. What are the benefits and limitations of using the payback method to choose between projects?
   b. Calculate the payback period for each of the three projects. Ignore income taxes. Using the payback method, which projects should Andrews choose?
2. Bart thinks that projects should be selected based on their NPVs. Assume all cash flows occur at the end of the year except for initial investment amounts. Calculate the NPV for each project. Ignore income taxes.
3. Which projects, if any, would you recommend funding? Briefly explain why.

1. Present value of terminal disposal of machine, 13,163

21-23 DCF, accrual accounting rate of return, working capital, evaluation of performance, no income taxes. Century Lab plans to purchase a new centrifuge machine for its Manitoba facility. The machine costs $137,500 and is expected to have a useful life of eight years, with a terminal disposal value of $37,500. Savings in cash operating costs are expected to be $31,250 per year. However, additional working capital is needed to keep the machine running efficiently. The working capital must continually be replaced, so an investment of $10,000 needs to be maintained at all times, but this investment is fully recoverable (will be "cashed in") at the end of the useful life. Century Lab's required rate of return is 14%. Ignore income taxes in your analysis. Assume all cash flows occur at year-end except for initial investment amounts.

REQUIRED

1. Calculate net present value.
2. Calculate internal rate of return.
3. Calculate accrual accounting rate of return based on net initial investment. Assume straight-line depreciation.
4. You have the authority to make the purchase decision. Why might you be reluctant to base your decision on the DCF methods?

21-24 Net present value, internal rate of return, sensitivity analysis. Muskoka Landscaping Ltd. is planning to buy equipment costing $25,000 to improve its services. The equipment is expected to save $8,000 in cash operating costs per year. Its estimated useful life is five years, and it will have zero terminal disposal price. The required rate of return is 12%.

1. a. Discount factor, 3.6048

REQUIRED

1. Compute (a) the net present value and (b) the internal rate of return.
2. What is the minimum annual cash savings that will make the equipment desirable on a net present value basis?
3. When might a manager calculate the minimum annual cash savings described in requirement 2 rather than use the $8,000 savings in cash operating costs per year to calculate the net present value or internal rate of return?

21-25 DCF, accrual accounting rate of return, working capital, evaluation of performance. Edilcan Inc. has been offered an automated special-purpose welder (robot) for $60,000. The machine is expected to have a useful life of eight years with a terminal disposal price of $12,000. Savings in cash operating costs are expected to be $15,000 per year. However, additional working capital is needed to keep the welder running efficiently and without stoppages. Working capital includes mainly argon gas, wires, and tips. These items must continually be replaced, so an investment of $5,000 must be maintained in them at all times, but this investment is fully recoverable (will be "cashed in") at the end of the useful life. Edilcan's required rate of return is 14%.

1. a. Present value of annuity of savings in cash operating costs, $69,583

REQUIRED

1. a. Compute the net present value.
   b. Compute the internal rate of return.
2. Compute the accrual accounting rate of return based on the net initial investment. Assume straight-line amortization.
3. You have the authority to make the purchase decision. Why might you be reluctant to base your decision on the DCF model?

21-26 Equipment replacement, net present value, relevant costs, payback. Edgeley Inc., a logistics operator located in Concord, Ontario, is considering replacing one of its tractor trailers (informally known as a 53' truck). The truck was purchased for $64,800 two years ago, has a current book value of $45,600, and a remaining useful life of four years. Its current disposal price is $31,200; in four years its terminal disposal price is expected to be $7,200. The annual cash operating costs of the truck are expected to be $42,000 for each of the next three years and $48,000 in year 4.

1. NPV, keep old truck, $126,833

Edgeley is considering the purchase of a new 53' truck for $67,200. Annual cash operating costs for the new truck are expected to be $30,000. The new truck has a useful life of four years and a terminal disposal price of $9,600.

Edgeley Inc. amortizes all its trucks using straight-line amortization calculated on the difference between the initial cost and the terminal disposal price divided by the estimated useful life. Edgeley uses a rate of return of 12% in its capital budgeting decisions.

REQUIRED

1. Using a net present value criterion, should Edgeley Inc. purchase the new truck?
2. Compute the payback period for Edgeley Inc. if it purchases the new 53' truck.

21-27 NPV and customer profitability. Ready Ink and Paper Ltd. sells and distributes office supplies for printers and photocopy machines; its overall margin on sales is 10%. Ready Ink and Paper has customers of two kinds: low and high volume. Low-volume customers on average generate sales for $5,000 per year and the average tenure is four years. High-volume customers on average generate sales for $18,000. Their average tenure is seven years but they require an initial investment of $8,000 (comprised mostly of legal fees paid to lawyers to review the long-term contract and upgrades in the software to allow customers to place purchase orders online). Assume a 12% required rate of return.

1. Operating income, high-volume customer, year 1, $657

REQUIRED

1. Calculate operating income per customer in each year.
2. Ready Ink and Paper Ltd. estimates the value of each kind of customer by calculating the customer's projected NPV over the total expected time of the contract. Use the operating incomes calculated above to compute the value of each kind of customer.
3. Indicate which type of customer is more profitable for Ready Ink and Paper Ltd.

PROBLEMS

21-28 **NPV.** (CMA, adapted) Fox Valley Healthcare Inc. is a not-for-profit organization that operates eight nursing homes and ten assisted-living facilities. The company has grown considerably over the last three years and expects to continue to expand in the years ahead, particularly in the area of assisted-living facilities for seniors.

Jim Ruffalo, president of Fox Valley, has developed a plan to add a new building for top management and the administrative staff. He has selected a building contractor, Vukacek Construction Co., and has reached agreement on the building and its construction. Vukacek is ready to start as soon as the contract is signed and will complete the work in two years.

The building contractor has offered Fox Valley a choice of three payment plans:

◆ **Plan I:** Payment of $240,000 on the signing of the contract and $3,600,000 at the time of completion.
◆ **Plan II:** Payment of $1,200,000 on the signing of the contract and $1,200,000 at the end of each of the two succeeding years. The end of the second year is the completion date.
◆ **Plan III:** Payment of $120,000 on the signing of the contract and $1,200,000 at the end of each of the three succeeding years.

Ruffalo is not sure which payment plan he should accept. He has asked the treasurer, Lisa Monroe, for her assessment and advice. Fox Valley will finance the construction with a long-term loan and has a borrowing rate of 10%.

REQUIRED

1. Using the net present value method, calculate the comparative cost of each of the three payment plans being considered by Fox Valley Healthcare Inc.
2. Which payment plan should the treasurer recommend? Explain.
3. Discuss the financial factors, other than the cost of the plan, and nonfinancial factors that should be considered in selecting an appropriate payment plan.

21-29 **DCF, sensitivity analysis, no income taxes.** (CMA, adapted) Landom Corporation is an international manufacturer of fragrances for women. Management at Landom is considering expanding the product line to men's fragrances. From the best estimates of the marketing and production managers, annual sales (all for cash) for this new line is 1,000,000 units at $25 per unit; cash variable cost is $10 per unit; cash fixed cost is $5,000,000 per year. The investment project requires $30,000,000 of cash outflow and has a project life of five years.

At the end of the five-year useful life, there will be no terminal disposal value. Assume all cash flows occur at year-end except for initial investment amounts.

Men's fragrance is a new market for Landom, and management is concerned about the reliability of the estimates. The controller has proposed applying sensitivity analysis to selected factors. Ignore income taxes in your computations. Landom's required rate of return on this project is 14%.

REQUIRED

1. Calculate the net present value of this investment proposal.
2. Calculate the effect on the net present value of the following two changes in assumptions. (Treat each item independently of the other.)
   a. 5% reduction in the selling price.
   b. 5% increase in the variable cost per unit.
3. Discuss how management would use the data developed in requirements 1 and 2 in its consideration of the proposed capital investment.

21-30 **NPV, IRR, and sensitivity analysis.** Crumbly Cookie Company is considering expanding by buying a new (additional) machine that costs $42,000, has zero terminal disposal value, and has a ten-year useful life. It expects the annual increase in cash revenues from the expansion to be $23,000 per year. It expects additional annual cash costs to be $16,000 per year. Its cost of capital is 6%. Ignore taxes.

REQUIRED

1. Calculate the net present value and internal rate of return for this investment.
2. Assume the finance manager of Crumbly Cookie Company is not sure about the cash revenues and costs. The revenues could be anywhere from 10% higher to 10% lower than predicted. Assume cash costs are still $16,000 per year. What are NPV and IRR at the high and low points for revenue?
3. The finance manager thinks that costs will vary with revenues, and if the revenues are 10% higher, the costs will be 7% higher. If the revenues are 10% lower, the costs will be 10% lower. Recalculate the NPV and IRR at the high and low revenue points with this new cost information.
4. The finance manager has decided that the company should earn 2% more than the cost of capital on any project. Recalculate the original NPV in requirement 1 using the new discount rate.

21-31 **Relevance and DCF.** The Strubel Company currently makes as many units of Part No. 789 as it needs. David Lin, general manager of the Strubel Company, has received a bid from the Gabriella Company for making Part No. 789. Current plans call for Gabriella to supply 1,000 units of Part No. 789 per year at $60 a unit. Gabriella can begin supplying on January 1, 2013, and continue for five years, after which time Strubel will not need the part. Gabriella can accommodate any change in Strubel's demand for the part and will supply it for $60 a unit, regardless of quantity.

3

1. Present value if Part No. 789 is purchased, $(7,916)

Jack Tyson, the controller of the Strubel Company, reports the following costs for manufacturing 1,000 units of Part No. 789:

Direct materials	$26,400
Direct manufacturing labour	13,200
Variable manufacturing overhead	8,400
Amortization on machine	12,000
Product and process engineering	4,800
Rent	2,400
Allocation of general plant overhead costs	6,000
Total costs	$73,200

The following additional information is available:

a. Part No. 789 is made on a machine used exclusively for the manufacture of Part No. 789. The machine was acquired on January 1, 2012, at a cost of $72,000. The machine has a useful life of six years and zero terminal disposal price. Amortization is calculated on the straight-line method.
b. The machine could be sold today for $18,000.
c. Product and process engineering costs are incurred to ensure that the manufacturing process for Part No. 789 works smoothly. Although these costs are fixed in the short run, with respect to units of Part No. 789 produced, they can be saved in the long run if this part is no longer produced. If Part No. 789 is outsourced, product and process engineering costs of $4,800 will be incurred for 2013 but not thereafter.
d. Rent costs of $2,400 are allocated to products on the basis of the floor space used for manufacturing the product. If Part No. 789 is discontinued, the space currently used to manufacture it would become available. The company could then use the space for storage purposes and save $1,200 currently paid for outside storage.
e. General plant overhead costs are allocated to each department on the basis of direct manufacturing labour dollars. These costs will not change in total. But no general plant overhead will be allocated to Part No. 789 if the part is outsourced.
   Assume that Strubel requires a 12% rate of return for this project.

REQUIRED

1. Should David Lin outsource Part No. 789? Prepare a quantitative analysis.
2. Describe any sensitivity analysis that seems advisable, but you need not perform any sensitivity calculations.
3. What other factors should Lin consider in making a decision?
4. Lin is particularly concerned about his bonus for 2013. The bonus is based on Strubel's accounting income. What decision will Lin make if he wants to maximize his bonus in 2013?

5

1. 2013 Homebuilders cash
flow from operations, $16,764

21-32 Defensive strategy. Christen Granite sells granite counter tops to the construction industry. Christen Granite has three customers: Homebuilders, a small construction company that builds private luxury homes; Kitchen Constructors, a company that designs and builds kitchens for hospitals and hotels; and Subdivision Erectors, a construction company that builds large subdivisions in major metro suburbs. Following are Christen Granite's revenue and cost data by customer for the year ended December 31, 2012:

	Homebuilders	Kitchen Constructors	Subdivision Erectors
Revenues	$54,000	$390,000	$1,032,000
Cost of goods sold	26,400	216,000	660,000
Operating costs	12,000	90,000	282,000

Operating costs include order processing, sales visits, delivery, and special delivery costs. Christen estimates that revenue and costs will increase as follows on an annual basis:

	Homebuilders	Kitchen Constructors	Subdivision Erectors
Revenues	5%	15%	8%
Cost of goods sold	4%	4%	4%
Operating costs	4%	4%	4%

REQUIRED
1. Calculate operating income per customer for 2012 and for each year of the 2013–2017 period.
2. Christen estimates the value of each customer by calculating the customer's projected NPV over the next five years (2013–2017). Use the operating incomes calculated above to compute the value of all three customers. Christen uses a 10% discount rate.
3. Recently, Kitchen Constructors (KC), Christen's most valuable customer, has been threatening to leave. Lawson Tops, Christen's fiercest competitor, has offered KC a greater discount. KC demands a 20% discount from Christen if the latter wants to keep KC's business. At the same time, Christen reevaluates the KC account and anticipates annual revenue increases of only 5% thereafter. Should Christen grant KC the 20% discount? What is the five-year value of KC after incorporating the 20% discount? What other factors should Christen consider before making a final decision?
4. What are the possible adverse effects of caving in to KC's pressure?

1 2

1. Net annual cash inflow,
$30,000

21-33 Payback, even and uneven cash flows. You have the opportunity to expand your business by purchasing new equipment for $159,000. You expect to incur fixed costs of $96,000 per year to use this new equipment, and you expect to incur variable costs in the amount of approximately 10% of annual revenues.

REQUIRED
1. Calculate the payback period for this investment assuming you will generate $140,000 in cash revenues every year.
2. Assume you expect the following revenue stream for this investment:

Year 1: $ 90,000   Year 4: 155,000   Year 7: 140,000
Year 2: 115,000   Year 5: 170,000   Year 8: 125,000
Year 3: 130,000   Year 6: 180,000   Year 9: 80,000

Based on this estimated revenue stream, what is the payback period for this investment?

1 2 4

1. Present value of initial
investments, ($325,000)

21-34 NPV and AARR, goal-congruence issues. Nate Stately, a manager of the Plate division for the Great Slate Manufacturing Company, has the opportunity to expand the division by investing in additional machinery costing $320,000. He would amortize the equipment using the straight-line method, and expects it to have no residual value. It has a useful life of six years. The firm mandates a required rate of return of 16% on investments. Nate estimates annual net cash inflows for this investment of $100,000 and an investment in working capital of $5,000.

1. Calculate the net present value of this investment.
2. Calculate the accrual accounting rate of return for this investment.
3. Should Nate accept the project? Will Nate accept the project if his bonus depends on achieving an accrual accounting rate of return of 16%? How can this conflict be resolved?

21-35 Recognizing cash flows for capital investment projects, NPV. Met-All Manufacturing manufactures over 20,000 different products made from metal, including building materials, tools, and furniture parts. The manager of the Furniture Parts division has proposed that his division expand into bicycle parts as well. The Furniture Parts division currently generates cash revenues of $4,700,000 and incurs cash costs of $3,600,000, with an investment in assets of $12,090,000. One-quarter of the cash costs are direct labour.

1. Annual cash flow from operations with new equipment, $760,000

The manager estimates that the expansion of the business will require an investment in working capital of $45,000. Because the company already has a facility, there would be no additional rent or purchase costs for a building, but the project would generate an additional $390,000 in annual cash overhead. Moreover, the manager expects annual materials cash costs for bicycle parts to be $1,700,000, and labour for the bicycle parts to be about the same as the labour cash costs for furniture parts.

The Controller of Met-All, working with various managers, estimates that the expansion would require the purchase of equipment with a $5,000,000 cost and an expected disposal value of $400,000 at the end of its ten-year useful life. Depreciation would occur on a straight-line basis.

The CFO of Met-All determines the firm's cost of capital as 12%. The CFO's salary is $460,000 per year. Adding another division will not change that. The CEO asks for a report on expected revenue for the project, and is told by the marketing department that it might be able to achieve cash revenue of $3,750,000 annually from bicycle parts. Met-All Manufacturing has a tax rate of 30%.

REQUIRED

1. Separate the cash flows into four groups: (1) net initial investment cash flows, (2) cash flows from operations, (3) cash flows from terminal disposal of investment, and (4) cash flows not relevant to the capital budgeting problem.
2. Calculate the NPV of the expansion project and comment on your analysis.

21-36 Recognizing cash flows for capital investment projects. Ludmilla Quagg owns a fitness centre and is thinking of replacing the old Fit-O-Matic machine with a brand new Flab-Buster 3000. The old Fit-O-Matic has a historical cost of $50,000 and accumulated amortization of $46,000, but has a trade-in value of $5,000. It currently costs $1,200 per month in utilities and another $10,000 a year in maintenance to run the Fit-O-Matic. Ludmilla feels that the Fit-O-Matic can be used for another ten years, after which it would have no salvage value.

2. Annual cash flow from operations, $9,320

The Flab-Buster 3000 would reduce the utilities costs by 30% and cut the maintenance cost in half. The Flab-Buster 3000 costs $98,000, has a ten-year life, and an expected disposal value of $10,000 at the end of its useful life. Ludmilla charges customers $10 per hour to use the fitness centre. Replacing the fitness machine will not affect the price of service or the number of customers she can serve.

Ludmilla also looked at replacing the Fit-O-Matic with a Walk-N-Pull Series 3, which costs $78,000. However, she prefers the Flab-Buster 3000.

REQUIRED

1. Ludmilla wants to evaluate the Flab-Buster 3000 project using capital budgeting techniques, but does not know how to begin. To help her, read through the problem and separate the cash flows into four groups: (1) net initial investment cash flows, (2) cash flow savings from operations, (3) cash flows from terminal disposal of investment, and (4) cash flows not relevant to the capital budgeting problem.
2. Assuming a required rate of return of 8%, and straight-line amortization over remaining useful life of machines, should Ludmilla buy the Flab-Buster 3000?

21-37 Defensive and offensive strategies in capital budgeting. (CMA, adapted) The management of Kleinburg Industrial Bakery is analyzing two competing investment projects and they must decide which one can be done immediately and which one can be postponed for at least a year. The details of each proposed investment are shown on the next page.

1. Present value, years 1–9 cash inflows, increase capacity project, $2,131,200

The bakery has a 12% required rate of return to evaluate all investments that directly impact operations and amortizes the investment in plant and equipment using straight-line amortization over ten years on the difference between the initial investment and terminal disposal price.

1. Calculate the net present value of each proposal.
2. Which project should the bakery choose on the basis of the NPV calculations?
3. Mention which strategic factors must be considered by the managers when ranking the projects.

	Project: Increase Capacity to Serve New Markets	Project: Upgrade Customer Service
Proposed by	Production manager	Sales and marketing manager
Rationale	Assets are operating at full capacity and we are unable to attend to all the demand, therefore we need to expand our facilities to produce more kilograms.	The fleet of trucks and vans need to be upgraded with tracking devices and remote connections to flex the planning of routes. The new software will allow the company to be paperless and respond faster to customers' requests.
Investment	$600,000	$345,000
Working capital	$ 50,000	$150,000
Terminal disposal value	$60,000	None
Expected useful life	10 years	5 years
Expected increase in operating income	$400,000	$80,000
Expected savings in administrative costs	None	$40,000

COLLABORATIVE LEARNING CASES

1. Annual net cash inflows, periods 1–12, $74,000

21-38 Net present value, internal rate of return, sensitivity analysis. Francesca Freed wants a Burg-N-Fry franchise. The buy-in is $500,000. Burg-N-Fry headquarters tells Francesca that typical annual operating costs are $160,000 (cash) and that she can bring in "as much as" $260,000 in cash revenues per year. Burg-N-Fry headquarters also wants her to pay 10% of her revenues to them per year. Francesca wants to earn at least 8% on the investment, because she has to borrow the $500,000 at a cost of 6%. Use a 12-year window, and ignore taxes.

REQUIRED
1. Find the NPV and IRR of this investment, given the information that Burg-N-Fry has given Francesca.
2. Francesca is nervous about the "as much as" statement from Burg-N-Fry, and worries that the cash revenues will be lower than $260,000. Repeat requirement 1 using revenues of $240,000 and $220,000.
3. Francesca thinks she should try to negotiate a lower payment to the Burg-N-Fry headquarters, and also thinks that if revenues are lower than $260,000, her costs might also be lower by about $10,000. Repeat requirement 2 using $150,000 as annual cash operating cost and a payment to Burg-N-Fry of only 6% of sales revenues.
4. Discuss how the sensitivity analysis will affect Francesca's decision to buy the franchise. Why don't you have to recalculate the internal rate of return if you change the desired (discount) interest rate?

21-39 Relevant costs, capital budgeting, strategic decision. (M. Porporato, adapted) Wilcox is a family-owned company that has been making microwaves for almost 20 years. The company's production line includes ten models, ranging from a basic model to a deluxe stainless steel model. Most of its sales are through independently owned retailers in medium-sized towns in central Canada, giving the microwaves an image of high quality and price. However, industry sales have been stagnant and those of Wilcox have been falling in the past two years due to the Asian brands. Currently Wilcox sells 75,000 units per year at an average price of $120 each with variable unit costs of $60 (of which materials is $30). As a result Wilcox is operating its plant at about 75% of a one-shift capacity, although in their "golden years" in the early 1990s they were operating at 75% of a two-shift capacity.

In the spring of 2013, Oh Mart, a chain of large supermarkets, approached Wilcox's CEO and asked about the possibility of producing microwaves for them. The microwaves will

1. Top Line unit contribution margin, $20

be sold under the Oh Mart house brand, called Top Line. They are offering a five-year contract that could be automatically extended on a year-to-year basis, unless one party gives the other at least three months' notice that it does not wish to extend the contract. The deal is for 24,000 units per year with a unit price of $90 each. Oh Mart does not want title on a microwave to pass from Wilcox to Oh Mart until the microwave is shipped to a specific Oh Mart store. Additionally Oh Mart wants the Top Line microwaves to be somewhat different in appearance from Wilcox's other microwaves. These requirements would increase Wilcox's purchasing, inventorying, and production costs.

In order to be able to give an answer to Oh Mart, knowing that they had no room to negotiate, Wilcox managers gathered the following information:

1. First-year costs of producing Top Line microwaves:

Materials (includes items specific to Oh Mart models)	$40
Labour (same as with regular microwaves)	$20
Overhead at 100% of labour (50% is variable; the 100% rate is based on a volume of 100,000 units per year)	$20
Total unit cost	$80

2. Related added inventories (the cost of financing them is estimated to be close to 15% per year):

Materials:	two-month supply (a total of 4,000 units)
Work in process:	1,000 units, half completed (but all materials for them issued)
Finished goods:	500 units (awaiting next carload lot shipment to an Oh Mart central warehouse in Concord, Ontario)

3. Impact on Wilcox's regular sales. Wilcox's sales over the next two years are expected to be about 75,000 units a year if they forgo the Oh Mart deal, based on the CEO estimates after launching a new "top of the line" microwave. If Wilcox accepts the deal, it would lose about 5,000 units of the regular sales volume a year, since their retail distribution is quite strong in Oh Mart market regions. These estimates do not include the possibility that a few of Wilcox's current dealers might drop their line if they find out that Wilcox is making microwaves for Oh Mart with a lower selling price.

INSTRUCTIONS
Form groups of three students to complete the following requirements.

REQUIREMENTS
1. Determine if the proposal of Oh Mart will increase Wilcox's net income in the next year.
2. Calculate the total value of the contract (suppose there is no renewal after the fifth year).
3. On the basis of the net present value criterion, should Wilcox Microwaves accept the offer?
4. Estimate the strategic consequences of accepting the proposal (consider the current situation of the industry, Wilcox positioning, image, distribution, and production issues).

ANSWERS TO EXERCISES IN COMPOUND INTEREST (EXERCISE 21-16)
The general approach to these exercises centres on a key question: Which of the four basic tables in Appendix A should be used? No computations should be made until this basic question has been answered with confidence.

1. **From Table 1.** The $5,000 is the present value P of your winnings. Their future value S in ten years will be:

$$S = P(1 + r)^n$$

The conversion factor, $(1 + r)^n$, is on line 10 of Table 1.

Substituting at 6%: $S = 5,000 (1.791) = \$8,955$
Substituting at 14%: $S = 5,000 (3.707) = \$18,535$

2. **From Table 2.** The $89,550 is a future value. You want the present value of that amount. $P = S \div (1 + r)^n$. The conversion factor, $1 \div (1 + r)^n$, is on line 10 of Table 2. Substituting,

$$P = \$89,550(0.558) = \$49,969$$

3. **From Table 3.** The $89,550 is a future value. You are seeking the uniform amount (annuity) to set aside annually. Note that $1 invested each year for ten years at 6% has a future value of $13.181 after ten years, from line 10 of Table 3.

$$S_n = \text{Annual deposit } (F)$$
$$\$89,550 = \text{Annual deposit } (13.181)$$
$$\text{Annual deposit} = \frac{\$89,550}{13.181} = \$6,794$$

4. **From Table 3.** You need to find the future value of an annuity of $5,000 per year. Note that $1 invested each year for ten years at 12% has a future value of $17.549 after ten years.

$$S_n = \$5,000F, \text{ where } F \text{ is the conversion factor}$$
$$S_n = \$5,000 \, (17.549) = \$87,745$$

5. **From Table 4.** When you reach age 65, you will get $200,000, a present value at that time. You need to find the annuity that will exactly exhaust the invested principal in ten years. To pay yourself $1 each year for ten years when the interest rate is 6% requires you to have $7.360 today, from line ten of Table 4.

$$P_n = \text{Annual withdrawal } (F)$$
$$\$200,000 = \text{Annual withdrawal } (7.360)$$
$$\text{Annual withdrawal} = \frac{\$200,000}{7.360} = \$27,174$$

6. **From Table 4.** You need to find the present value of an annuity for ten years.

$$\text{At 6\%: } P_n = \text{Annual withdrawal } (F)$$
$$P_n = \$50,000 \, (7.360)$$
$$P_n = \$368,000$$

$$\text{At 20\%: } P_n = \$50,000 \, (4.192)$$
$$P_n = \$209,600, \text{ a much lower figure}$$

7. Plan B is preferable. The NPV of plan B exceeds that of plan A by $980 ($3,126 − $2,146): Even though plans A and B have the same total cash inflows over the five years, plan B is preferred because it has greater cash inflows occurring earlier.

		Plan A		Plan B	
Year	PV Factor at 6%	Cash Inflows	PV of Cash Inflows	Cash Inflows	PV of Cash Inflows
0	1.000	$(10,000)	$(10,000)	$(10,000)	$(10,000)
1	0.943	1,000	943	5,000	4,715
2	0.890	2,000	1,780	4,000	3,560
3	0.840	3,000	2,520	3,000	2,520
4	0.792	4,000	3,168	2,000	1,584
5	0.747	5,000	3,735	1,000	747
			$ 2,146		$ 3,126

Capital Budgeting: A Closer Look

Tax Is a Relevant Cost

Deciding to invest in a long-term project such as a major year-round destination resort requires that a management team consider external factors such as tourism trends, economic cycles, and the environment, and predict how they will affect discounted cash flows. One of the key considerations is the effect on cash of tax paid when investments are made in projects of this type. Intrawest ULC has developed year-round destination resorts such as Whistler-Blackcomb in British Columbia and Mont Tremblant in Quebec (pictured here), at costs exceeding $200 million. While tax rules change, the fundamental business concept does not. To benefit from tax shields provided by the Canada Revenue Agency on various investments, companies must have profits to begin with. Because most investments take years to pay for and finally generate a positive return, careful matching of investments to corporate strategy and positive operating cash flow are required by any top management team.

After studying this chapter, you should be able to

1. Analyze the impact of income taxes on operating and capital cash flows.

2. Apply the total-project approach and the differential approach appropriately to different capital budgeting decisions.

3. Apply the concepts of real and nominal rate of return to account for inflation in capital budgeting.

4. Analyze alternative approaches used to recognize the degree of risk in capital budgeting projects.

5. Explain the usefulness of excess present value index in capital budgeting, and explain why IRR and NPV may rank projects differently.

In this chapter, the focus is on an exceptionally important cash outflow—income tax. Companies must pay their quarterly tax bill in cash. Different tax regimes affect different types of capital investments. The Canada Revenue Agency (CRA) enforces the Canadian Income Tax Act. The management teams at any company must analyze the effects of both tax and inflation as they make capital budgeting decisions. Tax and inflation are considered external factors affecting corporate decisions to undertake investment projects. One reason is that no single corporation can initiate or change either the rate of taxation or the rate of inflation. We discuss risk and uncertainty in capital budgeting, capital budgeting in not-for-profit organizations, and issues when using the NPV and IRR decision methods in this chapter.

The Income War Tax Act became legislation in 1917. This was the first time in Canada's history that the federal government was given the legal right to tax income. In 1942, automatic deduction at source began. In 1946, the Income Tax Appeal Board was born, and by 1983 it had become the Tax Court of Canada, but it was 1993 before this court achieved sole jurisdiction over income tax appeals. Today, Canadian federal and most provincial governments impose both sales and value-added taxes (HST and GST), corporate surtax (a percentage of tax paid), land transfer tax, and large corporations tax. Our discussion will emphasize the effect of capital cost allowance (CCA) on cash paid in corporate income tax.

INCOME TAXES AND CAPITAL BUDGETING

1 Analyze the impact of income taxes on operating and capital cash flows.

Income taxes are mandatory cash disbursements and therefore are an important cash flow consideration. Income taxes almost always influence the amount and/or the timing of cash flows. Their basic role in capital budgeting is no different from that of any other cash disbursement. Payment of income tax tends to narrow the cash differences between projects. Income tax rates differ considerably, and thus overall corporate income tax rates can vary widely.

Income tax rates are progressive and depend on the amount of pretax income. Larger pretax income is taxed at higher rates. In capital budgeting, the relevant rate is the **marginal income tax rate**; that is, the tax rate paid on additional amounts of pretax income. Suppose corporations pay income taxes of 15% on the first $50,000 of pretax income and 30% on pretax income over $50,000. What is the *marginal income tax rate* of a company with $75,000 of pretax income? It is 30%, because 30% of any *additional* income over $50,000 will be paid in taxes. In contrast, the company's *average income tax rate* is only 20%, (15% × $50,000 + 30% × $25,000 = $15,000 ÷ $75,000 of pretax income). When we assess tax effects of capital budgeting decisions, we will always use the *marginal* tax rate because that is the rate applied to the incremental cash flows generated by a proposed project.

The result is commonly referred to as the average tax rate. But the more arithmetically accurate term is the *weighted* average corporate tax rate. As you can see, each increment of pretax income is weighted or multiplied by its respective tax rate to provide the dollar values. The dollar values are summed, then divided by the total pretax income.

Organizations that pay income taxes report their net income to the public, compliant with GAAP, to obtain a clean audit opinion. GAAP permits managers to choose among amortization methods and, when necessary, change from one method to another. The amortization expense deducted to calculate pretax income would be at the discretion of corporate managers. This is *not* permitted by the CRA. Governments have created tax laws that require corporations to deduct capital cost allowance (CCA), not amortization, when calculating their taxable income.

Legally, the taxable income reported to CRA on a confidential basis differs from mandatory public disclosure under CICA standards. This means that the tax expense on the statement of income, an accrual, will differ from the cash tax paid to the government. The difference between the accrual and the cash flow amounts

Tax Is Mandatory

The CRA is authorized to investigate and undertake both civil and criminal proceedings against those who fail to accurately report taxable income and pay the appropriate amount of tax. Criminal investigations in 2008–2009 achieved 257 convictions that resulted in approximately $19.8 million in fines and over 63.7 years of jail sentences. Fines imposed by the courts can be as high as 200% of the amount owing, and taxpayers must still pay the taxes owed and any other civil penalties and interest imposed by CRA. The Special Enforcements Program specializes in audits of people suspected of criminal activity. Proceeds from crime are also taxable. The 1,349 audits undertaken identified an additional $80 million in taxes owed. All prosecutions are public documents, and the CRA itself ensures media coverage of convictions to deter criminal activity.[1]

accumulates as future tax liabilities, which eventually must be paid.[2] The CCA gives rise to a cash outflow in the form of corporate income tax paid each year and is relevant to assessing investment projects. Amortization, however, is not. We will examine the effects on the cash outflows for taxes. We focus on the tax *reporting rules*, not the principles and standards that govern public financial reporting.

TAX EFFECT OF CAPITAL INVESTMENTS ON OPERATING CASH FLOWS

Recognizing the impact of income taxes on operating cash flows is straightforward. If a capital proposal results in a reduction in costs—for example, an annual cost saving of $60,000—then the company's taxable income will increase by $60,000, all other things being equal. If the company has a marginal tax rate of 40%, then the company's income taxes will increase by $24,000 ($60,000 × 0.40). A net annual after-tax savings of $36,000 results ($60,000 − $24,000). This means the after-tax savings can be calculated quickly as $60,000 × (1 − the tax rate) or $60,000 × 0.60 = $36,000. This will be true only if the company has positive taxable income.

If operating expenses increase by $250,000, then the taxable income will decrease by $250,000. If the company has a 40% marginal tax rate, then the tax saving will be $100,000 ($250,000 × 0.40). An after-tax cost increase of $150,000 results: [$250,000 × (1 − 0.40)]. Thus, to incorporate the impact of income taxes on operating cash flows poses no real difficulty. The difficulty occurs in the recognition of the tax effects of investment expenditures in capital equipment. This will be true only if the company has positive taxable income.

TAX EFFECT ON INVESTMENT CASH FLOWS

The expenditure on capital equipment results in recording an increase to the long term-asset account. The additional related amortization expense over the asset's useful economic life also must be recorded and reported in compliance with GAAP. Amortization rates and policies are selected by the management team within GAAP and vary from company to company even for the same asset.

To apply a consistent set of regulations and to provide a means to implement government initiatives, the federal government has its own laws on how to calculate

[1]Canada Revenue Agency Fact Sheet, http://www.cra-arc.gc.ca/gncy/lrt/crmnl-eng.html, accessed June 9, 2011.

[2]Future tax assets may also be accumulated in some cases, which must eventually be received by the company as a tax refund in cash.

capital cost allowance (CCA). The Income Tax Act (ITA) does not permit a company to deduct amortization expense in determining taxable income, but rather a company is allowed to deduct CCA. CCA is the legally required income tax counterpart to annual GAAP-required amortization expense in financial reporting.

The income tax statutes for intangible assets such as patents, copyrights, goodwill, and trademarks differ, as does the terminology. The **eligible capital expenditure** is the acquisition cost of the intangible asset. The **eligible capital property** is 75% of the acquisition cost of the intangible asset. The full cost is not deductible because the asset is considered to provide indefinite benefit. Intangible assets, by definition, have an indefinite useful life, and the annual deduction is called the **cumulative eligible capital amount (CECA)**, calculated at 7% on a declining balance basis. The balance remaining after deducting CECA is called the **cumulative eligible capital (CEC)** pool. If the intangible asset is assigned a definite life, then it is not an eligible capital property and CCA must be deducted for tax purposes.[3]

CAPITAL COST ALLOWANCE—DECLINING BALANCE CLASSES

The ITA assigns all depreciable capital purchases to a CCA class. For example, a desk would qualify as a Class 8 asset that includes furniture, tools costing $500 or more each, appliances, refrigeration equipment, photocopiers, fax machines, and telephone equipment. It also includes data network infrastructure equipment and systems software acquired prior to March 23, 2004, outdoor advertising signs, and other business equipment not specified as a different class.

Exhibit 22-1 depicts the calculation of CCA for a desk acquired after March 23, 2004, at a cost of $10,000. We assume no other transactions occur and simplify the terminology in this introductory level illustration.[4]

If the Class 8 equipment cost $1,000 or more, managers can chose to include each piece in a separate class and calculate the CCA for a five-year period. Any unamortized capital cost (UCC) after five years must be transferred back to the general class to which it otherwise would belong. When *all* items in this asset class have been disposed of, the remaining UCC is fully deductible as a terminal loss. Class 8 has a predetermined rate of 20% declining balance capital cost allowance.

The **half-year rule** assumes that all net additions are purchased in the middle of the year, and thus only one-half of the stated CCA rate is allowed in the first year. Therefore, in year 1 of the example in Exhibit 22-1, the CCA is $1,000 or one-half of the net capital expenditure multiplied by 20% (the one-half net expenditure rule). This leaves a balance of $9,000 ($10,000 − $1,000), which is known as the **unamortized capital cost (UCC)**.[5] In year 2 and all succeeding years, the rate of 20% is applied to the UCC of the previous year. This results in a declining amount of capital cost allowance for each year. Even after the 25 years shown in Exhibit 22-1, a UCC of $42 remains and will require 15 more years to get to a zero balance (which in practice can only be obtained by rounding to the nearest dollar).

This, as you could well imagine, would be a long and labourious task to perform for each capital proposal. An efficient way to calculate the present value of the tax savings is to use the following **tax shield formula:**

$$\begin{array}{l} \text{Present value} \\ \text{of tax savings} \end{array} = \left(\begin{array}{l} \text{Investment} \times \\ \text{marginal tax rate} \end{array} \right) \left(\dfrac{\text{CCA rate}}{\begin{array}{l}\text{CCA rate} + \text{required} \\ \text{rate of return}\end{array}} \right) \dfrac{(2 + \text{required rate of return})}{2(1 + \text{required rate of return})}$$

[3]Canada Revenue Agency, "What Is? Eligible Capital Property," http://www.cra-arc.gc.ca/tx/bsnss/tpcs/slprtnr/rprtng/ece-dca/whts-eng.html, accessed July 8, 2008.

[4]The experts in tax know that changes in CCA during year 1, for example, are reported as a change to the beginning balance of year 2, not to the ending balance of year 1.

[5]The terminology is confusing for managerial accounting students when the word *unamortized* is used to describe the remainder in the CCA pool after all additions and deductions for the year. CRA also uses the terms *amortization* and *depreciation* interchangeably. It is an unavoidable complication because, despite using a CRA rather than financial accounting method, the CRA still uses financial accounting terms to label the result from CCA calculations. But for experienced financial accountants who are responsible for doing these calculations, the use of financial accounting terms actually simplifies their task.

EXHIBIT 22-1
Capital Cost Allowance Illustration

CCA—Class 8
Rate is 20% Declining Balance
(rounded to the nearest dollar)

Year 1 (day 1) net addition	$10,000	Year 13 UCC	618
CCA year 1 (20% half-year rule applied)	1,000	CCA year 14 (20%)	124
Year end UCC	9,000	Year 14 UCC	494
CCA year 2 (20%)	1,800	CCA year 15 (20%)	99
Year 2 UCC	7,200	Year 15 UCC	395
CCA year 3 (20%)	1,440	CCA year 16 (20%)	79
Year 3 UCC	5,760	Year 16 UCC	316
CCA year 4 (20%)	1,152	CCA year 17 (20%)	63
Year 4 UCC	4,608	Year 17 UCC	253
CCA year 5 (20%)	922	CCA year 18 (20%)	51
Year 5 UCC	3,686	Year 18 UCC	202
CCA year 6 (20%)	737	CCA year 19 (20%)	40
Year 6 UCC	2,949	Year 19 UCC	162
CCA year 7 (20%)	590	CCA year 20 (20%)	32
Year 7 UCC	2,359	Year 20 UCC	130
CCA year 8 (20%)	472	CCA year 21 (20%)	26
Year 8 UCC	1,887	Year 21 UCC	104
CCA year 9 (20%)	377	CCA year 22 (20%)	21
Year 9 UCC	1,510	Year 22 UCC	83
CCA year 10 (20%)	302	CCA year 23 (20%)	17
Year 10 UCC	1,208	Year 23 UCC	66
CCA year 11 (20%)	242	CCA year 24 (20%)	13
Year 11 UCC	966	Year 24 UCC	53
CCA year 12 (20%)	193	CCA year 25 (20%)	11
Year 12 UCC	773	Year 25 UCC	$42*
CCA year 12 (20%)	155		

*CCA is discretionary (see p. 893).

The CCA of each year is deducted in the calculation of a company's taxable income. Thus, the CCA is not a cash flow. Rather we must multiply the CCA of each year by the company's marginal tax rate to calculate the actual cash flow tax savings in each year. In Chapter 21, we recognized the time value of money. Thus, to determine the present value of the tax savings, we would need to multiply the tax savings of each year by the present value factor from the CCA list for each year at the company's required rate of return (say 10%).

In the case of the $10,000 desk, the present value of the tax savings from deducting CCA, commonly referred to as the tax shield, is $2,548, computed as follows assuming a 10% required rate of return:

$$\text{Tax shield} = (\$10,000 \times 40\%)\left(\frac{20\%}{20\% + 10\%}\right)\left(\frac{(2 + 10\%)}{2(1 + 10\%)}\right)$$

$$= \$4,000 \times 0.667 \times 0.955$$
$$= \$2,668 \times 0.955$$
$$= \$2,548$$

Therefore, the net after-tax cost of the desk is $7,452, or $10,000 – $2,548.

A detailed proof of the tax shield formula is not necessary for our purposes, but some explanation will be useful. The first component of the formula, investment times the marginal tax rate, computes the total tax savings over the life of the asset from the CCA deduction. The $4,000, however, does not incorporate any time value of money considerations.

The second component, the CCA rate divided by the sum of the CCA rate plus the required rate of return, calculates the present values of all the annual tax savings assuming the half-year rule did not exist.

The third component incorporates an adjustment for the half-year rule. For example, in the above scenario the tax shield was reduced to 95.5% of the benefit that existed before the introduction of the half-year rule. Most CCA classes use the declining balance method. However, occasionally the straight-line method is used, in which the CCA is the same for each year except the first and last years, which have one-half of the CCA due to the half-year rule. It is also important to recall that CCA applies only to tangible assets.

CCA CLASSES AND RATES

Companies may claim up to the percentages shown of the UCC in any year for the specified class of tangible assets (see the table below[6]). The legislation regarding CCA allows this annual deduction only if the asset can be classified under the act; otherwise no deduction is permitted. In establishing the initial value of the asset, if the company has or is entitled to receive financial assistance to acquire the asset, then the dollar value of this assistance may reduce the asset's initial value. In addition, if during the useful life of the asset its value is reappraised downwards, then the UCC must also decrease.

Class	Maximum CCA Rate	Tangible Assets in This Class
Class 1	4%	Buildings acquired after 1987 unless they belong to a different class. Any non-residential building acquired after March 18, 2007 includes a 6% additional allowance if it is used to manufacture or process goods in Canada. Other non-residential buildings include an additional 2%.
Class 3	5%	Buildings acquired or under construction on June 18, 1987. Any alterations or additions made after June 18, 1987, up to the lesser of $500,000 or 25% of the cost or alterations made before 1988. Any additional amount of alterations is included in Class 1.
Class 8	20%	Most furniture, fixtures, appliances, electronic copying and telecommunications equipment and software acquired before March 23, 2004. If the property costs $1,000 or managers can elect to have the property as a separate CCA deduction and calculate the CCA for a five-year period. When all assets in the class are disposed of the UCC is fully deductible as a terminal loss. At the end of the fifth year, any UCC of property remaining in the class is transferred back to the class it would otherwise belong to.
Class 10	30%	General purpose electronic data-processing equipment and systems software if acquired before March 23, 2004, and managers made this election (instead of class 8). Other eligible property includes motor vehicles, automobiles, and some passenger automobiles.
Class 12	100%	China, cutlery, linen, uniforms, dies, jigs, moulds, cutting or shaping parts of a machine, tools (excluding any electronic communication devices and data processing equipment), computer software (except systems software), videocassettes, laserdiscs, rented digital video disks rented that you do not expect to re-rent for longer than 7 days in any 30-day period. The limit after which these must be Class 8 has increased to $500 from $200 for tools, medical or dental instruments, and kitchen utensils acquired after May 2, 2006.
Class 29	Straight-line	Eligible machinery and equipment used in manufacturing and processing in Canada, acquired after March 18, 2007, and before 2012 that would otherwise be Class 43. Eligible general purpose electronic data-processing equipment and systems software if acquired after March 18, 2007 and before January 28, 2009, used in manufacturing and processing. The half-year rule applies to the calculation of straight-line amortization with 25% available in year 1, 50% in year 2, and the remaining 25% in year 3.

[6]Canada Revenue Agency Classes of depreciable property: http://www.cra-arc.gc.ca/tx/bsnss/tpcs/slprtnr/rprtng/cptl/dprcbl-eng.html, accessed April 5, 2011.

EXHIBIT 22-2
Trade-in of a Capital Asset

CCA—Class 8	
Ending UCC—year 3	$50,000
Purchase	12,000
Less: Trade-in	(4,000)
Net change in UCC	8,000
Revised UCC	58,000
Year 4—CCA	
20% × $50,000	10,000
10% × $8,000	800
Total CCA	10,800
UCC—year 4	$47,200

TRADE-INS AND DISPOSALS OF CAPITAL ASSETS

When a capital asset is either traded in on another asset or is sold, we do not need to concern ourselves with the net tax book value of the asset. Assume that a company's Class 8 UCC for all of its furniture and fixtures is $50,000, as shown in Exhibit 22-2, at the end of year 3. Also assume that included in the $50,000 is the remaining UCC on the desk of $5,760.

If in year 4 the desk were traded in on a new desk, where the price of the new desk was $12,000, and $4,000 was allowed as a trade-in, the Class 8 UCC would increase by $8,000. Note that the CCA system works on a pool basis, in that we are not concerned with the UCC of the specific desk being sold. Rather we are concerned only with the effect of each transaction on the net cash flows of the Class 8 CCA and UCC. The UCC of the class that existed before the disposal is reduced only by the amount of the cash received. As a result, the actual amount of the UCC of the specific asset is irrelevant to the decision. In this example, the net capital expenditure of $8,000 is the relevant cash flow.

Continuing with the example in Exhibit 22-2, the CCA for year 4 is $10,800. To simplify the terminology, we refer to the beginning UCC balance of year 4 as the ending UCC for year 3. This is a combination of the CCA at the rate of 20% on the opening UCC of $50,000 ($10,000) and the CCA at the half-year-rule of 20% on one-half of the net addition, which equals $4,000 ($800). Assume no other transactions occur.

Thus, as shown in Exhibit 22-3, the net after-tax present value of the cost of the new desk is $5,964. This amount recognizes the fact that the tax shield of $2,036 on the net addition of $8,000 must recognize the half-year rule.

If in the above scenario a new desk had not been purchased, but rather the old desk were sold for $4,000, the CCA would be 20% of $46,000 or $9,200. Note the half-year rule does not apply to net disposals of assets—that is, where the amount of disposals exceeds the amount of additions during a given year.

From Exhibit 22-3, note that the sale of $4,000 reduces the future CCA and results in a lost tax shield of $1,067. Thus, the net after-tax present value of the sale is $2,933. Again, the tax shield is irrelevant if the company has no taxable income.

SIMPLIFYING ASSUMPTIONS

It is useful to note that a number of simplifying assumptions have been made when using the tax shield formula:

◆ We have assumed that the company's marginal tax rate will remain the same (at 40% in the above examples). Further, the above examples also assume that the company will have a taxable income each year.

◆ Although it is uncommon, governments can change the CCA rates that we have assumed to be constant.

EXHIBIT 22-3
Net Capital Cash Flow of Trade-ins and Disposals

Trade-in:	Purchase price	$12,000
	Trade-in	(4,000)
	Net cash payment	8,000
	Tax shield[a]	2,036
	NPV cash outflow	$ 5,964
Disposal:	Sales price	4,000
	Lost tax shield[b]	1,067
	NPV cash inflow	$ 2,933

[a]Includes the half-year adjustment:

$$(\$8,000 \times 40\%) \times \left(\frac{20\%}{20\%+10\%}\right) \times \left(\frac{2+10\%}{2(1+10\%)}\right)$$

[b]Excludes the half-year adjustment

$$(\$4,000 \times 40\%) \times \left(\frac{20\%}{20\%+10\%}\right)$$

◆ We have also assumed that all CCA tax savings occur at year-end. In reality, companies make monthly instalments. However, the additional cost of attempting to be more precise is not warranted, given the degree of uncertainty that already exists in the estimation of the cash flows.

CAPITAL GAINS AND LOSSES

This brief section on capital gains does not cover all CRA guidelines, which exceed 40 pages. Experienced management teams understand that tax law is tailored to specific circumstances and will request a CRA ruling in advance of the transaction if they are unsure of how to interpret the guideline. Obtaining advanced rulings avoids delay in important renewal of old assets should CRA disagree with the company's interpretation of the guidelines. Tax implications involve the consideration of significant sums of cash that can reverse a transaction from one with positive to one with negative cash flow early in the useful life of an asset.

When capital properties are purchased, CRA permits deductions from taxable income based on the **adjusted cost base (ACB)**, which is the sum of the purchase price *plus purchase expenses*. When the capital property is disposed of, the seller may receive cash greater or less than the ACB *plus sales expenses*. When the sales price of the capital property plus sales expenses is greater than the ACB, the difference is called a **capital gain**. When the sales price plus sales expenses is less than the ACB the difference is called a **capital loss**. The sales expenses of an asset are never deducted directly from business revenue. Capital gains and losses may also arise from the exchange, expropriation, theft, and destruction of capital property.

Business tax rules for capital gains and losses apply only to capital property acquired for purposes of earning income. This means, for example, that corporate portfolios of shares held for trading by a manufacturing company usually are not eligible for the tax treatment of capital gains and losses.[7] For some types of shares and corporations, as defined by CRA, special tax rules apply.

All capital gains and losses must be reported on the tax return filed for the calendar year in which the transaction occurred. Some capital gains are exempt up to a maximum lifetime exemption of $750,000 for residents of Canada. Usually, once this exemption is used, proceeds from the disposition of long-term assets are taxed at 50% of any capital gain. In addition, if the proceeds from the disposition of a long-term

---

[7]The CRA's detailed methods of classifying capital property and the treatment of the proceeds from disposition of an eligible capital property are complex and beyond the scope of this text. They can be found in full at http://www.cra-arc.gc.ca/E/pub/tg/t4037/t4037-103.pdf.

EXHIBIT 22-4

Proceeds on Disposition of the Last Capital Asset in an Asset Class

	A	B	C	D
Proceeds of disposition	$ 4,000	$ 7,000	$ 3,000	$ 12,000
Less: ACB	(10,000)	(10,000)	(10,000)	(10,000)
Capital gain				$ 2,000
Capital (loss)	$ (6,000)	$ (3,000)	$ (7,000)	
Calculation including CCA				
Recapture of CCA and/or Terminal Loss				
UCC Beginning Balance	10,000	10,000	10,000	10,000
Less accumulated CCA	(4,000)	(4,000)	(4,000)	(4,000)
UCC in year of disposition	$ 6,000	$ 6,000	$ 6,000	$ 6,000
Subtract lesser of ACB or Proceeds of disposition	(4,000)	(7,000)	$ (3,000)	(10,000)
Terminal loss (recapture of CCA)	$ 2,000	$ (1,000)	$ 3,000	$ (4,000)

A: The business has no capital gain. There is a capital loss of $6,000 that can be used in this tax year to offset any taxable capital gains. There is a terminal loss of $2,000 that is 100% deductible from taxable income on the filing for the calendar year.

B: The business has no capital gain but has a capital loss of $3,000 that can be used in this tax year to offset any taxable capital gain. This is also a recapture of CCA of $1,000 that must declared as business income for the calendar year.

C: The company has a capital loss of $7,000, of which 50% can be deducted from any taxable capital gain in the year. There is a terminal loss of $3,000 that is 100% deductible from taxable income in the filing for the calendar year.

D: The business has a capital gain of $2,000 that may be taxable. The business also has a recapture of CCA of $4,000 that must be declared as business income for the calendar year.

asset are used to replace the sold asset, the reporting of any capital gain can be deferred until the sale of the replacement within specific time frames as specified by the ITS.

If a capital loss is incurred, then 50% of the loss can be used as a deduction from any *taxable* capital gains for the year. The actual tax assessed, however, depends on the timing of payments by the purchaser to the seller. These items are only very general guidelines and are not applicable to all transactions. For example, the calculation of terminal losses and recapture of CCA described next do not apply to Class 10.1 passenger vehicles.

Businesses are not compelled to take 100% of their CCA each year, which is why, for every depreciable capital property disposed of, there is a CCA calculation. Either the *lesser* of the proceeds on disposition minus the sales expenses is deducted from UCC or the adjusted cost base of the property is deducted. When the last property in a specific asset class is sold but the calculation results in a positive UCC balance for the asset class, the remainder is called a **terminal loss**. Unlike capital losses, where only 50% of any capital loss is deductible in the year of the transaction, 100% of a terminal loss can be deducted from taxable income for the calendar year in which the transaction occurs. If, upon sale of the last of a specific asset class, the calculation results in a negative UCC balance, CRA deems this a **recapture of CCA** and it is taxed as normal business income for the calendar year of the transaction.

Exhibit 22-4 illustrates three simple examples of how a disposition of the last asset in an asset class could give rise to a recapture of CCA, a terminal loss, or a capital gain and recapture of CCA. The difference in tax treatment arises strictly because of the different amount of the proceeds from disposition of the depreciable asset. In this example two simplifying assumptions are as follows:

◆ None of the capital gain is exempt.

◆ The proceeds on disposition are *not* used to purchase a replacement asset.

INCOME TAX COMPLICATIONS

In the foregoing illustrations, we deliberately avoided many possible income tax complications. As all taxpaying citizens know, income taxes are affected by many intricacies, including eligibility, exemptions, progressive tax rates, loss carrybacks and carryforwards, varying provincial income taxes, capital gains, distinctions between capital assets and other assets, liquidation of a CCA class, exchanges of property of like kind, exempt income, and so on. Keep in mind that changes in the tax law occur each year. In practice, management teams find the experts on tax when creating their cash flow models and, if necessary, obtain an advance tax ruling before calculating the tax consequences of an investment in or disposition of eligible assets.

The meanings of *amortization* and *book value* are widely misunderstood because the terms are commonly used incorrectly. Neither amortization nor book value is about cash. Admittedly, the use of these terms by CRA adds to the confusion (see footnote 3 on page 888). These accruals have no role in investment decisions. Suppose a bank has some printing equipment with a book value of $30,000, an expected terminal disposal value of zero, a current disposal value of $12,000, and a remaining useful life of three years. For simplicity, assume that straight-line amortization of $10,000 yearly will be taken.

The inputs to the decision model are the predicted income tax effects on cash. The book loss of $18,000 or the amortization of $10,000 may be necessary for making *predictions*. By themselves, however, they are not inputs to DCF decision models because they have no cash effect. Because investment decisions are often done in stages, these accruals may be used as placeholders for all alternatives until the final few alternatives are being modelled. At that point, the cash effects will be calculated in detail. The following points summarize the role of amortization regarding the replacement of equipment:

◆ *Initial investment.* The amount paid for (and hence amortization on) old equipment is irrelevant except for its effect on tax cash flows. In contrast, the amount paid for new equipment is relevant because it is an expected future cost that will not be incurred if replacement is rejected.

◆ *Do not double-count.* The investment in equipment is a one-time outlay at time zero, so it should not be double-counted as an outlay in the form of amortization. Amortization by itself is irrelevant; it is not a cash outlay.

◆ *Relation to income tax cash flows.* Relevant quantities were defined in Chapter 4 as expected future data that will differ among alternatives. Given this definition, book values and past amortization are irrelevant in all capital budgeting decision models. The relevant item is the *income tax cash effect*, not the book value or the amortization.

ALTERNATIVE APPROACHES TO CAPITAL BUDGETING

2 Apply the total-project approach and the differential approach appropriately to different capital budgeting decisions.

We turn now to a fuller discussion of how income taxes can affect cash inflows and outflows and also how they influence managers' decisions. We focus on the information-acquisition and selection stages of capital budgeting, highlight the effect of income taxes, and use the net present value method for the formal financial analysis. When interpreting the data tables please recall that 0 is the beginning of the initial year of the investment, and at time 0 all cash outflows occur. Time 1 is the point at the end of the initial year of the investment when all cash flows in occur. This means there is a time value attributed to cash inflow but not cash outflow in the initial investment year.

Example: Potato Supreme produces potato products for sale to supermarkets and other retail outlets. It is considering *replacing* an old packaging machine (purchased three years ago) with a new, more efficient packaging machine that has recently been introduced. The new machine is less labour-intensive and has lower operating costs than the old machine. For simplicity, we assume the following:

1. All cash outflows or inflows occur at the end of the year (even though cash operating costs generally occur throughout the year).

2. The tax effects of cash inflows and outflows occur at the same time that the inflows and outflows occur.

3. The income tax rate is 30% each year.

4. The equipment is one of several assets that qualify as CCA Class 8, with a CCA rate of up to 20% declining balance. Potato Supreme takes the maximum rate each year.

5. Both the old and the new machine have the same working capital requirements and the same remaining useful life.

6. Potato Supreme is a profitable company.

Summary data for the two machines are as follows:

	Old Machine	New Machine
Original cost	$ 87,500	$200,000
Accumulated amortization	$ 37,500	—
Current book value	$ 50,000	—
Current disposal price	$ 26,000	—
Proceeds of disposition, 4 years from now	$ 6,000	$ 20,000
Annual cash operating costs	$250,000	$150,000
Remaining useful life	4 years	4 years
After-tax required rate of return	10%	10%
Capital cost allowance rate	20% (declining balance)	20% (declining balance)

Potato Supreme uses the net present value method to evaluate whether it should replace the old with the new packaging machine immediately or in four years' time. As in the Lifetime Care example in Chapter 21, the key point in net present value analysis is to identify the relevant cash flows. Assume the proceeds from disposition will be used to purchase the replacement machine. To emphasize the ideas of relevance, Chapter 21 used the **differential approach**, which analyzes only relevant cash flows—those future cash outflows and inflows that differ between alternatives. The differential approach is generally faster when there are only two alternatives.

When the number of alternatives is more than two, the differential approach becomes unwieldy because it forces the analyst into difficult calculations of differences among multiple alternatives. Companies then use the **total-project approach**, which calculates the present value of *all* future cash inflows and outflows under each alternative separately. It does not require the identification of cash flows that differ among alternatives. The total-project approach requires the following:

1. Calculate the present value of all cash inflows and outflows under the status quo alternative.

2. Separately calculate the present value of all cash inflows and outflows under another alternative.

We use the Potato Supreme example to illustrate the two steps of the total-project approach. We then use the differential approach to show that both approaches give the same net present value. Because the proceeds on disposition will be used to purchase a replacement we do not need to consider any tax effect of capital gains or losses. The following categories of cash flows are considered in both approaches:

a. Initial machine investment.

b. Tax shield on initial investment.

c. Cash flow from current disposal of old machine.

d. Lost tax shield from current disposal of old machine.

e. Recurring after-tax cash operating flows.

f. Cash flow from proceeds of disposition of old machine. Other assets remain in this asset class.

g. Lost tax shield from terminal disposal of machine.

TOTAL-PROJECT APPROACH

1. Calculate the present value of total cash flows of replacing the old packaging machine in four years' time. Under this alternative, cash flow categories that specifically pertain to the new machine are not relevant. But the purchase price is relevant when calculating item g, the lost tax shield. In four years, should the purchase price of new equipment exceed proceeds of disposition of the old equipment, **net addition**, the half-year rule applies. Capital gain, if any, can be deferred for the life of the replacement equipment when the proceeds of disposition are used to purchase replacement equipment.

   a. *Initial machine investment.* No new investment is necessary if Potato Supreme keeps the old packaging machine. Exhibit 22-5, item a, shows an initial machine investment of $0 in year 0.

   b. *Tax shield on initial investment.* As there is no new investment, there is no additional tax shield.

   c. *Cash flow from current disposal of old machine.* Since the old machine is kept and not disposed of, Exhibit 22-5, item c, shows after-tax cash flow from current disposal of old machine of $0 in year 0.

   d. *Lost tax shield from current disposal of old machine.* As the old machine is not sold, no tax shield adjustments are required.

   e. *Recurring after-tax cash operating flows.*

Recurring cash operating flows (costs) for the old machine	$(250,000)
Deduct: Income tax savings at 30% of $250,000	75,000
Recurring after-tax cash operating flows	$(175,000)

   After-tax cash operating flows of $(175,000) in years 1 to 4 appear as relevant cash outflows in Exhibit 22-5, item e. Our example assumes that Potato Supreme's income tax rate is 30% each year. When future tax rates are uncertain, analysts must predict the tax rate applicable for each year of a project.

   f. *Cash flow from proceeds of disposition of old machine. Other assets remain in this asset class.*

Proceeds of disposition at end of year 4	$6,000

   The cash flow of $6,000 from the proceeds of disposition of the old machine appears as a cash inflow in year 4 of Exhibit 22-5, item f.

   g. *Lost tax shield.* The proceeds of disposition of $6,000 would reduce the CCA pool by $6,000, and thus reduce the future cash savings from capital cost allowance deductions by $1,146.

   $$(\$6,000 \times 0.30) \times \frac{0.20}{(0.20 + 0.10)} \times \frac{(2 + 0.10)}{2(1 + 0.10)}$$

   $$= \$1,800 \times 2 \div 3 \times 0.955 = \$1,146$$

   Exhibit 22-5 presents all after-tax cash flows that would arise if Potato Supreme continued to use the old packaging machine. Each cash flow is multiplied by its corresponding present value discount factor to give its present value. The total present value is $(551,435).

2. Calculate the present value of total cash flows of immediately replacing the old packaging machine.

   a. *Initial machine investment.* The original cost of the new packaging machine is $200,000. This amount appears as a cash outflow in year 0 in Exhibit 22-6, item a.

EXHIBIT 22-5

Total-Project Approach for Potato Supreme: After-Tax Analysis of Replacing Old Machine in Four Years' Time

	Total Present Value	Present Value Discount Factors at 10%	**Sketch of Relevant After-Tax Cash Flows**				
End of Year:			**0**	**1**	**2**	**3**	**4**
Explanations for the after-tax cash flow amounts are given on pp. 896–898.							
a. Initial machine investment	$ 0 ← 1.000 ←		$0				
c. After-tax cash flow from immediate proceeds of disposition	0 ← 1.000 ←		0				
e. Recurring after-tax cash operating flows	(554,750) ← 3.170 ←			$(175,000)	$(175,000)	$(175,000)	$(175,000)
f. Cash flow from proceeds of disposition in four years' time	4,098 ← 0.683 ←						6,000
g. Lost tax shield from the disposal in four years' time	(783) ← 0.683 ←						($1,146)
Total present value of all cash flows if Potato Supreme replaces the old machine in four years' time	$(551,435)						

Note: Parentheses denote relevant cash outflows throughout all exhibits in this chapter.

EXHIBIT 22-6

Total-Project Approach for Potato Supreme: After-Tax Analysis of Immediately Purchasing the New Machine

	Total Present Value	Present Value Discount Factors at 10%	**Sketch of Relevant After-Tax Cash Flows**				
End of Year:			**0**	**1**	**2**	**3**	**4**
Explanations for the after-tax cash flow amounts are given on pp. 896–898.							
a. Initial machine investment	$(200,000) ← 1.000 ←		$(200,000)				
b. Net differential tax shield effect (no 1/2 year rule on disposition)	38,182 ← 1.000 ←		$ 38,182				
	$(161,818)						
c. Cash flow from immediate proceeds of disposition of old machine	26,000 ← 1.000 ←		$ 26,000				
d. Lost tax shield from immediate disposal of old machine (no 1/2 year rule)	$ (5,200) ← 1.000 ←		$ (5,200)				
Net investment ($161,818 − $26,000 + $5,200)	$(141,018)						
e. Recurring after-tax cash operating flows	(332,850) ← 3.170 ←			$(105,000)	$(105,000)	$(105,000)	$(105,000)
f. Cash flow from proceeds of disposition of the new machine in four years' time	13,660 ← 0.683 ←						$20,000
g. Lost tax shield from disposal of the new machine in four years' time	(3,552) ← 0.683 ←						(5,200)
Total present value of all cash flows if Potato Supreme immediately replaces the old machine	$(463,760)						

b. *Tax shield.* The original cost of $200,000 will generate a cash savings from capital cost allowance of $38,160. This amount is determined by using the tax shield formula.

$$(\$200{,}000 \times 0.30) \times \frac{0.20}{(0.20 + 0.10)} \times \frac{(2 + 0.10)}{2(1 + 0.10)}$$

$$= \$60{,}000 \times \frac{2}{3} \times \frac{2.1}{2.2}$$

$$= \$40{,}000 \times 0.9545 = \$38{,}182$$

Recall that the tax shield formula calculates the present value of the cash flows.

c. *Cash flow from immediate proceeds of disposition.*

Immediate proceeds of disposition	$26,000

Review what is included in the present value analysis. It is the immediate *cash inflow* from the proceeds of disposition of the asset. The book value of the old machine and the loss on disposal do not themselves affect cash flow. The book value, however, enters into the calculation of the loss on disposal of the asset, which in turn affects the accounting net income.

d. *Lost tax shield from immediate disposal of old machine.* The current disposal of $26,000 would reduce the cash savings from future capital cost allowance by $5,200. There are no capital gains tax considerations because the proceeds on disposition contribute to the payment of the replacement.

$$(\$26{,}000 \times 0.30) \times \frac{0.20}{(0.20 + 0.10)}$$

$$= \$7{,}800 \times \frac{2}{3}$$

$$= \$5{,}200$$

In this case, the half-year rule does not apply to the calculation of the tax shield formula because the net addition is a positive number ($200,000 − $26,000).

e. *Recurring after-tax cash operating flows.*

Recurring cash operating flows (costs) for the new machine	$(150,000)
Deduct: Income tax savings (30% × $150,000)	45,000
Recurring after-tax cash operating flows	$(105,000)

The after-tax cash operating flows of $(105,000) in years 1 to 4 appear as relevant cash outflows in Exhibit 22-6, item e.

f. *Cash flow from proceeds of disposition of new machine. Other assets remain in this asset class.*

Proceeds from disposition of new machine	$20,000

g. *Lost tax shield from disposition of new machine in four years' time.* Assume no future replacement for the new machine. Therefore, the net addition ($0 – $20,000) will be negative and the half-year rule will not apply. The proceeds of disposition of $20,000 would reduce the future cash savings from CCA at the maximum rate of 20% by $3,552.

$$(\$20{,}000 \times 0.30) \times \frac{0.20}{(0.20 + 0.10)}$$

$$= \$6{,}000 \times \frac{2}{3} = \$4{,}000$$

Exhibit 22-6 summarizes the relevant after-tax cash flows that would occur if Potato Supreme replaced its old machine immediately. Present values are derived by multiplying cash flows by the corresponding present value discount factors. The total present value of cash flows equals $(463,760). Recall from Exhibit 22-5 that the present value of after-tax cash flows of replacing the old machine in four years' time is $(551,435). The decision to replace the old machine with the new machine immediately has a positive net present value of $87,675 ($551,435 − $463,760) and is therefore preferred.

DIFFERENTIAL APPROACH

Unlike the two-step total-project approach, the differential approach is a one-step method that includes only those cash inflows and outflows that *differ* between the two alternatives. Assume that the equipment disposed of will be replaced. The differential approach compares the cash outflows arising from replacing the old machine with the savings in future cash outflows resulting from using the new machine rather than the old machine. We will now examine the differences in cash flows between the keep and replace alternatives in the Potato Supreme example using the categories of cash flows that we described earlier.

    a. *Initial machine investment* of $200,000 for the new machine (see Exhibit 22-6) appears as a cash outflow in year 0 in Exhibit 22-7, item a.

    c. *Cash flow from immediate proceeds of disposition of old machine* of $26,000 (see Exhibit 22-6) appears as a cash inflow in year 0 in Exhibit 22-7, item c. The initial machine investment, $200,000, minus the cash flow from current disposal of the old machine, $26,000, is the net initial investment of $174,000, shown as a cash outflow in year 0 in Exhibit 22-7. There are no capital gains tax effects.

b. net of d. *Tax shield.* The net initial investment of $174,000 would increase the CCA pool by this amount and thus would generate cash savings from CCA from now to infinity. The cash savings would be $32,982, a figure determined as the net of tax shield effects of the increase in CCA and decrease from the lost tax shield on disposal:

$$\$38,182 + \$(5,200) = \$32,982$$

    e. *Recurring after-tax cash operating flows.* Replacing the old machine results in lower after-tax cash operating costs, as follows:

Recurring after-tax cash operating costs if old machine kept (Exhibit 22-5, item e)	$175,000
Deduct: Recurring after-tax cash operating costs if machine replaced (Exhibit 22-6, item e)	105,000
Savings in recurring after-tax cash operating costs if machine replaced	$ 70,000

Exhibit 22-7, item e, shows this $70,000 increase in recurring after-tax cash operating flows in years 1–4.

f. net of g. *Cash flow from proceeds of disposition of each machine in four years' time, net of the lost tax shield of each respective disposal.* The immediate disposition of the old machine results in no disposition of this machine in four years' time. This opportunity cost for the old machine based on Exhibit 22-5 is $3,315 ($4,098 − $783) for the old machine. The opportunity cost for the new machine based on Exhibit 22-6 is $10,108 ($13,660 − $3,552).

In Exhibit 22-7 the terminal disposal of the new machine for $20,000 will result in a lost tax shield of $3,552, the net of which is $10,108.

    Both the total-project approach (Exhibits 22-5 and 22-6) and the differential approach (Exhibit 22-7) result in a net present value of $87,675 in favour of immediately replacing the old packaging machine with the new one. When comparing alternatives, these two approaches will always give the same net present value.

EXHIBIT 22-7
Differential Approach for Potato Supreme: After-Tax Analysis of Replacing Old Machine

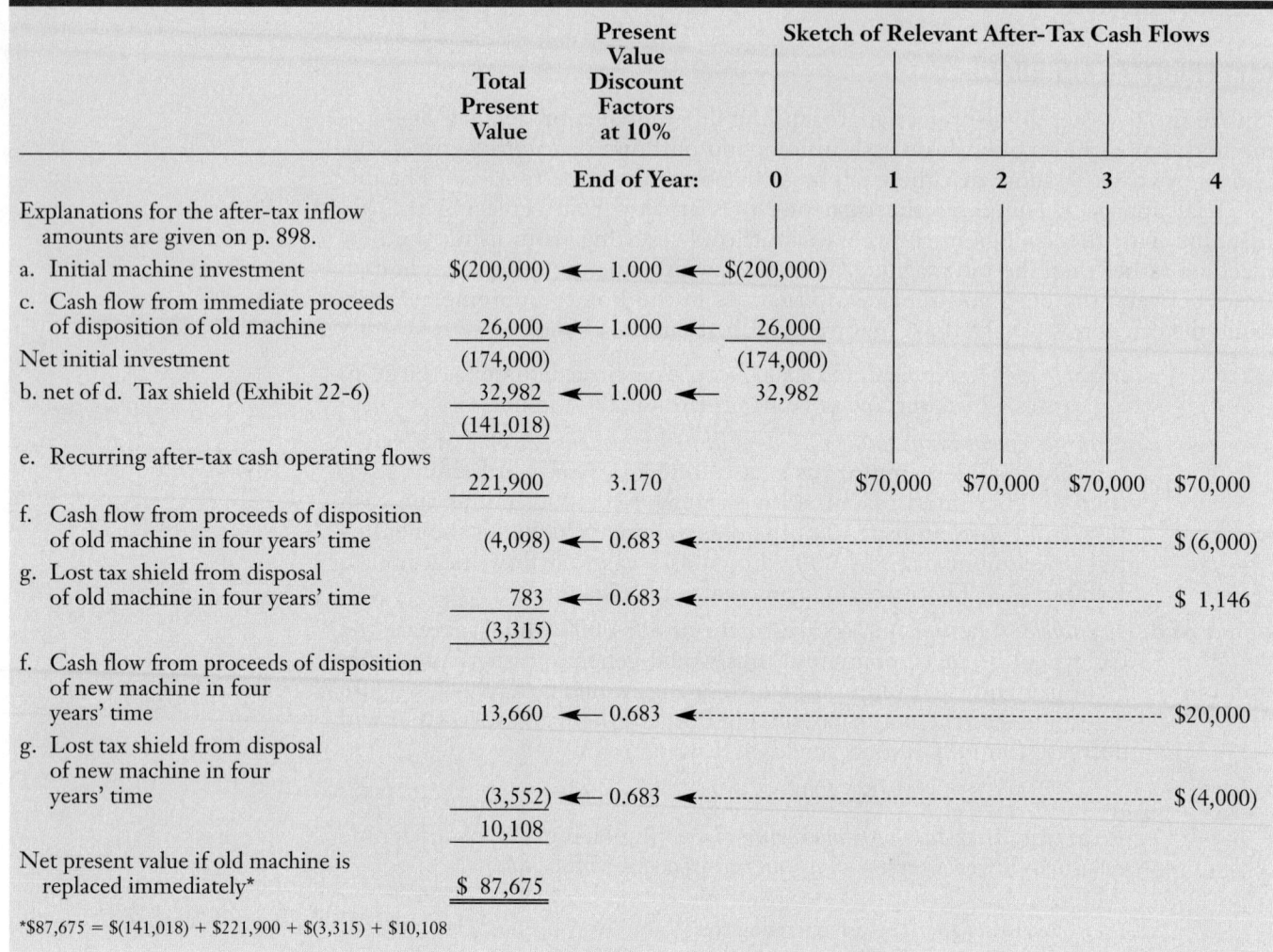

	Total Present Value	Present Value Discount Factors at 10%	Sketch of Relevant After-Tax Cash Flows

End of Year:			0	1	2	3	4
Explanations for the after-tax inflow amounts are given on p. 898.							
a. Initial machine investment	$(200,000) ◄— 1.000 ◄— $(200,000)						
c. Cash flow from immediate proceeds of disposition of old machine	26,000 ◄— 1.000 ◄— 26,000						
Net initial investment	(174,000)		(174,000)				
b. net of d. Tax shield (Exhibit 22-6)	32,982 ◄— 1.000 ◄— 32,982						
	(141,018)						
e. Recurring after-tax cash operating flows	221,900	3.170		$70,000	$70,000	$70,000	$70,000
f. Cash flow from proceeds of disposition of old machine in four years' time	(4,098) ◄— 0.683 ◄-----------						$ (6,000)
g. Lost tax shield from disposal of old machine in four years' time	783 ◄— 0.683 ◄-----------						$ 1,146
	(3,315)						
f. Cash flow from proceeds of disposition of new machine in four years' time	13,660 ◄— 0.683 ◄-----------						$20,000
g. Lost tax shield from disposal of new machine in four years' time	(3,552) ◄— 0.683 ◄-----------						$ (4,000)
	10,108						
Net present value if old machine is replaced immediately*	$ 87,675						

*$87,675 = $(141,018) + $221,900 + $(3,315) + $10,108

CAPITAL BUDGETING AND INFLATION

3 Apply the concepts of real and nominal rate of return to account for inflation in capital budgeting.

It is important to account for **inflation** in capital budgeting because declines in the general purchasing power of the monetary unit (say, dollars) will inflate future cash flows above what they would have been had there been no inflation. Inflation can be defined as the decline in the general purchasing power of the monetary unit (for example, the dollar in Canada or the yen in Japan). We present how inflation can be explicitly recognized in capital budgeting analysis. Because of inflation, the cash inflows for future periods will be measured in dollars that have less value than the dollars invested in the project in year 0. Failure to take inflation into account will overstate the financial return of the project.

An inflation rate of 10% in one year means that what you could buy with $100 (say) at the start of the year will cost you $110 [$100 + (10% × $100)] at the end of the year. Prices increase as more money chases fewer goods. Some countries—for example, Brazil, Israel, Mexico, and Russia—have experienced annual inflation rates of 15% to more than 100%. Even an annual inflation rate of 5% over, say, a five-year period can result in sizable declines in the general purchasing power of the monetary unit over that time.

REAL AND NOMINAL RATES OF RETURN

When analyzing inflation we need to distinguish between the real rate of return and the nominal rate of return:

◆ **Real rate of return** is the rate of return required to cover only investment risk.

◆ **Nominal rate of return** is the rate of return required to cover investment risk and the anticipated decline, due to inflation, in the general purchasing power of the cash that the investment generates. The rates of return (or interest) earned on the financial markets are nominal rates, because they compensate investors for both risk and inflation.

Assume that the real rate of return for investments in high-risk cellular data transmission equipment at Network Communications is 20% and that the expected inflation rate is 10%. The nominal rate of return is:[8]

$$\text{Nominal rate} = (1 + \text{Real rate})(1 + \text{Inflation rate}) - 1$$
$$= (1 + 0.20)(1 + 0.10) - 1$$
$$= [(1.20)(1.10)] - 1 = 1.32 - 1 = 0.32$$

The nominal rate of return is also related to the real rate of return and the inflation rate as follows:

Real rate of return	0.20
Inflation rate	0.10
Combination (0.20 × 0.10)	0.02
Nominal rate of return	0.32

Note that the nominal rate is slightly higher than the real rate (0.20) plus the inflation rate (0.10). The reason is that the nominal rate recognizes that inflation also decreases the purchasing power of the real rate of return earned during the year.

Foreign-currency exchange rates determine the domestic dollar value of cash flows from non-domestic investments. Foreign-currency exchange rates are based on nominal dollar values. The foreign-currency exchange rate tells you how much foreign money you can purchase with your Canadian dollar. The effect of inflation considered in this chapter applies to the erosion or improvement to the purchasing power of the domestic currency. There is a relationship, therefore, between inflation and the quantity of foreign currency a Canadian dollar will purchase because inflation erodes all purchasing power. If the cash flow from foreign investments has already been translated into nominal Canadian dollars, the quantity of Canadian-dollar-denominated foreign cash flow has already been calculated. What remains in the capital budgeting process is to convert the rate of return from nominal to the inflation-adjusted real rate of return.

NET PRESENT VALUE METHOD AND INFLATION

The watchword when incorporating inflation into the net present value (NPV) method is *internal consistency*. There are two internally consistent approaches:

◆ *Nominal approach*. Predict cash inflows and outflows in nominal monetary units and use a nominal rate as the required rate of return.

◆ *Real approach*. Predict cash inflows and outflows in real monetary units and use a real rate as the required rate of return.

Consider an investment that is expected to generate sales of 100 units and a net cash inflow of $1,000 ($10 per unit) each year for two years *absent inflation*. If inflation of 10% is expected each year, net cash inflows from the sale of each unit would be $11 ($10 × 1.10) in year 1 and $12.10 [$11 × 1.10 or $10 × (1.10)^2] in year 2—resulting in net cash inflows of $1,100 in year 1 and $1,210 in year 2. The net cash inflows of $1,100 and $1,210 are nominal cash inflows because they include the impact of inflation. *These are the cash flows recorded by the accounting system*. The cash inflows of $1,000 each year are real cash flows because they exclude inflationary effects. Note that the real cash flows equal the nominal cash flows discounted for inflation, $1,000 = $1,100 × 1.10 = $1,210 ÷ (1.10)^2. Many managers find the nominal

---

[8]The real rate of return can be expressed in terms of the nominal rate of return as follows:

$$\text{Real rate} = \frac{(1 + \text{Nominal rate})}{(1 + \text{Inflation rate})} - 1 = \frac{(1 + 0.32)}{(1 + 0.10)} - 1 = 0.20$$

EXHIBIT 22-8
Nominal Approach to Inflation for Network Communications: Predict Cash Inflows and Outflows in Nominal Dollars and Use a Nominal Discount Rate*

		Total Present Value	Present Value Discount Factors at 32%†	Sketch of Relevant After-Tax Cash Flows				
			End of Year:	0	1	2	3	4

1. Initial equipment investment

Year	Investment Outflows
0	$(750,000)

$(750,000) ◄—1,000000 ◄— $(750,000)

2. Cash savings from tax shield

$ 127,631‡ ◄—1,000000 ◄— $ 127,631

3. Recurring after-tax cash operating flows:

$(622,369)

Year (1)	Recurring Nominal Cash Operating Inflows (2)	Income Tax Outflows (3) = 0.40 × (2)	Recurring Nominal After-Tax Cash Operating Inflows (4) = (2) − (3)					
1	$550,000	$220,000	$330,000	250,000 ◄—0.757576 ◄·············· $330,000				
2	726,000	290,400	435,600	250,000 ◄—0.573921 ◄························· $435,600				
3	798,600	319,440	479,160	208,333 ◄—0.434789 ◄······································· $479,160				
4	439,230	175,692	263,538	86,805 ◄—0.329385 ◄··· $263,538				
				795,138				

Net present value — $ 172,769

*The nominal discount rate of 32% is made up of the real rate of interest of 20% and the inflation rate of 10%: [(1 + 0.20)(1 + 0.10)] − 1 = 0.32.
†Present value discount factors are shown to six decimal digits to emphasize that the approaches to inflation in Exhibits 22-8 and 22-9 are equivalent. The formula on Table 2 of Appendix A is used to compute the present value discount factor.

‡$(750,000 × 0.40) $\dfrac{0.30}{0.30 + 0.32}$ × $\dfrac{2 + 0.32}{2(1 + 0.32)}$ = $300,000 × 0.484 × 0.879 = $127,631.

approach easier to understand and use because they observe nominal cash flows in their accounting systems and the nominal rates of return on financial markets.

Let's revisit Network Communications, which is deciding whether to invest in equipment to make and sell a cellular data transmission product. The equipment would cost $750,000 immediately. It is expected to have a four-year useful life with a zero terminal disposal price. An annual inflation rate of 10% is expected over this four-year period. Network Communications requires an after-tax real rate of return of 20% from this project or an after-tax nominal rate of return of 32%.

The following table presents the predicted amounts of real (assuming no inflation) and nominal (after considering cumulative inflation) net cash inflows from the equipment over the next four years (excluding the $750,000 investment in the equipment and before any income tax payments):

Year	Before-Tax Cash Inflows in Real Dollars (1)	Cumulative Inflation Rate Factor* (2)	Before-Tax Cash Inflows in Nominal Dollars (3) = (1) × (2)
1	$500,000	$(1.10)^1 = 1.1000$	$550,000
2	600,000	$(1.10)^2 = 1.2100$	726,000
3	600,000	$(1.10)^3 = 1.3310$	798,600
4	300,000	$(1.10)^4 = 1.4641$	439,230

*1.10 = 1.00 + 0.10 inflation rate.

EXHIBIT 22-9
Real Approach to Inflation for Network Communications: Predict Cash Inflows and Outflows in Real Dollars and Use a Real Discount Rate

			Total Present Value	Present Value Discount Factors at 20%*	Sketch of Relevant After-Tax Cash Flows				
				End of Year:	0	1	2	3	4

1. Initial equipment investment:

Year	Investment Outflows
0	$(750,000)

$(750,000) ◄— 1.000000 ◄— $(750,000)

2. Cash savings from tax shield

127,631‡ ◄—1.000000 ◄—   127,631

3. Recurring after-tax cash operating flows:

$(622,369)

Year (1)	Recurring Real Cash Operating Inflows (2)	Income Tax Outflows (3) = 0.40 × (2)	Recurring Real After-Tax Cash Operating Inflows (4) = (2) − (3)						
1	$500,000	$200,000	$300,000	250,000 ◄— 0.833333 ◄------------$300,000					
2	600,000	240,000	360,000	250,000 ◄— 0.694444 ◄-------------------- $360,000					
3	600,000	240,000	360,000	208,333 ◄— 0.578704 ◄---------------------------- $360,000					
4	300,000	120,000	180,000	86,805 ◄— 0.482253 ◄--- $180,000					
				795,138					

Net present value $ 172,769

*Present value factors are shown to six decimal digits and the present value calculations rounded to emphasize that the approaches to inflation in Exhibits 22-8 and 22-9 are equivalent. The formula on Table 2 of Appendix A is used to compute the present value discount factor.
‡The tax shield formula has used the nominal rate of 32% for demonstration purposes. It is common for companies to use a nominal rate, even though capital cost allowance amounts are not inflated.

The income tax rate is 40%. For tax purposes, the equipment will be amortized using a capital cost allowance rate of 30%, declining balance method.

Exhibit 22-8 presents the capital budgeting approach for predicting cash flows in nominal dollars and using a nominal discount rate.[9] The calculations in Exhibit 22-8 exactly follow the calculations used in the Potato Supreme example for initial machine investment, tax shields, and recurring after-tax cash operating flows. Under the nominal approach, first express all amounts in terms of *future-year dollars* (using cumulative inflation rate factors), then discount the resulting amounts to their present value using *nominal discount-rate factors*.

Exhibit 22-9 presents the approach of predicting cash flows in real terms and using a real discount rate. The calculations for item 3, recurring after-tax cash operating flows, are basically the same as before except that the cash inflows are measured in real terms and discounted at real rates.

Both approaches show that the project has a net present value of $172,769 and should therefore be accepted. The two approaches give the same answer because, for example, in going from the real approach to the nominal approach, the cash flows

[9]The present value discount factors in the example are calculated using six decimal digits to eliminate doubt about the equivalence of the two approaches. In practice, the present value discount factors (to three decimal digits) can be obtained using Table 2 (present value of $1) in Appendix A at the end of the text. The Problem for Self-Study at the end of this chapter uses Table 2.

are multiplied by, and the discount rates are divided by, the same cumulative inflation factor.[10]

The most frequently encountered error when accounting for inflation in capital budgeting is stating cash inflows and outflows in real monetary units and using a nominal discount rate. This error understates the discounted present value of cash flows that occur in the future and therefore creates a bias against the acceptance of many worthwhile capital investment projects.

PROJECT RISK AND RATE OF RETURN

4 Analyze alternative approaches used to recognize the degree of risk in capital budgeting projects.

The *required rate of return (RRR)*, which we discussed in Chapter 21, is a critical variable in discounted cash flow analysis. It is the rate of return that the organization forgoes by investing in a particular project rather than in an alternative project of comparable risk. *Risk* here refers to the business risk of the project *independent* of the specific manner in which the project is financed—whether with debt or with equity. Here is a safe generalization: The higher the risk, the higher the required rate of return and the faster management would want to recover the net initial investment. The reason is that higher risk means a greater chance that the project may lose money. Management would be willing to take this added risk only if it were compensated with a higher expected return.

The RRR used in discounted cash flow analysis should be internally consistent with the approach applied to predict cash inflows and outflows. The options include various combinations of (1) the real rate and the nominal rate and (2) the pretax and the after-tax rate. The differences among these rates can be sizable, given estimates of inflation that may exceed 10% and corporate tax rates of 30% or more.

Organizations typically use at least one of the following approaches in dealing with the risk factor of projects:

1. *Varying the required payback time.* Companies such as Nissan that use payback as a project selection criterion vary the required payback to reflect differences in project risk. The higher the risk, the shorter the required payback time.

    When faced with higher risk, companies also evaluate how to minimize their downside risk if the project is prematurely abandoned before the full cash inflows can be realized. A reason for abandoning a project prematurely arises (as it did for Ontario Power Generation) when government policies regarding environmental protection change and affect current projects in operation, such as stopping the refurbishing of a coal-fired electricity-generating plant.[11]

2. *Adjusting the required rate of return.* Companies such as DuPont and Shell Oil use a higher required rate of return when the risk is higher. Estimating a precise risk factor for each project is difficult.

    Some organizations simplify the task by having three or four general-risk categories (for example, very high, high, average, and low). Each project under consideration is assigned to a specific category. Management uses a predetermined discount rate, assigned to each category, as the required rate of return for projects in that category.

3. *Adjusting the estimated future cash inflows.* Some companies, such as Dow Chemical, reduce the estimated future cash inflows of riskier projects. For example, they may systematically reduce the predicted cash inflows of very-high-risk projects by 30%, high-risk projects by 20%, average-risk projects by 10%, and make no change to the projected cash inflows of low-risk projects.

[10]For example, recurring after-tax *real* cash operating flow in year 2 of $360,000 in Exhibit 22-9 is multiplied by $(1.10)^2$ to give $435,600 in after-tax *nominal* cash operating flows in year 2 in Exhibit 22-8. The *real* discount rate of 0.694444 in year 2 in Exhibit 22-9 is divided by $(1.10)^2$ to give the nominal discount rate of 0.573921 in year 2 in Exhibit 22-8.

[11]See J. Grinyer and N. Daing, "The Use of Abandonment Values in Capital Budgeting—A Research Note," *Management Accounting Research 4* (1993).

Risk Analysis in Capital Budgeting at Consumers Energy Company

Consumers Energy Company (CEC) owns pipelines to distribute natural gas to its customers. About 1,609 of the 32,186 kilometres of CEC's main pipelines are cast iron, although most of the pipelines are made of cathodically protected coated and wrapped steel or of plastic. Gas leaks from cast-iron pipes are almost ten times higher than from the other materials.

An important capital budgeting decision for CEC is how much of the cast-iron pipes it should replace and when. The benefits of replacing the pipes include lower repairs and maintenance costs and fewer claims following gas leaks, but the dollar value is uncertain. CEC estimates a range of quantitative values for key factors—the number of times the pipeline might leak, the quantity of gas that may leak, the dollar claims that may have to be paid, and the repairs and maintenance costs that may be incurred—under each replacement alternative. Sensitivity analysis identifies the factors most likely to affect the decision and those that do not. Probability distributions for the key factors are based on actual data obtained from structured interviews with experts in different subject areas. Discounting expected returns by the risk-adjusted ROR gives the NPVs for the different alternatives. CEC computes NPVs on an after-tax basis, using nominal cash flows and nominal discount rates to consistently consider the effects of inflation.

CEC's analysis indicated that the optimal program was to replace the worst cast-iron pipes first and all cast-iron pipes over a 40-year period. In the absence of this detailed and thorough risk-based analysis, CEC's managers would have favoured replacing the cast-iron pipes sooner.

Source: Adapted from K. L. Elenbars and D. O'Neill, "Formal Decision Analysis Process Guides Maintenance Budgeting," *Pipeline Industry*, October 1994.

This approach is called the *certainty equivalent approach*. Since the cash flows for higher-risk projects have already been adjusted downward for their increased riskiness, the RRR used to evaluate those projects is the same as the RRR for low-risk projects. Note how this approach contrasts with adjusting the required rate of return. In that approach, the cash flows are not adjusted for risk, but the RRR is. Adjusting both the cash flows for risk *and* then using risk-adjusted RRRs would double-count the risk adjustment.

IMPLEMENTING CAPITAL BUDGETING

Discounted cash flow analysis applies to both profit-seeking and not-for-profit organizations. Almost all organizations must decide which investments in long-term assets will accomplish various tasks at the least cost.

Studies of the capital budgeting practices of government agencies at various levels (federal, provincial, and local) and in several countries report that, as in the profit-oriented sector, the following prevails:

> Explain the usefulness of excess present value index in capital budgeting, and explain why IRR and NPV may rank projects differently.

1. Urgency is an important factor when allocating funds. For example, capital budgeting for roads is often motivated by physical deficiencies in an existing highway rather than a systematic analysis of alternative road construction projects.

2. Project estimates are sometimes systematically biased. For example, studies report overestimates of the benefits, underestimates of the costs, and underestimates of the time it takes to construct dams and other irrigation infrastructures.

3. There is a tendency to cut capital-budget projects first when there is a strong push to balance a budget or reduce a deficit. Consider the effect of efforts to contain health-care costs in Canada. As a result of these changes and the increased emphasis on controlling hospital charges through competition and

regulation, hospitals are increasingly using analytical capital budgeting methods (such as discounted cash flow methods) and are also more carefully auditing the benefits of capital expenditures.

IMPLEMENTING THE NPV DECISION RULE

Executives in both profit-seeking and not-for-profit organizations must frequently work within an overall capital budget limit. This section discusses problems in using the net present value method when there is a restriction on the total funds available for capital spending.

The **excess present value index** (sometimes called the **profitability index**) is the total present value of future net cash inflows of a project divided by the total present value of the net initial investment. The following table illustrates this index for two software graphics packages—Superdraw and Masterdraw—that Business Systems is evaluating:

Project	Present Value at 10% (1)	Net Initial Investment (2)	Excess Present Value Index (3) = (1) ÷ (2)	Net Present Value (4) = (1) − (2)
Superdraw	$1,400,000	$1,000,000	140%	$400,000
Masterdraw	3,900,000	3,000,000	130%	900,000

The excess present value index or profitability index measures the cash flow return per dollar invested. The index is viewed as particularly helpful in choosing between projects when investment funds are limited. The reason is that profitability indexes can identify the projects that will generate the most money from the limited capital available.

Suppose the developers of each package require that Business Systems market only one software graphics package, so accepting one software package automatically means rejecting the other—that is, the packages are mutually exclusive. Which package should Business Systems choose?

Using the profitability index, Superdraw will be preferred over Masterdraw because it has a profitability index of 140%, which is higher than the 130% for Masterdraw. But the profitability index analysis assumes that all other things, such as risk and alternative use of funds, are equal. For example, it assumes that choosing between Superdraw and Masterdraw has no effect on the other projects that Business Systems plans to implement. If "all other things" are not "equal," which is often the case, the profitability index may not result in the optimal choice of investment projects.

Assume that Business Systems has a total capital budget limit of $5,000,000 for the coming year. It is considering investing in Superdraw or Masterdraw and in any one or more of eight other projects (coded B, C, . . . , H, I). Exhibit 22-10 presents two alternative combinations of these projects. Note that the project portfolio in alternative 2 is superior to that in alternative 1, despite the greater cash flow return per dollar invested in Superdraw than in Masterdraw. The reason is that the $2,000,000 incremental investment in Masterdraw increases net present value (NPV) by $500,000. The $2,000,000 would otherwise be invested in projects E and B, which have a lower combined NPV of $256,000:

	Present Value	Net Initial Investment	Increase in Net Present Value
Masterdraw	$3,900,000	$3,000,000	
Superdraw	1,400,000	1,000,000	
Increment	$2,500,000	$2,000,000	$500,000
Project E	$ 912,000	$ 800,000	
Project B	1,344,000	1,200,000	
Total	$2,256,000	$2,000,000	$256,000

Note that other than Superdraw, alternative 2 includes projects with the highest excess present value indexes and excludes those with the lowest excess present

EXHIBIT 22-10
Allocation of $5,000,000 Capital Budget: Comparison of Two Alternatives for Business Systems

	Alternative 1				Alternative 2		
Project	Net Initial Investment	Excess Present Value Index	Total Present Value at 10%	Project	Net Initial Investment	Excess Present Value Index	Total Present Value at 10%
C	$ 600,000	167%	$1,002,000	C	$ 600,000	167%	$1,002,000
Superdraw	1,000,000	140%	1,400,000				
D	400,000	132%	528,000	D	400,000	132%	528,000
				Masterdraw	3,000,000	130%	3,900,000
F	1,000,000	115%	1,150,000	F	1,000,000	115%	1,150,000
					$5,000,000*		$6,580,000‡
E	800,000	114%	912,000	E	$ 800,000	114%	Reject
B	1,200,000	112%	1,344,000	B	1,200,000	112%	Reject
	$5,000,000*		$6,336,000†				
H	$ 550,000	105%	Reject	H	550,000	105%	Reject
G	450,000	101%	Reject	G	450,000	101%	Reject
I	1,000,000	90%	Reject	I	1,000,000	90%	Reject

*Total budget constraint.
†Net present value = $6,336,000 − $5,000,000 = $1,336,000.
‡Net present value = $6,580,000 − $5,000,000 = $1,580,000.

value indexes. The excess present value index is a useful guide for identifying and choosing projects that will offer the best return on limited capital and that will thereby maximize net present value. But managers cannot base decisions involving mutually exclusive investments of different sizes solely on the excess present value index. The net present value method is the best general guide.

DIFFERENT METHODS GIVE DIFFERENT RANKINGS

The NPV method always indicates the project (or set of projects) that maximizes the NPV of future cash flows. However, surveys of practice report widespread use of the internal rate of return (IRR) method. The most probable reason is that managers find this method easier to understand and that, in most instances, their decisions would be unaffected by using one method or the other. In some cases, however, the two methods will not indicate the same decision.

Where mutually exclusive projects have unequal lives or unequal investments, the IRR method can rank projects differently from the NPV method. Consider Exhibit 22-11.[12] The ranking by the IRR method favours project X, while the ranking by the NPV method favours project Z. The projects ranked in Exhibit 22-11

EXHIBIT 22-11
Ranking of Projects Using Internal Rate of Return and Net Present Value.

				IRR Method		NPV Method $r = 10\%$*		
Project	Life	Net Initial Investment	Annual Cash Flow from Operations, Net of Income Taxes	IRR	Ranking	PV of Annual Cash Flow from Operations, Net of Income Taxes	NPV	Ranking
X	5	$286,400	$100,000	22%	1	$379,100	$ 92,700	3
Y	10	419,200	100,000	20	2	614,500	195,300	2
Z	15	509,200	100,000	18	3	760,600	251,400	1

*If the r is changed to 20%, the NPV rankings will change to $NPV_X = \$12,660$ (first); $NPV_Y = \$50$ (second); $NPV_Z = -\$41,650$ (not considered at all because it is negative).

[12]Exhibit 22-11 concentrates on differences in project lives. Similar conflicting results can occur when the terminal dates are the same but the sizes of the net initial investments differ.

Capital Budgeting Methods and the Balanced Scorecard (BSC)

Capital budgeting is about the financial perspective of the BSC. While those undertaking investment analyses must gather relevant information about the customer, internal business, and learning and growth perspective prior to estimating the cash inflows and outflows, the DCF and non-DCF methods of calculating the rate of return apply to these financial estimates. Most investment initiatives are motivated by an offensive strategy of growth; however, other strategies include harvest in a sunset industry or a defensive strategy to protect existing market share. Capital budgeting makes good strategic sense for a defensive strategy to provide information on the opportunity cost of undertaking a low ranking investment. In reality, ranking based on ROR will not be the sole factor in capital budgeting decisions.

differ in both life (5, 10, and 15 years) and net initial investment ($286,400, $419,200, and $509,200).

Managers using the IRR method implicitly assume that the reinvestment rate is equal to the indicated rate of return for the shortest-lived project. Managers using the NPV method implicitly assume that the funds obtainable from competing projects can be reinvested at the company's required rate of return. The NPV method is generally regarded as conceptually superior. Students should refer to corporate finance texts for more details on these issues, and on the problems of ranking projects with unequal lives or unequal investments.

PULLING IT ALL TOGETHER—PROBLEM FOR SELF-STUDY

This is a comprehensive review problem. It illustrates both income tax factors and capital budgeting with inflation.

(Try to solve this problem before examining the solution that follows.)

PROBLEM

Stone Aggregates (SA) operates 92 plants producing a crushed stone that is used in many construction projects. Transportation is a major cost item. A scale clerk weighs the products and, on a delivery ticket, records details of the product shipped: its weight, its freight charges, and whether or not it is taxed.

SA is considering a proposal to use computerized delivery ticket–writing equipment at each of its 92 plants. One plant has used the equipment as a pilot site for the past 12 months, generating cash operating cost savings (before taxes) of $300,000 by improving productivity and by reducing plant operating costs and excess shipments to customers. The cost analyst estimates that if the equipment had been in use at all of the company's plants for the past year, net cost savings would have been $25 million (expressed in today's dollars).

The cost of the equipment for all 92 plants is $45 million, which would be payable immediately. This equipment has an expected useful life of four years and a terminal disposal price of $10 million (expressed in today's dollars). The equipment qualifies for a capital cost allowance rate of 25% declining balance. Stone Aggregates expects a 30% income tax rate in each of the next four years.

REQUIRED

1. Does the proposal for the computerized delivery ticket-writing equipment meet SA's 16% after-tax required rate-of-return criterion? This rate of return includes an 8% inflation component. (The real rate of return is 7.4%; recall

that nominal rate of return = [(1 + 0.074)(1 + 0.08)] − 1 = 0.16.) This 8% inflation prediction applies to both the cost savings and the terminal disposal price of the equipment. Compute the NPV using nominal dollars and a nominal required rate of return.

2. What other factors would you recommend that SA consider when evaluating the computerized delivery ticket-writing equipment?

SOLUTION

1. Exhibit 22-12 shows the NPV computations. To illustrate an alternative presentation found in practice, the format of Exhibit 22-12 differs from that of Exhibits 22-5, 22-6, and 22-7 (pp. 897 and 900). The proposal for computerized delivery ticket-writing equipment has an NPV of $25,899 million, indicating that—on the basis of financial factors—it is an attractive investment.

2. The analysis in Exhibit 22-12 assumes that net cash savings are $25 million each year. However, operating and implementation costs in the year of changeover to new computerized equipment are often 200% higher than in subsequent years. Consequently, net cash savings may be lower in the first year.

EXHIBIT 22-12
Net Present Value Analysis of Computerized Delivery Ticket-Writing System for Stone Aggregates (in thousands; n.d. = Nominal Dollars)

	A	B	C	D	E	F
1		Total	End of	End of	End of	End of
2		Present Value	Year 1	Year 2	Year 3	Year 4
3	**Recurring After-Tax Cash Operating Flows**					
4	1. Recurring cash operating savings (real dollars)	$ —	$25,000	$25,000	$25,000	$25,000
5	2. Cumulative inflation factor (from Table 1, Appendix A for 8%)	—	1.080	1.166	1.260	1.360
6	3. Cash operating savings (n.d.): 1 × 2		$27,000	$29,150	$31,500	$34,000
7	4. Tax payments: 30% × 3		8,100	8,745	9,450	10,200
8	5. Recurring after-tax cash operating savings (n.d.): 3 − 4		$18,900	$20,405	$22,050	$23,800
9	6. Present value discount factor (16% nominal)		0.862	0.743	0.641	0.552
10	7. P.V. of recurring after-tax cash operating savings (n.d.): 5 × 6	$ 58,725	$16,292	$15,161	$14,134	$13,138
11						
12	**Initial Equipment Investment**					
13	New-equipment	$(45,000)				
14	Tax shield	7,664*				
15	After-tax cash flow effect of equipment investment	(37,336)				
16	Terminal disposal	10,000				
17	Lost tax shield	(1,829)†				
18	After-tax cash flow effect of terminal disposal	3,691				
19	Net present value	$ 25,080				
20						
21	*Tax shield = ($45,000 × 0.30) × $\dfrac{0.25}{0.25 + 0.16}$ × $\dfrac{(2 + 0.16)}{2(1 + 0.16)}$ = $7,664					
22	†Lost tax shield = ($10,000 × 0.30) × $\dfrac{0.25}{0.25 + 0.16}$ = $1,829					
23	(Half-year rule does not apply to disposals.)					

The following question-and-answer format summarizes the chapter's learning outcomes. Each point presents a key question, and the guidelines are the answer to that question.

LEARNING OUTCOMES	GUIDELINES
1. What is a tax shield?	Operating cash flows are multiplied by a rate of (1 – the tax rate) to obtain the after-tax operating cash flows. Capital cost allowance (CCA) is the Income Tax Act equivalent of amortization. It is the only legally allowable deduction when a corporation calculates the net taxable income on which income taxes will be based. The CCA on investments shields some taxable income from income tax.
2. What is the essential difference between the total-project approach and the differential approach to capital budgeting decisions?	The essential difference is that the total-project approach compares the sum of all the cash flows between two projects while the differential approach examines the differences in cash flows for each type of cash flow that varies between two projects.
3. What is included in the nominal rate of return that is not in the real rate of return?	The nominal rate of return includes the anticipated rate of inflation due to changes in the general purchasing power of the cash flows.
4. Why is it important to recognize risk when evaluating capital budgeting projects?	Risk is an important consideration because riskier projects should require a higher rate of return to compensate for the additional risk.
5. Under what condition can the internal rate of return (IRR) and the net present value (NPV) methods rank projects differently?	Different rankings of projects can arise when mutually exclusive projects have unequal lives or unequal investments.

TERMS TO LEARN

This chapter and the Glossary at the end of the book contain definitions of the following important terms:

adjusted cost base (ACB) (p. 892)
capital cost allowance (CCA) (p. 888)
capital gain (p. 892)
capital loss (p. 892)
cumulative eligible capital (CEC) (p. 888)
cumulative eligible capital amount
   (CECA) (p. 888)
differential approach (p. 895)

eligible capital expenditure (p. 888)
eligible capital property (p. 888)
excess present value index (p. 906)
half-year rule (p. 888)
inflation (p. 900)
marginal income tax rate (p. 886)
net addition (p. 896)
nominal rate of return (p. 901)

profitability index (p. 906)
real rate of return (p. 900)
recapture of CCA (p. 893)
tax shield formula (p. 888)
terminal loss (p. 893)
total-project approach (p. 895)
unamortized capital cost (UCC)
   (p. 888)

ASSIGNMENT MATERIAL

MyAccountingLab   Make the grade with MyAccountingLab: The questions, exercises, and problems marked in red can be found on MyAccountingLab at **www.myaccountinglab.com.** You can practise them as often as you want, and most feature step-by-step guided instructions to help you find the right answer. Exercises and problems with an Excel icon in the margin have an accompanying Excel template on MyAccountingLab.

SHORT-ANSWER QUESTIONS

22-1 Describe three types of cash flows affected by income taxes.

22-2 "It doesn't matter what accounting amortization method is used. The total-dollar tax bills are the same." Do you agree? Explain.

22-3 Give examples of categories of cash flows considered in capital budgeting analyses.

22-4 Distinguish between the total-project approach and the differential approach to choosing between two capital budgeting projects.

22-5 "Accounting amortization is an irrelevant factor in deciding whether to replace an existing delivery vehicle with a more energy-efficient vehicle." Do you agree? Explain.

22-6 Describe three ways income taxes can affect the cash inflows or outflows in a motor-vehicle-replacement decision by a taxpaying company.

22-7 What are the two basic types of capital cost allowance classes?

22-8 Distinguish between the nominal rate of return and the real rate of return.

22-9 How can capital budgeting tools assist in evaluating a manager who is responsible for retaining customers of a cellular telephone company?

22-10 What approaches might be used to recognize risk in capital budgeting?

22-11 "In practice there is no single rate that a given company can use as a guide for sifting among all projects." Do you agree? Explain.

22-12 "Discounted cash flow techniques are relevant only to profit-seeking organizations." Do you agree? Explain.

22-13 "The net present value method and the internal rate-of-return method always rank different projects identically." Do you agree? Explain.

EXERCISES

22-14 **Terminology.** A number of terms are listed below:

adjusted cost base (ACB)	amortization
capital cost allowance (CCA)	capital gain
capital loss	eligible capital expenditure
eligible capital property	excess present value index
half-year rule	marginal income tax rate
recapture of UCC	unamortized capital cost allowance (UCC)
terminal loss	

REQUIRED

Select the terms from the above list to complete the following sentences.

It is the _____ _____ ___ ____ that is important for planning investments because CRA income tax rates are progressive. It is the calendar year that is important to CRA, not the corporate fiscal year. All dispositions of _____ _____ _____ must be reported in the calendar year the transaction occurred. Tax law on eligible capital property is both complex and highly detailed. Financial accountants signal the decline in capacity of a long-term asset to generate revenue using one of three methods of _____. The CRA, however, has tax laws requiring companies to deduct _____ ____ _____(___) from the _____ _____ _____ made on an eligible capital property. Irrespective of when an eligible capital expenditure is made in a year, the _____ ____ means only half of the CCA can be deducted from taxable income in the year of acquisition of an eligible capital property. CRA calls the acquisition cost an _____ ____ ____ (___). When an eligible capital property is sold for more than the adjusted cost base plus sales expenses, the difference is a _____ ____. Once the exemption on taxable capital gains has been taken in full, CRA taxes 50% of the capital gain reported in the calendar year. If the property is sold for less than the adjusted cost base plus sales expenses, the difference is a _____ ____. Up to 50% of a capital loss can be deducted from a taxable capital gain for the same year. The _____ _____ _____ (___) is the relevant amount for calculating either a _____ ____ or a _____ __ ____. If the eligible capital property is the last of its class to be disposed of, there is a special calculation to determine if there is either a terminal loss or a recapture of unamortized UCC. Any recapture of UCC is reported as normal taxable income. Any terminal loss can be 100% deducted from income for the year. After adjusting cash flow for tax considerations the _____ _____ _____ _____ is calculated by dividing the present value of future net cash inflows by the present value of the initial investment. The index measures the cash flow return per dollar invested.

22-15 New equipment purchase. Presentation Graphics prepares slides and other aids for individuals making presentations. It estimates it can save $42,000 a year in cash operating costs for the next five years if it buys a special-purpose colour-slide workstation at a cost of $90,000. The workstation qualifies for a capital cost allowance rate of 25%, declining balance, and will have a zero terminal disposal price at the end of year 5. Presentation Graphics has a 12% after-tax required rate of return. Its income tax rate is 40% each year for the next five years.

REQUIRED
Compute (a) net present value, (b) payback period, and (c) internal rate of return.

22-16 Automated materials-handling capital project, income taxes, sensitivity analysis. Just-in-Time Distributors, an operator of a large distribution network of health-related products, is considering an automated materials-handling system for its major warehouse in Toronto to reduce storage space, labour costs, and product damage. The automation equipment will cost $7,375,000, payable at the time of acquisition. The equipment has a useful life of four years and no residual disposal price. The lease on the warehouse will expire in four years and is not expected to be renewed. The company has a marginal income tax rate of 40% and an after-tax required rate of return of 12%. Under existing tax laws, the $7,375,000 of the equipment cost will qualify for a capital cost allowance rate of 30%, declining balance. The before-tax net cash operating savings from the automation are estimated to be $3,000,000 a year.

REQUIRED
1. Compute (a) the net present value and (b) the payback period on the automated materials-handling project.
2. Calculate the minimum annual before-tax net cash operating savings that will make the automated material-handling equipment desirable from a net present value standpoint.
3. What other factors should Just-in-Time Distributors consider in its decision?

22-17 Total-project versus differential approach, income taxes. A specialized automobile parts manufacturer is considering the acquisition of a new machine. The new machine is far more efficient than the present machine. It would cost $87,600, would cut annual cash operating costs from $72,000 to $48,000, and would have zero terminal disposal price at the end of its useful life of three years. The applicable income tax rate is 30%. The after-tax required rate of return is 14%.

The current machine has been used for one year. It will have no useful economic life after three more years. It cost $105,600 when acquired, has a current disposal price of $39,200, and has a residual disposal price of $7,200.

These machines qualify for a capital cost allowance rate of 20%, declining balance.

REQUIRED
Using the net present value method, show whether the new machine should be purchased (a) under a total-project approach and (b) under a differential approach.

22-18 Capital budgeting methods, no income taxes. Saskatoon Hospital, a non-profit organization, estimates that it can save $28,000 a year in cash operating costs for the next ten years if it buys a special-purpose eye-testing machine at a cost of $110,000. No terminal disposal value is expected. Saskatoon Hospital's required rate of return is 14%. Assume all cash flows occur at year-end except for initial investment amounts.

REQUIRED
1. Calculate the following for the special-purpose eye-testing machine:
   a. Net present value.
   b. Payback period.
   c. Internal rate of return.
   d. Accrual accounting rate of return based on net initial investment. (Assume straight-line depreciation.)
2. What other factors should Saskatoon Hospital consider in deciding whether to purchase the special-purpose eye-testing machine?

22-19 Capital budgeting, income taxes. Assume the same facts as in Exercise 22-18, except that a different hospital, City Hospital, is a taxpaying entity. The income tax rate is 30% for all transactions that affect income taxes.

REQUIRED
1. Do requirement 1 of Exercise 22-18.
2. How would your computations in requirement 1 be affected if the special-purpose machine had a $10,000 terminal disposal value at the end of ten years? Assume depreciation deductions are based on the $110,000 purchase cost and zero terminal disposal value using the straight-line method. Answer briefly in words without further calculations.

22-20 Project risk, required rate of return. Northern Petroleum is considering two capital projects. The first project, viewed as a high-risk investment, is drilling equipment for oil exploration activities. Northern expects the drilling equipment to cost $1,185,000 and result in operating cash flows before taxes of $448,000 per year for five years. The drilling equipment has a five-year life and a terminal disposal price of zero.

1. Total present value of tax shield, $227,335

The second project, viewed as a low-risk investment, is for production equipment that will improve the yield in Northern's refinery. Northern expects the production equipment to cost $850,000 and result in operating cash flows before taxes of $355,000 per year for four years. The equipment has a four-year life and a terminal disposal price of zero. Northern's income tax rate is 30%. The production and drilling equipment capital cost allowance rate is 25%, declining balance.

REQUIRED
1. Which project has the higher net present value if Northern uses an after-tax required rate of return (RRR) of 12% for both projects?
2. A manager at Northern objects to the calculations in requirement 1, arguing that riskier investments should have a higher RRR. Suppose Northern requires an 18% after-tax RRR for high-risk investments and a 12% after-tax RRR for low-risk investments. Which project has the higher net present value?
3. Which project do you favour? Why?

22-21 Income taxes and inflation. An investment of $254,200 in special tools, with a life expectancy of four years and a residual price of $24,000, is being examined at December 31, 2012 by StrengthCo. The tools will enable StrengthCo to manufacture drill bits to very high tolerances without incurring any incremental costs, and to earn additional cash flows of $2.40 per unit in 2013, $2.54 in 2014, $2.70 in 2015, and $2.86 in 2016. StrengthCo expects to sell 37,500 units each year for the next four years. StrengthCo is subject to a 40% tax rate. The after-tax required rate of return determined by the plant manager, James Marco, is 18%. The tools qualify for a capital cost allowance rate of 35%, declining balance.

1. a. Total present value of recurring cash flows from drill bits, $156,974

REQUIRED
1. Compute the net present value of the project.
2. Marco feels that inflation will persist for the next four years at the rate of 6% per year. However, the 18% minimum desired rate of return already includes a return required to cover the effects of anticipated inflation. Repeat requirement 1 to take inflationary effects into consideration.
3. Could you have taken inflation into account in a way different from what you did in requirement 2? Broadly describe how without actually performing any calculations.

22-22 Inflation and not-for-profit institution, no tax aspects. KopiPro is considering the purchase of a photocopying machine for $5,500 on December 31, 2012. It has a useful life of five years and a zero residual disposal price. Amortization will be applied on a straight-line basis. The cash operating savings are expected to be $1,350 annually, measured in December 31, 2012, dollars. The discount factor is 18.8%, which includes the effects of anticipated inflation of 10%. KopiPro pays no taxes due to being a non-profit organization. The present values of $1 discounted at 18.8% received at the end of 1, 2, 3, 4, and 5 periods are 0.842, 0.709, 0.596, 0.502, and 0.423.

1. Present value of recurring cash operating savings, $5,390

REQUIRED
1. A KopiPro official computed the net present value of the project using an 18.8% discount rate without adjusting the cash operating savings for inflation. What net present value figure did he compute? Is this approach correct? If not, how would you redo the analysis?
2. (a) What is the real rate of return required by KopiPro for investing in the photocopying machine? (b) Calculate the net present value using the real rate of return approach to incorporating inflation.
3. Compare your analyses in requirements 1 and 2. Present generalizations that seem applicable about the analysis of inflation in capital budgeting.

22-23 Excess present value index. The ChipTech Company is considering the acquisition of four capital investment projects. The projects under consideration are mutually exclusive. The company is considering buying new design equipment for which each project is identified as Design Pro and Easychip. Also under consideration are two other capital investments which internally are referenced as projects C and D.

1. b. Excess present value index, Design Pro, 150%

The following table describes the financial characteristics of these projects:

Project	Present Value of Cash Inflows at 14% Required Rate of Return	Net Initial Investment
Design Pro	$ 900,000	$600,000
Easychip	1,260,000	900,000
Project C	702,000	540,000
Project D	384,000	240,000

REQUIRED

1. For each project, calculate (a) the net present value and (b) the excess present value index. On the basis of the excess present value index only, should ChipTech choose Design Pro or Easychip?
2. Supposing ChipTech must choose one of Design Pro or Easychip, and supposing ChipTech has a capital investment budget of $1,140,000, which projects should ChipTech choose?
3. Comment on your answers to requirements 1 and 2.

5

1. a. Total present value of recurring after-tax operating savings, $65,599

22-24 New equipment purchase, income taxes. Anna's Bakery plans to purchase a new oven for its store. The oven has an estimated useful life of four years. The estimated pretax cash flows for the oven are as shown in the table that follows, with no anticipated change in working capital. Anna's Bakery has a 12% after-tax required rate of return and a 40% income tax rate. Assume amortization is calculated on a straight-line basis for accounting purposes using the initial oven investment and estimated terminal disposal value of the oven. Assume all cash flows occur at year-end except for initial investment amounts. Equipment is subject to 20% CCA rate declining balance for income tax purposes.

	Relevant Cash Flows at End of Each Year				
	0	**1**	**2**	**3**	**4**
Initial machine investment	$(88,000)				
Annual cash flow from operations (excluding the amortization effect)		$36,000	$36,000	$36,000	$36,000
Cash flow from terminal disposal of machine					8,000

REQUIRED

1. Calculate (a) net present value, (b) payback period, and (c) internal rate of return.
2. Compare and contrast the capital budgeting methods in requirement 1.

1

1. a. Net present value, $19,882

22-25 New equipment purchase, income taxes. Innovation Inc. is considering the purchase of a new industrial electric motor to improve efficiency at its Fremont plant. The motor has an estimated useful life of five years. The estimated pretax cash flows for the motor are shown in the table that follows, with no anticipated change in working capital. Innovation has a 12% after-tax required rate of return and a 40% income tax rate. Assume amortization is calculated on a straight-line basis for tax purposes. Assume all cash flows occur at year-end except for initial investment amounts. Equipment is subject to 20% CCA rate declining balance for income tax purposes.

	Relevant Cash Flows at End of Each Year					
	0	**1**	**2**	**3**	**4**	**5**
Initial motor investment	$(62,500)					
Annual cash flow from operations (excluding the amortization effect)		$31,250	$31,250	$31,250	$31,250	$31,250
Cash flow from terminal disposal of motor						0

REQUIRED

1. Calculate (a) net present value, (b) payback period, and (c) internal rate of return.
2. Compare and contrast the capital budgeting methods in requirement 1.

1

1. a. Accounting income, $3,600

22-26 After-tax NPV. (CPA, adapted) The Apex Company is evaluating a capital budgeting proposal for the current year. Deal with operating cash flow, not operating income. The relevant data are as follows:

Year	Present Value of an Annuity of $1 in Arrears at 15%
1	$0.870
2	1.626
3	2.284
4	2.856
5	3.353
6	3.785

The initial equipment investment would be $36,000. Apex would amortize the equipment for accounting purposes on a straight-line basis over six years with a zero terminal disposal price. The before-tax annual cash inflow arising from this investment is $12,000. The income tax rate is 40%, and income tax is paid the same year as incurred. The capital investment qualifies for a capital cost allowance rate of 20%, declining balance. The after-tax required rate of return is 15%. Choose the best answer for each question and show your computations.

REQUIRED

1. What is the after-tax accrual accounting rate of return on Apex's initial equipment investment? (a) 10%, (b) 162/3%, (c) 262/3%, (d) 331/3%.
2. What is the after-tax payback period (in years) for Apex's capital budgeting proposal? (a) 5, (b) 2.6, (c) 3, (d) 2.
3. What is the net present value of Apex's capital budgeting proposal? (a) $(7,290), (b) $(1,056), (c) $7,850, (d) $11,760.
4. How much would Apex have had to invest five years ago at 15% compounded annually to have $36,000 now? (a) $12,960, (b) $17,892, (c) $20,592, (d) cannot be determined from the information given.

PROBLEMS

22-27 Equipment replacement, no income taxes. Pro Chips is a manufacturer of prototype chips based in Dublin, Ireland. Next year, in 2013, Pro Chips expects to deliver 552 prototype chips at an average price of $80,000. Pro Chips' marketing vice president forecasts growth of 60 prototype chips per year through 2019. That is, demand will be 552 in 2013, 612 in 2014, 672 in 2015, and so on.

2. Payback period, 3.04 years

The plant cannot produce more than 540 prototype chips annually. To meet future demand, Pro Chips must either modernize the plant or replace it. The old equipment is fully depreciated and can be sold for $3,600,000 if the plant is replaced. If the plant is modernized, the costs to modernize it are to be capitalized and depreciated over the useful life of the updated plant. The old equipment is retained as part of the modernize alternative. The following data on the two options are available:

	Modernize	Replace
Initial investment in 2013	$33,600,000	$58,800,000
Terminal disposal value in 2019	$6,000,000	$14,400,000
Useful life	7 years	7 years
Total annual cash operating costs per prototype chip	$62,000	$56,000

Pro Chips uses straight-line depreciation, assuming zero terminal disposal value. For simplicity, we assume no change in prices or costs in future years. The investment will be made at the beginning of 2013, and all transactions thereafter occur on the last day of the year. Pro Chips' required rate of return is 12%.

There is no difference between the modernize and replace alternatives in terms of required working capital. Pro Chips has a special waiver on income taxes until 2019.

REQUIRED

1. Sketch the cash inflows and outflows of the modernize and replace alternatives over the 2013 to 2019 period.
2. Calculate payback period for the modernize and replace alternatives.
3. Calculate net present value of the modernize and replace alternatives.
4. What factors should Pro Chips consider in choosing between the alternatives?

22-28 Equipment replacement, income taxes (continuation of 22-27). Assume the same facts as in Problem 22-27, except that the plant is located in Kamloops, B.C. Pro Chips has no special waiver on income taxes. It pays a 30% tax rate on all income. Proceeds from sales of equipment above book value are taxed at the same 30% rate.

1. After-tax cash flow from terminal disposal of equipment, $4,200,000

REQUIRED

1. Prepare a schedule of relevant after-tax cash inflows and outflows of the modernize and replace alternatives over the 2013 to 2019 period.
2. Calculate net present value of the modernize and replace alternatives.
3. Suppose Pro Chips is planning to build several more plants. It wants to have the most advantageous tax position possible. Pro Chips has been approached by Spain, Malaysia, and Australia to construct plants in their countries. Use the data in Problem 22-27 and this problem to briefly describe in qualitative terms the income tax features that would be advantageous to Pro Chips.

3

1. Net present value, $1,648

22-29 Inflation. (J. Fellingham, adapted) Sapna Patel is manager of the customer-service division of an electrical appliance store. Sapna is considering buying a repairing machine that costs $12,000 on December 31, 2012. The machine will last five years. Sapna estimates that the incremental pretax cash savings from using the machine will be $3,600 annually. The $3,600 is measured at current prices and will be received at the end of each year. For tax purposes, the machinery qualifies for a capital cost allowance rate of 25%, declining balance. Sapna requires a 10% after-tax real rate of return (that is, the rate of return is 10% when all cash flows are denominated in December 31, 2012, dollars). Use the 10% after-tax real rate of return when answering all four requirements.

REQUIRED

Treat each of the following cases independently.

1. Sapna lives in a world without income taxes and without inflation. What is the net present value of the machine in this world?
2. Sapna lives in a world without inflation, but there is an income tax rate of 40%. What is the net present value of the machine in this world?
3. There are no income taxes, but the annual inflation rate is 20%. What is the net present value of the machine? The cash savings each year will be increased by a factor equal to the cumulative inflation rate.
4. The annual inflation rate is 20%, and the income tax rate is 40%. What is the net present value of the machine?

4

1. Tax shield created by
CCA, $21,800

22-30 Assessing risk. (CMA, adapted) The WRL Company operates a snack food centre at the Hartsfield Airport. On January 2, 2013, WRL purchased a special cookie-cutting machine, which has been used for three years. WRL is considering purchasing a newer, more efficient machine. If purchased, the new machine would be acquired today on January 2, 2016. WRL expects to sell 300,000 cookies in each of the next four years. The selling price of each cookie is expected to average $0.60.

WRL has two options: (1) continue to operate the old machine or (2) sell the old machine and purchase the new machine. The seller of the new machine offered no trade-in.

The following information has been assembled to help management decide which option is more desirable:

	Old Machine	New Machine
Initial machine investment	$96,000	$144,000
Terminal disposal price at the end of useful life assumed for amortization purposes	$12,000	$24,000
Useful life from date of acquisition	7 years	4 years
Expected annual cash operating costs:		
Variable cost per cookie	$0.24	$0.168
Total fixed costs	$18,000	$16,800
Amortization method used for accounting purposes	Straight-line	Straight-line
Estimated disposal prices of machines:		
January 2, 2016	$48,000	$144,000
December 31, 2019	$12,000	$24,000
Capital cost allowance rate (declining balance)	25%	25%

WRL has a 40% income tax rate and an after-tax required rate of return of 16%.

REQUIRED

1. Use the net present value method to determine whether WRL should retain the old machine or acquire the new machine.
2. How much more or less would the recurring after-tax variable cash operating savings have to be for WRL to exactly earn the 16% after-tax required rate of return? Assume all other data about the investment do not change.
3. Assume that the financial differences between the net present values of the two options are so slight that WRL is indifferent between the two proposals. Identify and discuss the non-financial and qualitative factors that WRL should consider.

22-31 Capital budgeting, inventory changes. (M. Wolfson, J. Harris, adapted) Comfort Footwear Inc. is considering whether to add a new line of running shoes to be sold to its retail customers. To produce these shoes, special machines costing a total of $131,040 must be acquired. The machines will have a useful life of four years, with a combined terminal residual price of $21,600. The new line of shoes would be dropped at the end of four years. The estimates for the new product line are as follows:

①

1. Net cash flow after tax, year 1, $35,352

Year	Units Produced	Units Sold	Selling Price	Manufacturing Costs per Unit
1	7,000	6,000	$30.00	$14.40
2	6,500	6,200	30.00	15.60
3	6,500	7,700	28.80	16.80
4	3,000	3,100	26.40	18.00
	23,000	23,000		

For tax purposes, the machines qualify for a capital cost allowance rate of 25%, declining balance. Manufacturing costs are deductible for tax purposes in the year when the related goods are sold. The company uses the first-in, first-out inventory method for accounting purposes. Marketing, distribution, and customer-service costs are deductible for tax purposes in the year when they are incurred. Assume a 40% marginal tax rate. Also, assume that all operating cash flows and income tax payments occur at the end of the year. The after-tax nominal required rate of return is 16%.

Variable marketing, distribution, and customer-service costs are estimated at $3.60 per unit and are not expected to change over the four-year period. The selling-price data and all cost estimates are expressed in nominal dollars. Accounts receivable and current liabilities are expected to be minimal.

Absorption costing must be used for tax purposes. Amortization is allocated on the basis of the estimates of the units produced each year.

REQUIRED
1. Prepare a schedule of relevant cash flows, including income taxes, for each year.
2. Compute the net present value of adding the new line of running shoes.

22-32 Mining, income taxes, inflation, sensitivity analysis. (CMA, adapted) Frank Hart, Sparkling Enterprises' controller, has gathered the following data to analyze an investment in new mining equipment which will allow the company to extract gold ore from once inaccessible sections of the Mountain Creek Mining Facility.

③

1. Payback period, 3.60 years

Acquiring and installing the equipment will involve an investment of $3,600,000. The useful life of the specialized equipment is estimated to be five years with no residual value at the end of this period. Sparkling uses the straight-line amortization method for this equipment for financial reporting purposes.

Using the equipment, Sparkling estimates that an additional 400 troy pounds of gold (12 troy ounces per pound) will be extracted annually for the next five years. Hart plans to use an estimated market price of $490 per troy ounce of gold in his analysis based on expert information. A significant risk factor is represented by the price of gold projected due to the numerous factors that could influence the value per troy ounce.

Variable costs to extract, sort, and pack the gold are $175 per troy ounce. Allocated fixed overhead costs are $48 per ounce.

Three skilled technicians will be hired to operate the new equipment. The total salary and fringe benefit costs for these three employees will be $198,000 annually over the next five years. Periodic maintenance on the equipment is expected to cost $85,000 per annum.

Sparkling requires a 12% after-tax required rate of return and is subject to a 40% tax rate. The equipment qualifies for a 30% declining balance capital cost allowance rate.

REQUIRED
1. Determine the payback period.
2. Calculate the after-tax net present value for Sparkling's proposed acquisition of the extraction equipment.
3. Determine the revenue per ounce of gold at which Sparkling's acquisition of the extraction equipment will break even from a net present value perspective where Sparkling earns the 12% after-tax required rate of return.
4. Hart feels that inflation will occur and persist for the next five years at the rate of 2% per year. Assume all the data given in the problem are already in nominal dollars and that the 12% minimum desired rate of return already includes an element attributable to anticipated inflation. Repeat requirement 2, to take inflationary effects into consideration.

22-33 Alternative approaches. (CMA, adapted) Waterford Specialties Corporation, a clothing manufacturer, has a plant that will become idle on December 31, 2012. John Landry, corporate controller, has been asked to look at three options regarding the disposal of the plant.

♦ **Option 1:** The plant, which has been fully amortized for financial reporting, can be sold immediately for $10.8 million.

♦ **Option 2:** The plant can be leased to Auburn Mills, one of Waterford's suppliers, for four years. Under the terms of the lease, Auburn would pay Waterford $240,000 per month in rent and would grant Waterford a special 10% discount off the normal price of $2.40 per metre on 2.37 million metres of fabric purchased by another Waterford plant. Auburn would cover all the plant's ownership costs including property taxes. Waterford expects to sell this plant for $2.4 million at the end of the four-year lease.

♦ **Option 3:** The plant could be used for four years to make souvenir jackets for the Olympics. Fixed overhead, before any equipment upgrades, is estimated to be $240,000 annually for the four-year period. The jackets are expected to sell for $50.40 each. Unit variable costs are expected to be as follows: direct materials, $24.96; direct manufacturing, marketing, and distribution labour, $7.68; variable manufacturing, marketing, and distribution overhead, $6.96.

The following production and sales of jackets is expected: 2013, 200,000 units; 2014, 300,000 units; 2015, 400,000 units; 2016, 100,000 units. To manufacture the souvenir jackets, some of the plant equipment would have to be upgraded at an immediate cost of $1.8 million to be amortized for financial reporting purposes using straight-line amortization over the four years it will be in use. Because of the modernization of the equipment, Waterford could sell the plant for $3.6 million at the end of four years. The equipment qualifies for a 25% declining balance capital cost allowance rate.

Waterford treats all cash flows as if they occur at the end of the year and uses an after-tax cost of capital of 12%. Waterford is subject to a 40% tax rate.

REQUIRED

1. Would you use the total-project approach or the differential approach to choose among the three options? Why?
2. Calculate the net present value of each of the options available to Waterford and determine which option Waterford should select using the net present value criterion.
3. What nonfinancial and qualitative factors should Waterford consider before making its choice? Tax consideration and CAA credits should also be taken into consideration if applicable.

22-34 Ranking of capital budgeting projects, alternative selection methods, capital rationing. (CMA, adapted) Conglomerates has not yet told Sam Pilon what the total amount of funds available for capital projects at Firthing Manufacturing will be, except for the after-tax required rate of return being 12%.

Pilon, division president of Firthing, is preparing the 2013 capital budget for submission to corporate headquarters at Conglomerates Inc. Each project is considered to have the same degree of risk. Projects A and D are mutually exclusive: either one can be chosen, not both.

When analyzing projects, Firthing assumes that any budgeted amount not spent on the identified projects will be invested at the after-tax required rate of return, and funds released at the end of a project can be reinvested at the hurdle rate. Further information about each of these projects is presented in the following schedule:

Firthing Manufacturing Proposed Capital Projects

	Project A	Project B	Project C	Project D	Project E	Project F
Capital investment	$127,200	$240,000	$168,000	$192,000	$172,800	$156,000
Net present value at 12%	$ 83,620	$ 28,528	$(12,274)	$ 89,249	$ 7,232	$ 83,416
Excess present value index (profitability index)	1.66	1.12	0.93	1.46	1.04	1.53
Internal rate of return	35%	15%	9%	22%	14%	26%
Payback period	2.2 years	4.5 years	3.9 years	4.3 years	2.9 years	3.3 years
Economic life	6 years	8 years	5 years	8 years	6 years	8 years

REQUIRED

1. Assume that Firthing Manufacturing has no budget restrictions for capital expenditures and wants to maximize its value to Conglomerates. Identify the capital investment projects that Firthing should include in the capital budget it submits to Conglomerates Inc. Explain the basis for your selection.

2. Ignore your response to requirement 1. Assume that Conglomerates Inc. has specified that Firthing Manufacturing will have a restricted budget for capital expenditures, and that Firthing should select the projects that maximize the company's value. Identify the capital investment projects Firthing should include in its capital expenditures budget, and explain the basis for your selections, if the budget is (a) $540,000 and (b) $600,000.

22-35 NPV and inflation. Cost-Less Foods is considering replacing all of its old cash registers with new ones. The old registers are fully depreciated and have no disposal value. The new registers cost $600,000 (in total). Because the new registers are more efficient than the old registers, Cost-Less will have annual incremental cash savings from using the new registers in the amount of $140,000 per year. The registers have a six-year useful life, and are depreciated using the straight-line method with no disposal value. Cost-Less requires a 10% real rate of return. Ignore taxes.

3
1. Present value of annuity of annual cash savings, $609,700

REQUIRED
1. Given the information above, what is the net present value of the project?
2. Assume the $140,000 cost savings is in current real dollars, and the inflation rate is 5.5%. Find the NPV of the project assuming inflation.
3. Should Cost-Less buy the new cash registers?

22-36 NPV, inflation and taxes (continuation of 22-35). Refer to the information in the preceding problem, but now assume that the tax rate is 30% and that you are not ignoring taxes. Equipment is subject to 20% CCA rate declining balance for income tax purposes.

1 3
1. Total present value of tax shield, $114,545

REQUIRED
1. Calculate the NPV of the project without inflation.
2. Calculate the NPV of the project with inflation.
3. Should Cost-Less buy the new cash registers?

22-37 Governance, discounted cash-flow analysis. Claude Marchand, the manager of Homestead Products, a wholly owned division of Crosslink Inc., has asked Thandie Ng, the management accountant, to analyze the possibility of introducing a new product referenced as CL2009-6. Through the years the company has found that its products have a useful life of six years, after which the product is dropped and replaced by another new product.

4
1. Total present value of tax shield, $293,521

Marchand is trying to decide whether to launch the product. He is particularly excited about this proposal, because it calls for producing the product in the company's old plant at Kelowna, Marchand's home town. During the last recession, Crosslink had to shut down this plant and lay off its workers, many of whom had grown up with Marchand and were his friends. Marchand had been very upset when the plant was closed down. If CL2009-6 were produced in the new plant, most of the laid-off workers would be rehired.

Ng gathers the following data:
a. CL2009-6 will require new special-purpose equipment costing $1,275,000. The useful life of the equipment is six years, with a $360,000 estimated terminal disposal price at that time. The equipment qualifies for a capital cost allowance rate of 25%, declining balance.
b. The old plant has a book value of $300,000 and is being amortized for accounting purposes on a straight-line basis at $30,000 annually. The plant is currently being leased to another company. This lease has six years remaining at an annual rental of $60,000. The lease contains a cancellation clause whereby the landlord can obtain immediate possession of the premises upon payment of $42,000 cash (fully deductible for income tax purposes).
c. Certain nonrecurring market research studies and sales promotion activities will amount to a cost of $375,000 at the end of year 1. The entire amount is deductible in full for income tax purposes in the year of expenditure.
d. Additions to working capital will require $260,000 at the outset and an additional $240,000 at the end of two years. This total is fully recoverable at the end of six years.
e. Net cash inflow from operations before amortization and income taxes is expected to be $480,000 in years 1 and 2, $720,000 in years 3 to 5, and $400,000 in year 6.

The after-tax required rate of return is 12%. The income tax rate is 36%.

REQUIRED
1. Use a net present value analysis to determine whether Ng should recommend launching CL2009-6.
2. Ng subsequently learns that the new special-purpose equipment required to make CL2009-6 may only be available at a cost of $1.68 million. All other data would remain unchanged. He revises his analysis and presents it to Marchand. Marchand is very unhappy with what he sees. He tells Ng, "Try different assumptions and redo your analysis. I have no doubt that this project should be worth pursuing on financial grounds."

Ng is aware of Marchand's interest in supporting his hometown community. There is also the possibility that Marchand may be hired as a consultant by the new plant management after he retires next year. Why is Marchand unhappy with Ng's revised analysis? How should Ng respond to Marchand's suggestions? Identify the specific steps that Ng should take to resolve this situation.

22-38 Introduction of new product, income taxes. (W. Bruns, adapted) Sales of a new product line for Petrus S.A. as of December 2013 are forecast at SFr. 2,400,000 per year, from which a sales commission of 15% would be paid to sales agents. Actual sales are to be made in several different currencies, but all money measurements are stated in Swiss francs, the currency of the head office.

To add the new line of moulded plastic products to those already manufactured and distributed by Petrus S.A., the company, under the direction of Andre Andros, would have to buy new injection moulding equipment in order to maintain manufacturing quality control; none of the existing equipment could be adapted to perform the necessary operation.

Direct manufacturing costs are budgeted at SFr. 720,000 for materials and SFr. 1,080,000 for labour, leaving an annual cash flow before tax of SFr. 240,000. The new equipment would cost SFr. 720,000 delivered and installed, and was expected to have a useful life of 10 years, with a zero terminal disposal value. Petrus is able to borrow money at 8%.

REQUIRED

1. Ignoring the effect of taxes, what is the internal rate of return (IRR) on the proposed investment? Assume the new equipment would be installed by January 1, 2014, and begin producing on that date.
2. Assume for tax purposes, the equipment is amortized on a straight-line basis over ten years. The tax rate is expected to be 45%. What is the IRR on an after-tax basis?
3. Andros has stated that Petrus should be willing to purchase this machine as long as it yielded a return of 12% after taxation. Should he make the investment? Show your calculations.
4. Actually, to stimulate industrial development, the tax rules allow for amortization deductions up to one-third of the cost of any such investment to be deducted from reported earnings in the first year after the investment, and up to one-fifth of the remainder of the unamortized investment amount can be deducted in the second year. Thereafter, annual deductions are computed on a straight-line basis such that no more than the original cost of the equipment is amortized over its useful life. How, if at all, does this affect the attractiveness of the investment?
5. Petrus has learned that investment in working capital (receivables and inventories, less payables) amounts to approximately 15% of revenues. Will the additional SFr. 360,000 investment for the new line decrease the rate of return on investment to less than the 12% criterion Andros has been using?
6. In late December 2013, Petrus purchased the equipment, and the operating results turned out as forecast. A year later, Andros learned that the manufacturer of the new equipment had introduced new models that were more automated. The new equipment costs SFr. 1,200,000 and would permit labour savings of SFr. 240,000 per year, thus doubling the net operating cash flow on the product. As a result of the technological advance, Andros expected the one-year-old machine could be sold for only SFr. 240,000 despite the fact that its book value was SFr. 480,000. If Petrus buys the new machine and amortizes it using allowed tax amortization over ten years, would the investment meet the 12% after-tax criterion? Show your calculations.
7. If the one-year-old machine has a zero disposal price, would replacing it with the new machine still be desirable? Show your calculations.
8. Andros was loath to throw away a nearly new machine and thought he might be better off to keep it one more year and then replace it. Would he be better off? How would you go about addressing this issue? Explain.
9. During 2014 the rate of inflation remained low, and it was expected that it would average about 4% for the year. Andros wondered how Petrus's analysis should reflect this rate of inflation, which he expected might continue for several years. Should an assumed inflation rate change his decision? Explain.

COLLABORATIVE LEARNING CASE

22-39 Equipment replacement, income taxes, unequal project lives, governance. (CMA, adapted) Mark Hatcher, CFO, was instrumental in convincing the board of directors of Modern Food Services (MFS), preparers of microwaveable frozen foods, to open the Western Plant. Now, unless significant improvements in cost control and production efficiency are achieved, the Western Plant may be sold. Hatcher is anxious to have the Western Plant continue to operate to maintain his credibility with the board and also to help Western's production manager, a longtime friend of Hatcher.

1. Total present value of recurring operating cash flows, $4,881,600

MFS is considering purchasing an automated materials-handling system (AMHS) for its Western Plant. Hatcher has asked Simon Palmer, the assistant controller, to prepare a net present value analysis for the proposal.

The AMHS could replace a number of forklift trucks, eliminate the need for a number of materials handlers, and increase the output capacity of the Western Plant.

Hatcher has given Palmer the following information regarding the AMHS investment for the net present value analysis:

Projected useful life	10 years
Purchase/installation	$5,490,500
Increased working capital needed	1,125,000
Increased annual operating costs (excluding amortization) over current costs	240,000
Reduction in annual manufacturing costs over current costs	480,000
Reduction in annual maintenance costs over current costs	360,000
Increase in cash flow from higher sales revenue	840,000
Estimated disposal price at end of useful life	1,150,000
Estimated recovery of working capital at end of useful life	1,125,000

MFS uses the straight-line method of amortization for financial reporting purposes for all its equipment assuming a zero terminal disposal price. The forklift trucks have a net book value of $576,000 with a remaining useful life of eight years and a zero terminal disposal price. If MFS purchases an AMHS now, it can sell the forklift trucks for $155,000. To make the ten-year project life of the AMHS comparable to that of the forklift alternative, Palmer estimates that if MFS does not buy the AMHS, the company will lease new forklift trucks for the Western Plant for years 9 and 10 at a cost of $105,000 per year.

MFS has a 40% marginal tax rate and requires a 12% after-tax rate of return on this project. Assume that tax effects and cash flows from equipment acquisition and disposal occur at the time of the transaction and that tax effects and cash flows from operations occur at the end of each year. The equipment qualifies for a 30% declining balance capital cost allowance rate.

Hatcher was pleased with Palmer's initial analysis. After the initial analysis was completed and additional information became available, Palmer discovered that the estimated terminal disposal price of the AMHS should be $120,000, not $1,150,000, and that the useful life of the system was expected to be 8 years, not 10 years. Palmer prepared a revised, second analysis based on this new information. On seeing the second analysis, Hatcher told Palmer to discard the revised analysis and not to discuss it with anyone at MFS or with the board of directors.

INSTRUCTIONS
Assume that because the terminal disposal value is zero, there are no assets remaining in the pool.

REQUIRED
1. What is the net present value of the decision to replace forklifts with the AMHS based on the original estimates Hatcher gave to Palmer?
2. Using net present value analysis, determine whether MFS should purchase and install the AMHS on the basis of the revised estimates that Palmer obtained.
3. Explain how Palmer, a management accountant, should evaluate Hatcher's directives to conceal the revised analysis.
4. Identify the specific steps Palmer should take to resolve this situation.

22-40 Different methods, different ranking. (Adapted from NAA Research Report No. 35, pp. 83–85) Assume that six projects, A to F in the table that follows, have been submitted for inclusion in the coming year's budget for capital expenditures:

				Project Cash Flows			
	Year	A	B	C	D	E	F
Investment	0	$(120,000)	$(120,000)	$(240,000)	$(240,000)	$(240,000)	$(60,000)
	1	0	24,000	84,000	0	6,000	27,600
	2	12,000	24,000	84,000	0	18,000	24,000
	3	24,000	24,000	84,000	0	36,000	12,000
	4	24,000	24,000	84,000	0	60,000	12,000
	5	24,000	24,000	84,000	0	60,000	
Per year	6–9	24,000	24,000		240,000	60,000	
	10	24,000	24,000			60,000	
Per year	11–15	24,000					
Internal rate of return		14%	?	?	?	12.6%	12.0%

REQUIRED

1. Compute the internal rates of return (to the nearest half-percent) for projects B, C, and D. Rank all projects in descending order in terms of the internal rate of return. Show your computations.

2. On the basis of your answer in requirement 1, state which projects you would select, assuming a 10% required rate of return (a) if $600,000 is the limit to be spent, (b) if $660,000 is the limit, and (c) if $780,000 is the limit.

3. Assuming a 16% required rate of return and using the net present value method, compute the net present values and rank all the projects. Which project is more desirable, C or D? Compare your answer with your ranking in requirement 1.

4. What factors other than those considered in requirements 1 to 3 would influence your project rankings? Be specific.

Transfer Pricing and Multinational Management Control Systems

BUSINESS MATTERS

Global Governance and Transfer Pricing—It's Complicated

Transfer prices are the prices at which all assets and services among corporate subsidiaries are traded by related parties. Tax laws, as well as internal factors such as goal-congruence, incentives, and autonomy, are important considerations in transfer pricing. Transfer prices affect the profits reported in each division and are therefore of interest to both division managers, who may receive bonuses based on the division's financial performance, and tax officials in the different countries where multinational corporations operate, who must ensure their government receives its fair share of taxes.

LEARNING OUTCOMES

After studying this chapter, you should be able to

1. Integrate the accounting internal control system assurance framework with existing legislation.

2. Apply transfer-pricing processes.

3. Assess the market-based transfer price method.

4. Apply relevant costs and tax considerations to evaluate the selection of cost-based and negotiated transfer prices.

5. Analyze income tax considerations in multinational transfer pricing.

This chapter develops the link between strategy, internal control systems, and governance. With the global implementation of cooperative regulation and legislation, organizational structure is a response to mandated governance requirements. Transfer pricing is only one example of an area of corporate decision making in which legislation, in this case tax legislation, has severely curtailed managerial discretion. Global governance requirements for multinational corporations (MNCs) often make what used to be an internal decision a complex negotiation with tax authorities who wish to protect their country's tax revenue.

MANAGEMENT CONTROL SYSTEMS

① Integrate the accounting internal control system assurance framework with existing legislation.

To *organize* is to arrange elements into an orderly structure that is comprehensible to others. External legislation, regulation, and standards constrain decisions managers can make about how to structure their organizations. Legislation increasingly holds top managers accountable for organizing **management accounting control systems (MACS)** that ensure people within the organization have relevant information so they know what they are supposed to do and have the resources to complete their tasks. One part of a MACS is an internal control system. The internal control system is the foundation of any audit assurance to external parties. The internal control system is designed, implemented, and maintained to provide reasonable assurance about the achievement of a company's objectives.[1]

The control environment is pervasive and so too are the control activities. A strong control environment will influence how well the internal control system is designed, implemented, monitored, and maintained. The key elements are:

◆ Communication and enforcement of integrity and ethical values.
◆ Commitment to competence.
◆ Participation by those in charge of corporate governance.
◆ Management's approach to identifying, taking, and managing risks.
◆ Organizational structure.
◆ Assignment of authority and absence of override opportunities.
◆ Human resource policies and practices to support the control environment.

An important feature of the framework illustrated in Exhibit 23-1 is the emphasis on the interdependence of reliable financial reporting. The quality of reporting depends on coherent and directed organizational structures, and effective communication of relevant nonfinancial and financial information.

Internal control systems represent the best efforts of top management at ensuring good stewardship of resources under a company's control. The formal review of internal control systems provides assurance regarding the quality of financial reporting, the effectiveness and efficiency of operations, and compliance with all laws and regulations, which, done well, are indicators of good governance. This assurance is provided by financial accountants who conduct audits according to procedures found in the Canadian Institute of Chartered Accountants' *Canadian Professional Engagement Manual* (*CPEM*).

But Canadian legislation requires more of companies than assurance regarding the quality of their financial disclosure. The most recent legislation of publicly listed companies, National Instrument 52-109 (NI 52-109), formalizes the importance of a balanced scorecard (BSC) approach to management control.[2] The legislation was initially a response to difficulties enforcing fraud legislation. More recently it has been amended to include explicit requirements to detect and prevent bribery. The draft of amended legislation aligns Canada's corporate governance laws with those already in place in the United Kingdom and the United States and is scheduled to come into effect in the near future.[3]

---

[1] Canadian Institute of Chartered Accountants (CICA), *Canadian Professional Engagement Manual (CPEM)*, pp. 1–22.

[2] M. Ferris, *CMA Management*, 81.4 (2007): 30–34.

[3] At the moment, a new division of the RCMP is dedicated to the investigation and prosecution of alleged offences. Canada's Corrupt Foreign Public Officials Act (CFPOA) is the relevant legislation and has no statute of limitations.

EXHIBIT 23-1
Internal Control System Design: Assurance of the Quality of Financial Disclosure

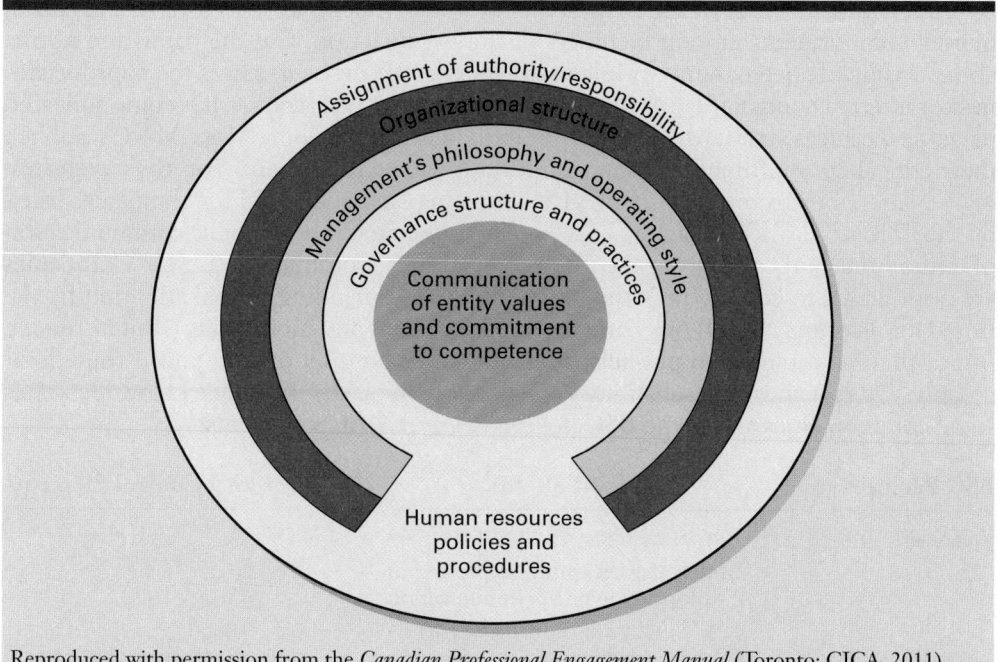

Reproduced with permission from the *Canadian Professional Engagement Manual* (Toronto: CICA, 2011), Vol. 1, p. 67: http://www.CAstore.ca.

The pending legislation holds the chief executive (CEO) and chief financial (CFO) officers responsible for ensuring the effectiveness of a company's internal control systems, without specifying what constitutes compliance. NI 52-109 will reinforce the need for high quality financial reporting by providing for specific enforcement action against individuals in the corporation. The top management team must evaluate the effectiveness of the corporate internal control systems annually and report deficiencies to their audit committee, the external auditors, and to the shareholders in the Management's Discussion and Analysis (MD&A) section of the annual report.

In effect, the CEO and CFO must sign a statutory declaration each year attesting that they have received all relevant information from others necessary to provide an opinion about the internal control system's design and operation. The accounting profession developed coherent compliance and control frameworks as well as formal and informal guidance regarding what constitutes compliance with NI 52-109.

While the CPEM guidance recommends in detail how to identify risks and provide the appropriate control over financial reporting, decisions about design are difficult. For an MNC, there is ample room for conflict over identification of the issues surrounding protection of the development of intellectual capital, customer intelligence, and internal process control as elements of competent stewardship. At step one of the decision framework there often exist differences among business units of the same corporation.

On the one hand, social responsibility and appropriate organizational identity require tolerance for and support of diversity. Indeed, belief systems, ethics, and values are diverse; thus there is an inherent conflict for MNCs in managing diversity and yet establishing core values. The implementation of effective internal control systems in itself raises profound ethical issues about what constitutes corporate social responsibility.

A MACS comprises formal and informal components. The MACS includes those explicit rules, procedures, performance measures, and incentive plans that guide the behaviour of managers and employees. The formal control system itself consists of several subsystems, including financial and management accounting systems, human resource systems (providing information on compensation, benefits, recruiting, training, absenteeism, and safety), and quality systems (providing information on scrap, defects, rework, and late deliveries to customers). This multidimensional approach was introduced along with the balanced scorecard with its specific measures of financial, learning, internal process, and customer outcomes.

The informal part of the MACS includes such aspects as shared values, loyalties, mutual commitments among members of the organization, and the unwritten norms about acceptable behaviour. Criteria used by external parties to assess the appropriateness of internal control include the extent to which the corporation has communicated its values, ethical standards, and corporate code of behaviour. Most MNCs publish their ethical commitment and their important values prominently on their websites.

National Instrument 58-201 (NI 58-201), in place since 2005 for companies listed on the Toronto Stock Exchange (TSX), includes guidance about public communication of ethical tone and codes from the Ontario Securities Commission (OSC). Companies are not obliged to comply with the OSC guidelines (including formal adoption by the Board of Directors (BOD) of a corporate code of ethics and monitoring). But to remain listed, they are obliged to publicly disclose if they comply or not, and if they don't comply, why not and what substitute guidelines are in place.[4] The table below illustrates some commonalities across the BSC, legislative, and MACS concepts:

BSC Perspectives	NI 58-201	Internal Control Elements
Financial	Purpose: indicators of achievement	Diagnostic control
	Monitoring, learning: appropriate information and communication systems	
Internal business	Purpose: mission, vision, strategy, policies, planning	Diagnostic control systems
		Interactive control systems
	Commitment: scope of responsibility, authority, accountability, HR policies	Boundary systems
	Capability: skill, tools, competence, communication, coordination	
	Monitoring, learning: challenge assumptions	
Customer	Monitoring, learning: feedback on external environment	Interactive control systems
Learning and growth (intellectual capital)	Commitment: ethics, mutual trust, HR policies	Boundary systems
		Belief systems
	Capability: knowledge, communication	

EVALUATING A MACS

An effective MACS is an intervention with the purpose of constraining behaviour. One constraint is **motivation**, the desire to attain a selected goal (the goal-congruence aspect) combined with the resulting drive or pursuit toward that goal (the effort aspect). Motivation implies, however, both that the goal is worthy and that the means to achieve it are known. In this context, the commitment by senior managers to goals and ethical practices, now formalized in *CPEM* and NI 58-201, are to some extent a means to adapt to new assumptions about inappropriate employee motivation and remedy new problems arising when motivation is absent.

Goal-congruence exists when individuals and groups work toward the publicly declared organization goals. Employees are expected to sacrifice their personal interest to achieve what is best for the organization as a whole. It is difficult to remember that organizations, whether profit, non-profit, or governmental, are entities whose existence is intended to benefit society as a whole. It is equally difficult to ignore opportunities to use the organizational structure for personal gain. Formal, public statements in an Annual Report of mission, vision, and code of ethics are a means to alert readers that there exist social goals for the corporation that have broader scope than immediate, corporate self-interest. Voluntary compliance is the least costly control process, but it depends in large part on consensus of beliefs, values, and ethics,

[4]C. Carnaghan and S. P. Gunz, "Recent Changes in the Regulation of Financial Markets and Reporting in Canada," *Accounting Perspectives*, 6.1 (2007): 55–94.

difficult to obtain in an MNC. The explosion of regulations, laws, certification, and attestation processes worldwide provide a more costly means to enforce behaviour.

Effort is defined as exertion toward a goal. Effort goes beyond physical exertion, such as a worker producing at a faster rate, to include all conscientious actions (physical and mental). Once people are formally advised of goals and expected behaviour, it takes effort to comply because formal legislation and regulation reduce individual discretion or freedom, a highly regarded value in Western democracies.

ORGANIZATIONAL STRUCTURE—CENTRALIZED OR DECENTRALIZED?

Control structures are interventions in the form of constraints, enforcement, and penalties. The interventions may be structural. For example, if the control issue is too broad a scope of discretion, then one remedy is to eliminate the **decentralization** that enables individual discretion. Decentralization itself is a strategic response made by organizations that face great uncertainties in their diverse environments, require detailed local knowledge for performing various jobs, and have few interdependencies among subunits, such as geographic divisions.

One way to manage the risks of a decentralized structure is to replace people with machines as a way to centralize an activity or sets of activities. Machines have a predetermined scope of activity and no discretion. Another structural remedy is to reduce an individual's scope of authority over the range of decisions that can be made without consulting and obtaining formal agreement from a higher level of management. A third remedy is to formalize processes through the implementation of new policies and procedures to document activity. Meetings, forms to authorize activity, and so on are structural responses to issues rising from decentralization. A fourth structural remedy is to provide formal incentives in employment contracts to reward the appropriate exercise of discretion. Rewards such as cash bonuses, perquisites (perks), and increased scope of discretion are positive incentives to behave appropriately in a decentralized structure within an organization.

Total decentralization means minimum constraints and maximum freedom for managers to make decisions at the lowest levels of an organization. Total centralization means maximum constraints and minimum freedom for managers at the lowest levels. Most corporate internal control structures fall somewhere in between these two extremes.

BENEFITS OF DECENTRALIZATION

From a practical standpoint, top managers can seldom quantify either the benefits or the costs of decentralization. Still, using a cost-benefit approach focuses on the central issues. Advocates of decentralized decision making and granting responsibilities to managers of subunits claim the following benefits:

◆ *Segregates duties.* Centralization, and in particular the grouping of key functions within one subunit, provides opportunities for people to intentionally or inadvertently make errors and then conceal them within the normal scope of their tasks and authority.

Segregation of duties is a principle of internal control that has been formalized in Generally Accepted Auditing Standards (GAAS). It is a mandatory element of good governance. Operating responsibility, reporting of asset transactions, and custody of assets must be segregated or decentralized. Limiting the scope of tasks performed by one subunit and one individual depends not only on capability but also on commitment to stewardship.

◆ *Creates greater responsiveness to local needs.* Information is the key to intelligent decisions. Compared with executives, subunit managers are better informed about their customers, competitors, suppliers, employees, and factors that affect the performance of their jobs, such as ways to decrease costs and improve quality in response to customer demand.

◆ *Leads to quicker decision making.* An organization that gives lower-level managers the responsibility for making decisions can make decisions quickly, creating a competitive advantage over organizations that are slower because they send the decision-making responsibility upward through layer after layer of management.

Structure Cannot Replace Commitment and Capability

Internal control failure costs are often embarrassingly public. One high-profile example occurred in 2008 in a London, Ontario, Tim Hortons when an employee exercised discretion and provided a $0.16 Timbit to a regular customer's child without charging the customer or paying for it herself.

Managers, reviewing stored video security data, called the employee into the office. They noted the store's policy was to give away no free food and dismissed the employee, who was rehired by the franchise owner a day later. Despite knowing the policy, the employee did not comply. But the franchisee who had hired the employee disagreed with the policy implemented by the managers.

This example illustrates the importance of both communication by the manager to the franchisee and capability or competence at management tasks. Boundary systems and centralized structures cannot replace common sense, belief systems, and commitment to core values.

Sources: http://www.cbc.ca/consumer/story/2008/05/08/timbit-lilliman. html?ref=rss, accessed July 11, 2008; www.theglobeandmail.com/ servlet/story/RTGAM.20080507.wtimbit0507/BNStory/National/home, accessed July 11, 2008.

Interlake, a manufacturer of materials-handling equipment, notes this important benefit of increased decentralization: "We have distributed decision-making powers more broadly to the cutting edge of product and market opportunity." Interlake's materials-handling equipment must often be customized to fit individual customers' needs. Delegating decision making to the sales force allows Interlake to respond quickly to changing customer requirements. Delegation must be accompanied, however, by capability and competence to ensure appropriate decisions are made.

◆ *Increases motivation.* Subunit managers are usually more highly motivated when they can exercise greater individual initiative.

Johnson & Johnson, a highly decentralized company, maintains that "Decentralization = Creativity = Productivity." Decentralization provides flexibility to deal with diversity in an MNC.

◆ *Aids management development and learning.* Giving managers more responsibility promotes the development of an experienced pool of management talent—a pool that the organization can draw from to fill higher-level management positions.

The organization also learns how to hone the skills of properly identifying issues of knowledge, storage of knowledge, and communication of knowledge. Intellectual capital management is enhanced by coherent control systems. Tektronix, an electronics instruments company, expressed this benefit as follows: "Decentralized units provide a training ground for general managers, and a visible field of combat where product champions may fight for their ideas."

◆ *Sharpens the focus of managers.* In a decentralized setting, the manager of a small subunit has a concentrated focus. A small subunit is more flexible and nimble than a larger subunit and is better able to adapt itself quickly to a fast-opening market opportunity. In a competitive environment where agility may be the optimal strategy, decentralization is essential. Also, top management, relieved of the burden of day-to-day operating decisions, can spend more time and energy on strategic planning for the entire organization.

COSTS OF DECENTRALIZATION

Advocates of more centralized decision making point out the following costs of decentralizing decision making:

◆ *Leads to suboptimal decision making.* **Suboptimal decision making** (also called either **goal-incongruent** or **dysfunctional decision making**) arises when a decision's benefit to one subunit is more than offset by the costs or loss of benefits to the organization as a whole.

This cost arises because top subunit management has lost sight of the interdependence among subunits. Interdependence means that subunit managers must cooperate with one another to realize organizational goals. Cooperation, however, best exists when relevant information is readily accessible and communicated effectively among subunits. The belief that each subunit serves a larger organizational purpose is also crucial to ensuring a functional team.

Suboptimal decision making may occur when (1) there is a lack of harmony or congruence among the overall organization goals, the subunit goals, and the individual goals of decision makers, (2) subunit managers lack competence, or (3) subunit managers lack the guidance necessary to evaluate the effects of their decisions on other parts of the organization. Suboptimal decision making is most likely to occur when the subunits in the organization are highly interdependent, such as when the end product of one subunit is the direct material of another subunit.

◆ *Results in redundant activities.* Several individual subunits of the organization may undertake the same activity separately. For example, there may be a duplication of staff functions (accounting, employee relations, and legal) if an organization is highly decentralized. Centralizing these support functions, which are crucial to effective management but non-value-added for a customer, helps to reduce their costs through internal operational redesign or downsizing.

◆ *Decreases loyalty toward the organization as a whole.* Individual subunit managers may regard the managers of other subunits in the same organization as external parties.

In a decentralized structure, managers may be unwilling to either share relevant information or assist when another subunit is in need. Instead of internal cooperation, managers act as if other managers were competitors. One remedy is to provide contractual incentives based on explicit performance criteria and reward managers for effective and efficient communication of relevant information.

◆ *Increases costs of gathering information.* Managers may spend too much time negotiating the prices for internal products or services transferred among subunits.

The outsourcing of resources as well as their internal transfer raises issues of not only cost but also revenue allocation among subunits. Many alternative allocation techniques have been presented in this text to remedy these issues. All rely on the availability of relevant information for excellent implementation.

The Canadian body of legislation and regulation is only one example of the increasing requirement of managers to account for their choices of organizational structures. These new constraints have been developed in cooperation with global regulatory and advisory agencies such as ISO and the Organisation for Economic Co-operation and Development (OECD). The nationally and provincially mandated governance practices are congruent with international benchmarks. This international cooperation among legislators and regulators helps establish a stable foundation for MNC governance.

Surveys of North American and European companies report that the decisions made most frequently at the decentralized level and least frequently at the corporate level are related to sources of supplies, products to manufacture, and product advertising. Decisions related to the type and source of long-term financing are made least frequently at the decentralized level and most frequently at the corporate level.[5]

DECISIONS ABOUT RESPONSIBILITY CENTRES

To measure the performance of subunits in centralized or decentralized organizations, the management accounting control system uses one or a mix of the four types of responsibility centres presented in Chapter 6:

◆ *Cost centre:* Manager accountable for costs only.
◆ *Revenue centre:* Manager accountable for revenues only.
◆ *Profit centre:* Manager accountable for revenues and costs.
◆ *Investment centre:* Manager accountable for investments, revenues, and costs.

Notice that a profit centre would require particular attention to desegregation of duties, which should reduce opportunities to manipulate both revenue and cost. With desegregation, however, comes the tendency to ignore interdependence and behave in ways that fail to achieve overall corporate objectives.

A common misconception is that the term *profit centre* (and, in some cases, *investment centre*) is a synonym for a decentralized subunit and that *cost centre* is a synonym for a centralized subunit. *Profit centres can be coupled with a highly centralized organization, and cost centres can be coupled with a highly decentralized organization.* For example, managers in a division organized as a profit centre may have little leeway in making decisions. They may need to obtain approval from corporate headquarters for any expenditure over, say, $10,000 and may be forced to accept central staff "advice." In another company, divisions may be organized as cost centres, but their managers may have great latitude on capital expenditures and on where to purchase materials and services. In short, the labels "profit centre" and "cost centre" are independent of the degree of decentralization in an organization.

TRANSFER PRICING

2 Apply transfer-pricing processes.

For both job and process costing, **intermediate products** in a multi-stage production process are transferred from one production stage to another. An intermediate product is an unfinished product transferred from one subunit to another subunit of the same organization. The cost of goods manufactured (COGM), a large proportion of which is allocated manufacturing overhead (MOH), is also transferred (see Chapter 2).

In large decentralized MNCs, individual subunits of an organization acting as autonomous units transfer intermediate goods not only among individual subunits at COGM but also across geographical boundaries at a transfer price (not at COGM). A **transfer price** is the price one subunit of an organization charges for a product (tangible or intangible) or service supplied to another subunit of the same organization. The transfer price more closely approximates absorption costs incurred from all business functions in the value chain.

Strategically, the goal within an MNC is good governance guided formally by the OECD pricing guidelines and known as the **arm's-length principle**. The principle maintains that a transfer price should be the same as it would be if the two subunits were independent companies.[6] In the age of supply-chain management, however, partnerships

---

[5] *Evaluating the Performance of International Operations* (New York: Business International, 1989), p. 4; and *Managing the Global Finance Function* (London: Business International, 1992), p. 31.
[6] M. E. Battersby, "Transfer Pricing Strategies Begin at Home," *The Bottom Line*, 3.1 (2008): 37–39.

to increase interdependence and reduce channel costs are often undertaken. Cooperation among subunits to maximize net profit could include deliberate over- or understatement of the transfer price to minimize tax.

The problem is that in this related-party transaction, the cost to the purchasing subunit is deductible from taxable income, and the transfer price received by the supplying subunit is revenue added to taxable income. Transfer prices affect the cash taxes collected by each country. A taxable income of $100 million in Canada would result in approximately $40 million in tax, but the same $100 million in Barbados would incur approximately $2.7 million of tax.

If the Barbados' subunit transferred nearly finished goods to Canada at, for example, $90 million, the MNC's taxable income in Canada would decrease to $10 million and the tax liability would be only $4 million, for a saving in Canada of approximately $36 million.[7] The CRA, along with other national tax authorities, is vitally interested in internal transfer prices for this reason. In the transfer-pricing process, national tax authorities are dominant partners and can enforce their opinion of the appropriate price.

ALTERNATIVE TRANSFER-PRICING METHODS

The CRA has adopted the OECD Hierarchy of Methods for transfer pricing, which ranks in preference the methods of transfer pricing. For a corporation, however, the goal when selecting a transfer-pricing method should be to reflect the economic facts of what has occurred. Internally, it is counterproductive to select a method that erodes the quality of data used by the management team to make important business decisions. For tax purposes it is not only counterproductive but expensive to select a method that the CRA deems is inappropriate.

First, we will discuss transfer of goods and services among divisions in the same country. Transfers of intellectual property, related-party loans, leases, and intragroup (centralized support) services are as subject to transfer pricing scrutiny by CRA when the transfers are interprovincial as are MNC transfers across national boundaries. For example, in 2005 the Ministry of Finance of Ontario noted that as a result of 25 Advanced Tax Rulings by the CRA, approximately $200 million in provincial tax revenue could be lost.[8] Increased scrutiny by Ontario is intended to prevent transfer pricing for the purpose of tax avoidance, which is not considered a good-faith intent, and penalize companies that do so.

There are three general methods for determining transfer prices:

1. *Market-based transfer prices.* Upper management may choose to use the price of a similar product or service publicly listed in, say, a trade journal.

   Also, upper management may select, for the internal price, the external price that a subunit charges to outside customers. Notice that the CRA method is consistent with current pricing methods that are the basis of many financial accounting valuation standards. Only when market prices are unavailable is a fair-value model used. In principle, the CRA and GAAP can be readily reconciled by professional accountants.

2. *Cost-based transfer prices.* Upper management may choose a transfer price based on the costs of producing the product in question.

   Examples include variable manufacturing costs, manufacturing (absorption) costs, and full product costs. "Full product costs" include all production costs as well as costs from other business functions (R&D, design, marketing, distribution, and customer service). The costs used in cost-based transfer prices can be actual costs or budgeted costs.

3. *Negotiated transfer prices.* In some cases, the subunits of a company are free to negotiate the transfer price between themselves and then to decide whether to buy and sell internally or deal with outside parties.

[7]D. C. Hill, *CMA Management*, 81.1 (2007): 36–39.

[8]M. Przysuski, "Canada Begins Provincial Transfer Pricing Enforcement," *Corporate Business Taxation Monthly*, 7.2 (2005): 17–20.

US$3.4 Billion Is an Incentive

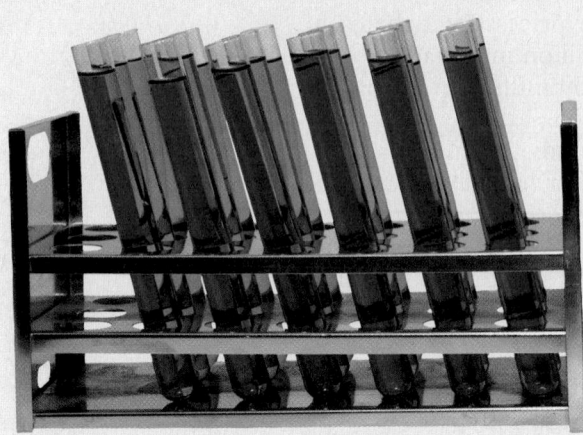

On May 30, 2008, the Tax Court of Canada decided that the Canadian subsidiary GlaxoSmithKline Inc. (GSKI), of the UK parent company Glaxo Group Ltd., had used an inappropriate transfer-pricing method during the years 1990–1993. The values involved decreased GSKI's taxable Canadian income by hundreds of millions of dollars.

The active ingredient of the drug product Zantac was purchased by GSKI from a Swiss affiliate. The Canadian manufacturers produced the drug for approximately $190 to $305 per kilogram, whereas the price paid to the Swiss affiliate was approximately $1,500 to $1,650 per kilogram. A 6% royalty on each purchase was remitted by GSKI to the U.K. parent under a licensing agreement. The U.K. parent then paid a 25% withholding tax to the U.K. government. This exceeds the U.K./Canada tax treaty amount of 10%.

The Canada Revenue Agency (CRA) successfully argued that the comparable uncontrolled price (CUP) method should have applied to the transfer price estimate where GSKI had applied the resale price method (RSP).

The decision hinged on two facts: first, what a reasonable price would have been in an arm's-length transaction; second, if the additional 6% royalty paid to the U.K. parent should be included in the transfer price.

In this case, it was successfully argued by CRA that "reasonable" meant the highest generic price for which the ingredient was sold in Canada. It also argued successfully to separate the supply and licensing contracts to consider the supply contract on its own and exclude the royalty from the total transfer price. The CRA has proposed an adjustment of $51.5 million payable by GSKI, which has appealed the decision to the Federal Court of Appeal.

The U.S. Internal Revenue Service (IRS) has already settled a 14-year claim against the U.S. affiliate of this company. At issue again was the use of inappropriate transfer pricing for ingredients for various drugs, including Zantac. This case was settled on September 11, 2006, with a negotiated settlement of $3.4 billion.

First, the decision upholds the use of the OECD hierarchy of transfer-pricing methods. Second, the court successfully narrowed the case to a decision on the supply price and excluded other contracts as irrelevant in assessing the appropriate transfer price. Third, the court decided that the analysis by GSKI's Canadian tax experts was unreasonable, relying instead on US and Canadian Crown experts.

Sources: The Economist, January 29, 2004; KPMG, "GlaxoSmithKline—Tax Court Prescribes Bitter Pill in Transfer Pricing Case," http://www.kpmg.ca/en/services/tax/tp60/tp60_0803.html, June 13, 2008; Fasken Martineau, "Tax Court of Canada issues *GlaxoSmithKline* decision," http://www.fasken.com/tax-court-of-canada-issues-iglaxosmithklinei-decision-07-11-2008/, July 2008; Fraser Milner Casgrain LLP, "Focus on Tax—*GlaxoSmithKline Inc. v. The Queen,*" http://www.fmc-law.com/Publications/Tax_SteevesC_Focus_On_Tax_June2008.aspx, June 17, 2008.

Subunits may use information about costs and market prices in these negotiations, but there is no requirement that the chosen transfer price bear any specific relationship to either cost or market price data. Negotiated transfer prices are often employed when market prices are volatile and change occurs constantly. The negotiated transfer price is the outcome of a bargaining process between the selling and the buying divisions. Ideally, the chosen transfer-pricing method should lead each subunit manager to make optimal decisions for the organization as a whole.

We present an example of internal transfer-pricing policies, Northern Petroleum of Calgary, Alberta, which operates its Transportation and Refining Divisions as profit centres. The Transportation Division manages the operation of a pipeline that transports crude oil from the Calgary area to the Refining Division in Sarnia, Ontario. The Refining Division processes crude oil into gasoline. (For simplicity, assume that gasoline is the only saleable product the refinery makes and that it takes two barrels of crude oil to yield one barrel of gasoline.)

EXHIBIT 23-2
Operating Data for Northern Petroleum

	A	B	C	D	E	F	G	H
1								
2				**Transportation Division**				
3	Contact price per barrel of crude oil supplied in Calgary =	$72	→	Variable cost per barrel of crude oil	$1			
4				Fixed cost per barrel of crude oil	3			
5				Full cost per barrel of crude oil	$4			
6								
7								
8				Barrels of crude oil transferred				
9								
10				↓				
11				**Refining Division**				
12	Market price per barrel of crude oil supplied to Sarnia refinery =	$85	→	Variable cost per barrel of gasoline	$ 8		Market price per barrel of gasoline sold =	$190
13				Fixed cost per barrel of gasoline	6	→	to external parties	
14				Full cost per barrel of gasoline	$14			
15								

Variable costs in each division are assumed to be variable with respect to a single cost driver in each division: barrels of crude oil produced by the Production Division, barrels of crude oil transported by the Transportation Division, and barrels of gasoline produced by the Refining Division. The fixed costs per unit are based on the budgeted annual output of crude oil to be produced and transported and the amount of gasoline to be produced. Northern Petroleum reports all costs and revenues of its non-Canadian operations in Canadian dollars using the prevailing exchange rate.

◆ The Production Division can sell crude oil to outside parties in the Calgary area at $72 per barrel.

◆ The Transportation Division "buys" crude oil from the Production Division, transports it to Sarnia, and then "sells" it to the Refining Division. The pipeline from Calgary to Sarnia has the capacity to carry 40,000 barrels of crude oil per day.

◆ The Refining Division has been using its total practical capacity, operating at 30,000 barrels of crude oil a day, using oil delivered by both the Transportation Division (an average of 10,000 barrels per day) and other external suppliers who also deliver to the Sarnia Refinery (an average of 20,000 barrels per day, at $85 per barrel).

◆ The Refining Division sells the gasoline it produces at $190 per barrel.

Exhibit 23-2 summarizes Northern Petroleum's variable and fixed costs per unit of the cost driver in each division, the external market prices of buying and selling crude oil, and the external market prices of selling gasoline. Consider the division operating income resulting from three transfer-pricing methods applied to a series of transactions involving 100 barrels of crude oil produced by Northern's Production Division:

◆ **Method A.** Market-based transfer prices.

◆ **Method B.** Cost-based transfer prices at 105% of full costs, where full costs are the cost of the transferred-in product plus the division's own variable and fixed costs.

◆ **Method C.** Negotiated transfer prices.

The transfer prices per barrel of crude oil under each method are as follows:

◆ **Method A:** Market-Based Transfer Prices
   ◆ From Production Division to Transportation Division = $72
   ◆ From Transportation Division to Refining Division = $85[9]

[9]Oil prices are notoriously volatile, and the price per barrel of crude oil on September 25, 2011, in Canadian dollars was $81.75. On June 25, 2011, it was $93.55 per barrel.

◆ **Method B:** Cost-Based Transfer Prices at 105% of Full Costs
   ◆ Full cost of crude oil plus the Transportation Division's = 1.05 ($72 + $1 + $3)
      full costs = $79.80

◆ **Method C:** Transfer Prices Negotiated by Divisions to Be between Market-
   Based and Cost-Based Transfer Prices
   ◆ Negotiated transfer price of $83.00 per barrel of crude oil (a price within the
      range of the market-based and cost-based transfer prices).

Exhibit 23-3 presents division operating incomes per 100 barrels of crude oil reported under each transfer-pricing method. Transfer prices create income for the "selling" division and corresponding costs for the "buying" division that cancel out when divisional results are consolidated. The Exhibit assumes that the different transfer-pricing methods have no effect on the decisions made and actions taken by the division managers. Northern Petroleum's total operating income from producing, transporting, and refining the 100 barrels of crude oil is therefore the same, $1,200, regardless of internal transfer prices used:

$$\text{Operating income} = \text{Revenues} - \frac{\text{Cost of}}{\text{crude oil}} - \frac{\text{Transporation}}{\text{costs}} - \frac{\text{Refining}}{\text{costs}}$$

$$= (\$190 \times 50 \text{ barrels of gasoline}) - (\$72 \times 100 \text{ barrels of crude oil})$$
$$- (\$4 \times 100 \text{ barrels of crude oil}) - (\$14 \times 50 \text{ barrels of gasoline})$$

$$= 9,500 - \$7,200 - \$400 - \$700 = \$1,200$$

When operating income is constant, we can focus on the effects of different transfer-pricing methods on division operating incomes. These incomes differ under the three methods. Analyzing the high and low operating incomes for each division, Exhibit 23-3 readily shows that the operating income of the Transportation Division benefits most when the market-based method is used ($900 − $380 = $520), whereas the Refining Division benefits most when the full-cost method is used ($820 − $300 = $520). This means that each division would choose a different transfer-pricing method if its sole criterion were to maximize its own division operating income: the Transportation Division would favour market pricing, and the Refining Division would choose 105% of full costs. Clearly, this is why managers whose compensation or promotion directly depends on operating-division income take considerable interest in the setting of transfer prices.

Exhibit 23-3 maintains companywide operating income at $1,200 and illustrates how the choice of a transfer-pricing method divides the companywide operating income pie among individual divisions. The transfer-pricing methods do not change the size of the total pie but rather how it is divided between the two divisions. If Northern Petroleum failed to obtain a long-term contract for the crude oil transported to its refinery, then the revenues and operating income would also fluctuate for each division and for the company as a whole, although the proportions or operating income for each division under each transfer-pricing method would not fluctuate.

The more volatile the market price, the more difficult it would be for Northern Petroleum to predict its future revenues upon which to base its strategic and operating plans. Subsequent sections of this chapter illustrate that the choice of a transfer-pricing method can also affect the decisions that individual division managers make and hence the size of the operating income pie itself. We consider this effect as we expand our discussion of market-based, cost-based, and negotiated transfer prices.

INTERPROVINCIAL TRANSFERS AND TAXES

Top management at Northern Petroleum transferred intermediate goods interprovincially. The corporate tax rates in Alberta are the lowest in Canada, whereas Ontario has the highest provincial corporate tax rates in the country. From the company's perspective, the split of taxable income between the provinces would make a difference in both operating cash flow and net income. It would also make a difference to the taxes collected by each province.

The operating margin if the market price is used will be 10.59% for the Transportation Division in Alberta and 3.16% for the Refining Division in Ontario.

EXHIBIT 23-3
Division Operating Income of Northern Petroleum for 100 Barrels of Crude Oil under Alternative Transfer-Pricing Methods

	A	B	C	D	E	F	G
1	**Production and Sales Data**						
2	Barrels of crude transferred =	100					
3	Barrels of gasoline sold =	50					
4		**Internal Transfers**			**Internal Transfers at**		**Internal Transfers at**
5		**at Market Price of**			**105% of Full Cost =**		**Negotiated Price of**
6		**$85.00**			**$79.80**		**$83.00**
7		**per Barrel**			**per Barrel**		**per Barrel**
8	**Transportation Division**						
9	Revenue: 100 × $85; $79.80; $83.00	$8,500			$7,980		$8,300
10	Costs						
11	Crude oil						
12	$72 × 100 barrels of crude oil	7,200			7,200		7,200
13	Division variable costs						
14	$1 × 100 barrels of crude oil	100			100		100
15	Division fixed costs						
16	$3 × 100 barrels of crude oil	300			300		300
17	Total division costs	7,600			7,600		7,600
18	Division operating income	$ 900			$ 380		$ 700
19	Operating margin	10.59%			4.76%		8.43%
20							
21	**Refining Division**						
22	Revenues: $190 × 50	$9,500			$9,500		$9,500
23	Costs						
24	Transferred-in costs: 100 × $85; $79.80; $83.00	8,500			7,980		8,300
25	Division variable costs						
26	$8 × 50 barrels of gasoline	400			400		400
27	Division fixed costs						
28	$6 × 50 barrels of gasoline	300			300		300
29	Total division costs	9,200			8,680		9,000
30	Division operating income	$ 300			$ 820		$ 500
31	Operating margin	3.16%			8.63%		5.26%
32	Total operating income for Northern Petroleum	$1,200			$1,200		$1,200

This would be the best after-tax choice for Northern Petroleum. The second-best choice would be at the negotiated transfer price, which will leave 8.43% of the operating income in Alberta and transfer 5.26% to Ontario. The least preferred choice from the company's perspective is to use full cost because that leaves only 4.76% of operating income in the provincial jurisdiction with the lowest tax rates (Alberta) and transfers 8.63% to the provincial jurisdiction with the highest tax rates in Canada (Ontario).

Fortunately, the first choice from the company's perspective also ranks first in the transfer price hierarchy of the OECD. The national and provincial governments prefer transfer prices at the market price because it is assured this transfer price is an arm's-length price. In this situation there is no need for Northern Petroleum to approach either tax authority to obtain an **advance transfer price arrangement (APA)**. APAs are a substitute for dispute resolution wherein the company and the tax authority can cooperate to prospectively agree on a transfer price method.[10]

[10]M. Przysuski, "Advance Pricing Arrangements (APAs) in Canada," *Corporate Business Taxation Monthly*, 6.2 (2004): 11–16.

APAs are exceptionally important to sustain good corporate governance. In disputes between the tax authorities and corporations, fines alone can reach billions. This excludes legal expenses and opportunity costs of diverting resources to dispute resolution. Most MNCs will approach the tax authorities in all countries (or provinces) where related-party transfers of intermediate goods will occur. Most tax authorities, including CRA, will negotiate a tax method acceptable to them for some specified future time period. Companies voluntarily undertake APAs, but the agreement is legally binding.

The APA process is costly; however, complex, high-dollar-value related-party transactions should be negotiated in advance because it is exactly these transactions that tax authorities will most likely audit. The opportunity cost of a CRA transfer price audit is very high, especially if the company has failed internally to produce ongoing documentation. All related-party transfers are reportable in the corporate tax return. The maximum late-filing penalty is $10,000 and the maximum failure to file penalty is $12,000 for *each* infraction. Legislation authorizes provinces to levy the same penalties domestically.[11] When companies fail to provide acceptable documentation, a 10% penalty can be added to any transfer-pricing adjustment. The penalty is applied only if the transfer-pricing adjustment exceeds 10% of the gross revenue prior to any transfer-pricing adjustments or $5 million.[12]

MARKET-BASED TRANSFER PRICES

3 Assess the market-based transfer price method.

Transferring products or services at market prices generally leads to optimal decisions when three conditions are satisfied: (1) the intermediate market is perfectly competitive, (2) interdependencies of subunits are minimal, and (3) there are no additional costs or benefits to the corporation as a whole in using the market instead of transacting internally. A **perfectly competitive market** exists when there is a homogeneous product with equivalent buying and selling prices and no individual buyers or sellers can affect those prices by their own actions. By using market-based transfer prices in perfectly competitive markets, a company can meet the criteria of goal-congruence, management effort, optimal subunit performance, and (if desired) subunit autonomy.

Reconsider the Northern Petroleum example, assuming that there is a perfectly competitive market for crude oil in the Calgary area and that the market price is $85 per barrel. As a result, the Transportation Division can sell and the Refining Division can buy as much crude oil as each wants at $85 per barrel. Northern, however, would like its managers to buy or sell crude oil internally. Think about the decisions that Northern's division managers would make if each had the option to sell or buy crude oil externally.

If the transfer price between Northern's Transportation and Refining Divisions is set below $85, the manager of the Transportation Division will be motivated to sell all production to outside buyers at $85 per barrel. If the transfer price is set above $85, the manager of the Refining Division will be motivated to purchase all its crude oil requirements from outside suppliers. A current market value transfer price of $85 could motivate both the Transportation and Refining Division to buy and sell internally.

Suppose each division manager is motivated to maximize his or her own division operating income. The Transportation Division will sell (either internally or externally) as much crude oil as it can profitably sell, and the Refining Division will buy (either internally or externally) as much crude oil as it can profitably transport. At a transfer price of $85, the actions that maximize division operating income are also the actions that maximize operating income of Northern Petroleum as a whole. Market prices also serve to evaluate the economic performance and profitability of each division individually.

---

[11]M. Przysuski, S. Lalapet, and H. Swaneveld, "Transfer Pricing Filing in Canada," *Corporate Business Taxation Monthly*, 6.7 (2005): 25–28.

[12]S. J. Smith and P. L. Kelley, "It's an Art, Not a Science," ca*magazine*, 138.8 (2005): 44–46.

In perfectly competitive markets, the minimum price the selling division is willing to accept from the buying division is the market price, because the selling division can always sell its output in the external market at that price. The maximum price the buying division is willing to pay to the selling division is the market price, because the buying division can always buy its input in the external market at that price.

DISTRESS PRICES

When supply outstrips demand, market prices may drop well below their historical average. If the drop in prices is expected to be temporary, these low market prices are sometimes called *distress prices*. Deciding whether a current market price is a distress price is often difficult. The market prices of several agricultural commodities, such as wheat and oats, have stayed for many years at what observers initially believed were temporary distress levels.

Which transfer-pricing method should be used for judging performance if distress prices prevail? Some companies use the distress prices themselves, but others use long-run average prices, or "normal" market prices. In the short run, the manager of the supplier division should meet the distress price as long as it exceeds the incremental costs of supplying the product or service; if not, the supplying division should stop producing, and the buying division should buy the product or service from an outside supplier. These actions would increase overall companywide operating income. If the long-run average market price is used, forcing the manager to buy internally at a price above the current market price will hurt the buying division's short-run performance and understate its profitability. If, however, prices remain low in the long run, the manager of the supplying division must decide whether to dispose of some manufacturing facilities or shut down and have the buying division purchase the product from outside.

Be aware of the conflict distress prices can cause. Because the selling division receives very low revenues from distress prices, managers may decide to produce other products that would not be in the company's best interest in the long run. Alternatively, if the transfer price is based on the long-run average market price, the buying division will prefer to buy externally or outsource. If top management requires buying internally (at the long-run average market price), subunit autonomy is violated in a decentralized structure.

COST-BASED AND NEGOTIATED TRANSFER PRICES

Cost-based transfer prices are helpful when market prices are unavailable, inappropriate, or too costly to obtain. For example, the product may be specialized or unique, price lists may not be widely available, or the internal product may be different from the products available externally in terms of quality and service.

Apply relevant costs and tax considerations to evaluate the selection of cost-based and negotiated transfer prices.

FULL-COST BASES

In practice, many companies use transfer prices based on full costs. These prices, however, can lead to suboptimal decisions. Assume that Northern Petroleum makes internal transfers at 105% of full cost. The Sarnia Refining Division purchases, on average, 30,000 barrels of crude oil per day from a local Sarnia supplier, who delivers the crude oil to the refinery. Freight-on-board (FOB) cost is $85 per barrel. To reduce crude oil costs, the Refining Division has located an independent producer in Calgary who is willing to sell 30,000 barrels of crude oil per day at $79 per barrel, delivered to Northern's pipeline in Calgary.

Given Northern's organization structure, the Transportation Division would purchase the 20,000 barrels of crude oil in Calgary, transport it to Sarnia, and then sell it to the Refining Division. The pipeline has excess capacity and can ship the 20,000 barrels at its variable costs of $1 per barrel. Will Northern Petroleum incur lower costs by purchasing crude oil from the independent producer in Calgary or by purchasing crude oil from the Sarnia supplier? Will the Refining Division show lower crude oil purchasing costs by using oil from the Calgary producer or by using its current Sarnia supplier?

The following analysis shows that operating income of Northern Petroleum as a whole would be maximized by purchasing oil from the independent Calgary producer. The analysis compares the incremental costs in all divisions under the two alternatives:

- ◆ **Alternative 1:** Buy 20,000 barrels from the Sarnia supplier at $85 per barrel. Total costs to Northern Petroleum = 20,000 × $85 = $1,700,000.
- ◆ **Alternative 2:** Buy 20,000 barrels in Calgary at $79 per barrel and transport it to Sarnia at $1 per barrel variable costs or $80 per barrel. Total costs to Northern Petroleum = 20,000 × $80 = $1,600,000.

There is a reduction in total costs to Northern Petroleum of $100,000 by using the independent producer in Calgary ($1,700,000 – $1,600,000).

In turn, suppose the Transportation Division's transfer price to the Refining Division is 105% of full cost. The Refining Division will see its reported division costs increase if the crude oil is purchased from the independent producer in Calgary:

$$\frac{\text{Transfer}}{\text{price}} = 1.05 \times \left(\begin{array}{c} \text{Purchase price} \\ \text{from Calgary} \\ \text{producer} \end{array} + \begin{array}{c} \text{Unit variable cost} \\ \text{of Transportation} \\ \text{Division} \end{array} + \begin{array}{c} \text{Unit fixed cost} \\ \text{of Transportation} \\ \text{Division} \end{array} \right)$$

$$= 1.05 \times (\$79 + \$1 + \$3) = 1.05 \times \$83 = \$87.15 \text{ per barrel}$$

- ◆ **Alternative 1:** Buy 20,000 barrels from the Sarnia supplier at $85 per barrel. Total costs to Refining Division = 20,000 × $85 = $1,700,000 (constant).
- ◆ **Alternative 2:** Buy 20,000 barrels from the Transportation Division of Northern Petroleum that are purchased from the independent producer in Calgary. Total costs to Refining Division = 20,000 × $87.15 = $1,743,000.

As a profit centre, the Refining Division can maximize its short-run division operating income by purchasing from the Sarnia supplier ($1,700,000 versus $1,743,000).

The transfer-pricing method has led the Refining Division to regard the fixed cost (and the 5% markup) of the Transportation Division as a variable cost. The reason is that the Refining Division looks at each barrel that it obtains from the Transportation Division as a variable cost of $87.15—if 10 barrels are transferred, it costs the Refining Division $871.50; if 100 barrels are transferred, it costs $8,715. From the point of view of Northern Petroleum as a whole, its variable costs per barrel are $80 ($79 to purchase the oil from the independent producer and $1 to transport it to Sarnia).

The remaining $7.15 ($87.15 – $80) per barrel is seen by the Refining Division as a fixed cost and markup of the Transportation Division. Buying crude oil in Sarnia costs Northern Petroleum $85 per barrel. For the company, it is cheaper to buy from Calgary. Goal-incongruence is induced by the transfer price based on full cost plus a markup.

Should Northern's top management interfere and force the Refining Division to buy from the Transportation Division? Top management interference would undercut the philosophy of decentralization, so Northern's top management would probably view the decision by the Refining Division to purchase crude oil from external suppliers as an inevitable cost of decentralization and not interfere. Of course, some interference may occasionally be necessary to prevent costly blunders. But recurring interference and constraints would simply transform Northern from a decentralized company into a centralized company.

What transfer price will promote goal-congruence for both the Transportation Division and the Refining Division? The minimum transfer price is $80 per barrel; a transfer price below $80 does not provide the Transportation Division with an incentive to purchase crude oil from the independent producer in Calgary while a transfer price above $80 generates contribution margin to cover fixed costs.

The maximum transfer price is $85 per barrel; a transfer price above $85 will cause the Refining Division to purchase crude oil from the external market rather than from the Transportation Division.

A transfer price between the minimum and maximum transfer prices of $80 and $85 respectively will promote goal-congruence—both divisions will increase their own reported division operating income by purchasing crude oil from the independent producer in Calgary. In particular, a transfer price based on the full costs of $83 without a markup will achieve goal-congruence. The Transportation Division will show no operating income and will be evaluated as a cost centre. Surveys indicate that managers prefer to use full-cost transfer pricing because it yields relevant costs for long-run decisions and because it facilitates pricing on the basis of full product costs.

Using full-cost transfer prices that include an allocation of fixed overhead costs raises other issues. How are indirect costs allocated to products? Have the correct activities, cost pools, and cost drivers been identified? Are the chosen overhead rates actual or budgeted rates? The issues here are similar to the issues that arise in allocating fixed costs (Chapter 14). Full-cost-based transfer prices calculated using ABC cost drivers can provide more refined allocation bases for allocating costs to products. Using budgeted costs and budgeted rates lets both divisions know the transfer price in advance.

Some companies calculate budgeted rates based on practical capacity rather than master-budget capacity utilization levels (Chapter 9). For tax purposes, however, the CRA requires the use of normal capacity, a long-term measure of demand. Using budgeted rates and practical capacity overcomes the problem of inefficiencies in actual costs and costs of unused capacity being passed along from the selling to the buying division. In negotiation with the CRA, the use of normal capacity as the allocation base for a fixed cost pool is unlikely to provide the same cost allocation rate. To maximize tax revenue, the CRA prefers the lower cost allocation rate to maximize taxable income. For CRA purposes, using budgeted fixed-cost allocation rates based on normal capacity will eliminate variations in full-cost transfer prices caused by variation in the actual quantity of units produced.

VARIABLE COST BASES

Transferring 20,000 barrels of crude oil from the Transportation Division to the Refining Division at the variable cost of $80 per barrel achieves goal-congruence, as shown in the preceding section. The Refining Division would buy from the Transportation Division because the Transportation Division's variable cost (which is also the relevant incremental cost for Northern Petroleum as a whole) is less than the $85 price charged by outside suppliers.

At the $80 per barrel transfer price, the Transportation Division would record an operating loss and the Refining Division would show large profits because it would be charged only for the variable costs of the Transportation Division. One approach to addressing this problem is to have the Refining Division make a lump-sum transfer payment to cover fixed costs and generate some operating income for the Transportation Division while the Transportation Division continues to make transfers at variable cost. The fixed payment is the price the Refining Division pays for using the capacity of the Transportation Division. The income earned by each division can then be used to evaluate the performance of each division and its manager.

PRORATING THE DIFFERENCE BETWEEN MINIMUM AND MAXIMUM TRANSFER PRICES

An alternative cost-based approach is for Northern Petroleum to choose a transfer price that splits the $5 difference between the maximum transfer price the Refining Division is willing to pay and the minimum transfer price the Transportation Division wants on some equitable basis. Suppose Northern Petroleum allocates the $5 difference on the basis of the budgeted variable costs incurred by the Transportation

Division and the Refining Division for a given quantity of crude oil. Using the data in Exhibit 23-3 (p. 935), the variable costs are as follows:

Transportation Division's variable costs to transport 100 barrels of crude oil ($1 × 100)	$100
Refining Division's variable costs to refine 100 barrels of crude oil and produce 50 barrels of gasoline ($8 × 50)	400
Total variable costs	$500

The Transportation Division gets to keep $100/$500 × $5 = $1.00, and the Refining Division gets to keep $400/$500 × $5 = $4.00 of the $5 difference. That is, the transfer price between the Transportation Division and the Refining Division would be $81 per barrel of crude oil ($79 purchase cost + $1 variable costs + $1 that the Transportation Division gets to keep). Essentially, this approach is a budgeted variable cost plus transfer price; the "plus" indicates the setting of a transfer price above variable costs.

To decide on the $1 and $4 allocation of the $5 contribution to total corporate operating income per barrel, the divisions must share information about their variable costs. In effect, each division does not operate (at least for this transaction) in a totally decentralized manner. Because most organizations are hybrids of centralization and decentralization anyway, this approach deserves serious consideration when transfers are significant. Note, however, that each division has an incentive to overstate its variable costs to receive a more favourable transfer price.

DUAL PRICING

There is seldom a *single* transfer price that simultaneously meets the criteria of goal-congruence, management effort, and subunit autonomy. Some companies turn to **dual pricing**, using two separate transfer-pricing methods to price each interdivision transaction. An example of dual pricing arises when the selling division receives a full cost plus markup–based price and the buying division pays the market price for the internally transferred products. Assume that Northern Petroleum purchases crude oil from the independent producer in Calgary at $79 per barrel. One way of recording the journal entry for the transfer between the Transportation Division and the Refining Division is as follows:

1. Credit the Transportation Division (the selling division) with the 105%-of-full-cost transfer price of $87.15 per barrel of crude oil.

2. Debit the Refining Division (the buying division) with the market-based transfer price of $85 per barrel of crude oil.

3. Debit a corporate cost account for the $2.15 ($87.15 – $85.00) difference between the two transfer prices for the cost of crude oil borne by corporate rather than the Refining Division.

The dual-price method promotes goal-congruence because it makes the Refining Division no worse off if it purchases the crude oil from the Transportation Division rather than from the outside supplier. In either case, the Refining Division's cost is $85 per barrel of crude oil. This dual-price system essentially gives the Transportation Division a corporate subsidy. One result of dual pricing is that the operating income for Northern Petroleum as a whole is less than the sum of the operating incomes of the divisions.

Managers, regardless of how decentralized their corporate structure is, must conform to tax legislation. It is unlikely the CRA would object as long as there was no decrease in corporate taxable income and the method complied with legislation. The OECD hierarchy of preference, however, places current market value as the most preferred method, and a competitive market is assumed where there is only one homogeneous price, not two. Interprovincially, and in an MNC situation, when dual rates do affect taxable income in more than one jurisdiction there is risk. Overall, the consolidated taxable income would be unaffected, but the distribution of tax revenue would be affected by dual rates. The amounts are not trivial. Nations as well as provinces will dispute what are perceived as tax avoidance strategies, especially if a current market price can be used instead.

Dual pricing is not widely used in practice even though it reduces the goal-congruence problems associated with a pure cost plus–based transfer-pricing method. One concern of top management is that the manager of the supplying division does not have sufficient incentive to control costs with a dual-price system. A second concern is that the dual-price system confuses division managers about the level of decentralization top management seeks. Above all, dual pricing tends to insulate managers from the frictions of the marketplace. Managers should know as much as possible about their subunits' buying and selling markets, and dual pricing reduces the incentive to gain this knowledge.

NEGOTIATED TRANSFER PRICES AND MNC ISSUES

Negotiated transfer prices arise as the outcome of a bargaining process between selling and buying divisions. Consider again the choice of a transfer price between the Transportation and Refining Divisions of Northern Petroleum. The Transportation Division has excess capacity that it can use to transport oil from Calgary to Sarnia. The Transportation Division will be willing to "sell" oil to the Refining Division only if the transfer price equals or exceeds $80 per barrel of crude oil (its variable costs). The Refining Division will be willing to "buy" crude oil from the Transportation Division only if the cost equals or is below $85 per barrel (the price at which the Refining Division can buy crude oil in Sarnia).

Given the Transportation Division's unused capacity, Northern Petroleum as a whole maximizes operating income if the Refining Division purchases from the Transportation Division rather than from the Sarnia market (incremental costs of $80 per barrel versus incremental costs of $85 per barrel). Both divisions would be interested in transacting with each other if the transfer price is set between $80 and $85. For example, a transfer price of $83 per barrel will increase the Transportation Division's operating income by $83 – $80 = $3.00 per barrel. It will increase the Refining Division's operating income by $85 – $83 = $2.00 per barrel because Refining can now "buy" the oil for $83 inside rather than for $85 outside.

The key question is where between $80 and $85 the transfer price will be. The answer depends on the bargaining strengths of the two divisions. The Transportation Division has more information about the price less incremental marketing costs of supplying crude oil to outside refineries, while the Refining Division has more information about its other available sources of oil. Negotiations become particularly sensitive if Northern evaluates each division's performance on the basis of divisional operating income.

The price negotiated by the two divisions will, in general, have no specific relationship to either costs or market price. But cost and price information are often useful starting points in the negotiation process. Exhibit 23-4 compares the three methods of transfer pricing discussed. The full-cost-based transfer price is the most used and negotiated prices are the least frequently used transfer-pricing method worldwide.

A GENERAL GUIDELINE FOR TRANSFER-PRICING SITUATIONS

There exists no pervasive rule for transfer pricing that leads toward optimal decisions for the organization as a whole because the three criteria of goal-congruence, management effort, and subunit autonomy must all be considered simultaneously. The following general guideline, however, has proven to be a helpful first step in setting a minimum transfer price in many specific situations:

$$\begin{matrix} \text{Minimum} \\ \text{transfer price} \end{matrix} = \begin{matrix} \text{Additional } \textit{incremental} \text{ or } \textit{outlay costs} \text{ per unit} \\ \text{incurred up to the point of transfer} \end{matrix} + \begin{matrix} \textit{Opportunity costs} \text{ per unit} \\ \text{to the supplying division} \end{matrix}$$

The term *incremental* or *outlay costs* in this context represents the additional costs that are directly associated with the production and transfer of the products or services. *Opportunity costs* are defined here as the maximum contribution forgone by the

EXHIBIT 23-4
Comparison of Different Transfer-Pricing Methods

Criteria	Market-Based	Cost-Based	Negotiated
Achieves goal-congruence	Yes, when markets are competitive	Often but not always	Yes
Useful for evaluating subunit performance	Yes, when markets are competitive	Difficult unless transfer price exceeds full cost and even then is somewhat arbitrary	Yes, but transfer prices are affected by bargaining strengths of the buying and selling divisions
Motivates management effort	Yes	Yes, when based on budgeted costs; less incentive to control costs if transfers are based on actual costs	Yes
Preserves subunit autonomy	Yes, when markets are competitive	No, because it is rule based	Yes, because it is based on negotiations between subunits
Other factors	Market may not exist, or markets may be imperfect or in distress	Useful for determining full cost of products and services; easy to implement	Bargaining and negotiations take time and may need to be reviewed repeatedly as conditions change

supplying division if the products or services are transferred internally. For example, if the supplying division is operating at capacity, the opportunity cost of transferring a unit internally rather than selling it externally is equal to the market price minus variable costs. We distinguish incremental costs from opportunity costs because the accounting system typically records incremental costs but not opportunity costs. We illustrate the general guidelines in some specific situations using data from the Production and Transportation Divisions of Northern Petroleum.

1. *A perfectly competitive market for the intermediate product exists, and the selling division has no unused capacity.* If the market for crude oil in Calgary is perfectly competitive, the Transportation Division can sell all the crude oil it transports to the external market at $85 per barrel, and it will have no unused capacity.

   The Transportation Division's incremental cost (as shown in Exhibit 23-2, p. 933) is either $73 per barrel (purchase cost of $72 per barrel plus variable transportation cost of $1 per barrel) for oil purchased under the long-term contract or $80 per barrel (purchase cost of $79 plus variable transportation cost of $1) for oil purchased at current market prices from the Calgary producer. The Transportation Division's opportunity cost per barrel of transferring the oil internally is the contribution margin per barrel forgone by not selling the crude oil in the external market: $12 for oil purchased under the long-term contract (market price, $85, minus variable cost, $73) and $5 for oil purchased from the Calgary producer (market price, $85, minus variable cost, $80). In either case,

$$\begin{array}{ccc} \text{Minimum transfer} & \text{Incremental} & \text{Opportunity} \\ \text{price per barrel} = \text{cost per barrel} + \text{costs per barrel} \end{array}$$

$$= \$73 + 12 = \$85$$

or

$$= \$80 + \$5 = \$85$$

Market-based transfer prices are ideal in perfectly competitive markets when there is no idle capacity.

2. *An intermediate market exists that is not perfectly competitive, and the selling division has unused capacity.* In markets that are not perfectly competitive, capacity utilization

can be increased only by decreasing prices. Unused capacity exists because decreasing prices is often not worthwhile—it decreases operating income. If the Transportation Division has unused capacity, its opportunity cost of transferring the oil internally is zero because the division does not forgo any external sales or contribution margin from internal transfers. In this case:

$$
\begin{array}{c}
\text{Minimum} \\
\text{transfer price} \\
\text{per barrel}
\end{array}
=
\begin{array}{c}
\text{Incremental} \\
\text{cost per barrel}
\end{array}
+
\begin{array}{c}
\text{\$73 per barrel for oil purchased under the} \\
\text{long-term contract or \$80 per barrel for oil} \\
\text{purchased from the Calgary producer}
\end{array}
$$

Any transfer price above incremental cost but below \$85—the price at which the Refining Division can buy crude oil in Sarnia—motivates the Transportation Division to transport crude oil to the Refining Division and the Refining Division to buy crude oil from the Transportation Division. In this situation, the company could either use a cost-based transfer price or allow the two divisions to negotiate a transfer price between themselves.

In general, though, in markets that are not perfectly competitive, the potential to influence demand and operating income through prices makes measuring opportunity costs more complicated. The transfer price depends on constantly changing levels of supply and demand. There is not just one transfer price; rather, a transfer-pricing schedule yields the transfer price for various quantities supplied and demanded, depending on the incremental costs and opportunity costs of the units transferred.

Consider the following situation: Suppose the Refining Division receives an order to supply specially processed gasoline. The Refining Division will profit from this order only if the Transportation Division can supply crude oil at a price not exceeding \$82 per barrel. Suppose the incremental cost to purchase and supply crude oil is \$80 per barrel. In this case, the transfer price that would benefit both divisions must be greater than \$80 but less than \$82 (rather than \$85).

3. *No market exists for the intermediate product.* This would occur, for example, in the Northern Petroleum case if oil from the production well flows directly into the pipeline and cannot be sold to outside parties.

Here, the opportunity cost of supplying crude oil internally is zero because the inability to sell crude oil externally means no contribution margin is forgone. At the Transportation Division of Northern Petroleum, the minimum transfer price under the general guideline would be the incremental costs per barrel of either \$73 or \$80. As in the previous case, any transfer price between the incremental cost and \$85 will achieve goal-congruence. Knowledge of the incremental cost per barrel of crude oil would be helpful to the Refining Division for many decisions, such as short-run pricing.

In transfer-pricing situations, opportunity cost is the profit the selling division (SD) forgoes by selling internally rather than externally. Assume the SD has no idle capacity for a particular product and can sell all it produces at \$4 per unit. Incremental cost is \$1 per unit. If the SD sells internally, the opportunity cost is \$3 per unit (\$4 revenue per unit – \$1 incremental cost per unit). In contrast, if the SD has unused capacity with no alternative use, no profit is forgone by selling internally (opportunity cost is \$0).

MNC TRANSFER PRICING AND TAX CONSIDERATIONS

Now we will consider factors affecting transfer prices among corporate subunits in different countries. Sales between corporate subunits are called sales between **related parties**, in contrast to external sales between a subunit and a nonrelated party termed **arm's-length transactions**. The transfer prices have tax implications and therefore affect the government revenues of each country involved. Tax factors include income taxes, payroll taxes, customs duties, tariffs, sales taxes, value-added

Once Again—Tax Is Mandatory—They Will Get You

Transfer pricing requires one subunit manager to earn revenues and another subunit manager to incur costs. Managers are frequently evaluated on the basis of subunit profits. Little wonder, then, that subunit managers care deeply about how transfer prices are set. It is natural for subunit managers to argue for transfer prices that make their own performance look good. Management accountants must ensure that the transfer prices set are in the best interests of the company as a whole. This requires management accountants to understand business issues and the external market environment within which the businesses function. They must also never cave in to pressure from managers that will make a subunit's performance look good while hurting the corporation as a whole.

Consider Motorola, the electronics products manufacturer. In 2004, the U.S. Internal Revenue Service (IRS) notified the company that it was disputing the way Motorola calculated earnings from 1996 to 2000, resulting in an additional tax liability of US$500 million. The underlying issue was related to transfer pricing involving Motorola's 67 tax entities around the world. The IRS claimed too much profit was left in the company's tax entities abroad and that not enough income was recognized in the United States. Motorola must convince the IRS that its practices are within the law.

Source: R. Crockett, "Motorola's Taxing Dispute," *Business Week Online,* August 12, 2004, http://www.businessweek.com/bwdaily/dnflash/aug2004/nj20040812_8175_db016.htm, accessed September 17, 2004.

taxes, environment-related taxes, and other government levies. We focus on income tax factors as a key consideration in transfer-pricing decisions.

The Income Tax Act of Canada (section 247) sets out the laws regarding transfer pricing. The most recent rules were introduced in 1998 after legislative changes in the United States and the publication of transfer price guidelines by the OECD. The CRA intends to achieve harmonization with OECD and US laws to reduce the costs of tax compliance for multinational corporations. The most important laws limit how companies set transfer prices to one of five methods.

Transfer prices also have tax implications, particularly when products are transferred across country borders. Setting transfer prices is almost always a matter of judgment. At no time, however, should management accountants choose transfer prices that do not adhere to the tax codes of different countries. The time and cost to resolve transfer-pricing disputes can be very high.

Traditional transaction methods include the **comparable uncontrolled price (CUP) method, resale price method (RPM),** and **cost-plus method (CPM).** The CUP is analogous to the internal market-based price. The related-party transfer price reported by a corporation is compared to prices for similar transactions among arm's-length (nonrelated) parties and must fall within the middle two quartiles of this range of prices. The CRA has confidential comparable tables in its ever-growing database that it uses to make these comparisons.

The RPM requires a company calculate the arm's-length resale price. Distributors of finished goods typically use this method when the cost of distribution is low relative to the value of the finished goods (that is, almost non-value-added). Again the CRA compares the estimated transfer price to a range of prices for similar arm's-length transactions and usually accepts transfer prices in the two mid-quartiles of this range.

The CPM highlights the effect of the transfer price on the pretax income of each subunit. This method permits corporations the greatest discretion and most readily justified transfer price to the CRA because of the quality of information provided by management accounting and control systems.

The transactional profit methods of setting a transfer price are the **profit split method (PSM)** and **transactional net margin method (TNMM)**. The PSM requires understanding the value added by the functions performed by each related party and the resulting allocation of profit and loss to each subunit. The fifth method, TNMM, is based on the return on assets (ROA) of the corporation as a whole and provides maximum discretion for establishing a transfer price.

Establishing the arm's-length price for value-added services such as marketing or intangible contributions such as research and development knowledge is difficult. The role of the management accountant has increased in importance as has the role of the internal data on pricing already produced by the management accounting and control system because companies must produce contemporaneous documentation for every transfer price transaction or be subject to an automatic financial penalty for failing to do so. Companies are obligated to comply with Canada's tax laws. This audit trail, which justifies in detail the transfer price used, provides the CRA with evidence companies have made reasonable effort to do what they should to establish the price is arm's length. The CRA auditors may still disagree with and adjust the transfer price despite the documentation provided, but no penalty will be imposed for failing to make a reasonable effort to establish an arm's-length transfer price.

Corporations may choose a tax minimization strategy by establishing a legitimate subsidiary in a tax haven (e.g., Andorra, Liechtenstein, Monaco). **Tax havens** have no tax agreements with Canada and share no information, which will increase the costs to the company of any tax audit. A second strategy is to establish a legitimate subsidiary in an **international financial centre** with very low income tax rates (e.g., Barbados or Ireland). These centres have tax treaties with Canada.

Consider an example of a Canadian company that manufactures and sells products from Ireland. Tax and other incentives offered there result in the Irish division paying lower taxes on its income in Ireland. Therefore, the company has an incentive to set the transfer price for transfers into Canada as high as possible. Why? To maximize income reported in Ireland where tax rates are lower and reduce income reported in Canada that is taxed at rates as high as 40%. Nevertheless, to make sound transfer-pricing decisions, managers must remember that penalties for non-compliance with transfer-pricing tax laws can be substantial.

In Canada, the CRA has indicated it will aggressively challenge transfer prices based on costs allocated proportionally to revenues of the related parties, management services to Canadian companies at cost plus, and any dual product prices. While the CRA has published transfer-pricing guidelines (IC87-2R), when disputes arise the final decision on the transfer price is often negotiated among the tax authorities involved in the dispute. This resolution process is not only costly but can also take as long as two years, and any penalties imposed are retroactive and accumulate interest during the process. To avoid costly disputes, companies may choose a third strategy—to request an advance pricing arrangement with all involved tax authorities.

Consider the Northern Petroleum data in Exhibit 23-3 (p. 935). Assume that Northern operates a Transportation Division in Mexico that pays Mexican income taxes at 30% of operating income and that both the Transportation and Refining Divisions based in Canada pay income taxes at 20% of operating income. Northern Petroleum would minimize its total income tax payments with the 105% of full costs transfer-pricing method, as shown in the following table:

Transfer-Pricing Method	Operating Income for 100 Barrels of Crude Oil			Income Tax on 100 Barrels of Crude Oil		
	Transportation Division (Mexico) (1)	Refining Division (Canada) (2)	Total (3) = (1) + (2)	Transportation Division (Mexico) (4) = 0.30 × (1)	Refining Division (Canada) (5) = 0.20 × (2)	Total (6) = (4) + (5)
Market price	$900	$300	$1,200	$270	$ 60	$330
105% of full costs	380	820	1,200	114	164	278
Negotiated price	700	500	1,200	210	100	310

Tax considerations raise additional issues that may conflict with other objectives of transfer pricing. Suppose that the market for crude oil in Calgary is perfectly competitive. In this case, the market-based transfer price achieves goal-congruence and provides effort incentives. It also helps Northern to evaluate the economic profitability of the Transportation Division. But it is costly from an income tax standpoint.

Northern Petroleum would favour using 105% of full costs for tax reporting, but tax laws in Canada and Mexico constrain this option. In particular, the Mexican tax authorities are fully aware of Northern Petroleum's incentives to minimize income taxes by reducing the income reported in Mexico. They would challenge any attempts to shift income to the Refining Division through a low transfer price.

The perfectly competitive market for crude oil in Mexico would probably force Northern Petroleum to use the market price for transfers from the Production Division to the Transportation Division. Northern Petroleum might successfully argue that the transfer price should be set below the market price because the Production Division incurs no marketing and distribution costs when "selling" crude oil to the Transportation Division. Northern Petroleum could obtain advance approval of the transfer-pricing arrangements from the appropriate tax authorities.

To meet multiple transfer-pricing objectives, a company may choose to keep one set of accounting records for tax reporting and a second set for internal management reporting. The difficulty here is that tax authorities may interpret two sets of books as suggestive of the company manipulating its reported taxable income to avoid tax payments. Additional factors that arise in multinational transfer pricing include tariffs and customs duties levied on imports of products into a country. The issues here are similar to the income tax considerations discussed earlier—companies will have incentives to lower transfer prices for products imported into a country to reduce the tariffs and customs duties that those products will attract. MNC transfer prices are sometimes influenced by restrictions that some countries place on the payment of income or dividends to parties outside their national borders. By increasing the prices of goods or services transferred into divisions in these countries, companies can increase the funds paid out of these countries without appearing to violate income or dividend restrictions.

PULLING IT ALL TOGETHER—PROBLEM FOR SELF-STUDY

(Try to solve this problem before examining the solution that follows.)

PROBLEM
The Pillercat Corporation is a highly decentralized company. Each division manager has full authority for sourcing and selling decisions. The Machining Division of Pillercat has been the major supplier of the 2,000 crankshafts that the Tractor Division needs each year.

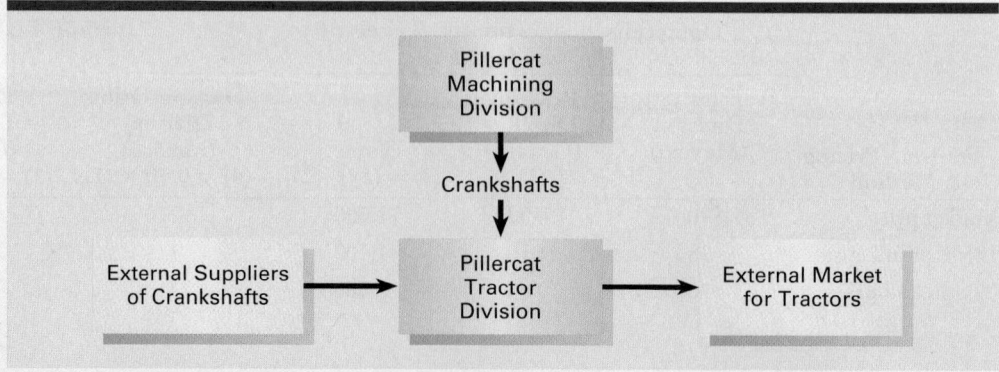

The Tractor Division, however, has just announced that it plans to purchase all its crankshafts in the forthcoming year from two external suppliers at $200 per crankshaft. The Machining Division of Pillercat recently increased its price for the forthcoming year to $220 per unit (from $200 per unit in the current year).

Juan Gomez, manager of the Machining Division, feels that the 10% price increase is fully justified. It results from a higher amortization charge on some new specialized equipment used to manufacture crankshafts and an increase in labour costs. Gomez wants the president of Pillercat Corporation to direct the Tractor Division to buy all its crankshafts from the Machining Division at the price of $220. The additional incremental costs per unit that Pillercat incurs to produce each crankshaft are the Machining Division's variable costs of $190. Fixed cost per crankshaft in the Machining Division equals $20.

	A	B
1	Number of crankshafts purchased by Tractor Division	2,000
2	External supplier's market price per crankshaft	$ 200
3	Variable cost per crankshaft in Machining Division	$ 190
4	Fixed cost per crankshaft in Machining Division	$ 20

REQUIRED
1. Compute the advantage or disadvantage (in terms of monthly operating income) to the Pillercat Corporation as a whole if the Tractor Division buys crankshafts internally from the Machining Division under each of the following cases:
   a. The Machining Division has no alternative use for the facilities used to manufacture crankshafts.
   b. The Machining Division can use the facilities for other production operations, which will result in monthly cash operating savings of $29,000.
   c. The Machining Division has no alternative use for the facilities, and the external supplier drops its price to $185 per crankshaft.
2. As the president of Pillercat, how would you respond to Juan Gomez's request to order the Tractor Division to purchase all of its crankshafts from the Machining Division? Would your response differ according to the scenarios described in parts (a), (b), and (c) of requirement 1? Why?
3. Discuss the tax implications if the Machining and Tractor division were located in different countries. Pillercat management's best transfer price choice would be the current market price or CUP because it conforms with the OECD hierarchy. The managers would be wise to negotiate an advance transfer price arrangement with tax authorities in both countries (APA). If there were no market for the intermediate product, then profit split (PSM) or transactional net margin methods (TNMM) could be negotiated.
4. The best transfer price for performance evaluation may not be the most acceptable to tax authorities. In terms of good governance what option is available to managers?

SOLUTION

1. Computations for the Tractor Division buying crankshafts internally for cases (a), (b), and (c) are:

	A	B	C	D
1			Case	
2		a	b	c
3	Number of crankshafts purchased by Tractor Division	2,000	2,000	2,000
4	External supplier's market price per crankshaft	$ 200	$ 200	$ 185
5	Incremental cost per crankshaft in Machining Division	$ 190	$ 190	$ 190
6	Opportunity costs of the Machining Division supplying	—	$ 29,000	—
7	crankshafts to the Tractor Division			
8				
9	Total purchase costs if buying from an external supplier			
10	(2,000 shafts × $200, $200, $185 per shaft)	$400,000	$400,000	$370,000
11	Incremental costs of buying from the Machining Division			
12	(2,000 shafts × $190 per shaft)	380,000	380,000	380,000
13	Total opportunity costs of the Machining Division	—	29,000	—
14	Total relevant costs	380,000	$409,000	380,000
15	Annual operating income advantage (disadvantage) to			
16	Pillercat of buying from the Machining Division	$ 20,000	$ (9,000)	$ (10,000)
17				

The general guideline introduced on page 941 as a first step in setting a transfer price highlights the alternatives:

	A	B	C	D	E	F	G
1		Incremental Cost		Opportunity Cost			External
2		per Unit Incurred to		per Unit to the		Transfer	Market
3	Case	Point of Transfer	+	Supplying Division	=	Price	Price
4	a	$190	+	$ 0	=	$190.00	$200
5	b	$190	+	$14.50[a]	=	$204.50	$200
6	c	$190	+	$ 0	=	$190.00	$185
7							
8	[a]Opportunity cost per unit = Total opportunity costs ÷ Number of crankshafts = $29,000 ÷ 2,000 = $14.50						

The Tractor Division will maximize monthly operating income of Pillercat Corporation as a whole by purchasing from the Machining Division in case (a) and by purchasing from the external suppliers in cases (b) and (c).

2. Pillercat Corporation is a highly decentralized company. If no forced transfer were made, the Tractor Division would use an external supplier, resulting in an optimal decision for the company as a whole in cases (b) and (c) of requirement 1, but not in case (a).

Suppose that in case 1(a), the Machining Division refuses to meet the price of $200. This decision means that the company will be $20,000 worse off in the short run. Should top management interfere and force a transfer at $200? This interference would undercut the philosophy of decentralization. Many top management teams would not interfere because they would view the $20,000 as an inevitable cost of a suboptimal decision that occasionally occurs under decentralization. But how high must this cost be before the temptation to interfere would be irresistible? $30,000? $40,000?

Any top management interference with lower-level decision making weakens decentralization. Of course, such interference may occasionally be necessary to prevent costly blunders. But recurring interference and constraints simply transform a decentralized organization into a centralized organization.

3. Pillercat management's best transfer price choice would be the current market price or CUP because it conforms with the OECD hierarchy. The managers would be wise to negotiate an advance transfer price arrangement with tax authorities in both countries (APA). If there were no market for the intermediate product, then profit split (PSM) or transactional net margin methods (TNMM) could be negotiated.

4. Assuming that managers do achieve satisfactory standards of good governance, they will have access to relevant information as described in the CPEM and NI 52-109. This implies the presence of coordinated information systems that enable the development of dual accounting records. One management accounting system reports values used for performance evaluation purposes over which tax authorities have no concern. The second reports performance according to methods of transfer pricing acceptable to tax authorities.

SUMMARY POINTS

The following question-and-answer format summarizes the chapter's learning outcomes. Each point presents a key question, and the guidelines are the answer to that question.

LEARNING OUTCOMES	GUIDELINES
1. What is a control system and how should it be designed?	A control system is a means to organize or arrange elements into an orderly structure. Choices of organizational structure are constrained by legislation such as NI 52-109 and NI 58-201 in Canada as well as CRA tax legislation. The goal of control systems is to nurture and sustain good governance.
2. How are transfer-pricing methods ranked?	To ease the compliance burden on MNCs, most countries worldwide have adopted the OECD Hierarchy of Methods for transfer pricing. The principle upon which the ranking is based is the arm's-length principle. The most preferred transfer price is current market price of intermediate products. Other alternatives for internal control include cost-based and negotiated prices.
3. What are the benefits of transferring products at current market price?	Optimal internal management decisions to benefit the entire corporation are made if the intermediate market is perfectly competitive (homogeneous product and prices) and interdependencies among subunits are minimal.
4. How does cost-plus transfer pricing lead to suboptimal internal management decisions?	A transfer price based on full cost plus a markup may lead to suboptimal decisions because it leads the buying division to regard the fixed costs and the markup of the selling division as variable costs. The buying division may then purchase products from an outside vendor expecting savings in variable costs that, in fact, will not occur.
5. What constraints are externally imposed to internal guidelines for determining a minimum transfer?	Transfer prices can reduce income tax payments by recognizing more income in low-tax-rate countries and less income in high-tax-rate countries. However, tax regulations of different countries restrict the transfer prices that companies can choose. Internal guidelines state that the minimum transfer price equals the incremental cost per unit incurred up to the point of transfer plus the opportunity cost per unit to the supplying division resulting from transferring products or services internally.

This chapter and the Glossary at the end of the book contain definitions of the following important terms:

advance transfer price arrangement (APA) (p. 935)
arm's-length principle (p. 930)
arm's-length transaction (p. 943)
comparable uncontrolled price method (CUP) (p. 944)
cost-plus method (CPM) (p. 944)
decentralization (p. 927)
dual pricing (p. 940)

dysfunctional decision making (p. 929)
effort (p. 927)
goal-congruence (p. 926)
goal-incongruent decision making (p. 929)
intermediate products (p. 930)
international financial centre (p. 945)
management accounting control system (MACS) (p. 924)
motivation (p. 926)

perfectly competitive market (p. 936)
profit split method (PSM) (p. 945)
related parties (p. 943)
resale price method (RPM) (p. 944)
suboptimal decision making (p. 929)
tax haven (p. 945)
transactional net margin method (TNMM) (p. 945)
transfer price (p. 930)

ASSIGNMENT MATERIAL

MyAccountingLab | Make the grade with MyAccountingLab: The questions, exercises, and problems marked in red can be found on MyAccountingLab at **www.myaccountinglab.com**. You can practise them as often as you want, and most feature step-by-step guided instructions to help you find the right answer. Exercises and problems with an Excel icon in the margin have an accompanying Excel template on MyAccountingLab.

SHORT-ANSWER QUESTIONS

23-1 What is a management control system?

23-2 Describe three criteria you would use to evaluate whether a management control system is effective.

23-3 What is the relationship among motivation, goal-congruence, and effort?

23-4 Name three benefits and two costs of decentralization.

23-5 "Organizations typically adopt a consistent decentralization or centralization philosophy across all their business functions." Do you agree? Explain.

23-6 "Transfer pricing is confined to profit centres." Do you agree? Why?

23-7 What are the three general methods for determining transfer prices?

23-8 What properties should transfer-pricing systems have?

23-9 "All transfer-pricing methods give the same division operating income." Do you agree? Explain.

23-10 Under what conditions is a market-based transfer price optimal?

23-11 What is one potential limitation of full-cost-based transfer prices?

23-12 Give two reasons why a dual-price approach to transfer pricing is not widely used.

23-13 "Under the general transfer-pricing guideline, the minimum transfer price will vary depending on whether or not the supplying division has idle capacity." Do you agree? Explain.

23-14 Why should managers consider income tax issues when choosing a transfer-pricing method?

EXERCISES

23-15 **Terminology.** A number of terms are listed below:

advance transfer price arrangement (APA)
comparable uncontrolled price
negotiated
cost-plus method (CPM)
goal-congruence
related-party transactions
tax haven

market-based price
cost-based
cost-plus
dual pricing
profit split
resale price
transactional net margin

Select the terms from the above list to complete the following sentences.

The CRA constrains global transfer-pricing choices and provincial tax authorities constrain the interprovincial transfer-pricing choice of management teams. A wise team will undertake an _____ _____ ____ _____ (___) to avoid future tax liabilities. There are two interprovincial transfer-price alternatives when no _____ ____ ____ exists. The alternatives are either ____ _____, which is a cost-plus approach, or _____ transfer prices that fall between a market and cost-plus price. Of course a _____ price may be either full absorption or variable cost-based, and in the transfer the same company may use ____ _____. The transferring division charges at a cost-based price while the receiving division pays at a market-based price. The difference is billed to a common corporate account rather than to the divisions. This method reduces ____ _____ problems between transferring divisions. There are three multinational corporate transfer-price alternatives. The respective tax authorities scrutinize these _____ ____ _____ very carefully to ensure their jurisdictions receive the appropriate tax payments from each party in the transfer. The alternatives are the _____ ___ _____ (CUP), _____ ____ (___), _____ (___), _____(___) and _____ ___ _____ _____ (___). In addition to negotiating APA with governments, corporations also minimize taxes by establishing legitimate subsidiaries in ___ _____ that share information with other governments.

23-16 **Management control systems, balanced scorecard.** Greystone Corporation manufactures stone tiles for kitchen counters and floors. Its strategy is to manufacture high-quality products at reasonable prices, and to rapidly deliver products following sales. Greystone sells to both hardware stores and contractors. To avoid holding large inventories of finished goods, Greystone manufactures products based on orders from customers. The factory setup enables workers to perform multiple functions, including receiving orders, running different machines, inspecting for quality, packaging, and shipping the final product.

REQUIRED

Given Greystone's strategy, describe the financial and nonfinancial measures that you would include in its balanced scorecard-based management control system.

23-17 **Decentralization, goal-congruence, responsibility centres.** Hexton Chemicals consists of seven independent operating divisions. The operating divisions are assisted by a number of support groups, such as R&D, human resources, and environmental management. The environmental-management group consists of 20 environmental engineers. These engineers must seek business from the operating divisions—that is, the projects they work on must be mutually agreed to and paid for by one of the operating divisions. Under Hexton's rules, the environmental group is required to charge the operating divisions for environmental services at cost.

REQUIRED

1. Is the environmental-management group centralized or decentralized?
2. What type of responsibility centre is the environmental-management group?
3. What benefits and problems do you see in structuring the environmental-management group in this way? Does it lead to goal-congruence and motivation? Explain.

23-18 **Cost centres, profit centres, decentralization, transfer prices.** Fenster Corporation manufactures windows with wood and metal frames. Fenster has three departments: Glass, Wood, and Metal. The Glass Department makes the window glass and sends it to either the Wood or Metal Department, where the glass is framed. The window is then sold. Upper management sets the production schedules for the three departments and evaluates them on output quantity, cost variances, and product quality.

REQUIRED

1. Are the three departments cost centres, revenue centres, or profit centres?
2. Are the three departments centralized or decentralized?
3. Can a centralized department be a profit centre? Why or why not?
4. Suppose the upper management of Fenster Corporation decides to let the three departments set their own production schedules, buy and sell products in the external market, and have Wood and Metal negotiate with Glass for the glass panes using a transfer price.
   a. Will this change your answers to requirements 1 and 2?
   b. How would you recommend upper management evaluate the three departments if this change is made?

23-19 **Multinational transfer pricing, effect of alternative transfer-pricing methods, global income tax minimization.** User Friendly Computer Inc., with headquarters in Nepean, Ontario, manufactures and sells a premium desktop computer system. User Friendly has three divisions, each of which is located in a different country:

a. China Division—manufactures memory devices and keyboards.

1. a. China to South Korea, $450 per subunit

Transfer Pricing and Multinational Management Control Systems

b. South Korea Division—assembles desktop computers using internally manufactured parts and memory devices and keyboards from the China Division.

c. Canada Division—packages and distributes desktop computer packages.

Each division is run as a profit centre. The costs for the work done in each division for a single desktop computer system are as follows:

China Division	Variable costs = 1,000 yuan
	Fixed costs = 1,800 yuan
South Korea Division	Variable costs = 360,000 won
	Fixed costs = 480,000 won
Canada Division	Variable costs = 100 CAD
	Fixed costs = 200 CAD

Chinese income tax rate on China Division's operating income	40%
South Korean income tax rate on South Korea Division's operating income	20%
Canadian income tax rate on Canada Division's operating income	30%

Each desktop computer package is sold to retail outlets in Canada for $3,200. Assume that the current foreign exchange rates are:

$$8 \text{ yuan} = \$1 \text{ Cdn.}$$
$$1,200 \text{ won} = \$1 \text{ Cdn.}$$

Both the China and South Korea Divisions sell part of their production under a private label. The China Division sells the comparable memory/keyboard package used in each User Friendly desktop computer to a Chinese manufacturer for 3,600 yuan. The South Korea division sells the comparable desktop computer package to a South Korean distributor for 1,560,000 won.

REQUIRED

1. Calculate the after-tax operating income per unit earned by each division under each of the following transfer-pricing methods: (a) market price, (b) 200% of full cost, and (c) 300% of variable cost. (Income taxes are not included in the computation of the cost-based transfer prices.)

2. Which transfer-pricing method(s) will maximize the after-tax operating income per unit of User Friendly Computer Inc.?

1. Incremental loss $(50) per 100 board feet

23-20 Transfer-pricing methods, goal-congruence. British Columbia Lumber has a Raw Lumber Division and a Finished Lumber Division. The variable costs are:

◆ Raw Lumber Division: $100 per 100 board feet of raw lumber.
◆ Finished Lumber Division: $125 per 100 board feet of finished lumber.

Assume that there is no board feet loss in processing raw lumber into finished lumber. Raw lumber can be sold at $200 per 100 board feet. Finished lumber can be sold at $275 per 100 board feet.

REQUIRED

1. Should British Columbia Lumber process raw lumber into its finished form? Show your calculations.

2. Assume that internal transfers are made at 110% of variable cost. Will each division maximize its division operating-income contribution by adopting the action that is in the best interests of British Columbia Lumber as a whole? Explain.

3. Assume that internal transfers are made at market prices. Will each division maximize its division operating-income contribution by adopting the action that is in the best interests of British Columbia Lumber as a whole? Explain.

1. Mining Division operating income, $6,000,000

23-21 Effect of alternative transfer-pricing methods on division operating income. (CMA, adapted) Ajax Corporation has two divisions. The Mining Division makes toldine, which is then transferred to the Metals Division. The toldine is further processed by the Metals Division and sold to customers at a price of $150 per unit. The Mining Division is currently required by Ajax to transfer its total yearly output of 200,000 units of toldine to the Metals Division at 110% of full manufacturing cost. Unlimited quantities of toldine can be purchased and sold on the outside market at $90 per unit.

The following table gives the manufacturing cost per unit in the Mining and Metals divisions for 2013:

	Mining Division	Metals Division
Direct material cost	$12	$ 6
Direct manufacturing labour cost	16	20
Manufacturing overhead cost	32[a]	25[b]
Total manufacturing cost per unit	$60	$51

[a] Manufacturing overhead costs in the Mining Division are 25% fixed and 75% variable.
[b] Manufacturing overhead costs in the Metals Division are 60% fixed and 40% variable.

REQUIRED

1. Calculate the operating incomes for the Mining and Metals divisions for the 200,000 units of toldine transferred under the following transfer-pricing methods: (a) market price and (b) 110% of full manufacturing cost.
2. Suppose Ajax rewards each division manager with a bonus, calculated as 1% of division operating income (if positive). What is the amount of bonus that will be paid to each division manager under the transfer-pricing methods in requirement 1? Which transfer-pricing method will each division manager prefer to use?
3. What arguments would Brian Jones, manager of the Mining Division, make to support the transfer-pricing method that he prefers?

23-22 Transfer pricing, general guideline, goal-congruence. (CMA, adapted) Quest Motors Inc. operates as a decentralized multidivision company. The Tivo Division of Quest Motors purchases most of its airbags from the Airbags Division. The Airbag Division's incremental cost for manufacturing the airbags is $90 per unit. The Airbag Division is currently working at 80% of capacity. The current market price of the airbags is $125 per unit.

5

1. Minimum transfer price, $90

REQUIRED

1. Using the general guideline presented in the chapter, what is the minimum price at which the Airbag Division would sell airbags to the Tivo Division?
2. Suppose that Quest Motors requires that whenever divisions with unused capacity sell products internally, they must do so at the incremental cost. Evaluate this transfer-pricing policy using the criteria of goal-congruence, evaluating division performance, motivating management effort, and preserving division autonomy.
3. If the two divisions were to negotiate a transfer price, what is the range of possible transfer prices? Evaluate this negotiated transfer-pricing policy using the criteria of goal-congruence, evaluating division performance, motivating management effort, and preserving division autonomy.
4. Do you prefer the transfer-pricing policy in requirement 2 or requirement 3? Explain your answer briefly.

23-23 Multinational transfer pricing, global tax minimization. The Zanello Company manufactures telecommunications equipment at its plant in Ottawa, Ontario. The company has marketing divisions throughout the world. A Zanello marketing division in Vienna, Austria, imports 1,000 units of Product 4A36 from Canada. The following information is available:

1. Canadian division Method A operating income, $0

Canadian income tax rate on the Canadian division's operating income	40%
Austrian income tax rate on the Austrian division's operating income	44%
Austrian import duty	10%
Variable manufacturing cost per unit of Product 4A36	$350
Full manufacturing cost per unit of Product 4A36	$500
Selling price (net of marketing and distribution costs) in Austria	$750

Suppose the Canadian and Austrian tax authorities only allow transfer prices that are between the full manufacturing cost per unit of $500 and a market price of $650, based on comparable imports into Austria. The Austrian import duty is charged on the price at which the product is transferred into Austria. Any import duty paid to the Austrian authorities is a deductible expense for calculating Austrian income taxes due.

REQUIRED

1. Calculate the after-tax operating income earned by the Canadian and Austrian divisions from transferring 1,000 units of Product 4A36 (a) at full manufacturing cost per unit and (b) at market price of comparable imports. (Income taxes are not included in the computation of the cost-based transfer prices.)

2. Which transfer price should the Zanello Company select to minimize the total of company import duties and income taxes? Remember that the transfer price must be between the full manufacturing cost per unit of $500 and the market price of $650 of comparable imports into Austria. Explain your reasoning.

④

1. Canadian division at 200% of full cost, $5,900,000

23-24 Multinational transfer pricing, global tax minimization. Industrial Diamonds, Inc., based in Montreal, Quebec, has two divisions:

◆ South African Mining Division, which mines a rich diamond vein in South Africa.
◆ Canadian Processing Division, which polishes raw diamonds for use in industrial cutting tools.

The Processing Division's yield is 50%: It takes two pounds of raw diamonds to produce one pound of top-quality polished industrial diamonds. Although all of the Mining Division's output of 4,000 pounds of raw diamonds is sent for processing in Canada, there is also an active market for raw diamonds in South Africa. The foreign exchange rate is 7 ZAR (South African Rand) = $1 CAD. The following information is known about the two divisions:

	A	B	C
1	**South African Mining Division**		
2	Variable cost per pound of raw diamonds	560	ZAR
3	Fixed cost per pound of raw diamonds	1,540	ZAR
4	Market price per pound of raw diamonds	3,150	ZAR
5	Tax rate	18%	
6			
7	**Canadian Processing Division**		
8	Variable cost per pound of polished diamonds	150	CAD
9	Fixed cost per pound of polished diamonds	700	CAD
10	Market price per pound of polished diamonds	5,000	CAD
11	Tax rate	30%	

REQUIRED

1. Compute the annual pre-tax operating income, in Canadian dollars, of each division under the following transfer-pricing methods: (a) 200% of full cost and (b) market price.
2. Compute the after-tax operating income, in Canadian dollars, for each division under the transfer-pricing methods in requirement 1. (Income taxes are not included in the computation of cost-based transfer price, and Industrial Diamonds does not pay Canadian income tax on income already taxed in South Africa.)
3. If the two division managers are compensated based on after-tax division operating income, which transfer-pricing method will each prefer? Which transfer-pricing method will maximize the total after-tax operating income of Industrial Diamonds?
4. In addition to tax minimization, what other factors might Industrial Diamonds consider in choosing a transfer-pricing method?

③ ⑤

1. Net cost (benefit) of purchasing from an external supplier, $15,000

23-25 Transfer-pricing dispute. The Allison-Chambers Corporation, manufacturer of tractors and other heavy farm equipment, is organized along decentralized product lines, with each manufacturing division operating as a separate profit centre. Each division manager has been delegated full authority on all decisions involving the sale of that division's output both to outsiders and to other divisions of Allison-Chambers. Division C has in the past always purchased its requirement of a particular tractor-engine component from Division A. However, when informed that Division A is increasing its selling price to $150, Division C's manager decides to purchase the engine component from external suppliers.

Division C can purchase the component for $135 per unit in the open market. Division A insists that, because of the recent installation of some highly specialized equipment and the resulting high depreciation charges, it will not be able to earn an adequate return on its investment unless it raises its price. Division A's manager appeals to top management of Allison-Chambers for support in the dispute with Division C and supplies the following operating data:

C's annual purchases of the tractor-engine component	1,000 units
A's variable cost per unit of the tractor-engine component	$120
A's fixed cost per unit of the tractor-engine component	$ 20

1. Assume that there are no alternative uses for internal facilities of Division A. Determine whether the company as a whole will benefit if Division C purchases the component from external suppliers for $135 per unit. What should the transfer price for the component be set at so that division managers acting in their own divisions' best interests take actions that are in the best interest of the company as a whole?

2. Assume that internal facilities of Division A would not otherwise be idle. By not producing the 1,000 units for Division C, Division A's equipment and other facilities would be used for other production operations that would result in annual cash-operating savings of $18,000. Should Division C purchase from external suppliers? Show your computations.

3. Assume that there are no alternative uses for Division A's internal facilities and that the price from outsiders drops $20. Should Division C purchase from external suppliers? What should the transfer price for the component be set at so that division managers acting in their own divisions' best interests take actions that are in the best interest of the company as a whole?

23-26 Transfer-pricing problem (continuation of 23-25). Refer to Exercise 23-25. Assume that Division A can sell the 1,000 units to other customers at $155 per unit, with variable marketing cost of $5 per unit.

1. Contribution margin from selling units to other customers, $30,000

REQUIRED

1. Determine whether Allison-Chambers will benefit if Division C purchases the 1,000 units from external suppliers at $135 per unit. Show your computations.

23-27 General guideline, transfer pricing. Shamrock Company manufactures and sells television sets. Its Assembly Division (AD) buys television screens from the Screen Division (SD) and assembles the TV sets. The SD, which is operating at capacity, incurs an incremental manufacturing cost of $80 per screen. The SD can sell all its output to the outside market at a price of $120 per screen, after incurring a variable marketing and distribution cost of $5 per screen. If the AD purchases screens from outside suppliers at a price of $120 per screen, it will incur a variable purchasing cost of $3 per screen. Shamrock's division managers can act autonomously to maximize their own division's operating income.

1. Minimum transfer price per screen, $115

REQUIRED

1. What is the minimum transfer price at which the SD manager would be willing to sell screens to the AD?
2. What is the maximum transfer price at which the AD manager would be willing to purchase screens from the SD?
3. Now suppose that the SD can sell only 80% of its output capacity of 10,000 screens per month on the open market. Capacity cannot be reduced in the short run. The AD can assemble and sell more than 10,000 sets per month.
   a. What is the minimum transfer price at which the SD manager would be willing to sell screens to the AD?
   b. From the point of view of Shamrock's management, how much of the SD output should be transferred to the AD?
   c. What transfer-pricing policy will achieve the outcome desired in requirement 3b?

23-28 Pertinent transfer price. Europa, Inc., has two divisions, A and B, which manufacture expensive bicycles. Division A produces the bicycle frame, and Division B assembles the rest of the bicycle onto the frame. There is a market for both the subassembly and the final product. Each division has been designated as a profit centre. The transfer price for the subassembly has been set at the long-run average market price. The following data are available for each division:

1. Contribution margin per unit, $30

Selling price for final product	$300
Long-run average selling price for intermediate product	200
Incremental cost per unit for completion in Division B	150
Incremental cost per unit in Division A	120

The manager of Division B has made the following calculation:

Selling price for final product		$300
Transferred-in cost per unit (market)	$200	
Incremental cost per unit for completion	150	350
Contribution (loss) on product		$(50)

1. Should transfers be made to Division B if there is no unused capacity in Division A? Is the market price the correct transfer price? Show your computations.
2. Assume that Division A's maximum capacity for this product is 1,000 units per month and sales to the intermediate market are now 800 units. Should 200 units be transferred to Division B? At what transfer price? Assume that for a variety of reasons, Division A will maintain the $200 selling price indefinitely. That is, Division A is not considering lowering the price to outsiders even if idle capacity exists.
3. Suppose Division A quoted a transfer price of $150 for up to 200 units. What would be the contribution to the company as a whole if a transfer were made? As manager of Division B, would you be inclined to buy at $150? Explain.

23-29 Pricing in imperfect markets (continuation of 23-28). Refer to Problem 23-28.

1. Opportunity cost per unit to the supplying division by transferring internally, $55

REQUIRED

1. Suppose the manager of Division A has the option of (a) cutting the external price to $195, with the certainty that sales will rise to 1,000 units or (b) maintaining the external price of $200 for the 800 units and transferring the 200 units to Division B at a price that would produce the same operating income for Division A. What transfer price would produce the same operating income for Division A? Is that price consistent with that recommended by the general guideline in the chapter so that the resulting decision would be desirable for the company as a whole?
2. Suppose that if the selling price for the intermediate product were dropped to $195, sales to external parties could be increased to 900 units. Division B wants to acquire as many as 200 units if the transfer price is acceptable. For simplicity, assume that there is no external market for the final 100 units of Division A's capacity.
   a. Using the general guideline, what is (are) the minimum transfer price(s) that should lead to the correct economic decision? Ignore performance-evaluation considerations.
   b. Compare the total contributions under the alternatives to show why the transfer price(s) recommended lead(s) to the optimal economic decision.

PROBLEMS

23-30 Effect of alternative transfer-pricing methods on division operating income. Crango Products is a cranberry cooperative that operates two divisions: a Harvesting Division and a Processing Division. Currently, all of Harvesting's output is converted into cranberry juice by the Processing Division, and the juice is sold to large beverage companies that produce cranberry juice blends. The Processing Division has a yield of 1,900 litres of juice per 1,000 kilograms of cranberries. Cost and market price data for the two divisions are as follows:

2. a. Total operating income, $159,920

	A	B	C	D	E
1	**Harvesting Division**			**Processing Division**	
2	Variable costs per kg of cranberries	$0.2205		Variable processing cost per litre of juice produced	$0.05263 per litre
3	Fixed cost per kg of cranberries	$0.5511		Fixed Costs per litre of juice produced	$0.1053 per litre
4	Selling price per kg of cranberries	$1.3228		Selling price per litre of juice	$0.55263 per litre

REQUIRED

1. Compute Crango's operating income from harvesting 181,440 kilograms of cranberries during June 2013 and processing them into juice.
2. Crango rewards its division managers with a bonus equal to 5% of operating income. Compute the bonus earned by each division manager in June 2013 for each of the following transfer-pricing methods:
   a. 200% of full cost   b. Market price
3. Which transfer-pricing method will each division manager prefer? How might Crango resolve any conflicts that may arise on the issue of transfer pricing?

23-31 Goal-congruence problems with cost-plus transfer-pricing methods, dual-pricing system (continuation of 23-30). Assume that Pat Borges, CEO of Crango, has mandated a transfer price equal to 200% of full cost. Now he decides to decentralize some management decisions and sends around a memo that states: "Effective immediately, each division of Crango is free to make its own decisions regarding the purchase of direct materials and the sale of finished products."

2. Harvesting Division 200% full costs operating income, $139,998

1. Give an example of a goal-congruence problem that will arise if Crango continues to use a transfer price of 200% of full cost and Borges's decentralization policy is adopted.
2. Borges feels that a dual transfer-pricing policy will improve goal-congruence. He suggests that transfers out of the Harvesting Division be made at 200% of full cost and transfers into the Processing Division be made at market price. Compute the operating income of each division under this dual transfer-pricing method when 181,440 kilograms of cranberries are harvested during June 2013 and processed into juice.
3. Why is the sum of the division operating incomes computed in requirement 2 different from Crango's operating income from harvesting and processing 181,440 kilograms of cranberries?
4. Suggest two problems that may arise if Crango implements the dual transfer prices described in requirement 2.

23-32 Transfer pricing, utilization of capacity. (J. Patell, adapted) The Ottawa Valley Instrument Company (OVIC) consists of the Semiconductor Division and the Process-Control Division, each of which operates as an independent profit centre. The Semiconductor Division employs craftsmen who produce two different electronic components: the new high-performance Super-chip and an older product called Okay-chip. These two products have the following cost characteristics:

1. Contribution margin per hour for Super-chip, $15

	Super-chip	Okay-chip
Direct materials	$ 2	$1
Direct manufacturing labour, 2 hours × $14; 0.5 hour × $14	28	7

Annual overhead in the Semiconductor Division totals $400,000, all fixed. Due to the high skill level necessary for the craftsmen, the Semiconductor Division's capacity is set at 50,000 hours per year.

One customer orders a maximum of 15,000 Super-chips per year, at a price of $60 per chip. If OVIC cannot meet this entire demand, the customer curtails its own production. The rest of the Semiconductor Division's capacity is devoted to the Okay-chip, for which there is unlimited demand at $12 per chip.

The Process-Control Division produces only one product, a process-control unit, with the following cost structure:
◆ Direct materials (circuit board): $60
◆ Direct manufacturing labour (5 hours × $10): $50

Fixed overhead costs of the Process-Control Division are $80,000 per year. The current market price for the control unit is $132 per unit.

A joint research project has just revealed that a single Super-chip could be substituted for the circuit board currently used to make the process-control unit. Using Super-chip would require an extra one hour of labour per control unit for a new total of six hours per control unit.

REQUIRED

1. Calculate the contribution margin per hour of selling Super-chip and Okay-chip. If no transfers of Super-chip are made to the Process-Control Division, how many Super-chips and Okay-chips should the Semiconductor Division sell? Show your computations.
2. The Process-Control Division expects to sell 5,000 process-control units this year. From the viewpoint of OVIC as a whole, should 5,000 Super-chips be transferred to the Process-Control Division to replace circuit boards? Show your computations.
3. If demand for the process-control unit is certain to be 5,000 units but its *price is uncertain*, what should the transfer price of Super-chip be to ensure that the division managers' actions maximize operating income for OVIC as a whole? (All other data are unchanged.)
4. If demand for the process-control unit is certain to be 12,000 units, but its *price is uncertain*, what should the transfer price of Super-chip be to ensure that the division managers' actions maximize operating income for OVIC as a whole? (All other data are unchanged.)

23-33 International transfer pricing, taxes, goal-congruence. Argone Division of Gemini Corporation is located in the United States. Its effective income tax rate is 20%. Another division of Gemini, Calcia, is located in Canada, where the income tax rate is 38%. Calcia manufactures, among other things, an intermediate product for Argone called IP-2007. Calcia operates at capacity and makes 20,000 units of IP-2007 for Argone each period, at a variable cost of $80 per unit. Assume that there are no outside customers for IP-2007. Because the IP-2007 must be shipped from Canada to the United States, it costs Calcia an additional $2 per unit to ship the IP-2007 to Argone. There are no direct fixed costs for IP-2007. Calcia also manufactures other products. A product similar to IP-2007 that Argone could use as a substitute is available in the United States for $100 per unit.

1. Minimum transfer price, $82

1. What are the minimum and maximum transfer prices that would be acceptable to Argone and Calcia for IP-2007, and why?
2. What transfer price would minimize income taxes for Gemini Corporation as a whole? Would Calcia and Argone want to be evaluated on operating income using this transfer price?
3. Suppose Gemini uses the transfer price from requirement 2, and each division is evaluated on its own after-tax division operating income. Now suppose Calcia has an opportunity to sell 10,000 units of IP-2007 to an outside customer for $95 each. Calcia will not incur shipping costs because the customer is nearby and offers to pay for shipping. Assume that if Calcia accepts the special order, Argone will have to buy 10,000 units of the substitute product in the United States at $100 per unit.
   a. Will accepting the special order maximize after-tax operating income for Gemini Corporation as a whole?
   b. Will Argone want Calcia to accept this special order? Why or why not?
   c. Will Calcia want to accept this special order? Explain.
   d. Suppose Gemini Corporation wants to operate in a decentralized manner. What transfer price should Gemini set for IP-2007 so that each division acting in its own best interest takes actions with respect to the special order that are in the best interests of Gemini Corporation as a whole?

4

1. Revenue, company as a whole, $1,378,000

23-34 Dual pricing. A company has two divisions. The Bottle Division produces products that have variable costs of $3 per unit. Its 2012 sales were 150,000 to outsiders at $5 per unit and 40,000 units to the Mixing Division at 140 percent of variable costs. Under a dual transfer-pricing system, the Mixing Division pays only the variable cost per unit. The fixed costs of Bottle Division were $125,000 per year.

Mixing sells its finished products to outside customers for $11.50 per unit. Mixing has variable costs of $2.50 per unit in addition to the costs from Bottle. The annual fixed costs of Mixing were $85,000. There were no beginning or ending inventories during the year.

1. What are the operating incomes of the two divisions and the company as a whole for the year?
2. Explain why the company operating income is less than the sum of the two divisions' total income.

2 5

1. Benefit, $20,000

23-35 Transfer pricing, goal-congruence, governance. Whengon Manufacturing makes electronic hearing aids. Department A manufactures 10,000 units of part HR-7 and Department B uses this part to make the finished product. HR-7 is a specific part for a patented product that cannot be purchased or sold outside of Whengon, so there is no outside demand for this part. Variable costs of making HR-7 are $12 per unit. Fixed costs directly traced to HR-7 equal $30,000.

Upper management has asked the two departments to negotiate a transfer price for HR-7. The manager of Department A, Henry Lasker, is worried that Department B will insist on using variable cost as the transfer price because Department A has excess capacity. Lasker asks Joe Bedford, his management accountant, to show more costs as variable costs and fewer costs as fixed costs. Lasker says, "There are grey areas when distinguishing between fixed and variable costs. I think the variable cost of making HR-7 is $14 per unit."

1. If Lasker is correct, calculate the benefit to Department A from showing a variable cost of $14 per unit rather than $12 per unit.
2. What cost-based transfer-price mechanism would you propose for HR-7? Explain briefly.
3. Evaluate whether Lasker's comment to Bedford about the variable cost of HR-7 is ethical. Would it be ethical for Bedford to revise the variable cost per unit? What steps should Bedford take to resolve the situation?

1 5

1. Operating income, $2,580

23-36 Apply transfer-pricing methods. Blue Ribbon Fisheries is a fishing company located on the Canadian Pacific coast. It has three divisions:

a. Harvesting—operates a fleet of 20 trawling vessels.
b. Processing—processes the raw fish into fillets.
c. Marketing—packages fillets in two-kilogram packets that are sold to wholesale distributors at $15 each on average.

The Processing Division has a yield of 500 kilograms of processed fish fillets from 1,000 kilograms of raw fish provided by the Harvesting Division. The Marketing Division has a yield of 300 two-kilogram packets from every 500 kilograms of processed fish fillets provided

REQUIRED

by the Processing Division (the weight of the packaging material is included in the two-kilogram weight). Cost data for each division are as follows:

Fish Harvesting Division

Variable costs per kilogram of raw fish	$0.24
Fixed costs per kilogram of raw fish	$0.48

Fish Processing Division

Variable costs per kilogram of processed fish	$0.96
Fixed costs per kilogram of processed fish	$0.72

Fish Marketing Division

Variable costs per two-kilogram packet	$0.36
Fixed costs per two-kilogram packet	$0.84

Fixed costs per unit are based on the estimated quantity of raw fish, processed fish, and two-kilogram packets to be produced during the current fishing season.

Blue Ribbon Fisheries has chosen to process internally all raw fish brought in by the Harvesting Division. Other fish processors on the Pacific Coast purchase raw fish from boat operators at $1.70 per kilogram on average. Blue Ribbon has also chosen to process internally all fish fillets into the two-kilogram packets sold by the Marketing Division. Several fish marketing companies on the Pacific Coast purchase fish fillets at $7 per kilogram on average.

REQUIRED

1. Compute the overall operating income to Blue Ribbon Fisheries of harvesting 1,000 kilograms of raw fish, processing it into fillets, and then selling it in two-kilogram packets.
2. Compute the transfer prices that will be used for internal transfers (i) from the Harvesting Division to the Processing Division and (ii) from the Processing Division to the Marketing Division under each of the following transfer-pricing methods:
   a. 200% of variable costs. Variable costs are the costs of the transferred-in product (if any) plus the division's own variable costs.
   b. 150% of full costs. Full costs are the costs of the transferred-in product (if any) plus the division's own variable and fixed costs.
   c. Market price.
3. Blue Ribbon Fisheries rewards each division manager with a bonus, calculated as 1% of division operating income (if positive). What is the amount of the bonus that will be paid to each division manager under each of the three transfer-pricing methods in requirement 2? Which transfer-pricing method will each division manager prefer to use?

23-37 Market-based transfer-price method. Mark's division has been judged on the basis of its profit and return on investment. Top management has been working to gain effective results from a policy of decentralizing responsibility for all decisions except those relating to overall company policy. Top management feels that the concept of decentralization has been successfully applied and that the company's profits and competitive position have definitely improved in the last two years.

Mark is considering two alternative bids to submit for a very large project that will represent 50% of his division's activity. He plans to apply the usual 10% profit markup on full costs to both bids.

◆ **Alternative 1:** Price of $55 per piece (will yield a ROI of 20% and the probability of winning the bid is 80%)

About 60% of Mark's cost represents the cost of parts manufactured by another division of the same company that has been running below capacity and has excess inventory but has quoted the market price. The costs of the supplying division are about 50 percent of the selling price quoted to Mark.

◆ **Alternative 2:** Price of $52.80 per piece (will yield a ROI of 18% and the probability of winning the bid is 90%)

A reduction in prices can be obtained if part of the job is outsourced. The parts that Mark's division needs can be bought at $28 from an external supplier.

Mark knows that they sell in a very competitive market, where higher costs cannot be passed on. His preference for alternative 2 is opposite to company's guidelines of buying internally, so he asks the CEO, "How can we be expected to show a decent profit and return on investment if we have to buy our supplies internally at more than the market price?"

Knowing that the supplying division has on occasion in the past few months been unable to operate at capacity, Mark asserts that it is odd to add the full overhead and profit charge to his costs. In particular, the portion that belongs to corporate overhead that is allocated to all divisions at a rate of 10% of total own costs.

REQUIRED

1. Calculate the profit per piece in dollars for Mark's division under each alternative.
2. Calculate the transfer price at which the parts are being transferred from the internal supplier to Mark's division. Explain if it is the most adequate in this situation.
3. Explain which alternative is best for Mark.
4. Explain which alternative is best for the whole corporation.

23-38 Transfer prices and excess capacity. Italian Sausages Inc. is still a family-owned company located in Maple, Ontario. It has experienced significant growth in the last 10 years, and nowadays it employs more than 100 persons in production-related activities and another 20 persons in support activities such as selling, administrative, health and safety, and so on. Italian Sausages manufactures and sells high-quality sausages and is organized along two divisions: (Meat) Grinding/Mixing and (Sausage) Stuffing.

The first step in the production of sausages is done in the Grinding/Mixing Division, where the meat is ground in special machines and then several spices and additives are added to the mixture. The mixture is transferred to the Stuffing Division in 50-kilogram metal containers. Each container is directed to a particular stuffing machine, whether vertical or horizontal, where sausages of different diameters are assembled. In Maple and vicinity there are active markets for both the mixture and the sausages. Each division is evaluated as a profit centre. The transfer price for the mixture has been set at the long-run average market price. The following data per kilogram are available to each division:

Estimated selling price of 1 kg of sausages	$5.00
Long-run average selling price for 1 kg of mixture	$3.25
Incremental costs for completion in Stuffing Division	$2.00
Incremental costs for preparing the mixture in Grinding/Mixing Division	$1.00

The manager of the Stuffing Division has made the following calculation:

Estimated selling price of 1 kg of sausages	$ 5.00
Transferred-in costs at market price	$ 3.25
Incremental costs for completion in Stuffing Division	$ 2.00
Contribution (loss) on 1 kg of sausage	$(0.25)

REQUIRED

1. Should transfers be made to Stuffing if there is no excess capacity in Grinding/Mixing? Is the market price the correct transfer price?
2. Assume that Grinding/Mixing's maximum capacity is 10,000 kilograms per week and sales to the intermediate market are now 5,000 kilograms. Should 5,000 kilograms be transferred to Stuffing? At what transfer price? Assume that for a variety of reasons, Grinding/Mixing will maintain the $3.25 selling price indefinitely; that is, Grinding/Mixing is not considering lowering the price to outsiders even if idle capacity exists.
3. Suppose Grinding/Mixing quoted a transfer price of $3 for up to 5,000 kilograms. What would be the contribution to the company as a whole if the transfer were made? As manager of Stuffing, would you be inclined to buy at $3?

COLLABORATIVE LEARNING CASES

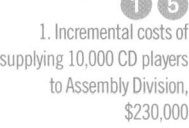

1. Incremental costs of supplying 10,000 CD players to Assembly Division, $230,000

23-39 Transfer pricing, goal-congruence. The Orsilo Corporation makes and sells 10,000 multisystem music players each year. Its Assembly Division purchases components from other divisions of Orsilo or from external suppliers and assembles the multisystem music players. In particular, the Assembly Division can purchase the CD player from the Compact Disc Division of Orsilo or from Johnson Corporation. Johnson agrees to meet all of Orsilo's quality requirements and is currently negotiating with the Assembly Division to supply 10,000 CD players at a price between $38 and $45 per CD player.

A critical component of the CD player is the head mechanism that reads the disc. To ensure the quality of its multisystem music players, Orsilo requires that if Johnson wins the contract to supply CD players, it must purchase the head mechanism from Orsilo's Compact Disc Division for $20 each.

The Compact Disc Division can manufacture at most 12,000 CD players annually. It also manufactures as many additional head mechanisms as can be sold. The incremental cost of manufacturing the head mechanism is $15 per unit. The incremental cost of manufacturing a CD player (including the cost of the head mechanism) is $25 per unit, and any number of CD players can be sold for $35 each in the external market.

REQUIRED

1. What are the incremental costs minus revenues from sales to external buyers for the company as a whole if the Compact Disc Division transfers 10,000 CD players to the Assembly Division and sells the remaining 2,000 CD players on the external market?
2. What are the incremental costs minus revenues from sales to external buyers for the company as a whole if the Compact Disc Division sells 12,000 CD players on the external market and the Assembly Division accepts Johnson's offer at (a) $38 per CD player or (b) $45 per CD player?
3. What is the minimum transfer price per CD player at which the Compact Disc Division would be willing to transfer 10,000 CD players to the Assembly Division?
4. Suppose that the transfer price is set to the minimum computed in requirement 3 plus $1, and the division managers at Orsilo are free to make their own profit-maximizing sourcing and selling decisions. Now, Johnson offers 10,000 CD players for $40.50 each.
   a. What decisions will the managers of the Compact Disc Division and Assembly Division make?
   b. Are these decisions optimal for Orsilo as a whole?
   c. Based on this exercise, at what price would you recommend the transfer price be set?

23-40 Goal-congruence, taxes, different market conditions. TECA Halifax makes kids' bicycles. The Frames Division makes and paints the frames and supplies them to the Assembly Division where the bicycles are assembled. TECA is a successful and profitable corporation that attributes much of its success to its decentralized operating style. Each division manager is compensated on the basis of division operating income.

① ② ③ ④ ⑤
1. Contribution margin from new frame, $272

The Assembly Division currently acquires all its frames from the Frames Division. The Assembly Division manager could purchase similar frames in the market for $480.

The Frames Division is currently operating at 80% of its capacity of 4,000 frames (units) and has the following particulars:

Direct materials ($150 per unit × 3,200 units)	$480,000
Direct manufacturing labour ($60 per unit × 3,200 units)	192,000
Variable manufacturing overhead costs ($30 per unit × 3,200 units)	96,000
Fixed manufacturing overhead costs	624,000

All the Frames Division's 3,200 units are currently transferred to the Assembly Division. No frames are sold in the outside market.

The Frames Division has just received an order for 2,000 units at $450 per frame that would utilize half the capacity of the plant. The order has to be either taken in full or rejected totally. The order is for a slightly different frame than what the Frames Division currently makes but takes the same amount of manufacturing time. To produce the new frame would require direct materials per unit of $100, direct manufacturing labour per unit of $48, and variable manufacturing overhead costs per unit of $30.

INSTRUCTIONS

Form groups of two or three students to complete the following requirements.

REQUIRED

1. From the viewpoint of TECA Halifax as a whole, should the Frames Division accept the order for the 2,000 units?
2. What range of transfer prices result in achieving the actions determined to be optimal in requirement 1, if division managers act in a decentralized manner?
3. The manager of the Assembly Division has proposed a transfer price for the frames equal to the full cost of the frames including an allocation of overhead costs. The Frames Division allocates overhead costs to engines on the basis of the total capacity of the plant used to manufacture the frames.
   a. Calculate the transfer price for the frames transferred to the Assembly Division under this arrangement.
   b. Do you think that the transfer price calculated in requirement 3a will result in achieving the actions determined to be optimal in requirement 1, if division managers act in a decentralized manner?

c. Comment in general on one advantage and one disadvantage of using full costs of the producing division as the basis for setting transfer prices.

4. Now consider the effect of income taxes.

   a. Suppose the Assembly Division is located in a country that imposes a 10% tax on income earned within its boundaries, while the Frames Division is located in a country that imposes no tax on income earned within its boundaries. What transfer price would be chosen by TECA to minimize tax payments for the corporation as a whole? Assume that only transfer prices that are greater than or equal to full manufacturing costs and less than or equal to the market price of "substantially similar" engines are acceptable to the taxing authorities.

   b. Suppose that TECA announces the transfer price computed in requirement 4a to price all transfers between the Frames and Assembly Divisions. Each division manager then acts autonomously to maximize division operating income. Will division managers acting in a decentralized manner achieve the actions determined to be optimal in requirement 1?

5. Consider your responses to requirements 1 to 4 and assume the Frames Division will continue to have opportunities for outside business as described in requirement 1. What transfer-pricing policy would you recommend TECA use and why? Would you continue to evaluate division performance on the basis of division operating incomes?

Multinational Performance Measurement and Compensation

Qualitative and Nonfinancial Measures Are Relevant

BCE, Canada's largest telecommunications service provider, reports performance data in its 2010 annual report. BCE's purpose is to be recognized as Canada's leading communications company. The five strategic imperatives are to improve customer service to its 20 million customers; accelerate the availability of and improve its wireless network services; improve market share in bundled wireline Internet and TV services; invest in broadband Fibre TV, internet, and Bell wireless services; and achieve a competitive cost structure. BCE reported 9 million fewer customer service calls and an improvement in customer satisfaction and installation success for same-day service, and a shorter installation cycle. BCE increased wireless access to 33 new devices, including BlackBerry, Apple, Android, and Windows smartphones. Innovative service bundling has won back 14% of lost customers in one year and reduced customer switching by 17%. In financial terms, BCE has invested $3 billion in the company and saved $290 million in costs compared to 2009.

The company has a pay-for-performance executive compensation structure based on these financial and nonfinancial performance measures of achievement. In advance of the adoption of new legislation, the company provides a separate Compensation Discussion and Analysis report.

After studying this chapter, you should be able to

1. Analyze and evaluate alternative measures of financial performance.

2. Evaluate current-cost and historical-cost asset measurement methods.

3. Analyze the technical difficulties that arise when comparing the performance of divisions operating in different countries.

4. Evaluate the behavioural effects of salaries and incentives in compensation arrangements.

5. Apply strategic concepts to analyze the four levers of control and evaluate their usefulness.

This chapter examines technical, governance, and behavioural issues in designing and implementing appropriate financial and nonfinancial performance measures. We have discussed multi-dimensional BSC performance measurement as a strategy. Performance measures are also a central component of a management accounting control system (MACS). To be effective, however, MACS must motivate not only internal goal congruence but also external governance achievements.

Performance measurement of managers is used in decisions about their salaries, bonuses, future assignments, and career advancement. Moreover, the very act of measuring their performance can motivate managers to strive for the goals used in their evaluation and ignore achieving other equally important goals. At a higher level of analysis, performance measurement of an organization's subunits is a prerequisite for allocating resources within that organization. At the highest corporate level of analysis, the corporation forecasts revenue, costs, and investments and periodically compares actual achievements with pro forma expected targets. Feedback then guides top management's decisions about future allocations.

FINANCIAL AND NONFINANCIAL PERFORMANCE MEASURES

1 Analyze and evaluate alternative measures of financial performance.

Chapters 13 and 23 noted how the information used in a MACS can be financial or nonfinancial. Many common financial performance measures, such as operating income, rely on internal financial and accounting information. Increasingly complex governance legislation, however, means companies must supplement internal financial with nonfinancial measures (for example, manufacturing lead time) and external nonfinancial information (such as customer satisfaction). In addition, companies often benchmark their financial and nonfinancial measures against other companies that are regarded as "best performers." To compete effectively in the global market, companies need to perform at or near the "best of the breed."

Corporations adopting a *balanced scorecard* (BSC; see Chapter 13)[1] approach to performance measurement have progressed to include risk measures. Incorporating risk is most often in the form of probable financial outcomes. Enterprise risk planning software includes automated collection of hundreds of possible financial and non-financial measures of performance. The advantage of enterprise risk planning software over a BSC is that more refined data discloses important interdependencies. There is less chance that either subunits or individuals will be unfairly rewarded or penalized for performance that depends on outcomes of other subunits or individuals.

Some performance measures, such as the number of new patents developed, are structural changes to intellectual capital, which have a long-run time horizon. It is sensible to provide a form of deferred compensation to individuals responsible to assure expected benefits are realized. Other measures, such as direct materials efficiency variances, overhead spending variances, and yield, have a short-run time horizon. Immediate cash or non-cash compensation elements are sensible. We focus on the most widely used performance measures covering an intermediate to long-run time horizon. These are internal financial measures based on accounting numbers routinely maintained by organizations.

GOVERNANCE AND COMPENSATION DECISIONS

Performance measurement is another example of a complex decision process wherein each decision informs and is interdependent with others. As has been explained in earlier chapters, there are very few direct causal relationships in a business compared to cost-benefit relationships. The relationship between corporate performance measurement and executive compensation is one prominent example.

The corporate management team must decide on performance measures upon which executive and other compensation will be based. But we live in a time of

---

[1] R. S. Kaplan and D. P. Norton, *The Strategy-Focused Organization: How Balanced Scorecard Companies Thrive in the New Business Environment* (Boston: Harvard Business School Press, 2001); and R. S. Kaplan and D. P. Norton, *Strategy Maps: Converting Intangible Assets into Tangible Outcomes* (Boston: Harvard Business School Press, 2004).

increased scrutiny of executive compensation. When the financial meltdown of 2007–2009 threatened global economic prosperity, employees who had lost their jobs because companies declared bankruptcy reacted with anger to news of executive salary, bonus, and severance payments in the millions of dollars. Compensation policies appear to have systematically enriched a handful of executive billionaires at the expense of all other stakeholders.

By June 2010, the U.S. Federal Reserve Bank had issued formal guidance to the financial industry on executive compensation. Financial services corporations in the industry must disclose how compensation policy and practice balance risk and return to prevent imprudent risk-taking. Various global stock exchanges have proposed sweeping changes to corporate governance to require independence of the Board of Directors (BOD), the Compensation Committee, and procedures of the committee. The Canadian Securities Association (CSA) plans to put legislation in place similar to that of the United States, applicable to companies with a year-end on or after October 31, 2011. Government oversight agencies and private shareholder activist groups such as the Canadian Coalition for Good Governance (CCGG) and Institutional Shareholder Services Inc. (ISS) have intensified their scrutiny of corporate performance measures and compensation policies.

With respect to government watchdog agencies, by October 2010 the U.S. Securities and Exchange Commission (SEC) had released proposed new legislation for all publicly listed corporations. By January 25, 2011, the Dodd-Frank Wall Street Reform and Consumer Protection Act mandated **say on pay**, which requires that shareholders vote for or against executive compensation packages. There are now many stakeholders involved in what used to be a purely corporate internal decision on performance and executive compensation, as illustrated in Exhibit 24-1.

EXHIBIT 24-1
Constraints on Board of Directors' (BOD) Performance Measurement Decisions

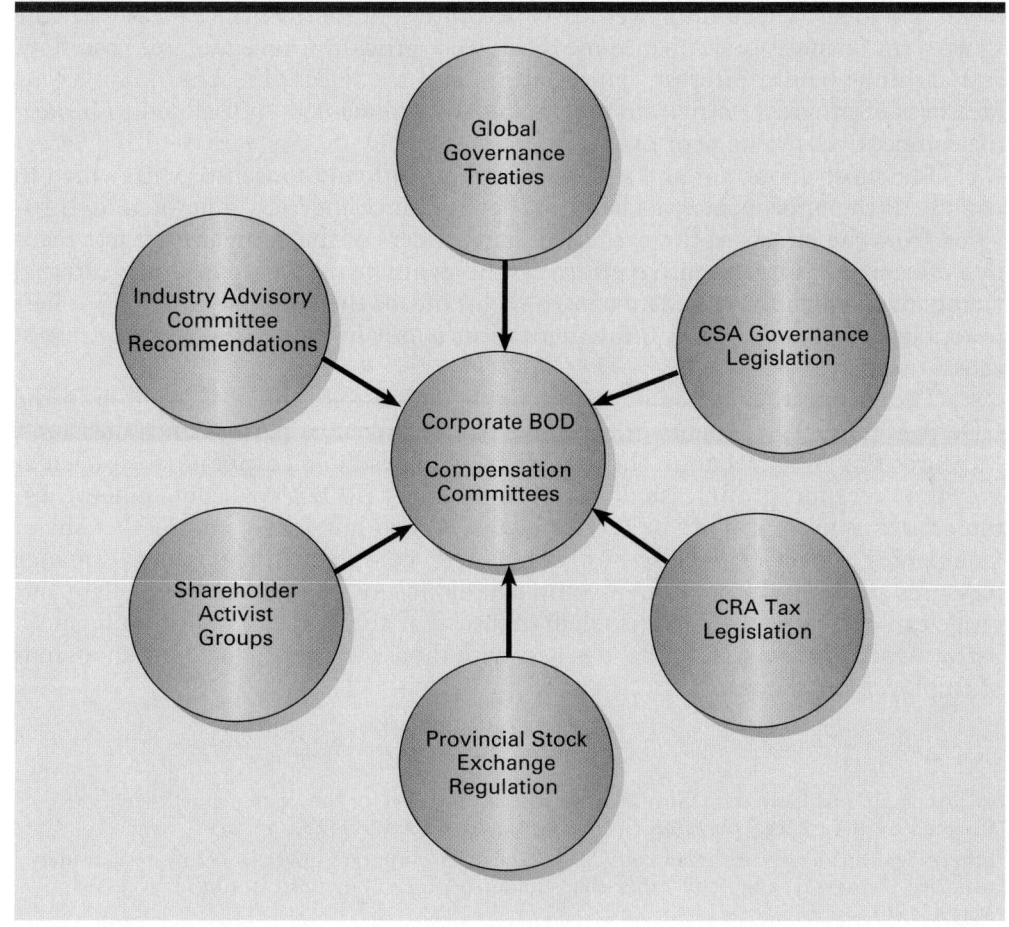

In response to the increasing presence of multinational corporations (MNC), agencies such as the Organisation for Economic Co-operation and Development (OECD) have established global treaties and guidelines for corporate governance, of which Canada is a signatory. There also exist global corporate governance indices (CGI) enabling investors to review the stringency of governance practices required in different countries.[2] The higher the stringency and rate of successful enforcement, the lower the risk to an investor's return.

In Canada, the CSA and Canada Revenue Agency (CRA) are discussing new legislation. The provincial Ontario Securities Commission (OSC), Toronto Stock Exchange (TSX), and private watchdogs such as the Institute of Corporate Directors (ICD) Blue Ribbon Panel on the Governance of Executive Compensation in Canada have also weighed in, making recommendations to improve decisions made by BOD. The ICD has recommended, among other things, that practice of **malus**, or clawback, of previously awarded compensation be instituted when performance has been poor, along with full disclosure of any severance compensation known as a golden parachute.

At the beginning of 2011, the OSC, which regulates companies listed on Canada's largest stock exchange, the TSX, published a staff notice that it was considering the introduction of mandatory say on pay regulations in Canada. To be meaningful, say on pay regulation requires expanded corporate disclosure. The OSC proposed this in the form of a Compensation Disclosure and Analysis (CD&A) section required in annual report. The CD&A would disclose the corporate philosophy on executive pay, specific performance measures, all elements of compensation, and any interdependencies among them.[3] The Canadian Institute of Chartered Accountants (CICA) has noted that the proposed CSA legislation is included within the scope of responsibility for corporate governance under the existing NI 52-109 legislation.

Some corporations, like BCE Inc., have already started disclosing compensation details in their annual reports. BCE Inc. provided a 62-page CD&A for named executive officers of the company in their 2010 annual report. All compensation elements and total compensation were disclosed with some performance measures. The short-term financial performance measures were growth in revenue, free cash flow, and earnings before interest, depreciation, and tax (EBIDT). The nonfinancial measures of progress on five strategic imperatives remained undisclosed to protect the competitive advantage of BCE.

The most important and perhaps the most difficult consensus with which to comply is the appropriate decision on performance metrics. The benefits provided from the efforts of the executives and officers of the company are not readily determined. The executive effort can be overwhelmed by change in external factors over which they have no control. This means the recommendation for best practices are apparent, but implementation is not because the metrics are not causal measures.

The proposed increase in plain-language disclosure of compensation in the CD&A requires all elements of executive pay be linked to performance measures. Measures should correlate to the achievement of desirable corporate goals such as growth in revenue, profit, cash flow, return on equity (ROE), cost containment, customer satisfaction, product or service quality, green initiatives, and market share. Companies must also disclose how non-GAAP-compliant financial performance measures are derived from GAAP-compliant disclosure. But no amount of plain language can overcome the basic problem of just what correlates to improved financial performance in a complex global business with thousands of products and thousands of employees on the team.

---

[2]C. Strenger, "The Corporate Governance Scorecard: A Tool for the Implementation of Corporate Governance," *Corporate Governance* (January 2004): 11–15.

[3]http://www.canadiansecuritieslaw.com/2011/01/articles/corporate-governance/osc-to-consider-majority-voting-sayonpay-and-other-shareholder-democracy-issues/print.html, accessed May 15, 2011.

One form of compensation is the award of stock options, which provide reward in the short term. But many factors out of the executive's control could generate a short-term price appreciation in shares that are independent of the executive's performance. The bonus awarded fails to reflect good management and any malus based on share price will fail to reflect bad management, especially if the executive is a new appointment. Under specific criteria, CRA permits the executive to shelter half of the benefit received from the stock option compensation.

There also exists conflict between recommended best governance practices to focus on short-term over long-term performance measures. The nature of investment, as explained in Chapters 21 and 22, is to obtain return over the lifetime of the investments made in excess of the cost of the investments. But this entails risk because the future cannot be known. Pay for performance measures in the best interests of shareholders would, logically, include long-term achievement and deferred compensation.

Deferred compensation implies the award of restricted stock options that executives would forfeit should they fail to meet the performance criteria within the specified time period. In theory, the executive who owns the right to purchase shares in the long term will work hard to improve the price of the shares. But CRA immediately taxes restricted stock options with a deferral of longer than three years as compensation in the year they are awarded. A short-term increase is as likely as not to have dissipated by the time executives can actually purchase or forfeit the shares. The current federal tax laws, if left unchanged, obstruct the implementation of the recommended best governance and compensation policies.

From the management team's perspective, there is a set of interdependent decisions to be made in a dynamic legislative environment. Each decision will influence those before and those made after it. The decisions are by no means sequential and the team must often retrace previous decisions before implementation of a compensation policy and selection of performance measures can be finalized. By and large, despite the availability of nonfinancial performance measures and the principles of BSC, compensation remains determined by accounting measures. A typical series of decisions could be:

◆ *Decide which accounting measures are best aligned with the executive team's financial goals.* For example, does operating income, net income, return on assets (ROA), or revenue best measure a subunit's financial performance?

◆ *Decide on the time horizons of each performance measure, short or long term, strategic or operating.* For example, should performance measures such as ROA be calculated for one year or for a multiyear horizon?

◆ *Decide how to define the components of performance measure.* For example, should assets be defined as total assets or net assets (total assets minus total liabilities)?

◆ *Decide on the appropriate measurement method.* For example, should assets be measured at historical cost, current cost, or present value?

◆ *Decide on the criteria—the target against which to gauge the level of performance.* For example, should all subunits have as a target the same required ROR on assets?

◆ *Decide on the timing of feedback.* For example, should manufacturing performance reports be sent to top management daily, weekly, or monthly?

◆ *Decide on the elements of the compensation package.* For example, the percentage of fixed and variable salary, share awards, option grants, pension, medical benefits, and perquisites such as personal accommodation and travel may all be elements of executive compensation.

Issues with which a decision team must cope will depend on top management's beliefs about how well proposed measures achieve both cost-effectiveness and goal-congruence. On the one hand, measures must isolate incentives to measure individual and team effort and whether they preserve an appropriate level of subunit autonomy, as discussed in Chapter 23. On the other hand, decisions must achieve benefit for shareholders, not merely executives. Formal structures such as statements of mission, vision, strategy, and beliefs all clarify how coherent the corporate foundations are for selecting robust performance measures.

The Compensation Analysis and Discussion—Barrick Gold

At their annual meeting, the agenda for companies such as Barrick Gold include shareholder voting on important matters such as executive compensation. Disclosure for Barrick's 2011 annual meeting included a formal notice and the Management Proxy Circular disclosing relevant data on voting matters. Of the 66-page document, 54 pages disclosed details of corporate governance practices and executive compensation. Specific remuneration elements and their cash value, termination agreements, and short-term and deferred compensation elements were disclosed.

The financial performance measures included earnings per share, operating cash flow per share, and return on equity, along with the threshold, target, and maximum goal, and the rating and weight attributed to each measure. Similar detail was provided measuring growth in millions of ounces of production and for cost per ounce of production as well as increase in reserves. The Dow Jones Sustainability Ranking was the measure of performance for environment, health, and safety along with lost time from injury.

Other financial metrics were growth in net income, cash flow, and net asset growth. Barrick's measure of share price appreciation relative to U.S., international, and Canadian measures of overall growth in stock market value and the markets for precious metals were also part of the performance measures. Barrick discloses the measures not only by business unit but also by individual. The individual measures are customized to reflect scope of control.

Barrick, by providing more disclosure than required, is following a strategy to take a first-mover advantage. It will gain benefits from being the leader in exceeding the current minimum governance requirements. In so doing, it reduces the risk of a legal challenge to its corporate governance practices.

Sources: http://www.barrick.com/Theme/Barrick/files/docs_annual/2011/Management-Proxy-Circular.pdf, accessed May 16, 2011; http://www.barrick.com/Theme/Barrick/files/docs_annual/2008% 20Annual%20Report%20-%20English.pdf, accessed May 16, 2011.

ACCOUNTING PERFORMANCE MEASURES

Four measures are commonly used to evaluate the financial performance of organization subunits. These performance measures all use financial accounting information:

◆ Return on investment (ROI).
◆ Residual income (RI).
◆ Economic value added (EVA).
◆ Return on sales (ROS).

We illustrate these measures using the example of Hospitality Inns, which owns and operates three motels located in Saskatoon, Saskatchewan; Brandon, Manitoba; and Hull, Quebec. Exhibit 24-2 summarizes data for each of the three motels for the most recent year (2013). At present, Hospitality Inns does not allocate to the three separate motels the total long-term debt of the company.

Exhibit 24-2 indicates that the Hull motel generates the highest operating income, $510,000. The Brandon motel generates $300,000; the Saskatoon motel, $240,000. But can the results be reliably interpreted that the Hull motel is the most "successful"? Actually, the comparison of operating income ignores potential differences in the size of the investments in the different motels. An investment is a long-term cash allocation decision intended to realize returns (see Chapter 21). The question is how large the return should be, given the resources that were used to earn it. When the CEO of a company like Thomson Reuters Corp. can earn in excess of $36 million, of which over $28 million is in shares, the expense is significant.

EXHIBIT 24-2
Annual Financial Data for Hospitality Inns for 2013

	A	B	C	D	E
1		Saskatoon	Brandon	Hull	Total
2		(1)	(2)	(3)	(4) = (1) + (2) + (3)
3	Motel revenue	$1,200,000	$1,400,000	$3,185,000	$5,785,000
4	Motel variable costs	310,000	375,000	995,000	1,680,000
5	Motel fixed costs	650,000	725,000	1,680,000	3,055,000
6	Motel operating income	240,000	300,000	510,000	1,050,000
7	Interest costs on long-term debt at 10%				450,000
8	Income before income taxes				600,000
9	Income tax at 30%				180,000
10	Net income				$ 420,000
11	Net book values at the end of 2013:				
12	Current assets	$ 400,000	$ 500,000	$ 600,000	$1,500,000
13	Long-term assets	600,000	1,500,000	2,400,000	4,500,000
14	Total assets	$1,000,000	$2,000,000	$3,000,000	$6,000,000
15	Current liabilities	$ 50,000	$ 150,000	$ 300,000	$ 500,000
16	Long-term debt	—	—	—	4,500,000
17	Shareholders' equity	—	—	—	1,000,000
18	Total liabilities and shareholders' equity				$6,000,000

RETURN ON INVESTMENT (ROI)

Return on investment (ROI) is an accounting measure of income divided by an accounting measure of investment. ROI tells managers how much income each dollar of investment generates. Here is the intuition for the two ROI components:

1. Income ÷ Revenues (return on sales, or ROS) tells how much of each revenue dollar becomes income; the goal is to get higher income per revenue dollar. Depending on the accounting accrual used to measure income, either operating or net margin comprises this component of ROI.

2. Revenues ÷ Investment (investment turnover) tells how many revenue dollars are generated by each dollar of investment; the goal is to make each investment dollar "work harder" to generate more revenues.

$$\text{Return on investment (ROI)} = \frac{\text{Income}}{\text{Investment}}$$

ROI is the most popular approach to incorporating the investment base into a performance measure. ROI appeals conceptually because it blends all the major ingredients of profitability (revenues, costs, and investment) into a single number. ROI can be compared with the rate of return on opportunities elsewhere, inside or outside the company. Like any single performance measure, however, ROI should be used cautiously and in conjunction with other performance measures.

ROI is also called the accounting rate of return or the accrual accounting rate of return (see Chapter 21) because accruals are included in both the numerator and denominator of this performance measure. Managers usually use the term *ROI* in the context of evaluating the performance of a division or subunit, and *accrual accounting rate of return* (AARR) when evaluating a project. Companies vary in the way they define both the numerator and the denominator of the ROI. For example, some firms use operating income for the numerator; other firms use net income. Some firms use total assets in the denominator; others use total assets minus current liabilities.

Hospitality Inns can increase ROI by increasing revenues or decreasing costs (both these actions increase the numerator), or by decreasing investments (which decreases the denominator). ROI can often provide more insight into performance when it is divided into the following components:

$$\frac{\text{Revenues}}{\text{Investment}} \times \frac{\text{Income}}{\text{Revenues}} = \frac{\text{Income}}{\text{Investment}}$$

This approach is widely known as the *DuPont method of profitability analysis.* The DuPont approach recognizes that there are two basic ingredients in profit making: using assets to generate more revenue and increasing income per dollar of revenue. An improvement in either ingredient without changing the other increases return on investment.

Consider the ROI of each of the three Hospitality motels in Exhibit 24-2. For our calculations, we are using the operating income of each motel for the numerator and total assets of each motel for the denominator.

Motel	Operating Income	÷	Total Assets	=	ROI
Saskatoon	$240,000	÷	$1,000,000	=	24%
Brandon	$300,000	÷	$2,000,000	=	15%
Hull	$510,000	÷	$3,000,000	=	17%

Using these ROI figures, the Saskatoon motel appears to make the best use of its total assets.

Assume that the top management at Hospitality Inns adopts a 30% target ROI for the Saskatoon motel. How can this return be attained? The DuPont method illustrates the present situation and three alternatives:

	Operating Income (1)	Revenue (2)	Total Assets (3)	Operating Income ÷ Revenue (4) = (1) ÷ (2)	×	Revenue ÷ Total Assets (5) = (2) ÷ (3)	=	Operating Income ÷ Total Assets (6) = (1) ÷ (3)
Current Situation	$240,000	$1,200,000	$1,000,000	0.20	×	1.2	=	24%
Alternatives								
A. Decrease assets (e.g., receivables). Revenue and operating income per dollar of revenue remain constant	$240,000	$1,200,000	$ 800,000	0.20	×	1.5	=	30%
B. Increase revenues (e.g., sell more rooms). Assets and operating income per dollar of revenue remain constant.	$300,000	$1,500,000	$1,000,000	0.20	×	1.5	=	30%
C. Decrease costs (e.g., efficient maintenance) to increase operating income per dollar of revenue; assets remain constant.	$300,000	$1,200,000	$1,000,000	0.25	×	1.2	=	30%

Other alternatives, such as increasing the selling price per room, could increase both the revenue per dollar of total assets and the operating income per dollar of revenue. Managers vary in their judgment of how best to define income (for example, operating income or net income) and investment (for example, total assets employed or total assets employed minus current liabilities).

ROI highlights the benefits that managers can obtain by reducing their investments in current or fixed assets. Some managers are conscious of the need to boost revenues or to control costs but pay less attention to reducing their investment base. Reducing investments means decreasing idle cash, managing credit judiciously, determining proper inventory levels, and spending carefully on fixed assets.

Operating income or earnings before interest and taxes (EBIT) is a measure of how well managers have deployed assets to generate an operating return. Incurring interest is not a result of any operating decisions made from day to day but rather a strategic decision made by the CFO and the team in the finance subunit. The expanded DuPont measure of ROI does contain a specific ratio to measure the effectiveness and efficiency of financial management. Tax is also the responsibility of the CFO and the management team in finance, not the operating managers. The expanded DuPont measure of ROI contains another specific ratio to measure the effectiveness and efficiency of tax management.

To use net income (after-tax earnings) in the numerator of an ROI measure could misstate by a material amount the actual operating return generated by the operating investments. This is why the operating income is more appropriate than either earnings before tax or net income.

RESIDUAL INCOME (RI)

Residual income (RI) is income minus a required dollar return on the investment:[4]

$$\text{Residual income} = \text{Income} - (\text{Required rate of return} \times \text{Investment})$$

The required rate of return (ROR) multiplied by investment is also called the **imputed cost** of the investment. Imputed costs are costs recognized in particular situations that are not regularly recognized by accrual accounting procedures. An imputed cost is not recognized in accounting records because it is not an incremental cost but instead represents the return forgone by Hospitality Inns as a result of tying up cash in various investments of similar risk. The ROR management should use to calculate residual income is the company's **weighted-average cost of capital (WACC)**. WACC equals the after-tax average cost of all the long-term funds used.

Conceptually, it would be better to use the cost of capital based on each subunit's risk level. For example, an oil-exploration division would warrant a higher required rate of return than an oil-refining division because the risk of failing to find oil is far higher than the risks of refining oil already being produced. Generally, the cost of capital based on each subunit's risk level is not externally available.

Assume that each motel faces similar risks. Hospitality Inns defines residual income for each motel as motel operating income minus a required rate of return of 12% of the total assets of the motel:

Motel	Operating Income	−	Required Rate of Return	×	Investment	=	Residual Income
Saskatoon	$240,000	−	12%	×	$(1,000,000)	=	$120,000
Brandon	$300,000	−	12%	×	$(2,000,000)	=	$ 60,000
Hull	$510,000	−	12%	×	$(3,000,000)	=	$150,000

Given the 12% ROR, the Hull motel is performing best in terms of residual income. Generally, residual income is more likely than ROI to induce goal-congruence. This preference for RI over ROI parallels the preference for NPV over IRR when managers produce a capital budget.

Some firms favour the residual-income approach because managers will concentrate on maximizing an absolute amount (dollars of residual income) rather than a percentage (return on investment). The objective of maximizing residual income assumes that as long as a division earns a rate in excess of the ROR, that specific division should expand.

[4]Just as in the case of ROI, companies using RI vary in the way they define income (for example, operating income, pretax income, or net income) and investment (for example, total assets or total assets minus current liabilities).

The objective of maximizing ROI may induce managers of highly profitable divisions to reject projects that, from the viewpoint of the organization as a whole, should be accepted. To illustrate, assume that Hospitality's required ROR is 12%. Assume also that an expansion of the Saskatoon motel will increase its operating income by $160,000 and increase its total assets by $800,000. The ROI for the expansion is 20% ($160,000 ÷ $800,000), which makes it attractive to Hospitality Inns as a whole. By making this expansion, however, the Saskatoon manager will see the motel's ROI decrease:

$$\text{Pre-expansion ROI} = \frac{\$240,000}{\$1,000,000} = 24\%$$

$$\text{Post-expansion ROI} = \frac{(\$240,000 + \$160,000)}{(\$1,000,000 + \$800,000)} = \frac{\$400,000}{\$1,800,000} = 22.2\%$$

The annual bonus paid to the Saskatoon manager may decrease if ROI is a key component in the bonus calculation and the expansion option is selected. In contrast, if the annual bonus is a function of residual income, the Saskatoon manager will view the expansion favourably:

$$\text{Pre-expansion residual income} = \$240,000 - (12\% \times \$1,000,000) = \$120,000$$
$$\text{Post-expansion residual income} = \$400,000 - (12\% \times \$1,800,000) = \$184,000$$

Goal-congruence is more likely to be promoted by using residual income rather than ROI as a measure of the division manager's performance.

ECONOMIC VALUE ADDED (EVA)

Economic value added (EVA) is a specific type of residual income calculation that attracted considerable attention during the dot-com boom of the late 1990s.[5] The difference between this and other accounting performance measures is that this measure does not use a reported GAAP accrual in the numerator. Economic value added substitutes the following numbers in the residual-income calculations: (1) income equal to after-tax operating income, (2) a required rate of return equal to the weighted-average cost of capital, and (3) investment equal to total assets minus current liabilities.[6] We use the Hospitality Inns data in Exhibit 24-2 to illustrate EVA.

$$\begin{matrix} \text{Economic} \\ \text{value added} \\ \text{(EVA)} \end{matrix} = \begin{matrix} \text{After-tax} \\ \text{operating income} \end{matrix} - \left[\begin{matrix} \text{Weighted-average} \\ \text{cost of capital} \end{matrix} \times \left(\begin{matrix} \text{Total} \\ \text{assets} \end{matrix} - \begin{matrix} \text{Current} \\ \text{liabilities} \end{matrix} \right) \right]$$

The key calculation is the weighted-average cost of capital (WACC). Hospitality Inns has two sources of long-term funds—long-term debt with a market and book value of $4.5 million issued at an interest rate of 10%, and equity capital that has a market value of $3 million (and a book value of $1 million).[7] Because interest costs are tax-deductible, the after-tax cost of debt financing equals 0.10 (1 − tax rate) = 0.10 × (1 − 0.30) = 0.10 × 0.70 = 0.07, or 7%. The cost of equity capital is the opportunity cost to investors of not investing their capital in another investment

[5]O'Byrne and D. Young, *EVA and Value-Based Management: A Practical Guide to Implementation* (New York: McGraw-Hill, 2000); J. Stein, J. Shiely, and I. Ross, *The EVA Challenge: Implementing Value Added Change in an Organization* (New York: John Wiley and Sons, 2001).

[6]When implementing EVA, companies make several adjustments to the operating income and asset numbers reported under generally accepted accounting principles. For example, when calculating EVA, costs such as R&D, restructuring costs, and leases that have long-run benefits are recorded as assets (which are then amortized), rather than as current operating costs. The goal of these adjustments is to obtain a better representation of the economic assets, particularly intangible assets, used to earn income. Of course, the specific adjustments applicable to a company will depend on its individual circumstances.

[7]The market value of Hospitality Inns' equity exceeds book value because book value, based on historical cost, does not measure the current value of the company's assets, and because various intangible assets, such as the company's brand name, are not shown at current value in the balance sheet under GAAP.

that is similar in risk to Hospitality Inns. Suppose that Hospitality's cost of equity capital is 15%.[8] The WACC computation, which uses market values of debt and equity, is as follows:

$$\text{WACC} = \frac{(0.07 \times \$4,500,000) + (0.15 \times \$3,000,000)}{\$4,500,000 + \$3,000,000}$$

$$= \frac{(\$315,000 + \$450,000)}{\$7,500,000} = \frac{\$765,000}{\$7,500,000}$$

$$= 0.102 \text{ or } 10.2\%$$

The company applies the same WACC to all its motels, since each motel faces similar risks.

Total assets minus current liabilities (see Exhibit 24-2, p. 969) can also be computed as:

Total assets − Current liabilities = Long-term assets + Current assets − Current liabilities
= Long-term assets + Working capital

where working capital = current assets – current liabilities. After-tax motel operating income is:

$$\frac{\text{Motel operating}}{\text{income}} \times (1 - \text{Tax rate}) = \frac{\text{Motel operating}}{\text{income}} \times (1 - 0.30) = \frac{\text{Motel operating}}{\text{income}} \times 0.70$$

EVA calculations for Hospitality Inns are as follows:

Motel	After-Tax Operating Income −	Weighted-Average Cost of Capital ×	Total Assets	Current − Liabilities =	EVA
Saskatoon	$240,000 × 0.70 −	[10.2%	× ($1,000,000 −	$ 50,000)] =	$71,100
Brandon	$300,000 × 0.70 −	[10.2%	× ($2,000,000 −	$150,000)] =	$21,300
Hull	$510,000 × 0.70 −	[10.2%	× ($3,000,000 −	$300,000)] =	$81,600

The Hull motel has the highest EVA. EVA, like residual income, charges managers for the cost of their investments in long-term assets and working capital. Value is created only if after-tax operating income exceeds the cost of investing the capital. To improve EVA, managers must earn more operating income with the same capital, use less capital, or invest capital in high-return projects.

After implementing EVA, CSX, a railroad company, began running trains with three locomotives instead of four by scheduling arrivals just in time for unloading, rather than having trains arrive at their destination several hours in advance. The idle time decreased as the capital utilization rate increased, without affecting service to the customer. The result was higher profits because of lower fuel costs, and less capital invested in locomotives. Chief executive officers of companies such as AT&T, Briggs & Stratton, Coca-Cola, CSX, Equifax, FMC, and Quaker Oats credit the EVA concept with motivating decisions that have increased shareholder value.

RETURN ON SALES

The income-to-revenue (sales) ratio—often called **return on sales (ROS)**—is a frequently used financial performance measure. ROS is one component of ROI in the DuPont method of profitability analysis. To calculate the ROS of each of Hospitality's motels, we use operating income divided by revenues. The ROS for each motel is:

Motel	Operating Income	÷	Revenues	=	ROS
Saskatoon	$240,000	÷	$1,200,000	=	20.00%
Brandon	$300,000	÷	$1,400,000	=	21.43%
Hull	$510,000	÷	$3,185,000	=	16.01%

[8]For details on calculating cost of equity capital adjusted for risk, see J. Van Horne, *Financial Management and Policy*, 12th ed. (Upper Saddle River, NJ: Prentice Hall, 2002).

The Brandon motel has the highest ROS, whereas its performance is rated worse than the other motels using performance measures such as ROI, RI, and EVA.

The following table summarizes the performance and ranking of each motel under each of the four performance measures:

Motel	ROI	Rank	Residual Income	Rank	EVA	Rank	ROS	Rank
Saskatoon	24%	1	$120,000	2	$71,100	2	20.00%	2
Brandon	15%	3	$ 60,000	3	$21,300	3	21.43%	1
Hull	17%	2	$150,000	1	$81,600	1	16.01%	3

The residual-income and EVA rankings differ from the ROI and ROS rankings. Consider the ROI and residual-income rankings for the Saskatoon and Hull motels. The Hull motel has a smaller ROI. Although its operating income is only slightly more than twice that of the Saskatoon motel ($510,000 versus $240,000), its total assets are three times as large ($3 million versus $1 million). The return on assets invested in the Hull motel is not as high as the return on assets invested in the Saskatoon motel. The Hull motel has a higher residual income because it earns a higher operating income after covering the 12% required return on investment.

The Brandon motel has the highest ROS but the lowest ROI, because although it earns very high income per dollar of revenue, it generates very low revenues per dollar of assets invested. None of the methods is superior to the others because each evaluates a slightly different aspect of performance. For example, in markets where revenue growth is limited, return on sales is the most meaningful indicator of a subunit's performance.

ROS measures how effectively costs are managed; ROI measures which investment yields the highest return. To evaluate overall aggregate performance, ROI or residual-income-based measures are more appropriate, since they consider both income earned and investments made. Residual-income and EVA measures overcome some of the goal-congruence problems that ROI measures might introduce. Some managers favour EVA because it explicitly considers tax effects, while pretax residual-income measures do not. Other managers favour pretax residual-income because it is easier to compute and because it often leads to the same conclusions as EVA. Generally, companies use multiple financial measures to evaluate performance.

SELECTING THE TIME HORIZON

Another consideration in designing accounting-based performance measures is choosing the time horizon of the measures. The ROI, RI, EVA, and ROS calculations represent the results for a single time period, a year in our example. Managers could take actions that cause short-run increases in these measures but are in conflict with the long-run interests of the organization. For example, managers may curtail R&D and plant maintenance in the last three months of a fiscal year to achieve a target level of annual operating income. For this reason, many companies evaluate subunits on the basis of ROI, RI, EVA, and ROS over multiple years.

Another reason for evaluating subunits over a multiyear time horizon is that the benefits of actions taken in the current period may not show up in short-run performance measures such as the current year's ROI or RI. For example, the investment in a new motel may adversely affect ROI and RI in the short run but benefit ROIs and RIs in the long run.

A multiyear analysis highlights another advantage of the RI measure. The net present value of all the cash flows over the life of an investment equals the net present value of RIs.[9] This means that if managers use net present value analysis to make investment decisions (as prescribed in Chapter 21), using multiyear RI to evaluate managers' performances achieves goal-congruence.

Another way that companies motivate managers to take a long-run perspective is by compensating them on changes in the market price of the company's shares (in addition to using multiyear accounting-based performance measures). Why does this approach help to extend managers' time horizons? Because share prices more rapidly incorporate the expected future period effects of current decisions.

DEFINING "INVESTMENT"

We use the different definitions of investment that companies use to illustrate the second phase of designing accounting-based performance measures. Definitions include the following:

◆ *Total assets available.* Includes all business assets, regardless of their particular purpose.

◆ *Total assets employed.* Defined as total assets available minus idle assets and minus assets purchased for future expansion. For example, if the Hull motel in Exhibit 24-2 (p. 969) has unused land set aside for potential expansion, the total assets employed by the motel would exclude the cost of that land.

◆ *Working capital (current assets minus current liabilities) plus long-term assets.* This definition excludes that portion of current assets financed by short-term creditors.

◆ *Shareholders' equity.* Use of this definition for each individual motel in Exhibit 24-2 requires allocation of the long-term liabilities of Hospitality Inns to the three motels, which would then be deducted from the total assets of each motel.

Most companies that employ ROI, residual income, or EVA for performance measurement use either total assets available or working capital plus long-term assets as the definition of investment. However, when top management directs a division manager to carry extra assets, total assets employed can be more informative than total assets available. The most common rationale for using working capital plus long-term assets is that the division manager often influences decisions on the short-term debt of the division.

[9]We are grateful to S. Reichelstein for pointing this out. To see this equivalence, suppose a $400,000 investment in the Brandon motel increases operating income by $70,000 per year as follows: Increase in operating cash flows of $150,000 each year for five years minus amortization of $80,000 per year ($400,000 ÷ 5), assuming straight-line amortization and zero terminal disposal price. Amortization reduces the investment amount by $80,000 each year. Assuming a required rate of return of 12%, net present values of cash flows and residual incomes are as follows:

Year	0	1	2	3	4	5	Net Present Value
(1) Cash flow	−$400,000	$150,000	$150,000	$150,000	$150,000	$150,000	
(2) Present value of $1 discounted at 12%	1	0.89286	0.79719	0.71178	0.63552	0.56743	
(3) Present value: (1) × (2)	−$400,000	$133,929	$119,578	$106,767	$ 95,328	$ 85,115	$140,717
(4) Operating income		$ 70,000	$ 70,000	$ 70,000	$ 70,000	$ 70,000	
(5) Assets at start of year		$400,000	$320,000	$240,000	$160,000	$ 80,000	
(6) Capital charge: (5) × 12%		$ 48,000	$ 38,400	$ 28,800	$ 19,200	$ 9,600	
(7) Residual income: (4) − (6)		$ 22,000	$ 31,600	$ 41,200	$ 50,800	$ 60,400	
(8) Present value of RI: (7) × (2)		$ 19,643	$ 25,191	$ 29,325	$ 32,284	$ 34,273	$140,716

To illustrate the decision on performance measurement alternatives, we examine present value and accrual methods of historical cost, current cost, and current disposal price. We also examine the relevance of gross book value in contrast to net book value for depreciable assets. Managers have already chosen the accrual method of ROI, RI, or EVA and now must select the most appropriate, relevant accruals to estimate dollar values in the numerator and denominator. Companies such as Barrick Gold distinguish between measures of subunit and individual accomplishment. The individual spans of control along with the measure for its officers are described in the CD&A portion of the Management Proxy Circular.

CURRENT COST

Current cost is the cost of purchasing an asset today identical to the one currently held. It is the cost of purchasing the services provided by that asset if an identical asset cannot currently be purchased. Of course, measuring assets at current costs will result in different ROIs compared to the ROIs calculated based on historical costs.

We illustrate the current-cost ROI calculations using the Hospitality Inns example (see Exhibit 24-2) and then compare current- and historical-cost-based ROIs. Assume the following information about the long-term assets of each motel:

	Saskatoon	Brandon	Hull
Age of facility (at end of 2013)	8 years	4 years	2 years
Gross book value of long-term assets	$1,400,000	$2,100,000	$2,800,000
Accumulated amortization (straight-line)	800,000	600,000	400,000
Net book value (at end of 2013)	$ 600,000	$1,500,000	$2,400,000
Amortization expense for 2013	$ 100,000	$ 150,000	$ 200,000

Hospitality Inns assumes a 14-year estimated useful life, assumes no terminal disposal price for the physical facilities, and calculates amortization on a straight-line basis.

An index of construction costs for the eight-year period that Hospitality Inns has been operating (year 0 = 100) is as follows:

Year	1	2	3	4	5	6	7	8
Construction cost index	110	122	136	144	152	160	174	180

Earlier in this chapter we computed an ROI of 24% for Saskatoon, 15% for Brandon, and 17% for Hull (see p. 970). One possible explanation for the high ROI of Saskatoon is that this motel's long-term assets are expressed in terms of year 0 construction price levels (eight years ago) and that the long-term assets for the Brandon and Hull motels are expressed in terms of the higher, more recent construction price levels, which depress ROIs for these motels.

Exhibit 24-3 illustrates a step-by-step approach for incorporating current-cost estimates for long-term assets and amortization into the ROI calculation. The aim is to approximate what it would cost today to obtain assets that would produce the same expected operating income as the subunits currently earn. (Similar adjustments to represent current costs of capital employed and amortization can also be made in the residual income and EVA calculations.) The current-cost adjustment dramatically reduces the ROI of the Saskatoon motel:

	Historical-Cost ROI	Current-Cost ROI
Saskatoon	24%	10.81%
Brandon	15%	11.05%
Hull	17%	14.70%

Step 1: Restate long-term assets from gross book value at historical cost to gross book value at current cost as of the end of 2013:

Motel	Gross Book Value of Long-Term Assets at Historical Cost	×	Construction Cost Index in 2013	÷	Construction Cost Index in Construction Year	=	Gross Book Value of Long-Term Assets at Current Cost at End of 2013
Saskatoon	$1,400,000	×	(180	÷	100)	=	$2,520,000
Brandon	$2,100,000	×	(180	÷	144)	=	$2,625,000
Hull	$2,800,000	×	(180	÷	160)	=	$3,150,000

Step 2: Derive net book value of long-term assets at current cost as of the end of 2013. (Assume estimated useful life of each motel is 14 years.)

Motel	Gross Book Value of Long-Term Assets at Current Cost at End of 2013	×	(Estimated Remaining Useful Life	÷	Estimated Total Useful Life)	=	Net Book Value of Long-Term Assets at Current Cost at End of 2013
Saskatoon	$2,520,000	×	(6	÷	14)	=	$1,080,000
Brandon	$2,625,000	×	(10	÷	14)	=	$1,875,000
Hull	$3,150,000	×	(12	÷	14)	=	$2,700,000

Step 3: Calculate the current cost of total assets at the end of year 8. (Assume the current assets of each motel are expressed in year 8 dollars.)

Motel	Current Assets at end of 2013 (from Exhibit 24-2)	+	Long-Term Assets Derived in Step 2 (above)	=	Current Cost of Total Assets at End of 2013
Saskatoon	$400,000	+	$1,080,000	=	$1,480,000
Brandon	$500,000	+	$1,875,000	=	$2,375,000
Hull	$600,000	+	$2,700,000	=	$3,300,000

Step 4: Calculate current-cost amortization expense in 2013 dollars.

Motel	Gross Book Value of Long-Term Assets at Current Cost at End of 2013	÷	Estimated Total Useful Life	=	Current Cost of Amortization Expense in 2013 Dollars
Saskatoon	$2,520,000	÷	14	=	$180,000
Brandon	$2,625,000	÷	14	=	$187,500
Hull	$3,150,000	÷	14	=	$225,000

Step 5: Calculate year 8 operating income using year 8 current cost amortization.

Motel	Historical Cost Operating Income	−	Current Cost of Amortization Expense in 2013 Dollars	−	Historical Cost Amortization Expense	=	Operating Income for 2013 Using Current Cost Amortization Expense in 2013 Dollars
Saskatoon	$240,000	−	($180,000	−	$100,000)	=	$160,000
Brandon	$300,000	−	($187,500	−	$150,000)	=	$262,500
Hull	$510,000	−	($225,000	−	$200,000)	=	$485,000

Step 6: Calculate ROI using current cost estimates for long-term assets and amortization expense.

Motel	Operating Income for 2013 Using Current Cost Amortization Expense in 2013 Dollars	÷	Current Cost of Total Assets at End of 2013	=	ROI Using Current Cost Estimate
Saskatoon	$160,000	÷	$1,480,000	=	10.81%
Brandon	$262,500	÷	$2,375,000	=	11.05%
Hull	$485,000	÷	$3,300,000	=	14.70%

Adjusting for current costs negates differences in the investment base caused solely by differences in construction price levels. Consequently, compared to historical-cost ROI, current-cost ROI is a better measure of the current economic returns from the investment. For example, current-cost ROI indicates that taking into account current construction price levels, investing in a new motel in Saskatoon will result in an ROI closer to 10.8% than to 24%. If Hospitality Inns were to invest in a new motel today, investing in one like the Hull motel offers the best ROI.

A drawback of the current-cost method is that obtaining current-cost estimates for some assets can be difficult because the estimate requires a company to consider technological advances when determining the current cost of assets needed to earn today's operating income.[10]

LONG-TERM ASSETS: GROSS OR NET BOOK VALUE?

Because historical-cost investment measures are used often in practice, there has been much discussion about the relative merits of using gross book value (original cost) or net book value (original cost minus accumulated amortization). Using the data in Exhibit 24-2 on page 969, the ROI calculations using net book values and gross book values of plant and equipment are as follows:

	Operating Income (from Exhibit 24-2)	Net Book Value of Total Assets (from Exhibit 24-2)	Accumulated Amortization (from p. 976)	Gross Book Value of Total Assets	2013 ROI Using Net Book Value of Total Assets	2013 ROI Using Gross Book Value of Total Assets
	(1)	(2)	(3)	(4) = (2) + (3)	(5) = (1) ÷ (2)	(6) = (1) ÷ (4)
Saskatoon	$240,000	$1,000,000	$800,000	$1,800,000	24%	13.33%
Brandon	$300,000	$2,000,000	$600,000	$2,600,000	15%	11.54%
Hull	$510,000	$3,000,000	$400,000	$3,400,000	17%	15.00%

Using the gross book value, the ROI of the older Saskatoon motel (13.33%) is lower than that of the newer Hull motel (15%). Those who favour using gross book value claim that it enables more accurate comparisons across subunits. For example, using gross book value calculations, the return on the original plant and equipment investment is higher for the newer Hull motel than for the older Saskatoon motel. This probably reflects the decline in earning power of the Saskatoon motel. In contrast, using the net book value masks this decline in earning power, because the constantly decreasing base results in a higher ROI (24%); this higher rate may mislead decision makers into thinking that the earning power of the Saskatoon motel has not decreased.

The proponents of using net book value as a base maintain that it is less confusing because (1) it is consistent with the total assets shown on the conventional balance sheet and (2) it is consistent with net income computations that include deductions for amortization. Surveys of company practice report net book value to be the dominant asset measure used by companies in their internal performance evaluations. When using net book value, the declining denominator increases ROI as an asset ages, all other things being equal. Evaluating managers based on assets at net book value rather than gross book value increases incentives for retaining old property, plant, and equipment. Because older assets valued at net book value inflate ROI (particularly if investment is defined as net book value rather than gross book value), top management may set higher target ROIs for divisions with older assets.

SELECTING PERFORMANCE GOALS AND TIMING OF FEEDBACK

We next consider the selection of criteria, those accounting-based measures against which to compare actual performance. Recall that book value accounting measures are often inadequate for evaluating economic returns on new investments and sometimes create disincentives for new expansion. Despite these problems,

---

[10] When a specific cost index (such as the construction cost index) is not available, companies use a general index (such as the consumer price index) to approximate current costs.

book value ROIs can be used to evaluate current performance by adjusting target ROIs. Consider our Hospitality Inns example. The key is to recognize that the motels were built at different times, which in turn means they were built at different levels of the construction cost index. Top management could adjust the target accordingly, perhaps setting Saskatoon's ROI at 26%, Brandon's at 18%, and Hull's at 19%.

Nevertheless, the alternative of comparing actual to target performance is frequently overlooked in the literature. Critics of book value have indicated how high rates of return on old assets may erroneously induce a manager not to replace assets. Regardless, the manager's mandate is often "Go forth and attain the budgeted results." The budget, then, should be carefully negotiated with full knowledge of book value measurement bias. *The desirability of tailoring a budget to a particular subunit and a particular accounting system cannot be overemphasized.* For example, many problems of asset valuation and income measurement (whether based on book value or current cost) can be satisfactorily solved if top management gets everybody to focus on what is attainable in the forthcoming budget period—regardless of whether the financial measures are based on book value or some other measure, such as current costs.

Top management often sets continuous improvement targets. Consider companies implementing EVA. These companies have generally found it cost-effective to use net book value rather than estimates of market or replacement values. Why? Because top management evaluates operations on year-to-year changes in EVA, not on absolute measures of EVA. Evaluating performance on the basis of improvements in EVA makes the initial method of calculating EVA less important.

SELECTING THE LEVEL OF RELEVANCE—THE TIMING OF FEEDBACK

The final selection is the timing of feedback. Timing of feedback depends largely on how critical the information is for the success of the organization, the specific level of management that is receiving the feedback, and the sophistication of the organization's information technology. For example, motel managers responsible for room sales will want information on the number of rooms sold each day on a daily or, at most, weekly basis. A large percentage of motel costs are fixed costs, so achieving high room sales and taking quick action to reverse any declining sales trends are critical to the financial success of each motel. Supplying managers with daily information about room sales would be much easier if Hospitality Inns had a computerized room reservation and check-in system. Senior management, on the other hand, in their oversight role may look at information about daily room sales only on a monthly basis. In some instances (for example, because of concern about the low sales to total assets ratio of the Brandon motel), they may want the information weekly.

PERFORMANCE MEASUREMENT IN MULTINATIONAL COMPANIES

Comparing the performance of divisions of a company operating in different countries creates additional difficulties:[11]

> **Analyze the technical difficulties that arise when comparing the performance of divisions operating in different countries.** ③

- ◆ The economic, legal, political, social, and cultural environments differ significantly across countries.
- ◆ Governments in some countries limit selling prices and impose controls on a company's products. For example, developing countries in Asia, Latin America, and Eastern Europe impose tariffs and duties to restrict the import of certain goods. Beginning in 2005, the General Agreement on Tariffs and Trade (GATT) seeks to reduce and eliminate tariffs and duties imposed.

[11]M. Z. Iqbal, T. Melcher, and A. Elmallah, *International Accounting—A Global Perspective* (Cincinnati: Southwestern ITP, 2002).

- Availability of materials and skilled labour, as well as costs of materials, labour, and infrastructure (power, transportation, and communication) may also differ significantly across countries.
- Divisions operating in different countries keep score of their performance in different currencies. Issues of inflation and fluctuations in foreign currency exchange rates then become important.

We focus on the last of these issues next.

CALCULATING THE FOREIGN DIVISION'S ROI IN THE FOREIGN CURRENCY

Suppose Hospitality Inns invests in a motel in Mexico City. The investment consists mainly of the costs of buildings and furnishings. The following information is available:

- The exchange rate at the time of Hospitality's investment on December 31, 2012, is 3 pesos = $1.
- During 2013, the Mexican peso suffers a steady and steep decline in value.
- The exchange rate on December 31, 2013, is 6 pesos = $1.
- The average exchange rate during 2013 is [(3 + 6) ÷ 2] = 4.5 pesos = $1.
- The investment (total assets) in the Mexico City motel = 9,000,000 pesos.
- The operating income of the Mexico City motel in 2013 = 1,800,000 pesos.

What is the historical-cost-based ROI for the Mexico City motel in 2013? Some specific questions arise. Should we calculate the ROI in pesos or in dollars? If we calculate the ROI in dollars, what exchange rate should we use? How does the ROI of Hospitality Inns Mexico City (HIMC) compare with the ROI of Hospitality Inns Hull (HIH), which is also a relatively new motel of roughly the same size? Hospitality Inns may be interested in this information for making future investment decisions.

$$\text{HIMC's ROI (calculated using pesos)} = \frac{\text{Operating income}}{\text{Total assets}} = \frac{1{,}800{,}000 \text{ pesos}}{9{,}000{,}000 \text{ pesos}} = 20\%$$

HIMC's ROI of 20% is higher than HIH's ROI of 17% (computed on p. 970). Does this mean that HIMC outperformed HIH on the ROI criterion? Not necessarily, because HIMC operates in a very different economic environment than does HIH.

The peso has declined steeply in value relative to the dollar in 2013. Research studies show that the peso's decline is correlated with correspondingly higher inflation in Mexico relative to Canada.[12] A consequence of the higher inflation in Mexico is that HIMC will charge higher prices for its motel rooms, which will increase HIMC's operating income and lead to a higher ROI. Inflation clouds the real economic returns on an asset and makes ROI calculated on historical cost of assets unrealistically high. The reason is that had there been no inflation, HIMC's room rates and hence operating income would have been much lower. Differences in inflation rates between the two countries make a direct comparison of HIMC's peso-denominated ROI with HIH's dollar-denominated ROI misleading.

CALCULATING THE FOREIGN DIVISION'S ROI IN CANADIAN DOLLARS

One way to achieve a more meaningful comparison of historical-cost-based ROIs is to restate HIMC's performance in dollars. But what exchange rate(s) should be used to make the comparison meaningful? Assume operating income was earned evenly throughout 2013. We use the average exchange rate of 4.5 pesos = $1 to convert the

---

[12]W. Beaver and M. Wolfson, "Foreign Currency Translation Gains and Losses: What Effect Do They Have and What Do They Mean?" *Financial Analysts Journal* (March–April 1984); F. D. S. Choi, "Resolving the Inflation/Currency Translation Dilemma," *Management International Review*, Vol. 34, Special Issue, 1994; H. Louis, "The Value Relevance of the Foreign Translation Adjustment," *The Accounting Review* (October 2003).

operating income from pesos to dollars: 1,800,000 pesos ÷ 4.5 = $400,000. The effect of dividing the operating income in pesos by the higher pesos-to-dollars exchange rate is that any increase in operating income in pesos as a result of inflation is undone when converting back to dollars.

At what rate should we convert HIMC's total assets of 9,000,000 pesos? At the exchange rate prevailing when the assets were acquired on December 31, 2012, namely 3 pesos = $1, because HIMC's book value of assets is recorded at the December 31, 2012, cost and is not revalued as a result of inflation in Mexico in 2013. Since the book value of assets is unaffected by subsequent inflation, so should be the exchange rate used to convert it into dollars. Total assets would be converted to 9,000,000 pesos ÷ 3 = $3,000,000. Then:

$$\text{HIMC's ROI (calculated using dollars)} = \frac{\text{Operating income}}{\text{Total assets}} = \frac{\$400,000}{\$3,000,000} = 13.33\%$$

These adjustments make the historical-cost-based ROIs of the two motels comparable because they negate the effects of any differences in inflation rates between the two countries. HIMC's ROI of 13.33% is less than HIH's ROI of 17%.

Residual income calculated in pesos suffers from the same problems as ROI calculated using pesos. Instead, calculating HIMC's residual income in dollars adjusts for changes in exchange rates and facilitates comparisons with Hospitality's other motels:

$$\begin{aligned} \text{HIMC's residual income} &= \$400,000 - (12\% \times \$3,000,000) \\ &= \$400,000 - \$360,000 \\ &= \$40,000 \end{aligned}$$

This is also less than HIH's residual income of $150,000. In interpreting HIMC's and HIH's ROI and residual income, note that they are historical-cost-based calculations. They do, however, pertain to relatively new motels.

LEVELS OF ANALYSIS DIFFER BETWEEN MANAGERS AND SUBUNITS[13]

The performance evaluation of a manager should be distinguished from the performance evaluation of an organization subunit, such as a division of a company. For example, historical-cost-based ROIs for a particular division can be used to evaluate a manager's performance relative to a budget or over time, even though historical-cost ROIs may be unsatisfactory for evaluating economic returns earned by the subunit. But using historical-cost ROIs to compare the performance of managers of different subunits can be misleading.

In the Hospitality Inns example, Hospitality Inns Hull's (HIH's) ROI of 17% exceeds Hospitality Inns Mexico City's (HIMC's) ROI of 13.33% after adjusting for the higher inflation in Mexico. The ROIs may give some indication of the economic returns from each motel but do not mean that the manager of HIH performed better than the manager of HIMC. The reason is that, among other factors, HIMC's ROI may have been adversely affected relative to HIH's ROI because of externalities beyond the HIMC manager's control, such as legal, political, and government regulations as well as economic conditions in Mexico.

Consider another example. Companies often put the most skillful division manager in charge of the weakest division in an attempt to change its fortunes. Such an effort may take years to bear fruit. Furthermore, the manager's efforts may result merely in bringing the division up to a minimum acceptable ROI. The division may continue to be a poor profit performer in comparison with other divisions, but it would be a mistake to conclude from the poor performance of the division that the manager is necessarily performing poorly.

What dictates the intensity of the incentives? That is, how large should the incentive component be relative to salary? A key question is: How well does the performance measure capture the manager's ability to influence the desired results?

[13]The presentations here draw (in part) on teaching notes prepared by S. Huddart, N. Melumad, and S. Reichelstein.

Measures of performance that are superior change significantly with the manager's performance and not very much with changes in factors that are beyond the manager's control. We presented this justification for using operating margin instead of either pretax or net margin when measuring ROI.

Superior performance measures motivate the manager but limit the manager's exposure to uncontrollable risk and hence reduce the cost of providing incentives to get the manager to accept the incentive program. When possible, owners use performance evaluation measures that are tightly linked to managers' efforts. Managers are evaluated based on things they can affect, even if they are not completely controllable. For example, salespeople often earn commissions based on the amount of sales revenues they generate. Salespeople can affect the amount of sales they generate by working harder, but they cannot control other factors (such as the economy and competitors' products) that also affect the amount of their sales.

Sally Fonda owns the Hospitality Inns chain of motels. Roger Brett manages the Hospitality Inns Saskatoon (HIS) motel. Suppose Brett has no authority to determine investments. Further, suppose revenue is determined largely by external factors such as the local economy. Brett's actions influence only costs. Using RI as a performance measure in these circumstances subjects Brett's bonus to excessive risk, because two components of the performance measure (investments and revenues) are unrelated to his actions. The management accountant might suggest that, to create stronger incentives, Fonda consider using a different performance measure for Brett—perhaps HIS's costs—that more closely captures Brett's effort. Note that in this case, RI may be a perfectly good measure of the economic viability of HIS, but it is not a good measure of Brett's performance.

The salary component of compensation dominates when performance measures sensitive to a manager's effort are unavailable (as in the case of some corporate staff and government officials). This is not to say, however, that incentives are completely absent; promotions and salary increases do depend on some overall measure of performance, but the incentives are less direct. Employers give stronger incentives when superior measures of performance are available to them and when monitoring the employee's effort is very difficult (real estate agencies, for example, reward employees mainly on commissions on houses sold).

In evaluating Brett, Fonda uses measures from multiple perspectives of the BSC because nonfinancial measures on the BSC—employee satisfaction and the time taken for check-in, cleaning rooms, and providing room service—are more sensitive to Brett's actions. Financial measures such as RI are less sensitive to Brett's actions because they are affected by external factors such as local economic conditions that are beyond Brett's control.

Another reason for using nonfinancial measures in the BSC is that these measures follow Hospitality Inns' strategy and are drivers of future performance. Evaluating managers on these nonfinancial measures motivates them to take actions that will sustain long-run performance. Therefore, evaluating performance in all four perspectives of the BSC promotes both short- and long-run actions. Surveys show that division managers' compensation plans include a mix of salary, bonus, and long-term compensation tied to earnings and share price of the company. The goal is to balance division and companywide, as well as short-term and long-term, incentives.

If managers are evaluated on a single performance measure, they will treat other critical success factors as secondary to that single measure. For example, managers might curtail advertising and maintenance to increase the current year's ROI. This is why performance evaluation needs to be based on a variety of critical success factors such as those sustained by the BSC strategy.

BENCHMARKS AND RELATIVE PERFORMANCE EVALUATION

Owners can use benchmarks to evaluate performance. Benchmarks representing best practice may be available inside or outside the overall organization. In our Hospitality Inns example, benchmarks could be other similar motels, either within or outside the Hospitality Inns chain. Suppose Brett has authority over revenues, costs, and investments. In evaluating Brett's performance, Fonda would want to use as a benchmark a motel of a similar size that is influenced by the same uncontrollable factors—for example, location, demographic trends, and economic conditions—that affect HIS. *Differences* in performances of the two motels occur only because of differences in the two managers' performances, not because of random factors. Thus, benchmarking, also called *relative performance evaluation*, "filters out" the effects of the common noncontrollable factors.

Can the performance of two managers responsible for running similar operations within a company be benchmarked against one another? Yes, but one problem is that the use of these benchmarks may reduce incentives for these managers to help one another. That is, a manager's performance-evaluation measure improves either by doing a better job or by making the other manager look bad. Failing to work together as a team is not in the best interests of the organization as a whole. In this case, using benchmarks for performance evaluation can lead to goal-incongruence.

EXECUTIVE PERFORMANCE MEASURES AND COMPENSATION

The performance evaluation of managers and employees often affects their compensation. Compensation arrangements run the range from a flat salary with no direct performance-based bonus (as in the case of government officials) to rewards based only on performance (as in the case of employees of real estate agencies). Most often, however, a manager's total compensation includes some combination of salary and a performance-based bonus. An important consideration in designing compensation arrangements is the tradeoff between creating incentives and imposing risk. We illustrate this tradeoff in the context of our Hospitality Inns example.

Insurance companies possess extraordinary expertise at modelling risk because their core business is to profitably enter into contracts to share risk. All other things being equal, some people purchase insurance while others do not. One explanation is difference in risk preference. Risk-averse people want to minimize the probability of enduring financial or other harms and are willing to pay to avoid bearing risk alone. Some people, however, are not risk averse. What this means is that in a competitive market, when faced with the same array of probabilities, outcomes, and financial penalties or rewards, people with different risk preferences will make different choices.

People who become entrepreneurs (owners) are generally more risk-tolerant than those who decide to work for others (managers). The reason is that an entrepreneur has no guaranteed return on investment. Entrepreneurs assume that, all other things being equal, their reward is linked to their effort—the harder they work, the higher the reward. What the entrepreneur receives is the residual after all contracted obligations have been paid.

Managers or employees, on the other hand, prefer the security of a salary and are willing to accept a lower but certain return for their hard work. Unfortunately, effort is no guarantee because uncontrollable factors also affect return. Whether or not compensation is well designed depends in large part on how well the performance measures reflect the manager's efforts. For example, Home Depot shareholders complained that former CEO Bob Nardelli was collecting rewards for misdirected effort that failed to produce increases in the price of their shares when his compensation package increased (to $38.1 million) even though Home Depot's share price had decreased by 6%. The shareholders' wealth is represented in the residual after all contracted obligations are paid. The more Mr. Nardelli received, the smaller was their residual.

It is more cost-efficient for owners to bear risk than managers, because managers demand a premium (extra compensation) for bearing risk. For risk-averse managers, an incentive is required to take the same level of risk as would an entrepreneurial owner. The objective of many compensation plans is to provide managers with incentives to work hard while minimizing the risk placed on them.

Assume that Fonda uses RI to measure performance. To achieve good results as measured by RI, Fonda would like Brett to control costs, provide prompt and courteous

Evaluate the behavioural effects of salaries and incentives in compensation arrangements.

service, and reduce receivables. But even if Brett did all those things, good results are by no means guaranteed. HIS's RI is affected by many factors outside Fonda's and Brett's control, such as a recession in the Saskatoon economy, or weather that might negatively affect HIS. Alternatively, noncontrollable factors might have a positive influence on HIS's RI. Either way, noncontrollable factors make HIS's profitability uncertain and risky.

Fonda is an entrepreneur (the owner) who does not mind bearing risk, but Brett does not like being subject to risk; that is why he chose to be an employee rather than an owner. One way of insuring Brett against risk is to pay Brett a flat salary, regardless of the actual amount of residual income attained. All the risk would then be borne by Fonda. There is a problem here, however, because the effort that Brett puts in is difficult to monitor. The absence of performance-based compensation provides Brett with no incentive to work harder or undertake extra physical and mental effort beyond the minimum necessary to retain his job or to uphold his own personal values.

Moral hazard[14] describes contexts in which, once risk is shared, the individual fails to make as much effort to avoid harm as when risk is not shared. Effort is generally not observable in employees in management because it is primarily mental, not physical. Assume that managers prefer to exert less effort (or report biased measures of effort) than the effort (or unbiased measures) desired by the owner because the employee's effort (or reported measures) cannot be accurately monitored and enforced. In employment contracting with managers, what the owner wants is performance measures highly correlated with effort (see Chapter 10). The finer the measures, the more completely will variation in those measures explain variation in effort.

Paying no salary and rewarding Brett *only* on the basis of some performance measure—RI, in our example—raises different concerns. Brett would now be motivated to strive to increase RI because his rewards would increase with increases in RI. But compensating Brett on RI also subjects Brett to risk because HIS's RI depends not only on Brett's effort, but also on external factors such as inflation or other changes in the economy over which Brett has no control. More succinctly, Brett's management effort may be overwhelmed by good or bad luck associated with these changes in externalities.

To compensate Brett, who is risk averse, for taking on the consequences of uncontrollable risk, Fonda must pay Brett some extra compensation within the structure of the RI-based arrangement. Thus, using performance-based incentives will cost Fonda more money, *on average*, than paying Brett a flat salary. "On average" is appropriate because Fonda's compensation payment to Brett will vary with RI outcomes. The motivation for having some salary and some performance-based bonus in compensation arrangements is to balance the benefits of incentives against the extra costs of imposing uncontrollable risk on the manager.

The BSC approach is important because Brett can be compensated for satisfactory performance measured in more than one way. This means that if, due to an uncontrollable factor, performance decreases according to one measure it may increase on another and Brett will be spreading his risk of financial loss over several measures. As a manager, moreover, Brett performs many business functions in the value chain. While the functions may be interdependent, if he excels at them all he should be rewarded more than another manager who excels at only a few. From Fonda's perspective, greater reliance can be placed on a performance report where several measures converge to report the same level of performance.

---

[14] The term *moral hazard* originated in insurance contracts to represent situations in which insurance coverage, which relieves the owner of assets of part of the risks of loss and/or damage, caused insured parties to take less care of their properties than they would if they bore the full costs of replacement and/or repair. One response to moral hazard in insurance contracts is the system of deductibles (that is, the insured pays for damages below a specified amount). You are familiar with the concept if you have worked in teams to obtain marks for your output. The presence of a team spreads the risk of a low mark among the team's members.

TEAM-BASED COMPENSATION ARRANGEMENTS

Many manufacturing, marketing, and design problems require employees with multiple skills, experiences, and judgments to pool their talents. In these situations, a team of employees achieves better results than employees acting on their own.[15]

Team-based incentive compensation encourages employees to work together to achieve common goals. This approach encourages cooperation among interdependent subunits. Individual-based incentive compensation rewards employees for their own performance, consistent with responsibility accounting. This approach encourages competition to excel and be the best. A mix of both types of incentives encourages employees to maximize their own performance while working together in the best interest of the company as a whole.

Some companies balance the need for competition among employees to excel against cooperation by giving incentives and bonuses to individuals on the basis of team performance. Team incentives encourage cooperation, with individuals helping one another as they strive toward a common goal. The blend of knowledge and skills needed to change methods and improve efficiency puts a team in a better position than a lone individual to respond to incentives.[16] TRW, Whirlpool, and Monsanto in the United States, Novartis (a Swiss pharmaceutical company), and Nissan Motors in Japan are examples of companies that use some form of team-based incentives.

Whether team-based compensation is desirable depends, to a great extent, on the culture and management style of a particular organization. One criticism of teams is that individual incentives to excel are dampened, harming overall performance. This problem becomes more acute when effort cannot be monitored. Unproductive team members contribute less than the effort expected (shirk); nevertheless, they share equally in the team's reward. Shirking is a pervasive problem and you have probably experienced shirking at least once when you have worked with teams of students to obtain shared marks for output.

The principles of performance evaluation apply to executive compensation plans at the total-organization level. Executive compensation plans are based on both financial and nonfinancial performance measures and consist of a mix of (1) base salary; (2) annual incentives (for example, cash bonus based on yearly net income); (3) long-term incentives (for example, stock options based on achieving a specified return by the end of a five-year period); and (4) fringe benefits (for example, life insurance, an office with a view, or a personal secretary).[17] Designers of executive compensation plans emphasize three factors: achievement of organizational goals, administrative ease, and the likelihood that affected managers will perceive the plan as fair.

Well-designed plans use a compensation mix that carefully balances risk and short- and long-term incentives. For example, evaluating performance on the basis of annual ROI would sharpen an executive's short-term focus. Using ROI and stock option plans over, say, five years would motivate the executive to take a long-term view as well. Stock options give executives and employees the right to buy company shares at a specified price (called the exercise price) within a specified period. Suppose that on September 16, 2012, BP gave its CEO the option to buy 200,000 shares of the company at any time before June 30, 2015, at the September 16, 2012, market price of $49 per share. Let's say BP's share price rises to $69 per share on March 24, 2013; these options are "in the money." If the CEO exercises share options on all 200,000 shares, the CEO would earn $20 ($69 – $49) per share on 200,000 shares, or $4 million. If BP's share price remains below $49 during the entire period, these shares will be "out of the money" and the CEO will simply forgo the right to buy the shares.

[15]J. Katzenbach and D. Smith, *The Wisdom of Teams* (Boston: The Harvard Business School Press, 1993).

[16]*Teams That Click: The Results-Driven Manager Series* (Boston: Harvard Business School Press, 2004).

[17]*The Wall Street Journal*/Mercer Human Resource Consulting, *2003 CEO Compensation Survey and Trends* (May, 2004).

By linking CEO compensation to increases in the company's share price, the stock option plan motivates the CEO to improve the company's long-run performance and share price. Accounting rules require Canadian companies to recognize stock option expense in their income statements according to standards published by the CICA. The International Accounting Standards Board requires the same disclosure, as does the Financial Accounting Standards Board (FASB) in the United States. Companies also provide full note disclosure of how the equivalent value of compensation expense for stock options was calculated as at the grant date of compensation. All relevant assumptions must also be disclosed.[18]

The Ontario Securities Commission (OSC) and the U.S. Securities and Exchange Commission (SEC) require detailed disclosures of the compensation arrangements of top-level executives. Investors use this information to evaluate the relationship between compensation and performance across companies generally, across companies of similar sizes, and across companies operating in similar industries. In recent years both regulators have investigated companies that backdated stock option exercise prices prior to the contract date. The executives and boards of directors signing these contracts knew at the date of signing what their profits would be. This is not legal, and convicted companies have paid multi-million-dollar fines for this practice.

STRATEGY AND LEVERS OF CONTROL[19]

5 Apply strategic concepts to analyze the four levers of control and evaluate their usefulness.

Given the management accounting focus of this book, this chapter has emphasized the role of quantitative financial and nonfinancial performance evaluation measures that companies use to implement their strategies. These measures—such as ROI, RI, EVA, ROS, customer satisfaction, and employee satisfaction—monitor critical performance factors that help managers monitor progress toward attaining the company's strategic goals. Because these measures help diagnose whether a company is performing to expectations, they are collectively called **diagnostic control systems**.

Companies motivate managers to achieve these goals by holding managers accountable for and by rewarding them for meeting these goals. Recently, however, it has become clear that sometimes one consequence of the pressure to perform is that managers materially misstate financial measures to obscure actual performance (e.g., Nortel, Parmalat, WorldCom). Avoiding unethical and illegal behaviour requires that companies balance the push for performance resulting from diagnostic control systems, the first of four levers of control, with three other levers: *boundary systems*, *belief systems*, and *interactive control systems*.

Boundary systems describe standards of behaviour and codes of conduct expected of all employees, especially actions that are off-limits. Ethical behaviour on the part of managers is paramount. In particular, numbers that subunit managers report should be free of overstated assets, understated liabilities, fictitious revenues, and understated costs. In Canada, the Canadian Securities Administrators (CSA) withdrew their proposed guidelines, Multilateral Instrument 52–111, covering corporate governance and internal control regulations for any company listed on a Canadian stock exchange.

The CSA reasoned that most large Canadian companies were already compliant with the **Sarbanes-Oxley Act**, which became law in the United States in 2002, because these companies are listed on both U.S. and Canadian stock exchanges. Currently, the CICA has proposed it will adopt the International Accounting Standards Board standards. For these reasons and others, the CSA amended its Multilateral Instrument 52–109 to include internal control regulations effective 2007 (see Chapter 23).

---

[18]If the exercise price is less than the market price of the shares on the date the options are granted, the company must recognize compensation cost equal to the difference between the two prices. This difference is less than the fair market value of the options. See http://asc.fasb.org.

[19]For a more detailed discussion see R. Simons, "Control in an Age of Empowerment," *Harvard Business Review* (March–April 1995).

Most large Canadian companies are already listed on U.S. stock exchanges and, because they have taken the steps needed to comply with Sarbanes-Oxley, will not have to incur additional costs. Costs of compliance have averaged approximately US$4.3 million, but have been reported as high as US$40 million.[20] The broad scope of Canadian legislation on corporate governance includes the requirement that the CEO accept full responsibility for any material misstatement of financial information. Under Sarbanes-Oxley, companies must publish their codes of ethics and conduct as part of the material audited for their annual report. Regulations are one set of boundary systems that mandate specific actions.

Belief systems articulate the mission, purpose, and core values of a company. They describe the accepted norms and patterns of behaviour expected of all managers and employees with respect to each other, shareholders, customers, and communities. Johnson & Johnson describes its values and norms in its credo statement:

> We believe our first responsibility is to the doctors, nurses and patients, to mothers and fathers and all others who use our products and services. . . . Everything we do must be of high quality.
>
> We are responsible to our employees. . . . We must respect their dignity and recognize their merit. They must have a sense of security in their jobs. . . . We must be mindful of ways to help our employees fulfill their family responsibilities and provide opportunity for development and advancement. . . . Our actions must be just and ethical.
>
> We are responsible to the communities in which we live. . . . We must support good works and charities and bear our fair share of taxes. . . . We must encourage better health and education.
>
> Our final responsibility is to our stockholders. Business must make a sound profit. . . . We must experiment with new ideas . . . develop innovative programs and pay for mistakes.

Johnson & Johnson's credo is intended to inspire managers and employees to do their best. Values and culture generate organizational commitment, pride, and belonging and are an important source of **intrinsic motivation**, which is the desire to achieve self-satisfaction from good performance regardless of external rewards such as bonuses or promotion. Intrinsic motivation comes from being given greater responsibility, doing interesting and creative work, having pride in doing that work, establishing commitment to the organization, and developing personal bonds with co-workers. High intrinsic motivation enhances performance because managers and workers have a sense of achievement, feel satisfied with their jobs, and see opportunities for personal growth.

Codes of business conduct signal appropriate and inappropriate individual behaviour. The following is a portion of Caterpillar Tractor's "Code of Worldwide Business Conduct and Operating Principles":

> We must not engage in activities that create, or even appear to create, conflict between our personal interests and the interests of the company. [. . .] A conflict of interest or the appearance of a conflict of interest very often arises where an employee is offered a gift, favour, or entertainment. While some of this activity is part of a normal business relationship, we do not accept gifts, favours, or entertainment that have a value greater than we could reasonably reciprocate or that obligate or appear to obligate us to act in any way contrary to the law, Caterpillar business interests or Caterpillar's ethical business practices.[21]

Division managers often cite enormous pressure from top management "to make the budget" as excuses or rationalizations for not adhering to ethical accounting policies and procedures. A healthy amount of motivational pressure is desirable,

---

[20]"SOX Causes Jump in Audit Costs, But Benefits Seen," http://www.accountingweb.com/item/100788, accessed August 2, 2011.

[21]Caterpillar, "Caterpillar's Worldwide Code of Conduct: Integrity: Conflicts of Interest," http://www.cat.com/cda/layout?m=209561&x=7, accessed April 16, 2008.

Courage—Boundaries and Beliefs

The managers of for-profit corporations face intense pressures. Not the least of these are the contractual requirements to achieve performance measures such as those specified in long-term debt covenants and compensation contracts and the more informal requirements in operating and capital budgets. Banks and bondholders are not charitable institutions, and the intent of covenants is to alert creditors of possible risk to their investment. These covenants are often based on ratios derived from accrual accounting such as times interest earned, operating cash flow, and debt to equity.

What can be the harm in, say, calling a supplier and asking for a few days' delay in sending an invoice to prevent reporting the additional expense in a quarterly statement of earnings if it avoids contravening a times interest earned ratio and gives the corporation another 90 days to recover? It would postpone recognizing the expense on the actual operating performance report as well and avoid a negative variance. If the cause of the shortfall is uncontrollable, surely the company's owners and managers should not be penalized by a contract rigidity, especially if the only issue is one of timing.

This type of reasoning leads to earnings management, whereby managers use their discretion to bias both internal and external performance reports. The ethical problem is clear—it is the professional duty of accountants to present unbiased reports—but their managers, who may not be accountants, are not bound to the same ethical standard. The logical problem is also clear—if uncontrollable factors have caused the shortfall in revenue over expenses, how can managers be assured time will fix the problem? They cannot be sure, nor can accountants avoid their professional duty to act in the best interests of the public, not the corporate managers. Where boundary systems fail, professional belief systems can prevail.[a]

[a]For a full discussion of earnings management refer to Chapter 11 of W. R. Scott, *Financial Accounting Theory* 6th edition (Toronto: Prentice Hall, 2012).

as long as both the "tone from the top" and the codes of conduct communicate the absolute need for all managers to behave ethically at all times. Managers should train employees to behave ethically, and promptly and severely reprimand unethical conduct, regardless of the benefits that might accrue to the company from unethical actions. Some companies, such as Lockheed-Martin, emphasize ethical behaviour by routinely evaluating employees against a business code of ethics.

Many organizations also set explicit boundaries precluding actions that harm the environment. Environmental violations (such as water and air pollution) carry heavy fines and are prison offences under Canadian laws and those of other countries. But in many companies, environmental responsibilities extend beyond legal requirements. There are also many international indices of environmental performance, such as the Dow Jones Sustainability Index. Some companies, such as TransCanada Corporation (a Canadian natural gas transportation company) and Unilever Group (a U.S. manufacturer of consumer products) believe that a high ranking on this index is sufficiently important to positively affect share price, and they announce their rankings on the Internet and in formal press releases.

Socially responsible companies, such as Starbucks, also report specific performance measures to affirm their commitment to human rights and fair pricing. German, Swiss, Dutch, and Scandinavian companies also provide social responsibility disclosures such as employee welfare and community development activities. Many existing sets of global principles, such as the **Sullivan Principles**, can be used to compare corporate performance in the area of social responsibility.

Interactive control systems are formal information systems that managers use to focus organization attention and learning on key strategic issues. An excessive focus on diagnostic control systems and critical performance variables can cause an organization to ignore emerging threats and opportunities—changes in technology, customer preferences, regulations, and industry competition that can undercut a business.

Interactive control systems track strategic uncertainties that businesses face, such as the emergence of digital imaging in the case of Kodak and Fujifilm, airline deregulation in the case of American Airlines and Southwest Airlines, and the shift in customer preferences for mini- and microcomputers in the case of IBM. The result is ongoing discussion and debate about assumptions and action plans. New strategies emerge from the dialogue and debate surrounding the interactive process. Interactive control systems force busy managers to step back from the actions needed to manage the business today and to shift their focus forward to positioning the organization for the opportunities and threats of tomorrow.

Measuring and rewarding managers for achieving critical performance variables is an important driver of corporate performance. But these diagnostic control systems must be counterbalanced by the other levers of control—boundary systems, belief systems, and interactive control systems—to ensure that proper business ethics, inspirational values, and attention to future threats and opportunities are not sacrificed to achieve business results.

PULLING IT ALL TOGETHER—PROBLEM FOR SELF-STUDY

(Try to solve this problem before examining the solution that follows.)

PROBLEM
Budgeted data of the baseball manufacturing division of Home Run Sports for February 2013 are as follows:

Current assets	$ 400,000
Long-term assets	600,000
Total assets	$1,000,000
Production output	200,000 baseballs per month
Target ROI (operating income ÷ total assets)	30%
Fixed costs	$ 400,000 per month
Variable costs	$ 4 per baseball

REQUIRED
1. Compute the minimum unit selling price necessary to achieve the 30% target ROI, assuming ROI is based on total assets.
2. Using the selling price from requirement 1, separate the target ROI into its two components using the DuPont method.
3. Pamela Stephenson, division manager, receives 5% of the monthly residual income of the baseball manufacturing division as a bonus. Compute her bonus for February 2013, using the selling price from requirement 1. Home Run Sports uses a 12% required rate of return on total division assets when computing division residual income.
4. What behavioural issues arise from compensation contracts based on a single performance measure?
5. If Pamela recommends an investment in new equipment and for reasons beyond her control revenue is not realized but she has the opportunity to postpone recognition of expenses until the next reporting period, what levers of control can reduce the likelihood she will do so?

SOLUTION

1.

$$\text{Target operating income} = 30\% \text{ of } \$1,000,000$$
$$= \$300,000$$
$$\text{Let } P = \text{Selling price}$$
$$\text{Sales} - \text{Variable costs} - \text{Fixed costs} = \text{Operating income}$$
$$200,000P - (200,000 \times \$4) \quad \$400,000 = \$300,000$$
$$200,000P = \$300,000 + \$800,000 + \$400,000 = \$1,500,000$$
$$P = \$7.50$$

Proof:	Sales, 200,000 × $7.50	$1,500,000
	Variable costs, 200,000 × $4	800,000
	Contribution margin	700,000
	Fixed costs	400,000
	Operating income	$ 300,000

2.

$$\frac{\text{Revenues}}{\text{Investment}} \times \frac{\text{Income}}{\text{Revenues}} = \frac{\text{Income}}{\text{Investment}}$$
$$\frac{\$1,500,000}{\$1,000,000} \times \frac{\$300,000}{\$1,500,000} = \frac{\$300,000}{\$1,000,000}$$
$$1.5 \quad \times \quad 0.2 \quad = 0.30 \text{ or } 30\%$$

3.

$$\text{Residual income} = \text{Operating income} - \text{Required return on investment}$$
$$= \$300,000 - (0.12 \times \$1,000,000)$$
$$= \$300,000 - \$120,000$$
$$= \$180,000$$

Stephenson's bonus is $9,000 (5% of $180,000)

4. This bonus is a cash bonus based on short-term operations. Should Pamela have the opportunity to invest in more efficient equipment, the investment will reduce ROI in the short term in two ways. First, the operating costs will increase before the revenues are realized because there is a lag between production and sales. Operating income will decrease and it is possible revenue will also decrease. Investment will increase, and in combination with reduced revenue and income it is unlikely that the 30% ROI will be achieved. If Pamela cares about her bonus, she will not invest.

5. If Pamela is a professional accountant, the belief system embodied in the professional ethical code is one lever of control to constrain the likelihood she will manage earnings. If she is not, then a public statement of the corporate code of ethics, its core values, and the tone at the top from examples set by top management, can also constrain her.

SUMMARY POINTS

The following question-and-answer format summarizes the chapter's learning outcomes. Each point presents a key question, and the guidelines are the answer to that question.

LEARNING OUTCOMES	GUIDELINES
1. What financial and nonfinancial measures do companies use to evaluate performance?	Financial measures such as return on investment (ROI), residual income (RI), and economic value added (EVA) measure aspects of both manager performance and organization-subunit performance. In many cases, financial measures are supplemented with nonfinancial measures of performance, such as customer satisfaction ratings, number of defects, and productivity.

2. What is the current cost of an asset?	The current cost of an asset is the cost now of purchasing an asset identical to the one currently held. Historical-cost measurement methods consider the original cost of the asset net of accumulated amortization.
3. What difficulties arise when comparing the performance of divisions in different countries?	Comparing the performance of divisions operating in different countries is difficult because of legal, political, social, economic, and currency differences. ROI calculations for subunits operating in different countries need to be adjusted for differences in inflation between the two countries and changes in exchange rates.
4. How do salaries and incentives work together in compensation arrangements?	Organizations create incentives by rewarding managers on the basis of performance. But managers may face risks because random factors beyond the managers' control may also affect performance. Owners choose a mix of salary and incentive compensation to trade off the incentive benefit against the cost of imposing risk.
5. What are the levers of control and why does a company need to implement them?	The four levers of control are diagnostic control systems, boundary systems, belief systems, and interactive control systems. Implementing the four levers of control helps a company simultaneously strive for performance, behave ethically, inspire employees, and respond to strategic threats and opportunities.

TERMS TO LEARN

This chapter contains definitions of the following important terms:

belief systems (p. 987)
boundary systems (p. 986)
current cost (p. 976)
diagnostic control systems (p. 986)
economic value added (EVA) (p. 972)
imputed cost (p. 971)

interactive control systems (p. 988)
intrinsic motivation (p. 987)
malus (p. 966)
moral hazard (p. 984)
residual income (RI) (p. 971)
return on investment (ROI) (p. 969)

return on sales (ROS) (p. 973)
Sarbanes-Oxley Act (p. 986)
say on pay (p. 965)
Sullivan Principles (p. 988)
weighted-average cost of capital (WACC) (p. 971)

ASSIGNMENT MATERIAL

MyAccountingLab   Make the grade with MyAccountingLab: The questions, exercises, and problems marked in red can be found on MyAccountingLab at **www.myaccountinglab.com**. You can practise them as often as you want, and most feature step-by-step guided instructions to help you find the right answer. Exercises and problems with an Excel icon in the margin have an accompanying Excel template on MyAccountingLab.

SHORT-ANSWER QUESTIONS

24-1 Give two examples of financial performance measures and two examples of nonfinancial performance measures.

24-2 What are the six steps in designing an accounting-based performance measure?

24-3 What factors affecting ROI does the DuPont method highlight?

24-4 "Residual income is not identical to ROI although both measures incorporate income and investment into their computations." Do you agree? Explain.

24-5 Describe economic value added.

24-6 Give three definitions of investment used in practice when computing ROI.

24-7 Distinguish among measuring assets based on present value, current cost, and historical cost.

24-8 What special problems arise when evaluating performance in multinational companies?

24-9 Why is it important to distinguish between the performance of a manager and the performance of the organization subunit for which the manager is responsible? Give examples.

24-10 Describe moral hazard.

24-11 Explain the management accountant's role in helping organizations design stronger incentive systems for their employees.

24-12 Explain the role of benchmarking in evaluating managers.

24-13 Explain the incentive problems that can arise when employees have to perform multiple tasks as part of their jobs.

24-14 Describe each of the levers of control and their interrelation with strategy.

EXERCISES

24-15 Terminology. A number of terms are listed below:

belief systems	boundary systems
economic value added (EVA)	imputed cost of investment
interactivity	intrinsic motivation
malus	return on investment (ROI)
say on pay	social responsibility
weighted-average cost of capital (WACC)	

REQUIRED
Select the terms from the above list to complete the following sentences.

Governance, or the management stewardship of assets management does not own, according to laws and regulations is more closely scrutinized than before. Legal reform in the United States now mandates a shareholder vote on any executive compensation packages, referred to as a ___ __ ___. While we are very familiar with executive bonus, a new clawback of previous compensation, or a _____, is becoming a feature of compensation. One important performance measure that could determine a bonus or malus is the accounting _____ __ _____ (___), calculated by dividing the net income by the investment made. Another measure is the ROR, also called the _____ ____ __ _____, which represents a return forgone from tying up cash in existing investments. A third measure is the _____ _____ _____ (___), which is calculated by subtracting the total assets minus current liabilities multiplied by the _____ _____ ____ __ _____ (___) from the after-tax operating income. But executive performance is not the only factor or even the most important factor affecting corporate profitability, excellent governance, and corporate _____ _____. Good management control systems will separate the effects of good luck from good management on performance. Additional considerations when designing a good management control system include _____ _____, _____ _____, _____ _____, and _____.

24-16 ROI, comparisons of three companies. (CMA, adapted) Return on investment (ROI) is often expressed as follows:

2. Revenue C, $ 10,000,000

$$\frac{\text{Income}}{\text{Investment}} = \frac{\text{Income}}{\text{Revenue}} \times \frac{\text{Revenue}}{\text{Investment}}$$

REQUIRED
1. What advantages are there in the breakdown of the computation into two separate components?
2. Fill in the following blanks:

	Companies in Same Industry		
	A	**B**	**C**
Revenue	$1,000,000	$500,000	?
Income	$ 100,000	$ 50,000	?
Investment	$ 500,000	?	$5,000,000
Income as a percentage of revenue	?	?	0.5%
Investment turnover	?	?	2
ROI	?	1%	?

After filling in the blanks, comment on the relative performance of these companies as thoroughly as the data permit.

24-17 Analysis of return on invested assets, comparison of two divisions, DuPont method. Learning World, Inc. has two divisions: Test Preparation and Language Arts. Results (in millions) for the past three years are partially displayed here:

	A	B	C	D	E	F	G
		Operating Income	Operating Revenue	Total Assets	Operating Income/ Operating Revenue	Operating Revenue/ Total Assets	Operating Income/ Total Assets
1							
2	Test Preparation Division						
3	2011	$ 680	$ 7,960	$1,920	?	?	?
4	2012	840	?	?	10%	?	42%
5	2013	1,160	?	?	11%	5	?
6	Language Arts Department						
7	2011	$ 620	$ 2,360	$1,280	?	?	?
8	2012	?	3,000	1,800	22%	?	?
9	2013	?	?	2,340	?	2	25%
10	Learning World Inc.						
11	2011	$1,300	$10,320	$3,200	?	?	?
12	2012	?	?	?	?	?	?
13	2013	?	?	?	?	?	?

REQUIRED

1. Complete the table by filling in the blanks.
2. Use the DuPont method of profitability analysis to explain changes in the operating-income-to-total-assets ratios over the 2011 through 2013 period for each division and for Learning World as a whole. Comment on the results.

24-18 ROI and RI. (D. Kleespie, adapted) The Outdoor Sports Company produces a wide variety of outdoor sports equipment. Its newest division, Golf Technology, manufactures and sells a single product: AccuDriver, a golf club that uses global positioning satellite technology to improve the accuracy of golfers' shots. The demand for AccuDriver is relatively insensitive to price changes. The following data are available for Golf Technology, which is an investment centre for Outdoor Sports:

Total annual fixed costs	$30,000,000
Variable cost per AccuDriver	$ 500
Number of AccuDrivers sold each year	150,000
Average operating assets invested in the division	$48,000,000

REQUIRED

1. Compute Golf Technology's ROI if the selling price of AccuDrivers is $720 per club.
2. If management requires an ROI of at least 25% from the division, what is the minimum selling price that the Golf Technology Division should charge per AccuDriver club?
3. Assume that Outdoor Sports judges the performance of its investment centres on the basis of RI rather than ROI. What is the minimum selling price that Golf Technology should charge per AccuDriver if the company's required rate of return is 20%?

24-19 ROI and RI with manufacturing costs. Superior Motor Company makes electric cars and has only two products, the Simplegreen and the Superiorgreen. To produce the Simplegreen, Superior Motor employed assets of $13,500,000 at the beginning of the period, and $13,400,000 of assets at the end of the period. Other costs to manufacture the Simplegreen include:

1. ROI, 16.0%

Direct materials	$3,000 per unit
Setup	$1,300 per setup-hour
Production	$ 415 per machine-hour

General administration and selling costs total $7,340,000 for the period. In the current period, Superior Motor produced 10,000 Simplegreen cars using 6,000 setup-hours and 175,200 machine-hours. Superior Motor sold these cars for $12,000 each. The company bases its ROI on average invested capital.

REQUIRED

1. Assuming that Superior Motor defines investment as average assets during the period, what is the return on investment for the Simplegreen division?
2. Calculate the residual income for the Simplegreen if Superior Motor has a required rate of return of 12% on investments.

24-20 Financial and nonfinancial performance measures, goal-congruence. (CMA, adapted) Summit Equipment specializes in the manufacture of medical equipment, a field that has become increasingly competitive. Approximately two years ago, Ben Harrington, president of Summit, decided to revise the bonus plan (based, at the time, entirely on operating income) to encourage division managers to focus on areas that were important to customers and that added value without increasing cost. In addition to a profitability incentive, the revised plan includes incentives for reduced rework costs, reduced sales returns, and on-time deliveries. Bonuses are calculated and awarded semi-annually on the following basis. A base bonus is calculated at 2% of operating income; this amount is then adjusted as follows:

a. i. Reduced by excess of rework costs over and above 2% of operating income.
   ii. No adjustment if rework costs are less than or equal to 2% of operating income.
b. i. Increased by $5,000 if more than 98% of deliveries are on time, and by $2,000 if 96% to 98% of deliveries are on time.
   ii. No adjustment if on-time deliveries are below 96%.
c. i. Increased by $3,000 if sales returns are less than or equal to 1.5% of sales.
   ii. Decreased by 50% of excess of sales returns over 1.5% of sales.

Note: If the calculation of the bonus results in a negative amount for a particular period, the manager simply receives no bonus, and the negative amount is not carried forward to the next period.

Results for Summit's Charter Division and Mesa Division for 2013, the first year under the new bonus plan, follow. In 2012, under the old bonus plan, the Charter Division manager earned a bonus of $27,060 and the Mesa Division manager a bonus of $22,440.

	Charter Division		Mesa Division	
	January 1, 2013 to June 30, 2013	July 1, 2013 to Dec. 31, 2013	January 1, 2013 to June 30, 2013	July 1, 2013 to Dec. 31, 2013
Revenue	$4,200,000	$4,400,000	$2,850,000	$2,900,000
Operating income	$ 462,000	$ 440,000	$ 342,000	$ 406,000
On-time delivery	95.4%	97.3%	98.2%	94.6%
Rework costs	$ 11,500	$ 11,000	$ 6,000	$ 8,000
Sales returns	$ 84,000	$ 70,000	$ 44,750	$ 42,500

REQUIRED

1. Why did Harrington need to introduce these new performance measures? That is, why does Harrington need to use these performance measures in addition to the operating-income numbers for the period?
2. Calculate the bonus earned by each manager for each six-month period and for 2013.
3. What effect did the change in the bonus plan have on each manager's behaviour? Did the new bonus plan achieve what Harrington desired? What changes, if any, would you make to the new bonus plan?

24-21 Goal-incongruence and ROI. Bleefl Corporation manufactures furniture in several divisions, including the Patio Furniture division. The manager of the Patio Furniture division plans to retire in two years. The manager receives a bonus based on the division's ROI, which is currently 11%.

One of the machines that the Patio Furniture division uses to manufacture the furniture is rather old, and the manager must decide whether to replace it. The new machine would cost $30,000 and would last ten years. It would have no salvage value. The old machine is fully amortized and has no trade-in value. Bleefl uses straight-line amortization for all assets. The new machine, being new and more efficient, would save the company $5,000 per year in cash operating costs. The only difference between cash flow and net income is amortization. The internal rate of return of the project is approximately 11%. Bleefl Corporation's weighted-average cost of capital is 6%. Bleefl is not subject to any income taxes.

Margin notes:

2. Charter Division semi-annual instalment, $(3,520)

2. ROI end of t1, 7.02%

1. Should Bleefl Corporation replace the machine? Why or why not?
2. Assume that "investment" is defined as average net long-term assets after amortization. Compute the project's ROI for each time period t1 to t5 when each time period is 1 year. If the Patio Furniture manager is interested in maximizing his bonus, would he replace the machine before he retires? Why or why not?
3. What can Bleefl do to entice the manager to replace the machine before retiring?

24-22 ROI, RI, EVA. Performance Auto Company operates a New Car Division (that sells high-performance sports cars) and a Performance Parts Division (that sells performance improvement parts for family cars). Some division financial measures for 2012 are as follows:

1. ROI New Car Division, 7.5%

	File Edit View Insert Format Tools Data Window Help	
	A	B	C
1		New Car Division	Performance Parts Division
2	Total assets	$33,000,000	$28,500,000
3	Current liabilities	$ 6,600,000	$ 8,400,000
4	Operating income	$ 2,475,000	$ 2,565,000
5	Required rate of return	12%	12%

REQUIRED

1. Calculate return on investment for each division using operating income as a measure of income and total assets as a measure of investment.
2. Calculate residual income for each division using operating income as a measure of income and total assets minus current liabilities as a measure of investment.
3. William Abraham, the New Car Division manager, argues that the Performance Parts Division has "loaded up on a lot of short-term debt" to boost its RI. Calculate an alternative RI for each division that is not sensitive to the amount of short-term debt taken on by the Performance Parts Division. Comment on the result.
4. Performance Auto Company, whose tax rate is 40%, has two sources of funds: long-term debt with a market value of $18,000,000 at an interest rate of 10%, and equity capital with a market value of $12,000,000 and a cost of equity of 15%. Applying the same weighted-average cost of capital (WACC) to each division, calculate EVA for each division.
5. Use your preceding calculations to comment on the relative performance of each division.

24-23 ROI, RI, measurement of assets. (CMA, adapted) Carter Corporation recently announced a bonus plan to be awarded to the manager of the most profitable division. The three division managers are to choose whether ROI or RI will be used to measure profitability. In addition, they must decide whether investment will be measured using gross book value or net book value of assets. Carter defines income as operating income and investment as total assets. The following information is available for the year just ended:

Radnor ROI using gross book value, 11.84%

Division	Gross Book Value of Assets	Accumulated Amortization	Operating Income
Radnor	$1,200,000	$645,000	$142,050
Easttown	1,140,000	615,000	137,550
Marion	750,000	420,000	92,100

Carter uses a required rate of return of 10% on investment to calculate RI.

REQUIRED

Each division manager has selected a method of bonus calculation that ranks his or her division number one. Identify the method for calculating profitability that each manager selected, supporting your answer with appropriate calculations. Comment on the strengths and weaknesses of the methods chosen by each manager.

24-24 Multinational performance measurement, ROI, RI. The Grandlund Corporation manufactures similar products in Canada and Norway. The Canadian and Norwegian operations are organized as decentralized divisions. The following information is available for 2014; ROI is calculated as operating income divided by total assets:

1. a. Operating income, $1,200,000

	Canadian Division	Norwegian Division
Operating income	?	8,100,000 kroner
Total assets	$8,000,000	52,500,000 kroner
ROI	15%	?

Both investments were made on December 31, 2013. The exchange rate at the time of Grandlund's investment in Norway on December 31, 2013, was 6 kroner = $1. During 2014, the Norwegian kroner increased steadily in value so that the exchange rate on December 31, 2011, is 7 kroner = $1. The average exchange rate during 2014 is [(6 + 7)/2] = 6.5 kroner = $1.

REQUIRED

1. **a.** Calculate the Canadian division's operating income for 2014.
   b. Calculate the Norwegian division's ROI for 2014 in kroner.
2. Top management wants to know which division earned a better ROI in 2014. What would you tell them? Explain your answer.
3. Which division do you think had the better RI performance? Explain your answer. The required rate of return on investment (calculated in Canadian dollars) is 12%.

24-25 ROI, RI, EVA and performance evaluation. Eva Manufacturing makes fashion products and competes on the basis of quality and leading-edge designs. The company has $3,000,000 invested in assets in its clothing manufacturing division. After-tax operating income from sales of clothing this year is $600,000. The cosmetics division has $10,000,000 invested in assets and an after-tax operating income this year of $1,600,000. Income for the clothing division has grown steadily over the last few years. The weighted-average cost of capital for Eva is 10% and the previous period's after-tax return on investment for each division was 15%. The CEO of Eva has told the manager of each division that the division that "performs best" this year will get a bonus.

REQUIRED

1. Calculate the ROI and residual income for each division of Eva Manufacturing, and briefly explain which manager will get the bonus. What are the advantages and disadvantages of each measure?
2. The CEO of Eva Manufacturing has recently heard of another measure similar to residual income called EVA. The CEO has the accountant calculate EVA-adjusted incomes of Clothing and Cosmetics, and finds that the adjusted after-tax operating incomes are $720,000 and $1,430,000, respectively. Also, the Clothing Division has $400,000 of current liabilities, while the Cosmetics Division has only $200,000 of current liabilities. Using the above information, calculate EVA, and discuss which division manager will get the bonus.
3. What nonfinancial measures could Eva use to evaluate divisional performances?

24-26 Evaluate behavioural effects. The Dexter Division of AMCO sells car batteries. AMCO's corporate management gives Dexter management considerable operating and investment autonomy in running the division. AMCO is considering how it should compensate Jim Marks, the general manager of the Dexter Division. Proposal 1 calls for paying Marks a fixed salary. Proposal 2 calls for paying Marks no salary and compensating him only on the basis of the division's ROI (calculated on the basis of operating income before any bonus payments). Proposal 3 calls for paying Marks some salary and some bonus based on ROI. Assume that Marks does not like bearing risk.

REQUIRED

1. **a.** Evaluate each of the three proposals, specifying the advantages and disadvantages of each.
   b. Suppose that AMCO competes against Tiara Industries in the car battery business. Tiara is roughly the same size and operates in a business environment that is very similar to Dexter's. The senior management of AMCO is considering evaluating Marks on the basis of Dexter's ROI minus Tiara's ROI. Marks complains that this approach is unfair because the performance of another firm, over which he has no control, is included in his performance evaluation measure. Is Marks's complaint valid? Why or why not?
2. Now suppose that Marks has no authority for making capital investment decisions. Corporate management makes these decisions. Is return on investment a good performance measure to use to evaluate Marks? Is return on investment a good measure to evaluate the economic viability of the Dexter Division? Explain.
3. Dexter's salespersons are responsible for selling and providing customer service and support. Sales are easy to measure. Although customer service is very important to Dexter in the long run, the company has not yet implemented customer service measures. Marks wants to compensate his sales force only on the basis of sales commissions paid for each unit of product sold. He cites two advantages to this plan: (a) it creates very strong incentives for the sales force to work hard, and (b) the company pays salespersons only when the company itself is earning revenues and has cash. Do you like his plan? Why or why not?

24-27 Residual income and EVA, timing issues. Doorwhistle Company makes doorbells. It has a weighted-average cost of capital of 8%, and total assets of $5,690,000. Doorwhistle has current liabilities of $700,000. Its operating income for the year was $649,000. Doorwhistle does not have to pay any income taxes. One of the expenses for accounting purposes was a

$100,000 advertising campaign. The entire amount was deducted this year, although the Doorwhistle CEO believes the beneficial effects of this advertising will last four years.

REQUIRED
1. Calculate residual income, assuming Doorwhistle defines investment as total assets.
2. Calculate EVA for the year. Adjust both the assets and operating income for advertising assuming that for the purposes of economic value added the advertising is capitalized and amortized on a straight-line basis over four years.
3. Discuss the difference between the outcomes of requirements 1 and 2 and which measure is preferred.

24-28 ROI performance measures based on historical cost and current cost. Nature's Elixir Corporation operates three divisions that process and bottle natural fruit juices. The historical-cost accounting system reports the following information for 2013:

2

1. ROI Kiwi, 19.13%

	Passion Fruit Division	Kiwi Fruit Division	Mango Fruit Division
Revenues	$1,000,000	$1,400,000	$2,200,000
Operating costs (excluding plant amortization)	600,000	760,000	1,200,000
Plant amortization	140,000	200,000	240,000
Operating income	$ 260,000	$ 440,000	$ 760,000
Current assets	$ 400,000	$ 500,000	$ 600,000
Long-term assets—plant	280,000	1,800,000	2,640,000
Total assets	$ 680,000	$2,300,000	$3,240,000

Nature's Elixir estimates the useful life of each plant to be 12 years, with no terminal disposal value. The straight-line amortization method is used. At the end of 2013, the Passion Fruit plant is 10 years old, the Kiwi Fruit plant is 3 years old, and the Mango Fruit plant is 1 year old. An index of construction costs over the 10-year period that Nature's Elixir has been operating (2003 year-end = 100) is:

2003	2010	2012	2013
100	136	160	170

Given the high turnover of current assets, management believes that the historical-cost and current-cost measures of current assets are approximately the same.

REQUIRED
1. Compute the ROI ratio (operating income to total assets) of each division using historical-cost measures. Comment on the results.
2. Use the approach in Exhibit 24-3 (p. 977) to compute the ROI of each division, incorporating current-cost estimates as of 2013 for amortization expense and long-term assets. Comment on the results.
3. What advantages might arise from using current-cost asset measures as compared with historical-cost measures for evaluating the performance of the managers of the three divisions?

24-29 Evaluating managers, ROI, DuPont method, value-chain analysis of cost structure. Peach Computer Corporation is the largest personal computer company in the world. The CEO of Peach is retiring, and the board of directors is considering external candidates to fill the position. The board's top two choices are CEOs Peter Diamond (current CEO of NetPro) and Norma Provan (current CEO of On Point). As a board member on the search committee, you collect the following information (in millions):

3

1. NetPro 2012 ROI = 29%

File Edit View Insert Format Tools Data Window Help				
A	B	C	D	E
1	NetPro		On Point	
2	2012	2013	2012	2013
3 Revenues	$ 600.0	$ 480.0	$300.0	$525.0
4 Costs				
5 R&D	71.2	40.2	35.9	76.1
6 Production	132.6	145.6	107.6	128.2
7 Marketing and distribution	173.2	193.7	96.4	153.8
8 Customer service	65.5	40.0	30.4	67.6
9 Total costs	442.5	419.5	270.3	425.7
10 Operating income	$ 157.5	$ 60.5	$ 29.7	$ 99.3
11 Total assets	$540.00	$510.0	$240.0	$360.0

In early 2014, a leading computer magazine gave On Point's main product five stars, its highest rating. NetPro's main product received three stars, down from five stars a year earlier. In the same article, On Point's new products received praise; NetPro's new products were judged as "mediocre."

REQUIRED

1. Use the DuPont method to calculate NetPro's and On Point's ROIs in 2012 and 2013. Comment on the results. What can you tell from the DuPont analysis that you might have missed from calculating ROI itself?
2. Compute the percentage of costs in each of the four business-function cost categories for NetPro and On Point in 2012 and 2013. Comment on the results.
3. Relate the results of requirements 1 and 2 to the comments made by the computer magazine. Of Diamond and Provan, whom would you suggest to be the new CEO of Peach?

1. RI France in dollars, $58,320

24-30 ROI, RI, and multinational firms. Konekopf Corporation has a division in Canada and another in France. The investment in the French assets was made when the exchange rate was $1.20 per euro. The average exchange rate for the year was $1.30 per euro. The exchange rate at the end of the fiscal year was $1.38 per euro. Income and investment for the two divisions are:

	Canada	France
Investment in assets	$3,490,000	2,400,000 euros
Income for current year	$ 383,900	266,400 euros

REQUIRED

1. The required return for Konekopf is 10%. Calculate ROI and RI for the two divisions. For the French division, calculate these measures using both dollars and euros. Which division is doing better?
2. What are the advantages and disadvantages of translating the French division information from euros to dollars?

1. New Zealand, $696,800

24-31 Multinational firms, differing risk, comparison of profit, ROI, and RI. Zzwuig Multinational Inc. has divisions in Canada, Germany, and New Zealand. The Canadian division is the oldest and most established of the three, and has a cost of capital of 6%. The German division was started three years ago when the exchange rate for euros was 1 € = $1.25. Although it is a large and powerful division of Zzwuig Inc., its cost of capital is 10%. The New Zealand division was started this year, when the exchange rate was 1 New Zealand Dollar (NZD) = $0.64. Its cost of capital is 13%. Average exchange rates for the current year are 1 € = $1.32 and 1 NZD = $0.67. Other information for the three divisions includes:

	Canada	Germany	New Zealand
Long-term assets	$14,845,000	9,856,000 euros	9,072,917 NZD
Operating revenues	$10,479,000	5,200,000 euros	4,800,000 NZD
Operating expenses	$ 7,510,000	3,600,000 euros	3,500,000 NZD
Income tax rate	40%	30%	20%

REQUIRED

1. Translate the German and New Zealand information into dollars to make the divisions comparable. Find the after-tax operating income for each division and compare the profits.
2. Calculate ROI using after-tax operating income. Compare the results among divisions.
3. Use after-tax operating income and the individual cost of capital of each division to calculate and compare residual income of each division.
4. Redo requirement 2 using pretax operating income instead of net income. Why is there a big difference, and what does it mean for performance evaluation?

PROBLEMS

2. ROI 2013 with proposal, 22.2%

24-32 ROI, RI, DuPont method, investment decisions, balanced scorecard. News Mogul Group has two major divisions: Print and Internet. Summary financial data (in millions) for 2012 and 2013 are as follows:

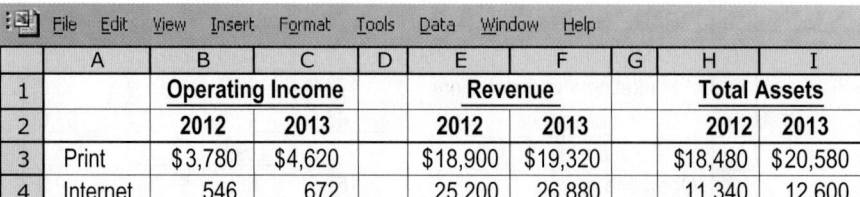

	A	B	C	D	E	F	G	H	I
1		**Operating Income**			**Revenue**			**Total Assets**	
2		**2012**	**2013**		**2012**	**2013**		**2012**	**2013**
3	Print	$3,780	$4,620		$18,900	$19,320		$18,480	$20,580
4	Internet	546	672		25,200	26,880		11,340	12,600

The two division managers' annual bonuses are based on division ROI (defined as operating income divided by total assets). If a division reports an increase in ROI from the previous year, its management is automatically eligible for a bonus; however, the management of a division reporting a decline in ROI has to present an explanation to the News Mogul Group board and is unlikely to get any bonus.

Carol Mays, manager of the Print Division, is considering a proposal to invest $800 million in a new computerized news reporting and printing system. It is estimated that the new system's state-of-the-art graphics and ability to quickly incorporate late-breaking news into papers will increase 2014 division operating income by $120 million. News Mogul Group uses a 15% required rate of return on investment for each division.

REQUIRED

1. Use the DuPont method of profitability analysis to explain differences in 2013 ROIs between the two divisions. Use 2013 total assets as the investment base.
2. Why might Mays be less than enthusiastic about accepting the investment proposal for the new system, despite her belief in the benefits of the new technology?
3. Murdoch Turner, CEO of News Mogul Group, is considering a proposal to base division executive compensation on division RI.
   a. Compute the 2013 RI of each division.
   b. Would adoption of an RI measure reduce Mays's reluctance to adopt the new computerized system investment proposal?
4. Turner is concerned that the focus on annual ROI could have an adverse long-run effect on News Mogul Group's customers. What other measurements, if any, do you recommend that Turner use? Explain briefly.

24-33 Division managers' compensation (continuation of 24-32). Murdoch Turner seeks your advice on revising the existing bonus plan for division managers of News Mogul Group. Assume division managers do not like bearing risk. Turner is considering three ideas:

◆ Make each division manager's compensation depend on division RI.
◆ Make each division manager's compensation depend on companywide RI.
◆ Use benchmarking, and compensate division managers on the basis of their division's RI minus the RI of the other division.

REQUIRED

1. Evaluate the three ideas Turner has put forth using performance-evaluation concepts described in this chapter. Indicate the positive and negative features of each proposal.
2. Turner is concerned that the pressure for short-run performance may cause managers to cut corners. What systems might Turner introduce to avoid this problem? Explain briefly.
3. Turner is also concerned that the pressure for short-run performance might cause managers to ignore emerging threats and opportunities. What system might Turner introduce to prevent this problem? Explain briefly.

24-34 Executive compensation, balanced scorecard. Community Bank recently introduced a new bonus plan for its business unit executives. The company believes that current profitability and customer satisfaction levels are equally important to the bank's long-term success. As a result, the new plan awards a bonus equal to 1% of salary for each 1% increase in net income or 1% increase in the company's customer satisfaction index. For example, increasing net income from $3 million to $3.3 million (or 10% from its initial value) leads to a bonus of 10% of salary, while increasing the bank's customer satisfaction index from 70 to 73.5 (or 5% from its initial value) leads to a bonus of 5% of salary. There is no bonus penalty when net income or customer satisfaction declines. In 2012 and 2013, Community Bank's three business units reported the following performance results:

	Retail Banking		Business Banking		Credit Cards	
	2012	2013	2012	2013	2012	2013
Net income	$2,800,000	$3,220,000	$2,900,000	$3,016,000	$2,750,000	$2,722,500
Customer satisfaction	73	73	70	75.6	69	79.35

REQUIRED

1. Compute the bonus as a percent of salary earned by each business unit executive in 2013.
2. What factors might explain the different improvement rates for net income and customer satisfaction in the three units?

1. Retail banking percentage change to net income, 15%

3. Community Bank's board of directors is concerned that the 2013 bonus awards may not actually reflect the executives' overall performance. In particular, it is concerned that executives can earn large bonuses by doing well on one performance dimension but underperforming on the other. What changes can it make to the bonus plan to prevent this from happening in the future? Explain briefly.

24-35 Incentives in compensation. (A. Spero, adapted) Hamilton Semiconductors manufactures specialized chips that sell for $20 each. Hamilton's manufacturing costs consist of variable cost of $2 per chip and fixed costs of $9,000,000. Hamilton also incurs $400,000 in fixed marketing costs each year.

Hamilton calculates operating income using absorption costing—that is, Hamilton calculates manufacturing cost per unit by dividing total manufacturing costs by actual production. Hamilton costs all units in inventory at this rate and expenses the costs in the income statement at the time when the units in inventory are sold. Next year, 2014, appears to be a difficult year for Hamilton. It expects to sell only 500,000 units. The demand for these chips fluctuates considerably, so Hamilton usually holds minimal inventory.

REQUIRED
1. Calculate Hamilton's operating income in 2014 (a) if Hamilton manufactures 500,000 units and (b) if Hamilton manufactures 600,000 units.
2. Would it be unethical for Randy Jones, the general manager of Hamilton Semiconductors, to produce more units than can be sold in order to show better operating results? Jones's compensation has a bonus component based on operating income. Explain your answer.
3. Would it be unethical for Jones to ask distributors to buy more product than they need? Hamilton follows the industry practice of booking sales when products are shipped to distributors. Explain your answer.

24-36 Incentives in compensation. (Ronald L. Madison). United Forest Products (UFP) is a large timber and wood processing plant. UFP's performance-evaluation system pays its managers substantial bonuses if the company achieves annual budgeted profit numbers. In the last quarter of 2013, Amy Kimbell, UFP's controller, noted a slight increase in output and a significant decrease in the purchase cost of raw timber.

One day when Kimbell was at the log yard where timber is received and scaled (weighed and checked for quality) to determine what UFP pays for it, she noted that a timber contractor was quite aggravated when he was given the scale report (board feet and quality). When she asked one of the scale employees what was bothering the contractor, he revealed that the scalers had received instructions from their supervisors to deliberately "lowball" evaluations of timber quantity and quality. This reduced the price paid to timber suppliers, which also reduced direct material costs, helping UFP to meet its profit target.

REQUIRED
1. What should Kimbell do?
2. Which lever of control is UFP emphasizing? What changes, if any, should be made?

24-37 Various measures of profitability. When the Coronet Company formed three divisions a year ago, the president told the division managers that an annual bonus would be paid to the most profitable division. However, absolute division operating income as conventionally computed would not be used. Instead, the ranking would be affected by the relative investments in the three divisions. Options available include ROI and residual income. Investment can be measured using gross book value or net book value. Each manager has now written a memorandum claiming entitlement to the bonus. The following data are available:

Division	Gross Book Value of Division Assets	Division Operating Income
Mastex	$480,000	$57,000
Banjo	456,000	55,200
Randal	300,000	36,960

All the assets are fixed assets that were purchased ten years ago and have ten years of useful life remaining. A zero terminal disposal price is predicted. Coronet's required rate of return on investment used for computing residual income is 10% of investment.

Which method for computing profitability did each manager choose? Make your description specific and brief. Show supporting computations. Where applicable, assume straight-line amortization.

24-38 **Evaluate accrual measures.** Mineral Waters Ltd. operates three divisions that process and bottle sparkling mineral water. The historical-cost accounting system reports the following data for 2013:

	Calistoga Division	Alpine Springs Division	Rocky Mountains Division
Revenues	$600,000	$ 840,000	$1,320,000
Operating costs (excluding amortization)	360,000	456,000	720,000
Plant amortization	84,000	120,000	144,000
Operating income	$156,000	$ 264,000	$ 456,000
Current assets	$240,000	$ 300,000	$ 360,000
Fixed assets—plant	168,000	1,080,000	1,584,000
Total assets	$408,000	$1,380,000	$1,944,000

Mineral Waters estimates the useful life of each plant to be 12 years with a zero terminal disposal price. The straight-line amortization method is used. At the end of 2013, the Calistoga plant is 10 years old, the Alpine Springs plant is 3 years old, and the Rocky Mountains plant is 1 year old.

An index of construction costs of plants for mineral water production for the 10-year period that Mineral Waters has been operating (2003 year-end = 100) is:

2003	2010	2011	2012	2013
100	136	149	160	170

Given the high turnover of current assets, management believes that the historical-cost and current-cost measures of current assets are approximately the same.

REQUIRED
1. Compute the ROI (operating income to total assets) ratio of each division using historical-cost measures. Comment on the results.
2. Use the approach in Exhibit 24-3 (p. 977) to compute the ROI of each division, incorporating current-cost estimates as of 2013 for amortization and fixed assets. Comment on the results.
3. What advantages might arise from using current-cost asset measures as compared with historical-cost measures for evaluating the performance of the managers of the three divisions?

24-39 **Financial and nonfinancial performance measures, goal-congruence.** (CMA, adapted) Leader Automotive Canada is a Tier 1 supplier in the automotive industry (direct supplier to car assemblies), an industry that is considered the most competitive in the manufacturing sector. A couple of years ago the CEO decided to revise the bonus plan (based, at the time, entirely on operating income) to encourage plant managers to focus on areas that were important to customers and that added value without increasing cost. In addition to a profitability incentive, the revised plan also includes incentives for reduced rework costs, reduced rejections (sales returns), and on-time deliveries. Bonuses are calculated and awarded semi-annually on the following basis. A base bonus is calculated at 2% of operating income. The bonus amount is then adjusted by the following amounts:

a. i. Reduced by excess of rework costs over 2% of operating income.
   ii. No adjustment if rework costs are less than or equal to 2% of operating income.
b. Increased by $6,000 if over 98% of deliveries are on time, by $2,400 if 96% to 98% of deliveries are on time, and by $0 if on-time deliveries are below 96%.
c. i. Increased by $3,600 if rejections are less than or equal to 1.5% of sales.
   ii. Decreased by 50% of excess of rejections over 1.5% of sales.

Note: If the calculation of the bonus results in a negative amount for a particular period, the manager simply receives no bonus, and the negative amount is not carried forward to the next period.

Results for Leader Automotive Canada's plants for the year 2013, the first year under the new bonus plan, follow. In the previous year, 2012, under the old bonus plan, the Alliston Plant manager earned a bonus of $32,472 and the Oshawa Plant manager a bonus of $26,928.

	Alliston Plant		Oshawa Plant	
	January 1, 2013 to June 30, 2013	**July 1, 2013 to Dec. 31, 2013**	**January 1, 2013 to June 30, 2013**	**July 1, 2013 to Dec. 31, 2013**
Revenues	$5,040,000	$5,280,000	$3,420,000	$3,480,000
Operating income	$ 554,400	$ 528,000	$ 410,400	$ 487,000
On-time delivery	95.4%	97.3%	98.2%	94.6%
Rework costs	$ 13,800	$ 13,200	$ 7,200	$ 8,600
Sales returns	$ 100,800	$ 84,000	$ 53,750	$ 51,000

REQUIRED

1. Why did the Leader Automotive CEO introduce these new performance measures? That is, why does he need to use these performance measures over and above the operating income numbers for the period?
2. Calculate the bonus earned by each manager for each six-month period and for the year 2013.
3. What effect did the change in the bonus plan have on each manager's behaviour? Did the new bonus plan achieve what the CEO desired? What changes, if any, would you make to the new bonus plan?

1. Expected net income, $29,312,500

24-40 Financial performance measures with uncertainty. (CMA, adapted) The following forecast variable costing income statement was prepared for Electric Machines Ltd. for the year ending April 2013:

Sales	$100,000,000
Variable costs	45,000,000
Contribution margin	55,000,000
Fixed costs	25,000,000
Net income	30,000,000

The general manager is interested in buying a leisure boat with a tag price of $30,000 with the bonus he will collect in May 2013 (based on the net income of the year ending in April 2013). To estimate his bonus, he developed a probabilistic model for a range of possible outcomes for these financial parameters. He collected the following information from various managers within the firm:

i. The likelihood that the worst-case scenario for sales would occur (drop of 25%) was set at 15%. The likelihood that the best-case scenario for sales would occur (an increase of 25%) was set at 10%. Finally, the likelihood that the most likely scenario would occur (sales of $100,000,000) was set at 75%.
ii. The likelihood that the worst-case scenario for fixed costs would occur (increase of 20%) was set at 20%. The likelihood that the best-case scenario for fixed costs would occur (a decrease of 20%) was set at 20%. Finally, the likelihood that the most likely scenario would occur (fixed costs of $25,000,000) was set at 60%.
iii. Variable costs will always run at 45% of sales.

The general manager's compensation is composed of a flat salary of $75,000 plus 1% of net income that is in excess of the target for the year. The target for the year ending April 2013 was $26,500,000.

REQUIRED

1. Calculate the expected outcome and determine if the manager will be able to buy the boat with the bonus he will collect in May 2013.
2. Suppose the owners of Electric Machines propose to change the remuneration to the general manager and they offer a flat salary of $100,000. Explain why the general manager would be interested in accepting the offer or not. What is more convenient in the long term for the general manager?

24-41 Historical-cost and current-cost ROI measures. World of 1 Dollar Ltd. owns and manages three convenience stores. The following information has been collected for the year 2013:

2

1. Jane and Rutherford
ROI (hist. cost), 56%

	Jane and Rutherford	Major Mackenzie and Keele	Weston and Langstaff
Operating income	28,000	33,000	15,000
Historical cost of investment	50,000	100,000	30,000
Current cost of investment	120,000	135,000	80,000
Age of store	5	2	4

REQUIRED

1. Compute the ROI for each store, where investment is measured at (a) historical cost and (b) current cost.
2. How would you judge the performance of each store?

24-42 Risk-sharing, incentives, benchmarking, multiple tasks. Acme Inc. is a diversified multidivisional corporation. One of its business units manufactures and sells industrial pumps. Acme's corporate management gives Industrial Pumps management considerable operating and investment autonomy in running the division. Cynthia Franco is an exceptional manager with a brilliant career within Industrial Pumps division and Acme will offer her the opportunity to become the new vice-president of industrial products. Acme has a handful of candidates to become the general manager of Industrial Pumps, but all of them lack the internal motivation that Cynthia has shown. Acme Inc. is considering how it should compensate the new general manager of the division.

♦ *Proposal 1:* Pay a fixed salary.
♦ *Proposal 2:* Pay no salary and compensate the manager only on the basis of the division's RI (calculated on the basis of operating income before any bonus payments).
♦ *Proposal 3:* Pay some salary and some bonus based on ROI.
♦ *Proposal 4:* Pay some salary and some bonus based on the difference between the ROI of Industrial Pumps division and the ROI of Pumps-for-All Ltd. Pumps-for-All is roughly the same size, operates in a very similar business environment, and half of its customers also buy from Industrial Pumps division of Acme Inc.

REQUIRED

1. Evaluate each of the four proposals, specifying the advantages and disadvantages of each.
2. One of the candidates complains that the fourth proposal is unfair because the performance of another firm, over which he has no control, is included in his performance evaluation measure. Is his complaint valid? Why or why not?
3. Now suppose the Industrial Pumps manager has no authority for making capital investment decisions. Corporate management makes these decisions. Is return on investment a good performance measure to use to evaluate the divisional manager? Is return on investment a good measure to evaluate the economic viability of the Industrial Pumps division? Explain.
4. Industrial Pumps's salespersons are responsible for selling and providing customer service and support. Sales are easy to measure. Although customer service is very important to Industrial Pumps in the long run, it has not yet implemented customer-service measures. Cynthia Franco recommended compensating her sales force only on the basis of sales commissions paid for each pump sold. She cites two advantages to this plan: (a) it creates very strong incentives for the sales force to work hard and (b) the company pays salespersons only when the company itself is earning revenues and has cash. Do you like her plan? Why or why not?

24-43 Nonfinancial performance and levers of control. (CMA, adapted) Light Seating Canada produces recliners, the device inside car seats that allows the seats to recline to a position comfortable to the driver but prevents the seat from trapping the driver in the case of a front crash. The company has always been associated with high-quality, expensive products, but this has limited their sales to manufacturers of sports cars.

About one year ago, the production manager, Bill Jones, identified an opportunity for Light Seating Canada to enter the low-cost, high-volume segment of the market. Up to that point, Light Seating Canada had used expensive materials assembled automatically using a special-purpose machine. Jones, considered a competent manager, felt certain a new, cheaper machine with intensive use of direct labour would allow for the manufacture of an inexpensive recliner, enabling the firm to enter the low-cost, high-volume segment of the market. Jones vocally championed this idea and eventually received permission to purchase one of these machines to begin stamping recliner parts and assembling them manually on a trial basis. If the trial were successful, about ten more of these machines would have to be purchased for Light Seating Canada to be an effective competitor.

The test machine had been installed approximately eight months ago, and it was time for senior management to review its performance and consider the decision to make the additional investment necessary to enter this new market segment. To aid in this review the vice-president of operations asked Emily Chang, the assistant controller, to conduct a post-audit report on the operations of the stamping machine and manual assembly.

Chang collected information from numerous sources in the preparation of her report. Her efforts unearthed a number of items that were in contrast with the original estimates provided by Jones to justify this investment. For example, the amount of time necessary to train production staff on the use of the stamping machine and manual assembly was more than four times greater than the one month originally forecast. Even then, with Jones describing the staff as now fully competent on the stamping machine and assembly process, the quality of the output was far below the acceptable level, and scrap rates were running double from the original plan. In addition to scrap rates, the throughput volume had failed to meet the levels expected. Chang concluded the report by describing all of these issues as significant and clearly sufficient grounds to reconsider the viability of the new initiative that would redirect the firm's market strategy.

As was standard practice at Light Seating Canada, Chang's report was reviewed by the Controller, Paul James, in advance of its presentation to senior management. The day after James had received a copy of Chang's report, he approached her to discuss its findings. James and Jones had both been with Light Seating Canada for many years, and James was Jones's brother-in-law. He explained to Chang that he had reviewed the findings of her report with Jones. He explained that while she had certainly identified some disappointing events in the past, he was unconvinced that these items warranted the cautionary tone of the report. He raised the issue of training delays and suggested that this entire item could be dropped from the report, as it was unlikely that training delays would persist since some staff were now familiar with the stamping machine and assembly process. Additionally, he asked Chang to rewrite the sections of the report dealing with scrap rates and throughput, as they were quite negative, and Jones believed that both of these items were likely to improve with more organizational experience with the machine and manual assembly process.

Finally, James mentioned that Jones was widely seen as the champion of this new initiative. He suggested to Chang that perhaps she should be particularly cautious in producing a report that might reflect negatively on Jones and impact his career and subjective portion of the bonus. James reminded Chang that at Light Seating Canada all managers and employees have an annual bonus that is mostly subjective and determined by his or her immediate superior.

REQUIRED

1. Put yourself in Emily Chang's position and consider the governance dimensions of the situation in which you find yourself. How would you resolve this situation?
2. Which levers of control need to be activated at Light Seating Canada?

24-44 **Various measures of profitability.** As a way to incent competition between divisions, the president of Industrial Products told the division managers that a quarterly bonus would be paid only to the most profitable division. However, absolute division operating income as conventionally computed would not be used. Instead, the ranking would be affected by the relative investments in the three divisions. Options available include ROI and residual income. Investment can be measured using gross book value or net book value. Each manager has now written a memorandum claiming entitlement to the bonus. The following data are available:

Division	Gross Book Value of Division Assets	Division Operating Income
Ontario	$1,000,000	$150,000
Quebec	$1,000,000	$120,000
Alberta	$ 350,000	$ 55,000

All the assets are fixed assets that were purchased ten years ago and have ten years of useful life remaining. A zero terminal disposal price is predicted. Industrial Products' required rate of return on investment used for computing residual income is 12% of investment.

1. Quebec division RI using net book value, $60,000

REQUIRED

Which method for computing profitability did each manager choose? Make your description specific and brief. Show supporting computations. Where applicable, assume straight-line amortization.

COLLABORATIVE LEARNING CASES

24-45 ROI, RI, division manager's compensation, nonfinancial measures. In 2013, the Mandarin Division of Key Products Corporation generated an operating income of $3,000,000 from $20,000,000 of sales revenues and using assets worth $15,000,000.

Mandarin managers are evaluated and rewarded on the basis of ROI defined as operating income divided by total assets. Key Products Corporation expects its divisions to increase ROI each year.

The year 2014 appears to be a difficult year for Mandarin. Mandarin Division had planned new investments to improve quality but, in view of poor economic conditions, has postponed the investment. ROI for 2013 was certain to decrease had Mandarin made the investment. Management is now considering ways to meet its target ROI of 22% for next year. It anticipates revenue to be steady at $20,000,000 in 2013.

INSTRUCTIONS

Form groups of two or more students to complete the following requirements:
1. Calculate Mandarin Division return on sales (ROS) and ROI for 2013.
2. **a.** By how much would Mandarin have to cut costs in 2014 to achieve its target ROI of 22% in 2014, assuming no change in total assets between 2013 and 2014?
   b. By how much would Mandarin have to decrease total assets in 2014 to achieve its target ROI of 22% in 2014, assuming no change in operating income between 2013 and 2014?
3. Calculate Mandarin's RI in 2013 assuming a required rate of return on investment of 18%.
4. Mandarin wants to increase RI by 30% in 2014. Assuming it could cut costs by $30,000 in 2014, by how much would Mandarin have to decrease total assets in 2014?
5. Key Products Corporation is concerned that the focus on cost cutting and asset sales will have an adverse long-run effect on Mandarin's customers. Yet Key Products Corporation wants Mandarin to meet its financial goals. What other measurements, if any, do you recommend that Key Products use? Explain briefly.

24-46 ROI, RI, division manager's compensation, nonfinancial measures. (CGA, adapted) General Appliance (GA) builds coffeemakers and battery-powered small tools. For a long time, GA held a reputation for strong, durable, and reliable appliances. This reputation began to decline, however, when increased competition forced GA to cut costs, and this was handled poorly. For a moderate period following the cost cutting, as long as they were able to take advantage of their reputation, GA's sales remained relatively steady. This effect then all but disappeared. The loss of reputation, coupled with increased overseas competition, caused GA's sales to plummet sharply.

On January 1, 2012, GA began a massive effort directed toward rewarding for quality. In the two years that followed, sales failed to go up, but remained steady at around $10 million per year. A significant amount of money was spent on testing equipment, increasing inspection, setting up a statistical process control system, reworking or throwing out defective items, and paying incentives. The results of the effort are presented in the following table:

Quality Costs as a % of Sales for the Years Ended:	2011	2012	2013
External failure costs	8.20	2.40	1.15
Internal failure costs	2.80	4.00	3.40
Appraisal costs	2.00	3.20	3.39
Prevention costs	1.20	2.60	2.79
Total quality costs	14.20	12.20	10.73

Also on January 1, 2012, GA organized into three divisions: electronic circuits, coffeemakers, and battery-powered small tools. Electronic circuits were used by the other two divisions, and 100% of its production was transferred at full cost plus an 8% markup (this is the standard practice in the electronic components industry) to coffeemakers and battery-powered small tools. All rejections made by coffeemakers and small tools were treated in the

Total bonus Electronic Circuits, $75,000

Multinational Performance Measurement and Compensation | **1005**

quality control system as internal failures, but most of the time they were not reported simply because electronic circuits replaced them immediately in the production lines.

Each division had a bonus pool with 50% based on quality performance and 50% based on financial performance. The 50% based on financial performance is equal to 20% of the divisional residual income (the minimum required rate of return is the ROI of the worst-performing division). The 50% based on quality performance is calculated as: (Internal Failures as % of sales − External Failures as % of sales) × GA's net profit.

Given the results of last year, the manager of the coffeemaker division asked the top managers to review the current compensation system, because he was having the feeling that his division had been subsidizing those "lazy" fellows of electronic circuits. He supported his claim with the following:

2013	Electronic Circuits	Coffeemakers	Battery-Powered Small Tools
Net profit	$ 500,000	$ 700,000	$ 660,000
Investment	$2,500,000	$7,000,000	$6,000,000
External failures	0% of sales	1.2% of sales	2.4% of sales
Internal failures	5% of sales	2% of sales	3.2% of sales
Appraisal costs	0% of sales	5.2% of sales	3.1% of sales
Prevention costs	1% of sales	7% of sales	4.2% of sales

INSTRUCTIONS

Form groups of two or more students to complete the following requirement.

Calculate the bonus paid to each division. Explain to the upper management if the money is being spent effectively and if the claims of the divisional manager are correct.

Notes on Compound Interest and Interest Tables

Interest is the cost of using money. It is the rental charge for funds, just as renting a building and equipment entails a rental charge. When the funds are used for a period of time, it is necessary to recognize interest as a cost of using the borrowed ("rented") funds. This requirement applies even if the funds represent ownership capital and if interest does not entail an outlay of cash. Why must interest be considered? Because the selection of one alternative automatically commits a given amount of funds that could otherwise be invested in some other alternative.

Interest is generally important, even when short-term projects are under consideration. Interest looms correspondingly larger when long-run plans are studied. The rate of interest has significant enough impact to influence decisions regarding borrowing and investing funds. For example, $100,000 invested now and compounded annually for 10 years at 8% will accumulate to $215,900; at 20%, the $100,000 will accumulate to $619,200.

INTEREST TABLES

Many computer programs and pocket calculators are available that handle computations involving the time value of money. You may also turn to the following four basic tables to compute interest.

TABLE 1—FUTURE AMOUNT OF $1

Table 1 shows how much $1 invested now will accumulate in a given number of periods at a given compounded interest rate per period. Consider investing $1,000 now for three years at 8% compound interest. A tabular presentation of how this $1,000 would accumulate to $1,259.70 follows:

Year	Interest per Year	Cumulative Interest Called Compound Interest	Total at End of Year
0	$ —	$ —	$1,000.00
1	80.00 (0.08 × $1,000)	80.00	1,080.00
2	86.40 (0.08 × $1,080)	166.40	1,166.40
3	93.30 (0.08 × $1,166.40)	259.70	1,259.70

This tabular presentation is a series of computations that could appear as follows, where S is the future amount and the subscripts 1, 2, and 3 indicate the number of time periods.

$$S_1 = \$1,000(1.08)^1$$
$$S_2 = \$1,000(1.08)^2$$
$$S_3 = \$1,000(1.08)^3$$

The formula for the "amount of 1," often called the "future value of $1" or "future amount of $1," can be written

$$S = P(1 + r)^n$$
$$S = \$1,000(1 + 0.08)^3 = \$1,259.70$$

S is the future value amount; P is the present value, $1,000 in this case; r is the rate of interest; and n is the number of time periods.

Fortunately, tables make key computations readily available. A facility in selecting the *proper* table will minimize computations. Check the accuracy of the preceding answer using Table 1.

TABLE 2—PRESENT VALUE OF $1

In the previous example, if $1,000 compounded at 8% per year will accumulate to $1,259.70 in 3 years, then $1,000 must be the present value of $1,259.70 due at the end of 3 years. The formula for the present value can be derived by reversing the process of *accumulation* (finding the future amount) that we just finished.

If $$S = P(1 + r)^n$$

then $$P = \frac{S}{(1 + r)^n}$$

$$P = \frac{\$1,259.70}{(1.08)^3} = \$1,000$$

Use Table 2 to check this calculation.

When accumulating, we advance or roll forward in time. The difference between our original amount and our accumulated amount is called *compound interest*. When discounting, we retreat or roll back in time. The difference between the future amount and the present value is called *compound discount*. Note the following formulas (where $P = \$1,000$):

$$\text{Compound interest} = P[(1 + r)^n - 1] = \$259.70$$

$$\text{Compound discount} = S\left[1 - \frac{1}{(1 + r)^n}\right] = \$259.70$$

TABLE 3—AMOUNT OF ANNUITY OF $1

An (ordinary) *annuity* is a series of equal payments (receipts) to be paid (or received) at the end of successive periods of equal length. Assume that $1,000 is invested at the end of each of 3 years at 8%:

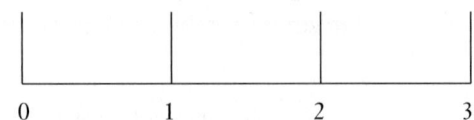

End of Year	Amount
1st payment	$1,000.00 ➤ $1,080.00 ➤ $1,166.40, which is $1,000(1.08)^2$
2nd payment	$1,000.00 ➤ 1,080.00, which is $1,000(1.08)^1$
3rd payment	1,000.00
Accumulation (future amount)	$3,246.40

The preceding arithmetic may be expressed algebraically as the amount of an ordinary annuity of $1,000 for 3 years = $1,000(1 + r)^2 + $1,000(1 + r)^1 + $1,000.

We can develop the general formula for S_n, the amount of an ordinary annuity of $1, by using the example above as a basis:

1. $S_n = 1 + (1 + r)^1 + (1 + r)^2$

2. Substitute: $S_n = 1 + (1.08)^1 + (1.08)^2$

3. Multiply (2) by $(1 + r)$: $(1.08)S_n = (1.08)^1 + (1.08)^2 + (1.08)^3$

4. Subtract (2) from (3): $1.08S_n - S_n = (1.08)^3 - 1$
   Note that all terms on the right-hand side are removed except $(1.08)^3$ in equation (3) and 1 in equation (2).

5. Factor (4): $S_n(1.08 - 1) = (1.08)^3 - 1$

6. Divide (5) by $(1.08 - 1)$: $S_n = \dfrac{(1.08)^3 - 1)}{1.08 - 1} = \dfrac{(1.08)^3 - 1}{.08}$

7. The general formula for the amount of an ordinary annuity of $1 becomes: $S_n = \dfrac{(1 + r)^n - 1}{r}$ or $\dfrac{\text{Compound interest}}{\text{Rate}}$

This formula is the basis for Table 3. Look at Table 3 or use the formula itself to check the calculations.

TABLE 4—PRESENT VALUE OF AN ORDINARY ANNUITY OF $1

Using the same example as for Table 3, we can show how the formula of P_n, *the present value of an ordinary annuity*, is developed.

End of Year

1st payment	$\dfrac{1,000}{(1.08)^1} = \$\ 925.93$ ⟵	$1,000	
2nd payment	$\dfrac{1,000}{(1.08)^2} = \$\ 857.34$ ⟵		$1,000
3rd payment	$\dfrac{1,000}{(1.08)^3} = \underline{\$\ 793.83}$ ⟵		
Total present value	$\underline{\$2,577.10}$		

For the general case, the present value of an ordinary annuity of $1 may be expressed as:

1. $P_n = \dfrac{1}{1 + r} + \dfrac{1}{(1 + r)^2} + \dfrac{1}{(1 + r)^3}$

2. Substitute: $P_n = \dfrac{1}{1.08} + \dfrac{1}{(1.08)^2} + \dfrac{1}{(1.08)^3}$

3. Multiply by $\dfrac{1}{1.08}$: $P_n\dfrac{1}{1.08} = \dfrac{1}{(1.08)^2} + \dfrac{1}{(1.08)^3} + \dfrac{1}{(1.08)^4}$

4. Subtract (3) from (2): $P_n - P_n\dfrac{1}{1.08} = \dfrac{1}{1.08} - \dfrac{1}{(1.08)^4}$

5. Factor: $P_n\left(1 - \dfrac{1}{(1.08)}\right) = \dfrac{1}{1.08}\left[1 - \dfrac{1}{(1.08)^3}\right]$

6. or $P_n\left(\dfrac{0.08}{1.08}\right) = \dfrac{1}{1.08}\left[1 - \dfrac{1}{(1.08)^3}\right]$

7. Multiply by $\dfrac{1.08}{0.08}$:
$$P_n = \frac{1}{0.08}\left[1 - \frac{1}{(1.08)^3}\right]$$

The general formula for the present value of an annuity of $1.00 is:

$$P_n = \frac{1}{r}\left[1 - \frac{1}{(1 + r)^n}\right] = \frac{\text{Compound discount}}{\text{Rate}}$$

Solving,

$$P_n = \frac{0.2062}{0.08} = 2.577$$

The formula is the basis for Table 4. Check the answer in the table. The present value tables, Tables 2 and 4, are used most frequently in capital budgeting.

The tables for annuities are not essential. With Tables 1 and 2, compound interest and compound discount can readily be computed. It is simply a matter of dividing either of these by the rate to get values equivalent to those shown in Tables 3 and 4.

TABLE 1
Compound Amount of $1.00 (The Future Value of $1.00)
$S = P(1 - r)^n$. In this table $P = \$1.00$.

Periods	2%	4%	6%	8%	10%	12%	14%	16%	18%	20%	22%	24%	26%	28%	30%	32%	40%	Periods
1	1.020	1.040	1.060	1.080	1.100	1.120	1.140	1.160	1.180	1.200	1.220	1.240	1.260	1.280	1.300	1.320	1.400	1
2	1.040	1.082	1.124	1.166	1.210	1.254	1.300	1.346	1.392	1.440	1.488	1.538	1.588	1.638	1.690	1.742	1.960	2
3	1.061	1,125	1.191	1.260	1.331	1.405	1.482	1.561	1.643	1.728	1.816	1.907	2.000	2.097	2.197	2.300	2.744	3
4	1.082	1.170	1.262	1.360	1.464	1.574	1.689	1.811	1.939	2.074	2.215	2.364	2.520	2.684	2.856	3.036	3.842	4
5	1.104	1.217	1.338	1.469	1.611	1.762	1.925	2.100	2.288	2.488	2.703	2.932	3.176	3.436	3.713	4.007	5.378	5
6	1.126	1.265	1.419	1.587	1.772	1.974	2.195	2.436	2.700	2.986	3.297	3.635	4.002	4.398	4.827	5.290	7.530	6
7	1.149	1.316	1.504	1.714	1.949	2.211	2.502	2.826	3.185	3.583	4.023	4.508	5.042	5.629	6.275	6.983	10.541	7
8	1.172	1.369	1.594	1.851	2.144	2.476	2.853	3.278	3.759	4.300	4.908	5.590	6.353	7.206	8.157	9.217	14.758	8
9	1.195	1.423	1.689	1.999	2.358	2.773	3.252	3.803	4.435	5.160	5.987	6.931	8.005	9.223	10.604	12.166	20.661	9
10	1.219	1.480	1.791	2.159	2.594	3.106	3.707	4.411	5.234	6.192	7.305	8.594	10.086	11.806	13.786	16.060	28.925	10
11	1.243	1.539	1.898	2.332	2.853	3.479	4.226	5.117	6.176	7.430	8.912	10.657	12.708	15.112	17.922	21.199	40.496	11
12	1.268	1,601	2.012	2.518	3.138	3.896	4.818	5.936	7.288	8.916	10.872	13.215	16.012	19.343	23.298	27.983	56.694	12
13	1.294	1.665	2.133	2.720	3.452	4.363	5.492	6.886	8.599	10.699	13.264	16.386	20.175	24.759	30.288	36.937	79.371	13
14	1.319	1.732	2.261	2.937	3.797	4.887	6.261	7.988	10.147	12.839	16.182	20.319	25.421	31.691	39.374	48.757	111.120	14
15	1.346	1.801	2.397	3.172	4.177	5.474	7.138	9.266	11.974	15.407	19.742	25.196	32.030	40.565	51.186	64.359	155.568	15
16	1.373	1.873	2.540	3.426	4.595	6.130	8.137	10.748	14.129	18.488	24.086	31.243	40.358	51.923	66.542	84.954	217.795	16
17	1.400	1.948	2.693	3.700	5.054	6.866	9.276	12.468	16.672	22.186	29.384	38.741	50.851	66.461	86.504	112.139	304.913	17
18	1.428	2.026	2.854	3.996	5.560	7.690	10.575	14.463	19.673	26.623	35.849	48.039	64.072	85.071	112.455	148.024	426.879	18
19	1.457	2.107	3.026	4.316	6.116	8.613	12.056	16.777	23.214	31.948	43.736	59.568	80.731	108.890	146.192	195.391	597.630	19
20	1.486	2.191	3.207	4.661	6.727	9.646	13.743	19.461	27.393	38.338	53.358	73.864	101.721	139.380	190.050	257.916	836.683	20
21	1.516	2.279	3.400	5.034	7.400	10.804	15.668	22.574	32.324	46.005	65.096	91.592	128.169	178.406	247.065	340.449	1171.356	21
22	1.546	2.370	3.604	5.437	8.140	12.100	17.861	26.186	38.142	55.206	79.418	113.574	161.492	228.360	321.184	449.393	1639.898	22
23	1.577	2.465	3.820	5.871	8.954	13.552	20.362	30.376	45.008	66.247	96.889	140.831	203.480	292.300	417.539	593.199	2295.857	23
24	1.608	2.563	4.049	6.341	9.850	15.179	23.212	35.236	53.109	79.497	118.205	174.631	256.385	374.144	542.801	783.023	3214.200	24
25	1.641	2.666	4.292	6.848	10.835	17.000	26.462	40.874	62.669	95.396	144.210	216.542	323.045	478.905	705.641	1033.590	4499.880	25
26	1.673	2.772	4.549	7.396	11.918	19.040	30.167	47.414	73.949	114.475	175.936	268.512	407.037	612.998	917.333	1364.339	6299.831	26
27	1.707	2.883	4.822	7.988	13.110	21.325	34.390	55.000	87.260	137.371	214.642	332.955	512.867	784.638	1192.533	1800.927	8819.764	27
28	1.741	2.999	5.112	8.627	14.421	23.884	39.204	63.800	102.967	164.845	261.864	412.864	646.212	1004.336	1550.293	2377.224	12347.670	28
29	1.776	3.119	5.418	9.317	15.863	26.750	44.693	74.009	121.501	197.814	319.474	511.952	814.228	1285.550	2015.381	3137.935	17286.737	29
30	1.811	3.243	5.743	10.063	17.449	29.960	50.950	85.850	143.371	237.376	389.758	634.820	1025.927	1645.505	2619.996	4142.075	24201.432	30
35	2.000	3.946	7.686	14.785	28.102	52.800	98.100	180.314	327.997	590.668	1053.402	1861.054	3258.135	5653.911	9727.860	16599.217	130161.112	35
40	2.208	4.801	10.286	21.725	45.259	93.051	188.884	378.721	750.378	1469.772	2847.038	5455.913	10347.175	19426.689	36118.865	66520.767	700037.697	40

TABLE 2 (*Place a clip on this page for easy reference.*)
Present Value of $1.00

$$P = \frac{S}{(1+r)^n}. \text{ In this table } S = \$1.00.$$

Periods	2%	4%	6%	8%	10%	12%	14%	16%	18%	20%	22%	24%	26%	28%	30%	32%	40%	Periods
1	0.980	0.962	0.943	0.926	0.909	0.893	0.877	0.862	0.847	0.833	0.820	0.806	0.794	0.781	0.769	0.758	0.714	1
2	0.961	0.925	0.890	0.857	0.826	0.797	0.769	0.743	0.718	0.694	0.672	0.650	0.630	0.610	0.592	0.574	0.510	2
3	0.942	0.889	0.840	0.794	0.751	0.712	0.675	0.641	0.609	0.579	0.551	0.524	0.500	0.477	0.455	0.435	0.364	3
4	0.924	0.855	0.792	0.735	0.683	0.636	0.592	0.552	0.516	0.482	0.451	0.423	0.397	0.373	0.350	0.329	0.260	4
5	0.906	0.822	0.747	0.681	0.621	0.567	0.519	0.476	0.437	0.402	0.370	0.341	0.315	0.291	0.269	0.250	0.186	5
6	0.888	0.790	0.705	0.630	0.564	0.507	0.456	0.410	0.370	0.335	0.303	0.275	0.250	0.227	0.207	0.189	0.133	6
7	0.871	0.760	0.665	0.583	0.513	0.452	0.400	0.354	0.314	0.279	0.249	0.222	0.198	0.178	0.159	0.143	0.095	7
8	0.853	0.731	0.627	0.540	0.467	0.404	0.351	0.305	0.266	0.233	0.204	0.179	0.157	0.139	0.123	0.108	0.068	8
9	0.837	0.703	0.592	0.500	0.424	0.361	0.308	0.263	0.225	0.194	0.167	0.144	0.125	0.108	0.094	0.082	0.048	9
10	0.820	0.676	0.558	0.463	0.386	0.322	0.270	0.227	0.191	0.162	0.137	0.116	0.099	0.085	0.073	0.062	0.035	10
11	0.804	0.650	0.527	0.429	0.350	0.287	0.237	0.195	0.162	0.135	0.112	0.094	0.079	0.066	0.056	0.047	0.025	11
12	0.788	0.625	0.497	0.397	0.319	0.257	0.208	0.168	0.137	0.112	0.092	0.076	0.062	0.052	0.043	0.036	0.018	12
13	0.773	0.601	0.469	0.368	0.290	0.229	0.182	0.145	0.116	0.093	0.075	0.061	0.050	0.040	0.033	0.027	0.013	13
14	0.758	0.577	0.442	0.340	0.263	0.205	0.160	0.125	0.099	0.078	0.062	0.049	0.039	0.032	0.025	0.021	0.009	14
15	0.743	0.555	0.417	0.315	0.239	0.183	0.140	0.108	0.084	0.065	0.051	0.040	0.031	0.025	0.020	0.016	0.006	15
16	0.728	0.534	0.394	0.292	0.218	0.163	0.123	0.093	0.071	0.054	0.042	0.032	0.025	0.019	0.015	0.012	0.005	16
17	0.714	0.513	0.371	0.270	0.198	0.146	0.108	0.080	0.060	0.045	0.034	0.026	0.020	0.015	0.012	0.009	0.003	17
18	0.700	0.494	0.350	0.250	0.180	0.130	0.095	0.069	0.051	0.038	0.028	0.021	0.016	0.012	0.009	0.007	0.002	18
19	0.686	0.475	0.331	0.232	0.164	0.116	0.083	0.060	0.043	0.031	0.023	0.017	0.012	0.009	0.007	0.005	0.002	19
20	0.673	0.456	0.312	0.215	0.149	0.104	0.073	0.051	0.037	0.026	0.019	0.014	0.010	0.007	0.005	0.004	0.001	20
21	0.660	0.439	0.294	0.199	0.135	0.093	0.064	0.044	0.031	0.022	0.015	0.011	0.008	0.006	0.004	0.003	0.001	21
22	0.647	0.422	0.278	0.184	0.123	0.083	0.056	0.038	0.026	0.018	0.013	0.009	0.006	0.004	0.003	0.002	0.001	22
23	0.634	0.406	0.262	0.170	0.112	0.074	0.049	0.033	0.022	0.015	0.010	0.007	0.005	0.003	0.002	0.002	0.000	23
24	0.622	0.390	0.247	0.158	0.102	0.066	0.043	0.028	0.019	0.013	0.008	0.006	0.004	0.003	0.002	0.001	0.000	24
25	0.610	0.375	0.233	0.146	0.092	0.059	0.038	0.024	0.016	0.010	0.007	0.005	0.003	0.002	0.001	0.001	0.000	25
26	0.598	0.361	0.220	0.135	0.084	0.053	0.033	0.021	0.014	0.009	0.006	0.004	0.002	0.002	0.001	0.001	0.000	26
27	0.586	0.347	0.207	0.125	0.076	0.047	0.029	0.018	0.011	0.007	0.005	0.003	0.002	0.001	0.001	0.001	0.000	27
28	0.574	0.333	0.196	0.116	0.069	0.042	0.026	0.016	0.010	0.006	0.004	0.002	0.002	0.001	0.001	0.000	0.000	28
29	0.563	0.321	0.185	0.107	0.063	0.037	0.022	0.014	0.008	0.005	0.003	0.002	0.001	0.001	0.000	0.000	0.000	29
30	0.552	0.308	0.174	0.099	0.057	0.033	0.020	0.012	0.007	0.004	0.003	0.002	0.001	0.001	0.000	0.000	0.000	30
35	0.500	0.253	0.130	0.068	0.036	0.019	0.010	0.006	0.003	0.002	0.001	0.001	0.000	0.000	0.000	0.000	0.000	35
40	0.453	0.208	0.097	0.046	0.022	0.011	0.005	0.003	0.001	0.001	0.000	0.000	0.000	0.000	0.000	0.000	0.000	40

TABLE 3
Compound Amount of Annuity of $1.00 in Arrears* (Future Value of Annuity)

$$S_n = \frac{(1+r)^n - 1}{r}$$

Periods	2%	4%	6%	8%	10%	12%	14%	16%	18%	20%	22%	24%	26%	28%	30%	32%	40%	Periods
1	1.000	1.000	1.000	1.000	1.000	1.000	1.000	1.000	1.000	1.000	1.000	1.000	1.000	1.000	1.000	1.000	1.000	1
2	2.020	2.040	2.060	2.080	2.100	2.120	2.140	2.160	2.180	2.200	2.220	2.240	2.260	2.280	2.300	2.320	2.400	2
3	3.060	3.122	3.184	3.246	3.310	3.374	3.440	3.506	3.572	3.640	3.708	3.778	3.848	3.918	3.990	4.062	4.360	3
4	4.122	4.246	4.375	4.506	4.641	4.779	4.921	5.066	5.215	5.368	5.524	5.684	5.848	6.016	6.187	6.362	7.104	4
5	5.204	5.416	5.637	5.867	6.105	6.353	6.610	6.877	7.154	7.442	7.740	8.048	8.368	8.700	9.043	9.398	10.946	5
6	6.308	6.633	6.975	7.336	7.716	8.115	8.536	8.977	9.442	9.930	10.442	10.980	11.544	12.136	12.756	13.406	16.324	6
7	7.434	7.898	8.394	8.923	9.487	10.089	10.730	11.414	12.142	12.916	13.740	14.615	15.546	16.534	17.583	18.696	23.853	7
8	8.583	9.214	9.897	10.637	11.436	12.300	13.233	14.240	15.327	16.499	17.762	19.123	20.588	22.163	23.858	25.678	34.395	8
9	9.755	10.583	11.491	12.488	13.579	14.776	16.085	17.519	19.086	20.799	22.670	24.712	26.940	29.369	32.015	34.895	49.153	9
10	10.950	12.006	13.181	14.487	15.937	17.549	19.337	21.321	23.521	25.959	28.657	31.643	34.945	38.593	42.619	47.062	69.814	10
11	12.169	13.486	14.972	16.645	18.531	20.655	23.045	25.733	28.755	32.150	35.962	40.238	45.031	50.398	56.405	63.122	98.739	11
12	13.412	15.026	16.870	18.977	21.384	24.133	27.271	30.850	34.931	39.581	44.874	50.895	57.739	65.510	74.327	84.320	139.235	12
13	14.680	16.627	18.882	21.495	24.523	28.029	32.089	36.786	42.219	48.497	55.746	64.110	73.751	84.853	97.625	112.303	195.929	13
14	15.974	18.292	21.015	24.215	27.975	32.393	37.581	43.672	50.818	59.196	69.010	80.496	93.926	109.612	127.913	149.240	275.300	14
15	17.293	20.024	23.276	27.152	31.772	37.280	43.842	51.660	60.965	72.035	85.192	100.815	119.347	141.303	167.286	197.997	386.420	15
16	18.639	21.825	25.673	30.324	35.950	42.753	50.980	60.925	72.939	87.442	104.935	126.011	151.377	181.868	218.472	262.356	541.988	16
17	20.012	23.698	28.213	33.750	40.545	48.884	59.118	71.673	87.068	105.931	129.020	157.253	191.735	233.791	285.014	347.309	759.784	17
18	21.412	25.645	30.906	37.450	45.599	55.750	68.394	84.141	103.740	128.117	158.405	195.994	242.585	300.252	371.518	459.449	1064.697	18
19	22.841	27.671	33.760	41.446	51.159	63.440	78.969	98.603	123.414	154.740	194.254	244.033	306.658	385.323	483.973	607.472	1491.576	19
20	24.297	29.778	36.786	45.762	57.275	72.052	91.025	115.380	146.628	186.688	237.989	303.601	387.389	494.213	630.165	802.863	2089.206	20
21	25.783	31.969	39.993	50.423	64.002	81.699	104.768	134.841	174.021	225.026	291.347	377.465	489.110	633.593	820.215	1060.779	2925.889	21
22	27.299	34.248	43.392	55.457	71.403	92.503	120.436	157.415	206.345	271.031	356.443	469.056	617.278	811.999	1067.280	1401.229	4097.245	22
23	28.845	36.618	46.996	60.893	79.543	104.603	138.297	183.601	244.487	326.237	435.861	582.630	778.771	1040.358	1388.464	1850.622	5737.142	23
24	30.422	39.083	50.816	66.765	88.497	118.155	158.659	213.978	289.494	392.484	532.750	723.461	982.251	1332.659	1806.003	2443.821	8032.999	24
25	32.030	41.646	54.865	73.106	98.347	133.334	181.871	249.214	342.603	471.981	650.955	898.092	1238.636	1706.803	2348.803	3226.844	11247.199	25
26	33.671	44.312	59.156	79.954	109.182	150.334	208.333	290.088	405.272	567.377	795.165	1114.634	1561.682	2185.708	3054.444	4260.434	15747.079	26
27	35.344	47.084	63.706	87.351	121.100	169.374	238.499	337.502	479.221	681.853	971.102	1383.146	1968.719	2798.706	3971.778	5624.772	22046.910	27
28	37.051	49.968	68.528	95.339	134.210	190.699	272.889	392.503	586.481	819.223	1185.744	1716.101	2481.586	3583.344	5164.311	7425.699	30866.674	28
29	38.792	52.966	73.640	103.966	148.631	214.583	312.094	456.303	669.447	984.068	1447.608	2128.965	3127.798	4587.680	6714.604	9802.923	43214.343	29
30	40.568	56.085	79.058	113.263	164.494	241.333	356.787	530.312	790.948	1181.882	1767.081	2640.916	3942.026	5873.231	8729.985	12940.859	60501.081	30
35	49.994	73.652	111.435	172.317	271.024	431.663	693.573	1120.713	1816.652	2948.341	4783.645	7750.225	12527.442	20188.966	32422.868	51869.427	325400.279	35
40	60.402	95.026	154.762	259.057	442.593	767.091	1342.025	2360.757	4163.213	7343.858	12936.535	22728.803	39792.982	69377.460	120392.883	207874.272	1750091.741	40

*Payments (or receipts) at the end of each period.

TABLE 4 *(Place a clip on this page for easy reference.)*
Present Value of Annuity $1.00 in Arrears*

$$P_n = \frac{1}{r}\left[1 - \frac{1}{(1+r)^n}\right]$$

Periods	2%	4%	6%	8%	10%	12%	14%	16%	18%	20%	22%	24%	26%	28%	30%	32%	40%	Periods
1	0.980	0.962	0.943	0.926	0.909	0.893	0.877	0.862	0.847	0.833	0.820	0.806	0.794	0.781	0.769	0.758	0.714	1
2	1.942	1.886	1.833	1.783	1.736	1.690	1.647	1.605	1.566	1.528	1.492	1.457	1.424	1.392	1.361	1.331	1.224	2
3	2.884	2.775	2.673	2.577	2.487	2.402	2.322	2.246	2.174	2.106	2.042	1.981	1.923	1.868	1.816	1.766	1.589	3
4	3.808	3.630	3.465	3.312	3.170	3.037	2.914	2.798	2.690	2.589	2.494	2.404	2.320	2.241	2.166	2.096	1.849	4
5	4.713	4.452	4.212	3.993	3.791	3.605	3.433	3.274	3.127	2.991	2.864	2.745	2.635	2.532	2.436	2.345	2.035	5
6	5.601	5.242	4.917	4.623	4.355	4.111	3.889	3.685	3.498	3.326	3.167	3.020	2.885	2.759	2.643	2.534	2.168	6
7	6.472	6.002	5.582	5.206	4.868	4.564	4.288	4.039	3.812	3.605	3.416	3.242	3.083	2.937	2.802	2.677	2.263	7
8	7.325	6.733	6.210	5.747	5.335	4.968	4.639	4.344	4.078	3.837	3.619	3.421	3.241	3.076	2.925	2.786	2.331	8
9	8.162	7.435	6.802	6.247	5.759	5.328	4.946	4.607	4.303	4.031	3.786	3.566	3.366	3.184	3.019	2.868	2.379	9
10	8.983	8.111	7.360	6.710	6.145	5.650	5.216	4.833	4.494	4.192	3.923	3.682	3.465	3.269	3.092	2.930	2.414	10
11	9.787	8.760	7.887	7.139	6.495	5.938	5.453	5.029	4.656	4.327	4.035	3.776	3.543	3.335	3.147	2.978	2.438	11
12	10.575	9.385	8.384	7.536	6.814	6.194	5.660	5.197	4.793	4.439	4.127	3.851	3.606	3.387	3.190	3.013	2.456	12
13	11.348	9.986	8.853	7.904	7.103	6.424	5.842	5.342	4.910	4.533	4.203	3.912	3.656	3.427	3.223	3.040	2.469	13
14	12.106	10.563	9.295	8.244	7.367	6.628	6.002	5.468	5.008	4.611	4.265	3.962	3.695	3.459	3.249	3.061	2.478	14
15	12.849	11.118	9.712	8.559	7.606	6.811	6.142	5.575	5.092	4.675	4.315	4.001	3.726	3.483	3.268	3.076	2.484	15
16	13.578	11.652	10.106	8.851	7.824	6.974	6.265	5.668	5.162	4.730	4.357	4.033	3.751	3.503	3.283	3.088	2.489	16
17	14.292	12.166	10.477	9.122	8.022	7.120	6.373	5.749	5.222	4.775	4.391	4.059	3.771	3.518	3.295	3.097	2.492	17
18	14.992	12.659	10.828	9.372	8.201	7.250	6.467	5.818	5.273	4.812	4.419	4.080	3.786	3.529	3.304	3.104	2.494	18
19	15.678	13.134	11.158	9.604	8.365	7.366	6.550	5.877	5.316	4.843	4.442	4.097	3.799	3.539	3.311	3.109	2.496	19
20	16.351	13.590	11.470	9.818	8.514	7.469	6.623	5.929	5.353	4.870	4.460	4.110	3.808	3.546	3.316	3.113	2.497	20
21	17.011	14.029	11.764	10.017	8.649	7.562	6.687	5.973	5.384	4.891	4.476	4.121	3.816	3.551	3.320	3.116	2.498	21
22	17.658	14.451	12.042	10.201	8.772	7.645	6.743	6.011	5.410	4.909	4.488	4.130	3.822	3.556	3.323	3.118	2.498	22
23	18.292	14.857	12.303	10.371	8.883	7.718	6.792	6.044	5.432	4.925	4.499	4.137	3.827	3.559	3.325	3.120	2.499	23
24	18.914	15.247	12.550	10.529	8.985	7.784	6.835	6.073	5.451	4.937	4.507	4.143	3.831	3.562	3.327	3.121	2.499	24
25	19.523	15.622	12.783	10.675	9.077	7.843	6.873	6.097	5.467	4.948	4.514	4.147	3.834	3.564	3.329	3.122	2.499	25
26	20.121	15.983	13.003	10.810	9.161	7.896	6.906	6.118	5.480	4.956	4.520	4.151	3.837	3.566	3.330	3.123	2.500	26
27	20.707	16.330	13.211	10.935	9.237	7.943	6.935	6.136	5.492	4.964	4.524	4.154	3.839	3.567	3.331	3.123	2.500	27
28	21.281	16.663	13.406	11.051	9.307	7.984	6.961	6.152	5.502	4.970	4.528	4.157	3.840	3.568	3.331	3.124	2.500	28
29	21.844	16.984	13.591	11.158	9.370	8.022	6.983	6.166	5.510	4.975	4.531	4.159	3.841	3.569	3.332	3.124	2.500	29
30	22.396	17.292	13.765	11.258	9.427	8.055	7.003	6.177	5.517	4.979	4.534	4.160	3.842	3.569	3.332	3.124	2.500	30
35	24.999	18.665	14.498	11.655	9.644	8.176	7.070	6.215	5.539	4.992	4.541	4.164	3.845	3.571	3.333	3.125	2.500	35
40	27.355	19.793	15.046	11.925	9.779	8.244	7.105	6.233	5.548	4.997	4.544	4.166	3.846	3.571	3.333	3.125	2.500	40

*Payments (or receipts) at the end of each period.

Cost Accounting in Professional Examinations

This appendix describes the role of cost accounting in professional examinations. We use professional examinations in Canada, the United States, Australia, Japan, and the United Kingdom to illustrate the role. A conscientious reader who has solved a representative sample of the problems at the end of the chapters will be well prepared for the professional examination questions dealing with cost accounting. This appendix aims to provide perspective, instill confidence, and encourage readers to take the examinations.

CANADIAN PROFESSIONAL EXAMINATIONS

CERTIFIED GENERAL ACCOUNTANT (CGA), CERTIFIED GENERAL ACCOUNTANTS' ASSOCIATION (CGA)

The designation of CGA represents an internationally recognized membership in excess of 75,000 members and students. The designation is obtained through a competency-based experience, learning, and examination process. The Professional Applications and Competence Evaluations (PACE) focus on ethics, critical thinking, professional judgment, communication, and leadership as well as development of practical accounting skills. The PACE program of courses and experience must be taken through the CGA and is a flexible, online study program.

CGA-Canada has mutual recognition agreements with CPA Australia, Ireland, and France and the Association of Chartered Certified Accountants (ACCA). CGA-Canada represents not only Canadian CGAs and students but also those in Bermuda, the nations of the Caribbean, the People's Republic of China, and Hong Kong. Detailed information may be accessed at www.cga-canada.org/en-ca/Programs/Pages/ca_ become_CGA.aspx.

CHARTERED ACCOUNTANT (CA), CANADIAN INSTITUTE OF CHARTERED ACCOUNTANTS (CICA)

The provincial institutes of the CICA educate and examine all those in Canada and members of the Bermuda Institutes/Ordre of Chartered Accountants who pursue a CA. In July 2011, the CICA welcomed 3,046 new members who had successfully completed the Uniform Final Examination (UFE) and acquired the experience necessary to meet the requirements of the profession. The Institute publishes exposure drafts and updates on the conceptual framework, generally accepted accounting principles (GAAP), and standards affecting publicly listed, privately owned, not-for-profit, and government organizations.

The CICA has recently initiated negotiations with the Certified Management Accountants to explore the merits of uniting their national and professional organizations. It has also signed a memorandum of understanding on Reciprocal Membership Arrangements with the Institute of Chartered Accountants of India to expedite recognition of ICAI accountants in Canada as CAs. Monthly, the CICA publishes *CAMagazine*. The magazine informs the membership of important economic, legal, and accounting issues. Detailed information may be accessed at www.cica.ca/about-the-profession/vision-and-mission/indes.aspx.

CERTIFIED MANAGEMENT ACCOUNTANT (CMA) SOCIETY OF MANAGEMENT ACCOUNTANTS OF CANADA (SMAC)

The SMAC is a partnership structure of provincial institutes that provide professional development programs in many business areas and grant accreditation to qualified CMAs. The courses are available online and through professional conferences, and through specialized educational programs for university graduates. A combination of experience, competencies, and educational achievement is required of CMAs. The qualified CMA has unique competencies in cost management, strategic performance measurement, process management, risk management and assurance services, and stakeholder reporting.

The CMA has formal international relationships with the American Institute of Certified Public Accountants (AICPA), Certified Practising Accountants of Australia (CPA Australia), and Chartered Institute of Public Finance and Accountancy (CIPFA), among others. CMA Canada publishes *CMA magazine* monthly. This magazine includes details of courses that assist students in preparing for the CMA examination. Detailed information may be accessed at www.cma-canada.org.

UNITED STATES PROFESSIONAL EXAMINATIONS

CPA AND CMA DESIGNATIONS

Many American readers may eventually take the Certified Public Accountant (CPA) examination or the Certified Management Accountant (CMA) examination. Certification is important to professional accountants for many reasons, such as:

1. Recognition of achievement and technical competence by fellow accountants and by users of accounting services.

2. Increased self-confidence in one's professional abilities.

3. Membership in professional organizations offering programs of career-long education.

4. Enhancement of career opportunities.

5. Personal satisfaction.

The CPA certificate is issued by individual states; it is necessary to obtain a state's licence to practice as a Certified Public Accountant. A prominent feature of public accounting is the use of independent (external) auditors to give assurance about the reliability of the financial statements supplied by managers. These auditors are called Certified Public Accountants in the United States and Chartered Accountants in many other English-speaking nations. The major US professional association in the private sector that regulates the quality of external auditing is the American Institute of Certified Public Accountants (AICPA).

The CMA designation is offered by the Institute of Management Accountants (IMA). The IMA is the largest association of management accountants in the world.

The major objective of the CMA certification is to enhance the development of the management accounting profession. In particular, focus is placed on the modern role of the management accountant as an active contributor to, and a participant in, management. The CMA designation is gaining increased stature in the business community as a credential parallel to the CPA designation.

The CMA examination is given in a computer-based format and has four parts. The questions are carefully constructed multiple-choice and written-response questions that test all levels of cognitive skills. The U.S. CMA exam consists of:

Part 1: Business Analysis
◆ Global Business
◆ Internal Controls
◆ Quantitative Methods
◆ Financial Statement Analysis
◆ Business Economics

Part 2: Management Accounting and Reporting
◆ Budget Preparation
◆ Cost Management
◆ Information Management
◆ Performance Measurement
◆ External Financial Reporting

Part 3: Strategic Management
◆ Strategic Planning
◆ Strategic Marketing
◆ Corporate Finance
◆ Decision Analysis
◆ Investment Decision Analysis

Part 4: Business Application
◆ All topics from Parts 1, 2, and 3, plus
◆ Organization Management
◆ Organization Communication
◆ Behavioural Issues
◆ Ethical Considerations

A person who has successfully completed the U.S. CPA examination is exempt from Part 1. For more information, visit the IMA website at www.imanet.org.

Cost management accounting questions are prominent in the CMA examination. The CPA examinations also include such questions, although they are less extensive than questions regarding financial accounting, auditing, and business law. This book includes many questions and problems used in past CMA and CPA examinations. In addition, a supplement to this book, *Student Guide and Review Manual* [John K. Harris (Upper Saddle River, NJ: Prentice Hall, 2009)], contains over 100 CMA and CPA questions and explanatory answers. Careful study of appropriate topics in this book will give candidates sufficient background for succeeding in the cost accounting portions of the professional examinations.

The IMA publishes *Strategic Finance* monthly. Each issue includes advertisements for courses that help students prepare for the CMA examination.

AUSTRALIAN PROFESSIONAL EXAMINATIONS

In Australia, the designation of CPA is awarded to those university graduates who have the required work experience and pass the CPA program. The ICAA awards the designation of CA to those who complete the professional training program. There are three compulsory core segments in the program: Reporting and Professional Practice,

Corporate Governance and Accountability, and Business Strategy and Leadership. Candidates must also take three of nine elective subjects. These subjects are assurance services and auditing, financial accounting, financial reporting and disclosure, financial risk management, insolvency and reconstruction, knowledge management, personal financial planning and superannuation, strategic management accounting, and taxation.

The strategic management accounting segment topics include:

1. Management accounting: supporting the value creation process.

2. Creating organizational value.

3. Managing performance measures.

4. Techniques for managing value.

5. Project management.

INTHEBLACK, published monthly, includes advertisements for courses that help students prepare for the CPA examination.

The Institute of Chartered Accountants in Australia (ICAA) offers the Chartered Accountant (CA) certification that has membership requirements including passing five modules: Financial Accounting and Reporting, Management Accounting and Analysis, Audit and Assurance, Taxation, and Ethics and Business Application.

The Management Accounting&Analysis module includes topics such as forecasting and budgeting with decision tools, investment analysis tools and techniques, risk management, strategic planning and analysis, ethics, and performance reporting.

JAPANESE PROFESSIONAL EXAMINATIONS

There are three major management accounting organizations in Japan—Japanese Industrial Management and Accounting Association (JIMMA); Enterprise Management Association (EMA); and Japanese Institute of Certified Public Accountants (JICPA)

JIMMA directs a School of Cost Control and a School of Corporate Tax Accounting where university professors and executives from member corporations teach. The EMA is the Japanese chapter of the U.S. IMA. JICPA is the CPA professional organization in Japan.

UNITED KINGDOM PROFESSIONAL EXAMINATIONS

The Chartered Institute of Management Accountants (CIMA) is the largest professional management accounting body in the U.K.. It provides a range of services to its members in commerce, education, government, and the accounting profession. Other accounting bodies include the Institute of Chartered Accountants in England and Wales (ICAEW) and the Institute of Chartered Accountants of Scotland (ICAS). The international body of accountants is the Association of Chartered Certified Accountants (ACCA).

The syllabus for the CIMA examination consists of three learning streams:

◆ *Business Management:* includes papers on organizational management and information systems, integrated management, and business strategy.
◆ *Management Accounting:* includes papers on performance evaluation, decision making, and risk control and strategy.
◆ *Financial Management:* includes papers on financial accounting and tax principles, financial analysis, and financial strategy.

Management Accounting, published monthly by CIMA, includes details of courses assisting students in preparing for their examinations. Management accounting topics are also covered by several other professional bodies. The syllabus for the examinations of the Association of Chartered Certified Accountants (ACCA) has three distinct parts. Skills examined include information for control, decision making, management, strategy, reporting, taxation, and overall strategic financial management.

GLOSSARY

Abnormal spoilage Spoilage that would not arise under efficient operating conditions; it is not inherent in a particular production process.

Absorption costing (or *full absorption costing*) A method of inventory valuation in which inventory "absorbs" both variable and fixed manufacturing costs as inventoriable costs, but all nonmanufacturing costs are classified as period costs.

Account analysis method Cost accounts are classified in the ledger as variable, fixed, or mixed with respect to the cost driver.

Accounting rate of return Also known as *accrual accounting rate of return (AARR)*, or *return on investment (ROI)*; an accounting measure of income divided by an accounting measure of investment.

Accrual accounting rate of return (AARR) Also known as *accounting rate of return*, or *return on investment (ROI)*; an accounting measure of income divided by an accounting measure of investment.

Activity An event, task, or unit of work with a specified purpose.

Activity-based budgeting A strategy to identify and control costs that focuses on the cost of activities necessary to produce and sell products and services.

Activity-based costing (ABC) A refined costing system that focuses on activities as the fundamental cost objects.

Activity-based management (ABM) A cost leadership strategy to eliminate non-value-added activities, which are those activities failing to add value for which customers will pay.

Activity cost driver In activity-based costing (ABC) systems, these are cost allocation bases.

Activity cost pool The dollar value of the cost of activities at a specified level.

Activity cost rate The activity cost pool divided by the total quantity consumed of the activity cost driver.

Activity level The cost object that specifies the scope of changes in cost, which may cause a change in the cost of single units, batches, and entire products.

Actual cost Cost incurred (a historical or past cost), as distinguished from a budgeted or forecasted cost.

Actual costing Tracing direct costs to each job by multiplying each actual unit direct cost rate by the quantity of the direct input used.

Actual indirect cost allocation rate The average cost per unit of shared resources used by all types of jobs calculated by dividing the actual MOH cost pool by the actual total quantity of the cost allocation base.

Adjacencies Opportunities to expand to markets related to the core business.

Adjusted allocation rate approach This approach restates all overhead entries in the general ledger and subsidiary ledgers using actual cost rates rather than budgeted cost rates.

Adjusted cost base (ACB) The cost of a property plus any expenses to acquire it.

Advance transfer price arrangement (APA) A substitute for dispute resolution wherein the company and the tax authority can cooperate to prospectively agree on a transfer price method.

Agility The ability for a service company to excel simultaneously in quality, delivery time, customization, and cost in a coordinated way.

Allowable cost A cost that the contract parties agree to include in the costs to be reimbursed.

Appraisal costs Costs incurred to detect which of the individual units of products do not conform to specifications.

Arm's-length principle A transfer price should be the same as it would be if the two subunits were independent companies.

Arm's-length transactions Transactions between a corporate subunit and a nonrelated party.

Artificial costs (also called *complete reciprocated costs*) The actual costs incurred by a support department plus a part of the costs of the other support departments that provide service to it.

Autocorrelation A type of systematic dependence that arises when the current value of X depends upon the value of X either immediately prior (lagged) to it or immediately after (leading) it in time.

Average cost Also called a *unit cost*, average cost is calculated by dividing the total prime cost pool by physical units consumed.

Average waiting time The average amount of time that an order will wait in line before it is set up and processed.

Backflush costing A costing system that omits recording some or all journal entries relating to the cycle from purchase of direct materials to the sale of finished goods.

Balanced scorecard (BSC) A document that translates an organization's mission and strategy into a comprehensive set of performance measures that provide the framework for implementing its strategy.

Batch-level costs Resources sacrificed on activities that are related to a group of units.

Belief systems   An articulation of the mission, purpose, and core values of a company.

Behavioural considerations   Considerations that motivate managers and other employees to aim for the goals of the organization.

Benchmark   The best possible performance achieved anywhere in any industry using a similar process.

Benchmarking reports   Based on the costs of other companies and can be developed for many activities and products

Board of directors   The independent group who hold the external auditors, CEO, CFO, and COO accountable for both the quality of financial information and organizational outcomes.

Book value   The original acquisition cost of a long-term asset minus accumulated amortization.

Bottleneck   An operation where the work required to be performed approaches or exceeds the available capacity.

Boundary systems   An articulation of standards of behaviour and codes of conduct expected of all employees, especially actions that are off-limits.

Breakeven point (BEP)   Quantity of output at which total revenues and total costs are equal; that is, where the operating income is zero.

Breakeven point (BEP), revenue   Level of sales in dollars at which total revenues and total costs are equal; that is, where the operating income is zero.

Breakeven point (BEP), volume   Level of sales in units at which total revenues and total costs are equal; that is, where the operating income is zero.

Breakeven revenue   Level of sales in dollars at which total revenues and total costs are equal; that is, where the operating income is zero.

Breakeven volume   Level of sales in units at which total revenues and total costs are equal; that is, where the operating income is zero.

Budget   A quantitative expression for a set time period of a proposed (future) plan of action by management.

Budget constraint   The combination of limitations on nonfinancial and financial resources within a company's management control.

Budgetary slack   The practice of underestimating budgeted revenues (or overestimating budgeted costs) to make budgeted targets easier to achieve.

Budgeted cost   Predicted or forecasted cost (future cost) as distinguished from an actual or historical cost.

Budgeting cycle   The process of budgeting: planning performance, providing a frame of reference, investigating variations from plans, and adjusting plans as necessary.

Business function costs   The sum of all the costs (variable costs and fixed costs) in a particular business function in the value chain.

Byproduct   A product that has a low sales value compared with the sales value of the main or joint product(s).

Canadian Institute of Chartered Accountants (CICA)   A body that licenses and certifies Canadian chartered accountants.

Capacity   The quantity of outputs that can be produced from long-term resources available to the company.

Capacity cost   The cost of maintaining a certain plant capacity—a fixed overhead cost. It is often a cost pool grouping all fixed overhead costs.

Capital budgeting   The process of collating information in a familiar pro forma financial accounting format.

Capital intensive companies   Companies with a high percentage of fixed costs in their cost structure.

Capital cost allowance (CCA)   The legally required income tax counterpart to annual amortization expense in financial reporting.

Capital gain   Arises when the selling price of a capital property exceeds the total ACB plus sales' expenses.

Capital loss   Arises when the selling price of a capital property is less than the total ACB plus sales' expenses.

Carrying costs   These costs arise when a business holds inventories of goods for sale.

Cash budget   A schedule of expected cash receipts and disbursements.

Cash cycle   Also known as a *self-liquidating cycle*, *working capital cycle*, or *operating cycle*; the movement of cash to inventories, to receivables, and back to cash.

Cause-and-effect diagram   A diagram that identifies potential causes of failures or defects.

Certified General Accountants (CGA)   The designation given by the Certified General Accountants to those who have passed admission and licensing criteria.

Certified Management Accountant (CMA)   The designation given by the Society of Management Accountants of Canada (SMAC) to management accountants who have passed admission criteria and demonstrated the competency of technical knowledge and skills required by the SMAC.

Chief executive officer (CEO)   This person is independent of and legally accountable to the Board of Directors for all organizational outcomes.

Chief financial officer (CFO)   Also called the *finance director*, this is the senior officer empowered with overseeing the financial operations of an organization.

Chief operating officer (COO)   This person is accountable to the CEO for all operating results.

Coefficient a   Coefficient a represents the fixed cost component in the linear cost function $Y = a + bX$, which is constant and unavoidable even if the value of X is 0. b is the coefficient of the slope, or rate of change in y (or Y) when X changes by 1 unit.

Coefficient of determination r^2   Measures the percentage of variation in an outcome variable explained by one or more predictor variables.

Coefficient matrix   Summarizes the cost allocation percentages to solve the equations of each complete reciprocated cost.

Collusive pricing   Companies in an industry conspire in their pricing and output decisions to achieve a price above the competitive price.

Combined-variance analysis   (also called *three-variance analysis*) Combines variable-cost and fixed-cost variances when reporting overhead cost variances.

Common cost   A cost of operating a facility, operation, activity, or like cost object that is shared by two or more users.

Comparable uncontrolled price method (CUP) A transfer price that is analogous to the internal market-based price.

Composite unit A hypothetical unit with weights based on the mix of individual units.

Conference method Develops cost estimates based on analysis and opinions gathered from various departments of an organization.

Confidence level The probability that the conclusion based on the student *t*-statistic is wrong.

Conformance quality The performance of a product or service according to design and production specifications.

Constant gross margin percentage NRV method The gross margin (based on the overall gross margin percentage) and separable costs deducted from the final sales value of units produced for each product. The residual amount for each product is its allocation of joint costs.

Constraint In linear programming techniques, a mathematical inequality or equality that must be satisfied by the variables in a mathematical model.

Continuous improvement A strategy whereby a budgeted cost is successively reduced over succeeding time periods.

Contribution income statement Income statement that groups line items by cost-behaviour pattern to highlight the contribution margin.

Contribution margin (TCM) Revenues minus all costs of the output (a product or service) that vary with respect to the number of output units.

Contribution margin percentage (CM%, contribution margin ratio) Contribution margin per unit divided by unit selling price, or total contribution margin divided by total revenue.

Contribution margin per unit The difference between selling price and variable cost per unit.

Contribution margin ratio The contribution margin per unit divided by the selling price per unit. Also called *contribution margin percentage*.

Control Coordinated action that companies take to implement their planning decisions, evaluate actual against expected performance, and provide timely feedback on current results.

Control chart Graphs a time series of successive observations of a particular step, procedure, or operation taken at regular time intervals. In addition to actual results, the expected range of specified results is also presented.

Controllability The degree of authority that a specific manager has over costs, revenues, or other items in question.

Controllable cost Any cost that is primarily subject to the authorization of a specific manager of a specific responsibility centre for a specific time span.

Controller The financial executive primarily responsible for both management accounting and financial accounting.

Conversion cost Any manufacturing cost (may include direct labour) other than direct material cost.

Core competence A unique combination of human and captial resources that provides the corporation with a competitive advantage in its economic environment. Also called *distinctive competence*.

Core (operating) division (department, production department) This core division or department, also called an *operating division*, or, in manufacturing companies, a *production division or department*, adds value that is observable by a customer to a product or service.

Corporate governance Mandatory compliance with existing laws, regulations, and standards.

Corporate social responsibility (CSR) The voluntary integration by companies of social and environmental concerns into their business operation.

Correlation (or *covariance*) Identifies two events that systematically vary together.

Cost Resource sacrificed or forgone to achieve a specific objective.

Cost accounting Measures, analyzes, and reports financial and nonfinancial information relating to the costs of acquiring or using resources in an organization. It provides information for both management accounting and financial accounting.

Cost accumulation The collection (accumulation) of actual cost data in an organized way.

Cost allocation (or *cost application*) A method to attribute or assign relevant indirect costs to each job.

Cost allocation base (or *cost application base*) An input factor that systematically links some proportion of each indirect cost pool to each job or cost object.

Cost allocation rate A unit average cost of an input common to all jobs. It is the result of dividing a cost pool by its cost-allocation base.

Cost application (or *cost allocation*) A method to attribute or assign relevant indirect costs to each job.

Cost application base A synonym for *cost allocation base*.

Cost assignment The multiplication of the cost-allocation rate by the specific quantity of inputs in the denominator that is consumed by the specific job.

Cost-benefit approach Promotes decision making in which the perceived net benefits from spending corporate resources should exceed their perceived expected costs.

Cost centre A responsibility centre for which managers are accountable for costs only, not revenue lost or gained.

Cost cross-subsidization (or *cross-subsidization*) A result that arises when at least one miscosted product results in miscosting at least one other product in the organization.

Cost driver A variable, such as the level of activity or volume, that causally affects costs over a given time span.

Cost incurrence Costs are incurred when a resource is sacrificed or consumed.

Cost hierarchy The name given to the management-accounting logic used to separate one indirect cost pool into one of four possible cost pools according to the level at which activities contribute to producing output.

Cost leadership An organization's ability to achieve low costs relative to competitors through productivity and efficiency improvements, elimination of waste, and tight cost control.

Cost management The approaches and activities of managers who undertake both short-run and long-run planning and control decisions to increase value to customers and to achieve organizational goals.

Cost object Anything for which it is desirable to measure the costs.

Costs of goods manufactured (COGM) Cost of goods brought to completion, whether they were started before or during the current accounting period.

Costs of goods sold (COGS) The accumulation of all costs incurred to manufacture the finished products that have been sold during a specific time period.

Costs of sales (COS) The accumulated purchase costs for merchandise sold by merchandising companies.

Cost-plus method (CPM) A method of determining a transfer price that highlights the effect of the transfer price on the pretax income of each subunit.

Cost-plus pricing Pricing in which the gross margin equals a certain percentage of the price.

Cost pool The accumulation of relevant costs from general ledger accounts.

Cost smoothing A costing system that spreads the costs of conversion and inputs uniformly.

Cost tracing The method of assigning direct costs to a distinct cost object.

Cost-volume-profit (CVP) analysis Examines the behaviour of total revenues, total costs, and operating income as changes occur in the output level, selling price, variable costs per unit, or fixed costs; a single revenue driver and a single cost driver are used in this analysis.

Costs of quality (COQ) Costs incurred to prevent or rectify the production of a low-quality product.

Critical value A benchmark value for the student *t*-statistic such that if the calculated value of *t* for the values of the coefficients *a*, and *b* exceed the critical value, then at a specific confidence level, the values of *a* and *b* are not due to chance.

Cross-secctional data Data that has been systematically collected simultaneously at many different locations.

Cross-subsidization (or *cost cross-subsidization*) The situation that, when a simple average method is used, one output, batch, or product will be undercosted and at least one output, batch, or product will be overcosted.

Cumulative average time learning model Depicts a relationship such that the cumulative average time per unit declines by a constant percentage each time the cumulative quantity of units produced doubles.

Cumulative eligible capital (CEC) This pool is the balance of the eligible capital property remaining after deducting CECA.

Cumulative eligible capital amount (CECA) The annual CRA deduction permitted on intangible assets, calculated at 7% on a declining-balance basis.

Current cost The cost of purchasing an asset today identical to the one currently held.

Curvilinear cost function Depicts in arithmetic notation a nonlinear relationship between consumption of a resource and a cost. When the data points are joined they form a curve.

Cushion Excess capacity.

Customer life-cycle costing Costing that focuses on the external customer's costs to acquire, maintain, and dispose of the product or services.

Customer perspective This perspective identifies the targeted market segments and measures the company's success in these segments.

Customer profitability analysis The reporting and analysis of customer revenues and customer costs.

Customer-response time The amount of time between when a customer places an order for a product or requests a service and when the product or service is delivered to the customer.

Customer service Providing after-sale support to customers.

Decentralization A strategic response made by organizations that enables individual discretion. Primarily useful to organizations that face great uncertainties in their diverse environments, require detailed local knowledge for performing various jobs, and have few interdependencies among subunits.

Degree of operating leverage Contribution margin divided by operating income.

Degrees of freedom, df A way to properly classify a critical value for each sample size.

Denominator-level variance A production-volume or output-level variance equal to the difference between budgeted fixed overhead and the assigned fixed overhead for the actual quantity of outputs.

Design of products, services, or processes The detailed planning and engineering of products, services, or processes.

Designed-in costs (or *locked-in costs*) Costs that have not yet been incurred but that will be incurred in the future on the basis of decisions that have already been made.

Diagnostic control systems Measures that help diagnose whether a company is performing to expectations.

Differential approach This approach analyzes only relevant cash flows—those future cash outflows and inflows that differ between alternatives.

Differential cost (or *net relevant cost*) The difference in total cost between two alternatives.

Differential revenue The difference between the total revenue of two or more alternatives.

Direct allocation method This cost allocation method applies each support division's costs directly to the operating divisions.

Direct cost A cost related to a particular cost object that can be traced to that object in an economically feasible way.

Direct costing Inaccurately describes the inventory costing (valuation) method we call *variable costing*.

Direct labour cost (DL) The compensation of all period labour that can be traced to a cost object in an economically feasible way but are *not* part of cost of goods sold.

Direct machine-hour costs The quantity of machine-hours used when a product is manufactured.

Direct manufacturing labour cost (DML) The compensation of all manufacturing labour that can be traced to a cost object (work in process and then finished goods) in an economically feasible way.

Direct materials cost (DM) Acquisition costs of all materials that eventually become part of the cost object (work in process and then finished goods), and that can be traced to the cost object in an economically feasible way.

Direct materials inventory Materials in stock and awaiting use in the manufacturing process.

Direct materials mix variance The difference between two amounts: (1) the budgeted cost for the actual mix of the total quantity of direct materials used, and (2) the budgeted cost of the budgeted mix of the actual total quantity of direct materials used.

Direct materials yield variance The difference between two amounts: (1) the budgeted cost of direct materials based on the actual total quantity of all direct materials inputs used, and (2) the flexible-budget cost of direct materials based on the budgeted total quantity of direct materials inputs for the actual output, holding the budgeted input mix constant.

Direct method (also called the *direct allocation method*) Allocates each support department's costs directly to the operating departments.

Discontinuous cost functions (or *step fixed cost*) Arises when, within the relevant range of production inputs, the graph of total costs with a single resource consumed does not form a straight line with a constant slope.

Discount rate Also known as *hurdle rate, (opportunity) cost of capital*, or *required rate of return (RRR)*; the minimum acceptable rate of return on an investment.

Discounted cash flow (DCF) Two methods are net present value (NPV) and internal rate of return (IRR).

Discretionary costs These costs arise from periodic (usually yearly) decisions regarding the maximum amount to be incurred; they have no clearly measurable cause-and-effect relationship between output and resources used.

Distinctive competence A unique combination of human and captial resources that provides the corporation with a competitive advantage in its economic environment. Also called *core competence*.

Distribution Delivering products or services to customers.

Downside risk (also called *upside potential risk/return, cost/benefit*) Used to make resource allocations such that the expected benefits exceed the expected costs.

Downsizing (or *rightsizing*) An integrated approach to configure processes, products, and people to match costs to the activities needed to be performed to operate efficiently and effectively in the present and future.

Downstream costs Costs incurred after production.

Downward demand spiral A progressive reduction in sales and production that leads to an increase in the fixed overhead rate. As sales decrease, the realized quantity in the denominator of any fixed overhead cost rate decreases but the fixed cost pool is constant. Diminishing sales must bear higher costs per unit, which leads to diminishing sales.

Dual pricing Using two separate transfer pricing methods to price each interdivision transaction.

Dual-rate method This method first classifies costs in the cost pool into two pools (typically into a variable-cost pool and a fixed-cost pool), and each pool has a different allocation rate or base.

Dumping A non-Canadian company sells goods in Canada at a price below the market value in the home country or receives a government subsidy and this action materially injures or threatens to materially injure an industry in Canada.

Dysfunctional decision making Also known as *goal-incongruent decision making*, or *suboptimal decision making*; arises when a decision's benefit to one subunit is more than offset by the costs or loss of benefits to the organization as a whole.

Economic order quantity (EOQ) A decision model that calculates the optimal quantity of inventory to order.

Economic plausibility The cost drivers X_i under consideration as predictor variables are actually consumed when the indirect costs are incurred.

Economic substance The financial outcome of the all the different types of business transactions that happened in a specified time period.

Economic value added (EVA) A calculation that substitutes the following numbers in the residual-income calculations: (1) income equal to after-tax operating income, (2) a required rate of return equal to the weighted-average cost of capital, and (3) investment equal to total assets minus current liabilities.

Economies of scale Given a specific fixed cost of capacity, the greater the volume of output in the relevant range, the lower the unitized fixed cost of any one output.

Economies of scope These economies are achieved if a company designs different products that can be produced using the same equipment and plant.

Effectiveness The degree to which a predetermined objective or target is met.

Efficiency The relative amount of inputs used to achieve a given level of output.

Efficiency variance The difference between the actual quantity of input used and the budgeted quantity of input that should have been used multiplied by the budgeted input price.

Effort Exertion toward a goal. Effort goes beyond physical exertion, such as a worker producing at a faster rate, to include all conscientious actions (physical and mental).

Eligible capital expenditure The acquisition cost of an intangible asset.

Eligible capital property 75% of the acquisition cost of an intangible asset.

Engineered costs These costs arise specifically from a clear cause-and-effect relationship between output (or cost driver) and the (direct or indirect) resources used to produce that output.

Enterprise resource planning (ERP) Systems that improve internal business process flows of information enabling effective inventory cost control.

Enterprise risk management (ERM) Aligns strategy with risk management and evaluates how management initiatives have improved the overall risk profile of the company.

Equivalent units (EU) Derived amount of output units that (a) takes the quantity of each input (factor of production) in units completed and in incomplete units of work in process and (b) converts the quantity of input into the amount of completed output units that could be produced with that quantity of input.

Estimated net realizable value (NRV) method A method that allocates joint costs on the basis of the *relative estimated net realizable value* (expected final sales value in the ordinary course of business minus the expected separable costs of production and marketing of the total production of the period).

Ethical guidelines Guidelines that help members of a profession reason through an appropriate response to an ethical issue.

Ethics Agreed-upon standards of honesty and fairness that apply to everyone in all their dealings with one another.

Excess present value index (or *profitability index*) The total present value of future net cash inflows of a project divided by the total present value of the net initial investment.

Expected monetary value The sum of the weighted outcomes as measured in monetary terms.

Expected value The sum of multiplying each cash inflow, a_i, by the probability or $\sum_{a=1}^{i} E(a) = \sum (p_i) \times a_i$.

Experience curve A cost function that shows how full product costs per unit (including manufacturing, marketing, distribution, and so on) decrease as total quantity produced increases.

Explanatory power A change in the quantity of an activity cost driver will explain the change in cost of a distinct type of output.

External failure costs Costs incurred to detect a nonconforming product after it is shipped to customers.

Facility-sustaining costs The cost of activities that cannot be traced to individual products or services but support the organization as a whole.

Favourable (F) variance A favourable variance results when actual operating income exceeds the budgeted amount.

Finance director (or *chief financial officer*) The senior officer empowered with overseeing the financial operations of an organization.

Financial accounting Measures and records business transactions and provides financial statements that are based on generally accepted accounting principles. It focuses on reporting to external parties such as investors and banks.

Financial budget That part of the master budget that comprises the capital budget, cash budget, budgeted balance sheet, and budgeted statement of cash flows.

Financial perspective This perspective highlights achievement of financially strategic goals.

Fineness A characteristic of reliable information that enables users of that information to better predict how one factor will change with a change in another factor.

Finished goods inventory Unsold finished goods.

First-in, first-out (FIFO) process-costing method A method of process costing that assigns the cost of the previous accounting period's equivalent units in beginning work-in-process inventory to the first units completed and transferred out of the process, and assigns the cost of equivalent units worked on during the current period first to complete beginning inventory, next to start and complete new units, and finally to units in ending work-in-process inventory.

Fixed cost A cost that remains unchanged in total for a particular time period despite wide changes in the related level of total activity or volume.

Fixed overhead rate variance The difference between the budgeted fixed manufacturing overhead cost minus the actual fixed manufacturing overhead cost.

Flexible budget A budget that is adjusted in accordance with ensuing changes in either actual output or actual revenue and cost drivers.

Flexible-budget variance The difference between the actual (realized) results and the flexible-budget (pro forma) amount for the actual levels of the revenue and cost drivers.

Full absorption costing A method of inventory valuation in which inventory "absorbs" both variable and fixed manufacturing costs as inventoriable costs, but all nonmanufacturing costs are classified as period costs.

Full product costs The sum of all the costs in all the business functions in the value chain (R&D, design, production, marketing, distribution, and customer service).

Goal-congruence Exists when individuals and groups work towards the publicly declared organization goals.

Goal-incongruent decision making Also known as *dysfunctional decision making*, or *suboptimal decision making*; arises when a decision's benefit to one subunit is more than offset by the costs or loss of benefits to the organization as a whole.

Goodness of fit The term statisticians use to describe the proportion of change in an outcome variable Y that is explained by a predictor variable X. r^2 is the statistic or measure of goodness of fit.

Gross margin Revenue minus cost of goods sold (or cost of sales); Rev – COGS (or COS).

Gross margin percentage (GM%) The result obtained from dividing the gross margin by the total revenue.

Gross profit percentage See *operating margin percentage*.

Half-year rule Assumes that all net additions are purchased in the middle of the year, and thus only one-half of the stated CCA rate is allowed in the first year.

Heterogeneous cost pool A mix of different types of costs caused by different cost drivers that may contain both variable and fixed costs.

High-low method Uses only the highest and lowest observed values of the common input within the relevant range. The line connecting these two points becomes the estimated cost function.

Human capital The value added by people with skill and experience gained from working together.

Hurdle rate Also known as *discount rate*, *(opportunity) cost of capital*, or *required rate of return (RRR)*; the minimum acceptable rate of return on an investment.

Hybrid-costing system Costing system that blends characteristics from both job-costing systems and process-costing systems.

Idle time Wages paid for unproductive time caused by lack of orders, machine breakdowns, material shortages, poor scheduling, and the like that interrupt production.

Imputed costs Costs recognized in particular situations that are not regularly recognized by accrual accounting procedures.

Incremental cost allocation method This method ranks the individual cost objects and then uses this ranking to allocate costs among those cost objects.

Incremental costs Also known as *out-of-pocket costs*, or *outlay costs*; additional costs made to obtain either additional resources or sales.

Incremental revenue Any additional total revenue from one alternative.

Incremental revenue-allocation method A method that ranks the individual products in a bundle and then uses this ranking to allocate the bundled revenues to these individual products. The first-ranked product is termed the *primary product* in the bundle.

Incremental unit time learning model The incremental unit time (the time needed to produce the last unit) declines by a constant percentage each time the cumulative quantity of units produced doubles.

Indirect cost A cost related to a particular cost object that cannot be traced to that object in an economically feasible way.

Indirect cost allocation rate The result of dividing an indirect cost pool by the quantity of resources in the indirect cost-allocation base. It is the estimated unit or average cost of indirect inputs.

Industrial engineering method This work measurement begins with an analysis of the relationship between quantities of physical inputs and physical outputs.

Inflation The decline in the general purchasing power of the monetary unit.

Infrastructure costs These costs arise from having property, plant, and equipment and a functioning organization.

Input mix The determination of the *standard* combination and proportion of very similar direct material inputs that may be substituted for one another.

Input-efficiency variance The difference between the actual quantity of input used and the budgeted quantity of input that should have been used multiplied by the budgeted input price.

Input-price variance The difference between the actual price and the budgeted price multiplied by the actual quantity of input in question.

Insource To produce goods or provide services within the organization.

Inspection point Stage of the production process at which products are examined to determine whether they are acceptable or unacceptable units. In the situation of process costing, spoilage is typically assumed to occur at the stage of completion where inspection takes place.

Intellectual capital This is comprised of human, structural, and relational capital.

Interactive control systems Formal information systems that managers use to focus organization attention and learning on key strategic issues.

Intermediate products Unfinished products transferred from one subunit to another subunit of the same organization in a multi-stage production process.

Internal business process perspective This perspective requires analysis of how to improve internal operations, which implicates the entire value chain of business functions.

Internal failure costs Costs incurred to detect a nonconforming product before it is shipped to customers.

Internal rate of return (IRR) (or *time-adjusted rate of return*) The discount rate at which the present value of expected cash inflows from a project equals the present value of expected cash outflows of the project.

International financial centres Countries with very low income tax rates that have tax treaties with Canada.

Intrinsic motivation The desire to achieve self-satisfaction from good performance regardless of external rewards such as bonuses or promotion.

Inventoriable cost All costs of a product that are considered as assets in the balance sheet when they are incurred and that become cost of goods sold only when the product is sold.

Inventory management The planning, coordinating, and control activities related to the flow of inventory into, through, and from the organization.

Invested capital Total assets plus current assets required to fund a specific project.

Investment centre A responsibility centre for which managers are accountable for investments, revenues, and costs.

Investment decision Also known as *investment program*, or *investment project*; a long-term cash allocation decision.

Investment program Also known as *investment*, or *investment project*; a long-term cash allocation decision.

Investment project Also known as *investment*, or *investment program*; a long-term cash allocation decision.

Job A distinct output unit or set of units.

Job-cost record (or *job-cost sheet*) The document where the costs for a job are recorded and accumulated. Jobs usually require some type of direct materials input.

Job-cost sheet See *job-cost record*.

Job-costing system A system where costs are assigned to a distinct unit, or set of units, of a product or service called a job.

Joint costs The costs of a production process that yields multiple main products simultaneously.

Joint products Products that have relatively high sales value but are not separately identifiable as individual products until the splitoff point.

Just-in-time (JIT) production (or *lean production*) A demand-pull system in which each component in a production line is produced immediately as the next step in the production line needs the component.

Just-in-time (JIT) purchasing A strategy to purchase goods or materials such that a delivery immediately precedes demand or use.

Kaizen budgeting Budgeting to implement a strategy of systematic elimination of waste in every business process.

Key performance factor Interdependent BSC factors most relevant to implementing a strategy successfully. Also called *key success factors (KSF)*.

Key success factor A strategic factor that requires close attention and control to assure an organization will survive and thrive.

Labour intensive Labour costs are a significant proportion of total costs.

Labour time record A source document recording the type of labour, quantity of time, unit labour rate, and total cost of labour for each job.

Lagged relationship The cost driver activity occurred the time period $(t-1)$ before the costs were recorded in the cost pool.

Leading relationship Costs were prepaid or incurred the time period before the cost driver activity occurred in the time period $(t+1)$.

Lean production (or *JIT production*) A demand-pull system in which each component in a production line is produced immediately as the next step in the production line needs the component.

Learning Arises from examining actual performance and systematically exploring how to make better informed predictions, decisions, and plans in the future.

Learning and growth perspective A field of study on the identification, development, retention, and valuation of intellectual capital, which comprises human, structural, and relational capital.

Learning curve   A curvilinear mathematical production function that shows how the ratio of quantity produced increases at a faster rate than the rate at which the time spent in activities of production decreases (Q_t output $\div$ Q_t DLH).

Life-cycle budgeting   A form of budgeting that requires that managers estimate full product costs across the entire value chain of business functions.

Life-cycle costing   This process tracks and accumulates the actual costs attributable to each product from start to finish.

Life-cycle pricing   Cradle-to-grave pricing that includes the environmental costs of production, reclamation, recycling, and reuse of materials.

Line management   Managers (for example, in production, marketing, or distribution) who are directly responsible for attaining the goals of the organization.

Linear cost function   Can be depicted on a graph as a straight line of the equation $y = a + bX$.

Linear programming   An *optimization technique* used to maximize total contribution margin (the objective function) given multiple constraints.

Locked-in costs   (or *designed-in costs*) Costs that have not yet been incurred but that will be incurred in the future on the basis of decisions that have already been made.

Main product   One product with a high sales value relative to the other products that a single process yields.

Make/buy decision   The decision whether to insource or outsource a business service or product.

Malus   The clawback of previously awarded compensation from an executive because of poor performance.

Management accountants   Accountants who measure, analyze, and report financial and nonfinancial information to internal managers.

Management accounting   Measures, analyzes, and reports financial and nonfinancial information that helps managers make decisions to fulfill the goals of an organization. It focuses on internal reporting.

Management accounting control system (MACS)   A system that provides relevant information as a basis for assurance of effective control.

Management by exception   The practice of focusing management attention on areas not operating as expected (such as a cost overrun on a project) and giving less attention to areas operating as expected.

Management information system (MIS)   Sometimes called a data warehouse or infobarn, these databases consist of small, detailed bits of information that can be used for several purposes.

Manufacturing cells   A grouping of all the different types of equipment used to make a given product.

Manufacturing cycle efficiency (MCE)   The ratio of value-added manufacturing cycle time divided by the total manufacturing cycle time.

Manufacturing cycle time   The sum of waiting time plus production cycle time.

Manufacturing lead time   The sum of waiting time plus manufacturing time for the order.

Manufacturing overhead   See *indirect cost*.

Manufacturing overhead allocated   The amount of manufacturing overhead costs allocated to distinct types of jobs based on the budgeted rate multiplied by the actual quantity of the allocation base used. Also called *manufacturing overhead applied*.

Manufacturing overhead applied   See *manufacturing overhead allocated*.

Manufacturing-sector companies   Companies that purchase materials and components and convert them into various finished goods.

Margin of safety   The excess of forecasted or budgeted revenues over the breakeven revenues.

Marginal income tax rate   The tax rate paid on additional amounts of pretax income.

Market-share variance   The difference between two amounts: (1) the budgeted amount based on actual market size in units, *actual market share*, and budgeted contribution margin per composite unit for the budgeted mix, and (2) the budgeted amount based on actual market size in units, *budgeted market share*, and budgeted contribution margin per composite unit for the budgeted mix.

Market-size variance   The difference between two amounts: (1) the budgeted amount based on *actual market size in units*, budgeted market share, and budgeted contribution margin per composite unit for budgeted mix, and (2) the static budget amount based on the *budgeted market size in units*, budgeted market share, and budgeted contribution margin per composite unit for budgeted mix.

Marketing   Promoting and selling products or services to customers or prospective customers.

Master budget   Summarizes the financial projections of all the organization's individual schedules and sub-unit budgets required to produce an operating budget.

Master-budget capacity   The level of output that will satisfy customer demand for a single budget cycle and complies with Canada Revenue Agency (CRA) for tax purposes.

Materials requirements planning (MRP)   A demand push-through system that manufactures finished goods for inventory on the basis of demand forecasts.

Materials-requisition record   A source document recording the job for which materials are needed.

Matrix   A way of succinctly communicating relevant information in rows and columns.

Merchandising-sector companies   Companies that purchase and then sell tangible products without changing their basic form.

Mix variance   A measurement of the variance of actual from expected input mix.

Mixed cost   A cost pool that comprises both variable and fixed costs.

Moral hazard   Describes contexts in which, once risk is shared, the individual fails to make as much effort to avoid harm as when risk was not shared.

Motivation   The desire to attain a selected goal (the goal-congruence aspect) combined with the resulting drive or pursuit towards that goal (the effort aspect).

Multicollinearity   When two or more predictor variables are highly correlated with each other.

Multiple linear regression   The technique used to measure the strength of relationships among at least two predictor variables and the outcome variable.

Net addition   Arises when the purchase price of new equipment exceeds proceeds of disposition of the old equipment.

Net income margin   (or *net profit margin*) An alternative technical term for *net* income.

Net income margin percentage   Net income divided by revenue.

Net present value (NPV) method   A method that calculates the expected net monetary gain or loss from a project by discounting all expected future cash inflows and outflows to the present point in time, using the required rate of return.

Net relevant cost   (or *differential cost*) The difference in total cost between two alternatives.

Nominal rate of return   The rate of return required to cover investment risk and the anticipated decline, due to inflation, in the general purchasing power of the cash that the investment generates.

Nonfinancial budget   Budgets that report on both the timing and quantity of resources required to achieve predicted financial results.

Nonlinear cost function   Arises when, within the relevant range of production inputs, the graph of total costs with a single cost driver does not form a straight line.

Non-productive idle capacity   A capacity level that incorporates downtime for setups.

Non-value-added activity   An activity that fails to contribute to the customer's value proposition.

Non-value-added cost   A cost that, if eliminated, would not reduce the value customers obtain from using the product or service.

Normal capacity   The level of output that will satisfy average customer demand over a specified time period and complies with GAAP.

Normal costing   The use of standard or predetermined or budgeted indirect cost-allocation rates to assign overhead costs but actual direct cost rates to assign direct costs.

Normal spoilage   Spoilage inherent in a particular production process that arises even under efficient operating conditions; often a locked-in cost.

Objective function   The objective or goal to be maximized expressed by a linear program.

Off-limits idle capacity   A capacity level that accounts for unavoidable operating interruptions such as scheduled maintenance time, shutdowns for holidays, safety inspections, and so on.

On-time performance   Situations in which the product or service is actually delivered at the time it is scheduled to be delivered.

Operating budget   (or *pro forma net income statement*) When the income statement refers to the future and not the past, it is an *operating budget*, also referred to as a *pro forma net income statement*. The operating budget presents the results of operations in many value-chain business functions prior to financing and taxes.

Operating cycle   Also known as a *self-liquidating cycle*, *working capital cycle*, or *cash cycle*; the movement of cash to inventories, to receivables, and back to cash.

Oprerating (core) division (department, production department)   This core division or department, also called in manufacturing companies, a *production division or department*, adds value that is observable by a customer to a product or service.

Operating leverage   The effects that different fixed costs (FC) have on changes in operating income (OI) as changes occur in the quantity (Q) available and sold, and hence either the unit or total contribution margin.

Operating margin (OM)   Total revenues from operations minus total costs from operations (excluding interest and income tax expenses) including inventoriable and period costs.

Operating margin percentage   (or *gross profit percentage*) The result obtained from dividing the operating income by the total revenue.

Operation   A standardized method or technique that is performed repetitively, often on different materials, resulting in different finished goods. Operations are usually conducted within departments.

Operations   The activities that convert various resources into a product or service ready for sale.

Opportunity cost   The contribution to income that is forgone (rejected) by not using a limited resource in its next-best alternative use.

(Opportunity) cost of capital   Also known as *discount rate*, *hurdle rate*, or *required rate of return (RRR)*; the minimum acceptable rate of return on an investment.

Optimization technique   A way to find the best answer using a mathematical model.

Order delivery time   The time it takes distribution to pick up the order from manufacturing and deliver it to the customer.

Order receipt time   The time it takes the Marketing Department to send engineering and other specifications to the Manufacturing Department.

Ordering costs   The costs to prepare and issue a purchase order.

Ordinary least squares (OLS) linear regression   A method that computes a formal measure of goodness of fit, called the *coefficient of determination*.

Organic revenue growth   Growth obtained without mergers or acquisitions.

Organizational structure   An arrangement of centres of responsibility within an entity.

Out-of-pocket costs   Also known as *incremental costs*, or *outlay costs*; additional costs made to obtain either additional resources or sales.

Outcome variable   Any value (Y), that increases and decreases after a change in the value of another factor (X).

Outcomes   Refer to the company and are uncertain if they are possible-but-unidentified consequences from different combinations of actions and events.

Outlay costs   Also known as *incremental costs*, or *out-of-pocket costs*; additional costs made to obtain either additional resources or sales.

Outliers   Actual observations outside the specified limits that are ordinarily regarded as nonrandom and worth investigating.

Output-level overcosting   A unit, batch, or product consumes a relatively low level of input materials and conversion activities but is reported to have a relatively high total cost.

Output-level overhead variance   A production-volume or denominator-level variance equal to the difference between budgeted fixed overhead and the assigned fixed overhead for the actual quantity of outputs.

Output-level undercosting   A unit, batch, or product consumes a relatively high level of input materials and conversion activities but is reported to have a relatively low total cost.

Output unit-level costs   Costs that arise when activities contribute to the cost of each unit of a product or service.

Outsource   The process of purchasing goods and services from outside vendors rather than producing the same goods or providing the same services within the organization.

Overallocated indirect costs   Also known as *overapplied indirect costs* or *overabsorbed indirect costs*; costs that occur when the allocated amount of indirect costs in an accounting period is greater than the actual (incurred) amount in that period.

Overtime premium   The wage rate paid to workers for any labour in excess of their straight-time wage rates.

P-value   The probability that, regardless of the statistical significance of the *t*-Stat, we are wrong to conclude that either a or b are not random.

Padding   The practice of underestimating budgeted revenues (or overestimating budgeted costs) to make budgeted targets easier to achieve.

Paralysis by analysis   A phrase that describes situations where managers delay making a decision because they decide to wait for more information.

Pareto diagram (frequency chart)   This diagram indicates how frequently each type of failure (defect) occurs.

Pareto principle   Expresses materiality in a straightforward way—for many events, 80% of effects arise from 20% of the causes.

Partial productivity   This most frequently used productivity measure compares the quantity of output produced with the quantity of an individual input used.

Payback method   A method that measures the time it will take to recoup, in the form of net cash inflows, the net initial investment in a project.

Peak-load pricing   The practice of charging a higher price for the same product or service when demand approaches physical capacity limits.

Peanut butter costing   A costing system that spreads the costs of conversion and inputs uniformly.

Perfectly competitive market   Exists when there is a homogeneous product with equivalent buying and selling prices and no individual buyers or sellers can affect those prices by their own actions.

Period costs   All costs incurred to generate revenue during a specific time period except the costs of manufacturing accumulated as cost of goods sold.

Perverse incentive   Rewards inappropriate management behaviour to present the appearance of cost-effective performance instead of to achieve actual cost-effective performance.

Physical measure method   This method allocates joint costs on the basis of their relative proportions at the splitoff point, using a common physical measure such as weight or volume of the total production of each product.

Planning   Selecting organizational goals, predicting results under various ways of achieving those goals, deciding how to attain the desired goals, and communicating the goals and how to attain them to the entire organization.

Practical capacity   The amount of output possible if idle time for maintenance, safety inspections, and holidays is scheduled.

Predatory pricing   A company sells products at unreasonably low prices that either tend to substantially lessen competition or were designed to have that effect.

Predictor variable(s) X Measured first for changes then associated changes are measured for the outcome variable Y.

Prevention costs   Costs incurred to preclude the production of products that do not conform to specifications.

Previous department costs   (or *transferred-in costs*) Costs incurred in previous departments that are carried forward as the product's costs when it moves to a subsequent process in the production cycle.

Price discounting   The reduction of selling prices below listed levels to encourage an increase in purchases by customers.

Price discrimination   The practice of charging some customers a higher price than is charged to other customers.

Prime cost   May include only direct materials, or may include all direct manufacturing costs including direct labour.

Production (core, operating) division (department, production department)   This core division or department, also called an *operating division*, or, in manufacturing companies, a *production department*, adds value that is observable by a customer to a product or service.

Pro forma net income statement   See *operating budget*.

Probability   Likelihood an actual or realized value, event or outcome will differ from an expected or budgeted value, event, or outcome.

Process-costing system   A system where costs are assigned to masses of similar units produced during a specific time period.

Product   Any output that has a positive sales value (or an output used internally that enables an organization to avoid incurring costs).

Product bundle   A combination of two or more different products, two or more different services, or products combined with services.

Product cost   Sum of the costs assigned to a product for a specific purpose.

Product differentiation   A company's ability to offer products or services perceived by its customers as being superior and unique relative to those of its competitors.

Product life cycle   From the viewpoint of the producer, the product life cycle spans the time from initial R&D to the time at which support to customers is withdrawn.

Product-sustaining costs   (or *service-sustaining costs*) Resources sacrificed on activities undertaken to support product lines, not batches of product lines or units of product.

Production   Acquiring, coordinating, and assembling resources to produce a product or deliver a service.

Production denominator level   (or *production denominator volume*) A measure of capacity. The denominator can be one of four choices.

Production division (or *core or operating division*) In manufacturing companies, a division that adds value that is observable by a customer to a product or service.

Production-volume variance A denominator-level or output-level variance equal to the difference between budgeted fixed overhead and the assigned fixed overhead for the actual quantity of outputs.

Productivity Measurement of the relationship between actual inputs used (both quantities and costs) and actual outputs produced.

Professional codes of conduct Codes that specify how the professions must behave in professional practice.

Profit centre A responsibility centre for which managers are accountable for revenues and costs and have some authority over others who decide upon key factors affecting both revenue and cost.

Profit split method (PSM) A transactional profit method of setting a transfer price that requires understanding the value added by the functions performed by each related party and the resulting allocation of profit and loss to each subunit.

Profitability index (or *excess present value index*) The total present value of future net cash inflows of a project divided by the total present value of the net initial investment.

Proration An allocation method that uses the percentages of manufacturing overhead allocated based on normal costing to allocate the underallocation or overallocation among the relevant accounts.

Purchase order lead time The time between the placement of an order and its delivery.

Purchasing costs The acquisition costs of goods acquired from suppliers including freight in, the transportation costs.

Qualitative factors Outcomes that cannot be measured in numerical terms.

Quality of design Measures how closely the characteristics of products or services match the needs and wants of customers.

Quantitative factors Outcomes that are measured in numerical terms.

r^2 (or *coefficient of determination* r^2); measures the percentage of variation in an outcome variable explained by one or more predictor variables.

Rate of return (ROR) The ratio of the predicted cost inflow minus outflow divided by the total outflow for the investment.

Rate variance The difference between the actual price and the budgeted price multiplied by the actual quantity of input in question.

Real rate of return The rate of return required to cover only investment risk.

Recapture of CCA If, upon sale of the last of a specific asset class, the calculation results in a negative UCC balance, CRA deems this a *recapture of CCA* and it is taxed as normal business income for the calendar year of the transaction.

Reciprocal allocation method Allocates costs by explicitly including the mutual services provided among all support departments.

Reciprocated cost This is also known as an artificial cost pool for each support services division. It identifies the output from an intermediate step used in Excel Solver and in Excel matrix calculations to eventually calculate the results of reciprocal cost allocation.

Redesigning The fundamental rethinking and redesign of business processes to achieve improvements in critical measures such as cost, quality, speed, and customer satisfaction. Also called *reengineering*.

Reengineering The fundamental rethinking and redesign of business processes to achieve improvements in critical measures of performance such as cost, quality, service, speed, and customer satisfaction.

Refined costing system A costing system that improves the measure of non-uniformity in the use of an organization's shared resources.

Related parties Corporate subunits conducting sales activity between one another.

Relevant costs Forecast future costs that *differ* because of a decision.

Relevant range Band of normal activity level or volume in which there is a specific relationship between the level of activity or volume and the cost in question.

Relevant revenues Forecast future revenues that *differ* because of a decision.

Refined costing system A costing system that results in a better measure of the nonuniformity in the use of an organization's resources by products and customers.

Reorder point The quantity level of the inventory on hand that triggers a new order.

Required rate of return (RRR) Also known as *discount rate, hurdle rate,* or *(opportunity) cost of capital*; the minimum acceptable rate of return on an investment.

Resale price method (RPM) This transaction method requires a company calculate the arm's-length resale price.

Research and development (R&D) Generating and experimenting with ideas related to new products, services, or processes.

Residual Also called the *disturbance* or the *error* term. The residual is calculated as $e = Y - y$ and graphically it appears as the vertical deviation of the actual data point (X,Y) from the estimated data point (X, y).

Residual income (RI) Income minus a required dollar return on the investment.

Responsibility accounting A system that measures the plans (by budgets) and actions (by actual results) of each responsibility centre.

Responsibility centre A part, segment, or sub-unit of an organization whose manager is accountable for a specified set of activities.

Return on investment (ROI) Also known as *accounting rate of return,* or *accrual accounting rate of return (AARR)*; an accounting measure of income divided by an accounting measure of investment.

Return on sales (ROS) The income-to-revenue (sales) ratio and a frequently used financial performance measure.

Revenue allocation Allocation that occurs when revenues must be assigned to distinct types of sales, but it is not economically feasible to trace the revenue (which would result in a more accurate assignment of revenues to products).

Revenue centre A responsibility centre for which managers are accountable for revenues only, not costs incurred to generate the revenues.

Revenue driver Any factor that affects revenues.

Rework   Unacceptable units of production that are subsequently reworked into good units and sold.

Rightsizing   (or *downsizing*) An integrated approach to configure processes, products, and people to match costs to the activities needed to be performed to operate efficiently and effectively in the present and future.

Risk   The probability that actual future results will differ from budgeted or expected results. Risk is uncertainty quantified as a probability.

Risk aversion   Low risk tolerance.

Risk loving   High risk tolerance.

Risk neutral   The decision maker will feel as much pain at losing a dollar as joy at gaining a dollar.

Risk tolerance   The risk of loss measured in percent that a person or team is willing to take.

Risk-weights   Probabilities of a particular outcome occurring; that is, the probability of receiving a financial payout from pursuing a specific course of action.

Rolling budget   A budget or plan that is always available for a specified future period by adding a month, quarter, or year in the future as the month, quarter, or year just ended is dropped.

Safety stock   Inventory held at all times regardless of inventory ordered using EOQ.

Sales mix   The relative contribution of quantities of products or services that constitutes total revenues.

Sales-mix variance   The difference between two amounts: (1) the budgeted amount for the actual sales mix and (2) the budgeted amount for the budgeted sales mix.

Sales-quantity variance   The difference between two amounts: (1) the budgeted contribution margin based on actual units sold of all products and the budgeted mix, and (2) the contribution margin in the static budget (which is based on the budgeted units to be sold of all products and the budgeted mix).

Sales value at splitoff method   This method allocates joint costs on the basis of the relative sales value at the splitoff point of the total production in the accounting period for each product.

Sales-volume variance   The difference between the flexible-budget amount and the static-budget amount; unit selling prices, unit variable costs, and fixed costs are held constant.

Sarbanes-Oxley Act   A law that took effect in the US in 2002 and that is the US equivalent of Canada's NI52-109.

Say on pay   A requirement that shareholders vote for or against executive compensation packages.

Scaleability   Adding one computer chip to another in a single circuit to increase the speed and power of the device.

Scrap   Outputs that have minimal sales value, or, residual material left over when making a product. Some outputs can have a negative revenue when their disposal costs are considered.

Self-liquidating cycle   Also known as a working *capital cycle*, *cash cycle*, or *operating cycle*; the movement of cash to inventories, to receivables, and back to cash.

Sensitivity analysis   Uses percentage changes to understand what changes cause the largest effect on profit.

Separable costs   Costs incurred beyond the splitoff point that can be assigned to one or more individual products.

Sequential method   Often called the *step-down* or *step allocation method*; allows for *partial* recognition of the services rendered by support departments to other support departments.

Sequential tracking   (or *synchronous tracking*) Any product costing method in which the accounting system entries occur in the same order as actual purchases and production.

Service-sector companies   Companies that provide services (intangible products)—for example, legal advice or audits—to their customers.

Service-sustaining costs   Resources sacrificed on activities undertaken to support service lines, not batches of service lines or units of service.

Shrinkage costs   Costs that arise from theft, embezzlement, misclassifications, and clerical errors.

Simple linear regression analysis   An analysis of the relationship between alternative cost drivers X_i, and the total indirect cost pool y, one at a time.

Single-rate method   Pools all costs in one cost pool and allocates them to cost objects using the same rate per unit of the single allocation base.

Slope coefficient b   Represents the rate of change in total variable cost Y, when the variable cost driver X changes by one unit.

Society of Management Accountants of Canada (SMAC) The largest association of management accountants in Canada.

Source document   An original record, such as a time sheet for an employee where the hours worked per job are recorded as well as the cost per hour.

Splitoff point   The juncture in the process when one or more products in a joint cost setting become separately identifiable.

Spoilage   Units of production that do not meet the specifications required by customers for good units and that are discarded or sold at reduced prices. Partially completed or fully completed units of output may be spoiled.

Spurious correlation   A repetitive but useless coincidence.

Staff management   Staff, such as management accountants and human resources managers, who provide advice and assistance to line management.

Stand-alone cost-allocation method   Uses information pertaining to each cost object as a separate operating entity to determine the cost-allocation weights.

Stand-alone revenue-allocation method   An allocation method that uses product-specific information pertaining to products in the bundle to determine the weights used to allocate the bundled revenues to those individual products. The term *stand-alone* refers to the product as a separate (nonsuite) item.

Standard   A carefully determined price, cost, or quantity used for judging performance; frequently refers to amounts estimated from either engineering or time-motion studies. Standard and budgeted amounts are often interchangeable for the purpose of calculating variance.

Standard cost   A carefully predetermined cost. Standard costs can relate to units of inputs or units of outputs.

Standard-costing method   A predetermined average cost per input or a predetermined average total input cost per unit of output.

Standard input   A carefully predetermined quantity of inputs (such as kilograms of materials or hours of labour time) required for one unit of output.

Static budget A budget that is based on one level of output; it is not adjusted or altered after it is set, regardless of ensuing changes in either actual output or actual revenue and cost drivers.

Step allocation method See *step-down method*.

Step-down method Sometimes called the *step allocation method*, or *sequential method*; allows for *partial* recognition of the services rendered by support departments to other support departments.

Step fixed (discontinuous) cost function (or *discontinuous cost function*) Arises when, within the relevant range of production inputs, the graph of total costs with a single resource consumed does not form a straight line with a constant slope.

Step variable cost function A function in which the cost is constant over various ranges of the predictor variable, but the cost increases by discrete amounts (that is, in steps) as the range of the predictor variable changes from one set of values to another set of values.

Stockout costs Costs that occur when a company runs out of an item for which there is customer demand.

Strategic analysis Evaluation of how well an organization has combined its own capabilities with the competitive environment to progress towards its future.

Stretch goals Goals that challenge managers to achieve excellent performance rather than maintain the status quo.

Strategic management Cost management that focuses on strategic issues.

Strategy Specifies how an organization matches its own capabilities with the opportunities in the marketplace to accomplish its objectives.

Student's t (or *t-Stat, test of statistical significance*) The ratio of how large the estimated value of the coefficient *a* or *b* is relative to its standard error.

Suboptimal decision making Also known as *dysfunctional decision making*, or *goal-incongruent decision making*; arises when a decision's benefit to one subunit is more than offset by the costs or loss of benefits to the organization as a whole.

Substitutable inputs Inputs for which the manufacturer can readily replace one with the other.

Sullivan Principles A set of principles that can be used to compare corporate performance in the area of social responsibility.

Sunk costs Past costs that cannot be changed, no matter what action is taken.

Super-variable costing (or *throughput costing*) A costing method that treats all costs except variable direct materials as period costs that are expensed when they are incurred. Only variable direct materials costs are inventoriable.

Supply chain An integrated system of suppliers, subcontractors, manufacturers, distributors, and retailers collaborating with the purpose of adding value to the output for the customer.

Supply-chain strategy A strategy that transforms external suppliers into internal partners with the buyer.

Synchronous tracking Any product costing method in which the accounting system entries occur in the same order as actual purchases and production. Also called *sequential tracking*.

***t*-Stat** (or *Student's t, test of statistical significance*) The ratio of how large the estimated value of the coefficient *a* or *b* is relative to its standard error.

Target cost per unit The estimated long-run cost per unit of a product (or service) that, when sold at the target price, enables the company to achieve the target operating income per unit.

Target margin percentage Determined by management teams based on the target price. Then the costs must be such that the target price minus costs equals the target margin percentage.

Target operating income per unit The operating income that a company wants to earn on each unit of a product (or service) sold.

Target price per unit The estimated price for a product or service that potential customers will pay.

Target pricing Pricing based on what customers are willing to pay.

Target rate of return on investment (ROI) The target operating income that an organization must earn divided by invested capital.

Tax havens Countries that have no tax agreements with Canada and share no information, which will increase the costs of any tax audit for the company.

Tax shield formula An efficient way to calculate the present value of the tax savings as a result of deducting CCA.

Technical considerations Considerations that help managers make wise economic decisions by providing them with costs in the appropriate format and at the preferred frequency.

Terminal loss When the last property in a specific asset class is sold but the calculation results in a positive UCC balance for the asset class, the remainder is called a *terminal loss*.

Test of statistical significance (also known as *t-Stat* or *student's t*) The ratio of how large the estimated value of the coefficient *a* or *b* is relative to its standard error.

Theoretical capacity The amount of output theoretically possible if there were never any delays or interruptions; a 24/7/365 quantity.

Theory of constraints (TOC) This theory describes methods to maximize operating income when faced with some bottleneck and some nonbottleneck operations.

Throughput costing (or *super-variable costing*) A costing method that treats all costs except variable direct materials as period costs that are expensed when they are incurred. Only variable direct materials costs are inventoriable.

Time-adjusted rate of return (or *internal rate of return (IRR)*) The discount rate at which the present value of expected cash inflows from a project equals the present value of expected cash outflows of the project.

Time driver Any factor where change in the factor causes a change in the speed with which an activity is undertaken.

Time-series data The collection of historical data over a long time horizon about the same process.

Total factor productivity (TFP) The ratio of the quantity of output produced to the costs of all inputs used, where the inputs are combined on the basis of current period prices.

Total-project approach Calculates the present value of *all* future cash inflows and outflows under each alternative separately.

Traditional costing Also known as *cost smoothing*, or *peanut butter costing*; a costing system that spreads the costs of conversion and inputs uniformly.

Transactional net margin method (TNMM) A transactional profit method of setting a transfer price that is based on the return on assets (ROA) of the corporation as a whole and provides maximum discretion for establishing a transfer price.

Transfer price The price one subunit of an organization charges for a product (tangible or intangible) or service supplied to another subunit of the same organization.

Transferred-in costs (or *previous department costs*) Costs incurred in previous departments that are carried forward as the product's costs when it moves to a subsequent process in the production cycle.

Trigger point A stage in the cycle going from purchase of direct materials (Stage A) to sale of finished goods (Stage D) at which journal entries are made in the accounting system.

Triple bottom line This type of reporting is a formal response to the Global Reporting Initiative (GRI) and augments standard financial reports with specific environmental and social sustainability reports.

Unamortized capital cost (UCC) The balance of a capital expenditure after the allowable CCA has been deducted.

Underallocated indirect costs (or *underapplied indirect costs, underabsorbed indirect costs*) Costs that occur when the allocated amount of indirect costs in an accounting period is less than the actual (incurred) amount in that period.

Unfavourable (U) variance A variance that results in an actual operating income that is less than the budgeted amount.

Unit cost Also called the *average cost*, it is calculated by dividing the total prime cost pool by physical units consumed.

Upside potential Also called *downside risk, risk/return, cost/benefit;* used to make resource allocations such that the expected benefits exceed the expected costs.

Upstream costs Costs incurred prior to production.

Usage variance The difference between the actual quantity of input used and the budgeted quantity of input that should have been used multiplied by the budgeted input price.

Value-added activity An activity that contributes directly to the customer's value proposition.

Value-added cost A cost that, if eliminated, would reduce the value customers obtain from using the product or service.

Value analysis With the purpose of reducing costs, an analysis that focuses on the product design stage, where there is the greatest opportunity to change design, materials, and manufacturing processes.

Value chain The sequence of business functions in which customer usefulness is added to products or services.

Value engineering An analysis of the entire value chain of all business functions to determine where non-value-added costs can be eliminated.

Value leadership A strategy of developing and sustaining the unique characteristics of a product or service for which consumers will pay because there is a price inelasticity of demand.

Value proposition A distinct benefit for which customers will pay.

Variable cost A cost that changes in total in proportion to changes in the related level of total activity or volume.

Variable costing A method of inventory valuation in which only *variable manufacturing* costs are included as inventoriable costs. All fixed and all nonmanufacturing costs are classified as period costs expensed during the specific time period they are incurred.

Variable overhead efficiency variance A measure of the efficiency with which the cost allocation base is used.

Variable overhead rate variance The difference between actual variable overhead cost per unit of the cost allocation base and budgeted variable overhead cost per unit of the cost allocation base.

Variance The difference between actual (realized) and budgeted (pro forma) results.

Variance analysis An exceptions-based approach to management.

Vector A matrix with one or more rows and one single column.

Vertical integration A company that incorporates as much of the value chain as possible within itself is vertically integrated.

Weighted-average cost of capital (WACC) Equals the after-tax average cost of all the long-term funds used.

Weighted-average process-costing method Method of process costing that assigns the equivalent-unit cost of the work done to date (regardless of the accounting period in which it was done) to equivalent units completed and transferred out of the process and to equivalent units in ending work-in-process inventory.

Work-in-process inventory Goods partially worked on but not yet completed. Also called *work in progress*.

Work in progress Goods partially worked on but not yet completed. Also called *work-in-process inventory*.

Work measurement method This *industrial engineering* method begins with an analysis of the relationship between quantities of physical inputs and physical outputs.

Working capital cycle Also known as a *self-liquidating cycle, cash cycle,* or *operating cycle;* the movement of cash to inventories, to receivables, and back to cash.

Yield The proportion of output obtained from a specified quantity of input.

Yield variance A measurement of the variance of the actual from expected yield of outputs obtained from expected quantity of inputs.

Zero-sum game A game in which what one gains the other loses.

NAME INDEX

decision making
  see also decision framework
  accounting and, 9
  advertising decision, 74
  alternative fixed- and variable-cost structures, 76–77
  and book value, 441–443
  capacity-level choices, 341
  carrying costs of inventory, 439–440
  compensation decisions, 964–967
  complex decisions, and CVP analysis, 73–80
  compliance with generally accepted accounting principles (GAAP), 48
  and confusing terminology, 451
  decision table, 80
  dysfunctional decision making, 929
  equipment replacement decisions, 441–443
  expected value, 79–80, 80*f*
  goal-incongruent decision making, 929
  governance decisions, 964–967
  implementation of, 8–9
  investment decisions, 846
  and joint costs, 609
  long-term output decisions, 432–437
  make/buy decision, 434–437, 439*f*
  margin of safety and risk, 75–76
  negative effects and conflict, reduction of, 451–453
  and opportunity cost, 438–443
  opportunity-cost approach, 438, 439*f*
  output-level decisions, 432–437
  outsourcing decision, 434–437, 576*n*
  and performance evaluation, 452–453
  vs. performance evaluation, 610–611
  pricing decisions. *See* pricing decisions
  product costs, 46–48
  product mix decisions, 48, 443–450
  qualitative factors, 440–441
  reduction of selling price, 74–75
  relevance, 559–560
  relevant-cost analysis, pitfalls of, 451
  risk-return trade-off, 77
  sell or process further decision, 604–610
  short-term output decisions, 432–437
  strategic factors, 440–441
  suboptimal decision making, 929
  total-alternatives approach, 438, 439*f*
  unit costs, misleading, 451
decision-making process. *See* decision framework
defence contracts, 578
deferred compensation, 967
defrauding the government, 47
degree of operating leverage, 77
degrees of freedom (df), 405
demand inelasticity, 494
demand-pull system, 811
Deming Prize, 754
denominator-level variance, 302

denominator levels
  capacity costs, and denominator-level issues, 351–352
  complex decision with complex effects, 342–346
  costing, effects on, 346–349
  decision framework and denominator choice, 344–346
  demand measures, 345–346
  inventory valuation, 352–363
  master-budget denominator, 350
  performance evaluation, effects on, 346–349, 350–351
  practical capacity as denominator, 350
  pricing, effects on, 346–350
  product costing, 349
  product pricing, 349–350
  recoverable costs in strategic pricing, 350
  reporting, effects on, 346–352
  stage in denominator level choice process, 343*f*
  supply measures, 344–345
design of operations, 30
design of products, services, or processes, 5
design quality, costs of, 769
designed-in costs, 485
diagnostic control systems, 986–989
differential approach, 895, 899, 900*f*
differential cost, 430, 437
differential revenue, 430
direct allocation method, 569–570, 570*f*
direct cost tracing, 159
direct costing, 356
  see also variable costing
direct costs, 28–30, 29
  assignment of, 106–108
  cost tracing, 29
  direct cost tracing, 159
  vs. indirect costs, 30
direct labour (DL) cost, 29
direct labour hours (DLH), 106
  identification of, 107
  manufacturing jobs, 108
direct machine-hour (DMH) costs, 29, 106
  identification of, 107
  manufacturing jobs, 108
direct manufacturing labour budget, 202
direct manufacturing labour (DML) cost, 29, 41
direct materials (DM) costs, 29, 40, 43, 106
  identification of, 107
  manufacturing jobs, 108
direct materials efficiency variance, 261
direct materials inventory (DM), 40
direct materials mix variance, 262
direct materials mix yield variance, 262–263
direct materials partial productivity, 537
direct materials purchases budget, 201–202

direct materials rate variance, 261
direct materials usage budget, 201–202
direct materials yield variance, 262–263
direct method, 569–570, 570*f*
direct variable efficiency variance, 253
direct variable rate variance, 253
dirty data, cleaning up, 399–401
discontinuous cost function, 393, 393*f*
discount rate, 853, 853*n*
discounted cash flow (DCF), 852–853
  internal rate of return (IRR), 855–858, 856*f*
  net present value (NPV), 853–855, 854*f*, 857–858, 858*f*
  relevance, assessment of, 861–864
  sensitivity analysis, 857–858
discretionary costs, 540, 540*f*
disposal price, 862, 863
disposals of capital assets, 891, 892*f*, 893*f*
distinctive competence, 518
distress prices, 937
distribution, 5
distribution-channel costs, 641
documentation, 107
Dodd-Frank Wall Street Reform and Consumer Protection Act, 965
double-count, 894
Dow Jones Sustainability Index, 988
downside risk, 10
downsizing, 542
downstream costs, 29, 30*f*, 41, 475
downward demand spiral, 349–350
dual pricing, 940–941
dual-rate method, 561–565
dumping, 496
Durbin-Watson d calculation, 401, 408, 408*n*
dysfunctional decision making, 929

E

e-business, 4
early warning, 216
economic order quantity (EOQ), 805–807
economic order quantity procurement model, 805–807, 810–813, 815
economic plausibility, 388, 390, 393, 400
economic sectors, 40
economic substance, 2
economic value added (EVA), 972–973
economies of scale, 519
economies of scope, 520
effectiveness, 267
efficiency, 267
  analysis of, 264
  customer response, 320
  as key success factor, 6
  manufacturing cycle efficiency (MCE), 773
efficiency variance, 253–254, 256–259
  direct materials efficiency variance, 261
  direct variable efficiency variance, 253
  favourable efficiency variances, 565–567
  flexible-budget variance, 266

insurance companies, 983
integrated cost information systems, 30
intellectual capital, 528
interactive control systems, 988–989
intercept value, 389
interdependencies, 319
intermediate market, 942–943
intermediate products, 930
internal business process perspective, 527
internal business processes, 765–767, 769–770
internal consistency, 901
internal control failure, 928
internal control systems, 683, 924, 925f
internal evaluation, 357
internal failure costs, 757
internal quantitative data, 152
internal rate of return (IRR), 855–858, 856f, 907–908
internal reporting, 11
International Accounting Board regulations, 868
international financial centre, 945
International Financial Reporting Standards (IFRS), 32n
international standards, 754
International Standards Organization (ISO) certification, 754
Internet, 821n, 822
interprovincial transfers and taxes, 934–936
intrinsic motivation, 987
inventoriable costs, 40, 41–44, 567
inventory
    carrying costs of inventory, 439–440
    direct materials inventory (DM), 40
    ending inventory budget, 203
    ending WIP inventory, 680
    finished goods inventory (FG), 38, 40
    and GAAP, 822n
    generally accepted accounting principles (GAAP), 38
    information technology, 805
    inventoriable costs, 40, 41–44
    investments (inventory), 777
    pro forma inventory valuation, 348
    stockouts, 805
    types of, 40
    undesirable buildup of inventories, 361–363
    valuation. *See* inventory valuation
    variance analysis, 270
    work-in-process inventory (WIP), 40
    see also work-in-process inventory (WIP)
inventory management, 804
    backflush costing, 821–830
    costs associated with goods for sale, 804–805
    economic order quantity procurement model, 805–807, 810–813
    enterprise resource planning (ERP), 820–821
    just-in-time (JIT) purchasing, 810–813

materials requirements planning (MRP), 819–820
reorder point, 808
safety stock, 809–810, 809f
supply-chain management. *See* supply-chain management
inventory valuation
    absorption costing, 355f, 365–366, 365f, 430f
    absorption inventory valuation assumptions, 352–356
    and balance sheet, 40–44
    comparison of inventory costing systems, 365–366, 365f
    corporate governance, 830
    denominator levels, 352–363
    overstatement of inventory value, 830
    super-variable costing, 363–366
    throughput costing, 363–366, 364f
    variable costing, 355f, 365–366, 365f
    variable inventory valuation assumptions, 352–356
invested capital, 488
investment, 777, 975
investment cash flows, 887–888
investment centre, 215, 930
investment decisions, 846
    see also capital budgeting
    long-term investments, 846, 850
    and relevant costs, 845
investment programs, 846
investment projects, 846
investor relations, 11
irrelevant costs, 429–431
irrelevant data, 428
ISO 9004, 754
ISO 14001, 754
ISO 14064, 754
ISO 22000, 754
ISO 22005, 754
ISO 26000, 754, 755f
ISO 28000, 754
ISO 31000, 754, 755f

J

job, 109, 111
job-cost record, 111, 116f, 123
job-cost sheet, 111
job costing
    see also job-costing system
    actual cost assignment to distinct product, 115–118
    actual cost assignment to distinct service, 112–114
    actual costing, 119–120
    budgeted costing, 120
    cost flows, 122f
    cost rate calculation methods, 119–122, 119f
    information technology, 117
    job cost assignment methods, 119–122, 119f
    non-manufacturing costs, 127–128
    normal costing, 121–122

scrap, 737
and spoilage, 735
job-costing system, 109–112
    see also job costing
    adjusted allocation-rate approach, 129
    assignment of costs to jobs, 111–112
    budgeted indirect costs, 128–129
    choice among approaches, 131
    end-of-accounting-year adjustments, 128–129
    examples, 110f
    general ledger, 123–124, 123f
    generic job-costing system, 107f
    key elements, 106–107
    normal job-costing system, and cost flow, 122–131, 122f
    proration, 129–131
    service sector, 110f, 112, 114f
    subsidiary ledgers, 125–128, 125f, 126f
    transactions, explanations of, 124–125
    write-off to cost of goods sold approach, 131
joint cost allocation
    approaches, 600–604
    constant gross margin percentage of NRV method, 600, 606–609
    decision framework, 600–602
    estimated net realizable value (NRV) method, 600, 604–605, 607–609
    overcoming the challenges of, 611
    physical measure method, 600, 603–604
    reasons to allocate joint costs, 599
    sales value at splitoff method, 600, 602–604
joint costs, 598
    allocation of. *See* joint cost allocation
    basics of, 598–599
    industries incurring, 599f
    irrelevance, for decision making, 609
joint products, 598
just-in-time (JIT) production, 811–813, 815–819
just-in-time (JIT) purchasing, 810–813
just-in-time (JIT) strategy, 811–813, 815–819, 830
justification
    of reimbursement costs, 578
    of relevance, 560–561

K

Kaizen budgeting, 212–213
key performance factors (KPF), 523
key success factors (KSF), 6–7, **523**
knowledge, and production costs, 761

L

labour costs, 45–46
labour intensive, 111
labour-time record, 115, 116f
lagged relationship, 408, 521n
land transfer tax, 886
large corporations tax, 886

laws and regulations
    corporate governance, 13, 219, 924
    cost assignment, 166
    management accounting control
        systems (MACS), 924
    organizational structures, 929
leading relationship, 408
lean, demand-pull manufacturing
    system, 821
lean production, 811–813
learning, 9
learning and growth nonfinancial
    measures, 770
learning and growth perspective, 528,
    759–765
learning curve, 759–765, 764*f*
legislation. *See* laws and regulations
levers of control, 986–989
life-cycle budgeting, 491
life-cycle costing, 492, 851
life-cycle pricing, 474, 491–499
life-cycle reports, 493–494
line management, 11
linear cost function, 387–388, 387*f*, 389
linear equation method, 573
linear programming, 444–447
linearity, 393
locked-in costs, 485, 486*f*
long-run budgets, 194*f*
long-run customer profitability, 654
long-term assets, 978
long-term contracts, 866
long-term investments, 846, 850
    see also capital budgeting
long-term output decisions, 432–437
long-term pricing, 481–491

M

main products, 598
make/buy decision, 434–437, 439*f*
Malcolm Baldrige Quality Award, 754
malus, 966
management
    investment activity, control of, 866–867
    judgment of, 640
    line management, 11
    project, control of, 867–868
    staff management, 11
management accountants, 2
    accountability, 13
    challenges for, 610–611
    decision making *vs.* performance
        evaluation, 610–611
    as internal auditors, 830
    liability of, 13
management accounting, 2
    behavioural considerations, 10
    and control, 9*f*
    and corporate governance laws, 219
    cost-benefit approach, 10
    data, 2–4
    and decision making, 9*f*

different costs for different purposes,
    10–11
vs. financial accounting, 3*f*
high-quality, reliable information, 10
key guidelines, 10–11
operating decisions, 2–3
organization structure, 11
and planning, 9*f*
and strategic decisions, 3–4
technical considerations, 10
management accounting control
    systems (MACS), 924–927, 964
management by exception, 246
management control systems, 924–930
management information system
    (MIS), 2, 152
Management's Discussion and Analysis
    (MD&A), 925
manufacturing cells, 812
manufacturing costs, 40–41
    overhead costs. *See* manufacturing
        overhead (MOH)
    total manufacturing costs, 43
manufacturing cycle efficiency
    (MCE), 773
manufacturing cycle time, 773
Manufacturing Department overhead
    records, 127
manufacturing lead time, 773
manufacturing overhead (MOH),
    29, 41, 106
    actual manufacturing overhead
        rate, 117
    capacity cost, 299
    cost allocation methods, 566–567
    different purposes of manufacturing
        overhead cost analysis, 320
    fixed overhead costs, 298, 298*n*,
        299–306
    and GAAP, 386
    indirect manufacturing overhead, 386
    indirect manufacturing overhead cost
        pools, 390–391
    indirect manufacturing overhead
        costs, 477
    infrastructure cost, 540
    linear cost function, 387–388, 387*f*
    overhead cost variances. *See* overhead
        cost variances
    period overhead costs, 299
    variable overhead costs, 298, 298*n*,
        306–313
manufacturing overhead allocated,
    124, 128
manufacturing overhead applied, 124
manufacturing overhead budget, 202–203
Manufacturing Overhead Control, 128
manufacturing-sector companies, 40
    cost allocation base, 108
    income statement terminology, 44*f*
    job costing, 115–118
    job-costing system, 110*f*

merchandising *vs.* manufacturing
    ledgers, 44*f*
process-costing system, examples
    of, 110*f*
product-sustaining costs, 157
margin of safety, 75–76
marginal income tax rate, 886
market-based measures, 607
market-based transfer prices, 931, 936–937
market changes, 865
market share, 649
market-share growth, 652
market-share variance, 649–650
market-size growth, 652
market-size variance, 650–652
marketing, 5
master budget, 192
    see also master operating budget
master-budget capacity, 342,
    345–346, 351
master-budget denominator, 350
master-budget fixed overhead rate, 350
master operating budget, 195–206, 197*f*
    basic data and requirements, 198–200
    preparation of, 200–206
    steps in development of, 196–197
    time period, 195–196
Materials Records, 125–126
materials requirements planning
    (MRP), 819–820
materials-requisition record, 115, 116*f*
matrix, 449, **581**
matrix algebra, 572*n*, 573, 580–583
matrix multiplication, 582–583
measurement of costs, 45–48
merchandising-sector companies, 40
    activity-based costing (ABC)
        system, 169
    income statement terminology, 44*f*
    inventoriable costs, 41, 44
    job-costing system, examples of, 110*f*
    merchandising *vs.* manufacturing
        ledgers, 44*f*
    period costs, 41, 44
    process-costing system, examples
        of, 110*f*
    product-sustaining costs, 157
missing data entry, 400
mix and yield level 4 variances, 259–264
mix variance, 260
mixed cost, 34–35, 35*f*
mixed linear cost function, 387*f*, 389
monopoly, 520
monopsony, 519–520
moral hazard, 984, 984*n*
motivation, 926, 928
Multi-Lateral Instruments (MI), 13
multicollinearity, 414–415
Multilateral Instrument 52-109, 986
Multilateral Instrument 52-111, 986
multinational corporations
    arm's length principle, 930–931

performance goals, 978–979
performance measures
    see also performance evaluation
    accounting performance measures, 968
    control, 819
    corporate governance, 988
    current cost, 976–978
    diagnostic control systems, 986–989
    economic value added (EVA),
      972–973
    evaluation of performance
      measurement alternatives, 976–979
    executive performance measures and
      compensation, 983–986
    financial performance measures,
      267–268, 320, 363, 525–526,
      964–975
    governance and compensation
      decisions, 964–967
    gross *vs.* net book value, 978
    level of relevance, 979
    long-term assets, 978
    multinational companies, 979–983
    nonfinancial BSC measures, 528–529,
      769–770
    nonfinancial performance measures,
      267–268, 320–323, 363, 525–526,
      819, 964–975
    performance goals and timing of
      feedback, 978–979
    residual income (RI), 971–972
    return on investment (ROI), 969–971
    return on sales (ROS), 973–974
    time horizon, 974–975
performance report, 9*f*
period costs, 41, 44
    common costs, allocation of, 576–578
    cost allocation, 558*f*
    direct allocation method, 569–570, 570*f*
    dual-rate method, 561–565
    favourable efficiency variances, 565–567
    reciprocal allocation method, 572–576,
      575*f*, 580–583
    relevance criterion, 558–561
    single-rate method, 561–565
    step-down method, 570–572, 572*f*
    unfavourable efficiency variances,
      565–567
period overhead costs, 299
physical measure method, 600, 603–604
physical units, 637, 692
planned growth, 168–169
planned unused capacity, 351
planning, 8, 9*f*
Poisson distribution, 774
Porter's five forces analysis, 518–522
post-investment audit, 867–868
practical capacity, 342, 344–345, 350, 351
predatory pricing, 495
Predatory Pricing and Enforcement
    Guidelines, 495
prediction error, cost of, 814–815
predictions, 7–8

predictor variable, 395, 401
Premio Nacional de Calidad, 754
present value discount factors, 903*n*
prevention costs, 757
previous department costs, 701
price
    see also pricing decisions
    arm's length price, 945
    cost-plus price, 480
    disposal price, 862, 863
    distress prices, 937
    oil prices, 933*n*
    regulated prices, 489
    selling price, 74–75, 636
    setting prices, 764–765
    target price per unit, 480
    terminal disposal price, 863
    transfer price, 930
price discounting, 644
price discrimination, 494
price recovery
    cost effect, 533–534
    operating income, 533–534, 535–536
    revenue effect, 533
price-setting power
    of customers, 519–520
    of input suppliers, 520
price stability, 490
pricing decisions, 48
    alternative cost-plus methods, 489–490
    collusive pricing, 496
    Competition Act, 494–497
    competitors, influence of, 474
    cost-plus pricing, 157, 474, 487–489,
      489–491
    costs, influence of, 474
    cross-functional teams, 485–487
    customers, influence of, 474
    and denominator levels, 346–350
    dumping, 496
    environmental sustainability,
      497–499
    fair business, 494–497
    highball bid target pricing, 481
    life-cycle pricing, 474, 491–499
    long-term pricing, 481–491
    major influences on, 474–475
    peak-load pricing, 496
    predatory pricing, 495
    price discrimination, 494
    product cost categories, 475
    product pricing, 349–350
    qualitative factors, 491–499
    recoverable costs in strategic
      pricing, 350
    reduction of selling price, 74–75
    relevant costs in short-run pricing,
      475–479
    ROI cost-plus pricing method, 489
    target costing, 479–481
    target margin percentage, 480
    target pricing, 474, 479–481, 488,
      490–491

    time horizon, 475
    value-analysis teams, 485–487
primary party, 577
primary product, 637
prime cost pool, 678
prime costs, 31–32
pro forma statements, 192, 205–206
problem identification, 7
process activities, 168
process costing
    alternative methods, 680
    calculations, 678–684
    conversion costs, assignment of,
      681–684, 681*f*
    first-in, first-out (FIFO) process-
      costing method, 680, 692–697,
      725–730
    journal entries, 688–689
    and spoilage, 724, 725–734
    standard-costing method, 680,
      697–698, 730–734
    transferred-in costs, 700–706
    weighted-average process-costing
      method, 680, 725–730
    see also weighted-average process-
      costing method
process-costing system, 109
    decision framework, 678–680
    examples, 110*f*
    flow of costs, 688*f*
    generic process cost allocation, 110*f*
    service sector, 110*f*
    variances, accounting for, 698–700
product, 598
    byproducts, 598, 611–614
    first incremental product, 637
    intermediate products, 930
    joint production process, 598*f*
    joint products, 598
    main product, 598
    primary product, 637
    second incremental product, 637
    substitute products, 519
product bundle, 559, 635–640
product cost, 46–48, 47*f*
product cost categories, 475
product costing, 349
product differentiation, 520
product life cycle, 344*f*, 491
product mix decisions, 48, 443–450
    Excel Solver®, 448–450
    linear programming, 444–447
    sensitivity analysis, 447–448
product output, 265–266
product pricing, 349–350
product-sustaining costs, 157–158
production, 5
    costs, 30*f*
    just-in-time (JIT) production, 811–813
    lean production, 811–813
    operating income, effect on, 360–361
production budget, 200–201
production costs, 761

PHOTO CREDITS

LIST OF ABBREVIATIONS